Papyri Copticae Magicae

Archiv für Papyrusforschung
und verwandte Gebiete

Begründet von
Ulrich Wilcken

Herausgegeben von
Lajos Berkes   Jean-Luc Fournet
Demokritos Kaltsas   Brian McGing
Fabian Reiter   Giuseppe Ucciardello
Marja Vierros

Beiheft 48

De Gruyter

Papyri Copticae Magicae

Coptic Magical Texts
Volume 1: Formularies

Edited by
Korshi Dosoo and Markéta Preininger

In collaboration with
Roxanne Bélanger Sarrazin, Edward O. D. Love,
Selina Schuster, and Julia Schwarzer

De Gruyter

ISBN 978-3-11-221513-5
e-ISBN (PDF) 978-3-11-108010-9
ISSN 1868-9337

Library of Congress Control Number: 2023944027

Bibliographic information published by the Deutsche Nationalbibliothek
The Deutsche Nationalbibliothek lists this publication in the Deutsche Nationalbibliografie;
detailed bibliographic data are available on the Internet at http://dnb.dnb.de.

© 2025 Walter de Gruyter GmbH, Berlin/Boston
This volume is text- and page-identical with the hardback published in 2023.

Printing and binding: CPI books GmbH, Leck

www.degruyter.com

Cum nuper tecum (reverende pater) in cœnobio tuo apud Herbipolim aliquandiu conversatus, multa de chymicis, multa de magicis, multa de cabalisticis caeterisque; quae adhuc in occulto delitescunt arcanis scientiis atque artibus una contulissemus: magna inter cæteras questio erat (...) magia ipsa...
Heinrich Cornelius Agrippa to Johannes Trithemius (1509/1510)

KD: *Dedicated to the memory of Deirdre Jill McGarry*

MP: *Dedicated to the memory of Jacqueline Trak, who taught me how to learn*

Foreword

It has become increasingly common to see "magic" as a negative word, primarily designating illicit religion and ritual. But while this was often true in antiquity, in the modern day it tends to conjure up different associations—the promise of romance and excitement ("magical adventures") or of miraculous ease and efficiency ("it works like magic!"). This may be why magical texts are often of such interest, even—and perhaps especially—to non-scholars; they seem to embody the distance between our own mundane present and the past, in its alien distance and possibility. Yet the reality is that magical texts are often inaccessible or obtuse—difficult in their language, and drawing deeply from a reservoir of cultural references unfamiliar to most modern readers.

 The present volume is the product of the project *The Coptic Magical Papyri: Vernacular Religion in Late Roman and Early Islamic Egypt* (2018–2023), whose goal was to make one group of these texts, those written in Coptic, more accessible to scholars and laypeople. This project was funded by, and housed at, the Julius Maximilian University Würzbug through the Excellent Ideas programme. We must in particular thank Martin Stadler and Daniel Schwemer for supporting the initial proposal, made by the project leader Korshi Dosoo; without their advocacy, and later guidance, the project, and this volume, would never have come to be.

 When the project began in 2018, Dosoo worked alongside Edward O.D. Love and Markéta Preininger, respectively the post-doctoral and doctoral research fellows. In 2021, Love moved on from the project, while Preininger became the post-doctoral research fellow, and Julia Schwarzer in turn joined the team as doctoral research fellow. Throughout the course of the project, the core team was assisted by numerous co-workers and collaborators, notably Matouš Preininger, who worked as information technician from 2020–2022, and Stella Türker and Selina Schuster, who joined as research assistants in 2020 and 2022 respectively. While we continually received invaluable support from the Coptological, Papyrological, and Egyptological communities, a number of colleagues were recognised as contributors to the project based on their valuable input: Roxanne Bélanger Sarrazin, Anne Grons, Krisztina Hevesi, Bill Manley, Ortal-Paz Saar, Anne Sieberichs, Simon St-Arnault Chiasson, and David Tibet.

 The initial goal of the project was to develop a database which would facilitate the study of the corpus within its larger context, by including data on magical texts in Coptic, Greek, Demotic, and other relevant languages. This materialised in the *Kyprianos Database of Ancient Ritual Texts and Objects*, launched online in October 2020. The database initially focused on metadata—that is, physical and bibliographical descriptions of manuscripts—but, over the five years of the project, we continually edited published and unpublished Coptic texts and made them available through the *Kyprianos* database. From the beginning of the project, we envisaged its culmination in a published volume. It is now clear that the full corpus will require an extensive series of volumes, and it is the first of these which you are reading now.

Our original conception of the volume was of something like a *Sammelbuch*, a volume that would bring together and present editions and translations with minimal commentary. Our reasons for this were simple—while we are confident that we have made significant progress in understanding these texts, major unanswered questions remain, and we thus preferred to separate the presentation of the texts from their interpretation. Consultation with colleagues nonetheless convinced us that something more complete was required. As a result, this volume does contain extensive commentary, and, while we are certain that it will become outdated over time, we nonetheless hope that it will allow readers an initial basis on which to develop their own understandings and interpretations.

This volume offers editions of 37 manuscripts from Egypt, written in Coptic, dating to between the fourth and eleventh centuries of the common era. These are of the type known as formularies, handbooks describing numerous rituals for accomplishing diverse goals, such as obtaining health, love, success, and cursing enemies. In a sense, it is here that we see a link between our modern conceptions of magic as a domain of infinite possibility, and past conceptions, in which 'magical' texts offered one way of dealing with the dangers, conflicts, and frustrations of life. While all ancient texts are valuable in providing windows onto the past, our experience has been that magical texts are often particularly rich sources; we find in them everything from the structure of the angelic hierarchy of the highest heavens to names for and descriptions of cooking pots.

Acknowledgments

This project is heavily indebted to the work of previous and contemporary scholars who have worked on Coptic magic, figures such as Angelicus Kropp, Marvin Meyer, Jacques van der Vliet, and David Frankfurter, who have been a great inspiration to us over the last five years, and readers will see their names regularly cited.

Of more immediate relevance for the project, we must thank again Martin Stadler and Daniel Schwemer, as well as Roland Baumhauer, the former dean of the Faculty of Philosophy, and Alfred Forchel, former president of the Julius Maximilian University Würzbug for financing and supporting the project. Korshi Dosoo would like to thank Malcolm Choat, Rachel Yuen Collingridge, Jennifer Cromwell, and Victor Ghica, his first papyrological and Coptological mentors; Iain Gardner and Jay Johnston, on whose project he first began to explore

Coptic magical texts in depth; and Davide, for his constant support. We thank those who read and commented on the manuscript of this first volume of *Papyri Copticae Magicae* at various stages of its production, who improved its quality immeasurably—Yasmine Amory, Roxanne Bélanger Sarrazin, Lajos Berkes, Anne Boud'hors, Dylan Burns, Nathan Carlig, Anna Cherkashina, Eyob Derillo, Christopher Faraone, David Frankfurter, Krisztina Hevesi, Tea Ghigo, Anne Grons, Ursula Hammed, Eliza Jacobi, Frederic Krueger, Ágnes Mihálykó, Ivan Miroshnikov, Marijn van Putten, Ortal-Paz Saar, Joseph Sanzo, Valérie Schram, Sofía Torallas Tovar, Jacques van der Vliet, Vincent Walter, and Michael Zellmann-Rohrer. The inevitable mistakes which remain are our own. We thank also the curators and staff of the various collections which hold the manuscripts studied here, who kindly allowed us access to them, provided us with photographs, and answered our questions about their materiality and acquisition—Andrea Jördens and Elke Fuchs at the University of Heidelberg; Jan Moje at the Ägyptisches Museum und Papyrussammlung of the Staatliche Museen zu Berlin; Daniel Soliman, Lara Weiss, Jeroen Rensen, and Eliza Jacobs at the National Museum of Antiquities in Leiden; Claudio Gallazzi at the University of Milan; Gisela Bélot at the Bibliothèque nationale et universitaire in Strasbourg; Charles Powers at the Los Angeles County Museum of Art; Julie Scott at the Rosicrucian Egyptian Museum; Charikleia Armoni at the Kölner Papyrussammlung, and Anna Maria Donadoni Roveri and Giovanna Donadoni. We would also like to thank Nadja Aboulenein, Adrienn Almásy-Martin, Paola Buzi, Jean-Charles Coulon, Jennifer Cromwell, Frank Feder, Jean-Luc Fournet, Marius Gerhardt, Gianluigi Galli, Massimo Giuseppetti, Arcangela Carbone Gross, Colin Hope, Raquel Martín Hernández, Beatrice Melchiorri, So Miyagawa, Ahmed Nakshara, Luigi Prada, Joachim Quack, Sebastian Richter, Stefanie Schmidt, Alin Suciu, and Alexandros Tsakos, as well as the *Coptic Scriptorium, Database and Dictionary of Greek Loanwords in Coptic, PAThs*, and *Thesaurus Linguae Aegyptiae* projects and their members, all of whom helped us in innumerable ways in the course of our work on the volume and the project which lay behind it. We would like to thank our present and former teammates, whose hard work can be seen on every page—Edward O.D. Love, Matouš Preininger, Selina Schuster, Julia Schwarzer, and Stella Türker. Finally, we would like to thank those whose names escape us for now, but whose contributions were no less real and valuable.

Coptic text in this volume is typeset in Antinoou, developed by Michael Everson. Greek text is typeset in IFAO Grec, conceived by Jean-Luc Fournet for the Institut français d'archéologie orientale, and developed by Ralph Hancock with the assistance of Adam Bülow-Jacobsen. Arabic text is typeset in Scheherazade, developed by the SIL. Ethiopic text is typeset in Ethiopic Lessan, developed by the Senamirmir Project. Syriac text is typeset using East Syriac Adiabene, part of the Meltho fonts package from Beth Mardutho: The Syriac Institute.

Contributors to this volume

This volume was produced under the direction of Korshi Dosoo, who is also the primary author of the introduction. Both he and Markéta Preininger, the second author, were involved in every aspect of the volume, from initial conception to publication, and are jointly responsible for all of the manuscript introductions, editions, notes, and the glossary. Edward O.D. Love was involved in some way in the work which lies behind all of the manuscript editions in the volume, either collecting their metadata, producing tracings, working on apparatuses, or as one of the primary text editors. Julia Schwarzer participated in the editions of several of the manuscripts, worked extensively as a researcher on various aspects of the volume, including the identification of Biblical passages, produced most of the tracings, and was involved with many of the practical aspects of the volume's creation, including the *index locorum*, the index of Arabic words and, with Markéta Preininger, the indices of Greek words and abbreviations. Selina Schuster was responsible for most of the initial work of layout, as well as the formatting and the bibliography. Roxanne Bélanger Sarrazin cooperated with the team externally to produce several editions in this publication. For some of the more complex tracings (those on pp. 310, 320, 366), automatic binarisation was carried out by Raquel Martín Hernández using the techniques described in Martín Hernández/Shaus 2022, before being manually touched up by Julia Schwarzer.

Using this volume

The volume is intended to accommodate a broad audience. For students and enthusiasts without knowledge of Coptic, we provide English translation and commentaries to the texts. For experts in Coptic and papyrology and other specialists, we provide detailed information on acquisition of the manuscripts, hands, dialect, and a detailed apparatus and index of Greek and Coptic words and abbreviations at the end. A glossary at the end of the book gives brief definitions of some of the most common concepts and expressions found in the manuscripts.

This volume exists in a symbiotic relationship with the *Kyprianos* online database. Every manuscript has an ID number in this database, given in the section "other references" in the introduction to each papyrus in the form KYP M(anuscript) followed by the number; each individual textual unit also has a reference, KYP T(ext) + number. These allow the manuscripts and their constituent texts to be consulted online, and doing so will allow readers to see any updates or corrections, or additional bibliography, which has appeared since the publication of this volume.

Table of Contents

Introduction
1. Situating Coptic Magical Texts 1
   1.1. The Christian Magical Tradition in History 1
   1.2. The Coptic Language 9
2. The Study of Coptic Magical Texts 11
3. The Corpus of Coptic Magical Texts 15
   3.1. Contexts of Production and Deposition 15
   3.2. Categories of Texts 20
   3.3. Materiality 26
   3.4. Language 29
   3.5. Structure 30
4. The Presentation of Texts in this Volume 37
   4.1. Principles of Edition 37
   4.2. Layout, Notes and Apparatus 38
   4.3. Palaeographical Descriptions 41
5. The Contents of *Papyri Copticae Magicae* I 43

Text Editions
PCM I 1. *P.Kell.* V *Copt.* 35: Letter of Oualēs to Psais containing separation spell 47
PCM I 2. P.Vindob. K 5520: Healing prescription to stop uterine bleeding ... 54
PCM I 3. P.Mich.Inv. 1190: Two aggressive procedures targeting women 58
PCM I 4. P.Mil.Vogl.Copt. 16: Miniature codex 68
PCM I 5. P.Berol. 11918: Procedure for the healing of internal organs 77
PCM I 6–8. The Schmidt Coptic Magical Dossier 80
  PCM I 6. Hs.Schmidt 1: Horus-Isis narrative charm for sleep or love 82
  PCM I 7. Hs.Schmidt 2: Love spell using Horus-Isis narrative charm 87
  PCM I 8. P.Mich.Inv. 4932f: Love spell invoking oil 93
PCM I 9. *BKU* I 22: Formula for sleep 99
PCM I 10. *P.Morgan Copt.* 10: Prayer for pregnancy 103
PCM I 11. AMS 9: Leiden Anastasy Codex 109
PCM I 12. Rossi's Tractate 172
PCM I 13. Rossi's Fragmentary Tractate 221
PCM I 14. LACMA MA 80.202.214: Invocation for unclear purposes 225
PCM I 15. O.Brit.Mus.Copt. 27: Narrative charm for healing the eye 228

PCM I 16. *O.BYU Mag.* 1–3: Ostraca containing Horus-Isis narrative
    love charm 232
PCM I 17. P.CtYBR inv. 1791: Spell for a good singing voice and love spell 238
PCM I 18. P.CtYBR inv. 1800 qua: Curse to cause sickness. 247
PCM I 19. *P.Rosicrucian Mag.Copt.*: Adjuration to protect virginity
    and marriage 251
PCM I 20. P.Donadoni: Love spell in the form of a Horus-Isis
    narrative charm 254
PCM I 21–29. The Heidelberg Coptic Magical Library 259
    PCM I 21. *P.Bad.* V 141: Parchment formulary containing curse (?) 265
    PCM I 22. *P.Bad.* V 139: Parchment sheet with procedures for favour and
        cursing 269
    PCM I 23. *P.Bad.* V 137: Parchment sheet with two curses 274
    PCM I 24. *P.Bad.* V 140: Parchment sheet with silencing curse and a love
        spell 281
    PCM I 25. *Pap.Heid. N.F.* IX: Book of Mary and the Angels 287
    PCM I 26. P.Heid.Inv. Kopt. 686: *Endoxon* of the Archangel Michael. . . . 324
    PCM I 27. *P.Bad.* V 142: Curses of hatefulness and separation 362
    PCM I 28. *P.Bad.* V 122: Love spell of Cyprian 369
    PCM I 29. *P.Bad.* V 138: Curse using narrative charm and further
        prescription(s) 398
PCM I 30. *P.Heid.Kopt.* 4: Two curses drawing on the *Testament of Solomon* 405
PCM I 31. P.Heid.Äg.Slg.inv. Kopt. 1030: Two separation spells 413
PCM I 32. *P.Bad.* V 131: Parchment bifolio with two preserved love spells . 421
PCM I 33. *P.Bad.* V 133: Formulary with healing procedures 432
PCM I 34. *P.Stras.Copt.* 9: Bifolio with bowl divination procedure
    and silencing curses 436
PCM I 35. *P.Bad.* V 135: Fragmentary formulary with various curses 447
PCM I 36. P.Köln. XV 641: Three healing prescriptions on paper 454
PCM I 37. Leiden F 1964/4.14: Parchment sheet with various prescriptions . 459

Indices
Glossary 471
Concordance of texts in this volume 489
Index locorum 491
    Books of the Hebrew Bible and New Testament 491
    Manuscripts and Papyri 493
    Literary Works 502
Bibliography 505
    Abbreviations 505
    Works Cited 507
Word Indices for *PCM* I 555

I. Personal names and *voces magicae* 555
II. Place-names and Ethnonyms. 564
III. Numbers. 565
IV. Calendrical Vocabulary 566
V. Abbreviations. 566
VI. Words of Arabic Origin 568
VII. Words of Greek Origin. 569
VIII. Words of Egyptian Origin. 579
Plates 605

List of Plates

Plate I. *PCM* I 9 (*BKU* I 22) front. © Staatliche Museen zu Berlin – Ägyptisches Museum und Papyrussammlung, Inv. Nr. 5565.

Plate II. *PCM* I 20 (P.Donadoni) front. Photography: Massimo Giuseppetti. Image courtesy of the Donadoni family.

Plate III. *PCM* I 20 (P.Donadoni) back. Photography: Massimo Giuseppetti. Image courtesy of the Donadoni family.

Plate IV. *PCM* I 28 (*P.Bad.* V 122) pages 16 & 1. Photography: Elke Fuchs © Institut für Papyrologie, Universität Heidelberg.

Plate V. *PCM* I 28 (*P.Bad.* V 122) pages 2 & 15. Photography: Elke Fuchs © Institut für Papyrologie, Universität Heidelberg.

Plate VI. *PCM* I 28 (*P.Bad.* V 122) pages 14 & 3. Photography: Elke Fuchs © Institut für Papyrologie, Universität Heidelberg.

Plate VII. *PCM* I 28 (*P.Bad.* V 122) pages 4 & 13. Photography: Elke Fuchs © Institut für Papyrologie, Universität Heidelberg.

Plate VIII. *PCM* I 28 (*P.Bad.* V 122) pages 12 & 5. Photography: Elke Fuchs © Institut für Papyrologie, Universität Heidelberg.

Plate IX. *PCM* I 28 (*P.Bad.* V 122) pages 6 & 11. Photography: Elke Fuchs © Institut für Papyrologie, Universität Heidelberg.

Plate X. *PCM* I 28 (*P.Bad.* V 122) pages 10 & 7. Photography: Elke Fuchs © Institut für Papyrologie, Universität Heidelberg.

Plate XI. *PCM* I 28 (*P.Bad.* V 122) pages 8 & 9. Photography: Elke Fuchs © Institut für Papyrologie, Universität Heidelberg.

Plate XII. *PCM* I 32 (*P.Bad.* V 131) page 2. Photography: Elke Fuchs © Institut für Papyrologie, Universität Heidelberg.

Plate XIII. *PCM* I 34 (*P.Stras.Copt.* 9) pages 4 & 1. Coll. and photogr. Bnu de Strasbourg.

Plate XIV. *PCM* I 34 (*P.Stras.Copt.* 9) pages 2 & 3. Coll. and photogr. Bnu de Strasbourg.

Plate XV. *PCM* I 35 (*P.Bad.* V 135) front. Photography: Elke Fuchs © Institut für Papyrologie, Universität Heidelberg.

Plate XVI. *PCM* I 35 (*P.Bad.* V 135) back. Photography: Elke Fuchs © Institut für Papyrologie, Universität Heidelberg.

List of Critical Signs

[ ]	Gap due to damage in the writing surface
[…]	Presumed number of lost letters
⟦ ⟧	Deletion by copyist
\αβγ/	Letters written above the line
/αβγ\	Letters written below the line
{ }	Deletion by the editor
⟨ ⟩	Addition or emendation by editor
( )	Resolution of an abbreviation
. . . .	Unreadable letters
α̣β̣γ̣	Damaged or uncertain letters
|⁵	Line change
- - - - -	Papyrus broken
*Iao	Word appears in the glossary
Iao?	Translation uncertain
vac.	Vacat (unwritten space)

Introduction

The texts presented in this volume are those defined by scholars as 'magical', written in the Coptic language on papyrus and other supports (parchment, paper, wood, ostraca). Both of these terms—"magical" and "Coptic"—require some explanation. This introduction will begin by offering brief presentations of what it means for a text to be defined as "magical" in the context of papyrology, and then give an overview of the Coptic language. This will be followed by a short history of the study of Coptic magical texts. The next part of the introduction will provide a summary of the manuscripts and texts contained in this volume in terms of their materiality and structure, before we end by presenting the volume's conception and principles—how the editions of texts are organised and how they may be understood.

1. Situating Coptic Magical Texts
1.1. The Christian Magical Tradition in History

In the context of papyrology, the term "magic" refers to manuscripts containing a specific genre of ritual texts. These are texts attesting to a range of private, non-institutional ritual traditions, whose typical features (more fully discussed in 3.5 below) include the use of "magical words" (*voces magicae*), "magical symbols" (*kharaktēres*), and particular verbal and ritual practices.[1] Likewise, the texts reflect a recurrent set of concerns—they aim to achieve specific goals, including healing disease, casting out demons, protecting their user from hostile magic, cursing enemies, manipulating relationships (gaining social success, separating friends or couples, causing men and women to be attracted to one another), and divining the future through the consultation of superhuman beings.[2]

The use of the term "magic" to refer to such texts in the context of papyrology began in the early nineteenth century in reference to Greek magical papyri.[3] Thus, it predates and does not relate directly to questions of the relationship of magic and religion, magic as marginal religion, or magic as a specific mode of rationality which became key concerns in the wake of the work of late nineteenth and early twentieth century scholars such as James Frazer, Henri Hubert and Marcel Mauss,

---

[1] For other introductions to Coptic magical texts and their wider context, see van der Vliet 2014 & 2019b; Bélanger Sarrazin 2017; Dosoo/Love/Preininger 2022: 51–56.

[2] For an overview of the types of rituals found in these texts, see Dosoo/Love/Preininger 2022: 58–62.

[3] *Cf.* Dosoo 2021a: 677–679 & forthcoming a.

and Bronisław Malinowski.⁴

These older magical Greek and Demotic papyri are today understood as one piece of evidence for a larger Graeco-Egyptian magical tradition.⁵ Such texts survive from the first century BCE to around the fifth century CE, and seem to represent an innovative textual and ritual tradition which draws upon older Egyptian and Greek, and to a lesser extent Jewish and Mesopotamian, ritual practices. These traditions existed alongside one another in the multi-ethnic Egypt of the Ptolemaic and Roman periods, in which the native Egyptian majority lived under the rule of Greek-speaking elites, and alongside large numbers of immigrants from around the Mediterranean, including the Near East.⁶ The earliest examples of Coptic-language magical texts occur in a few of the predominantly Greek manuscripts of the Graeco-Egyptian magical tradition, but these are generally non-Christian, centred on traditional Egyptian deities, and written in a form of the language different from the standard Coptic used by Christians.⁷

The Graeco-Egyptian magical papyri were produced in a period of dramatic historical changes. Within Egypt, the traditional temple cults show a precipitous decline from the third century onwards, so that few temples lasted beyond the second half of the fourth century CE.⁸ The reasons for this are still imperfectly understood, but seem to be linked to changes in the Roman policy, which restricted the temples' economic base while reducing the amount of direct support that they received from the imperial administration. The second major event was the rise of Christianity; Egyptian Christians claim that their faith arrived in Egypt in the mid-first century CE with Saint Mark, the author of the gospel of the same name. More concretely, Egyptian Christian authors are known from the second century, but the community was likely small, and restricted to the area around Alexandria.

---

⁴ *Cf.* Dosoo 2021a: 677–679; Dosoo forthcoming a. The key works associated with each of these authors are Frazer's *Golden Bough* (in particular, the 1925 abridged edition), Hubert/Mauss' *Esquisse d'une théorie générale de la magie* (1902–1903, translation in Mauss 1972), and Malinowski's *Coral Gardens and their Magic* (1935). Helpful overviews of these theoretical approaches may be found in Tambiah 1990 and Sørensen 2007: 9–28. See also the reflections on the function of the term "magic" in Bohak 2009: 110–112; Sanzo 2020.

⁵ For overviews of the Graeco-Egyptian corpus, see Brashear 1995; Dieleman 2005; Dieleman 2019. For texts from this corpus, see Preisendanz/Henrichs 1973–1974; Betz 1986; Daniel/Maltomini 1990–1992; Faraone/Torallas Tovar 2022a, b.

⁶ *Cf.* Dieleman 2005: 285–294; Dosoo forthcoming b.

⁷ Magical texts written in Old Coptic script include BM EA 10808/*GEMF* 14 (KYP M545); *PGM* III/*GEMF* 55 (KYP M154) ll. 410–423, 633–731; *PGM* IV/*GEMF* 57 (KYP M3) ll. 1–21, 81–153 (*cf.* the Egyptian passage written purely in Greek characters in ll. 1231–1239 (*cf.* n. 13 below)); compare also *GEMF* 16/*PDM* xiv (KYP M162), which uses Old Coptic script for glosses, and the Old Coptic Schmidt Papyrus (KYP M524), a letter to a god written in Old Coptic (for which see Love 2022e: 225–456, with further references *ad loc.*). For discussions, see Satzinger 1994; Love 2016.

⁸ On the decline of the Egyptian temples, see Bagnall 1988; Bagnall 2008; Dijkstra 2008; Fournet 2020b; *cf.* Monson 2012: 131–141; Connor 2022; Sippel 2022.

This changed in the third century, when Demetrius (r. 188–230 CE), the bishop of Alexandria, began to appoint other bishops in the *khōra* (Egypt outside Alexandria), and the first mentions of Christians in surviving papyri occur shortly afterwards.[9] Christians nonetheless remained a sporadically persecuted minority until the fourth century,[10] when the Emperor Constantine and his successors made Christianity first a licit religion (313 CE), and then the state religion of the Roman Empire. Christians in Egypt went from being a small minority (perhaps *ca.* 10%) at the beginning of the fourth century to a majority (*ca.* 70%) by the end of it, and virtually the entire population of Egypt by the middle of the fifth.[11]

This had a major consequence for the magical tradition, which had continued to exist and evolve alongside Christianity. Magic, like Christianity, was distrusted and punished by the Roman state; early Christian rituals may often have looked like magic to non-Christians.[12] One of the earliest surviving Christian ritual texts, an exorcism written in a non-standard version of Coptic, is found in a fourth-century magical manual which otherwise primarily consists of texts belonging to the Graeco-Egyptian tradition. The manual's compiler must have considered the exorcism as part of the same broad category of ritual practice.[13] The pre-existing distrust of magic among some members of the Graeco-Roman elite was taken up by Christians and combined with the Jewish injunction against rituals defined as *kišuf* ("sorcery") to create a strong anti-magic discourse within Christianity.[14] Early canons and council proceedings defining how Christians should behave forbade the baptism of "magicians" (*magoi*) and similar figures, and prescribed penance for those who practiced or made use of magic.[15]

By the fourth century, the "Great Church"—that form of Christianity sponsored by the Imperial authorities and headed by bishops—had developed its own suite of rituals, known as the Christian liturgical tradition. This included the regularly-performed anaphora—the consecration of bread and wine for the communion ritual—as well as others for more specific needs, such as exorcising demons and healing illness.[16] These latter practically-oriented rituals could overlap in terms of function with those of the magical tradition and were promoted by bishops as

---

[9] See Wipszycka 2015: 60–74. On Christianity in Egypt more generally, see Choat 2012a.

[10] For a recent discussion, see Luijendijk 2008: 155–226.

[11] Depauw/Clarysse 2013; *cf.* the reflections in Choat 2006: 52–55; Frankfurter 2014; Depauw/Clarysse 2015.

[12] For the Roman legal measures against the practice of "magic", see Pharr 1932; Phillips 1991; Kippenberg 1997; Rives 2003; Rives 2006; for the association of magic with Christians, see Origen, *Against Celsus* 1.6, 29, 38, 68, 6.38–41; *cf.* Stratton 2007: 117–120; Bremmer 2002: 54–56.

[13] *PGM* IV/*GEMF* 57.1227–1264; see the discussion in Rist 1938: 289–303.

[14] Harari 2019.

[15] On Christian opposition to magic, see Dickie 2001: 251–272; de Bruyn 2017: 17–42; Sanzo 2019b: 221–223; van der Vliet 2019a; Dosoo 2021b: 49–50, 52–54.

[16] For the Christian liturgical tradition, see Johnson 1995: 111–277; Johnson 2010; Mihálykó 2019, and for the relationship of magic to liturgical texts, see Kropp 1930: III 180–244.

alternatives to them. Yet the magical tradition did not disappear, despite the efforts of the Christian hierarchy; rather it underwent what we can characterise as a series of parallel and overlapping processes of Christianisation.[17]

The first way in which the magical tradition might become Christian is simply related to context. A few texts were transmitted with little change for centuries; these included narrative charms containing stories of the traditional Egyptian gods, which circulated in Egypt until the ninth century or so.[18] Yet, merely by virtue of existing in a primarily Christian context, they began to reflect this context—the degree of traditional religious content atrophied, so that the divine protagonists became little more than names, while references to the Christian God began to be incorporated.[19]

This changed context likely also led to the preferential survival and transmission of texts which circulated prior to Christianity, but which were already amenable to a Christian audience.[20] While many of the magical texts dating to before the fifth century contain mention of the deities of Greek and Egyptian cults (Osiris, Anubis, Selene, Hekate, and so on), this is not true of all of them. The magical tradition also made extensive use of Jewish names—the personal name and titles of the Jewish God, *Iao Sabaoth Adonai, and the names of angels such as Michael and Gabriel.[21] It is often unclear whether these were used by Jews, Christians, or gentiles—or most likely all three—but they become more frequent in texts from Egypt from around the third century, perhaps as a result of the rise in prominence of Christianity. Likewise, many of the "magical names" were not linked to any real cults and so could be reinterpreted by Jews and Christians. 'Abrasax', a name with solar associations within the Graeco-Egyptian tradition, was reinterpreted as the name of the angel of the sun in Jewish and Christian magic.[22] Many magical texts which circulated before the Christianisation of the Roman Empire could thus continue to be used in an only slightly modified form.

Another way in which magic could be made Christian is in the composition of new texts, which drew upon the techniques of the magical tradition—the use of *voces magicae*, *kharaktēres*, and so on—but called exclusively upon figures from the Jewish-Christian tradition, and which made use of the ritual techniques of the Christian liturgical tradition.[23] This process seems to have begun in the early centuries CE, when the first stages of the handbook known as the *Testament of Solomon* may have been composed.[24] But many of the texts which survive in

---

[17] *Cf.* de Bruyn 2017.

[18] These are discussed below at 3.2.3.

[19] *Cf.* Blumell/Dosoo 2018: 244–250 *et passim*; van der Vliet 2018a: 158–160; Zellmann-Rohrer/Love 2022: 61–64.

[20] On this process, *cf.* Bélanger Sarrazin forthcoming a.

[21] Bohak 2008: 194–214.

[22] See *Abrasax in the glossary.

[23] Compare the discussions in de Bruyn 2017; van der Vliet 2020.

[24] See the introduction to *PCM* I 38 for a fuller discussion of the *Testament of Solomon* and

the Coptic magical tradition seem to be later compositions, dating to the period between the fifth and seventh centuries.

In the earlier Graeco-Egyptian tradition, works were often attributed to famous authors—the Persian priests called *magoi*, Egyptian kings and priests, or Greek philosophers and sages[25]—and this continued in the Christian texts, which could be attributed to Biblical figures, famous saints, and even angels.[26] Just as in the Graeco-Egyptian tradition, however, these longer pseudepigraphal texts are complemented by shorter, anonymous recipes of a similar type, which constitute the majority of surviving texts.

The Christian magical tradition seems to originally have been Greek in language, but in Egypt it was translated very quickly into Coptic, the contemporary written form of the native Egyptian language. It is in Coptic that the vast majority of Christian magical texts from the Egypt of the first millennium CE survive. The papyrological evidence from Egypt suggests that Christian magical texts flourished in the centuries following the Christianisation of Egypt, but clerical opposition remained. We continue to find church canons and sermons from bishops from this period denouncing the practice of magic, even when it appeared to be Christian. The sixth-century *Gelasian Decree*, a list of forbidden books from the Western Roman Empire, lists among them "all amulets which have been composed, not by angels, as they pretend, but by the magical arts of demons".[27] Yet the need to repeat bans on magic demonstrates that, like the apocryphal literary works which also appear in the *Decree*, Christian magic continued to enjoy considerable popularity among both laypeople and clerics.

While we have been discussing Christianity as a monolithic object, the textual and material evidence from Egypt demonstrates its great diversity. Relevant for us here is the phenomenon of Sethian Gnosticism, a movement within Christianity which saw Jesus as a revealer sent by the true God to unveil the saving "knowledge" (*gnōsis*) that the world was a creation of the lesser deity of the Hebrew Bible, which could be escaped through secret rituals.[28] The only primary sources for Sethian Gnosticism come from Egypt, primarily fourth and fifth-century Coptic codices, including those of the famous Nag Hammadi Library. Another religion related to Christianity, Manichaeism, developed in Mesopotamia in the middle of

---

further references.

[25] See Dieleman 2005: 263–275; Suárez de la Torre 2014.

[26] In this volume, see for example the *Prayer of Mary 'in Bartos'* (*PCM* I 25 pp. 2–9), the *Endoxon of the Archangel Michael* (*PCM* I 26), the *Love Spell of Cyprian* (*PCM* I 28), and the texts based on the *Testament of Solomon* (*PCM* I 30 & *PCM* I 36 ll. 13–15).

[27] *Gelasian Decree* 244–245, in von Dobschütz 1912: 74–75.

[28] See Brakke 2010; Burns 2019, for helpful overviews. Note that while here we present 'Sethian Gnosticism' as a Christian movement, other scholars see it as having a more complex relationship to Christianity, either being originally derived directly from Jewish sources and only later taking on Christian trappings, or existing in a border space between Christian and Jewish traditions; see *inter alia* Yamauchi 2003; Burns 2014.

the third century, reaching Egypt via missionaries towards the end of that century.[29] It saw itself as the culmination of previous revelations by Zoroaster, Moses, the Buddha, and Jesus, and envisaged the world as a battleground between the forces of light and darkness, in which human beings would be reborn until they were able to return to the realm of light through ritual purification and good deeds. Well-attested in Egypt by papyri in Greek, Coptic, and Syriac, Egyptian Manichaeism disappears from the archaeological record in the fifth century, likely a victim to Imperial and Christian hostility.[30] Both of these movements have left traces in the papyri published here—the earliest Coptic magical text we publish (*PCM* I 1) comes from a Manichaean household, and many of the others contain names taken from, or reminiscent of, the divinities of Sethian Gnosticism, a feature shared by a few later Coptic apocryphal literary texts.[31]

While these 'alternative Christianities' left only traces, a major split in the Christian tradition in Egypt occurred at the Council of Chalcedon in 451 CE, at which the head of the Egyptian Church, Dioscorus I, Patriarch of Alexandria, was deposed. Dioscorus had supported the miaphysite position, that Jesus had one nature, at once human and divine, while the larger Imperial Church supported the dyophysite position that Jesus existed in two natures, one human, one divine.[32] This event would ultimately divide the Egyptian Church, creating a situation in which Alexandria has generally had two patriarchs, one Miaphysite, one Chalcedonian. The patriarchates of Peter IV (r. 576–78) and his successor Damian (r. 576–605) created a distinct Miaphysite hierarchy of bishops, existing in parallel to the Chalcedonian hierarchy (and, indeed, other, smaller factions).[33] This miaphysite church is the predecessor to the modern Coptic Orthodox Church, which expanded after the Muslim conquest of Egypt (642 CE), becoming the numerically dominant Christian church in Egypt.[34] Whether they were always the majority is unclear; the Chalcedonian Church (whose modern successors include the Greek Orthodox and Roman Catholic Churches) was supported by the Imperial state and many of the Egyptian elites; it has been suggested that they controlled the cities while the

---

[29] For brief overviews, see BeDuhn 2000; Teigen 2021: 1–21; Brand 2022: 5–12.

[30] *Cf.* the overview in Gardner/Lieu 1996; Gardner 2022: 295–305.

[31] For the relationship between Sethian Gnosticism and magic, see Burns 2018; Choat 2019; Piwowarczyk 2020.

[32] In the past the miaphysite churches were usually referred to as 'monophysite', but this term is generally rejected by modern members of non-Chalcedonian churches, who prefer 'miaphysite' (*cf.* Awad/Moawad 1999; Farag 2011). For a fuller discussion of the theological questions, see Farag 2014. The term 'miaphysite' has been strongly criticised by Luisier 2014 as being both misleading (since he finds the theological differences with dyophysitism minimal) and an unacceptable Greek formation, but it remains widely used; alternatives include simply 'non-Chalcedonian' and henophysite.

[33] Booth 2017; Dekker 2018: 4–9 *et passim*; *cf.* Mikhail 2016: 10–15.

[34] Mikhail 2016: 60–64.

Miaphysites controlled the countryside.³⁵ It is following the rift at Chalcedon that the Miaphysite Church started to develop a distinctively Egyptian identity—albeit one with close links to their Miaphysite brethren in Syria, Armenia, Nubia, and Ethiopia—and it is in the sixth century, around the time of the patriarchate of Damian that we begin to see major original literary compositions in Coptic rather than translations from Greek; it may be that many of the magical texts contained here belong to this same period of creativity.³⁶

In the seventh century, Egypt would be definitively severed from the Roman Empire when, in 642 CE, it was conquered by the Muslim armies under the successors of Muhammad. But cultural change seems to have been slow. The new rulers initially left much of the Late Roman administration in place, and made no concerted effort to convert the population to Islam.³⁷ It was only in the eighth century that Arabic gradually replaced Greek as the language of administration.³⁸ While an Arabic-Muslim magical tradition would develop—in part through contact with the older Greek tradition³⁹—the Christian magical tradition shows little hint of the changed cultural realities until the ninth century or so, when Arabic loanwords begin to appear, mainly as the names of ingredients, in texts which otherwise belong to the same tradition as those transmitted before the conquest.⁴⁰ This shift in the ninth century is likely due to the larger socio-political forces at work—it was in the ninth century that the last major revolts against Arab-Muslim rule took place, and in their wake, the rate of conversion of Egyptians to Islam increased, and even Christians began to use Arabic in their daily lives.⁴¹ This process culminated during the period of the Baḥrī Mamlūks (1250–1382 CE); Christians became a minority of about 10% of the population of Egypt, as they remain to today.⁴² Coptic became a primarily written, rather than spoken language, which had to be learned by priests for recital in the liturgy; no substantial original texts were composed between the fourteenth and twentieth centuries.⁴³ This period marks the end of the production of Coptic-language magical texts, which ceased

---

³⁵ Wipszycka 2015: 140–146 (arguing for the predominance of the Chalcedonians in the cities); Mikhail 2016: 14–15 (arguing for the numerical majority of the Miaphysites), 27–28, 38–39, 55 (on Chalcedonian adherence among elites); Booth 2017: 160 (arguing that whether the Miaphysites were always the majority is unknowable); Dekker 2018: 146–47, 278–279 *et passim* (arguing against the restriction of Miaphysite bishops to the countryside).

³⁶ Orlandi 1998; Orlandi 2005; Buzi 2021.

³⁷ Frantz-Murphy 2004; Sijpesteijn 2013: 48–111.

³⁸ Richter 2010: 214–215 *et passim*; Sijpesteijn 2013: 104.

³⁹ The literature on Arabic-language magic is extensive. For some works offering introductions, see Saif *et al.* 2020; Bsees 2019; Coulon 2017.

⁴⁰ Love 2022a: 182–195.

⁴¹ O'Sullivan 2006; Richter 2009: 417–434; Sijpesteijn 2013: 105–113; Wissa 2020; *cf.* Lev 2012; Mikhail 2016: 118–127.

⁴² Little 1976; Bulliet 1979: 92–99; O'Sullivan 2006.

⁴³ Richter 2009: 426–434; Zakrzewska 2014: 84–87.

to be copied and composed around the twelfth century, like most other types of Coptic-language texts.

Christian Egyptians continued to practice magic, often using texts translated or inspired by older Coptic-language texts, but also increasingly influenced by the Muslim magical tradition which existed around them.[44] The most prominent of the later texts are the *Guides to the Psalms* which contain ritual instructions for various purposes using the text of the Psalms as the spoken formulae.[45] Coptic-language magic, however, was just one branch of a larger Christian magical tradition, perhaps originally linguistically Greek, but translated into and then elaborated in many local languages. Magical texts which share close affinities with those in Coptic can be found in Mediaeval and/or early modern texts in languages such as Armenian, Greek, Syriac, Old Nubian, and Ge'ez (the liturgical language of Ethiopia), with a few texts sharing not only specific magical names or practices, but also representing parallel versions of especially popular texts which survive in Coptic.[46] The Coptic tradition, like all of these others, demonstrates particularities, the result of original composition as well as local Christian and pre-Christian specificities. One important aspect of the Coptic magical corpus is its early date. Thanks to the dry climate of Upper Egypt, many texts survive in Coptic which are many centuries older than the copies preserved in other Christian traditions. These copies allow us a privileged perspective on the complex process by which 'magic' became 'Christian'.

Before leaving behind the history of Coptic magic, it is worth briefly mentioning

---

[44] For examples of Copto-Arabic magical texts (*i.e.*, magical texts used by Egyptian Christians and written in Arabic), see Khater 1970; Viaud 1977; Henein/Bianquis 1975, and see the discussions in Fodor 1978; Viaud 1978; Budelli 2014.

[45] Published *Copto-Arabic examples include Khater 1970; Henein/Bianquis 1975; Viaud 1977; *cf.* Fodor 1978. For Greek examples, see Zellmann-Rohrer 2018a & 2022b, and for Ethiopian examples, see Strelcyn 1981. Earlier Coptic examples exist, but are currently unpublished; an early example on papyrus is P.Duke inv. 460 (KYP M404; *cf.* Zellmann-Rohrer 2022b: 1116 with n. 3), although the best-dated is Collège de France Ms. 3 (KYP M597), with a colophon dating to 1035 CE; *cf.* Pezin 1983.

[46] For Armenian magical texts, see Wingate 1930; Feydit 1986; Vardanyan 2012, and for a discussion see Russell 2011. For Christian Greek magic, see Delatte 1927; Marathakis 2012; Zellmann-Rohrer 2018a, and for discussions, see Greenfield 1988; Maguire 1995; Zellmann-Rohrer 2016 & 2019; Afentoulidou 2021. For Syriac magical texts, see Hazard 1893; Gollancz 1912; Lyavdansky 2011; Cherkashina (Nurullina) 2012 & 2021; Cherkashina/Kuzin 2022; Cherkashina/Lyavdansky 2021 & 2022; Dickens/Smelova 2021; Cherkashina/Cherkashin/Saar 2022, and for discussions see Hunter 1987 & 1990; Moriggi/Bhayro 2022. For Greek and Old Nubian magical texts from Christian Nubia, see Hägg 1993; Ruffini 2012; Łajtar/van der Vliet 2011 & 2017. For Ge'ez magical texts, see Basset 1892 & 1984; Worrell 1909, 1910 & 1915; Grohmann 1917–1918; Euringer 1928 & 1937; Griaule 1930; Strelcyn 1955; Strelcyn 1981; and for discussions and overviews, see Rodinson 1967; Young 1970 & 1975; Mercier/Mercier 1974; Mercier 1988; Chernetsov 2005 & 2006; Mulugetta 2015; Kebede 2017; de Ménonville 2018a & b; Derillo 2019; Malara 2022.

its complex relationship with medicine.⁴⁷ Coptic magical and medical texts can often be distinguished based on the practices they contain: medical texts aim to heal the body through the application of pharmacological agents or the use of basic surgical interventions. While magical texts for healing may involve such medical techniques as the use of plasters, fumigation, or salves, they often accompany them with other elements, such as spoken formulae and the wearing of amulets.⁴⁸ Coptic magical and medical texts are generally transmitted in different manuscripts, which contain recipes belonging primarily to one genre or the other, and magical healing recipes often occur alongside texts for other purposes, such as love spells, curses, and divination. Yet there is also overlap; as we note below (3.1.1), there is evidence of medical doctors using magical texts, and we do sometimes find magical and medical texts transmitted in the same manuscripts. In these cases, and those of recipes which involve the preparation of pharmacological agents similar to those found in medical texts, but simply add a spoken formula, the theoretical line between magic and medicine may be very fuzzy.

1.2. The Coptic Language

We have described Coptic-language magical texts as part of a larger, primarily Greek-language Christian tradition which developed in Late Antiquity and which existed both within and beyond Egypt. This does not mean that it is without unique characteristics; several texts feature Pharaonic Egyptian deities whom we would not expect to find in non-Coptic texts, while other texts reflect theological details particular to Egyptian Christianity. Furthermore the Coptic-language magical texts show an occasional but recurrent interest in adapting healing prayers into curses and love spells which we do not find in other traditions.⁴⁹

In this volume, "Coptic" is a linguistic designation, describing the written form of the native Egyptian language as it existed in the first millennium CE, descended from its older forms. Pre-Coptic Egyptian texts survive from the third millennium BCE to the fifth century CE, written in the native hieroglyphic, hieratic, and, later, demotic scripts. Coptic is thus the descendant of the older forms of Egyptian in the same way that modern Italian is descended from Latin. But with the arrival of the Greek language in Egypt around the time of the conquest of Alexander (332 BCE),

---

⁴⁷ For Coptic medical texts, see Till 1951; Richter 2014b; Richter 2016b; Grons 2021; Grons 2022; Grons forthcoming.

⁴⁸ For discussions of the distinction between medical and magical texts in Coptic, see van der Vliet 2019b: 334–335; Dosoo 2021b: 61–2; Grons 2021: 124; Dosoo 2022c: 521–22. Note that we are here making a distinction between textual genres, rather than a larger theoretical point about the difference between 'magic' and 'medicine' as cross-cultural categories.

⁴⁹ See *PCM* I 28 & 31, as well as the unpublished Montserrat, Abadia Inv. 604 + 1235 (KYP M30), which seems to represent a love spell drawing on the *Prayer of Mary* (for which see *PCM* I 25, pp. 1–9).

Egyptians began experimenting with writing their language in the Greek script, producing early instances of 'Graeco-Egyptian' writing, generally short texts such as graffiti or personal names.[50] By the early centuries CE, Egyptian priests were using mixed systems of Greek supplemented by Demotic signs, first to annotate texts written in older forms of the language, and later to write continuous texts; these various systems are known as 'Old Coptic'.[51] Sometime around the late third or early fourth century, one of these Old Coptic systems began to be used by Christians for purposes including the translation of the Greek Bible into Egyptian and the writing of private letters, creating the basis for standard Coptic.[52] This language remained Egyptian in grammar and basic vocabulary, but was written using the Greek alphabet of 24 letters, supplemented by 6–7 letters (depending on the dialect) drawn from Demotic to represent sounds not present in Greek. Coptic also incorporated a significant number of loanwords from Greek, the result of the influence of that language in the spheres of religion (as the language of Christianity) and political power (as the language of the Roman administration).[53]

It is likely that the Egyptian language was always made up of multiple dialects, but this diversity was concealed by older writing systems which tended to represent single dialectal varieties.[54] Coptic, by contrast, was very diverse, with different dialects representing standardised versions of the different forms of Egyptian spoken throughout the Nile Valley and the oases. It was also diverse in its use; in the third to fifth centuries, Coptic was also used to write Hermetic, Sethian and Valentinian Gnostic, and Manichaean texts translated from Greek (or, in the case of the Manichaeans, perhaps Syriac). A form of Egyptian is likely to have been the predominant spoken language of Egypt until the ninth century, when it was replaced by Arabic. Written Coptic would have been close, if not identical, to the spoken language of most Egyptians, making it the written language most readily learned and understood.

In both Coptic and Greek, the Coptic language was referred to simply as "Egyptian", and this holds more or less true for Arabic, in which the term *qubṭ* or *qibṭ* (from Greek Αἰγύπτιος *Aiguptios*) came to refer to non-Arab Egyptians, and thus their language (*al-qibṭiyya*), both contemporary Christians and their non-Christian ancestors.[55] As Arabic became the spoken language of all Egyptians between the ninth and twelfth centuries, Coptic became restricted in role to the liturgical language of the Miaphysite Egyptian church. Thus, when Europeans began to take an interest in Egyptian Christians from the late fifteenth century,

---

[50] On 'Graeco-Egyptian' writing, see Quack 2017.

[51] On Old Coptic, see Kasser 1991a; Satzinger 1991; Richter 2009: 406–416; Quack 2017; Love 2021a, 2021b, 2022d.

[52] Richter 2009: 414–417; Choat 2012b: 586–588; Fournet 2022: 7–16.

[53] For Greek loanwords in Coptic magical texts, see Hevesi 2022.

[54] Allen 2013: 4.

[55] Lane 1863: 2484a *s.v.* قبط; Omar 2013; Sijpesteijn 2021: 349, 355–356.

they encountered them as a minority within Egypt, and referred to them not simply as Egyptians, but as (in Latin) *copti*, an adaptation of the Arabic word. This single word thus came to refer simultaneously to the ethnic group, the Church to which they belonged, and the liturgical language of that Church.[56] Thus, in modern European languages, we often refer to Coptic people, a Coptic Church, and a Coptic language. But when we refer to Coptic magical texts, we are referring only to texts written in the Coptic language, generally at a time when it was the language of almost all Egyptians rather than of a religious minority. Although many of those who used these texts would have considered themselves Christian, and may have belonged to the miaphysite Church, their practices were not generally approved of by the Church hierarchy. In this sense, Coptic magic must be distinguished from the Coptic Church and modern Coptic people, and rather seen as the local Egyptian form of a broader ritual tradition common to contemporary Christians, and shared, to a considerable degree, with their Jewish and Muslim neighbours, who may even have used it at times.[57] Indeed, hundreds of magical texts produced and used by the Egyptian Jewish community from around the tenth century CE onwards survive in the archive known as the 'Cairo Genizah'.[58] Many of these show striking parallels to contemporary Coptic magical texts in their language, structure, and ritual practices. As more Arabic papyri from Egypt are published, we can expect to find comparable similarities with texts produced and used by Muslims.[59]

2. The Study of Coptic Magical Texts

The earliest Coptic magical text to be published by a Western scholar was a short invocation to angels for healing contained in a codex of largely pharmacological medical recipes, published by the Italian scholar Georges Zoega.[60] The first text

---

[56] Hamilton 2006: 24 *et passim*.

[57] For Arabic Muslim magic, see n. 39 above; for Arabic Christian ('Copto-Arabic') magic in Egypt, see n. 44 above. Some Coptic magical texts contain Arabic names, perhaps suggesting Muslim clients; see Love 2022a: 192; Dosoo forthcoming c. *Cf.* n. 58 below.

[58] For texts from the Cairo Genizah, see *MTKG* I–III; Schiffmann/Swartz 1992; Naveh/Shaked 1993: Geniza 9–29; Schäfer/Shaked 1994–1999, and for discussions, see Swartz 1990 & 2006; Wasserstrom 1992; Bohak 1999; Bohak 2005; Saar 2014; Bohak/Saar 2015; Bellusci 2016; Saar 2017 & 2019a. The presence of a few Coptic-language texts in the Genizah suggests the involvement of Jewish Egyptians with Coptic-language magic; these include *P.Lond.Copt.* 524 (KYP M359) and Cambridge UL T-S 12.207 (Crum 1902; KYP M534).

[59] *Cf.* Bsees 2019.

[60] This is Biblioteca Nazionale di Napoli I.B.14.06-07 (KYP M643), edited in Zoega 1810: no. 278; see Zellmann-Rohrer/Love 2022: 181 for a more recent translation. A new edition and commentary is in preparation by Anne Grons. For other overviews of the historiography of the study of Christian magic in Egypt, see van der Vliet 2019b: 323–328; Dosoo/Love/Preininger 2022: 44–48.

to receive major attention, however, was a long invocation of Gabriel and other angels which came to be known as "Rossi's Gnostic Tractate", held in Turin in Italy, and published by Francesco Rossi in 1894 (*PCM* I 12). In describing it as 'gnostic', Rossi—following his predecessor Bernardino Peyron—was responding to features such as magical names and *kharaktēres* similar to those known from recently published gnostic texts.[61]

At the same time, the developing study of Greek magical texts offered an alternative way of understanding similar Coptic texts. The earliest Greek magical texts arrived in Europe in the 1820s, and were published shortly thereafter by scholars who identified them as "magical", recognising in them documents of the practices of *mageia* and *theourgia* ("magic" and "theurgy") described by late antique authors.[62] While there was a brief, and inconsistent, tendency to understand them as evidence of a particularly 'gnostic' magic, this tendency was arrested by the publication of the corpus of the Greek Magical Papyri (*Papyri Graecae Magicae*, 1928–1931), led by the scholar Karl Preisendanz, which brought together all the examples then known, allowing them to be referred to conveniently, and conclusively establishing the label of 'magical', rather than 'gnostic', texts.[63]

As we have noted, most of the Coptic magical papyri seem to represent a Christian variety of the magical tradition represented by the Greek and Demotic magical texts, and scholars, recognising this, began to refer to Coptic magical texts as such, abandoning the label 'gnostic'. Over the next seventy years, most of the publications relating to Coptic magical texts consisted of editions of individual manuscripts, primarily in the context of larger publications of Coptic papyri from various European and American collections. Notable among these was Adolf Erman's publication of the Coptic manuscripts of the (then) Royal Museums of Berlin, which contained a large group of magical papyri, discussed further by him in a series of separate articles.[64]

The major exception to the practice of publication by collection was the work of Angelicus Kropp, a scholar who extensively studied Coptic magical texts as part of his 1930 doctoral dissertation in which he explored their relationship to the Christian liturgy. Kropp published the results of his thesis in the three volume *Ausgewählte koptische Zaubertexte* ("Selected Coptic Magical Texts", 1930–1931), containing one volume each of texts, translations, and interpretation. To

---

[61] These were the Bruce and Askew Codices, held in the United Kingdom, and containing texts from a variety of Gnostic literary traditions, for which see Schwartze/Petermann 1851; Amélineau 1891; *cf.* Dosoo/Love/Preininger 2022: 44–45.

[62] See, *e.g.*, Reuvens 1830: 1ère lettre 16–20, 25–27; Goodwin 1852: iii–vi; *cf.* the discussion in Dosoo forthcoming a.

[63] Preisendanz/Henrichs 1973–1974; Dosoo 2014: 43–44, 47–48; Choat 2019: 217–220.

[64] Erman 1904 (=*BKU* I), of which nos. 1–20, 22–28; no. 22 is republished in this volume as *PCM* I. 9. The magical texts published in *BKU* I are discussed in more detail in Erman 1895 & 1917.

this day, this remains the only real full study of the corpus. Kropp would later go on to publish studies of two major Coptic magical texts republished in this volume, the *Endoxon of Michael* (*PCM* I 26) and the *Prayer of Mary 'in Bartos'* (*PCM* I 25 pp. 2–9).[65] Alongside Kropp, mention should be made of Friedrich Bibabel and Adolf Grohmann, who in 1934 published many of the magical texts belonging to the Heidelberg University collection republished here, in part a result of Grohmann's interest in the story of Cyprian the repentant magician.[66] Another major editor was Walter Beltz, who, in a series of articles in the 1980s published most of the Coptic magical texts held in the German National Museum in Berlin.[67] Despite the interest of these manuscripts, the editions of Bilabel, Grohmann,[68] and Beltz[69] are often insufficiently accurate, and the original manuscripts generally need to be consulted to correct them. Other editors and commentators on Coptic magical texts represent a "who's who" of famous Coptologists, among them William H. Worrell (1879–1952), whose interest in Egyptian magic extended into the practical;[70] Walter E. Crum (1865–1944), who edited the definitive Coptic dictionary;[71] James Drescher (1902–1985), who wrote extensive corrections to that dictionary;[72] and Hans Jakob Polotsky (1905–1991), whose work revolutionised our knowledge of Coptic-Egyptian grammar.[73]

The study of Greek magic saw a renaissance in the late 1970s and 1980s. This was in part linked to a resurgence in interest in the study of the Graeco-Roman religious context of the New Testament, one of the original impetuses for the study of the Greek magical papyri at the turn of the twentieth century.[74] This saw the republication of the Preisendanz edition of the *Greek Magical Papyri*, and then a project of translation of these texts into English in the 1980s, led by Hans Dieter Betz.[75] Sensing a lacuna in the study of the later Christian magical texts, Marvin Meyer led the *Coptic Magical Texts* project in the 1990s,[76] which resulted in the publication—amongst other works—of *Ancient Christian Magic: Coptic Texts of*

---

[65] Kropp 1966 & 1965 respectively.
[66] Grohmann 1917–1918.
[67] Beltz 1980, 1983, 1984 & 1985.
[68] On the deficiencies of Bilabel and Grohmann's publication, see Polotsky 1935: 416, a prelude to a masterful series of corrections. His comments take on additional significance when one notes that Polotsky, born in Switzerland to Russian-speaking Jewish parents, was writing the year after fleeing Germany for Palestine as a result of Nazi persecution (Shisha-Halevy 1992: 208). On Bilabel's active membership in the Nazi party, see p. 325. On Grohmann, a member of the Nazi party from 1938 and a collaborator during the German occupation of Czechoslovakia, see Reinfandt 2013.
[69] On Beltz, *cf.* the comments of van der Vliet 2019b: 325.
[70] Worrell 1930, 1935a & b; for Worrell's practical interest in magic, see Worrell 1916.
[71] Crum 1896, 1902, 1922b, 1934a & b.
[72] Drescher 1948, 1950, 1958.
[73] Polotsky 1935 & 1937.
[74] *Cf.* Dosoo forthcoming a.
[75] Betz 1986.
[76] *Cf.* Dosoo/Love/Preininger 2022: 46.

Ritual Power (1994), which to this day remains the most consulted volume on Coptic magic, containing texts in Greek, Old Coptic, and standard Coptic, and a mixture of magical texts, Sethian Gnostic literature, oracle tickets, and other genres.

Since the publication of *Ancient Christian Magic*, much of the important work on Coptic magic has been carried out by Meyer's younger contemporaries, David Frankfurter and Jacques van der Vliet, who have contributed significantly to our understanding of these texts, both in terms of questions of basic comprehension, and of larger socio-historical and theoretical context.[77] The last decade has seen another wave of major work; we can see the beginning of this in the 2013 publication by Malcolm Choat and Iain Gardner of the Macquarie codex (*P.Macq.* I 1). Along with Jay Johnston, Iain Gardner subsequently launched an Australian Research Council Project focusing on magical images, which has enriched our understanding of the archive of texts known as the Heidelberg Library (*PCM* I 21–29).[78] In recent years, Joseph Sanzo has examined the boundary between licit and illicit ritual, beginning with his 2014 study of scriptural amulets, and continuing in his European Research Council project exploring the relationship between Jewish and Christian magical traditions.[79] The work of Edward Love has focused attention on Old Coptic—including, but not limited to, magical texts—confirming that it represents not a single dialect or chaotic blend of features, but rather a similar dialectal diversity to standard Coptic.[80] Of direct relevance to this volume is Roxanne Bélanger Sarrazin's 2017 checklist of published Coptic magical texts,[81] which took inspiration from a similar checklist of Christian Greek texts established by Jitse Dijkstra and Theodore van Bruyn to provide, for the first time, a synoptic view of magical material in Coptic.[82] Two forthcoming works by Roxanne Bélanger Sarrazin and Markéta Preininger—respectively on non-Christian divinities and conceptions of the body—will represent the first synthetic monographs on Coptic magic since that of Kropp.[83]

The project which lies behind this volume, *Coptic Magical Papyri: Vernacular Religion in Late Roman and Early Islamic Egypt* (2018–2023) at the University of

---

[77] See, *e.g.*, Frankfurter 1995, 1998, 2001, 2007, 2009, 2012, 2017, 2022; van der Vliet 1991, 1995, 1998, 2000, 2005a & b, 2011, 2014, 2018, 2019a & b, 2020.

[78] This project was titled *The Function of Images in Magical Papyri and Artefacts of Ritual Power from Late Antiquity* (ARC DP120102952). The project's research is published in Johnston/Gardner 2018, 2023; Gardner/Johnston 2019.

[79] *Early Jewish and Christian Magical Traditions in Comparison and Contact* (EJCM-851466; 2020–2025). *Cf.* Sanzo 2017, 2019a & 2020.

[80] Love 2016; *cf.* Love 2021a, b, d; Zellmann-Rohrer/Love 2022. Magical texts written partially in Old Coptic script include *GEMF* 14/*BM EA* 10808 (II CE); *GEMF* 16/*PDM* xiv (II CE); *GEMF* 55/*PGM* III (III–IV CE); *GEMF* 57/*PGM* IV (IV CE).

[81] Bélanger Sarrazin 2017a.

[82] De Bruyn/Dijsktra 2011.

[83] Bélanger Sarrazin forthcoming a; Preininger forthcoming c.

Würzburg, owes a deep debt to the work done by these scholars, and many others. Our work has attempted to record and describe the full corpus of surviving Coptic magical texts, and to develop deeper understandings of them, focusing in particular on questions of materiality and philology. In these goals, it has significant overlap with the project *The Transmission of Magical Knowledge* led by Christopher Faraone and Sofía Torallas Tovar, which aims to publish the corpus of Greek and Demotic formularies in the series *Greek and Egyptian Magical Formularies (GEMF)*. In a way, our project begins where theirs ends.[84]

3. The Corpus of Coptic Magical Texts

This volume contains texts drawn from 37 manuscripts of the approximately 600 known to us which have traditionally been classified as magical.[85] The texts and our principles of selection are discussed in more detail below (§5), but here we present the larger corpus from the perspectives of context, typology, materiality, and structure.

3.1. Contexts of Production and Deposition

3.1.1. Users and Findspots

A major question in the study of Coptic-language magical texts is that of their users. Literary texts which describe similar practices use terms such as μάγος (*magos*, "magician"), φάρμακος (*pharmakos*, "sorcerer"), and ⲣⲉϥⲙⲟⲩⲧⲉ (*refmoute*, "enchanter") to describe practitioners, but also mention the possibility that clerics might learn from these figures.[86] But do these terms refer to full-time 'magical' professionals? Something of a consensus has developed among many scholars that the primary practitioners of Coptic magic were monks.[87] There are indeed some literary texts mentioning monks as practitioners of something that looks like 'magic', and certain magical manuscripts have been found in monastic

---

[84] On this project, see the project website, https://voices.uchicago.edu/magicalpapyri/. Products of this project to date include Faraone/Torallas Tovar 2022a & b.

[85] The full corpus exists within the *Kyprianos Database of Ancient Ritual Texts and Objects*, created by the Coptic Magical Papyri project, online at https://www.coptic-magic.phil.uni-wuerzburg.de/index.php/manuscripts-search/

[86] For discussions of terms for magician in Coptic, see van der Vliet 2019a: 242–244; Dosoo 2021b: 49–51; *cf.* the discussion of terms in Greek and Latin in Dickie 2001: 12–17, 224–229 *et passim*.

[87] See, *e.g.*, Frankfurter 1997: 125–130; Frankfurter 1998: 257–264; Frankfurter 2017: 192–211; van der Vliet 2019b: 348.

contexts, such as hermitages.[88] Some of the manuscripts in this volume fall into this category: *PCM* I 10 was reused for an account of deliveries of wine to a monastery, perhaps the Monastery of Apa Apollo at Bawit in Middle Egypt, while the copyist of *PCM* I 15 seems to have been a monk from the Monastery of Apa Paulos near Thebes, who also copied a surviving liturgical prayer. Some of the later manuscripts are written on parchments which were originally used for literary or even Biblical texts of the type found in the monastic libraries of the Faiyum, and one of these magical texts even has a colophon of the type found in such monastic codices, in which the copyist identifies himself as the "Deacon Iōhannēs".[89] These manuscripts clearly demonstrate the implication of religious professionals, including monks, in the production and use of magical texts. Parallels can be drawn to other Christian cultures—in Syriac and Ethiopian Christianity, and the Mediaeval Latin West, magical texts seem to have been primarily owned and copied by clerics, who were the only figures with the skills in literacy required to produce and use them.[90] These "clerics" were not necessarily active members of the Church hierarchy, though; often "cleric" in these contexts had a relatively informal meaning, referring to someone who had acquired the skill of literacy, creating a somewhat circular relationship between clerical status and literacy.[91]

At the same time, we should be wary of assuming that all magical texts were produced, owned, or used by religious professionals affiliated with the church. Literacy in Egypt, at least before the decline of written Coptic between the tenth and twelfth centuries, seems to have been broader than it may have been in other Christian cultures; there were administrative scribes as well as artisans, including doctors, and small businessmen, who were also literate in Coptic.[92] The use of magical texts by, for example, doctors, is well attested in the Greek-speaking

---

[88] Examples include BnF Copte 129.20 fol. 178 (Preininger 2022; KYP M108), from the library of the White Monastery; Cairo JdE 45060 (Kropp 1931: I no. K; KYP M303), found in a jar buried in the floor of a monastic cell in Thebes; and Naqlun N. 78/93 (Kalchenko/van der Vliet 2022; KYP M1135), from the Monastery of the Archangel Gabriel in Naqlun.

[89] See the introduction to the 'Heidelberg Coptic Magical Library' on pp. 259–263

[90] For priests as practitioners in Syriac Christianity, see Moriggi 2018; Bhayro 2021, and the prominence of priests among owners and copyists of the *Books of Protection* in Zellmann-Rohrer 2021: 81–99. The Ge'ez word *däbtära* is often translated as "cleric", but the figures it refers to, including magical practitioners, are not necessarily ordained, and may not exercise any ecclesiastical function; see Young 1970 & 1975; Milkias 1976; de Ménonville 2018a & b; Malara 2022. For the Latin West, see Kieckhefer 2014: 151–156; *cf.* Dosoo/Torallas Tovar 2022b: 74–75.

[91] Milkias 1976; Mercier 1988: 461–462; Kieckhefer 2014: 154; Malara 2022.

[92] *Cf.* de Bruyn 2017: 7–8, 238–245; *pace* Frankfurter 1997: 128. For a discussion of professional scribes writing in Coptic, see Cromwell 2017: 14–21 *et passim*; Fournet 2022: 82–89 *et passim*; compare the discussion of official scribes under the Umayyad administration in Richter 2010: 211–218. Well-known dossiers produced by lay Coptic writers include the Kellis House A House 3 Archive (IV CE, discussed in the introduction to *PCM* I 1), and the Archive of Dioscorus of Aphrodito (see Vanderheyden 2012; Papaconstantinou 2015, with further references).

world,⁹³ and, as we have noted, we sometimes find medical and magical texts transmitted together in Coptic.⁹⁴ The Coptic magical text with the best understood context, *PCM* I 1, was owned by a lay Manichaean, whose family operated a small business involving weaving and the exploitation of fruit trees.⁹⁵ There is a similar case of a modern Christian Egyptian tailor who possessed and used one of the Arabic books of magic using the Psalms which derive ultimately from the Coptic-language tradition.⁹⁶ Some of the hands, and scribal features, found in the corpus here resemble those of scribes of the Roman and later Arab administration; others seem to have had very little training, and while these could be the hands of monks, they also resemble those of laypeople who had acquired basic literacy for their own particular needs.

A final point concerns the manner in which texts from Egypt are found and made accessible to scholars. The archaeological record of Late Antique Egypt is biased towards monastic settlements; these tended to be in the desert, where the dry sands preserve organic materials, rather than in the more densely populated towns in or on the border of the Nile Valley, which were annually flooded until the building of the Aswan High Dam, and have often been continuously inhabited down to the present day, destroying fragile texts and preventing archaeological excavation. Archaeology in Egypt has also historically focused on monumental Pharaonic sites—tombs and temples—and these were typically the same sites reused by Christian monks as hermitages, monasteries, and churches.

A still more fundamental problem is that, for the vast majority of papyri from Egypt, there is no record of their circumstances of discovery. While the situation has, fortunately changed, historically most of them were found in informal excavations—either by native Egyptians looking for artefacts to sell, or early European or North American archaeologists who did not value questions of materiality and context enough to record where their papyri came from. It is to be deeply regretted that, of the 37 manuscripts in this volume, only one has a well-recorded context, but this is not unusual in the case of Egyptian papyri. We have managed to recover, or propose, approximate provenances for 31 of the remaining 36, but we invite readers to compare the introduction to *PCM* I 1 to those of the other manuscripts to see how much precious information has been lost in the process of what was, essentially, looting.

---

⁹³ Bohak 2016: 367–368; Zellmann-Rohrer/Love 2022: 70–73.
⁹⁴ Dosoo 2021b: 61–62. In the checklist of medical texts provided in Richter 2014b: 189–191, at least nos. 11, 12, 16, 24, 27, 31 (of a total of 38 manuscripts) can be considered to contain magical recipes.
⁹⁵ For discussions of known historical owners and users of magical texts, see Dosoo/Torallas Tovar 2022a: 25–26; Dosoo forthcoming c.
⁹⁶ Henein/Bianquis 1975: x–xii.

3.1.2. Temporal Distribution

Coptic magical texts generally date to between the fourth and twelfth centuries CE, with peaks in the sixth to eighth and ninth to eleventh centuries, corresponding respectively to the peaks of surviving Coptic documentary and literary manuscripts.[97] Earlier Old Coptic magical texts date to the first to fourth centuries CE, and short Coptic phrases may be found in later, predominantly Arabic, Christian magical texts from Egypt.[98]

The dating of Coptic papyri is a major problem in Coptology; because most of them come from informal or illegal excavations, there is usually no archaeological context to help with dating, and, with the exception of a few notable manuscripts, there is insufficient interest and funding to use scientific dating techniques, such as radiocarbon dating, on papyri—which in any case, rely on destroying pieces of manuscripts as part of the process.[99] Coptic manuscripts very rarely contain internal absolute dates, and this is particularly true of magical texts; in a corpus of about 600 manuscripts, we are only aware of three which provide a date of production.[100] As a result, in most cases palaeography—the study of changes in handwriting—is the only means to date manuscripts. While this is generally accepted as broadly accurate for Greek papyri—within approximately fifty years to a century—Coptic palaeography remains poorly understood.[101] Similar styles may continue to be used for centuries,[102] and existing palaeographical tools are insufficient.[103] As a result, manuscripts may be dated very differently by different scholars, with discrepancies of hundreds of years. The association of magic with the "primitive" and "pagan" may have often led magical texts to be dated to inappropriately early dates; the carbon dating of the manuscripts purchased by Robert Hay has established an eighth or ninth century date for Coptic magical

---

[97] For overviews of the temporal distribution of Coptic magical texts, see Dosoo/Torallas Tovar 2022b: 66–67; Dosoo/Love/Preininger 2022: 63–65; Bélanger Sarrazin 2017a: 373–374.

[98] For a striking example, see Schulz/Kolta 1998, an amulet against a scorpion bite created in 1932 containing a mixture of Coptic and Arabic text. Shorter fragments of Coptic are often found among the *kharaktēres* of the Psalm guides discussed at n. 44.

[99] Carbon-dated Coptic papyri include the leather cover of Nag Hammadi Codex I (Lundhaug 2021); the Hay manuscripts, discussed at n. 104 below; Codex Tchacos, containing the *Gospel of Judas*, for which see Kasser *et al.* 2008: 134, 184; and a leaf from a medical codex, cat.no. 137 (98:Ms4) from excavations at the Monastery of St. Antony at the Red Sea, discussed in Blid *et al.* 2016: 191–193. The modern forgery generally known as the *Gospel of Jesus' Wife* was also subject to carbon dating; see Tuross 2014; *cf.* the comments of Mazza 2019.

[100] These include the amuletic wall inscriptions in the 'Anchorite's Grotto' at Pachoras (Griffith 1927; KYP M91), datable by a graffito to ca. 739 CE, as well as *PCM* I 23 and the unpublished Collège de France Ms. 3 (KYP M597), dated by colophons to 967 and 1035 CE respectively.

[101] *Cf.* the works listed at n. 201 below.

[102] Askeland 2018.

[103] The primary reference work for Coptic palaeography remains Stegemann 1936.

texts previously dated by palaeographic estimates to the sixth or seventh century.[104]

In this volume, we have endeavoured to propose dates for all of the manuscripts. We generally propose two or even three century ranges, reflecting our uncertainty, although in a few cases, we propose single centuries, if the parallels seem to cluster towards the middle of a particular century. We regularly indicate uncertainty with a question mark and here, as elsewhere in this volume, these question marks should be taken seriously as signs that more work needs to be done to definitively establish these points. Wherever possible, we have tried to find explicitly dated parallels for the hands of our manuscripts. We have also attempted to use parallels from geographical contexts close to the origin of the manuscripts, since hands may have varied considerably regionally, and we have also used broader criteria of manuscript formats (see below) to propose datings.

With these provisos in mind, the manuscripts in this volume can be dated to most of the span of the production of Coptic manuscripts—the fourth to eleventh centuries—although there is a slight bias towards the later end of the range, due to the inclusion of many texts from the Heidelberg University papyrus collection (*PCM* I 21–33, 35), which can be dated to the tenth to eleventh centuries. The earliest manuscript, *PCM* I 1, is dated to the late fourth century, while the intervening texts have been dated to between the fifth and ninth centuries.

3.1.3. Geographical Distribution

Like most papyrological manuscripts, all of the documents in this collection come from Egypt. Of the 32 for which a geographical origin can be proposed with certainty or likelihood (see fig. 1), 18 come from the Faiyum, a large, oasis-like depression fed by the canal Bahr Yussef emptying into Lake Moeris, to the west of the Nile Valley. In particular from the Ptolemaic onwards, this area was heavily populated, and became the site of numerous monasteries, whose remains provide many of the surviving Coptic literary manuscripts. The Faiyum has also been heavily excavated by treasure-hunters and archaeologists since the nineteenth century, when Egyptian farmers in search of fertiliser often visited the abandoned Roman-era cities to gather decaying mud-brick. While manuscripts from the Faiyum are generally well-represented in papyrology, they are somewhat over-represented here, as a result again of the many manuscripts from the University of Heidelberg collection.

Six texts come from Middle Egypt, defined here as the region south of the Faiyum, from Oxyrhynchus to Bawit. Again, these areas were the sites of several major towns (Hermopolis, Antinoopolis) and monasteries (Apa Apollo) which

---

[104] See Lucy-Anne Skinner, Rebecca Stacey, Caroline R. Cartwright, Craig Williams and Barbara Willshay in O'Connell 2022: 49–53.

were abandoned in late antiquity, leaving their remains to be preserved for later excavators. The area further south, notably containing Abydos, may have yielded another manuscript for this volume. From still further south, around Thebes (modern Luxor), we find another six. The Theban region, one of the richest in terms of surviving tombs and temples for excavation, has consistently yielded large quantities of artefacts for excavators. The final text with a known origin is again *PCM* I 1, from Kellis in the Dakhla Oasis, 350 kilometres west of the Nile valley; abandoned at the end of the fourth century, it is one of a small number of very well-preserved Egyptian urban settlements from the Roman Period.

3.2. Categories of Texts

3.2.1. The Formulary-Applied Text Distinction

Magical texts, almost without exception, fall into one of two types. The first is that of *formularies* (also known as 'handbooks', or 'models'), texts containing the information necessary for practitioners to carry out rituals.[105] The second type is the *applied text* (also known as the 'finished product', 'activated text', or 'documentary' magical text), which represents an object created in the course of a ritual for a specific purpose. These serve as protective and healing amulets, or as curses or love spells, which, depending on their function, would be worn on the body, deposited in a particular place, or used in other ways. There is some overlap—applied texts could be used as models for other applied texts, essentially serving as formularies. We also have examples of 'personalised formularies',[106] that is, formularies in which the generic name marker (see 3.5.3) is replaced by a personal name, so that the owner of the formulary could read it out loud more easily (an example of this probably lies behind *PCM* I 25 p. 13).

This volume contains only formularies, or manuscripts likely to have been formularies. At times it is difficult to distinguish the two categories; although they were quite different in the way in which they were used, they often contain the same types of texts (since applied texts were, at least theoretically, copied from formularies) and may both demonstrate other typical genre features, such as *kharaktēres* and *voces magicae*. Signs that a manuscript is a formulary rather than an applied text include the addition of titles, ritual instructions, the generic name marker, and multiple texts for different purposes (*cf.* 3.5.3 below). But formularies may also lack these features, and there are a few cases of applied texts including them—copyists creating applied texts might accidentally copy titles or instructions from formularies, or fail to include personal names in applied

---

[105] On this distinction, see Dosoo/Love/Preininger 2022: 56–58; Dosoo/Torallas Tovar 2022b: 66.
[106] On this format, see Saar 2007: 103–104 *et passim*.

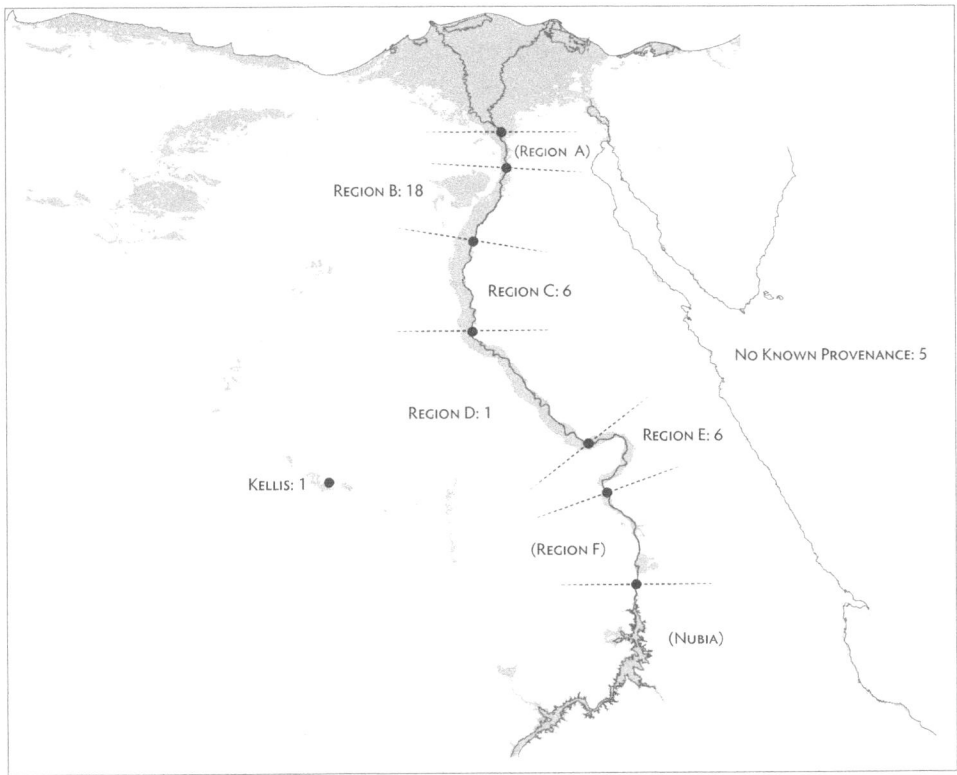

Fig. 1: Origins of manuscripts in *PCM* I (regions after Kahle 1954: 51). Figure by Davide Galli.

texts. Formularies might have been re-used as amulets by being worn or carried by individuals who attributed them a power of their own.[107] As a result, it may be that some of the manuscripts in this volume—although they contain features associated with formularies—served primarily or secondarily as applied texts.

3.2.2. Manuscript Structures

Formularies contain one or more recipes, thus the simplest kind of manuscript is a *single-text formulary*, which contains the information (formula to be spoken and/or ritual procedure) for only one goal. Within the Coptic magical corpus, there are about 200 formularies, of which about half only contain one recipe. The remainder are *multiple-text formularies* containing two or more recipes.[108] Graeco-Egyptian formularies with multiple texts tend to represent collections of recipes

---

[107] See the case of *P.Lond.Copt.* I 524 (KYP M359).
[108] For this terminology, compare Buzi 2016 & 2019 on single and multi-unit Coptic literary manuscripts.

from originally diverse sources, which circulated among and were collected by copyist-practitioners.[109] While some of the manuscripts in this collection represent similar collections (*e.g.*, *PCM* I 4, 11 & 25), Coptic multi-text collections more often represent groups of closely related recipes. These are often of a type which may be referred to as "polypractical texts", which contain a single spoken formula which can be used for multiple purposes depending on the ritual performed with them.[110] The beginnings of this format can be found among the Graeco-Egyptian magical corpus, but there are many more examples in Coptic, and it seems to have been a common format, to the extent that we have evidence of formulae originally intended for one purpose being adapted to serve multiple purposes by the addition of multiple additional recipes at the end.[111]

3.2.3. Genres

We distinguish three major genres or traditions within the larger category of 'magical texts'—invocations, narrative charms, and scriptural amulets—the first two of which are well-represented in this collection.[112]

The first category, *invocations*, represents the most common and prototypical type of text found in the Coptic magical corpus. This is likely the kind of text that most ancient authors had in mind when discussing terms translated as magic, such as *mageia* or *hik*.[113] These are centred on speech acts calling upon or commanding superhuman beings through direct addresses, which may make extensive use of features such as *voces magicae* and *kharaktēres*.

We should distinguish two further categories, which may be considered either sub-types of invocations, or related but separate genres. The first are what Jacques van der Vliet has described as "magical liturgies", long and complex invocations which show clear influence from the liturgical tradition of rituals such as the anaphora, which transforms the liturgical bread and wine into the flesh and blood of Christ.[114] The Coptic magical liturgies are likewise generally used to activate oil, wine and/or water to be used in healing, a process sometimes referred to

---

[109] *Cf.* Dosoo/Torallas Tovar 2022a: 9–11.

[110] For this terminology, see Dosoo 2014: 137; *cf.* Gordon 2022. Published Coptic examples include P.Mich.Inv. 593 (KYP M9; Worrell 1930); P.Mich.Inv. 594–599 (KYP M15; Worrell 1930); Cairo JdE 45060 (KYP M303; Kropp 1931: I no. K); *P.Macq.* I 1 (KYP M167); BM EA 10391 (Zellmann-Rohrer 2022a: no. 1; KYP M302); *PCM* I 26; *PCM* I 37.

[111] See Choat/Gardner 2013: 36; *cf.* the introduction to *PCM* I 26 for the case of the *Endoxon of Michael*.

[112] *Cf.* the discussion in Dosoo/Love/Preininger 2022: 54–55.

[113] *Cf.* Dosoo 2021b: 51–56.

[114] For the concept of the "magical liturgy", see van der Vliet 2019b: 340–343; van der Vliet 2020. On the relationship of magic to the anaphora, see Kropp 1930: III 217–244. For the anaphora in Egypt more generally, see Johnson 2010: 17–34; Mihálykó 2019: 60–64.

as "sealing".[115] The surviving examples show clear interdependence upon one another, using recurrent phraseology and references, suggesting that they belong to a single, narrower tradition—they may derive from the *Prayer of Mary 'in Bartos'*, which seems to be the earliest and most widely-diffused of the surviving examples.[116]

The second sub-type of invocation is the 'first-person exorcistic prayer'.[117] This is a type of text best preserved in mediaeval and early modern Greek manuscripts,[118] although related texts also exist in other languages, such as Armenian, Arabic, Ge'ez, and Syriac.[119] The only clear example in this volume is the *Prayer of Gregory* (PCM I 11 p. 1 l.1–p. 14 l. 14), although the *Prayer of Mary 'in Bartos'* (PCM I 25 pp. 2–9) and the *Love Spell of Cyprian* (PCM I 28) could be considered related texts. First-person exorcistic prayers are intended to provide healing and protection from demons and hostile magic, and are attributed to saints who speak in the first-person, often explicitly mentioning their own names in the prayer. They contain an interesting divergence from other invocations in that they often address harmful forces—acts of violence, magic, or demons—and command and adjure them to depart, rather than adjuring superhuman beings (God or the angels) to cast out these harmful forces. For this reason, they may have been more acceptable to the church hierarchy, and are often found in manuscripts with liturgical prayers.[120] The Coptic manuscript containing the *Prayer of Gregory* contains several canonical and apocryphal texts (the Jesus-Abgar correspondence, the incipits of the Gospels and Psalm 90 (91), two lists of saint names) rather than more markedly magical texts of the invocation-type, and so may not have been considered as "magical" either by its users or by Church authorities at the time.

Invocations—particularly the magical liturgies and exorcistic prayers—offer some of the best evidence for the transmission of magical texts over long periods and across languages; several of the examples contained in this volume can be attested as having been transmitted for over a thousand years, and across many of the languages of Christianity; as well as Coptic, and Greek (the original language of many of them), we find close parallels in, for example, Armenian, Ge'ez, and

---

[115] For references to this process as "sealing" (σφραγίζειν), see *e.g.*, PCM I 25 p. 8 l. 22; *P.Lond. Copt.* 1007 (KYP M361) l. 8. As noted in Mihálykó 2018b: 146, this refers specifically to the act of tracing the sign of the cross over the material. For a recent general discussion of liturgical healing practices, see Mihálykó 2021.

[116] See the introduction to *PCM* I 25 on pp. 288–289

[117] See the note to *PCM* I 11 p. 1 l.1–p. 14 l. 14 on p. 113.

[118] See Delatte 1927: 125, 230–263; Nesseris 2021: 91–97.

[119] For Armenian, see, for example, Feydit 1986: nos. LXXXVIII–XCI; for *Copto-Arabic texts, see Viaud 1978: 78–80; for a discussion of a similar Ge'ez genre, see Strelcyn 1955; for Syriac, see the discussions of the genre of *Anathema* in Hunter 1987 & 1990.

[120] *Cf.* Nesseris 2021: 91–97. This is not to say, of course, that other types of "magical" texts did not sometimes find their way into prayer books (*euchologia*); see Afentoulidou 2021.

Syriac.[121]

The next category is that of the 'narrative charm'. Within folklore studies, the term "charm" refers to spoken formulae used in popular ritual practices—usually for healing—which often have a primarily oral mode of transmission, but which are frequently preserved in written copies. These texts may demonstrate very extensive transmission in time—over periods of millennia—and between languages.[122] "Narrative charms" are a particular sub-group which, as their name suggests, are built around narratives, often called *historiolae* ('little stories').[123] These narratives serve as mythic precedents which both parallel the present problem, and offer a resolution of that problem.

The most common example in the Pharaonic tradition consists of the story of the infant god Horus being injured while he has been left alone, and his mother Isis rushing to help him in response to his cries.[124] These texts are used to heal injuries or illness, and so set up a parallel between events in the mythic past and the present. The resolution of the mythic past works to resolve the events of the present: just as Horus was healed, so should the patient be healed. Texts following this structure can be found in Egypt as early as the Middle Kingdom, but are relatively rare in the Graeco-Egyptian magical tradition.[125] In Coptic, by contrast, many examples survive. Most of them, like the older Pharaonic texts, centre on the adventures of the pre-Christian deities Horus and Isis, although several later examples instead involve Jesus as the primary protagonist.[126]

---

[121] See the notes for *PCM* I 11, p. 1 l.1–p. 14 l. 14;, *PCM* I 25 pp. 2–9; & *PCM* I 28.

[122] For overviews of charms, see Gaster 1900; Roper 2004, 2005 & 2009; Kapaló/Pócs/Ryan 2013. The term "charm" largely overlaps with the use of the term "incantation" in Zellmann-Rohrer 2016 (*cf.* 4 n. 16), 2019 & forthcoming.

[123] See Frankfurter 1995 for the classic study, and on narrative charms more generally, Roper 2005: 13–28; Bozóky 2013. For critiques of the term, see Zellmann-Rohrer 2020: 59; Zellmann-Rohrer/Love 2022: 186–197. Note that the overview in Zellmann-Rohrer/Love 2022: 187–189 is rather misleading; the term was already in use by Egyptologists before Frankfurter's study, and continues to be widely used within Egyptology; see *e.g.*, Sørensen 1984: 7, 9; Ritner 1993: 76, 96; Fischer-Elfert 2005: 120, 133.

[124] For discussions of these, see Sørensen 1984: 7–9; Ritner 1998; Fischer-Elfert 2005: 19; Frankfurter 2009: 231–232; Blumell/Dosoo 2018: 241–243; Bélanger Sarrazin forthcoming a: chapter 1 and appendix a.

[125] For a list of examples, see Blumell/Dosoo 2018: 243–244.

[126] Standard Coptic examples of narrative charms, with the principal protagonists in brackets, include *PCM* I 6 (Horus-Isis); *PCM* I 7 (Horus-Isis); *PCM* I 15 (pupil(?)-Jesus); *PCM* I 16 (Horus-Isis); *PCM* I 20 (Horus-Isis); *PCM* I 29 front (Jesus-worm); *P.Herm.Copt.* 67 (KYP M57, NN-Jesus); *BKU* I 1 (KYP M76; doe-Jesus & Horus-Isis); Mich.Ms. 136 pp. 5–6 (Zellmann-Rohrer/Love 2022; KYP M128; Amun-Isis); Naqlun N. 78/93 (Kalchenko/van der Vliet 2022; NN-Jesus; parallel in *P.Herm.Copt.* 67, republished in Kalchenko/van der Vliet 2022; KYP M57); a possible fragmentary narrative charm involving the Archangel Michael is *P.Herm.Copt.* 59 (KYP M49), and examples of texts with similarities to the narrative charms, without strictly following their structure, include *PCM* I 4 pp. 4–6; *PCM* I 9; BM EA 10391 front ll. 12–27 (Zellmann-Rohrer 2022a: no. 1; KYP M302); *BKU* I 7 (KYP M88).

A key event in all of the Coptic, and many of the European examples, is the *meeting*—the protagonist encounters another figure, which prompts the crisis in the narrative and then its resolution. In European examples, this second figure is often a harmful being who causes disease, and who is commanded to leave,[127] but in the Coptic examples the figure is usually either a beautiful woman whom Horus meets (in love spells), or else the encounter may be between an individual in need of healing and the healer. In German folklore studies, such texts are known specifically as *Begegnungssegen* ("encounter charms").[128]

Coptic narrative charms are often quite different from invocations—they do not typically contain *voces magicae* or *kharaktēres*, but at times show signs of interaction with them. They often end with one character speaking an invocation, and there are a few examples of narrative charms which include *voces magicae*.[129] Although narrative charms may be seen as a cross-cultural tradition, the Coptic examples may represent a rare case of the transmission of textual culture from pre-Coptic Egyptian to Coptic without a Greek intermediary.[130]

The next genre of text often studied as magical is the 'scriptural amulet'.[131] These are typically small papyrus amulets onto which passages from the Bible, or related apocryphal literature (such as the Jesus-Abgar correspondence) has been copied; the most common texts are the incipits of the canonical gospels and of Psalm 90 (91). Distinguishing these amulets from texts intended for other purposes can be difficult, but features indicating use (such as folding or piercing to allow them to be worn or carried), or the presence of common amuletic texts, may serve as criteria.[132] The earliest Christian examples of scriptural amulets appear in the papyrological record around the third century CE, but their use may derive from older Jewish practices of wearing passages of scripture as amulets,

---

[127] Compare the Sisinnios charms, well-attested in Armenian, Ge'ez, Greek, and Syriac, in which Saint Sisinnios meets and banishes a child-killing demoness; see Basset 1894: 351–353; Gaster 1900: 153–162; Worrell 1909: 158–173; Viaud 1978: 112–117; Feydit 1986: no. 107; Greenfield 1989; Schwartz 1996; Passalis 2014; Nurullina (Cherkashina)/Lyavdansky 2017. A now lost text from Karanog in Nubia apparently contained an example of a Coptic Sisinnios text, which may have been a charm of this type (see Woolley 1911: 4–5), and there is an unpublished Greek and Old Nubian example from Nubia (Qasr Ibrim 80.3.11/2 (NI 113), see DBMNT no. 2880). These examples from Nubia and Ethiopia imply the tradition also existed in Egypt in Coptic. Compare the fourteenth-century *Copto-Arabic exorcistic prayer of Sisinnios, published in Winkler 1931: 97–100.

[128] On the *encounter charm*, see Ohrt 1936; van der Vliet 2019b: 345–346; Kalchenko/van der Vliet 2022: 231, with further references. On the translation "charm" for *Segen*, see Roper 2005: 13–14.

[129] *Cf.* Blumell/Dosoo 2018: 254–255.

[130] On verbal parallels suggestive of such a transmission, see Blumell/Dosoo 2018: 240 n. 98; Zellmann-Rohrer/Love 2022: 184–264.

[131] For scriptural amulets, see Sanzo 2014; Jones 2016; de Bruyn 2017: 139–183; Bélanger Sarrazin 2020.

[132] See de Bruyn/Dijskstra 2011: 172–173; Jones 2016: 27–34.

attested as early as the seventh or sixth century BCE.[133] The use of scriptural amulets shows a clear parallel to the kinds of 'magical' amulets attested in the Graeco-Egyptian magical corpus and among Coptic invocation-type texts; all of these practices involve wearing a powerful written text as a means of protection. But it seems that scriptural amulets were not generally considered to belong to the category of *mageia* by most Christians; bishops such as Augustine and John Chrysostom considered them an acceptable Christian alternative to the wearing of 'magical' amulets.[134] Scriptural amulets are almost without exception applied texts, and we only find a single example of a formulary containing incipits to be copied as amulets.[135] They do not usually demonstrate the typical features of other categories of magical texts, such as *kharaktēres* or *voces magicae*, suggesting that they were conceived of in different terms, although there are a few exceptional cases which do display *kharaktēres*, and which thus draw upon what we call here the 'invocation' tradition.[136]

3.3. Materiality

We refer to the manuscripts in this collection generically as "papyri", following the papyrological usage in which the term can be used to refer to any movable support for writing. In practical terms, this means that the manuscripts in this volume are written not only on papyrus, but also on parchment, paper, ostraca, and wooden tablets.

In terms of temporal distribution, papyrus was used in Egypt from at least the Old Kingdom (*ca.* XXVI BCE), and continued to be used until the early to mid tenth century CE,[137] although the details of its use changed. Sheets of papyrus are produced by laying strips of the fibres of the plant over one another at ninety degrees, so that one side of each sheet has horizontal fibres, and the other vertical fibres.[138] For most of Egyptian history, papyrus was usually written with the text running parallel to the horizontal fibres, but in the fifth century CE it became common (for some kinds of texts) to rotate the roll so that the fibres on the side

---

[133] Barkay *et al.* 2004; Bohak 2008: 30, 114–15.

[134] Sanzo 2014: 159–165; de Bruyn 2017: 29–30.

[135] The incipits of the Gospels and Psalm 90 (91) are found in *PCM* I 11 p. 29 l. 23–p. 30 l. 28. As noted above, though, the contents of the codex are unusual within the corpus; only the second text (p. 14 l. 13–p. 20) clearly belongs to the invocation tradition, while the other texts include a first-person exorcistic prayer attributed to Saint Gregory (p. 1 l. 1–p. 14 l. 14), a prayer attributed to Judas Cyriacus drawn from the *Finding of the Holy Cross* (*Inventio sanctae crucis*) (p. 25 l. 24–p. 28 l. 21), and two lists of the names of saints (p. 28 l. 22–p. 29 l. 22).

[136] See, for example, *Stud.Pal.* 20 294 (KYP M544); *P.Mich.Copt.* 18 (KYP M681).

[137] Karabacek 1887: 89–100 (Anne Grons is thanked for this reference); Grob 2010: 11–14; Legendre 2014: 326–330.

[138] On the production of papyrus, see Bülow-Jacobsen 2009: 4–10.

prepared for writing were vertical, a format known as *transversa charta*. In all periods, though, copyists might choose to turn the papyrus over and continue writing on the less favoured side.[139]

Parchment is a writing surface created by preparing the skin of domestic animals, the techniques for whose preparation developed in the second half of the first millennium BCE; examples from Egypt tend to appear around the third century CE.[140] Like papyrus, the process of creating parchment resulted in two distinct surfaces—the 'hair' side, generally darker, and showing signs of hair follicles, and the smoother, lighter 'flesh' side. Paper—more specifically, rag paper—was invented in China in the second century BCE, but did not arrive in Egypt until the ninth century, and did not come into widespread use until the tenth, when it replaced papyrus.[141] Finally, the word 'ostracon' in the context of Egyptian papyrology refers to two different objects—the first, pottery fragments, the second limestone flakes—both of which could be found lying on the ground in Egypt, and were often used as readily available writing supports.[142]

In addition to the material they are made from, manuscripts can also be categorised based on their format.[143] Papyrus was produced in long rolls, typically 20–30 cm high and several metres wide; these rolls were produced by glueing together multiple smaller sheets, with the join between individual sheets being referred to as *kollēsis* ("glueing").[144] These could be written from right to left or left to right (depending on the writing system) in multiple columns to produce the format of the horizontal *book-roll* (*volumen* or simply, *roll*).

The roll could also be cut into smaller widths to produce individual sheets, which could also be used to write shorter texts, such as letters. Individual sheets are in fact the most common format of magical formularies, and of almost all applied texts.[145] An important point to mention in the context of sheets is that of folding. The presence of folding in the case of Biblical texts is often used as a criterion for classification as an amulet, since papyri which were folded could then be pierced with a thread or placed in a holder in order to be worn as amulets.[146]

---

[139] See Fournet 2009: 28–32; *cf.* Dosoo/Torallas Tovar 2022b: 101–107, and Sarri 2017: 91–95 for the use of this format in the Ptolemaic period.

[140] *Cf.* Bülow-Jacobsen 2009: 11.

[141] See the references at n. 137 above, Boud'hors 1999: 75–84; Bloom 2001: 74–85 *et passim*; *cf.* Dosoo/Torallas Tovar 2022b: 69; Dosoo/Love/Preininger 2022: 69.

[142] Martín Hernández/Torallas Tovar 2014b; Dosoo/Torallas Tovar 2022b: 108–109; Dosoo/Love/Preininger 2022: 69–70.

[143] On manuscript formats, *cf.* the discussions in Dosoo/Torallas Tovar 2022b; Dosoo/Love/Preininger 2022: 71–73.

[144] On the book roll format, see Turner 1978; Johnson 2004: 85–152; Dosoo/Torallas Tovar 2022b: 79–86.

[145] On sheets, see Dosoo/Torallas Tovar 2022b: 72–73, 101–108; Dosoo/Love/Preininger 2022: 73; Faraone 2022.

[146] *Cf.* n. 132 above.

Yet there are cases of manuscripts which are clearly formularies being extensively folded. While it is possible that these are formularies which were re-used as applied texts, there are so many that we suspect that folding was simply a way to make formularies written on sheets easier to store and transport; folding is thus not always an indicator of use as an amulet.[147]

As we have noted, from the fifth century it became increasingly common in Egypt to rotate the papyrus roll 90° to write across the horizontal fibres (*transversa charta*). This produced a new format, the vertical book-roll, or *rotulus*.[148] Although horizontal rolls do not disappear, they become far less common after the fourth century CE.

The last major format to be discussed here is the codex, produced by folding and binding together sheets of papyrus, parchment, or, later paper, to produce a book with a spine and individual pages of the type we know today.[149] This format was likely developed by Romans around the first century BCE or CE and adopted gradually in Egypt, finally becoming the predominant format for long texts by the fourth century. The use of the codex is often linked to Christianity, but, although Christians do seem to have favoured the use of the codex over the book-roll, codices become more popular even for non-Christian texts over the course of the third to fourth centuries.[150] There are some interesting cases in this volume of codices without hard covers which seem to have been folded to make them smaller; again, this may indicate re-use as an applied text, but more likely, it served as way to make them smaller for transport and storage.[151]

As this brief overview suggests, materiality offers additional criteria for dating; the use of a codex suggests a post-fourth century date, *transversa charta* writing suggests a post-fifth century date, the use of papyrus suggests a pre-tenth century date, and the use of paper a date in the tenth century at the earliest.

A final question is that of inks.[152] While we have not been able to obtain information on inks for all manuscripts, we are able to describe the probable composition of inks in the case of some of them, largely thanks to the work of Krisztina Hevesi on the papyrus collections of the Heidelberg University Library and Strasbourg National Library;[153] we also thank Tea Ghigo for her invaluable

---

[147] Dosoo/Torallas Tovar 2022b: 103, 107.

[148] Turner 1978: 26–53; Stroppa 2013; Mihálykó 2019: 164–166; Torallas Tovar 2021; Dosoo/Torallas Tovar 2022b: 83–86. Compare the practice of writing against the fibres of sheets, which became common at around the same time, discussed above (*cf.* n. 139 above).

[149] Turner 1977; Roberts/Skeat 1983; Skeat 1994; Bagnall 2009a: 70–90; Harnett 2017; Dosoo/Torallas Tovar 2022b: 76–79, 86–101.

[150] Roberts/Skeat 1983: 67–74; Bagnall 2009a: 70–90; Harnett 2017; Nongbri 2018: 21–46.

[151] These are *PCM* I 4, 28 & 34.

[152] The overview of inks given here is based on Rabin/Binetti 2014; Rabin 2015; Rabin/Krutsch 2019: 776–779; Ghigo/Rabin/Buzi 2020; Ghigo/Albarrán Martínez 2021.

[153] Krisztina Hevesi's work will be published in her forthcoming thesis, *Continuity and Discontinuity of Scribal Traditions in Coptic Magical Texts* (Freie Universität Berlin).

help in interpreting the evidence and accurately describing the results. For our purposes, inks can be classified as belonging to one of three types. The first, carbon ink, was produced by burning organic matter to produce a soot which would be mixed with gum arabic suspended in water; carbon ink was the most common, and oldest, type of ink in antiquity. The second type, iron-gall ink, was produced by mixing a source of iron (such as vitriol or iron filings) with tannins extracted from gall nuts. The earliest written evidence for this type of ink seems to be found in a recipe dating to the early fourth century CE, and it became established in the fifth century, at least for literary texts. The third type is plant ink, a heterogenous range of inks made from tannins obtained by boiling vegetable matter, such as gall nuts or tree barks. In this work, we identify inks by examining manuscripts using light of different wavelengths, in most cases using a Dino Lite AD4113T-I2V digital microscope. We compare the appearance of ink in the range of visible light, near-infrared (~940nm), and ultraviolet (~395nm). We base our interpretations on the fact that carbon inks are equally visible under all three wavelengths, iron gall ink is visible, but lighter, under infrared, and plant inks are visible in ultraviolet light, but disappear in the infrared spectrum.[154] We may also note that carbon inks tend to be very black, whereas plant inks are generally brown; degraded iron gall ink also tends to be brown, but is typically darker than plant inks, except where the superficial pigment layer has flaked or been rubbed off.

3.4. Language

The Coptic language is divided into a number of varieties, usually referred to as 'dialects', which likely originally represented the standardised written forms of local varieties, but which sometimes spread beyond their original range;[155] this is likely true both of Sahidic, the most common and widespread dialect until the ninth century, and of Lycopolitan, which was used for Manichaean texts in areas in which non-Manichaeans seem to have used Sahidic.[156] Coptic magical texts, like documentary texts, are often highly divergent from the literary standards used to define dialects, and so only a few manuscripts in this volume can be clearly defined as belonging to a standard dialect.[157] These are Lycopolitan (L4 or L*, originally from the region of Lycopolis or Assiut), and Faiyumic (F4/5), the

---

[154] Rabin/Binetti 2014: 467; Rabin 2015: 28; Ghigo/Rabin/Buzi 2020: 70.

[155] In popular usage the term 'dialect' may be associated with non-standard or non-prestigious language varieties, but we use it here in the neutral, strictly linguistic sense which has become established in Coptic studies; cf. Boberg/Nerbonne/Watt 2018. On Coptic dialectology, see, for example, Kasser 1980a & b; Funk 1988; Funk 1991; Kasser 1990; Kasser 1991a, c–e.

[156] On Sahidic, see Funk 1988; Shisha-Halevy 1991: 195; on Lycopolitan at Kellis, see Zakrzewska 2015.

[157] On dialects in the corpus of magical papyri, see Dosoo/Love/Preininger 2022: 74–78.

dialect associated with the region of the Faiyum.[158] Most of the manuscripts are written in a more or (usually) less standard form of Sahidic (S). In this volume, we usually describe such manuscripts as "Sahidic (non-standard)" and then provide a fuller description in the accompanying introduction, noting any features which may suggest a particular dialectal affiliation and hence geographical origin. We must note that the study of non-standard Sahidic is not deeply developed. We usually rely on the work of Paul Kahle (1954), who extensively described non-standard features and the geographical regions in which they are found. Despite the value of his work, however, his survey does not explicitly take into account statistical information on regional diversity, which often makes it seem as if nearly all non-standard features were equally common in most of Egypt. In a few cases, we define manuscripts simply as "Sahidic"; this is generally in the rare cases in which the surviving text does not show more divergence from the standard than would be expected in a contemporary literary text.

All of the manuscripts presented in this volume are primarily or exclusively Coptic in language. A few contain whole Greek phrases; in two cases, we do treat this as Greek text, printing it in Greek rather than in Coptic. In most instances, though, short passages of syntactic Greek seem to represent fixed phrases embedded within Coptic text, and so we print them in Coptic font, and give the Greek form in the apparatus at the foot of the page. The later manuscripts also contain the regular use of Arabic loanwords, particularly in the descriptions of ingredients.[159] In the larger corpus, there are a few cases of mixed Coptic-Arabic texts, but we do not have any examples in this volume.[160]

3.5. Structure

3.5.1. The Structure of Magical Rituals

The basic structure of a ritual (at least, within the context of the invocation tradition) seems to have consisted of three essential acts—the *recitation of a formula*, the *burning of an offering* (usually resins and other aromatics), and the *production of an applied object* which manifested the power of the ritual in an ongoing manner.[161] This process of activation may be described in a manner analogous to the liturgical *epiclesis* ("summoning"), the procedure in which the celebrant calls upon God to send his power (sometimes in the form of the Holy Spirit) upon the bread and wine—or, in the context of healing, exorcism, and baptism rituals,

---

[158] Lycopolitan: *PCM* I 1; Faiyumic: *PCM* I 2.
[159] On Arabic loanwords in Coptic, see Richter 2009: 422–426; Richter 2015b; Richter 2016a; Richter 2017a.
[160] Love 2022a: 182–192.
[161] *Cf.* Dosoo/Love/Preininger 2022: 62–63.

other liquids such as water and oil. In the same way, within the magical tradition, verbal formulae may call upon angels to descend and seal water or other liquids, or alight upon their images, thus creating applied objects.[162] The form of applied object most apparent in the archaeological record is the applied text—copies of formulae, images, and *kharaktēres* written onto supports such as papyrus in the course of rituals, often worn as amulets or deposited to serve as curses or love spells. These written texts might be transformed into liquids by being washed, so that the liquid would take on the power previously inherent in the applied text.

The use of the applied object depends upon the goal of the ritual; for rituals of healing, protection, exorcism, or favour, applied texts are typically worn by the patient or displayed in the home, or liquids may be drunk by patients, or used to anoint or wash them. In curses or love spells, applied texts are usually deposited at particular sites (a path which the target may use, or a crossroads; at the target's door or in a grave) or cast into fires, while liquid may be poured at the victim's door. In divinatory procedures, the activated object may be the bowl of water or oil used in divination, or else an object (usually a piece of salt) placed by the head when the practitioner goes to sleep in order to provoke a divinatory dream.

In this volume, we usually distinguish between the practitioner (who carries out the ritual) and the beneficiary or client (for whom the ritual is carried out), and, in the case of curses and love spells, the target(s), the people whom the ritual aims to effect. The situation was likely more complex, however; individuals who owned formularies could carry out rituals for themselves, and literary evidence in Coptic and parallels from modern Ethiopia suggest that ritual experts may have at times explained to their clients what to do, so that (parts of) the actual ritual performance would be carried out by the beneficiaries themselves.[163]

3.5.2. The Structure of Magical Texts

The basic structure of a Coptic magical formulary is highly practical, generally consisting of the following elements: *title*, *formula*, *ritual instruction*, and *tableau*. *Titles* are typically placed at the beginnings of texts, and specify the purpose of the ritual, often in highly abbreviated terms (such as ⲟⲩⲙⲉ "love" for a love spell), sometimes prefixed by the word "for" (ⲉ- or ⲉⲧⲃⲉ). In a few texts we also find the use of section titles such as "the procedure" (ⲛϭⲓⲛⲣ̄ϩⲱⲃ) to label other parts of the recipe, in this case, the ritual instructions (for instance, for the production of an applied object), or "offering" (ⲑⲩⲥⲓⲁ) to introduce lists of objects to be burned as offerings. The *formula* represents the text to be copied, and/or pronounced, and in many cases is the only information to be contained in Coptic formularies.

---

[162] Dosoo 2021d: 425–428.

[163] For Coptic evidence, see, for example, the passage from the *Canons of Basil* discussed in Dosoo 2021b: 53–54; for Ethiopia, see *e.g.*, Young 1970: 201.

Ritual instructions are usually highly abbreviated in comparison to those found in the earlier Graeco-Egyptian tradition.[164] They often consist simply of subheadings followed by lists of ingredients, which therefore require some knowledge of the basic ritual processes to decipher. The final elements are the image constructions referred to here as *tableaux*. These consist both of figurative drawings (of human beings, angels, demons, and so on), *kharaktēres*, and associated text—usually combinations of all three. These images are intended to be copied as part of the process of creating applied texts, which may consist only of such tableaux.

3.5.3. Elements of Magical Texts

Magical texts belonging to the invocation tradition (and sometimes those from other traditions) contain a range of recurrent features worth briefly explaining here.[165]

Spoken formulae are primarily structured around 'speech acts',[166] of which the most common are *invocations*, *adjurations*, and *requests*, representing different ways of addressing superhuman beings. Invocations are speech acts which call upon the addressed being to be present, and which may also request some specific action; they are translated in English as "I call upon you" or "I invoke you".[167] Adjurations are stronger speech acts which likewise call upon the addressed being to carry out an action, but do so by binding them in a process comparable to an oath; they are translated in English as "I adjure you".[168] Requests call upon the addressed being to carry out a specific act, but do so in a way which assumes less power, or demonstrates greater deference, on the part of the speaker than either invocations or adjurations; they are translated in English as by forms such as "I

---

[164] For a description of these text formats, see Dieleman 2011.

[165] Compare the discussion of the structure of Jewish magical texts from the Cairo Genizah in Swartz 1990.

[166] For the theory of speech acts, see Austin 1962; Searle 1969 & 1989; Sadock 2006; House/Kádár 2021. For the application of speech act theory to ancient magic, see, for example, Lesses 1995; Dosoo 2014: 321–325, 402–405; Frankfurter 2019; Janowitz 2019.

[167] The typical structures in Coptic for invocations are ϯⲉⲡⲓⲕⲁⲗⲉⲓ ⲙ̄ⲙⲟⲕ, ϯⲡⲁⲣⲁⲕⲁⲗⲉⲓ ⲙ̄ⲙⲟⲕ, ϯⲱϣ ⲉϩⲣⲁⲓ ⲉⲣⲟⲕ, translated in this volume respectively as "I invoke you", "I invoke you", and "I call upon you". The verb ⲡⲁⲣⲁⲕⲁⲗⲉⲓ poses problems for classification, since it might also be understood as a verb of request (see LSJ, Lampe *s.v.* παρακαλέω), and translated as "beseech" or "entreat", as is usually done in liturgical contexts. The occurrence of ⲡⲁⲣⲁⲕⲁⲗⲉⲓ in contexts where no specific request is made (see, *e.g.*, *PCM* I 5 front l. 1) suggests that it is better translated as "invoke", as we do in this volume, but further research on this point would be desirable. For further discussions of the relationship between the verbs of invocation, ἐπικαλέω and παρακαλέω, *cf.* Mihálykó 2015: 188; Dosoo 2018: 21–22; Blumell/Dosoo 2021: 141 n. 146.

[168] Adjurations in Coptic magical texts typically take the form ϯⲱⲣⲕ ⲉⲣⲟⲕ or ϯⲧⲁⲣⲕⲟ ⲙ̄ⲙⲟⲕ; much rarer are ϯ(ⲣ) ⲉⲝⲟⲣⲕⲓⲍⲉⲓ ⲙ̄ⲙⲟⲕ (*PCM* I 2 l. 1) and ϯⲣ̄ ⲁⲛⲁϣ ⲉⲣⲟⲕ (*PCM* I 4 p. 2 l. 3–4). These are all translated as "I adjure you". On adjurations in general, see Shauf 2005: 202–211.

entreat you" or "I beseech you".[169] These speech acts may be strengthened by the use of 'authorities', or *horkōmotoi*,[170] upon which the speaker calls during the speech act in the same way that modern legal witnesses might swear on the Bible: "I adjure you by your great name..." (*PCM* I 10 ll. 19–20).

Formulae may also include other recurrent phrases, such as "yea, yea, quickly, quickly!", usually found at the end of texts or speech acts. The injunction that the requested act be carried out "quickly" is found already in Egyptian ritual texts of the Late Period, and continues into the Graeco-Egyptian magical tradition before being taken up by other textual traditions dependent on it.[171] "Yea, yea" seems to have a similar effect; it translates the Coptic word (ϩ)ⲁ(ⲉ)ⲓⲟ (*haeio*) repeated twice, an interjection used to call for attention and insist upon what is being requested.[172]

Formularies usually contain places in which the names of particular individuals —the beneficiary and/or target(s)—should be named; these are marked with a placeholder which we refer to here as the "generic name marker", translated into English as NN, generally derived from the Latin *nomen nescio* ("I do not know the name").[173] In Coptic, the most common way of writing the generic name marker is with the Greek δεῖνα ("so and so"), usually abbreviated to its first letter, delta (ⲇ), often given a supralinear stroke indicating abbreviation, and a tail representing the vowel iota (ι, thus ⲇ̄); the sequence ει was not phonologically distinct from ι by the Roman period.[174] This is usually doubled to represent the Greek δεῖνα τῆς δεῖνα—"NN (child) of (the woman) NN". The tradition of identifying individuals in magic based on their mother's names derives once again from older Egyptian ritual practice.[175] Although the abbreviation is Greek, it is likely that Coptic readers

---

[169] The most common structures for requests are †ⲥⲟⲡ̄ⲥ̄ ("I entreat") and †ⲧⲱⲃ̄ϩ̄ ("I beseech"). The common speech acts of the form †ⲥⲟⲡ̄ⲥ̄ ⲁⲩⲱ †ⲡⲁⲣⲁⲕⲁⲗⲉⲓ ("I invoke and I entreat") are modelled on the liturgical pattern ⲧⲛ̄ⲥⲟⲡ̄ⲥ̄ ⲁⲩⲱ ⲧⲛ̄ⲡⲁⲣⲁⲕⲁⲗⲉⲓ, from the Greek δεόμεθα καὶ παρακαλοῦμεν ("we invoke and we entreat"); see Mihálykó 2019: 31. For the translation of παρακαλει, *cf.* n. 167 above.

[170] For this term, see Shauf 2005: 203, and the glossary, at *horkōmotos*.

[171] Dieleman 2019: 306–307.

[172] Crum CD 636b–637a.

[173] *Nomen nescio* (alternatively *nomen nominandum*, "name to be named", or *nomen notetur* "name may be noted") may itself represent a later, and perhaps originally German, reinterpretation of the original Latin *Numerius Negidius*, used in Roman jurisprudence to refer to the defendants in hypothetical lawsuits (see Berger 1968: 596; Hamann 1871: 26). Perhaps because of the German influence on the modern study of ancient magic, the term was in use to translate δεῖνα by at least the time of Albrecht Dieterich (1903: 5 *et passim*). In mediaeval Latin magical texts, N for *nomen* ("name") on its own seems more common (*e.g.*, CLM 849 in Kieckhefer 1998: 199), although NN is also found by at least the eighteenth century (*e.g.*, Skemer 2021: 40).

[174] Dieleman 2010.

[175] Curbera 1999; Dieleman 2010. In some cases, Coptic copyists act as if the doubled NN (ⲇⲇ) is a single NN (see *e.g.*, *PCM* I 24 l. 16; *PCM* I 28 p. 7 l. 10); for consistency, we translate this as "NN, child of NN" too. On the different forms of the δεῖνα-sign in Coptic, *cf.* Dosoo/Love/Preininger 2022: 83.

would have understood—and probably read it—as the Coptic equivalent ⲛⲓⲙ ⲡ/ⲧϣⲉ ⲛ̄ⲛⲓⲙ.[176] Similarly, the word "child of" is sometimes replaced in later texts by the sign ⳽, derived from a ligature of upsilon (υ) and iota (ι), an abbreviation of the Greek word υἱός ("son"), but used both for men and women; it was likely also read as ϣⲉ. Both abbreviations—ⲗ̄ and ⳽—are found in non-magical texts: ⲗ̄ most often in liturgical texts,[177] in which it likewise indicates where the name of an individual is to be inserted in prayers, and ⳽ most often in documentary texts following the Arab conquest in which individuals are identified by their fathers' names.[178]

Related to the generic name marker are the words "usual" (κοινά) and "request" (ἀπολογία). The former word is usually abbreviated (ⲕⲟⲩ), and has typically been misread in the past as ⲕⲟⲭ (*kokh*). The two words would seem to be generally equivalent, and both have been typically translated in the past as "spell".[179] The word κοινά is well-known from Graeco-Egyptian magic as an abbreviation for "(add the) usual", and both seem to serve as paratextual notes to the reader to fill in missing information as required.[180] This seems usually to have referred to the specific name to replace NN, or the specific goals of the ritual, which may not be given elsewhere in the formula.

Ritual procedures may be marked by the title ⲡϭⲓⲛⲣ̄ϩⲱⲃ ("the procedure"). The term ⲡϭⲱⲣϭ̄ ⲛ̄ⲧϭⲁⲗⲁϩⲧ̄ ("the preparation of the pot") may be used to refer more specifically to the preparation of liquids in a *pot in certain rituals.[181] Within the procedures, the term θυσία ("(burnt) offering", usually abbreviated to ⲑ̄ⲩ̄) is used to introduce lists of objects to be burned. Tableaux are referred to as "images" (ζῴδιον, often abbreviated), and may be referred to as such either in the formula or in the ritual instructions. Many texts end with the phrase "it is complete" (ⲁϥϫⲱⲕ ⲉⲃⲟⲗ), to let the reader know that they possess the full recipe or formula.

The final elements we note here are *voces magicae* and *kharaktēres*, two characteristic features of magical texts in Coptic and other traditions dependent on Graeco-Egyptian magic. Since Betz's translation of the *Greek Magical Papyri*, it has been common to print *voces magicae* in small caps, but they are not usually marked out in a comparable way in the manuscripts themselves. It is similarly difficult to decide what should be treated as a *vox magica* and what as simply a

---

[176] *Cf.* the comments of Crum CD 584b *s.v.* ϣⲏⲣⲉ on the abbreviation for υἱός.

[177] See, *e.g.*, Budde 2004: 166, 188; we thank Ágnes Mihálykó for providing us with this reference.

[178] See, *e.g.*, *CPR* IV 174b l. 12; *CPR* IV 4 l. 1. For a brief discussion of the form and origin of this abbreviation, see Berkes/Delattre/Vanthieghem 2021: 169. We thank Vincent Walter and Lajos Berkes for discussing this abbreviation with us.

[179] See Dosoo/Love/Preininger 2022: 84, with further references.

[180] *Cf.* Daniel/Maltomini 1992: II 225, and the note to PCM I 12 p. 9 l. 7.

[181] See, *e.g.*, BL Ms Or. 6796 (4) + 6796 (Kropp 1931: I no. J; KYP M308) l. 49. For a fuller list of occurrences, see the discussion in Choat/Gardner 2013: 100, but note that their own proposal to read ϭϭ as ϭⲱⲣϭ̄ ⲛ̄ⲧϭⲁⲗⲁϩⲧ̄ should be corrected to *ⲇⲇ*, to be read as (ἡμέραι) "days"; see Dosoo/Love/Preininger 2022: 84.

divine name, so we do not mark *voces magicae* differently from other text in this volume. We do attempt to break them up following the procedure of the copyist and normally add commas between them. As far as we can tell, *voces magicae* were usually understood as the secret names of superhuman beings, such as the Jewish-Christian god, although at times they are clearly understood as syntactic phrases in a special language—often divine, but at other times a sacred human language, such as Hebrew, or that of animals.[182] *Voces magicae* are generally understood to be phrases whose perceived power derived from their lack of comprehensibility, even if some of the words, or at least their elements, were ultimately derived from real words in real languages. Equally, they often show poetic qualities such as the repetition of sounds (such as *hrix hrax* in *PCM* I 16 ostracon 1 ll. 1–5), and sometimes form palindromes (such as *Ablanathanalba*, known in both Greek and Coptic magic), showing that they may have been valued for their aural and visual qualities. Editors of magical texts often spend considerable time gathering comparanda for *voces magicae* in an attempt to interpret them. We generally do not do this here, both because the meanings of most *voces magicae* are very uncertain, and because we believe that compiling such parallels is best carried out in the context of a dedicated project. Related to *voces magicae* are vowel sequences (repetitions of the seven Greek vowels) and *tekhnopaignia*, or text formations—these latter are shapes, such as squares and triangles, formed from names or letters, found in Greek magical texts, and in some of the traditions dependent on them, including those in Coptic, albeit not in the texts of this volume.[183]

Lastly, *kharaktēres* are magical signs which seem to represent a written form of the divine language, whose spoken form would likely be *voces magicae*.[184] While these may take many forms, in Coptic magic they are typically based on simple shapes: the letters of the Greek (and more rarely, Coptic) alphabet as well as geometric shapes such as crosses, circles, and squares. These are usually decorated with circles at their corners and terminal points, leading to them being known by names such as *signes pommetés* ("signs with 'little apples'")[185] or *Brillenbuchstaben* ("spectacle letters"). In this volume, we reproduce *kharaktēres* as tracings, and in the translations of the texts we generally provide the basic shapes upon which they are based in brackets. Coptic texts are somewhat different from the earlier Graeco-Egyptian magical texts in their use of *kharaktēres*. In Coptic manuscripts we sometimes find them simply used as Coptic letters to write

---

[182] On *voces magicae*, see Versnel 2002; Bohak 2003; Dosoo 2014: 108–110, 423–426. For *voces magicae* which supposedly represent Hebrew, see *PCM* 11 p. 25 l. 24–p. 26 l. 7.

[183] See Gordon 2002: 85–90; Bohak 2008: 265–270.

[184] See Gordon 2011; Mastrocinque 2012; Gordon 2014; Dosoo 2022a: 121–122, 132.

[185] The term 'pommeté' derives from heraldry, in which it usually describes a type of cross whose bars terminate in rounded balls, the 'croix pommetée' or 'bourdonnée' (from 'bourdon', a type of knobbed staff); see Geliot 1664: 103–104, 550. As noted in Gordon 2011: 18 n. 16, the term seems to have originated in Derchain 1964: 193.

words (often, but not always, divine names), the addition of circles simply serving to stylise or in some sense 'empower' the text.¹⁸⁶

3.5.4. Paratextual Signs

The structure of Coptic magical texts is apparent both in the specialist vocabulary used to designate particular textual or ritual components of the practices and in the range of paratextual signs used in the texts.

Many of the manuscripts begin with an initial cross (+) or staurogram (⳨). This was a frequent practice in texts produced in Christian contexts from the fourth century CE onwards, although, by the fifth century, it was not necessarily a clear sign of strong personal faith.¹⁸⁷ From the eighth century, this sign may be replaced by two strokes (//); this seems to have been a practice which emerged among scribes writing in Greek and Coptic for the Umayyad administration, and so may have represented a way to avoid writing the cross out of sensitivity to the new Muslim ruling class.¹⁸⁸ Such slashes are found in one manuscript in this volume (*PCM* I 17), and offer an additional dating criterion.

At a higher level, texts may be divided by horizontal strokes, which may be simple, or decorated. Decorated dividers may consist of two parallel stokes and/or be broken with dots, among other strategies for decoration. The *diple* is a wedge shape (>), usually drawn in the left margin, and marking breaks in textual units.

Coptic script is generally written continuously (*scriptio continua*), although scribes may (inconsistently) leave small spaces between words or word groups. Individual copyists may also use various signs—such as the mid dot (·), colon (:), tricolon (⁚), or two oblique strokes (⸗)—to mark breaks between words and word groups. These may sometimes break up units that we consider to be single groups.

Coptic also makes extensive use of supralineation, the practice of writing supralinear strokes above certain letters. In standard Sahidic Coptic, these are usually used above abbreviations, as well as consonants which were either pronounced with a preceding short vowel (*schwa*) or were autosyllabic, *i.e.*, the syllable to which they belonged may not have had any true vowel sound.¹⁸⁹ Supralinear strokes are used in this way (albeit inconsistently, as in other genres) in Coptic magical texts, but they are also used to mark the names of superhuman beings, and in particular, *voces magicae*. This practice continues that found in some Graeco-Egyptian magical texts, although it seems to ultimately derive from a non-magical context, in which Greek-literate scribes marked non-Greek words with a supralinear stroke in order to clearly mark where they began and ended

---

[186] Sanzo 2015: 79–82; Dosoo 2022a: 121–122.
[187] Choat 2006: 116–118; Blumell 2012: 43–46; de Bruyn 2017: 62–64; Carlig 2020.
[188] Richter 2003: 223–230; Cromwell 2023: 234–235; Amory 2023: 65–66.
[189] Peust 1999: 61–65; Layton 2000: 28–30, 31–32.

to aid in reading.[190] In this volume, we do not generally attempt to reproduce supralinear strokes exactly; if a stroke is partially above a letter, we mark it as being above that letter, rather than rendering a smaller stroke between two letters. Likewise, we do not generally indicate in transliteration if a supralinear stroke was rounded or flat, although in cases in which they are closer to sign known as the djinkim (`, used in the Bohairic dialect), we do reproduce this form schematically. We encourage readers to consult photographs of the original manuscripts—either in the plates, or at the links provided in the introductions to each entry—if the exact form of paratextual markers is of interest to them.

4. The Presentation of Texts in this Volume

4.1. Principles of Edition

The goal of this volume is to present Coptic magical texts in a way which enables readers—professional scholars but also students and interested laypeople—to access them as directly as possible. We provide basic notes to aid in the interpretation of these texts and to explain our decisions as translators, signalling uncertainties as clearly as possible using question marks. These uncertainties—of the meaning or interpretation of words, phrases and practices—should not be taken as admissions of defeat, but rather as signposts marking the extensive work that remains to be done on these understudied texts.

We have sought to follow modern papyrological norms, specifically those proposed by the Association of Papyrology in 2022,[191] but with some important deviations from these based on the particular features of magical texts. First, we understand the *mise en page* (layout) of magical texts to be significant:[192] the decision of copyists of where to place different text sections in relation to one another or to images, and the way in which they subsequently correct or add text provides us with important information as to their conceptions of the work, and the way in which they used and interacted with it. This means that, generally, each manuscript page or sheet side is reproduced on one printed page, schematically reproducing the original document as clearly as possible. Where there are two or more manuscript pages to a printed page, these are clearly signalled, and separated by a horizontal line which goes across the full width of the printed column (as opposed to shorter lines reproducing dividing lines in the original manuscripts). Translations of these texts are reproduced on facing pages. With the exception of common abbreviations, we avoid Latin in the apparatus, instead using English to

---

[190] Fournet 2020a: 154–157.
[191] See Fournet *et al.* 2022, online at https://aip.ulb.be//PDF/Guidelines_for_editing_papyri.pdf
[192] We use the term "significant" here as the equivalent of the French *signifiant* ("signifying"), inspired by the usage of Fournet 2007.

make the volume accessible to the largest number of readers.

In the past, the contexts of manuscripts have often been neglected; although, as explained above (3.1.1) we usually have no precise information on the circumstances of discovery of manuscripts, we have attempted to reconstruct these as accurately as possible from surviving records, and we have likewise attempted to date the manuscripts as precisely as possible based on the analysis of palaeography and other features. These processes are rarely conclusive, but we think that they are worth carrying out in order to ground texts in place and time. For this reason, we are occasionally quite daring in our proposals, but, as in other cases, we signal our uncertainty with the use of question marks; again, these question marks should be taken seriously, and readers should be sure to consult the rationales provided in the introductions to decide for themselves how plausible they find our suggestions. For reasons of space, only images of manuscripts which have not been published in the past, or which are not readily available online, are published in this volume.

4.2. Layout, Notes and Apparatus

Each manuscript begins with its number in this publication, followed by a modern title briefly describing its form and/or content. This is followed by basic information in the form of bullet points, and then an introduction. The following pages provide the text, accompanied by an apparatus below the text, with facing translation, below which are notes.

4.2.1. Basic information and Introduction

Each manuscript begins with a section of basic information, which first gives the provenance, dimensions (height, width, and where relevant, depth, in centimetres (cm)) and then proposed date. Edited volumes are referenced according to the standard *Checklist of Editions of Greek, Latin, Demotic, and Coptic Papyri, Ostraca, and Tablets*,[193] with the sigla italicised. We indicate the URL of the official online photo of the manuscript, the plate number for this volume, or in another printed publication. If the image is no longer accessible at the online address given, we advise readers to consult the *Kyprianos* or *Trismegistos* databases, where a more up-to-date link may be available. The linguistic description briefly discusses the dialect (or language, if the text contains more than simply Coptic text). The contents provide a list of the texts contained in the manuscript, numbered in order of writing, along with the *Kyprianos* text number associated with each entry.

---

[193] For the checklist, see https://papyri.info/docs/checklist

The basic information is followed by a discursive introduction, which provides further information on questions of materiality, including manuscript format, *kollēsis*, folding (described in terms of the number of visible creases), inks, and so on. This also includes information on provenance and acquisition, and then a description of the hand and a discussion of dating. In general, we do not discuss the contents of the manuscripts here, but rather in the notes accompanying the translation, although we make an exception in a few cases, notably those in which the manuscript contains texts with a complex history which cannot be adequately discussed in the notes printed below the translation.

4.2.2. Text and Apparatus

The text field contains the original language form of the text, with minimal interventions. At the top of each page or column, the fibre direction (↓/→) is noted for papyrus, and the same signs are used on ostraca to indicate the direction of wheel marks. Side (hair/flesh) is noted for parchment, as well as curvature (concave/convex) for ostraca, where we have access to this information.

Coptic words are generally divided following the scheme of Walter Till.[194] In Greek text, accents and breathings are added, but the transliteration contains only punctuation present in the original manuscript. We attempt to represent any text added above or below the line of text in a schematic manner which allows its relative position to the line to be appreciated without compromising legibility. *Eisthesis* and *ekthesis* (indentation and extension into the margin), as well as notably enlarged letters, may also be represented visually, with the format being described in the apparatus. Abbreviations are resolved in the apparatus, and any non-Coptic (Greek or Arabic) words are also noted in their original language form. For Greek verbs, we give the present infinitive form, which usually seems to have been that borrowed into Coptic, although in the case of a few verbs, we should probably understand them as imperatives.[195]

A solid horizontal line across the entire column marks a new page or side, but a shorter horizontal line marks dividers from the original text. A dashed line at the end of a page or side indicates a break in the writing surface, suggesting lost text.

Variant readings by previous editors are indicated in the apparatus according to line number, but only when these diverge from our own readings or interpretations. The previous editors' readings are indicated by providing their reading followed

---

[194] Till 1960; note that in a few cases we diverge from his schema for reasons of clarity.

[195] This is the case for γράφε and βοήθει, which appear as imperatives at the equivalent points in Greek magical texts. For γράφε, see *e.g.*, *GEMF* 15/*PGM* XII (KYP M160) l. 127 (78); *GEMF* 30/*PGM* II (KYP M152) l. 77 (30). For βοήθει, see *PGM* VI b (KYP M424) l. 3; *cf. PGM* XIII/*GEMF* 60 (KYP M161) l. 289; *PGM* LXXXIX/*SM* 13 (KYP M813) l. 5. On the general borrowing of infinitive forms of verbs, see Grossmann/Richter 2017: 221–223.

by their surname, at times abbreviated for space. The editors can be identified by consulting the list of editions and translations at the beginning of the introduction, where any abbreviations are also introduced. Alternative translations may also be noted, where they diverge significantly from those we offer, by giving the translation in inverted commas, followed by the translator's name. Coptic words which appear in a form not found in Crum's *Coptic Dictionary* (1939) are given in their standard Sahidic form in the apparatus,[196] prefixed by a superscript ^{S},[197] and broken into morphemes by dashes (the sign ⸗ precedes suffix pronouns). The apparatus also notes corrections and deletions made by the copyists, including a brief description of how the deletion or correction has been made. A full list of critical signs is available on p. xv.

4.2.3. Translation, Notes, and Glossary

Translations are largely continuous, although we indicate line breaks in the translation to aid in the comprehension of text structure. Paragraph breaks are used to indicate separate texts or text sections (such as the passage from formula to ritual instructions). We generally indicate line breaks in the original text at every five lines of the translation by a vertical stroke followed by the line number (|^5) but further line breaks are sometimes indicated where these aid in understanding the structure of the text. Words broken across lines, or which survive only partially, are not broken up either across line divisions or by square brackets in order to maximise legibility and searchability. Words broken across lines are assigned to the line which contains most of their letters, and if both lines have an equal number of letters, they are usually assigned to the first of the lines on which they appear. Words whose translation is uncertain, either because of damage, or for other reasons, are marked with a superscript question mark. Words marked by an asterisk appear in the glossary at the end of the volume (pp. 471–488).

For deities and culturally significant figures who are well known, we use the standard English (or at times Latin) equivalent, thus 'Jesus' (ⲓⲏⲥⲟⲩⲥ), 'Isis' (ⲏⲥⲉ), and 'John' (ⲓⲱϩⲁⲛⲛⲏⲥ, in the case of the Apostle or Evangelist). For historical people who were not famous, and superhuman beings whose names do not have a standard English form, we use a standard transliteration scheme, based on but modified from the Leipzig-Jerusalem transliteration system (fig. 2).[198] Thus, for example, the copyist responsible for *PCM* I 21–26, who has the same name as the Apostle John, is called in this work the Deacon Iōhannēs (ⲓⲱϩⲁⲛⲛⲏⲥ).

---

[196] In this case, we use *i.e.* ("that is") rather than *l.* ("read"), that is, we understand our intervention as an interpretation rather than a correction.

[197] Comparable signs are used when, more rarely, we compare forms in other dialects, such as Bohairic (^{B}) and Faiyumic (^{F}).

[198] Grossmann/Haspelmath 2015.

Introduction 41

Letter	Name[199]	Transl.	Value[200]	Letter	Name	Transl.	Value
ⲁ	alpha	a	/a/	ⲣ	rho	r	/r/
ⲃ	beta	b	/β/	ⲥ	sigma	s	/s/
ⲅ	gamma	g	/k/ or /g/	ⲧ	tau	t	/t/
ⲇ	delta	d	/t/ or /d/	ⲩ	upsilon	u	/u/ or /w/
ⲉ	epsilon	e	/ɛ/	ⲫ	phi	ph	/pʰ/
ⲍ	zeta	z	/z/	ⲭ	chi	kh	/kʰ/
ⲏ	eta	ē	/e/	ⲯ	psi	ps	/ps/
ⲑ	theta	th	/tʰ/	ⲱ	omega	ō	/o/
ⲓ	iota	i	/i/ or /j/	ϣ	shai	š	/ʃ/
ⲕ	kappa	k	/k/	ϥ	fai	f	/f/
ⲗ	lambda	l	/l/	ϧ	khai	ḫ	/x/
ⲙ	mu	m	/m/	ⳉ	barred hori	ẖ	/x/
ⲛ	nu	n	/n/	ϩ	hori	h	/h/
ⲝ	xi	x	/ks/	ϫ	djandja	č	/tʃ/
ⲟ	omicron	o	/ɔ/	ϭ	kjima	c	/kʲ/ or /tʃʰ/
ⲡ	pi	p	/p/	ϯ	ti	ti	/ti/

Fig. 2: Transliteration scheme used in this volume

Each translation ends with a list of the editors' initials (for which see the list of abbreviations), and a description of how the manuscript was examined, either via photograph alone or also through in-person inspection ('autopsy'), and who was responsible for producing tracings of tableaux, where relevant.

4.3. Palaeographical Descriptions

In our palaeographical descriptions, we try to make use of a regular vocabulary in order to standardise these as much as possible, despite the uniqueness of every hand.[201]

---

[199] The names of the Coptic letters here are those used by modern Copticists, corresponding to the Greek names in the cases where the alphabets overlap; for the Coptic names, see the initial entries for each letter in Crum CD; Peust 1999: 58–60.

[200] Given here are the approximate values for these letters in classical Sahidic; the actual pronunciation changed considerably across dialect and over time, and likely also depended upon their position in words and phrases. For discussions of Coptic phonology, see Sobhy 1915; Worrell 1934; Peust 1999: 56–65 *et passim*; Casey 2022.

[201] For discussions of Coptic palaeography, and the terminology used here, see Boud'hors 1997;

The term *majuscule* (generally equivalent to *uncial*) refers to the 'capital' forms of letters in which each has, in principle, the same height; these letterforms may also be referred to as *bilinear*, that is, they can be understood as being written between two lines, an upper line marking the height of all or nearly all letters, and a lower line, marking the lowest point of all letters. The term *minuscule* refers to letterforms similar to those of modern Greek lowercase letters. These may also be referred to as *quadrilinear*, since the letters can be understood as being written between four lines, with their bodies generally resting between two central lines, and the ascendant or descendant parts of certain letters reaching higher or lower boundary lines. The concept of *modus* refers to letter width; early majuscules tend to give all letters (with a few exceptions, such as ι) equal width, and are thus referred to as *unimodular*. By contrast, later *bimodular* hands, used from the sixth century or so, vary the width of letters, with є, ѳ, o, and c usually being markedly narrower than other letters.

A further point of description is *slope*; hands may be described as *upright*, or *slanting* or *inclined* to one side. *Cursivity* describes the degree to which hands make use of ligatures—if letters regularly join together, they may be described as cursive, or as making use of ligatures. Hands may furthermore be described more vaguely in terms of *regularity*, *formality*, and *training*. Regular hands consistently produce letters with the same shapes, sizes, and spacing. Formal hands are by definition regular, but also seem to consciously reproduce particular canonical styles, often associated with high-prestige texts, and aim for a high degree of legibility.[202] Informal or irregular hands tend to be more idiosyncratic, with more variation in letterform, sizing, spacing, and so on. While trained scribes might deliberately produce informal texts, some informal hands may be described as 'untrained', as 'literates with specific competences', or as 'functional semi-literates'.[203] In these cases we sometimes make use of Raffaella Criobiore's categories of learner hands, in particular the *alphabetic* and *evolving* hands.[204] Alphabetic hands describe writers who know the alphabet and the letterforms, but can only write individual letters slowly and with some difficulty, while evolving hands seem to write with more frequency, but are not able to write with absolute regularity or in a canonical style. *Shading* refers to the thickness of the

---

MacCoull 1997 (note that some of the dates given are incorrect); Delattre 2007: 127–132; Gardner/Choat 2004; Askeland 2018; Mihálykó 2019: 83–92; Boud'hors 2020; Krueger 2020: 166–183; Amory forthcoming. We also thank Yasmine Amory for her helpful advice on this section, and for her many invaluable comments on our palaeographical descriptions.

[202] Here we follow the definitions of formality and informality offered in Crisci/Degni 2011: 25–6. We thank Yasmine Amory for this reference.

[203] For this term, see Petrucci 2002: 20–21; Amory forthcoming.

[204] Cribiore 1996: 33, 112. As Yasmine Amory points out, the terminology is not ideal, since 'evolving', for example, implies a stage in training, whereas here we use it to describe an established writer. Nonetheless, the categories identified by Cribiore are useful in more narrowly defining types of non-expert writing, and may imply the highest level of scribal training attained by particular writers.

strokes which make up the letters, and whether there is variation in line thickness. *Flourishes* and *serifs* are terms which refer to decorative extensions or ticks which may be used at the ends of strokes.

In general, the hands contained in this collection are usually either highly informal, or represent the right-sloping majuscule common in *Kleinliteratur* ("minor literature")—technical texts such as medical, magical, and alchemical works—as well as in the colophons of literary texts.[205] Occasionally, we see examples of cursive documentary-type hands which evolve from the sixth century onwards. There are relatively few letterforms which we consider absolutely diagnostic of a date; one exception to this is the so-called "flat mu", which almost resembles an inverted π (ɯ); this form seems to appear only in the tenth century.[206]

Where more than one hand writes a single manuscript, we mark changes of hand by adding *m(anus)* + number in the left margin of the Coptic text. Where individual copyists use markedly different styles for different sections, we likewise mark *s(tyle)* + number in the left margin.[207]

5. The Contents of *Papyri Copticae Magicae* I

In choosing texts for this volume, it has been necessary to be selective, but we have been unable to use entirely objective criteria. The corpus as a whole is not yet well enough studied to propose a purely chronological arrangement, as is done for the *Greek and Egyptian Magical Formularies*; the work of dating the manuscripts is best carried out alongside their publication. We also see the Coptic magical papyri as an open corpus, which will grow as more texts are discovered or published. As a result, a strictly chronological arrangement would become incoherent over time. Instead, we divide the corpus first by basic type—formularies and applied texts (see 3.2)—then divide the latter category into texts which are 'aggressive' (broadly, curses and love spells) and 'amuletic' (healing, exorcistic, protective, and for gaining favour). This first volume contains formularies.

For this volume of formularies, we aim to provide a selection which gives readers a good idea of the general nature of the corpus, mixing long texts whose histories can be traced for centuries across multiple languages (*e.g.*, *PCM* I 11 & 25) with shorter and more idiosyncratic examples (*e.g.*, *PCM* I 2 & 35). We have deliberately picked some which we judge to be particularly important—*PCM* I 1, for example, is the earliest well-dated magical text in a standard Coptic dialect, and its archaeological context provides a rich idea of *Sitz im Leben* ("lived context") not possible for the other manuscripts.

We have also selected many texts which benefitted significantly from re-edition,

---

[205] Till 1942: 101; Boud'hors 1997; Mihálykó 2019: 85–92.
[206] *Cf.* Mihálykó 2019: 16–18.
[207] For the concept of 'style' in papyrology, see Fournet 2019: 572–575, 581.

including several from the University of Heidelberg papyrus collection (*PCM* I 21–33, 35), all of which date to the tenth or eleventh centuries CE. Nine of these (*PCM* I 21–29) provide us with an example of an archive containing magical texts, and even those which do not belong to this archive show striking similarities of format, content, and language. This is also true of three other manuscripts from other modern collections dating to the tenth and eleventh centuries (*PCM* I 34, 36, 37). Presenting these texts together has allowed us to bring out these shared features. We nonetheless exclude texts, including those from Heidelberg, with significant Arabic-language content, reserved for a future volume.

The Heidelberg group also includes some of the longest surviving texts, several belonging to the category of the 'magical liturgies'; for this reason we include other extensive exemplars, including the Leiden Anastasy Codex (*PCM* I 11) and Rossi's 'Gnostic' Tractate (*PCM* I 12), which offer both notable similarities and contrasts with the Heidelberg material. The inclusion of Rossi's famous 'tractate' suggested to us the inclusion of its largely forgotten sibling, the much more fragmentary second 'tractate', perhaps found with it (*PCM* I 13).

We also include in this volume most of the 'narrative charms' (*PCM* I 6, 7, 15, 16, 20, 29), and the related texts featuring Pharaonic deities (*PCM* I 4, 8, 9); these have attracted considerable attention in past research, and so we hope that presenting new editions of them will prove useful to their ongoing study.[208]

The remaining manuscripts contain the briefer and more idiosyncratic texts which constitute the majority of the corpus. *PCM* 2, 3 & 10 demonstrate the important place accorded to female reproductive health in magical texts: respectively, a procedure for healing uterine bleeding, a curse to cause it, and a prayer to allow a woman to become pregnant.[209] In the other texts of this volume we see a still wider range of purposes: *PCM* I 5 represents a typical example of a short healing recipe, which may be found both alone in individual sheets and as part of larger collections (*cf.* *PCM* I 33 & 36); *PCM* I 14, perhaps a love spell, demonstrates the use of figural images reminiscent of those on later and more complex formularies. *PCM* I 17 & 19 have more idiosyncratic goals—acquiring a good singing voice and maintaining the virginity of a woman. Finally, *PCM* I 18 contains a curse whose vivid description of the sickness it aims to bring about is accompanied by a brief but evocative account of the workings of the celestial hierarchy reminiscent of those found in a more extensive form in the 'magical liturgies'.

---

[208] Excluded manuscripts which could be counted among these include *BKU* I 1 (KYP M76), to be published with the other manuscripts of its archive (KYP A14); and four recently (re-) published manuscripts: Mich.Ms. 136 (Zellmann-Rohrer/Love 2022; KYP M128); Saqqara F.17.10 (SA.03/141) (van der Vliet 2018a; Zellmann-Rohrer/Love 2022; KYP M716); Naqlun N. 78/93 (KYP M1135) and *P.Herm.Copt.* 67 (KYP M57) (both Kalchenko/van der Vliet 2022).

[209] For another recently-published recipe to treat a gynaecological problem, see BnF Copte 129.20 fol. 178 (Preininger 2022; KYP M108) ll. 1–5.

Text Editions

PCM I 1. Letter of Oualēs to Psais containing separation spell

Kellis (Ismant al-Kharab)   23.7 (H) × 7.7 (W) cm   Late IV CE

Other references: Kellis Excavation no. P88 + P77B + P79 + P92.49; TM 85886; *P.Kell.* V *Copt.* 35; KYP M176; Bélanger Sarrazin #189.

Editions: Mirecki *et al.* 1997 (*ed. pr.*); Gardner *et al.* 1999.

Translations: Mirecki *et al.* 1997; Gardner *et al.* 1999; van der Vliet 2019b: 332–334; Hope/Bowen 2022: 423–424.

Additional commentary: Shisha-Halevy 2002; Mirecki 2013; Love 2016: 273–276; van der Vliet 2020: 263–265; Teigen 2021: 205–206, 248, 280; Brand 2022: 102, 104–105, 280–281; Dosoo/Torallas Tovar 2022a: 42–54; Love 2022a: 180–181.

Present location: Ismant al-Kharab magazine, Egypt.

Image: Gardner *et al.* 1999: plate 27.

Linguistic description: Written in Lycopolitan (L4); initial 3 lines of the formula (front ll. 1–3) and address (back ll. 11–12) in Greek.

Contents:

1. Front ll. 1–22: Separation spell (KYP T350)
2. Front ll. 23–42, back ll. 1–8: Letter from Oualēs to Psais (KYP T1506)
3. Back ll. 9–10: Address formula (KYP T1505)

A complete papyrus sheet with some damage along the folds. The text is a formulary copied as part of a letter from a man named Oualēs to another named Psais, found in room 6 of House 3 of Area A during the Dakhleh Oasis Project excavation of Kellis, with various fragments being found in the years between 1977 and 1992.[1] The letter begins with instructions for a separation spell taking up 22 lines on the front (→), followed by the contents of the letter—a resumé of the request which led to the sending of the letter, an apology for not finding the text requested, and a counter request that the addressee copy and send other texts in return. This letter takes up the remaining 20 lines of the front, and then 8 lines on the back, written at 90° counterclockwise to the text of the front. Finally, the address is written in Greek on the back in 2 lines on the opposite corner from the end of the letter, with the point where the seal would be attached (*locus sigilli*) indicated by a cross, broken where the string tying the letter closed would have been. 5 horizontal and 3 vertical creases are apparent (from the perspective of the front), indicating that it was folded before being sent. The tall, narrow format is typical of Greek and Coptic letters dating to before the fifth century, including examples from Kellis.[2]

---

[1] Specifically deposit 3 + deposit 4 north-west corner, east wall + deposit 5 west wall; see Gardner *et al.* 1999: 118.

[2] For the formats of Greek letters, see Fournet 2009; Sarri 2017. For similar letters from Kellis,

At several points, the scribe has left blank spaces (*vacats*) between words or lines, presumably to avoid imperfections in the papyrus' writing surface.[3]

The site of Kellis, modern Ismant al-Kharab, is in the Dakhla Oasis, 350 kilometres west of the Nile Valley. Area A House 3 is a particularly rich site, containing over 200 texts written in Coptic, Greek, and to a lesser extent, Syriac, testifying to the lives of one or more extended families who seem to have been Manichaean Hearers.[4] Alongside various epistolary, business, and administrative documents, the preserved manuscripts contain a number of ritual texts, including hymns, a prayer for the unction of the sick known from other Christian liturgical sources, a Greek magical formulary containing healing prescriptions, and three amulets against disease.[5] The texts document a period from the end of the third century into the 390s, at which point the house, along with the rest of the village, was abandoned, perhaps due to the encroachment of the desert. The inhabitants of the house at this period were involved in various businesses, primarily weaving, trading cloth and finished clothing as far as the Nile Valley, but also the maintenance of fruit trees (olive and perhaps jujube), some of which were leased out.[6] The house appears to have been stripped of valuable items when it was abandoned, so that the remaining texts are apparently those left behind in storage jars on the roof, which subsequently collapsed and fell into the ground-floor rooms.[7]

The writer of the letter, Oualēs (the Greek writing of the Latin *Valens*) lived outside Kellis, and is responsible for one other letter to the inhabitants of House 3 (*P.Kell.* V *Copt.* 36); it has been suggested that he was a member of the Manichaean monastic and clerical group known as the Elect, but this remains uncertain.[8] Psais (the Greek form of the Egyptian *Pšai*) was one of the younger members of the household of House 3, known from several other texts in the archive, and identified by Klaas Worp as Psais III, since this name was a recurrent one within the family.[9]

The hand of Oualēs is an accomplished, largely bilinear majuscule, inclined to the right and rather cursive; ⲁ, ⲉ, and ⲧ are regularly ligatured to the following letter. Bilinearity is broken by ⲃ, ⲣ, ⲭ, ϥ, and ϯ, which descend below the lower line,

---

cf. P.Kell. V *Copt.* 20, 25, 26, 31, 36, 39, 43, 50.

[3] *E.g.*, at front ll. 22, 29, 40–43; back ll. 4–5; *cf.* Jones 2015 for scribes avoiding damaged areas of papyrus.

[4] For recent overviews, see Teigen 2021: 53–80; Brand 2022: 40–90; Hope/Bowen 2022: 42–48.

[5] Prayer for the unction of the sick: *P.Kell.* I *Gr.* 88 (KYP M1105); Greek formulary: *.Kell.* I 85 (KYP M185); published Greek amulets: *P.Kell.* I 86 (KYP M2114) & *P.Kell.* I 87 (KYP M184). For a discussions of the magical and other ritual/technical texts, see Dosoo/Torallas Tovar: 2022a; Brand 2022: 98–105.

[6] For a recent overview, see Teigen 2021: 75–79.

[7] Bowen 2015: 235.

[8] For this proposal see Gardner *et al.* 1999: 34–35, Mirecki *et al.* 1997: 5–6; Teigen 2021: 248–249; *cf.* Brand 2022: 280–281.

[9] Worp 1995: 50–54; Gardner *et al.* 1999: 41, 57–58; *cf.* Mirecki *et al.* 1997: 6; Teigen 2021: 66–67; Brand 2022: 341.

and ⳰ which ascends above it. Most of the Demotic-derived letters (ϣ, ϥ, ϫ, ϭ), are compact, respecting the overall bilinearity. There are marked flourishes on many letters at the ends of the lines. The oblique stroke of ⲁ is short and considerably raised; the bulb often gives the impression of hanging from it. ⲉ is formed in two strokes: the rounded vertical followed by the horizontal. ⲏ generally takes its majuscule form, more rarely being written in a single stroke, in which it resembles a mirrored ⲛ (*e.g.*, front l. 33). ⲙ is rounded, as is the suprelinear stroke. ⲡ is written in a single stroke, without a distinct horizontal bar. ⲩ is in the form of a Latin V, also written in a single stroke. Letters are generally undecorated, although there are occasionally slight serifs, as on the vertical stroke of ϯ. As noted by Gardner and Choat, the degree of cursivity in this manuscript, and others from Kellis, is unusual in a Coptic text of the fourth century, as is the fact that Greek and Coptic text are not visually distinguished.[10] Similar hands are nonetheless common in the papyri from Kellis; see for example *P.Kell.* VII *Copt.* 78 and *P.Kell.* I *Gr.* 44, both by Pekusis (Pecoš), apparently the brother of Psais, as well as *P.Kell. Copt.* V 15, 17 & 22.[11] Similar features (albeit with less cursivity and greater formality) may also be seen in some of the literary manuscripts, such as *P.Kell.* II *Copt.* 53.

The circumstances behind the letter have been discussed numerous times. Briefly, Psais seems to have requested a specific separation procedure from Oualēs; Oualēs was unable to find it, but instead copied another he had access to in the present letter, noting that he would send the originally requested text if he found it. He specifies that the text should not be shown to a "Brother Kalliklēs"—perhaps suggesting the necessity of secrecy in the transmission of this text[12]—and asks, in return, that Psais copy for him some quaternions (*cf.* the note to front l. 37). The larger context of the letter allows it to be dated with some precision to the second half of the fourth century, when Psais III was active, between the years 351 and 390 CE; this is thus one of the earliest magical texts to be written in one of the standard Coptic dialects, as opposed to one of the forms of Old Coptic.

The magical text consists primarily of an invocation to the Jewish-Christian god. The ritual, alluded to in the invocation, and briefly described in the instructions which follow, seems to have consisted of burning mustard, which was mixed with Arabian natron, over which the formula was spoken before being deposited at the door of the house of the intended victims of the separation spell. Similar rituals are known from later Greek and Coptic-language sources.[13]

---

[10] Gardner/Choat 2004: 505–07.
[11] Brand 2022: 338, 341.
[12] *Cf.* Mirecki 2001.
[13] These include *SM* II 95/*PGM* CXXVI (V CE) and BM EA 10391 (Zellmann-Rohrer 2022a: no. 1; KYP M302; back ll. 76–78, 79–80, 82–84, 94–95; VIII–IX CE); *cf.* the discussion in Mirecki *et al.* 1997: 25–28.

front (→)

Ἐπικαλοῦμαί σε τὸν ἐπὶ ἀρχῆς
ὄντα τὸν καθήμενον ἐπάνω
χερουβὶν καὶ σαρουφὶν πεταϩαρετϥ
ⲁⲭⲛ̅ ⲙ̅ⲙⲓϣⲉ ⲙⲛ̅ ⲛ̅†ⲧⲱⲛ ⲡⲉⲧⲁϩⲱ-
5 ⲭ[ⲡ] ⲛ̅ⲛ̅ⲧⲏⲟⲩ ϩⲛ̅ ⲧϥⲛⲁϭ ⲛ̅ⲉⲝⲟⲩⲥⲓⲁ ⲛ̅-
ⲑ[ⲉ ⲉ]ⲧⲁⲕⲣ̅ ⲡⲕⲁϩ ⲛ̅ⲕⲏⲙⲉ ⲛ̅ⲭⲁⲓ̈ⲥ ⲁⲕⲛⲟⲩ-
[ⲭⲉ] ⲛ̅ϩⲛ̅†ⲧⲱⲛ ⲁⲭⲛ̅ ⲛ̅ⲭⲁⲗⲇⲁⲓⲟⲥ ⲛ̅ⲧⲱ-
[ⲧⲛ] ⲡⲉ†ⲧⲉⲟⲩⲟ ⲛ̅ⲛⲓⲣⲉⲛ ⲁⲭⲱⲧⲛ̅ ⲛ̅ⲧⲟ-
. . ⲓ̈ⲣ ⲉⲧϫⲡⲟ ⲉⲧⲕⲏⲙ · ⲙⲁⲣⲉⲛⲓⲙ ⲡϣⲏⲣⲉ
10 ⲣⲉ ⲛ̣ⲛⲓⲙ ⲙⲁⲣⲉⲡⲟⲩϩⲏⲧ ⲕⲙⲁⲙ ⲙⲛ̅ ⲛⲟⲩⲉⲣⲏⲟⲩ · ⲡϩⲁⲥⲃ̅ ⲛ̅ⲡⲓⲛⲉ ⲛ̅ⲧⲁⲣⲁⲃⲓⲁ ⲛ̅-
ⲑⲉ ⲉⲧⲕ̅ⲛⲁⲓ̈ϣⲉ ⲛ̅ϩⲛⲟ ⲛⲓⲙ ⲁⲃⲁⲗ ⲉⲕⲁ-
ⲓ̈ϣⲉ ⲙ̅ⲡⲟⲩⲱϣⲉ ⲉⲧⲟⲩⲧⲱⲟⲩ ϣⲁ ⲛⲟⲩⲉⲣⲏⲟⲩ ⲛ̅ⲧⲁⲕ ⲇⲉ ⲡⲭⲱϥ ⲙ̅ⲡⲁϣⲧⲉⲙ
15 ⲉⲕⲁ† ⲡⲭⲱϥ ⲙⲛ̅ ⲡⲣⲱⲭϩ ⲁⲡⲟⲩϩⲏⲧ
ϣⲁ ⲛⲟⲩⲉⲣⲏⲟⲩ ⲡⲏⲓ̈ ⲉ†ⲛⲁⲕⲁⲕ ⲛ̅ϩⲏ-
ⲧϥ ⲙ̅ⲡⲣⲉⲓ ⲁⲃⲁⲗ ⲛ̅ϩⲏⲧϥ ⲉⲙⲡⲕ̅-
ⲧⲟⲩⲛⲟⲩⲥ ⲛ̅ⲟⲩⲙⲓϣⲉ ⲙⲛ̅ ⲟⲩ†-
ⲧⲱⲛ ⲙⲛ̅ ⲟⲩϭⲉⲣⲁⲩⲛⲟⲥ ⲙⲛ̅ ⲇ
20 ⲏ̈ⲩ ⲇ ⲛ̅ⲧⲁⲥ ⲇ ⲟ̈ⲛ ⲇ ⲉⲕⲁⲧⲉⲟⲩ-
ⲟ ⲛⲓϣⲉϫⲉ ⲁⲭϣⲟⲩ
ⲁϥϫⲱⲕ

---

2 ὄντα Pap : + ὄντα Mirecki *et al.* : ὄντα Gardner *et al.* ‖ **3** πεταϩ‹ε› ⲁⲣⲉⲧϥ Mirecki *et al.* ‖ **4–5** *i.e.* ˢⲡ-ⲉⲛⲧ-ⲁϥ-ϩⲱⲭⲡ : ⲡⲉⲧⲁϩⲱ|ⲭ[ⲛ] Mirecki *et al.*, Gardner *et al.* ‖ **5** *i.e.* ˢⲧⲉϥⲛⲟϭ | *i.e.* ἐξουσία ‖ **7** *i.e.* Χαλδαῖος ‖ **8** *i.e.* ˢⲡ(ⲉ)-ⲉⲧ-†-ⲧⲁⲟⲩⲟ ‖ **8–9** "you (s.) [are the one who makes (?)] what is generated black (?)" Mirecki *et al.* : "by (?) ... who generates (?), who is black" Gardner *et al.* : "you, O dung (?) (*i.e.* ˢⲧ-ϩⲟⲉⲓⲣⲉ) of the black ..." van der Vliet ‖ **10** *l.* ‹ⲛⲛⲓⲙ ⲙⲛ ⲛⲓⲙ ⲧϣⲉⲉⲣⲉ ⲛⲛⲓⲙ ? : [ⲣⲉ ⲛ] ⲛⲓⲙ Mirecki *et al.* ‖ **11** *i.e.* ˢϩⲟⲥⲙ | *i.e.* ˢⲙ-ⲡ-ⲉⲓⲛⲉ ? : ⲛ̅ⲡⲓⲛⲟ *i.e.* ˢⲙ̅-ⲡⲉⲓ-ⲛⲁⲩ Mirecki *et al.*, Shisha-Halevy : *i.e.* πίνος, πιναρός, less likely πίνη/πινάριον or πίνινος (λίθος) "dirt", "dirty", "pearl", less likely "pearl" or "mother of pearl" Gardner *et al.* ‖ **13** *i.e.* ˢⲉⲧ-ⲟⲩ-ⲧⲱ ? | ⲉⲧⲟⲩⲧⲱⲟⲩ/ⲉⲧⲁⲣⲧⲱⲟⲩ Mirecki *et al.* ‖ **14** *i.e.* δέ | *i.e.* ˢⲁϣⲗⲟⲙ ‖ **15** ⲡⲣⲱⲭϩ Mirecki *et al.*, Gardner *et al.* ‖ **17** corrected from ⲙ̅ⲡϥ̅ⲉⲓ Mirecki *et al.* | *i.e.* ˢⲙ̅ⲡⲁⲧⲉⲕ- ‖ **19** *i.e.* κεραυνός : *l.* δ(ⲉ)ⲓ̈(ⲛⲁ) *cf.* van der Vliet : ⲇ Mirecki *et al.*, Gardner *et al.* ‖ **20** *l.* ⲏ̈ⲛ (ⲉ̈ⲧⲉⲕⲉⲛ ⲏ̈) δ(ⲉ)ⲓ̈(ⲛⲁ) ⲛ̅ⲧⲁⲥ δ(ⲉ)ⲓ̈(ⲛⲁ) ὄν (ⲉ̈ⲧⲉⲕⲉⲛ ⲏ̈) δ(ⲉ)ⲓ̈(ⲛⲁ) *cf.* van der Vliet : ⲕⲉ ⲇ | ⲛ̅ⲧⲁⲥ ⲇ ⲟⲛ ⲇ Mirecki *et al.*, Gardner *et al.* ‖ **21** ⲁⲭϣⲟⲩ ⲱ corrected from unclear letter by overwriting : ⲁⲭ⟦ⲱ⟧ ⲙⲟⲩ Mirecki *et al.* : ⲁⲭⲉϣⲟⲩ corrected from ⲁⲭ . . ⲟⲩ Gardner *et al.*

PCM I 1 (P.Kell. V Copt. 35) : Letter of Oualēs to Psais containing separation spell   51

|*Greek* "I invoke you who have existed from the beginning, who sit over *cherubim and *seraphim, |*Coptic* who stand over the conflicts and the strifes, who shut up |⁵ the winds through your great *authority; just as you made the land of Egypt lord and you cast strifes upon the Chaldaeans. It is you (pl.) upon whom I pronounce these *names, O ... that give birth?, that are black, may NN son |¹⁰ of NN, may their heart become black with one another! O natron in the likeness? of Arabia, just as you will wash away all things, may you wash ‹away› their desire that they have for one another! And you, O scorching of the mustard, |¹⁵ may you put scorching and burning in their hearts towards one another! The house in which I shall place you, do not leave it before you have awoken a conflict and a strife and a thunderbolt with NN, |²⁰ daughter of NN, she ‹and› NN, son of NN!"

You should pronounce these words over them. It is finished.

---

1. τὸν ἐπὶ ἀρχῆς : "**you who have existed from the beginning**" Mirecki *et al.* 1997 translate "the one who rules" (*cf.* LSJ *s.v.* ἐπί sense I.2; *s.v.* ἀρχή sense II); Gardner *et al.* 1999 translate "who has been from the beginning" (likewise van der Vliet 2019b); Zellmann-Rohrer/Love 2022: 277 translate "the one who presides over rule", comparing the aulic titles of officials of the Hellenistic monarchies which designate them as "the one responsible for" (ὁ ἐπί) various domains (Zellmann-Rohrer 2018b: 110; Zellmann-Rohrer 2020: 74); *cf. e.g., Shepherd of Hermas* 23.4–5 (II CE), in which the angel Thegri is "set over the beasts" (ἐπὶ τῶν θηρίων); *GEMF* 16/*PDM* (KYP M162) ll. 497–8: "the one who sits upon the mountain of Gabaon" (pꜣ nt ḥmsk ḥr pꜣ tw n Gꜣbꜣ.ꜥꜣ.n). The question hinges on the ambiguity of ἐπί ("upon" and various metaphorical extensions) and ἀρχή ("beginning" or "sovereignty"). Here we follow the translation of Gardner *et al.* 1999, apparently the usual sense in the Septuagint (Ezekiel 16.25, 21.24; Lamentations 2.19, 4.1; *cf.* Epiphanius, *Panarion* 31.5.2 in Holl 1915: 390.10).

4–5. ⲡⲉⲧⲁϩⲱⲭ[ⲡ] ⲛ̄ⲛ̄ⲧⲏⲟⲩ : "**who shut up the winds**" Mirecki *et al.* 1997 compare Jesus' miracle of *Calming the Storm* (Matthew 8.26; Mark 4.39; Luke 8.24). *Cf.* the references to the Jewish deity keeping the winds in storehouses in Psalm 134 (135) 7; Jeremiah 10.13, 51.16, perhaps more apposite here given the references elsewhere to the Hebrew Bible rather than the New Testament.

6. [ⲉ]ⲧⲁⲕⲣ̄ ⲡⲕⲁϩ ⲛ̄ⲕⲏⲙⲉ ⲛ̄ⲭⲁⲓ̈ⲥ : "**you made the land of Egypt lord**" Mirecki *et al.* 1997 compare the image of Egypt as the liberator of Israel from Chaldaea in Jeremiah 41 (37) 1–21; perhaps also consider the enslavement Israel by Egypt described in the book of Exodus (we thank Michael Zellmann-Rohrer for this suggestion).

6–7. ⲁⲕⲛⲟⲩ[ⲭⲉ] ⲛ̄ϩⲛ̄ⲧⲧⲱⲛ ⲁϫⲛ̄ ⲛ̄ⲭⲁⲗⲇⲁⲓⲟⲥ : "**you cast strifes upon the Chaldaeans**" *Cf.* the prophecy of the destruction of Chaldaea in Jeremiah 27 (50) 1–46. Mirecki *et al.* 1997 compare Jeremiah 44 (37) 5.

9–10. ⲙⲁⲣⲉⲛⲓⲙ ⲡϣⲏⲣⲉ ⲣⲉ ⲛ̄ⲛⲓⲙ : "**may NN son of NN**" As noted in Mirecki *et al.* 1997 and Gardner *et al.* 1999, something has almost certainly dropped out here, since we would expect two names; perhaps restore "NN, son ‹of NN, and NN, daughter› of NN" (ⲛⲓⲙ ‹ⲡϣⲏⲣⲉ ⲛ̄ⲛⲓⲙ ⲙⲛ̄ ⲛⲓⲙ ⲧϣⲉⲉⲣⲉ ⲛ̄ⲛⲓⲙ›); Ouales probably inadvertently skipped a line while copying.

19–20. ⲙⲛ̄ ⳲⲞ ϩⲩ Ⳳ ⲛ̄ⲧⲁⲥ Ⳳ ⲟⲩ Ⳳ : "**NN daughter of NN, she ‹and› NN, son of NN**" Mirecki *et al.* 1997 and Gardiner *et al.* 1999 understand the Ⳳ sign, standing for "NN", as the Greek numeral δ ("4"), interpreting this as a series of commands to speak the name of the male victim, then the female victim, the full text, and then another sequence of words four times each over the ingredients.

front (→) (continued)

ϯϣⲓⲛⲉ ⲁⲣⲁⲕ ⲧⲟⲛⲟⲩ ϯϣⲗⲏⲗ ϩⲁ
ⲡⲕⲟⲩϫⲉⲓⲧⲉ ⲛ̄ⲟⲩⲛⲁϭ ⲛ̄ⲟⲩⲁⲓϣ
25 ϣⲁϯⲟⲩⲁϣⲧⲕ̄ ⲛ̄ⲕⲉⲥⲁⲡ ϩⲛ̄ ⲡⲥⲱⲙⲁ
ⲛ̄ⲧⲉⲡⲁⲣⲉϣⲉ ϫⲱⲕ ⲁⲃⲁⲗ ϯⲱⲣⲕ ⲛⲉⲕ
ⲙ̄ⲡⲛ̄ϫⲁⲓⲥ ⲡⲁⲣⲁⲕⲗⲏⲧⲟⲥ ⲙⲛ̄ ⲡⲥⲁⲩⲛⲉ
ⲛ̄ⲧⲙⲏⲉ ϫⲉ ⲡⲉⲧⲁⲓ̈ϭⲛ̄ⲧϥ ⲡⲉ ⲡⲉⲓ ⲉϥϩⲏⲛ
ⲁⲣⲁⲓ̈ ⲁⲓ̈ⲧⲁⲭⲩ ⲁⲓ̈ⲥⲁϩϥ ⲁⲓ̈ⲧⲛ̄ⲛⲁⲩϥ
30 ⲛⲉⲕ ϫⲉ ⲉⲣⲉⲡⲕⲉⲟⲩⲉ ⲥⲏϩ ⲁⲩ[ⲕⲟ]ⲩⲓ ⲛ̄ⲗⲉⲕ-
ⲙⲉ ⲛ̄ⲭⲁⲣⲧⲏⲥ ⲙ̄ⲡⲓϭⲛ̄ⲧϥ ⲉⲓϣⲁϭⲛ̄ⲧϥ
ϯⲛⲁⲧⲛ̄ⲛⲁⲩϥ ⲛⲉⲕ ⲉⲓ̈ⲥⲁⲩⲛᵛᵃᶜⲉ ϩⲱⲧ o̞
ϫⲉ ⲛ̄ⲛⲟⲩⲛ̄ⲧϥ ⲁⲡⲥⲁⲛ ⲕⲁⲗᵛᵃᶜⲗⲓⲕⲗⲏ-
ⲧⲉⲓ ϯⲧⲛ̄ⲛⲁⲩϥ ϫⲉ ⲛ̄ⲧⲁⲓ̈ⲥⲉϩ ⲡⲉⲓ ⲙⲛ̄
35 ⲧⲟⲧ ⲁⲓ̈ⲧⲛ̄ⲛⲁⲩϥ ⲉⲓ̈ⲭⲱ ⲙ̄ⲙⲁⲥ ϫⲉ
ⲧⲁⲭⲁ ⲧⲕ̄ⲭⲣⲓⲁ ⲧⲉ ϯⲣ̄ ⲁⲍⲓⲟⲩ ⲙ̄ⲙⲁ̄ⲕ
ⲡⲁϫⲁⲓⲥ ⲡⲁⲥⲁⲛ ϫⲉⲕⲁⲥϩⲉⲓ̈ ⲛⲓⲧⲉⲧⲣⲁⲥ
ⲛⲏⲓ̈ ⲉⲧⲁⲓⲧⲛ̄ⲛⲁⲩⲥⲉ ⲛⲉⲕ ϯⲛⲁⲧⲣⲟⲩⲛ̄
ⲧⲉⲧⲥϩϩ ⲛⲉⲕ ⲁⲛ ϫⲉⲕⲁⲙ̄ⲙⲉ ϫⲉ ⲛ̄-
40 ⲧⲁⲩⲡⲱϩ ⲁⲧⲟ ⲁⲛⲟ ⲁᵛᵃᶜⲃⲁⲗ ⲙ̄-
ⲡϥⲣ ⲁⲙⲉⲗⲉⲓ ⲁⲥⲁϩⲟⲩ ⲧⲁᵛᵃᶜⲭⲩ ⲕⲧⲛ̣̄-
ⲛⲁ̣ⲩⲥⲉ ⲛⲏⲓ̣ ⲛ̄ⲧⲟⲧϥ ⲛ̄ⲟⲩⲉ ᵛᵃᶜ ⲉϥⲥⲙⲁⲙ[ⲁ]
                                              ⲧ

---

back (↓) *written at 90 degrees counterclockwise to front*

ϫⲉ ⲡⲁϫⲉⲩ ϫⲉ ⲉⲛⲟⲩⲱϣ ⲧⲣⲉⲕⲉⲟⲩⲉ ⲥϩⲉⲓ ⲛ̄ⲕⲉⲕⲉⲩⲉ ϯⲛⲟⲩ ⲙ̄-
ⲡⲣⲣ ⲁⲙⲉⲗⲉⲓ ⲁⲧⲛ̄ⲛⲁⲩⲥⲉ ⲛ̄ϭⲗⲁⲙ ⲙ̄ⲡⲱⲣ ⲁⲓ̈ⲉⲧϥ ⲛ̄ⲛⲁϭ ⲛ̄ⲥϩⲉⲓ̈ ϫⲉ
ⲡⲁϫⲉⲩ ϫⲉ ⲁⲛⲭⲁⲣⲧⲏⲥ ⲟⲩⲱ ⲁⲗⲗⲁ ⲟⲩⲥϩⲉⲓ ⲉϥⲣ̄ ϣⲉⲩ ⲁⲩⲱ ⲉⲕ-   45
ⲥⲁϩⲟⲩ ϯⲛⲁϭⲛ̄ ⲡⲕϣⲓⲃⲉ ϩⲱⲧ ⲁⲛⲁⲕ ⲟⲩⲥⲉϭⲉ ⲉⲛ ϣⲓⲛⲉ ⲛⲏⲓ
ᵛᵃᶜ
5 ⲧⲟⲛⲟⲩ ⲁⲛⲉⲧϯ ⲙ̄ⲧⲁⲛ ϩⲏⲧ ⲛⲉⲕ ϩⲛ̄ ⲡⲥⲉϫⲉ ⲙⲛ̄ ⲡϩⲱⲃ
ϩⲱⲃ ⲉⲕⲟⲩⲁϣϥ ⲛ̄ⲛⲓⲙⲁ ⲕⲉⲗⲉⲩⲉ ⲛⲏⲓ ϯⲛⲁⲉϥ ⲉⲓⲣⲉϣⲉ ⲱⲛϩ
ⲛ̄ⲕⲟⲩϫⲉⲓⲧⲉ ⲛ̄ⲟⲩⲛⲁϭ ⲛ̄-
ⲟⲩⲁⲓϣ ⲡⲁϫⲁⲓⲥ ⲡⲁⲥⲁⲛ   50

written 90 degrees clockwise to recto

τῷ δεσπότῃ μου   ✗   Ψάιτι

10   ἀδελφῷ   Οὐάλης ὁ ἀδελφός σο̣ι̣

---

front 25 *i.e.* σῶμα || 27 *i.e.* παράκλητος || 29 *i.e.* ταχύνειν || 36 *i.e.* τάχα | *i.e.* χρεία | *i.e.* ἀξιοῦν || 37 *i.e.* τετράς || 40 ᾱ *vac.* ⲃⲁⲗ *pap.* || 41–43 *vacats to avoid pre-existing damage* || 41 ἀμελεῖν | *i.e.* ταχύ || **back** 10 ἀδελφῶι Mirecki *et al.*, Gardner *et al.* | *l.* σου : omitted in Mirecki *et al.*

I greet you warmly, I pray for your wellbeing for a long time, |²⁵ until I embrace you again in the body, and my joy is completed. I swear to you by our Lord Paraclete and the Knowledge of the Truth that this is what I found close to me, and I hurried, I wrote it, and I sent it |³⁰ to you, because the other one is written on a small piece of papyrus, and I did not find it. If I find it, I will send it to you, for I know for my part that it will not be taken to Brother Kalliklēs. I send it to you for it is with my own hand that I wrote it, |³⁵ and I wrote it saying, "Perhaps it is what you need".

I ask you, lord brother, that you write these quaternions for me that I sent to you. I will also have them bring what is written to you so that you will know |⁴⁰ where they have reached ‹and› to see ‹that› he has not been neglectful in writing them, and quickly send them to me through a blessed one |*back* for they said, "We want someone else to write others!" Now, do not be neglectful to send them in haste. Please do not make it a long text, for they have said that the papyrus is finished, but rather a useful text, and if you write them, I will find your recompense myself —I am not an idiot!

Greet for me |⁵ warmly those who give your heart rest by word and deed. Anything you need, tell me and I will do it happily. Live and be well for a long time, my lord, my brother.

|⁹, *at 180° to the other text on the back* To my lord brother, Psais, from Oualēs, your brother.

KD, EL & MP, edited from photograph.

23–24. ϯϣⲗⲏⲗ ϩⲁ ⲡⲕⲟⲩϫⲉⲓⲧⲉ : **"I pray for your wellbeing"** Compare the similar phrase in *P.Kell.* VII *Copt.* 97.5–8: "I pray to the Father, the God of Truth for your wellbeing" (ϯϣⲗⲏⲗ ⲁⲡⲓⲱⲧ ⲡⲛⲟⲩⲧⲉ ⲛ̄[ⲧ]ⲉ ⲧⲙⲏⲉ ϩⲁ ⲡⲉⲧⲛ̄ⲟⲩϫⲉⲓⲧⲉ; 19.68–69; 50.2–3; VII *Copt.* 72.4–5). This is likely a calque of the common Greek phrase "I pray for your health for many years" (ἐρρῶσθαί σε εὔχομαι πολλοῖς χρόνοις; *cf.* Sarri 2017: 48–49), usually used as a farewell greeting, and found in several letters from Kellis, including *P.Kell.* V *Copt.* 12.17–18; 21.30–31; 22.51–52; VII *Copt.* 72 ll. 7–8; 103 ll. 50–51.

27. ⲡⲁⲣⲁⲕⲗⲏⲧⲟⲥ : **"Paraclete"** "The Intercessor", a title of Mani, the prophet of Manichaeism.

37. ⲛⲓⲧⲉⲧⲣⲁⲥ : **"quaternions"** Quaternion here likely refers to a small codex made of four bifolios, which often served as standardised notebooks. The contents of the texts to be copied are unspecified, but we see no reason to assume that they were magical; *cf.* Teigen 2021: 206; Dosoo/Torallas Tovar 2022a. Gardner *et al.* note the possiblity of a reference to quaternions, but prefer to understand a "4-fold spell", based on their interpretation of front ll. 19–20, where they read ⲇ as the numeral four.

40–41. ⲛ̄ⲟⲩⲉ ⲉϥⲥⲙⲁⲙ[ⲁ]ⲧ : **"a blessed one"** This term does not appear elsewhere in the corpus, but may refer to a member of the Manichaean monastic order, the Elect; see Mirecki *et al.* 1997: 32.

back **2** ⲙ̄ⲡⲱⲣ ⲁⲉⲓⲧϥ ⲛ̄ⲛⲁϭ ⲛ̄ⲥϩⲉⲓ : **"please do not make it a long text"** Mirecki *et al.* & Gardner *et al.* translate this difficult passage as "by no means! I did it for the great texts...". We understand ˢⲙ̄ⲡⲱⲣ ⲉ-ⲁⲁϥ, an emotive negative imperative (Layton 2000: 294; for the absent indefinite article before the following noun, *cf.* Shisha-Halevy 2002: 305–306). ⲥϩⲉⲓ in this corpus generally has the sense of "letter", but here it may translate the Greek γραφή, in the sense of "religious writing" (*cf.* Gardner/ BeDuhn/Dilley 2018: 74–75, 167–170; Crum CD 383a). On this reading, Oualēs is asking Psais to select a short, useful text to copy into the quaternions since papyrus is scarce.

9–10. This is the address, giving the name of the sender and the intended recipient. The *x*-shape is the *locus sigilli*, "the place of the seal". In this case, the letter was not sealed with wax, but, after the letter was folded and tied with string, the *x* was written across it so that any tampering would be apparent; see Vandorpe 1996: 241–243.

PCM I 2. Healing prescription to stop uterine bleeding

Arsinoites (Faiyum) ? 4.5 (H) × 23.5 (W) cm V–VI CE
Other references: P.Vindob. K 5520 Pap; TM 91401; KYP M241; Bélanger Sarrazin #289.
Editions: Stegemann 1933–1934: no. 8 (*ed. pr.*); Till 1935: no. 8.
Translations: Stegemann 1933–1934: no. 8 (German); Till 1935: no. 8 (German).
Present location: Vienna, Nationalbibliothek.
Image: http://data.onb.ac.at/rec/RZ00004836
Linguistic description: Faiyumic.
Contents:

1. Front ll. 1–5: Healing prescription to stop uterine bleeding (KYP T443)

Completely preserved healing formulary written on a rectangular papyrus sheet. The papyrus is very damaged, and the lower part is missing. The 5 surviving lines are written in black ink in a single column on the front (↓). The manuscript has no clearly visible folds, although some of the damage patterns may have been caused by folding. The provenance of this manuscript, now kept in the Nationalbibliothek in Vienna, is not recorded, although the dialectal features suggest an origin in the Faiyum. The majority of manuscripts in the Vienna Nationalbibliothek were acquired in the Faiyum, so that such a provenance would be unsurprising.[1]

The script is an informal and irregular upright majuscule whose idiosyncracies pose considerable problems for palaeographical dating. Notably, the ⲉ varies between a two stroke form consisting of a C with a middle stoke, and a form which resembles two Latin C written on top of each other, while ⲙ is deeply curved, the ⲁ pointed, and the ⲩ resembles Latin Y, written in a single stroke. Ligatures are used with certain letter combinations (ⲧⲓ, ⲉⲧ, *etc.*). The ⲛ occasionally has a dot above it where a supralinear stroke might be expected. The ⲥ displays a typically Faiyumic form, in which the ascender is written last, rising from the lower part of the bowl, something like the printed form of the Old Nubian *shima* (ϭ).[2] The hand's irregularity, showing some features typical of more highly trained scribes (the ligatures and elaborate serifs and flourishes), may imply that the copyist was working from a model written in a more formal hand.[3] Stegemann dated this hand to the fourth century,[4] while Till dated it to the seventh century, noting the

---

[1] Loebenstein 1983.
[2] *Cf.* Krall 1886–1887: 111.
[3] We are grateful to Yasmine Amory for this suggestion.
[4] Stegemann 1933–1934: 16, no. 8.

recurved tail of the ϣ as typical of older Faiyumic hands.⁵ The angularity of the alpha would seem to argue for an earlier date than that envisaged by Till, while the initial writing perpendicular to the fibres would suggest a fifth century date at the earliest.⁶ We thus tentatively propose a fifth to sixth century date for this piece.

The text is written in a fairly standard form of Faiyumic (F4/F5), although it is too fragmentary to determine which subdialect it should be assigned to. The text demonstrates ϲⲁⲛ/ⲡⲉⲛ vocalism, lambdacism, the writing of the unstressed final vowel as ⲓ, and lexical forms peculiar to this dialect (*e.g.*, ϣⲉϣⲧ⸗ for ˢϲⲉϣⲧ⸗; ⲙⲉϩⲓ for ˢⲁⲙⲁϩⲧⲉ).

Stegemann, reading only a few words, tentatively classified the text as a "Dämonenbeschwörung" ("demon adjuration"), but it belongs to the category of formularies treating uterine bleeding, as indicated by the first legible passage of the manuscript, "blood under her."⁷ The putative title is followed by an invocation of a being named "great Baōth", and ends with instructions for the production of an amulet.

---

⁵ Till 1935: 203, no. 8.

⁶ For the practice of writing on the vertical fibres first, see the introduction (p. 26–28). For the shape of the ⲁ, compare the examples in Stegemann 1936: 4–7 with those on later pages.

⁷ *Cf.* the discussion in the apparatus to l. 1 of this text.

front (↓)

[. ?]ⲥⲛⲁϥ ϩⲁⲗⲁⲥ ϣⲉϣⲧϥ ϩⲛ ⲧⲉⲥⲙⲏⲧⲣⲁ ϯⲉⲗⲉϩⲟⲣⲕⲓⲍⲓⲛ [ⲙⲁⲕ] ⲡⲓⲛⲁϭ ⲃ̅ⲁ̅ϣ̅ ⲙⲛ̀ ⲡⲓ[. ?
[. ? ⲉⲧϩ]ⲙ[ⲁ]ⲥ ⲉϩⲗⲁⲓ ϩⲛ ⲧⲡⲏ ⲙⲛ ⲡⲏ ⲉⲧϩⲙⲁⲥ ϩⲓⲭⲉⲛ ⲡⲕⲉ[ϩⲓ] ⲙⲛ ⲡⲏ ⲉⲧⲙⲉϩⲓ ⲉⲭⲉⲛ . [.
[. ?] Γ̅ . ⲫⲉⲣ / ⲫⲉⲩ̅ // ⲙ̅ⲟ̅ϣ̅ⲣ̅ⲏ̅ⲏ̅ⲥ̅ /// ⲡⲏ . . . . . [*ca.* 16]
[. ?] ⲡⲉⲓϩⲏⲃⲓ . . . ⲛ̀ⲡⲱⲧϩ̣ ⲡ̀ⲧⲉⲡ[ⲟⲥ *ca.* 14]
5 [. ? ⲡⲓ]ⲧⲁⲕⲓⲱⲛ ⲙⲁⲗⲃ ⲉⲗⲁⲥ // ⲫ̅ⲫ̅ⲫ̅ⲫ̅ⲫ̅ⲫ̅ⲫ̅ . . [. ?]

1].ⲁϥ ϩⲁⲗⲗⲥ Till | *l*. ⲉ-ϣⲉϣⲧ⸗ϥ ? : ϣⲉϣ ⲧⲏⲧⲛ̀ Till | ⲉϩⲟⲣⲕⲓⲍⲓⲛ ⲉ modified from ο *i.e.* ἐξορκίζειν : *ca.* 6 ϯⲉⲗⲉϩⲟⲣⲕⲓⲍⲓ . . . . ⲡⲛⲁ . . . . Stegemann : ⲛ̣[. ?]ⲡⲛⲁϭ [ⲓ]ⲁ̅ϣ̅ ⲙ̣ⲡ̣ⲧ̣ⲓ̣[?] Till | nothing lost at the end of the line ? || **2** .]ⲉϩⲗⲁⲓ ϩⲛ ⲧⲡⲏ ⲙⲛ ⲡⲏ ⲉⲧϩⲙ ⲡⲕⲉϩⲓ *ca.* 5 Stegemann :]ⲉ̣ ⲉϩⲗⲁⲓ ϩⲛ̀ ⲧⲡⲏ ⲙⲛ̀ ⲡⲏ ⲉⲧϩⲙⲁⲥ ϩⲓⲭⲉⲛ ⲡⲕ[ ] . . . ⲉⲙⲉϩ . . ϭⲃⲛ̣ . [Till || **3** .]ⲫⲉⲣ ⲫⲉⲩ̅ . ⲟ̅ϣ̅ⲣ̅ⲏ̅ⲏ̅ⲥ̅ Stegemann :]ⲫ̅ⲉ̅ⲣ̅ - ⲫ̅ⲉ̅ⲩ̅ = ⲙ̅ⲟ̅ϣ̅ⲣ̅ⲏ̅ⲏ̅ⲥ̅ ⲉⲡⲏ . ⲉ̣ . . . [Till || **4** Stegemann does not transliterate this line :]ⲡⲉⲓϩⲏⲃⲓ ⲛⲉⲩ ⲙⲛ ⲡⲱⲧϩ . . ⲧⲉⲧ[Till | *i.e.* τύπος ? || **5** *i.e.* πιττάκιον :]ⲁⲕⲓⲱⲗⲓ Till | *i.e.* ˢⲙⲟⲣ⸗ϥ ⲉⲣⲟ⸗ⲥ : ⲙⲁⲁⲃ ⲉ *ca.* 9 [Till | Stegemann does not transliterate this line.

PCM I 2 (P.Vindob. K 5520) : Healing prescription to stop uterine bleeding   57

[…] blood under her, ⟨to?⟩ stop it in her womb. "I adjure [you] O great Baōth and the [… who] sits up in heaven and he who sits upon the earth and he who rules over […]pher, Pheu, Moōrēēs, he? … […] this grief? … depict the model? […] |⁵ […] sheet, bind it to her. ☩☩☩☩☩☩☩ […]

KD, EL & MP, edited from photograph, with notes from autopsy by Ágnes Mihálykó.

---

1. [ⲥ]ⲛⲁϥ ϩⲁⲗⲁⲥ : **"blood under her"** Perhaps restore "For a woman with blood under her" ([ⲉⲧⲃⲉ ⲟⲩⲥϩⲓⲙⲓ ⲉⲗⲉⲡⲉⲥ]ⲛⲁϥ ϩⲁⲗⲁⲥ) *cf. PCM* I 33 front l. 7: "a [woman] who has blood under her" (ⲟⲩ[ⲥϩⲓⲙ]ⲉ ⲉⲣⲉⲡⲉⲥⲛⲟϥ ϩⲁⲣⲟⲥ); *PCM* I 36 col. 1 l. 1: ⲉⲧⲃⲉ ⲟⲩⲥϩⲓⲙⲉ ⲉⲣⲉⲟⲩⲥⲛⲟϥ ϩⲁⲣⲟⲥ; *BKU* I 25 (KYP M174) front l. 13: [ⲉⲧⲃⲉ] ⲟⲩⲥϩⲓⲙⲉ ⲉⲣⲉⲡⲉⲥⲛⲟϥ ϩⲁⲣⲟⲥ); P.Mich.Inv. 593 (Worrell 1930; KYP M9) p. 9 l. 3: ⲉⲧⲃⲉ ⲟⲩⲥϩⲓⲙⲉ ⲉⲣⲉⲡⲉⲥⲛⲟϥ ϩⲁⲣⲟⲥ (likewise P.Mich.Inv. 594 back l. 3, Worrell 1930; KYP M15). For another recipe with the goal of preventing uterine bleeding, see P.Vindob. K 11088 B ll. 4–7 (Hevesi 2015; KYP M374). For the description of blood being "under" someone as a way to express uterine bleeding, *cf. e.g.* Matthew 9.20 (Horner 1911: I 78) and Luke 8.43 (Horner 1911: II 160) "a woman with blood under her for twelve years" (ⲟⲩⲥϩⲓⲙⲉ ⲇⲉ ⲉⲣⲉⲡⲉⲥⲛⲟϥ ϣⲟⲟⲡ ϩⲁⲣⲟⲥ ⲙⲙⲛⲧⲥⲛⲟⲟⲩⲥⲉ ⲛⲣⲟⲙⲡⲉ). The same construction is used in Demotic, *e.g., GEMF* 16/*PDM* xiv (KYP M162) ll. 1197–1198: "a woman… whose blood is under her" (*sḥm.t… iw pꜣ snf ḥr-rꜣs-s*). For uterine bleeding and menstrual blood in Coptic magical papyri, see Preininger 2022; Preininger forthcoming a; Preininger forthcoming c: chapter 4, and compare curses to cause menstrual bleeding, discussed in the notes to *PCM* I 3 front col. 1 1–34.
1. ⲃⲁⲱⲑ : **"Baōth"** The initial ⲃ is very uncertain. The name Baōth occurs also in *P.Bad.* V 123 (KYP M315) front ll. 34, 49, although in the latter case it may be understood as as continutation of the previous name which ends at the end of the preceding line (*i.e.*, ⲥⲁⲗⲁⲃⲁⲱⲑ). The name is reminiscent of, and probably derived from, *Sabaoth.
2. [ⲉⲧⲉ]ⲙⲁⲥ ⲉϩⲗⲁⲓ ϩⲛ ⲧⲡⲏ ⲙⲛ ⲡⲏ ⲉⲧϩⲙⲁⲥ ϩⲓϫⲉⲛ ⲡⲕⲉ[ϩⲓ] : **"[who] sits up in heaven and he who sits upon the earth"** This passage finds conceptual parallels in two different textual traditions. The first is that of descriptions of deities sitting upon or set over various locations or abstract concepts (for which see the notes to *PCM* I 1 l. 1). The second conception is that of descriptions of cosmic beings whose magnitude is expressed in terms of stretching from heaven to earth. For further discussions of the first phenomenon, see Robert 1981: 9–14; Zellmann-Rohrer 2018b: 107–112; Dosoo 2022c: 524 n. 175. For discussions of the second, see Dosoo 2022c: 502.
4. ⲡⲱⲧϩ ⲛⲧⲉⲛ[ⲟⲥ]: **"depict the model?"** We are grateful to Ágnes Mihálykó for this suggestion, which would seem to fit the traces. This may mark an instruction to the reader to copy the amulet onto the sheet mentioned in l. 5, but the apparent use of the verb ⲡⲱⲧϩ ("to carve, depict") for the action is surprising; more often we find ⲥϩⲁⲓ or γράφειν (both "to write, draw").
5. [ⲡⲓ]ⲧⲁⲕⲓⲱⲛ : **"sheet"** The use of a sheet (πιττάκιον) as the support for an amulet is attested in *P.Macq.* I 1 (KYP M167), at p. 13 ll. 7, 9, 15, p. 15 ll. 12–13; in the first two cases it is bound (ⲙⲟⲩⲣ) to the beneficiary, as is the case here.
5. ⲙⲁⲗⲃ ⲉⲗⲁⲥ : **"Bind it to her"** "It" here refers to an amulet, probably consisting of the formula and the staurograms, which is to be bound to the woman's body to treat her.
5. ☩☩☩☩☩☩☩ : Traces of two letters are visible after the seven staurograms; although they are not sufficiently well-preserved to be certain, it is possible that there was a sequence of another seven shapes afterwards, such as 6-pointed stars; compare the seven five-pointed stars found at the ends of fever amulets, such as P.Heid.Inv. Kopt. 564a (Quecke 1963b: 255–256; KYP M513) l. 11; *P.Stras. Copt.* 6a (KYP M102) ll. 7–8; *P.Stras.Copt.* 6b (KYP M103) ll. 7–8.

PCM I 3. Two aggressive procedures targeting women

Abydos   29.9 (H) × 29.6 (W) cm   V–VI CE ?

Other references: P.Mich.Inv. 1190; TM 98058; KYP M72; Bélanger Sarrazin #162.
Editions: Worrell 1934: 145–150 (*ed. pr.*); Worrell 1935a: no. 2 [W]; van der Vliet 2000: 335–337.
Translations: Worrell 1935a: no. 2 [W]; Skiles in Meyer/Smith 1994: no. 66 [S]; Pernigotti 1995: no. 23 [P] (Italian); van der Vliet 2000: 335–337 [V].
Additional commentary: Preininger forthcoming c: chapter 4.
Present location: Ann Arbor, Michigan University Library.
Image: https://quod.lib.umich.edu/a/apis/x-1328/1190v.tif
Linguistic description: Sahidic (non-standard).
Contents:

1. Front col. 1 ll. 1–34: Curse to make a woman bleed (KYP T610)
2. Front col. 1 ll. 35–36, col. 2 ll. 1–38, back col. 1 ll. 1–19, col. 2 ll. 1–10: Love spell to fill a woman with fire (KYP T1705)

Complete papyrus roll, with significant damage in the middle of the height. According to the report of Harold I. Bell, the manuscript was bought through the antiquities dealer Maurice Nahman in July 1922 and acquired by the University of Michigan in the same year.[1] In the same report, Walter E. Crum gives a brief description of the manuscript and dates it to the fifth, perhaps even fourth century, noting that it came from El-Araba el-Madfuna (Abydos).[2]

The sheet is large and square, with generous margins, particularly on the left hand side, where *kollēsis* is visible in the margin. The front (→) is written in two columns, the first of 36 lines, the second of 38 lines, divided by a vertical line. The back is written in two further columns, one of 19 lines, the other of 10 lines, with the second column written at 90° clockwise to the first, on the lower right part of the papyrus. The extensive damage in the middle may be the result of a horizontal crease resulting from folding, but no other creases are clearly visible; the mirrored damage patterns rather indicate that it may have been rolled four times on the horizontal axis. Here we assume that no full lines are lost in the break, but this must be considered uncertain.

The hand is an informal alphabetic majuscule, rather regular, the script bilinear, unimodal and upright. Β is pointed, and respects the bilinearity of the script, while

---

[1] Bell 1922: 1; Crum 1922: 8, no. 115 B IV. On Maurice Nahman, see Hagen/Ryholt 2016: 253–255.

[2] Bell 1922: 2 (Lot IV). The manuscript was described by Crum as being two leaves ("2 cols. to a page") from a Coptic papyrus codex, apparently misinterpreting what is in fact a single leaf broken in half.

ⲁ, ᴢ, ϯ and sometimes ⲧ have simple serifs. ⲙ has a deep curve, ⲩ consistently resembles a Latin capital Y. Letters such as ϣ do not have elongated descenders, respecting the bilinearity of the script. The ascender of ϭ seems to rise from the lower part of the bowl, as is common in hands from the Faiyum (*cf.* the introduction to *PCM* I 2). The copyist makes extensive use of diaeresis on ⲓ, and sometimes uses supralineation to mark numerals, abbreviations and names; a colon is used to separate clauses and morphemes. Crum's dating to the fourth or fifth century seems too early.[3] A fifth-century date at the latest might be suggested by the initial writing on the horizontal fibres,[4] but the fact that the manuscript takes the form of a short horizontal roll—which continued to be used in some contexts until the eighth century—might explain this unusual choice in a later text.[5] A manuscript with a very similar hand, P.MMA 34.1.226 (Zellmann-Rohrer 2017; KYP M506), is likewise written on a short roll, dated by its editor to the sixth century, noting the absence of bimodularity (narrowing of letters such as ⲉ, ⲑ, ⲟ, ⲥ).[6] A few of the graffiti and ostraca from the Osireion at Abydos show similar hands;[7] these can be loosely dated to between the sixth and ninth centuries.[8] We thus tentatively propose a fifth, or more likely, sixth century date, but note that the hands of writers with little formal training may display striking similarities over long periods of time.

The dialect is a non-standard form of Sahidic; alongside common features—such as ⲃ for ^{S}ⲡ, ⲉ for the Sahidic supralinear stroke, haplography (in particular of ⲉ and ⲙ), and the writing of ⲓ in place of ^{S}ⲉⲓ—we see some more idiosyncratic divergences. Most notably, the sequence *vowel-ϩ* is regularly written in reverse (*e.g.*, ⲡϩⲱ, front col. 1, l. 3; ⲭϩⲁⲙ, front col. 1 l. 24). We also see the interchange of voiced/unvoiced and aspirated/unaspirated consonants: ᴢ for ⲥ, ⲑ for ⲧ, ⲭ for ϭ; this last likely suggests that ϭ was treated as the aspirated phoneme corresponding to the unaspirated ϫ, as in Bohairic.

We treat the initial staurogram of col. 1 as an independent line, so that in front col. 1, our l. 2 corresponds to l. 1 in Worrell and other editions. Where the date of Worrell is not noted in the apparatus, his reading is the same in both publications.

---

[3] Bell 1922: 2 (Lot IV).

[4] For the post-fifth century practice of writing on the vertical fibres first (*transversa charta*), see the introduction, pp. 26–28

[5] For magical rolls, see Dosoo/Torallas Tovar 2022a: 73, 79–83.

[6] Zellmann-Rohrer 2017: 242; *cf.* the similar hand of Cairo JdE 49547 (Girard 1927; KYP M297), undated by its editor, but assigned by Trismegistos (TM 102068; accessed 7/3/2023) to the ninth to eleventh centuries. Despite the striking similarity between *PCM* I I 3 and P.MMA 34.1.226 in hand and format, we hesitate to suggest a single copyist, based on the different apparent findspot (Abydos *vs.* Saqqara), and notable differences in the formation of certain letters (*e.g.*, ⲁ, ⲩ, ϭ).

[7] See *e.g.*, Murray 1904: 41, pl. 34, no. 36; 43, pl. 37 *ostracon*; *cf.* also BM EA58928 (TM 393509).

[8] For the dates of the inscriptions from Abydos, see Delattre 2003: 134. The mention of Shenoute and perhaps Severus of Antioch in Murray 1904: 41, pl. 34, no. 36 would suggest a sixth century date at the earliest for this text.

front, column 1 (→)

☩ ϯⲉⲡⲓⲕⲁⲗⲉ ⲙⲟⲕ ⲁⲑⲣⲁⲕ ⲡⲛⲟϫ
ⲛⲁⲅⲅⲉⲗⲟⲥ ⲉⲧⲁϩⲉⲣⲁⲑϥ ⲛⲥⲁ ⲟⲩ-
ⲛⲁⲙ̄ ⲙ̄ⲡⲣⲏ ⁚ ⲡⲉⲧⲉⲣⲉⲛⲉⲕϫⲟⲩⲓ̇ⲁ ⲧⲏ-
5 ⲣⲟⲩ ⲙ̄ⲡⲣⲏ · ⲉⲩϩⲏⲡⲟⲧⲁⲥⲉ ⲛⲁϥ ϫⲉⲓ̈-
ϣⲁⲛⲥⲁⲧⲕ ⲉⲡⲛⲟⲩⲛ ⁚ ⲉⲕⲉⲙⲟⲟⲩⲧϥ
ⲡ̄ϩⲁⲧ ϫⲉⲕⲉⲙⲟⲟⲩⲧϥ ⁚ ⲡⲗⲁⲓ̈ⲛ ϫⲉ-
ⲕⲉⲟⲩⲟⲗⲡϥ ⁚ ⲡⲉⲛⲓ̈ⲡⲉ ⲉⲕⲉ⟦ⲟ̣⟧ⲃⲟⲗ-
ⲉⲃ ⲉⲃⲟⲗ · ⲡⲱⲛⲉ ⲉⲕⲉⲡⲟϭϥ ⁚ ⲙ-
10 ⲟⲟⲩ ⲛⲛⲑⲁⲗⲗⲁⲥ ⁚ ⲉⲕⲉⲧⲣⲉⲩϣ-
ⲟⲟⲩⲉ ⁚ ⲛⲧⲟⲟⲩ ⲛⲕⲧⲉⲣⲉ[ⲩ]ⲕ̣ⲓ̈ⲙ ·
ⲙ̄ⲡⲉⲧⲣⲁ · ⲉⲕⲉⲧⲣⲉⲩⲃⲱⲗ ⲉⲃⲟⲗ ⁚
ⲟⲩⲥⲓⲙⲉ · ⲥⲉⲧ · ⲉⲕⲉⲡⲣϩ ⲙⲡⲉⲥⲡⲓ̈-
ⲣ ⲛⲟⲩⲛⲁⲙ ⁚ ⲛⲕⲓⲛⲉ ⲉⲃⲟⲗ ⲙⲡⲉ-
15 ϣⲏⲣⲉ · ⲛⲉⲓ̈ⲉϫⲓ ⲙⲟⲕ ⲛⲁⲓ̈ ⲁⲛ ⲟⲩⲇⲉ ⲛⲉⲕⲟⲟⲩⲉ ⲁⲗⲗ[ⲁ *ca.* 6]
ⲕ̣[*ca.* 6 ⲥ]ⲁ̣ⲃ̄ⲁ̣ⲱ̄ⲑ̄[*ca.* 7]
[*ca.* 10]ⲉ̣ ⁚ ⲧ[*ca.* 10]
[*ca.* 10]ⲡⲁ̣ⲓ̣ · [*ca.* 11]
20 [*ca.* 10]ⲟⲩⲏⲛ ⲉ[*ca.* 7]
.[*ca.* 7]ⲙ̣ⲏ̣ⲧⲣⲁ ⁚ ⲉⲡⲉⲥⲥⲡ[ⲓ]ⲣ ⁚ ⲉⲕ-
ⲟⲩⲛ̣ ⲓⲥ̣ϫⲓ̈ⲛ ⲥϩ[ⲟ]ⲩ ⲛ ⳓⲱⲥ ⁚ ⲉⲡⲉϩⲏ-
ⲧ · ⲉⲓ̈ⲃ ⲛⲉⲥⲟⲩⲉⲣⲏⲧⲉ · ⲛⲕⲓⲛⲉ ⲉⲃⲟⲗ ϩⲁⲣⲟⲥ · ⲛⲟⲩⲥⲛⲟϥ · ⲉⲩϩⲁⲙ
25 ⲙⲛ ⲟⲩⲙⲟ·ⲟⲩ ⁚ ⲉⲃⲟⲕⲉⲙ · ⲉϫⲉⲛ ⲡ-
ⲉϩⲡⲓⲣ ⲛⲟⲩⲛⲁⲙ ⁚ ϣⲁ ⲡⲉⲥⲡⲓⲣ ⁚ ⲛ-
ⲉϩⲃⲟⲩⲣ ⁚ ⲉⲕⲉⲧⲣⲉⲃϩⲉⲣⲟϣ ⁚ ⲉⲣⲟⲥ ⁚
ⲛⲧⲉ ⲛⲟⲩⲱⲛⲉ ⲛⲥⲓⲕⲉ ⁚ ⲉⲃⲉϩⲱ-
ⲕ ϩⲁⲣⲟⲥ ⁚ ⲛⲑⲉ ⲛⲧⲁⲣⲭⲏ ⲙⲡⲉϥ-

---

1 ☩ in *ekthesis* ‖ **2** *i.e.* ἐπικαλεῖν | *i.e.* ˢⲙⲙⲟ⸗ⲕ ‖ **3** *i.e.* ἄγγελος | *i.e.* ˢⲁϩⲉⲣⲁⲧ⸗ϥ ‖ **3–4** *i.e.* ˢⲟⲩⲛⲁⲙ ‖ **4** *i.e.* ἐξουσία : ⲛⲉⲕϫⲟⲩⲓⲁ W | ⲧⲏ- ⲧ corrected from unclear letter by overwriting ‖ **5** corrected from ϩⲏⲡⲟⲧⲁⲉⲉ by erasure, overwriting *i.e.* ὑποτάσσειν | *i.e.* ˢϫⲉ ⲉⲓ̈ W, P, S ‖ **5–6** *i.e.* ˢϫⲉ ⲉ⸗ⲓ-ϣⲁⲛ-ⲥⲉⲧ⸗ⲕ : ϣⲁⲛⲥⲁⲧⲕ ⲉⲡⲛⲟⲩⲛ : ϣⲁ ⲛⲥⲁ ⲧⲕⲉ ⲡⲛⲟⲩⲛ *i.e.* ˢϣⲁ ⲛⲥⲁ ⲧⲕⲏ ⲡⲛⲟⲩⲛ ⲙ̄-ⲡ-ⲛⲟⲩⲛ W, P, S ‖ **6** *i.e.* ˢⲙ̄-ⲡ-ⲛⲟⲩⲛ ‖ **7** *i.e.* ˢϫⲉ ⲉ⸗ⲕ-ⲉ-ⲙⲟⲟⲩⲧ⸗ϥ ‖ **7–8** *i.e.* ˢϫⲉ ⲉ⸗ⲕ-ⲉ-ⲟⲩⲟⲗⲡ̄⸗ϥ see CD 477b *cf.* CED 211 : *l.* ⲥⲟⲗⲡ W, P, S ‖ **8** *i.e.* ˢⲡ-ⲃⲉⲛⲓ̈ⲡⲉ ‖ **8–9** *i.e.* ˢⲉⲕⲉⲃⲟⲗ⸗ϥ : ⟦ⲟ⟧ deleted by erasure ‖ **9–10** *i.e.* ˢⲙ̄-ⲙⲟⲟⲩ ‖ **10** *i.e.* θάλασσα ‖ **11** *i.e.* ˢⲛ⸗ⲅ̄-ⲧⲣⲉ⸗ⲩ-ⲕⲓⲙ : ⲛⲕⲧⲉⲣⲉ[ⲩⲕ]ⲓ̈ⲙ W ‖ **12** *i.e.* ˢⲙ̄-ⲡⲉⲧⲣⲁ / *l.* ⲃⲟⲗ⸗ϥ ‖ **13** *i.e.* ˢⲟⲩ-ⲥϩⲓⲙⲉ ⲉ⸗ⲥ-ⲥⲉⲧ (hapolography) | *i.e.* ˢⲡⲱϩ ‖ **13–14** *l.* ⲙ̄-ⲡⲉ⸗ⲥ-ⲥⲡⲓⲣ ‖ **14–15** *l.* ⲙ̄-ⲡⲉ⸗ⲥ-ϣⲏⲣⲉ W, P, V ‖ **15** *i.e.* ˢⲛ̄-ⲉ⸗ⲓ-ⲁⲓⲧⲉⲓⲛ | *i.e.* ˢⲙⲙⲟ⸗ⲕ | ⲏ ⲛⲁ[ⲙ]ⲏ "in fact" W ‖ **15–16** *i.e.* οὔτε : "it is not I who ask you, nor [other] (humans)" S ‖ **16** ⲛⲉ̣ⲕⲟⲟⲩⲉ : [*ca.* 4]ⲟⲟⲩⲉ W | *i.e.* ἀλλ[ά] ‖ **17** [ⲥⲁ]ⲃ̄ⲁ̣ⲱ̄ⲑ̄ W ‖ **18**]ⲉ̣ ⁚ ⲧ[: [.]†[.] W ‖ **19** ⁚]ⲁⲓ[W ‖ **21** *i.e.* μήτρα :]ⲡⲣⲁ W ‖ **22** *i.e.* ᴮⲓⲥϫⲉⲛ : [. . .] ϫⲓⲛ W | *i.e.* ˢⲥⲟⲟⲩϩⲉ ⁚ ˢⲛ̄-ϫⲱ⸗ⲥ ‖ **22–23** *i.e.* ˢⲉ-ⲡ-ⲉⲥⲏⲧ ‖ **23** *i.e.* ˢⲉ-ⲛ-ⲉⲓ̈ⲃ | *i.e.* ˢⲛ̄-ⲛⲉ⸗ⲥ-ⲟⲩⲉⲣⲏⲧⲉ ‖ **24** *i.e.* ˢϩⲁⲣⲙ ‖ **25** ⲟⲩⲙⲟⲟⲩ W | *i.e.* ˢϣⲕⲙ̄ | *i.e.* ˢϫⲓⲛ ‖ **25–26** *i.e.* ˢⲡⲉ⸗ⲥ-ⲥⲡⲓⲣ ‖ **26** *i.e.* ˢⲡⲉ⸗ⲥ-ⲥⲡⲓⲣ ‖ **27** *i.e.* ˢϩⲃⲟⲩⲣ ‖ **28** *i.e.* ˢⲛⲑⲉ ‖ **28–29** *i.e.* ˢⲉ⸗ϥ-ⲉ-ⲥⲱⲕ ‖ **29** *i.e.* ἀρχή

☦ I invoke you Athrak, the great *angel who stands at the right side of the sun, he to whom all the *authorities |⁵ of the sun are subject, for if I sent you to the *abyss, you would destroy it; silver, that you would destroy it; steel, that you would break it; iron, you would melt it; stone, you would break it; |¹⁰ the waters of the seas, you would make them go dry; the mountains, you make them move; the rocks, you would make them dissolve; a pregnant woman, you would tear open her right side and you would bring out the |¹⁵ child. It is not these things that I ask you, nor other things, but […] *Sabaoth […] |²⁰ […] womb to her side, opening from the crown of her head down to the nails of her feet, may? you draw out from under her polluted blood |²⁵ and darkened water from her right side to her left side. May you cause it to weigh upon her like a millstone! May it flow under her like the source of the

---

1–34. Curse to cause menstrual bleeding: Worrell understands this as a ritual to cause childbirth through a caesarian section, while Skiles suggests that it is rather a call for angelic protection during childbirth. Ritner (in Meyer/Smith 1994: 126) suggests that it is a spell to induce abortion. All understand the whole manuscript as a single ritual. The description of a child being torn out of a pregnant woman in ll. 13–15 is explicitly not requested (*cf.* note to ll. 15–16), and instead the request is for "polluted blood and water" to come out of the woman. The negative force of this is clear: it is to weigh upon her like a millstone (*cf.* the imagery of a millstone as punishment in Matthew 18.6, Mark 9.42, Luke 17.2), the blood is to come from her entire body (ll. 21–22), and it is to be of an extreme quantity, compared to the source of the four rivers of Eden (*cf.* Genesis 2.10). For other curses to cause a woman to bleed, see *Crum ST* 399 (KYP M536); *P.Lond.Copt.* 1223 (KYP M533); *GEMF* 34/*PGM* LXII (KYP M526) ll. 75–105, perhaps also *BKU* I 11 (KYP M78). *Cf.* the curses to make a woman bleed pus in *PCM* I 35 front ll. 7–17, 21–23. Compare also the recipes to heal menstrual bleeding, discussed in the note to *PCM* I 2 l. 1; *cf.* Preininger forthcoming c: ch. 4.

5–6. ⲭⲉⲓϣⲁⲛⲥⲁⲧⲕ ⲉⲡⲛⲟⲩⲛ : **"for if I sent you to the abyss"** Worrell and Pernigotti translate "go even to the shore of the abyss" ("va' sulla riva dell'Abisso"), understanding ⲕⲉ as ⲕⲏ "shore (?)" (Crum CD 92a), and parsing the first part as ⳉⲉ ⟨ⲉⲕⲉ⟩ⲉⲓ. Skiles understands ϣⲁ ⲛⲥⲁ ⲧⲕⲉ "to the other", referring to a female client. For our reading, *cf.* Crum CD 360b; van der Vliet 2000: 336.

6, 7. ⲉⲕⲉⲙⲟⲟⲩⲧϥ : **"you would destroy it"** Worrell (1934, 1935a) mistakenly understands this as redundant. As noted in Crum CD 201a, ⲙⲟⲟⲩⲧ here may be equivalent to ⲧⲁⲕⲟ/ἀπόλλυμαι, "destroy".

7–9. Destruction of stone and metals: This represents a prototypical feat which demonstrates the power of a being or ritual. In the Coptic magical corpus *cf. PCM* I 26 p. 12 ll. 4–5, p. 15 ll. 5–7; *BKU* I 3 (KYP M77) ll. 21–24; *BKU* I 7 (KYP M88) ll. 20–21; 21–24; BM EA 10391 (Zellmann-Rohrer 2022a: no. 1; KYP M302) front ll. 23–24. Several instances are found in copies of the *Prayer of Mary 'in Bartos'*: *PCM* I 25 p. 2 l. 23–p. 3 l. 1; *P.Lond.Copt.* 368 (KYP M117) p. 4 ll. 4–6; *cf.* the brief discussion in Łajtar/van der Vliet 2017: 148–149; Bélanger Sarrazin forthcoming a: ch. 4.

13. ⲡⲱϩ : **"tear"** Worrell and Pernigotti translate "to break", whereas Skiles prefers "to reach". The context, and the use of ⲛ̄-/ⲙ̄ⲙⲟⲥ to indicate the object of the verb suggests the former to be correct.

15–16. ⲛⲉⲓ̈ⲉⳉⲓ ⲙⲟⲕ ⲛⲁⲓ̈ ⲁⲛ ⲟⲩⲇⲉ ⲛ̄[ⲉ]ⲕⲟⲟⲩⲉ : **"it is not these things that I ask you, nor [other things]"** *Cf. PCM* I 9 ll. 3–4; *BKU* I 7 (KYP M88) ll. 10–11: "for I do not ask for [these things], nor other things" (ⳉⲉ ⲉⲓ̈ⲉⲧⲓ [ⲛⲁⲓ̈] ⲁⲛ ⲟⲩⲧⲉ ⲟ̣[ⲩⲧⲉ ⲛ̄]ⲉⲕⲟⲟⲩⲉ); BM EA 10391 (Zellmann-Rohrer 2022a: no. 1; KYP M302) front l. 24: "I do not ask you for these things, nor..." (ⲉⲓⲏⲧⲉ ⲙ̄ⲙⲟⲕ ⲛ̄ⲛⲁⲓ ⲁⲛ ⲟⲩⲇⲉ ⲛ[). This represents a rhetorical structure in which the speaker initially lists difficult or impossible things which could be requested, only to deny them and ask instead for something which is claimed to be simpler; see the discussions in Bell *et al.* 1932: 30–31. In addition to the two Coptic examples given above, we find the same structure in the Greek texts *GEMF* 18/*PGM* LXI (KYP M183) col. 3 ll. 174–177; *GEMF* 42 (KYP M410) col. 1 ll. 10–11; *GEMF* 57/*PGM* IV (KYP M3) ll. 1505–1508.

30 ⲧⲟⲟⲩ ⲛⲓⲉⲣⲟ : ïⲇⲉ ⲙⲁⲕⲟⲥ : ïⲇⲉ
ⲫⲁⲣⲙⲁⲅⲟⲥ : ⲓⲇⲉ ⲡⲟⲩⲣⲁⲛⲓⲟⲛ
ïⲇⲉ ⲕⲁⲧⲁⲡⲧⲟⲛⲓⲟⲛ : ïⲇⲉ ϫⲓϭ
ⲛⲣⲱⲙⲉ ϭⲉⲙϭⲟⲙ ⲉⲱⲗ ⲙⲡ-
ⲓⲥⲛⲟϥ : ⲉⲧ︤ⲁ︥ ⲛⲓⲙ ⲇ̣ ⲉⲙⲓⲧⲉ ⲁⲛⲟ︤ⲕ︥
35 ⳩ ϯⲉⲡⲓⲕⲁⲗⲓ ⲙⲟⲕ : ⲙⲓⲭⲁⲏⲗ :
ⲡⲁⲅⲅⲉⲗⲟⲥ

---

front column 2 (→)

ⲉⲧϩⲁⲉⲣⲁϥ : ⲛⲥⲁ ⲟⲩⲛⲁⲙ ⲙⲡïⲱⲧ
ϫⲉⲕⲉï · ⲉⲭ :· ϯⲉⲡ : ⲅⲁⲃⲣⲓⲏⲗ ⲡⲁⲅⲅⲉⲗⲟⲥ : ⲉⲧϩⲁⲉⲣⲁⲧϥ ⲥⲁϩⲃⲟⲩⲣ ⲙ-
ⲡïⲱⲧ ϫⲉⲕⲉï ⲛⲁï ⲙⲛ ⲧⲉⲕⲥⲛⲏϥ-
5 ⲉ ⲛⲕϩⲱⲧ · ⲉϫⲉⲛ ⲡⲓⲥ : ϯⲉⲡ : ⲙⲟ- ·
ⲕ : ⲁⲇⲱⲛⲉ ⲡⲛⲟϭ ⲛⲁⲅⲅⲉⲗⲟⲥ
ⲉⲧϩⲁⲉⲣⲁⲧϥ : ϩïϫⲉⲛ ⲧⲙⲉ ⲓ︤ⲃ︥ · ⲛⲟⲩⲛⲟⲩ ⲙⲡⲉϩⲟⲟⲩ · ϫⲉⲕⲉï ⲛⲁï ⲉϫⲉⲛ
ⲡⲓⲥ : ϯⲉⲡ : ⲟⲩⲣï ⲡⲛⲟϭ ⲛⲁⲅⲅⲉⲗⲟ︤ⲥ︥
10 ⲉⲧϩⲁⲉⲣⲁⲧϥ ϩïϫⲛ : ⲓ︤ⲃ︥ : ⲛⲟⲩⲛⲟⲩ
ⲛⲧⲉⲩϣⲏ : ϫⲉⲕⲉï ⲛⲁï ⲉϫⲉⲛ ⲡⲓⲥ :
ϯⲉⲡⲓⲕⲁⲗⲉ ⲙⲟⲕ ⲃⲟⲣ . . . ⲱ :
ⲡϩⲟ ⲛϣⲁϩ ⲛⲕϩⲱⲧ ϫⲉⲕⲉï ⲛ-
ⲁ[ï] ⲉϫⲉⲛ : ϯⲉⲡ ⲙⲟⲕ : . [*ca.* 5]
15 ⲏⲗ ⲡⲁⲅ[ⲅⲉⲗⲟⲥ *ca.* 8]
[ⲧ]ⲟⲣⲅ[ⲏ *ca.* 13]
[.] . ⲃ[*ca.* 14]
. ϫ . [*ca.* 14]
ⲡⲉⲃⲥ . [*ca.* 14]
20 ϩⲛ ⲧⲁ . [. .] . ⲙ̣ⲡⲧⲁ[ⲣ]ⲧ̣ⲁ̣ⲣⲟⲩ-
ⲭⲟⲥ : ⲛⲁⲙⲉⲛⲧⲉ : ⲡⲉⲧⲉⲡⲗⲟ-

---

col. 1, 30 i.e. εἴτε (twice) | *i.e.* μάγος ‖ **31** *i.e.* εἴτε | *i.e.* φάρμακος | *i.e.* ἐπουράνιον ‖ **32** *i.e.* εἴτε (twice) | *i.e.* καταχθόνιον | *i.e.* ˢϭⲓϫ ‖ **33** ⲉⲱⲗ ⲱ corrected by washing and overwriting?| *l.* ⲉⲃⲟⲗ ϩⲓ ? W ‖ **34** *i.e.* δ(ε)ῖ(ν)α | *i.e.* εἰ μήτε : εἰμί τε "(NN) am I" W, P, S ‖ **35** *i.e.* ἐπικαλεῖν | *i.e.* ˢⲙⲙⲟ⸗ⲕ | ⲙⲓⲭⲁⲏⲗ : W omits in translation ‖ **36** *i.e.* ἄγγελος ‖ *col. 2,* **1** *i.e.* ˢⲉⲧ-ⲁϩⲉⲣⲁⲧ⸗ϥ ‖ **2** *i.e.* ˢϫⲉ ⲉ⸗ⲕ-ⲉ-ⲉï | ⲉϫ(ⲙ̅ ⲡⲓ-ζ(ῴδιον): *l.* ⲉϫⲙ ⲡⲓⲥⲡⲓⲣ W, P, S | l. ϯ-ἐπ(ικαλεῖν ⲙⲙⲟ⸗ⲕ) ‖ **3** *i.e.* ἄγγελος | *i.e.* ˢⲉⲧ-ⲁϩⲉⲣⲁⲧ⸗ϥ | *l.* ⲛ̅ⲥⲁ ‖ **4** *i.e.* ˢϫⲉ ⲉ⸗ⲕ-ⲉ-ⲉï ‖ **5** *i.e.* ˢⲕⲱϩⲧ | *i.e.* ζ(ῴδιον): *l.* ⲡⲓⲥⲡⲓⲣ W, P, S | *i.e.* ἐπ(ικαλεῖν) | *i.e.* ˢⲙⲙⲟ⸗ⲕ ‖ **6** *i.e.* ἄγγελος ‖ **7** *l.* ⲧ-ⲙⲛ̅ⲧ-ⲥⲛⲟⲟⲩⲥ ‖ **8** *i.e.* ˢϫⲉ ⲉ⸗ⲕ-ⲉ-ⲉï ‖ **9** *i.e.* ζ(ῴδιον) : *l.* ⲡⲓⲥⲡⲓⲣ W, P, S | *l.* ϯ-ἐπ(ικαλεῖν ⲙⲙⲟ⸗ⲕ) | *l.* ⲟⲩⲣⲓ(ⲏⲗ), *cf.* back col. 1 l. 3 | *i.e.* ἄγγελος ‖ **10** ⲉⲧϩⲁⲉⲣⲁⲧ[ϥ Worrell ‖ **11** *i.e.* ˢϫⲉ ⲉ⸗ⲕ-ⲉ-ⲉï | *i.e.* ζ(ῴδιον) : *l.* ⲡⲓⲥⲡⲓⲣ W, P, S ‖ **12** *i.e.* ἐπικαλεῖν | *i.e.* ˢⲙⲙⲟ⸗ⲕ | ⲃⲟⲣï[ⲏⲗ ⲡ]ⲱ *i.e.* ˢⲡⲁ- W, P, S ‖ **13** *i.e.* ˢϫⲉ ⲉ⸗ⲕ-ⲉ-ⲉï ‖ **14** *l.* ⲉϫⲙ̅ (ⲡⲓ-ζ(ῴδιον): *l.* ⲡⲓⲥⲡⲓⲣ W | *l.* ἐπ(ικαλεῖν) ‖ **15** *i.e.* ἄγ[γελος] : ⲡⲁⲅⲅⲉⲗⲟⲥ ⲉⲧ] W, P, S ‖ **16** *i.e.* ὀργ(ή) ‖ **19** ⲧⲉⲃⲥ W ‖ **20–21** *i.e.* ⲧⲁ[ⲣ]ⲧⲁⲣⲟⲩ̂ⲭⲟⲥ :]ⲡⲧⲁ[ⲣ]ⲧⲁⲣⲟⲩ̂ⲭⲟⲥ W

four rivers!

Neither magician nor sorcerer nor heavenly ⟨being⟩ nor underworld ⟨being⟩ nor ⟨the⟩ hand of man will be able to contain this blood which is under NN ⟨child of⟩ NN, except me!

|³⁵ ☩ I invoke you, *Michael, the *angel, |ᶜᵒˡ· ² who stands at the right side of the Father, that you come upon ⟨this image⟩!

I invoke ⟨you⟩, *Gabriel, the angel who stands at the left side of the Father that you come for me with your fiery sword |⁵ upon this image!

I invoke you, *Adonai, the great angel who stands over the twelve hours of the day that you come for me upon this *image!

I invoke you Uriel?, the great angel |¹⁰ who stands over ⟨the⟩ twelve hours of the night, that you come for me upon this image!

I invoke you, Bor...ō, the face of fiery flame, that you come for me upon ⟨this image⟩!

I invoke you, [...]ēl, |¹⁵ the angel [...] the wrath? [...] |²⁰ in the? [...] of? the *Tartaruchus of *hell, he

---

front, col. 1
30–32. ⲓⲇⲉ : **"neither ... nor"** Although εἴτε ("whether") is used, the sense, and parallels (see note to ll. 31–33 below) require us to understand οὔτε ("neither"). It is possible that an original structure of the form "whether magician *etc.* ... ⟨no-one⟩ will be able to..." has been miscopied; we thank Michael Zellmann-Rohrer for this suggestion. For the *topos* of magicians being unable to heal, compare *PCM* I 18 ll. 15–16, and see Dosoo 2021b: 51 for a brief discussion.
31–33. ⲓⲇⲉ ⲡⲟⲩⲣⲁⲛⲓⲟⲛ... ϫⲓϭ ⲛⲣⲱⲙⲉ : **"nor heavenly ⟨being⟩ nor underworld ⟨being⟩ nor ⟨the⟩ hand of man"** Skiles translates "whether heavenly or infernal or human hand", but this is not possible grammatically, since the genitive ⲛ̄ indicating the possessor of ϫⲓϭ can only apply to ⲣⲱⲙⲉ.
33–34. ϭⲉⲙϭⲟⲙ ⲉϭⲱⲗ ⲙ̄ⲡⲓⲥⲛⲟϥ : **"be able to contain this blood"** Worrell, Pernigotti, and Skiles translate "find strength from this blood", but this seems unlikely. For the trope of magicians and sorcerers being unable to undo curses, see *PCM* I 8 ll. 15–16.

front, col. 2
2, 5, 8–9, *etc.* ⲉϫ̄, ⲉϫⲉⲛ, ⲉϫⲉⲛ ⲡⲓⲥ *etc.* : **"upon this image"** Worrell, Pernigotti, and Skiles understand these as abbreviations for Standard Sahidic ⲉϫⲙ̄ ⲡⲓⲥⲡⲓⲣ "upon this side" (*cf.* col. 1 ll. 12–13), but this is a different invocation, and it seems more likely that the powers are being invoked to descend upon an image; ζῴδιον is commonly found written with devoiced consonants (e.g., ⲥⲱⲧⲓⲟⲛ), and appears in a variety of abbreviations; the closest to that here is ζ(ⲱⲇⲓⲟⲛ) in *PCM* I 27 front l. 15. This invocation is an example of an epiclesis, a call to God or an angelic being to descend in order to empower a physical object, a ritual act likely inspired by the epicleses of liturgical rituals such as the anaphora and the blessing of the oil to anoint the sick; *cf.* the discussion in Dosoo 2021d: 426–428.
12–14. ⲃⲟⲣ . . . ⲱ : ⲡⲣⲟ ⲛϣⲁϩ ⲛ̄ⲕⲣⲱⲧ : **"Bor...ō, the face of fiery flame"** Worrell, Pernigotti, and Skiles translate "Boriel, thou of the face of fiery flame" ("Boriel, tu che hai il volto fiammeggiante"), i.e. ⲡⲁ ⲡⲣⲟ ⲛ̄ϣⲁϩ ⲛ̄ⲕⲱϩⲧ, but ⲡⲱ for ⲡⲁ would be unexpected, and the traces do not obviously suggest ⲃⲟⲣⲓⲏⲗ, although the angel names here do typically end in ⲓⲏⲗ. Perhaps compare rather names such as ⲃⲟⲣⲁⲱ (*PCM* I 11 p. 26 ll. 1–2) and ⲃⲟⲣⲁⲩ (Mich.Ms. 136 p. 2 l. 4 (Zellmann-Rohrer/ Love 2022; KYP M128)), and for the whole phrase "Sabaho, the face of flaming fire" (ⲥⲁⲃⲁϩⲟ· ⲡⲓϩⲁ ⲛϣⲁ · ⲛⲕⲱϩⲧ (*P. Macq.* I 1; KYP M167)).

ο[υ] μπεϥϣ πορεϣ εβολ : εχ-
ν ⲧⲕⲟⲩⲙⲏⲛⲏ ⲧⲏⲣⲉⲥ : ⲉⲧⲉ ⲡ-
ⲉϥⲣⲁⲛ ⲡⲉ · ⲥⲓ̈ⲥⲓ̈ⲛⲁⲉⲓ ⲡⲁⲙⲓⲛ · ϫⲉ-
25 ⲕⲉⲓ̈ ⲛⲁⲓ̈ : ⲉⲭⲉ : ⲧ̄ⲉ ⲙⲟ ⲧⲉⲥⲡⲁⲣⲧ-
ⲏ · ⲧϣⲉⲣⲉ ⲙⲡⲧⲓⲁⲃⲟⲗⲟⲥ ⲧⲉⲛⲧⲁ-
ⲥϭⲱⲕ ⲉⲡⲉⲥⲏⲧ ⲉⲁⲙⲉⲛⲧⲉ ⲁⲥⲓⲛ-
ⲉ ⲙⲡⲧⲁⲣⲧⲁⲣⲟⲩⲭⲟⲥ ⲛⲁⲙⲉⲛⲧⲉ
ⲉϩⲣⲁⲓ̈ · ϫⲉⲣⲉⲓ̈ ⲛⲁⲓ̈ ⲉⲭⲉⲛ = ⲧ̄ⲉ ⲙⲱ-
30 ⲧⲉⲛ ⲓ̄ⲃ̄ : ⲛⲁⲣⲭⲁⲅⲅⲉⲗⲟⲥ : ⲉⲣⲉ-
ⲧⲉⲩⲙ̄ ⲓ̄ⲃ̄ : ⲙⲡⲓⲁⲗⲉ ⲙϩ ⲙⲟⲟⲩ
ϩⲛ ⲉⲩϫⲓϭ ⲙⲡⲛⲁⲩ ⲉⲧⲓ ⲛⲁⲥⲓ̈-
ⲧⲉ ⲙⲟϥ : ⲉϩⲟⲩⲛ ⲉⲡⲕϩⲱⲧ · ⲉⲧ-
ⲉⲧⲛⲉⲙϩⲟⲩ ⲛⲧⲉ ⲓ̄ⲃ̄ · ⲙⲡⲓⲁⲗⲉ
35 ⲛ̇ⲕϩⲱⲧ · ⲛⲧⲉⲧⲛⲟⲩϫⲉ ⲙⲟⲟⲩ
ⲉϩⲟⲩⲛ ⲉⲡⲉϩⲏⲧ : ⲡⲉⲥⲟⲩ̌ⲟϥ : ⲡⲉⲥϩⲏⲧ ⲡⲉϩⲏⲡⲁⲣⲟⲛ ⲡⲉⲥⲓ̇ⲕⲟⲩ-
ⲧⲟⲛ ⲡⲉϣⲉ ⲙϫⲉⲥ ⲧⲏ ⲙⲉⲗⲟⲥ

---

back column 1 (↓)

ⲧ̄ⲉⲡ : ⲙⲱⲧⲉⲛ ⲡⲓ̄ⲃ̄ ⲛⲁⲣⲭⲏ-
ⲁⲅⲅⲉⲗⲟⲥ ⲉⲧⲉ ⲛⲁⲓ̈ ⲛⲉ ⲙⲓⲭⲁⲏⲗ :
ⲅⲁⲃⲣⲓ̈ⲏⲗ = ⲟⲩⲣⲓⲏⲗ = ⲣⲁⲕⲟⲩⲏⲗ :
ⲥⲟⲩⲣⲓ̈ⲏⲗ = ⲁⲥⲟⲩⲏⲗ = ⲥⲁⲗⲁⲫⲟⲩⲏⲗ =
5 ⲛ̇ⲅⲓ ϩⲱⲕ ⲙⲓⲭⲁⲏⲗ ⲉϩⲣⲁⲓ̈ = ⲉⲭⲉ : ⲉⲧ-
ⲉⲧⲙⲥⲱⲧⲉⲙ ⲛⲥⲁ ⲛⲁⲣϣⲓ̈ ⲛⲧⲉ-
ⲧⲉⲛϭⲱⲕ ⲉⲃⲟⲗ ⲙⲡⲟⲩⲱϣ ⲙⲡ-
ⲁϩⲏⲧ · ⲡⲉⲧⲛⲙⲁ ⲛⲧⲁⲯⲩⲭⲏ
ⲧⲛⲁϫⲱⲧⲉ ⲙⲡⲓ̈ⲥⲁϣϥ ⲛⲓⲉⲣⲟ
10 ⲛⲕϩⲱⲧ : ⲛⲧⲁⲡⲱⲧ ⲉϩⲣⲁⲓ̈ · ⲉ-

---

22 i.e. ˢⲙ̄-ⲡⲉϥ-ϥⲱ | i.e. ˢⲡⲱⲣϣ̄ | [ⲉⲃⲟ]ⲗ W ǁ **23** i.e. οἰκουμένη ǁ **25** l. ⲉⲭ(ⲙ̄ ⲡⲓ-ζῴδιον) : ⲉⲭ l. ⲉⲭ(ⲙ̄ ⲡⲓⲥⲡⲓⲣ) W, P, S | l. ἐ(πικαλεῖν) i.e. ˢⲙ̄ⲙⲟϥⲕ **26** i.e. διάβολος ǁ **27** i.e. ˢⲃⲱⲕ : ϭⲱⲕⲉ i.e. ˢϭⲱϭⲉ W, S ǁ **28** i.e. ταρταροῦχος ǁ **29** i.e. ˢϫⲉ ⲉⲣⲉϥ-(ⲉ)ⲓ | l. ⲉⲭⲙ̄ (ⲡⲓ-ζῴδιον) : l. ⲉⲭⲉⲛ ⲡⲓⲥⲡⲓⲣ W, P, S | l. ἐ(πικαλεῖν) ǁ **30** i.e. ἀρχάγγελος ǁ **31** ⲧ-ⲙⲛ̄ⲧ-ⲥⲛⲟⲟⲩⲥ / i.e. φιάλη ǁ **31–32** i.e. ˢⲧⲉϥ-ⲙⲛ̄ⲧ-ⲥⲛⲟⲟⲩⲥⲉ ⲙ̄-ⲫⲓⲁⲗⲏ ⲙⲏϩ ⲙ̄ⲙⲟⲟⲩ ϩⲛ ⲛⲉϥ-ϭⲓϫ ǁ **33** i.e. ˢⲙ̄ⲙⲟϥ | i.e. ˢⲕⲱϩⲧ ǁ **34** i.e. ˢⲙⲟⲩϩ | i.e. φιάλη ǁ **35** i.e. ˢⲕⲱϩⲧ ⲛ perhaps corrected from unclear letter by overwriting ǁ **36** l. ⲉ-ⲡⲉⲥ-ϩⲏⲧ ǁ **37** i.e. ⲡⲉⲥ-ⲏ̂ⲡⲁⲣ ǁ **37–38** i.e. ˢⲡⲉⲥ-ⲥⲩⲕⲱⲧⲟⲛ : i.e. ⲡⲉⲥⲕⲟⲓⲧⲉ ⲟⲛ W 1934 ǁ **38** i.e. ˢⲡⲉⲥ-ϣⲉ ⲟⲩ-ϭⲟⲥ ⲙⲛ ⲧⲉ ⲙ̄-ⲙⲉⲗⲟⲥ ? : i.e. ⲡⲉⲥ-ϣⲉ ⲙ̄-ϩⲟⲩⲧⲛ̄ ⲙ̄-ⲙⲉⲗⲟⲥ Polotsky in W, S | i.e. μέλος ǁ
back col. 1, 1 l. ἐπ(ικαλεῖν) ǁ **2–3** i.e. ἀρχάγγελος ǁ **5** i.e. ⲉⲭⲙ̄ (ⲡⲓ-ζῴδιον) : l. ⲉⲭⲉ(ⲛ ⲡⲓⲥⲡⲓⲣ) W, P, S | ⲉⲧ- W ǁ **5–6** i.e. ˢⲉϥⲧⲉⲧⲛ̄-ⲧⲙ̄-ⲥⲱⲧⲙ̄ : ⲉϥ ⲧⲙⲥⲱⲧⲉⲙ "to give – not to hear" ("dare, non per ascoltare (altro)") W, P : "to give, without hearing" S ǁ **7** i.e. ˢϫⲱⲕ ǁ **8** i.e. αἴτημα | i.e. ψυχή ǁ **9** l. ⲙ̄-ⲡⲓ-ⲥⲁϣϥ : ⲙⲡϫⲁϣϥ W ǁ **10** i.e. ˢⲕⲱϩⲧ

whose lock of hair is spread out over the entire world, whose name is Sisinaei Pamin, that |²⁵ you come for me upon ⟨this image⟩!

I invoke you, Espartē, the daughter of the Devil, she who went down to *hell and brought up the *Tartaruchus of hell, that you come for me upon ⟨this image⟩!

I invoke you, |³⁰ twelve *archangels, your twelve bowls filled with water in your hands, in the moment I cast it into the fire, may you fill the twelve bowls |³⁵ with fire and may you cast them into her heart, her lung, her heart, her liver, her one hundred and fifty-five? parts! |^(back, col. 1) I invoke you, O seven *archangels, who are *Michael, *Gabriel, Uriel, Raguel, *Suriel, Asouēl, Salaphouēl, |⁵ that you (s.), yourself, Michael, come down!

If you (pl.) do not obey the ⟨words⟩ of my mouth and fulfill the desire of my heart, the demand of my soul, I will traverse the seven rivers of fire, |¹⁰ and I will run up to

---

front, col. 2 **24. ⲡⲁⲙⲏⲛ** : "**Pamin**" Worrell translates "the amin", understanding a word of Syriac or Arabic origin meaning "trustworthy", presumably ܐܡܝܢ (ʔamīn) or أمِن (amin).

25–26. ⲧⲉⲥⲡⲁⲣⲧⲏ : **Espartē** As noted by Worrell (1934: 12 n. 7), the name of the Devil's daughter is likely derived from Astarte (ⲁⲥⲧⲁⲣⲧⲏ in Judges 2.13), a Levantine goddess who is mentioned several times in the Hebrew Bible, reinterpreted here as a demonic figure. The form here is likely the result of a visual confusion of ⲧ and ⲡ in the name's transmission, and the change of the initial (likely unstressed) vowel. For the initial definite article ⲧ- with the names of divinities in Coptic, see Shisha-Halevy 1989: 13–15; Emmel 1994. The same figure appears in *P.Bad.* V 123 (KYP M315) front l. 76, a curse in which the victim is to be left without company, except "Devil and Spartē" (ⲧⲓⲁⲃⲟⲗⲟⲥ ϩⲓ ⲥⲡⲁⲣⲧⲏ). In this case the initial ⲉ has apparently been reanalysed as part of the definite article (ⲧⲉ-) and removed; note the comparable absence of article before ⲧⲓⲁⲃⲟⲗⲟⲥ.

30–32. ⲉⲣⲉⲧⲉⲩⲙⲓⲃ̄ : **ⲙⲡⲓⲁⲗⲉ ⲙⲉϩ ⲙⲟⲟⲩ ϩⲛⲉⲩϫⲓϭ** : "**your 12 bowls filled with water in your hands**" The Coptic here uses the third-person plural suffix pronoun, but a second-person translation seems more natural here (*cf.* Shisha-Halevy 1989: 52–53). The image is likely inspired by Revelation 16, in which seven angels carry bowls, in particular Revelation 16.1, in which the fourth angel has a bowl which is poured onto the sun in order to scorch men with fire. The twelve angels here may be those described in Cairo JdE 49547 (Girard 1927; KYP M297) ll. 29–32: "twelve small boys who watch over the body of the sun... twelve bowls which are filled with water; they filled their hands and threw (it) into the rays so that the sun would not burn the fruits" (ⲓ̄ⲃ̄ ⲕⲟⲩⲓ̈ ⲛⲁⲗⲟⲩ ⲉⲧⲥⲕⲉⲡⲁⲥⲉ ⲙⲟⲃ ⲡⲥⲱⲙⲉ ⲡⲣⲏ... ⲓ̄ⲃ̄ ⲛⲣⲓ̈ⲁⲗⲉ ⲉⲧⲙⲉϩ ⲙⲟⲟⲩ ⲁⲩⲙⲟⲩϩ ⲛⲛⲉⲩϭⲓϫ ⲁⲩⲛⲟⲩϫⲉ ϩⲟⲩⲛ ⲛⲁⲕⲧⲓⲛ ⲧⲙ ⲡⲣⲏ ϫⲉ ⲛⲟⲩⲣⲱⲕϩ ⲛⲉⲕⲁⲡⲱⲥ). The image seems to be of the angels who regulate the heat of the sun replacing the water of their bowls with fire, and directing the heat they usually moderate at the spell's victim; *cf.* the discussion in Dosoo 2021d: 423–433.

33–38. ⲉϩⲟⲩⲛ ⲉⲡⲕⲣⲱⲧ : "**into the fire …** " This is an example of the motif identified by Ortal-Paz Saar as LOVE IS FIRE, in which the burning of love is analogised to the burning of a fire; see Saar 2017: 194–195; Saar 2019b; Cherkashina/Lyavdansky 2021: 79–80, 86; Cherkashina/Lyavdansky 2022: 25, 35; and *cf. PCM* I 20 ll. 13–16; *PCM* I 28; *PCM* I 32; *PCM* I 37 front l. 22; and among Greek texts, *e.g.*, *SM* I 45 (KYP M822); *SM* I 48 (KYP M874). The ritual described here involves copying an image onto an object which is then cast into the fire while the formula is being spoken; the same ritual is described in, *e.g.*, *PCM* I 28 p. 9 ll. 10–13, *PCM* I 32 p. 1 ll. 16–17, 24–25, p. 2 ll. 11–12. While the object to be inscribed here is unspecified, other recipes often prescribe the use of an ostracon. Naveh/Shaked 1998: amulet 10 (V–VI CE), a series of fired shards written in Aramaic, represents a rare example of a surviving applied object from such a ritual; its text is paralleled in a later recipe from the Cairo Genizah (Naveh/Shaked 1993: Geniza 22 p. 1 ll. 1–6); for discussions see Bohak 2008: 156–157; Saar 2017: 116–120.

ⲧⲙⲉϩⲍⲁϣϥⲉ ⲙⲡⲉ ⲡⲙⲁ ⲉⲧ-
ⲉⲣⲉⲓⲁⲱ ⲥⲁⲃⲁⲱⲑ ⲉϩⲙⲟⲟⲥ
ⲛϩⲏ[ⲧ]ϥ ϯⲛⲁϫⲓⲛⲉ ⲙⲓⲭⲁⲏⲗ ⸗
ⲉⲃϩ[ⲁ]ⲉⲣⲁⲧϥ ⲛ̅[ⲥⲁ ⲟⲩ]ⲛⲁⲙ [ⲙⲡ-]
15 ⲉⲓⲱ[ⲧ *ca.* 11] . ⲥⲏ[. .]
    [*ca.* 15]ⲙ̣ⲡ̣ⲕ[. . .]
    [*ca.* 14]ⲉ̣ ⲙⲡⲉ-
    [*ca.* 15]ϥⲙⲁ
    [*ca.* 5] . ⲧⲁ̣ⲭⲏ ⲧⲁⲭⲏ

---

back, column 2 (at 90° to column 1)

[. ?]ⲱⲱⲱx   ⲱⲱⲱⲱx
[. ?]ⲱⲱⲱⲱx   ⲱⲱⲱⲱx
[. ?]ⲱⲱⲱⲱx   ⲱⲱⲱⲱx
[. ?]ⲱⲱⲱⲱx   ⲱⲱⲱⲱx
5 [. ?]ⲱⲱⲱⲱx ⲱⲱⲱⲱx
[. ?]ϕⲱⲱⲱx
[. ? ⲱ]ⲱⲱⲱx

10

---

11 *i.e.* ᶜⲥⲁϣϥ ‖ **col. 1, 12** ϩⲙ[ⲟ]ⲥ W ‖ **13** *i.e.* ᶜϭⲓⲛⲉ ‖ **15**]ⲥⲏ W ‖ **16**]ⲏ̣[W ‖ **17**]ⲙⲡⲉ W ‖ **18** *l.* ⲡⲉϥⲙⲁ ? :]ϥⲙⲁ[. . .] W ‖ **19** *i.e.* ταχύ (twice) ‖ **col. 2, 8, 10** *i.e.* κο(ινά) ? : understood as *kharaktēr* by W, P, S

the seventh heaven, the place in which *Iao *Sabaoth sits; I will find *Michael, standing [at the right] of [the] |¹⁵ Father [...] of the? [...] his? place? [...] Quickly, quickly!

|^(col. 2) [...]ōōōkh ōōōōkh, ōōōōkh ōōōōkh, ōōōōkh ōōōōkh, ōōōōkh ōōōōkh,
|⁵ ōōōōkh ōōōōkh, ōōōōkh, [ō]ōōōkh. ‹Add the› usual?.
    (*kharaktēres*: ZZZHHH ⌐ ⌐)
|¹⁰   (*kharaktēres*: ⌐BBBXXX) ‹Add the› usual?.

KD, EL & MP, edited from photograph, tracing by KD.

PCM I 4. Miniature codex

Middle Egypt ? 9.5 (H) × 9.1 (W) cm V–VI CE
Other references: P.Mil.Vogl.Copt. 16; TM 102252; KYP M126; Bélanger Sarrazin #230.
Editions: Pernigotti 1979 (*ed. pr.*) [P 1979]; Pernigotti 1993 [P 1993]; Bélanger Sarrazin forthcoming a: appendix 4, no. 5 [B-S].
Translations: Pernigotti 1995: 3707–3708: no. 9 (Italian) [P 1995]; Bélanger Sarrazin forthcoming a: appendix 4, no. 5 (French).
Additional commentary: Bélanger Sarrazin forthcoming a: chapter 3.
Present location: Milan, Università Statale.
Image: Pernigotti 1979: plates I–III; Pernigotti 1993: 100, 101, 107–109.
Linguistic description: Sahidic (non-standard).
Contents:

1. p. 1 ll. 1–10: Amulet (?) consisting of letters, *kharaktēres*, and *voces magicae* (KYP T1254)
2. p. 2 l. 1–17 – p. 3 ll. 1–5: Invocation of Prabaoth (KYP T1255)
3. p. 4 l. 1–17 – p. 6 ll. 1–2: Love spell mentioning Isis, Osiris, Apis, and Petbe (KYP T341)

Incomplete papyrus codex, originally of 12 pages (3 bifolios, all broken into individual sheets), of which two are now lost. Pernigotti's descriptions assume that the lost folio is the second part of the outermost,[1] corresponding to pages 11–12, but more recent photographs, demonstrating continuities across the fibres, show that it is in fact the second half of the innermost folio (corresponding to pages 7–8) which is lost. The text is written only on the first six pages, with the rest of the codex blank. The damage patterns of the codex, resembling a vertical crease, suggest that it may have been folded in half before deposition.[2]

The manuscipt was purchased by the Università Statale in Milan through the antiquities market in the early 1960s.[3] The purchase of the manuscript as part of a larger group of magical texts, written in Greek and Aramaic, suggests that it may have belonged to an ancient archive, which was deposited, discovered, and then sold together, known as the 'Multilingual Library' (KYP A17; TM Arch ID 380).[4] A drawing identical to that of page 3 of this codex is found in one of the Greek

---

[1] Pernigotti 1979: 19; Pernigotti 1993: 95.
[2] Pernigotti 1993: 96 n. 10; *cf. PCM I* 28 & 34, codices which also seem to have been folded before deposition.
[3] Gallazzi/Piacentini 1998: 5–6; Pernigotti 1979: 21.
[4] Daniel/Maltomini 1992: 231–232; Bohak 2008: 167–168. The archive consists of two Greek rotuli (*GEMF* 82, 84, 85=*PGM* CXXIII, CXXIV, CXXVa=KYP M180, M840, M902), and several fragments in Greek, Coptic and Aramaic (*PGM* CXXIIIb–f, *PGM* CXXVb–f). Some of these fragments may be applied texts, and repeat text found in the formularies.

manuscripts, *GEMF* 84/*PGM* CXXIV (KYP M840), strengthening the hypothesis of the existence of an archive (see notes to page 3).

The longest pages of the codex have 17 lines (pp. 2 & 4), the shortest, the final written page, only 2 (p. 6). A decorated horizontal line marks the end of a text on page 1, but the rest of the page is left blank; similarly long spaces are left at the ends of pages 3 and 5.[5]

The hand is an informal, trained bilinear, generally unimodal and upright majuscule. Ligature of ε with π, τ and other letters is common. The м is deeply curved, the γ resembles Latin Y, written in one stroke. Letter size is somewhat variable, with в, к, ө, and ф in particular at times larger than the other letters, and ʒ, x, ⲱ, ϭ tending towards quadralinearity. The hand is generally undecorated, with the exception of notable serifs on †, and marked loops on ⲁ and ф (which takes the form often described as "treble clef"). The writing on the last page is notably lighter in shading than on the other pages, suggesting the use of a different writing implement. A colon, sometimes extended into two short oblique strokes, marks paratextual divisions. The Greek manuscripts of the archive are dated to the fifth or sixth centuries,[6] and Pernigotti (1979: 21) suggested a similar date for this manuscript.[7] We note similarities to the Greek hands, in particular that of *PGM* CXXIIIa/*GEMF* 82 (KYP M180); although the single ϩ (l. 17) in that manuscript is quite different from that of *PCM* I 4, the forms of the ϥ and ϩ do seem close to those of *PGM* CXXVc/*SM* II 98.3 (KYP M540). We thus tentatively agree with Pernigotti's fifth to sixth century dating of this manuscript.

The dialect is Sahidic, with some inconsistent yet significant divergences from the literary standard. As well as common features such as the writing of schwa as ε, of doubled vowels as single vowels, of ^{S}ϥ as в, of τⲱ as ϫ (purely graphic), the lack of ⲛ › м assimilation, and the use of the strong article (пι- for expected ^{S}п(ε)-), we find indications of cⲁⲛ/peⲛ vocalism typical of the more conservative dialects (*i.e.*, those other than Sahidic and Bohairic)—^{S}e as ⲁ, ^{S}o as ⲁ, and the final tonic vowel written as -ι rather than -^{S}e. Pernigotti understood these these as a mixture of dialectal influences, principally Faiyumic and Lycopolitan. He thus suggested a possible origin in the region of Beni Suef (Heracleopolis), comparing Cairo JdE 49547 (Girard 1927; KYP M297), found in Mazura, near Beni Suef,[8] but we find this assessment overly optimistic; this latter text is not notably closer to *PCM* I 4 than many other non-standard manuscripts. Kahle does note that the lack of ⲛ › м assimilation is generally found north of Thebes, so we may cautiously suggest a more general Middle Egyptian provenance.[9]

---

[5] Extensive blank spaces occur in other manuscripts of this archive; see Daniel/Maltomini 1992: 231.
[6] See *SM* II nos. 96–98.
[7] Pernigotti 1979: 19 (V CE); Pernigotti 1993: 96 (V–VI CE).
[8] Pernigotti 1979: 45–46; Pernigotti 1993: 119–120.
[9] Kahle 1954: I 99–100.

page 1 (→)

ⲱ ⲱ ⲱ ⲱ ⲱ ⲱ ⲱ ⲱ ⲱ ⲱ ⲱ
ⲣ̣ ⲣ̣ ⲣ̣ ⲣ̣ ⲣ̣ ⲣ̣ ⲣ̣ ⲣ̣ ⲣ̣ ⲣ̣
ⲃ ⲃ ⲃ ⲃ ⲃ ⲃ ⲃ ⲃ ⲃ ⲃ ⲃ̣

    ⲁⲃⲓⲛⲓⲭⲟⲭ   ⲁⲃⲟⲩⲟⲩⲭ
5 ⲑⲁⲃⲟⲃⲩⲭ   ⲁⲙⲱⲙⲓⲭ
    ⲟⲣⲓⲥⲉⲕⲑⲣⲩⲃ   ⲑⲁⲣⲥⲟⲩⲭ
    ⲉⲙⲟⲩⲃⲓⲕ   ⲑⲉⲛⲉⲡⲑⲓⲙ̣
    ⲛ̣ . ⲛⲁⲣ   ⲟⲩⲫⲉⲗⲁ̣ⲕ-
    ⲟⲩⲭⲱⲑⲱⲙⲓⲭ   ⲧⲏⲣⲓⲟⲛ ⲛ.ⲉⲡ
10 ⲡⲣⲱⲑⲏⲙⲁⲥ   ⲡⲥⲉⲛⲁⲓⲱ

———»»»»»———«««———

page 2 (↓)

    ⸗ ϯⲉⲡⲓⲕ[ⲁ]ⲗⲓ ⲛⲙⲟⲕ ⲡⲣⲁⲃⲁⲱⲑ
    ⲡⲁⲓ ⲉⲑⲙ̣ⲙⲟⲟⲥ ϩⲛ ⲧⲉⲩⲭⲏ ⲛ̅ⲛϭⲟⲙ
    ⲧⲏⲣⲟⲩ ϯⲉ : ⲛⲉⲕⲙⲱⲣⲫⲩ ϯⲉⲣ ⲁⲛⲁⲱ
    ⲉⲣⲟⲕ ⲛ̅ⲡⲉⲕⲙⲛ̅ⲧⲓⲃ ⲛϩⲁⲣⲙⲁ
5 ⲉⲕⲧⲁⲗⲏⲟⲩ ⲉϫⲱⲟⲩ ⲥⲱⲧⲙ̅ ⲉⲣⲟⲓ
    ⲁⲃⲣⲁ ϯⲉⲡⲓ̈ ⲛⲙⲟⲕ ⲛⲡⲟⲟⲩ ϫⲉ ⲁⲛⲟⲕ
    ⲇⲇ ⲕⲟⲓ̈ ϯᵉ ⲑ̅ⲱ̅ⲣ̅ⲁ̅ⲑ̅ ϯᵉ ⲗ̅ⲁ̅ⲉ̅ⲗ̅ⲁ̅ⲙ̅ⲑ̅
    ϯᵉ ⲱ̅ⲣ̅ⲱ̅ⲙ̅ⲁ̅ⲛ̅ⲗ̅ : ϯᵉ ⲑ̅ⲁ̅ⲣ̅ⲁ̅ⲃ̅ⲭ̅ : ϯᵉ
    ⲗ̅ⲁ̅ⲑ̅ⲁ̅ⲑ̅ : ϯᵉ ⲛ̅ⲓ̅ⲏ̅ⲗ̅ : ⲕⲟⲣⲁⲑⲟⲑ : ϯᵉ
10 ⲁ̅ⲕ̅ⲣ̅ⲁ̅ⲙ̅ⲁ̅ⲭ̅[ⲁ̅]ⲙ̅ⲁ̅ⲣ̅ⲓ̅ : ϯᵉ ⲁⲣⲓⲱⲙⲁ : ϯᵉ
    ⲕ̅ⲟ̅ⲣ̅ⲁ̅ⲛ̅ⲓ̅ⲏ̅ⲗ̅ : ϯᵉ ⲃ̅ⲱ̅ⲣ̅ⲁ̅ⲃ̅ⲱ̅ⲏ̅ⲗ̅ ϯᵉ
    ⲥ̅ⲟ̅ⲩ̅ⲭ̅ⲱ̅ⲣ̅ⲁ̅ⲃ̅ⲑ̅ : ϯᵉ ⲕ̅ⲟ̅ⲩ̅ⲏ̅ⲗ̅ : ϯᵉ
    ⲥ̅ⲁ̅ⲣ̅ⲁ̅ⲙ̅ⲓ̅ⲏ̅ⲗ̅ : ϯᵉ ⲥ̅ⲁ̅ⲏ̅ⲗ̅ : ⲛⲉϩⲥⲉ ⲛ̅-
    ⲙⲱⲧⲛ ϫⲉⲕⲁⲁⲥ ⲉⲧⲉⲧ̣[ⲛ̅]ⲉⲉⲓ ϣⲁⲣⲟⲓ
15 ⲙ̣ⲡⲟⲟⲩ ⲃⲁⲗ ⲡⲁⲅⲅⲉⲗⲟⲥ ⲡⲁϯ-
    ⲙⲉ̣ⲥ ⲛϩⲏᵀⲛ ϩⲁⲙⲏ[ⲛ . . .] ϯϣ
    ᵛᵃᶜ·   [ca. 5 ?]ⲉ̣ ⸗

---

page 1, 1 ⲱ : [ⲱ] P || **2** ⲣ̣ : ⲃ P || **3** ⲃ : ⲁ P || **5** ⲑⲁⲃⲟⲣ... P || **6** ⲟⲣⲓⲥⲉⲕⲑⲣⲟⲃ 1979 P || **7** ⲑⲉⲛⲉⲟⲑⲓⲙ P || **8** [..]ⲛ̣ⲁⲣ P || **8–9** *i.e.* φυλακτήριον B-S : ⲟⲩⲫⲉⲗⲁⲭ|ⲧⲏⲣⲓⲟⲛ ⲛ.ⲉⲓ P || **10** or *l.* ⲡϭⲉⲛ ⲁⲓⲱ "Psen, yea!" ?
page 2, 1 *i.e.* ἐπικ[α]λεῖν : ϯⲉⲡⲓⲕ[ⲁⲗ]ⲓ P | *i.e.* ˢⲙ̅ⲙⲟ⸗ⲕ | ⲡⲣⲁⲃⲁⲱⲑ P || **2** *i.e.* ˢⲉⲧ-ϩⲙⲟⲟⲥ : ⲉⲑ{ⲙ}ⲙⲟⲟⲥ P | *i.e.* εὐχή || **3** *i.e.* ἐ(πικαλεῖν) | *i.e.* μορφή : ⲙⲟⲣⲫⲩ P || **4** *i.e.* ἅρμα || **5** ⲉⲧ⸗ⲕ-ⲧⲁⲗⲏⲩ | ⲥⲱⲧⲙ P || **6** *i.e.* ἐπι(καλεῖν) | *i.e.* ˢⲙ̅ⲙⲟⲕ | *i.e.* ˢⲙ̅ⲡⲟⲟⲩ || **7–13** *i.e.* ἐ(πικαλεῖν) (twice) || **7** *i.e.* δ(ε)ῖ(να) δ(ε)ῖ(να) κοι(νά) : ⲕⲟⲭ *i.e.* "ἀπολογία" P | ϯⲉ P || **8** ⲱ̅ⲣ̅ⲱ̅ⲙ̅ⲁ̅ⲛ̅[ⲗ̅] P || **11** bipunct read by P as a tripunct || **13–14** *i.e.* ˢⲙ̅ⲙⲱⲧⲛ || **15** ⲙⲡⲟⲟⲩ P | *vox magica* or ˢⲉⲃⲟⲗ ? with P | *i.e.* ἄγγελος : ⲡⲁⲅⲅ[ⲉ]ⲗⲟ[ⲥ] P || **15–16** *i.e.* ἄτιμος ? : ⲡⲁϯⲙⲉ[[ⲥ]] P 1979 *l.* ⲙ̅-ⲡ-ϯⲙⲉ or ⲡⲁ-ⲧ-ⲙⲉ ? || **16** ⲛϩⲏⲧⲛ P 1979 | *i.e.* ἀμήν | ϯϣ\ⲉ/[.]ⲱ *l.* ϯⲁⲉⲓⲱ ("I cry"), or "I invoke" + name of invoked being ? - ϯⲉ ⲁⲓⲱ or ϯⲉ ⲱⲃϣ P || **17** P does not read a line here, understanding the ⲉ as an addition to the previous line

|*p. 1* ō ō ō ō ō ō ō ō ō ō ō ō
　　　　ⲣ ⲣ ⲣ ⲣ ⲣ ⲣ ⲣ ⲣ ⲣ ⲣ ⲣ
　　　　B B B B B B B B B B B
　　　　Abinikhokh　　　Abououkh
|⁵　　　Thabobukh　　　Amōmikh
　　　　Orisekthrub　　　Tharsoukh
　　　　Emoubik　　　　Thenepthim
　　　　N.nar　　　　　　A phylactery
　　　　Oukhōthōmikh　Ndep
|¹⁰　　Prōthēmas　　　　Psenaiō

|*p. 2* "I invoke you, Prabaoth, he who dwells in the prayer of all the *powers! I invoke your forms, I adjure you by your twelve chariots |⁵ that you ride upon! Listen to me *Abra, I invoke you today, for I am NN (⟨add the⟩ usual)!

I invoke Thōrath! I invoke Laelamth! I invoke Ōrōmaēl! I invoke Tharabkh! I invoke Lalath! I invoke Niēl Korathoth! I invoke |¹⁰ Akramakhamari! I invoke Ariōma! I invoke Koraniēl! I invoke Bōraboēl! I invoke Soukhōrabth! I invoke Kouēl! I invoke Saramiēl! I invoke Saēl!

Awaken yourselves so that you come to me |¹⁵ today, Bal?, O *angel, you who are not honoured among us! Amen! … I call? […]

Note: In the apparatus, 'Pernigotti' [P] refers to his editions of 1979, 1993, and his translation of 1995; the date is only specified when these diverge from one another.

page 1
2–3. The ⲣ signs which occupy l. 2 and the в which occupy l. 3 are touching, and each pair might therefore be considered a single symbol.

page 2
7–13. *Voces magicae*: Pernigotti 1993 notes several parallels to the names here, including ⲑⲟⲩⲣⲁⲭ (*P.Lond.Copt.* 1008 l. 50; KYP M282); λαιλαμ (several Greek magical papyri; see Brashear 1995: 3590); ⲁⲣⲱⲙⲁⲛⲁⲛⲗ (*PCM* I 22 l. 15, 27), ⲑⲣⲁⲕⲁⲓ, ⲃⲱⲃⲱⲏⲗ, ⲥⲁⲏⲗ (*PCM* I 12, p. 11 l. 13, p. 39 page l. 17, p. 41 l. 10); ⲥⲁⲭⲱⲣⲁⲕ (BL Ms Or. 6795 l. 36; Kropp 1931: I no. F; KYP M307).

15. ⲙⲡⲟⲟⲩ ⲃⲁⲗ : "today, Bal?" Pernigotti (1979, 1993) understands this to have the sense of "from today forward" (Crum CD 731a), but this would not seem to make sense in a context in which the being is commanded to come to the practitioner. For ⲃⲁⲗ as the name of a superhuman being, *cf.* Cairo JdE 45060 l. 3 (Kropp 1931: I no. K; KYP M303); *PCM* I 33 l. 4 (ⲃⲁⲣ). It is tempting to see here a link to the Northwest Semitic deity (or divine title) Ba'al (בעל "lord"), who appears at numerous points in the Hebrew Bible, but the normal Coptic writing would be ⲃⲁϩⲁⲗ; see, *e.g.*, Jeremiah 7.9 (Feder 2002: 122).

15–16. ⲡⲁⲅⲅⲉⲗⲟⲥ ⲡⲁ†ⲙⲉⲥ ⲛϩⲏⲧⲛ : "**O angel, you who are not honoured among us**" Pernigotti 1979 translates "the angel of the village (or "in possession of justice") is in our midst?" ("l'angelo del villagio/possessore della giustizia è in mezzo a noi"). Pernigotti 1993 translates "the ignominious angel is among us" ("l'angelo ignominiosa è tra di noi").

page 3 (→)

ⲛⲡⲉⲛⲓⲡⲉ ⲡⲁ ⲛⲓⲃ̣ⲁ̣ⲗ ⲛⲕⲱϩⲧ
ⲕⲟⲩ : ⲉⲧⲓ ⲉⲧⲓ ⲧⲁⲭⲩ ⲃ : ϩⲛ ϭⲟⲙ :
ⲁⲥⲱⲧⲱⲑ : ⲁⲙⲓⲱⲏⲗ : ⲃⲱⲭⲱⲭ

5

page 4 (↓)

ⲧⲥⲟⲧⲉ ⲕ̣ⲱⲧⲉ ⲉⲡⲣⲏ ⲧⲭⲁⲗⲟⲟⲩ
ⲕⲱⲧⲉ ⲉⲡⲟⲟϩ ⲧϭⲓⲙⲟⲩⲧ ϩⲛ ⲧ-
ⲙⲏⲧⲓ ⲛⲡⲕⲱϩⲧ ⲡⲕⲱϩⲧ ⲟⲩ-
ⲱⲙ ⲛ̄ⲥⲁ ⲡϣⲙⲧ ⲉⲧⲏⲣ ⲥⲟⲩⲥⲁϩ-
5   ⲧⲉ ϩⲁ ⲛⲕⲉⲉⲥ ⲛ̄ϩⲁⲡⲉ ⲙⲛ ϩⲥⲉ̄ ⲙⲛ
ⲟⲩⲥⲓⲣⲉ ⲛ̄ⲛⲉⲧⲥⲟⲧⲉ ⲗⲟ ⲉⲥⲕⲱⲧⲉ
ⲉⲡⲣⲏ ⲛ̄ⲏⲭⲁⲗⲟⲟⲩ ⲗⲱ ⲉⲥⲕⲱⲧⲉ
ⲉⲡⲟⲟϩ ⲛ̄ⲛⲉⲧϭⲓⲙⲟⲩⲧ ⲗⲟ ϩⲛ ⲧⲙⲏⲧⲉ ⲛ̄ⲡⲕⲱϩⲧ ⲛ̄ⲉⲡⲕⲱϩⲧ ⲗⲟ : ⲉ-
10 ⲃⲟⲩⲟⲙ ⲛ̄ⲥⲁ ⲡϣⲙⲧ ⲉⲧⲏⲣ ⲛ̄ⲛ-
ⲉⲩⲗⲟ ⲉ[ⲩⲥ]ⲁϩⲧⲉ ϩⲁ ⲛⲕⲉⲉⲥ
ⲛ̄ϩⲁⲡⲉ ⲙⲛ ϩⲥⲉ ⲙⲛ ⲟⲩⲥⲓⲣⲉ
ⲛ̄ⲉⲁⲃⲣⲁⲥⲁⲝ ⲗⲟ ϩⲛ ⲧⲙⲏⲧⲉ ⲛ̄-
ⲡⲕⲱϩⲧ ⲉⲭⲱⲣⲙ ⲛⲥⲱⲥ ⲉⲃⲱϣ
15 ⲉⲃⲟⲗ ϫⲉ ⲛⲧⲓⲛⲁⲉⲓ ⲉϩⲣⲁⲓ ⲉⲛ
ϩⲛ ⲧⲙⲏⲧⲉ ⲛ̄ⲡⲓⲕⲱϩⲧ ⲉⲓⲭⲱ-
ⲣⲙ ⲛⲥⲁ ⲇ̣ⲇ̣ ϣⲁ[. . .] . .

page **3, 1** *i.e.* ˢⲙ̄-ⲃⲉⲛⲓⲡⲉ | ⲡⲁⲛⲓ[..] || **2** *i.e.* ⲕⲟⲓ(ⲛά) : ⲕⲟⲭ *i.e.* "ἀπολογία" P | *i.e.* ἤδη (twice) | *i.e.* ταχύ | *i.e.* ˢϩⲛ ⲧ-ϭⲟⲙ ⲛ̄- || **page 4, 1** [ⲕ]ⲱⲧⲉ P 1979 | *i.e.* ˢⲧ-ϣⲁⲗⲟⲟⲩ || **3** *i.e.* ˢⲙⲏⲧⲉ | *i.e.* ˢⲙ̄-ⲡ-ⲕⲱϩⲧ || **4** ⲉⲧⲛ̄ⲧⲏⲣ P 1979 | *i.e.* ˢⲥⲉ- || **5** ϩⲥⲉ P 1979 || **7** *i.e.* ⲛ̄ⲧⲉ-ⲧ-ϣⲁⲗⲟⲟⲩ | *i.e.* ˢⲗⲟ || **9** *i.e.* ˢⲙ̄-ⲡ-ⲕⲱϩⲧ : ⲛ̄ⲡⲕⲱϩ[ⲧ] P 1979 | *i.e.* ˢⲛ̄ⲛⲉ- || **10** ⲡϣⲙⲧ ⲉⲧⲛ̄ⲧⲏⲣ P 1979 || **13** *i.e.* ˢⲛ̄ⲛⲉ- || **14** ⲉϥ-ⲭⲱⲣⲙ || **15** *i.e.* ˢⲁⲛ || **16** ⲛ̄ⲡⲓⲕ[ⲱ]ϩ[ⲧ] P 1979 || **17** *i.e.* δ(ε)ῖ(να) δ(ε)ῖ(να) | *l. e.g.* ϣⲁⲛⲧⲉⲥⲃⲱⲕ ? : ϣⲁ[*ca.* 4]... P

|*p. 3* of iron, he with eyes? of fire—⟨add the⟩ usual—now, now, quickly (twice), by ⟨the⟩ power of Asōtōth, Amiōēl, Bōkhōkh!"
|*above tableau* (*kharaktēres:* ΠΧΚΗΑΓΝ) |⁵ ōōō iii sss
|*p. 4* The arrow goes around the sun, the water-wheel goes around the moon, the Pleiades are in the midst of the fire. The fire consumes the three deities, a fire is being kindled |⁵ under the bones of *Apis and *Isis and *Osiris. The arrow will not stop going around the sun, the water-wheel will not stop going around the moon, the Pleiades will not cease to be in the midst of the fire. The fire will not |¹⁰ stop consuming the three deities, they will not stop kindling fire under the bones of Apis, Isis, and Osiris. *Abrasax will not cease to be in the midst of the fire, driving it on, calling |¹⁵ out, "I am not going to come out from the midst of this fire, driving on NN until [she? goes?]

---

page 3 **1. ⲛⲡⲉⲛⲓⲡⲉ ⲡⲁ ⲛⲓⲃⲁⲗ ⲛⲕⲱϩⲧ** : **"of iron, he with eyes? of fire"** We thank Michael Zellmann-Rohrer for suggesting this reading. The oblique stroke of the ⲁ curls upwards more than expected, but perhaps the scribe anticipated a ligature (*cf.* ⲉϩⲣⲁⲓ on p. 5 l. 7). "Iron" presumably describes another attribute (perhaps a body part) of the invoked being. For similar descriptions of superhuman beings, compare *GEMF* 57/*PGM* IV (KYP M3) l. 109 "he of the bronze feet, he of the iron heels" (ⲡ[ⲁ] ⲧⲓϭⲁⲗⲁⲩϭ ⲛ̄ⲟⲙⲛⲧ ⲡⲁ ⲛⲓⲧⲓⲃⲥ ⲛ̄ⲃⲉⲛⲓⲡⲉ); *BKU* I 1 (KYP M76) front col. 2 l. 19: "(Isis) with an head of iron upon her" (ⲉⲣⲉⲟⲩⲕⲉⲫⲁⲗⲏ ⲛ̄ⲃⲓⲛⲓⲃⲉ ϩⲓⲭⲟⲥ); BM EA 10376 (Zellmann-Rohrer 2022a: no. 2; KYP M286) l. 1 "he of the iron staff, he of the … face" (ⲡⲁ ⲡⲉϭⲉⲣⲱⲃ ⲛⲡⲉⲛⲓⲡⲉ ⲡⲁ ⲡⲉϩⲟ .[..]); BM EA 10391 (Zellmann-Rohrer 2022a: no. 1; KYP M302) l. 13: "this one who stands upon the iron legs" (ⲡⲁⲓ ⲉⲧⲁϩⲉ ⲉⲣⲁⲧϥ ⲉϫⲛ ⲛⲕⲉⲗⲉ ⲃⲓⲛⲓⲡⲉ); P.Carlsberg 52 (Lange 1932; KYP M125) p. ll. 2–3 "he of the bronze head, he of the iron teeth" (ⲡⲁ †ⲁⲡⲏ ⲛ̄ϩⲁ̄ⲙⲉⲧ ⲡⲁ ⲛⲓⲁ̄ⲃⲁϩ ⲛ̄ⲃⲉⲛⲓⲡⲓ).
2. ϩⲛ ϭⲟⲙ : **"by ⟨the⟩ power"** For this phrase, *cf.* the notes to *PCM* I 16 o. 3 ll. 7–8.
4–6. Image: The figure of a man and the associated *kharaktēres* and vowels above it are identical to those at *GEMF* 84/*PGM* CXXIV (KYP M840) front ll. 10–33. This Greek recipe, though, seems to be a binding curse, and the image may depict an effigy to be made out of wax. Here, by contrast, it is associated with an invocation with no clear link to cursing or the use of effigies.
page 4 **1, 6. ⲧⲥⲟⲧⲉ** : **"the arrow"** Here we follow the translation "the arrow" (Crum CD 361b) proposed by Pernigotti (1979: 36; 1993: 112–113), although it is also possible to translate "the fire" (Crum CD 360a *s.v.* ⲥⲁⲧⲉ). Pernigotti 1979 understands it as the constellation of the same name (Sagitta, Greek Οἰστός, although Pernigotti refers to τόξον "the bow"); *cf. PCM* I 9 ll. 7–8.
1, 7. ⲧⲭⲁⲗⲟⲟⲩ : **"water wheel"** For this translation, see Crum CD 561a *s.v.* ϣⲁⲗⲟⲟⲩ. Pernigotti (1979: 36) proposes "scorpion", *i.e.* the constellation Scorpio, attested in Coptic as †ϭⲗⲏ (Spiegelberg 1911: 147). Pernigotti (1993: 113) later decided against this earlier interpretation, instead proposing to understand "water wheel" as the constellation Aquarius; *cf. PCM* I 9 ll. 7–8.
4–6. Fire consumes the bones of the three deities: For the "three deities" *cf.* Mich.Ms. 136 (Zellmann-Rohrer/Love 2022: commentary 125–126, 129; KYP M128) p. 5 ll. 3–4, but there apparently referring to the triune deity Amun. Threats against gods or the cosmic order are a common way of compelling deities in Pharaonic ritual and later Graeco-Egyptian magic (Sauneron 1951; Altenmüller 1977; Merkelbach/Totti 1991, 83–88; Maravela in Faraone/Torallas Tovar 2022a: 39 nn. 24–25). Threats are often against the vulnerable mummy of Osiris (*e.g.*, *GEMF* 8/*PGM* LVII (KYP M788) l. 47; *GEMF* 16/*PDM* xiv (KYP M162) ll. 451–458; *GEMF* 70/*PGM* V (KYP M141) l. 266; Audollent 1904: no. 270 ll. 21–24), here paralleled by the threat against his bones. Threats against the corpses of Apis and Isis do not seem to be otherwise attested; perhaps the composer of this formula was attempting to amplify the threat by adding other Pharaonic deities known to them.
15. ⲛ̄ⲧⲓⲛⲁⲉⲓ ⲉϩⲣⲁⲓ ⲉⲛ : **"I am not going to come out from"** More strictly "come up/down", but the implied meaning seems to be "come up/down out *of*". Pernigotti renders "come down" ("scendere").

page 5 (→)

ⲉⲣⲁⲧϥ ⲇⲇ ⲉⲓⲕⲁⲧⲓⲭⲉ ⲛⲧ-
ϭⲟⲙ ⲛⲥⲏⲑ ϣⲁⲛⲧⲉⲩⲉⲣ ⲡⲁⲟⲩ-
ⲱϣ ⲍⲏⲑ ⲓⲱ ⲥⲏⲑ ⲓⲱ ⲡⲁⲕⲉⲣ-
ⲃⲏⲑ ⲓⲱ ⲫⲉⲛⲓⲝ ⲓⲱ ⲡⲁⲫⲩⲗⲁⲝ
5 ⲃⲁϣⲧⲱⲣ ⲡⲉⲧⲃⲉ ⲛϩⲁ ⲛϭⲉⲙ
ⲡⲉⲧⲃⲟⲗⲃⲉⲗ ⲛ̄ⲥⲁ ⲛⲥⲛⲧⲉ ⲛⲡⲕⲁϩ
ⲕⲓⲙ ⲛ̄ⲙⲟⲕ ⲛⲉϩⲥⲉ ⲛⲙⲟⲕ ⲉϩⲣⲁⲓ
ⲉϫⲛ ⲛⲓⲙ ⲧϣⲉⲣⲓ ⲛⲓⲙ ⲃⲓⲧⲥ ⲉⲣⲁⲧϥ
ⲛⲇⲇ ϫⲉ ⲉⲕϣⲁⲛⲕⲓⲙ ⲛⲙⲟⲕ ϣⲁⲩ-
10 ϣⲧⲟⲣⲧⲣ ⲛ̄ϭⲓ ⲛⲥⲛⲧⲉ ⲛ̄ⲡⲕⲁϩ ⲉⲕϣⲁⲛⲕⲓⲙ ⲛⲙⲟⲕ ϣⲁⲩϣⲧⲟⲣⲧⲣ
ⲛ̄ϭⲓ ⲛⲉⲥⲧⲉⲣⲉⲩⲙⲁ ⲛ̄ⲧⲡⲉ ⲙ̄ⲛ
ⲛⲉⲑⲣⲟⲛⲟⲥ ⲙⲛ ⲛⲉⲧϩⲙⲟⲟⲥ ϩⲓⲭⲟ[ⲩ]
ⲛⲥⲉⲟⲩⲱϣⲡ ⲛⲉ ⲧⲏⲣⲟⲩ ⲛⲥⲉⲡⲱⲧ̣
15 ⲉⲡⲉⲥⲏ[ⲧ . . .]ⲁ̣ ⲛⲉⲩⲁⲣⲏⲟⲩ ⲛ̄-
ⲥⲉϣϣ [ⲉⲃⲟ]ⲗ ϩⲛ ⲟⲩⲛⲟϭ ⲛⲥⲙⲏ

page 6 (↓)

ϫⲉ ϩⲁⲣⲡⲁ[ⲥ]ⲥⲉ ⲛⲇⲇ ⲁⲛⲓⲧⲥ̣ ⲉⲣⲁⲧϥ
ⲛ̣ⲇⲇ ϩⲛ ϭⲟⲙ ⲓⲁⲱ ⲥⲁⲃⲁⲱⲑ ⲕⲟⲓ̸

***page* 5, 1** *i.e.* κατέχειν : κα[τ]ιχε P 1979 | *i.e.* ˢⲛ̄-δ(ε)ῖ(να) δ(ε)ῖ(να) || **5** ⲃⲁϣⲧⲱⲣ P 1979 | *i.e.* ˢϭⲁⲙ || **6** *i.e.* ˢⲃⲟⲗⲃⲗ | *i.e.* ˢⲛ̄-ⲡ-ⲕⲁϩ || **7–8** *i.e.* ˢⲙ̄ⲙⲟ= | **8** ⲛⲓ[ⲙ] P || **9** *i.e.* δ(εῖνα) δ(εῖνα) | ⲉⲕϣⲁⲛⲕⲓⲙ ⲛ corrected from ⲕ by overwriting : ⲉⲕϣⲁⲛⲕⲓⲙ P 1979 | *i.e.* ˢⲙ̄ⲙⲟ= | ϣⲁⲩ P 1979 || **10** ϣⲧⲟⲣⲧⲉⲣ P | *i.e.* ˢⲙ̄-ⲡ-ⲕⲁϩ || **11** *i.e.* ˢⲙ̄ⲙⲟ= || **12** *i.e.* στερέωμα || **13** *i.e.* θρόνος || **14** ⲛⲥⲉⲟⲩⲱϣⲡ ⲛⲉ corrected from ⲛϥⲟⲩⲱϣⲧ ⲛⲉ by overwriting ? *i.e.* ˢⲟⲩⲱϭⲡ ⲛⲁⲓ ? : ⲛⲥⲉⲟⲩⲱϣ [.]ⲉ "and they desire..." ("ed essi vogliono...") P || **16** ⲱ[ϣ] P || ***page* 6, 1** *i.e.* ἁρπάζειν | *i.e.* δ(ε)ῖ(να) δ(ε)ῖ(να) || **2** *i.e.* ˢⲛ̄-δ(ε)ῖ(να) δ(ε)ῖ(να) | *i.e.* ˢϩⲛ ⲧ-ϭⲟⲙ | *i.e.* κοι(νά) : ⲕⲟⲭ *i.e.* "ἀπολογία" P

|$^{p.5}$ to NN! I restrain the power of *Seth until he does my desire!" Seth, Iō Seth, Iō Pakerbeth, Iō Phenix, Iō Paphulax, |^5 Baōtōr! Bull-faced *Petbe, he who uproots the foundations of the earth, move yourself, awaken yourself against NN, the daughter of NN, carry her to NN, for if you move yourself, |^{10} the foundations of the earth will shake; if you move yourself the firmaments of the heaven and the *thrones and those who sit upon them will be shaken and they will break?, all of these?, and they will go |^{15} down ... one another, and they will call out in a great voice, |$^{p.6}$ "Seize NN, bring her to NN by ⟨the⟩ power of *Iao *Sabaoth!"
⟨Add the⟩ usual.

RBS, KD, EL & MP, edited from photograph; tracing by KD.

page 5
3–5. ⲍⲏⲑ ⲓⲱ ⲥⲏⲑ : "Seth Iō Seth..." This is a variant of the *Ērbeth*-logos, a sequence whose opening part, "Iō Seth", can perhaps be translated "Hail Seth!" (Dosoo 2021c: 209). The formula is associated with the god Seth-Typhon in the older Graeco-Egyptian corpus, and typically occurs in curses and love spells, where it is a compulsive formula intended to force the target or invoked beings to obey; *cf. PCM* I 14 l. 5; Martín Hernández 2019. The initial writing of Seth with a ⲍ rather than a ⲥ (*i.e.*, *Zēth*) is unlikely to be significant, since Coptic does not distinguish between voiced and unvoiced consonants.
4. ⲓⲱ ⲫⲉⲛⲓⲝ ⲓⲱ ⲡⲁⲫⲩⲗⲁⲝ : "Iō Phenix, Iō Paphulax" The recurrent Iō indicates that this is part of the *Ērbeth*-logos (see notes to ll. 3–5 above). Phenix resembles the Greek φοῖνιξ ("phoenix"), and Paphulax could be understood as "my guardian" (ⲡⲁ-φύλαξ), but both seem to function simply as *voces magicae* here.
page 6
2. ϩⲛ ϭⲟⲙ : "by ⟨the⟩ power" For this phrase, *cf.* the notes to *PCM* I p. 3 ll. 17–18.

PCM I 5. Procedure for the healing of internal organs

Hermopolis (El-Ashmunein)   9 (H) × 7.5 (W) cm   VI–VII CE
Other references: P.Berol. 11918; TM 107301; KYP M213; Bélanger Sarrazin #31.
Editions: Beltz 1984: no. III 26 (*ed. pr.*).
Translations: Beltz 1984: no. III 26 (German).
Present location: Berlin, Staatliche Museen.
Linguistic description: Sahidic (non-standard).
Contents:
1. Front ll. 1–12, back ll. 1–3: Procedure for the healing of internal organs (KYP T419)

Complete parchment sheet, inscribed in black ink on the front (flesh) and back (hair), containing a recipe for the healing of the internal organs. The sheet was rolled or folded multiple times on its vertical axis; approximately 10 horizontal creases are visible. The manuscript was excavated in 1902 in Hermopolis by the Deutsche Orient-Gesellschaft under the supervision of Otto Rubensohn,[1] and the manuscript is now kept in the Staatliche Museen in Berlin.

The hand is regular, bilinear, and unimodal, largely upright, but nonetheless occasionally sloping to the right, and displaying elongated descenders (on ⲁ, ⲕ, ⲗ, ⳉ, ⲣ, ⲩ, ⲫ, ϯ, ϣ) which descend below the baseline. The rounded letters, ⲑ and ⲟ, are sometimes written in such a way that the two strokes forming the circle do not meet, leaving gaps at the top and bottom. Likewise, ⲕ, ⲣ, and ⲃ are written in multiple strokes which often do not touch. Short vertical serifs are found on both sides of the horizontal stroke of the ⲧ and ϯ, while curved serifs are apparent on the ⳉ. Very fine supralinear strokes are used regularly, and the copyist marks word divisions with an apostrophe, a single stroke, or two oblique lines.

The closest parallels we have been able to find are in the hand of the priest Mark of the *Topos* of Saint Mark in Thebes, whose activity can be dated to the late sixth to early seventh centuries. Mark's hand is more clearly inclined to the right, and has bimodular traits not present in this manuscript, but the letterforms, in particular the notable serifs on ϯ and ⳉ, are strikingly close.[2]

The dialect is Sahidic, albeit with a few common non-standard features, such as haplography of ⲛ, and the use of ⲃ for ˢϥ.

---

[1] Beltz 1984: 100. Rubensohn 1903: 79 gives a brief mention of the excavation, but not of this particular piece.

[2] *Cf.* in particular *P.Mon.Epiph.* 592+49; *cf.* Boud'hors 2008: 154–155; Mihálykó 2019: 79. On Mark and his career, see Heurtel 2007 & 2010; Boud'hors/Heurtel 2015: 9–10, 19–22.

front (flesh)

ϯⲡⲁⲗⲁⲕⲁⲗⲓ ⲙⲙⲱⲧⲛ̄
ⲛⲉⲧⲛ̄ⲛⲟϭ ⲛⲣⲁⲛ` ⲛ̄ⲭⲱ-
ⲱⲣⲉ` ⲉⲧⲉ ⲛⲁⲓ̈ ⲛⲉ ⁒
ⲁⲥⲃⲓⲏⲧ – ⲁⲭⲓⲏⲗ –
5   ⲁⲥⲫⲟⲩⲏⲗ ⁒ ⲕⲁⲙⲟⲩⲥ
ⲁⲙⲧⲁⲧⲑ ⁒ ⲁϥⲗⲓ-
ⲃⲏⲗⲓⲍⲉ ⁒ ⲙⲁⲣⲙⲁⲣⲓⲱ^θ
ϯⲱⲣⲕ` ⲉⲣⲱⲧⲛ̄` ⲛⲉⲧⲛ̄-
ⲛⲟϭ ⲛⲣⲁⲛ` ⲙ̄ⲛ ⲛⲉⲧⲛ̄-
10 ⲙⲁ ⲛϣⲱⲡⲉ` ⲉⲧⲉⲧⲛ̄-
ⲟⲩⲏϩ ⲛ̄ϩⲏⲧⲟⲩ – ϫⲉⲕⲁⲥ
ⲉⲧⲉⲧⲛ̄ⲱⲗ` ⲙ̄ⲡⲙⲁϩⲧ

---

back (hair)

1   ⲇⲇ ⲙⲛ ⲛⲉϥϭⲗⲟⲧⲉ
ⲭⲁⲗⲃⲁⲛⲉⲓ ⁒ ⲃⲱⲧⲉ
ⲛⲁⲃ` ⲛⲉⲃⲓⲱ ⁒ ⲕⲉⲛⲧⲁ^ⲣ

---

front 1 *i.e.* παρακαλεῖν ‖ 2 *i.e.* ˢⲛ̄-ⲛⲉ⸗ⲧⲛ̄-ⲛⲟϭ ‖ 5 ⲁⲫⲟⲩⲏⲗ Beltz ‖ 8–9 *i.e.* ˢⲛ̄-ⲛⲉ⸗ⲧⲛ̄-ⲛⲟϭ ‖ 12 ⲉⲧⲉⲧⲛ̄ⲱϫ Beltz : ⲙ̄ⲡⲙⲁ ϩⲧ Beltz ‖ *back* 1 *i.e.* δ(ε)ῖ(να) δ(ε)ῖ(να) : . ⲙ Beltz ‖ 2 *i.e.* χαλβάνη : . ⲭⲁⲗⲃ` ⲁⲕⲓⲏ Beltz ‖ 3 *i.e.* ˢⲛ̄-ⲁϥ : . . ⲁⲃ . ⲛⲉⲣⲁⲩ Beltz | *i.e.* κενταύριον ? : ⲕⲉⲥ . . . Beltz

|^front I invoke you (pl.) ⟨by⟩ your great, mighty *names, which are these: Asbiēt, Akhiēl, |⁵ Asphouēl, Kamous, Amtatth, Aflibēlize, Marmariōth! I adjure you ⟨by⟩ your great names and your |¹⁰ *dwelling places in which you dwell, that you contain the bowels ⟨of⟩ |^back NN, son of NN, and his innards!

Galbanum, sweat of a honey-bee, centaury?.

KD, EL & MP, edited from photograph and autopsy.

---

front
12. ⲉⲧⲉⲧⲛⲱⲗ` : "contain" This word seems unexpected in reference to internal organs; it is usually used in the context of the prevention of bleeding by "gathering it in", and so may refer to healing internal bleeding or diarrhoea (cf. PCM I 25 p. 16 l. 24; P.Macq. I 1 (KYP M167) p. 16 l. 1). We might alternatively understand a metathesis of ⲗⲟ ("heal").
back
2–3. ⲭⲁⲗⲃⲁⲛⲉⲓ ⸗ ⲃⲱⲧⲉ ⲛⲁⲃ` ⲛⲉⲃⲓⲁ' : "galbanum, sweat of a honey-bee" Galbanum is the resin produced by the stem of the Galbanum plant (perhaps *Ferula gummosa* Boiss.). Dioscorides (*De materia medica* III.83) describes it as being used as a medicinal substance for various complaints, either inhaled, applied externally, or ingested, so that any of these may be the intended use here (cf. Lev/Amar 2008: 171–172; Macomber 2020: I 135 *s.v.* ⲭⲁⲗⲁⲃⲁⲛⲏ). The meaning of "sweat of a honey-bee" here is uncertain; presumably it refers to some kind of secretion from the insect, such as honey or wax (although this would not be the usual term for either of these), or else royal jelly or the pollen gathered on their legs.
3. ⲕⲉⲛⲧⲁⲣ : "centaury?" The spiny plant centaury (perhaps *Centaurea centaurium* L. or *Erythraea centaurium* L.; André 1985: 55) is mentioned by Dioscorides (*De materia medica* III.6–7), as well as mediaeval Arabic and Hebrew works, as suitable for various medical problems, including internal diseases (Lev/Amar 2008: 377–378). The plant seems to also be mentioned in a fragmentary recipe from the unpublished magico-medical handbook Collège de France Ms. 1 (KYP M572; XI CE?), where it appears as ⲕⲉⲧⲁⲩⲣⲟⲥ (p. 1 l. 3) and its juice is used to anoint the patient for an unclear complaint; in a recipe from the Cairo Genizah we find the drinking of centaury prescribed to provoke an abortion (*MTKG* I: T-S NS 322.10 p. 2b l. 13).

PCM I 6–8. The Schmidt Coptic Magical Dossier

Provenance unknown   VI–VII CE

Other references: Hs. Schmidt 1 & 2; P.Mich.Inv. 4932f; KYP A4.

Bibliography: Kropp 1931: I no. A, B; Bélanger Sarrazin forthcoming a: 159 n. 95, 236 n. 5, 264 n. 20.

Present location: Ann Arbor, Michigan University Library; Berlin, Private collection of Carl Schmidt (?).

Linguistic description: Sahidic (non-standard).

Manuscripts belonging to the archive: *PCM* I 6–8.

The putative 'Schmidt Coptic Magical Dossier' consists of three manuscripts; two sheets of parchment and one sheet of papyrus recognised by Bélanger Sarrazin as having been written in a very similar, if not the same, hand by a single copyist.[1] The manuscripts *PCM* I 6 & 7 were acquired together from a dealer in Cairo some time before 1931,[2] the date from which they are known to have belonged to the private collection of Carl Schmidt (1836–1938).[3] *PCM* I 8 was acquired from the Cairo antiquities dealer Maurice Nahman by Harold I. Bell and William L. Westermann at some point between 1926 and 1927;[4] it is therefore quite possible that Schmidt also acquired his pieces from Nahman. The role of Cairo as a hub for antiquities from all over Egypt prevents us from drawing any conclusions about provenance.

The 'Schmidt scribe' hand writes in a largely bilinear, bimodular majuscule, inclined slightly to the right. There are occasional serifs: τ and ϯ consistently have serifs on the left side of their horizontal bar, while ⲁ has a left facing serif at its apex, and usually a broad flat base. ⲩ, ϣ, and ϥ usually, but do not always, descend below the baseline of the bilinear letters, and may have flourishes on their descenders. Overall, the hand is irregular; while the ⲙ is consistently curved—the curve may be either shallow or deep—and the ⲩ varies between forms resembling the Latin Y and V, with the most common form being a two-stroke form with an oblique stem resembling a lowercase Latin y. The scribe's use of supralinear

---

[1] Bélanger Sarrazin forthcoming a: 159 n. 95, 264 n. 20.

[2] Kropp 1931: I 11.

[3] On Carl Schmidt, see Markschies 2009. We thank Vincent Walter for this reference.

[4] Bell 1927 describes the acquisition as follows: "The third lot consists of the papyri bought by Prof. Westermann and myself from Nahman. These were acquired in one lot but consist of very various papyri purchased by Nahman at different times and of different vendors. Some had arrived recently; others were selected by me from boxes of fragments which had apparently been in stock for a long time". On Maurice Nahman, see Hagen/Ryholt 2016: 253–255.

strokes is limited to the letters ⲙ and ⲛ, and the stroke is gently curved downwards. Occasionally, ⲡ resembles ⲅ due to its short vertical stroke on the right (*e.g.*, *PCM* I 7 l. 18 ⲡⲉⲛⲓⲡⲉ; *PCM* I 8 front l. 1 ⲡⲛⲉϩ, back l. 8 ⲡⲁⲙⲉ), while the ⲏ may in turn resemble a ⲡ due to the high horizontal bar sloping upwards to the right (*e.g.*, *PCM* I 6 l. 4 ⲩϣⲏ; *PCM* I 8 front l. 9 ϩⲏⲧ). Ligatures, in particular of ⲁ and ⲉ to the following letter (especially ⲓ) are common, but not consistent. The copyist begins all three texts by writing a staurogram, uses mid-points as paratextual markers, as well as an occasional rounded supralinear stroke. Diaeresis is used on ⲓ. The writing of *PCM* I 6 is noticeably thicker; presumably it was written using a larger or blunter pen.

Tonio Sebastian Richter tentatively dated the manuscript *PCM* I 8 to between the fifth and sixth centuries,[5] while Walter E. Crum suggested the seventh century at the latest for the other two manuscripts.[6] Parallels for the hand are difficult to come by, but we can see some similar features in *SB Kopt.* I 36 (TM 87781)—the rounded ⲁ and supralinear stroke, ⲕ with large, curved upper leg, the distinctive forms of the ⲏ, ⲧ and ⲩ. This text, a verbal process recording a dispute over the ownership of part of a house, mentions the Sasanian Persian conquest of Egypt (619–630 CE), and individuals known to have been active as late as 647 CE,[7] allowing it to be dated with some precision to between these dates. We thus propose a sixth to seventh century date for this copyist.

The texts are written in a form of Sahidic with only minor, and relatively common, divergences from the literary standard, such as the interchange of ⲉ/ⲏ and ⲟ/ⲱ (*e.g.*, *PCM* I 6 l. 7 ⲕⲉⲧ for [S]ⲕⲏⲧ; *PCM* I 8 front l. 10 ⲥⲱⲛ for [S]ⲥⲟⲛ), occasional haplography, and the writing of ⲛⲧ as ⲧ.[8] None of these are clearly suggestive of a geographical origin or of particular dialectal influence.

In terms of content, all three manuscripts are remarkable for mentioning Pharaonic Egyptian deities—Isis, Horus, and Osiris. *PCM* I 6 & 7 take the form of narrative charms of the common Horus-Isis type, while *PCM* I 8 is an invocation which simply mentions Isis and Osiris alongside Jewish-Christian figures. *PCM* I 7 & 8 are love spells, while *PCM* I 6 is either a narrative charm for causing sleep, or yet another love spell.

---

[5] Richter 2015a: 99.
[6] Crum in Kropp 1931: I x–xi.
[7] For the question of date, *cf.* Schiller 1968: 117–118. Several of the same individuals are mentioned in *SB* VI 8988 (TM 17841), dated to 16 July 647; *cf.* Schiller 1968: 113–116.
[8] *Cf.* Dosoo/Love/Preininger 2022: 75.

PCM I 6. Horus-Isis narrative charm for sleep or love

Provenance unknown   15 (H) × 15 (W) cm   VI–VII CE

Other references: Hs. Schmidt 1; Private collection Carl Schmidt 1; TM 98043; KYP M120; Bélanger Sarrazin #43.

Editions: Kropp 1931: I no. A (*ed. pr.*); Bélanger Sarrazin forthcoming a: appendix 3, no. 1.

Translations: Kropp 1931: II no. 1 (German); Kelsey in Meyer/Smith 1994: no. 48; Pernigotti 1995: no. 1 (Italian); Pernigotti 2000: no. 17 (Italian); Martín Hernández/Torallas Tovar 2012; Bélanger Sarrazin forthcoming a: appendix 3, no. 1 (French).

Additional commentary: Frankfurter 2009; Blumell/Dosoo 2018; Hevesi 2019; Bélanger Sarrazin forthcoming a: chapter 2.

Last known location: Berlin, private collection of Carl Schmidt.

Image: Kropp 1931: I Tafel I (A).

Linguistic description: Sahidic

Contents:

1. Front ll. 1–25: Horus-Isis narrative charm for sleep or love (KYP T74)

Completely preserved papyrus sheet containing 25 lines written in a single column (↓). The papyus was folded into a square of 3.5 × 4 cm.[1] The low quality of the surviving image of the manuscript does not allow us determine the precise number of folds, but at least 4 vertical and 6 horizonal creases seem to be visible. The manuscript was acquired by Carl Schmidt from a dealer in Cairo before 1931;[2] its present location is unknown. The papyrus seems to be written in the same hand as *PCM* I 7 & 8, thus forming part of the group referred to here as the 'Schmidt Coptic Magical Dossier'; a full description of the copyist's palaeographic and linguistic tendencies may be found in the introduction to the dossier (pp. 80–81).

There have been two suggestions as to the goal of this formula. The instructions to send the target to sleep implies that the purpose is to treat insomnia—it would be comparable perhaps to *PCM* I 9, a formula for sleep which also mentions the characters Horus, Isis, and Abdemelech. On the other hand, the text follows the narrative structure of love spells (*cf. PCM* I 7, 20, 24), perhaps implying that the goal is to cause the target to sleep so that they will be unable to resist the sexual advances of the user.[3] One point against this second possibility may be the

---

[1] Kropp 1931: I 11.

[2] Kropp 1931: I 11.

[3] Frankfurter 2009: 239 considers this a formula for sleep, suggesting a link to the genre of the lullaby. Martín Hernández/Torallas Tovar 2012 argue it to be a formulary against insomnia caused by lovesickness. Blumell/Dosoo 2018: 230–231 note both the possibility of a formula for sleep and of a love spell, albeit based on reading ⲅⲟⲧⲉ = ⲛ̄ⲕⲟⲧⲕ̄ "lie down" in *PCM* I 16 (ostracon 2 ll. 1, 11)

masculine gender of the target, since the generic targets of love spells are usually female, but there are exceptions in which the generic target is male.[4]

(not followed in this volume). Kelsey (in Meyer/Smith 1994: 94) hesistates between the insomnia and erotic readings of the text, while Kropp 1931: II 3–6, Pernigotti 2000: 52–53 and Bélanger Sarrazin forthcoming a: 109–111 follow the latter understanding. Kropp specifically suggests it may be a formula for insomnia adapted as a love spell, although the larger pattern of this narrative being used primarily for love spells makes this seem unlikely.

[4] On gender in love spells, see Pachoumi 2013: 301–303 *et passim*.

front (↓)

ϯ ⲥⲱⲧⲙ ⲉϩⲱⲣ ⲉϥⲣⲓⲙⲉ · ⲥⲱⲧⲙ ⲉϩⲱⲣ
ⲉϥⲁϣⲁϩⲟⲙ ϫⲉ ⲁⲓϩⲓⲥⲉ ⲟⲩⲟⲑ ⲉⲥⲁϣϥⲉ ⲛ̄-
ⲛⲟⲩⲥⲉ ϫⲓⲛ ⲉⲡϣⲟⲙⲧⲉ ⲙⲡⲉϩⲟⲟⲩ ϣⲁ ⲭⲡϥⲧⲟ ⲛ̄ⲧⲉⲩϣⲏ ⲙⲡⲉⲟⲩⲉⲓ ⲙⲙⲟⲩ ϩⲓⲛⲏⲃ
5   ⲙⲡⲉⲓⲟⲩⲉⲓ ⲙⲙⲟⲩ ϫⲓ ⲣⲉⲕⲣⲓⲕⲉ · ⲁⲛⲥⲉ ⲧⲉϥ-
ⲙⲁⲁⲩ ⲣ̄ ⲟⲩⲱ ⲛⲁϥ ⲛ̄ϩⲟⲩⲛ ⲉⲡⲣ̄ⲡⲉ ⲛ̄ϩⲁⲃⲓⲛ ·
ⲉⲣⲉⲡⲉⲥϩⲟ ⲕⲉⲧ ⲉϩⲟⲩⲛ ⲉϫⲛ̄ ⲥⲁϣϥⲉ ⲛⲟⲩⲥⲉ
ⲉⲣⲉⲥⲁϣϥⲉ ⲛⲟⲩⲥⲉ ⲕⲏⲧ ⲉϩⲟⲩⲛ ⲉϫⲙ ⲡⲉⲥ-
ϩⲟ · ϫⲉ ϩⲱⲣ ⲁϩⲣⲟⲕ ⲉⲕⲣⲓⲙⲉ ϩⲱⲣ ⲁϩⲣⲟⲕ ⲉⲕ-
10 ⲁϣⲁϩⲟⲙ ϫⲉ ⲛ̄ⲧⲉⲟⲩⲱϣ ⲧⲁⲣⲓⲙⲉ ⲁⲛ ⲛ̄ⲧⲉ-
ⲟⲩⲱϣ ⲧⲁⲁϣⲁϩⲟⲙ ⲁⲛ ϫⲓⲛ ⲉⲡⲭⲡϣⲟⲙⲧⲉ
ⲙⲡⲉϩⲟⲟⲩ ϣⲁ ⲭⲡϥⲧⲟ ⲛ̄ⲧⲉⲩϣⲏ · ⲉⲓⲟⲩⲱϣ
ⲉⲥⲁϣϥⲉ ⲛⲟⲩⲥⲉ ⲙⲡⲉⲟⲩⲉⲓ ⲙⲙⲟⲩ ϩⲓⲛⲏϥ
ⲙⲡⲉⲟⲩⲉⲓ ⲙⲙⲟⲩ ϫⲓ ⲣⲉⲕⲣⲓⲕⲉ · ⲕⲁⲉⲓ ⲙⲡⲉ[ⲕϭⲛⲧ]
15 ⲙⲡⲉⲕϭⲓⲛⲉ ⲙⲡⲁⲣⲁⲛ · ϫⲓ ⲛⲁⲕ ⲛⲟⲩⲁⲡⲟ[ⲧ ϩⲓ]
ⲟⲩϣⲏⲙ ⲙⲟⲟⲩ · ⲉⲓⲉ ⲟⲩⲕⲟ[ⲩⲓ ⲛⲛⲓ-]
ⲃⲉ ⲉⲓⲉ ⲛⲛⲓⲃⲉ ⲛ̄ⲣⲱⲕ ⲉⲓⲉ ⲛⲛⲓϥⲉ ⲛ̄ϣ[ⲁⲛⲧⲕ]
ⲛ̄ⲅⲙⲟⲩⲧⲉ ⲉⲡⲉⲥⲏⲧ ⲉϫⲱⲟⲩ ϫⲉ ⲡⲕⲉⲭⲏ[. . . .]
ⲡⲁⲅⲅⲉⲗⲟⲥ ⲥⲛⲁⲩ ⲛⲧⲁⲟⲩⲱϩ ⲉⲧⲟⲟⲧⲟⲩ ⲁⲩ[ϩⲓ-]
20 ⲛⲏϥ ⲉϫⲛ ⲁϥⲧⲓⲙⲉⲗⲉⲭ ⲛ̄ϣⲃⲉ ⲥⲛⲟⲟⲥ ⲉⲛ[ⲣⲟⲙⲡⲉ]
ⲟⲩⲱϩ ⲉⲧⲟⲟⲧⲧⲏⲩⲧⲛ ⲉϩⲣⲁⲓ ⲉϫⲙ̄ ⲁⲇ ⲛ̄ⲧⲉⲧ[ⲛ-]
ϩⲣⲟϣ ⲉϫⲛ̄ ⲧϥⲁⲡⲉ ⲛⲑⲉ ⲛⲟⲩⲕⲟⲧ ⲛ̄ⲥⲓⲕⲉ ⲉϫⲛ ⲛϥ-
ⲃⲁⲗ ⲛⲑⲉ ⲛⲟⲩϭⲟⲟⲩⲛⲉ ⲛϣⲱ ϣⲁⲛϯϫⲱⲕ ⲉⲃⲟⲗ
ⲙⲡⲁⲛⲧⲏⲙⲁ ⲧⲁⲉⲓⲣⲉ ⲙⲡⲟⲩⲱϣ ⲙⲡⲁϩⲏⲧ
25 ⲉⲧⲓ ⲉⲧⲓ ⲧⲁⲭⲏ ⲧⲁⲭⲏ

---

2 *i.e.* ˢⲟⲩⲱⲑ *l.* ⲉϊ̈-ⲟⲩⲱⲑ ? *cf.* l. 12 : "desiring" ? ("indem ich begehre", "di desiderio") *l.* ⲟⲩⲱϣ or ⲱⲧϩ ? Kropp, Pernigotti : *l.* ⲱⲧϩ Martín Hernández/Torallas Tovar : *l.* ⲟⲩⲁⲁⲧ≠Ø Blumell/Dosoo || **2–3** *l.* ⲛ̄-ⲟⲩⲥⲉ ? (dittography) || **3** *l.* ϫⲓⲛ ⲉ-ⲡ-ⲭⲡ-ϣⲟⲙⲧⲉ *cf.* the same in l. 11 | *i.e.* ˢⲙ̄-ⲡ-ϩⲟⲟⲩ || **5** *i.e.* ˢⲙ̄ⲡⲉ-ⲟⲩⲉⲓ || **7** *i.e.* ˢⲕⲏⲧ || **11** *l.* ϫⲓⲛ ⲉⲭⲡϣⲟⲙⲧⲉ Kropp || **12** *i.e.* ˢⲙ̄-ⲡ-ϩⲟⲟⲩ | *l.* ⲟⲩⲱϣ or ⲱⲧϩ ? "I desire" ? ("ich begehre", "io desiderio") Kropp, Pernigotti : *l.* ⲱⲧϩ Martín Hernández/Torallas Tovar || **14** *i.e.* κἄν ? || **17** ⲉⲓ[ⲉ] Kropp || **18** ⲡⲕⲉⲭⲡ̣[*l.* ⲡⲕⲉⲭⲉⲣⲟⲃ ⲃ̄ ? Kropp || **19** *i.e.* ἄγγελος || **19–20** *i.e.* ϣⲉ-(ⲟ)ⲩ-ϩⲓⲛⲏⲃ || **20** *i.e.* ˢⲛ̄-ⲣⲟⲙⲡⲉ || **21** *i.e.* δ(ε)ῖ(να) δ(ε)ῖ(να) || **22** *i.e.* ˢⲧⲉ≠ϥ-ⲁⲡⲉ | *i.e.* ˢⲛⲉ≠ϥ- || **24** *i.e.* αἴτημα || **25** *i.e.* ἤδη (twice) | *i.e.* ταχύ (twice).

☦ Listen to *Horus, crying, listen to Horus, groaning:

"I have suffered, melting for seven women? from the third ⟨hour⟩ of the day until the fourth hour of the night. Not one of them sleeps, |⁵ not one of them dozes."

*Isis, his mother, replied to him from within the temple of Habin, her face turned towards seven women?, seven women? turned towards her face:

"Horus, why are you crying? Horus, why are you |¹⁰ groaning?"

"Do you want me not to cry? Do you want me not to groan from the third hour of the day to the fourth hour of the night? I am melting for seven women?. Not one of them sleeps, not one of them dozes."

"Even if? [you] did not [find me], |¹⁵ and you did not find my name, take a *cup [and] a little water, whether a little breath or a breath of your mouth or a breath of [your nose], and recite down over them, 'O ... O two *angels through whom |²⁰ sleep was set upon Abdemelech for seventy-two [years], set sleep upon NN, child of NN; make his head heavy like a millstone, upon his eyes like a sack of sand, until I complete my demand, and I fulfil the desire of my heart, |²⁵ now, now, quickly quickly!'"

RBS, KD, EL & MP, edited from photograph, incorporating Kropp's edition.

Horus-Isis Narrative Charms: This text represents an example of a narrative charm in which the main protagonists are Horus and Isis; see the notes to *PCM* I 7 front.

2. ⲟⲩⲟⲉ : "melting" Kropp and Pernigotti translate "desiring" (ⲟⲩⲱϣ), Martín Hernández/Torallas Tovar "tied" (ⲱⲧϩ), and Blumell and Dosoo "alone" (ⲟⲩⲁⲁⲧ). Here we understand the stative form of the verb ⲟⲩⲱⲧϩ (Crum CD 498b), following Bélanger Sarrazin forthcoming a. For the motif of LOVE IS FIRE, upon which this would seem to draw, see the notes to *PCM* I 3 front col. 2 ll. 33–38.

3, 7, 8, 13. ⲛⲟⲩⲥⲉ : "women?" This word does not seem to be otherwise attested in Coptic. It may derive from the Demotic *nsy* ("prostitute (?)"); see Blumell/Dosoo 2018: 228–229, n. 76), or else represent a contraction of the Greek παρθένος ("maiden"). We here choose the neutral translation "women". Ritner (1998) suggests that the seven women derive from the seven scorpion wives of Horus who appear in earlier Egyptian healing charms, which seem to draw upon a myth in which Horus is stung by his wife during intercourse, and must be healed; here the drama of Horus' healing would be replaced by a narrative of his infatuation with the scorpion-women (*cf.* Blumell/Dosoo 2018: 229–231).

6. ⲉⲡⲣ̄ⲡⲉ ⲛ̄ϩⲁⲃⲓⲛ : "Habin" This is the temple of Hebenu, Alabastron Polis, modern Kom el-Ahmar (TM Geo ID 2684), where there was a temple to Isis (see Blumell/Dosoo 2018: 233 n. 89).

14. ⲕⲁⲉⲓ ⲙⲡⲉ[ⲕⲟⲛⲧ] : "even if? [you] did not [find me]" For this construction, see the notes to *PCM* I 16 o. 2 ll. 15–16.

16. ⲙⲟⲟⲩ · ⲉⲓⲉⲓ : "water, whether" There is a large space between the two words; from the only image available to us it is impossible to know if there is erased or damaged text here; there are traces of what might have been a vertical stroke approximately in the middle of the space, printed here as a mid-point.

20. ⲁϥⲧⲓⲙⲉⲗⲉⲭ : "Abdemelech" Abdemelech (Ἀβδεμέλεχ) is a Kushite official who appears in Jeremiah 45–46 (38–39), and in 4 Baruch/*Paraleipomena Ieremiou* and the *History of the Captivity in Babylon* (CAVT 227 (=CC 576?); see Kuhn 1970; Piovanelli 2000) as Abimelech (Ἀβιμέλεχ). In the latter works he is said to have been put to sleep for 66 or 70 years in order to be spared the destruction of Jerusalem; *cf.* Martín Hernández/Sofía Torallas Tovar 2012: 311. Abdemelech also appears in *PCM* I 9 ll. 11–12.

PCM I 7. Love spell using Horus-Isis narrative charm

Provenance unknown   26 (H) × 10.5 (W) cm   VI–VII CE

Other references: Hs. Schmidt 2; Private collection Karl Schmidt 2; TM 98063; KYP M121; Bélanger Sarrazin #44.

Editions: Kropp 1931: I no. B (*ed. pr.*); Bélanger Sarrazin forthcoming a: appendix 3 no. 2.

Translations: Kropp 1931: II no. 2 (German); Kelsey in Meyer/Smith 1994: no. 72; Pernigotti 1995: no. 2 (Italian); Pernigotti 2000: no. 18 (Italian); Richter 2005: no. 98 (German); Bélanger Sarrazin forthcoming a: appendix 3 no. 2 (French).

Additional commentary: Frankfurter 2009; Martín Hernández/Torallas Tovar 2012; Blumell/Dosoo 2018; Hevesi 2019; Bélanger Sarrazin forthcoming a: chapter 2.

Last known location: Berlin, Private collection of Carl Schmidt.

Image: Kropp 1931: I Tafel I (B).

Linguistic description: Sahidic (non-standard).

Contents:

1. Front ll. 1–38: Horus and Isis narrative love charm (KYP T340)

Complete formulary written on a parchment sheet, inscribed on the front in a single column of 38 lines. The shape of the sheet and the folding pattern is unclear, due to the low quality of the only surviving incomplete photograph of the manuscript.[1] The manuscript was acquired from a dealer in Cairo,[2] and belonged to Carl Schmidt's private collection by 1931. The manuscript seems to have been written by the same scribe as *PCM* I 6 & 8, thus forming part of the part 'Schmidt Magical Dossier', an archive of three manuscripts; the hand and linguistic characteristics of the group are more fully described in its introduction (pp. 80–81).

The present location of this manuscript is unknown. The only surviving image is printed in Kropp 1931, vol. I, as Tafel I (B), and shows only ll. 1–20, with the leftmost parts of ll. 15–20 hidden by the overlapping Hs. Schmidt 1. We accept Kropp's readings in all cases for parts not visible in the image, except where he has restored text.

---

[1] Kropp 1931: I Tafel I (B). Kropp does not provide any details on folding, or on whether the manuscript is written on the hair or flesh side.

[2] Kropp 1931: I 11.

front

```
    ⳨ ⲁⲛⲟⲕ ⲇⲇ ⲁⲓⲃⲱⲕ ⲉϩⲟⲩⲛ
    ϩⲛ̄ ⲟⲩⲣⲟ ⲛⲱⲛⲉ ⲁⲉⲓ ⲉⲃⲟⲗ ϩⲛ ⲟⲩ-
    ⲣⲟ ⲙⲡⲉⲛⲓⲡⲉ ⲁⲓⲃⲱⲕ ⲉϩⲟⲩⲛ ⲛⲥⲁ ⲭⲱⲓ̈
    ⲁⲓⲉⲓ ⲉⲃⲟⲗ ⲛ̄ⲥⲁ ⲣⲁⲧ ⲁⲓϭⲓ̈ⲛⲉ ⲛ̄ⲥⲁϣϥ
5   ⲙ̄ⲡⲁⲣⲑⲉⲛⲟⲥ ⲉⲩϩⲙⲟⲟⲥ ϩⲓⲭⲛ̄ ⲟⲩ-
    ⲡⲩⲅⲏ ⲙ̄ⲙⲟⲟⲩ ⲁⲓⲟⲩⲱϣ ⲙ̄ⲡⲟⲩⲱϣ
    ⲁⲓⲡⲓⲑⲉ ⲙ̄ⲡⲟⲩⲡⲓⲑⲉ · ⲁⲓⲟⲩⲱϣ ⲉ-
    ⲙⲉⲣⲉ ⲛⲓⲙ̄ ⲧⲱϣ ⲛ̄ⲛⲓⲙ · ⲧⲟⲥ ⲇⲉ ⲙ̄-
    ⲡⲉⲥⲟⲩⲱϣ ⲉⲭⲓ̈ ⲛ̄ⲧⲁⲡⲓ · ⲁⲓⲧⲟⲕⲧ ⲁⲓ-
10  ⲁϩⲉⲣⲁⲧ ⲁⲓⲣⲓⲙⲉ ⲁⲓⲁϣⲁϩⲟⲙ ϣⲁⲛ-
    ⲧⲉⲛⲣⲙⲉⲓⲟⲟⲩⲉ ⲛⲁⲃⲁⲗ ϩⲱⲃⲥ ⲛ̄ϭⲟⲡ
    ⲛ̄ⲣⲁⲧ ⲁⲛ̄ⲥⲉ ⲣ̄ ⲟⲩⲱ ϫⲉ ⲁϩⲣⲟⲕ ⲡⲣⲱⲙⲉ
    ⲡϣⲏⲣⲉ ⲙ̄ⲡⲣⲉ · ⲉⲕⲣⲓⲙⲉ ⲉⲕⲁϣⲁϩⲟⲙ
    ϣⲁⲛⲧⲉⲛⲣⲙⲉⲓⲟⲟⲩ ⲛⲉⲕⲃⲁⲗ ϩⲱⲃⲥ
15  ⲛ̄ϭⲟⲡ ⲛ̄ⲣⲁⲧⲕ̄ · ϫⲉ ⲛⲥⲁ ⲟⲩ ⲛ̄ⲥⲉ
    ⲛ̄ⲧⲉⲟⲩⲱϣ ⲧⲁⲣⲓⲙⲉ ⲁⲛ̄ · ⲛ̄ⲧⲁⲓⲃⲱⲕ
    ⲉϩⲟⲩⲛ̄ ϩⲛ ⲟⲩⲣⲱ ⲛⲱⲛⲉ · ⲁⲓⲉⲓ ⲉⲃⲟⲗ
    ϩⲛ ⲟⲩⲣⲟ ⲙ̄ⲡⲉⲛⲓⲡⲉ · ⲁⲓⲃⲱⲕ ⲉϩⲟⲩⲛ
    ⲛⲥⲁ ⲭⲱⲓ̈ ⲁⲓⲉⲓ ⲉⲃⲟⲗ ⲛ̄ⲥⲁ ⲣⲁⲧ ⲁⲓϭⲓⲛⲉ
20  ⲛ̄ⲥⲁϣϥⲉ ⲙ̄ⲡⲁⲣⲑⲉⲛⲟⲥ ϩⲓⲭⲛ ⲟⲩⲡⲏⲅⲏ
    ⲙ̄ⲙⲟⲟⲩ ⲁⲓⲟⲩⲱϣ ⲙ̄ⲡⲟⲩⲱ̄ϣ ⲁⲓⲡⲓⲑⲉ
    ⲙ̄ⲡⲟⲩⲡⲓⲑⲉ ⲁⲓⲟⲩⲱϣ ⲉⲙⲉⲣⲉ ⲛⲓⲙ
    ⲧⲱϣ ⲛⲛⲓⲙ ⲛ̄ⲧⲟⲥ ϭⲉ ⲙ̄ⲡⲉⲥⲟⲩⲱϣ ⲉⲭⲓ
    ⲛ̄ⲧⲁⲡⲓ · ϫⲉ ⲕⲁⲃⲱⲕ ⲉϩⲟⲩⲛ ϩⲛ ⲟⲩⲣⲟ
25  ⲛⲱⲛⲉ ⲛ̄ⲥⲁ ⲟⲩ ⲛ̄ⲅⲉⲓ ⲉⲃⲟⲗ ϩⲛ̄ ⲟⲩⲣⲟ ⲙ̄ⲡⲉ-
```

---

1 *i.e.* δ(ε)ῖ(να) δ(ε)ῖ(να) || **3** ⲛⲥⲁⲭⲱⲓ̈ Kropp | **4** *i.e.* ˢⲥⲁϣϥⲉ || **5** *i.e.* παρθένος || **6** *i.e.* πηγή | ⲙ̄ⲙⲟⲟⲩ Kropp | *i.e.* ˢⲙ̄ⲡ=ⲟⲩ-ⲟⲩⲱϣ || **7** *i.e.* πείθειν (twice) || **8** ⲧⲟⲥ corrected from ⲧⲟⲟ by modification *i.e.* ⲛ̄ⲧⲟⲥ | *i.e.* δέ || **9** ⲡⲉⲥⲟⲩⲱϣ ⲥ corrected from ⲟ by overwriting | ⲁⲓⲧⲟⲕⲧ : "I threw myself down" ("Ich warf mich hin") Kropp, Richter || **11** *i.e.* ˢⲛ̄-ⲛⲁ-ⲃⲁⲗ (haplography) | *i.e.* ˢⲛ̄-ⲛ-ϭⲟⲡ (haplography) || **12** ⲁⲛⲥⲉ Kropp || **14** *i.e.* ˢⲣⲙⲉⲓⲟⲟⲩⲉ | *i.e.* ˢⲛ̄-ⲛⲉ=ⲕ-ⲃⲁⲗ (haplography) || **15** *i.e.* ˢⲛ̄-ⲛ-ϭⲟⲡ (haplography) | ⲛⲥⲉ ⲛ corrected from unclear letter by overwriting || **20** *i.e.* πηγή || **21** *l.* ⲙ̄ⲡⲟⲩⲱ̄ϣ *i.e.* ˢⲙ̄ⲡ=ⲟⲩ-ⲟⲩⲱϣ | *i.e.* πείθειν || **22** *i.e.* πείθειν || **24** *l.* ⲁⲕⲃⲱⲕ ? : *l.* ⲉ=ⲕ-ⲁ-ⲃⲱⲕ Richter (*cf.* note to l. 24).

☧ "I, NN, child of NN, went in through a door of stone, I came out through a door of iron. I went in headfirst, I came out feet first. I found seven |⁵ maidens sitting by a well of water. I desired, ⟨but⟩ they did not desire. I was seduced ⟨but⟩ they were not seduced. I wanted to love NN, the daughter of NN, but she, she did not want me to kiss her. I fortified myself, I |¹⁰ stood, I cried and I groaned until the tears of my eyes covered ⟨the⟩ soles of my feet."

*Isis replied, "What is wrong with you, O man, O child of the sun, crying and groaning until the tears of your eyes cover |¹⁵ the soles of your feet?"

"Why, Isis, do you not want me to cry? I went in through a door of stone, I came out through a door of iron. I went in headfirst, I came out feet first. I found |²⁰ seven maidens by a well of water. I desired ⟨but⟩ they did not desire. I was seduced ⟨but⟩ they were not seduced. I wanted to love NN, the daughter of NN, but she, she did not want me to kiss her."

"Why did you go in through a door of |²⁵ stone, and come out through a door of

Horus-Isis Narrative Charms: This text represents an example of a narrative charm in which the main characters are *Horus and Isis; for other examples in Coptic, see *PCM* I 6, *PCM* I 16, *PCM* I 20; *BKU* I 1 (KYP M76) col. 2, and *cf. PCM* I 9, *BKU* I 7 (KYP M88) and BM EA 10391 (Zellmann-Rohrer 2022a: no. 1; KYP M302) ll. 12–16, which incorporate aspects of these charms. For discussions of these texts, see Frankfurter 2009; Blumell/Dosoo 2018; Zellmann-Rohrer 2022a: 97–99; Bélanger Sarrazin forthcoming a. The basic structure of the texts consists of the sequence *encounter between protagonist and antagonist* (A), *protagonist turns to helper* (B), *protagonist recites initial events* (A'), *helper provides solution* (C) (Kalchenko/van der Vliet 2022: 216–217; Blumell/Dosoo 2018: 221–241). In the variants included in this volume, the primary protagonist is the young god Horus, who travels into *hell where he encounters the antagonist(s) in the form of one or more women (*cf.* the notes to *PCM* I 6 l. 3 for their identity) who refuse his attempts at seduction. He turns to his mother Isis as a helper, who provides ritual instructions which may be carried out both in the mythic narrative past and in the ritual present.

2–3. ⲟⲩⲣⲟ ⲛⲱⲛⲉ ... ⲟⲩⲣⲟ ⲙⲡⲉⲛⲓⲡⲉ : **"a door of stone... a door of iron"** This passage describes a descent to hell; the door of stone would be the tomb, or the door to the underworld depicted on late antique funerary stelae. *Tartarus in the Iliad 8.15 is said to have "gates of iron iron and a bronze threshold" (σιδήρειαί τε πύλαι καὶ χάλκεος οὐδός), while the description of the Lord shattering "bronze gates and iron bars" (τὰς πύλας τὰς χαλκᾶς καὶ τοὺς μοχλοὺς τοὺς σιδηροῦς; Psalm 106 (107) 14–16) was taken by Christians as referring to Jesus' destruction of the gates of hell prior to his resurrection (see Blumell/Dosoo 2018: 222–227). For parallels, *cf. PCM* I 16 p. 1 ll. 5–9; *PCM* I 20 l. 1 (in which the destination is explicitly hell); *BKU* I 7 (KYP M88), and BM EA 10391 (Zellmann-Rohrer 2022a: no. 1; KYP M302) ll. 14–15 (ⲡⲉⲗⲗⲱⲛⲓⲁ likely from ⲡⲩⲗⲏ ⲛ̄ⲱⲛⲉ). The "doors of iron" (ⲛⲉⲣⲟ ⲡⲉⲛⲓⲡⲉ) recur in *BKU* I 3 (KYPM77), a love spell in which a being threatens to destroy them.

7. ⲁⲓⲡⲓⲑⲉ ⲙⲡⲟⲩⲡⲓⲑⲉ : **"I was seduced, but they were not seduced"** For πείθειν with the sense of "be seduced" *cf.* Pseudo-Chrysostom, *On Susannah* 26 (CC 178): "be seduced, then; it is good for you to sleep with us" (ⲡⲉⲓⲑⲉ ϭⲉ ⲛⲁⲛⲟⲩ ⲛⲧⲉϣⲱⲡⲉ ⲛⲙⲙⲁⲛ; Budge 1910: 51 l. 17; *cf.* Crum CD 578b).

13. ⲡϣⲏⲣⲉ ⲙⲡⲣⲉ : **"O child of the sun"** Kropp and Richter translate "son of Re" ("Sohn des Re").

24. ϫⲉ ⲕⲁⲃⲱⲕ : **"did you go"** We translate this as a first perfect, understanding ϫⲉ ⲁⲕⲃⲱⲕ, since this is the tense used throughout for this narrative section, which recurs in the juxtaposed negative first perfect in ll. 29–30 (ⲙⲡⲉⲕⲧⲟⲕ), and used in the texts which offer the closest parallels to this narrative (see Blumell/Dosoo 2018: 234–235 *et passim*). The form however resembles a third future (*l.* ϫⲉ⟩ ⲉⲕ⟨ⲛ⟩ⲁⲃⲱⲕ); this is how it is translated in Richter. It is possible that the discrepancy is caused by a typo in Kropp, since he also translates this in the past tense.

front (continued)

ⲛⲓⲡⲉ ⲛⲅϭⲓⲛⲉ ⲛ̄ⲥⲁϣϥ ⲙⲡⲁⲣⲑⲉⲛⲟⲥ
ⲛⲅⲟⲩⲱϣ ⲛⲥⲉⲧⲙ̄ⲟⲩⲱϣ ⲛⲅⲟⲩⲱϣ
ⲉⲙⲉⲣⲉ ⲛⲓⲙ̄ ⲧϣ ⲛ̄ⲛⲓⲙ ⲛ̄ⲧⲟⲥ ⲇⲉ ⲛⲥ-
ⲧⲙⲟⲩⲱϣ ⲉϫⲓ ⲛⲧⲉⲕⲡⲓ · ⲙⲡⲉⲕ-
30 ⲧⲟⲕ ⲛ̄ⲅⲁϩⲉⲣⲁⲧⲕ ⲛ̄ⲅ̄ⲧⲉⲕ ⲥⲁϣϥ
ⲛ̄ⲗⲁⲥ ⲉⲃⲟⲗ ϫⲉ ⲑⲏⲧϥ̄ · ⳍ
ⲡⲛⲟϭ ⲉϩⲛ̄ ⲛⲉⲡ̄ⲛ̄ⲁ̄ ⲉⲓ̈ⲟⲩⲱϣ ⲉⲧⲣⲉ-
ⲛⲓⲙ̄ ⲧϣ ⲛ̄ⲛⲓⲙ ⲣ̄ ϩⲙⲉ ⲛ̄ϩⲟⲟⲩ
ⲙⲛ̄ ϩⲙⲉ ⲛⲟⲩϣⲏ ⲉⲥⲁϣⲉ ⲉⲃⲟⲗ
35 ⲛ̄ⲥⲱⲓ ⲛⲑⲉ ⲛⲟⲟⲩϩⲟⲣᵉ ϩⲁ ⲟⲩϩⲟⲣ
ⲛⲑⲉ ⲛⲟⲩϣⲟⲩ ϩⲁ ⲟⲩⲕⲁⲡ̄ⲣ̄ⲥ
ϫⲉ ⲁⲛⲟⲕ ⲡⲉⲧⲙⲟⲩⲧⲉ ⲛⲧⲟⲕ ⲉⲧ-
[ⲣ̄] ⲡⲉⲟⲩⲱϣ ·

---

26 i.e. παρθένος ‖ **28** i.e. δέ ‖ **30** i.e. ⲧⲟⲕ⸗ⲕ (haplography) : "throw yourself down" ("dich … hingeworfen") Kropp, Richter ‖ **32** i.e. ˢⲉⲧ-ϩⲛ̄ ? ‖ *l.* πν(εῦμ)α ‖ **35** i.e. ˢⲛ̄-ⲟⲩ-ⲟⲩϩⲟⲣⲉ ‖ **36** i.e. κάπρος ‖ **37–38** cf. *PCM* I 8 back l. 10: ⲛⲧⲟⲕ ⲡⲉⲧⲉⲣⲉ ⲡⲟⲩⲱϣ : ⲛⲧⲟⲕ ⲉⲧ[ⲭ]ⲡⲉ ⲟⲩⲱϣ "you are the one who produces love" ("der Liebe erzeugt") ? Kropp : or *l.* ⲛⲧⲟⲕ ⲉⲧ-ⲭⲡⲓ-ⲟⲩⲱϣ "you are the one who must obey" ("der willfahren muß") ? Kropp, Crum in Kropp : "you are the one who must desire" Kelsey

iron, and find seven maidens, and desire, and they did not desire, want to love NN, the daughter of NN, but she did not want you to kiss her, ⟨why⟩ did you not |³⁰ fortify yourself and stand up and cast out seven tongues, saying 'Thētf' (seven ⟨times⟩), O great one among the spirits, I want to make NN, the daughter of NN, spend forty nights and forty days clinging |³⁵ to me like a female dog under a male dog, like a sow under a boar, for it is I who recites, you who [does] the wish!"

RBS, KD, EL & MP, edited from photograph and readings of Kropp.

---

31. ⲐⲎⲦϤ̄ : "thētf" Usually understood as a *vox magica,* perhaps understand instead a writing of the archaic phrase *ti ḥ3.t⸗f* "give/cause his heart"; compare *GEMF* 16/*PDM* xiv (KYP M162) l. 772: "a procedure to put the heart of a woman after a man" (*wꜥ ky r ti ḥ3.t sḥm.t m-s3 ḥwṯ*). The form ⲧ- for ϯ is well attested from Coptic causative verbs (*cf.* Vycichl *DELC* 209). We would expect ⲈⲦⲚϤ rather than ⲈⲚⲦϤ for "his heart", although note the Akhmimic form ⲚⲦ⸗ in Crum *CD* 714a.

35–36. Animal Analogies: For similar references to animal behaviour as a metaphor for passionate love and desire, compare *PCM* I 17 back l. 17–front l. 1; *PCM* I 28 p. 6 ll. 3–14; *PCM* I 32 back ll. 16–18; *BKU* I 3 ll. 8–9 (KYP M77): "the desire... of a black dog, whose children he is about to take away before her eyes" (ⲠⲞⲨⲰϢ... ⲚⲞⲨⲞⲨϨⲞⲢ ⲔⲀⲘⲈ ⲈϤⲚⲀⲂⲒ ⲚⲈⲤϢⲎⲢⲈ ⲈϨⲞⲚ ⲒⲀⲦⲤ); London Hay 10414a (Zellmann-Rohrer 2022a: no. 3; KYP M287) ll. 11–13: "... (may) she cling to me like a drop of water clinging to a jar, and may she become a (honey-)bee seeking, a female dog wandering, a female cat going from house to house, a mare going under mad (horses)" (ⲚⲤⲈⲒϢ ⲈⲂⲞⲖ ⲚⲤⲰⲒ ⲚⲐⲈ ⲚⲞⲨⲦⲀⲦⲒⲖⲈ ⲘⲘⲞⲨ ⲈⲤⲀϨⲈ ⲚⲤⲀⲞⲨⲔⲀⲆⲞⲤ ⲚⲤⲢ ϨⲚ ⲞⲨⲂⲒⲰ ⲈⲤϢⲒⲚⲈ ⲞⲨϨⲞⲞⲢ ⲈⲤⲖⲈⲖⲈ ⲞⲨⲈⲘⲞⲨⲈ ⲈⲤⲂⲰⲔ ϨⲚ ⲞⲨⲎⲒ ⲀⲨⲎⲒ ϨⲚ ⲞⲨϨⲦⲰⲢⲈ ⲈⲤⲂⲰⲔ ϨⲀ ⲚⲈⲦⲞⲂⲖⲈ). Some of these extend the analogies to inanimate objects: *P.Herm.Copt.* 55 + 71 (KYP M45) p. 5 ll. 2–5: "and may they love him like a drop of water clinging to the edge of a jar" (ⲀⲨⲰ ⲚⲤⲈⲘⲈⲢ[ⲒⲦϤ ⲚⲐⲈ] ⲚⲞⲨⲦⲈⲖⲦⲒⲖⲈ Ⲙ[ⲘⲞⲞⲨ] ⲈⲤⲀϢⲈ ⲚⲤⲀ ⲠⲂⲒⲦ [Ⲛ]ⲞⲨⲔⲀⲦⲞⲨⲤ). For these analogies, *cf.* Frankfurter 2001; Saar 2017: 36–37, 39; Dosoo 2020: 266–267 (noting that the common reference to female horses is due to the belief that they were "the most sexually eager of all animals"); Zellmann-Rohrer 2022a: 137–138; Dosoo 2022c: 531–533. A similar analogy is found in the Demotic *GEMF* 16/*PDM* xiv (KYP M162) ll. 1029–1031: "the desire which a female cat feels for a male cat, desire which a female wolf feels for a male wolf, desire that a female dog feels for a male dog, the desire which the god, the son of Sothis?, felt for Moses..." (*p3? wḥ3e iw ḥr ire im(y).t? y.t⸗f r im (y)-mw wḥ3e iw ḥr ire wnše.t iy r wnše wḥ3e iw ḥr ire wḥr.t iy.t⸗f p3 wḥ3e r wḥr nt r p3 nṯr šr Spt.t? iy.yt⸗f r Mw.s.t.s*).

36–37. ⲀⲚⲞⲔ ⲠⲈⲦⲘⲞⲨⲦⲈ ⲚⲦⲞⲔ ⲈⲦ[Ⲣ̄] ⲠⲈⲞⲨⲰϢ : "it is I who recites, you who [does] the wish!" Compare *PCM* I 8 back ll. 9–10; *BKU* 1 1 (KYP M76) front col. 1 ll. 17–18: "it is I who speaks, the Lord Jesus is the one who gives healing" (ⲀⲚⲞⲔ ⲈⲦϢⲀϪⲈ ⲠϪⲞⲈⲒⲤ Ⲓ̄Ⲥ̄ ⲠⲈⲦϮ [ⲚⲠⲦⲀⲖϬ]Ⲟ), col. 2 back l. 8: "it is I who recites, the Lord Jesus is the one who gives healing" (ⲀⲚⲞⲔ ⲈⲦⲘⲞⲨⲦⲈ ⲠϪⲞⲈⲒⲤ Ⲓ̄Ⲥ̄ ⲠⲈⲦϮ ⲚⲠⲦⲀⲖϬⲞ).

PCM I 8. Love spell invoking oil

Provenance unknown 14.4 (H) × 13.2 (W) cm V–VI CE

Other references: P.Mich.Inv. 4932f; TM 99569; KYP M129; Bélanger Sarrazin #165.
Editions: Worrell 1935b: no. 5 (*ed. pr.*); Bélanger Sarrazin forthcoming a: appendix 4, no. 6.
Translations: Worrell 1935b: no. 5; Polotsky 1937: 127–130 (German); Skiles in Meyer/Smith 1994: no. 82; Pernigotti 1995: no. 18 (Italian); Bélanger Sarrazin forthcoming a: appendix 4, no. 6.
Additional commentary: Frankfurter 2009: 230, n. 7; Richter 2015a: 99; Hevesi 2019: 45; Bélanger Sarrazin forthcoming a: chapter 3.
Present location: Ann Arbor, Michigan University Library.
Image: https://quod.lib.umich.edu/a/apis/x-2349/4932fr.tif
Linguistic description: Sahidic.
Contents:
1. Front ll. 1–20, back ll. 1–10: Love spell invoking oil (KYP T343)

Parchment sheet with its lower margin lost and some damage to the left margin. The text nonetheless seems to be complete, since it continues and ends in the middle of the back; the manuscript contains a single formula. The rounded corner of the surviving upper right part of the sheet suggests that it may be a leaf from a codex. The parchment is very fine, and the text on one side can be seen through the other. The manuscript was acquired between 1926 and 1927 by Harold I. Bell and William L. Westermann from the Cairo antiquities dealer Maurice Nahman,[1] and is currently kept in the University of Michigan Library.

The text is written in black ink in a single column of 20 lines on the front (hair side), and in a single column of 10 lines on the back (flesh side). 1 vertical and 5 horizontal creases are visible; it is probable that the manuscript broke at the bottom along a fold, suggesting that the original manuscript was at least *ca.* 2.5 cm taller. The hand of the text seems to belong to the same copyist responsible for *PCM* I 6–7, making it part of the group designated here as the 'Schmidt Coptic Magical Dossier' (see pp. 80–81).

---

[1] Bell 1927. On Maurice Nahman, see Hagen/Ryholt 2016: 253–255.

front (hair)

ⲡⲛⲉϩ ⲡⲛⲉϩ ⲡⲛⲉϩ · ⲡⲛⲉϩ ⲉⲧⲟⲩⲁⲁⲃ
ⲡⲛⲉϩ ⲉⲧϩⲁⲧⲉ ⲉⲃⲟⲗ ϩⲁ ⲡⲉⲑⲣⲟⲛⲟⲥ ⲛⲓⲁⲱ
ⲥⲁⲃⲁ*vac*ⲱⲑ · ⲡⲛⲉϩ ⲛ̄ⲧⲁⲛⲥⲉ ⲧⲁϩⲥϥ ⲛ̄ⲕⲉ-
ⲉⲥ ⲛⲉⲩⲥⲓⲣ · †ⲙⲟⲩⲧⲉ ⲉⲣⲟⲕ ⲡⲛⲉϩ · ⲡⲣⲏ ⲙⲛ̣
5 ⲡⲟⲟϩ · ⲙⲟⲩⲧⲉ ⲉⲣⲟⲕ · ⲛ̄ⲥⲓⲟⲩ ⲛ̄ⲧⲡⲉ ⲙⲟⲩⲧⲉ
ⲉⲣⲟⲕ · ⲛ̄ⲣⲉϥⲡⲱϣⲛ ⲙⲡⲣⲏ ⲙⲟⲩⲧⲉ ⲉⲣⲟⲕ
†ⲟⲩⲱϣ ⲉϫⲟⲟⲩⲕ ⲉⲕⲉⲃⲱⲕ · ⲧⲁⲛⲧⲕ ⲛ̄ⲅ-
ⲉⲓⲛⲉ ⲇⲇ ⲉⲣⲁⲧ ⲁⲛⲟⲕ ⲇⲇ ⲛ̄ⲅⲧⲣⲉⲡⲁⲙⲏ
ϣϣ[ⲡⲉ] ϩⲙ ⲡⲉⲥϩⲛⲧ ⲛ̄ⲧⲉⲡⲱⲥ ϣⲱⲡⲉ ϩⲙ ⲡⲱⲓ
10 [ⲛⲑⲉ] ⲛⲟⲩⲥⲱⲛ ⲙⲛ ⲟⲩⲥⲱⲛⲉ · ⲙⲛ̄ ⲟⲩⲗⲁⲃⲟⲓ
[ⲉⲥⲟⲩ]ⲱϣ ⲉϯ ϫⲓ ⲛⲉⲥϣⲏⲣⲉ · ⲁⲓⲟ ⲁⲓⲟ †-
[ⲧⲁⲣ]ⲕⲁ ⲙⲙⲟⲕ ⲡⲉⲧⲉⲣⲉⲭⲱϥ ϩⲛ ⲧⲡⲉ
ⲉⲣⲉⲣⲁⲧϥ ϩⲙ ⲡⲛⲟⲩⲛ ⲉⲣⲉϩⲛ ⲙⲙⲟϥ ⲟ ⲛϩⲁ
ⲛⲉⲥⲟⲟⲩ ⲉⲣⲉⲡⲁϩⲟⲩ ⲙⲙⲟϥ ⲟ ⲛϩⲁ ⲇⲣⲁⲕⲱ̄
15 ⲡⲉⲧⲉⲣⲉⲧⲡⲉ ⲧⲏ ⲛ̄ⲕⲁˈⲕⲓ ⲛⲓⲙ ⲁϣⲉ ⲛ̄ⲥⲟ̣ⲕ
ⲉⲣⲉⲡⲣⲓⲕⲉ ⲛⲉ[.] . [*ca.* 17]
ⲛⲉ̣ϩⲓⲟⲙⲉ ⲉⲧ[*ca.* 18]
[.] . ⲥ ⲉⲧϩⲓϫ[ⲛ *ca.* 17]
[. .]ⲭⲟⲩⲃⲁ . [*ca.* 18]
20 [. . . .] . . [*ca.* 20]
- -

2 i.e. θρόνος ǁ **3** ⲥⲁⲃ ⲁϣⲉ *pap. vacat* due to hole in parchment ǁ **3–4** i.e. ˢⲛ̄-ⲛ-ⲕⲉⲉⲥ ǁ **4** ⲙ i.e. ˢⲙⲛ̄ Worrell ǁ **8** i.e. δ(ε)ῖ(να) δ(ε)ῖ(να) (twice) ǁ **9** ϣ[ⲱⲡⲉ] Worrell ǁ **11** [ⲉⲥⲟⲩ]ⲱϣ Crum CD 752a : [†ⲟⲩ]ⲱϣ Worrell | *l.* ⲛ̄ⲛⲉⲥϣⲏⲣⲉ (haplography) ǁ **12** [ⲡⲁⲣⲁ]ⲕⲁ i.e. παρακαλεῖν Worrell ǁ **13** ⲉⲣⲉϩⲛ corrected from ⲉⲣⲉⲓⲛ by overwriting | ⲟⲛ ϩⲁ Worrell, Skiles ǁ **14** ⲟⲛ ϩⲁ Worrell, Skiles | *l.* ⲛ̄-δράκω(ν) ǁ **15** *l.* ⲡⲉⲧⲉⲣⲉⲧⲡⲉ ⲧⲏⲣⲥ ⲙⲛ ⲕⲁⲕⲉ ? : i.e. ⲛ̄ⲧⲉ Worrell : i.e. Old Coptic ⲧⲏ "underworld" Crum CD 392a, Polotsky | ⲛ̄ⲕⲁⲕⲓ Worrell | i.e. ˢⲛ̄ⲥⲱ⸗ⲕ but ⲛ̄ⲥⲱ⸗ϥ expected : ⲛ̄ⲛ[ⲁϩⲣⲁϥ] : Worrell ǁ **17** [.] ⲉϩⲓⲟⲙⲉ Worrell ǁ **19** ⲭⲟⲩⲃⲁ corrected from ⲃⲟⲩⲃⲁ by overwriting

✝ O oil, O oil, O oil, O holy oil! O oil which flows from beneath the throne of *Iao *Sabaoth! O oil with which *Isis anointed the bones of *Osiris! I call to you, O oil! The sun and |⁵ the moon call to you. The stars of the sky call to you. The servants of the sun call to you. I want to send you; you will go and I will bring you so that you will bring NN, child of NN, to me, I, NN, child of NN, and you will cause my love to be in her heart, and hers to be in mine |¹⁰ [like] a brother and a sister, and ⟨like⟩ a she-bear [who] wants to suckle her offspring, yea, yea!

I adjure you, he whose head is in heaven, whose feet are in the *abyss, whose forepart has the appearance of a sheep, whose hindpart has the appearance of a serpent, |¹⁵ he from whom the whole? sky and? of all darkness hangs, while the turning … the women who … which is upon […] … khouba …

2–3. ⲡⲛⲉϩ ⲉⲧⲣⲁⲧⲉ ⲉⲃⲟⲗ ϩⲁ ⲡⲉⲑⲣⲟⲛⲟⲥ ⲛⲓⲁⲱ ⲥⲁⲃⲁⲱⲑ : "**O oil which flows from beneath the throne of Iao Sabaoth**" *Cf.* Gessel 1988, discussing stone reliquaries from Apamaea (Syria) constructed so that oil poured into the top flows out of the bottom, sanctified by proximity to the saint. For formulae directly addressing materia, compare *GEMF* 4/*PGM* CXXII (KYP M488) ll. 31–52; *GEMF* 57/*PGM* IV (KYP M3) ll. 1496–1595; *GEMF* 68/*PGM* XXXVI (KYP M181) ll. 333–360 (all addressing myrrh burnt in offerings); *BKU* I 3 (KYP M77); *GEMF* 18/*PGM* LXI (KYP M183) ll. 159–196 (both oil); *GEMF* 156/*PGM* VII (KYP M156) ll. 643–651 (wine).

3–4. ⲡⲛⲉϩ ⲛ̄ⲧⲁⲏⲥⲉ ⲧⲁϩⲥϥ ⲛⲕⲉⲉⲥ ⲛⲉⲩⲥⲓⲣ : "**oil with which Isis anointed the bones of Osiris**" The love of Isis and Osiris serves as a paradigm in many Graeco-Egyptian love spells, as does the claim that Isis used a particular procedure (Dosoo 2021c: 212 nn. 93, 94). The reference here seems to be to the resurrection of Osiris by Isis and Anubis, god of embalming, followed by her conception of their son *Horus. The oil used to anoint Osiris' bones is implicitly powerful enough both to raise the dead, and to ensure love beyond death. Compare *GEMF* 4/*PGM* CXXII (KYP M488) ll. 31–32, adressing myrrh as that with which Isis anointed herself when she went to Osiris; *GEMF* 16/*PDM* xiv (KYP M162) ll. 610–620 in which Isis addresses oil in order to anoint and heal her son Anubis. In the Coptic magical corpus, Isis is also mentioned in *PCM* I 4 p. 4; *PCM* I 6, 7, 9, 16, 20; *BKU* I 1 front col. 2 & back; Mich.Ms. 136 (Zellman-Rohrer/Love 2022; KYP M128) p. 5 l. 1–p. 6 l. 5.

10. ⲙⲛ̄ ⲟⲩⲗⲁⲃⲟⲓ : "**and ⟨like⟩ a she-bear**" Worrell (following Youtie) sees a translation of an originally Greek καὶ γὰρ οὕτως ("and indeed thus") miscopied as καὶ ἄρκτος; he reconstructs ll. 9–11 as "and make my love arise in her heart and hers in mine, in the manner of a brother and a sister, and indeed thus I desire to beget (ⲉϯϫⲓ) her children". This seems unnecessary, however, given the frequent use of animal metaphors to describe emotion; *cf.* the notes to *PCM* I 7 ll. 35–36. Polotsky proposes "a lioness whose children one wants to take" ("eine Löwin, deren Junge man [sic] wegnehmen will", [ⲉⲩⲟⲩ]ⲱϣ ⲉ{ϯ}ϫⲓ ⲛⲉⲥϣⲏⲣⲉ). Here we translate "she-bear", but the word ⲗⲁⲃⲟⲓ originally, and still, had the alternative meaning of "lioness".

13–14. ⲉⲣⲉϩⲏ ⲙⲙⲟϥ ⲟ ⲛϩⲁ ⲛⲉⲥⲟⲟⲩ ⲉⲣⲉⲡⲁϩⲟⲩ ⲙⲙⲟϥ ⲟ ⲛϩⲁ ⲇⲣⲁⲕⲱ̄ : "**whose forepart has the appearance of a sheep, whose hindpart has the appearance of a serpent**" Worrell translates "in front of him being (what is) under the Sheep, behind him being (what is) under Draco", with Skiles following him ("before whom is (what) is also under the Sheep (pl.), behind whom is (what) is also under Draco"). Both understand "the Sheep" to be a constellation, paralleling Draco. This seems unnecessary, since descriptions of such polymorphic cosmic beings are common in Coptic magical texts; see Dosoo 2022c: 501–503; Bélanger Sarrazin forthcoming a: chapter 4.

16. ⲉⲣⲉⲡⲣⲓⲕⲉ ⲛⲉ[: "**while the turning**" Polotsky and Pernigotti read ⲡⲣⲓⲕⲉ ⲛⲛⲉ[ϥⲃⲁⲗ] and translate "while the winking of his eyes…" ("mentre l'ammiccare dei suoi occhi…").

back (flesh)

☧ ϯⲛⲁⲡⲟⲣⲕϥ ⲟⲩⲡⲉⲛⲓⲡⲉ ϯⲛⲁⲃⲟⲗϥ
ⲉⲃⲟⲗ · ⲙⲡⲱⲣ ⲡⲁϫⲟⲉⲓⲥ · ⲙⲡⲣⲧⲁⲁⲧ
ⲉⲧⲟⲟⲧϥ ⲛ̄ⲇⲓⲙⲉⲗⲟⲩⲭⲟⲥ ⲡⲉⲧϩⲣⲁⲓ
ⲉϫⲛ̄ ⲧⲕⲣⲓⲥⲓⲥ · ⲁⲗⲗⲁ ϯⲟⲩⲱϣ ⲉⲧ-
5 ⲣⲉⲕⲃⲱⲕ ⲉⲡⲉⲥⲏⲧ ⲉⲁⲙⲛ̄ⲧⲉ ⲛ̄ⲅⲡⲱ-
ⲣ̄ⲕ ⲛ̄ⲙ̄ⲙⲉⲉⲩⲉ ⲧⲏⲣⲟⲩ ⲙⲡⲇⲓⲁⲃⲟⲗⲟⲥ
ⲉϩⲣⲁⲓ ⲉϫⲛ̄ ⲙⲉϣⲉ ⲛⲓⲙ ⲡⲇⲇ ·
ⲛ̄ⲅ̄ⲧⲣⲉⲡⲁⲙⲉ ϣⲱⲡⲉ ϩⲙ ⲡⲉⲥϩ[ⲏⲧ]
ⲛ̄ⲧⲉⲡⲱⲥ ϣⲱⲡⲉ ϩⲙ ⲡⲁⲓ̈ ϫⲉ ⲁⲛ[ⲟⲕ]
10 ⲡ[ⲉ]ⲧⲙⲟⲩⲧⲉ ⲛ̄ⲧⲟⲕ ⲡⲉⲧⲉⲣⲉ ⲡⲟⲩⲱϣ

---

1 *l.* ⲛ̄ⲟⲩⲡⲉⲛⲓⲡⲉ Worrell, Skiles ‖ **4** *i.e.* κρίσις | *i.e.* ἀλλά ‖ **6** *i.e.* διάβολος ‖ **7** *l.* π‹ϣ›ⲉ ⲛ̄-δ(ε)ῖ(να) {δ(ε)ῖ(να)} ‖ **8** ⲛ̄ⲅ̄ⲧⲣⲉⲡⲁⲙⲉ corrected from ⲛ̄ⲅ̄ⲧϩⲉⲡⲁⲙⲉ by overwriting ‖ **10** [ⲡⲉ]ⲧⲙⲟⲩⲧⲉ Worrell | *i.e.* ˢⲡ-ⲉⲧ-ⲣ̄ : *l.* ⲡⲉⲧⲉⲓⲣⲉ Worrell | *l.* ⲙⲡⲟⲩⲱϣ Worrell.

☧ I will tear it out; iron, I will dissolve it".

"No, my lord, do not hand me over to *Temeluchus, he who is set over the judgement, rather I want |⁵ you to go down to *hell and tear out all the thoughts of the Devil concerning NN, the ⟨child of⟩ NN and cause my love to be in her [heart] and hers to be in mine, for it is I |¹⁰ who recites, ⟨and⟩ you are the one who does the wish."

RBS, KD, EL & MP, edited from photograph.

1–2. ⲟⲩⲡⲉⲛⲓⲡⲉ ϯⲛⲁⲃⲟⲗϥ ⲉⲃⲟⲗ : **"iron, I will dissolve it"** For the *topos* of destroying stone and metal, *cf.* the notes to *PCM* I 3 front col. 1 ll. 7–9.

3. ⲡ̄ⲇⲓⲙⲉⲗⲟⲩⲭⲟⲥ : **"Temeluchus"** For this figure, see *hell in the glossary, and *cf.* P.Berol. 10587 (Beltz 1983: no. I 555; KYP M510) ll. 3–7: "send Temeluchus to me, he who is over the punishment of the (pl.)... he who tortures the lawless and the liars and those who swear falsely, that he wreak vengeance for me upon them!" (ⲙⲁⲧⲛⲟⲟⲩ ⲛ̄ⲛⲁⲓ̈ ⲧⲉⲙⲉⲗⲟⲩⲭⲟⲥ ⲡⲉⲧϩⲓⲭⲛ ⲛ̄ⲕⲟⲗⲁⲥⲓⲥ ⲛ̄ⲛ . . . ⲁ ⲡⲉⲧⲃⲁⲥⲁⲛⲓⲍⲉ ⲛ̄ⲛⲁⲛⲟⲙⲟⲥ ⲙⲛ̄ ⲛ̄ⲣⲉϥϫⲓϭⲟⲗ : ⲙⲛ̄ ⲛ̄ⲛⲣⲉϥⲱⲣⲕ ⲛ̄ⲛⲟⲩϫ ⲉⲧⲣⲉϥⲣ̄ ⲡⲁⲕⲃⲁ ⲛ̄ⲙⲙⲁⲩ).

4. ⲁⲗⲗⲁ ϯⲟⲩⲱϣ : **"rather I want..."** Compare the rhetorical device described in the notes to *PCM* I 3 front col. 1 ll. 15–16, although the construction of the argument here is less clear. The example here may rather represent a threat in which the speakers have become confused; we might expect (i) the first speaker to threaten to hand the second to Temeluchus, (ii) the second to beg for this not to happen, and (iii) the first to reply with a command based upon the threat. Here parts ii and iii of this hypothetical dialogue seem to have been merged together.

5–7. ⲛ̄ⲅⲡⲱⲣⲕ ⲛ̄ⲙⲙⲉⲉⲩⲉ ⲧⲏⲣⲟⲩ ⲙ̄ⲡⲇⲓⲁⲃⲟⲗⲟⲥ ⲉϩⲣⲁⲓ̈ ⲉϫⲛ̄ ⲙⲉϣⲉ ⲛⲓⲙ̄ ⲡⲁⲁ : **"tear out all the thoughts of the Devil concerning NN, the ⟨child of⟩ NN"** Polotsky understands this phrase to mean something like "fill NN, child of NN, with thoughts snatched from the Devil", comparing *PCM* I 28 p. 5, ll. 22–23: "her mind will have devilish thoughts" (ⲡⲉⲥⲛⲟⲩⲥ ⲉⲣ ⲙⲉⲟⲩⲉ ⲛ̄ⲧⲓⲁⲃⲱⲗⲓⲕⲱⲛ), but this would seem to require the addition of another verb, such as ϯ ("give") rather than "tear out". As Michael Zellmann-Rohrer points out (private communication), this passage may imply that the goal of the ritual is not to create a new sexual or romantic relationship, but rather to maintain an existing one, in this passage by preventing one partner from having negative thoughts concerning the other. This would correspond to the Greek rituals identified by Faraone (2009: 27–30 *et passim*) which have the goal of "maintain[ing] or increas[ing] affection" used by social inferiors (including women) on higher status men.

9–10. ⲁⲛ[ⲟⲕ] ⲡ[ⲉ]ⲧⲙⲟⲩⲧⲉ ⲛⲧⲟⲕ ⲡⲉⲧⲉⲣⲉ ⲡⲟⲩⲱϣ : **"for it is I who recites, ⟨and⟩ you are the one who does the wish"** For parallels, see the notes to *PCM* I 7 ll. 36–37.

PCM I 9. Formula for sleep

Thebes	18 (H) × 31 (W) cm	VI–VIII CE

Other references: P.Berol. 5565; TM 98042; *BKU* I 22; KYP M122; Bélanger Sarrazin #73.
Editions: Erman 1904: no. 22 (*ed. pr.*); Bélanger Sarrazin forthcoming a: appendix 3, no. 3.
Translations: Erman 1895: 50–51 (German); Kropp 1931: II no. 4 (German); Meyer in Meyer/Smith 1994: no. 47; Pernigotti 2000: no. 22 (Italian); Bélanger Sarrazin forthcoming a: appendix 3, no. 3 (French).
Additional commentary: Hevesi 2019; Bélanger Sarrazin forthcoming a: chapter 2.
Present location: Berlin, Staatliche Museen.
Image: Plate I.
Linguistic description: Sahidic (non-standard).
Contents:
  1. Front ll. 1–13: Formula for sleep mentioning Isis, Nephthys, and Horus (KYP T179)

Complete papyrus sheet, generally well-preserved but slightly damaged on the edges and along the folds. The manuscript was likely folded to form a small package; approximately 6 horizontal and 11 vertical folds are visible. The sheet was acquired in 1887 in Thebes,[1] and is held in the Staatliche Museen in Berlin.

The text is written in black ink on the vertical fibres in a highly informal and irregular hand. The writing is bimodular, largely bilinear, and right-sloping, with significant variation in letter height and shading. The ⲩ varies in shape between Y, V, and y, with the last being the most common. ⲩ, ϥ, and ϣ have long descenders, while ⲭ and ⳉ have flourishes on the upper part of the left oblique stroke. The supralinear stroke is either curved, or resembles an acute accent or later djinkim, and the scribe makes use of diaeresis on ⲓ. Erman noted that the hand's idiosyncrasies prevented a precise dating.[2] We may note some approximate parallels to manuscripts from the Monastery of Epiphanius in Thebes—ⲁ with a closed, rounded bulb but straight oblique stem; bilinear ⲃ and ϩ, narrow ⲉ and ⲥ, rounded ⲙ, rounded ⲧ with serifs, y-shaped ⲩ, some decoration of ⲭ and ⳉ (*P.Mon. Epiph.* 164, 230, 436, 482), datable to the seventh century—although we propose a more cautious sixth to eighth century date for this text.

The dialect is Sahidic, but with some highly idiosyncratic features; alongside frequent haplography and dittography (especially of ϩ), we occasionally find ⲁ for Sahidic ⲉ or ⲟ (*e.g.*, ll. 2, 8), as well as more unexpected substitutions, such as ⲟⲓ › ⲩ (l. 2) and ϣ › ⲥ (l. 12).

---

[1] Erman 1904: 21.
[2] Erman 1895: 50.

front (↓)

ⲁϥⲃⲟⲩⲣⲉ ⲁϥⲃⲟⲩⲣⲉ ⲉⲓⲥ ⲡⲁⲡⲁⲧ ⲛ̄ⲛⲟⲩⲃ ⲛ̄ⲧⲟⲟᵀⲕ ⲉⲓϫⲟⲟⲩⲕ ⲙ̄ⲡⲁϩⲱⲃ ⲕⲛ̄ⲁⲉⲓ ⲁⲉⲓ ⲉⲡⲁϣ
ⲕⲛⲁⲙ̄ⲙⲟⲩϩⲥ ⲉⲧⲃⲉ ⲡⲁⲓ̈ ⲉⲕϫⲟⲟⲩⲧ ⲉⲡⲙⲟⲟⲩ ⲧⲁⲡⲁⲅⲕⲱϫ ⲁⲡⲣⲉⲓⲟ ⲧⲁⲉⲓⲛ ⲡϥ̄ⲗⲩϩϩⲉ
ⲙ̄ⲡⲉ ⲙ̄ⲡⲉⲓ̈ϫⲟⲟⲩⲕ ⲛ̄ⲥⲁ ⲛⲁⲓ̈ ⲙ̄ⲡⲉⲓ̈ϩⲁⲃⲕ̄ ⲛ̄ⲥⲁ ⲛⲓⲕⲟⲟⲩⲉ ⲉⲓⲓⲁϫⲟⲩⲕ ⲉϩⲟⲩⲛ ⲉⲛⲓⲙ
ⲡϣⲏ ⲛ̄ⲛⲓⲙ ϫⲉ ⲉⲕⲁⲛⲧ ⲕⲓⲧⲉ ⲁϫⲱϥ ⲙⲛ̄ ⲡϥⲓⲛⲏⲃ ϣⲁⲛⲧⲉⲡⲣⲏ ⲙ̄ⲡⲭⲟⲩⲥⲓ ⲉⲓ̈ ⲉϩⲣⲁⲓ̈
5 ϫⲉ ⲡⲣⲁⲛ ⲙ̄ⲙⲏⲧ ⲡⲁⲡⲗⲏⲩ ⲡⲉ ⲁϫⲉ ⲉⲥⲥⲉ ⲧⲉ ⟦ⲧⲃ⟧ : ⲥⲃ̄ⲱ ⲧⲉ ⲧⲁⲓ̈ ⲧⲁⲓ̈ⲥⲛ̄ⲧⲉ ⲛ̄ⲥⲱⲛⲉ
ⲉⲧⲙⲟⲟⲩⲕ ⲛ̄ϩⲏⲧ ⲉⲧⲁϥ⁽ϣ⁾ϣⲉ ⲉϩⲣⲁⲓ̈ ϩⲁ ⲧⲡⲉ ⲙⲛ ⲡⲕⲁϩ ⲉⲧϩⲙ̄ ⲡⲛⲟⲩⲛ
ϫⲉ ⲉⲓ̈ᶜ ϩⲱⲣ ⲡϣⲏⲣⲉ ⲉⲛ̄ⲛⲉⲓⲥⲉ ϩϥ   ⲛ̄ⲁϩⲛ̄ⲟⲩ ⲉⲓᶜⲉ ⲥⲟⲩⲟⲩⲉ ⲙ̄ⲙⲟϥ ⲁϩⲣⲱ ⲧⲁ ⲧⲥ .. ᵗᶜ··
                    ⲕⲱⲧⲉ ⲁⲡⲟϩ
ⲉⲥⲕⲱⲧⲉ ⲁⲡⲣⲏ ⲉϫⲁⲗⲁⲩ ⲛ̄ⲧⲙⲏⲧⲉ ⲛ̄ⲧⲡⲉ · ⲉⲧⲕⲛ̄ⲙⲟⲩⲧ ⲛ̄ⲧⲙⲏⲧⲉ ⲛ̄ⲧⲡⲉ ⲉⲥⲥⲉ
ⲙⲛ ⲥⲃ̄ⲱ ⲧⲉⲥᵉⲛ̄ⲧⲉ ⲛ   ᵛᵃᶜ·   ⲥⲱⲛⲉ ⲉⲧⲙⲟⲟⲩⲕϩ ⲛ̄ϩⲏⲧ ⲉⲧⲗⲩⲡⲏ ⲛ̄ϩⲏ
10 ⲉⲧϩⲙ̄ ⲡⲛⲟⲩⲛ ϫⲉ ⲛ̄ⲧⲟⲕ ⲡⲉ ⲁϩ ⲛ̄ⲧⲟⲕ ⲡⲉ ⲁⲃⲣⲁⲍⲁⲝ ⲡⲁⲅⲅⲓ̈ⲗⲟⲥ
ⲉⲧϩⲙⲙⲟⲟⲥ ϩⲓϫⲙ̄ ⲡϣⲏⲛ ⲙ̄ⲡⲡⲁⲣⲁⲇⲓⲥⲟⲥ ⲉⲧⲁϩⲉ ⲛ̄ⲧⲕⲓⲧⲉ ϫⲛ ⲁⲃⲧⲓⲙⲉⲗⲗⲉⲭ ⲛ̄ⲥϩⲃⲩⲧⲏ ⲛ̄ⲣⲙ̄ⲡⲉ ⲉⲕⲁⲉⲓⲛ ⲧⲕⲓⲧⲉ ⲉϫⲛ̄ ⲛⲓⲙ ⲡϣⲏ ⲛⲓⲙ
ᵛᵃᶜ·   ⲉⲧⲏ ⟦· ·⟧ ⲉⲧⲏ ⲧⲁⲭⲏ ⲧⲁⲭⲏ

---

1 ⲁϥⲃⲟⲩⲣⲉ unidentified verb ? Erman 1904 : -ⲃⲟⲩⲣⲉ *l.* ⲡⲱⲱⲣⲉ "he dreamed" ? Crum CD 42a | ⲉⲓⲥ Erman 1904 | ⲡⲁⲡⲁⲧ Erman 1904 | *l.* ⲛ̄ⲧⲟⲟⲧ⟦ⲕ⟧ ? : *l.* ⲛ̄ⲧⲟⲟⲧⲕ "your hand" Erman, Meyer, Pernigotti | ⲉ . ϫⲟⲟⲩⲕ Erman 1904 | ⲙ̄ⲡⲁϩⲱⲃ Erman 1904 | *i.e.* ˢⲕ-ⲛⲁ-ⲉⲓ ⲉⲓⲉ or dittography ? : ⲕⲛ̄ⲁⲉⲓⲁⲉⲓ Erman 1904 : {ⲁⲉⲓ} Bélanger Sarrazin | ⲉⲡⲁϣⲱⲧ or correct to ⲧ-ϣⲱⲧⲉ "the well" ? : *l.* ⲉⲡϣⲟⲓ Erman 1904 || **2** *i.e.* ˢⲙⲁϩϩⲥ Bélanger Sarrazin : *l.* ϩⲙⲟⲟⲥ Erman 1895 : ⲙ̄ⲙⲟⲟⲥ Erman 1904 : "stay" ("sitzen", "niedersetzen") Kropp, Meyer | ⲡⲁⲓ̈ Erman 1904 | *i.e.* ˢⲡⲟⲛⲕ= | *i.e.* ˢⲉ-ⲡ-(ⲉ)ⲓⲉⲣⲟ : ⲁⲡⲣⲉⲓⲟ Erman 1904 | *i.e.* ˢ(ⲉ)ⲓⲉⲣⲟ | *i.e.* ˢⲡⲉϥ-ⲗⲟⲓϩⲉ || **3** ⲉⲓⲓⲁϫⲟⲩⲕ ⲩ resembling ϥ, or small raised ⲟ added before (suggestion of Michael Zellmann-Rohrer) ? : *i.e.* ϫⲟⲟⲩⲕ Erman 1904 | *i.e.* ˢⲉϩⲓ-ⲛⲁ- | **4** ⲡϣⲏ ⲡ corrected from ⲛ by overwriting? | *l.* ⲡ-ϩⲓⲛⲏⲃ | *i.e.* Χουσί ? *cf.* note || **5** ⲡⲣⲁⲛ or *l.* ⲡⲁⲣⲁⲛ ? | *cf.* ⲡⲁⲡⲗⲉⲟⲩ in *P.Lond.Copt.* 524 (KYP M359) l. 132 | *l.* ⲛ̄ⲥⲉ | *l.* ⲁϫⲓ ? | ⟦ⲧⲃ⟧ deleted with strokes : *l.* ⲧⲁⲓ ? Kropp : ⲧⲃⲁ̄ Erman 1904 | *i.e.* ˢⲧⲉⲓ-ⲥⲛ̄ⲧⲉ | **6** *i.e.* ˢⲙⲟⲕϩᵠ *cf.* ⲙⲟⲟⲩⲕϩ in l. 9 | ⲛ̄ϩⲏⲧ Erman 1904 | *i.e.* λυπεῖν | *i.e.* ˢⲛ̄ⲧⲁ-ⲩ-ϣⲉ || **7** ⲉⲓ̈ᶜ/ ⲓ corrected from ⲥ and ⲥ added subsequently : ⲉⲥ Erman 1904 | \ⲉ/ⲛ̄ⲛⲉⲓⲥⲉ ⲓ corrected from ⲥ : \ⲟ/ⲛ̄ⲛⲉⲥⲥⲉ Erman 1904 | ⲁϥ *vac.* ⲛ . ⲟ ⲛ̄ⲟⲩⲥⲓⲥⲉ Erman 1904 | *i.e.* ˢⲥⲟⲩ-ⲟⲩⲛ(ⲏ)ⲩ (haplography) | ⲙ̄ⲙⲟ . Erman 1904 : ⲙⲙⲟϥ Crum 1904 | *i.e.* ˢⲁϩⲣⲟ≠∅ Kropp, Crum | *l.* {ⲧⲥⲁ} \ⲧⲥⲁⲧⲉ/ or \ⲧⲥⲟⲧⲉ/ ? *cf. PCM* I 4 p. 4 l. 1 || **8** *i.e.* ˢⲉ-ⲡⲣⲏ | *i.e.* ˢⲉ-ⲧ-ϣⲁⲗⲁⲩ : *l.* ⲉ-ϫⲱⲗⲉ-ⲩ "to confine them" ? Crum CD 769a, Meyer | *i.e.* ˢϭⲓⲛⲙⲟⲩⲧ | ⲛ̄ⲧⲙⲏⲧⲉ Erman 1904 | *l.* ⲛⲥⲉ || **9** ⲙⲛ̄ Erman 1904 | ⲥⲃ̄ⲱ Erman 1904 | *i.e.* ˢⲙⲟⲕϩᵠ | ⲛ̄ϩⲏⲧ Erman 1904 | *i.e.* λυπεῖν || **10** ⲉⲧϩ⟦ⲙ⟧ Erman 1904 | *i.e.* ἄγγελος || **11** *i.e.* ˢⲉⲧ-ϩⲙⲟⲟⲥ | *i.e.* παράδεισος : ⲙ̄ⲡⲁⲣⲁⲧⲟⲓⲥⲟⲥ Erman 1904 | *i.e.* ˢⲉⲛⲧ-ⲁ≠ϥ-ⲟⲩⲱϣ *cf. PCM* I 6 ll. 19, 21 : Erman does not translate : "who sent" ("der... sandte", "che inviò") Kropp, Meyer, Pernigotti | *i.e.* ˢⲉϫⲛ̄ (haplography) || **12** *i.e.* ˢϣϥⲉⲧⲏ ? | ˢⲣⲟⲙⲡⲉ : ⲛⲉⲙⲡⲉ Erman 1904 | *i.e.* ˢⲉⲕⲉⲉⲓⲛⲉ ⲛ̄ⲛⲕⲟⲧⲕ | ⲛ[ⲓ]ⲙ Erman 1904 || **13** *i.e.* ἤδη (twice) | ⟦· ·⟧ erased by wiping | *i.e.* ταχύ (twice).

"Afboure, Afboure! Look, the golden *cup is in my? hand! If I send you on my work, you will go, yea?, to ⟨my⟩ need, you will fulfil it."

"Because of this, if you send me to the water, I will draw it, ⟨if⟩ to the river, I will bring its mud."

"No, I did not send you concerning those things, I did not send you concerning those other things; I shall send you to NN, the son of NN, so that you might bring sleep upon him and slumber until the sun of the Kushite? rises, |⁵ because the true name is Paplēu."

Say, "It is *Isis [[the two]], this is *Sephthys, these two sisters who are afflicted within, who are grieved within, who have gone up to heaven and earth, who are in the *abyss, for, behold, *Horus, the son of Isis … find them?, behold, they are far from him. What is wrong with you (f.s.)? … The arrow goes around the sun, the water-wheel goes around the moon in the midst of the sky, as the Pleiades are in the midst of the sky, Isis and Sephthys, the two sisters who are afflicted within, who are grieved within, |¹⁰ who are in the abyss, for you are *Ax, you are *Abrazakh, the *angel who sits upon the Tree of Paradise, who set sleep upon Abdemelech for seventy-five? years; you will bring sleep upon NN, the son of NN, now, now, quickly, quickly!"

RBS, KD, EL & MP, edited from photograph and autopsy.

1–2. Erman 1895, Kropp, and Pernigotti understand this first phrase as a question "If I send you to my work, will you go…?"; Meyer notes this as a possibility. Previous editors translate "your hand"; here we propose that the inserted ⲧ represents a correction. On this understanding, possession of the "golden cup" permits the first speaker to command the second. Alternatively, if we translate "your hand", the second speaker may be implicitly requested to fill it with water or mud.

3. ⲙ̄ⲡⲉⲓ̈ⲭⲟⲟⲩⲕ ⲛ̄ⲥⲁ ⲛⲁⲓ̈ : "I did not send you concerning those things" For this rhetorical construction, see *PCM* I 3 front col. 1 15–16 and the accompanying note.

4. ⲭⲟⲩⲥⲓ : "Kushite?" Previous translators have understood ⲭⲟⲩⲥⲓ as a *vox magica*, although we may note two more concrete possibilities. ⲭⲟⲩⲥⲓ is the Coptic spelling of Hushai the Archite, the friend of King David who appears in 2 Samuel. The meaning of the phrase "sun of Hushai" is not clear, however, and the definite article before ⲭⲟⲩⲥⲓ would imply another word. Χους is the Greek writing of Cush, the eldest son of Ham in (*inter alia*) Genesis 10.6, and Χουσι is the transliteration of Hebrew כושי (*kûšî*), "Kushite", generally translated in Greek as Αἰθίοψ. Awareness of this meaning among Greek-language authors appears in *e.g.* John Chrysostom, *Exposition of Psalm* 7 (καὶ ἀντὶ τοῦ Χουσὶ, Αἰθίοπός φησιν). Alternatively we might understand χοῦς ("soil", "dust"), or in Psalm 21 (22) 16 "the grave" (as χοῦς θανάτου) as a masculine noun.

7–8. ⲁϩⲣⲱ… : "What is wrong with you…" Bélanger Sarrazin suggests to understand ⲁϩⲣⲟⲧⲁⲧⲥ and ⲭⲁⲗⲁⲩ as constellations, by analogy with the Pleiades mentioned later, with the later as ⳉⲁⲗⲁⲁⲩ ("water wheel"), perhaps "Aquarius", although Aquarius in Demotic was "the water" (*pꜣ mw i.e.* ˢⲡ-ⲙⲟⲟⲩ); an alternative might be Scorpio, attested in Coptic as ϯⲟ̄ⲗⲏ (Spiegelberg 1910: 147). If it were a stellar body, ⲁϩⲣⲟⲧⲁⲧⲥ might refer to one of the planets or constellations identified with Horus, whose name might be found in -ϩⲣ-. Here we interpret ⲁϩⲣⲱ as a question, and propose to read the following word as ⲧⲥⲟⲧⲉ (*cf. PCM* I 4 p. 4 l. 1), "arrow", which, if a constellation, might refer to Sagittarius (Bélanger Sarrazin forthcoming a).

11–12. ⲁⲃⲧⲓⲙⲉⲗⲗⲉⲭ : "Abdemelech" Perhaps the "Kushite" referred to in l. 4; the target of the spell is to sleep until the sun of the Kushite (*i.e.*, Abdemelech) rises, that is, until he awakens; *cf.* the note to *PCM* I 6 l. 20.

PCM I 10. Prayer for pregnancy

Bawit ? 28.6 (H) × 21.7 (W) cm VII CE

Other references: Pierpont Morgan Library MS M.662B.22; Pierpont Morgan Library B1 363 D MS M.0662 Box 3; TM 99570; *P.Morgan Copt.* 10; *SB Kopt.* V 2356; KYP M290; Bélanger Sarrazin #83.

Editions: MacCoull 1982: no. 10 (*ed. pr.*); Hasitzka 2020: no. 2356.

Translations: MacCoull 1982: no. 10; Meyer in Meyer/Smith 1994: no. 83.

Additional commentary: Friedman 1989: no. 108; Depuydt 1993: no. 306; Preininger forthcoming c: chapter 4.

Present location: New York, Pierpont Morgan Library.

Image: http://corsair.themorgan.org/vwebv/holdingsInfo?bibId=351423

Linguistic description: Sahidic (non-standard); first line in Greek.

Contents:

Original use:

1. Front ll. 1–22: Prayer for pregnancy (KYP T482)

Re-use:

2. Back ll. 1–20: Account of wine (KYP T1563; TM 85366)

A well-preserved papyrus sheet, with some damage to the lower left, containing a prayer for pregnancy on the front and an account of wine on the back. The manuscript was part of a lot bought from the Cairo-based dealer Maurice Nahman by Francis Willey Kelsey, who brought it to Rome in 1920. It was then purchased by Henri Hyvernat on behalf of John Pierpont Morgan (Jr.), and is now kept in the Pierpont Morgan Museum.[1]

The prayer is written in black ink, with crosses marking the beginning and the end of the text. The account on the back is written in two different hands at 180° to the front. The rough surface of the manuscript led the copyists on both sides to jump across sections of pre-existing damage,[2] and makes it difficult to be sure of the extend of folding; 10 horizontal creases may be visible. *Kollēsis* is apparent on the left side of the sheet (viewed from the front). The order of the writing of the two sides is not immediately apparent; the writing of the accounts on the vertical fibres does not follow the normal practice for such documents, and suggests that this was the later re-use. In this case, it may be that the copyist of the prayer

---

[1] *The Morgan Library and Museum*, http://corsair.themorgan.org/vwebv/holdingsInfo?bibId=351423 (accessed 10/7/2023; additional bibliography concerning the manuscript is accessible through this link); MacCoull 1982: 1. On Maurice Nahman, see Hagen/Ryholt 2016: 253–255.

[2] *Cf.* Jones 2015.

decided to begin on the horizontal fibres of this sheet since the damaged surface, worse on the vertical fibres, made this the more sensible choice.

The hand is fairly, but not entirely, regular, with varying letterforms and sizes, a right-sloping bimodal majuscule, with ⲃ, ⲕ, ⲣ, ⲧ, and ⳉ showing a tendency towards quadrilinearity. Letters are sometimes deliberately enlarged, as where one marks a divine name at the beginning of l. 18. ⲁ has a rounded bowl, with a short oblique stroke, sometimes with a slight serif at its lower end. ⲃ and ⲕ are large, and ⲇ, ⲗ, and ⲝ have curling serifs at their tips. The points of ⲙ are rounded, the central downward point clearly marked rather than flattened. ⲧ is highly mannered, with a right-facing serif on its descender, and often another on the left side of its horizontal bar, so that it can at times resemble a ⳉ. ⲧ is also regularly ligatured to the following letter, as is ⲉ. ⲩ is very small, shaped like a Latin minuscule y. ⲱ has a flattened central apex, at times resembling ⳇ. Parallels to this hands can be found in manuscripts dated by their editors to the seventh or eighth centuries,[3] although we cannot point to any specific dated parallels. Alain Delattre suggests that the account on the back shows features typical of seventh-century examples, suggesting that the earlier magical text should also be dated to this century.[4]

The dialect is a non-standard Sahidic, with some common features—haplography of ⲛ & ⲙ, and the writing of ⲃ for ⳇ. The absence of ⲛ › ⲙ assimilation before labial consonants is perhaps indicative of a broadly Middle Egyptian origin,[5] and we find occasional aphaeresis of an initial ⲉ (*e.g.*, l. 22), doubling of consonants, with the unmarked consonant preceding the aspirated or voiced variant (ⲭ › ⲕⲭ, ⲍ › ⲥⲍ in ll. 8, 12), and omission of a nasal before a stop (ⲛ̄ⲧ › ⲧ, ll. 15, 16).

The account on the back is of considerable interest for determining the context of the earlier prayer;[6] it consists of a series of records of deliveries and payments of wine made on the 9th and 10th Koiak (6th & 7th December), written on the left in one hand, with a second hand copying the figures and writing totals and additions to the right. Similar accounts have been found at the monasteries of Apa Apollo at Bawit and Apa Thomas at Wadi Sarga.[7] Two monks are mentioned as recipients of wine in ll. 16–17, Ounobre and Apollō, both referred to by the title "my brother" (ⲡⲁⲥⲟⲛ) typical of texts from Bawit,[8] and Apollō is described as coming from the

---

[3] *Cf. CPR* II 226 (VII CE); *CPR* II 233 (VIII).

[4] Personal communication 15/2/2023.

[5] *Cf.* Kahle 1954: I 99–100.

[6] Republished recently as *SB Kopt.* V 2344. We are very grateful to Alain Delattre for reading this text with us during a seminar, aiding us in understanding its content and context; we are equally grateful for corrections suggested by him to l. 11 of the magical text.

[7] For similar accounts, see *e.g.*, *O.BawitIFAO* 31, 33–37, 40, 42; *P.Brux.Bawit* 5, 9, 22, 28, 30; *P.Mon.Apollo* I 47 (Bawit); *SB* XVIII 13422, 13423, 13448, 13477, 13478, 13504, 13505, 13542, 13371 (Wadi Sarga). For these sites, see Wipszycka 2009: 86–87, 90, 143–150, 155–157; Wegner 2016.

[8] Delattre 2007: 147–148.

nearby city of Assiut. The prayer therefore likely belonged to one of the inhabitants of the monastery of Bawit, and was re-used for accounts when it was no longer needed; papyri from Bawit are known to be among those acquired by the Pierpont Morgan from Nahman in 1920.[9]

---

[9] Delattre/Pilette/Vanthieghem 2015: 33–34.

front (→)

+ δέσποτα παντωκράτωρ κυρίου ὦ θεός ⲛⲧⲟⲕ
ⲅⲁⲣ ϫⲓⲛ ⲉϣⲟⲣⲡ ⲁⲕⲧⲁⲙⲓⲟ ⲡⲣⲱⲙⲉ ⲕⲁⲧⲁ
ⲡⲉⲕⲛⲓⲛⲉ ⲁⲩⲱ ⲕⲁⲧⲁ ⲧⲉⲕϩⲓⲕⲱⲛ ⲛⲧⲟⲕ ⲟⲛ
ⲁⲕⲧⲁⲓⲉⲓ ⲧⲁϭⲛⲏⲛ ⲙⲛ ⲧⲉⲧⲙⲓⲥⲉ ⲛⲧⲟⲕ
5   ⲁⲕϫⲟⲟⲥ ⲉⲧⲉⲛⲙⲁⲁⲩ ⲥⲁⲁⲣⲁ ϫⲉ ϩⲛ ⲡⲓⲟⲉⲓϣ
ⲛⲧⲕⲉⲣⲟⲙⲡⲉ ⲟⲩⲛ ⲟⲩϣⲏⲣⲉ ⲛⲁϣⲱⲡⲉ ⲛⲉ
ⲛⲧⲓϩⲉ ⲟⲛ ϯⲥⲟⲡⲟⲡⲥ ⲁⲩⲱ ϯⲡⲁⲣⲁⲕⲁⲗⲓ ⲙⲟⲕ
ⲡⲉⲧϩⲙⲟⲟⲥ ⲉϩⲣⲁⲓ ⲉϫⲛ ⲛⲉⲕⲭⲣⲉⲣⲓⲃⲓⲛ ⲉⲧⲣⲉⲕ-
ⲥⲱⲧⲙ ⲉⲡⲁⲧⲱⲃϩ ⲙⲡⲟⲟⲩ ⲁⲛⲟⲕ ⲛⲓⲙ ⲡϣⲉ ⲛⲓⲙ
10 ⲉϫⲛ ⲡⲓⲁⲡⲟⲧ ⲛⲉⲣⲡ ⲉⲧϩⲛ ⲧⲁϭⲓϫ ϫⲉⲕⲁⲥ
ⲉⲓϣⲁⲛⲧⲁⲁⲃ ⲛⲙⲉϣ ⲛⲓⲙ ⲧϣⲉ ⲛⲛⲓⲙ ⲉⲕⲉ-
ⲭⲁⲣⲓⲥⲍⲉ ⲛⲁⲥ ⲛⲟⲩⲥⲡⲉⲣⲙⲁ ⲛⲣⲱⲙⲉ ⲁⲓⲱ ⲡⲭ̅ⲥ̅
ⲡⲉⲧⲥⲱⲧⲙ ⲉⲟⲩⲟⲛ ⲛⲓⲙ ⲉⲧⲱϣ ⲉϩⲣⲁⲓ ⲉⲣⲟϥ
ⲁ̅ⲇ̅ⲱ̅ⲛ̅ⲉ̅ ⲉⲗ̅ⲱ̅ⲛ̅ ⲥⲁⲃⲁⲱ̅ⲑ̅ ⲡⲛⲟⲩⲧⲉ ⲛⲉⲛⲟⲩⲧⲉ
15 ⲁⲩⲱ ⲡϫⲟⲉⲓⲥ ⲛⲉϫⲟⲉⲓⲥ ⲅⲁⲛ ⲧⲁⲩⲣⲱⲙⲉ ⲙⲟⲩⲣ
ⲛⲟⲩⲫⲩⲗⲁⲕⲧⲏⲣⲓⲟⲛ ⲉⲣⲟⲥ ⲅⲁⲛ ⲧⲁⲟⲩⲁ ϯ ⲛⲁⲥ
ⲛⲟⲩⲁⲡⲟⲧ ⲙⲟⲩⲧⲉ ⲅⲁⲛ ⲟⲩ ⲉⲃⲟⲗ ϩⲓⲧⲟⲟⲧⲕ ⲡⲉ
ⲙⲁⲣⲉⲥϣⲱⲗ ⲉⲃⲟⲗ ϭⲓ ⲧⲙⲉⲣⲉ ⲛⲧⲉⲥⲟⲟⲧⲉ ⲙⲛ
[ⲧⲉⲥ]ⲛⲉⲡⲏⲗ ⲙⲛ [ⲧⲉⲥ]ⲕⲁⲗⲁϩⲉ ⲉⲓⲱⲣⲕ ⲉⲣⲟⲕ
20 ⲙⲡⲉⲕⲛⲟϭ ⲛⲣⲁⲛ ⲙⲛ ⲛⲉϩⲓⲥⲉ ⲛⲧⲁⲕϣⲟⲡⲟⲩ
ϩⲓϫⲛ ⲡⲉⲥⲧⲁⲩⲣⲟⲥ ⲉⲕⲉϫⲱⲕ ⲉⲃⲟⲗ ⲛϣⲁϫⲉ ⲛ[ⲓⲙ]
ⲛⲧⲁⲩϫⲟⲟⲩ ⲉϫⲛ ⲡⲓⲁⲡⲟⲧ ⲧϩⲓ ⲧⲁϭⲓϫ +

---

1 ⲇⲉⲥⲡⲟⲧⲁ ⲡⲁⲛⲧⲱⲕⲣⲁⲧⲱⲣ ⲕⲩⲣⲓⲟⲩ ⲱ ⲑⲉⲟⲥ *pap. i.e.* δέσποτα παντοκράτωρ κύριος ὁ θεός ‖ **2** *i.e.* γάρ | *i.e.* κατά ‖ **3** *i.e.* ˢⲡⲉⲕ-ⲉⲓⲛⲉ : ⲧⲉⲕⲛⲓⲛⲉ MacCoull, Hasitzka | *i.e.* εἰκών ‖ **4** *i.e.* ˢⲧⲁⲉⲓⲉ⸗ | *i.e.* ˢⲁϭⲣⲏⲛ ‖ **5** *i.e.* ˢⲟⲩⲟⲉⲓϣ ‖ **7** ⲥⲟⲡⲟⲡⲥ corrected from ⲥⲟⲡⲟⲥⲥ by overwriting *i.e.* ˢⲥⲟⲡⲥ : ϯⲥⲟⲡ ⲟ ⲉⲓⲥ MacCoull | *i.e.* παρακαλεῖν | *i.e.* ˢⲙ̅ⲙⲟ⸗ⲕ ‖ **8** *i.e.* ⲛⲉ-ⲭⲉⲣⲟⲩⲃⲓⲙ ‖ **9** *i.e.* ˢⲙ̅-ⲡⲟⲟⲩ : ⲙⲡⲟⲟⲩ MacCoull, Hasitzka ‖ **10** ⲛⲉⲣⲡ ⲡⲉⲧϩⲛ MacCoull : ⲛⲉⲣⲡ Hasitzka ‖ **11** ⲉⲓϣⲁⲛϩⲁⲁⲃ ⲛⲙⲉϥ ⲉⲛⲓⲙ ⲧϣⲉ ⲛⲓⲙ MacCoull : ⲉⲓϣⲁⲛⲧⲁⲁⲃ ⲛⲙⲉϣ ⲛⲓⲙ Hasitzka ‖ **12** *i.e.* χαρίζειν : ⲭⲁⲣⲓⲥⲉ MacCoull | *i.e.* σπέρμα | ⲁⲩⲱ MacCoull, Hasitzka | *l.* ϫ(ⲟⲉⲓ)ⲥ ‖ **14** or ⲉⲗⲱⲗⲓ ? : ⲉⲗⲱ̅ ⲛⲭⲁⲃⲁⲱ̅ⲑ̅ MacCoull : ⲉⲗⲱ̅ ⲛⲥⲁⲃⲁⲱ̅ⲑ̅ Hasitzka | *i.e.* ˢⲛ̅-ⲛ-ⲛⲟⲩⲧⲉ ‖ **15** *i.e.* ˢⲛ̅-ⲛ-ϫⲟⲉⲓⲥ | *i.e.* κἄν : ⲅⲁ *i.e.* ˢϫⲉ Hasitzka | *i.e.* ˢⲛ̅ⲧⲁ-(ⲟ)ⲩ-ⲣⲱⲙⲉ : ⲛⲧⲁⲩⲣⲱⲙⲉ Hasitzka ‖ **16** *i.e.* φυλακτήριον | *i.e.* κἄν : ⲅⲁ *i.e.* ˢϫⲉ Hasitzka | *i.e.* ˢⲛ̅ⲧⲁ-ⲟⲩⲁ : ⲛⲧⲁⲟⲩⲁ Hasitzka | ϯⲛⲟⲥ MacCoull ‖ **17** *i.e.* ˢⲙ̅-ⲙⲟⲩⲧⲉ | *i.e.* κἄν : ⲅⲁ *i.e.* ˢϫⲉ Hasitzka | ⲛⲟⲩ ⲉⲃⲟⲗ Hasitzka ‖ **18** *i.e.* ˢⲃⲱⲗ | *l.* ⲛϭⲓ | ϭⲓ ⲧⲙⲉⲣⲉ ⲛⲧⲉⲥⲟⲟⲧⲉ translate "through redeeming love" MacCoull, Meyer ‖ **19** . . . ⲡⲉⲙⲱⲗⲏⲛ MacCoull, Hasitzka | *i.e.* ˢⲕⲁⲗⲁϩⲏ : [. ?] MacCoull : . . . . ⲁⲗⲁⲥⲉ Hasitzka | ⲉⲣⲟⲕ [MacCoull ‖ **20** *i.e.* ˢⲙ̅-ⲡⲉ⸗ⲕ-ⲛⲟϭ | ⲛⲧⲁⲕϣⲟⲡⲟⲩ [Hasitzka ‖ **21** *i.e.* σταυρός | ⲛ[MacCoull ‖ **22** ⲛⲧⲉⲩϫⲟⲟⲩ MacCoull | *i.e.* ˢⲉⲧ-ϩⲛ̅ ⲧⲁ-ϭⲓϫ : ⲡⲣⲓⲧⲁϭⲓϫ MacCoull : [ⲉ]ⲧϩⲓ ⲧⲁϭⲓϫ Hasitzka

| ^{Greek} + O Master, Almighty Lord God, | ^{Coptic} since from the beginning, you created man according to your likeness and according to your image, and you also honoured the barren woman and the one who gives birth, you |⁵ yourself said to our mother Sarah: "By this time next year you will have a child". Again in this way, I entreat you and I invoke you, you who sit upon the *cherubim, that you listen to my prayer today, I, NN, son of NN, |¹⁰ over this *cup of wine that is in my hand, so that when I give it to NN, the daughter of NN, you will grace her with a seed of man! Yea, Lord, you who listen to anyone who calls upon you, *Adonai Elon *Sabaoth, god of gods |¹⁵ and lord of lords, even if a man has bound a phylactery to her, even if someone has given her an enchanted cup, even if it is from you, may the *binding of her womb be released, and [of her] navel? and of her belly!

I adjure you |²⁰ by your great name and by the sufferings you received upon the cross, that you accomplish every word which has been spoken over this cup which is in my hand! +

KD, EL, MP & SVS, edited from photograph.

2–3. ⲕⲁⲧⲁ ⲡⲉⲕⲛⲓⲛⲉ ⲁⲩⲱ ⲕⲁⲧⲁ ⲧⲉⲕϩⲓⲕⲱⲛ : "according to your likeness and according to your image" An allusion to Genesis 1.26: "God said, "Let us make a man according to our image and according to our likeness" (ⲡⲉϫⲁϥ ⲛϭⲓ ⲡⲛⲟⲩⲧⲉ ϫⲉ ⲙⲁⲣⲉⲛⲧⲁⲙⲓⲟ ⲛⲟⲩⲣⲱⲙⲉ ⲕⲁⲧⲁ ⲧⲉⲛϩⲓⲕⲱⲛ · ⲁⲩⲱ ⲕⲁⲧⲁ ⲡⲉⲛⲉⲓⲛⲉ; Staatsbibliothek zu Berlin Ms. or. fol. 1605 fol. 1v col. 1 ll. 10–15). For other references to this passage, see *PCM* I 26 p. 3 ll. 25–26, p. 4 l. 12, p. 5 l. 1, p. 9 31–32, p. 11 l. 17, p. 15 ll. 19–20.

5. ⲁⲕϫⲟⲟⲥ ⲉⲧⲉⲛⲙⲁⲁⲩ ⲥⲁⲁⲣⲁ : "(you), yourself said to our mother Sarah" A reference to Genesis 17.15–18.15, 21.1–3, in which God promises Abraham that his wife Sarah will bear a child, Isaac, despite the fact that Abraham is one hundred years old and Sarah ninety; the miraculous pregnancy of Sarah serves as a model for God's capacity to allow women to conceive. For a similar Jewish text from the Cairo Genizah intended to make a woman give birth quickly, drawing upon the prototype of Sarah and other Biblical mothers (including Eve, Hagar, Rebecca, Lea, Rachel, and Zipporah), see *MTKG* I T.-S. NS 322.10 1a ll. 12–28.

14. ⲉⲗⲱⲛ : "Elon" *Cf. PCM* I 34 p. 3 l. 3 [.]ⲗⲱⲛ, and *Eloei in the glossary.

15. ⲛⲟⲩⲫⲩⲗⲁⲕⲧⲏⲣⲓⲟⲛ : "a phylactery" The reference to "binding a phylactery" as a possible cause of infertility is surprising; normally a "phylactery" refers to an amulet which would itself represent a source of healing. It is possible that this therefore represents a case in which anti-'magic' discourse is being deployed; the woman may have previously sought out the use of a phylactery which has harmed her and may itself constitute the source of the problem. Compare the story reported in Augustine, *City of God* 22.8, in which a woman receives a miraculous cure from a long illness when she throws away an amuletic belt which she had been given by a Jewish practitioner. The other possible causes for infertility envisaged here are clearer—that someone has given her a curse in the form of a potion (*cf.* note to *PCM* I 26 p. 16 l. 9), or that God himself has caused it.

19. [ⲧⲉⲥ]ⲛⲉⲡⲏⲗ : "navel?" Perhaps understand ^{S}ϩⲗⲡⲉ, "navel" with a loss of the initial ϩ and ⲗ-ⲡ metathesis; compare the additional ⲛ added in ll. 3, 4 (ⲡⲉⲕⲛⲓⲛⲉ, ⲧⲁϭⲛⲏⲛ).

PCM I 11. Leiden Anastasy Codex

Thebes ?   22 (H) × 14.5 (W) × 5.3 (D) cm   late VI–VIII CE

Other references: P.Leiden I 385; AMS 9; Leiden Anastasy 9 (1828); TM 100023; CML 3355; KYP M171; Bélanger Sarrazin #139.

Editions: Pleyte/Boeser 1897: 441–479 (*ed. pr.*).

Translations: Boeser 1922 (French); Lexa 1925: nos. XVIII–XXI (French); Kropp 1931: II nos. 22–23, 27, 45–46, 63B, 64A (German); Smith in Meyer/Smith 1994: no. 134; Pernigotti 1995: nos. 4, 5, 7 (Italian); Pernigotti 2000: nos. 37–38 (Italian).

Additional commentary: Crum 1899: 17–21; Raven 1982: no. 25; Geerard 1992; Raven 1996: 13, plate 6; Szirmai 1999: 34, 37, 41, 43, fig. 3.3, 3.8; Raven 2010: plate 137; Sanzo 2014: 82–83; Given 2016: 177–222; Boud'hors 2017a: 175–212; de Bruyn 2017: 87, 219; Sanzo 2019a: 230–254; Bélanger Sarrazin 2020: 192; Bélanger Sarrazin forthcoming c; Jacobi/Scheper/Menei forthcoming; Preininger forthcoming b.

Present location: Leiden, National Museum of Antiquities (Rijksmuseum van Oudheden).

Image: https://hdl.handle.net/21.12126/21319

Linguistic description: Sahidic.

Contents:

1. p. 1 l. 1 – p. 14 l. 13: Prayer of Gregory (KYP T61)
2. p. 14 l. 14 – p. 20 l. 5: Prayer for protection (KYP T1478)
3. p. 20 l. 6 – p. 23 l. 26: Letter of Abgar to Jesus (KYP T1479)
4. p. 24 l. 1 – p. 25 l. 23: Letter of Jesus to Abgar (KYP T1606)
5. p. 25 l. 24 – p. 28 l. 21: Prayer of Judas Cyriacus (KYP T991)
6. p. 28 ll. 22–27: Names of Seven Sleepers of Ephesus (KYP T1480)
7. p. 29 ll. 1–22: Names of Forty Martyrs of Sebaste (KYP T1481)
8. p. 29 l. 23 – p. 30 l. 28: Incipits of the canonical gospels and Psalm 90 (91) (KYP T1482)

Complete papyrus codex with binding intact, consisting of 30 pages (15 folios), each page inscribed in single columns of 27–30 lines in black ink. The codex consists of 3 quires: quire 1 is a ternion (folios 1–6), quire 2 a quaternion (folios 7–14), quire 3 a singleton (folio 15). The folios are numbered on the verso (even pages), except for folio 1, which is numbered on both sides; the numbering goes directly from ⲋ (6, p. 12) to ⲏ (8, p. 14) so that the final folio is numbered 16 (ⲓⲋ) instead of 15.[1] The quires are likewise numbered from 1–3 on their rectos (odd pages). The stitching was reinforced by slim parchment guards, visible along the spines of pages 6–7 and 20 (*i.e.*, between quires 1 and 2); the parchment can be identified as the remains of a Psalter, preserving portions of Psalms 96 (97) 7 and

---

[1] The manuscript is described as 16 folios on the collection website (*Rijksmuseum van Oudheden*, https://hdl.handle.net/21.12126/21319; accessed 14/10/2022) as a result of the error in folio numbering; *cf.* Sanzo 2019a: 232 n. 8.

93 (94) 8.² There is considerable damage to the lower right parts of the first two folios (pp. 1–4, viewed from the front), as well as to the eighth folio (pp. 15–16) perhaps caused by worms. Damage on the other pages is generally restricted to the margins (as on fol. 3, 14–15=pp. 5–6, 27–30), or to abrasion of the ink.

The covers are intact, formed by a papyrus leaf wrapped around chunks of papyrus and other organic material to form thick boards, then covered by two separate pieces of leather. A light coloured parchment strip was interleaved through slits cut in the leather to create decoration on the front and back cover—a circle inside a square inside a rectangle. Four loops of leather on the back (one each at top and bottom, two on the outside edge), probably corresponding to lost clasps on the front, would have served to close the codex when it was not in use; a surviving leather strand on the upper outside corner of the back cover may be the remains of a bookmark.³

The manuscript was acquired by the National Museum of Antiquities of Leiden as part of the 1828 purchase from Jean d'Anastasy (1765–1860), Consul General of Sweden and Norway in Egypt.⁴ It appears in the sale catalogue (RMO inv. 3.1.6), on p. 95 as no. 9. In their edition, Pleyte and Boeser state that that it was found in Thebes by d'Anastasy in January 1829, but this is impossible based on the timeline of the sale; the catalogue was prepared in 1827, and January 1829 is in fact the date of the shipment's arrival in Leiden.⁵ Although no provenance is given in the catalogue, many of the manuscripts from this sale did come from Thebes,⁶ and its format closely resembles that of other codices from the Theban region.⁷

The manuscript is written in a very consistent formal literary hand, an upright unimodular, bilinear Coptic majuscule characterised by PAThs as a "mixed" hand, and by Boud'hors as tending towards the Biblical majuscule.⁸ Supralinear strokes are short and curved, and diaeresis is often written as a single flattened dot. *Ekthesis* and enlargement of the first letter occurs at the beginning of certain texts, often also marked by dashed horizontal lines and diplai in the margins; on several

---

² We are grateful to Anne Boud'hors and Frank Feder for their help in identifying these passages. For similar parchment fragments likely used as guards, see Boud'hors/Garel 2016: 48–49.

³ For discussions of the binding, see Jacobi/Scheper/Menei forthcoming; Petersen 1954: 60 n. 18, 61; Szirmai 1999: 40–43 with n. 6.

⁴ For Jean d'Anastasy, see Dosoo/Torallas Tovar 2022a: 5 n. 5; Chrysikopoulos 2015. For an overview of the sale with further references, see Dosoo 2016: 252–253.

⁵ Pleyte/Boeser 1897: v; *cf.* Dosoo/Torallas Tovar 2022b: 98.

⁶ Notably three of the texts of the famous 'Theban Magical Library', nos. 65, 66, and 75 in the catalogue; *cf.* Dosoo 2016. Other manuscripts are noted in the catalogue as coming not only from Thebes, but also from Memphis, Philae, and Elephantine.

⁷ Boud'hors 2017a; *cf.* Dosoo/Torallas Tovar 2022b: 98. The closest parallels of format and hand seem to be found in BM EA 71005 (CLM 860), *P.Lond.Copt.* 275 (CLM 852), *P.Lond.Copt.* 279 (CLM 854; also owned by Anastasy), *P.Lond.Copt.* 325 (CLM 844); *cf.* the discussion in O'Connell 2018: 86–88.

⁸ Boud'hors 2017a: 189.

pages more elaborate decoration divides texts and marks titles. Before writing, the scribe marked the corners of the textblock with pinpricks to serve as guides.⁹ The ink, very opaque under ultraviolet light but less so under near-infrared light, may be identified as an iron gall ink (a mixture of iron and tannins).¹⁰

Trismegistos and Sanzo 2014 (82) date the text to the sixth century, while PATHs, following Proverbio (1997: 161–162) date it to the fifth to sixth centuries. Sanzo 2019a (236) has more recently followed a later, sixth to eighth century dating. The dating of the closest parallels, from Thebes, rests uncertain, but we follow Sanzo 2019a in proposing a date from the late sixth to eighth centuries, based on the analysis of the best studied of the manuscripts with similar hands and formats, and the archaeological context of other Theban codices.¹¹

The dialect is a form of Sahidic very close to the literary standard. The non-standard forms we find are generally the most common—haplography, dittography, and the occasional exchange of schwa/ⲉ, ⲉ/ⲏ, ⲃ/ϥ.

The manuscript contains a number of amuletic texts, most known from other contexts. The first text of the manuscript is the *Prayer of Gregory*, a protective prayer with later parallels in Greek.¹² The second text is likewise an amuletic prayer, without a title or known parallels. The third and fourth texts consist of the well-known Jesus-Abgar correspondence, while the fifth is a prayer attributed to Judas Cyriacus taken from the literary text known as the *Finding of the Holy Cross*. The sixth and seventh texts are lists of the names of saints, while the final text consists of the incipits of the canonical gospels and Psalm 90 (91). These texts are more fully discussed in the accompanying notes, in particular those of their first pages.

Note that Pleyte and Boeser use the sign = in their edition to indicate words which continue over multiple lines, but this is not present in the codex.

---

⁹ Jacobi/Scheper/Menei forthcoming.
¹⁰ Jacobi/Scheper/Menei forthcoming.
¹¹ *Cf.* n. 6 above for close parallels. Behlmer/Alcock (1996: 3) date BM EA 71005 to the seventh century, without excluding a late sixth century date; on the larger context see Boud'hors 2008; Boud'hors 2017a, who notes that most papyrus codices from the Theban region date to the seventh or eighth centuries.
¹² Strittmatter 1930: 169–178; Strittmatter 1932: 125–144.

page 1 (1r) (↓)

/:ⲁ̣:/ /:ⲁ̣:/
ⲟⲩⲉⲩⲭⲏ ⲁⲩⲱ ⲟⲩⲉⲝⲟⲣⲅⲓⲥ-
ⲙⲟⲥ : ⲉⲁⲓⲥϩⲁⲓ̈ⲉϥ ⲁⲛⲟⲕ ⲅⲣⲏ-
ⲅⲟⲣⲓ̈ⲟⲥ ⲡϩⲙ̄ϩⲁⲗ ⲙⲡⲛⲟⲩⲧⲉ
ⲉⲧⲟⲛϩ̄ ⲉⲧⲣⲉϥϣⲱⲡⲉ ⲙ̄-
5 ⲫⲩⲗⲁⲕⲧⲏⲣⲓ̈ⲟⲛ ⲛⲟⲩⲟⲛ ⲛⲓⲙ
ⲉⲧⲛⲁϫⲓⲧⲥ̄ ⲁⲩⲱ ⲛ̄ⲥⲉⲟϣϥ̄
ⲉⲧⲣⲉⲥⲃⲱⲗ ⲉⲃⲟⲗ ⲛⲉ́ⲛⲉⲣⲅⲓ̈ⲁ
ⲛⲓⲙ ⲉⲧⲉϣⲁⲩϣⲱⲡⲉ ϩⲓⲧⲛ̄
ⲛⲉⲣⲱⲙⲉ ⲙ̄ⲡⲟⲛⲏⲣⲟⲥ : ⲉ-
10 ⲧⲉ ⲙⲙⲛ̄ⲧⲣⲉϥϩⲓⲕ ⲛⲉ :
ⲙⲛ̄ ⲙ̄ⲙⲛ̄ⲧⲣⲉϥⲙⲟⲩⲧⲉ : ⲙⲛ̄
ϩⲉⲛⲙⲛ̄ⲧⲣⲉϥⲙⲟⲩⲣ ⲛ̄ϩⲉⲛ-
ⲣⲱⲙⲉ ϩⲛ̄ ϩⲉⲛϣⲱⲛⲉ ⲉⲩ-
ϣⲟⲃⲉ : ⲙⲛ̄ ϩⲉⲛⲫⲑⲟⲛⲟⲥ
15 ⲙⲛ̄ ϩⲉⲛⲕⲱϩ : ⲙⲛ̄ ϩⲉⲛⲙⲛ̄ⲧ-
ⲁⲡⲣⲁⲕⲧⲟⲥ : ⲉⲧⲉ ⲡⲁⲓ̈ ⲡⲉ
ⲉⲧⲙ̄ⲧⲣⲉⲩϭⲛ̄ ϩⲱⲃ ⲉⲉⲓⲣⲉ
ϩⲁⲡⲁⲝ ϩⲁⲡⲗⲱⲥ ⲡⲣ[ⲁⲅⲙⲁ]
ⲛⲓⲙ ⲉⲧⲉⲛⲥⲟⲟⲩⲛ [ⲉⲣⲟϥ]
20 ⲙⲛ̄ ⲛⲉⲧⲉⲛⲥⲟⲟ[ⲩⲛ ⲉⲣⲟ-]
ⲟⲩ ⲁⲛ ⲙⲛ̄ ϩⲱⲃ ⲛ[ⲓⲙ ⲉⲧ-]
ϣⲱⲡⲉ ϩⲓⲧⲛ̄ ϩ[ⲛ̄ⲣⲱⲙⲉ ⲙ-]
ⲡⲉⲣⲓ̄ⲉⲣⲅⲟⲥ · ⲙ[ⲛ ϩⲛⲣⲱⲙⲉ ⲛ-]
ⲥⲁⲛⲕⲟⲧⲥ̄ ⲛ̄ⲧ[ca. 5]
25 ⲙ̄ⲡⲟⲛⲏⲣⲟⲥ : †[ⲡⲁⲣⲁⲕⲁ-]
ⲗⲉⲓ̄ ⲙ̄ⲙⲟⲕ ⲡⲭⲟ[ⲉⲓⲥ ⲡⲛⲟⲩ-]
ⲧⲉ ⲡⲡⲁⲛⲧⲱ[ⲕⲣⲁⲧⲱⲣ]
ⲁⲛⲟⲕ ⲅⲣⲏⲅⲟⲣ[ⲓⲟⲥ ⲡⲉⲕ-]

---

1 i.e. εὐχή ‖ **1–2** i.e. ἐξορκισμός ‖ **5** i.e. φυλακτήριον ‖ **7** i.e. ἐνέργεια ‖ **9** i.e. πονηρός ‖ **14** i.e. φθόνος ‖ **16** i.e. ἄπρακτος ‖ **18** i.e. ἅπαξ ἁπλῶς πρ[ᾶγμα] : ⲡ[ⲉϩⲱⲃ] Pleyte/Boeser, Kropp, Smith ‖ **21** [ⲉⲧ-] : [. . .] Pleyte/Boeser ‖ **23** i.e. περίεργος | [ⲛ-] : Boeser does not restore ‖ **25** i.e. πονηρός ‖ **25–26** i.e. παρακαλεῖν ‖ **26** ⲡⲭ[ⲟⲉⲓⲥ] Pleyte/Boeser ‖ **27** i.e. παντο[κράτωρ] ‖ **28** ⲅⲣⲏⲅⲟ[ⲣⲓⲟⲥ] Pleyte/Boeser | [ⲡⲉⲕ-] : Pleyte/Boeser, Boeser, Kropp, Smith do not restore anything here : "servant of God" ("serviteur du Dieu") Lexa

A prayer and an adjuration which I wrote, I, Gregory, the servant of the living God, so that it might be a |⁵ phylactery to all who will take it and read it, that it might undo every working that comes about through evil men, |¹⁰ that is sorceries and enchantments and *bindings of men through terrible sicknesses, and jealousy |¹⁵ and envy and idleness, that is not finding any work to do, and in general every [matter] that we know about |²⁰ and that we do not know about, and every thing [that] comes about through meddlesome men and cunning [men ...] |²⁵ evil.

I invoke you, O Lord God almighty, I, Gregory, [your]

---

p. 1 l.1–p. 14 l. 14. Prayer of Gregory: As first noted by Crum (1899), parallel versions of the *Prayer of Gregory* are attested in several Greek codices dating from at least the eleventh to sixteenth centuries CE, suggesting that this was its original language (Strittmatter 1930: 178; Strittmatter 1932: 141–144; Nesseris 2021: 93–94 with n. 12; Kropp 1931: II 169). This text belongs to a larger genre of exorcistic prayers attributed to saints which are common in Greek magical and liturgical handbooks; parallels exist in other languages, notably Syriac (see the discussion on p. 23). Other examples are attributed to figures such as John Chrysostom, Basil of Caesarea, Athanasius of Alexandria, and Ephraim the Syrian (Delatte 1927: 125, 230–263; Nesseris 2021: 91–97). Like the later Greek examples, the *Prayer of Gregory* makes extensive use of adjurations ("I adjure you..."), but only against negative external forces (demons, diseases, and evil acts), unlike many of the other magical texts in this collection, which also adjure God and his subordinate beings, such as the saints and the angels. The Gregory to whom the prayer is attributed is unclear; the versions published by Strittmatter (1932: 141–144) are attributed to Gregory Thaumaturgus (*ca.* 213–270 CE), while that first noted by Crum (Kropp 1931: II 169) is attributed to Gregory the Theologian, *i.e.*, Gregory of Nazianzus (*ca.* 329–390 CE).

24–25. N̄T[*ca.* 5 | M̄ΠΟΝΗΡΟC : "[...] evil" Boeser translates "depraved men" ("hommes dépravés"), Lexa "cowardly" ("lâches"), and Kropp "bad [men?]" ("böse [Menschen?]").

page 2 (1v) (→)

ⲁ
ϩⲙϩⲁⲗ : ⲁⲩⲱ ϯⲥⲟⲡⲥ ⲙ-
ⲙⲟⲕ ⲡⲉⲓⲱⲧ ⲙⲡⲉⲛⲭⲟⲉⲓⲥ
ⲓⲥ ⲡⲉⲭⲥ · ⲡⲛⲟⲩⲧⲉ ⲛⲉⲛ-
ⲛⲟⲩⲧⲉ ⲡⲣⲣⲟ ⲛⲣⲣⲱⲟⲩ ⲧⲏ-
5 ⲣⲟⲩ : ⲡⲁⲧⲧⲁⲕⲟ : ⲡⲁⲧⲧⲱ-
ⲗⲉⲙ · ⲡⲁⲧⲥⲟⲛⲧϥ : ⲡⲁⲧ-
ϭⲙϭⲱⲙⲉϥ : ⲡⲥⲟⲩ ⲛϩⲧⲟ-
ⲟⲩⲉ · ⲧϭⲓⲭ ⲉⲧⲁⲙⲁϩⲧⲉ ·
ⲁⲇⲱⲛⲁⲓ ⲉⲗⲱⲉⲓ ⲉⲗⲉⲙⲁⲥ
10 ⲥⲁⲃⲁⲱⲑ · ⲡⲛⲟⲩⲧⲉ ⲛⲉ- —
ⲛⲟⲩⲧⲉ ⲡⲣⲣⲟ ⲉⲧϭⲙϭⲱⲙ
ϩⲛ ϩⲱⲃ ⲛⲓⲙ · ⲡⲉⲧϩⲁ ⲉⲟ-
ⲟⲩ : ⲡⲉⲓⲱⲧ ⲛⲧⲙⲉ : ⲡⲉⲧⲉ-
ⲛⲁϣⲉ ⲛⲉϥⲙⲛⲧϣⲁⲛϩ-
15 ⲧⲏϥ · ⲡⲉⲧⲁⲣⲭⲉⲓ ⲙⲁⲩⲁⲁϥ
ⲉⲭⲛ ⲥⲁⲣⲝ ⲛⲓⲙ : ⲁⲩⲱ ⲉⲭⲛ
ⲉⲝⲟⲩⲥⲓⲁ ⲛⲓⲙ ⲡⲓⲱⲧ ⲙ-
[ⲡⲉ]ⲛϫⲟⲉⲓⲥ ⲓⲥ ⲡⲉⲭⲥ : ⲉⲕⲉ-
[ⲧⲁⲛ]ϩⲉ ⲟⲩⲟⲛ ⲛⲓⲙ ⲉⲧⲛⲁ-
20 [ⲧⲁⲟⲩⲟ] ⲛ̣ⲧ̣ⲓⲡⲣⲟⲥⲉⲩⲭⲏ : ⲏ
[ⲉⲧⲛⲁ]ⲕⲁⲁⲥ ⲛⲁϥ ⲙ̄ⲫⲩ-
[ⲗⲁⲕⲧⲏ]ⲣⲓⲟⲛ : ϯⲡⲁⲣⲁⲕⲁ-
[ⲗⲉⲓ ⲙⲙⲟ]ⲕ ⲡϫⲟⲉⲓⲥ ⲡⲛⲟⲩ-
[ⲧⲉ ⲡⲡⲁ]ⲛⲧⲱⲕⲣⲁⲧⲱⲣ
25 [ⲉⲕⲉϯ] ⲛⲟⲩⲟⲩϫⲁⲓ : ⲙⲛ
[ⲟⲩⲧⲁⲗϭ]ⲟ : ⲙⲛ ⲟⲩⲧⲃⲃⲟ
[ⲉⲡⲙⲁ ⲉ]ⲧⲟⲩⲛⲁⲕⲱ ⲧⲓ̈ⲡ-
[ⲣⲟⲥⲉⲩⲭ]ⲏ̣ ⲛϩⲏⲧϥ : ⲉⲓⲧⲉ

---

1 ⲛⲛ̄ⲁⲁ Pleyte/Boeser : *l.* ⲡϩⲙϩⲁⲗ ⲙⲡⲛⲟⲩⲧⲉ ⲉⲧⲟⲛϩ, "⟨the⟩ servant ⟨of the God almighty⟩" ("der Diener des allmächtigen Gottes") Kropp, Boeser, Smith ‖ **3** *l.* ⲓ(ⲏⲥⲟⲩ)ⲥ ⲡⲉ-χ(ριστό)ς : ⲓⲥ ⲡⲉⲭⲥ Pleyte/Boeser ‖ **10–11** ⲛⲉⲛⲛⲟⲩⲧⲉ Pleyte/Boeser ‖ **15** *i.e.* ἄρχειν | ⲙⲁⲩⲁⲁϥ · Pleyte/Boeser ‖ **16** *i.e.* σάρξ : ⲥⲁⲣⲝ Pleyte/Boeser ‖ **17** *i.e.* ἐξουσία ‖ **17–18** ⲡⲓⲱⲧ ⲙ[ⲡⲏⲩⲉ ⲡ]ϫⲟⲉⲓⲥ Pleyte/Boeser : "Father in the heavens" ("Père aux cieux") Boeser : "father of the heavens" (père des cieux) Lexa : "father of our Lord Jesus Christ" ("Vater unseres Herrn Jesu Christi") Kropp ‖ **18** [ⲡⲏⲩⲉ ⲡ]ϫⲟⲉⲓⲥ Pleyte/Boeser | *l.* ⲓ(ⲏⲥⲟⲩ)ⲥ ⲡⲉ-χ(ριστό)ς ‖ **20** *i.e.* προσευχή : ⲛϯⲡⲣⲟⲥⲉⲩⲭⲏ Pleyte/Boeser | *i.e.* ἤ ‖ **21** [ⲉⲧⲛⲁⲕ]ⲁⲁⲥ Pleyte/Boeser ‖ **21–22** *i.e.* φυ[λακτή]ριον : ⲫⲩ[ⲗⲁⲕⲧⲏⲣ]ⲓⲟⲛ Pleyte/Boeser ‖ **22–23** *i.e.* παρακα[λεῖν] ‖ **24** *i.e.* [πα]ντοκράτωρ ‖ **25** [ⲉⲕⲉϯ] : [. . . .] Pleyte/Boeser ‖ **26** [ⲟⲩⲧⲁⲗϭ]ⲟ : [. . .]ⲟ Pleyte/Boeser ‖ **27** [ⲉⲡⲙⲁ] : [. . .] Pleyte/Boeser : "the body" ("le corps") restores Lexa | ⲉⲧⲟⲩⲛⲁⲕⲱ Pleyte/Boeser | ⲧⲓ̈ⲡ- Pleyte/Boeser ‖ **27–28** *i.e.* [προσευχ]ή ‖ **28** *i.e.* εἴτε

servant, and I entreat you, O Father of our Lord Jesus Christ, god of gods, king of all kings, |⁵ the imperishable, unpolluted, uncreated, untouchable, the morningstar, the hand that rules, *Adonai *Eloei *Elemas |¹⁰ *Sabaoth, god of gods, the king who is mighty in every work, the glorious one, the father of truth, he whose mercies are many, |¹⁵ who rules alone over all flesh and over every *authority, the Father of [our] Lord Jesus Christ, may you preserve all who will |²⁰ [recite] this prayer or who will place it for themselves as a phylactery!

I invoke [you], O Lord God almighty |²⁵ [may you give] salvation and [healing] and purity [to the place in] which this [prayer] is placed, whether

---

7–8. ⲡⲥⲟⲩ ⲛϩⲧⲟⲟⲩⲉ : "**the morningstar**" Here a reference not to the Devil as the morningstar (cf. Isaiah 14.12), but rather Jesus' self-identification as such in Revelation 22.16.
8. ⲧϭⲓϫ ⲉⲧⲁⲙⲁϩⲧⲉ : "**the hand that rules**" Lexa translates "elusive hand" ("main insaisissable").

page 3 (2r) (→)

ϩⲟⲟⲩⲧ ⲉⲓⲧⲉ ⲥϩⲓⲙⲉ :
ⲛ̄ⲣⲙϩⲉ ⲙⲛ̄ ⲛⲉϩⲙϩⲁⲗ : ⲛⲉ-
ϣⲏⲣⲉ ⲕⲟⲩⲓ ⲙⲛ̄ ⲛⲉⲧϫⲓ ⲉ-
ⲕⲓⲃⲉ : ⲙⲛ̄ ⲛⲉⲕⲉⲧⲃ̄ⲛⲟⲟⲩⲉ
5 ⲧⲏⲣⲟⲩ : ⲉⲕⲉϩⲁⲣⲉϩ ⲉⲧⲉ-
ϩⲓⲏ ⲛⲓ ⲉϩⲟⲩⲛ : ⲙⲛ̄ ⲧⲉϩⲓⲏ
ⲛⲓ ⲉⲃⲟⲗ : ⲙⲛ̄ ⲛⲉϥⲙⲁ ⲛ̄ϣⲱ-
ⲡⲉ ⲧⲏⲣⲟⲩ : ⲙⲛ̄ ⲛⲉϥϣⲟⲩ-
ϣⲧ : ⲙⲛ̄ ⲛⲉϥⲁⲩⲗⲏ : ⲙⲛ̄
10 ⲛⲉϥⲕⲟⲓⲧⲱⲛ : ⲙⲛ̄ ⲛⲉϥ-
ⲙⲁ ⲉⲧϭⲟⲗⲉⲡ ⲉⲃⲟⲗ : ⲙⲛ̄
ⲛⲉϥⲭⲱⲣⲏⲙⲁ ⲉⲧⲏⲡ̄ ⲉ-
ⲣⲟϥ · ⲙⲛ̄ ⲛⲉϥⲥⲛ̄ⲧⲉ ⲙⲛ̄
ⲛⲉϥϣⲛ̄ⲏ : ⲙⲛ̄ ⲛⲉϥϣⲏⲓ
15 ⲙⲛ̄ ⲛⲉϥϣⲏⲛ ⲉⲧϯ ⲕⲁⲣ-
ⲡⲟⲥ : ⲙⲛ̄ ⲛⲉⲧⲉⲛⲥⲉϯ
ⲕⲁⲣⲡⲟⲥ ⲁⲛ : ϯⲡⲁⲣⲁⲕⲁ-
ⲗⲉⲓ ⲙ̄ⲙⲟⲕ ⲡⲛⲟⲩⲧⲉ ⲛⲉⲛ-
ⲛⲟⲩⲧⲉ ⲡ̄ⲣⲣⲟ ⲛⲉⲛϭⲟⲙ
20 ⲧⲏⲣⲟⲩ : ⲡⲉⲧϩ̄ⲙⲟⲟⲥ ⲉϩ-
ⲣⲁⲓ ⲉϫⲛ̄ ⲛⲉⲭⲉⲣⲟⲩⲃⲓⲛ ⲙ̣[ⲛ̄]
ⲛⲉⲥⲉⲣⲁⲫⲓⲛ ⲉⲧⲣⲉⲕⲱϣ[ⲗ]
ⲉⲃⲟⲗ ⲛ̄ϫⲓⲛϭⲟⲛⲥ ⲛⲓⲙ̣ [ⲉⲧ-]
ϣⲟⲟⲡ ⲟⲩϥⲏ ⁿⲙⲁ ⲛⲓ[ⲙ ⲉ-]
25 ⲧⲟⲩⲛⲁⲧⲁⲟⲩⲟ ⲛ̄ϩⲏ[ⲧϥ]
ⲛ̄ϯⲡⲣⲟⲥⲉⲩⲭⲏ : ⲏ [ⲉⲧ-]
ⲙ̄ⲡⲁⲧⲉϥϣⲱⲡⲉ : ⲏ ⲉ̣[ⲧ-]

---

1 *i.e.* ⲉⲓⲧⲉ || **9** *i.e.* αὐλή || **10** *i.e.* κοιτών || **12** *i.e.* χώρημα || **15–17** *i.e.* καρπός (twice) || **17–18** *i.e.* παρακαλεῖν || **21** *i.e.* χερουβίμ | [ⲙⲛ̄] Pleyte/Boeser || **22** *i.e.* σεραφίμ | ⲉⲧⲣⲉⲕⲕ[ⲱ] Pleyte/Boeser || **24** *i.e.* ˢⲟⲩⲃⲉ | ⲛ[ⲓⲙ] Pleyte/Boeser || **25** ⲛ̄ϩ[ⲏⲧϥ] Pleyte/Boeser || **26** *i.e.* προσευχή || **26, 28** *i.e.* ἤ

male or female, free and slave, the little children and those who are suckling, and also all livestock, |⁵ may you watch over the entrance and the exit and all its dwelling places and its windows and its courtyards and |¹⁰ its bedrooms and its open places and and its lands that belong to it and its foundations and its gardens and its wells |¹⁵ and its trees which bear fruit and its trees which do not bear fruit!

I invoke you, O god of gods, O king of all the powers, |²⁰ the one who sits upon the *cherubim and the *seraphim, that you undo every act of violence that has been done against every place |²⁵ in which this prayer will be recited, or that has yet to happen, or that

---

5–7. ⲕⲉϩⲁⲣⲉϩ ⲉⲧⲉϩⲓⲏ ⲛⲓ ⲉϩⲟⲩⲛ : ⲙⲛ̄ ⲧⲉϩⲓⲏ ⲛⲓ ⲉⲃⲟⲗ : **"may you watch over the entrance and the exit"** Compare Psalm 120 (121).8: "He (the Lord) will watch over your coming and going forever and ever" (ϥⲛⲁϩⲁⲣⲉϩ` ⲉⲧⲉⲕϭⲓⲛⲉⲓ ⲉϩⲟⲩⲛ ⲙⲛ̄ ⲧⲉⲕϭⲓⲛⲉⲓ ⲉⲃⲟⲗ ϣⲁ ⲉⲛⲉϩ ⲛ̄ⲉⲛⲉϩ; Budge 1898: 135); Anna Cherkashina is thanked for identifying this allusion.

10–13. ⲛⲉϥⲙⲁ ⲉⲧϭⲟⲗⲉⲡ ⲉⲃⲟⲗ : ⲙⲛ̄ ⲛⲉϥⲭⲱⲣⲏⲙⲁ ⲉⲧⲏⲡ ⲉⲣⲟϥ : **"its open places and and its lands that belong to it"** Boeser translates, "its fields and lands, with their surrounding areas" ("ses champs et ses terres, avec leurs dépendances"). Lexa translates "their visible and hidden places, their fields and gardens" ("leurs lieux visibles et leurs lieux cachés, leurs champs et leurs jardins").

23–24. ⲛ̄ϫⲓⲛϭⲟⲛⲥ ⲛⲓⲙ [ⲉⲧ]ϣⲟⲟⲡ ⲟⲩϥⲏ \ⲉ/ⲙⲁ ⲛⲓ[ⲙ] : **"every act of violence that has been done against every place"** Here and elsewhere, Boeser translates "malicious spirits, which are (hidden everywhere) in the place" ("esprit malins qui sont, (cachés partout) en l'endroit"). Lexa translates "violence that could arise at any location" ("violence qui pourrait naître à n'importe quel lieu"). The term "acts of violence" (ⲛ̄ϫⲓⲛϭⲟⲛⲥ) translates the Greek ἀδικήματα, and seems to refer broadly to any intentional evil carried out against the text's beneficiary (cf. Strittmatter 1932: 141.20 *et passim*).

page 4 (2v) (↓)

-: β̄ :-

ⲧⲏϣ ⲉϣⲱⲡⲉ : ⲏ̄ ⲉϣⲭⲉ
ⲁⲟⲩⲁ ⲙⲟⲩⲣ ⲛⲟⲩⲙⲁ : ⲉⲁϥ-
ⲕⲱ ⲛ̄ϩⲏⲧϥ̄ ⲛ̄ⲧⲙ̄ⲣⲣⲉ ⲙ̄-
ⲡⲉⲕⲣⲟϥ : ⲉϥϩⲏⲡ ϩⲛ̄ ⲛⲉϥ-
5 ⲥⲛ̄ⲧⲉ : ⲏ̄ ϩⲛ̄ ⲛⲉϥⲙⲁ ⲉⲧⲟⲩ-
ⲟⲟ̄ϩⲥ ⲉⲃⲟⲗ : ⲏ ϩⲛ̄ ⲧⲉϥϩⲓⲏ ⲛ̄-
ⲃⲱⲕ ⲉϩⲟⲩⲛ : ⲏ̄ ϩⲛ̄ ⲧⲉϥϩⲓⲏ
ⲛⲓ ⲉⲃⲟⲗ : ⲏ̄ ϩⲙ̄ ⲡⲣⲟ : ⲏ̄ ϩⲙ̄ ⲡ-
ϣⲟⲩⲁ̄ⲧ : ⲏ̄ ϩⲙ̄ ⲡⲙⲁ ⲛⲉⲛ-
10 ⲕⲟⲧⲕ : ⲏ̄ ϩⲙ̄ ⲡⲟϩⲉ : ⲏ̄ ϩⲙ̄
ⲡⲉⲧⲣⲓ̈ⲕⲗⲓ̈ⲛⲟⲛ · ⲏ̄ ϩⲛ̄ ⲧⲁⲩ-
ⲗⲏ ⲉⲧϩⲛ̄ ⲧⲙⲏⲧⲉ : ⲏ̄ ϩⲛ̄ ⲧ-
ⲥⲱϣⲉ : ⲏ̄ ϩⲛ̄ ⲛⲉⲕⲁⲣⲡⲟⲥ
ⲏ̄ ϩⲛ̄ ⲛ̄ⲕⲏⲡⲟⲥ : ⲏ̄ ϩⲛ̄ ⲟⲩϩⲉ
15 ⲉⲥⲟ ⲛⲥⲛ̄ⲧⲉ : ⲏ̄ ϣⲟⲙⲧⲉ
ⲛ̄ϩⲏ : ⲏ̄ ϩⲛ̄ ⲛ̄ϣⲏⲛ ⲛ̄ⲛⲁⲧ-
ⲕⲁⲣⲡⲟⲥ : ⲏ̄ ϩⲛ̄ ⲛⲉⲙⲟⲩⲛⲉⲓ-
ⲟⲟⲩⲉ ⲉⲧϩⲛ̄ ⲛⲉⲓ̈ⲉⲣⲱⲟⲩ :
ⲏ̄ ϩⲛ̄ ⲛ̄ϩⲟⲓ̈ : ⲏ ϩⲛ̄ ⲛ̄ϭⲟⲟⲙ : ⲏ̄
20 ϩⲛ̄ ⲧⲟⲡⲟⲥ ⲛⲓ̄ⲙ ⲛ̄ⲭⲓ̈ⲛϭⲟ-
[ⲛ]ⲥ : ⲟⲩⲟⲛ ⲛⲓⲙ ⲛ̄ⲧⲁⲩϣⲱ-
[ⲡ]ⲉ : ⲏ̄ ϩⲛⲉⲧⲧⲏϣ ⲉϣⲱⲡⲉ
[ϯⲧⲁ]ⲣⲕⲟ ⲙ̄ⲙⲱⲧⲛ̄ ⲁⲛⲟⲕ
[ⲅⲣⲏ]ⲅⲟⲣⲓ̄ⲟⲥ ⲡϩⲙ̄ϩⲁⲗ ⲛⲓ̄ⲥ̄
25 [ⲡⲉⲭ̄]ⲥ̄ · ⲡⲛⲟϭ ⲛ̄ⲣⲁⲛ ⲉⲧ-
[ϩⲁ ϩⲟ]ⲧⲉ : ⲁⲩⲱ ⲉⲧⲙⲉϩ ⲛ̄-
[ⲥ]ⲧⲱⲧ ϩⲓ ⲛⲉϩϣⲉⲗϥ̄ ⲡⲉⲧ-

5–22 *i.e.* ἤ ‖ 11 *i.e.* τρίκλινον/τρικλίνιον ‖ 11–12 *i.e.* αὐλή ‖ 13 *i.e.* καρπός ‖ 14 *i.e.* κῆπος ‖ 14–15 *i.e.* ˢⲟⲩ-ϩⲓⲏ ⲉ̳ⲥ-ⲟ *cf.* ϩⲛ for ϩⲓⲏ Kasser CDC 95a *cf.* note : *l.* ϩⲉⲃⲥⲱ *i.e.* ˢϩⲃⲥⲱ Boeser, Kropp, Lexa, Smith ‖ 15 ⲛⲥⲛ̄ⲧⲉ *i.e.* ἤ ⲥⲛⲧⲉ Pleyte/Boeser, Boeser, Kropp, Lexa, Smith ‖ 16 *i.e.* ˢⲛ̄-ϩⲓⲏ ? *cf.* note : *l.* ⲏ̄ ϩⲛ̄ ⟨ⲛϣⲏⲛ ⲛⲕⲁⲣⲡⲟⲥ⟩ Boeser, Kropp, Lexa, Smith ‖ 17 *i.e.* καρπός ‖ 20 *i.e.* τόπος ‖ 22 *i.e.* ˢϩⲛ̄ ⲛ-(ⲏⲥⲟⲩ)-ⲧⲏϣ (haplography) ? ‖ 24–25 *l.* ⲓ(ⲏⲥⲟⲩ)ⲥ ⲡⲉ-ⲭ(ⲣⲓⲥⲧⲟ́)ⲥ ‖ 26 [ϩⲁ ϩⲟ]ⲧⲉ *cf.* p. 8 ll. 4–5 ‖ [. . .]ⲧⲉ Pleyte/Boeser ‖ 27 . ⲧⲱⲧ Pleyte/Boeser, Boeser | *i.e.* ˢⲛ̄-ϣⲗϩϥ̄

is ordained to happen, or if someone *bound a place, having placed in it the bond of deceit, hidden in its |⁵ foundations, or in its extended places, or in its entrance or in its exit, or in the door, or in the window, or in the |¹⁰ bedroom or in the yard, or in the dining-room or in the courtyard in the middle of it, or in the field, or among the fruits, or in the garden, or at a |¹⁵ forked road or crossroad, or in a fruitless tree, or in the waters that are in the rivers or in the canals, or in vineyards, or |²⁰ in any place!

O acts of violence, every one that has happened, or that is among those ordained to happen, [I] adjure you, I, Gregory, the servant of Jesus |²⁵ Christ?, the great name that [is fearful] and that is filled with trembling and terror, that is

---

3–20. The "bond of deceit" and list of sites: The "bond of deceit" here seems to refer to a binding curse (Greek κατάδεσμος, "binding, bond") which has been buried either somewhere in the home of the victim, or in one of the common sites of deposition, in a body of water or a crossroad; not mentioned here, but present in one of the partial Greek parallels (Reitzenstein 294 n. 3, *cf.* note to ll. 14–16) is a grave, another common site for depositing curses. In the Classical Greek tradition which was transmitted to Egypt, curses were often written on lead tablets and folded before deposition, but in Egypt papyrus and other supports, such as ostraca, were also often used. For a discussion of depositing curses, *cf.* Gager 1992: 18–21, and *cf.* *Binding and Releasing in the glossary. In addition to the mediaeval Greek parallels, similar lists of potential means of cursing are found in Syriac Christian and mediaeval Jewish magic; for a Syriac example see Dickens/Smelova 2021: 120, 127–130; for Jewish magic, see T-S K 1.168, ll. 108–112, in Schiffmann/Swartz 1992: 143–159. In comments published in Dickens/Smelova 2021, Gideon Bohak compares such lists to those found in the "Spell-loosener of Hanina ben Dosa", a late antique Jewish Aramaic text which continued to be used into the 20th century, in which he sees a Judaised version of older Mesopotamian anti-witchcraft texts, such as the *Maqlû* ("burning") series, attested by the ninth century BCE. For the "spell-loosener", see Bohak 2019, and for similar lists in the *Maqlû*, see Abusch 2015: esp. tablet IV 10–73 (317–323), with discussions in Abusch 2011; Schwemer 2014: 274–276.

10. ⲡⲟϩⲉ : **"yard"** Respectively, Boeser, Lexa, and Kropp translate "stable" ("écurie", "Stall").

14–16. ⲟⲩϩⲉ ⲉⲥⲟ ⲛⲥⲛ̄ⲧⲉ : ϩ̄ ϣⲟⲙⲧⲉ ⲛϩⲏ : **"or in a forked road or crossroad"** Previous translators (Boeser, Kropp, Lexa, Pernigotti, Smith) have translated as "in two or three items of clothing", but there is no tradition of placing curses in items of clothing. The solution is provided by a partial Greek parallel in BnF Gr. 2316 (KYP M3784) fol. 435v l. 14, which gives ἐν διοδίᾳ ἢ ἐν τριοδίᾳ ("at a fork or crossroads"; Reitzenstein 294 n. 3), these terms literally referring to a place where three or four roads meet, a common place to leave curses in the Greek binding tradition and it successors. The putative ⲃ read by previous editors seems rather to be an ⲉ. Compare also the instructions to bury a curse at "a crossroads" (ⲟⲩϩⲓⲣ ⲉⲥ̄ϯ̄ⲟⲥ̄) in P.Vindob. K 880 (Stegemann 1933–1934: no. 3; KYP M239) l. 49. For the form, *cf.* ϩⲏ for ϩⲓⲏ Kasser CDC 95a.

16. ⲛ̄ϩⲏ : **"road"** We understand this as part of the preceding clause (ϣⲟⲙⲧⲉ ⲛ̄ϩⲏ). Previous translators have read ϩ̄ ϩⲛ with Boeser, and restored ⲛϣⲏⲛ ⲛⲕⲁⲣⲡⲟⲥ afterwards, *i.e.* "fruit trees", assuming that the scribe forgot to copy the clause. The traces do not seem to fit this, however, and the text already includes "fruits and gardens/orchards" (ϩ̄ ϩⲛ̄ ⲛⲉⲕⲁⲣⲡⲟⲥ ϩ̄ ϩⲛ̄ ⲛⲕⲏⲡⲟⲥ) in ll. 13–14.

19. ϩⲛ ⲛ̄ϩⲟⲓ : ⲏ ϩⲛ ⲛ̄ϭⲟⲟⲙ : **"or in the canals, or in vineyards"** Kropp and Lexa translate "in the fields or in the gardens ("dans les champs ou dans les jardins", "in den Wiesen oder in den Gärten"). Boeser translates "or in the terrains" ("soit dans les terrains").

page 5 (3r) (↓)

ϩⲁ ⲉⲟⲟⲩ : ⲁⲩⲱ ⲡⲉⲧⲧⲁ-
ⲓⲏⲩ ⲛ̄ϭⲟⲩ ⲡⲣⲟⲥⲕⲩⲛⲉⲓ̈
ⲛⲁϥ : ⲡⲁⲧⲧⲁⲅⲟϥ : ⲡⲁⲧⲭⲟ-
ⲟⲛϥ̄ : ⲡⲣⲁⲛ ⲉⲧⲟⲩⲁⲁⲃ : ⲁⲩ-
5 ⲱ ⲉⲧⲥ̄ⲙⲁⲙⲁⲁⲧ : ⲁⲇⲱⲛⲁⲓ̄
ⲉⲗⲱⲉⲓ̄ : ⲉⲗⲉⲙⲁ̄ⲥ · ⲥⲁⲃⲁⲱ̄ⲑ
ϫⲉⲕⲁⲥ ⲉⲧⲉⲧⲛⲉⲃⲱⲗ ⲉ-
ⲃⲟⲗ : ⲛ̄ⲧⲉⲧⲛ̄ⲁⲛⲁⲭⲱⲣⲏ
ⲛ̄ⲥⲁⲃⲟⲗ ⲛⲟⲩⲟⲛ ⲛⲓ̈ⲙ ⲉⲧⲟⲩ-
10 ⲛⲁⲧⲁⲟⲩⲟ ⲛ̄ϩⲏⲧϥ̄ ⲛ̄ⲧⲉⲓ̈ⲡ-
ⲣⲟⲥⲉⲩⲭⲏ : ⲏ̄ ⲙⲁ ⲛⲓ̈ⲙ ⲉⲧⲟⲩⲛⲁⲕⲁⲁⲥ ⲛ̄ϩⲏⲧϥ ⲙⲛ̄ ⲛⲉ-
ⲧⲏⲡ ᵉⲣⲟϥ ⲧⲏⲣⲟⲩ · ⲁⲩⲱ ⲛ-
ⲧⲉⲧⲛ̄ⲃⲱⲕ ⲡⲟⲩⲁ ⲡⲟⲩⲁ
15 ⲙ̄ⲙⲱⲧⲛ̄ ⲉϫⲛ̄ ⲧⲁⲡⲉ ⲙ̄-
ⲡⲉⲛⲧⲁϥⲧ̄ⲛⲉⲩⲧⲏⲩⲧⲛ̄
ⲉⲉⲓⲣⲉ ⲛ̄ⲛⲉⲓ̄ⲃⲟⲧⲉ : ⲁⲩⲱ ⲉ-
ϫⲛ̄ ⲧⲁⲡⲉ ⲛ̄ⲛⲉⲧⲥⲩⲛⲉⲩ-
ⲇⲟⲕⲉⲓ̄ ⲛⲙ̄ⲙⲁⲩ : ⲉⲓⲧⲉ ⲟⲩ-
20 ϣ̄ⲙⲙⲟ ⲡⲉ : ⲉⲓ̄ⲧⲉ ⲟⲩⲁ ⲡⲉ
ⲛ̄ⲛⲉⲧⲏⲡ ⲉⲣⲟϥ : ⲉⲓ̄ⲧⲉ ⲟⲩⲁ
ⲡⲉ ⲉϥⲡⲁⲣⲁⲕⲉ : ⲉⲓ̄ⲧⲉ ⲟⲩ-
ϩⲙ̄ϩⲁⲗ ⲡⲉ : ⲏ ⲟⲩⲣⲙ̄ϩⲉ
ⲡⲉ : ⲏ̄ ⲟⲩⲙⲁⲅⲟⲥ ⲡⲉ : ⲏ̄ ⲟⲩ-
25 ⲙⲁⲅⲟⲥ ⲛ̄ⲥ̄ϩⲓ̄ⲙⲉ ⲧⲉ : ⲏ̄ ⲟⲩⲡⲉⲣⲥⲟⲥ ⲛ̄ϩⲟⲟⲩⲧ ⲡⲉ :
ⲏ̄ ⲟⲩⲡⲉⲣⲥⲟⲥ ⲛ̄ⲥ̄ϩⲓ̄ⲙⲉ ⲧⲉ :

---

2 *i.e.* προσκυνεῖν ‖ **3–4** *i.e.* ˢⲁⲧ-ϫⲱ ? Boeser : *i.e.* ˢⲁⲧϫⲱⲛϥ Smith : "not succumbing to chance" ("ne succombant au hasard") Lexa : "unreachable" ("unerreichbar") Kropp ‖ **8** *i.e.* ἀναχωρεῖν ‖ **10–11** *i.e.* προσευχή ‖ **11** *i.e.* ἤ ‖ **18–19** *i.e.* συνευδοκεῖν ‖ **19–22** *i.e.* εἴτε ‖ **20–22** ⲉⲓ̄ⲧⲉ ⲟⲩⲁⲡⲉ ⲛ̄ⲛⲉⲧⲏⲡ ⲉⲣⲟϥ : ⲉⲓ̄ⲧⲉ ⲟⲩⲁⲡⲉ ⲉϥⲡⲁⲣⲁⲕⲉ Pleyte/Boeser: "whether the person is … a boss of those belonging to him, or is one who leads" Smith : "whether it be the head of those who belong to him, or the head of one who dwells beside him" ("sei es ein Haupt der zu ihm Gehörigen, sei es das Haupt eines, der daneben wohnt") Kropp ‖ **22** *i.e.* παράγειν : *i.e.* παροικεῖν or παράγειν Kropp ‖ **23–27** *i.e.* ἤ ‖ **25** *i.e.* μάγος ‖ **26–27** *i.e.* Πέρσης

glorious, and the honoured one, worthy of prostration, the indescribable one, the ..., the name that is holy and |⁵ blessed, *Adonai *Eloei *Elemas *Sabaoth, that you release and you withdraw from everyone who |¹⁰ will recite in themselves this prayer, and every place in which it will be put, and all those belonging to it, and that you go, each one |¹⁵ of you, upon the head of the one who sent you to do these abominations, and upon the head of the ones who consented to them, whether it is a |²⁰ foreigner, or it is someone who is related to him, or a it is someone who is passing by, or a slave, or a free person, or it is a magician, or a |²⁵ female magician, or a Persian man, or a Persian woman,

---

3–4. ⲁⲧϫⲟⲟⲛϥ : " ... " The meaning of this word is unclear; Boeser suggested either reading ⲁⲧϫⲱ ("ineffable"), or the (unattested) ⲁⲧϫⲱⲛϥ (cf. Crum CD 776b–777a), which he translates as "inaccessible" ("inabordable"), followed by Kropp as "unreachable" ("unerreichbar"), and Smith as "unencounterable". One of the Greek parallel texts has ἀχράντου in this place (Strittmatter 1932: 142 n. ll. 1–2), so it is possible that this is an error for ⲁⲧϫⲱϩⲙ ("undefiled"), its Coptic equivalent (cf. Crum CD 798b).

8–12. ⲛ̄ⲧⲉⲧⲛ̄ⲁⲛⲁⲭⲱⲣⲏ ⲛ̄ⲥⲁⲃⲟⲗ ⲛⲟⲩⲟⲛ ⲛⲓⲙ ⲉⲧⲟⲩⲛⲁⲧⲁⲟⲩⲟ ⲛ̄ϩⲏⲧϥ̄ ⲛ̄ⲧⲉⲓ̈ⲡⲣⲟⲥⲉⲩⲭⲏ : ⲏ̄ ⲙⲁ ⲛⲓⲙ ⲉⲧⲟⲩⲛⲁⲕⲁⲁⲥ ⲛ̄ϩⲏⲧϥ̄ : "and you withdraw from everyone who will recite in themselves this prayer, and every place in which it will be put" Smith translates "withdraw from every one near whom this prayer shall be recited". Kropp translates "from every 'place' where this prayer is said, or from every prayer, or from any place where it is laid down" ("zurückweichet von einem jeden 'Orte' an dem man dieses Gebet aussprechen wird, oder von einem jeden Orte, an dem man es niederlegt").

p. 5 l. 17–p. 6 l. 7. List of Potential Culprits: A list of all potential enemies who might have harmed the beneficiary of the ritual through magic, the evil eye, or some other means, expressed in terms of relationship to the beneficiary (foreigner/relation/passer-by), social status (enslaved/free person), socio-ethnic identity (magician, Persian, Chaldaean, Hebrew, Egyptian), and gender (male/female). Our translation of the initial lines, which posed problems for previous translators (see apparatus) is confirmed by the Greek versions gathered in Strittmatter 1932 (142.4–8); these later lists give different socio-ethnic options—magician, Persian, Syrian, Egyptian, Anatolian, Hebrew, Indian, French, and African (μάγος/μάγισσα, Πέρσης/Πέρσισσα, Σύρος/Σύραινα Αἰγύπτιος/Αἰγυπτία, Ἀσιανός/Ἀσιανή, Ἑβραῖος/Ἑβραία, Ἰνδός, Γάλλος, Ἀφρός/Ἀφρά)—demonstrating the tendency of such lists to expand according to the horizons of the redactor. Similar lists of ethnic identities appear in other Christian amuletic texts, with many of the most striking examples in Ge'ez: "undo the spells of Arabs and of Romans... of Jews and Ethiopians... of Muslims and Christians... of foreign Muslims and Europeans..." (Streclyn 1955: 119, cf. pp. xix–xx, 13, 37, 55, 119 etc.). Similar lists of potential enemies can be found in older Egyptian ritual texts, such as the execration texts listing national enemies (e.g., Fischer-Elfert 2005: 60, cf. the discussion of lists in amulets on pp. 22–23), and in the amulet P.Berol. 3027 ro col. 2 ll. 6–10, against a female enemy who may be a Levantine (ꜥꜣm.t), Nubian (nḥsy.t), slave (ḥm.t), or noble (šps.t; Borghouts 1978: no. 66; XVIII Dynasty). Similar lists also appear in the Mesopotamian anti-witchcraft *Maqlû* ("burning") series (cf. note to p. 4 ll. 3–20); see Abusch 2015: tablet IV 80–92 (324), which likewise lists possible adversaries in terms of relationship to the beneficiary, ethnic identity, and profession. For the listing of both genders of each ethnic group, cf. the note to *PCM* I 12 p. 37 ll. 18–20.

page 6 (3v) (→)

-: ̄г ̄ :-

ⲏ ⲟⲩⲭⲁⲗⲇⲁⲓⲟⲥ ⲡⲉ : ⲏ ⲟⲩ-
ⲭⲁⲗⲇⲁⲓⲟⲥ ⲛ̄ⲥϩⲓⲙⲉ : ⲏ ⲟⲩ-
ϩⲉⲃⲣⲁⲓⲟⲥ ⲡⲉ : ⲏ ⲟⲩϩⲉⲃⲣⲁⲓ-
ⲟⲥ ⲛ̄ⲥϩⲓⲙⲉ ⲡⲉ : ⲏ ⲟⲩⲣ̄ⲙ-
5 ⲛ̄ⲕⲏⲙⲉ ⲡⲉ : ⲏ ⲟⲩⲣ̄ⲙⲛ̄ⲕⲏ-
ⲙⲉ ⲛ̄ⲥϩⲓⲙⲉ ϩⲁⲡⲁⲝ ϩⲁⲡ-
ⲗⲱⲥ ⲡⲉⲧⲉⲛⲧⲟϥ ⲡⲉ ⲙⲁ-
ⲣⲉⲭⲓⲛⲅⲟⲛⲥ̄ ⲛⲓⲙ ⲃⲱⲗ ⲉ-
ⲃⲟⲗ ϩⲓⲧⲛ̄ ⲡⲓⲉⲝⲟⲣⲅⲓⲥⲙⲟⲥ
10 ⲁⲩⲱ ϩⲓⲧⲛ̄ ⲧⲉⲥⲫⲣⲁⲅⲓⲥ ⲉ-
ⲧⲟⲩⲁⲁⲃ ⲙ̄ⲡⲉⲧⲛⲏⲩ ⲉⲕ-
ⲣⲓⲛⲉ ⲛ̄ⲛⲉⲧⲟⲛϩ̄ ⲙⲛ̄ ⲛⲉⲧ-
ⲙⲟⲟⲩⲧ : ⲉⲧⲉ ⲡⲁⲓ̈ ⲡⲉ
ⲡⲣ̄ⲣⲟ : ⲁⲩⲱ ⲡⲛⲟⲩⲧⲉ
15 ⲛ̄ⲧⲁⲩⲥ̄ⲣ̄ⲟⲩ ⲙ̄ⲙⲟϥ ϩⲁ-
ⲣⲟⲛ : ⲙⲓⲭⲁⲏⲗ : ⲅⲁⲃⲣⲓⲏⲗ
ϩ̄ⲣⲁⲫⲁⲏⲗ ⲟⲩⲣⲓ̈ⲏⲗ ⲛⲁⲅ-
ⲅⲉⲗⲟⲥ ⲉⲧⲟⲩⲁⲁⲃ ⲉⲧⲁ̄ϩⲉ-
ⲣⲁⲧⲟⲩ ⲙ̄ⲡⲉⲙⲧⲟ ⲉⲃⲟⲗ
20 ⲙ̄ⲡⲉⲧⲟⲩⲏϩ ϩⲛ̄ ⲛⲉⲙ-
ⲡⲏⲩⲉ : ⲡⲡⲉⲧⲟⲩⲁⲁⲃ
ⲁⲩⲱ ⲡⲉⲧϫⲟⲥⲉ : ϩⲁⲣⲉϩ
ⲉⲙⲙⲉⲗⲟⲥ ⲧⲏⲣⲟⲩ ⲛ̄ⲛⲉ-
ⲧⲉⲟⲩⲉⲛⲧⲁⲩ ⲙ̄ⲙⲁⲩ
25 ⲛ̄ⲧⲉⲓⲡⲣⲟⲥⲉⲩⲭⲏ ⲛⲉⲧ-
ⲧⲁⲟⲩⲟ ⲙ̄ⲙⲟⲥ ⲁⲛ ⲙ̄ⲙⲁ-
ⲧⲉ : ⲁⲗⲗⲁ ⲛⲉⲧⲉⲥⲉⲛⲧⲟ-

1–5 *i.e.* ἤ || 1–2 *i.e.* Χαλδαῖος || 3–4 *i.e.* Ἑβραῖος || 4 *l.* ⲧⲉ || 6–7 *i.e.* ἅπαξ ἁπλῶς || 9 *i.e.* ἐξορκισμός || 10 *i.e.* σφραγίς || 15 *i.e.* στ(αυρ)οῦν || 17–18 *i.e.* ἄγγελος || 23 *i.e.* μέλος || 25 *i.e.* προσευχή || 27 *i.e.* ἀλλά

or a Chaldaean, or a Chaldaean woman, or a Hebrew, or a Hebrew woman, or an |⁵ Egyptian, or an Egyptian woman, and in short whoever it is!

Let all violence be undone through this adjuration |¹⁰ and through the holy seal of the one who is coming to judge the living and the dead, who is King and God, |¹⁵ who was crucified for us!

*Michael, *Gabriel, *Raphael, Uriel, O holy *angels standing before |²⁰ the one who dwells in the heavens, the holy and exalted one, guard all the body parts of the ones who possess |²⁵ this prayer, not only those who recite it, but those who

---

11–13. ⲘⲠⲈⲦⲚⲎⲨ ⲈⲔⲢⲒⲚⲈ ⲚⲚⲈⲦⲞⲚϨ ⲘⲚ ⲚⲈⲦⲘⲞⲞⲨⲦ : "the one who is coming to judge the living and the dead" *Cf.* e.g., 2 Timothy 4.1 "Christ Jesus the one who will judge the living and the dead" (ⲠⲈⲬⲤ ⲒⲤ ⲠⲀⲒ ⲈⲦⲚⲀⲔⲢⲒⲚⲈ ⲚⲚⲈⲦⲞⲚϨ ⲘⲚⲚⲈⲦⲘⲞⲞⲨⲦ; Thompson 1932: 243).

page 7 (4r) (→)

ΟΤΟΥ ΟΝ ⲘⲪⲨⲖⲀⲔⲦⲎⲢⲒ-
ΟΝ ⲚⲦⲞⲨⲬⲞⲞⲨ ⲈⲈⲰⲂ
ⲚⲒⲘ ⲘⲠⲞⲚⲎⲢⲞⲤ · ⲀⲨⲰ
ⲈⲠⲈⲐⲞⲞⲨ ⲚⲒⲘ : ⲠⲀⲖⲒⲚ Ⲟ̄
5 ϮⲦⲀⲢⲔⲞ ⲘⲘⲰⲦⲚ ⲚϪⲒⲚ-
ϬⲞⲚⲤ ⲚⲒⲘ ⲘⲠⲚⲞϬ ⲚⲢⲀⲚ
ⲈⲦϨⲀ ⲈⲞⲞⲨ ⲠⲚⲞⲨⲦⲈ · Π-
ⲠⲀⲚⲦⲰⲔⲢⲀⲦⲰⲢ : ⲠⲈⲚ-
ⲦⲀϤⲈⲚ ⲠⲈϤⲖⲀⲞⲤ ⲈⲂⲞⲖ
10 ϨⲘ ⲠⲔⲀϨ ⲚⲔⲎⲘⲈ ϨⲚ ⲞⲨ-
ϬⲒϪ ⲈⲤϪⲞⲞⲢ ⲘⲚ ⲞⲨϬⲂⲞⲒ
ⲈϤϪⲞⲤⲈ : ⲠⲈⲚⲦⲀϤⲠⲀ-
ⲦⲀⲤⲤⲈ ⲘⲪⲀⲢⲀⲰ ⲘⲚ ⲦϤ-
ϬⲞⲘ ⲦⲎⲢⲤ : ⲠⲈⲚⲦⲀϤ-
15 ϢⲀϪⲈ ⲘⲚ ⲘⲰⲨⲤⲎⲤ ϨⲘ
ⲠⲦⲞⲞⲨ ⲚⲤⲒⲚⲀ : ⲈⲀϤϮ
ⲘⲠⲈϤⲚⲞⲘⲞⲤ ⲘⲚ ⲚⲈϤ-
ⲠⲢⲞⲤⲦⲀⲄⲘⲀ ⲚⲈⲚϢⲎ-
ⲢⲈ ⲘⲠⲒⲎⲖ : ⲀⲨⲰ ⲀϤⲦⲢⲈϤ-
20 ⲞⲨⲰⲘ ⲘⲠⲘⲀⲚⲚⲀ : ϪⲈ-
ⲔⲀⲤ ⲈⲦⲈⲦⲚⲈⲠⲰⲦ Ⲉ-
ⲠⲞⲨⲈ ⲚⲦⲈⲦⲚⲦⲘⲞⲨⲰϨ
ⲈⲦⲞⲞⲦⲦⲎⲨⲦⲚ ⲈⲀϨⲈ-
ⲢⲀⲦⲦⲎⲨⲦⲚ ϨⲞⲖⲰⲤ :
25 ϨⲘ ⲠⲘⲀ ⲈⲦⲞⲨⲚⲀⲔⲀ
ⲦⲈⲒⲠⲢⲞⲤⲈⲨⲬⲎ ⲚϨⲎⲦϤ
ⲀⲒⲦⲒ ΟΝ : ⲀⲚⲞⲔ ⲄⲢⲎⲄⲞⲢⲒⲞⲤ

---

p. 6 l. 27–p. 7 l. 1 ⲚⲈⲦⲈⲤⲈⲚⲦⲞⲞⲦⲞⲨ : *l.* ⲚⲈⲦⲈⲚⲦⲞⲞⲨ ⲈϨⲢⲀⲒ ϨⲒϪⲰⲤ Boeser || **1–2** *i.e.* φυλακτήριον || **3** *i.e.* πονηρός || **4** *i.e.* πάλιν | *l.* ο(ν) : ον Pleyte/Boeser || **8** *i.e.* παντοκράτωρ || **9** *i.e.* λαός || **12–13** *i.e.* πατάσσειν || **13** *i.e.* Φαραώ || **17** *i.e.* νόμος || **19** *l.* ι(σρα)ηλ || **18** *i.e.* πρόσταγμα || **20** *i.e.* μάννα || **22–23** ⲚⲦⲈⲦⲚⲦⲘⲞⲨⲰϨ ⲈⲦⲞⲞⲦⲦⲎⲨⲦⲚ for the sense of ⲞⲨⲰϨ ⲈⲦⲞⲞⲦ⸗ as "to repeat", *cf.* Crum CD 506 || **24** *i.e.* ὅλως || **26** *i.e.* προσευχή || **27** *i.e.* ἔτι : ⲀⲒⲦⲒⲞⲚ *i.e.* αἴτιον Pleyte/Boeser, Smith.

have it in their hand as a phylactery, and save them again from every evil thing and every evil!

Again, |⁵ I adjure you, every act of violence, by the great name that is glorious, God Almighty—the one who brought his people out from |¹⁰ the land of Egypt with a strong hand and an exalted arm, the one who struck Pharaoh and all his power, the one who |¹⁵ spoke with Moses on the mountain of Sinai as he gave his law and his ordinance to the children of Israel, and he caused him to |²⁰ eat manna—that you flee far away, and you do not return at all to stand |²⁵ in the place in which is placed this prayer!

Yet again, I, Gregory,

10–12. ⲟⲩϭⲓϫ ⲉⲥϫⲟⲟⲣ ⲙ̄ⲛ ⲟⲩϭⲃⲟⲓ̈ ⲉϥϫⲟⲥⲉ : **"a strong hand and an exalted arm"** These are recurrent phrases in the Hebrew Bible; *cf.* Exodus 13.16 "For with a strong hand the Lord brought you out of the land of Egypt" (ϩⲣⲁⲓ ϩⲛ̄ ⲟⲩϭⲓϫ ⲉⲥϫⲟⲟⲣ ⲁⲡϫⲟⲉⲓⲥ ⲛ̄ⲧⲛ̄ ⲉⲃⲟⲗ ϩⲙ̄ ⲡⲕⲁϩ ⲛ̄ⲕⲏⲙⲉ; Kasser 1961: 164); Exodus 32.11 "you brought them (*i.e.*, the Israelites) out of the land of Egypt with your great power and your exalted arm" (ⲛ̄ⲧⲁⲕⲛ̄ⲧⲟⲩ ⲉⲃⲟⲗ ϩⲙ̄ ⲡⲕⲁϩ ⲛ̄ⲕⲏⲙⲉ ⲉϩⲣⲁⲓ ϩⲛ̄ ⲧⲉⲕⲛⲟϭ ⲛ̄ϭⲟⲙ ⲙⲛ̄ ⲡⲉⲕϭⲃⲟⲓ ⲉⲧϫⲟⲥⲉ; Maspero 1892: 46).

page 8 (4v) (↓)

-:ⲁ̄̇:-

ⲡⲣⲙϩⲁⲗ ⲙ̄ⲡⲛⲟⲩⲧⲉ ⲉⲧⲟ-
ⲛϩ̄ : †ⲡⲁⲣⲁⲕⲁⲗⲉⲓ̈ ⲙ̄ⲙⲱ-
ⲧⲛ̄ ⲛ̄ⲧⲱⲧⲛ̄ ⲛ̄ϫⲓⲛϭⲟⲛⲥ
ⲛⲓ̈ⲙ : ⲙ̄ⲡⲛⲟϭ ⲛ̄ⲣⲁⲛ ⲉⲧϩⲁ
5 ϩⲟⲧⲉ ⲙ̄ⲡⲉⲓ̈ⲱⲧ ⲙ̄ⲡⲉⲛ-
ϫⲟⲉⲓ̄ⲥ ⲓ̄ⲥ ⲡⲉⲭ̄ⲥ̄ · ⲡⲛⲟⲩⲧⲉ
ⲛⲁⲃⲣⲁϩⲁⲙ ⲙ̄ⲛ̄ ⲓ̈ⲥⲁⲕ ⲙ̄ⲛ̄
ⲓ̈ⲁⲕⲱⲃ ⲛ̄ⲑⲉ ⲉⲧⲉⲧⲛ̄ⲟ ⲙ-
ⲙⲟⲥ ϩⲓ̈ ⲟⲩⲥⲟⲡ : ⲕⲁⲛ ⲟⲩ-
10 ⲙ̄ⲛ̄ⲧⲙⲁⲅⲟⲥ ⲧⲉ : ⲏ̄ ϩⲉⲛ-
ⲉⲓ̄ⲇⲱⲗⲟⲛ : ⲏ̄ ϩⲙ̄ ⲙⲁ ⲛϣ̄ⲙ-
ϣⲉ ⲛⲉ ⲛ̄ ϩⲙ̄ ⲙⲁ ⲛⲓⲙ ⲛ̄ⲧⲁⲩ-
ⲧⲛⲉⲩⲧⲏⲩⲧ̄ⲛ̄ ⲛ̄ϩⲏⲧⲟⲩ
ⲉⲧⲣⲉⲧⲉⲧ̄ⲛ̄ⲉⲓⲣⲉ ⲛ̄ϩⲉⲛ-
15 ⲙ̄ⲛ̄ⲧⲛⲉϩϣ̄ⲗϥ : ⲙ̄ⲛ̄ ϩⲉⲛ-
ⲙ̄ⲛ̄ⲧⲣⲉϥϩⲓ̄ⲧⲉ ⲙ̄ⲛ̄ ϩⲉⲛ-
ⲙ̄ⲛ̄ⲧⲉⲙⲡⲟ : ⲁⲩⲱ ⲛⲁⲗ :-
ⲙ̄ⲛ̄ ϩⲉⲛⲙ̄ⲛ̄ⲧⲁⲧϣⲁϫⲉ :
ⲙ̄ⲛ̄ ϩⲉⲛⲙ̄ⲛ̄ⲧϭⲁⲓ̈ⲉ ϩⲣⲁϥ
20 ⲙ̄ⲛ̄ ϩⲉⲛⲧⲕⲁⲥ ⲙ̄ⲙⲓ̈ⲛⲉ
ⲛⲓⲙ ⲕⲁⲛ ⲉⲧⲉⲧⲛ̄ϩⲏⲛ ⲉ-
ϩⲟⲩⲛ : ⲕⲁⲛ ⲉⲧⲉⲧ̄ⲛ̄ⲟⲩ-
ⲏⲩ ⲉⲃⲟⲗ ⲁⲣⲓ̄ ϩⲟⲧⲉ ⲉϩⲣⲏⲧ̄ϥ̄
ⲙ̄ⲡⲣⲁⲛ ⲙ̄ⲡϫⲟⲉⲓ̈ⲥ : ⲛ̄ⲧⲉ-
25 ⲧ̄ⲛ̄ⲁⲛⲁⲭⲱⲣⲉⲓ̈ ⲛⲏⲧⲛ̄ ⲥⲁⲃⲟⲗ ⲙ̄ⲙⲁ ⲛⲓⲙ ⲉⲧⲟⲩⲛⲁ-
ϣ ⲛ̄ⲧⲉⲓ̈ⲡⲣⲟⲥⲉⲩⲭⲏ

---

2 *i.e.* παρακαλεῖν || **4** ⲛ̄ⲣⲁⲛ Pleyte/Boeser || **6** *l.* ι(ηϲου)ϲ πε-χ(ριϲτο)ϲ || **9** *i.e.* κἄν | ⲕⲁ ⲛⲟⲩ- Pleyte/Boeser | *i.e.* μάγος || **10–11** *i.e.* ἤ || **11** *i.e.* εἴδωλον || **12** ⲛ̄ *l.* ⲏ̄ *i.e.* ἤ || **21–22** *l.* ⲉϩⲟⲩⲛ (dittography) || **22** *i.e.* κἄν || **25** *i.e.* ἀναχωρεῖν || **27** *i.e.* προσευχή

the servant of the living God, I invoke you, you, every act of violence, by the great name that |⁵ is fearful of the Father of our Lord, Jesus Christ, the god of Abraham and Isaac and Jacob, just as you acted together, whether |¹⁰ it was magic, or idols, or from places of worship, or any place you were sent from to cause |¹⁵ terror and torments and dumbness and deafness and speechlessness and disgrace of his face? |²⁰ and all types of pain, whether you have come near or are far away, be afraid before the name of the Lord, |²⁵ and withdraw yourselves from every place in which this prayer will be read

---

8–9. ⲛ̄ⲑⲉ ⲉⲧⲉⲧⲛ̄ⲟ ⲙ̄ⲙⲟⲥ ϩⲓ ⲟⲩⲥⲟⲡ : **"just as you acted together"** Smith translates "all at once." Kropp translates "according to what you all are" ("gemäss dessen, was ihr allzumal seid"). For our translation, *cf.* Crum CD 350a.

10. ⲙ̄ⲛ̄ⲧⲙⲁⲅⲟⲥ : **"a magic"** Boeser translates "magic objects" ("objets magiques").

12–13. ⲛ̄ⲧⲁⲩⲧⲛⲉⲩⲧⲏⲩⲧⲛ̄ ⲛ̄ϩⲏⲧⲟⲩ : **"you were sent from"** Smith translates "to which you have been sent" Smith but *cf.* Crum CD 420a.

19. ϩⲉⲛⲙ̄ⲛ̄ⲧⲥⲁⲓⲉ ⲉⲡⲣⲁϥ : **"disgrace of his face"** We are unable to find a parallel for this phrase; the literal translation is "disgrace/ugliness of his face/voice" (ⲉⲡⲣⲁ= from either ϩⲟ or ϩⲣⲟⲟⲩ), and in the past the phrase has been translated by Boeser as "deformity of the face" ("la difformité de face"), by Smith as "disgrace", by Kropp as "ugliness of the speech ("Hässlichkeit der Sprache"), and by Lexa as "paralysis of the face" ("la paralysie de face"). The phrase probably refers to something specific. We might understand a concept inversely related to that of the "favour of the face" (ⲡⲭⲁⲣⲓⲥ ⲙ̄ⲡϩⲟ), the quality that makes one socially popular and successful; in this case, this would be a reference to a curse to make someone hated, for examples of which see *PCM I 22* ll. 27–50; *PCM I 27*; *P.Bad. V 123* (KYP M315) front ll. 52–84; and *cf.* Dosoo 2018: 21; Dosoo 2023a: 174–176. See also Preininger forthcoming c: chapter 2.

page 9 (5r) (↓)

ⲛ̄ϩⲏⲧϥ̄ · ⲏ ⲛ̄ⲥⲉⲕⲁⲥ ⲛ̄-
ϩⲏⲧϥ̄ : ⲙ̄ⲛ ⲛⲉⲧⲏⲡ ⲉⲣⲟ-
ⲟⲩ ⲧⲏⲣⲟⲩ : ⲛ̄ⲧⲉⲧⲛ̄ⲃⲱⲕ
ⲡⲟⲩⲁ ⲡⲟⲩⲁ ⲉϫⲛ̄ ⲧⲁⲡⲉ
5   ⲛⲟⲩⲛ ⲛⲓⲙ ⲛ̄ⲧⲁϥⲉⲓⲛⲉ
ⲙ̄ⲙⲱⲧⲛ̄ ⲏ ⲡⲉⲛⲧⲁϥⲧⲉ-
ⲛⲉⲩⲧⲏⲩⲧⲛ̄ : ⲛ̄ⲧⲟⲟⲩ
ⲙⲛ̄ ⲛⲉⲧⲥⲩⲛⲉⲩⲇⲟⲕⲉⲓ
ⲛⲙ̄ⲙⲁⲩ : ⲡⲛⲟⲩⲧⲉ ⲡⲉ
10 ϯⲣⲏⲛⲏ : ⲡⲛⲟⲩⲧⲉ ⲡⲉ ⲡ-
ⲧⲁⲗϭⲟ : ⲡⲛⲟⲩⲧⲉ ⲡⲉ ⲧ-
ⲇⲓⲕⲁⲓⲟⲥⲩⲛⲏ · ⲡⲛⲟⲩⲧⲉ
- ⲡⲉ ⲡⲟⲩⲟⲉⲓⲛ : ⲡϫⲟⲉⲓⲥ
ⲡⲛⲟⲩⲧⲉ ⲛⲉⲛϭⲟⲙ : ⲙⲓ-
15 ⲭⲁⲏⲗ ⲡⲉ ϣⲁⲩⲟⲩⲁϩⲙⲉϥ
ϫⲉ ϯⲣⲏⲛⲏ · ⲉⲧⲉ ⲡⲁⲓ ⲡⲉ ⲡ-
ⲛⲟⲩⲧⲉ ⲡⲟⲩⲟⲉⲓⲛ : ⲅⲁⲃ-
ⲣⲓⲏⲗ ϫⲉ ⲛⲟⲩⲧⲉ ϩⲓ ⲣⲱⲙⲉ
ϩⲣⲁⲫⲁⲏⲗ ϫⲉ ⲡⲧⲁⲗϭⲟ
20 ⲟⲩⲣⲓⲏⲗ ϫⲉ ⲧϭⲟⲙ : ⲥⲉⲇⲉⲕⲓⲏⲗ ϫⲉ ⲧⲇⲓⲕⲁⲓⲟⲥⲩⲛⲏ ·
ⲁⲛⲁⲏⲗ ϫⲉ ⲧⲙⲏⲧⲥ̄ⲧⲙⲏⲧ
ⲁϩⲁⲏⲗ ϫⲉ ⲧⲙ̄ⲛ̄ⲧϣⲁⲛϩ̄-
ⲧⲏϥ : ⲉⲧⲉ ⲛⲁⲓ ⲧⲏⲣⲟⲩ ⲛⲉ
25 ⲛ̄ⲣⲁⲛ ⲙ̄ⲡⲛⲟⲩⲧⲉ : ⲁⲩⲱ
ⲛⲁⲓ ⲧⲏⲣⲟⲩ ⲛⲉ ⲛⲣⲁⲛ ⲛⲁⲣ-
vac. ⲭⲁⲅⲅⲉⲗⲟⲥ : ⲁⲩⲱ

---

1 *i.e.* ἤ : ⲏ̄ Pleyte/Boeser || **6** *i.e.* ἤ || **6–7** *i.e.* ˢⲡ-ⲉⲛⲧⲁ=ϥ-ⲧⲛⲛⲉⲩ-ⲧⲏⲩⲧⲛ̄ || **8** *i.e.* συνευδοκεῖν || **10** *i.e.* εἰρήνη || **12** *i.e.* δικαιοσύνη || **14** *l.* ⲛ̄-ⲛ̄-ϭⲟⲙ || **15** *i.e.* ˢⲉ-ϣⲁ=ⲩ-ⲟⲩⲁϩⲙⲉ=ϥ || **16–17** *l.* ⲡⲛⲟⲩⲧⲉ ⲡⲉ ⲡⲟⲩⲟⲉⲓⲛ *cf.* Strittmatter 1932: 143 ll. 9–10: φῶς ὁ θεός : *l.* ⲡⲛⲟⲩⲧⲉ ⲙ̄ⲡⲟⲩⲉⲓⲛ Boeser, Kropp, Smith, Lexa || **21** *i.e.* δικαιοσύνη || **22** *i.e.* ˢⲙⲛ̄ⲧ̄-ⲥⲧⲙⲏⲧ || **26–27** *i.e.* ἀρχάγγελος || **27** *vac.* of *ca.* 4 letters at beginning of line.

or placed in, and all those belonging to them, and go, each of you, upon the head |⁵ of every one who brought you, or that sent you, them and those who consented to them!

God is |¹⁰ peace. God is healing. God is justice. God is light, the Lord God of powers. |¹⁵ *Michael is interpreted as "peace", that is "God ⟨is⟩ light", *Gabriel as "god and man", *Raphael as "healing", |²⁰ Uriel as "power", Sedekiēl as "justice", Anaēl as "obedience", Azael as "mercy"; these are all |²⁵ the names of God and these are all the names of *archangels, and

---

5–6. ⲛ̅ⲧⲁϥⲉⲓⲛⲉ ⲙ̅ⲙⲱⲧⲛ̅ : "who brought you" Smith translates "who is like you."

12–24. List of angel names and interpretations: Several of the interpretations here demonstrate genuine knowledge of Hebrew on the part of the composer (cf. Davidson 1967: 117, 240, 324). Gabriel's name is indeed composed of the Hebrew elements "man" (גבר *geber*) and "god" (אל *ēl*); compare the *Scala Magna*, whose definition of Gabriel is likewise "Man and God" (ⲫⲣⲱⲙⲓ ⲟⲩⲟϩ ⲫϯ; Macomber 2020: 198). See also *PCM* I 26 p. 3 l. 20, in which Michael claims "my name is God and man" (ⲡⲁⲣⲁⲛ ⲋ ⲡⲛⲟⲩⲧⲉ · ϩⲓ ⲣⲱⲙⲉ). The first element of Raphael similarly derives from the root "to heal" (רפא *rāpā'*), while that of Sedekiēl is "justice" (צדק *ṣedeq*). Anael may be derived here from the verb "to answer, respond" (ענה *'ānāh*; we thank Ortal-Paz Saar for this suggestion). The rationale behind the other derivations given here is less obvious to us. A similar list of angel names and their interpretations may be found in *PGM* P 14 (KYP M435; we thank Michel Zellmann-Rohrer for the reference). For other Coptic lists of angels and their associated attributes, see *The Book of Bartholomew* (CC 27; ed. Westerhoff 1999: 136–139); *P.Lond.Copt.* 524 (KYP M359) front ll. 116–19.

page 10 (5v) (→)

-: ⲉ̄ :-

ⲟⲩⲟⲛ ⲛⲓⲙ ⲉⲧⲉⲟⲩⲉⲛⲧⲁⲩ
ⲙ̄ⲙⲁⲩ ⲛ̄ⲛⲁⲓ̈ ⲉⲩⲧⲱⲟⲩⲛ
ϩⲁⲣⲟⲟⲩ ⲟⲩⲉⲛⲧⲁⲩ ⲙ̄ⲙⲁⲩ
ⲛⲟⲩⲛⲟϭ ⲛ̄ⲃⲟⲏⲑⲓ̈ⲁ ⲉⲥⲙⲉϩ
5   ⲛ̄ⲛⲁⲅⲁⲑⲟⲛ ⲛⲓⲙ ⲉⲃⲟⲗ ϫⲉ
ⲡⲛⲟⲩⲧⲉ ⲛ̄ⲙⲙⲁⲛ : ⲥⲱ-
ⲧⲙ ⲛⲁ ϫⲓ̄ⲛ ⲁⲣⲏⲭ̄ϥ ⲙ̄ⲡⲕⲁϩ
ϫⲉ ⲡⲛⲟⲩⲧⲉ ⲛ̄ⲙⲙⲁⲛ
ϩⲟⲧⲁⲛ ⲅⲁⲣ ⲉⲧⲉⲧⲛ̄ϣⲁⲛ-
10 ϭⲙϭⲟⲙ : ⲡⲁⲗⲓ̈ⲛ ⲟⲛ ⲧⲉⲧ-
ⲛⲁϭⲱⲧⲡ̄ ϫⲉ ⲡⲛⲟⲩⲧⲉ
ⲛⲙⲙⲁⲛ : ⲁⲩⲱ ⲡϣⲟϫⲛⲉ
ⲉⲧⲉⲧⲛ̄ⲙⲉⲉⲩⲉ ⲉⲣⲟϥ ⲡ-
ϫⲟⲉⲓ̄ⲥ ⲛⲁϫⲟⲟⲣⲉϥ ⲉⲃⲟⲗ : -
15 ⲁⲩⲱ ⲛⲉϣⲁϫⲉ ⲉⲧⲉⲧⲛⲁ-
ϫⲟⲟⲩ ⲉⲛⲉⲩϭⲱ ⲛ̄ϩⲏⲧⲧⲏⲩ-
ⲧⲛ̄ ϫⲉ ⲡⲛⲟⲩⲧⲉ ⲛ̄ⲙⲙⲁⲛ
ⲟⲩⲱⲛⲉ ⲛ̄ϫⲣⲟⲡ ⲙ̄ⲛ ⲟⲩ-
ⲡⲉⲧⲣⲁ ⲛ̄ⲥⲕⲁⲧⲁⲗⲟⲛ ⲙ̄-
20 ⲡⲉⲣⲧⲣⲉⲩⲧⲟⲗⲙⲁ ⲉϩⲱ-
ⲛⲉ ⲉϩⲟⲩⲛ ⲉⲛⲉⲧⲉⲟⲩⲉⲛ-
ⲧⲁⲩ ⲙ̄ⲙⲁⲩ ⲛ̄ⲧⲓ̈ⲡⲣⲟⲥ-
ⲉⲩⲭⲏ ϫⲉ ⲡⲛⲟⲩⲧⲉ ⲛ̄ⲙ-
ⲙⲁⲛ : ⲟⲩⲟⲛ ⲅⲁⲣ ⲛⲓⲙ ⲉⲧ-
25 ⲛⲁϫⲓ̄ ⲛ̄ⲧⲉⲓ̈ⲡⲣⲟⲥⲉⲩⲭⲏ :
ⲛ̄ⲡ̄ⲙⲁ ⲉⲧⲟⲩⲛⲁⲕⲱ ⲛ̄-
ϩⲏⲧϥ̄ ⲛ̄ⲧⲓ̈ⲡⲣⲟⲥⲉⲩⲭⲏ
ⲛ̄ⲥⲉⲛⲁⲉⲣ ϩⲟⲧⲉ ⲁⲛ ϩⲏⲧϥ

---

1 *i.e.* ˢⲉⲧⲉ-ⲟⲩⲛⲧⲁ⸗ⲩ ‖ **3** *i.e.* ˢⲟⲩⲛⲧⲁ⸗ⲩ ‖ **4** *i.e.* βοήθεια ‖ **5** *i.e.* ἀγαθόν ‖ **7** *i.e.* ˢⲛⲁ⸗ⲓ ? "(obey) me" Smith : *i.e.* ˢⲛⲁⲓ "these" ("cela", "dies") Boeser, Lexa, Kropp ‖ **9** *i.e.* ὅταν γάρ ‖ **10** *i.e.* πάλιν ‖ **10–11** *i.e.* ˢⲉ-ⲧⲉⲧⲛ̄-ⲛⲁ-ⲥⲱⲧⲡ̄ ‖ **16** *i.e.* ˢⲛ̄ⲛⲉ⸗ⲩ-ϭⲱ ? ‖ **19** *i.e.* πέτρα | *i.e.* σκάνδαλον ‖ **20** *i.e.* τολμᾶν ‖ **21–22** *i.e.* ˢⲉ-ⲛ-ⲉⲧⲉ-ⲟⲩⲛⲧⲁ⸗ⲩ ‖ **22–23, 25** *i.e.* προσευχή ‖ **24** *i.e.* γάρ ‖ **25** *i.e.* προσευχή ‖ **27** *i.e.* προσευχή

everyone who has these with them, carrying them, have with them a great help, which is filled |⁵ with every good thing, for God is with us.

Listen, you ⟨who come⟩ from the end of the earth, for God is with us, for when you |¹⁰ are strong, again, you will be defeated, for God is with us, and the scheme that you prepare, the Lord will bring it to naught, |¹⁵ and the words that you will say, they shall not remain within you, for God is with us. A stone of stumbling and a rock of offence, |²⁰ do not permit them to dare approach those who have this prayer with them, for God is with us, for everyone who |²⁵ will bring this prayer to the place within which the prayer will be put will not fear

---

6, 8, 11–12, 17, 23–24. ⲡⲛⲟⲩⲧⲉ ⲛ̄ⲙⲙⲁⲛ : **"God is with us"** A citation of Matthew 1.23 (Horner 1911: I 8) and Isaiah 7.14 (Bąk 2020: 536); *cf.* the note to *PCM* I 25 p. 11 l. 7.

18–19. ⲟⲩⲱⲛⲉ ⲛ̄ϫⲣⲟⲡ ⲙⲛ̄ ⲟⲩⲡⲉⲧⲣⲁ ⲛ̄ⲥⲕⲁⲧⲁⲗⲟⲛ : **"A stone of stumbling and a rock of offence"** *Cf.* I Peter 2.8: "And a stone of stumbling and a rock of offence to those who stumble in the word, being unbelieving, since they have been delivered to this" (ⲁⲩⲱ ⲟⲩⲱⲛⲉ ⲛ̄ϫⲣⲟⲡ ⲙⲛ̄ ⲟⲩⲡⲉⲧⲣⲁ ⲛ̄ⲥⲕⲁⲛⲇⲁⲗⲟⲛ ⲛ̄ⲛⲁⲓ ⲉⲧϫⲓ ϫⲣⲟⲡ ⲉⲡϣⲁϫⲉ ⲉⲩⲟ ⲛ̄ⲁⲧⲛⲁϩⲧⲉ ⲉⲁⲩⲕⲁⲁⲩ ⲉⲡⲁⲓ; Horner 1924: 20).

page 11 (6r) (→)

ⲛ̄ⲧⲉⲧⲛ̄ϩⲟⲧⲉ : ⲟⲩⲇⲉ ⲛ̄-
ⲥⲉⲛⲁϣⲧⲟⲣⲧⲣ̄ ⲁⲛ ϫⲉ ⲡⲛⲟⲩ-
ⲧⲉ ⲛⲙⲙⲁⲛ ⲛ̄ⲧⲱⲧⲛ̄ ⲇⲉ
ϩⲱⲧⲧⲏⲩⲧⲛ̄ ⲟⲩⲟⲛ
5 ⲛⲓⲙ ⲉⲧⲉⲟⲩⲉⲛⲧⲁⲩ ⲙ̄-
ⲙⲁⲩ ⲙⲡⲉϣⲗⲏⲗ ⲛ̄ⲧⲉⲓ̈ⲡ-
ⲣⲟⲥⲉⲩⲭⲏ ⲡϫⲟⲉⲓⲥ ⲡ-
ⲛⲟⲩⲧⲉ ⲙⲁⲧⲃ̄ⲃⲟϥ ⲛ̄ϩⲏⲧ-
ⲧⲏⲩⲧⲛ̄ ⲁⲩⲱ ϥⲛⲁϣⲱ-
10 ⲡⲉ ⲛⲙ̄ⲙⲁⲛ ⲛ̄ⲣⲉϥϩⲁⲣⲉϩ
ⲁⲩⲱ ⲛϥ̄ⲧⲟⲩϫⲟⲛ ⲉⲛϩⲟ-
ⲧⲉ ⲧⲏⲣⲟⲩ ⲙ̄ⲡϫⲁϫⲉ : ⲙⲛ̄
ⲛⲉϥⲉⲛⲉⲣⲅⲓ̈ⲁ ⲛ̄ⲇⲁⲓⲙⲟ-
ⲛⲓ̈ⲟⲛ : ⲁⲩⲱ ⲉⲛϣⲁⲛϣⲱ-
15 ⲡⲉ ⲉⲛⲛⲁϩⲧⲉ ϩⲙ ⲡⲉⲛϩⲏⲧ
ⲧⲏⲣϥ̄ : ⲡϫⲟⲉⲓⲥ ⲡⲛⲟⲩ-
ⲧⲉ ϥ̄ⲛⲁϣⲱⲡⲉ ⲛⲁⲛ ⲉⲩ-
ⲧⲃⲃⲟ ϫⲉ ⲡⲛⲟⲩⲧⲉ ⲛⲙ̄- .
ⲙⲁⲛ : ⲉⲧⲃⲉ ⲡⲁⲓ̈ ⲧⲉⲛⲁ-
20 ϫⲱ ⲙ̄ⲡϣⲁϫⲉ ⲙ̄ⲡϫⲟⲉⲓⲥ
ϫⲉ ⲉⲓ̈ⲥ ϩⲏⲏⲧⲉ ⲁⲛⲟⲕ ⲙⲛ
ⲛⲉϣⲏⲣⲉ ϣⲏⲙ ⲛ̄ⲧⲁⲡ-
ⲛⲟⲩⲧⲉ ⲧⲁⲁⲩ ⲛⲁⲓ̈ : ⲡⲗⲁ-
ⲟⲥ ⲉⲧϩⲙⲟⲟⲥ ϩⲙ̄ ⲡⲕⲁⲕⲉ
25 ⲁⲩⲛⲁⲩ ⲉⲩⲛⲟϭ ⲛⲟⲩⲟⲉⲓⲛ
ϫⲉ ⲡⲛⲟⲩⲧⲉ ⲛⲙ̄ⲙⲁⲛ :
ⲡⲉⲭⲥ̄ ⲓ̄ⲥ̄ ⲛⲙⲙⲁⲛ : ⲡⲁⲓ̈ ⲛ̄-
ⲧⲁⲩⲥϩⲁⲓ̈ ⲉⲧⲃⲏⲏⲧϥ̄ :-

---

1 *i.e.* οὐδέ ∥ **2** ⲥⲉⲛⲁϣⲧⲟⲣⲧⲣ̄ ⲥⲉ added in *ekthesis* at the beginning of the line ∥ **3** *i.e.* δέ ∥ **6–7** *i.e.* προσευχή ∥ **8** *l.* ⲛⲁⲧⲃ̄ⲃⲟϥ ∥ **11–12** *i.e.* ˢⲛ̄-ⲛ-ϩⲟⲧⲉ : ⲛϥ̄ⲧⲟⲩϫⲟ ⲛⲉⲛϩⲟⲧⲉ Pleyte/Boeser ∥ **13** *i.e.* ἐνέργεια ∥ **13–14** *i.e.* δαιμόνιον ∥ **21** ⲉⲓ̄ⲥ ϩⲏⲏⲧⲥ Pleyte/Boeser ∥ **23–24** *i.e.* λαός ∥ **27** *l.* ⲡⲉ-χ(ριστό)ϲ ι(ⲏⲥⲟⲩ)ⲥ

your fear, nor will they be disturbed, for God is with us.

But you, yourselves, every one |⁵ who has with them this prayer of this entreaty, the Lord God will purify him of you, and he will be |¹⁰ with us as a guardian and he will deliver us from the fears of the Enemy and his demonic works, and if we are |¹⁵ faithful in all our heart, the Lord God will be a purification for us, for God is with us. For this reason, we will |²⁰ speak the word of the Lord: "Behold, I am with the children of God whom he gave to me. The people that dwell in darkness |²⁵ saw a great light, for God is with us". Christ Jesus is with us, the one of whom they wrote concerning him,

---

1. ⲛ̄ⲧⲉⲧⲛ̄ϩⲟⲧⲉ : ⲟⲩⲇⲉ : **"your fear, nor"** Smith translates "they shall (neither) be afraid...."

2–3, 18–19, 25–26. ⲡⲛⲟⲩⲧⲉ ⲛⲙⲙⲁⲛ : **"God is with us"** *Cf.* the note to p. 10 ll. 6, 8, 11–12, 17, 23–24.

7–9. ⲡϫⲟⲉⲓⲥ ⲡⲛⲟⲩⲧⲉ ⲙⲁⲧⲃⲃⲟϥ ⲛ̄ϩⲏⲧⲧⲏⲩⲧⲛ̄ : **"the Lord God will purify him of you"** Smith translates "the Lord god purifies it in you". For our translation, see Crum CD 400a.

19–20. ⲧⲉⲛⲁϫⲱ ⲙ̄ⲡϣⲁϫⲉ ⲙ̄ⲡϫⲟⲉⲓⲥ : **"we will speak the word of the Lord"** Kropp compares Joshua 24: "But I and my household, we will serve the Lord" (ⲁⲛⲟⲕ ⲇⲉ ⲙⲛ ⲡⲁϩⲓ ⲉⲛⲛⲁϣⲙϣⲉ ⲙ̄ⲡϫⲟⲉⲓⲥ; Thompson 1911: 124).

21–23. ⲉⲓⲥ ϩⲏⲏⲧⲉ ⲁⲛⲟⲕ ⲙⲛ ⲛⲉϣⲏⲣⲉ ϣⲏⲙ ⲛ̄ⲧⲁⲡⲛⲟⲩⲧⲉ ⲧⲁⲁⲩ ⲛⲁⲓ̄ : **"behold, I am with the children of God whom he gave to me"** This is a direct citation of Isaiah 8.18/Hebrews 2.13 (Horner 1920: 14).

23–25. ⲡⲗⲁⲟⲥ ⲉⲧϩ̄ⲙⲟⲟⲥ ϩ̄ⲙ ⲡⲕⲁⲕⲉ ⲁⲩⲛⲁⲩ ⲉⲩⲛⲟϭ ⲛⲟⲩⲟⲉⲓⲛ : **"the people that dwell in darkness saw a great light"** A direct citation of Isaiah 9.2, quoted in Matthew 4.16: "The people that dwell in the darkness saw a great light" (ⲡⲗⲁⲟⲥ ⲉⲧϩ̄ⲙⲟⲟⲥ ϩ̄ⲙ ⲡⲕⲁⲕⲉ ⲁϥⲛⲁⲩ ⲉⲩⲛⲟϭ ⲛⲟⲩⲟⲉⲓⲛ; Horner 1911: I 26).

page 12 (6v) (↓)

-:ⲋ̄:-

ϫⲉ ⲥⲉⲛⲁⲙⲟⲩⲧⲉ ⲉⲡⲉϥ-
ⲣⲁⲛ ϫⲉ ⲡⲁⲅⲅⲉⲗⲟⲥ ⲙ̄ⲡ-
ⲛⲟϭ ⲛ̄ϣⲟϫⲛⲉ : ⲡⲛⲟⲩⲧⲉ
ⲉⲧϭⲙϭⲟⲙ · ⲡⲛⲟⲩⲧⲉ ⲙ̄-
5 ⲡⲛⲟϭ ⲛ̄ϣⲟϫⲛⲉ ⲛ̄ϣⲏⲣⲉ
ⲙⲁⲣⲉⲛϥⲓⲟⲩ ⲛ̄ⲛⲉⲛ̄ⲃⲁⲗ ⲉϩ-
ⲣⲁⲓ ⲉⲧⲡⲉ ⲛ̄ⲧⲛ̄ⲥⲙⲟⲩ ⲉ-
ⲣⲟϥ ϩⲛ̄ ⲟⲩⲣⲁϣⲉ ⲙ̄ⲯⲩⲭⲏ
ⲉⲛⲱϣ ⲉⲃⲟⲗ ⲉⲛϫⲱ ⲙ̄ⲙⲟⲥ
10 ϫⲉ ⲡⲉⲟⲟⲩ ⲙⲛ̄ ⲧⲉⲡⲣⲟⲥ-
ⲕⲩⲛⲏⲥⲓⲥ ⲙⲛ̄ ⲧⲙⲛ̄ⲧⲛⲟϭ
ⲡⲣⲉⲡⲓ ⲛⲁⲕ : ⲡⲉⲓⲱⲧ ⲙⲛ̄ ⲡ-
ϣⲏⲣⲉ ⲙⲛ̄ ⲡⲉⲡ̄ⲛ̄ⲁ̄ ⲉⲧⲟⲩ-
ⲁⲁⲃ ⲉⲧϩⲛ̄ ⲟⲩⲙⲛ̄ⲧⲟⲩⲁ
15 ⲙⲛ̄ ⲟⲩⲙⲛ̄ⲧⲟⲩⲁ ⲉⲥϩⲛ̄ ⲟⲩⲧⲣⲓⲁⲥ : ⲟⲩⲙⲛ̄ⲧⲛⲟⲩⲧⲉ ⲛⲟⲩ-
ⲱⲧ ⲧⲉ ⲛ̄ⲧϣⲟⲙⲧⲉ ⲛ̄-
ϩⲩⲡⲟⲥⲧⲁⲥⲓⲥ : ⲙⲛ̄ ⲟⲩ-
ⲙⲛ̄ⲧϫⲟⲉⲓⲥ ⲛⲟⲩⲱⲧ : ⲙⲛ̄
20 ⲟⲩⲁⲣⲭⲏ ⲛⲟⲩⲱⲧ : ⲙⲛ̄ ⲟⲩ-
ϭⲟⲙ ⲛⲟⲩⲱⲧ : ⲙⲛ̄ ⲟⲩⲉ-
ⲛⲉⲣⲅⲓⲁ ⲛⲟⲩⲱⲧ ⲙⲛ̄ ⲉ-
ⲝⲟⲩⲥⲓⲁ ⲛⲓⲙ : ⲙⲛ̄ ⲟⲩⲡ-
ⲣⲟⲥⲱⲡⲟⲛ ⲛⲟⲩⲱⲧ : ⲙⲛ̄
25 ⲟⲩⲃⲁⲡⲧⲓⲥⲙⲁ ⲛⲟⲩⲱⲧ
ⲟⲩϫⲟⲉⲓⲥ ⲛⲟⲩⲱⲧ : ⲟⲩ-
ⲛⲟⲩⲧⲉ ⲛⲟⲩⲱⲧ : ⲡⲓ̄ⲱⲧ
ⲙⲛ̄ ⲡϣⲏⲣⲉ ⲙⲛ̄ ⲡⲉⲡ̄ⲛ̄ⲁ̄

---

2 *i.e.* ἄγγελος ‖ **8** *i.e.* ψυχή ‖ **10–11** *i.e.* προσκύνησις ‖ **12** *i.e.* πρέπειν : "distinguish" Smith ‖ **13** *i.e.* πνεῦμα ‖ **15–16** *i.e.* τρίας ‖ **18** *i.e.* ὑπόστασις : "substances" ("substances") Lexa : "persons" ("Personen") Kropp : Boeser does not translate ‖ **20** *i.e.* ἀρχή ‖ **21–22** *i.e.* ἐνέργεια ‖ **22–23** *i.e.* ἐξουσία ‖ **23–24** *i.e.* πρόσωπον ‖ **25** *i.e.* βάπτισμα ‖ **28** *i.e.* πνεῦμα

"For they will call his name the *angel of great counsel, God who is strong, God of |⁵ great and wondrous counsel."

Let us lift our eyes up to heaven and bless him with joy in our souls, crying out, saying, |¹⁰ "Glory and adoration and greatness are fitting for you, O Father and Son and Holy Spirit who exist in unity, |¹⁵ and a unity in a trinity; he is a single divinity in three hypostases and a single lordship and |²⁰ a single rule and a single power and a single energy and every authority, and a single person, and |²⁵ a single baptism, a single lord, a single god, the Father, and the Son and the Spirit!"

1–4. ϲⲉⲛⲁⲙⲟⲩⲧⲉ ⲉⲡⲉϥⲣⲁⲛ ϫⲉ ⲡⲁⲅⲅⲉⲗⲟϲ ⲙ̄ⲡⲛⲟϭ ⲛ̄ϣⲟϫⲛⲉ : ⲡⲛⲟⲩⲧⲉ ⲉⲧϭⲙϭⲟⲙ : "they will call his name the angel of great counsel, God who is strong" *Cf.* Isaiah 9.6–7: "they will call his name the angel of great counsel" (ⲉⲩⲛⲁⲙⲟⲩⲧⲉ ⲉⲡⲉϥⲣⲁⲛ ϫⲉ ⲡⲁⲅⲅⲉⲗⲟϲ ⲙⲡⲛⲟϭ ⲛϣⲟϫⲛⲉ; Bąk 2020: 544), *cf.* the addition "wondrous counsellor, mighty god" (θαυμαστὸς σύμβουλος θεὸς ἰσχυρός) found in some copies of the Septuagint (Rahlfs 1935: 574 note to l. 5).

12–26. Credal Statement: We have been unable to find an exact parallel for this credal statement, but it seems to be an adapted citation of the Greek pseudopigraph known as the *Instruction of the 318 Nicene Fathers (Didascalica CCCXVIII Patrum Nicaenorum)*, which claims to be the doctrinal teaching of the bishops present at the Council of Nicaea (325 CE). The work existed by ca. 435/436 CE, when it was cited by the Armenian Catholikos Sahak (Blumell 2017: 613 *et passim*). Specifically, it draws from the passage anathematising the Sabellian claim that God had a single hypostasis: "for we know Father is Father, and Son, Son, and Holy Spirit, Holy Spirit: one essence, one kingdom, one divinity (πατέρα γὰρ οἴδαμεν πατέρα καὶ υἱὸν υἱόν καὶ πνεῦμα ἅγιον πνεῦμα ἅγιον, μίαν βασιλείαν, μίαν οὐσίαν, μίαν θεότητα; Riedinger/Thurn 1985: 84). Compare the similar passage in the fourth century *Ancoratus* of Epiphanius of Salamis, which adds "a single baptism" (βάπτισμα μία; Holl 1915: 146 (118.3–4)), also present here (*cf.* Ephesians 4.5). One of the surviving Coptic versions of the *Instruction* (CC 19; CLM 359, 1002–1003 CE) records the variant: "We confess the Father is the Father, the Son is the Son, and the Holy Spirit is the Holy Spirit, three names, three hypostases, a single kingdom, a single essence, a single divinity, a single energy" (ⲧⲛ̄ϩⲟⲙⲟⲗⲟⲅⲉⲓ ⲙ̄ⲡⲉⲓⲱⲧ ⲉⲡⲉⲓⲱⲧ ⲡⲉ ⲁⲩⲱ ⲡϣⲏⲣⲉ ⲉⲡϣⲏⲣⲉ ⲡⲉ ⲁⲩⲱ ⲡⲉⲡ̅ⲛ̅ⲁ̅ ⲉⲧⲟⲩⲁⲁⲃ ⲉⲡⲉⲡ̅ⲛ̅ⲁ̅ ⲉⲧⲟⲩⲁⲁⲃ ⲡⲉ ϣⲟⲙⲛ̄ⲧ ⲛ̄ⲣⲁⲛ ϣⲟⲙⲛ̄ⲧⲉ ⲛ̄ϩⲩⲡⲟⲥⲧⲁⲥⲓⲥ ⲟⲩⲙ̄ⲛ̄ⲧⲉⲣⲟ ⲛ̄ⲟⲩⲱⲧ ⲟⲩⲟⲩⲥⲓⲁ ⲛ̄ⲟⲩⲱⲧ ⲟⲩⲙ̄ⲛ̄ⲧⲛⲟⲩⲧⲉ ⲛ̄ⲟⲩⲱⲧ ⲟⲩⲉⲛⲉⲣⲅⲓⲁ ⲛ̄ⲟⲩⲱⲧ; Revillout 1875: 222, corrected by reference to the original). A similar, certainly dependent, statement is found in Pseudo-Alexander of Alexandria, *On Peter of Alexandria* (CC 15), in which Peter, bishop of Alexandria, denies the Sabellians, saying: "We say, 'Father and the Son and the Holy Spirit, three hypostases or persons, and a single divinity and a single essence and a single lordship, a trinity in a unity'" (ⲁ̄ⲛⲟⲛ ⲉ̄ϣⲁⲛϫⲟⲥ ϫⲉ ⲫⲓⲱⲧ ⲛⲉⲙ ⲡϣⲏⲣⲓ ⲛⲉⲙ ⲡⲓⲡ̅ⲛ̅ⲁ̅ ⲉⲑⲟⲩⲁⲃ ⲅ̄† ⲛ̄ϩⲩⲡⲟⲥⲧⲁⲧⲓⲥ ⲓ̅ⲉ̅ ⲙ̄ⲡⲣⲟⲥⲱⲡⲟⲛ ⲟⲩⲙⲉⲑⲛⲟⲩ† ⲇⲉ ⲛ̄ⲟⲩⲱⲧ ⲟⲩⲟⲩⲥⲓⲁ̄ ⲛ̄ⲟⲩⲱⲧ ⲟⲩⲙⲉⲧⲟ̅ⲥ̅ ⲛ̄ⲟⲩⲱⲧ ⲟⲩⲧⲣⲓⲁⲥ ⲉⲥϧⲉⲛ ⲟⲩⲙⲉⲧⲟⲩⲁⲓ; Hyvernat 1886: 254.9–13). "Energy" (ἐνέργεια/ⲉⲛⲉⲣⲅⲉⲓⲁ *energeia*) here refers the activity of the divinity; the term might be seen to point to a seventh-century date of composition or redaction for this text, linked to the Emperor Heraclius' (r. 610–641) attempt to resolve the Chalcedonian schism with the compromise of Christ's single energy ('monoenergism'), but we consider this uncertain, since the teaching was already present in the sixth century. A letter from the miaphysite patriarch Damian of Alexandria (r. 578–605 CE) preserved in the *Chronicle* of Michael the Syrian (Patriarch of Antioch, r. 1166–1199) proclaims "one single Son and one single nature of the incarnate Word, one single hypostasis, one single person, and one single activity" (Hovorun 2008: 50 *et passim*).

page 13 (7r) (→)

-: ⲃ̇ :-
ⲟⲩⲙⲉⲉⲩⲉ ⲛ̄ⲕⲁⲧⲁⲗⲁⲗⲓ̈ⲁ ·
ⲟⲩⲙⲉⲉⲩⲉ ⲛ̄ⲕⲱϩ : ϩⲓ̈ ⲙⲟⲥ-
ⲧⲉ : ϩⲓ̈ ⲙ̄ⲛ̄ⲧⲭⲁϫⲉ : ϩⲓ̈ ⲙ̄ⲛ̄ⲧ-
ⲭⲁⲥⲓ̈ϩⲏⲧ : ϩⲓ̈ ⲙ̄ⲛ̄ⲧⲁⲟⲩ-
5 ⲱϣⲟ : ϩⲓ̈ ⲙ̄ⲛ̄ⲧⲁⲧⲥⲱⲧⲙ̄ : ϩⲓ̈
ⲙ̄ⲛ̄ⲧⲗⲁⲙⲁϩ̄ⲧ : ϩⲓ̈ ⲙ̄ⲛ̄ⲧ-
ⲙⲁⲓ̈ϩⲟⲙⲛ̄ⲧ ⲧⲛⲟⲩⲛⲉ ⲙ̄-
ⲡⲉⲑⲟⲟⲩ ⲛⲓⲙ : ϩⲓ̈ ⲙⲛⲧⲃⲁ-
ⲃⲉⲣⲱⲙⲉ : ⲙ̄ⲛ ⲇⲓ̈ⲁⲃⲟⲗⲏ
10 ⲛⲓ̈ⲙ : ϩⲓ̈ ⲙⲉⲉⲩⲉ ⲛⲓ̈ⲙ ⲉⲧ-
ⲭⲁϩ̄ⲙ : ϩⲓ̈ ⲉⲡⲓ̄ⲕⲣⲓ̈ⲁ ⲛⲓ̈ⲙ :
ⲧⲉⲧⲣⲓ̈ⲁⲥ ⲉⲧⲟⲩⲁⲁⲃ † ⲥⲟ
ⲉⲟⲩⲟⲛ ⲛⲓ̈ⲙ : ⲧⲉⲧⲣⲓ̈ⲁⲥ ⲉ-
ⲧⲟⲩⲁⲁⲃ ⲧⲉⲃⲟ ⲙ̄ⲡⲣⲱⲙⲉ
15 ϩⲓ̈ϩⲟⲩⲛ ⲁⲩⲱ ⲉⲧϩⲓ̈ⲃⲟⲗ
ⲥⲛ̄ⲧⲛ̄ ⲉⲃⲟⲗ ϩⲁⲣⲟⲥ ⲙ̄ⲡ̄ⲣⲁⲥ-
ⲙⲟⲥ ⲛⲓ̈ⲙ ⲉⲧⲙⲟⲕϩ̄ : ⲛⲓ̈ ⲉ-
ⲃⲟⲗ ϩⲁⲣⲟⲥ ⲙ̄ⲛ̄ ⲉⲛⲉⲣⲅⲓ̈ⲁ
ⲛⲓ̈ⲙ ⲛ̄ⲧⲉⲡⲇⲓ̈ⲁⲃⲟⲗⲟⲥ :
20 ⲙ̄ⲛ̄ ⲉⲛⲉⲣⲅⲓ̈ⲁ ⲛⲓ̈ⲙ ⲛ̄ⲧⲉⲡ-
ⲡⲟⲛⲏⲣⲟⲥ · ⲙ̄ⲛ̄ ⲉⲡⲓ̈ⲃⲟⲩ-
ⲗⲓ̈ⲁ ⲛⲓ̈ⲙ ⲛ̄ⲣⲱⲙⲉ ⲙ̄ⲡⲟⲛⲏ-
ⲣⲟⲛ : ⲧⲉⲧⲣⲓ̈ⲁⲥ ⲉⲧⲟⲩⲁ-
ⲁⲃ † ⲥⲟ ⲉⲟⲩⲟⲛ ⲛⲓ̈ⲙ ⲉⲧⲉ-
25 ⲟⲩⲉⲛⲧⲁⲩ ⲙ̄ⲙⲁⲩ ⲛ̄ⲧⲉⲓ̈-
ⲥⲫⲣⲁⲅⲓ̈ⲥ ⲙ̄ⲛ̄ ⲛⲉⲧⲉⲟⲩ-
ⲉⲛⲧⲁⲩ ⲙ̄ⲙⲁⲩ ⲛ̄ⲧⲉⲓ̈-
ⲡⲣⲟⲥⲉⲩⲭⲏ : ⲙⲛ ⲙⲁ
ⲛⲓⲙ ⲉⲧⲟⲩⲛⲁⲧⲟϭⲥ ⲉⲃⲟⲗ

---

1 *i.e.* καταλαλία ‖ **9** *i.e.* διαβολή ‖ **11** *i.e.* πικρία ‖ **12, 13** *i.e.* τρίας ‖ **16–17** *i.e.* πειρασμός ‖ **17** ⲛⲓ̈ *i.e.* ⁵ⲛ̄-ⲉⲓ ‖ **18** *l.* ϩⲁⲣⲟϥ (referring back to ⲡⲣⲁⲥⲙⲟⲥ) ? | *i.e.* ἐνέργεια ‖ **19** *i.e.* διάβολος ‖ **20** *i.e.* ἐνέργεια ‖ **21** *i.e.* πονηρός ‖ **21–22** *i.e.* ἐπιβουλία ‖ **22–23** *i.e.* πονηρόν ‖ **23** *i.e.* τρίας ‖ **24–25** *i.e.* ⁵ⲉⲧⲉ-ⲟⲩⲛⲧⲁⲤⲩ ‖ **26** *i.e.* σφραγίς ‖ **28** *i.e.* προσευχή : προ[ⲥ]ⲉⲩⲭⲏ Pleyte/Boeser

A slanderous thought, a thought of envy and hate and enmity and arrogance and pride |⁵ and disobedience and gluttony and greed, the root of every evil, and boastfulness and every slander |¹⁰ and every defiled thought and every bitterness! The Holy Trinity spares everyone, the Holy Trinity, purifies the man |¹⁵ from within and from without, it brings us to itself from every temptation that is difficult to get out of, and every work of the Devil |²⁰ and every work of evil and every treachery of evil men. The Holy Trinity spares everyone who |²⁵ has with them this seal, and those who have with them this prayer, and every place in which it will be affixed,

---

12–13. ⲧⲥⲟ ⲉⲟⲩⲟⲛ ⲛⲓⲙ : "**spares everyone**" Lexa translates "turns them away from everyone ("les détourne de chacun"). Kropp translates this passage up to p. 14 l. 5 as a series of imperatives, "spare each one ‹…›!" ("verschone einen jeden ‹…›!").

17–18. ⲛⲓ̈ ⲉⲃⲟⲗ ϩⲁⲣⲟⲥ : "**that is difficult to get out of**" Boeser assumes something is missing here. Kropp translates "that we come out of it" ("dass wir aus ihr hervorgehen"), Smith "from them". Πειρασμός is apparently treated as a feminine noun in l. 18, perhaps a mistake conditioned by the same preposition with feminine pronoun in l. 16 (ϩⲁⲣⲟⲥ, referring to the grammatically feminine word τρίας "Trinity").

23–24. ⲧⲉⲧⲣⲓ̈ⲁⲥ ⲉⲧⲟⲩⲁⲁⲃ ⲧⲥⲟ : "**the Holy Trinity spares**" Smith translates "Holy trinity, spare …"

page 14 (7v) (↓)

-:⳨:-
ⲛ̄ϩⲏⲧϥ̄ : ⲛ̄ⲥϣⲱⲡⲉ ⲛⲁⲩ ⲙ̄-
ⲫⲩⲗⲁⲕⲧⲏⲣⲓ̈ⲟⲛ : ⲁⲩⲱ ⲛ̄ⲃⲟ-
ⲏⲑⲏⲙⲁ : ϩⲓ̄ ⲧⲁⲗϭⲟ ⲛⲓ̄ⲙ :
ϩⲓ̄ ⲧⲕⲁⲥ ⲛⲓⲙ ⲙ̄ⲙⲓ̈ⲛⲉ ⲛⲓ̄ⲙ
5 ⲧⲉⲧⲣⲓ̄ⲁⲥ ⲉⲧⲟⲩⲁⲁⲃ ⲉⲥⲉ-
ϣⲱⲡⲉ ⲛ̄ⲙ̄ⲙⲁⲛ : ⲡⲉⲟⲟⲩ
ⲙ̄ⲛ̄ ⲡⲧⲁⲓ̈ⲟ : ⲙ̄ⲛ̄ ⲧⲙ̄ⲛ̄ⲧ-
ⲛⲟϭ : ⲙ̄ⲛ̄ ⲧϭⲟⲙ ⲛ̄ⲧⲉⲧⲣⲓ̄ⲁⲥ
ⲉⲧⲟⲩⲁⲁⲃ ⲛ̄ϩⲟⲙⲟⲟⲩⲥⲓ̈ⲟⲛ
10 ⲁⲩⲱ ⲛ̄ⲣⲉϥⲧⲁⲛϩⲟ ⲧⲉⲛⲟⲩ
ⲁⲩⲱ ⲛⲟⲩⲟⲉⲓ̄ϣ ⲛⲓ̄ⲙ ϣⲁ ⲉ-
ⲛⲉϩ ⲉⲛⲉⲛⲉϩ ϩⲁⲙⲏⲛ : —
ⲡⲣⲟⲥⲉⲩⲭⲏ ⲁⲅⲓⲟⲥ ⲉⲣⲅⲟⲣⲓ̈ⲟⲩ
ⲛⲓ̄ⲥⲱⲛⲧ̄ ⲉⲧⲛⲏⲩ ⲉϩⲣⲁⲓ̈
15 ⲙ̄ⲛ̄ ⲡⲟⲟϩ ⲁⲙⲏⲓ̄ⲧⲛ̄ ϣⲁⲣⲟⲓ̈
ⲥⲱⲧⲙ̄ ⲉⲡⲁⲉⲝⲟⲣⲅⲓ̈ⲥⲙⲟⲥ
ⲉⲧⲉ ⲛⲁⲓ̄ ⲛⲉ ⲛⲉⲩⲛⲟϭ ⲛ̄ⲣⲁⲛ
ⲁⲣⲁ̄ⲙ : ⲁⲣⲁ̄ⲙ : ⲁⲣⲓ̄ⲙⲁⲑⲁ
ⲁⲓ̄ⲟⲩ̄ⲑⲁ : ⲁⲑⲁ̄ⲏⲗ : ⲡⲛⲟϭ
20 ⲛⲭⲉⲣⲟⲩⲃⲓ̄ⲛ ⲉⲧⲉⲣⲟⲩⲟⲉⲓ̄ⲛ
ⲉⲧⲛⲏⲩ ⲉϩⲣⲁⲓ̈ ⲙ̄ⲛ̄ ⲡⲣⲏ
ⲁⲙⲏⲓ̄ⲧⲛ̄ ϣⲁⲣⲟⲓ̈ ⲥⲱⲧⲙ̄
ⲉⲡⲁⲉⲝⲟⲣⲅⲓ̈ⲥⲙⲟⲥ : ⲁⲣⲁⲭ̄ⲁ
ⲁⲣⲁⲭⲁ : ⲁⲣⲁⲭⲁⲏⲗ : ⲛⲓ̄ⲥⲱ-
25 ⲛⲧ̄ ⲉⲧⲛⲏⲩ ⲉϩⲣⲁⲓ̈ ⲙ̄ⲛ̄
ⲛⲉⲥⲓ̄ⲟⲩ ⲛ̄ⲧⲡⲉ ϩⲙ̄ ⲡⲥⲁ

---

2 *i.e.* φυλακτήριον ǀǀ **2–3** *i.e.* βοήθημα ǀǀ **5, 8** *i.e.* τρίας ǀǀ **9** *i.e.* ὁμοούσιον ǀǀ **12** *i.e.* ἀμήν ǀǀ
13 *i.e.* προσευχή ǀ *i.e.* ἅγιος ǀ *i.e.* Γρηγορίου ǀǀ **16** *i.e.* ἐξορκισμός ǀǀ **20** *i.e.* χερουβίμ ǀǀ
23 *i.e.* ἐξορκισμός

so that it will be for them a phylactery and a remedy and every healing in? every pain of every sort. |⁵ Let the Holy Trinity be with us, the glory and honour and greatness |⁸ and the power of the consubstantial and life-giving Holy Trinity, now and |¹¹ at all times, forever and ever, amen!

The Prayer of Saint Gregory.

O creatures rising |¹⁵ with the moon, come to me! Listen to my adjuration which is their great names, Aram, Aram, Arimatha, Aioutha, Athaēl! O great |²⁰ shining *cherubim, rising with the sun, come to me! Lsisten to my adjuration, Arakha, Arakha, Arakhaēl! O |²⁵ creatures rising up with the stars of heaven in the

---

13. προсєγχн ᴀгιoc єргoρϊoγ : "The Prayer of Saint Gregory" This is an end title, referring to the preceding text, as is clear from the parallels discussed in the notes to p. 1. Pleyte/Boeser, Boeser, Kropp, Pernigotti (1995), and Smith, mistakenly consider this line and the decorative lines surrounding it to be the title of the next prayer, which is in fact without a title.

page 15 (8r) (→)

```
    ⲛ̄ⲧⲁⲛⲁⲧⲟⲗⲏ ⲁⲙⲏⲓ-
    ⲧⲛ̄ ϣⲁⲣⲟⲓ̈ ⲙ̄ⲡⲟⲟⲩ ⲥⲱ-
    ⲧⲙ̄ ⲉⲡⲁⲉⲍⲟⲣⲅⲓ̈ⲥⲙⲟⲥ
    ⲁⲣⲁⲏ̄ⲗ̄ : ⲁⲣⲁⲏ̄ⲗ̄ : ⲁⲣⲁⲧⲁⲭⲁ-
5   ⲏ̄ⲗ̄ : ⲟⲩⲣⲓ̄ⲏ̄ⲗ̄ : ⲁⲣⲁⲭⲁⲏ̄ⲗ̄
    ⲛⲓ̈ⲥⲱⲱⲛ̄ⲧ ⲉⲧⲛⲏⲩ ⲉϩ-
    ⲣⲁⲓ̈ ⲙ̄ⲛ ⲡⲟⲩⲟⲉⲓ̈ⲛ · ⲁⲙⲏⲓ̄-
    ⲧⲛ̄ ϣⲁⲣⲟⲓ̈ ⲥⲱⲧⲙ̄ ⲉⲡⲁ-
    ⲉⲍⲟⲣⲅⲓ̈ⲥⲙⲟⲥ : ⲁⲙⲁⲛⲁ̄-
10  ⲏ̄ⲗ̄ : ⲁⲙⲁⲣⲁ̄ⲏ̄ⲗ̄ : ⲛⲁⲛⲟ̄ⲏ̄ⲗ̄ :
    [ . . ] . ⲁⲏ̄ⲗ̄ · ⲁⲛⲁⲛⲓⲏ̄ⲗ̄ · ⲛⲓ̈ⲥⲱ-
    [ⲛ]ⲧ̣ ⲉⲧⲛⲏⲩ ⲉϩⲣⲁⲓ̈ ⲙ̄ⲛ ⲡ-
    ⲣⲏ̣ · ⲁⲙⲛⲏⲓ̄ⲧⲛ̄ ⲥⲱⲧⲙ̄ ⲉⲡⲁ-
    ⲉⲍⲟⲣⲅⲓ̈ⲥⲙⲟⲥ · ⲁⲑⲁ̄ · ⲁⲑⲁ̄
15  ⲁⲑⲁ̄ⲏ̄ⲗ̄ · ⲛⲓ̈ⲥⲱⲛⲧ ⲉⲧ-
    ⲛⲏⲩ ⲉϩⲣⲁⲓ̈ ⲙ̄ⲛ ⲡⲛⲟϭ ⲛ̣ⲥⲓ̈-
    ⲟⲩ : ⲁⲙⲏⲓⲧⲛ ϣⲁⲣⲟⲓ̈ ⲥⲱ-
    ⲧⲙ̄ ⲉⲡⲁⲉⲍⲟⲣⲅⲓ̈ⲥⲙⲟⲥ : ⲏ̄ⲣ̄
    ⲏ̄ⲣ̄ · ⲏ̄ⲣ̄ · ⲏ̄ⲣ̄ · ⲏ̄ⲣ̄ · ⲏ̄ⲣ̄ · ⲏ̄ⲣ̄ · ⲛⲓ̈-
20  ⲥⲱⲛ̄ⲧ ⲉⲧⲛⲏⲩ ⲉϩⲣⲁⲓ̈ ⲉⲩ-
    ϩⲩⲡⲟⲩⲣⲅⲓ̈ⲉ ⲡⲥⲁϣϥ̄ ⲛ̄-
    ⲛⲁⲣⲭⲁⲅⲅⲉⲗⲟⲥ : ⲁⲙⲏⲓ̄-
    ⲧⲛ̄ ϣⲁⲣⲟⲓ̈ ⲥⲱⲧⲙ̄ ⲉⲡⲁ-
    ⲉⲍⲟⲣⲅⲓ̈ⲥⲙⲟⲥ : ⲁⲣⲓ̄ⲙⲁⲑⲁ
25  ⲙⲁⲣⲓ̈ⲛⲑⲁⲏ̄ⲗ̄ : ⲉⲇⲉⲕⲓ̄ⲏ̄ⲗ̄ :
    ⲛⲓ̈ⲥⲱⲛⲧ ⲉⲧⲛⲓ̄ ϩⲛ ⲧⲡⲉ
    ⲉⲩϣⲟⲟⲡ ϩⲁ ⲧⲉⲍⲟⲩⲥⲓ̈ⲁ
```

---

1 *i.e.* ἀνατολή ‖ **3** *i.e.* ἐξορκισμός ‖ **6** *i.e.* ˢⲥⲱⲛ̄ⲧ̄ : ⲥⲱⲛ̄ⲧ̄ Pleyte/Boeser ‖ **9** *i.e.* ἐξορκισμός ‖ **11** [. .] . ⲏ̄ⲗ̄ : ⲁⲛⲁⲏ̄ⲗ̄ Pleyte/Boeser, Pleyte, Kropp, Smith, Lexa ‖ **11–12** ⲥⲱⲛⲧ Pleyte/Boeser ‖ **13** ⲁⲙⲛⲏⲓ̄ⲧⲛ̄ ⟨ϣⲁⲣⲟⲓ̈⟩ Pleyte ‖ **14** *i.e.* ἐξορκισμός ‖ **15** ⲁⲑⲁ̄ⲏ̄ⲗ̄ Pleyte/Boeser ‖ **21** *i.e.* ὑπουργεῖν ‖ **22** *i.e.* ἀρχάγγελος ‖ **24** *i.e.* ἐξορκισμός ‖ **27** ⲉⲩϣⲟⲟⲡ ≠ⲩ- expected, but resembles ϥ : ⲉⲩϣⲟⲟⲧ Pleyte/Boeser | *i.e.* ἐξουσία

east, come to me today! Listen to my adjuration, Araēl, Araēl, Aratakhaēl, |⁵ Ouriēl, Arakhaēl! O creatures rising up with the light, come to me! Listen to my adjuration, Amanaēl, |¹⁰ Amaraēl, Nanoēl, …ēl, Ananiēl! O creatures rising up with the sun, come! Listen to my adjuration, Atha, Atha, |¹⁵ Athaēl! O creatures rising up with the great star, come to me! Listen to my adjuration, Ēr, Ēr, Ēr, Ēr, Ēr, Ēr, Ēr! O |²⁰ creatures rising up, serving the seven *archangels, come to me! Listen to my adjuration, Arimatha, |²⁵ Marinthaēl, Edekiēl! O creatures who come through heaven, being under the authority

---

14. ⲁⲑⲁ · ⲁⲑⲁ : **"Atha Atha"** Pleyte translates "Atha" only once.

25. ⲉⲇⲉⲕⲓⲏⲗ : **"Edekiēl"** Understood as "Sedekiel" by Pleyte/Boeser, Pleyte, Kropp, Smith, and Lexa.

26–27. ⲛⲓⲥⲱⲛⲧ ⲉⲧⲛⲓ ϩⲛ ⲧⲡⲉ ⲉⲩϣⲟⲟⲡ ϩⲁ ⲧⲉⲝⲟⲩⲥⲓⲁ : **"O creatures who come through heaven, being under the authority"** Pleyte translates "O Beings who are in heaven … under the power of" ("O Êtres qui êtes au ciel … sous la puissance"), Smith translates "O creatures who … in heaven, who … under the authority", Kropp translates "You creatures, you … in heaven, slaughtered?, under the power" ("Ihr Geschöpfe, die ihr … in den Himmel, geschlachtet?, unter der Macht"), and Lexa translates "beings, who are in heaven, being accredited with the power"("êtres, qui êtes au ciel, étant accrédités de la puissance").

page 16 (8v) (↓)

-: θ̄ :-

ⲙ̄ⲡⲉⲓⲱⲧ ⲥⲱⲧⲙ · ⲉⲡⲁⲉ-
ⲝⲟⲣⲅⲓⲥⲙⲟⲥ · ⲙⲁⲛⲟⲩⲏ̄ⲗ̄ :
ⲙⲁⲛⲟⲩⲏ̄ⲗ̄ · ⲥⲉⲙⲁⲛⲟⲩⲏⲗ
ⲙⲁⲛⲟⲩⲏ̄ⲗ̄ : ⲧⲉϥⲧⲟ ⲙ̄ⲡⲩ-
5 ⲗⲏ ⲛ̄ⲑ̄ⲓ̄ⲉⲣⲟⲩⲥⲁⲗⲏⲙ ⲛ̄ⲧⲡⲉ
ⲁⲙⲏⲓ̄ⲧ̄ⲛ̄ ϣⲁⲣⲟⲓ̈ ⲙⲡⲟⲟⲩ
ⲥⲱⲧ̄ⲙ̄ ⲉⲡⲁⲉⲝⲟⲣⲅⲓⲥⲙⲟⲥ
ϯⲧⲁⲣⲕⲟ ⲙ̄ⲙⲟⲧ̄ⲛ̄ ⲛ̄ⲧϣⲟⲣ-
ⲡⲉ ⲙ̄ⲡⲏⲗⲏ ⲛ̄ⲧⲡⲉ · ⲧⲁ
10 ⲡⲉⲙ̄ϩⲓ̄ⲧ : ⲙ̄ⲛ̄ ⲛⲉⲥⲱⲛⲧ
ⲧⲏⲣⲟⲩ ⲉⲧⲁϩⲉⲣⲁⲧⲟⲩ ⲉ-
ⲧⲉⲝⲟⲙⲟⲗⲟⲅⲉⲓ̈ ⲉⲡⲣⲁⲛ [ⲙ̄-]
ⲡϫⲟⲉⲓ̄ⲥ ⲡⲓ̄ⲱⲧ ⲙ̄ⲡⲕ[ⲟⲥ-]
ⲙⲟⲥ ⲧⲏⲣϥ̄ : ⲁⲇⲱⲛⲁ̣ⲓ̣̄
15 ⲉⲗⲱ̄ⲉⲓ : ⲉⲗⲉⲙⲁⲥ · ⲥⲁⲃⲁ̄ⲱ̄ⲑ̄
ⲛⲁⲓ̈ ⲛⲉ ⲛⲉⲩⲣⲁⲛ · ⲏ̄ⲣ̄ · ⲏ̄ⲣ̄ · ⲏ̄ⲣ̄
ⲏ̄ⲣ̄ · ⲏ̄ⲣ̄ · ⲏ̄ⲣ̄ · ⲏ̄ⲣ̄ · ⲛⲓ̄ⲥⲱⲛⲧ ⲉⲧⲛⲏⲩ ϩ̄ⲛ̄ ⲧ̄ⲡⲩⲗⲏ ⲙ̄ⲡⲣⲏⲥ
ⲁⲙⲏⲓ̄ⲧ̄ⲛ̄ ϣⲁⲣⲟⲓ̈ ⲙ̄ⲛ̄ ⲡⲁⲉ-
20 ⲝⲟⲣⲅⲓⲥⲙⲟⲥ · ⲙⲁⲣⲟⲩⲑ̄ⲁ̄ :
ⲙⲁⲣⲟⲩⲑ̄ⲁ̄ · ⲙⲁⲣⲟⲩⲑⲁⲏⲗ :
ⲛⲓ̄ⲥⲱⲛⲧ̄ ⲉⲧⲛⲏⲩ ⲉϩⲣⲁⲓ̈
ϩ̄ⲛ̄ ⲧⲡⲩⲗⲏ ⲙ̄ⲡⲓ̄ⲏ̄ⲃⲧ̄ · ⲁ-
ⲙⲏⲓ̄ⲧ̄ⲛ̄ ϣⲁⲣⲟⲓ̈ ⲙⲡⲟⲟⲩ
25 ⲥⲱⲧⲙ̄ ⲉⲡⲁϣⲁϫⲉ ⲛⲉⲗⲁ-
ⲭⲓⲥⲧⲟⲥ · ⲁⲣⲁⲑ̄ⲁ̄ · ⲁⲣⲁ̄ⲑ̄ⲁ̄
ⲁⲣⲁⲑⲁⲏ̄ⲗ̄ · ⲁⲛⲁⲧⲏ̄ⲗ̄ · ⲙⲁ-
ⲛⲟⲩⲏ̄ⲗ̄ · ⲉⲇⲉⲕⲓ̄ⲏ̄ⲗ̄ · ⲛⲓ̄ⲥⲱ-
ⲛⲧ̄ ⲉⲧⲛⲏⲩ ⲉϩⲣⲁⲓ̈ ϩ̄ⲛ̄ ⲧ-

1–2 *i.e.* ἐξορκισμός ‖ **4–5** *i.e.* πύλη ‖ **7** *i.e.* ἐξορκισμός ‖ **9** *i.e.* πύλη ‖ **12** *i.e.* ἐξομολογεῖν ‖
13–14 *i.e.* κ[όσ]μος ‖ **18** *i.e.* πύλη ‖ **19–20** *i.e.* ἐξορκισμός ‖ **23** *i.e.* πύλη ‖ **25–26** *i.e.* ἐλάχιστος ‖
28 *l.* ⲥⲉⲇⲉⲕⲓⲏⲗ "Sedekiel" Pleyte/Boeser, Pleyte, Kropp, Smith, Lexa

of the Father, listen to my adjuration, Manouēl, Manouēl, Semanouēl, Manouēl, the four gates |⁵ of the Heavenly Jerusalem! Come to me today, listen to my adjuration!

I adjure you by the first gate of heaven, that |¹⁰ of the north, with all the creatures who stand praising the name [of] the Lord, the Father of the whole world, *Adonai |¹⁵ *Eloei *Elemas *Sabaoth! These are their names: Ēr, Ēr, Ēr, Ēr, Ēr, Ēr, Ēr. O creatures rising in the gate of the south, come to me and to my |²⁰ adjuration, Maroutha, Maroutha, Marouthaēl! O creatures rising up in the gate of the east, come to me today! |²⁵ Listen to my humble word, Aratha, Aratha, Arathaēl, Anatēl, Manouēl, Edekiēl! O creatures rising in the

---

2–4. ⲙⲁⲛⲟⲩⲏⲗ : ⲙⲁⲛⲟⲩⲏⲗ · ⲥⲉⲙⲁⲛⲟⲩⲏⲗ ⲙⲁⲛⲟⲩⲏⲗ : "Manouēl, Manouēl, Semanouēl, Manouēl" These names are probably to be understood as deriving from Emmanuel, from Hebrew עמנואל (*Īmmānū'ēl*, "God is with us"), from Isaiah 7.14: "Behold, the virgin will become pregnant and she will give birth to a boy, and they will call him 'Emmanuel' (ⲉⲓⲥ ⲧⲡⲁⲣⲑⲉⲛⲟⲥ ⲛⲁⲱⲱ ⲛⲥϫⲡⲟ ⲛⲟⲩϣⲏⲣⲉ ⲛⲧⲉⲧⲛⲙⲟⲩⲧⲉ ⲉⲡⲉϥⲣⲁⲛ ϫⲉ ⲉⲙⲙⲁⲛⲟⲩⲏⲗ; Bąk 2020: 536). In Matthew 1.22–23 this prophecy is explicitly made to refer to Jesus, so that 'Emmanuel' can be understood as another name of Jesus. The form 'Manouēl' may have arisen from a reanalysis in Coptic in which the initial ⲉ is understood as part of ϫⲉ. Manouēl is also found as a name of Jesus in p. 17 l. 4 of this manuscript, as well as *PCM* I 12 p. 31 l. 8, p. 37 l. 8; *PCM* I 25 p. 17 ll. 34–35; *PCM* I 26 p. 12 l. 13; BL Ms Or. 6796 (Kropp 1931: I no. H; KYP M118) l. 21; *P.Bad.* V 123 (KYP M315) front l. 41; EES 39 5B.125/A (Alcock 1982; KYP M280) l. 19; *P.Macq.* I 1 (KYP M167) p. 2 l. 16; P.Vindob K 8301 (Stegemann 1934: no. 45; KYP M 364) l. 6. 'Emmanuel' also appears in full in *e.g.*, *PCM* I 25 p. 11 l. 6; *P.Lond.Copt.* 1223 (KYP M553) l. 10; *P.Macq.* I 1 (KYP M167) p. 1 l. 14; P.Stras. K 204 + 205 + 282 §2.27 l. 8 (Hevesi 2018; KYP M92). Compare also the name 'Methemōn', based on the Greek translation of the name in Matthew 1.23, for which see *PCM* I 25 p. 11 l. 6. Ortal-Paz Saar points out that Semanouēl might be understood as a writing of the Hebrew שמענו אל (*šəmā'ēnû 'ēl* "hear us, God").

22. ⲉⲧⲛⲏⲩ ⲉϩⲣⲁⲓ : "rising up" Lexa hesitantly translates "descend" ("descendez en bas (?)").

page 17 (9r) (→)

ⲡⲩⲗⲏ ⲙ̄ⲡⲉⲙⲛ̄ⲧ · ⲁⲙ-
ⲙⲏⲓⲧⲛ̄ ϣⲁⲣⲟⲓ̈ ⲥⲱⲧⲙ̄ ⲉ-
ⲡⲁϣⲁϫⲉ ⲛⲉⲗⲁⲭⲓ̈ⲥⲧⲟⲛ ·
ⲁⲭⲁⲏ̄ⲗ̄ · ⲁⲏ̄ⲗ̄ · ⲙⲁⲛⲟⲩⲏ̄ⲗ̄
5 ⲉⲇⲉⲕⲓⲏ̄ⲗ̄ · ⲥⲛ̄ⲧⲁⲏ̄ⲗ̄ · ⲭⲉ-
ⲣⲟⲩⲃⲓ̈ⲛ · ⲭⲉⲣⲓ̈ⲛⲁⲏ̄ⲗ̄ · ⲥⲁⲣⲓ̈-
ⲛⲁⲏ̄ⲗ̄ · ⲁⲣⲓ̈ⲛⲁⲧⲁⲏ̄ⲗ̄ · ⲛⲉ-
ⲭⲉⲣⲟⲩⲃⲓ̈ⲛ ⲙ̄ⲛ ⲛⲉⲥⲉⲣⲁ-
ⲫⲓ̈ⲛ ⲉⲧⲁϩⲉⲣⲁⲧⲟⲩ ϩⲁ ⲡ-
10 ϩⲟ ⲙ̄ⲡⲉⲭ̄ⲥ̄ · ⲁⲙⲏⲓⲧⲛ̄ ϣⲁ-
ⲣⲟⲓ̈ ⲙ̄ⲡⲟⲟⲩ · ⲥⲱⲧⲙ̄ ⲉⲡⲁ-
ⲉⲍⲟⲣⲅⲓ̄ⲥⲙⲟⲥ · ⲛ̄ⲓ̄ⲥⲱⲛ̄ⲧ̄
ⲛ̄ⲧⲉⲛⲁⲣⲭⲁⲅⲅⲉⲗⲟⲥ · ⲙⲓ̄-
ⲭⲁⲏ̄ⲗ̄ · ⲅⲁⲃⲣⲓ̄ⲏ̄ⲗ̄ · ϩ̄ⲣⲁⲫⲁ-
15 ⲏ̄ⲗ̄ · ⲟⲩⲣⲓ̄ⲏⲗ · ⲥⲉⲇⲉⲕⲓ̄ⲏⲗ
ⲁⲛⲁⲏⲗ · ⲥⲉⲧⲏ̄ⲗ̄ · ⲁⲍⲁⲏⲗ ·
ⲛⲁⲓ̈ ⲉⲧⲁϩⲉⲣⲁⲧⲟⲩ ⲙ̄ⲡϩⲟⲧ
ⲉⲃⲟⲗ · ⲡⲉⲧⲟⲩⲏϩ ϩⲛ ⲛⲉⲙ-
ⲡⲏⲩⲉ · ⲡⲥⲁϣϥ̄ ⲛ̄ⲣⲁⲛ ⲛ̄-
20 ϣⲟⲩ ⲥⲱⲧⲙ̄ ⲉⲣⲟⲟⲩ · ⲛⲁⲓ̈
ⲉϣⲁⲣⲉⲟⲩⲟⲛ ⲛⲓ̈ⲙ ϩⲛ ⲛⲁⲅ-
ⲅⲉⲗⲟⲥ ⲙ̄ⲛ ⲛⲉϥⲥⲱⲟⲛ ⲧⲏ-
ⲣⲟⲩ · ⲟⲛⲟⲙⲁⲍⲉ ⲙ̄ⲙⲟϥ ·
ϣⲁⲣⲉⲡⲕⲁϩ ⲥ̄ⲧⲱⲧ · ⲛ̄-
25 ⲧⲉⲛⲧⲟⲟⲩ ⲛⲟⲉⲓⲛ · ⲛ̄ⲧⲉⲙ-
ⲙⲟⲟⲩ ⲉⲩⲫⲣⲁⲛⲉ · ⲉϫⲙ̄ ⲡ-
ⲛⲟϭ ⲛⲟⲩⲟⲉⲓⲛ ⲙ̄ⲡⲉϥⲣⲁⲛ ·
ⲁⲇⲱⲛⲁⲓ̈ · ⲉⲗⲱⲉⲓ̈ · ⲁⲗⲫⲁ
⸤ⲙⲓⲏ̄ⲗ̄⸥

---

1 *i.e.* πύλη ‖ 1–2 *l.* ⲁⲙⲏⲓⲧⲛ̄ ‖ 3 *i.e.* ἐλάχιστος ‖ 5 *l.* ⲥⲉⲇⲉⲕⲓⲏⲗ Pleyte/Boeser ‖ 8 *i.e.* χερουβίμ ‖ 8–9 *i.e.* σεραφίμ ‖ 10 *i.e.* ⲙ̄ⲡⲉ-χ(ριστό)ς ‖ 12 *i.e.* ἐξορκισμός ‖ 13 *i.e.* ἀρχάγγελος ‖ 18–19 *i.e.* ˢⲛ̄-ⲙ̄-ⲡⲏⲩⲉ ‖ 21–22 *i.e.* ἄγγελος ‖ 22 *i.e.* ζῷον : *l.* ⲥⲱⲛⲧ Pleye/Boeser, Pleyte ‖ 23 *i.e.* ὀνομάζειν ‖ 26 *i.e.* εὐφραίνειν ‖ 28–29 *l.* ⲁⲗⲫⲁⲙⲓⲏ̄ⲗ̄, line below ⲙⲓⲏ̄ⲗ̄ in papyrus : "Miel, Alpha" Boeser, Lexa, Kropp, Smith, Pernigotti 1995

gate of the west, come to me, listen to my humble word, Akhaēl, Aēl, Manouēl, |⁵ Edekiēl, Sntaēl, Kheroubin, Kherinaēl, Sarinaēl, Arinataēl! O *cherubim and *seraphim who stand before the |¹⁰ face of Christ, come to me today!

Listen to my adjuration, O creatures of the archangels, *Michael, *Gabriel, *Raphael, |¹⁵ Uriel, Sedekiēl, Anael, Setēl, Azael, those who stand in the presence of he who dwells in heavens, the seven names |²⁰ worthy of hearing, they that, when any among the *angels and all his living creatures name them, the earth trembles, |²⁵ the mountains shake, the waters rejoice on account of the great light of his name: *Adonai *Eloei Alphamiēl,

---

28–29. αλφαμιηλ : "Alphamiēl" We are grateful to Agnes Mihálykó for her suggestion to understand this as a single angelic name built upon the Greek word "alpha", in reference to the Lord God's self-identification as alpha and omega in Revelation 1.8; *cf.* p. 19 ll. 14–15 of this manuscript.

page 18 (9v) (↓)

-: ī̇ :-
ⲡⲉϥⲛⲟϭ ⲛ̄ⲣⲁⲛ · ⲁⲩⲱ ⲡⲉϥ-
ⲣⲁⲛ ⲙ̄ⲙⲏⲧ : ϯⲧⲁⲣⲕⲟ ⲙ̄ⲙⲱ-
ⲧⲛ̄ ⲙ̄ⲡⲉϥⲛⲟϭ ⲛ̄ⲣⲁⲛ : ⲥⲱ-
ⲛⲧ̄ ⲛⲓⲙ ⲉⲧⲛⲁⲟⲛⲟⲙⲁⲍⲉ
5   ⲙ̄ⲡⲓⲉⲝⲟⲣⲅⲓⲥⲙⲟⲥ : ϫⲉⲕⲁⲥ
ⲉⲧⲉⲧⲛⲁⲕⲁⲧⲁⲗⲏ ⲛ̄ⲧϭⲟⲙ
ⲧⲏⲣⲥ̄ ⲙ̄ⲡⲇⲓⲁⲃⲟⲗⲟⲥ : ⲛ̄-
ⲧⲉⲧⲛ̄ⲃⲱⲗ ⲉⲃⲟⲗ ⲙ̄ⲙⲣ̄ⲣⲉ
ⲛⲓⲙ : ⲙⲛ̄ ϫⲓⲛϭⲟⲛⲥ̄ ⲉⲧϣⲟ-
10 ⲟⲡ ⲛ̄ϩⲏⲧⲟⲩ · ⲙⲁⲣⲉⲡⲁⲁⲓ-
ⲧⲏⲙⲁ ϫⲱⲕ ⲉⲃⲟⲗ ⲉⲩⲛⲁ-
ⲱϣ ⲙ̄ⲡⲁⲉⲝⲟⲣⲅⲓⲥⲙⲟⲥ
ⲉⲙⲡⲁⲧⲉⲟⲩⲛⲟⲩ ϣⲱⲡⲉ
ⲁⲓⲧⲓ ⲙⲛ̄ⲛⲥⲱⲥ ⲧⲁⲡⲱ-
15 ⲣⲉⲕ ⲛⲉⲛⲛⲟⲩⲛⲉ ⲙ̄ⲡⲥⲁⲧⲁ-
ⲛⲁⲥ : ⲙⲛ̄ ⲙ̄ⲙⲣ̄ⲣⲉ ⲧⲏⲣⲟⲩ
ⲙ̄ⲡⲇⲓⲁⲃⲟⲗⲟⲥ · ⲛ̄ⲧⲉⲡⲁ-
ⲥⲟⲡⲥ̄ ϫⲱⲕ ⲉⲃⲟⲗ ϩⲓⲧⲙ̄
ⲡⲉⲕⲣⲁⲛ ⲡϫⲟⲉⲓⲥ ⲥⲁⲃⲁ-
20 ⲱⲑ · · ⲉⲗⲱⲉⲓ · ⲉⲗⲱⲉⲓ
ⲉⲗⲱⲉⲓ : ⲓⲁⲱ · ⲉⲓⲁⲱϩ ⲉⲓⲁⲱ
ⲥⲁⲃⲁⲱⲑ : ϩⲣⲁⲃⲟⲩⲛⲉⲓ
ⲡⲉⲧϣⲁⲟⲩⲁϩⲙⲉϥ
ϫⲉ ⲡⲥⲁϩ : ⲡⲁⲓ ⲉϣⲁⲣⲉⲛ-
25 ⲥⲱⲛⲧ̄ ⲧⲏⲣⲟⲩ ⲛ̄ⲛⲁⲅ-
ⲅⲉⲗⲟⲥ · ⲙⲛ̄ ⲛⲁⲣⲭⲁⲅⲅⲉ-
ⲗⲟⲥ ⲧⲉⲗⲏⲗ ⲙ̄ⲙⲟⲟⲩ ⲛ̄-
ϩⲏⲧϥ̄ · ϫⲉ ⲁⲅⲓⲟⲥ · ⲁⲅⲓⲟⲥ :-

---

6 *i.e.* καταλύειν ǁ **7** *i.e.* διάβολος ǁ **10–11** *i.e.* αἴτημα ǁ **12** *i.e.* ἐξορκισμός ǁ **14** *i.e.* ἔτι ǁ **15** *i.e.* ˢⲛⲉ-ⲛⲟⲩⲛⲉǁ **15–16** *i.e.* σατανᾶςǁ **17** *i.e.* διάβολοςǁ **25–26** *i.e.* ἄγγελοςǁ **26–27** *i.e.* ἀρχάγγελοςǁ **28** *i.e.* ἅγιος (twice)

his great name and his true name!

I adjure you by his great name, every creature which will pronounce |⁵ this adjuration, so that you will destroy the whole power of the Devil, and you will undo every *bond and violence that has come about |¹⁰ through them! Let my demand be fulfilled when my adjuration will be read, before ⟨the⟩ hour comes, furthermore, after this, I will pluck out |¹⁵ the roots of Satan and all the bonds of the Devil, and my prayer will be accomplished through your name, O Lord *Sabaoth |²⁰ *Eloei Eloei Eloei *Iao Eiaōh Eiaō Sabaoth Hrabounei—which is interpreted as "teacher"—the one in whom all |²⁵ creatures of the *angels and the *archangels rejoice, saying: "*Holy, holy,

---

11–14. ⲉⲩⲛⲁϣⲱ ⲙ̄ⲡⲁⲉⲝⲟⲣⲅⲓⲥⲙⲟⲥ ⲉⲙⲡⲁⲧⲉⲟⲩⲛⲟⲩ ϣⲱⲡⲉ ⲁⲓⲧⲓ ⲙ̄ⲛ̄ⲛ̄ⲥⲱⲥ : "when my adjuration will be read before ⟨the⟩ hour comes. Furthermore, after this" This passage is difficult to translate; perhaps understand "before an hour (ⲟⲩⲟⲩⲛⲟⲩ) has passed", although we have been unable to find an instance of ϣⲱⲡⲉ being used to describe an hour passing rather than coming; *cf.* Crum CD 484b, which would lead us to expect ϫⲱⲕ for the sense "to pass", and Luke 22.14: "when the time came..." (ⲛ̄ⲧⲉⲣⲉⲧⲉⲩⲛⲟⲩ ϣⲱⲡⲉ; Horner 1911: II 410). *Cf.* perhaps the copy of the *Prayer of Mary* in *BKU* I 6 l. 22–25 (KYP M119): "I invoke your names... before the hour comes and you are distant, so that I might undo the bonds of the Adversary" (ϯⲱⲣⲕ ⲛ̄ⲛⲉⲧⲉⲛⲣⲁⲛ ⲙⲡⲁⲧⲉⲟⲩⲛⲟⲩ ϣⲱⲡⲉ ⲛ̄ⲧⲉⲕⲉⲟⲩⲉⲓⲉⲓ̈ ⲛ̄ⲧⲁⲃⲟⲗ ⲉⲃⲟⲗ ⲛⲉⲙⲏⲣⲉ ⲧⲏⲣⲟⲩ ⲛ̄ⲡⲁⲛⲧⲓⲕⲓ̈ⲙⲉⲛ̣[ⲟⲥ]).

22–24. ϩ̄ⲣⲁⲃⲟⲩⲛⲉⲓ̈ ⲡⲉⲧⲉϣⲁⲩⲟⲩⲁϩⲙⲉϥ ϫⲉ ⲡⲥⲁϩ : "Hrabounei—which is interpreted as 'teacher'" *Cf.* John 20.16: "she (Mary Magdalene) said in Hebrew, "Rabbounei", which is interpreted as 'teacher'" (ⲡⲉϫⲁⲥ ⲙ̄ⲙⲛ̄ⲧϩⲉⲃⲣⲁⲓⲟⲥ ϫⲉ ⲣⲁⲃⲃⲟⲩⲛⲉⲓ ⲡⲉϣⲁⲩⲟⲩⲁϩⲙⲉϥ ϫⲉ ⲡⲥⲁϩ; Quecke 1984: 213).

page 19 (10r) (→)

ⲁⲅⲓⲟⲥ · ⲕⲩⲣⲓⲟⲥ · ⲥⲁⲃⲁⲱⲑ :
ⲙ̄ⲡⲏⲩⲉ ⲙ̄ⲛ̄ ⲡⲕⲁϩ ⲙⲉϩ ⲉⲃⲟⲗ
ϩⲙ̄ ⲡⲉⲕⲉⲟⲟⲩ · ⲙ̄ⲛ̄ ⲡⲉⲕⲥ̄-
ⲙⲟⲩ : ⲣⲁϣⲉ ⲛⲏⲧ̄ⲛ̄ ⲛⲉⲥⲱ-
5 ⲛⲧ̄ ⲧⲏⲣⲟⲩ ϫⲉ ⲁⲡϫⲟⲉⲓⲥ
ⲧⲱⲟⲩⲛ ⲉⲃⲟⲗ ϩⲛ̄ ⲛⲉⲧⲙⲟ-
ⲟⲩⲧ · ϩⲙ̄ ⲡⲙⲉϩϣⲟⲙⲛ̄ⲧ
ⲛ̄ϩⲟⲟⲩ : ⲁϥⲉⲗⲉⲩⲑⲉⲣⲟⲩ
ⲙ̄ⲡⲕⲉⲛⲟⲥ ⲧⲏⲣϥ̄ ⲛⲁⲇⲁⲙ :-
10 ⲁϥϣⲱⲗ ⲛ̄ⲛⲓ̈ⲟⲩⲇⲁⲓ̈ ⲛ̄ⲧⲁⲩ-
ϫⲓ̈ ϣⲓ̈ⲡⲉ ⲉϫⲙ̄ ⲡⲉⲛⲧⲁⲩ-
ⲁⲁϥ · ⲁϥⲁⲡⲁⲛⲧⲁ ⲉⲛⲉϥ-
ⲙⲁⲑⲏⲧⲏⲥ · ⲁϥϯ ⲛⲁⲩ ⲙ̄ⲡ-
ϣⲙ̄ⲛⲟⲩϥⲉ · ⲡⲛⲟϭ ⲛ̄ⲛⲁⲗ-
15 ⲫⲁ ⲉⲧⲧⲁϫⲣⲏⲩ ⲉϫⲛ̄ ⲛⲁⲓ̈
ⲧⲏⲣⲟⲩ : †ⲡⲁⲣⲁⲕⲁⲗⲉⲓ̈ ⲙ̄-
ⲙ̄ⲙⲱⲧⲛ̄ · ⲛ̄ⲧⲉⲧⲛ̄ⲁϩⲉ-
ⲣⲁⲧⲧⲏⲩⲧⲛ̄ ⲛⲙ̄ⲙⲁⲓ̈ ⲙ̄-
ⲡⲟⲟⲩ · ⲛ̄ⲧⲉⲧⲛ̄ϫⲱⲕ ⲉ-
20 ⲃⲟⲗ ⲛ̄ⲙⲡⲉⲧⲛⲁⲛⲟⲩⲟⲩ
ⲙ̄ⲡⲁϩⲏⲧ · ⲙⲁⲣⲟⲩϫⲓ̈ ϣⲓ̈-
ⲡⲉ ⲛ̄ϭⲓ̈ ⲛⲉⲧⲙⲉ ⲙ̄ⲡⲇⲓ̈ⲁ-
ⲃⲟⲗⲟⲥ : ⲁⲩⲱ ⲛ̄ⲥⲉϩⲉ ϩⲁ-
ⲣⲁⲧⲥ̄ ⲛ̄ⲧⲉⲓ̈ⲡⲟⲣⲥⲉⲩⲭⲏ
25 ⲡ̄ⲛ̄ⲁ ⲛⲓ̈ⲙ ⲙ̄ⲡⲟⲛⲏⲣⲟⲛ ·
ⲡ̄ⲛ̄ⲁ ⲛⲓ̈ⲙ ⲛⲁⲅⲁⲑⲁⲣⲧⲟⲛ :
ϩⲓ̈ⲕ ⲛⲓ̈ⲙ · ϣⲁϥⲧⲉ ⲛⲓ̈ⲙ
ⲁⲛⲁⲭⲱⲣⲉⲓ̈ ⲛⲏⲧⲛ̄ ⲡⲉⲭ̄ⲥ̄
        ⲓ̄ⲥ̄ ⲡⲉⲧⲇⲓⲱⲕⲉⲓ

---

1 *i.e.* ἅγιος κύριος ‖ **8** *i.e.* ἐλευθεροῦν ‖ **9** *i.e.* γένος ‖ **12** *i.e.* ἀπαντᾶν ‖ **13** *i.e.* μαθητής ‖ **14–15** *i.e.* ˢⲛ̄-ἄλφα ‖ **16** *i.e.* παρακαλεῖν ‖ *l.* ⲙ̄ⲙⲱⲧⲛ̄ (dittography) ‖ **22–23** *i.e.* διάβολος ‖ **24** *i.e.* προσευχή ‖ **25** *i.e.* πν(εῦμ)α | *i.e.* πονηρόν ‖ **26** *i.e.* πν(εῦμ)α | *i.e.* ἀκάθαρτον ‖ **28** *i.e.* ἀναχωρεῖν | *l.* ⲡⲉ-ⲭ(ⲣⲓⲥⲧⲟ́)ⲥ ⲓ(ⲏⲥⲟⲩ)ⲥ | *i.e.* διώκειν ‖ **29** line below in *pap.*

holy, Lord *Sabaoth, the heavens and the earth are full of your glory and your blessing!"

Rejoice, |⁵ all you creatures, for the Lord rose from the dead on the third day and he freed the entire race of Adam, |¹⁰ and he despoiled the Jews, who were ashamed of what they had done, and he met his disciples and gave them the good news, the great Alpha |¹⁵ who is established by all these things. I invoke you that you stand with me today and fulfil |²⁰ that which is good in my heart! Let them be ashamed, those who love the Devil, and fall down before this prayer. |²⁵ Every evil spirit, every unclean spirit, every sorcery, every impiety, withdraw yourselves; it is Christ Jesus who chases

---

3–4. ϩⲙ ⲡⲉⲕⲉⲟⲟⲩ · ⲙⲛ ⲡⲉⲕⲥⲙⲟⲩ : "your glory and your blessing" The *Sanctus usually ends with the phrase "your glory" (Greek δόξης σου, Coptic ⲡⲉⲕⲉⲟⲟⲩ). The ending "your blessing" added here seems to attest to a variant also found in the sixth/seventh century BM EA 54036 (Quecke 1971; for the date see Mihálykó 2019: 294), a Coptic copy of the Anaphora of Mark containing the end of the reprise of the Sanctus by the priest. In this reprise "your blessing" (ⲡⲉⲕⲥⲙⲟⲩ) replaces "your glory" (ⲡⲉⲕⲉⲟⲟⲩ) at the end of the Sanctus, perhaps anticipating the following request to "fill this offering too... with your blessing" (ⲙⲉϩ ⲧⲉⲓⲑⲩⲥⲓⲁ ⲟⲛ : ⲙⲡⲛⲟⲩⲧⲉ ϩⲙ ⲡⲉⲕⲥⲙⲟⲩ). The inclusion of both here may imply that the composer of this text was aware of this variant and chose to harmonise it with the more common "your glory". Note that the version here combines the Greek and Coptic versions of the Sanctus. We are very grateful to Ágnes Mihálykó for suggesting this possibility to us.

14–15. ⲡⲛⲟϭ ⲛⲛⲁⲗⲫⲁ : "the great Alpha" Pleyte translates "he, the great Alpha", Lexa translates similarly ("lui le grand Alpha").

15–16. ⲉⲧⲧⲁϫⲣⲏⲩ ⲉϫⲛ ⲛⲁⲓ ⲧⲏⲣⲟⲩ : "who is established by all these things" Smith translates "that is stronger than anything", but the comparative would be expressed with ⲉ-/ⲉⲣⲟϥ; *cf.* Crum CD 463a, and, for example, Sirach 22.18: "a heart established by a wise thought will never be afraid" (ⲟⲩϩⲏⲧ ⲉϥⲧⲁϫⲣⲏⲩ ⲉϫⲛ ⲟⲩⲙⲉⲉⲩⲉ ⲙⲙⲛⲧⲣⲙⲛϩⲏⲧ ⲉⲛϥⲛⲁⲣϩⲟⲧⲉ ⲁⲛ ⲉⲛⲉϩ; de Lagarde 1883: 144).

27. Pleyte omits this line in his translation.

page 20 (10v) (↓)

-: ι̅α̅ :-
ⲙⲙⲱⲧⲛ̅ · ⲡⲉⲥⲛⲟϥ ⲙ̅ⲡⲉ-
ⲭ̅ⲥ̅ ϩⲁⲣⲉϩ ⲉⲟⲩⲟⲛ ⲛⲓⲙ ⲉⲧ-
ⲫⲟⲣⲓ̈ ⲛ̅ⲧⲡ̅ⲡⲣⲟⲥⲉⲩⲭⲏ ·
ⲧⲉⲧⲣⲓ̅ⲁⲥ ⲉⲧⲟⲩⲁⲁⲃ ⲛⲉ-
5 ⲙⲁⲛ ⲧⲏⲣⲛ̅ ϩⲁⲙⲏⲛ -
>>>>>>>>>>>>>>>>>>

ⲁ̀ⲅⲕⲁⲣⲟⲥ ⲡ̅ⲡⲣⲟ ⲛⲉⲧⲉⲥ-
ⲥⲁ ⲧⲡⲟⲗⲓ̅ⲥ · ⲉϥⲥ̅ϩⲁⲓ̈ ⲙ̅ⲡ-
ⲛⲟϭ ⲛ̅ⲡ̅ⲣⲟ · ⲡϣⲏⲣⲉ ⲙ̅ⲡⲛⲟⲩ-
ⲧⲉ ⲉⲧⲟⲛϩ̅ · ⲓ̅ⲥ̅ ⲡⲉⲭ̅ⲥ̅ ⲭⲉⲣⲉ
10 ⲁⲩⲁⲛⲁⲛⲁⲅⲉ ⲛⲁⲓ̅ ⲉⲧⲃⲏ-
ⲏⲧⲕ̅ ⲛ̅ϭⲓ̅ ϩⲉⲛⲣⲱⲙⲉ ⲉⲩⲧⲁ-
ⲓⲏⲩ : ⲁⲩⲱ ⲛ̅ϣⲟⲩ · ⲡⲓⲥⲧⲉⲩ-
ⲉ ⲛⲁⲩ · ϫⲉ ⲁⲡⲕⲟⲥⲙⲟⲥ ⲉⲙ-
ⲡϣⲁ ϩ̅ⲙ̅ ⲡⲉⲛⲟⲩⲟⲉⲓϣ ⲙ̅-
15 ⲙⲁⲧⲉ : ⲙ̅ⲡⲉⲕϭ̅ⲙ̅ⲡϣⲓ-
ⲛⲉ ⲉⲧⲛⲁⲛⲟⲩϥ ϩⲓⲧⲙ̅ ⲡⲉ-
ⲕⲟⲩⲱⲛϩ̅ ⲉⲃⲟⲗ · ⲡⲁⲓ̅ ⲛ̅-
ⲧⲁⲕϭ̅ⲙ̅ⲡⲉⲛϣⲓ̈ⲛⲉ ⲛ̅ϩⲏⲧϥ̅
ϩ̅ⲛ̅ ⲧⲉⲛⲅⲉⲛⲉⲁ ⲉⲧⲥⲟϫϥ̅
20 ϩⲓⲧⲛ̅ ⲧⲉⲕⲙ̅ⲛ̅ⲧⲙⲁⲓ̈ⲣⲱ-
ⲙⲉ ⲉⲧϣⲟⲟⲡ ϫⲓ̅ⲛ ⲉⲛⲉϩ
ⲉⲩⲟⲩϫⲁⲓ̈ ⲙ̅ⲡ̅ⲧⲏⲣϥ̅ · ⲛ̅-
ⲧⲉⲣⲓ̅ⲥⲱⲧⲙ̅ ⲇⲉ ⲉⲛⲁⲓ̅ ⲁⲓ̅-
ⲡⲓⲥⲧⲉⲩⲉ ϩ̅ⲛ̅ ⲟⲩⲱⲣⲭ̅ :
25 ⲭⲱⲣⲓ̈ⲥ ⲧ̅ⲓ̅ⲥⲧⲁⲍⲉ : ϩⲁⲙⲁ
ⲇⲉ ⲁⲩϫⲟⲥⲉ ϫⲉ ⲕⲉⲓⲣⲉ ⲛ̅-
ϩ̅ⲛ̅ⲛⲟϭ ⲛ̅ⲧⲁⲗϭⲟ : ⲭⲱⲣⲓ̅ⲥ

---

2 *i.e.* χ(ριστό)ς ‖ **3** *i.e.* φορεῖν | *i.e.* προσευχή ‖ **4** *i.e.* τρίας ‖ **5** *i.e.* ἀμήν ‖ **6** ⲁⲅⲕⲁⲣⲟⲥ enlarged capital ⲁ in *ekthesis* ‖ **7** *i.e.* πόλις ‖ **9** *l.* ι(ηⲥⲟⲩ)ⲥ ⲡⲉ-χ(ριστό)ς | *i.e.* χαῖρε ‖ **10** *i.e.* ἀναγαγεῖν *cf.* LBG *s.v.* ἀναγάγω : *i.e.* ἀνάγειν Kropp ‖ **12–13** *i.e.* πιστεύειν ‖ **13** *i.e.* κόσμος ‖ **19** *i.e.* γενεά ‖ **23** *i.e.* δέ ‖ **24** *i.e.* πιστεύειν ‖ **25** *i.e.* χωρίς | *i.e.* διστάζειν | *i.e.* ἅμα ‖ **26** *i.e.* δέ | *i.e.* ˢϫⲟⲟ=ⲥ ‖ **27** *i.e.* χωρίς

you away!

O blood of Christ, guard everyone who carries this prayer! The Holy Trinity is |⁵ with us all, amen.

Abgar, the king of the city of Edessa writes to the great king, the son of the living God, Jesus Christ, greetings! |¹⁰ Some people, honoured and worthy of belief, have reported about you saying that the world has been most worthy in our time |¹⁵ of your good coming through your appearance, that in which you have come to us, in our humble generation |²⁰ through your love of humanity which has existed since eternity, all enduring. So, when I heard these things, I believed firmly, |²⁵ without hesitation. And also they said that you perform great healings without

---

1–2 пєсноϥ ⲙ̄ⲡⲉ-ⲭ̄ⲥ̄ : "**O blood of Christ**" The 'blood of Christ' (sometimes mentioned alongside his 'body') is commonly invoked in both amuletic and liturgical texts, referring simultaneously to the blood spilled during the crucifixion and its representation in the eucharistic ritual; for a recently discussion see Chepel 2017.

p. 20 l. 6–p. 25 l. 23. The Jesus-Abgar Correspondence: The pseudepigraphal letter of King Abgar of Edessa to Jesus, and Jesus' response, are first recorded in the early fourth century *Ecclesiastical History* of Eusebius (13.1–20), while the evidence of Etheria (*Itinerary* 17.1, 19.19), a pilgrim from the Western Roman Empire, suggests the text was in circulation, perhaps as an amulet, by the 380s (Bradshaw 2020: 9–11). The version here, found in most Coptic witnesses, represents a variant adapted to be used as an amulet, as is clear from the promise that it will protect anyone who wears it or puts it in their house (p. 25 ll. 10–21). The incipit of the Jesus-Abgar correspondence is the only non-Biblical text commonly attested on scriptural amulets, demonstrating its importance as the sole text attributed directly to Jesus himself, and it is often juxtaposed with the incipits of the Gospels and Psalm 90 (91), as is the case here; *cf.* Sanzo 2014: 77–131, nos. 1, 4, 5, 59, 153–154, 174. For further discussion of these texts as amulets, see von Dobschütz 1900; Given 2016; Henry 2016; Polański 2016; Bélanger Sarrazin 2020; Bélanger Sarrazin forthcoming c; Preininger forthcoming b. Other attestations of the correspondence in Coptic include: *O.Crum* 22 (KYP M670); *O.Crum ST* 36 (KYP M671); *O.Gurna Górecki* 108 (KYP M2135); *O.Saint-Marc* 398 (KYP M2136); *P.Lond.Copt.* 316 (KYP M739); *P.Lond.Copt.* 317 (KYP M411); *P.Mon.Epiph.* 50 (KYP M598); *P.MoscowCopt.* 88 (KYP M644); *P.Oxy.* LXV 4469 (KYP M654); *P.PalauRib.Copt.* 5 (KYP M509); Al-Suryan MS 383/Al-Suryan MS 266 Lit. ('Abd Al-Masiḥ 1947; KYP M3782); 'Anchorite's Grotto' texts 25-26 (Griffith 1927: no. 25–26; KYP M91); Bawit, Courtyard 47, East wall, text IV. (Clédat 1999: 98–100; KYP M3783); BM EA 19967 (von Lemm 1910: no. 11; KYP M695); Mich.Ms.Copt. 166 ('Abd Al-Masiḥ 1954: 21–28; KYP M3780); P.Mich.Inv. 6213 ('Abd Al-Masiḥ 1954: 25–26; KYP M543); P.Vindob. K 78 (Stegemann 1933–1934: no. 50; KYP M278); P.Vindob. K 3151a (Stegemann 1933–1934: no. 46; KYP M274); P.Ryl.Copt.Suppl.No. 50 (Giversen 1959: 71–82; KYP M734); PSI inv. C 55 (Proverbio 1997: 1170; KYP M3756); P.Vindob. K 8302 (Stegemann 1933–1934: no. 45; KYP M364); P.Vindob.K 8636 Pap (Stegemann 1933–1934: no. 26; KYP M257); P.Antinoopolis 1966–224 (to be published by Alain Delattre); P.Vindob. G 1329 back (unpublished). We are grateful to Roxanne Bélanger Sarrazin for her assistance in finding these references.

19. ⲧⲉⲛⲅⲉⲛⲉⲁ ⲉⲧϭⲟⲝϥ̄ : "**our humble generation**" Smith translates "our inferior race".

page 21 (11r) (↓)

ⲡⲁϩⲣⲉ ϩⲓ ⲃⲏⲧⲁⲛⲓⲁ · ⲁⲩⲱ
ⲛⲉⲛⲧⲁⲩⲱⲥⲕ ϩⲙ · ⲡⲉⲭ-
ⲣⲟⲛⲟⲥ · ⲛ̄ⲃⲉⲗⲉⲉⲩⲉ · ⲙⲛ̄
ⲛⲉϭⲁⲗⲉⲉⲩⲉ · ⲙⲛ̄ ⲛⲉⲙⲡⲟ
5 ⲙⲛ̄ ⲛⲁⲗ · ⲁⲩⲱ ⲛⲉⲧⲥⲟ-
ⲃⲉϩ ⲕ̄ⲧⲃ̄ⲃⲟ ⲙ̄ⲙⲟⲟⲩ ϩⲙ̄
ⲡϣⲁϫⲉ ⲛ̄ⲣⲱⲕ ⲙ̄ⲙⲁⲧⲉ : —
ⲁⲩⲱ ⲛⲉⲇⲁⲓⲙⲟⲛⲓⲟⲛ ⲥⲉ-
ⲛⲏⲩ ⲉⲃⲟⲗ ϩⲛ̄ ⲟⲩϩⲟⲧⲉ ⲙⲛ̄
10 ⲟⲩⲥⲧⲱⲧ ⲉⲩⲉⲝⲟⲙⲟⲗⲟ-
ⲅⲓ̄ ⲙ̄ⲡⲉⲕⲣⲁⲛ ⲉⲧϩⲁ ⲉⲟⲟⲩ
ⲇⲏⲙⲟⲥⲓⲁ̄ : ⲁⲩⲱ ⲕⲟⲩⲉϩ-
ⲥⲁϩⲛⲉ ⲛ̄ⲛⲉⲧⲙⲟⲟⲩⲧ
ϩⲛ̄ ⲟⲩⲁⲩⲑⲉⲛⲧⲓⲁ̄ ⲥⲉⲛⲏⲩ
15 ⲉⲃⲟⲗ ϩⲛ̄ ⲛⲉⲙϩⲁⲁⲩ ⲙⲛ̄-
ⲛ̄ⲥⲁ ⲧⲣⲉⲩⲧⲟⲙⲥⲟⲩ :
ⲛ̄ϩⲃⲏⲩⲉ ⲟⲩⲱⲛϩ̄ ⲙ̄ⲙⲟⲕ
ⲉⲃⲟⲗ ⲉⲧⲣⲉⲥⲁⲣⲝ̄ ⲛⲓⲙ ⲥⲟⲩ-
ⲱⲛⲅ̄ : ϫⲉ ⲛⲧⲟⲕ ⲡⲉ ⲡⲙⲟ-
20 ⲛⲟⲅⲉⲛⲏⲥ ⲛ̄ϣⲏⲣⲉ ⲛ̄ⲧⲉⲡ-
ⲛⲟⲩⲧⲉ ⲙⲛ̄ ⲕⲉⲟⲩⲁ ⲛⲃⲗ̄-
ⲗⲁⲕ : ⲉⲧⲃⲉ ⲡⲁⲓ̄ ⲁⲓⲁⲝⲓ̄ⲟⲩ
ⲙ̄ⲙⲟⲕ : ⲡϫⲟⲉⲓⲥ ϩⲓⲧⲛ̄ ⲟⲩⲥ-
ϩⲁⲓ̄ ⲉⲧⲣⲉⲕⲉⲣ ⲡⲙⲉⲉⲩⲉ
25 ϩⲱⲱⲥ ⲛⲁⲓ̄ⲇⲉⲥⲥⲁ ϩⲓⲧⲛ̄
ⲡⲣⲟⲟⲩϣ ⲛ̄ⲧⲉⲕⲙⲛ̄ⲧⲛⲟⲩ-
ⲧⲉ ⲙⲛ̄ ⲧⲉⲕⲙⲛ̄ⲧⲣⲱⲙⲉ :

---

1 *i.e.* βοτάνια ‖ **2–3** *i.e.* χρόνος ‖ **3** *i.e.* ˢⲃⲗⲗⲉⲉⲩ ‖ **4** ⲛⲉⲙⲧⲡⲟ Pleyte/Boeser ‖ **5–6** *i.e.* ˢⲥⲱⲃϩ ‖ **8** *i.e.* δαιμόνιον ‖ **10–11** *i.e.* ἐξομολογεῖν ‖ **12** *i.e.* δημοσίᾳ ‖ **14** *i.e.* αὐθεντία ‖ **18** *i.e.* σάρξ ‖ **19–20** *i.e.* μονογενής ‖ **21–22** *i.e.* prepronominal form of ˢⲛⲃⲗ- ‖ **22** *i.e.* ἀξιοῦν ‖ **25** *i.e.* Ἔδεσσα

medicines or herbs and that those who have for a long time been blind, and the lame and the mute |⁵ and the deaf and the lepers, you purify them greatly by the word of your mouth, and the demons leave in fear and |¹⁰ trembling, confessing your glorious name publicly. And you command the dead with authority, and they |¹⁵ depart the tombs after having been buried. These deeds reveal you, so that all flesh might know you, that you are the |²⁰ only-begotten son of God, there is no other except you. Because of this, I have asked of you, O Lord, in writing, that you remember |²⁵ for its part Edessa in the care of your divinity and your humanity,

page 22 (11v) (→)

-: ⲓⲃ :-

ⲕⲁⲓ ⲅⲁⲣ ⲛ̄ϩⲉⲑⲛⲟⲥ ⲧⲏⲣⲟⲩ
ⲥⲉϣⲟⲟⲡ ⲛⲁⲕ ⲛ̄ⲣⲟⲟⲩϣ :
ⲁⲩⲱ ⲙⲛ̄ϣ ϭⲟⲙ ⲉⲧⲣⲉⲗⲁ-
ⲁⲩ ⲉⲣ ⲃⲟⲗ ⲛ̄ⲧⲟⲟⲧⲕ̄ · ⲧⲛ̄-
5 ⲥⲟⲡⲥ̄ ϭⲉ ⲙ̄ⲙⲟⲕ ⲁⲛⲟⲕ ⲙⲛ̄
ⲡⲗⲁⲟⲥ ⲉⲛⲡⲣⲟⲥⲕⲩⲛⲉⲓ
ⲛⲁⲕ ⲉⲧⲣⲉⲕⲥ̄ⲕ̄ⲏⲗⲗⲓ̈ ⲙ̄-
ⲙⲟⲕ ⲛ̄ⲅ̄ⲉⲓ ϣⲁⲣⲟⲛ · ⲉⲧ-
ⲃⲉ ⲡⲉⲛⲟⲩϫⲁⲓ : ⲙⲛ̄ ⲡ-
10 ⲧⲁⲗϭⲟ ⲛⲉⲛϣⲱⲛⲉ ⲉⲧⲟϣ
ⲁⲩⲱ ϫⲉⲕⲁⲥ ⲉⲩⲉⲧⲁⲟⲩⲉ
ⲡⲉⲕⲣⲁⲛ ⲉϩⲣⲁⲓ̈ ⲉϫⲱⲛ ⲡ-
ϫⲟⲉⲓ̈ⲥ · ⲁⲩⲱ ⲧⲁⲡⲟⲗⲓ̄ⲥ
ⲛⲁϣⲱⲡⲉ ⲉⲥϣ̄ⲙϣⲉ ⲙ̄-
15 ⲡⲉⲕⲑⲣⲟⲛⲟⲥ ⲛⲛⲉϩⲟⲟⲩ
ⲧⲏⲣⲟⲩ ⲙ̄ⲡⲉⲥⲱⲛϩ̄ : ⲁⲓ̄-
ⲥⲱⲧⲙ̄ ϫⲉ ⲁⲡⲉⲕϩⲉⲑⲛⲟⲥ
ⲁⲑⲉⲧⲓ̄ ⲛ̄ⲧⲉⲕⲙⲛ̄ⲧϫⲟ-
ⲉⲓⲥ̄ · ⲉⲩϣⲟⲟⲡ ϩⲛ̄ ⲟⲩⲕⲁ-
20 ⲕⲓ̄ⲁ ⲙ̄ⲛ ⲟⲩⲫⲑⲟⲛⲟⲥ ·
ⲁⲩⲱ ⲥⲉϯⲱⲕⲉ ⲙ̄ⲙⲟⲕ
ⲛ̄ⲥⲉⲟⲩⲱϣ ⲁⲛ ⲉⲧⲣⲉ-
ⲕⲉⲣ ⲉⲣⲣⲟ ⲉϩⲣⲁⲓ̈ ⲉϫⲱⲟⲩ
ⲉⲩⲟ ⲛⲁⲧⲥⲟⲟⲩⲛ ⲙ̄ⲡⲁⲓ̈
25 ϫⲉ ⲛ̄ⲧⲟⲕ ⲡⲉ ⲡ̄ⲣ̄ⲣⲟ ⲛⲉⲧ-
ϩⲛ̄ ⲛⲉⲙⲡⲏⲩⲉ ⲙⲛ̄ ⲛⲉⲧ-
ϩⲓ̈ϫⲙ̄ ⲡⲕⲁϩ ⲉⲧϯ ⲙ̄ⲡⲱ-

---

1 *i.e.* καί | *i.e.* γάρ | *i.e.* ἔθνος || **6** *i.e.* λαός | *i.e.* προσκυνεῖν || **7** *i.e.* σκύλλειν || **10** *i.e.* ˢⲛ̄-ⲛⲉ=ⲛ-ϣⲱⲛⲉ || **13** *i.e.* πόλις || **15** *i.e.* θρόνος || **17** *i.e.* ἔθνος || **18** *i.e.* ἀθετεῖν || **19–20** *i.e.* κακία || **20** *i.e.* φθόνος || **21** *i.e.* διώκειν || **25** *i.e.* ˢⲛ̄-ⲛⲉⲧ-

for indeed, all the nations are your concern and no one is able to escape from you. We |⁵ entreat you, therefore, I and the people, prostrating ourselves before you, that you trouble yourself and come to us for the sake of our salvation and the |¹⁰ healing ⟨of⟩ our numerous illnesses, and so that your name will be pronounced over us, O Lord, and my city will serve |¹⁵ your throne for all the days of its life. I heard that your nation rejected your lordship, being |²⁰ wicked and envious, and they persecute you, and they do not want to let you reign over them, being ignorant of this: |²⁵ that you are the king ⟨of⟩ those in the heavens and those upon the earth, who gives

page 23 (12r) (↓)

ⲛϩ̅ ⲛⲟⲩⲟⲛ ⲛⲓⲙ · ⲁⲩⲱ ⲛⲓⲙ
ϩⲱⲱϥ ⲡⲉ ⲡⲗⲁⲟⲥ ⲙⲡⲓⲏ̅ⲗ̅
ⲡⲟⲩϩⲟⲣ ⲉⲧⲙⲟⲟⲩⲧ ϫⲉ
ⲁⲩⲥⲧⲟ ⲉⲃⲟⲗ ⲙ̅ⲡⲛⲟⲩⲧⲉ
5   ⲉⲧⲟⲛϩ̅ · ⲕⲁⲓ̈ ⲅⲁⲣ ϩⲛ̅ⲁⲧ-
ⲉⲙⲡϣⲁ ⲛⲉ ⲛ̅ⲧⲉⲕⲇⲱⲣⲉ-
ⲁ ⲉⲧⲟⲩⲁⲁⲃ : †ⲧⲁⲙⲟ ⲇⲉ
ⲙ̅ⲙⲟⲕ ⲡⲁϫⲟⲉⲓⲥ ϫⲉ ⲉⲛ-
ϣⲁⲛⲕⲁⲧⲁⲝⲓ̈ⲟⲩ ⲣⲱ ⲉⲛⲉϩ
10 ⲉⲧⲣⲉⲕⲥ̅ⲕⲏⲗⲗⲓ ⲛ̅ⲅⲉⲓ ϣⲁ-
ⲣⲟⲓ̈ · ⲉⲧⲕⲟⲩⲓ̈ ⲙ̅ⲡⲟⲗⲓⲥ ⲉⲧ-
ⲁⲣⲭⲓ ⲉⲣⲟⲥ · ⲥ̅ⲣⲱϣⲉ ⲉⲣⲟⲛ
ϩⲓ ⲟⲩⲥⲟⲡ ϩⲛ̅ ⲟⲩⲁⲅⲁⲡⲏ :
ⲭⲱⲣⲓ̈ⲥ ⲕⲱϩ ϩⲓ ⲫⲑⲟⲛⲟⲥ
15 ⲉⲧⲣⲉⲕϣⲱⲡⲉ ⲉⲕⲟ ⲛ̅ⲣ̅ⲣⲟ
ⲉϫⲱⲛ : ⲁⲛⲟⲕ ⲙⲛ̅ ⲡⲗⲁⲟⲥ
ⲧⲛ̅ⲛⲁⲥⲱ ϩⲁⲣⲁⲧⲕ̅ · ⲉⲛⲟⲩ-
ⲱϣ̅ⲧ ⲉⲡϩⲩⲡⲟⲡⲟⲇⲓ̈ⲟⲛ
ⲛ̅ⲛⲉⲕⲟⲩⲉⲣⲏⲧⲉ : ⲁⲩⲱ
20 ⲉⲛϣ̅ⲙϣⲉ ⲉⲡⲉⲕⲑⲣⲟⲛⲟⲥ
ⲉⲧⲟⲩⲁⲁⲃ : ⲡⲉⲟⲟⲩ ⲛⲁⲕ
ⲡⲉⲟⲟⲩ ⲙ̅ⲡⲉⲕⲉⲓⲱⲧ ⲛ̅ⲁ-
ϩⲟⲣⲁⲧⲟⲛ ⲛ̅ⲧⲁϥⲧⲛ̅ⲛⲟ-
ⲟⲩⲕ ⲛⲁⲛ · ⲡⲉⲟⲟⲩ ⲙ̅ⲡⲕ̅-
25 ⲡ̅ⲛ̅ⲁ̅ ⲉⲧⲟⲩⲁⲁⲃ ⲉⲧϭⲙ̅-
ϭⲟⲙ ϣⲁ ⲉⲛⲉϩ ϩⲁⲙⲏⲛ —

---

2 *i.e.* λαός | *i.e.* Ἰ(σρα)ήλ || **5** *i.e.* καί | *i.e.* γάρ || **6–7** *i.e.* δωρεά || **7** *i.e.* δέ || **9** *i.e.* καταξιοῦν || **10** *i.e.* σκύλλειν || **11** *i.e.* πόλις | *i.e.* ˢⲉⲧ†- || **12** *i.e.* ἄρχειν || **13** *i.e.* ἀγάπη || **14** *i.e.* χωρίς | *i.e.* φθόνος || **16** *i.e.* λαός || **17** ⲧⲛ̅ⲛⲁⲭⲱ Pleyte/Boeser || **18** *i.e.* ὑποπόδιον || **20** *i.e.* θρόνος || **21** ⲡⲉⲟⲟⲩ ⲛⲁⲕ Kropp does not translate || **22–23** *i.e.* ἀόρατον || **25** *i.e.* πν(εῦμ)α || **26** *i.e.* ἀμήν

life to everyone. And what indeed is the people of Israel? The dead dog, because they have rejected the living God. |⁵ For indeed, they are not worthy of your holy gift. But I tell you, my Lord, that if indeed we are ever deemed worthy |¹⁰ for you to trouble ⟨yourself⟩ and come to me, to the small city which I rule, it is enough for us together, and in love without envy or jealousy, |¹⁵ that you be king over us. I, and the people, we shall remain beneath you, worshipping the footstool of your feet, and |²⁰ serving your holy throne. Glory to you! Glory to your invisible father who sent you to us! Glory to your |²⁵ Holy Spirit, which is mighty forever! Amen.

3. ⲡⲟⲩϩⲟⲣ ⲉⲧⲙⲟⲟⲩⲧ : **"the dead dog"** As noted by Sanzo (2017: 241), this piece of anti-Jewish invective is absent from the other known versions of the Abgar letter. It may draw upon a tradition of associating Jews with dogs based on an interpretation of Paul's warning to "beware the dogs" (ϯϩⲧⲏⲧⲛ̄ ⲉⲛⲉⲩϩⲟⲟⲣ) in Philippians 3.2, already understood by John Chrysostom as referring to Jews and Judaising Christians (Sanzo 2017: 241; Nanos 2009: 454–455 *et passim*). This in turn draws upon the general Near Eastern use of "dog" as an insult or term of self-abasement (Thomas 1960: 416–417 *et passim*); the phrase "dead dog" specifically appears in, for example, 2 Samuel 16.9: "Who is this dead dog that he should curse my lord the king? I will go to him and take his head" (ⲟⲩ ⲡⲉ ⲡⲉⲓⲟⲩϩⲟⲣ ⲉⲧⲙⲟⲟⲩⲧ ϫⲉ ⲉϥⲉⲥⲁϩⲟⲩ ⲙ̄ⲡⲁϫⲟⲉⲓⲥ ⲡ̄ⲣ̄ⲣⲟ ϯⲛⲁⲃⲱⲕ ⲉⲣⲟϥ ⲛ̄ⲧⲁϥⲓ ⲛ̄ⲧⲉϥⲁⲡⲉ; Drescher 1970: 153).

page 24 (12v) (→)

-: ⲓ̅ⲃ̅ :-

ⲧⲉⲡⲓ̅ⲥⲧⲟⲗⲏ ⲛⲓ̅ⲥ̅ ⲡⲉⲭ̅ⲥ̅ ⲡⲛ̅-
ⲭⲟⲉⲓⲥ ϣⲁ ⲁⲩⲕⲁⲣⲟⲥ ϩⲁⲙⲏⲛ
ⲡⲁⲛⲧⲓ̈ⲅⲣⲁⲫⲟⲛ ⲛⲧⲉⲡⲓ̅ⲥ-
ⲧⲟⲗⲏ ⲛⲓ̅ⲥ̅ ⲡⲉⲭ̅ⲥ̅ ⲡϣⲏⲣⲉ
5 ⲙ̅ⲡⲛⲟⲩⲧⲉ ⲉⲧⲟⲛϩ̅ : ⲉϥⲥ-
ϩⲁⲓ̈ ⲛ̅ⲛⲁⲩⲕⲁⲣⲟⲥ ⲡ̅ⲣ̅ⲣⲟ
ⲛⲉⲧⲉⲥⲥⲁ : ⲭⲁⲓ̈ⲣⲉⲧⲉ :
ⲛⲁⲓ̈ⲁⲧⲕ̅ ⲁⲩⲱ ⲡⲡⲉⲧⲛⲁ-
ⲛⲟⲩϥ ⲛⲁϣⲱⲡⲉ ⲙ̅ⲙⲟⲕ :
10 ⲁⲩⲱ ⲛⲁⲓ̈ⲁⲧⲥ̅ ⲛ̅ⲧⲉⲕⲡⲟ-
ⲗⲓⲥ · ⲧⲁⲓ̈ ⲉⲡⲉⲥⲣⲁⲛ ⲡⲉ ⲉ-
ⲧⲉⲥⲥⲁ · ⲉⲡⲓⲇⲏ ⲙⲡⲉⲕ-
ⲛⲁⲩ ⲁⲕⲡⲓ̅ⲥⲧⲉⲩⲉ · ⲕⲛⲁ-
ϫⲓ ⲕⲁⲧⲁ ⲧⲉⲕⲡⲓ̅ⲥⲧⲓ̅ⲥ
15 ⲁⲩⲱ ⲧⲉⲕⲡⲣⲟϩⲉ-
ⲣⲏⲥⲓ̈ⲥ : ⲛⲉⲕ-
ϣⲱⲛⲉ ⲥⲉⲛⲁⲧⲁⲗϭⲟⲟⲩ :
ⲁⲩⲱ ⲉϣϫⲉ ⲁⲕⲉⲣ ϩⲁϩ ⲛ̅ⲛⲟ-
ⲃⲉ ϩⲱⲥ ⲣⲱⲙⲉ ⲥⲉⲛⲁⲕⲁ-
20 ⲁⲩ ⲛⲁⲕ ⲉⲃⲟⲗ · ⲁⲩⲱ ⲉⲧⲉⲥ-
ⲥⲁ ⲛⲁϣⲱⲡⲉ ⲉⲥⲥ̅ⲙⲁⲙⲁ-
ⲁⲧ ϣⲁ ⲉⲛⲉϩ · ⲛⲧⲉⲡⲉⲟ-
ⲟⲩ ⲙⲡⲛⲟⲩⲧⲉ ⲁϣⲁⲓ̈ ϩⲙ̅
ⲡⲉⲥⲗⲁⲟⲥ · ⲁⲩⲱ ⲧⲡⲓⲥ-
25 ⲧⲓ̅ⲥ ⲙⲛ̅ ⲧⲁⲅⲁⲡⲏ ⲛⲁⲉⲣ
ⲟⲩⲟⲉⲓ̈ⲛ ϩⲛ̅ ⲛⲉⲥⲡⲗⲁⲧⲓ̈ⲁ
ⲁⲛⲟⲕ ⲓ̅ⲥ̅ ⲁⲛⲟⲕ ⲉⲧϩⲱⲛ
ⲁⲩⲱ ⲁⲛⲟⲕ ⲉⲧϣⲁϫⲉ ·
ⲉⲃⲟⲗ ϫⲉ ⲁⲕⲙⲉ ⲉⲙⲁⲧⲉ

---

1 *i.e.* ἐπιστολή | *l.* ι(ησου)ς πε-χ(ριστό)ς || **2–3** diple in margin | **2** *i.e.* ἀμήν || **3** *i.e.* ἀντίγραφον || **3–4** *i.e.* ἐπιστολή || **4** *l.* ι(ησου)ς πε-χ(ριστό)ς || **7** *i.e.* χαίρετε || **10–11** *i.e.* πόλις || **12** *i.e.* ἐπειδή || **13** *i.e.* πιστεύειν || **14** *i.e.* κατά | *i.e.* πίστις || **15–16** *i.e.* προαίρεσις || **19** *i.e.* ὡς || **24** *i.e.* λαός : "your people" Smith || **24–25** *i.e.* πίστις || **25** *i.e.* ἀγάπη || **26** *i.e.* πλατεῖα

The letter of Jesus Christ our Lord to Abgar. Amen.

The copy of the letter of Jesus Christ, the son |⁵ of the living God, writing to Abgar, the king of Edessa:

Greetings! You are blessed, and that which is good will happen to you, |¹⁰ and blessed is your city, whose name is Edessa, for you have not seen ⟨but⟩ you have believed, you will receive according to your faith |¹⁵ and according to your good intention. Your illnesses will be healed, and if you have committed many sins as ⟨a⟩ man, they will be forgiven |²⁰ for you, and Edessa will be blessed forever, and the glory of God will multiply among its people, and faith |²⁵ and love will shine in its streets. I, Jesus, it is I who commands and it is I who speak. Because you have loved greatly,

---

12–13. ⲉⲡⲓⲇⲏ ⲙⲡⲉⲕⲛⲁⲩ ⲁⲕⲡⲓⲥⲧⲉⲩⲉ : **"for you have not seen ⟨but⟩ you have believed"** A reference to John 20.29: "blessed are those who have not seen (me) and who have believed" (ⲛⲁⲓⲁⲧⲟⲩ ⲛ̄ⲛⲉⲧⲉⲙ̄ⲡⲟⲩⲛⲁⲩ ⲁⲩⲡⲓⲥⲧⲉⲩⲉ; Quecke 1984: 216).

page 25 (13r) (↓)

ϯⲛⲁⲕⲱ ⲙ̄ⲡⲉⲕⲣⲁⲛ ⲉⲩⲉⲣ-
ⲡⲙⲉⲉⲩⲉ ⲛ̄ϣⲁ ⲉⲛⲉϩ · ⲁⲩ-
ⲱ ⲟⲩϯⲙⲏ ⲙ̄ⲛ ⲟⲩⲥⲙⲟⲩ
ϩⲛ̄ ⲛ̄ⲅⲉⲛⲉⲁ ⲉⲧⲛⲏⲩ ⲙ̄ⲛ̄-
5 ⲛ̄ⲥⲱⲕ · ϩⲛ̄ ⲧⲉⲕⲡⲁⲧⲣⲓ̈ⲁ
ⲧⲏⲣⲥ̄ · ⲁⲩⲱ ⲛ̄ⲥⲉⲥⲟⲧ-
ⲙⲉϥ ϣⲁ ⲁⲣⲏⲭ̄ϥ ⲙ̄ⲡ-
ⲕⲁϩ · ⲁⲛⲟⲕ ⲓ̄ⲥ̄ ⲡⲉⲛⲧⲁⲓ̈ⲥ-
ϩⲁⲓ̈ ⲛ̄ⲧⲉⲓ̈ⲉⲡⲓ̈ⲥⲧⲟⲗⲏ ϩⲛ̄
10 ⲧⲁϭⲓ̄ϫ ⲙ̄ⲙⲓ̄ⲛⲉ ⲙ̄ⲙⲟⲓ · ⲡ-
ⲙⲁ ⲉⲧⲟⲩⲛⲁⲧⲱϫⲉ ⲉⲃⲟⲗ
ⲛ̄ϩⲏⲧϥ̄ ⲛ̄ⲧⲓ̄ϭⲓ̄ϫ ⲛ̄ϭϩⲁⲓ
ⲛ̄ⲛⲉⲗⲁⲁⲩ ⲛ̄ⲇⲏⲛⲁⲙⲓ̈ⲥ
ⲛ̄ⲧⲉⲡⲁⲛⲧⲓ̄ⲕⲓ̈ⲙⲉⲛⲟⲥ
15 ⲟⲩⲇⲉ ⲗⲁⲁⲩ ⲙ̄ⲡ̄ⲛ̄ⲁ̄ ⲛⲁⲕⲁⲑⲁⲣⲧⲟⲛ · ⲉϣϭⲙϭⲟⲙ ⲉ-
ϩⲱⲛⲉ ⲉϩⲟⲩⲛ · ⲟⲩⲇⲉ ⲉ-
ϫⲱϩ ⲉϩⲟⲩⲛ ⲉⲡⲧⲟⲡⲟⲥ
ⲉⲧⲙ̄ⲙⲁⲩ · ⲁⲩⲱ ⲛ̄ϣⲁ ⲉ-
20 ⲛⲉϩ : ⲟⲩϫⲁⲓ̈ ϩⲛ̄ ⲟⲩⲉⲓ̄ⲣⲏ-
ⲛⲏ ϩⲁⲙⲏⲛ   ·———·———

ϯⲉⲡⲓ̄ⲥⲧⲟⲗⲏ ⲙ̄ⲡⲉⲛϫⲟⲉⲓ̄ⲥ
ⲓ̄ⲥ̄ ⲡⲉⲭ̄ⲥ̄ ϣⲁ ⲁⲩⲅⲁⲣⲟⲥ ϩⲁⲙⲏⲛ :
ⲁϥϥⲓ̄ ⲛ̄ⲧⲉϥⲥ̄ⲙⲏ ⲉϩⲣⲁⲓ̈ ⲙ̄-
25 ⲙⲛ̄ⲧϩⲉⲃⲣⲁⲓ̄ⲟⲥ ⲁϥϣⲗⲏⲗ
ⲛ̄ϯϩⲉ ⲉϥϫⲱ ⲙ̄ⲙⲟⲥ : ϫⲉ
ⲁⲕⲣⲁⲃⲓ̄ : ⲁⲕⲣⲁⲃⲉⲓ̈ : ⲙⲓⲗⲁⲥ̄
ⲫⲓ̄ⲛⲁⲇⲱⲛ : ⲁⲉⲓ̇ⲣ : ⲉⲗϣⲉⲓ : –

---

3 *i.e.* τιμή ‖ 4 *i.e.* γενεά ‖ 5 *i.e.* πατριά ‖ 9 *i.e.* ἐπιστολή ‖ 13 *i.e.* δύναμις ‖ 14 *i.e.* ἀντικείμενος ‖ 15 *i.e.* οὐδέ | *i.e.* πν(εῦμ)α ‖ 15–16 *i.e.* ἀκάθαρτον ‖ 17 *i.e.* οὐδέ ‖ 18 *i.e.* τόπος ‖ 20–21 *i.e.* εἰρήνη ‖ 21 *i.e.* ἀμήν ‖ 22 *i.e.* ἐπιστολή ‖ 23 *l.* ι(ηϲου)ϲ πε-χ(ριϲτό)ϲ | *i.e.* ἀμήν ‖ 25 *i.e.* Ἑβραῖος

I shall preserve your name as an eternal memory and an honour and a blessing among the generations who come after |⁵ you through your entire lineage, and they will hear it to the end of the earth. It is I, Jesus, who has written this letter with |¹⁰ my very own hand. The place to which this manuscript will be affixed, no power of the Adversary |¹⁵ nor unclean spirit will be able to approach nor to reach into that place, and forever. |²⁰ Be well in peace, amen!

The letter of our Lord Jesus Christ to Abgar. Amen.

He raised his voice in |²⁵ Hebrew and he prayed in this way, saying:
"Akrabi, Akrabei, Milas, Phinadōn, Aeir, *Eloei,

---

p. 25 l. 24–p. 28 l. 21. The Prayer of Judas Cyriacus: No title is given in this manuscript, but the text is recognisable as an extract from the fifth-century *Finding of the Holy Cross* (*Inventio sanctae crucis*), in which the Empress Helena, mother of Constantine the Great (r. 306–337 CE), travels to Jerusalem to find the remains of the True Cross on which Jesus had been crucified. She enlists the help of the local Jewish population, torturing one particularly learned man named Judas Cyriacus by having him thrown into a dry well to starve until after seven days he prays to God to reveal the cross. This prayer is said to be in Hebrew, and causes the place where the cross is to make a loud sound and let forth the smell of incense. The prayer alone is excerpted here; a second Coptic copy is found on *T.Varie* 13 (KYP M107). The relationship between the two versions is unclear; some of the divergences between the copies are replicated in the Greek tradition, leading Pernigotti to propose that they represent independent translations of different Greek recensions (Pernigotti 1983: 86–87; Pernigotti 1989: 67). But as Ivan Miroshnikov (forthcoming) points out, the two Coptic versions begin and end at the same points, show agreements not found in the Greek witnesses, and contain some divergences best explained as miscopying from a Coptic model resembling the other copy, so that it is more likely that they represent two independent branches of a single Coptic translation. Below we provide some notes highlighting divergences between the published Coptic and Greek copies, but these are not exhaustive; a synoptic critical edition of all manuscripts is a desideratum. The text of the prayer is given first in 'Hebrew'—in reality, a series of words resembling *voces magicae* with little genuine Hebrew vocabulary—followed by its translation (here, Coptic). The function of the prayer in this manuscript is unclear; it may be intended to be copied as an amulet or recited for another purpose, or it may be included simply because the opening Hebrew words could be used in other ritual contexts. Note that the Syriac version and some of the Greek manuscripts (*e.g.*, Athens, National Library of Greece, 343 fol. 15v–25r; Delatte 1927: 289–298, at 295) lack the initial 'Hebrew' words, which are also absent in a re-telling of the story in the hymn found in the Coptic *Difnar* (XVIII CE, perhaps copy of XIV CE manuscript; O'Leary 1927: 15b); these omissions may indicate a discomfort with their potentially 'magical' associations. For the *Finding of the Holy Cross* and its textual history, see Borgehammar 1991: 145–303; Drijvers 1992: 165–180; Drijvers/Drijvers 1997: 44–45, 64; de Bruyn 2017: 87. A fragmentary Faiyumic Coptic version of the *Finding of the Holy Cross*, preserved as P.Berol. 5731 + 5732 (VI–VIII CE?), is under preparation for publication by Ivan Miroshnikov (forthcoming), whom we thank for discussing this text with us and helping us to improve our translation.

p. 25 l. 27–p. 28 l. 7. 'Hebrew' Version of the Prayer: For variants of the opening 'Hebrew' words in the Latin and Greek manuscripts, see Borgehammar 1991: 272–278. The words and their divisions vary significantly; most versions (including *T.Varie* 13 ll. 5–6) contain the genuine Hebrew sequence *baroukh aththa Adonai* (ברוך אתה אדני; "blessed are you, Lord"). The version here, however, retains only *Adonai, split between adjacent words to give "Phinadōn Aeir" (the second Baroukh below is a different part of the sequence). The version here is also unusually short, preserving only 24 words compared to 26 in *T.Varie* 13 and Sinai gr. 493 (Nestle 1895: 328).

page 26 (13v) (→)

-: ιδ :-

ⲁⲁⲙⲉⲕⲧⲱⲗ · ⲁⲍⲁⲥⲏⲗ ⲃⲟⲣ-
ⲁⲱ · ⲁⲃⲣⲁⲝⲓⲱ · ⲁⲑⲏⲑⲁⲗ :
ⲃⲁⲣⲟⲩⲭ · ⲍⲓⲁⲙⲟⲩⲣ : ⲙⲗⲙⲟⲩⲑ :
ⲁⲭⲗⲉ · ⲃⲓⲣⲟⲃⲁ · ⲉⲣⲙⲟⲩ · ⲕⲁ-
5   ⲑⲁⲇⲱ : ⲇⲁⲩⲗⲁ · ⲙⲉⲗⲙⲱⲛ :
ⲥⲉⲥⲏⲛ · ⲅⲏⲙⲛⲁⲛ : ⲓⲗⲏⲙ ·
ⲓⲏⲗ : ϩⲁⲙⲏⲛ : ⲉⲧⲉ ⲡⲁⲓ ⲡⲉ
ⲡⲉⲩⲃⲱⲗ · ⲡⲛⲟⲩⲧⲉ ⲡⲉⲧ-
ϩⲙⲟⲟⲥ ⲉϩⲣⲁⲓ ⲉϫⲛ ⲛⲉⲭⲉⲣⲟⲩ-
10 ⲃⲓⲛ · ⲉⲣⲉϥⲧⲟⲟⲩ ⲛⲍⲱⲟⲩⲛ
ϩⲁⲣⲟϥ · ⲁⲩⲱ ⲛⲧⲟⲟⲩ ⲛⲉⲧ-
ϩⲏⲗ ⲉⲃⲟⲗ ϩⲙ ⲡⲉⲇⲣⲟⲙⲟⲥ
ⲙⲡⲁⲏⲣ ϩⲛ ⲟⲩϩⲟⲧⲉ · ⲡⲛⲟⲩ-
ⲧⲉ ⲉⲧϩⲙ ⲡⲟⲩⲟⲉⲓⲛ ⲛⲁⲧⲁ-
15 ⲣⲏⲭϥ : ⲡⲉⲧⲉⲙⲛⲫⲩⲥⲓⲥ
ⲛⲣⲱⲙⲉ · ⲛⲁϣ ⲟⲩⲱϩ ⲙ-
ⲙⲁⲩ · ϫⲉ ⲛⲧⲟⲕ · ϫⲉ ⲛⲧⲁⲕ-
ⲧⲁⲙⲓⲟⲟⲩ ⲛⲁⲕ · ⲉⲩϩⲩ-
ⲡⲉⲣⲣⲏⲥⲓⲁ ⲛⲁⲕ · ϥⲧⲟⲟⲩ
20 ⲛⲍⲱⲟⲛ · ⲛϥⲧⲟⲟⲩ ⲛⲍⲱϩ ·
ⲛⲁⲓ ⲉⲧⲗⲓⲧⲟⲩⲣⲅⲓ ⲛⲛⲁⲩ
ⲛⲓⲙ · ⲉⲩⲱϣ ⲉⲃⲟⲗ ϩⲛ ⲟⲩⲥ-
ⲙⲏ ⲛⲁⲧⲕⲁⲣⲱⲥ · ϫⲉ ϩⲁ-
ⲅⲓⲟⲥ · ϩⲁⲅⲓⲟⲥ · ϩⲁⲅⲓⲟⲥ :—
25 ⲡⲉⲥⲛⲁⲩ ⲇⲉ ⲁⲩⲕⲁ ⲧⲟⲟ-
ⲧⲟⲩ ⲉⲡⲡⲁⲣⲁⲇⲓⲥⲟⲥ
ⲉⲧⲣⲉⲩⲣⲟⲉⲓⲥ ⲉⲡⲡⲁⲣⲁ-
ⲇⲓⲥⲟⲥ ⲉⲧⲣⲉⲩⲣⲟⲉⲓⲥ ⲉⲡ-

4–5 ⲕⲁⲑⲁⲭⲱ Pleyte/Boeser || 7 *i.e.* ἀμήν || 9–10 *i.e.* χερουβίμ || 10 *i.e.* ζῷον || 12 *i.e.* δρόμος || 13 *i.e.* ἀήρ || 15 *i.e.* φύσις || 18–19 *i.e.* ὑπηρεσία || 20 *i.e.* ζῷον | *l.* ⲧⲛϩ ? *cf. note* || 21 *i.e.* λειτουργεῖν || 23–24 *i.e.* ἅγιος || 25 *i.e.* δέ || 26, 27–28 *i.e.* παράδεισος

Aamektōl, Azasēl, Boraō, Abraxiō, Athēthal, Baroukh, Ziamour, Mlmouth, Akhle, Biroba, Ermou, Kathadō, |⁵ Daula, Melmōn, Sesēn, Gēmnan, Jerusalem, Israel, Amen!"—whose interpretation is this:

"O God who is seated upon the cherubim, |¹⁰ *Four Living Creatures beneath him, and it is they who fly fearfully in the course of the air! O God who is in the limitless light, |¹⁵ that in which no human nature shall be able to dwell, for you, that is, you have created them for yourself as servants for your, four |²⁰ living, four-winged? creatures, they who serve at every moment, calling out in an unceasing voice, 'Holy, Holy, Holy!', |²⁵ but the hands of two have been assigned? to Paradise that they might guard Paradise, that they might guard the

---

p. 26 p. 8–p. 27 l. 3. Description of God, the Cherubim, and Seraphim: There are numerous divergences between the Greek and Coptic versions of the prayer (for a discussion of the manuscripts and some of the variation presented below, see Miroshnikov forthcoming, who is thanked for his observations). The Greek versions begin by addressing God as creator of heaven, earth, and/or humankind, and describe his act of measuring heaven (Gretser 1734: 428a; Wotke 1891: 307–308; Nestle 1895: 329; Olivieri 1898: 417–418; Delatte 1927: 295; references below by name alone) *T.Varie* 13 (front l. 12) and several of the Greek versions refer to God being seated on the chariot of the cherubim rather than the cherubim themselves (ⲉϫⲛ ⲛ̄ϩⲁⲣⲙ[ⲁ]; ἐπὶ ἅρματος, Nestle, Olivieri; ἅρματι in Wotke). The Greek texts describe the cherubim as "swimming in the airy courses in limitless light" (νηχόμενα ἀερίοις δρόμοις φωτὶ ἀμετρήτῳ in Wotke, Nestle, Olivieri, variations in Gretser, Delatte); in the two Coptic versions this clause is split, so that God is said to be in the limitless light, and while *T.Varie* 13 (l. 13) retains the description of the cherubim swimming (ⲉⲩⲛⲏⲏⲃⲉ), the version in this manuscript has been emended to the more expected "fly". The Greek versions also describe the limitless light as unreachable for human nature (ὅπου ἀνθρωπίνη φύσις παρελθεῖν οὐ δύναται in Wotke, Nestle, Olivieri, Delatte; παρέρχεται in Gretser), with *T.Varie* 13 (l. 15) following (ⲙⲛ ⲫⲏⲥⲓⲥ ⲛⲣⲱⲙⲉ ⲛⲁϣ ⲡⲱϩ ϣ[ⲁⲣⲟϥ]). As Miroshnikov notes, "dwell" (ⲟⲩⲱϩ) in this manuscript edited here likely derives from a visual miscopying of an earlier ⲡⲱϩ. The Greek versions describe God as having created six six-winged creatures (ἓξ ζῷα ἑξαπτέρυγα; absent in Delatte), of whom four, the cherubim, carry the throne of God, and two, the seraphim, have been assigned to guard the Tree of Life ("the path of the Tree of Life" (τὴν ὁδὸν τοῦ ξύλου τῆς ζωῆς) in Gretser). *T.Varie* 13 (ll. 16–17) likewise describes "six creatures with six wings each" (ⲥⲟⲟⲩ ⲛ̄[ⲍ]ⲱⲟⲛ ⲉⲩⲛ ⲥⲟ[ⲟⲩ] ⲛ̄ⲧⲛϩ ⲙ̄ⲙⲟⲟⲩ ⲉⲡⲟⲩⲁ ⲡⲟⲩⲁ), but does not specify that four of them carry the chariot. The manuscript here describes four creatures with four ⲍⲱϩ; here we translate this as ⲧⲛϩ ("wing"), but it may also represent a confused copying of ϥⲧⲟⲟⲩ ⲛ̄ⲍⲱⲟⲛ ("four creatures"), paralleling the Greek ἅτινα μὲν τέσσαρα ζῷα (Wotke; Gretser, Nestle, Olivieri without ζῷα; absent in Nestle). *T.Varie* 13 (ll. 19–20) and the Greek texts note that they are called cherubim (ⲛⲁⲓ ⲉⲧⲟⲩⲙⲟⲩⲧⲉ ⲉⲣⲟⲟⲩ ϫⲉ ⲭⲁⲓⲣⲟⲩⲃⲓⲛ; χερουβὶμ καλεῖται Wotke; καλοῦνται Nestle, Delatte; λαβοῦνται Olivieri). The repetition for the 'seraphim' is present in this manuscript (p. 27 ll. 1–3), suggesting that the first instance simply dropped out in the process of transmission. *T.Varie* 13 (front ll. 20–21) and the Greek versions have "you placed (them) in Paradise" (ⲁⲕⲕⲁⲁⲩ ϩⲙ̄ ⲡⲡⲁⲣⲁⲇⲓⲥⲟⲥ; ἔθου ἐν (τῷ) παρασδείσῳ), but the version here uses the phrase ⲁⲅⲕⲁ ⲧⲟⲟⲧⲟⲩ, literally "their hands have been placed". Kropp translates "they who have not ceased" ("die nicht aufgehört haben"), but this makes the sentence negative, and would normally require the adverb ⲉⲃⲟⲗ to follow (*cf.* Crum 426a–b). As suggested by Ivan Miroshnikov, this is likely another error in transmission, originating in the ⲁⲕⲕⲁⲁⲩ of *T.Varie* 13. Finally, all of the other Coptic and Greek versions note simply that the seraphim were placed in Paradise to protect the (path leading to) the Tree of Life; it is likely that the repetition of "that they might guard" (ⲉⲧⲣⲉⲩⲣⲟⲉⲓⲥ) in ll. 27 & 28 here is an instance of dittography.

page 27 (14r) (↓)

ϣⲏⲛ ⲙ̄ⲡⲱⲛ︤ϩ︥ · ⲛⲁⲓ̈ ⲉϣⲁⲩ-
ⲙⲟⲩⲧⲉ ⲉⲣⲟⲟⲩ ϫⲉ ⲥⲉⲣⲁ-
ⲫⲓ̄ⲛ · ⲛ̄ⲧⲟⲕ ⲅⲁⲣ ⲉⲧⲟ ⲛ̄ϫⲟ-
ⲉⲓ̈ⲥ ⲉϫⲛ ⲟⲩⲟⲛ ⲛⲓ̄ⲙ · ⲁⲛⲟⲛ
5 ⲛⲉⲧⲉⲛⲟⲩⲕ · ⲁⲩⲱ ⲡⲉⲕ-
ⲧⲁⲙⲓ̄ⲟ ⲡⲛⲟⲩⲧⲉ · ⲡⲉⲛ-
ⲧⲁϥⲡⲁⲣⲁⲇⲓ̄ⲇⲟⲩ ⲛ̄ⲛⲁⲅ-
ⲅⲉⲗⲟⲥ ⲛ̄ⲧⲁⲩⲡⲁⲣⲁⲃⲉ
ⲉⲡϣⲓ̈ⲕ ⲙ̄ⲡⲧⲁⲣⲧⲁⲣⲟⲥ
10 ⲁⲩⲱ ⲛ̄ⲧⲟⲟⲩ ⲛⲉⲧⲟⲩϩⲁ-
ⲣⲉϩ ⲉⲣⲟⲟⲩ : ϩ︤ⲛ︥ ⲙ̄ⲙⲟⲩⲭⲗⲟⲥ
ⲛⲁⲙ︤ⲛ︥ⲧⲉ · ⲉⲩⲕⲟⲗⲁⲥⲓ̄ⲥ
ⲛⲁⲩ ϣⲁ ⲉⲛⲉϩ · ⲉϣϫⲉ
ⲡⲁⲓ̈ ⲡⲉ ⲡⲉⲕⲟⲩⲱϣ ⲉⲧ-
15 ⲣⲉϥⲉⲣ ⲉⲣⲟ ⲛ̄ϭⲓ̈ ⲡϣⲏⲣⲉ
ⲙ̄ⲙⲁⲣⲓ̈ⲁ ⲧⲉϭⲣⲟⲟⲙⲡⲉ
ⲙ̄ⲙⲉ · ⲡⲁⲓ̄ ⲛ̄ⲧⲁⲕϫⲟ-
ⲟⲩϥ ⲉⲃⲟⲗ ϩⲓ̄ⲧⲟⲟⲧ︤ⲕ︥ · ⲉⲧ-
ⲣⲉϥⲟⲩⲱⲛ︤ϩ︥ ⲉⲃⲟⲗ ⲛ̄ⲛⲉⲕ-
20 ϣⲡⲏⲣⲉ · †ⲥⲟⲟⲩⲛ ⲡϫⲟ-
ⲉⲓⲥ ϫⲉ ⲛ̄ⲥⲁⲃⲏⲗϫⲉ ⲛ̄ⲧⲁ-
ϥⲉⲓ̄ ⲉⲃⲟⲗ ϩⲓ̄ⲧⲟⲟⲧ︤ⲕ︥ : ⲉ-
ⲛⲉϥⲛⲁⲉⲓ̄ⲣⲉ ⲁⲛ ⲛ̄ⲛⲉⲓ̈ϣ-
ⲡⲏⲣⲉ · ⲁⲩⲱ ⲛ̄ⲥⲁⲃⲏⲗϫⲉ
25 ⲡⲉⲕⲙⲉⲣⲓ̄ⲧ ⲛ̄ϣⲏⲣⲉ ⲡⲉ
ⲛ︤ϥ︥ⲛⲁⲧⲱⲟⲩⲛ ⲁⲛ ⲡⲉ ⲉ-
ⲃⲟⲗ ϩ︤ⲛ︥ ⲛⲉⲧⲙⲟⲟⲩⲧ · ÷

2–3 *i.e.* σεραφίμ ‖ **3** *i.e.* γάρ ‖ **7** *i.e.* παραδιδόναι ‖ **7–8** *i.e.* ἄγγελος ‖ **8** *i.e.* παραβαίνειν ⲃ corrected from ⲇ by overwriting ‖ **9** ⲧⲁⲣⲧⲁⲣⲟⲥ corrected by overwriting from ⲧⲁⲣⲟⲣⲟⲥ *i.e.* τάρταρος ‖ **11** *i.e.* μοχλός ‖ **12** *i.e.* κόλασις

Tree of Life, they who are called *seraphim. For you are Lord over all, we are |⁵ those who are yours, and your creation, God, you who handed over the angels who transgressed to the depth of *Tartarus, |¹⁰ and they are those who are guarded by the bolts of *hell as a punishment for them forever. If this is your will, |¹⁵ that the son of Mary, the true dove, rule, the one whom you sent by your hand to have him reveal your |²⁰ wonders—I know, O Lord, that unless he had come from you, he would not have performed these wonders, and unless |²⁵ he was your beloved son, he would not have arisen from the dead—

8–13. The Punishment of the Fallen Angels: We find again here minor differences between the different Coptic and Greek versions of the *Prayer*. In this version and the Greek versions, the fallen angels are said to be in the "depths of Tartarus" (βυθῷ ταρτάρῳ Gretser 1734, Wotke 1891, Delatte 1927; βυθῷ ταρτάρου Nestle 1895, Olivieri 1898; following references by name only), but *T.Varie* 13 (front l. 25) has "the depths of hell" (ⲡϣⲓⲕ ⲛⲁⲙⲛⲧⲉ). In this version they are "guarded by the bolts of hell", while the Greek versions and *T.Varie* 13 (front ll. 26–27) have "the abyss" (ⲥⲉϩⲁⲣⲉϩ ⲉⲣⲟⲟⲩ ϩⲛ ⲛⲙⲟⲭⲗⲟⲥ ⲙ̄ⲡⲛⲟⲩⲛ; αὐτοί εἰσιν ὑπὸ τὰ ἐνθυρώματα τῶν μοχλῶν τῆς ἀβύσσου Wotke, Nestle; τῶν μοχλῶν absent in Gretser, Olivieri; ὀχυρώματα τῶν μοχλευμάτων in Delatte). *T.Varie* 13 (front ll. 27–28) and some of the Greek versions end this section by noting that the fallen angels are "unable to gainsay to your command" (ⲉⲙⲛ̄ ϣϭⲟⲙ ⲙ̄ⲙⲟⲟⲩ ⲉⲁⲛⲧⲓⲗⲓⲅⲉ ⲛⲛⲉⲕⲟⲩⲉϩⲥⲁϩⲛⲉ; τῷ σῷ προστάγματι ἀντειπεῖν οὐ δύνανται, Wotke, Olivieri, Delatte; δυνάμενοι in Nestle; absent in Gretser), a passage absent in the copy here. Again, these differences demonstrate the fluidity of the text; *cf.* the first notes to pp. 25 & 26.

13–21. Address to God concerning Jesus: Before "if this is your will", *T.Varie* 13 (front l. 29) and the published Greek versions include the address "now, O Lord" (ⲧⲉⲛⲟⲩ ϭⲛ ⲡϫⲟⲉⲓⲥ; καὶ τανῦν κύριε Gretser 1734, Nestle 1895; νῦν in Wotke 1891; δέσποτα κύριε in Delatte 1927); these versions also describe Mary as the "beautiful" rather than "true" dove, as in this text (καλῆς περιστερᾶς; Wotke 1891, Nestle 1895, Delatte 1927; absent in Gretser 1734, Olivieri 1898; ⲧⲉϭⲣⲟⲟⲙⲡⲉ ⲧⲛⲉⲥⲱⲥ; *T.Varie* 13 front l. 30). The specification that Jesus came in order to reveal God's wonders is absent in *T.Varie* 13 and all of the published Greek versions. The following parenthetical note ("I know, O Lord, that") is likewise absent in all of the other published Greek and Coptic versions, who instead begin directly with "unless he had come"; *cf.* the first note to pp. 25 & 26.

page 28 (14v) (→)

-: ⲓⲉ̄ :-   -: ⲃ̄ :-

ⲁⲣⲓⲣⲉ ϭⲉ ⲛ̄ⲛⲉⲕⲙⲁⲉⲓⲛ ⲛ̄ⲅ-
ⲧⲥⲁⲃⲟⲛ ⲉⲣⲟⲟⲩ ⲡϫⲟⲉⲓⲥ
ⲁⲩⲱ ⲕⲁⲧⲁ ⲑⲉ ⲛ̄ⲧⲁⲕⲥⲱ-
ⲧⲙ̄ ⲉⲡⲉⲕϩ̄ⲙϩⲁⲗ ⲙⲱⲩ-
5 ⲥⲏⲥ · ⲁⲕⲧⲥⲁⲃⲟϥ ⲉⲛⲕⲉⲉⲥ
ⲙ̄ⲡⲉⲛⲥⲟⲛ ⲓ̈ⲱⲥⲏⲫ : ⲧⲉ-
ⲛⲟⲩ ϭⲉ ⲡϫⲟⲉⲓⲥ ⲟⲩⲱⲛϩ̄
ⲉⲃⲟⲗ ⲙ̄ⲡⲙⲁ ⲉⲧⲉϥⲕⲏ ⲛ̄-
ϩⲏⲧϥ ⲛ̄ϭⲓ ⲡⲉⲥ̄ⲝ̄ⲟⲥ ⲙ̄ⲡⲉ-
10 ⲭ̄ⲥ̄ : ⲁⲩⲱ ⲛ̄ⲅⲕⲉⲗⲉⲩⲉ ⲛⲟⲩ-
ⲕⲁⲡⲛⲟⲥ ⲉⲧⲣⲉϥϣⲱ-
ⲡⲉ : ϫⲉⲕⲁⲥ ⲉⲓⲛⲁⲡⲓⲥ-
ⲧⲉⲩⲉ ⲉⲡⲉⲥ̄ⲝ̄ⲟⲥ ⲙ̄ⲡⲉⲭ̄ⲥ̄
ⲁⲩⲱ ⲛ̄ⲅⲕⲉⲗⲉⲩⲉ ⲛⲟⲩⲕⲁⲡ-
15 ⲛⲟⲥ ⲉⲧⲣⲉϥϣⲱⲡⲉ ϫⲉ-
ⲕⲁⲥ ⲉⲓ̈ⲛⲁⲡⲓⲥⲧⲉⲩⲉ ⲉ-
ⲡⲉⲥ̄ⲝ̄ⲟⲥ ⲙ̄ⲡⲉⲭ̄ⲥ̄ · ϫⲉ ⲛ̄-
ⲧⲟϥ ⲡⲉ ⲡⲣ̄ⲣⲟ ⲙ̄ⲡⲓ̄ⲏ̄ⲗ̄ :
ⲁⲩⲱ ⲡⲟⲩϫⲁⲓ̈ ⲙ̄ⲡⲕⲟⲥ-
20 ⲙⲟⲥ · ⲙⲛ̄ ⲑⲓ̄ⲗ̄ⲏ̄ⲙ̄ ϣⲁ ⲉⲛⲉϩ
ⲉⲛ ⲉⲛⲉϩ ϩⲁⲙⲏⲛ :——

ⲛⲁⲓ̈ ⲛⲉ ⲛⲣⲁⲛ ⲙ̄ⲡⲥⲁϣϥ
ⲛϣⲏⲣⲉ ϣⲏⲙ ⲛ̄ⲛⲉⲙⲫⲉⲥⲟⲥ
ⲁⲣⲭⲓ̈ⲗⲗⲓ̈ⲧⲟⲥ · ⲇⲓ̈ⲟⲙⲏⲧⲟⲥ ·
25 ⲁⲗⲗⲁⲧⲓⲟⲥ · ⲡⲣⲟⲃⲁⲧⲓⲟⲥ ·
ⲥⲧⲉⲫⲁⲛⲟⲥ · ⲕⲩⲣⲓⲁⲕⲟⲥ :
ⲥⲁⲃⲃⲁⲧⲓ̈ⲟⲥ   ·——

---

3 *i.e.* κατά ‖ **8** ⲉⲧⲉϥⲕⲏ corrected by overwriting from ⲉⲧⲧϥⲕⲏ ‖ **9** *i.e.* σ(ταυρ)ός ‖ **10** *i.e.* χ(ριστό)ς | *i.e.* κελεύειν ‖ **11** *i.e.* καπνός ‖ **12–13** *i.e.* πιστεύειν ‖ **13** *i.e.* σ(ταυρ)ός | *i.e.* χ(ριστό)ς ‖ **14** *i.e.* κελεύειν ‖ **14–15** *i.e.* καπνός ‖ **16** *i.e.* πιστεύειν ‖ **17** *i.e.* σ(ταυρ)ός | *i.e.* χ(ριστό)ς ‖ **18** *i.e.* Ἰ(σρα)ήλ ‖ **19–20** *i.e.* κόσμος ‖ **20** *i.e.* Ἰ(ερουσα)λήμ ‖ **21** *i.e.* ἀμήν ‖ **23** *i.e.* ˢⲛ̄-ⲉⲫⲉⲥⲟⲥ : ⲛ̄ⲛⲉⲫⲉⲥⲟⲥ Pleyte/Boeser ‖ **24** ⲁⲣⲭⲓ̈ⲗⲗⲓ̈ⲧⲟⲥ enlarged capital ⲁ in *ekthesis*

then perform your signs and show them to us, O Lord, and just as you listened to your servant Moses, |⁵ and you showed him the bones of our brother Joseph, now, therefore, O Lord, reveal the place in which the cross of Christ lies, |¹⁰ and command that there be smoke so that I shall believe in the cross of Christ, {and command that there be smoke |¹⁵ so that I shall believe in the cross of Christ} because he is the King of Israel and the salvation of the world |²⁰ and Jerusalem forever and ever, amen."

|²² These are the names of the seven children of Ephesus: Archillides, Diomedes, |²⁵ Allatios, Probatios, Stephanos, Cyriacus, Sabbatios.

---

1. ⲁⲣⲓⲣⲉ ⲟⲉ ⲛⲛⲉⲕⲙⲁⲉⲓⲛ ⲛ̄ⲅ̄ⲧⲥⲁⲃⲟⲛ ⲉⲣⲟⲟⲩ ⲡⲭⲟⲉⲓⲥ : **"then perform your signs and show them to us, O Lord"** *T.Varie* 13 (front ll. 33–34) has the similar "perform then, your great wonders" (ⲉⲓⲣⲉ ⲟⲩⲛ ⲛⲛⲉⲕⲛⲟϭ ⲛ̄ϣⲡⲏⲣⲉ). The Greek versions, by contrast, have "perform for us this sign" (ποίησον ἡμῖν τὸ σημεῖον τοῦτο, Gretser 1734; τὸ τεράστιον τοῦτο in Wotke 1891, Nestle 1895, Delatte 1927; τὸ τέρας τοῦτο in Olivieri 1898). As Ivan Miroshnikov suggests (personal communication), the vaguer, plural reference in the Coptic versions, modified from the singular, more specific, and deictic Greek original, may indicate light editing to allow this prayer to be used in a more general, and recurrent, ritual context.

3–6. ⲕⲁⲧⲁ ⲑⲉ ⲛ̄ⲧⲁⲕⲥⲱⲧⲙ̄ ⲉⲡⲉⲕⲣ̅ⲙ̅ϩⲁⲗ ⲙⲱⲩⲥⲏⲥ · ⲁⲕⲧⲥⲁⲃⲟϥ ⲉⲛⲕⲉⲉⲥ ⲙ̄ⲡⲉⲛⲥⲟⲛ ⲓⲱⲥⲏⲫ : **"just as you listened to your servant Moses, and you showed him the bones of our brother Joseph"** A reference to a tradition recorded in the *Book of Mary's Repose* 32–35, extant in Ge'ez and partially in Syriac (see the translation in Shoemaker 2002: 306–309). According to this tradition, Joseph's bones had been hidden by Pharaoh so that when the Israelites wished to leave Egypt they could not find them (*cf.* Exodus 13.19). Moses and the people of Israel reproach God, who causes the Archangel Michael to strike the river, causing the water to part to reveal a box in which he finds the bones of Joseph. Similar traditions appear in the Babylonian Talmud; see Borgehammar 1991: 176–77.

17–18. ϫⲉ ⲛⲧⲟϥ ⲡⲉ ⲡⲣ̄ⲣⲟ : **"he is the king"** Smith translates "you are the king."

19–20. ⲡⲟⲩϫⲁⲓ̈ ⲙ̄ⲡⲕⲟⲥⲙⲟⲥ : **"the salvation of the world"** This title is absent in *T.Varie* 13, and all but one of the published Greek texts, which has "saviour of the world" (σωτὴρ τοῦ κόσμου; Olivieri 1898).

22–27. The Seven Sleepers of Ephesus: The Seven Sleepers of Ephesus are a group of third-century Christians said to have been put into a miraculous sleep by God to save them from the persecution of Decius (249–251 CE), awakening nearly two hundred years later during the reign of Theodosius II (401–450 CE); they testify before the emperor before passing away and having a church built over the cave in which they slept. The earliest attestations of the legend are found in the Syriac writings of Jacob of Sarug (*ca.* 450–521 CE), dependent upon an older, likely Greek, source (Honigmann 1953: 125–168; van der Horst 2015). These names here were probably intended to be copied onto an amulet to protect the wearer or the place; *cf.* the walls of the eighth-century anchorite's grotto in Pachora, Nubia, whose walls are decorated with several of the texts included in this manuscript, including the names of the Sleepers of Ephesus (see Griffith 1927: no. 29; Sanzo 2014: 77–78: no. 1). Compare the different tradition of the names of the Sleepers alluded to in *PCM* I 21 p. 9 ll. 24–25.

page 29 (15r) (→)

-: ⲅ̄ :-

ⲡⲉϩⲙⲉ ⲙ̄ⲙⲁⲣⲧⲏⲣⲟⲥ ⲛ̣[ⲥⲉ-]
ⲃⲁⲥⲏⲧⲏ ⲧⲡⲟⲗⲓⲥ :-
ⲇⲟⲙⲏⲇⲓ̈ⲁⲛⲟⲥ · ⲟⲩⲁⲗⲗⲏⲥ :
ⲏⲥⲏⲭⲓ̄ⲟⲥ : ⲥⲙⲁⲣⲁⲕⲧⲟⲥ :
5   ⲥⲓ̄ⲥⲓ̄ⲛⲛⲓ̄ⲟⲥ : ⲥⲉⲩⲏⲣⲓ̄ⲁⲛⲟⲥ :-
ⲫⲓ̈ⲗⲟⲕⲧⲏⲙⲱⲛ : ⲏ̄ⲗⲁⲕⲓ̄ⲟⲥ
ⲕⲩⲣⲓ̈ⲱⲛ : ⲁⲗⲉⲝⲁⲛⲇⲣⲟⲥ :
ⲟⲩⲁⲗⲗⲉⲣⲓ̄ⲟⲥ · ⲉⲩⲧⲏⲭⲓ̄ⲟⲥ
ⲃⲉⲃⲓ̄ⲁⲛⲟⲥ : ⲗⲉⲥⲓ̄ⲙⲁⲭⲟⲥ
10 ⲕⲩⲣⲓ̈ⲗⲗⲟⲥ · ⲉⲩⲧⲩⲭⲓ̄ⲟⲥ :
ⲉⲩⲛⲟⲉⲓ̄ⲕⲟⲥ : ⲫⲗⲁⲩⲉⲓ̈ⲟⲥ
ⲝⲁⲛⲑⲓ̄ⲁⲥ : ⲗⲉⲟⲛⲧⲓ̈ⲟⲥ :
ⲙⲉⲧⲱⲛ · ⲏⲅⲓ̄ⲁⲥ :
ⲉⲕⲇⲓ̄ⲕⲁⲓ̄ⲟⲥ : ⲁⲕⲁⲕⲓ̄ⲟⲥ
15 ⲁⲉⲇⲓ̄ⲟⲥ : ⲛⲓ̄ⲕⲟⲗⲁⲟⲥ : -
ⲓ̈ⲱϩⲁⲛⲛⲏⲥ · ⲭⲟⲩⲇⲓ̈ⲱⲛ : -
ⲕⲁⲓ̄ⲟⲥ · ⲕ̄ⲗⲁⲩⲇⲓ̄ⲟⲥ : -
ⲩⲗⲓ̄ⲧⲟⲙⲛⲟⲥ : ⲁⲑⲁⲛⲁⲥⲓ̄ⲟⲥ :
ⲡⲣⲓ̄ⲥⲕⲟⲥ : ⲕⲁⲛⲧⲓ̄ⲧⲟⲥ :
20 ⲥⲁⲕⲉⲣⲧⲱⲛ : ⲕⲟⲣⲕⲟⲛⲓ̄ⲟⲥ :
ⲑⲉⲟⲇⲟⲩⲗⲟⲥ : ⲑⲉⲟⲫⲓ̄ⲗⲟⲥ :-
ⲧⲟⲙⲛⲟⲥ : ⲁⲕⲗⲁⲉⲓ̄ⲕⲟⲥ :-

ⲡⲁⲓ̈ ⲡⲉ ⲡⲧⲱϣ ⲛ̄ⲧⲁⲣⲭⲏ
ⲙ̄ⲡⲉϥⲧⲟⲟⲩ ⲛⲉⲩⲁⲅⲅⲉ-
25 ⲗⲓ̄ⲟⲛ : ⲙⲁⲑⲑⲁⲓⲟⲥ ⲉⲩⲁⲅⲅⲉⲗⲓⲟⲩ
ⲡⲭⲱⲱⲙⲉ ⲙⲡⲉϫⲡⲟ
ⲛⲓ̄ⲥ ⲡⲉⲭ̄ⲥ ⲡϣⲏⲣⲉ ⲛ̄-
ⲇⲁⲩⲉⲓⲇ ⲡϣⲏⲣⲉ ⲛⲁⲃⲣⲁ-
ϩⲁⲙ

The Forty Martyrs of the city of Sebaste: Domitian, Valens, Hesychius, Smaragdus, |⁵ Sisinnius, Severianus, Philoctimon, Heraclius, Cyrion, Alexander, Valerius, Eutychius, Vibianus, Lysimachus, |¹⁰ Cyril, Eutychius, Eunoicus, Flavius, Xantheas, Leontius, Meton, Aggius, Ecdicius, Acacius, |¹⁵ Aetius, Nicholas, John, Chudion, Gaius, Claudius, Ulitomnos, Athanasius, Priscus, Candidus, |²⁰ Sacerdon, Gorgonius, Theodulus, Theophilus, Domnus, Aglaius.

This is the order of the beginning of the four Gospels.
|²⁵ Gospel ‹of› Matthew.
The book of the birth of Jesus Christ, the son of David, the son of Abraham.

---

p. 29 ll. 1–22. The Forty Martyrs of Sebaste: The Martyrs of Sebaste were forty Christian soldiers belonging to the *Legio XII Fulminata* said to have been martyred by Licinius around the year 320 by being abandoned on a frozen lake. The earliest mention of the Martyrs is in the homily on them by Basil of Caesarea dating to 373 CE (*PG* XXXI: 508–525); see Karlin-Hayter 1991. Their names appear in several contexts as amulets; in addition to the hermitage at Pachora (see note to p. 28 ll. 22–27), they are found in three manuscripts belonging to the 'Berlin Library' (KYP A14; VIII CE)—*BKU* I 8, 19 front, & 20—as well as *O.Eleph. Wagner* 322 (KYP M1122; IV–V CE); *P.Lat.Bat.* XIII 25 (KYP M1072); *P.Ryl.Copt.* 101 (KYP M323), *SB* VI 9615 (KYP M1056), *SB* XXVIII 17249 (KYP M1076); none of these seems to preserve the same sequence of names as that present here. *Cf.* de Bruyn 2017: 218–220; Dosoo 2023b: 75–76.
3. ογαλληc : **"Valens"** Smith misreads as "Onalles."
5. ceγηρῐανοc : **"Severianus"** Smith misreads as "Seuepianos."
8. ογαλλερῐοc : **"Valerius"** Smith misreads as "Onallerios."
p. 29 l. 23–p. 30 l. 28. Incipits of the Four Gospels and Psalm 90 (91): The incipits of the four canonical gospels and of Psalm 90 (91) are the most common texts copied onto scriptural amulets. Their arrangement here follows the 'canonical order', found in most, but far from all, incipit amulets with multiple gospels; see Sanzo 2014: 102–104 *et passim*. The amuletic use of Psalm 90 (91) seems to pre-date Christianity, being found in a first-century CE text from Qumran (11QPsAp[a]; see Puech 1990; Kraus 2005; Chapa 2011; Sanzo 2014: 106–130). These incipits, like the other texts in this manuscript, were likely intended to be copied as amulets.
25–26. *i.e.* Matthew 1.1 (Horner 1911: I 2).

page 30 (15v) (↓)

-: ⲓ̅ⲥ̅ :-

𝈒 ⲡⲉⲩⲁⲅⲅⲉⲗⲓ̅ⲟⲛ ⲛ̅ⲕⲁⲧⲁ ⲙⲁⲣⲕⲟⲥ ——— · ———————
ⲧⲁⲣⲭⲏ ⲙ̅ⲡⲉⲩⲁⲅⲅⲉⲗⲓⲟⲛ
ⲛⲓ̅ⲥ̅ ⲡⲉⲭ̅ⲥ̅ ⲡϣⲏⲣⲉ ⲙ̅ⲡⲛⲟⲩ-
5   ⲧⲉ ⲉⲧⲟⲛϩ̅ · ⲕⲁⲧⲁ ⲑⲉ ⲉⲧⲥⲏϩ ϩ̅ⲛ̅ ⲏⲥⲁⲓ̅ⲁⲥ : ⲡⲉⲡⲣⲟ-
ⲫⲏⲧⲏⲥ : ——————— — —
ⲡⲉⲩⲁⲅⲅⲉⲗⲓ̅ⲟⲛ ⲛⲕⲁⲧⲁ ⲗⲟⲩ-
ⲕⲁⲥ ——— · ———————
10 𝈒 Ⲉⲡⲓⲇⲏⲡⲉⲣ ⲉϩⲁϩ ϩⲓⲧⲟⲟ-
ⲧⲟⲩ ⲉⲥϩⲁⲓ̅ ⲛⲉⲛϣⲁϫⲉ
ⲉⲧⲃⲉ ⲛⲉϩⲃⲏⲩⲉ ⲛ̅ⲧⲁⲩ̈ⲧⲱⲧ
ⲛ̅ϩⲏⲧ ⲉϩⲣⲁⲓ̅ ⲛ̅ϩⲏⲧⲛ̅ : ———
ⲡⲉⲩⲁⲅⲅⲉⲗⲓ̅ⲟⲛ ⲛ̅ⲕⲁⲧⲁ ⲓ̅ⲱ-
15   ϩⲁⲛⲛⲏⲥ : ——— · ———
𝈒 Ϩ̅ⲛ̅ ⲧⲉϩⲟⲩⲉⲓ̅ⲧⲉ ⲉⲛⲉϥϣⲟ-
ⲟⲡ ⲛ̅ϭⲓ̅ ⲡϣⲁϫⲉ ⲁⲩⲱ ⲡ-
ϣⲁϫⲉ ⲉⲛⲉϥϣⲟⲟⲡ ⲛ̅ⲛⲁϩ-
ⲣⲙ̅ ⲡⲛⲟⲩⲧⲉ · ⲁⲩⲱ ⲉⲛⲉⲩ-
20 ⲛⲟⲩⲧⲉ ⲡⲉ ⲡϣⲁϫⲉ : ———
-: Ϥ ⲡⲉⲥⲙⲟⲩ ⲛ̅ⲇⲱⲇⲏ ⲛ̅ⲇⲁⲩ-
ⲉⲓ̈ⲇ ⲡⲉⲧⲟⲩⲏϩ ϩⲁ ⲧⲃⲟⲏ-
ⲑⲓ̅ⲁ ⲙ̅ⲡⲉⲧϫⲟⲥⲉ · ϥⲛⲁ-
ϣⲱⲡⲉ ϩⲁ ⲑⲁⲓ̅ⲃⲉⲥ ⲙ̅ⲡ-
25   ⲛⲟⲩⲧⲉ ⲛ̅ⲧⲡⲉ · ϥⲛⲁ-
ϫⲟⲟⲥ ⲉⲡϫⲟⲉⲓ̅ⲥ ϫⲉ ⲛ̅-
ⲧⲉⲕ ⲡⲁⲣⲉϥϣⲟⲡⲧ ⲉ-
ⲉⲣⲟⲕ ⲁⲩⲱ ⲡⲁⲙⲁ ⲛ̅ⲡⲱⲧ :-

1, 10, 16 diplai in margin ‖ **1** *i.e.* εὐαγγέλιον | *i.e.* κατά ‖ **3** *i.e.* ἀρχή | *i.e.* εὐαγγέλιον ‖ **4** *l.* ι(ηⲥⲟⲩ)ⲥ ⲡⲉ-χ(ριστό)ⲥ ‖ **5** *i.e.* κατά ‖ **6–7** *i.e.* προφήτης ‖ **8** *i.e.* εὐαγγέλιον | *i.e.* κατά ‖ **10** *i.e.* ἐπειδήπερ enlarged ⲉ in *ekthesis* ‖ **14** *i.e.* εὐαγγέλιον | *i.e.* κατά ‖ **16** ϩ̅ⲛ̅ enlarged and in *ekthesis* ‖ **21** ϥ̅ enlarged and in *ekthesis* | *l.* ⲧ-ⲱⲇⲏ *i.e.* ᾠδή ‖ **22–23** *i.e.* βοήθεια ‖ **27–28** *l.* ⲉⲣⲟⲕ (dittography)

The Gospel according to Mark.
The beginning of the Gospel of Jesus Christ, the son of the |⁵ living God, as it is written in Isaiah the prophet...

The Gospel according to Luke.
|¹⁰ Inasmuch as many have undertaken to write the words concerning the things which have been agreed among us...

The Gospel according to |¹⁵ John.
In the beginning was the word and the word was in the presence of God and |²⁰ the word was a god...

Ninety, the blessing of the song of David.
The one who dwells in the help of the exalted one will be in the shade of |²⁵ God of heaven. He will say to the Lord, "You are my helper and my refuge"...

KD, EL & MP, edited from photograph and autopsy.

1–7. *i.e.* Mark 1.1 (Horner 1911: I 354).
10–13. *i.e.* Luke 1.1 (Horner 1911: II 2).
16–20. *i.e.* John 1.1 (Förster *et al.* 2021: 35).
21–28. *i.e.* Psalm 90 (91) 1–2 (Budge 1898: 98–99).

PCM I 12. Rossi's Tractate

Theban region   16 (H) × 16 (W) cm   VII–VIII CE ?

Other references: P.Biblioteca Nazionale Turin, a.IV.27; TM 98062; CLM 5754; KYP M283; Bélanger Sarrazin #140.

Editions: Rossi 1894 (*ed. pr.*); von Lemm 1901: 306–307 (p. 1 ll. 1–5); Kropp 1931: I no. R; Meyer 1988.

Translations: Rossi 1894 (Italian); Amélineau 1895 (French); von Lemm 1901: 306–307 (p. 1 ll. 1–5; German); Kropp 1931: II no. 47 (German); Müller 1959: no. 211 (German); Meyer in Meyer/Smith 1994: no. 71.

Additional commentary: Rossi 1899; Gabrieli 1930; Orlandi 1974; Peyron 1876: 65–66; Sperber 1985; Preininger forthcoming c: chapter 7.

Present location: Lost.

Image: Kropp 1931: I 87 (R) (hand sample).

Linguistic description: Sahidic (non-standard).

Contents:

1. pp. 1–45: Invocation of God and the Archangel Gabriel for protection from demons (KYP T359)

Papyrus codex, lost in a fire in 1904.[1] The earliest description of the codex, by Bernardino Peyron in 1876, describes it as consisting of 46 pages, of which two (the second folio) were blank.[2] The next description, by Francesco Rossi, describes it as consisting of 44 pages, implying that the second folio had been lost.[3] Both authors note its very unusual format, with the folios inscribed on the right-hand side only.[4] Kropp (1931), who had never seen the manuscript, misunderstood the two pages as being missing between the second and third surviving pages (corresponding to our pp. 5 & 7), but this is not noted by Rossi, and the text that survives does not imply lost pages. Kropp does not seem to have realised that the codex consisted of 44 pages of which only 22 were written, instead understanding it to have 22 surviving pages.

The codex was acquired by Bernardino Drovetti (1776–1852), consul general

---

[1] Kropp 1931: I 63.

[2] Peyron 1876: 65.

[3] Peyron 1876: 65 notes that they are written on only one side ("una sola facciata"). Rossi 1894: 22 (*cf.* Rossi 1899: 121) is more explicit, saying they are written on the "diritto". As noted in Turner 1978: 8–13, the papyrological concept of the recto as the horizontal fibres only began to develop in the work of Ulrich Wilcken from the late 1880s, and so "diritto" here certainly refers to the right-hand page of the codex (*i.e.*, the recto of the folio). We would like to thank Alin Suciu for discussing this question with us.

[4] Rossi 1894: 22.

of France in Egypt, likely between 1804 and 1818, and sometime between then and 1821 his collection was sent to Livorno in Italy for sale.[5] Drovetti donated the Tractate to the philologist Amedeo Peyron (1785–1870) at some point after 1841, and after Peyron's death his nephew, Bernardino Peyron (1818–1903), donated it to the Biblioteca Nazionale ("National Library") in Turin.[6] Rossi published the manuscript in 1894, and in 1896 Carl Schmidt examined and transcribed it; this transcription was used as the basis of the edition of his student, Kropp.[7] The manuscript was lost in the fire, of unknown causes, of the night of 25th to 26th January 1904, which resulted in the destruction of 67% of the Library's manuscripts, and 78% of its printed volumes.[8]

Prior to the manuscript's loss, a handwriting sample was produced by Crum, which Kropp published alongside his edition.[9] This is the only surviving image of the manuscript known to us, posing considerable challenges to palaeographic dating. The sample demonstrates a bilinear, largely unimodal hand with a rounded ⲁ, slightly enlarged and angular ⲃ, slight serifs on ⲍ and ⲧ, curved ⲙ, slightly narrow ⲥ, and ⲩ shaped like a Latin Y. Very similar letterforms may be seen in the literary codex Turin cat. 63000, codex 3 (CLM 47) from the This (or *Thinis*) group (TM Arch ID 498), purchased by Drovetti at around the same time as the Tractate.[10] This codex, and the other *ca.* 16 codices of the archive, were sold by Drovetti to the Egyptian Museum in Turin on the 24th January 1824,[11] but at least one leaf from the archive was among those given by him to Peyron as part of his later gift to the scholar along with the Tractate,[12] making a link between them more likely. Based on material considerations, the This group can be dated to the late seventh or eighth century,[13] and evidence from two codices (a book-list and a colophon) suggest that the group belonged to the church of the *topos* ("place", probably monastery) of John the Baptist in This.[14] These seem to have been the only other Coptic papyrus codices in Drovetti's collection. We thus tentatively

---

[5] Marro 1952: 124; Buzi 2015–2016: 71; Orlandi 1974: 115.

[6] Peyron 1876: 64 notes that Drovetti donated the manuscript to his uncle Amedeo after the completion of his lexicon and grammar (Peyron 1835 & 1841 respectively); *cf.* Rossi 1899: 121.

[7] Kropp 1931: I 5, 192.

[8] Gorrini 1904: 18, 21, 26, 29, 34, 38, 41; 1,500 of a total of 4,500 manuscripts were saved; of printed volumes, 6,800 were saved, and 23,711 destroyed. Gabrieli 1930: 51 does not list the Tractate among the manuscripts rescued, and Kropp 1931: I 63 confirms that it was destroyed.

[9] Kropp 1931: I 5, 87 (R). Crum seems to have begun by copying the letters from p. 23 l. 16, before continuing with a sequence of random letters chosen to provide a wide range of letterforms; unfortunately the sample does not constitute a full alphabet.

[10] On this group, see Orlandi 1974; Orlandi 2013; Buzi 2018; Buzi 2023; *cf.* the comment in Rossi 1899: 121 that the manuscripts in the Library and Museum constitute a single collection ("una sola Raccolta"). We thank Alin Suciu for this suggestion; *cf.* Suciu 2012.

[11] Marro 1952: 125; Buzi 2015–2016: 70; Buzi 2018: 39.

[12] Buzi 2015–2016: 78.

[13] Orlandi 2013: 525; Buzi 2018: 47.

[14] Orlandi 1974: 116; Buzi 2018: 42.

propose a similar, seventh or eighth century date for the Tractate, and note that it too may have come from This, perhaps even the collection of the church. While this is highly speculative, it is almost certain that the manuscript derives from the general region of Thebes, to which This belongs, and from where nearly all of Drovetti's manuscripts derive.[15] Among the other manuscripts given by Drovetti to Peyron were a sheet of papyrus containing a formulary, perhaps for favour (*PCM* I 13, also lost in the fire),[16] and an unpublished Coptic magical rotulus. This latter was sold by his family to the National Library in Turin in 1969, and the hand is different to that of the Tractate.[17]

The scribe uses supralineation to mark names, *voces magicae*, and autosyllabic consonants. The dialect is a highly standard but not entirely consistent form of Sahidic, with occasional common non-standard features, such as haplography, and the interchange of ⲃ/ϥ. More unusual is the occasional interchange of ⲍ/ⲥ and ϫ/ϭ, and the presence of a single Faiyumic form (ⲱⲛⲁϩ, p. 35 l. 5)

The text consists of long invocation of God and (from p. 13) the archangel Gabriel, with notable similarities to other extensive 'magical liturgies' such as the *Prayer of Mary 'in Bartos'* (see *PCM* I 25 pp. 2–9), the *Endoxon of the Archangel Michael* (see *PCM* I 26), and the prayer to the Baktiotha preserved in three manuscripts.[18] Peyron described it as a "gnostic tractate on the particular virtues which the celestial spirits possess from God" ("trattato gnostico delle particolari virtù, che hanno da Dio gli spiriti celesti"), referring specifically to the content on p. 7 l. 1–p. 9 l. 6.[19] This title was taken up by Rossi, so that it has become traditional to refer to the text as as 'Rossi's "Gnostic" Tractate'. While the text is neither meaningfully 'gnostic' nor a tractate, we retain the distinctive name of 'Tractate' here in deference to history, removing the word 'gnostic', which is liable to mislead those encountering the text for the first time.

Since the manuscript is lost, our edition makes use of the edition of Rossi as the base text, sometimes preferring the readings of Schmidt (in Kropp) where these seem more plausible. At places we suggest alternative readings, marked 'CMPT' (for *Coptic Magical Papyri Team*). Since the text is written only on the recto of each sheet, we number the pages first by their ordinal number of writing (*first, second*, and so on), corresponding to folio numbers in Rossi and page numbers in Kropp, followed by the actual page number, including blank pages in the count, thus, the second page written is the fifth page of the codex: "*second page*

---

[15] Peyron 1824: 7–8; Töpfer 2018: 74–75. Of the forty papyri from Drovetti on the online Turin catalogue (https://collezioni.museoegizio.it; accessed 10/3/2023) all are listed as certainly or probably from Thebes ("Tebe" or "Deir el-Medina").

[16] Rossi 1894: 24 says that this fragment was "united with this papyrus" ("unito a questo papiro").

[17] Mss. Peyron 158–159 (KYP M3761); *cf.* Buzi 2015–2016: 76; Buzi 2018: 43.

[18] *BKU* I 23 (KYP M194); *P.Lond.Copt.* 1008 (KYP M282); *P.Macq.* I 1 (KYP M167); *cf.* Choat/Gardner 2013. For the concept of 'magical liturgies', see van der Vliet 2019b: 342–343 and pp. 22–23 of this volume.

[19] Peyron 1876: 66; *cf.* Rossi 1894: 21; Rossi 1899: 121.

(page 5)". Since earlier publications do not count the first page, which contains the ritual instructions, our 'second page' corresponds to earlier folio/page 1, and so on. In cross-references throughout this volume, we refer to the absolute page number, *i.e.*, p. 5 for the *second page*.

first page (page 1)

+ ⲥϩⲁⲓ ϫⲉ ⲡⲉϥⲧⲟⲟⲩ ⲛⲁⲅⲅⲉⲗⲟⲥ ϩⲓⲑⲏ ⲙⲡⲕⲁⲧⲁⲡⲉⲧⲁⲥⲙⲁ ⲙ̄ⲡⲓⲱⲧ ⲉⲕⲫⲟⲣⲓ
ⲛ̄ⲟⲩⲕⲗⲟⲙ ⲛ̄ⲟⲩⲉⲣⲧ ⲉⲣⲉⲟⲩⲕ[ⲗ]ⲁⲧⲟⲥ
ⲙ́ⲙⲟⲣⲥⲏⲛⲏ ϩⲛ̄ ⲧⲉ[ⲕ]ϫⲓϭ ⲉⲣⲉⲟ[ⲩ]ⲁⲙⲟⲩⲛⲓ-
5 ⲁⲕⲟⲩ ϩⲛ̄ ⲣⲱⲕ

vac.

θ λι/ . . . ⲥⲧⲏ/ - ⲥⲧⲁⲕ/ ⲙⲁϩ/
ⲱⲧⲛⲉⲥ - ⲟ . . . ⲣⲟⲙ̄ⲡⲉ · ⲕⲓⲛ̄ⲁ[ⲙ]ⲱⲙⲟⲛ . .
ⲛ̄ⲉϩ ⲛⲟⲩⲉⲓⲧ/ . . . ϩ/ ⲕⲁⲣⲃⲱⲛⲉ ⲧ . . ⲍⲏⲗ[ⲟⲛ] .
ⲛⲗⲉⲩⲕⲟ[ⲛ] . [ⲍⲏ]ⲗⲟⲛ̄ ⲛ̄ϫⲟⲉⲓⲧ/

---

1 † Rossi, Lemm : ⳨ Kropp, Meyer 1988 | *i.e.* ἄγγελος ‖ **2** *i.e.* καταπέτασμα | *i.e.* φορεῖν ‖ **3** *i.e.* κ[λ]άδος : κ . . ⲁⲧⲟⲥ Rossi : ⲕⲗ[ⲁ]ⲧⲟⲥ Lemm ‖ **4** *i.e.* μυρσίνη Kropp : ⲙⲙⲟⲣⲥ . . . Rossi : ⲙⲟⲣⲥ[ⲩⲛⲉ] Lemm | *i.e.* ˢϭⲓϫ ‖ **4–5** *i.e.* ἀμμωνιακός : ⲟ . . ⲁⲙⲟⲩ ⲛⲕⲁⲕⲟⲩ Rossi ‖ **6** *i.e.* θ(υσία) : θ̄ Kropp, Meyer | *i.e.* λί(βανος) | [ⲕⲣⲓ]ⲥⲧⲏ Lemm : omitted by Kropp, Meyer 1988, 1994 | *i.e.* στύ(ραξ) | *i.e.* στακ(τή) : "stac(te)" Meyer 1988, 1994 | ⲙⲁϩ/ Rossi : *l.* ⲙⲁⲥ/ *i.e.* μασ(τίχη) ? CMPT : *l.* ⲙⲁϩⲃⲁⲗ "(dove nest)" ("[Tauben]nest") Kropp, Meyer 1988, 1994 ‖ **7** ⲱⲧ ⲙⲉ ⲥⲛⲟϥ ⲛ̄ϭⲣⲟⲙⲡⲉ ? CMPT : ⲱⲧⲛⲉⲥⲟⲟⲩ ⲛ̄ϭⲣⲟⲙⲡⲉ "butcher the (?) six doves" ("Schlachte die (?) sechs Tauben") Schmidt in Kropp, Meyer 1988, 1994 *cf.* note | *i.e.* κιννά[μ]ωμον ‖ **8** *l.* ⲛⲟⲩⲉⲣⲧ ? CMPT, Kropp, Meyer : ⲛϫⲟⲉⲓⲧ Lemm | ⲃϩ Schmidt in Kropp, Meyer 1988 : *l.* [ϣⲟⲩⲣⲏ ⲛ̄ⲁⲙ]ϩ "brazier" ("Rauchfaß") Kropp ? | *i.e.* κάρβων | ⲧ . . ⲍⲏⲗ . . . Rossi : ⲍⲏⲗ[ⲟⲛ] Kropp, Meyer : [ⲕ]ⲗⲟⲙ ⲛ- Lemm | *i.e.* ξύλ[ον] ‖ **9** *i.e.* λευκόν | *i.e.* [ξύ]λον : ⲍⲏⲗ[ⲟ]ⲛ Meyer 1988

Draw the four *angels in front of the *veil of the Father while wearing a crown of roses, with a branch of myrtle in your hand and some ammoniac |⁵ in your mouth.

Offering: *frankincense, flea-wort?, *styrax, oil of *myrrh, *mastic?, fat? and blood? of a dove?, cinnamon, rose? oil … charcoal … white wood, olive wood.

First page: This page is not given a folio or page number in Rossi, Kropp, or Meyer. It seems possible that this page should be placed at the end of the manuscript, rather than the beginning; compare the similar invocations in *PCM* I 25, 26 & 28, which have illustrations and ritual instructions after the spoken formulae. The initial cross may suggest, however, that this is indeed the beginning.

2–5. ⲕⲫⲟⲣⲓ ⲛ̄ⲟⲩⲕⲗⲟⲙ ⲛ̄ⲟⲩⲉⲣⲧ ⲉⲣⲉⲟⲩⲕ[ⲗ]ⲁⲧⲟⲥ ⲙ̄ⲙⲟⲣⲥⲏⲛⲏ ϩⲛ̄ ⲧⲉ[ⲕ]ϫⲓϭ ⲉⲣⲉⲟ[ⲩ]ⲁⲙⲟⲩⲛⲓⲁⲕⲟⲩ ϩⲛ̄ ⲣⲱⲕ "while wearing a crown of roses, with a branch of myrtle in your hand and some ammoniac in your mouth" As Lemm 1901: 306–307 points out, a close parallel to this passage may be found in chapter 47 of the Gnostic text known as the 'Second Book of Ieou': "and Jesus performed this mystery (baptism with the Holy Spirit) while all his disciples were wearing linen garments, crowned with myrtle, with a *kunokephalon* of *kristē* in their mouths, and a branch of artemisia in their two hands" (ⲓ̄ⲥ̄ ⲇⲉ ⲁϥⲉⲓⲣⲉ ⲙ̄ⲡⲉⲓ̈ⲙ̄ᴾ ⲉⲣⲉⲛⲉϥⲙⲁⲑⲏ ⲧⲏⲣⲟⲩ ϭⲟⲟⲗⲉ ⲛ̄ϩⲉϩⲃⲟⲟⲥ ⲛ̄ⲉⲓⲁⲁⲩ ⲉⲩⲥⲧⲉⲫⲁⲛⲟⲩ ⲙ̄ⲙⲟⲣⲥⲩⲛⲏ ⲉⲣⲉⲟⲩⲕⲩⲛⲟⲕⲉⲫⲁⲗⲟⲛ ⲛ̄ⲧⲉⲧⲉⲕⲣⲏⲥⲧⲏ ϩⲛ̄ⲟⲩⲛ ⲛ̄ⲣⲱⲟⲩ · ⲉⲣⲉⲟⲩⲙⲟⲛⲟⲕⲗⲁⲇⲟⲥ ⲛ̄ⲁⲣⲧⲉⲙⲓⲥⲓⲁⲥ ϩⲛ̄ ⲧⲉⲩϭⲓϫ ⲥⲛ̄ⲧⲉ; Crégheur 2019: 218.23–28, 219 (trans.), 373 (commentary)). *Kunokephalon* seems to refer to some kind of plant; *cf.* Dioscorides, *Materia Medica* 4.69, perhaps referring to fleawort (*Plantago indica* L.; *cf.* LSJ *s.v.* ψύλλιον) or weasel's-snout (*Antirrhinum orontium* L.; see André 1985: 83). The meaning of *kristē* is similarly difficult, although Dioscorides notes that another name for the *kunokephalon* is κρυστάλλιον (*cf.* André 1985: 79), so that this may simply be a construction that combines the two names. Crégheur (2019: 373), following Amélineau (1891: 192), notes that it might refer to the island of Crete (Κρήτης ?), giving "Cretan *kunokephanon*". Lemm suggests reading ⲕⲣⲓⲥⲧⲏ (his reading of ⲕⲣⲏⲥⲧⲏ) in l. 6 of our manuscript, and so we tentatively follow him.

6. … ⲥⲧⲏ : "fleawort" *Cf.* the note to ll. 2–5 above.

7. ⲱⲧⲛⲉⲥ - ⲟ … ⲣⲟⲙ̄ⲡⲉ : "fat? and blood? of a dove" Kropp and Meyer translate "butcher the six (?) doves", but this kind of animal sacrifice would be otherwise unattested in the Coptic magical corpus. Instead we suggest that the blood (and perhaps fat) of a dove is offered up; dove blood is often used in rituals for positive purposes, such as favour, or as in the case here, protection; *cf.* the note to *PCM* I 17 back ll. 1–5, and Dosoo 2022c: 517–519.

9. ⲕⲁⲣⲃⲱⲛⲉ ⲧ . . ϩⲏⲗ[ⲟⲛ] . ⲛ̄ⲗⲉⲩⲕⲟ[ⲛ] . [ϩⲏ]ⲗⲟⲛ ⲛ̄ϫⲟⲉⲓⲧ/ : "charcoal … white wood, olive wood" Perhaps understand "charcoal from white wood or olive wood"; the incenses listed above were probably intended to be placed on the burning charcoals.

second page (page 5)

[†παρακα]λι̣ ⲙⲙⲟⲕ ⲙ̄ⲡ[ⲟⲟⲩ] ⲡⲉⲧⲇⲓ̈-
[ⲟⲓⲕⲉⲓ] ϭⲓⲛ ⲉⲧⲡⲉ ϣⲁ ⲡ[ⲕⲁϩ] ϭⲓⲛ ⲉ-
[ⲡⲕⲁϩ] ϣⲁ ⲧⲡⲉ · ⲡⲛⲟϭ ⲙ̄ⲙⲟⲛⲟ-
ⲅⲏⲛⲏⲥ · ⲥⲱⲧⲙ̄ ⲉⲣⲟⲓ ⲙⲡⲟⲟⲩ ⲉⲓ-
5   ⲱϣ ⲉϩⲣⲁⲓ̈ ⲉⲣⲟⲕ · ⲡⲓⲱⲧ ⲙⲙⲁ[ⲩ]ⲁⲁϥ
ⲡⲡⲁⲛⲇⲱⲕⲣⲁⲇⲱⲣ · ⲡⲛⲟⲩⲥ ⲉⲧ-
ϩⲏⲡ ϩⲙ̄ ⲡⲓⲱⲧ · ⲡϣⲉⲣⲡⲙⲓⲥⲉ
ⲛ̄ⲥⲱⲛⲧ ⲛⲓⲙ ⲙⲛ̄ ⲉⲱⲛ ⲛⲓⲙ
ⲁⲃⲗⲁⲛ[ⲁⲑ]ⲁⲛⲁⲁϥⲗⲁ · ⲥⲱⲧⲙ
10 ⲉⲣⲟⲓ ⲙ̄ⲡⲟⲟⲩ ⲉⲓⲱϣ ⲉϩⲣⲁⲓ̈ ⲉⲣⲟⲕ
ⲡⲉⲑⲓⲭⲛ̄ ⲉⲱⲛ ⲛⲓⲙ · ⲡϣⲉⲣⲡⲙⲓⲥⲉ
ⲛⲓⲣⲁⲛ̄ ⲛ̄ⲁⲅⲅⲉⲗⲟⲥ ⲧⲏⲣⲟⲩ · ⲙⲁ-
ⲣⲉⲩⲥⲱⲧⲙ̄ ⲉⲣⲟⲓ ⲛ̄ϭⲓ ⲛ̄ⲁⲅⲅⲉ-
ⲗⲟⲥ ⲧⲏⲣⲟⲩ ⲙⲛ̄ ⲛ̄ⲁⲣⲭⲏⲁⲅⲅⲉⲗⲟⲥ
15 ⲛ̄ⲥⲉϩⲩⲡⲟⲧⲁⲥⲥⲉ ⲛⲁⲓ · ⲛ̄ϭⲓ ⲫⲏⲥⲓⲥ ⲛⲓⲙ ⲡ̄ⲛ̄ⲁ̄ · ⲉⲧϩ̄ⲛ̄ ⲡⲉⲓⲧⲟⲡⲟⲥ
ϩⲛ̄ ⲟⲩϭⲉⲡⲏ · ⲡⲁⲓ ⲅⲁⲣ ⲡ[ⲉ ⲡ]ⲟⲩ-
ⲱϣ ⲛ̄ⲥⲁⲃⲁⲱⲑ · ⲁⲣⲓ ⲃⲟ[ⲏ]ⲑⲓⲁ
ⲉⲣⲟⲓ̈ · ⲛ̄ⲓ̈ϩⲁⲅⲓⲟⲥ ⲛ̄ⲛⲁⲅ[ⲅⲉ]ⲗⲟⲥ
20 [ⲙ]ⲁⲣⲉⲩⲡⲱⲧ ⲉⲃⲟⲗ ⲙ[ⲙⲟⲓ̈]
[ⲛ̄]ⲁϫⲁϫⲉ ⲧⲏⲣⲟⲩ ⲙⲛ̄ . . .
. . . .

---

1 *i.e.* [παρακα]λεῖν *cf.* Dosoo 2018: 21–22 on verbs of invocation : or †[ⲉⲡⲓⲕⲁ]ⲗⲓ Kropp | ⲙ̄ⲡ[ⲟⲟⲩ] Kropp, Meyer 1988 : ⲙ̄ⲡ[ⲟⲟⲩ . .] Rossi ‖ **1–2** *i.e.* δι(οικεῖν) Schmidt in Kropp, Meyer 1988 : ⲧⲉⲧⲇⲓ . . . Rossi ‖ **2–3** ϭⲓⲛ ⲉⲧⲡⲉ ϣⲁ ⲡ . . . ϭⲓⲛ ⲉ . . . Rossi : ϭⲓⲛ ⲉⲧⲡⲉ ϣⲁ ⲡⲕⲁϩ ϭⲓⲛ ⲉ[ⲡⲕⲁ]ϩ Kropp, Meyer 1988 ‖ **3–4** *i.e.* μονογενής ‖ **4** *i.e.* ˢⲥⲱⲧⲙ ‖ **6** *i.e.* παντοκράτωρ | *i.e.* νοῦς ‖ **7** *l.* ⲡ-ϣⲉⲣⲡ-ⲙⲓⲥⲉ ‖ **8** *i.e.* αἰών ‖ **9** ⲁⲃⲗⲁⲛ[. . .]ⲁⲛⲁ ⲁⲓⲗⲁ Rossi : ⲁⲃⲗⲁⲛⲁⲑⲁⲛⲁϥⲗⲁ Kropp, Meyer 1988 : ⲁⲃⲗⲁⲛ[ⲁⲑ]ⲁⲛⲁⲁϥⲗⲁ CMPT | *i.e.* ˢⲥⲱⲧⲙ : ⲥⲱⲧⲙ̄ Meyer 1988 ‖ **11** *i.e.* αἰών ‖ **11–12** ⲡϣⲉⲣⲡⲙⲓⲥⲉ ⲛⲓⲣⲁⲛ̄ ⲛ̄ⲁⲅⲅⲉⲗⲟⲥ "the firstborn of all the angels" ("le premier né de tous les anges") Amélineau ‖ **12** *i.e.* ˢⲛ̄-ⲛⲓ-ⲣⲁⲛ ⲛ̄-ⲛ̄-ⲁⲅⲅⲉⲗⲟⲥ ⲧⲏⲣ⸗ⲟⲩ : ⲛⲓⲣⲁ ⲛ̄ⲛⲁⲅⲅⲉⲗⲟⲥ Rossi, Kropp : "of the names of all the angels!" Meyer 1988, 1994 | *i.e.* ἄγγελος ‖ **13** *i.e.* ˢⲥⲱⲧⲙ ‖ **13–14** *i.e.* ἄγγελος | *i.e.* ἀρχάγγελος ‖ **15** *i.e.* ὑποτάσσειν ‖ **15–16** *i.e.* φύσις : *l.* φύσεις Kropp | ⲫⲏⲥⲓⲥ ⲛⲓⲙ ⲡ̄ⲛ̄ⲁ̄ "all, physical and spiritual" ("tutte, fisiche e spirituali") Rossi ‖ **16** *i.e.* ˢⲛⲓⲙ ⲙ̄-ⲡⲛ(ⲉⲩⲙ)ⲁ (haplography) *i.e.* πνεῦμα | *i.e.* τόπος : "aions" ("Æons") Amélineau ‖ **17** *i.e.* γάρ ‖ **18** *i.e.* βο[ή]θεια ‖ **19** *i.e.* ἅγιος | *i.e.* ˢⲛ̄-ⲁⲅ[ⲅⲉ]ⲗⲟⲥ *i.e.* ἄγγελος

I invoke you today, you who govern from heaven to the [earth], from the [earth] to heaven, the great Only-Begotten One, listen to me today as I call |⁵ upon you, the only Father, Almighty, the mind that is hidden in the Father, the Firstborn of every creature and every aion, Ablanathaanaafla!

Listen |¹⁰ to me today, as I call upon you, you who are over every aion, the Firstborn, ⟨by⟩ the names of all ⟨the⟩ angels! Let all the *angels and *archangels listen to me, |¹⁵ and let every being ⟨of⟩ spirit that is in this place be subjected to me quickly, for this is the wish of *Sabaoth!

Help me, O holy angels; |²⁰ let them flee from me, all my enemies and…

7–8. πϣρπμιcε ⲛⲥⲱⲛⲧ ⲛⲓⲙ ⲙⲛ ⲉⲱⲛ ⲛⲓⲙ ⲁⲃⲗⲁⲛ[ⲁⲑ]ⲁⲛⲁⲁϥⲗⲁ : "**the Firstborn of every creature and every aion, Ablanathaanaafla**" A reference to and an expansion of the description of the Son in Colossians 1.15 as the "firstborn of every creature" (πϣρπμμιcε ⲛⲥⲱⲛⲧ ⲛⲓⲙ; Horner 1920: 324, we are grateful to Ágnes Mihálykó for recognising this citation). The following name is a variant of Ablanathanalba, a palindromic name common in Graeco-Egyptian and Coptic magic; see Brashear 1995: 3577.

third page (page 7)

[... ϩⲛ ⲟ]ⲩϭⲉⲡⲏ · ⲙⲁⲣⲉⲩⲡⲱ-
[ⲧ ⲉⲃⲟⲗ ⲉ]ⲡⲁϩⲟ ϩⲛ ⲟⲩⲕⲁⲣⲱϥ
ⲙⲓⲭ[ⲁ]ⲏⲗ ⲡⲉⲑⲓⲭⲛ ⲛⲉϭⲟⲙ ⲧⲏ-
ⲣⲟⲩ ⲉⲧⲧⲁⲭⲣⲏⲩ · ϩⲣⲁⲫⲁⲏⲗ
5   ⲡⲉⲑⲓⲭⲙ ⲡⲉⲩⲭⲁⲓ · ⲅⲁⲃⲣⲓⲏⲗ
ⲡⲉⲑⲓⲭⲛ ⲛⲉϭⲟⲙ · ⲁⲣⲛⲁⲏⲗ
ⲡⲉⲧⲇⲓ ⲙⲯⲱⲧⲙ · ⲟⲩⲣⲓⲏⲗ ⲡⲉ-
ⲑⲓⲭⲛ ⲛⲉⲕⲗⲟⲙ · ⲛⲉⲫⲁⲏⲗ ·
ⲡⲉⲑⲓⲭⲛ ⲧⲃⲟⲏⲑⲓⲁ · ⲁⲕⲉⲛⲧⲁⲏⲗ
10 ⲡⲉⲑⲓⲭⲛ ⲛⲉⲥⲓⲟⲩ · ⲁⲥⲉⲛⲧⲁⲏⲗ
ⲡⲉⲑⲓⲭⲙ ⲡⲣⲏ · ⲏⲣⲁⲫⲁⲏⲗ
ⲡⲉⲑⲓⲭⲙ ⲡⲉϩⲟⲟⲩ · ⲓⲉⲣⲉⲙⲓⲏⲗ
ⲡⲉⲑⲓⲭⲛ ⲛⲉⲕⲣⲏⲕⲧⲏⲣⲓⲟⲛ ·
ⲏⲣⲓⲏⲗ ⲡⲉⲑⲓⲭⲛ ⲛⲉⲙⲙⲟⲟⲩ
15 ⲫⲁⲛⲟⲩⲏⲗ ⲡⲉⲑⲓⲭⲛ ⲛⲉⲅⲁⲣⲡⲟⲥ
ⲁⲫⲁⲏⲗ ⲡⲉⲑⲓⲭⲙ ⲡⲉⲭ[ⲓ]ⲱⲛ
ⲁⲕⲣⲁⲏⲗ ⲡⲉⲑⲓⲭⲛ ⲑⲁⲗⲁ[ⲥ]ⲥⲁ
. ⲉⲓⲗⲁⲏⲗ · ⲡⲉⲑⲓⲭⲛ ⲛⲉⲙ[ⲟⲟⲩ] ⲛϩⲱⲟⲩ
. . ⲁⲃⲟⲩⲏⲗ · ⲡⲉⲑⲓⲭⲛ ⲛⲉⲗⲏ[ⲙ]ⲛⲏ . .
20 . . . ⲁⲑⲓⲏⲗ · ⲡⲉⲑⲓⲭⲛ ⲛⲁⲡⲁ . . . . .
. . . . ⲡⲉ[ⲑⲓⲭⲙ] ⲡ . . . . . .

---

2 ⲟⲩ ⲕⲁϩ Rossi : "pain" ("douleur") Amélineau ‖ **3** ⲱ ⲭⲓⲏⲗ Rossi ‖ **7** *i.e.* ˢⲡ-ⲉⲧ-ϯ ⲙ̄-ⲡ-ⲥⲱⲧⲙ Kropp : "the one who is over hearing" Meyer ‖ **9** *i.e.* βοήθεια ‖ **12** ⲓⲉⲣⲉⲙⲓⲏⲗ Kropp : ⲓⲉⲣⲉⲱⲏⲗ Rossi ‖ **13** *i.e.* ˢⲛ-ⲛⲩⲕⲧⲉⲣⲓⲟⲛ ? (haplography?) suggestion of Ágnes Mihálykó : *i.e.* κρατήριον "(mixing) bowls" ("die Mischkrüge") Kropp, Meyer : "volcanoes" ("vulcani") Rossi : κρηστήριον Schmidt in Kropp ‖ **14** *i.e.* ˢⲛ(ⲉ)-ⲙⲟⲟⲩ ‖ **15** *i.e.* καρπός ‖ **16** *i.e.* χ[ι]ών ‖ **17** [ⲁⲕ]ⲣⲁⲏⲗ Rossi | *i.e.* θάλα(σ)σα ‖ **18** . . ⲓⲗⲁⲏⲗ Rossi | ⲛⲉ[ⲙⲱⲟⲩ] Rossi ‖ **19** *i.e.* λί[μ]νη ? : ⲛⲉⲗⲏ . . . ⲛⲏ . . Rossi, Kropp, Meyer : *l.* ⲗⲏ[ⲕⲁ]ⲛⲏ [ⲛ̄-ⲁⲗ] "the vessels of hail" ("die Gefäße des Hagels") *i.e.* λεκάνη Kropp : *l.* ⲗⲏ[ⲕⲁ]ⲛⲏ *i.e.* λεκάνη "vessels" ? Meyer 1988, 1994 ‖ **20** ⲛⲁⲡⲁ Kropp : *l.* ⲁⲡⲁⲣⲭⲏ *i.e.* ἀπαρχή ? CMPT : ⲛⲁⲧⲁ Rossi

… [in] haste! Let them flee [from] my face in silence!

*Michael, the one who is over all the powers that are strong! *Raphael, |[5] the one who is over salvation! *Gabriel, the one who is over the powers! Arnaēl, the one who gives obedience! Uriel, the one who is over the crowns! Nephaēl, the one who is over help! Akentaēl, |[10] the one who is over the stars! Asentaēl, the one who is over the sun! Ēraphaēl, the one who is over the day! Ieremiēl, the one who is over the nocturnal? ⟨matters⟩! Ēriēl, the one who is over the waters! |[15] Phanouēl, the one who is over the fruits! Aphaēl, the one who is over the snow! Akraēl, the one who is over the sea! .eilaēl, the one who is over the rainwaters! ..abouēl, the one who is over the lakes?! |[20] ...athiēl, the one who is over the first-fruits?! … who is over the …

---

third page l. 3–fourth page l. 7. Angels and their spheres of competence: For the concept of *angels being set "over" various phenomena, *cf.* the note to *PCM* I front l. 1.

fourth page (page 9)

ⲭⲁ ... ⲏ ⲑⲁⲩⲣⲟⲩⲏⲗ · ⲡⲉⲑⲓⲭⲛ ⲛⲉⲕ-
ⲗⲟ[ⲟⲗⲉ] ⲁⲇⲣⲁⲥⲁⲍⲁⲏⲗ · ⲡⲉⲑⲓⲭⲛ
ⲛ̅ⲛⲉⲃ[ⲣ]ⲏⲭⲉ · ⲓ̅ⲁ̅ⲱ̅ⲏ̅ⲗ̅ · ⲡⲉⲑⲓⲭⲛ
ⲧⲟⲡⲟⲥ ⲛⲓⲙ · ⲥⲁⲃⲁⲏⲗ · ⲡⲉⲑⲓⲭⲙ
5   ⲡⲡⲉⲧⲛⲁⲛⲟⲩϥ · ⲁ̅ⲇ̅ⲱ̅ⲛ̅[ⲁ̅]ⲏ̅ⲗ̅
ⲡⲉⲑⲓⲭⲙ ⲡⲓ ⲉϩⲟⲩⲛ ⲙ̅ⲡⲓⲱⲧ ⲙ̅ⲛ̅
ⲡⲉϥⲉⲓ ⲉⲃⲟⲗ · ⲁ̅ⲡⲟ̅ⲗ̅ₒ/ ϫⲉⲕⲁⲥ
ⲉⲧⲉⲧⲛ̅ⲛⲉⲉⲓ ⲛⲁⲓ · ⲛ̅ⲧⲉⲧⲛ̅ⲁϩⲉ-
ⲣⲁⲧⲧⲏⲩⲧⲛ ⲛⲉⲙⲁⲓ · ⲛ̅ⲧⲉⲧⲛ̅-
10 ⲛ̅ⲟⲩϫ ⲉⲃⲟⲗ ϩⲓⲑⲏ [ⲙ]ⲡⲁϩⲟ ⲙⲡ̅ⲛ̅ⲁ̅
ⲛⲓⲙ ⲛ̅ⲁⲕⲁⲑⲁⲣⲧⲟⲛ · ⲙⲁⲣⲉⲩⲁ-
ⲛⲁⲭⲱⲣⲓ ⲉⲃⲟⲗ ϩⲓⲑⲏ ⲙⲡⲁϩⲟ
ⲧⲏⲣⲟⲩ ϫⲉ ⲛⲛⲉⲩϫⲟⲟⲥ ϫⲉ ⲉϥ-
ⲧⲱⲛ ⲡⲉϥⲛⲟⲩⲧⲉ · ⲙⲁⲣⲉⲩ-
15 ⲥⲧⲱⲧ ⲛ̅ⲥⲉⲡⲱⲧ ⲙ̅ⲡⲁⲙⲧⲟ
ⲉⲃⲟⲗ ⲧⲏⲣⲟⲩ · ϩⲙ̅ ⲡⲣⲁⲛ ⲙⲡⲓⲱⲑ
ⲙ̅ⲛ̅ ⲡϣⲏⲣⲉ ⲙ̅ⲛ̅ ⲡⲉⲡ̅ⲛ̅ⲁ̅ ⲉⲧⲟⲩⲁⲁⲃ ⲁⲁⲁⲁⲁⲁⲁⲁⲁⲁⲁⲁ · ⲁⲅⲓⲟⲥ
ⲁ̅ⲅ̅ⲓ̅ⲟ̅ⲥ̅ ⲁ̅ⲅ̅ⲓ̅ⲟ̅ⲥ̅ · ⲕ̅ⲩ̅ⲣ̅ⲓ̅ⲟ̅ⲥ̅ ⲥⲁ[ⲃⲁⲱ]ⲑ
20 [ⲡⲗ]ⲏⲣⲟⲥ ⲟ ⲟ̅ⲩ̅ⲣ̅ⲁ̅ⲛ̅ⲟ̅ⲥ̅ ⲕⲏ ⲉ ⲕⲣ · ⲧⲏⲥ ϩⲁ-
[ⲅⲓⲁⲥ ⲇⲟⲍⲏⲥ ⲥ]ⲟⲩ [ⲧⲛ̅]ϯ ⲉⲟⲟⲩ ⲛⲁⲕ [ⲧ]ⲛ̅ϯ ⲉⲟⲟⲩ

---

1 ⲭⲁ ... ⲏ Kropp, Meyer : ...... Rossi ‖ **2** ⲗⲟ[ⲙ ..] Rossi | ⲁⲇⲣⲁⲥⲁⲍⲁⲏⲗ Rossi : ⲁⲃⲣⲁⲥⲁⲍⲁⲏⲗ Kropp, Meyer 1988, 1994 ‖ **4** *i.e.* τόπος : "aion" ("Æon") Amélineau ‖ **3** *i.e.* ˢⲉⲃⲣⲏϭⲉ ‖ **6** *i.e.* ˢⲡ-ⲉⲓ ⲉϩⲟⲩⲛ : "the entrance" ("den Eingang") Kropp ‖ **7** *i.e.* ἀπο(λογία) : *l.* ⲁⲡⲟⲗ(ⲗⲱⲛ) Rossi : "Apolo" Amélineau *cf.* note ‖ **10** *i.e.* πν(εῦμ)α ‖ **11** *i.e.* ἀκάθαρτον ‖ **11–12** *i.e.* ἀναχωρεῖν ‖ **16** *i.e.* ˢⲉⲓⲱⲧ ‖ **17** *i.e.* πν(εῦμ)α ‖ **18** "Amen. 12 times" Kropp ‖ **18–21** *i.e.* ἅγιος ἅγιος ἅγιος κύριος Σα[βαω]θ [πλ]ήρης ὁ οὐρανὸς καὶ ἡ γῆ τῆς ἁ[γίας δόξης σ]ου ‖ **20** . . ⲏⲣⲟⲥ Rossi | ⲕⲏ ⲉ ⲕⲏ Kropp ‖ **21** [ⲅⲓⲟⲥ ⲇⲟⲍⲏⲥ ⲥ]ⲟⲩ Kropp : ...... ⲟⲩ Rossi

... Thaurouēl, the one who is over the clouds! Adrasaxaēl, the one who is over the flashes of lightning! Iaōēl, the one who is over every place! Sabaēl, the one who is over |⁵ what is good! Adōnaēl, the one who is over the coming in of the Father and his coming out—request—so that you (pl.) will come to me and you will stand with me and you will |¹⁰ cast away before my face every unclean spirit! Let them all withdraw before my face so that they will not say, "Where is his God?" Let them all |¹⁵ tremble and flee from my presence, in the name of the Father, and the Son and the Holy Spirit!

AAAAAAAAAAAA, |^{Greek} *holy, holy, holy, Lord *Sabaoth, |²⁰ the heaven and the earth are full of your holy glory! |^{Coptic} [We] give glory to you, we give glory

---

7. ⲁⲡⲟⲗⲟ/ : "request" This abbreviation likely indicates the point at which the reader was to insert specific information. Rossi understood it as an abbreviation of the name of the god Apollo (ἀπολλων), while Amélineau (1895: 15) prints *Apolo* in italics and suggests that it indicates the responses to be made by assistants, presumably imagining a call and response situation akin to a liturgy. We instead understand a writing of ἀπολογία (usually "defence") whose nuances we still do not fully understand (*cf.* p. 34), but translate as "request". This text displays some of the most extensive use of this word. We propose that, like κοινά, it marks where the recipe is to be personalised, although its position—often breaking running text—might seem to challenge this theory. In most cases, such as p. 21 ll. 15–16, it would nonetheless fit well: "let them all flee before my face—mine, NN", allowing the formula to be personalised (*cf. e.g.*, PCM I 17 l. 21 for this very common construction). On this page our interpretation faces greater difficulties, since the nearest first person pronoun which it could supplement is in the following line, rather than before it, as we might expect. It is possible that ἀπολογία here does indeed supplement the ⲛⲁⲓ ("to me") in l. 8. More probably, perhaps, it may stand in this case for a fuller formula, such as "I, NN, invoke you". This would work quite well given that the following "so that" (ⲭⲉⲕⲁⲁⲥ) is not otherwise preceded by a verb of invocation or adjuration, as we would generally expect.

13–14. ⲛⲛⲉⲩⲭⲟⲟⲥ ⲭⲉ ⲉϥⲧⲱⲛ ⲡⲉϥⲛⲟⲩⲧⲉ : "so that they will not say, 'Where is his God?'" *Cf.* Psalm 113 (115) 10: "... lest the nations say "Where is their god?" (ⲙⲏ ⲡⲟⲧⲉ ⲛ̄ⲧⲉ ⲛ̄ϩⲉⲑⲛⲟⲥ ⲭⲟⲟⲥ ⲭⲉ ⲉϥⲧⲱⲛ ⲡⲉⲩⲛⲟⲩⲧⲉ; Budge 1898: 123).

fifth page (page 11)

ⲛ̅[ⲛⲉ]ⲕ︦ϩⲁⲅⲓⲟⲥ ⲧⲏⲣⲟⲩ · ⲓ̅ⲁ̅ⲱ̅ ⲧ̅ⲛ̅ϯ ⲉ-
ⲟⲟ[ⲩ] ⲛⲁⲕ ⲡⲓ̅ϩ̅ⲁⲕⲓⲟⲥ ⲥⲁⲃⲁⲱⲑ ·
ⲡϣⲟⲣ[ⲡ] ⲛ̅ⲧⲡⲉ ⲙ̅ⲛ̅ ⲡⲕⲁϩ · ⲧ̅ⲛ̅ϯ ⲉ-
ⲟⲟⲩ ⲛⲁⲕ · ⲁ̅ⲇ̅ⲱ̅ⲛ̅ⲁ̅ⲓ̅ · ⲉ̅ⲗ̅ⲟⲉⲓ ⲡⲡⲁⲛ-
5 ⲇ̅ⲱ̅ⲕ̅ⲣ̅ⲁ̅ⲧ̅ⲱ̅ⲣ̅ · ⲡϣⲟⲣⲡ ⲉⲛⲉⲭⲉ-
ⲣⲟⲩⲃⲓⲛ ⲙ̅ⲛ̅ ⲛⲉⲥⲉⲣⲁⲫⲓⲛ · ⲧ̅ⲛ̅-
ϯ ⲉⲟⲟⲩ ⲛⲁⲕ ⲙ̅ⲁ̅ⲣ̅ⲙ̅ⲁ̅ⲣ̅ⲁ̅ⲱ̅ⲑ̅ ·
ⲡⲉⲧϣⲟⲟⲡ ϩⲁⲑⲏ ⲛⲁⲅⲅⲉⲗⲟⲥ
ⲙ̅ⲛ̅ ⲛⲁⲣⲭⲏⲁⲅⲅⲉⲗⲟⲥ · ⲧ̅ⲛ̅ϯ ⲉ-
10 ⲟⲟⲩ ⲛⲁⲕ · ⲭ̅ⲁ̅ⲙ̅ⲁ̅ⲣ̅ⲙ̅ⲁ̅ⲣ̅ⲓ̅ⲁ̅ⲱ̅
ⲡⲉⲧϩⲁⲑⲏ ⲙ̅ⲡⲓ̅ⲙ̅ⲛ̅ⲧⲁϥⲧⲉ
ⲛ̅ⲥⲧⲉⲣⲉⲩⲙⲁ · ⲧ̅ⲛ̅ϯ ⲉⲟⲟⲩ ⲛⲁⲕ
ⲑ̅ⲣ̅ⲁ̅ⲕ̅ⲁ̅ⲓ̅ · ⲡⲉⲛ̅ⲧⲁϥϩⲱ̅ⲃ̅ⲥ̅ ⲙ̅ⲡ-
ⲕⲁϩ ϩⲓϫⲙ̅ ⲡⲛⲟⲩⲛ · ⲁϥⲁϣ [ⲧⲡⲉ]
15 ⲛ̅ⲑⲉ ⲛ̅ⲟⲩⲕⲁⲙⲁⲣⲁ · ⲧ̅ⲛ̅ϯ ⲉⲟⲟⲩ
ⲛⲁⲕ ⲙ̅ⲁ̅ⲛ̅ⲁ̅ⲭ̅ⲱ̅ⲑ̅ · ⲡⲉⲛⲧⲁϥ-
ⲥⲙⲛ ⲥ̅ⲛ̅ⲧⲉ ⲛ̅ⲧⲡⲉ ⲙ̅ⲛ̅ ⲡⲕⲁϩ
ⲁϥⲧⲁϫⲣⲟ ⲙ̅ⲡⲓ̅ⲙ̅ⲛ̅ⲧⲁϥⲧⲉ ⲛⲥ-
ⲧⲉⲣⲉⲩⲙⲁ · ϩⲓϫⲙ̅ ⲡⲓⲃⲧⲟⲟⲩ ⲛ̅ⲥ-
20 [ⲧ]ⲏⲗⲟⲥ · ⲧ̅ⲛ̅ϯ ⲉⲟⲟⲩ ⲛ[ⲁⲕ .]ⲛ
. . . ⲣ̅ⲁ̅ⲱ̅ⲙ̅ · ⲡⲉⲛⲧⲁϥⲉⲓ ⲛ̅[ⲭⲱ]ⲗ

---

1 *i.e.* ἅγιος | ⲛ̅[ⲛⲉ]ⲕ︦ϩⲁⲅⲓⲟⲥ ⲧⲏⲣⲟⲩ : "all your holinesses" Meyer 1994 ‖ **2** *i.e.* ἅγιος ‖ **4–5** *i.e.* παντοκράτωρ : ⲡⲛ̅ⲁ̅ⲇ̅ⲱ̅ⲕ̅ⲣ̅ⲁ̅ⲧ̅ⲱ̅ⲣ̅ Kropp, Meyer ‖ **5–6** *i.e.* χερουβίμ ‖ **6** *i.e.* σεραφίμ ‖ **8** *i.e.* ἄγγελος ‖ **9** *i.e.* ἀρχάγγελος ‖ **12** *i.e.* στερέωμα ‖ **15** *i.e.* καμάρα ‖ **17** ⲥ̅ⲙ̅ⲉ̅ⲥ̅ⲛ̅ⲧⲉ Kropp, Meyer ‖ **18–19** *i.e.* στερέωμα ‖ **19** *i.e.* ˢϥⲧⲟⲟⲩ ‖ **19–20** *i.e.* στῦλος ‖ **20** [ⲙ̅]ⲛ Rossi : ⲁⲛ Kropp, Meyer ‖ **21** ⲣ̅ⲁ̅ⲱ̅ⲙ̅ Rossi : ⲃ̅ⲁ̅ⲱ̅ⲙ̅ Kropp, Meyer | ⲛ̅[ⲭⲱ]ⲗ "gird" ("gürten") Kropp, Meyer 1988, 1994 : *i.e.* ˢⲭⲱⲣ ? CMPT : ⲛ . . ⲗ . . Rossi

to all your saints, *Iao! We give glory to you, O holy *Sabaoth, the first of heaven and earth! We give glory to you, *Adonai *Eloei Almighty |⁵ the first of the *cherubim and *seraphim! We give glory to you, Marmaraōth, the one who existed before *angels and *archangels! We give |¹⁰ glory to you Khamarmariaō, the one who existed before the fourteen firmaments! We give glory to you Thrakai, the one who covered the *abyss with the earth, and suspended [heaven] |¹⁵ like a vault! We give glory to you Manakhōth, the one who established ⟨the⟩ foundations of heaven and earth and made fast the fourteen firmaments upon the four |²⁰ pillars! We give glory to [you] …raōm, the one who has come to sharpen?

14–15. ⲁϥⲱ [ⲧⲡⲉ] ⲛ̄ⲑⲉ ⲛ̄ⲟⲩⲕⲁⲙⲁⲣⲁ : **"suspended [heaven] like a vault"** A reference to Isaiah 40.22: "he who erected heaven like a vault" (ⲡⲉⲛⲧⲁϥⲧⲁϩⲉ ⲧⲡⲉ ⲉⲣⲁⲧⲥ̄ ⲛ̄ⲑⲉ ⲛ̄ⲟⲩⲕⲏⲡⲉ; Bąk 2019: 82). Note that ⲕⲏⲡⲉ in this version translates καμάρα from the Septuagint, so that *PCM* I 12 may either be relying directly on the Greek text, or on a different Coptic translation.

21. ⲛ̄[ⲭⲱ]ⲗ : **"sharpen"** We might expect here a verb meaning "sheath" or "gird", but we have been unable to find any word which would fit the reported traces.

sixth page (page 13)

ⲛⲧ[ⲉϥ]ⲥⲏⲃⲉ ⲛⲧⲙⲏⲧⲉ ⲙ̄ⲡⲉϥⲁⲗⲟⲥ
ⲥⲛⲁⲩ ⲛ̄ⲁⲣⲥⲏⲧⲟⲩ · ⲧⲛ̄ϯ ⲉⲟⲟⲩ ⲛⲁⲕ
ⲑⲣⲁⲕⲁⲓⲙ · ⲡⲁⲓ ⲛⲧⲁϥϫⲓ ⲙ̄ⲡⲉⲡⲣⲟ-
ⲥⲟⲡⲟⲛ ⲛ̄ⲅⲁⲩⲣⲓⲏⲗ · ⲧⲛ̄ϯ ⲉⲟⲟⲩ ⲛⲁⲕ
5 ⲗⲁⲩⲣⲓⲏⲗ · ⲡⲉⲕⲟⲛⲟⲙⲟⲥ ⲛ̄ⲛⲣⲁⲫⲁⲏⲗ
ⲧⲛ̄ϯ ⲉⲟⲟⲩ ⲛⲉⲧⲡⲉ · ⲧⲛ̄ϯ ⲉⲟⲟⲩ ⲛⲁⲕ
ⲡⲕⲁϩ ⲧⲛ̄ϯ ⲉⲟⲟⲩ ⲛⲁⲕ ⲡⲣⲏ · ⲧⲛ̄ϯ ⲉⲟⲟⲩ
ⲛⲁⲕ ⲡⲟϩ ⲧⲛ̄ϯ ⲉⲟⲟⲩ ⲛⲁⲕ ⲥⲁⲃⲁⲱⲑ
ⲙⲛ ⲛⲉⲥⲓⲟⲩ ⲧⲏⲣⲟⲩ · ⲧⲛ̄ϯ ⲉⲟⲟⲩ ⲛⲁⲕ
10 ⲁⲣⲁⲕⲧⲟⲥ ⲧⲛ̄ϯ ⲉⲟⲟⲩ ⲛⲁⲕ ⲓⲁⲱ
ⲧⲛ̄ϯ ⲉⲟⲟⲩ ⲛⲁⲕ ⲁⲇⲱⲛⲁⲓ ⲉⲗⲟⲉⲓ · ⲡⲡⲁ-
ⲇⲱⲕⲣⲁⲇⲱⲣ ⲍⲱⲧⲙ̄ ⲉⲣⲟⲓ · ⲁⲙⲟⲩ
ϣⲁⲣⲟⲓ ⲡⲁⲕⲁⲑⲟⲥ ⲅⲁⲩⲣⲓⲏⲗ · ϩⲱⲥⲇⲉ ⲛ̄ⲕⲥⲱⲧⲙ̄ ⲉⲣⲟⲓ ⲙⲡⲟⲟⲩ ⲉⲧⲃⲉ
15 ⲧⲉⲓⲥⲫⲣⲁⲕⲓⲥ ⲛⲧⲉ ⲁⲇⲱⲛⲁⲓ · ⲡⲓⲱϣ
ⲙⲛ ⲡⲓⲙⲛ̄ⲧⲁϥⲧⲉ ⲙ̄ⲫⲏⲗⲁⲕⲧⲏ-
ⲣⲓⲟⲛ ⲉⲧϩ̄ⲛ ⲧⲁϭⲓϫ ⲛⲟⲩⲛⲁⲙ ·
ⲉⲧⲣⲉⲕⲉⲓ ϣⲁⲣⲟⲓ ⲉⲡⲉⲓⲧⲟⲡⲟⲥ ⲛ̄ⲅ-
ϣⲱⲡⲉ ⲛⲁⲓ ⲙⲡⲣⲟⲥⲧⲁⲧⲏⲥ · ⲛⲉ-
20 [ⲕⲟ]ⲛⲟⲙⲟⲥ · ⲛ̄ⲃⲟⲏⲑⲓⲁ ⲛ̄ⲛⲉϩⲟⲟⲩ
[ⲧⲏ]ⲣⲟⲩ ⲙ̄ⲡⲁⲱⲛϩ ·
[ⲛ̄ⲅⲛ̄]ⲱϫϭ ⲉⲃⲟⲗ ⲙ̄ⲡ̄ⲛ̄ⲁ̄ ⲛⲓ[ⲙ ⲙⲡⲟ]ⲛⲏ[ⲣⲟⲛ]

---

2 *i.e.* ἄρρητος ? Kropp || **3–4** *i.e.* πρόσωπον || **5** *i.e.* οἰκονόμος | *l.* ⲛ-ⲣⲁⲫⲁⲏⲗ : *l.* ⲛ̄-ⲛ-ⲣⲁⲫⲁⲏⲗ "of the Raphaels" ("dei ⲣⲁⲫⲁⲏⲗ") Rossi || **6** *i.e.* ˢⲛ̄-ⲧ-ⲡⲉ || **10** *i.e.* ἄρκτος "Bear, Wagon" *i.e.* Ursa Major ("Bär, Wagen") ? Kropp *cf.* note | ⲓⲁⲱ Kropp, Meyer 1988, 1994 : ⲁⲱ Rossi || **11–12** *i.e.* πα(ν)τοκράτωρ : ⲡⲁⲛⲇⲱⲕⲣⲁⲇⲱⲣ Rossi || **12** *i.e.* ˢⲥⲱⲧⲙ || **13** *i.e.* ἀγαθός || **13–14** *i.e.* ὥστε || **15** *i.e.* σφραγίς || **16–17** *i.e.* φυλακτήριον || **18** *i.e.* τόπος || **19** *i.e.* προστάτης || **19–20** *i.e.* οἰ[κο]νόμος || **20** *i.e.* βοήθεια : "and (a) help" ("und Hilfe") Kropp : "and help" Meyer 1988, 1994 || **21** ⲁ[..] at the end of the line Kropp, Meyer || **22** *i.e.* ˢⲛⲟⲩϫⲉ : ... ⲱϫϭ Rossi : [. . ⲛ]ⲟⲩϭ Schmidt in Kropp : [ⲛ̄ⲅⲛ̄]ⲟⲩϭ Kropp, Meyer | *i.e.* πν(εῦμ)α | *i.e.* πονηρόν CMPT : ⲛⲓ[ⲙ̄ⲡⲟ]/ⲛⲏ[ⲣⲟⲥ]\ Rossi : ⲛⲓ[ⲙ ⲙ̄ⲡⲟ]ⲛⲏⲣⲟ̣ⲛ̣ Kropp, Meyer

[his] sword in the middle of his two thighs. We give glory to you Thrakaim, the one who received the appearance of *Gabriel! We give glory to you today, |⁵ Lauriel, the steward of *Raphael! We give glory to heaven! We give glory to you, O earth! We give glory to you, O sun! We give glory to you, O moon! We give glory to you, *Sabaoth, and all the stars! We give glory to you, |¹⁰ Araktos! We give glory to you, *Iao! We give glory to you, *Adonai *Eloei Almighty!

Listen to me! Come to me, O good Gabriel, so that you listen to me today because of |¹⁵ this seal of Adonai, the Father, and the fourteen phylacteries that are in my right hand, so that you come to me, to this place, so that you become for me a benefactor ⟨and⟩ |²⁰ ⟨a⟩ helping steward for all the days of my life, [and you?] cast out? every evil

---

10. ⲁⲣⲁⲕⲧⲟⲥ : **"Araktos"** Kropp understands a reference to ἄρκτος, that is, Ursa Major, or the constellation of the Great Bear, which would make sense in the context of the mention of several other celestial bodies. In Egyptian astrology, Ursa Major is called the Foreleg (𓄟𓂺𓃀 *msḫ.tyw*) and is associated with the god *Seth (Neugebauer/Parker 1969: 190–191). It is is frequently invoked in association with Seth-Typhon in the Graeco-Egyptian magical papyri (Gundel 1968: 59–64), although the context here would seem to be rather different, mentioning it simply as part of the natural world created by the Christian god.

seventh page (page 15)

ϩⲓ [ⲁ]ⲕ[ⲁⲑⲁ]ⲣⲧⲟⲛ · ⲉⲓⲧⲉ ϩⲟⲟⲩⲧ
ⲉⲓⲧⲉ ⲥϩⲓⲙⲉ · ⲉⲓⲧⲉ ⲡⲟⲩⲣⲁ[ⲛ]ⲓⲟⲛ ·
ⲉⲓⲧⲉ ⲛⲁ ⲡⲕⲁϩ · ⲉⲓⲧⲉ ⲛⲁ ⲡⲁⲏⲣ
ⲛⲉⲩⲉϣ ϭⲙϭⲟⲙ ⲉⲁϩⲉⲣⲁⲧⲟⲩ ⲙⲡⲁⲙ-
5 ⲧⲟ ⲉⲃⲟⲗ ⲟⲩⲧⲉ ⲙⲡⲉⲙⲧⲟ ⲉⲃⲟⲗ
ⲛⲧⲉⲕⲛⲟϭ ⲛϭⲟⲙ ⲡⲛⲟⲩⲧⲉ · ϩⲁⲙⲏ[ⲛ] ⲅ̅
†† ⲉⲟⲟⲩ ⲛⲁⲕ · ⲡⲉⲡⲣⲟⲥ[ⲱ]ⲡⲟⲛ
ⲛⲁⲇⲱⲛⲁⲓ ⲉⲗⲟⲉⲓ · ⲡⲡⲁⲛⲇⲱⲕ-
ⲣⲁⲇⲱⲣ ϩⲱⲥⲇⲉ ⲛⲅⲥⲱⲧⲙ̅ ⲉⲣⲟⲓ
10 ⲙⲡⲉⲓϩⲟⲟⲩ ⲛⲅ̅ⲧⲉⲛⲟⲟⲩ ⲛⲁⲓ ⲛ̅-
ⲅⲁⲩⲣⲓⲏⲗ · ⲡⲁⲅⲅⲉⲗⲟⲥ ⲛ̅ⲧⲇⲓ-
ⲕⲁⲓⲟⲥⲏⲛⲏ · ⲛ̅ⲃⲓ ϣⲁⲣⲟⲓ · ⲉⲧⲃⲉ ⲧⲉⲓⲥⲫⲣⲁⲕⲓⲥ · ⲛ̅ⲧⲉⲡⲓϣⲑ ⲡⲡⲁⲛⲇⲱⲕⲣⲁⲇⲱⲣ ⲉⲑⲉⲛ̅ ⲧⲁϭⲓϫ ⲛⲟⲩⲛⲁⲙ · ⲛ̅ⲅ-
15 ⲁϩⲉⲉⲣⲁⲧⲕ̅ ⲥⲁ ⲟⲩⲛⲁⲙ ⲙⲟⲓ · ⲛ̅ⲅⲃⲟ-
ⲏⲑⲓⲁ ⲉⲣⲟⲓ · ⲥⲟⲟⲩⲧⲛ̅ ⲉⲃⲟⲗ ⲙⲡⲉⲕ-
ⲥⲟⲧⲉ ⲉϫⲙ̅ ⲡⲁⲣⲭⲏⲡⲗⲁⲥⲙⲁ ⲙⲛ
ⲛⲉϥⲧⲏⲛⲁⲙⲓⲥ ⲧⲏⲣⲟⲩ · ⲙⲛ ⲛⲉϥ-
[ⲧ]ⲉⲙⲟⲛⲓⲟⲛ ⲛ̅ⲁⲕⲁⲑⲁⲣⲧⲟⲛ ⲙⲛ̅ ⲙⲡⲟ-
20 [ⲛⲏⲣ]ⲟⲛ · ⲟⲩⲱⲛϩ ⲧⲉⲕϭⲓϫ ⲉⲣⲟⲓ ⲙ-
[ⲡⲟⲟⲩ · ⲛ̅ⲅ]ⲟⲩⲱⲛϩ ⲛⲁⲓ [ⲉⲃⲟⲗ] ⲙ̅ⲡⲟⲟⲩ

---

1 i.e. [ἀ]κ[άθα]ρτον : [ⲛⲁⲕⲁⲑⲁ]ⲣⲧⲟⲛ Rossi || **1–3** i.e. εἴτε || **2** i.e. οὐρά[ν]ιον || **3** i.e. ἀήρ || **4** i.e. ˢⲛ̅ⲛⲉ=ⲩ-ϣ ϭⲙϭⲟⲙ || **5** i.e. οὔτε || **6** i.e. ἀμή[ν] || **7** i.e. πρόσ[ω]πον || **8–9** i.e. παντοκράτωρ | i.e. ὥστε || **11** i.e. ἄγγελος || **11–12** i.e. δικαιοσύνη || **12** i.e. ˢⲛ̅=ϥ-ⲉⲓ || **13** i.e. σφραγίς | i.e. ˢⲡ-ⲉⲓⲱⲧ || **13–14** i.e. παντοκράτωρ || **15** ⲁϩⲉⲣⲁⲧⲕ̅ Rossi || i.e. ˢⲛ̅ⲥⲁ | i.e. ˢⲙ̅ⲙⲟ=ⲓ || **15–16** i.e. βοηθεῖν || **17** i.e. ἀρχίπλασμα || **18** i.e. δύναμις || **19** i.e. [δ]αιμόνιον | i.e. ἀκάθαρτον | ⲙⲛ̅ omitted Kropp, Meyer 1988 || **19–20** ⲙⲛ̅ ⲡⲟ[ⲛⲏⲣ]ⲟⲛ Rossi | i.e. πο[νηρ]όν || **21** ⲛ̅ⲅ]ⲟⲩⲱⲛϩ ⲛⲁⲕ [ⲉⲃⲟⲗ] Rossi

and unclean spirit, whether male or female, whether heavenly or those of the earth or those of the air! They will not be able to stand in my |⁵ presence nor in the presence of your great power, God! Amen (thrice)!

I give glory to you, O countenance of *Adonai *Eloei Almighty, so that you listen to me |¹⁰ in this day and you send to me *Gabriel, the angel of righteousness and he comes to me because of this seal of the Father Almighty that is in my right hand, and you |¹⁵ stand ⟨at⟩ my right side, and you help me!

Draw your bow against the First-Formed One and all his powers and his unclean and evil demons! |²⁰ Reveal your hand to me [today] and reveal to me today

---

17. ⲡⲁⲣⲭⲏⲡⲗⲁⲥⲙⲁ : "the First-Formed One" A reference to the Devil, understood to have been the first and foremost of all created beings, inspired by the description of the Behemoth as the first created being (ἀρχὴ πλάσματος) in Job 40.19; see van der Vliet 1995: 402, 406, 410.

eighth page (page 17)

ⲛⲧ[ⲉⲕⲧⲏⲛ]ⲁⲙⲓⲥ ⲙⲛ̄ ⲡⲉⲕⲉⲟⲟⲩ · ⲉⲓ-
ⲧⲁⲣⲕⲟ ⲙⲙⲟⲕ ⲙ̄ⲡⲟⲟⲩ ⲅ̄ⲁ̄ⲩ̄ⲣ̄ⲓ̄ⲏ̄ⲗ̄
ⲛⲕⲁⲧⲁ ⲥ̄ⲁ̄ⲃ̄ⲉ̄ⲣ̄ · ⲃ̄ⲗ̄ⲁ̄ⲣ̄ⲁ̄ⲣ̄ⲟ̄ ⲡⲓϣⲟ-
ⲙⲛⲧ ⲙ̄ⲡⲣⲟⲥⲱⲡⲟⲛ · ⲉⲧϩⲛ̄ ⲧⲙⲏ-
5 ⲧⲉ ⲙⲡⲓϥⲧⲟⲟⲩ ⲛ̄ⲥⲧⲏⲗⲟⲥ ⲉⲧⲧⲱⲟⲩⲛ ϩⲁ ⲧⲡⲉ ⲙⲛ̄ ⲡⲕⲁϩ
ⲑ̄ⲁ̄ⲗ̄ⲁ̄ⲙ̄ⲱ̄ⲣ̄ⲁ̄ · ⲑ̄ⲏ̄ⲥ̄ⲟ̄ϩ̄ⲁ̄ ⲑ̄ⲁ̄ⲓ̄ⲥ̄ⲁ̄ⲣ̄ⲁ̄
†ⲧⲁⲣⲕⲟ ⲙⲙⲟⲕ ⲅ̄ⲁ̄ⲩ̄ⲣ̄ⲓ̄ⲏ̄ⲗ̄ · ⲙⲡⲉⲓ-
ϥⲧⲟⲟⲩ ⲛⲁⲅⲅⲉⲗⲟⲥ ⲉⲧⲁϩⲉ-
10 ⲉⲣⲁⲧⲟⲩ ⲉϫⲙ̄ ⲡⲓϥⲧⲟⲟⲩ ⲛ̄ⲥⲧⲏ-
ⲗⲟⲥ · ⲉⲣⲉⲣⲁⲧⲟⲩ ⲧⲁⲭⲣⲏⲟⲩ ⲉϫⲛ̄ ⲛⲉ-
ⲥⲛ̄ⲧⲉ ⲙⲡⲛⲟⲩⲛ · ⲡⲉⲧⲟⲩⲁⲁϥ ⲉⲧ-
ⲧⲱⲟⲩⲛ̄ ϩⲁⲑⲏ ⲛ̄ⲧⲡⲉ · ⲑ̄ⲏ̄ⲣ̄ⲓ̄ⲏ̄ⲗ̄ ·
ⲑ̄ⲣ̄ⲟ̄ⲏ̄ⲗ̄ · ⲃ̄ⲁ̄ⲏ̄ⲗ̄ · †ⲡⲁⲣⲁⲕⲁⲗⲓ ⲙ̄-
15 ⲙⲱⲧⲛ̄ ⲡⲉϥⲧⲟⲟⲩ ⲛⲟϭ ⲛⲁⲅⲅⲉⲗⲟⲥ
ⲛ̄ⲧⲉⲧⲁⲡⲉ ⲙⲡ̄ⲡ̄ϣ̄ⲑ̄ · ϫⲉⲕⲁⲥ ⲉⲧⲉ-
ⲧⲛ̄ⲛⲉⲧⲉⲛⲟⲟⲩ ⲛⲁⲓ ⲛ̄ⲅⲁⲩⲣⲓⲏⲗ ⲡⲁⲅⲅⲉⲗⲟⲥ ⲛ̄ⲧⲇⲓⲕⲁⲓⲟⲥⲏⲛⲏ · ⲛⲃⲓ ϣⲁ-
[ⲣ]ⲟⲓ ⲛ̄ⲃⲟⲩⲱⲛ̄ϩ ⲛ̄ⲁⲓ ⲉⲃⲟⲗ ⲛⲧⲉϥ-
20 [ϭⲟ]ⲙ̣ ⲙⲛ̄ ⲡⲉϥⲉⲟⲟⲩ · ⲁ̄ⲡ̄ⲟ̄ⲗ̄ⲟ̄/ ⲡⲁⲓ ⲅⲁⲣ
[ⲡⲟⲩ]ⲱϣ ⲙ̄ⲡⲡⲁⲛⲇⲱⲕ̄ⲣ̄ⲁ̄ⲇ̄ⲱ̄ⲣ̄ · ⲥ̄ⲁ̄-
[ⲃ̄ⲁ̄ⲱ̄ⲑ̄] · ϫⲉⲕⲁⲥ ⲉⲃⲉⲉⲓ ϣⲁⲣ[ⲟⲓ ⲙⲡⲟ]ⲟⲩ
. . . . . †ⲧⲁⲣⲕⲟ ⲙⲙⲟⲕ [ⲅ̄ⲁ̄ⲩ̄ⲣ̄]ⲓ̄ⲏ̄ⲗ̄

---

1 *i.e.* δύναμις : [ⲇⲩⲛ]ⲁⲙⲓⲥ Rossi || **3** *i.e.* κατά : "by Katasaber" ("par Katasaber") Amélineau | ⲃ̄ⲗ̄ⲁ̄ⲣ̄ⲁ̄ⲣ̄ⲟ̄ : "remove from me" ("éloigne de moi") Amélineau || **3–4** *l.* ⲙ̄-ⲡⲓ-ϣⲟⲙⲛⲧ || **4** *i.e.* πρόσωπον || **5** *i.e.* στῦλος || **9** *i.e.* ἄγγελος || **9–10** *i.e.* ^{S}ⲉⲧ-ⲁϩⲉ-ⲣⲁⲧ≠ⲟⲩ (dittography) || **10** ⲡ[ⲉ]ϥⲧⲟⲟⲩ Rossi || **10–11** *i.e.* στῦλος || **12** *i.e.* ^{S}ⲡ-ⲉⲧ-ⲟⲩⲁⲁⲃ : "the saints" ("die Heiligen") ? Kropp : "the holy one(s?)" Meyer 1994 || **14** *i.e.* παρακαλεῖν || **15** ⲡⲉϥⲧⲟⲟⲩ Rossi : ⲡⲓϥⲧⲟⲟⲩ Kropp | *i.e.* ^{S}ⲛ̄-ⲛⲟϭ | *i.e.* ἄγγελος || **16** *i.e.* ^{S}ⲡ-ⲉⲓⲱⲧ || **16–17** *i.e.* ^{S}ⲉ≠ⲧⲉⲧⲛ̄-ⲉ-ⲧⲛ̄ⲛⲟⲩ : ⲉⲧⲉⲧⲛ̄ⲛⲉⲧⲉⲛⲟⲟⲩ Kropp || **17–18** *i.e.* ἄγγελος || **18** *i.e.* δικαιοσύνη | *i.e.* ^{S}ⲛ̄≠ϥ-ⲉⲓ || **19** *i.e.* ^{S}ⲛ̄≠ϥ-ⲟⲩⲱⲛϩ || **20** *i.e.* ἀπο(λογία) | *i.e.* γάρ || **21** *i.e.* παντοκράτωρ || **22** *i.e.* ^{S}ⲉ≠ϥ-ⲉ-ⲉⲓ

your *power and your glory!

I adjure you today, *Gabriel, by Saber, Blararo, the three countenances that are in the |⁵ midst of the four pillars that bear the heaven and the earth, Thalamōra, Thēsoha, Thaisara! I adjure you Gabriel, by these four *angels who |¹⁰ stand upon the four pillars, whose feet are firmly planted upon the foundations of the *abyss, the holy one who bears heaven, Thēriēl, Throēl, Baēl!

I invoke |¹⁵ you, O four great angels by the head of the Father, that you send to me Gabriel, the angel of righteousness, so that he comes to me and he reveals to me his |²⁰ power and his glory—request— for this ⟨is⟩ [the] wish of Almighty *Sabaoth, that he come to [me] today [...]

I adjure you Gabriel,

ninth page (page 19)

ⲛ̄ⲧⲁ[ⲡⲉ ⲛ̄ⲃ]ⲁ̅ⲑ̅[ⲟ̅]ⲩⲣⲓⲏⲗ ⲡⲛⲟϭ ⲛⲓⲱⲧ
ϫⲉⲕⲉ[ⲉⲓ ϣ]ⲁⲣⲟⲓ̈ ⲛ̄ⲕⲟⲩⲱⲛⲁϩ ⲉⲣⲟⲓ ⲧⲁⲭⲏ
†ⲧⲁⲣⲕⲟ ⲙ̄ⲙⲟⲕ ⲅⲁⲩ̅ⲣⲓⲏⲗ · ⲙⲡⲉϥⲧⲟⲟⲩ
ⲛ̄ⲕⲟϩ ⲙ̄ⲡⲙ̄ⲛ̄ⲧⲁϥⲧⲉ ⲛ̄ⲥⲧⲉⲣⲉⲩⲙⲁ
5 ϫⲉⲕⲉⲉⲓ ϣⲁⲣⲟⲓ ⲛ̄ⲅ̄ϣⲱⲡⲉ ⲛⲉⲙⲁⲓ · ϩⲙ̄
ⲡⲉⲓϩⲟⲟⲩ ⲙⲛ̄ ⲧⲉⲓⲟⲩⲛⲟⲩ · ⲛ̄ⲅⲃⲟⲏⲑⲓⲁ
ⲉⲣⲟⲓ ϩⲛ̄ ⲧⲉⲕϭⲟⲙ ⲙⲛ̄ ⲡⲉⲕⲉⲟⲟⲩ ϩⲛ̄ ⲟⲩⲧⲁⲭⲏ †ⲧⲁⲣⲕⲟ ⲙⲙⲟⲕ ⲓ̅ⲱⲣⲓⲏⲗ ⲕⲁⲧⲁ †ϭⲏⲡⲉ ⲛ̄ⲟⲩⲟⲉⲓⲛ̄ ⲉⲧϩⲁⲧⲙ̄ ⲡⲱⲧ
10 ⲉϥϩⲏⲡ ⲛ̄ϩⲏⲧⲟⲩ ⲙ̄ⲡⲁⲧⲉϥⲧⲁⲙⲓⲉ
ⲗⲁⲁⲩ · ⲧⲁⲓ ⲉⲡⲉⲥⲣⲁⲛ ⲡⲉ ⲙⲁⲣⲙⲁⲣⲁⲙⲓ
ⲡⲛⲟϭ · ⲡⲙⲁ ⲙ̄ⲡⲉⲡ̅ⲛ̅ⲁ̅ · ⲛⲁⲇⲱⲛⲁⲓ
ⲉ̅ⲗⲟⲉⲓ · ⲡⲡⲁⲛⲇⲱⲕⲣⲁⲇⲱⲣ · ⲉⲕⲉ-
ⲟⲩⲱⲛⲁϩ ⲉⲣⲟⲓ ⲛ̄ⲅ̄ⲧⲉⲛⲟⲟⲩ ⲛⲁⲓ ⲛ̄ⲅⲁⲩ-
15 ⲣⲓⲏⲗ ⲡⲁⲅⲅⲉⲗⲟⲥ ⲛ̄ⲧⲇⲓⲕⲁⲓⲟⲥⲏⲛⲏ
ⲙⲡⲟⲟⲩ ⲛ̄ϥϫⲱⲱⲣ ⲉⲃⲟⲗ ϩⲁⲑⲏ ⲙ̄ⲙⲟⲓ ⲙ̄ⲡ̅ⲛ̅ⲁ̅
ⲛⲓⲙ ⲛ̄ⲧⲉ ⲯⲁⲧⲁⲛⲁⲥ · ⲛ̄ⲧⲁⲩⲧⲁ-
ⲙⲓⲟⲟⲩ ⲧⲏⲣⲟⲩ ⲙ̄ⲡⲉⲥⲛⲁⲩ ⲛⲟⲩϩⲟⲟⲩ ⲛ̄-
[ⲟ]ⲩⲱⲧ · ⲡϫⲟⲉⲓⲥ ⲡⲛⲟⲩⲧⲉ ⲡⲡⲁⲛⲇⲱⲕ-
20 [ⲣ]ⲁⲇⲱⲣ ⲟⲩⲱⲛⲁϩ ⲛⲁⲓ ⲉⲃⲟⲗ ⲛ̄ⲧⲉⲕⲧⲏ-
ⲛⲁⲙⲓⲥ ⲧⲉⲛⲟⲟⲩ ⲛⲁⲓ ⲛ̄ⲅⲁⲩⲣⲓⲏⲗ ⲡⲁⲅⲅⲉⲗⲟⲥ ⲛ̄ⲧⲇⲓⲕⲁⲓⲟⲥⲏ̣ⲛ̣ⲏ · ⲛ̄ⲃⲓ
[ϣⲁⲣⲟⲓ] ϩⲛ̄ ⲟⲩϭⲉⲡⲏ ϩⲁ[ⲙⲏⲛ] ⲅ̄ ·

---

1 ⲛ̄ⲧⲁ[ⲡⲉ ⲛ̄ⲃ]ⲁ̅ⲑ̅[ⲟ̅]ⲩⲣⲓⲏⲗ ⲡⲛⲟϭ ⲛⲓⲱⲧ Kropp *cf.* p. 20 ll. 6–7, p. 35 l. 16 : [ⲛ̄ϭⲟⲙ] . . ⲁ̅ . ⲩⲣⲓⲏⲗ ⲡ . . . Rossi || **2** *i.e.* ^{S}ϫⲉ ⲉ꞊ⲕ-ⲉ-ⲉⲓ̈ | *i.e.* ταχύ || **4** *i.e.* στερέωμα || **5** *i.e.* ^{S}ϫⲉ ⲉ꞊ⲕ-ⲉ-ⲉⲓ̈ || **6** *i.e.* βοηθεῖν || **8** *i.e.* ταχύ || **8–9** *i.e.* κατά || **10** *l.* ⲛ̄ϩⲏⲧ꞊ⲥ̅ ? || **12** *i.e.* πν(εῦμ)α || **13** *i.e.* παντοκράτωρ || **15** *i.e.* ἄγγελος | *i.e.* δικαιοσύνη || **16** ϩⲁⲑⲏ corrected from ϩⲓⲑⲏ by overwriting Kropp || *i.e.* πν(εῦμ)α || **17** *i.e.* Σατανᾶς || **19–20** *i.e.* παντοκράτωρ || **20–21** *i.e.* δύναμις || **21–22** *i.e.* ἄγγελος || **22** *i.e.* δικαιοσύνη : ⲇⲓⲕⲁⲓⲟⲥⲏ̣ⲛ̣ⲏ Kropp : ⲇⲓⲕⲁⲓⲟⲥ[ⲩⲛⲏ] Rossi | *i.e.* ^{S}ⲛ̄꞊ϥ-ⲉⲓ̈ || **23** *i.e.* ἀ[μήν]

by the head [of] Bathouriel, the great father, that you come to me and appear to me, quickly! I adjure you, *Gabriel, by the four corners of the fourteen firmaments, |⁵ that you come to me and you be with me, in this day and this hour, and you help me, in your power and your glory, quickly!

I adjure you Iōiriēl, by the cloud of light that is beside the Father, |¹⁰ in which he was hidden before he had created anything—that whose name is Marmarami, the great, the place of the spirit of *Adonai *Eloei Almighty—may you appear to me, and send me Gabriel, |¹⁵ the *angel of righteousness today, so that he will annihilate before me every spirit of Satan, all of which were created together in a single day!

O Lord God Almighty, |²⁰ reveal to me your power, send to me Gabriel, the angel of righteousness, so that he comes [to me] in haste, amen (three ‹times›),

---

18. ⲙ̄ⲡⲉⲥⲛⲁⲩ : "together" For this translation cf. Crum CD 347a.

tenth page (page 21)

ⲉⲧⲃ[ⲉ ⲧϭⲟ]ⲙ ⲙ̄ⲡⲉⲕⲣⲁⲛ ⲉⲧⲟⲩⲁⲁⲃ
ⲓ̄ⲁ̄ⲱ̄ · ⲥ̄[ⲁⲃ]ⲁ̄ⲱ̄ⲑ̄ · ⲁ̄ⲇ̄ⲱ̄ⲛ̄ⲁ̄ⲓ̄ · ⲉ̄ⲗ̄ⲟ̄ⲉ̄ⲓ̄
ⲡⲡⲁⲛⲇⲱⲕⲣⲁⲇⲱⲣ · ⲙ̄ⲡⲟⲟⲩ ⲉⲓⲱϣ
ⲉϩⲣⲁⲓ ⲉⲣⲟⲕ · ⲓ̄ⲁ̄ⲱ̄ ⲥ̄ⲁ̄ⲃ̄ⲁ̄ⲱ̄ⲑ̄ · ⲁ̄ⲇ̄ⲱ̄ⲛ̄ⲁ̄ⲓ̄
5 ⲉ̄ⲗ̄ⲟ̄ⲉ̄ⲓ̄ ⲡⲛⲟϭ ⲛⲟⲩⲧⲉ ⲙⲁⲅⲁⲁϥ ⲉⲧⲥⲁ-
ϩⲟⲩⲛ ⲙ̄ⲡⲥⲁϣϥ ⲛ̄ⲕⲁⲧⲁ፥ⲡⲉⲧⲁⲥⲙⲁ
ⲡⲉⲧϩⲙⲟⲟⲥ ϩⲓⲭⲙ̄ ⲡⲉϥⲑⲣⲟⲛⲟⲥ
ⲛ̄ⲛⲉⲟⲟⲩ ⲉⲧⲟⲩⲁⲁⲃ · ⲉⲕⲉⲧⲛ̄ⲛⲟⲩ
ⲛⲁⲓ ⲛ̄ⲅⲁⲩⲣⲓⲏⲗ ⲡⲁⲅⲅⲉⲗⲟⲥ ⲛ̄ⲧ-
10 ⲇⲓⲕⲁⲓⲟⲥⲏⲛⲏ · ⲉⲣⲉⲧⲉϥⲥⲛⲃⲏ
ⲃⲏϣ ⲛ̄ⲧⲟⲟⲧϥ · ⲉⲥϩⲛ̄ ⲧⲉϥϭⲓⲭ
ⲛⲟⲩⲛⲁⲙ ⲛ̄ⲃⲛⲟⲩⲭ ⲥⲁⲃⲟⲗ ⲙⲟ̄ⲓ ⲙ̄ⲡ-
ⲛ̄ⲁ̄ ⲛⲓⲙ ⲛ̄ⲁⲕⲁⲑⲁⲣⲧⲟⲛ · ⲛⲉⲩϣ ⲁ-
ⲁϩⲉⲣⲁⲧⲟⲩ ⲙ̄ⲡⲁⲙ̄ⲧⲟ ⲉⲃⲟⲗ · ⲁⲗ-
15 ⲗⲁ ⲙⲁⲣⲟⲩⲡⲱⲧ ϩⲓⲑⲏ ⲙ̄ⲡⲁϩⲟ ⲧⲏⲣⲟⲩ
ⲁⲡⲟⲗ₀/ · †ⲡⲁⲣⲁⲕⲁⲗⲓ ⲙ̄ⲙⲟⲕ ⲛ̄ⲛⲉⲕⲣⲁⲛ
ⲉⲧⲧⲁⲓⲏⲩ · ⲁ̄ⲇ̄ⲱ̄ⲛ̄ⲁ̄ⲓ̄ ⲉ̄ⲗ̄ⲟ̄ⲉ̄ⲓ̄ · ⲉⲗⲉⲙⲁ
ⲥ̄ⲁ̄ⲃ̄ⲁ̄ⲕ̄ⲧ̄ⲁ̄ⲛ̄ⲓ̄ · ⲡⲉϣⲁϥⲭⲱϣⲧ ⲉⲭⲛ̄
ⲛ̄ⲛⲉⲙⲡⲏⲩⲉ ⲛ̄ⲥⲉⲥⲧⲱⲧ · ϣⲁⲣⲉ-
20 ⲡⲕⲁϩ ⲡⲟⲟⲛⲉϥ · ⲥ̄ⲁ̄ⲃ̄ⲁ̄ · ⲥ̄ⲁ̄ⲃ̄ⲁ̄ⲃ̄ · ⲥ̄ⲁ̄ⲃ̄ⲁ̄-
ⲱ̄ⲑ̄ ⲓ̄ⲁ̄ⲱ̄ · ⲓ̄ⲁ̄ⲱ̄ⲑ̄ · ⲛⲁ - ⲫⲏⲣ ⲡⲁⲓ ⲡⲉ
ⲡⲉⲕⲣⲁⲛ ⲉⲑⲏⲡ · ⲡⲛⲟⲩⲧⲉ ⲉⲧϩ-
ⲙⲟⲟⲥ ϩⲛ̄ ⲛⲉⲧϫⲟⲥⲉ ⲉ̄ⲥ̄ⲁ̄ⲉ̄ⲥ̄
ⲁ̄ⲃ̄[ca. 7]ⲙ̄ⲟ̄ⲩ̄ ⲡⲙⲟⲩ ·

---

1 ⲉⲧⲃ[ⲉ ⲧϭⲟ]ⲙ Kropp : ⲉⲧⲃ . . . . . Rossi ‖ **3** *i.e.* παντοκράτωρ ‖ **5** *i.e.* ˢⲡ-ⲛⲟϭ ⲛ̄-ⲛⲟⲩⲧⲉ (haplography) ‖ **6** *i.e.* καταπέτασμα ‖ **7** *i.e.* θρόνος ‖ **8** *i.e.* ˢⲛ̄-ⲉⲟⲟⲩ (dittography) ‖ **9** *i.e.* ἄγγελος ‖ **10** *i.e.* δικαιοσύνη | *i.e.* ˢⲥⲛϥⲉ ‖ **12** *i.e.* ˢⲛ̄-ϥ-ⲛⲟⲩϫⲉ | *i.e.* ˢⲙ̄ⲙⲟ፥ⲓ ‖ **12–13** *i.e.* πν(εῦμ)α ‖ **13** *i.e.* ἀκάθαρτον ‖ **13–14** *i.e.* ˢⲛ̄ⲛⲉ፥ⲩ-ϣ-ⲁϩⲉⲣⲁⲧ፥ⲟⲩ ‖ **14–15** *i.e.* ἀλλά ‖ **16** *i.e.* ἀπολο(γία) : *l.* ⲁⲡⲟⲗ(ⲗⲱⲛ) Rossi : "Apolo" Amélineau *cf.* note to p. 9 l. 7 | *i.e.* παρακαλεῖν ‖ **18** *i.e.* ˢⲡ-ⲉⲧ-ϣⲁ፥ϥ-ϭⲱϣⲧ̄ ‖ **19** *i.e.* ˢⲛ̄-ⲙ̄-ⲡⲏⲩⲉ ‖ **20** ⲡⲟⲟⲛⲉϥ : "moves" Meyer 1988, 1994 ‖ **23** ⲛⲉⲧϫⲟⲥⲉ : "the heights" ("in den Höhen") Kropp, Meyer 1988, 1994 ‖ **24** .]ⲙ̄ⲟ̄ⲩ̄ Rossi : [. ⲡ]ⲙ̄ⲟ̄ⲩ̄ Kropp

because of [the] power of your holy name, *Iao *Sabaoth *Adonai *Eloei Almighty!

Today I call upon you, Iao Sabaoth Adonai |⁵ Eloei, the great, only god, who is within the seven *veils, you who sit upon your glorious, holy *throne; may you send to me *Gabriel, the *angel of |¹⁰ righteousness with his sword unsheathed in his right hand, so that he casts away from me every unclean spirit! May they be unable to stand in my presence, |¹⁵ but rather let them all flee before my face—request!

I invoke you by your honoured names, Adonai Eloei *Elema Sabaktani, you who look upon the heavens and they tremble |²⁰ ⟨and⟩ the earth is overturned; Saba Sabab Sabaoth Iao Iaōth Naphēr: this is your hidden name, O God who sits over the exalted ones, Esaes Ab… mou, Pmou,

---

17–18. ⲉⲗⲟⲉⲓ · ⲉⲗⲉⲙⲁ ⲥⲁⲃⲁⲕⲧⲁⲛⲓ : **"Eloei Elema Sabaktani"** *Cf.* words of Jesus on the cross found in Matthew 27.46 (ηλι ηλι λεμα σαβαχθανι) and Mark 15.34 (ελωι ελωι λεμα σαβαχθανι); *cf.* Kropp 1930: III p. 128 (§218).

eleventh page (page 23)

ⲟⲛⲟⲉⲣⲟⲥ · ⲧⲟⲩⲱⲣⲁ . . . . . [ⲁ]ⲕⲁⲑⲟ[ⲥ]
ϥⲡⲁⲕⲁⲗⲉ · ⲭⲉⲃⲟⲩⲑⲁⲛⲓⲉ ⲁ[ⲙ]ⲁⲙⲓⲏⲗ
ⲧⲁⲙⲁⲭ · ⲙⲁⲙⲓⲏⲗ · ⲙⲁⲣⲓⲏⲕ ⲧⲱⲁⲕ
ⲉⲧⲱⲁⲕ · ⲁϥⲣⲁⲕ · ⲓⲟⲁⲕ · ⲡⲉⲧϩⲙⲟⲟⲥ
5   ϩⲓϫⲛ ⲛⲉⲭⲉⲣⲟⲩⲃⲓⲛ ϯⲡⲁⲣⲁⲕⲁⲗⲓ
ⲙⲙⲟⲕ ⲛⲧⲁⲡⲉ ⲛⲃⲁⲑⲟⲩⲣⲓⲏⲗ ⲡⲛⲟϭ
ⲛⲓⲱⲧ ⲙⲛ ⲧⲉϥϭⲓϫ ⲛⲟⲩⲛⲁⲙ ⲧⲁⲓ
ⲉⲧⲁⲙⲁϩⲧⲉ ⲛⲧⲉⲕⲙⲛⲧⲛⲟⲩⲧⲉ
ⲧⲏⲣⲥ · ϩⲱⲥⲇⲉ ⲛⲅⲥⲱⲧⲙ ⲉⲣⲟⲓ ⲁⲛⲟⲕ
10 ⲇ ⲇ · ⲛⲅⲧⲉⲛⲟⲟⲩ ⲉⲃⲟⲗ ϩⲛ ⲧⲡⲉ ⲛⲁⲓ
ⲛⲁⲑⲱⲛⲁⲑⲁⲑⲱⲛⲁⲑ ⲉⲧⲉ ⲡⲉϥⲣⲁⲛ
ⲅⲁⲩⲣⲓⲏⲗ ⲡⲁⲅⲅⲉⲗⲟⲥ ⲛⲧⲓⲧⲓⲕⲁⲓ-
ⲟⲥⲩⲛⲏ ⲛϥⲓ ϣⲁⲣⲟⲓ ⲛϥⲓⲣⲉ ⲙⲡⲁϩⲱϥ
ⲉϯⲡⲁⲣⲁⲕⲁⲗⲓ ⲙⲙⲟⲕ ⲉⲧⲃⲏⲧϥ · ⲁⲡⲟⲗⲟ/
15 ϫⲱⲗⲕ ⲛⲧⲉⲕⲡⲓⲧⲉ ⲉϫⲙ ⲡⲁⲣⲭⲏⲡⲗⲁⲥⲙⲁ ⲙⲛ ⲛⲉϥⲧⲏⲛⲁⲙⲓⲥ ⲧⲏⲣⲟⲩ
ⲧⲱⲕⲙ ⲛⲧⲉⲕⲥⲛⲏⲃⲏ ⲉϫⲙ ⲡⲁⲣⲭⲏ-
ⲡⲗⲁⲥⲙⲁ ⲙⲛ ⲛⲉϥϭⲟⲙ ⲧⲏⲣⲟⲩ ·
ⲕⲁⲑⲁⲣⲓⲍⲉ ⲛⲁⲓ ⲙⲡⲉⲓⲧⲟⲡⲟⲥ ⲛⲥⲉ
20 ⲛⲧⲃⲁ ⲙⲙⲁϩⲉ · ⲕⲁⲑⲁⲣⲓⲍⲉ ⲛⲁⲓ
ⲙⲡⲛⲟⲩⲛ ⲛⲥⲉ ⲛⲧⲃⲁ ⲙⲙⲁϩⲉ
ⲕⲁⲑⲁⲣⲓⲍⲉ ⲛⲁⲓ ⲙⲡⲉⲓⲉⲃⲧ ⲛⲥⲉ
ⲛⲧⲃⲁ ⲙⲙⲁϩⲉ ⲕⲁⲑⲁⲣⲓⲍⲉ ⲛⲁⲓ
ⲙⲡⲉⲙϩ[ⲓ]ⲧ ⲛⲥⲉ ⲛⲧⲃⲁ [ⲙⲙⲁϩⲉ] ·

---

1 cf. ἀγαθός (?) ‖ **2** ϥⲡⲁⲕⲁⲗⲉ : "Efpakale" Meyer 1994 | ⲭⲉⲃⲟⲩⲑⲁⲛⲓⲉ Rossi : ⲭⲉⲃⲟⲩⲑⲁⲛⲓⲥ Kropp, Meyer | ⲁ[ⲙ]ⲁⲙⲓⲏⲗ Kropp : . . ⲁⲙⲓⲏⲗ Rossi ‖ **5** i.e. χερουβίμ | i.e. παρακαλεῖν ‖ **9** i.e. ὥστε ‖ **10** i.e. δ(ε)ῖ(να) δ(ε)ῖ(να) ‖ **11** "Athonas Athonas" Kropp : "Athonath Athonath" Meyer 1988, 1994 | i.e. ˢⲉⲧⲉ ⲡⲉ=ϥ-ⲣⲁⲛ ⲡⲉ ‖ **12** i.e. ἄγγελος ‖ **12–13** i.e. δικαιοσύνη ‖ **14** i.e. ˢⲉⲧ-ϯ-ⲡⲁⲣⲁⲕⲁⲗⲉ i.e. παρακαλεῖν | i.e. ἀπολο(γία) ‖ **15–16** i.e. ἀρχίπλασμα cf. note ‖ **16** i.e. δύναμις ‖ **17** i.e. ˢⲥⲛϥⲉ ‖ **17–18** i.e. ἀρχίπλασμα cf. note ‖ **19, 20, 22, 23** i.e. καθαρίζειν ‖ **19** i.e. τόπος

Onoeros, Touōra, Akathos, Fpakale, Khebouthanie, Amamiēl, Tamakh, Mamiēl, Mariēk, Tōak, Etōak, Afrak, Ioak, the one who sits |⁵ upon the *cherubim!

I invoke you by the head of Bathouriēl, the great father, and his right hand, that which possesses all your divinity, that you listen to me, me, |¹⁰ NN, and that you send forth from heaven to me Athōnathathōnath, whose name ⟨is⟩ *Gabriel, the *angel of righteousness, so that he comes to me and does my work concerning that which I am invoking you—request!

|¹⁵ Draw your bow against the First-Formed One and all his powers! Draw your sword against the First-Formed One and all his powers! Purify for me this place for six |²⁰ hundred thousand cubits! Purify for me the *abyss for six hundred thousand cubits! Purify for me the east for six hundred thousand cubits! Purify for me the north for six hundred thousand cubits!

15–16, 17–18. ⲡⲁⲣⲭⲏⲡⲗⲁⲥⲙⲁ : "the First-Formed One" *cf.* the note to p. 15 l. 17.

twelfth page (page 25)

ⲕⲁⲑⲁⲣⲓⲍⲉ ⲛⲁⲓ ⲙⲡⲣ[ⲏ]ⲥ̣ ⲛ̄[ⲥⲉ ⲛ̄ⲧ]ⲃⲁ ⲙⲁϩⲉ · ⲕⲁⲑⲁⲣⲓⲍⲉ ⲛⲁⲓ ⲙ̄ⲡⲉⲙ[ⲛ̄]ⲧ ⲛ̄ⲥⲉ
ⲛ̄ⲧⲃⲁ ⲙⲙⲁϩⲉ · ⲕⲁⲑⲁⲣⲓⲍⲉ ⲛⲁⲓ ⲙ̄ⲡⲁ-
ⲏⲣ ⲛ̄ⲥⲉ ⲛ̄ⲧⲃⲁ ⲙⲙⲁϩⲉ ϫⲉ ⲛⲉϥⲉⲓ ⲉ-
5   ⲣⲟⲓ · ⲁⲡⲟⲗⲟ/ ⲁⲓⲟ ⲁⲓⲟ ϫⲉ †ⲡⲁⲣⲁⲕⲁ-
ⲗⲓ ⲙⲙⲟⲕ ⲅⲁⲩⲣⲓⲏⲗ ⲛ̄ⲧⲁⲡⲉ ⲛ̄ⲃⲁ-
ⲑⲟⲩⲣⲓⲏⲗ ⲡⲛⲟϭ ⲛⲓⲱⲧ ⲛ̄ⲕⲁϣⲱⲡⲉ
ⲛⲁⲓ ⲙ̄ⲡⲣⲟⲥⲧⲁⲧⲏⲥ · ⲛⲉⲕⲟⲛⲟⲙⲟⲥ
ⲛ̄ⲃⲟⲏⲑⲟⲥ · ϩⲛ̄ ϩⲱⲃ ⲛⲓⲙ · †ⲥⲟⲡ̄ⲥ̄
10   †ⲡⲁⲣⲁⲕⲁⲗⲓ ⲙⲙⲟⲕ ⲁⲛⲟⲕ ⲡⲉ
ⲡⲉⲡⲣⲟⲥⲟⲡⲟⲛ ⲛⲓⲁⲱ ⲥⲁⲃⲁⲱⲑ
ⲁⲇⲱⲛⲁⲓ ⲡⲡⲁⲛⲧⲱⲕⲣⲁⲇⲱⲣ
ⲛ̄ⲅⲥⲱⲧⲙ̄ ⲉⲣⲟⲓ ⲛ̄ⲅⲓ ϣⲁⲣⲟⲓ ⲙⲡⲟⲟⲩ ⲉⲧⲃⲉ ⲧⲉⲥⲫⲣⲁⲕⲓⲥ ⲙ̄ⲡⲓⲱⲧ
15   ⲉⲧϩⲙ̄ ⲡⲉⲓⲫⲏⲗⲁⲕⲧⲏⲣⲓⲟⲛ ϩⲛ̄ ⲧⲁϭⲓϫ ⲛⲟⲩⲛⲁⲙ ⲡϫⲟⲩⲧⲁϥⲧⲉ ⲛ̄ⲥ-
ϩⲁⲓ ⲉⲧϩⲙ̄ ⲡⲉⲓⲫⲏⲗⲁⲕⲧⲏⲣⲓⲟⲛ
ⲙ̄ⲡⲓⲱⲧ · ϩⲱⲥ ⲛ̄ⲅⲥⲱⲧⲙ̄ ⲉⲣⲟⲓ
ϩⲛ̄ ⲟⲩϭⲉⲡⲏ · †ⲡⲁⲣⲁⲕⲁⲗⲓ ⲙⲙⲟ[ⲕ]
20   ⲅⲁⲩⲣⲓⲏⲗ · ⲙ̄ⲡⲛⲟϭ ⲛ̄ⲣⲁⲛ ⲙ̄ⲡⲓⲱⲧ
ⲙⲛ̄ ⲡⲉϥⲉⲟⲟⲩ ⲉⲧⲟⲩⲁⲁⲃ ⲙⲛ̄ ⲛⲉⲧ-
ⲁϩⲉⲉⲣⲁⲧⲟⲩ ⲙ̄ⲡⲉϥⲉⲙⲧⲟ ⲉⲃⲟⲗ
ⲁ̄[ⲑ̄]ⲱ̄[ⲛ̄]ⲁ̄ⲥ̄ · ⲥ̄ⲓ̄ⲁ̄ⲕ̄ · ⲕ̄ⲥ̄ⲁ̄ⲥ̄ · ⲥ̄ⲁ̄ⲃ̄ⲁ̄ⲕ̄
ⲕ̄ⲁ̄ⲁ̄ⲃ̄ · ⲕ̄ⲁ̄ⲛ̄ⲥ̄ⲁ̄ⲥ̄ · ⲉ̄ⲕ̄ⲱ̄ⲉ̄ · . . . †ⲡⲁ-

---

1 *i.e.* καθαρίζειν ‖ **1–2** *i.e.* ˢⲙ̄-ⲙⲁϩⲉ ‖ **2, 3** *i.e.* καθαρίζειν ‖ **3–4** *i.e.* ἀήρ ‖ **5** *i.e.* ἀπολο(γία) : *l.* ἀπολ(λων) Rossi : "Apolo" Amélineau *cf.* note to p. 9 l. 7 ‖ **5–6** *i.e.* παρακαλεῖν ‖ **4** *i.e.* ˢⲛ̄ⲛⲉϥⲩ-ⲉⲓ ‖ **8** *i.e.* προστάτης | *i.e.* οἰκονόμος ‖ **9** *i.e.* βοηθός ‖ **10** *i.e.* παρακαλεῖν ‖ **11** *i.e.* πρόσωπον ‖ **12** *i.e.* παντοκράτωρ ‖ **14** *i.e.* σφραγίς ‖ **15** *i.e.* φυλακτήριον ‖ **16** ⲡϫⲟⲩⲧⲁϥⲧⲉ Rossi : ⲡⲓϫⲟⲩⲧⲁϥⲧⲉ Kropp ‖ **17** *i.e.* φυλακτήριον ‖ **18** *i.e.* ὡς ‖ **19** *i.e.* παρακαλεῖν ‖ **21–22** *i.e.* ˢⲛ̄-ⲛⲉⲧⲁϩⲉ ⲉⲣⲁⲧ=ⲟⲩ

Purify for me the south for six hundred thousand cubits! Purify for me the west for six hundred thousand cubits! Purify for me the air for six hundred thousand cubits, so that they will not come to |⁵ me—request—yea, yea, for I entreat you *Gabriel, by the head of Bathouriēl, the great father, that you become for me a benefactor, a steward, a helper in every matter! I entreat you, |¹⁰ I invoke you—I am the countenance of *Iao *Sabaoth *Adonai Almighty—that you listen to me and come to me today because of the seal of the Father |¹⁵ which is on this phylactery in my right hand, the twenty-four letters which are on the phylactery of the Father, so that you listen to me, quickly!

I invoke you, |²⁰ Gabriel, by the great name of the Father and his holy glory and those who stand before him, Athōnas, Siak, Ksas, Sabak, Kaab, Kaēsas, Ekōe ... I

thirteenth page (page 27)

ρακαλι μμοκ γαυριηλ [ντ]απε
μμιχαηλ · ραφαηλ · ανληλ ϲαριηλ
γαυριηλ · αυριηλ · φαριηλ · ϲαϲαηλ
νεχιηλ · αδονιηλ · θριηλ · αθιηλ
5 ακουταηλ ναι εταϩερατου μπκω-
τε μπιωτ νατναυ εροϥ μν τεϥ-
καθετρα · ϫεκεει ϣαροι νκροιϲ
εροι νεϩοου τηρου μπαωναϩ
απολ₀/ · †παρακαλι νκαυριηλ
10 μπεϥϲαϣϥ ναρχηαγγελοϲ
τοφου · μν ραφαηλ · μν βαριηλ
αρθαμιηλ · αρωφτηβηλ · λαναχ
εφνιξ ναι εταϩεερατ μπμ-
το εβολ μπιωτ ευϲωτμ ενετ-
15 ννηυ εβολ ϩν ρωϥ · ται τε ταϩε
ϩω ϩωτμ ενετννηυ εβολ ϩν
ρωι · ϩαμην ζ αιο αιο ϫε †-
παρακαλι μμοκ γαυριηλ
πακαθοϲ μπεοου μπνοϭ
20 νθρο[νοϲ] μπιωθ ϫε ουϣα[ϩ]
νκω[ϩ]τ ενεϥτροχοϲ

---

1 *i.e.* παρακαλεῖν | [ντ]απε Kropp or *l.* [νν]απε ? CMPT : [ντ]απ[ε] Rossi ‖ **2** ανληλ *l.* αναηλ ? Kropp : αν[η]λ Rossi ‖ **7** *i.e.* καθέδρα | *i.e.* ˢεϥκ-ε-εϊ | *i.e.* ˢροειϲ ‖ **8** *i.e.* ˢν-ν-ϩοου ‖ **9** *i.e.* ἀπολο(γία) | *i.e.* παρακαλεῖν ‖ **10** *i.e.* ἀρχάγγελος ‖ **16** *i.e.* ˢϲωτμ ‖ **17** *i.e.* ἀμήν ‖ **18** *i.e.* παρακαλεῖν ‖ **19** *i.e.* ἀγαθός ‖ **20** *i.e.* θρό[νος] | *i.e.* ˢειωτ | ουϣα[ϩ] Kropp : ουϣα Rossi ‖ **21** *l.* ν-κωϩτ πε εϥϥ-τ[? : νκω .... νεϥτ Rossi : νκω[ϩ]τ ⟨ⲛ⟩ⲉ νεϥτ[ροχοϲ] Kropp, Meyer 1988, 1994

invoke you, *Gabriel, [by the] head of *Michael, *Raphael, Anlēl, Sariēl, Gabriel, Auriēl, Phariēl, Sasaēl, Nekhiēl, Adoniēl, Thriēl, Athiēl, |⁵ Akoutaēl, they who stand around the invisible Father and his seat, that you come to me and protect me for all the days of my life—request!

I invoke you Gabriel, |¹⁰ by his seven *archangels, Tophou and Raphael and Bariēl, Arthamiēl, Arōphtēbēl, Lanax, Ephnix, they who stand before the Father, listening to the ⟨words⟩ that |¹⁵ come out of his mouth; this is my manner, too—listen to the ⟨words⟩ that come out from my mouth!

Amen (seven ⟨times⟩), yea, yea, for I invoke you, Gabriel, the good one, by the glory of the great |²⁰ *throne of the Father—⟨it is⟩ a flaming fire whose wheels

---

p. 27 l. 20–p. 29 l. 3. The Throne of God and the River of Fire: A reference to the vision of God as the Ancient of Days in Daniel 7.9–10: "his throne was a flaming fire, its wheels were flaming fires which burned, there was a river of fire which flowed from his presence" (ⲡⲉϥⲑⲣⲟⲛⲟⲥ ⲛⲉⲟⲩⲱϩ ⲛ̄ⲕⲱϩⲧ ⲡⲉ · ⲉⲣⲉⲛⲉϥⲧⲣⲟⲭⲟⲥ ⲟ ⲛ̄ⲕⲱϩⲧ ⲉⲧⲙⲟⲩϩ ⲁⲩⲱ ⲛⲉⲣⲉⲟⲩⲉⲓⲉⲣⲟ ⲛ̄ⲕⲱϩⲧ ⲉⲧⲥⲱⲕ ⲙ̄ⲡⲉϥⲙ̄ⲧⲟ ⲉ̄ⲃⲟⲗ; Ciasca 1889: 317). In Coptic apocryphal texts the river of fire surrounding the judgement throne of God had to be crossed by the human dead before they were judged, and would burn sinners but not the just; see Zandee 1960: 307–309.

fourteenth page (page 29)

ϩⲛⲱϣ ⲛⲕⲱϩⲧ ⲛⲉ ⲉⲩⲙⲟⲩϩ ϩⲛ̄-
ⲡⲟⲧⲁⲙⲟⲥ ⲛ̄ⲕⲱϩⲧ ⲛⲉ ⲉⲩⲕⲱⲧⲉ
ⲉⲣⲟϥ ⲉⲩⲥⲱⲕ ϩⲁ ⲧⲉϥϩⲏ ϫⲉⲕⲉⲉⲓ
ϣⲁⲣⲟⲓ ⲧⲁⲭⲏ ⲁⲓⲟ ⲅⲁⲩ̄ⲣⲓⲏⲗ̄ ϫⲉ †ⲡⲁ-
5 ⲣⲁⲕⲁⲗⲓ ⲙⲙⲟⲕ ⲙ̄ⲡⲉϥⲧⲟⲟⲩ ⲛ̄-
ⲥⲱⲛⲧ ⲉⲧⲥⲱⲕ ϩⲁⲣⲟϥ · ⲟⲩϩⲟ ⲙⲟⲩ̄ⲓ̄
ⲟⲩϩⲟ ⲙ̄ⲙⲁⲥⲉ · ⲟⲩϩⲟ ⲛ̄ⲁⲉⲧⲟⲥ · ⲟⲩϩⲟ ⲛ̄-
ⲣⲱⲙⲉ · ϫⲉ ⲕⲉⲉⲓ ϣⲁⲣⲟⲓ ⲙ̄ⲡⲟⲟⲩ · ⲁⲡⲟⲗₒ/
†ⲡⲁⲣⲁⲕⲁⲗⲓ ⲙⲙⲟⲕ ⲙ̄ⲡⲟⲟⲩ ⲅⲁⲩ̄ⲣⲓⲏⲗ̄
10 ⲛ̄ⲉⲓⲫⲏⲗⲁⲕⲧⲏⲣⲓⲟⲛ ⲉⲧϩⲁ ⲛ̄ⲉⲩⲉⲣⲏⲧⲉ
ⲙ̄ⲡⲓⲱⲧ ⲛⲁⲓ ⲉⲣⲉϩⲛ̄ⲁϣⲟ ⲛ̄ⲁϣⲟ ⲛ̄ⲧⲉ ⲧⲡⲉ
ⲙⲛ ⲡⲕⲁϩ ⲥⲧⲱⲧ ϩⲁ ⲧⲉϥϩⲏ · ϫⲉⲕⲉⲉⲓ ϣⲁⲣⲟⲓ ⲁⲡⲟⲗₒ/ · †ⲡⲁⲣⲁⲕⲁⲗⲓ
ⲙⲙⲟⲕ ⲕⲁⲩ̄ⲣⲓⲏⲗ̄ ⲙ̄ⲡⲓⲛⲟϭ ⲥⲛⲁⲩ ⲛ̄ⲥⲉⲣⲁ-
15 ⲫⲓⲛ · ⲉⲣⲉⲥⲟⲟⲩ ⲛ̄ⲧⲛⲁϩ ϩⲓ ⲡⲟⲩⲁ ⲡⲟⲩⲁ
ⲙ̄ⲙⲟⲩ · ⲥⲛⲁⲩ ⲉⲩϩⲱⲃⲥ ⲙ̄ⲡⲉⲩϩⲟ
ⲥⲛⲁⲩ ⲉⲩϩⲱⲃⲥ ⲛ̄ⲉⲩⲉⲣⲏⲧⲉ · ⲉⲩϩⲏⲗ
ⲉⲃⲟⲗ ϩⲛ̄ ⲥⲛⲁⲩ ⲟⲩⲁ ⲛⲥⲁ ⲟⲩⲁ ⲙ̄ⲙⲟⲟⲩ
ⲉⲩⲱϣⲉ ⲉⲃⲟⲗ ⲉⲩⲭⲱ ⲙⲙⲟⲥ ϫⲉ
20 ϩⲁⲅⲓⲟⲥ ϩⲁⲅⲓⲟⲥ ϩⲁⲅⲓⲟⲥ ⲕⲩ̄[ⲣⲓⲟⲥ]
ⲥⲁⲃⲁⲱ[ⲑ] [ⲡ]ⲗⲏⲣⲟⲥ ⲟⲩⲣⲁⲛ̄ⲟⲥ [ⲕⲁⲓ ⲏ]
ⲕⲏ [ⲧⲏⲥ ϩⲁⲅⲓ]ⲁⲥ ⲉⲩ ⲧⲁ[ϩⲏⲥ . . . . .]
. . . ⲧⲡⲉ ⲙⲏ ⲡⲕⲁ[ϩ ⲙⲉϩ ⲉⲃⲟⲗ]

---

1 *i.e.* ˢϩⲉⲛ-ⲱⲁϩ | ⲛⲕⲱϩⲧ Kropp : ⲛⲕ . . ⲧ Rossi | ⲉⲩⲙⲟⲩϩ ϩⲛ̄ Kropp : ⲉⲩⲙⲟⲩ . . ϩⲛ̄ Rossi | *i.e.* ˢϩⲉⲛ- ‖ **2** *i.e.* ποταμός ‖ **3** ⲉⲩⲥⲱⲕ Kropp : ⲉⲩ[ⲥ]ⲱⲕ Rossi | *i.e.* ˢⲉ=ⲕ-ⲉ-ⲉⲓ̈ ‖ **3–5** ⲕⲉⲉⲓ ϣⲁⲣⲟⲓ ⲅⲁⲗ . . ⲁⲓⲟ ⲅⲁⲩ̄ⲣⲓⲏⲗ̄ [ϫⲉ †]ⲡⲁⲣⲁⲕⲁⲗⲓ Rossi : ⲕⲉⲉⲓ ϣⲁⲣⲟⲓ ⲧⲁⲭⲏ ⲁⲓⲟ ⲅⲁⲩ̄ⲣⲓⲏⲗ̄ ϫⲉ †ⲡⲁⲣⲁⲕⲁⲗⲓ Kropp ‖ **4** *i.e.* ταχύ : ⲅⲁⲗ Rossi ‖ **4–5** *i.e.* παρακαλεῖν ‖ **6** ⲉⲧⲥⲱⲕ ϩⲁⲣⲟϥ : "that draw it" Meyer 1988, 1994 | *i.e.* ˢⲙ̄-ⲙⲟⲩⲓ̈ (haplography) ‖ **7** *i.e.* ἀετός ‖ **8** *i.e.* ˢⲉ=ⲕ-ⲉ-ⲉⲓ̈ | *i.e.* ἀπολο(γία) : *l.* ἀπολ(λων) Rossi : "Apolo" Amélineau *cf.* note to p. 9 l. 7 ‖ **9** *i.e.* παρακαλεῖν ‖ **10** *l.* ⲛ̄-ⲛⲉⲓ̈-ⲫⲏⲗⲁⲕⲧⲏⲣⲓⲟⲛ *i.e.* φυλακτήριον ‖ **11** ⲙ̄ⲡⲓⲱⲧ Kropp : ⲙ̄ⲡⲕⲟⲧ Rossi : "wheel (?)" ("roue (?)") Amélineau | *i.e.* ˢϩⲉⲛ- ‖ **12** ⲥⲧⲱⲧ Kropp : . . ⲙⲧ Rossi ‖ **13** *i.e.* ˢⲉ=ⲕ-ⲉ-ⲉⲓ̈ | *i.e.* ἀπολο(γία) | *i.e.* παρακαλεῖν ‖ **14–15** *i.e.* σεραφίμ ‖ **17** *i.e.* ˢⲛ̄-ⲛⲉ=ⲩ-(ⲟⲩ)ⲉⲣⲏⲧⲉ ‖ **19** *i.e.* ˢⲉ=ⲩ-ⲱϣ ⲉⲃⲟⲗ ‖ **20–22** *i.e.* ἅγιος ἅγιος ἅγιος κύριος Σαβαώθ πλήρης ὁ οὐρανὸς καὶ ἡ γῆ τῆς ἁγίας σου δό[ξης, ἀληθῶς ?] *cf. PCM* I 9 p. 6 l. 9 & BM EA 54036 l. 1 (Quecke 1971) : ϩⲁⲅⲓⲟⲥ ϩⲁⲅⲓⲟⲥ ϩⲁⲅⲓⲟⲥ ⲕⲩ̄[ⲣⲓⲟⲥ] ⲥⲁⲃⲁⲱ[ⲑ] [ⲡ]ⲗⲏⲣⲟⲥ ⲟⲩⲣⲁⲛ̄ⲟⲥ [ⲕⲁⲓ ⲏ] ⲕⲏ [ⲧⲏⲥ ϩⲁⲅⲓ]ⲁⲥ ⲉⲩⲧⲁ[ⲃ] Kropp : *l.* ... [ϩⲁⲅⲓ]ⲁⲥ ⲇⲟϫⲏⲥ ⲥⲟⲩ ? Kropp, Meyer 1988, 1994 : ⲥⲁⲃⲁⲱ[ⲑ . . ⲗⲏⲣⲟⲥ] ⲟⲩⲣⲁⲛ̄ⲟⲥ . . ⲕⲏ *ca.* 7 ⲉⲩⲧⲁ *ca.* 5 Rossi ‖ **23** ⲧⲡⲉ ⲙⲏ ⲡⲕⲁ[ϩ ⲙⲉϩ ⲉⲃⲟⲗ] CMPT : *ca.* 10 ⲡⲕⲁ[ϩ *ca.* 5] Kropp : *ca.* 13 Rossi

are flaming fires which burn, it is rivers of fire which surround it, flowing beneath it—that you come to me, quickly, yea, *Gabriel, for I |⁵ invoke you by the *Four Creatures which fly beneath him—one lion-faced, one calf-faced, one eagle-faced, one human-faced—that you come to me today—request—!

I invoke you today, Gabriel, |¹⁰ ⟨by⟩ these *phylacteries that are under the feet of the Father, those before which thousands of thousands of the heaven and ⟨of⟩ the earth tremble, that you come to me—request!

I invoke you, Gabriel, by the two great |¹⁵ *seraphim, each one of them having six wings, two covering their face, two covering their feet, flying with two, one after the other, crying out, saying: |²⁰, Greek "*Holy, holy, holy, Lord *Sabaoth, the heaven and the earth are full [of] your [holy glory, truly] |Coptic the heaven and the earth [are full]

fifteenth page (page 31)

ϩⲙ ⲡⲉⲕⲉⲟⲟⲩ ⲉⲧⲟⲩⲁⲁⲃ · ϫⲉ ⲕ[ⲉ]ⲉⲓ ϣⲁⲣⲟⲓ
ⲁⲡⲟⲗₒ/ ϯⲡⲁⲣⲁⲕⲁⲗⲓ ⲙⲙⲟⲕ ⲅⲁⲩⲣⲓⲏⲗ
ⲛ̄ⲙ ⲡⲣⲁⲛ̄ ⲛ̄ⲟⲣⲫⲁ · ⲡⲥⲱⲙⲁ ⲧⲏⲣϥ̄ ⲙ̄ⲡⲓⲱⲧ
ⲙⲛ̄ ⲟⲣⲫⲁⲙⲓⲏⲗ ⲡⲛⲟϭ ⲛ̄ⲧⲏⲏⲃⲉ ⲉⲧϩⲛ̄
5   ⲧϭⲓϫ ⲛ̄ⲟⲩⲛⲁⲙ ⲙ̄ⲡⲓⲱⲧ ⲙⲛ̄ ⲧⲁⲡⲉ ⲙⲡⲉ-
ⲭ̄ⲥ̄ ϫⲉⲕⲉⲉⲓ ϣⲁⲣⲟⲓ ⲙ̄ⲡⲟⲟⲩ ⲁⲡⲟⲗₒ/
ϯⲡⲁⲣⲁⲕⲁⲗⲓ ⲙⲙⲟⲕ ⲅⲁⲩⲣⲓⲏⲗ ⲛ̄ⲧ-
ⲇⲏⲛⲁⲙⲓⲥ ⲙⲙⲁⲛⲟⲩⲏⲗ ⲥⲁⲃⲁⲱⲑ
ϯⲡⲁⲣⲁⲕⲁⲗⲓ ⲙ̄ⲙⲟⲕ ⲅⲁⲩⲣⲓⲏⲗ ⲛ̄ⲧϭⲓϫ
10 ⲛⲟⲩⲛⲁⲙ ⲡⲓⲱⲧ ⲙⲛ̄ ⲧⲉⲥⲫⲣⲁⲕⲓⲥ
ⲉⲧϩⲛ̄ ⲕⲟⲩⲛϥ ⲙ̄ⲡⲓⲱⲧ ⲙⲛ̄ ⲛ̄ⲉⲓ-
ⲫⲏⲗⲁⲕⲧⲏⲣⲓⲟⲛ ⲉⲧⲥⲏϩ ⲉⲧⲙⲏⲥⲧⲛ̄-
ϩⲏⲧ ⲙ̄ⲡⲓⲱⲧ · ϫⲉⲕⲉⲉⲓ ϣⲁⲣⲟⲓ
ⲙ̄ⲡⲟⲟⲩ ϩⲛ̄ ⲟⲩϭⲉⲡⲏ · ⲁⲡⲟⲗₒ/ ϯⲡⲁ-
15 ⲣⲁⲕⲁⲗⲓ ⲙⲙⲟⲕ ⲅⲁⲩⲣⲓⲏⲗ ⲛ̄ⲧϣⲟⲣ-
ⲡⲉ ⲙ̄ⲫⲱⲛⲏ ⲛ̄ⲧⲁⲥⲉⲓ ⲉⲃⲟⲗ ϩⲛ̄ ⲣⲱϥ
ⲙ̄ⲡⲓⲱⲧ · ⲙⲛ̄ ⲡⲛ̄ⲓⲃⲉ ⲛ̄ⲧⲁϥⲉⲓ ⲉⲃⲟ[ⲗ]
ϩⲛ̄ ⲛⲉϥϫⲉϥϣⲁ ⲙⲙⲛ̄ ⲧⲉϥⲙⲛ̄ⲧ-
ⲁⲕⲁⲕⲁⲑⲟⲥ ⲙⲛ̄ ⲡⲉⲟⲟⲩ ⲉⲧⲕⲱⲧⲉ
20 ⲉⲣⲟϥ ϫⲉⲕⲉⲉⲓ ϣⲁⲣⲟⲓ ⲙ̄ⲡⲟⲟⲩ ⲁ[ⲡⲟⲗₒ/]
ϯⲡⲁⲣⲁⲕⲁⲗⲓ ⲙⲙⲟⲕ ⲅⲁⲩⲣⲓ[ⲏⲗ]
ⲙ̄ⲡⲛⲟ[ϭ ⲛ̄ⲥ]ⲧⲏⲗⲗⲟⲥ ⲛ̄ⲟⲩ[ⲟⲉⲓⲛ]
ⲡⲁⲓ . . . . ⲏⲥⲓⲥ . . .

---

1 ϫⲉ ⲕ[ⲉ]ⲉⲓ Kropp *i.e.* ᔅϫⲉ ⲉ⸗ⲕ-ⲉ-ⲉⲓ̈ (haplography) : ϫⲉⲉ[ⲕⲉ]ⲉⲓ Rossi ‖ **2** *i.e.* ἀπολο(γία) : *l.* ⲁⲡⲟⲗ(ⲱⲛ) Rossi : "Apolo" Amélineau *cf.* note p. 9 l. 7 | *i.e.* παρακαλεῖν ‖ **3** *i.e.* σῶμα ‖ **6** *i.e.* χ(ριστό)ς | *i.e.* ᔅϫⲉ ⲉ⸗ⲕ-ⲉ-ⲉⲓ̈ (haplography) | *i.e.* ἀπολο(γία) : *l.* ⲁⲡⲟⲗ(ⲱⲛ) Rossi : "Apolo" Amélineau *cf.* note to p. 9 l. 7 ‖ **7** *i.e.* παρακαλεῖν ‖ **8** *i.e.* δύναμις ‖ **9** *i.e.* παρακαλεῖν ‖ **10** *l.* ⲛ̄-ⲟⲩⲛⲁⲙ ⲙ̄-ⲡ-ⲓⲱⲧ (haplography) | *i.e.* σφραγίς ‖ **12** *i.e.* φυλακτήριον ‖ **12–13** *i.e.* ᔅⲙⲉⲥⲑⲛ̄ⲧ, *cf.* ⲙⲉⲥⲧⲛ̄ϩⲏⲧ ‖ **13** *i.e.* ᔅϫⲉ ⲉ⸗ⲕ-ⲉ-ⲉⲓ̈ (haplography) ‖ **14** *i.e.* ἀπολο(γία) : *l.* ⲁⲡⲟⲗ(ⲱⲛ) Rossi : "Apolo" Amélineau *cf.* note to p. 9 l. 7 ‖ **16** *i.e.* φωνή ‖ **17** ⲉⲃⲟ[ⲗ] Kropp : [ⲉⲃⲟⲗ] Rossi ‖ **18** *l.* ⲙⲛ̄ (dittography) | ⲧⲉϥⲙⲛ̄ⲧ- Kropp : ⲧⲉϥⲙ . . Rossi ‖ **18–19** ⲧⲉϥⲙⲛ̄ⲧⲁⲕⲁⲕⲁⲑⲟⲥ : "the goodness" Meyer ‖ **19** *i.e.* ᔅⲁⲅⲁⲑⲟⲥ *i.e.* ἀγαθός ‖ **20** *i.e.* ᔅϫⲉ ⲉ⸗ⲕ-ⲉ-ⲉⲓ̈ (haplography) | ⲙ̄ⲡⲟⲟⲩ Kropp : ⲙ̄ⲡⲟ[ⲟⲩ] Rossi | *i.e.* ἀπολο(γία) ‖ **21** *i.e.* παρακαλεῖν ‖ **22** *i.e.* [σ]τύλος | ⲙ̄ⲡⲛⲟ[ϭ ⲛ̄ⲥ]ⲧⲏⲗⲗⲟⲥ ⲛ̄ⲟⲩ[ⲟⲉⲓⲛ] : ⲙ̄ⲡ . . . . ⲧⲏⲗⲗⲟⲥ ⲛ̄ⲟⲩ . . . Rossi ‖ **23** *l.* ⲉⲧϥⲓ ϩⲁ ⲧⲕⲧⲏⲥⲓⲥ ⲧⲏⲣϥ *i.e.* κτίσις CMPT : Rossi dots entire line

of your holy glory!", that you come to me—request!

I invoke you, *Gabriel, in the name of Orpha, the whole body of the Father, and Orphamiēl, the great finger which is on |⁵ the right hand of the Father and the head of Christ, that you come to me today—request!

I invoke you, Gabriel, by the power of Manouēl *Sabaoth! I invoke you, Gabriel, by the right hand |¹⁰ ⟨of⟩ the Father and the seal which is on the bosom of the Father and these *phylacteries which are written on the chest of the Father, that you come to me today, quickly—request!

I |¹⁵ invoke you, Gabriel, by the first sound which came forth from the mouth of the Father, and the breath which came forth from his nostrils, and his goodness and the glory which surrounds |²⁰ him, that you come today—request!

I invoke you, Gabriel by the great pillar of light, that [supports all] creation?

3–6. The body of God: Descriptions of the body of God the Father are recurrent in the 'magical liturgies'; compare *PCM* I 25 p. 14 ll. 11–24, *PCM* I 26 p. 7 l. 12–p. 8 l. 17. These descriptions are reminiscent of the Jewish *Shiʿur Qomah* ("Measure of the Body") literature, which seems to have existed by the sixth century CE. In these texts the body of God is described in detail in terms of its enormous size, the names of the different body parts, and the ministering angels assigned to each of them. A systematic comparison between the *Shiʿur Qomah* and the descriptions in Coptic magical texts remains a desideratum. On the body of God in Coptic literature, *cf.* Fauth 2014: 72; Dosoo 2021d: 418, Preininger forthcoming c: chapter 7, and on the *Shiʿur Qomah*, see Fossum 1983; Cohen 1983 & 1985; Bohak 2008: 328–329; Gruenwald 2014: 245–248.

4–5. ⲟⲣⲫⲁⲙⲓⲏⲗ ⲡⲛⲟϭ ⲛⲧⲏⲏⲃⲉ ⲉⲧϩⲛ ⲧϭⲓⲝ ⲛⲟⲩⲛⲁⲙ : "Orphamiēl, the great finger which is on the right hand" Orphamiel, the "finger of the Father", is mentioned several times in the Coptic magical corpus; the reference is likely to the "finger of God" (δάκτυλος Θεοῦ) by which Jesus claims to cast out demons in Luke 11.20, drawing upon the language of Exodus 8.15 (8.19). For other mentions of Orphamiel, see *PCM* I 25 p. 14 ll. 11–13, p. 15 ll. 18–19; *PCM* I 26 p. 8 ll. 11–12; 'Nahman' Amulet (Drescher 1950; KYP M 529) ll. 14–15; BL Ms Or 6796 (Kropp 1931: I no. J; KYP M308) ll. 41–42; Fribourg AeT 2006.5 (Müller 2009; KYP M398) front col. 2 ll. 18–21; Moen Inv. no 34/607 (Clarysse 1986; KYP M4), and *cf.* Dosoo 2021d: 418.

11–13. ⲛⲉⲓⲫⲏⲗⲁⲕⲧⲏⲣⲓⲟⲛ ⲉⲧⲥⲏϩ ⲉⲧⲙⲏⲥⲧⲛϩⲏⲧ ⲙⲡⲓⲱⲧ : "phylacteries which are written on the chest of the Father" This likely refers to a breastplate worn by God the Father, upon which a vowel sequence is written. The breastplate is comparable to that of the Jewish high priest Aaron described from Exodus 28:15–21. This is made most explicit in BL Ms. Or. 6794 (Kropp 1931: I no. E; KYP M 306), in which seven rows of seven letters decorate the chest of God; in the Exodus, the breastplate is described as having four rows of stones. See Preininger forthcoming c: chapter 7.

13. ⲙⲙⲁⲛⲟⲩⲏⲗ : "of Manouēl" Likely a name for Jesus, specifically a variant writing of Emmanuel; *cf. PCM* I 11 p. 16 ll. 2–4 and accompanying note.

23–24. ⲙⲡⲛⲟ[ϭ ⲛⲥ]ⲧⲏⲗⲗⲟⲥ ⲛⲟⲩ[ⲟⲉⲓⲛ] ⲡⲁⲓ .... ⲏϭⲓϭ ... : "by the great pillar of light, that [supports all] creation?" We are grateful to Frederic Krueger for suggesting this reading. For the concept of pillars (usually four) supporting parts of the cosmos, *cf.* p. 17 ll. 5–6 & p. 43 ll. 1–3 of this manuscript, and *PCM* I 25 p. 14 ll. 25-26; *PCM* I 26 p. 6 ll. 17-18. As these examples show, we would expect ⲧⲱⲟⲩⲛ ϩⲁ rather than ϥⲓ ϩⲁ, but there does not seem to be space for the former. The concept of a singular pillar of light is reminiscent of the pillars of cloud and fire which guided the Israelites by day and night respectively (Exodus 13.21–22), described in Christian sources as a pillar of light (στύλος φωτός/ⲥⲧⲩⲗⲟⲥ ⲛⲟⲩⲟⲉⲓⲛ) by at least the second century (*e.g.* Justin Martyr, *Dialogue with Trypho* 131.3; *History of the Captivity in Babylon* (Kuhn 1970: 108; CAVT 227 (=CC 576?)); *cf.* Krueger forthcoming for 'pillar of light' as an epithet for monastic leaders.

sixteenth page (page 33)

ⲙⲛ̄ ⲧⲕⲏⲫⲁⲗⲓⲥ ⲛ̄ⲛⲟⲩϥ ⲉⲣⲉ[ⲡ]ⲣ[ⲁⲛ] ⲙ̄ⲡⲓⲱⲧ
ⲥⲏϩ ⲉⲣⲟⲥ ϫⲉⲕⲉⲉⲓ ϣⲁⲣⲟⲓ ⲙ̄ⲡⲟⲟⲩ ⲁⲡⲟⲗₒ/
†ⲡⲁⲣⲁⲕⲁⲗⲓ ⲙ̄ⲙⲟⲕ ⲅⲁϥⲣⲓⲏⲗ ⲙ̄ⲡⲟⲩⲟⲉⲓⲛ
ⲙ̄ⲡⲓⲱⲧ ⲉⲩⲟ ⲛ̄ⲟⲩⲟⲉⲓⲛ ⲛ̄ϩⲏⲧϥ̄ ⲛ̄ϭⲓ ⲛⲉ-
5   ⲭⲉⲣⲟⲩⲃⲓⲛ ⲙⲛ̄ ⲛⲉⲥⲉⲣⲁⲫⲓⲛ · ⲙⲛ̄ ⲛⲉⲙ̄-
ⲡⲏⲩⲉ ⲧⲏⲣⲟⲩ ⲙⲛ̄ ⲡⲕⲟⲥⲙⲟⲥ ⲧⲏⲣϥ̄
ϫⲉⲕⲉⲉⲓ ϣⲁⲣⲟⲓ ⲙ̄ⲡⲟⲟⲩ ⲁⲡⲟⲗₒ/
†ⲡⲁⲣⲁⲕⲁⲗⲓ ⲙⲙⲟⲕ ⲅⲁϥⲣⲓⲏⲗ ⲛ̄ⲧⲉⲥ-
ⲧⲟⲗⲏ ⲉⲥⲟⲩⲟϥϣ ⲛ̄ⲑⲉ ⲛ̄ⲟⲩⲭⲓⲱⲛ
10 ⲉⲣⲉⲡⲓⲱⲧ ϫⲟⲟⲗⲉ ⲙ̄ⲙⲟⲥ · ⲙⲛ̄
ⲡⲃⲟ ⲛ̄ⲧⲉϥⲁⲡⲉ ⲉⲃⲟ ⲛ̄ⲑⲉ ⲛ̄ⲟⲩ-
ⲥⲟⲣⲧ ⲛ̄ⲟⲩⲱϥϣ ⲛ̄ⲕⲁⲑⲁⲣⲟⲛ ⲙⲛ̄
ⲡⲉⲛ̄ⲧⲏⲙⲁ ⲙ̄ⲡⲉⲕⲗⲟⲙ ⲙⲁⲣ-
ⲕⲁⲣⲓⲧⲏⲥ ⲉⲧϩⲓϫⲛ ⲧⲁⲡⲉ ⲙ̄ⲡⲓⲱⲧ
15 ϫⲉ ⲕⲉⲉⲓ ϣⲁⲣⲟⲓ ⲙ̄ⲡⲟⲟⲩ ⲁⲡⲟⲗₒ/
†ⲡⲁⲣⲁⲕⲁⲗⲓ ⲙ̄ⲙⲟⲕ ⲅⲁϥⲣⲓⲏⲗ
ⲙ̄ⲡⲙⲟⲩ ⲛ̄ⲃⲉⲉⲃⲉ ⲉⲧϩⲁⲧⲉ ⲉⲃⲟⲗ
ϩⲓϫⲛ̄ ⲧⲁⲡⲉ ⲙ̄ⲡⲓⲱⲧ · ⲙⲛ̄ ⲡⲛⲟϭ
ⲛⲁⲉⲧⲟⲥ ⲉⲣⲉⲛⲉϥⲧⲉⲛⲁϩ ⲡⲟⲣϣ
20 ⲉⲃⲟⲗ ϩⲓϫⲛ̄ ⲧⲁⲡⲉ ⲙⲡⲓⲱⲧ
ϫⲉ ⲕⲉⲉⲓ ϣⲁⲣⲟⲓ ⲙ̄ⲡⲟⲟⲩ ⲁⲡⲟⲗₒ/
†ⲡⲁⲣ[ⲁⲕⲁ]ⲗⲓ ⲙⲙⲟⲕ ⲅⲁϥ[ⲣⲓⲏⲗ]
ⲛ̄ⲧ[ca. 5] ⲛ̄ⲟⲩⲟⲉⲓ[ⲛ ca. 8]

---

1 *i.e.* κεφαλίς | ⲉⲣⲉ[ⲡ]ⲣ[ⲁⲛ] Kropp : ⲉⲣⲉ . . . Rossi ‖ **2** *i.e.* ˢϫⲉ ⲉ≠ⲕ-ⲉ-ⲉⲓ̈ (haplography) | *i.e.* ἀπολο(γία) : *l.* ⲁⲡⲟⲗ(ⲗⲱⲛ) Rossi : "Apolo" Amélineau *cf.* note to p. 9 l. 7 ‖ **3** *i.e.* παρακαλεῖν ‖ **5** *i.e.* χερουβίμ | *i.e.* ˢⲛ-ⲥⲉⲣⲁⲫⲓⲛ *i.e.* σεραφίμ ‖ **6** *i.e.* κόσμος ‖ **7** *i.e.* ἀπολο(γία) *cf.* note to p. 9 l. 7 ‖ **8** *i.e.* παρακαλεῖν ‖ **8–9** *i.e.* στολή ‖ **9** *i.e.* ˢⲟⲩⲟⲯϣQ | *i.e.* χιών ‖ **11** *i.e.* ˢϣⲱ | ⲉⲃⲟ Kropp : ⲉ[ϥ]ⲟ Rossi ‖ **12** *i.e.* ˢⲟⲩⲃⲁϣ | *i.e.* καθαρόν ‖ **13** ἔνδυμα Kropp, Amélineau, Meyer 1988, 1994 : "necklace" ("collana") Rossi ‖ **13–14** *i.e.* ˢⲙ̄-ⲡⲉ-ⲕⲗⲟⲙ ⲙ̄-ⲙⲁⲣⲕⲁⲣⲓⲧⲏⲥ (haplography) *i.e.* μαργαρίτης ‖ **15** *i.e.* ˢϫⲉ ⲉ≠ⲕ-ⲉ-ⲉⲓ̈ (haplography) | *i.e.* ἀπολο(γία) : *l.* ⲁⲡⲟⲗ(ⲗⲱⲛ) Rossi : "Apolo" Amélineau *cf.* note to p. 9 l. 7 ‖ **16** *i.e.* παρακαλεῖν ‖ **17** *i.e.* ˢⲡ-ⲙⲟⲟⲩ ⲛ̄-ⲃⲉⲉⲃⲉ : "springwater" ("eau de source") Amélineau ‖ **19** *i.e.* ἀετός | ⲛⲉϥⲧⲉⲛⲁϩ ⲧ corrected from ⲡ Rossi : ⲡⲉϥⲧⲉⲛⲁϩ Kropp, Meyer 1988, 1994 ‖ **21** *i.e.* ˢϫⲉ ⲉ≠ⲕ-ⲉ-ⲉⲓ̈ (haplography) | *i.e.* ἀπολο(γία) ‖ **22** *i.e.* παρ[ακα]λεῖν ‖ **23** ⲛ̄ⲧ[*ca.* 5] ⲛ̄ⲟⲩⲟⲉⲓ[ⲛ *ca.* 8] Kropp : *ca.* 7 ⲛ̄ⲟⲩⲟⲉⲓ *ca.* 9 Rossi

and the golden capital on which the name of the Father is written, that you come to me today—request!

I invoke you, *Gabriel, by the light of the Father, in which shine the |⁵ *cherubim and the *seraphim and all the heavens and the entire world, that you come to me today—request!

I invoke you, Gabriel, by the garment which is white as snow |¹⁰ with which the Father is clothed, and the hair of his head, which is like pure white wool and the garment? of the crown ‹of› pearls which is upon the head of the Father, |¹⁵ that you come to me today—request!

I invoke you, Gabriel, by the rainwater which flows from from the head of the Father and the great eagle whose wings are spread |²⁰ out over the head of the Father, that you come to me today—request!

I invoke you, Gabriel, by the [...] of light [...]

---

1. ⲧⲕⲏⲫⲁⲗⲓⲥ : "capital" The Greek word κεφαλίς may refer to either the capital of a column, or a chapter or scroll of a book. Here we opt for the former meaning, since a column has been mentioned shortly before; cf. Exodus 26.32, which describes the pillars of the *tabernacle as having gold capitals.

8–12. ⲛ̄ⲧⲉⲥⲧⲟⲗⲏ ⲉⲥⲟⲩⲟϥϣ̄ ⲛ̄ⲑⲉ ⲛ̄ⲟⲩⲭⲓⲱⲛ ⲉⲣⲉⲡⲓⲱⲧ ϫⲟⲟⲗⲉ ⲙ̄ⲙⲟⲥ · ⲙⲛ̄ ⲡⲃⲟ ⲛ̄ⲧⲉϥⲁⲡⲉ ⲉⲃⲟ ⲛ̄ⲑⲉ ⲛ̄ⲟⲩⲥⲟⲣⲧ̄ ⲛ̄ⲟⲩⲱϥϣ ⲛ̄ⲕⲁⲑⲁⲣⲟⲛ : "by the garment which is white as snow, with which the Father is clothed, and the hair of his head, which is like pure white wool" Cf. Daniel 7.9: "the ancient of days was sitting; his garment was white like snow, and his hair was like pure wool" (ⲛⲉⲣⲉⲡⲁⲡⲁⲥ ⲡⲛ ⲛⲉϥϩⲟⲟⲩ ϩⲙⲟⲟⲥ ⲡⲉ ⲧⲉϥϩⲃⲥⲱ ⲇⲉ ⲛⲉⲥⲟⲩⲱⲃϣ̄ ⲛ̄ⲑⲉ ⲛ̄ⲟⲩⲭⲓⲱⲛ ⲁⲩⲱ ⲛⲉⲣⲉⲡϣⲱ ⲛ̄ⲧⲉϥⲁⲡⲉ ⲟ ⲛ̄ⲑⲉ ⲛ̄ⲟⲩⲥⲟⲣⲧ̄ ⲉϥⲧⲃⲃⲏⲩ; Ciasca 1889: 317); Revelation 1.14: "his head was white and his hair was like white wool and like snow, and his eyes were like a burning flame" (ⲉⲣⲉⲧⲉϥⲁⲡⲉ ⲟⲩⲟⲃϣ̄ ⲙⲛ ⲡⲉϥϥⲱ ⲛ̄ⲑⲉ ⲛ̄ⲟⲩⲥⲟⲣⲧ̄ ⲛ̄ⲟⲩⲟⲃϣ̄ ⲁⲩⲱ ⲛ̄ⲑⲉ ⲛ̄ⲟⲩⲭⲓⲱⲛ ⲉⲣⲉⲛⲉϥⲃⲁⲗ ⲟ ⲛ̄ⲑⲉ ⲛ̄ⲟⲩϣⲁϩ ⲛ̄ⲕⲱϩⲧ; Budge 1912: 273).

seventeenth page (page 35)

ϫⲉⲕⲉⲉⲓⲣⲉ ⲛ̄ϩⲱϥ ⲛⲓⲙ ⲉⲧ[ⲉⲓ ⲉ]ⲃⲟⲗ ϩ̄ⲛ ⲣⲱⲓ
ⲁⲡⲟⲗₒ/ ϯⲡⲁⲣⲁⲕⲁⲗⲓ ⲙⲙⲟⲕ ⲅⲁⲩⲣⲓⲏⲗ
ⲛ̄ⲧⲛⲟϭ ⲙ̄ⲡⲁⲣⲑⲉⲛⲟⲥ ⲉⲧⲧⲁⲓⲏⲩ ⲉⲣⲉⲡⲓⲱⲧ ϩⲏⲡ ⲛϩⲏⲧⲥ̄ ⲛ̄ϭⲓⲛ ⲉϣⲟ-
5 ⲣⲡ̄ ⲙⲡⲁⲧⲉϥⲧⲁⲙⲓⲉ ⲗⲁⲁⲩ ϫⲉⲕⲉⲉⲓ
ϣⲁⲣⲟⲓ ⲙ̄ⲡⲟⲟⲩ ⲁⲡⲟⲗₒ/ ϯⲡⲁⲣⲁⲕⲁⲗⲓ ⲙ-
ⲙⲟⲕ ⲅⲁⲩⲣⲓⲏⲗ ⲙ̄ⲡϣⲟⲙⲧ ⲛ̄ϩⲟⲟⲩ
ⲛ̄ⲧⲁⲡⲓⲱⲧ ⲁⲁⲩ ⲉⲃⲁϩⲉⲣⲁⲧϥ ⲙ̄ⲡⲁ-
ⲧⲉϥⲕⲓⲙ ⲉⲧⲉⲕⲧⲏⲥⲓⲥ ⲧⲏⲣⲥ̄ · ⲁⲡⲟⲗₒ/
10 ϯⲡⲁⲣⲁⲕⲁⲗⲓ ⲙⲙⲟⲕ ⲅⲁⲫⲣⲓⲏⲗ
ⲙ̄ⲡϫⲱⲕⲙ ⲛ̄ⲧⲁⲡⲓⲱⲧ ϫⲓⲧϥ
ⲉϥⲛⲁⲡⲗⲁⲥⲥⲉ ⲛ̄ⲁⲇⲁⲙ ⲙ̄ⲛ ⲧⲉϥ-
ⲣⲏⲣⲉ ⲛ̄ⲧⲁⲥϯ ⲟⲩⲱ ⲉⲃⲟⲗ ϩ̄ⲛ ⲧⲉϥϭⲓϫ
ⲛ̄ϩⲃⲟⲩⲣ ⲙ̄ⲛ ⲡⲁⲡⲟⲧ ⲉⲧϩ̄ⲛ ⲧⲉϥ-
15 ϭⲓϫ ⲛⲟⲩⲛⲁⲙ · ⲛ̄ⲧⲁϥⲧⲥⲟ ⲛ̄-
ⲛⲉϥⲁⲅⲅⲉⲗⲟⲥ ⲛ̄ϩⲏⲧϥ ⲙ̄ⲛ
ⲕⲟⲥⲙⲟⲥ ⲧⲏⲣϥ̄ ϫⲉⲕⲉⲉⲓ ϣⲁ-
ⲣⲟⲓ ⲙ̄ⲡⲟⲟⲩ · ⲁⲡⲟⲗₒ/ · ϯⲡⲁⲣⲁⲕⲁⲗⲓ ⲙⲙⲟⲕ ⲅⲁⲩⲣⲓⲏⲗ ⲛ̄ⲧⲡⲁⲧ-
20 ⲥⲉ ⲛ̄ⲧⲁⲥⲉⲓ ⲉⲃⲟⲗ ϩ̄ⲛ ⲣⲱϥ ⲙ̄ⲡⲓⲱⲧ
ⲁⲥϣⲱⲡⲉ ⲛ̄ⲟⲩⲡⲏⲅⲏ ⲙⲙⲟⲟⲩ ⲛⲱ-
ⲛⲁϩ · ϫⲉ [ⲕⲉ]ⲉⲓ ϣⲁⲣⲟⲓ ⲙ̄ⲡⲟⲟⲩ
ϯⲡ[ⲁⲣⲁⲕⲁⲗⲓ] ⲙⲙⲟⲕ ⲅⲁϥ[ⲣⲓⲏⲗ]
. . . . ⲛ̄ⲧⲉϥ[ϣⲟⲣⲡ]

---

1 *i.e.* ˢϫⲉ ⲉ=ⲕ-ⲉ-ⲉⲓⲣⲉ (haplography) | ⲉⲧ[ⲉⲓ ⲉ]ⲃⲟⲗ Kropp : ⲉⲧⲕ . . . [ⲉⲃ]ⲟⲗ Rossi || **2** *i.e.* ἀπολο(γία) : *l.* ⲁⲡⲟⲗ(ⲱⲛ) Rossi : "Apolo" Amélineau *cf.* note to p. 9 l. 7 | *i.e.* παρακαλεῖν || **3** *i.e.* παρθένος || **4** ϩⲏⲡ Kropp : ϩⲏ[ⲡ] Rossi || **4–5** *i.e.* ˢϫⲓⲛ ⲛ-ϣⲟⲣⲡ̄ *cf.* Crum CD 587b || **5** *i.e.* ˢϫⲉ ⲉ=ⲕ-ⲉ-ⲉⲓ (haplography) || **6** *i.e.* ἀπολο(γία) *cf.* note to p. 9 l. 7: *l.* ⲁⲡⲟⲗ(ⲱⲛ) Rossi : "Apolo" Amélineau *cf.* note to p. 4 l. 7 | *i.e.* παρακαλεῖν || **8** *i.e.* ˢⲉ=ϥ-ⲁϩⲉⲣⲁⲧ=ϥ || **9** *i.e.* κτίσις | *i.e.* ἀπολο(γία) : *l.* ⲁⲡⲟⲗ(ⲱⲛ) Rossi : "Apolo" Amélineau *cf.* note to p. 9 l. 7 || **10** *i.e.* παρακαλεῖν || **11** ϫⲓⲧϥ Kropp : ϫ[ⲓ]ⲧϥ Rossi || **12** *i.e.* πλάσσειν || **13** ⲛⲧⲁⲥϯⲟⲩⲱ ⲉⲃⲟⲗ Rossi : ⲛⲧⲁⲥϯⲟⲩ ⲉⲃⲟⲗ Kropp || **15** ⲛ̄ⲧⲁϥⲧⲥⲟ ⲛ̄- Kropp : ⲛ̄ⲧⲁϥ . . . . *l.* ⲛ̄ⲧⲁϥ[ⲧⲁⲙⲓⲉ] "and he shaped you" ("e vi formò") Rossi : "with which he created" ("dont il a crée ?") Amélineau || **16** *i.e.* ἄγγελος || **17** *l.* ⲡ-ⲕⲟⲥⲙⲟⲥ *i.e.* κόσμος | *i.e.* ˢϫⲉ ⲉ=ⲕ-ⲉ-ⲉⲓ (haplography) || **18** *i.e.* ἀπολο(γία) || **18–19** *i.e.* παρακαλεῖν || **19** ⲛ̄ⲧⲡⲁⲧ- Kropp : ⲛ̄ⲧⲁⲡⲁ[ⲧ] Rossi || **21** *i.e.* πηγή | ⲛⲱ- Kropp : . . . Rossi || **22** *i.e.* ˢϫⲉ ⲉ=ⲕ-ⲉ-ⲉⲓ (haplography) || **23** ϯⲡⲁ[ⲣⲁⲕⲁⲗⲓ] Kropp : ϯ[ⲡⲁⲣⲁⲕⲁⲗⲓ] Rossi | *i.e.* π[αρακαλεῖν] || **24** *ca.* 7 ⲛ̄ⲧⲉϥ[ϣⲟⲣⲡ] CMPT, *cf.* PCM I 26 p. 13 l. 15: ⲛⲧϣⲁⲣⲉⲡⲓ ⲛⲣⲉⲙⲉ = ⲛⲧⲁⲥⲓ ⲉⲃⲁⲗ : *ca.* 7 ⲛ̄ⲧⲉϥⲛ̄ⲧⲉϥ . . . Rossi

that you do everything which [comes] forth from my mouth—request!

I invoke you, *Gabriel, by the great honoured virgin, in whom the Father was hidden from the beginning, |⁵ before he had created anything, that you come to me today—request!

I invoke you, Gabriel, by the three days which the Father spent standing before he set all creation in motion—request!

|¹⁰ I invoke you, Gabriel, by the bath which the Father took when he was about to mould Adam, and the flower which sprouted in his left hand and the *cup which is in |¹⁵ his right hand, from which he had his *angels drink, and ⟨the⟩ entire world, that you come to me today—request!

I invoke you, Gabriel, by the spittle |²⁰ which came from the mouth of the Father and became a spring of water of life, that you come to me today! I [invoke] you, Gabriel, ... his first

---

14–16. ⲡⲁⲡⲟⲧ ⲉⲧϩⲛ̄ ⲧⲉϥϭⲓϫ ⲛⲟⲩⲛⲁⲙ · ⲛ̄ⲧⲁϥⲧⲥⲟ ⲛ̄ⲛⲉϥⲁⲅⲅⲉⲗⲟⲥ ⲛ̄ϩⲏⲧϥ : "the cup which is in his right hand, from which he had his angels drink" For the concept of a eucharistic ritual carried out by the angels in heaven, *cf. PCM* I 25 p. 7 ll. 23–24 and the accompanying note.

eighteenth page (page 37)

ⲛ̄ⲣⲉⲙⲓⲏ ⲛ̄ⲧⲁⲥⲓ ⲉⲃⲟⲗ ϩ︦ⲛ︦ ⲛⲉ[ⲃⲁ]ⲗ ⲙ̄ⲡⲓⲱⲧ
ⲉϫⲉⲙ̄ ⲡⲉϥϣⲏⲣⲉ ϩⲓϫⲙ̄ ⲡⲉⲥϯⲟⲥ
ϫⲉⲕⲉⲓ ϣⲁⲣⲟⲓ ⲙ̄ⲡⲟⲟⲩ ⲁⲡⲟⲗₒ/ ϯⲡⲁⲣⲁⲕⲁⲗⲓ ⲙ̄ⲙⲟⲕ ⲅⲁⲩⲣⲓⲏⲗ ⲉⲧⲃⲉ ⲛⲉⲓ-
5 ⲣⲁⲛ ⲉⲧⲟⲩⲁⲁⲃ ⲛ̄ⲧⲉⲡⲓⲱⲧ · ⲙⲁⲣⲓ ⲛⲁⲃ
ⲙⲁⲣⲙⲁⲣⲟⲩ · ⲃⲁⲃⲁⲙ ⲫⲓϣⲟⲩ
ⲃⲁⲑⲟⲩⲣⲓⲏⲗ · ⲓⲁⲱ ⲥⲁⲃⲁⲱⲑ ⲁⲇⲱⲛⲁⲓ
ⲡⲡⲁⲛⲇⲱⲕⲣⲁⲇⲱⲣ ⲙⲁⲛⲟⲩⲏⲗ
ⲥⲁⲃⲁⲱⲑ ⲁⲃⲁⲑⲟⲩ · ⲓⲁⲭⲁⲟⲓ ⲓⲭⲁⲟϥ
10 ⲥⲁⲃⲁⲑⲱ · ⲛⲁⲓ ⲉⲣⲉⲇⲁⲛⲓⲏⲗ ϩⲏⲡ
ⲛ̄ϩⲏⲧϥ ϩⲱⲥⲇⲉ ⲛ̄ⲅⲓ ϣⲁⲣⲟⲓ ⲉⲡⲉⲓⲧⲟⲡⲟⲥ ⲉⲓϣⲟⲟⲡ ⲛ̄ϩⲏⲧϥ ⲉⲧⲃⲉ
ϩⲱϥ ⲛⲓⲙ ⲛ̄ⲧⲁⲓⲡⲁⲣⲁⲕⲁⲗⲓ ⲙ̄ⲙⲟⲕ
ⲉⲧⲃⲏⲧⲟⲩ ⲉⲕⲉⲧⲁϫⲣⲟⲓ ⲛ̄ϩⲏⲧⲟⲩ
15 ⲧⲏⲣⲟⲩ ⲛ̄ⲉϩⲟⲟⲩ ⲧⲏⲣⲟⲩ ⲙ̄ⲡⲁⲱ-
ⲛⲁϩ · ϩⲁⲙⲏⲛ ⲓ︦ⲃ︦ ⲙⲁⲣⲉⲩⲕⲁⲑⲁ-
ⲣⲓⲍⲉ ⲙ̄ⲡⲁⲥⲱⲙⲁ ϩⲙ̄ ⲡ︦ⲛ︦ⲁ︦ ⲛⲓⲙ
ⲛ̄ⲁⲕⲁⲑⲁⲣⲧⲟⲛ · ⲉⲓⲧⲉ ⲡ︦ⲛ︦ⲁ︦ ⲛ̄ⲧⲉ-
ⲙⲟⲛⲓⲟⲛ ⲛ̄ϩⲟⲟⲩⲧ · ⲉⲓⲧⲉ ⲡ︦ⲛ︦ⲁ︦
20 ⲛ̄ⲧⲉⲙⲟⲛⲓⲟⲛ ⲛ̄ⲥϩⲓⲙⲉ · ⲉⲓⲧⲉ
ⲡ︦ⲛ︦ⲁ︦ ⲛ̄ⲁⲕⲉⲗⲓⲕⲏ ⲛ̄ⲧⲉ . . . . . .
ⲉⲓⲧⲉ ⲡ︦ⲛ︦ⲁ︦ ⲛ̄ⲧⲉ ⲡⲁⲣⲭⲏⲡⲗ[ⲁⲥ]-
ⲙⲁ ⲙ[ⲡ︦ⲣ︦ⲧ]ⲉⲩⲭⲙϭⲟⲙ ⲁϩⲉ-
ⲉⲣⲁ[ⲧⲟⲩ ⲙⲡ]ⲁⲙⲧⲟ ⲉⲃ[ⲟⲗ]

---

1 *i.e.* ˢⲣⲙⲉⲓⲏ : "tears" ("Tränen") Kropp, Meyer 1988, 1994 | *i.e.* ˢⲛ̄ⲧⲁ꞊ⲥ-ⲉⲓ ⲉⲃⲟⲗ | ⲛⲉ[ⲃⲁ]ⲗ Kropp : . . . ⲗ Rossi || **2** ⲡⲉⲥϯⲟⲥ Rossi, Meyer 1988 *i.e.* ⲥⲧ(ⲁⲩ)ⲣόⲥ : ⲡⲉⲥⲥϯⲟⲥ Kropp || **3** *i.e.* ˢϫⲉ ⲉ꞊ⲕ-ⲉ-ⲉⲓ̈ (haplography) | *i.e.* ἀⲡⲟⲗⲟ(γία) : *l.* ⲁⲡⲟⲗ(ⲱⲛ) Rossi : "Apolo" Amélineau *cf.* note to p. 9 l. 7 || **3–4** *i.e.* ⲡⲁⲣⲁⲕⲁⲗⲉῖⲛ || **5** ⲙⲁⲣⲓ ⲛⲁⲃ : "Marinab" parse Kropp, Meyer 1988, 1994 || **6** ⲃⲁⲃⲁⲙ : "Balam" Kropp || **8** *i.e.* ⲡⲁⲛⲧⲟⲕⲣάⲧⲱⲣ || **9** ⲓⲭⲁⲟϥ Kropp : ⲓⲭⲁⲓⲭϥ Rossi || **11** *i.e.* ὥⲥⲧⲉ | *i.e.* ˢⲛ̄꞊ⲅ-ⲉⲓ̈ || **12** *i.e.* ⲧόⲡⲟⲥ || **13**. *i.e.* ⲡⲁⲣⲁⲕⲁⲗⲉῖⲛ || **14** ⲉⲕⲉⲧⲁϫⲣⲟⲓ ⲛ̄ϩⲏⲧⲟⲩ : "you must be strong in all of them" Meyer 1994 || **16** *i.e.* ἀⲙⲏⲛ || **16–17** *i.e.* ⲕⲁⲑⲁⲣίⲍⲉⲓⲛ || **17** *i.e.* ⲥῶⲙⲁ | *i.e.* ⲡⲛ(ⲉῦⲙ)ⲁ || **18** *i.e.* ἀⲕάⲑⲁⲣⲧⲟⲛ | *i.e.* ⲉἴⲧⲉ | *i.e.* ⲡⲛ(ⲉῦⲙ)ⲁ || **18–19** *i.e.* ⲇⲁⲓⲙόⲛⲓⲟⲛ | *i.e.* ⲉἴⲧⲉ | *i.e.* ⲡⲛ(ⲉῦⲙ)ⲁ || **20** *i.e.* ⲇⲁⲓⲙόⲛⲓⲟⲛ | *i.e.* ⲉἴⲧⲉ || **21** *i.e.* ⲡⲛ(ⲉῦⲙ)ⲁ | *i.e.* ἀⲅⲅⲉⲗⲓⲕⲏ́ | . . . . . . Kropp : . . . . Rossi || **22** *i.e.* ⲉἴⲧⲉ | *i.e.* ⲡⲛ(ⲉῦⲙ)ⲁ || **22–23** ⲡⲁⲣⲭⲏⲡⲗ[ⲁⲥ]ⲙⲁ Kropp : ⲡⲁⲣⲭⲏⲡ[ⲗⲁⲥ]ⲙⲁ Rossi | *i.e.* ἀⲣⲭίⲡⲗ[ⲁⲥ]ⲙⲁ *cf.* note || **23** ⲙ[ⲡ︦ⲣ︦ⲧ]ⲉⲩⲭⲙ ϭⲟⲙ ⲁϩⲉ Kropp : ⲙ . . . ⲣⲉⲩⲭⲙ ϭⲟⲙ ⲁϩⲉ . . . Rossi | *i.e.* ˢϭⲙ̄ϭⲟⲙ || **24** ⲉⲣⲁ[ⲧⲟⲩ ⲙⲡ]ⲁⲙⲧⲟ ⲉⲃ[ⲟⲗ] Kropp : ⲉⲣⲁ *ca.* 5 ⲙⲧⲟ ⲉ . . . Rossi

tear which came forth from the [eyes] of the Father over his son upon the cross, that you come to me today—request—!

I invoke you, *Gabriel, because of these |⁵ holy names of the Father: Mari, Nab, Marmarou, Babam, Phiōou, Bathouriēl, *Iao *Sabaoth, *Adonai, Almighty, Manouēl, Sabaoth, Abathou, Iakhaoi, Ikhaof, |¹⁰ Sabathō, these in which Daniel was hidden, that you come to me at this place in which I am, concerning everything about which I have invoked you! You shall strengthen me in all of them |¹⁵ all the days of my life, amen (12 ⟨times⟩)! Let my body be purified of every unclean spirit, whether a male demonic spirit |²⁰ or female demonic spirit or angelic spirit of ... or spirit of the First-Formed One! Do not allow them to be able to stand [in] my presence

---

8. ⲙⲁⲛⲟⲩⲏⲗ : "**Manouēl**" Likely a name for Jesus derived from Emmanuel; *cf. PCM* I 11 p. 16 ll. 2–4 and accompanying note.

18–20. ⲉⲓⲧⲉ ⲡⲛⲁ ⲛ̄ⲧⲉⲙⲟⲛⲓⲟⲛ ⲛ̄ϩⲟⲟⲩⲧ · ⲉⲓⲧⲉ ⲡⲛⲁ ⲛ̄ⲧⲉⲙⲟⲛⲓⲟⲛ ⲛⲥϩⲓⲙⲉ : "**whether a male demonic spirit or female demonic spirit**" As noted by Frankfurter (in Meyer/Smith 1994: 108), such lists of possible demonic attackers, listing both male and female variants, find echoes in older Pharaonic Egyptian amuletic texts. See, for examples, Pap.Athen.Nat.-Bibl. 1826 ro col. x + 5 l. 12: "Book for driving off... male and female revenants" (*mḏꜣ.t n.t dr... mwt mwt⟨.t⟩*; XIX–XX Dynasty; Fischer-Elfert 2005: no. 15); P.BM EA 10688 vo. col. 4.1–2: "every male revenant, every female revenant, every male enemy, every female enemy, every male opponent, every female opponent, every male *akh*-spirit, every female *akh*-spirit" (*mwt nb mwt.t nb.t ḫft.y nb ḫft.t nb.t ḏꜣy nb ḏꜣy.t nb.t ꜣḫ nb ꜣḫ.t nb.t*; XIX–XX Dynasty; Fischer-Elfert 2005: no. 18). Similar listing of potential male and female witches is also a principle in Mesopotamian anti-witchcraft rituals; see, for example, the *Maqlû* ("burning") series (*cf.* note to *PCM* I 11 p. 4 ll. 3–20) edited in Abusch 2015: tablet I 78–86 (288–289), tablet II 42–50 (294–295), tablet IV 86 (324).

22–23. ⲡⲁⲣⲭⲏⲡⲗⲁⲥⲙⲁ : "**the First-Formed One**" *Cf.* the note to p. 15 l. 17.

nineteenth page (page 39)

ⲁⲗⲗⲁ ⲙⲁⲣⲉⲩⲡⲱⲧ ϩⲁ[ⲑⲏ ⲙ̄ⲙⲟⲓ] ⲧⲏⲣⲟⲩ
ϩⲁⲙⲏⲛ ⲓ̄ⲃ̄ ⲉⲕⲉⲕⲁⲑⲁⲣ[ⲓⲍⲉ ⲙ]ⲡⲉⲓ-
ⲧⲟⲡⲟⲥ ⲉⲡⲛ̄ⲁ̄ ⲛⲓⲙ ⲛⲁⲕⲁⲑⲁⲣⲧⲟⲛ
ⲣⲟⲉⲓⲥ ⲉⲣⲟⲓ ⲉⲛ̄ⲉⲑⲟⲟⲩ ⲧⲏⲣⲟⲩ ⲛ̄ⲉϩⲟⲟⲩ
5   ⲧⲏⲣⲟⲩ ⲙ̄ⲡⲁⲱⲛⲁϩ ⲕⲁⲑⲁⲣⲓⲍⲉ
ⲛⲁⲓ ⲙ̄ⲡⲉϥⲧⲟⲟⲩ̀ ⲥⲁ ⲉⲧⲕⲱⲧⲉ
ⲉⲣⲟⲓ ⲛ̄ⲥⲉ ⲛ̄ⲧⲃⲁ ⲙ̄ⲙⲁϩⲉ ⲉϥⲕⲱⲧⲉ
ⲕⲁⲑⲁⲣⲓⲍⲉ ⲛⲁⲓ ⲙ̄ⲡⲛⲟⲩⲛ ⲛ̄ⲥⲉ ⲛ̄-
ⲧⲃⲁ ⲙ̄ⲙⲁϩⲉ ϩⲓ ⲧⲡⲉ ⲙ̄ⲙⲟⲓ ⲛ̄-
10 ⲥⲉ ⲛ̄ⲧⲃⲁ ⲙ̄ⲙⲁϩⲉ ϫⲉ ⲛⲉⲩⲉⲓ ⲉ-
ⲡⲉⲥⲏⲧ ⲉⲣⲟⲓ ⲁⲡⲟⲗο/ †ⲡⲁⲣⲁⲕⲁ-
ⲗⲓ ⲙ̄ⲙⲟⲕ ⲅ̄ⲁ̄ⲩⲣⲓⲏⲗ · ⲙ̄ⲡⲥⲁ⟨ϣ⟩ϥ ⲛ̄-
ⲛ̄ⲃⲁⲗ ⲙ̄ⲡⲓⲱⲧ · ⲥⲉⲣⲛⲉⲩⲱ
ⲡⲁⲃⲁⲱⲑⲟⲩ · ⲁⲩⲣⲓⲧⲱⲛ · ⲁⲙⲓⲧⲱⲛ
15 ⲑⲉⲱⲑⲁⲛⲁⲩⲧⲏⲣⲓ · ϩ̄ⲁ̄ ϩ̄ⲁ̄ ϩ̄ⲁ̄ ϩ̄ⲁ̄ ϩ̄ⲁ̄ ϩ̄ⲁ̄ ϩ̄ⲁ̄
ⲃⲁⲑⲟⲩⲣⲓⲏⲗ ⲡⲛⲟϭ ⲛ̄ⲓⲱⲧ ⲃⲁⲑⲟⲩⲣⲓⲏⲗ
ⲥⲁⲃⲁⲱⲑ · ⲃⲱⲃⲱⲏⲗ · ⲁⲑⲁⲱⲣ ⲙⲁⲩⲉ
ⲡⲛⲟⲩⲧⲉ ⲛ̄ⲉⲛⲟⲩⲧⲉ ⲉⲕⲉⲧⲉⲛⲟⲟⲩ ⲛⲁⲓ
ⲛ̄ⲅⲁⲩⲣⲓⲏⲗ · ⲡⲁⲅⲅⲉⲗⲟⲥ ⲛ̄ⲧⲇⲓⲕⲁⲓ-
20 ⲟⲥⲏⲛⲏ · ϫⲉⲃⲉⲉⲓⲣⲉ ⲛ̄ϩⲱϥ ⲛⲓⲙ
ⲉ†ⲡⲁⲣⲁⲕⲁⲗⲓ ⲙ̄ⲙⲟⲕ ⲉⲧⲃⲏⲧⲟⲩ
ϩⲁⲙⲏⲛ̄ ⲁ̄ ⲍ̄ ⲉ̄ ⲍ̄ ⲏ̄ ⲍ̄ ⲓ̄ ⲍ̄ ⲟ̄ ⲩ̄ ⲍ̄ ⲱ̄ ⲍ̄
ⲙ̄ ⲍ̄ ⲭ̄ ⲍ̄ [ⲡ̄ ⲍ̄] †ⲡⲁⲣⲁⲕⲁⲗⲓ ⲙ̄ⲙⲟⲕ
ⲅⲁⲩⲣⲓ[ⲏⲗ ⲙ̄]ⲡⲛⲟϭ ⲛ̄ⲣⲁⲛ ⲛⲁ . . .
25 . . . . ⲉⲧϩ . . . .

---

1 *i.e.* ἀλλά | ⲙⲁⲣⲉⲩⲡⲱⲧ ϩⲁ[ⲑⲏ ⲙ̄ⲙⲟⲓ] Kropp : ⲙⲁⲣ[ⲟⲩ]ⲡⲱⲧ ϩ[ⲓⲑⲏ ⲙ̄ⲡⲁϩⲟ] Rossi || **2** *i.e.* ἀμήν | *i.e.* καθαρ[ίζειν] || **3** *i.e.* τόπος | *i.e.* πν(εῦμ)α | *i.e.* ἀκάθαρτον || **5** *i.e.* καθαρίζειν || **5–7** ⲕⲁⲑⲁⲣⲓⲍⲉ ⲛⲁⲓ ⲙ̄ⲡⲉϥⲧⲟⲟ\ⲩ/ ⲥⲁ ⲉⲧⲕⲱⲧⲉ ⲉⲣⲟⲓ : "purify for me this place that surrounds me" ("purifichi per me questo luogo che mi circonda") Rossi || **6** ⲙ̄ⲡⲉϥⲧⲟ\ⲩ/ⲟⲥⲁ ⲉⲧⲕⲱⲧⲉ Kropp : ⲙ̄ⲡⲉϥⲧⲟⲡⲟⲥ ⲁⲉⲧⲕⲱⲧⲉ Rossi || **8** *i.e.* καθαρίζειν || **9** ϩⲓⲧⲡⲉ ⲙ̄ⲙⲟⲓ : "heaven above me" Meyer 1988, 1994 || **10** *i.e.* ᶳⲛ̄ⲛⲉ=ⲩ-ⲉⲓ (haplography) || **10–11** ϫⲉ ⲛⲉⲩⲉⲓ ⲉⲡⲉⲥⲏⲧ ⲉⲣⲟⲓ "beneath me" ("sotto di me") Rossi || **11** *i.e.* ἀπολο(γία) || **11–12** *i.e.* παρακαλεῖν || **12–13** *l.* ⲛ̄-ⲃⲁⲗ (dittography over the line) || **15** *l. i.e.* ἀ(μήν) (seven times) Kropp, Meyer 1988, 1994 || **18** *i.e.* ᶳⲡ-ⲛⲟⲩⲧⲉ ⲛ̄-ⲛ̄-ⲛⲟⲩⲧⲉ || **19** *i.e.* ἄγγελος || **19–20** *i.e.* δικαιοσύνη || **20** *i.e.* ᶳⲉ=ϥ-ⲉⲓⲣⲉ (haplography) || **21** *i.e.* παρακαλεῖν || **22** *i.e.* ἀμήν || **23** [ⲡ̄ⲍ̄] Kropp : ⁻. . Rossi | *i.e.* παρακαλεῖν || **24** ⲅⲁⲩⲣⲓ[ⲏⲗ ⲙ̄]ⲡⲛⲟϭ ⲛ̄ⲣⲁⲛ ⲛⲁ. . . Kropp : ⲅⲁ[ⲩⲣⲓⲏⲗ] . . . ⲡⲛⲟϭ ⲛ̄ⲣⲁⲛⲛⲁ . . . Rossi || **25** *ca.* 13 ⲉⲧϩ *ca.* 10 Kropp : *ca.* 14 Rossi

but rather let them all flee before [me,] amen (12 ‹times›)! May you purify this place of every unclean spirit! Protect me from all evil, all of the days |⁵ of my life!

Purify for me the four sides around me, for six hundred thousand cubits around! Purify for me the *abyss for six hundred thousand cubits, above me for |¹⁰ six hundred thousand cubits, so that they will not come down upon me—request!

I invoke you, *Gabriel, by the seven eyes of the Father, Serneuō, Pabaōthou, Afritōn, Amitōn, |¹⁵ Theōthanautēri, Ha Ha Ha Ha Ha Ha Ha! Bathouriel, the great Father, Bathouriel *Sabaoth Bōbōēl Athaōr Maue, God of gods, may you send to me Gabriel, the *angel of righteousness, |²⁰ so that he does every work concerning which I invoke him, amen! A (7 ‹times›) E (7 ‹times›) Ē (7 ‹times›) I (7 ‹times›) O (7 ‹times›) U (7 ‹times›) Ō (7 ‹times›) M (7 ‹times›) Kh (7 ‹times›) [P (7 ‹times›)]!

I invoke you, Gabriel, by the great *name of? |²⁵ ... which is ...

12-13. ⲙ̄ⲡⲥⲁϣϥ̄ ⲛ̄ⲃⲁⲗ ⲙ̄ⲡⲓⲱⲧ : **"by the seven eyes of the Father"** *Cf.* Revelation 5.6: "there was a lamb standing there who had been slain, who had seven horns and seven eyes" (ⲉⲩϩⲓⲉⲓⲃ ⲉϥⲁϩⲉⲣⲁⲧϥ̄ ⲉⲁⲩⲕⲟⲛⲥϥ̄ ⲉⲟⲩⲛⲧϥ̄ ⲥⲁϣϥ̄ ⲛ̄ⲧⲁⲡ ⲁⲩⲱ ⲥⲁϣϥ̄ ⲛ̄ⲃⲁⲗ; Budge 1912: 283).

15. ϩⲁ ϩⲁ ϩⲁ ϩⲁ ϩⲁ ϩⲁ ϩⲁ : **"Ha Ha Ha Ha Ha Ha Ha"** Or understand seven 'amens' with Kropp and Meyer; *cf.* p. 27 l. 17.

twentieth page (page 41)

ⲥⲁⲃⲁⲱⲑ · ⲃⲁⲑⲟⲩⲣⲓⲏⲗ . . . . ⲙⲁⲭⲁ
ⲙⲁⲣⲓⲏⲗ ⲭⲉⲧⲉⲧⲛ̄ⲛⲉⲧⲉⲛⲟⲟⲩ ⲛⲁⲓ
ⲛ̄ⲅⲁⲩⲣⲓⲏⲗ ⲡⲁⲅⲅⲉⲗⲟⲥ ⲛ̄ⲧⲧⲓⲕⲁⲓ-
ⲟⲥⲏⲛⲏ · ⲉⲣⲉⲧⲉϥⲥⲏⲃⲉ ⲃⲏϣ ⲉⲥϩⲛ
5   ⲧⲉϥϭⲓϫ ⲛⲟⲩⲛⲁⲙ · ⲉϫⲛ̄ ⲡⲛⲉⲩⲙⲁ
ⲛⲓⲙ ⲛⲁⲕⲁⲑⲁⲣⲧⲟⲛ · ⲉⲓⲧⲉ ⲧⲉⲙⲟⲛ
ⲛ̄ϩⲟⲟⲩⲧ ⲉⲓⲧⲉ ⲧⲉⲙⲟⲛ ⲛ̄ⲥϩⲓⲙⲉ
ⲉⲓⲧⲉ ⲉⲛⲧⲏⲣ ⲛ̄ϩⲟⲟⲩⲧ ⲉⲓⲧⲉ ⲉⲛⲧⲏⲣ ⲛ̄ⲥϩⲓⲙⲉ · ⲁⲡⲟⲗₒ/ · ⲑⲁⲏⲗ · ⲓⲱⲏⲗ
10 ⲑⲁⲏⲗ · ⲑⲣⲟⲏⲗ · ⲥⲁⲏⲗ · ⲃⲁⲏⲗ · ⲑⲟⲕ
ⲑⲏⲗ ⲑⲁⲃⲟⲩⲏⲗ ⲑⲁⲩⲣⲓⲏⲗ · ⲥⲁⲣⲟⲁⲏⲗ
ⲁⲃⲟⲑⲏⲗ · ⲑⲁⲙⲓⲏⲗ · ⲑⲁⲩⲏⲗ · ⲟⲩⲏⲗ
ⲧⲁⲙⲃⲏⲗ · ⲑⲁⲣⲟⲓⲉⲗ · ⲁⲭⲉ ⲁⲭⲏ ⲧⲁⲭⲁⲏⲗ
ⲥⲁⲣⲥⲁⲏⲗ · ⲥⲁⲣⲥⲟⲙⲱⲏⲗ · ⲥⲁⲣ-
15 ⲥⲁⲃⲁⲏⲗ · ⲡϫⲟⲩⲧⲁϥⲧⲉ ⲛ̄ⲁⲅⲅⲉ-
ⲗⲟⲥ ⲉⲧⲁϩⲉⲉⲣⲁⲧⲟⲩ ⲉⲡⲉϫⲟⲩⲧⲁϥⲧⲉ
ⲙ̄ⲡⲣⲏⲥⲃⲏⲧⲉⲣⲟⲥ ⲃⲟⲏⲑⲓ ⲉⲣⲟⲓ
ⲧⲁⲭⲏ ⲧⲁⲭⲏ · ⲁ̄ ⲍ̄ ⲉ̄ ⲍ̄ ⲏ̄ ⲍ̄ ⲓ̄ ⲍ̄ ⲟ̄ ⲍ̄ ⲩ̄ ⲍ̄ ⲱ̄ ⲍ̄
ⲙ̄ ⲍ̄ ⲭ ⲍ̄ ⲡ ⲍ̄ · ⲧⲱⲟⲩⲛ̄ ⲭⲱⲗ̄ⲕ ⲛ̄ⲧⲉⲕ-
20 ⲡⲓⲧⲉ ⲉϫⲛ̄ ⲡⲁⲣⲭⲏⲡⲗⲁⲥⲙⲁ [ⲙⲛ̄]
ⲡⲉϥⲧⲏ[ⲛⲁ]ⲙⲓⲥ ⲧⲏⲣⲟⲩ . . . .
ⲑⲉⲃⲱⲏⲗ . . ⲱⲏⲗ . . . .

1–2 . . . . ⲙⲁⲭⲁ ⲙⲁⲣⲓⲏⲗ Kropp : . . . . . ⲙⲁⲣⲓⲏⲗ Rossi | [ⲁⲅⲣⲁ]ⲙⲁ ⲭⲁⲙⲁⲣⲓⲏⲗ ? parse Kropp, Meyer 1988, 1994 || **2** *i.e.* ˢⲉⲧⲉⲧⲛ̄-ⲉ-ⲧⲛ̄ⲛⲟⲟⲩ || **3** *i.e.* ἄγγελος || **3–4** *i.e.* δικαιοσύνη || **5** *i.e.* ˢϭⲓϫ | *i.e.* πνεῦμα || **6** *i.e.* ἀκάθαρτον | *i.e.* εἴτε | *i.e.* δαίμων || **7** *i.e.* εἴτε | *i.e.* δαίμων || **8** *i.e.* εἴτε || **9** *i.e.* ἀπολο(γία) : *l.* ⲁⲡⲟⲗ(ⲱⲛ) Rossi : "Apolo" Amélineau *cf.* note to p. 9 l. 7 || **15–16** *i.e.* ἄγγελος || **17** *i.e.* πρεσβύτερος | *i.e.* βοηθεῖν || **18** *i.e.* ταχύ (twice) || **20** *i.e.* ἀρχίπλασμα || **21** ⲧⲏ[ⲛⲁ]ⲙⲓⲥ Kropp *i.e.* δύναμις : ⲧⲏ[ⲛⲁⲙ]ⲓⲥ Rossi | *ca.* 8 Kropp : *ca.* 5 Rossi || **22** ⲑⲉⲃⲱⲏⲗ . . ⲱⲏⲗ *ca.* 13 Kropp : ⲑⲉⲃⲱⲏⲗ *ca.* 7 ⲏⲗ *ca.* 5 Rossi

*Sabaoth Bathouriel ... Makha Mariēl, that you (pl.) send to me *Gabriel the *angel of righteousness, with his sword drawn in |⁵ his right hand against every unclean spirit, whether a male demon or a female demon, whether a male deity or a female deity—request!

Thaēl, Ioēl, |¹⁰ Thaēl, Throēl, Saēl, Baēl, Thok, Thēl, Thabouēl, Thafriēl, Saroaēl, Abothēl, Thamiēl, Thauēl, Ouēl, Tambēl, Tharoiel, Ače, Ačē, Takhaēl, Sarsaēl, Sarsomoēl, |¹⁵ Sarsabaēl, the twenty-four angels who stand by the *Twenty-Four Presbyters, help me, quickly, quickly! A (7 ‹times›) E (7 ‹times›) Ē (7 ‹times›) I (7 ‹times›) O (7 ‹times›) U (7 ‹times›) Ō (7 ‹times›) M (7 ‹times›) Kh (7 ‹times›) P (7 ‹times›)!

Arise, draw your |²⁰ bow against the First-Formed One [and] all of his power ... Theboēl ... oēl ...

8–9. ⲉⲓⲧⲉ ⲉⲛⲧⲏⲣ ⲛ̄ϩⲟⲟⲩⲧ ⲉⲓⲧⲉ ⲉⲛⲧⲏⲣ ⲛ̄ⲥϩⲓⲙⲉ : "whether a male deity or a female deity" For the word ⲉⲛⲧⲏⲣ, translated here as "deity", *cf.* the note to *PCM* I 25 p. 4 l. 25.

20. ⲡⲁⲣⲭⲏⲡⲗⲁⲥⲙⲁ : "the First-Formed One" *cf.* the note to p. 15 l. 17.

twenty-first page (page 43)

ⲉⲡⲉϥⲧⲟⲟⲩ ⲛ̄ⲥⲧⲏⲗⲟⲥ ⲙ̄[ⲡⲛⲟ]ⲩⲛ ·
ⲉⲧⲃⲉ ⲧⲉϥϩⲧⲟ ⲛ̄ⲁⲡⲉ · ⲉⲧⲧⲱⲟⲩⲛ
ϩⲁ ⲧϣⲟⲣⲡⲉ ⲙ̄ⲡⲉ ⲁⲡⲟⲗₒ/ · ⲅⲁⲩⲣⲓⲏⲗ
ⲡⲁⲅⲅⲉⲗⲟⲥ ⲛ̄ⲧⲇⲓⲕⲁⲓⲟⲥⲏⲛⲏ ⲧⲱⲕⲙ
5   ⲛ̄ⲧⲉⲕⲥⲛⲃⲉ ϩⲛ̄ ⲧⲉⲕϭⲓϫ ⲛ̄ⲟⲩⲛⲁⲙ
ⲡⲱⲧ ⲛ̄ⲥⲁ ⲡ̄ⲛ̄ⲁ̄ ⲛⲓⲙ ⲡⲟⲛⲏⲣⲟⲛ
ⲁⲡⲟⲗₒ/ ⲃⲁⲏⲗ ⲫⲱⲏⲗ ⲑⲁⲏⲗ ⲑⲣⲟⲏⲗ
ⲑⲁⲃⲁⲏⲗ ⲑⲱⲏⲗ ⲃⲁⲭⲱⲱⲗ ⲑⲓⲏⲗ
ⲁⲣⲟⲏⲗ ⲁϥⲫⲏⲗ · ⲁⲣⲟⲩⲱⲏⲗ · ⲥⲁⲙⲓⲏⲗ
10 ⲁⲩⲏⲗ · ⲟⲩⲏⲗ · ⲟⲃⲙⲓⲏⲗ ⲑⲁⲣⲓⲙⲓⲏⲗ
ⲁⲭⲏⲗ ⲁⲁⲣⲟⲁⲃⲇⲏⲗ · ⲥⲱⲧⲙ̄ ⲉⲣⲟⲓ
ⲛⲁⲅⲅⲉⲗⲟⲥ ⲛ̄ϫⲱⲱⲣⲉ · ϫⲉ †ⲡⲁ-
ⲣⲁⲕⲁⲗⲓ ⲙ̄ⲙⲱⲧⲛ ⲙ̄ⲡϫⲟⲉⲓⲥ ⲡⲓ-
ϫⲟⲩⲧⲁϥⲧⲏ ⲛⲁⲣⲭⲁⲅⲅⲉⲗⲟⲥ
15 ⲛ̄ⲧⲉⲡⲥⲱⲙⲁ ⲛ̄ⲓⲁⲱ ⲓⲉⲭⲁ ϩⲱⲥ
ⲛ̄ⲧⲉⲧⲛ̄ⲥⲱⲧⲙ̄ ⲉⲣⲟⲓ ⲛ̄ⲧⲉⲧⲛ̄-
ⲧⲉⲛⲟⲟⲩ ⲛⲁⲓ ⲛ̄ⲁⲑⲱⲛⲁⲑ ⲁⲑⲱⲛⲁⲑ
ⲉⲧⲉ ⲡⲁⲓ ⲡⲉ ⲅⲁⲩⲣⲓⲏⲗ ⲡⲁⲅⲅⲉ-
ⲗⲟⲥ ⲛ̄ⲧⲇⲓⲕⲁⲓⲟⲥⲏⲛⲏ ⲛϥⲓ ϣⲁⲣⲟⲓ
20 ⲛ̄ⲃⲓⲣⲉ ⲙ̄ⲡⲁϩⲱϥ ⲁⲡⲟⲗₒ/ ϩⲁⲙⲏⲛ ⲅ
.....

---

1 *i.e.* στῦλος || **2** · [ⲉⲧ]ⲧⲱⲟⲩⲛ Rossi || **3** *i.e.* ἀπολο(γία) : *l.* ⲁⲡⲟⲗ(ⲗⲱⲛ) Rossi : "Apolo" Amélineau *cf.* p. 9 l. 7 || **4** *i.e.* ἄγγελος | *i.e.* δικαιοσύνη || **6** *i.e.* πν(εῦμ)α | *i.e.* πονηρόν || **7** *i.e.* ἀπολο(γία) : *l.* ⲁⲡⲟⲗ(ⲗⲱⲛ) Rossi : "Apolo" Amélineau *cf.* note to p. 9 l. 7 || **9** ⲥⲁⲙⲓⲏⲗ Kropp, Meyer 1988, 1994 : ⲥⲁⲱⲏⲗ Rossi || **10** ⲟⲃⲙⲓⲏⲗ Kropp, Meyer 1988, 1994 : ⲟⲃⲱⲏⲗ Rossi || **12** *i.e.* ἄγγελος || **12–13** *i.e.* παρακαλεῖν || **14** *i.e.* ἀρχάγγελος || **15** *i.e.* σῶμα | *i.e.* ὡς || **18–19** *i.e.* ἄγγελος || **19** *i.e.* δικαιοσύνη || **20** *i.e.* ἀπολο(γία) : *l.* ⲁⲡⲟⲗ(ⲗⲱⲛ) Rossi : "Apolo" Amélineau *cf.* note p. 9 l. 7 | *i.e.* ἀμήν | ⲅ or ⲓ Rossi || **21** Kropp notes a line here, Rossi does not

to the four pillars of the *abyss, because of their four heads which support the first heaven—request!

*Gabriel, O *angel of righteousness, draw |⁵ your sword in your right hand, pursue every evil spirit—request!

Baēl, Phoēl, Thaēl, Throēl, Thabaēl, Thōēl, Bakhōōl, Thiēl, Aroēl, Afphēl, Arouōēl, Samiēl, |¹⁰ Auēl, Ouēl, Obmiēl, Tharimiēl, Akhēl, Aaroabdēl, listen to me, O mighty angels, for I invoke you by the Lord, O twenty-four *archangels |¹⁵ of the body of Iao Iekha, that you listen to me and send to me Athōnath Athōnath, that is Gabriel, the angel of righteousness, so that he comes to me |²⁰ and he does my work—request—amen (3 ‹times›)! [...]

twenty-second page (page 45)

......ιс...παϥω..
μгρα...αмωθαм в · θα · ⳝ αнωω
αмαι . · ραмωθαм · αϥρωмωθαм
гαυριηλ αθωнαθ αθωнαθ

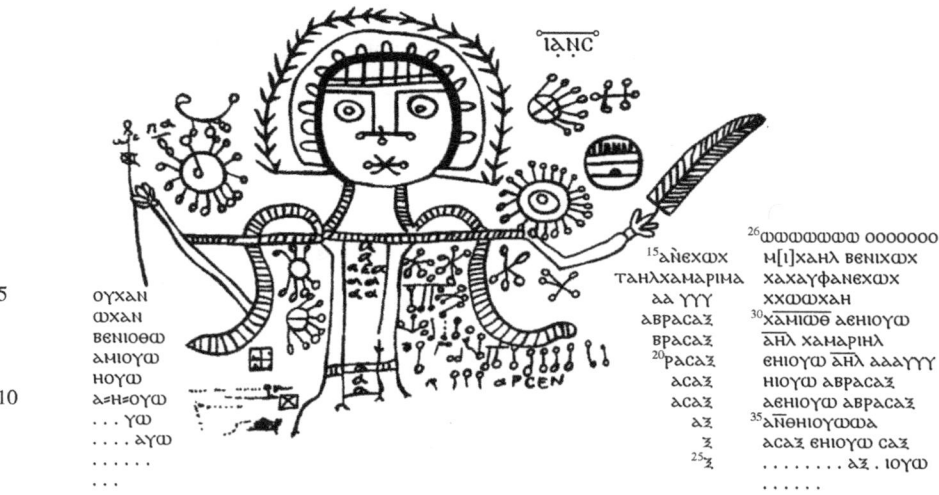

5 ογχαν
   ωχαν
   вενιοθω
   αмιογω
   ηογω
10 α≠η≠ογω
   ...γω
   ....αγω
   ......
   ...

15 αν̄εχωχ
   таηλχαмαριηλ
   αα γγγ
   αвραcαξ
20 вραcαξ
   αcαξ
   αcαξ
   αξ
25 ξ

26 ωωωωωω οοοοοοο
   м[ι]χαηλ вενιχωχ
   χαχαγϥανεχωχ
   χχωωχαη
30 χαмιωθ αεηιογω
   αη̄λ χαмαριηλ
   εηιογω αη̄λ αααγγγ
   ηιογω αвραcαξ
   αεηιογω αвραcαξ
35 αν̄θηιογωωα
   αcαξ εηιογω cαξ
   ....αξ . ιογω
   ......

---

1 ......ιс...παϥω.. Kropp : ......ιс...παϥω.. Rossi ‖ **3** αмαι . Rossi : αмαι · Kropp ‖ **11** cαξ Meyer 1988 ‖ *Above figure* ιαης Kropp does not note ‖ **27** χαχαγϥανεχωχ Kropp : [χα]χαγϥανεχωχ Rossi ‖ **35** αν̄θηιογωωα Kropp : αν̄ εηιογωωα Rossi ‖ **36** αcαξ εηιογω αcαξ Rossi : αcαξ εηιογω cαξ Kropp

... is ... paōō ... mgra ... amōtham, b, Tha, [*kharaktēr*: C]anōō Amai., Ramōtham, Afrōmōtham, *Gabriel, Athōnath, Athōnath.

|above figure Ians

|5, left of figure Oukhan, Ōkhan, Beniothō, Amiouō, Ēouō, |10 aēouō, ...uō, ...auō, ..., ...

|15, right of figure Anekhōkh, Taēlkhamarima, Aauuu,
*Abrasax,
brasax, |20
rasax,
asax,
asax,
ax,
x, |25
x

|26, far right of figure ōōōōōōō, ooooooo,
*Michael, Benikhōkh,
Khakhauphanekhōkh,
Khkhōōkhaē,
|30 Khamiōth, aeēiouō,
Aēl, Khamariēl,
eēiouō, Aēl, aaauuu,
ēiouō, Abrasax,
aeēiouō, Abrasax,
|35 Anthēiouōōa,
Asax, eēiouō, sax,
...ax, ...iouō,
...

KD, EL & MP, edited from Rossi and Kropp; tracing after Rossi 1894.

Image: Since the manuscript no longer survives, we are dependent on the copy made by Rossi, whose general accuracy is nonetheless suggested by its strong resemblance to similar images from surviving Coptic magical manuscripts. The figure is of an angel, holding in his right hand a staff surmounted by a cross or staurogram, and in his left hand a sword or palm branch. His head is surmounted by curly hair and a halo, and two wings, represented as striated tubes, emerge from his shoulders. See Dosoo 2022a: 139–151 for images of angels in Coptic magical manuscripts, and for superhuman beings carrying palm branches in the context of Babylonian incantation bowls (VI–VIII CE) see Vilozny 2015: 147–150, who notes that the motif denotes "positive or protective entities". This image was perhaps to be copied four times to represent the four angels described on p. 1 ll. 1–2, likely to be worn as an amulet during the performance of the ritual and thereafter.

PCM I 13. Rossi's Fragmentary Tractate

Theban region ?　　　　　　　　33 (H) × 12 (W) cm　　　　　　　　VII–VIII CE ?

Other references: P. Biblioteca Nazionale Turin [number unknown]; KYP M3723.
Editions: Rossi 1894: 44 (*ed. pr.*).
Additional commentary: Amélineau 1895: 26; Peyron 1876: 66.
Present location: Lost.
Linguistic description: Sahidic (?).
Contents:
  1. Front ll. 1–29: Invocation for favour (?) (KYP T6571)

Papyrus sheet, now presumably lost. The sheet was found with the text described by Peyron and, following him, Rossi, as a "Gnostic" Tractate (*PCM* I 12). Peyron (1876: 66) describes this as a second, fragmentary, "Gnostic Tractate" (*Trattato gnostico*); as with the larger and better-known manuscript, this is not really an appropriate name for text that is neither a tractate nor 'gnostic', but again we retain the name in deference to this history. Rossi's somewhat confusing presentation of the manuscripts led Amélineau (1895: 26) to mistakenly understand this manuscript as the last page of the larger Tractate codex (*PCM* I 12).

The manuscript was likely acquired along with the larger Tractate codex by Bernardino Drovetti between 1804 and 1818, then sent to Egyptian Museum in 1821. Drovetti would have gifted it to Amedeo Peyron between 1841 and 1870, before his nephew, Bernardino Peyron, gave it to the National Library in Turin prior to 1876. Like the larger Tractate, it seems to have been lost in the fire of 1904.[1]

Rossi (1894: 24) describes it as being "united with" (*unito a*) the Tractate codex, implying that the two belonged together; we thus tentatively propose that it, too, may come from the Theban region, and be dated to the seventh or eighth century. Nothing in its content would speak against this, but both points must be understood as extremely speculative. The dialect of the manuscript, as far as can be determined given its fragmentary state, is Sahidic; in l. 1 ⲙⲉ for ˢⲙⲛ̄ may suggest the influence of a Middle Egyptian dialect of the type demonstrated in the 'Heidelberg Library' (see pp. 261–262).

Since the manuscript has been lost, we reproduce here the edition of Rossi, suggesting alternative readings based on parallels where appropriate.

---

[1] *Cf.* the discussion of the origin of *PCM* I 12 (pp. 171–174) for fuller details and references.

front

```
         . . . . . . ΟΥ ΝΑΙ ΙΑⲰ ΜΕ ΤΕΚϬΟΜ . . .
         . . . . . ΤΕΚΧΑΡ . Α . . . . ΑΔⲰΝΑΙ . . .
         . . . . . . . . ΕΛΟΕΙ . . . ΜΠΕΚϬΟΜ . . .
         . . . . . . . . . ΝΤΑϨⲰΒ Ε . . .
  5      . . . . . . . . . ϤΝΝΕΥΝ . . . ΧΕ . . .
         . . . . . . . . . . ΝΤΕ . . . Ε . . .
         . . . . . . . . . . . . . . . . . . . . .
         . . . . . . . . . . . . . . . . . . . . .
         . . . . . . . . . . . . ΒⲰΛ . . .
 10      . . . . ΝΕ . . . ΑΥⲰ ΤΟΥΜΕΡ . Τ ΘΕ . . .
         . . . ΜΕΡΙΤ ΝϢΕΕΡΕ ΑΥⲰ ΤΑ . . ΑΡ . ΝΑ
         . ΑΚ . . ΧΑΡΙⲤ . . . ΝΕΚΑΓΑΘΟⲤ M̄N̄ N
         . . . . . ΑΥⲰ ΡⲰΜΕ ΝΙΜ ΕΤ . . ⲤⲰ ΕΒΟΛ . . .
         . . . ΝΕΤΝ . . . . . . . . . . . . ΤΝ . . .
 15      . . . . . ΑϢΤ ΤΗΡΟΥ ϨΙ ΟΥⲤΟΠ Ν . . .
         . . . . . . . . . . ΧΕ ϯΟΥΚΕ . . ΚΝ . . .
         . . . . . . . . . . ΑΝ [ ca. 14 ] ΕΡΧΙ
         . . . . . . . . . . . . . . . . . . . . .
         . . . . . . . . . . . . . . . . Β . Ϩ . . Κ
 20      . . . . . . . . . . . . . . Ε . ΙⲰ ΙⲰ ΑϨ . . .
         . . . . . . . . . . ⲤΑϨ ΙⲰΑ ΙⲰΑ
         ϯⲤΑϨ . Ε . . . . . . . . ΤΕΝΕΤ . . M̄N̄ ΝΕΤΕ . . .
         . . . Ν . . Ο . . . . . . . . ΕΤΟΥΑΑΒ ΕΤϢ . . .
         . . . Ν . ΕΙΚΑ . . ΧΕ ΕΜ . Τ . . ΕΠ . . .
 25      . . . . . ΡⲰΜΕ ΝΙΜ ΕΤΝΑΥ . . .
         . . . . . . ΟΟΥϨ . . . Α . ΕΝΟ . M̄N̄ Χ . . .
         . . . . M̄N̄ Ν . ϢΠΡΕ . . . ΚΕ Ν̄Ⲱ . . .
```

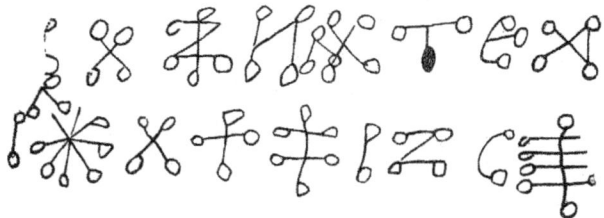

---

1 *l.* ΑΜΟΥ ? ‖ **2** *l.* ΤΕΚ-ΧΑΡΙⲤ ? ‖ **10** *l.* ΤΟΥΜΕΡΙΤ | *i.e.* ⁵N̄-Τ-Ϩε ‖ **12** *i.e.* ΧΑΡΙⲤ | *i.e.* ἀγαθός ‖ **13** *l.* ⁵ΕΤ-ΝΑ-ⲤⲰ ΕΒΟΛ Ν̄Ϩ̄ΗΤ=Ϥ ? ‖ **15** *l.* ⁵Ν̄=ⲤΕ-ΟΥΑϢ=Τ ? ‖ **16** *i.e.* διώκειν ? ‖ **22** *l.* ϯⲰϢ ΕϨΡΑΙ ΕΡΟΚ ΝΤΕΤΕΝΡΑΝ M̄N̄ ΝΕΤΕΝ… ? ‖ **23** *l.* ΝΕΤΕΝΦΥΛΑΚΤΗΡΙΟΝ ΕΤΟΥΑΑΒ ? ‖ **26** *i.e.* ⁵ⲤⲰΟΥϨ ? ‖ **27** *l.* ϢΗΡΕ ?

... come? to me, *Iao with your *power ... your favour? ... *Adonai ... *Eloei ... of your power ... my? work? ... |⁵ ... |¹⁰ ... and they love me like ... beloved daughter and ... favour ... your good ones and ... and everyone who will? drink [from? it?] your (pl.)... |¹⁵ ... [and they will all] desire? me? at once... drive away? ... |²⁰ Iō Iō Ah ... Iōa Iōa ... and your? ... the holy ... that ... |²⁵ everyone who sees ... and ... and ... child? ...

(*kharaktēres*: IXⰜИMTEXI)
(*kharaktēres*: I✶X+ ǂ IZC ≢)

KD, EL & MP, edited from Rossi 1894; tracing after Rossi 1894.

1–3. "... come? to me, Iaō with your power ... your favour? ... Adonai ... Eloei ... of your power" *Cf.* the love spell in P.Köln Inv. 1470 (Weber 1975; KYP M353) ll. 1–2 "Come to me, come to me, O holy unique one! Come to me Iao in his power, Adonai in his beauty, king in his grace, *Sabaoth in his peace!" (ⲁⲙⲟⲩ ⲛⲁⲓ ⲁⲙⲟⲩ ⲛⲁⲓ ⲡⲓϩⲁⲅⲓⲟⲥ ⲛⲁⲑⲁⲛⲁⲧⲟⲥ ⲙⲛⲙⲁⲁϥ ⲁⲙⲟⲩ ⲛⲁⲓ ⲓⲁⲱ ϩⲛ- ⲧⲉϥϭⲟⲙ ⲁⲇⲱⲛⲏ ϩⲙ ⲡⲉϥⲥⲁ ⲡⲉⲣⲟ ϩⲛ ⲧⲉϥⲭⲁⲣⲓⲥ ⲥⲁⲃⲁⲱⲑ ϩⲛ ⲧⲉϥⲉⲓⲣⲏⲛⲏ). Compare the similar, earlier (fourth century) Greek and Coptic favour spells discussed in Zellmann-Rohrer/Love 2022: 272–274.

27. ⲙⲛ ⲛ . ϣⲏⲣⲉ : **"and ... child?"** Perhaps restore something like "the entire race of Adam and all the children of Zoe"; *cf.* the note to *PCM* 25 p. 7 ll. 12–14.

PCM I 14. Invocation for unclear purposes

Provenance unknown   18.8 (H) × 7.5 (W) cm   VII–VIII CE ?

Other references: LACMA MA 80.202.214;[1] TM 642006;[2] KYP M8; Bélanger Sarrazain #88.
Editions: Dieleman 2006 (*ed. pr.*); Bélanger Sarrazin forthcoming a: appendix 4, no. 9.
Translations: Dieleman 2006; Bélanger Sarrazin forthcoming a: appendix 4, no. 9.
Additional commentary: Martín-Hernández/Torallas Tovar 2014: 796, no. 10; Dosoo 2022a: 142; Love 2022c: 630, n. 44.
Present location: Los Angeles County Museum of Art (LACMA).
Image: https://collections.lacma.org/node/245077.
Linguistic description: Sahidic.
Contents:
1. Front ll. 1–14: Invocation (KYP T617)

Incomplete oblong fragment of a pottery plate. The top, bottom, and right side are missing and the faded text is written along the remaining surface, with the right and upper margin lost. The plate was of high quality craftsmanship, likely flat, with a red, polished surface.[3] The ostracon's fragmentary state makes it unclear if it should be considered a recipe or an applied text. The object was a gift of Jerome F. Snyder to the LACMA, acquired by the collection on the 31st December 1980.[4]

The script, written in a faded black ink, is an undecorated, alphabetic, largely bilinear uncial, at times sloping to the right. ⲩ resembles a Latin V; the ⲁ is rounded, with the upper part of the bowl somewhat separated from the stalk, and the ⲙ very wide and curved; the ⲃ is enlarged, with a very flat base. The highly informal nature of the hand makes dating difficult; Dieleman does not attempt to date the piece. The combination of the rounded ⲁ and enlarged, flat-bottomed ⲃ leads us to tentatively suggest a seventh or eighth century date for this piece, since these are both typical of documentary texts from this period.[5] The text would seem to be written in standard Sahidic; no dialectal irregularities are present in the surviving text.

---

[1] On the LACMA website, the photograph of the manuscript can be found under the siglum MA 80.202.213. This siglum and the description of the object, however, belong to another object than the one depicted.

[2] The siglum provided by TM, MA 80.202.192, is invalid.

[3] Dieleman 2006: 20.

[4] Personal communication with the LACMA, information from internal museum database, 27/9/2022; *cf.* Dieleman 2006: 20.

[5] See the plates in Stegemann 1936: 9–13; *cf. P.Pisentius* 35 (late VI–early VII CE) for an example of a broadly similar hand.

front

ⲥⲟⲩⲭ ⲙ̣[… ?]
ⲫⲣⲓⲝ : ⲫⲣⲱ[… ?]
ⲁⲣ ⲁⲑⲁ ⲫ[… ?]
ⲥⲁⲣⲙⲁⲧⲁⲣ ⲁⲑⲁ[… ?]
5   ⲓⲱⲃⲏⲑ ⲓⲱⲫ[… ?]
ⲟⲥ †ⲡⲁⲣⲁⲕⲁⲗ[ⲉⲓ … ?]
ϫⲉⲕⲁⲁⲥ ϩⲛ̄ ⲧ[ⲉⲩⲛⲟⲩ … ?]
ⲣⲉ ⲡⲕ̄ⲩ̄ⲃⲁⲕ[… ?]
ⲥⲱ̄ ⲙ̄ⲡⲁⲡⲁⲧ [… ?]
10 ⲙⲟⲟⲩ † ⲛⲟⲩ[… ?]
ϩⲏⲧ ϫⲟⲩⲉ .. [… ?]
[… ?]
[… ?]
.. ⲛⲏⲍⲉ̣

3 ⲁ̄ⲣ̄ . Dieleman ‖ **5** ⲓ̄ⲱ̄ⲫ[ⲟⲃⲏⲑ] cf. *GEMF* 31/*PGM* I.253–254 Dieleman ‖ **6** i.e. παρακαλεῖν : *l.* †ⲡⲁⲣⲁⲕⲁⲗ[ⲉⲓ ⲙⲙⲟⲕ/ⲙⲙⲱⲧⲛ] Dieleman ‖ **7** *l.* ϫⲉ ⲕⲁⲁ⸗ⲥ ϩⲛ ⲧ-… ? Dieleman ‖ **8** or ⲡⲕ̄ⲩ̄ⲃⲁⲕ ? ⲕ̣ very narrow: *l.* ⲣⲉⲡ-ⲕⲩⲣⲓ(ⲟⲩ) or ⲣⲉⲡ-ⲕⲩ́(ⲣⲓⲉ) Dieleman ‖ **9** ⲥⲱ̄ ⲙ̄ⲡⲁⲡⲁⲧ or *i.e.* ζῴ(διον) : ⲥⲱⲏ . ⲁⲡⲁⲧ *i.e.* Ζωή Dieleman ‖ **10** *l.* † ⲛ-ⲟⲩ- : or †-ⲛⲟⲩϫⲉ ⲉⲃⲟⲗ Dieleman ‖ **11** ϫⲟⲩⲉ or ϫ̣ⲟⲩⲉ Dieleman.

Soukh M[...] Phrix Phrō[...] ar Atha Ph[...] Sarmatar Atha[...] |⁵ Iōbēth Iōph[...]os, I invoke [you ...] that as [soon as ...] ... drinks from the *cup ... |¹⁰ water? give a... (*kharaktēres*: ✴✹ H...)

KD, EL & MP, edited from photograph; tracing by KD and JS.

1. ⲥⲟⲩⲭ : "**Soukh**" The name Soukh also appears in the curse *PCM* I 27 front l. 24, 26, back l. 4.
3. ⲁⲣ ⲁⲑⲁ : "**]ar Atha**" There is a dark spot in the gap between the two words, noted by Dieleman as an unidentified letter. We interpret it as a smudge, but it may be a small letter, such as an o or an ⲁ, or else a mid-point.
5. ⲓⲱⲃⲏⲉ ⲓⲱⲫ : "**Iōbēth Iōph[**" Perhaps the opening of the *Ērbeth*-logos, for which see the notes to *PCM* I 4 p. 5 ll. 3–5; this may suggest this is a curse or love spell. The reference to someone drinking water in ll. 9–10 may suggest a love spell in which the target is to drink empowered water.
9–10. ⲙ̄ⲡⲁⲡⲁⲧ [. ?] ⲙⲟⲟⲩ : "**from the cup ... water?**" Perhaps restore, for example, "the cup that is filled with water" (ⲙ̄ⲡⲁⲡⲁⲧ [ⲉⲧⲙⲏϩ ⲙ̄]ⲙⲟⲟⲩ); *cf. PCM* I 3 front col. 2 l. 31: "their twelve bowls filled with water" (ⲧⲉⲩⲙ̄·ⲓ̄ⲃ̄ : ⲙ̄ⲡⲓⲁⲗⲉ ⲙⲉϩ ⲙ̄ⲟⲟⲩ).
12–13. Dieleman describes these lines as "washed out".
Image: The damaged image here is of an angel, holding a staff topped with a cross in its right hand, one wing and one foot visible before the break; *cf.* Dosoo 2022a: 139–151.

PCM I 15. Narrative charm for healing the eye

Deir el Bakhit, Thebes ? 8.6 (H) × 25.2 (W) × 0.9 (D) cm VII–VIII CE

Other references: BM EA 29528; TM 82864; *O.Brit.Mus.Copt.* 27; *P.Rain.UnterrichtKopt.* (*MPER N.S.* 18) 198; KYP M335; Bélanger Sarrazin #153.

Editions: Hall 1905: no. 27; von Lemm 1908: no. LIV; Kosack 1974: no. 68; Hasitzka 1990: no. 198; Zellmann-Rohrer forthcoming.

Translations: Hall 1905: no. 27; Kropp 1931: II no. 18 (German); Zellmann-Rohrer forthcoming.

Additional commentary: Bélanger Sarrazin forthcoming a: chapter 2.

Present location: London, British Museum.

Image: https://www.britishmuseum.org/collection/object/Y_EA29528

Linguistic description: Sahidic (non-standard).

Contents:

1. Front ll. 1–8, back ll. 1–5: Jesus-pupil narrative charm for healing the eye (KYP T392)

Broken wooden tablet with a narrative charm written as a palimpsest. At most half of the original height remains; the breakage took place prior to the writing of the charm, which seems to be complete. The manuscript was acquired by the British Museum from Jean d'Anastasy in 1839. The tablet has raised edges, and one remaining drilled hole each on the left and right-hand sides for binding it to other tablets to form a codex. Three hands are discernible (m^{1-3}): m^1 is responsible for line 5 of the back (presumably the only surviving line of the original text), m^2 wrote the charm, and m^3 wrote line 8 of the front, perhaps in an attempt to copy the contents of line 7.

M^2 is a right-sloping bimodal majuscule with some tendencies towards quadrilinearity. ⲏ has its minuscule form, while ⲙ is angular, with a shallow vertex. ⲉ is often ligatured to preceding and following letters, with a distinctive, enlarged form where ligatured to a previous letter. ⲃ is very large, and the oblique strokes of ⲕ are separated from the vertical. Supralineation is used inconsistently for abbreviations and autosyllabic consonants.

We accept the proposal of Agnes Mihálykó[1] that the hand of this manuscript is identical to that found on a liturgical prayer for the vesting of a monk from the Monastery of Apa Paulos (Deir el-Bakhīt) on the west bank of Thebes.[2] Alongside

---

[1] Private communication (11/5/2023).

[2] This manuscript is an ostracon made up of BM EA 5892 + EA14241 + *O.Bachit.* 929. The British Museum pieces are published in Hall 1905: 23, plate 17 no. 2, with a translation in Winlock/ Crum 1929: 139–140. *O.Bachit.* 929 may be consulted online at https://www.koptolys.gwi.uni-muenchen.de/showOstraka.php?id=520. A publication of both pieces is in preparation by Agnes Mihálykó; *cf.* Mihálykó 2019: 130, 148, 293, 304. As noted by Winlock and Crum, the prayer for

the general similarity of letterforms, we note the specific ⲉϯ and ⲁ/ⲭ+ⲉ ligatures found in both manuscripts.³ This shared scribal hand strongly implies that this manuscript also comes from that site, although this cannot be proven through what remains of the acquisition history of the two pieces.⁴ It is therefore likely that the copyist was a monk belonging to the monastery.

The pottery from Deir el-Bakhit can be dated to between the sixth and tenth centuries,⁵ but the ostracon in the same hand as *PCM* I 15 has been dated more narrowly to the seventh to eighth centuries. We likewise propose the same range for this manuscript, noting similar hands in dated or dateable manuscripts from this range.⁶

The text is Sahidic with some common deviations from the literary standard, such as ⲃ for ϥ; there are a few surprising or unattested writings of words which would not seem to be dialectal, but rather idiosyncrasies of the copyist. The use of the word ⲗⲁϭⲉ with the sense "to heal" in back l. 2, if read correctly, may imply specifically southern dialectal influence (*cf.* Crum CD 151b).

Note that Hall & Hasitzka incorrectly begin l. 6 at the word ⲡⲟⲟϩ, assigning earlier words to l. 5. Hasitzka numbers the lines continuously, so that our verso l. 1 corresponds to her l. 9.

We note with particular gratitude the comments of Michael Zellmann-Rohrer on an earlier draft of this edition.

---

vesting finds a close parallel in the Bohairic prayer published in Tuki 1761: ⲡϥ–ⲡϥⲁ. On ostraca from Deir el-Bakhīt more generally, see Hodak 2012.

³ ⲉϯ: *PCM* I 15 front ll. 2, 3, back ll. 2, 4; BM EA 5892 + EA142411. 13; ⲁ/ⲭ+ⲉ: *PCM* I 15 front ll. 1, 2, 7, back l. 3; *O.Bachit.* 929 l. 3.

⁴ Anastasy's sale catalogue, held in the British Museum (AES Ar.246), records provenances only for papyri, and thus not for *PCM* I 15; *cf.* Zellmann-Rohrer forthcoming, who nonetheless proposes a Theban origin for this piece. For Anastasy's sale, *cf.* Dosoo 2016: 253 (with further references). *O.Bachit.* 929 was excavated in situ at Deir el-Bakhīt in 2008 (*cf.* n. 2 above), while BM EA 5892 + EA14241 was acquired by the British Museum from the dealer Joseph Sams (1784–1860) in 1934; Sams himself likely purchased it in Egypt during his visit of 1832–1833 (*cf.* Bierbrier 2012: 485).

⁵ Hodak 2012: 735.

⁶ *Cf. P.Pisentius* 21 (*ca.* 590–632 CE); *P.Mon.Phoib.Test.* 2 (634 CE); IFAO P.Edfou Jarre 13, 19 (both late VII CE; TM 900981 & 874490).

front

m² ☧ ⲁϥⲡⲁⲣⲁⲅⲉ ⲇⲉ ⲛ̄ϭⲓ ⲓ̄ⲥ̄ ϩⲓⲃⲟⲗ ⲙ̄ⲡⲣⲟ ⲙ̄ⲡⲡⲁⲣⲁⲇⲓⲥⲟⲥ
[ⲁ]ϥⲛⲁⲩ ⲉⲩⲉⲗⲟⲟⲗⲉ ⲉⲥⲣⲓⲙⲉ ⲉⲥϯ ⲣⲙⲉⲓⲉⲓ · ⲡⲉϫⲁϥ ϫⲉ ⲁ-
ϩⲣⲟ ⲧⲉⲗⲟⲟⲗⲉ ⲉⲧⲉⲣⲓⲙⲉ ⲧⲉϯ [ⲣ]ⲙⲉⲓⲉ ⲡⲉϫⲁⲥ ϫⲉ ⲡⲁϫⲟⲉⲓⲥ
ⲁⲩⲛ̄ⲧ̣ⲧⲁⲧ ⲉϩⲣⲁⲓ ϩⲙ̄ ⲡⲕⲁϩ ⲁϥⲙⲁϣⲧ ⲉⲡⲁⲃⲁⲗ ⲡⲣⲱⲣ ϩⲉ-
5 ⲛ ⲉⲓⲧ` ⲧⲁϭⲟ ⲙ̄ⲡⲁⲟⲩⲟⲉⲓⲛ ⲁⲓ̈ⲃⲓ ⲛ̄ⲛⲁⲃⲁⲗ ⲉϩⲣⲁⲓ̈ ⲉⲧⲡⲉ ⲡⲉ-
ϫⲁⲓ̈ ϫ̣ⲉ ⲡⲣⲏ ⲙ̄ⲡⲣ̄ⲧⲱⲣⲉ ⲡⲟⲟϩ ⲙ̄ⲡⲣⲱ̄ϣⲁ ⲉⲛⲱⲭ ⲡⲉⲅⲣⲁⲙⲙⲁⲧⲉⲩⲥ ⲙ̄ⲡ̄ⲣⲛⲟⲩϫⲉ ⲙ̄ⲡⲉⲕⲕⲁϣ ⲉⲡⲉⲕ-
m³   ⲙ̄ⲡⲣⲛⲟⲩϫⲉ̣ ⲟⲕⲥⲁⲟⲓ . ⲁⲛ . . . . .

---

back

m² ⲙⲉⲗⲁ ϣⲁⲛⲧⲉⲙⲓⲭⲁⲏⲗ ⲉⲓ ⲉⲃⲟⲗ ϩⲛ̄ ⲧⲡⲉ ⲛϥⲗⲁϭ̣ⲉ̣ ⲉⲡⲁ-
[ⲃ]ⲁ̣ⲗ ⲛ̄ⲧⲉⲩⲛⲟⲩ ⲉⲧⲙ̄ⲙⲁⲩ ⲁⲙⲓⲭⲁⲏⲗ ⲉⲓ ⲉⲃⲟⲗ ϩⲛ̄ ⲧⲡⲉ
[ⲡⲉϫ]ⲁϥ ϫⲉ ⲡϫⲓ ϥⲛⲁⲗⲟ ⲡⲉϩⲗⲟⲥⲧⲛ̄ ϥⲛⲁⲃⲱⲗ ⲉ̣[ⲃⲟⲗ]
ϩⲙ ⲡⲣⲁⲛ ⲙ̄ⲡⲉⲓⲱⲧ ⲙⲛ̄ ⲡϣⲏⲣⲉ ⲙⲛ̄ ⲡⲉⲡ̄ⲛ̄ⲁ̄ ⲉⲧⲟⲩⲁⲁⲃ

5 m¹   ⟦☧ . . . . ⟧ # . . ϥ̣ . . . ϩⲙ̄ⲙ̄ ⲡⲣⲁ̣ⲛ

---

front **1** *i.e.* παράγειν δέ : . . . . Hasitzka : "stepped out" Hall : *i.e.* παραβαίνειν Kropp : ….ⲡⲁⲣⲁ.. von Lemm : [ⲁ]ϥⲡⲁⲣⲁⲕⲉ Zellmann-Rohrer | *l.* ⲓ(ⲏⲥⲟⲩ)ⲥ | *i.e.* παράδεισος ‖ **2** [ⲁϥⲛ]ⲁⲩ Hasitzka : [ⲁϥⲛⲁⲩ] von Lemm | ⲟⲩⲉⲗⲟⲟⲗⲉ Hall, Hasitzka : *i.e.* ᵂⲟⲩ-ⲉⲓⲟⲩⲗ Kropp, von Lemm, Zellmann-Rohrer | *i.e.* ᵂⲣⲙⲉⲓⲏ : ⲣⲙⲉ[ⲓⲉ] Hall, Hasitzka : ⲣⲙ̄ⲉ[ⲓⲉ] von Lemm ‖ **3** [ϩⲣⲟ] von Lemm | ⲧⲉⲗⲟⲟⲗⲉ *cf.* note : "vine (or grape)" Hall : *l.* ⲧ-ⲉⲓⲟⲩⲗ von Lemm, Kropp, Zellmann-Rohrer : [ⲧⲉⲗⲟⲟⲗⲉ] von Lemm | ⲧⲉⲣⲓⲙⲉ Zellmann-Rohrer | *i.e.* ᵂⲛ̄ⲧⲉ⸗ᵒ-ϯ ᵂⲣⲙⲉⲓⲏ : ⲣⲙⲉⲓⲉⲓ Hall : ⲣⲙⲉⲓⲉ von Lemm ‖ **4** *i.e.* ᵂⲁ⸗ϥ-ⲛⲧ⸗ⲟ ? *cf.* ⲛⲧⲁ⸗ in Kasser CDC p. 177a *s.v.* ⲉⲓⲛⲉ : ⲁⲩⲛⲧ[…] "cast down" Hall : ⲁⲩⲛ̄ ⲡ[ⲥⲟⲧⲉ] ? "… was cast upon the earth" ("… auf die Erde herabgeworfen") Kropp ? : *l.* ⲁⲩⲛ ⲡϫⲓ "they cast down a splinter ("ein Splitter wurde hinabgeworfen") Hasitzka : [ⲁⲩⲛⲧ . . .] von Lemm : ⲁⲩⲛ̄ ⲡϫ̣ⲓ "the mote was kicked (up)" Zellmann-Rohrer | *i.e.* ᵂⲁ⸗ϥ-ⲙⲁϣ⸗ⲧ (‹ ⲙⲓϣⲉ) ⲉ-ⲡⲁ-ⲃⲁⲗ : "he pierced my eye" ("Er durchbohrte mein Auge") Hall, Kropp | ⲡⲣⲱⲣ ϩⲉ : ⲡⲣⲱⲙⲉ Hall, Hasitzka, Kropp, von Lemm, Zellmann-Rohrer ‖ **4–5** *i.e.* ᵂϩⲛ̄ ? ‖ **5** *i.e.* ᵂⲉⲓⲁⲧ⸗ⲟ ⲧⲁⲕⲟ ? : ⲛⲉⲓⲧⲧⲁϭⲱ : *i.e.* -ⲧⲁⲗϭⲟ Hall : *l.* ⲛⲉ⸗ⲓ-ⲧⲁⲗϭⲟ "I healed" ("ich heilte") Hasitzka : [ⲛⲉⲓⲧⲧⲁϭⲱ] von Lemm : *i.e.* ᵂⲛⲉ⸗ϥ-ⲧⲁⲗϭⲟ "(he) could not heal" Zellmann-Rohrer | *i.e.* ᵂⲙ̄-ⲡⲁ-ⲟⲩⲱⲧⲛ "in my wound" Hall, Hasitzka : ⲙⲡⲁⲟⲩⲟⲧⲛ von Lemm ‖ **6** [ϫⲁⲓ̈ ϫⲉ] von Lemm | *i.e.* ᵂⲙ̄ⲡⲣ-ⲧⲱⲣϣ *cf.* Crum CD 432b : "set" Hall ‖ **7** *i.e.* γραμματεύς ‖ **8** ⲙ̄ⲡⲣⲛⲟⲩϫⲉ ("followed by confused letters") Hall, Hasitzka : ⲙ̄ⲡⲣⲛϩ . . ⲁⲛⲟⲕ ⲥⲁϩ . ⲛⲛϣ . . . . . von Lemm : ⲙ̄ⲡⲣⲛⲟⲩϫⲟ ⲕⲥⲁⲁⲥ ⲉⲡⲉⲕⲙⲉⲗⲁ Zellmann-Rohrer
back **1** *i.e.* μέλαν | ⲗⲁϭⲉ *cf.* Crum CD 151b : *l.* ⲧⲁⲗϭⲟ "healed" ("heilte") Hall, Kropp, Hasitzka : ⲛϥⲧⲁⲗϭ̣ⲟ̣ Zellmann-Rohrer | ⲉⲡⲁ- : ⲉⲡ[ⲁ] von Lemm ‖ **2** [ⲃⲁⲗ] von Lemm ‖ **3** ⲡϫⲓ *cf.* Crum CD 747b *s.v.* ϫⲏ : "wound" (Wunde) Kropp : Hall does not translate ‖ **4** *i.e.* πν(εῦμ)α | ⲉⲧⲟⲩⲁⲁⲃ corrected from ⲉⲧⲣⲩⲁⲁⲃ ‖ **5** Hall, Hasitzka, von Lemm do not transcribe

|^(m2) ⳨ And Jesus went out from the door of Paradise. He saw a pupil? crying, shedding tears. He said, "What is wrong with you, O pupil?, that you are crying, that you are shedding tears?"

She said, "My Lord, I was brought down upon the earth. He struck me in my eye, the *binding? in |⁵ my eye destroys? my light. I raised my eyes up to heaven, I said, 'O sun, do not redden?; O moon, do not rise; Enoch the scribe, do not put your pen in your |⁸, ᵐ³ {do not put} ... |^(back, m2) ink until *Michael comes out from heaven and heals my eye!' At that moment, Michael came out from heaven. He said, 'The mote will heal, the darkness will be undone, in the name of the Father and the Son and the Holy Spirit!'"

|⁵, ᵐ¹ [erased passage] ⳨ ... in the name.

RBS, KD, EL, MP & JS, edited from photograph.

---

front 2. ⲉⲩⲉⲗⲟⲟⲗⲉ : "a pupil?" Hall and Hasitzka opt for the translation "vine" or "grape" (Crum CD 54b). Here we translate "pupil" (κόρη), a sense attested in the unpublished glossary P.Mich. inv. 4949 (Crum CD 55a); the word may be a metaphorical extension of the sense "grape", or else related to (or an error for) ⲁⲗⲱ ("pupil"), literally "maiden". Von Lemm understands ⲉⲓⲟⲩⲗ ("deer", Crum CD 77a), *cf.* the similar story in *BKU* I 1 (KYP M76) front col. 1 ll. 1–18 in which Jesus heals a doe in labour. Vycichl (CED 41a) understands this specifically as a hypothetical female form, ⲉⲓⲟⲟⲗⲉ, with ⲓ replaced by (miscopied as?) ⲗ. Kropp and Zellmann-Rohrer follow him. Given this parallel, it is possible that ⲉⲗⲟⲟⲗⲉ represents a transmission error.

4–5. ⲁϥⲙⲁϣⲧ ⲉⲡⲁⲃⲁⲗ ⲡⲣⲱⲣ ϩⲉ : "he struck me in my eye, the binding?" This passage presents several difficulties of comprehension. Hall translates "it has pierced my eye; the man ...". Kropp translates likewise, suggesting that "the man" here refers to a hunter who has left the deer injured. Hasitzka translates "O Man, I healed my piercing" ("O Mensch, ich heilte meine Durchbohrung"). Zellmann-Rohrer translates "mankind (could not heal my sight)" (*i.e.*, ⲛⲉϥⲧⲁⲗϭⲟ), suggesting that the praeterite has a negative sense here. The word ⲣⲱⲣ, which we translate as "binding", is attested as a verb in Kasser CDC 49a *s.v.* ⲣⲟⲣ, and also in Westendorf HWB p. 534 *s.v.* ⲣⲱⲣ.

6. ⲙ̄ⲡⲣ̄ⲧⲱⲣⲉ : "redden" Probably implying "to set" (that is, the sun reddens as it sets).

6–7. ⲉⲛⲱⲭ ⲡⲉⲅⲣⲁⲙⲙⲁⲧⲉⲩⲥ : "Enoch the scribe" Enoch is often referred to as the "scribe of righteousness" (ⲡⲉⲅⲣⲁⲙⲙⲁⲧⲉⲩⲥ ⲛ̄ⲇⲓⲕⲁⲓⲟⲥⲩⲛⲏ) in Coptic literature, a title which first appears in 1 Enoch 12.4 (Isaac in Charlesworth 1983: 19). Pseudo-Chrysostom, *On the Four Bodiless Living Creatures* 11, 27 (CC 177; Wasink 1991: 30, 34 (text), 30–31, 34–35 (trans.)) describes how God translated Enoch into an immortal being (*cf.* Genesis 5.24), giving him the "pen-case of salvation" and the books of the angel Mefriel, his predecessor as scribe, which he copied in six days (*cf.* 2 Enoch 22.8–23.6, in which Mefriel is named 'Vrevoil'; Isaac in Charlesworth 1983: 138–141) before returning to heaven, where he has since recorded the deeds of humankind. Pseudo-Theodosius of Alexandria, *On Saint Michael* (CC 387; Budge 1915: 345, 909 (trans.)) repeats this outline, noting in addition that the Archangel Michael presents the record to God; *cf.* Pearson 2000: 226–228.

7. ⲉⲡⲉⲕ- : "in your" There are traces of one or two letters at the end of this line, perhaps belonging to an underlying text over which the present one is written as a palimpsest.

8. ⲙ̄ⲡⲣⲛⲟⲩϫⲉ ⲟⲕⲥⲁⲟⲓ . ⲁⲛ... : "{do not put} ..." This line seems to have been added after the writing of the preceding by a different, less regular hand. It apparently copies the text in the line above it, although the letters following ⲙ̄ⲡⲣⲛⲟⲩϫⲉ are too idiosyncratic to be certain that this is the case.

back 5. [[+ . . . .]] ⳨ . . ϛ . . . ϩⲙ̄ ⲡⲣⲁⲛ : "[erased passage] ⳨ ... in the name" This seems to be written in a different hand, and partially erased, in parts by washing, in parts by striking through the text. This may have been the original text of the tablet, before the current main text (in m²) was added, likely after the tablet was broken.

PCM I 16. Ostraca containing Horus-Isis narrative love charm

Provenance unknown   H × W: 21.5 × 12 cm (1); 22.5 × 19 (2); 19.5 × 11 (3)   VII–VIII CE

Other references: Brigham Young University Harold B. Lee Library inv. 76, 77, 81; TM 756246; *O.BYU Mag.* 1–3; KYP M109.

Editions: Blumell/Dosoo 2018 (*ed. pr.*) [B/D].

Translations: Blumell/Dosoo 2018.

Additional commentary: Richter 2015a: 87, n. 5; Hevesi 2019; Bélanger Sarrazin forthcoming a: chapter 2.

Present location: Provo, Brigham Young University.

Image: Blumell/Dosoo 2018: 213–215.

Linguistic description: Sahidic (non-standard).

Contents:

1. Ostraca 1–3 (ll. 1–40): Love spell containing Horus-Isis narrative charm (KYP T298)

Complete formulary written continuously over the convex sides of three separate pottery ostraca with black ink. The ostraca were inscribed only after the vessels to which they belonged were broken.[1] Each ostracon is fully covered with a single column of legible text with no significant margins or blank spaces, except for *O.BYU Mag.* 3—the ostracon containing the end of the text—whose lower half is blank. The provenance of the manuscript is unknown. Aziz Atiya, professor of Languages and History at the University of Utah, likely acquired the ostraca in Egypt before donating them to the Harold B. Lee Library, Brigham Young University, where the ostraca are kept today. According to the catalogue records of the library, they were donated in 1980, however Atiya himself signed the catalogue only on the 31st of December 1981.[2]

The text is written in an upright majuscule, bilinear and bimodal, without ligatures. Although the scribe generally respects the space between letters and lines, the letterforms are irregular; the hand can be described as an alphabetic or evolving hand, according to Cribiore's typology.[3] ⲁ is written as a curved vertical line open to the right, with a small rounded bowl attached to its upper part. ⲩ is written as Latin V and ⲗ as an inverted V. The ⲙ and ⲉ are very curved, and the oblique strokes of ⲕ, written in a single stroke, touch the vertical stroke. The letters are undecorated and unligatured. As in *PCM* I 20, the copyist does not use supralineation, but does make use of diaeresis above the iota. The copyist makes

---

[1] Blumell/Dosoo 2018: n. 12.
[2] For acquisition information, see Blumell/Dosoo 2018: 202–203, n. 11.
[3] Cribiore 1996: 112; *cf.* Blumell/Dosoo 2018: 204 n. 16.

use of the tricolon to separate *voces magicae* at the beginning of the text, and begins each ostracon by marking a simple cross.

The informality of the hand makes dating very difficult; as Blumell and Dosoo (2018: 204) note, the hand is very similar to that of Tsie, preserved in the archive of the monk Frange from the eighth century.[4] It is also similar to a group of informal hands found in other Coptic magical texts, discussed by Choat and Gardner in their publication of *P.Macq.* I 1, which they date to the seventh or eighth centuries.[5] At the same time, informal hands can display considerable similarities over large spans of time; Naqlun N. 45/95 (van der Vliet 2000; KYP M64) also shows many similar features, despite being dated to the fifth century based on its archeological context. We thus tentatively agree with Blumell and Dosoo's proposal of a seventh or eighth century date.

The dialect is a highly non-standard form of Sahidic, with several surprising features noted by Blumell and Dosoo (2018: 204–205). There is considerable haplography, confusion of visually similar letters (*e.g.*, ⲉ/ⲥ ostracon 1 l. 6), interchange of ⲃ/ϥ, omission of ϩ, the writing of two consonants with the same point of articulation with a single letter (ⲙⲃ/ⲙⲡ > ⲙ, ⲛⲧ > ⲛ/ⲧ, ⲧⲥ > ⲥ), the writing of /ti/ as ⲧϯ, and the regular use of the strong article (ϯ). Although none of these are particularly indicative of a geographical origin, Blumell and Dosoo (2018: 205, 209–210) suggest a possible origin north of Thebes; the other ostraca from Atiya's donation with known provenances come from Bawit, Wadi Sarga, and Edfu.[6] At certain points (in particular ostracon 2 ll. 1, 2, 5) the text seems to be significantly abbreviated, perhaps implying either miscopying, or that the manuscript was intended to serve as a prompt for a text well known to the reader.

---

[4] *O.Frange* nos. 247–62, 265, 266, 294–318.
[5] Choat/Gardner 2013: 3–4.
[6] Blumell 2013; Blumell/Dosoo 2018: 209–210 n. 50.

Ostracon 1 (inv. no. 81, convex, →)

+ ϣαειμ ː вλικα-
воу ː λαвιϣ ː αλⲱμ ː
λαχ ː ⲙαλαχ ː ⲙαλα-
ⲅα ː λααⲅουⲙ ː ϩριζ ː
5 ϩραζ ː αⲅουακ ː ανοκ π-
ⲉ ϩⲱρ ⲡϣⲉ ⲛⲏ⟦ⲉ⟧ⲥⲉ
αϊвⲱκ ⲉϩουⲛ ϩⲛ ου-
ⲡⲏλⲏ ⲛⲱⲛⲉ αϊ ⲉвολ
ⲛουⲡⲏλⲏ ⲙⲉⲛιⲡⲉ ː
10 αϭⲓⲛⲉ ϊⲥⲓ̈ⲙⲉ ⲧⲁ̈ϊⲉαιⲛ
ⲧϯουⲟϣⲉ ⲧϯκα вαλ
ⲧϯαλ ⲙϫⲱв ⲧⲉⲛ-
αⲧαⲯⲭⲏ ⲙⲉρι-
ⲥ ⲡⲉϫαι ⲛ-

---

6 ⲛⲏ⟦ⲉ⟧ⲥⲉ ⲉ deleted by rubbing out ∥ **8** *i.e.* πύλη ∣ *i.e.* ᔆαϥι-ⲉⲓ ∥ **9** *i.e.* πύλη ∣ *i.e.* ᔆⲙ̄-вⲉⲛιⲡⲉ ∥
10 *i.e.* ᔆⲛ-ϯ-ⲥϩιⲙⲉ δ(ε)ῖ(να) δ(ε)ῖ(να) ∣ *i.e.* ᔆϯ-ⲥαιⲛ ∥ **11** *i.e.* ᔆϯ-*ουⲟвϣⲉ, *cf.* ᴮουⲟϣвι Crum CD 576b, *i.e.* feminine of ουⲟвϣ, see B/D ∣ *i.e.* ᔆⲛ̄-ϯ-καⲙ ː or *i.e.* ᔆⲧα-ϯ-καⲙ B/D ∥
12 ⲧϯαλ ⲙϫⲱв *i.e.* ᔆⲛ̄-ϯ-αλου ⲛ-ϫουϥ ∥ **12–13** *i.e.* ᔆⲧ-ⲉⲛⲧα- ∥ **13** *i.e.* ψυχή ∥ **13–14** *i.e.* ᔆⲙⲉριⲧ≠ⲥ

+ Šaeim, Blikabou, Labiš, Alōm, Lakh, Malakh, Malaha, Laagoum, Hrix, |⁵ Hrax, Agouak.

I am *Horus the son of *Isis. I went into a gate of stone, I came out from a gate of iron. |¹⁰ I found the woman NN, child of NN, the beautiful one, the white one with the black eyes, with the burning? pupils?, the one that my soul loved. I said to

---

Horus-Isis Narrative Charms: This text represents an example of a narrative charm in which the main protagonists are Horus and Isis; for a discussion of structure and parallels, see the notes to *PCM* I 7 front. For a discussion of the doors of stone and iron, see the notes to *PCM* I 7 ll. 2–3, and for the woman encountered by Horus in ll. 10–11, see the notes to *PCM* I 6 l. 3.

Ostracon 2 (inv. no. 77; convex, →)

+ ⲁ·ⲥ ϫⲉ ⲅⲟ ⲧⲉ ⲩⲡⲓ ⲛⲟⲥ ⳓ ⲉⲙⲉⲥⲟⲩⲱϣ
ⲟⲩⲧⲉ ⲙⲉⲥⲉⲣ ϩⲛⲁⲥ ⲉⲃⲉ^ⲡⲓ ⲁⲓ̈ⲣⲓⲙⲉ
ⲛⲁⲣⲉ ⲏⲥⲉ ⲧⲁⲙⲁⲟⲩ ⲡⲉϫⲉ ⲏⲥⲉ ⲛ-
ⲁⲓ̈ ϫⲉ ⲁⲣⲟⲕ ⲉⲕⲣⲓ̈ⲙⲡⲉ ϩⲱⲣ ⲡⲁϣ-
5 ⲏⲣⲉ ϫⲉ ⲛⲉⲟⲩⲱϣ ⲧⲛ ⲛⲉ ⲧⲁⲙⲁⲟⲩ ⲛⲁⲓ̈ⲃⲱⲕ ⲉϩⲟⲩⲛ ⲛⲟⲩⲏⲗⲏ ⲛ̄-
ⲛⲱⲛⲉ ⲁⲓ̈ ⲉⲃⲟⲗ ⲛⲟⲩⲡⲏⲗⲏ ⲙⲉ-
ⲛⲓ̈ⲡⲉ ⲁⲓ̈ϭⲛ ⲧϯⲥⲓ̈ⲙⲉ ⳓⳓ ⲧϯⲥⲁⲓ-
ⲏ ⲧϯⲟⲩⲟⲃϣⲉ ⲧϯⲕ̄ ⲃⲁⲗ ⲧϯⲁⲗ ⲙ-
10 ϫⲱⲃ ⲧⲏⲛⲁⲧⲁⲯⲭⲏ ⲙⲉⲣⲓⲥ
ⲡⲉϫⲁⲓ ⲛⲁⲥ ϫⲉ ⲕⲟ ⲧⲉ ⲩⲡⲓ
ⲛⲟⲥ ⳓ ⲉⲙⲉⲥⲟⲩⲱϣ ⲟⲩ-
ⲧⲉ ⲙⲉⲥⲣ ⲛⲁⲥ ⲡⲉ-
ϫⲉ ⲏⲥⲉ ⲛⲁⲓ̈ ϫⲉ
15 ⲉϫⲉ ⲙⲉⲕ-
ⲉⲓⲙⲉ ϭⲛ
ⲁⲙⲟⲩ
[ⲉ]ⲡⲁ[ⲡ-]

Ostracon 3 (inv. no. 76, convex, →)

+ ⲁⲧ ϫⲉⲕⲁⲥ
ⲓ̈ⲉⲟⲩⲱⲙ ⲉⲃⲟⲗ
ⲛⲕⲁⲓ ⲙⲉϣⲟⲡ ⲛ-
ⲁⲥ ⲛⲥⲭⲱ ⲉⲃⲟⲗ
5 ⲙⲁⲟⲩⲱϣ ⲧⲏⲣ⟦..⟧-
ⲃ ⲉⲧϯ ⲧⲁⲭⲏ ⲧⲁ-
ⲭⲏ ϩⲛ ϭⲟⲙ ⲓⲁ-
ⲱ ⲥⲁⲃⲁⲱⲑ

ostracon 2, 1 *i.e.* ^Sⲕⲱ (ⲛⲁ=ⲓ) ⲉ-ϯ ⲟⲩ-ⲡⲓ (ⲛⲉ) ⲛ̄ⲧⲟⲥ ? : *i.e.* ^Sⲛ̄ⲕⲟⲧⲕ ⲉ-ⲩ-πίνος or ὕπνος ? "lie on the dirt" or "go to sleep" B/D | *i.e.* δ(ε)ῖ(να) | *i.e.* ^Sⲙ̄ⲡⲉ=ⲥ-ⲟⲩⲱϣ=ⲧ || **2** *i.e.* οὐδέ | *i.e.* ^Sⲙ̄ⲡⲉ=ⲥ-ⲣ̄ | *i.e.* ^Sⲉ=ϥ-ϯ-ⲟⲩ-ⲡⲓ (ⲛⲁ=ⲥ) ? : ⲉⲃⲉⲙ meaning unclear or *l*. ϩⲉⲛ ἀσέβημα ? B/D || **3** *i.e.* ^Sⲛ̄ⲛⲁϩⲣⲛ- | *i.e.* ^Sⲙⲁⲁⲩ || **4** *i.e.* ^Sⲁϩⲣⲟ=ⲕ | *i.e.* ^Sⲣⲓⲙⲉ || **5** *i.e.* ^Sⲛ̄ⲧⲉ=ⲑ-ⲟⲩⲱϣ | ⲧⲛ *l*. ⲧⲁ-ⲣⲓⲙⲉ ⲁⲛ ? *cf*. *PCM* I 6 l. 10, *PCM* I 7 l. 16 B/D | *l*. ⲏⲥⲉ || **5–6** *i.e.* ^Sⲙⲁⲁⲩ || **6** *l*. ⲛ̄ⲧⲁ=ⲓ̈-ⲃⲱⲕ | *i.e.* ^S(ⲉ)ⲛ̄ ⲟⲩ-ⲡⲩ́ⲗⲏ || **6–7** ⲛ-ⲱⲛⲉ (dittography) || **7** *i.e.* ⲡⲩ́ⲗⲏ || **7–8** *i.e.* ^Sⲙ-ⲃⲉⲛⲓⲡⲉ || **8** *i.e.* ^Sϯ-ⲥϩⲓⲙⲉ | δ(ε)ῖ(να) δ(ε)ῖ(να) || **9** *i.e.* ^Sϯ-ⲟⲩⲟⲃϣⲉ *cf*. ostracon 1 l. 11 | *i.e.* ^Sⲛ̄-ϯ-ⲕⲁⲙ : or *i.e.* ^Sⲧⲁ-ϯ-ⲕⲁⲙ ? B/D | *i.e.* ^Sⲛ̄-ϯ-ⲁⲗⲟⲩ : or *i.e.* ^Sⲧⲁ-ϯ-ⲁⲗⲟⲩ ? || **10** *i.e.* ^Sⲧ-ⲉⲛⲧⲁ-ⲧⲁ-ψυχή | *i.e.* ^Sⲙⲉⲣⲓⲧ=ⲥ || **11–12** *i.e.* ^Sⲕⲱ (ⲛⲁ=ⲓ) ⲉ-ϯ ⲟⲩ-ⲡⲓ (ⲛⲉ) ⲛ̄ⲧⲟⲥ ? : *i.e.* ^Sⲛ̄ⲕⲟⲧⲕ ⲉ-ⲩ-πίνος or ὕπνος "lie on the dirt" or "go to sleep" ? B/D *cf*. l. 1 || **12** *i.e.* δ(ε)ῖ(να) | *i.e.* ^Sⲙ̄ⲡⲉ=ⲥ-ⲟⲩⲱϣⲧ || **12–13** *i.e.* οὐδέ || **13** *i.e.* ^Sⲙ̄ⲡⲉ=ⲥ-ⲣ̄ ϩⲛⲁⲥ || **15** *i.e.* ^Sⲉϣϫⲉ || **16** *i.e.* ⲉ-ϭⲛ=ⲧ (haplography) ||
ostracon 3, 1 ϫⲉⲕⲁⲥ ⲕ corrected from . by overwriting || **2** *i.e.* ^Sⲉ=ⲓ-ⲉ-ⲟⲩⲱⲙ || **3–4** *l*. ⲛⲛⲉ=ⲕ-ⲕⲁⲁ=ⲓ ⲉ-ⲙⲡⲉ=ⲥ-ϣⲱⲡⲉ ⲛⲁ=ⲥ : or *i.e.* ^Sⲛ̄-ⲧ-ⲛⲕⲁ ⲉ=ⲥ-ϣⲟⲟⲡ ⲛⲁ=ⲥ B/D || **4** *i.e.* ^Sⲛ̄=ⲥ-ϫⲱⲕ || **5** *i.e.* ^Sⲙ̄-ⲡⲁ-ⲟⲩⲱϣ | ⲧⲏⲣ⟦..⟧- erasure or smudge? || **5–6** *i.e.* ^Sⲧⲏⲣϥ̄ || **6** *i.e.* ἤδη || **6–7** *i.e.* ταχύ || **7** *i.e.* ^S ⲧ-ϭⲟⲙ

|^(o. 2) + her, "Let ⟨me⟩ kiss ⟨you⟩!" She, NN, did not want ⟨me⟩, neither was she willing for him [sic] to kiss ⟨her⟩. I cried before *Isis, my mother.

Isis said to me, "Why are you crying, *Horus, my |^5 son?"

⟨I said⟩, "Do you not want ⟨me to cry?⟩, Isis, my mother? I went into a gate of stone, I came out of a gate of iron. I found the woman NN, child of NN, the beautiful one, the white one with the black eyes, with the burning pupils?, |^10 the one my soul loved. I said to her, "Let ⟨me⟩ kiss ⟨you⟩!" She, NN, did not want ⟨me⟩, neither was she willing."

Isis said to me, |^15 "⟨Even⟩ if you did not know how to find me, ⟨say?⟩ "Come to [my] *cup? |^(o. 3) + that I might eat?, do not leave me until it happens that she shall fulfill |^5 all my desire, now, quickly, quickly, by ⟨the⟩ power of *Iao *Sabaoth!"

KD, EL & MP, edited from photographs.

---

ostracon 2 l. 1. ⲅⲟ ⲧⲉ ⲩⲡⲓ : "Let ⟨me⟩ kiss ⟨you⟩!" *Cf.* l. 11 (ⲕⲟ ⲧⲉ ⲩⲡⲓ), perhaps l. 2 (ⲉⲃⲉⲡⲓ). Blumell and Dosoo propose to understand the command "sleep" or "lie down" (ⲛ̄ⲕⲟⲧⲕ) followed by the word for "sleep" or "dirt" (πίνος/ὕπνος, using the following ⲛⲟⲥ). By comparison with *PCM* I 7 l. 9 and *PCM* I 20 l. 5, we suggest that Horus is here asking the woman to let him kiss her, with an initial imperative ⲕⲱ (for the sense "permit" see Crum CD 95a) followed by ϯ ("give", imperative or infinitive), then ⲟⲩⲡⲓ "a kiss". Here, as often in the narrative charms, the difficulty of parsing the text syntactically may suggest either the writing of a primarily oral text, or that the written form served as an abbreviated *aide memoire* (compare in particular ⲧⲛ̄ in l. 5.).

15–16. ϫⲉ ⲙⲉⲕⲉⲓⲙⲉ ⲟⲛ : "⟨even⟩ if you did not know how to find me" A recurrent phrase in the final section of narrative charms, this serves as a kind of 'charter' for the performance of the ritual in the present. In the mythic past it was possible for Horus to appeal to Isis directly, but even if this had not been possible the ritual she describes would still be sufficient. For parallels to this phrase, see *PCM* I 6 l. 14; *PCM* I 20 ll. 11–12; *BKU* I 7 (KYP M76) back ll. 3–4; *BKU* I 7 (KYP M88) ll. 29–30; Naqlun N. 78/93 (Kalchenko and van der Vliet 2022; KYP M1135) ll. 22–26; Mich.Ms. 136 (Zellmann-Rohrer/Love 2022; KYP M128) p. 5 ll. 18–19. By contrast, in *PCM* I 7 ll. 25–31 Isis asks Horus why he did not originally perform the ritual instead of seeking her help first, a variant which leads Kalchenko and van der Vliet (2022: 231–235) to see such phrases as formulas of reproach.

ostracon 2 l. 17–*ostracon 3* l. 1. ⲁⲙⲟⲩ [ⲉ]ⲡⲁ[ⲡ]ⲁⲧ : "Come to [my] cup?" This phrase is uncertain; if the reconstruction "cup" is correct, this would represent an epiclesis, calling on a supernatural being to empower liquid in a cup, which the practitioner would presumably drink, although the verb used, ⲟⲩⲱⲙ, rather means "to eat"; *cf.* the discussion in Blumell/Dosoo 2018: 237–238.

ostracon 3 7–8. ϩⲛ ϭⲟⲙ ⲓⲁⲱ ⲥⲁⲃⲁⲱⲑ : "by ⟨the⟩ power of Iao Sabaoth" The phrase "by the power of…" recurs in many Coptic magical texts; in this volume, compare *PCM* I 4 p. 3 l. 2, p. 6 l. 2; *PCM* I 25 p. 15 l. 12, p. 16 l. 2, p. 18 l. 6. This construction (*e.g., ḥn tꜣ gm*) does not seem to appear in older Egyptian texts, but rather to derive from the Greek ἐν δυνάμει + genitive, first clearly attested in Hellenistic Jewish texts (*e.g., Testament of Levi* 16.3 "by the power of the Most High" (ἐν δυνάμει ὑψίστου); Charles 1908: 59.3) and to become common in early Christian writings, in particular the Pauline letters (Romans 15.13, 19; I Corinthians 2.5; II Corinthians 6.7). The phrase does not occur in the Graeco-Egyptian magical corpus, rather appearing with the names of Jewish-Christian deities as an addition to Coptic narrative charms from around the fourth century (*e.g.,* Mich.Ms. 136 p. 6 l. 5 (Zellmann-Rohrer/Love 2022; KYP M128), suggesting that it derives from a Christian context. *Cf.* the comments of Zellmann-Rohrer and Love (2022: 61–62, 237–238) who prefer to see an origin among Graeco-Egyptian magical texts.

PCM I 17. Spell for a good singing voice and a love spell

Middle Egypt ?   37.3 (H) × 25.4 (W) cm   VIII CE
Other references: P.CtYBR inv. 1791; TM 98065; KYP M284; Bélanger Sarrazin ##7, 8.
Editions: Emmel in Meyer/Smith 1994: appendix 2, 3 (*ed. pr.*).
Translations: Emmel in Meyer/Smith 1994: nos. 74, 122.
Additional commentary: Petersen 1964: no. 53.
Present location: New Haven, Beinecke Library (Yale University).
Image: http://hdl.handle.net/10079/digcoll/2759562
Linguistic description: Sahidic (non-standard).
Contents:
1. Front ll. 1–35, back ll. 1–28: Spell for good singing voice (KYP T329; hand 1)
2. Back ll. 29–46, front ll. 36–38: Love spell (KYP T330; hand 2)

A complete and well-preserved papyrus sheet containing two recipes written in different hands, the first a spell for a good singing voice, the second a love spell. The manuscript was purchased by Yale University from Hans P. Kraus, the rare book dealer, in New York on the 1ˢᵗ May 1964, using funds donated by Edwin John Beinecke.[1] The provenance of the manuscipt is unknown, although Petersen notes that the references to place names in papyri from the same collection point to Middle Egypt, an origin that would agree with the dialectal features.[2]

The sheet is rectangular, with damage along the folds. 2 horizontal creases, as well as approximately 10 vertical creases, are visible. The manuscript was produced by cutting a length from a papyrus roll and turning it 90° to write the first recipe on the front (↓), before completing the recipe by copying the associated image and instructions onto the back (→). Subsequently, a second hand added the second recipe in the space remaining on the back, finishing in the narrow space at the bottom of the front, writing on the back at 180° to the other text on the object. Note that this interpretation reverses that of Emmel, who understood the text as beginning on the horizontal fibres; this would mean that the original scribe left an unusually large upper margin of 13.8 cm before beginning to write. Emmel thus begins the text on what we understand to be the back, numbering lines 1–28, before turning to what we consider as the recto, counting the first line as 29.

The first hand is highly informal and irregular, with letters varying in shape,

---

[1] Beinecke Rare Book and Manuscript Library, "Guide to the Yale Papyrus Collection", online at https://beinecke.library.yale.edu/research-teaching/doing-research-beinecke-library/introduction-yale-papyrus-collection/guide-yale (accessed 17/10/2022).

[2] Petersen 1964: "Introductory Note".

shading, and size. Notable is the ⲡ, which may be written in either one or three strokes, and the ⲥ, which may be either very narrow, or very extended. The overall impression is of a sloping majuscule, with no serifs, although the ⲗ has a characteristic shape, with the longer stroke (which may be written in either orientation) often demonstrating a marked leftwards curl at its top. The ⳉ is tightly curled, and the ascender of ϭ is rather short. The impression is of a writer of the type classified by Cribiore as possessing an "alphabetic hand", demonstrating knowledge of letterforms but clumsiness of coordination;[3] a lack of experience may also be demonstrated by the extensive interlinear correction. The informality of this hand makes it extremely difficult to date.

The second hand is written with a thinner pen, generally using bilinear letterforms, but sometimes employing quadrilinear forms (notably the ⲏ), showing marked descenders on the ⲓ, ⲣ, ⲧ, and ⲫ, and an enlarged ⲃ typical of post-seventh century documentary texts, of which this hand would seem to represent a good example. The ⲩ is bilinear, and the ⲧ shows a marked serif on the left part of its horizontal bar. In general the letters are separated, with only occasional ligatures (usually of ⲉ or ⲧ to the following letter); diaeresis is written as a single supralinear stroke, while supralineation indicating a schwa or autosyllabic consonant is usually marked by a dot. The hand becomes noticeably more upright, and uses thicker strokes, in the later lines of the back and on the front. Emmel suggested a seventh- or eight-century date for this manuscript, but the presence of the scribal mark of two oblique strokes (//), first attested in documentary texts of the eighth century, may allow us a more precise dating.[4] Similar hands can be seen in *SB Kopt.* II 946 (TM 23156; 737 CE) and *P.CLT* 1 (TM 85755; 698 CE). Among the hands of this volume, it is comparable to nos. 10 and 18.

Both texts are written in non-standard Sahidic; the first shows the common writing of ⲉ in place of the supralinear stroke, as well as alternation of ⲓ/ⲉⲓ. More unusual features, such as the insertion of ⲏ where no letter or a schwa would be expected, the absence of ⲉ or its replacement by ⲩ, and the addition of unexpected vowels, suggests either considerable confusion about vowel qualities, or the phonetic writing of a non-standard variety. The second hand is far closer to standard Sahidic, but nonetheless occasionally displays the same general tendencies, notably the use of ⲏ for ⲉ, and of ⲉ for schwa, suggesting a dialectal affinity between the two writers. Kahle notes similar features as typical of dialects north of Thebes, with the use of ⲏ in particular being suggestive of Middle Egyptian dialectal influence.[5]

---

[3] Cribiore 1996: 33, 112.

[4] *Cf.* Richter 2003: 223–230; Cromwell 2023: 234–235.

[5] *E.g.*, ⲏ=ⲉ: ⲧⲏⲥⲕⲩⲛⲏ (f.3), ⲟⲩⲙⲏ (b.29, 40); ⲏ=∅: ⲛⲏⲡⲉⲩⲉ (f.10), ⲛⲏⲥⲓⲟⲩ (f.13), ⲥⲏⲛⲟϥ (b.1); ∅=ⲉ: ⲧⲣⲉⲛ (f.10), ⲧⲕⲱⲧⲉ (f.13), ϫ (f.26), ϫⲕⲁⲁⲥ (f.29); ⲩ=ⲉ: ⲛⲩⲧϣⲟⲟⲡ (f.4), ⲧⲩⲕⲗⲉⲥⲓⲁ (f.6-7, 9-10), ⲛⲩⲭⲉⲣⲟⲩⲃⲉⲛ (f.8), ⲉⲕⲩⲕⲱ (8); ⲩ=∅: ⲡⲙⲏⲛⲧⲥⲩⲛⲟⲟⲥ (15); *cf.* Kahle 1954: 54–57. Instances of ⲉ=∅ are too numerous to list here.

front (↓)

m¹ [*ca.* 22] . . ⲉⲕⲟⲩⲙⲉⲛⲟⲥ ⲉⲙ-
   [*ca.* 20]ⲥⲟ ⲙ̄ⲫⲟ ⲉⲙⲡⲓⲱⲧ
3 [*ca.* 6 ⲇ]ⲓⲕⲁⲓⲟⲥⲩⲛⲏ ⲭⲉⲣⲉ ⲧⲏⲥⲕⲩⲛⲏ ⲉⲙⲡⲓⲱⲧ ⲙⲛ
                                          ⲙⲛ ⲡϣⲏⲣⲉ ⲙⲛ ⲡⲛⲉⲙⲁ ⲧ̣
4 ⲛⲩⲧϣⲟⲟⲡ ⲉⲛϩⲏⲧⲥⲉ ⲭⲉⲣⲉ ⲉⲥϣⲁϥⲉ ⲛⲛⲁⲣⲭⲏⲁⲅⲅⲉⲗⲟⲥ
5 ⲉⲧⲧⲁϩⲉⲣⲁⲧⲟⲩ ⲉⲡⲉⲟⲟⲩ ⲉⲙ[ⲡ]ⲓ̈ⲱⲧ ⲭⲉⲣⲉ ⲛⲁⲣⲭⲏ ⲙⲛ
   ⲛⲏⲕⲝⲟⲥⲓⲁ ⲙⲛ ⲉⲛϭⲟⲙ [ⲉ]ⲧϩⲉⲙ ⲡⲭ̄ⲓ̈ⲥⲉ ⲭⲉⲣⲉ ⲧⲩⲕⲗⲉⲥⲓⲁ ⲛ̄ⲛⲉϣⲉⲣⲉⲡⲙⲉⲥⲉ ⲛⲛⲉⲧϣⲟⲟⲡ ⲉⲛϩⲏⲧⲥⲉ
   ⲭⲉⲣⲉ ⲉⲛⲧⲩⲛⲁⲙⲉⲥ ⲭⲉⲣⲉ ⲛⲩⲭⲉⲣⲟⲩⲃⲉⲛ ⲭⲉⲣⲉ ⲉⲛⲥⲩⲣⲁ-
   ⲡⲫⲉⲛ ⲭⲉⲣⲉ ⲉⲡⲭⲟⲩⲧⲁⲃⲧⲉ ⲙ̄ⲡⲣⲉⲥⲃⲏⲧⲏⲣⲟⲥ ⲉⲛⲧⲩⲕ-
10 ⲗⲉⲥⲓⲁ ⲧ̄ϩⲉⲛ ⲛⲏⲏⲡⲉⲩⲉ ⲙⲛ ⲛⲟⲩⲛ ⲛⲓⲙ ⲉⲧϣⲟⲟⲡ ⲉⲛϩⲏⲧⲉⲥ
   ⲭⲉⲣⲉ ⲉⲧⲡⲁⲣⲁⲇⲓⲥⲱⲥ ⲙⲛ ⲛⲟⲩⲟⲛ ⲛⲓⲙ ⲉⲧϣⲟⲟⲡ ⲛ̄ϩⲏⲧⲥ̄ ⲭⲉⲣⲉ
   ⲉⲡⲡⲣⲏ ⲉⲧⲧⲉⲣ ⲟⲩⲉⲓⲛ ⲭⲉⲣⲉ ⲉⲧⲙⲏ̣ⲧⲥⲩⲛⲟⲟⲥ ⲉⲛⲧⲏⲛⲁ-
   ⲙⲓ̈ⲥ ⲧ̄ⲕⲱⲧⲉ ⲉⲣⲟϥ ⲭⲉⲣⲉ ⲉⲡⲟϩⲉ ⲙⲛ ⲛⲏⲥⲓⲟⲩ ⲧⲏⲣⲟⲩ ⲭⲉⲣⲉ
   ⲡⲙⲏⲧⲥⲩⲛⲟⲟⲥ ⲉⲛⲁⲣⲭⲱⲛ ⲉⲧⲧⲛϣ ⲛ̄ⲉⲩⲛⲟⲟⲩⲉ ⲛⲧⲩϣⲏ
15 ⲭⲉⲣⲉ ⲡⲙⲏⲧⲥⲩⲛⲟⲟⲥ ⲉⲛⲁⲣⲭⲱⲛ ⲉⲧⲧⲛϣ ⲉⲛⲛⲉⲩⲛⲟⲩⲉ ⲙ̄ⲡⲉ-
   ϩⲟⲟⲩ ⲭⲉⲣⲉ ϩⲱⲣⲙⲟⲥⲉⲏⲗ ⲡⲛⲟϭ ⲉⲛⲁⲣⲭⲱⲛ ⲉϥⲥⲱⲩϩⲉ ⲉⲛ-
   ⲛᵀⲁ ⲡⲉ ⲙⲛ ⲛⲁ ⲡⲕⲁϩ ⲡⲁⲓ ⲉϣⲁⲣⲉⲛⲁ ⲡⲉⲩ ⲥⲱⲧⲉⲙ ⲉⲧⲉϥⲥⲉⲙⲏ
   ⲥⲩⲛⲧⲟⲩⲛⲏ ⲉⲛⲥⲱϥ ⲧⲓⲛⲟⲩ ⲧⲉⲥⲟⲡⲥ̄ ⲙ̄ⲙⲟⲕ ⲙ̄ⲡⲟⲟⲩ ⲁⲩⲱ
   ⲧⲓⲡⲁⲣⲁⲅⲁⲗⲉ ⲉⲙⲟⲕ ϩⲟⲣⲙⲟⲥⲉⲏⲗ ⲡⲁ ⲡⲓ̄ⲣⲟⲟⲩ ⲉⲧϩⲟⲗⲉϭ
20 ⲉⲧⲛⲟⲧⲉⲙ ᵉᴺⲑⲉ ⲙⲫⲓⲗⲉⲙⲟⲛ ⲡⲁⲧⲉⲥⲙⲏ ⲉⲧϩⲟⲗⲉϭ ϫⲉⲕⲁⲁⲥ
   ⲉⲕⲁⲉⲓ̈ ϣⲁⲣⲟⲓ ⲉⲙⲡⲟⲟⲩ ⲁⲛⲟⲕ ⲇⲇ ⲛ̄ⲉⲅⲁϩⲉⲣⲁⲧ ϩⲉϫⲉ-
   ⲛ ⲡⲓⲁⲡⲟⲧ ⲉⲧⲕⲏ ⲉⲣⲁⲓ ⲉⲙⲡⲁⲛⲧⲟⲩ ⲉⲃⲟⲗ ⲛⲉϥⲙⲁϩⲉϥ ⲛⲁⲓ̈
   ⲉⲛϩⲉⲣⲟⲟⲩ ⲉϥϩⲟⲗⲉϭ ⲉϥⲛⲟⲧⲉ[ⲙ] ⲉϥⲃ[ⲏⲕ] ⲉⲣⲁⲓ ⲉϥⲛⲏⲩ ⲉⲡⲉⲥⲏⲧ ⲉϥⲕⲱⲧⲉ ⲛ̄ⲑⲉ ⲛⲟⲩⲧⲣ[ⲟ]ⲭⲟⲥ ⲉϥⲙⲏϩ ⲉⲛⲛⲟⲩⲉⲗⲗⲉ ⲛⲓⲙ
25 ⲉϥϩⲟⲗⲉϭ ⲉϥⲥⲱⲕ ⲑⲉ ⲛⲟⲩⲧⲏⲩ ⲛⲁⲧⲟⲗ ⲛⲁⲧⲑⲉⲙⲛⲉϥⲉ
   ⲛⲁⲧⲛⲉϫ ⲑⲁⲃ ⲉⲃⲟⲗ ϩⲁⲉⲓⲟ ϩⲁⲉⲓ ϫ ⲧⲉϣⲣⲉⲕ ᵉⲣᵒᵏ ⲛ̄ⲧⲟⲩ-
   ⲛⲁⲙ ⲙ̄ⲡⲓⲱⲧ ⲧⲓϣⲣⲉⲕ ⲉⲣⲟⲕ ⲧⲁⲡⲉ ⲉⲙⲡϣⲏⲣⲉ

---

1 . . ⲟⲩⲙⲉⲛⲟⲥ Emmel ‖ **2** . ⲟ Emmel | *i.e.* ˢⲡ-ϩⲟ ‖ **3** *et passim i.e.* χαῖρε ‖ **3** *i.e.* δικαιοσύνη suggestion of Agnes Mihálykó : . ⲛ̣ⲁⲓⲟⲩⲛⲏ Emmel | ⲙⲛ ⲡϣⲏⲣⲉ ⲙⲛ ⲡⲛⲉⲙⲁ inserted below the line, to be read after ⲉⲙⲡⲓⲱⲧ | *i.e.* σκηνή | ⲛ̣ⲁⲓⲟⲩⲛⲏ Emmel | *i.e.* πνεῦμα (ⲉ)ⲧ(ⲟⲩⲁⲁⲃ) : ⲡⲛⲉⲙⲁⲧⲓ Emmel ‖ **4** *i.e.* ˢⲛⲉⲧ-ϣⲟⲟⲡ | *i.e.* ˢⲛ̄-ϩⲏⲧ=ⲥ | *i.e.* ˢⲡ-ⲥⲁϣϥⲉ | *i.e.* ἀρχάγγελος ‖ **5** *i.e.* ἀρχή ‖ **6** *i.e.* ἐξουσία ‖ **7** *l. i.e.* ἐκκλησία | *i.e.* ˢ-ⲙⲓⲥⲉ | *l.* ⲙⲛ ⲛⲉⲧϣⲟⲟⲡ | *i.e.* ˢⲛ̄-ϩⲏⲧ=ⲥ̄ ‖ **8** *l.* δύναμις | *i.e.* χερουβίμ ‖ **8–9** *i.e.* σεραφίμ ‖ **9** *i.e.* πρεσβύτερος ‖ **9–10** *i.e.* ἐκκλησία ‖ **10** *i.e.* ˢⲙ-ⲡⲏⲩⲉ | *i.e.* ˢⲡⲏⲩⲉ | *i.e.* ˢⲛ̄-ϩⲏⲧ=ⲥ̄ ‖ **11** *i.e.* παράδεισος ‖ **12** *l.* ⲡⲣⲏ | *l.* ⲉⲧⲉⲣ- ‖ **12–13** *i.e.* δύναμις ‖ **13** *i.e.* ˢⲉⲧ-ⲕⲱⲧⲉ | *i.e.* ˢⲟⲟϩ | *i.e.* ˢⲛ̄-ⲥⲓⲟⲩ ‖ **14** *i.e.* ἄρχων | *i.e.* ˢⲛ̄-ⲛ-ⲟⲩⲛⲟⲟⲩⲉ | *i.e.* ˢⲛ̄-ⲧ-ⲟⲩϣⲏ ‖ **15** *i.e.* ˢⲡ-ⲙⲛⲧ-ⲥⲛⲟⲟⲩⲥ | *i.e.* ἄρχων | *i.e.* ˢⲛ̄-ⲛⲉ-ⲟⲩⲛⲟⲟⲩⲉ ‖ **16** *i.e.* ἄρχων | *i.e.* ˢⲥⲱⲟⲩϩ ‖ **17** *l.* ⲛⲁ ⲧⲡⲉ | *i.e.* ˢⲥⲙⲏ ‖ **18** *i.e.* ˢⲛ̄ⲥⲉ-ἡδύνειν | *l.* ⲛ̄ⲥⲟⲩⲁⲧⲟⲩ {ⲙⲛ̄-} "and it sends them" Emmel | *i.e.* ˢⲧⲉⲛⲟⲩ ‖ **19** *i.e.* παρακαλεῖν | *i.e.* ˢⲙ̄ⲙⲟ=ⲕ | *i.e.* ˢϩⲟⲗⲟ̄ ‖ **20** *i.e.* ˢⲛⲟⲧⲙ̄ | *i.e.* ˢϩⲟⲗⲟ̄ ‖ **21** *i.e.* ˢⲉ=ⲕ-ⲛⲁ-ⲉⲓ | *i.e.* δ(εῖνα) δ(εῖνα) | *i.e.* ˢⲛ̄ⲅⲁϩⲉⲣⲁⲧ | *l.* ⲡⲁ ⲡⲓϩⲣⲟⲟⲩ | *i.e.* ˢϩⲓϫⲛ̄ ‖ **22** corrected from ⲛⲡⲓⲁⲡⲧⲧ by overwriting | *i.e.* ˢⲉϩⲣⲁⲓ | *i.e.* ˢⲛ̄ϥ-ⲙⲉϩ=ϥ ‖ **23** *i.e.* ˢϩⲣⲟⲟⲩ | *i.e.* ˢϩⲟⲗⲟ̄ | *i.e.* ˢⲛⲟⲧⲙ̄ ‖ **24** *i.e.* τροχός : ⲧⲣ . . ⲟⲥ Emmel | *i.e.* ˢⲛ̄-ⲟⲩⲗⲗⲉ ‖ **25** *i.e.* ˢϩⲟⲗⲟ̄ | *i.e.* ˢⲁⲧ-ϩⲱⲗ | *l.* ⲁⲧ-ϩⲉⲙⲛⲉϥⲉ : *i.e.* ˢⲁⲧ-ϩⲙ-ⲛⲓϥⲉ Emmel *cf.* Crum CD 239b ‖ **26** *i.e.* ˢⲛ̄-ⲁⲧ-ⲛⲉϫ ⲧⲁ=ϥ | *l.* ϩⲁⲉⲓⲟ | *l.* ϫⲉ | *i.e.* ˢϯ-ⲱⲣⲕ̄ ‖ **27** *i.e.* ˢⲛ̄-ⲧ-ⲁⲡⲉ

...the face of the Father... righteousness?... Hail, *tabernacle of the Father and the Son and the Spirit and those who are within it! Hail, seven *archangels |⁵ who stand before the glory of the Father! Hail, *Principalities and *Authorities and *Powers that are on high! Hail, Church of the Firstborn and those who are within it! Hail, Powers! Hail, *cherubim! Hail, *seraphim! Hail, *Twenty-Four Presbyters of the |¹⁰ Church that is in the heavens, and all who are in it! Hail, Paradise, and all who are in it! Hail, sun that shines! Hail, twelve powers that surround it! Hail, moon and all the stars! Hail, twelve rulers that appoint the hours of the night! |¹⁵ Hail, twelve rulers that appoint the hours of the day! Hail, Hormosiel, the great ruler who gathers those of the heaven and those of the earth, he to whose voice those of the heavens listen, and they delight in it!

Now, I entreat you today, and I invoke you, Hormosiel, the one with the sweet voice |²⁰ that is pleasant like ⟨that of⟩ Philemon, the one with the sweet voice, that you come to me today, me, NN, child of NN, and you stand over this *cup that is placed before me and you fill it for me with a voice which is sweet, which is pleasant, which [goes] up, which comes down, turning like a wheel, filled with all music, |²⁵ which is sweet, which flows like a wind, which is not hoarse, does not breathe with difficulty, does not spit, yea, yea, for I adjure you by the right hand of the Father, I adjure you by the head of the Son,

---

General notes: Spells for a good singing voice are rare in the surviving corpus; there are no examples in Greek or Demotic, and only four others in Coptic: BL Ms. Or. 6794 (Kropp 1931: I no. E; KYP M306); *BKU* I 8 (KYP M81) ll. 1–39; P.PalauRib. 137 (KYP M719; unpublished); Turin Biblioteca Nazionale Ms. Peyron 158 c.1r (KYP M3761; unpublished).

19. ϩορⲙⲟⲥⲓⲏⲗ : "**Hormosiel**" Hormosiel is one of the Four Luminaries known from Sethian Gnostic cosmologies; *cf.* the note to *PCM* I 25 p. 8 ll. 8–9. For Hormosiel as a celestial trumpeter, *cf.* BM EA 10122 (Zellmann-Rohrer 2022a: no. 4; KYP M289) front ll. 20–24: "Hormosiel the angel, the one in whose hands is the trumpet, who gathers the angels to the greeting of the Father, of the whole council of the Lord" (ϩⲟⲣⲙⲟⲥⲓⲏⲗ ⲡⲁⲅⲅⲉⲗⲟⲥ ⲡⲁⲓ ⲉⲧⲉⲣⲉⲧⲥⲁⲗⲡⲓⲝ ⲛⲧⲟⲧϥ ⲉϥⲥⲱⲟⲩϩ ⲉϩⲟⲩⲛ ⲛⲁⲅⲅⲉⲗⲟⲥ ⲉⲡⲁⲥⲡⲁⲥⲙⲟⲥ ⲙⲡⲓⲱⲧ ⲛⲡⲉⲭⲉⲣⲱⲥⲓⲁ ⲧⲏⲣϥ ⲙⲡⲓⲱⲧ); Cairo JdE 49547 (Girard 1927; KYP M297) ll. 23–24: "Hail Hormosiel, the one who trumpets within the *veil of the Father" (ⲭⲉⲣⲁ ϩⲟⲣⲙⲟⲥⲓⲏⲗ : ⲡⲉⲧⲥⲁⲗⲉ ⲡϩⲟⲩⲛ ⲙⲡⲕⲁⲧⲁⲡⲉⲧⲁⲥⲙⲁ ⲙⲡⲓⲱⲧ). Hormosiel recurs as an angelic trumpeter in Coptic apocrypha, such as the *Investiture of Gabriel* (CC 378; Müller 1962: 67.19–20) and *Book of Bartholomew* (CC 27; Westerhoff 1999: 136.10); *cf. BKU* I 8 (KYP M81), another spell for a good singing voice, in which Daueithe, another luminary, appears as an angelic lute player; Burns 2018.

20. ⲉⲛⲑⲉ ⲙⲫⲓⲗⲉⲙⲟⲛ : "**like Philemon**" *Cf. Acts of Andrew and Philemon* (CC 562) in which Philemon, disciple of Andrew, sings in the church of Lydda. His voice is "pleasing" and "sweet" (ⲛⲟⲧⲙ̄, ϩⲟⲗϭ̄), causing the pagan priests who come to kill the apostles to break into tears and convert to Christianity when they hear it. The sweetness of his voice is mentioned again when he is tortured by the governor Rufus; see Miroshnikov 2017: 22, 33–36, 43, 53, 65–67, 70 (trans.); Miroshnikov 2023 (translation of Coptic and Arabic versions); and compare the summary in the *Copto-Arabic Synaxarium*, 14ᵗʰ Khoiak (Basset 1909: 376–377). The description of the pagan priests "delighting" (ἡδύνειν; Miroshnikov 2017: 60, 66 (trans.)) in his voice is reminiscent of l. 18 of this text. Compare also the boy with five loaves and two fish in John 6.8–9, called Philemon in Pseudo-Cyril of Jerusalem's *On Mary Magdalene* (CC 118), described as having been given by God "a voice which is pleasant" (ⲟⲩⲥⲙⲏ ⲉⲥⲛⲟⲧⲙ̄), likely the same figure (Coquin/Gordon 1990: 177 col. 1 ll. 21–22, 201 (trans.); Burke/Landau 2016: 206 (English trans.); *cf.* Miroshnikov 2017: 22).

front (↓) (continued)

ⲧⲓⲱⲣⲉ ⲉⲣⲟⲕ ⲉⲙⲧⲉⲃⲟ ⲉⲙⲡⲉⲛⲉⲩⲙⲁ ⲉⲧⲟⲩⲁⲁⲃ
ϫⲉ ϫⲕⲁⲁⲥ ⲉⲕⲩⲕⲱ ⲉⲛⲥⲱⲕ ⲛ̄ⲧⲟⲡⲟⲥ ⲛⲓⲙ ⲉⲛ̄ⲛⲉ-
30 ⲕⲕⲉ ϣⲁⲣⲟⲓ ⲉⲡⲉⲧⲟⲡⲟⲥ ⲡⲁⲓ ⲉⲓϣⲟⲟⲡ ⲉⲛϩⲏⲧϥ̄ ⲁⲛⲟⲕ
ⲇⲇ ⲛⲉⲕϫⲱⲕ ⲛⲁⲓ ⲉⲃ[ⲟ]ⲗ ⲉⲙⲡⲟⲩⲱϣ ⲉⲙⲡⲁϩⲏⲧ
ⲙⲛ ⲛⲁⲡⲟⲩⲗⲉⲅⲓⲁ ⲉⲛⲡ[ⲁ]ⲗ[ⲁ]ⲥ ϩⲛ̄ ⲟⲩⲧⲁⲭⲏ ⲧⲁⲭⲏ
ϩⲁⲉⲓⲟ ϫⲉ ⲧⲓⲱⲣⲉⲕ ⲧⲟⲩⲛⲁⲙ ⲉⲙⲡϣⲏⲣⲉ ⲧⲁⲓ ⲉⲧ-
ⲧⲁⲙⲁϩⲧⲉ ⲉⲙⲡⲥⲁϣⲉϥ ⲉⲛⲥⲓⲟⲩⲉ ⲉⲣⲉⲙⲏⲧⲥⲛⲟⲟⲥ
35 ⲉⲛⲥⲓⲟⲩ ⲟ ⲛ̄ⲛⲟⲩⲕⲗⲟⲙ ⲉⲛϫⲉⲛ ⲧⲉϥⲁⲡⲉ

back (→)

ⲥⲛⲟϥ
ⲉⲛϭⲉ-
ⲣⲟⲡⲉ
ⲉⲛⲗⲉ-
5 ⲩⲕⲱⲛ
ⲥⲧⲏⲣⲉϩ
ⲛⲁⲡⲟⲩⲕⲁ-
ⲗⲁⲙⲱⲛ
ⲙⲁⲥⲭⲉ
10 ϩⲟⲉⲓⲧ
ⲕⲟϣ
ⲗⲉⲩⲕⲱⲛ

15

ⲉⲕⲥⲁⲓ ⲉⲛ-
ⲛⲁⲓ
ⲉⲛϫⲉⲛ [ⲧ-]
ⲃⲁⲥⲓⲥ ⲉⲙⲡⲁ-
ⲁⲡⲟⲧ ⲛⲁⲧⲧⲱϣⲉⲙ
ⲉϥϣⲱ ⲗⲉⲩⲕⲱⲛ
ⲉⲣⲏⲡ ⲕⲱⲛ
20 ⲙⲟⲩ ⲧⲱⲃ
ⲕⲁⲓⲣⲉ ⲕⲁ
ϭⲉⲙⲟϥ ⲕⲁ
ⲡⲁⲓ ⲡⲉ ϭⲱⲣⲉϫ
ⲉⲛⲡⲁⲡⲟⲧ

25 ⲁϣⲧⲟϥ ⲉⲡⲉⲕ-
ⲙⲟⲧⲉ

at 180° 27 ⲟⲩⲫⲓⲁⲗⲉ ⲛ̄ⲕⲁⲙ..ⲉϩ ⲕⲟⲩϣⲧ
28 ⲛⲁⲗⲁⲩ

---

28 *i.e.* ˢϯⲱⲣ=ⲕ̄ | *i.e.* ˢⲙ̄-ⲡ-ⲧⲃⲃⲟ : *i.e.* ˢⲙ-ⲡ-ϥⲱ "by the hair" Emmel | *i.e.* πνεῦμα ‖
front **29** *l.* ϫⲉⲕⲁⲁⲥ | *i.e.* ˢⲉ=ⲕ-ⲉ-ⲕⲱ | *i.e.* ˢⲛ̄ⲥⲱ=ⲕ | *i.e.* τόπος ‖ **29–30** *i.e.* ˢⲛ̄=ⲅ-ⲉⲓ ? ‖ **30** *i.e.* τόπος |
i.e. ˢⲛ̄ϩⲏⲧ=ϥ ‖ **31** *i.e.* δ(εῖνα) δ(εῖνα) | *i.e.* ˢⲛ̄=ⲅ-ϫⲱⲕ ‖ **32** ⲁⲡⲟⲩⲗⲉⲅⲓⲁ corrected from
ⲛⲁⲡⲟⲩⲗⲉⲗⲓⲁ by overwriting *i.e.* ἀπολογία | *i.e.* ταχύ (twice) ‖ **33** *i.e.* ˢⲛ̄-ⲧ-ⲟⲩⲛⲁⲙ ‖
33–34 *l.* ⲉⲧ-ⲁⲙⲁϩⲧⲉ (dittography over the line) ‖ **34** *i.e.* ˢⲙⲛⲧ-ⲥⲛⲟⲟⲩⲥ ‖ **35** *i.e.* ˢⲛ̄-ⲟⲩ-ⲕⲗⲟⲙ
(dittography) | *i.e.* ˢⲉϫⲛ̄ ‖ **back 1** *i.e.* ˢⲥⲛⲟϥ ‖ **2–3** *i.e.* ˢϭⲉⲣⲟⲙⲡⲉ ‖ **5** *i.e.* λευκόν ‖ **6** *i.e.* στύραξ ‖
7–8 *i.e.* ὁποκάλαμος, *cf.* CDO *s.v.* ⲁⲡⲟⲕⲁⲗⲁⲙⲱⲛ ‖ **9** *i.e.* μόσχος or μαστίχη ‖ **10** *l.* ⲛ̄-ϩⲟⲟⲩⲧ ? :
ϩⲥⲉⲓ . Emmel ‖ **11** *l.* ⲕⲟⲩϣⲧ ‖ **13** *i.e.* ˢⲉ=ⲕ-ⲉ-ⲥϩⲁⲓ ‖ **16** *i.e.* βάσις ‖ **17** *i.e.* ˢⲁⲧ-ⲱϣⲙ ‖
18 *i.e.* ˢ ⲉⲃⲓⲱ | *i.e.* λευκόν : λογκⲱⲛ Emmel ‖ **19** *i.e.* ˢⲏⲣⲡ̄ ⲛ̄-ⲗⲉⲩⲕⲟⲛ : ⲉⲣⲉⲡ ⲗⲉⲕⲱⲛ Emmel ‖
20. *l.* ⲙⲟⲩ-ⲧⲱⲃⲉ : ⲙⲟⲟⲩ ⲛ̄ⲧⲱⲃⲉ ? Emmel ‖ **21** *i.e.* ˢⲕⲁⲣⲩⲁ ? see CDO *s.v.* ⲕⲁⲣⲟⲓⲁ or χαῖρε? : χαιρε or ⲕⲁⲓⲣⲉ
"offer greetings (?) 21 times (?)" Emmel ‖ **22** *i.e.* ˢϫⲟⲟⲩϥ ? *cf.* ᴮϭⲟⲙϥ see Crum CD 795a : verb + -ϥ
"... it" ? Emmel ‖ **23** *i.e.* ˢϭⲱⲣϭ ‖ **24** *i.e.* ˢⲛ̄-ⲡ-ⲁⲡⲟⲧ ‖ **25** *i.e.* ˢⲁϣⲧ=ϥ ‖ **27** *i.e.* φιάλη | ⲛ̄ⲕⲁⲙⲉ Emmel

I adjure you by the purity of the Holy Spirit, that you leave behind you every place and you |30 come to me, to this place in which I am, I, NN, child of NN, and you accomplish for me the desire of my heart and the requests of my tongue, quickly, quickly, yea, for I adjure you by the right hand of the Son who rules the seven stars, while the twelve |35 stars are the crown upon his head!

|back, left of figure Blood of a white dove, |6 *styrax, calamus juice, male? *musk?, |11 white *costus.

|13, right of figure You should draw these things |15 upon the base of the unfired *cup. White honey, white wine, |20 water ⟨from the month of⟩ Tobi, 21 nuts?, 21 papyrus? ⟨plants⟩?; this is the preparation of the cup.

|25, further right Hang it on your neck.

|27, at 180° degrees, hand 1? A ... bowl, white costus.

back Image: This depicts the angel Hormosiel, his curly hair framed by a halo, with two tube-like wings, standing on a platform to blow his trumpet; the letters ⲁ and ⲱ are written on his throat and body respectively; for a discussion of similar images of angels, see Dosoo 2022a: 139–151.

1–5. ⲥⲛⲟϥ ⲉⲛⲟⲉⲣⲟⲡⲉ ⲉⲛⲗⲉⲩⲕⲱⲛ : **"blood of a white dove"** The blood of white doves is commonly used in rituals with a positive goal, such as acquiring favour or good business; cf. PCM I 25 p. 17 ll. 20–24; PCM I 26 p. 15 l. 32; Cairo JdE 45060 (Kropp 1931: I no. K; KYP M303) l. 59; BL Ms. Or. 6796 (2, 3) (Kropp 1931: I no. H; KYP M118) back l. 112; P.Stras. K 204 + 205 + 282 §2.22 l. 9 (Hevesi 2018; KYP M92); BM EA 10414a (Zellmann-Rohrer 2022a: no. 3; KYP M287) back l. 17; cf. PCM I 12 p. 1 l. 7. For a discussion, see Dosoo 2022c: 517–519.

9. ⲙⲁⲥⲭⲉ : **"musk"** For this word, see Dosoo 2018: 17–18; alternatively understand "mastic".

16–17. ⲉⲛⲡⲁⲁⲡⲟⲧ ⲛⲁⲧⲧⲱⲉϭⲉⲙ : **"the unfired cup"** Literally "unslaked", in this context perhaps understand a cup made from clay dried in the sun rather than fired in a kiln. Emmel suggests to translate "pristine", that is, one which has not been used for cooking; cf. Crum CD 535a.

18–19. ⲉϥⲓⲱ ⲗⲉⲩⲕⲱⲛ ⲉⲣⲏⲡ ⲗⲉⲕⲱⲛ : **"white honey, white wine"** These ingredients recur in other recipes for a good singing voice (BL Ms. Or. 6794 (Kropp: I no. E; KYP M306), front ll. 56–58; BKU I 8, front ll. 33, 39; P.PalauRib. 137 (KYP M719; unpublished) front l. 3), demonstrating that they belong to the same ritual tradition. The colour white likely has a positive connotation (cf. Dosoo 2022c: 518), while the honey has the quality of sweetness desired for the user's voice (cf. front ll. 23, 25). See also Preininger forthcoming c: chapter 2.

20. ⲙⲟⲩ ⲧⲱⲃ : **"water ⟨from the month of⟩ Tobi"** Water blessed during the feast of Epiphany on 11th Tobi (19th January), the feast celebrating the baptism of Jesus, in a ritual called the 'Sanctification of the Waters' carried out the night before, during which the priest calls upon God to endow it with powers of purification. The ritual originally took place at the Nile, but from the tenth century was moved within the church building. The water is used to baptise the congregation (symbolically, by anointing the head in the modern rite), while participants may also take it home to use throughout the year (Basset 1915: 573–574; Drescher 1958: 60–61; Burmester 1967: 250–256; Grossmann 1991; Denysenko 2016; cf. the Coptic prayer for the sanctification in SPP XVIII 276 L.12–M.3). For other examples in the Coptic magical corpus, see BKU I 8 (KYP M81) l. 33; BL Ms. Or. 6796 (2), (3) back (Kropp 1931: I no. H; KYP M118) back ll. 104–105; P.Mich.Inv. 593 (Worrell 1930: 245, translating "brick water"; KYP M9) p. 6 l. 5–7 (cf. the same recipe in P.Mich.Inv. 594 front ll. 3–4; KYP M15). For examples of its use in later *Copto-Arabic magic, see the rituals for Psalms 4, 27, 31, 35, 74, 88 in Henein/Bianquis 1975; for Mediaeval and early Modern Greek magic (as ἁγιασμὸν τῶν Θειοφανείων/Φώτων etc.), see Delatte 1927: 43.15, 49.3, 50.22–23, 101.1–2, 127.32, 129.3, 137.11, 597.19–20, 620.22; for examples from Ethiopian magic, see Strelcyn 1981: 60.

back (→) (continued)

m² // ετβε ογмн nсϊмε ογднρanoc εчnaϫτ καλως ·
30 εκсгaϊ nnaϊ εγπεταλωn nκасϊτнρn : θγ г̅ асπаρτοn
ογвнτε nτε ρωч νογгτο [n]κамн тнρч̅ · мn ογбιнбλω εκ-
τωмεс m̅мος επρο nτεсϊмε κnαναγ ετεчбoм гn ογταχн //
/ εριβιετϊοдγθч̅ϕοραρεθа θτλοαποαε
 дικων aaaaaaa εεεεεεε нннннннн
35 ιιιιιιιι οοοοοοο γγγγγγγ ωωωωωωω аεнιογ ταενι //

τϊω̅ρκ ερωτn̅ n̅nετn̅ραn ετογααβ τнρογ мn̅ nετn̅θεсῒ
мn̅ nετn̅ϕнλακτнριοn мn̅ nετn̅θρονος ετετn̅гмοος
гϊχοογ мn̅ nετn̅cτωλн ετбoλε m̅мωτn̅ мn̅ n̅ετn̅-
cτнλн ετχнκ εβoλ [мn̅ nετn̅]τ[ο]πος ετn̅τn̅ϣοοπ n̅гнτο[γ]
40 τϊω̅ρκ ερωτn nnaϊ τнρογ ετβε ογмн n̅гнτ мn ογλнπε
мn ογλιβε n̅гнτ гn̅ πг[н]τ̅ nаȷаȷ гn̅ ογταχн τϊω̅ρκ n̅nε-
τn̅ᵀnοб nбoм n̅τεβ[ε]ρсεβογρ πρρω n̅n̅днмοnϊοn
... πογχαι n̅гογ .... m̅nτρмn̅гнτ τϊω̅ρκ ερωτn
nnaϊ τнρογ m̅περκααс εογωm ογдε [εсω ογдε ....]
45 ογдε гемοος ϣan̅τεсερ θε n̅nιογгωρ nκ[амε]
ετλοβε n̅cа nεϣ[н]ρε αγω n̅θε n̅ογτελτιλ [*nothing lost?*]

---

front (↓), *below and at 180° to ll. 1–35*

36 / m̅мοογ εсαϣε n̅cа ογκατος n̅θε nογгοч εсαϣε n̅[...]
 ⳩γχн nдаа ϣan̅τεсει ϣа nιм а, гn̅ ογταχн . мn̅ [...]
 τϊθнм . сεθ [..] . [*ca.* 5] . [. ?]

---

29 *i.e.* ˢмε | *i.e.* ˢcгιмε | *i.e.* τύραννος | *i.e.* ˢnαϣτ | *i.e* καλῶς || **30** *i.e.* ˢε꞊κ-ε-сгαι | *i.e.* πέταλον | *i.e.* κασσίτερος | *i.e.* θυ(σία) | *i.e.* ἄσφαλτος : ἄσπαρτον or ἄσφαλτος ? Emmel || **31** *i.e.* ˢε꞊κ-ε- || **32** *i.e.* ˢτωм꞊ | *i.e.* ˢcгιмε | *i.e.* ταχύ || **34** *cf.* τ-εἰκών ? || **36** *i.e.* θυσία || **37** *i.e.* φυλακτήριον | *i.e.* θρόνος | *i.e.* ˢετ-τετn̅- || **38** *i.e.* στολή || **39** *i.e.* στήλη | *i.e.* ˢετ-τετn̅- || **40** *i.e.* λύπη || **41** *i.e* δ(ε)ῖ(να) δ(ε)ῖ(να) : *i.e.* ταχύ || **41–42** n̅nετn̅nοб corrected to n̅τnοб Emmel || **42** *i.e.* ˢp̅ρο | *i.e.* δαιμόνιον || **43** .ογχαι n̅.ογ Emmel || **44** [εсω ογдε ....] Emmel || **44, 45** *i.e.* οὔτε || **45** *i.e.* ˢгмοος | *i.e.* ˢογгορ | n̅κ[амε] Emmel, *cf.* ογгορε καмε εчnαβι nεсϣнρε in *BKU* I 3 ll. 8–9 (KYP M77) || **front 36** *i.e.* κάδος | Emmel suggests to read εn̅cατε at the end of the line | "snake desperate [for] the soul of NN" Emmel || **37** *i.e.* δ(ε)ῖ(να) (three times) || *i.e.* ψυχή | *i.e.* ταχύ | perhaps restore мn ογбнπε or similar : ...[...] Emmel || **38** τεθнмιсεθ [...].[*ca.* 6]α[.] Emmel

|*back, 29* For a woman's love: A "tyrant" which is very strong. |30 You should write these on a leaf of tin. Offering: three? ⟨measures of⟩ bitumen, foam of the mouth of a horse which is all black, and a bat. You should bury it at the door of the woman. You will see its power quickly.

Eribetioduthfpharorethathtloapoae (*kharaktēres*: ⵞB××Δʒ⊠)
(*kharaktēres*: ⊠EƵ+) ... Dikōn (?) AAAAAAA EEEEEEE ĒĒĒĒĒĒĒ |35 IIIIIIII OOOO OOO UUUUUUU ŌŌŌŌŌŌŌ AEĒIOU Taeni

I adjure you (pl.) by your all your holy *names and your offerings and your *phylacteries and your *thrones, which you sit upon, and by your garments, which cover you, and by your stelae, which are perfect, [and by your] *places in which you dwell! |40 I adjure you by all of these, concerning a love of the heart, and grief and madness of the heart in the heart of NN, child of NN, quickly! I adjure you by your great power, Beelzebub, the king of demons, ... the *wellbeing ... wisdom?; I adjure you by all of these! Do not let her eat or ... |45 or sit, until she becomes like [black] dogs mad for their children, and like a drop |*front, 36* of water hanging from a jar, like a snake hanging from? ... soul of NN, child of NN, until she comes quickly to NN, child of NN ...

KD, EL & MP, edited from photograph, tracings by KD & JS.

Image: The figures here seem to constitute a performative depiction of the ritual; on the left a man and a woman stand side by side, while in the middle a figure, likely representing the practitioner, is depicted in the orant position, surrounded by *kharaktēres* representing his power. On the right, the man is now kissing the woman, with the *kharaktēres* beside him representing the force of the spell; see Dosoo 2018: 30–31 for a discussion.

29. ⲟⲩⲇⲏⲣⲁⲛⲟⲥ : "a 'tyrant'" This seems to be a technical term for a type of love spell which takes control of its target, but it is otherwise unattested in our corpus.

30. ⲅ : "three" Emmel proposes an uncertain abbreviated word modified by following ἄσπαρτον rather than a numeral here.

45. ⲛ̄ⲛⲓⲟⲩϩⲱⲱⲣ : "dogs" Literally "these (black) dogs", but an instance of the affective demonstrative (or 'strong article') being used in a generalisation, equivalent to a noun without an article in English (Layton 2000: 49).

***back* l. 44–*front* l. 36.** ⲙ̄ⲡⲉⲣⲕⲁⲁⲥ ⲉⲟⲩⲱⲙ : "Do not let her eat..." This passage draws upon the common motifs of love as the inability to eat, or drink (LOVE IS ABSTINENCE), and of love as animal behaviour; see the notes to *PCM* I 7 ll. 32–36 for parallels for animal behaviour in the Coptic corpus. For parallels to the inability to eat or drink in the context of Greek magic, see Martinez 1995, in the context of Jewish magic, see Saar 2017: 126–128, and in the context of Syriac magic, see Cherkashina/Lyavdansky 2021: 78–81; Cherkashina/Lyavdansky 2022: 29–31. Compare Isaiah 40.15 for the analogy of a "drop of water in a jar" (ⲟⲩⲧⲉⲗⲧ̄ⲗⲉ ⲉⲃⲟⲗ ϩⲛ ⲟⲩⲕⲁⲇⲟⲥ); *cf.* the discussion in Jernstedt 1929: 125–128; a near exact parallel to this phrase may be found in *PCM* I 28 p. 6 ll. 11–12. For other instances of the motif of LOVE IS ABSTINENCE in this volume, see *PCM* I 28 p. 5 ll. 11–13; *PCM* I 32 p. 1 l. 16.

PCM I 18. Curse to cause sickness

Middle Egypt ?	32.4 (H) × 24.1 (W) cm	VIII CE

Other references: P.CtYBR inv. 1800 qua; TM 99993; KYP M294; Bélanger Sarrazin #9.
Editions: Emmel in Meyer/Smith 1994: appendix 4 (*ed. pr.*).
Translations: Emmel in Meyer/Smith 1994: no. 106.
Additional commentary: Petersen 1964: no. 62; MacCoull 1975: 219; Friedman 1989: 198; Krueger 2022: 294–296.
Present location: New Haven, Beinecke Library (Yale University).
Image: https://hdl.handle.net/10079/digcoll/2759462
Linguistic description: Sahidic (non-standard).
Contents:
1. Front ll. 1–20: Curse to cause sickness (KYP T483)

Complete sheet of papyrus with damage along the folds and a piece of the bottom-right missing, containing a curse intended to cause sickness. It is rectangular in shape, with 3 vertical and 8 horizontal creases visible. The back is uninscribed. The manuscript was purchased in New York, from Hans P. Kraus, the rare book dealer,[1] and acquired by Yale University on the 1st May 1964 with funds donated by Edwin John Beinecke. Its provenance is unknown, although Petersen notes that place names in papyri from the same collection point to Middle Egypt.[2]

The sheet is written in black ink in a single column of 20 lines (↓). The hand is a regular, bimodal majuscule, respecting intralinear space. The script demonstrates a slight slant to the right, particularly in the final seven lines. The horizontal and right vertical stroke of the ⲏ are sometimes written in a single movement, leading it to resemble the minuscule form. There are occasional ligatures, in particular ⲧ + ⲓ. ⲉ, ⲟ, and ⲥ are very narrow, while ⲗ and ⲧ are wide, and ⲃ is tall, extending beyonds the bounds of the general bilinearity. Supralineation is only used with *voces magicae*. Petersen (1964) hesitantly suggested a sixth or seventh century date, but close hands may be found in *P.Ryl.Copt.* 175 (TM 87349; 721 CE) and *PSI Com.* XI 2 (TM 65033; 743–769 CE); we thus suggest an eighth century date.[3]

The dialect is Sahidic, only slight diverging from the literary standard, writing the supralinear stroke as ⲉ and lacking ⲛ › ⲙ assimilation before a labial; while these are both common, the latter is particularly characteristic of Middle Egypt.[4]

---

[1] "Guide to the Yale Papyrus Collection."
[2] Petersen 1964: "Introductory note".
[3] We are very grateful to Ágnes Mihálykó for suggesting these comparanda.
[4] *Cf.* Kahle 1954: I 100.

front (↓)

[.] . [. . . .] . . ⲛⲁⲥ ⲡⲥⲁⲧⲁⲏⲗ ⲧⲓⲱⲣⲉⲕ ⲉⲣⲟⲕ ⲉⲛⲛⲁⲏⲗ
ⲡⲁⲓ ⲉⲧ[ⲉ]ⲣⲉ ⲧⲉϥⲟⲩⲛⲁⲙ ⲧⲁⲗⲏⲩ ⲉϩⲣⲁⲓ ⲉϫⲉⲛ ⲫⲁⲣⲙⲁ
ⲉⲛⲡⲓⲱⲧ ⲉⲧⲟⲩⲁⲁⲃ ⲙⲉⲛ ⲁⲥⲁⲣⲱⲑ ⲡⲛⲟϭ ⲉⲛⲭ[ⲉ]ⲣⲟⲩⲃⲓⲛ
ⲡⲁⲓ ⲉⲧⲣⲟⲉⲓⲥ ⲉⲧⲉⲥⲕⲩⲛⲏ ⲉⲛⲡⲓⲱⲧ ⲡⲡⲁⲛⲧⲱⲕⲣⲁⲧⲱⲣ
5   ⲧⲓⲱⲣⲉⲕ ⲉⲛⲡ[ⲟ]ⲩ ⲡⲁⲅⲅⲉⲗⲟⲥ ⲉⲛⲡⲉⲑⲛⲥⲓⲁⲥⲧⲏⲣⲓⲟⲛ ⲉⲧⲟⲩⲁⲁⲃ
ϫⲉ ⲛⲕⲟ ⲛⲣⲉⲙϩⲉ ⲁⲛ ⲟⲩⲇⲉ ⲛⲉⲅⲃⲏⲗ ⲉⲃⲟⲗ ⲉⲃⲱⲕ ⲉϩⲣⲁⲓ ϣⲁ ⲡⲛⲟⲩ[ⲧⲉ]
ⲟⲩⲇⲉ ⲧⲉⲕⲑⲛⲥⲓⲁ ⲉϩⲣⲁⲓ ⲏ ⲉⲟⲩⲱϣⲧ ⲉⲛⲡⲉⲕⲣⲓⲧⲏⲥ ⲉⲙⲙⲏ[ⲧ]
ⲟⲩⲇⲉ ⲉⲁⲡⲁⲛⲧⲁ ⲉⲡϫⲟⲉⲓⲥ ⲉⲛⲡⲉⲕⲁϩⲉⲣⲁⲧⲉⲕ ⲉϩⲣⲁⲓ ⲉϫⲉⲛ
ⲡⲥⲱ[ⲙⲁ] ⲁⲗⲗⲁ ⲛⲉϥⲉⲓⲛⲉ ⲉϩⲣⲁⲓ [ⲉ]ϫⲱϥ ⲉⲛⲟⲩϩⲓⲥⲉ ⲙⲉⲛ ⲟⲩϣⲱ[ⲛⲉ]
10 ⲙⲉⲛ ⲟⲩⲗⲟϭⲗⲉϭ ⲙⲉⲛ ⲟⲩϩⲣⲉⲩⲙⲁ ⲙⲉⲛ ⲟⲩⲁⲥⲓⲕ ⲙⲉⲛ ⲟⲩⲕⲁⲥ
ⲙⲉⲛ ⲟⲩϩⲗⲟⲡⲗⲉⲡ ⲙⲉⲛ ⲟⲩⲙⲉⲧⲕⲟⲩⲓ ⲉⲛϩⲏⲧ ⲙⲉⲛ ⲟⲩⲉⲣⲙⲟ-
ⲉⲧ ⲙⲉⲛ ⲟⲩϣⲃⲉ ⲙⲉⲛ ⲟ[ⲩⲧ]ⲉⲙⲟⲛⲓⲟⲛ ⲉⲛⲗⲓⲃⲉ ⲙⲉⲛ
ϣⲃⲉ ⲉⲛϭⲓ ⲉⲛϣⲱⲛⲉ ⲉⲣ[ⲉⲛⲁⲓ] ϣⲟⲃⲉ ⲉⲩⲉⲓ ⲉⲛⲕⲉⲛⲧⲟⲩ ⲉϩⲣⲁⲓ
ⲉϫⲉⲛ ⲡ[ⲥⲱ]ⲙⲁ ⲁⲗⲗⲁ ⲉⲛⲛ[ⲉ]ϩⲟⲟⲩ ⲧⲏⲣⲟⲩ ⲉⲛⲡⲉϥⲱⲛⲉϩ
15 ϫⲉ ⲛⲉⲙⲁⲕⲟⲥ ⲉⲛϩⲟⲟⲩⲧ ⲟⲩⲇⲉ ⲫⲁⲣⲙⲁⲅⲟⲥ ⲉⲛⲥϩⲓⲙⲉ ⲉϣ ⲛⲁ
ⲛⲁϥ ⲟⲩⲇⲉ ⲉⲣ ⲡⲁϩⲣⲉ ⲉⲣⲟϥ ⲉⲃⲟⲗ ϩⲉⲛ ⲛⲁϭⲓϫ ⲁⲛⲟⲕ ⲇⲁ ϣⲁⲛ-
ⲧⲓⲛⲁ ⲛⲁϥ ⲉⲓⲣⲉ ⲁⲩⲱ ⲛⲉϭϫⲱⲕ ⲛⲁⲓ ⲉⲃⲟⲗ ⲉⲛⲡⲟⲩⲱϣ ⲧⲏⲣⲉϥ
ⲉⲛⲡⲁϩⲏⲧ ⲡⲉⲧⲉⲙⲁ ⲉⲛⲧⲁⲯⲩⲭⲏ ϩⲉⲛ ⲧⲉⲕⲛⲟϭ ⲉⲛϭⲟⲙ ⲁⲥⲙⲟⲧⲉⲟⲥ ⲧⲉⲙⲟⲛⲓⲁⲕⲟⲥ ⲁⲓ[ⲟ ⲁⲓ]ⲟ ⲧⲁⲭⲏ ⲧⲁⲭⲏ . . . [.] . [.]ⲑ
20 ⲫⲉⲗⲗⲱⲑ ⲁⲑⲉⲥ ⲧⲁⲭⲏ ⲧ[ⲁⲭⲏ . . . ?]

[…] Psataēl. I adjure you, Ennaēl, he whose right hand is lifted over the chariot of the holy Father, and Asarōth, the great *cherub, he who guards the *tabernacle of the Almighty Father!

|⁵ I adjure ⟨you⟩ today, O *angel of the holy altar, that you will not be free, nor will you be released to go up to God, nor ⟨to take⟩ your offering up, nor to worship the true judge, nor to meet the Lord, until you have stood upon the body ⟨of⟩ NN and you have brought upon him suffering and disease |¹⁰ and sickness and a discharge and a fever and a pain and a weariness and a dejection and a shivering and a swelling and a demon of madness and seventy diseases, each one being different, and you bring them down upon the [body] ⟨of⟩ NN for all the days of his life, |¹⁵ so that neither a male magician nor a female sorcerer will be able to take pity on him, nor heal him from my hands, I, NN, child of NN, until I have mercy upon him!

Act and complete for me the entire desire of my heart, the demand of my soul through your great power, demoniac Asmodeus, yea, yea, quickly, quickly! … |²⁰ Phellōth, Athes, quickly, quickly!

KD, EL & MP, edited from photograph.

---

2. ⲧⲉϥⲟⲩⲛⲁⲙ : "right hand" Emmel mistakenly translates "left hand".

3. ⲡⲛⲟϭ ⲉⲛ̅ⲭ[ⲉ]ⲣⲟⲩⲃⲓⲛ : "the great cherub" Emmel translates "great guardian angel". The title "great cherub" is applied in Pseudo-Chrysostom, *On the Four Bodiless Living Creatures* (CC 177) to the chief of the *Four Living Creatures who draw the chariot of god, in which he is named Kherubiēl (Wasink 1991); he is likely the lion-faced creature (Hagen 2007). Asarōth is mentioned as the mount of God in *PCM* I 26 p. 10 l. 27 and P. Vindob. K 8301 (Stegemann 1933–1934: no. 44; KYP M273) ll. 1–5, and the name also appears in *P.Lond.Copt.* 524 (KYP M359) l. 115, without further context, but with three other names (ⲓⲁⲑⲁⲧⲁⲃⲓⲣ, ⲓⲕⲉⲅⲅⲓⲏⲗ, and ⲥⲉⲃⲣⲓⲏⲗ) perhaps the other three Living Creatures; *cf.* Dosoo 2021d: 417.

5. ⲡⲁⲅⲅⲉⲗⲟⲥ ⲉⲛⲡⲉⲑⲛⲥⲓⲁⲥⲧⲏⲣⲓⲟⲛ ⲉⲧⲟⲩⲁⲁⲃ : "O angel of the holy altar" As discussed in Krueger 2022, the "angel of the altar" (also "angel of the sacrifice" or "angel of the *topos*") is the guardian angel of the church altar in Egyptian Christianity, attested from the fourth century. One of the angel's tasks, alluded to here, is to convey the prayers and offerings of the congregation to God. The prominence of the angel of the altar here is perhaps a sign that the written curse was to be deposited at the altar; *cf.* BM EA 10391 (Zellmann-Rohrer 2022a: no. 1; KYP M302) back ll. 80–82, a curse which is to be buried under the altar of a *topos* (*i.e.*, a monastery, church or shrine; ⲡⲉⲑⲛⲥⲓⲁⲥⲧⲏⲣⲓⲟⲛ ⲛⲟⲩⲧⲟⲡⲟⲥ).

15. ⲛⲉⲙⲁⲕⲟⲥ ⲉⲛϩⲟⲟⲩⲧ ⲟⲩⲇⲉ ⲫⲁⲣⲙⲁⲅⲟⲥ ⲉⲛⲥϩⲓⲙⲉ : "neither a male magician nor a female sorcerer" For the claim that (other?) "magicians" will be unable to heal a curse, compare *PCM* I 3, front col. 1 ll. 30–33, and *cf.* the discussion in Dosoo 2021b: 51.

18–19. ⲁⲥⲙⲟⲧⲉⲟⲥ : "Asmodeus" A demonic figure known from Tobit 3.8, 16 *etc.*, in which he murders seven husbands of Sarah before he is banished and bound by the intervention of the angel Raphael. He recurs in the *Testament of Solomon* 5 in an account clearly inspired by Tobit (McCown 1922: 21*–25*; Charlesworth 1983: 965–967 (trans.)). Since the demon here seems to be under the command of the angel of the altar, Krueger (2022: 295–296) suggests that this text may have been associated with a church dedicated to Raphael. For other instances of angels commanding demons in curses, see P.Berol. 10587 (Beltz 1983: no. I 555; KYP M510) col. 1 ll. 21–23; Bodleian MS. Copt. c (P) 4 (Crum 1896; KYP M412) back l. 6.

PCM I 19. Adjuration to protect virginity and marriage

Upper Egypt ? 8 (H) × 24 (W) cm late VIII–early X CE
Other references: RC-2643; TM 874221; *P.Rosicrucian Mag.Copt.*; KYP M574.
Editions: Blumell/Dosoo 2021 (*ed. pr.*).
Translations: Blumell/Dosoo 2021.
Present location: San José, Rosicrucian Museum.
Image: https://s3.amazonaws.com/pastperfectonline/images/museum_698/001/rc2643-2.jpg
Linguistic description: Sahidic.
Contents:
1. Front ll. 1–5: Invocation to protect virginity and marriage (KYP T659)

Complete rectangular sheet of papyrus, slightly damaged on the right side, leaving some of the individual fibres visible. The presence of the generic name marker likely indicates that this was a formulary, an invocation to protect the 'purity' of a woman, perhaps in the context of a celibate marriage. The manuscript was folded or rolled; vertical creases are apparent *ca.* every 2 cm, about 14 in all.

The manuscript was purchased as part of a lot of six Coptic manuscripts for $150 on the 13th October 1952 from Ulrich Steindorff Carrington, the son of the Egyptologist Georg Steindorff, who had died in August of the previous year. The papyrus had been part of his father's collection.[1]

The text is written in black ink on the front (→) of the papyrus; the back was left blank. Between the third and fourth line, there is a wider interlinear space of about 1 cm, separating possessive article from noun.[2] The script is an informal bilinear, bimodal, right-sloping majuscule. ⲑ, ⲧ, ⲩ, ⳉ have serifs, and there is a distinctive ⲑ-ⲉ ligature. The ⲃ is significantly larger than other letters, the ⲙ appears deeply curved; we follow the original editors in proposing a date in the late eighth to early tenth centuries.[3] The dialect is non-standard Sahidic, displaying the lack of ⲛ › ⲙ assimilation before labials, the writing of the supralinear stroke as ⲉ, and of ⲱ for ^{S}ⲟ; the original editors suggest an Upper Egyptian origin, primarily because of the use of the ⲉⲣⲉ-SUBJECT-ⲛⲁ future with ϫⲉⲕⲁⲁⲥ in l. 3.[4]

---

[1] Rosicrucian Museum Master Artifact Record Database; Blumell/Dosoo 2021: 120, n. 7.
[2] Blumell/Dosoo 2021: 121, n. 10.
[3] Blumell/Dosoo (2021: 122) compare the script to Pierpont Morgan M636 (*post* 795–797 CE) and *P.Lond.Copt.* 514 (*ca.* 880–907 CE; TM 99548).
[4] Blumell/Dosoo 2021: 128; *cf.* Depuydt 2017.

front (→)

ⲧⲓⲱⲣⲉⲕ ⲉⲣⲱⲧⲉⲛ ⲛⲡⲱⲟⲩ ϫⲉ ⲛⲑⲉ ⲛⲧⲁϩⲁⲣⲉϩ
ⲉⲧⲟⲩⲡⲁⲣⲑⲉⲛⲓⲁ ⲙⲉⲛ ⲡⲟⲩⲧⲉⲃⲱ ⲙⲉⲛ ⲡⲟⲩⲕⲁⲙⲟⲥ
ⲉⲣⲉⲇ︦ⲇ︦ ⲛⲁϩⲁⲣⲉϩ ⲉⲧⲉⲥ-

vac.

    ⲡⲁⲣⲑⲉⲛⲓⲁ ⲙⲉⲛ ⲡⲉⲥⲕⲁⲙⲟⲥ
5   ⲙⲉⲛ ⲡⲉⲥⲧⲉⲃⲱ

---

1 *i.e.* ˢϯ-ⲱⲣⲕ̄ | *i.e.* ˢⲙ̄-ⲡⲟⲟⲩ || **2** *i.e.* παρθενία | *i.e.* ˢⲧⲃ̄ⲃⲟ | *i.e.* γάμος || **3** *i.e.* δ(ε)ῖ(να) δ(ε)ῖ(να) || **3–4** *vacat* in papyrus || **4** *i.e.* παρθενία | *i.e.* γάμος || **5** *i.e.* ˢⲧⲃ̄ⲃⲟ.

I adjure you (pl.) today, that, just as you (f.s.) guarded your virginity and your purity and your marriage, may NN, child of NN, guard her virginity and her marriage |⁵ and her purity!

KD, EL & MP, edited from photograph.

---

1. "**you, (pl.)... you (f.s.)**" A rare case in which the adjured being is female; for other examples see *PCM* I 25 p. 1 ll. 25–26 (adressing a female demon), *PCM* I 29 l. 10 (adressing a scorpion); BnF Suppl.Grec. 1340 (unpublished; KYP M39) l. 9 (adressing Artemis). The apparent alternation between plural and singular may be either an error, or indicate the use of the plural to indicate respect, an example of the phenomenon known in linguistics as the 'T-V distinction', in which V pronouns indicate greater formality or express a hierarchical relationship between speaker and addressee. For the first possibility, compare, for example, *PCM* I front ll. 1, 7–8 and *PCM* I 27 ll. 4, 9, in which singular and plural forms alternate. For the possibility of the T-V distinction, see the discussion in Blumell/Dosoo 2021: 124. The likely addressee here is Mary, in her role as the "ever-virgin" (ἀειπάρθενος), who is called upon to help the target to maintain her virginity in marriage just as Mary did (Blumell/Dosoo 2021: 139).

2. ⲉⲧⲟⲩⲡⲁⲣⲑⲉⲛⲓⲁ ⲙⲉⲛ ⲡⲟⲩⲧⲉⲃⲱ ⲙⲉⲛ ⲡⲟⲩⲕⲁⲙⲟⲥ : "**your virginity and your purity and your marriage**" "Virginity" here likely refers straightforwardly to lack of sexual experience, rather than being 'faithful' to one's spouse. "Purity" (ˢⲧⲃ̄ⲃⲟ) in this context translates Greek ἁγνεία, with the more specific meaning of "chastity". The pairing of the two nouns is attested from around the fourth century in reference to Christian celibate ascetics, both male and female, and the Virgin Mary, who "guard" (ϩⲁⲣⲉϩ/φυλάσσειν) their virginity and chastity. The reference to "marriage" is less expected; Blumell/Dosoo (2021) suggest the context of celibate marriage, in which couples agreed to cohabit without engaging in sexual intercourse (to be distinguished from spiritual marriage, in which celibate ascetic couples lived together without formally marrying). Such marriages are attested in Egypt in literary sources which date from the fourth century, but are particularly common in Egypt around the ninth (Mikhail 2017: 42). On this understanding, this text would represent a short adjuration of Mary to be used by an individual in a celibate marriage—likely the husband, since it refers to the woman in the third person—to ensure that the wife remains celibate. Alternatively, it might be possible to understand the text as being intended to protect an unmarried woman from losing her virginity, and thus marriageability; this seems to be a concern in two other surviving texts, *PCM* I 23 ll. 21–49 and P.Stras. K 135 (Crum 1922b; KYP M474). The first of these texts also mentions the virginity of Mary, although both include the binding of the virility of a specific man, and neither mention marriage. Compare the discussion of these texts in Blumell/Dosoo 2021: 129–131 who suggest that young women's parents might be the most likely commissioners of such a ritual.

PCM I 20. Love spell in the form of a Horus-Isis narrative charm

Arsionites (Faiyum) ? 14 (H) × 16 (W) cm VIII–IX CE
Other references: P.Donadoni; TM 102259; KYP M127; Bélanger Sarrazin #1.
Editions: Donadoni 1965–1966 (*ed. pr.*) (repr. in Donadoni 1986: 545–552); Bélanger Sarrazin forthcoming a: appendix 3 no. 4.
Translations: Donadoni 1965–1966 (Italian) (repr. in Donadoni 1986: 545–552); Pernigotti 1995: no. 20 (Italian); van der Vliet 2019b: 334; Bélanger Sarrazin forthcoming a: appendix 3, no. 4. (French).
Additional commentary: Martín Hernández/Torallas Tovar 2014; Blumell/Dosoo 2018; Hevesi 2019; Bélanger Sarrazin forthcoming a: chapter 2.
Present location: Rome, private collection family Donadoni.
Image: Plates II–III.
Linguistic description: Sahidic with Faiyumic features.
Contents:
1. Front ll. 1–16: Love spell in the form of Horus-Isis *historiola*-based charm (KYP T342)
2. Back l. 1: Name of target (?) (KYP T6890)

Complete sheet of papyrus, damaged on the left, and along the fold line in the top third of the sheet, resulting in damage to lines 5 and 6. At least 5 vertical and 2 horizontal creases are visible. The papyrus is of uncertain provenance, having been gifted before 1965 to Sergio Donadoni (1914–2015) by his former student Carla Burri, perhaps acquired during her time as cultural attachée to the Italian Embassy in Cairo (1964–1981).[1] The papyrus remains in the private collection of the Donadoni family in Rome.

The hand of the front is an irregular, generally upright majuscule; letter heights are inconsistent and there is little interlinear space. The ⲁ has a rounded bowl separated from a straight oblique stem, ⲇ and ⲝ are narrow and highly angular. ⲉ, ⲑ, and ⲥ are also narrow, although ⲉ has a long middle stroke. ⲕ is written in two movements, the first resembling a Latin V, with the lower oblique stroke drawn separately in a second movement. ⲙ is curved but not deeply, and ⲟ is small; ⲩ is written like a Latin V. The bottom stroke of the ⲱ is straight and sloped to the left, while ϩ is bilinear. There is no supralineation or punctuation, but diaeresis

---

[1] Donadoni 1965–1966: 285 n. 1. On Burri, see Orsenigo 2020, who notes (p. 53) that she was a "regular visitor to auction houses and dealers authorized by the Egyptian government... she could often be found at the Sale Room of the Cairo Egyptian Museum making purchases on her own or on friend's behalf". While the late Donadoni's records do not record the date of the gift, a time shortly after her arrival in Egypt in 1964 seems likely.

is always used on ι. The hand's idiosyncrasy makes dating difficult, but similar letterforms may be found in a few private legal documents from the Faiyum (*CPR* IV 55, 66, & 88). Although dated by their original editor to the eighth century, this is somewhat arbitrary; documents from the Faiyum tend to date to the late eighth to ninth centuries, a range we likewise propose for this papyrus. We may note that like this magical manuscript, Faiyumic legal texts tend to be wider than they are tall.[2]

A single word is written on the lower left part of the back, at 90° counterclockwise to the front, in a second, alphabetic, hand suggestive of an even lower level of scribal training. ⲁ consists of a short vertical stroke with a rounded second stroke written in nearly in the centre. o resembles a mirrored ⲁ with a flat left-hand side, apparently written in a second stroke.

The dialect is broadly Sahidic, heavily influenced by what are best understood as Faiyumic features. The hypercorrection of ⲗ to ⲣ suggests a writer whose own dialect was lambdicistic. There is a similar, albeit non-dialectal hypercorrection of ⲧ to ⲁ, ⲃ to ϥ, and use of the long form of the vowels ⲉⲓ and ⲟⲩ where their reduced forms would be expected in Sahidic. We also see the occasional omission of the circumstantial ⲉ- (apocope), and the writing of ⲉ for schwa or ⲛ̄. There are examples of the exchange of the vowels ⲉ/ⲏ and ⲟ/ⲱ, as well as, once (l. 1), ⲉ for ⁵ⲟ. The use of ⲙⲉϫⲉ-/ⲙⲉϫⲁ⸗ for ⁵ⲡⲉϫⲉ-/ⲡⲉϫⲁ⸗ is likewise associated by Quecke (1970: 373–374) with the Faiyum, although Kahle (1954: I 123–124) associates it with regions B–E, that is, from the Faiyum to Armant.

---

[2] Garel 2018: 201–203, 206–207.

front (↓)

m¹ ⳨ ⲁⲉⲓⲙⲟⲟϣⲉ ϩⲓⲣⲉⲛ ⲉⲡⲉⲣⲉ ⲛⲁⲙⲉⲛⲧⲉ ⲁⲓϩⲉ ⲟⲩⲥⲁⲓⲉ
ⲛⲁⲣⲁⲩ ⲛⲕⲁⲙ ϥⲁⲣ ⲉⲥϩⲙⲟⲟⲥ ϩⲉⲭⲉ ⲟⲩϣⲱⲧⲉ ⲛϣⲛⲉ
ⲉⲣⲉⲟⲩϥⲉⲥⲉⲕⲓⲛ ϩⲓϫⲱⲥ ⲉⲥⲥⲱⲕ ⲙⲟⲩ ⲉⲕⲁⲧⲉⲥ ⲛϩⲟ-
ⲙⲉⲧ ⲉⲥ . . . ⲣϭ . ϲ ⲙⲡⲛⲓⲡⲉ ⲙⲉⲭⲁⲓ ⲛⲁⲥ ϫⲉ ⲇⲥⲁ-
5   ⲓⲉ ⲇⲓ ⲟⲩⲡⲉ ⲉⲣϣⲓ ⲙⲉⲭⲁⲥ ⲛⲁⲓ ϫⲉ ⲥⲁϩⲱⲕ ⲥⲁⲃⲁ-
ⲣ ⲙϥⲓ ⲡⲉⲥⲁϣ ⲡⲁϩⲉⲧ ⲙ . ⲓ . . . ϩⲓⲣⲉⲛ ⲉⲡⲉⲣⲉ ⲛⲁⲙⲉ-
[ⲛⲧⲉ] ⲁⲓⲡⲱⲧ ⲥⲁⲃⲟⲣ ⲙⲟⲥ ⲁⲓϩⲓⲥⲉ ⲁⲓϩⲓⲙⲉ ⲁⲓⲁϣⲁϩⲟⲙ ⲙⲉ-
[ⲭⲉ] ⲛⲥⲉ ⲛⲁⲓ ϫⲉ ⲁϩⲣⲟⲕ ⲕⲣⲓⲙⲉ ⲕⲁϣⲁϩⲟⲙ ϫⲉ ⲁϩⲣⲟⲓ ⲁⲛ
[ⲧⲁⲣ]ⲓⲙⲉ ⲛⲇⲁⲓϭⲓⲛ ⲟⲩⲥⲁⲓⲉ ⲛⲥϩⲓⲙⲉ ⲉⲓⲟⲩⲱϣ ⲉⲇⲓ ⲟⲩⲡ-
10   [ⲉ ⲉ]ⲣⲱⲥ ⲙⲡⲉⲥⲁϣ ⲡⲁϩⲉⲧ ⲙⲉⲭⲁⲥ ϫⲉ ⲕⲁⲛ ⲙⲡⲉⲕϩⲉ
[ⲉⲣⲱ]ⲓ ⲙⲡⲉϩⲉ ⲡⲁⲣⲁⲛ ⲙⲡⲉⲕϩⲉ ⲡⲣⲁⲛ ⲙⲡⲉⲓϣⲟⲙⲉ-
[ⲧ] ⲛⲁⲛⲕⲉⲣⲟⲥ ⲕⲓⲣⲓⲉ ⲕⲓⲣⲓⲉ ⲡⲣⲱⲥⲕⲉⲉⲩⲛⲓ ϯ-
[. .] . ⲉⲧⲛⲓⲛⲉ ⲉⲣⲁⲧ ⲇ ⲛⲓⲙ ⲇϣⲉ ⲛⲛⲓⲙ ⲇⲁϣⲱ-
[ⲡⲉ] ⲛⲉⲙⲁⲥ ⲇⲁⲛⲟⲩϫⲉ ⲛⲇⲁⲉⲡⲉⲑⲉⲙⲓ ⲉⲣⲟⲥ ⲛⲥ-
15   [. .]ⲩ ⲉϩⲟⲩⲛ ⲉⲇⲉⲥⲟⲟⲇⲉ ⲡⲉϣϥⲉ ⲙⲟⲩⲧ ⲉⲩⲕⲱⲧⲉ
[ⲉ]ⲣⲟⲥ ⲉⲡⲕⲱⲧⲉ ⲧⲁⲭⲉ ⲧⲁⲭⲉ

back (→) *(written at 90° counterclockwise to front)*

m² ⲥⲟⲫⲓⲁ

---

1 *i.e.* ˢⲁⲓⲙⲟⲟϣⲉ | *i.e.* ˢϩⲓⲣⲙ̄ ⲡ-ⲣⲟ | *i.e.* ˢⲁ-ⲓ̈-ϩⲉ ⲉ-(ⲟ)ⲩ-ⲥⲁⲓⲉ (haplography) ‖ **2** *i.e.* ˢⲁⲗⲁⲩ | *i.e.* ˢⲃⲁⲗ : or *l.* ϣⲁⲣ Donadoni, Pernigotti | ⲉⲥϩⲙⲟⲟⲥ corrected from ⲉⲉϩⲙⲟⲟⲥ by overwriting | *i.e.* ˢϩⲓⲭⲛ-ⲟⲩϣⲱⲧⲉ corrected from ⲟⲩ . ⲱⲧⲉ ? ‖ **3** ϥⲉⲥⲉⲕⲓⲛ *i.e.* βισάκκιον ? see note | *i.e.* ˢⲉⲥⲥⲱⲕ ⲙ̄ⲙⲟⲟⲩ | *i.e.* ˢⲛ̄-κάδος Förster WBGW 357 ‖ **3–4** ϩⲟⲙⲉⲧ corrected from ϩⲉⲙⲉⲧ : ⲛ̄ϩⲟⲙⲉⲧ Donadoni ‖ **4** ⲉⲥ . . . ⲣϭ . ϲ *i.e.* ˢϩⲁⲗⲟⲥⲓⲥ ? : ⲉⲥ[. . . .]ⲣⲁϩⲉ Donadoni | *i.e.* ˢⲡⲉⲭⲁ⸗ | *i.e.* ˢⲧ- ‖ **4–5** ⲇⲥⲁⲓⲉ Donadoni ‖ **5** *i.e.* ˢϯ | *i.e.* ˢⲡⲉⲭⲁ⸗ | ϫⲉ ⲥⲁϩⲱⲕ ⲥⲁⲃⲁ- : [. . .] Donadoni ‖ **6** *i.e.* ˢⲙ̄ⲡⲉ⸗ⲥ-ⲧⲱⲡ ? *cf.* l. 10 | for this line . ⲛⲟⲓⲡⲉⲥⲇ . . . . . ϥⲉⲙ [. .] . . [*ca.* 7] . . . . ⲉⲣⲉⲡⲁⲙⲉ Donadoni ‖ **7** *i.e.* ˢⲁⲓ-ⲡⲱⲧ ⲉⲃⲟⲗ ⲙ̄ⲙⲟ⸗ⲥ : [ⲧⲁⲗ]ⲁⲓⲡⲱⲣ[ⲟ]ⲥ ⲁⲫⲟⲣⲙⲟⲥ *i.e.* ταλαίπωρος ἄφορμος "wretched wanderer" ("[mis]ero vagante") ? Donadoni, Pernigotti ‖ **7–8** *i.e.* ˢⲡⲉⲭⲉ- ‖ **9** *i.e.* ˢⲛ̄ⲧⲁ- | *i.e.* ˢⲉ-ϯ- ‖ **10** *l.* ⲙⲡⲉⲥⲁϣⲱⲡ Donadoni | *i.e.* ˢϩⲏⲧ | *i.e.* ˢⲡⲉⲭⲁ⸗ | *i.e.* κἄν ‖ **11** [ⲉⲣⲟ]ⲓ Donadoni | *i.e.* ˢⲙ̄ⲡⲉ⸗ⲕ-ϩⲉ ⲉ-ⲡⲁ-ⲣⲁⲛ | *i.e.* ˢⲙ̄ⲡⲉ⸗ⲕ-ϩⲉ ⲉ-ⲡⲁ-ⲣⲁⲛ | ϣⲟⲙⲉ "subtlety" ("sottigliezza") Donadoni, Pernigotti ‖ **12** *i.e.* ἄγγελος van der Vliet : [.]ⲛⲁⲛⲕ ⲉⲣⲟⲥ Donadoni | *i.e.* κύριε ? (twice) *cf.* note | *i.e.* προσκυνεῖν : ⲡⲣⲱⲥⲕⲉ ⲉⲩⲛⲓϯ Donadoni ‖ **13** *i.e.* ˢⲉ⸗ⲧⲉⲧⲛ̄-ⲉ-ⲉⲓⲛⲉ : [. . .]ⲁⲉⲧⲛⲓⲛⲉ Donadoni | *l.* δ(εῖνα) ⲧ-ϣⲉ ⲛ̄-ⲛⲓⲙ or *l.* ⲙⲉϣⲉ ⲛⲓⲙ ? | *i.e.* ˢ(ⲛ̄)ⲧⲁ- ‖ **14** *i.e.* ˢ(ⲛ̄)ⲧⲁⲛⲟⲩϫⲉ : ⲇ ⲁⲙⲟⲩ ϫⲉ Donadoni | ⲛⲥ- Roxanne Bélanger Sarrazin (private communication 26/3/2020) : ⲛⲅ Donadoni | *i.e.* ˢ(ⲛ̄)ⲧⲁ-ἐπιθυμία ‖ **14–15** ⲛⲅ[ⲛⲟ]ⲩ Donadoni, Pernigotti ‖ **15** *i.e.* ˢⲉ-ⲧⲉ⸗ⲥ-ⲟⲟⲧⲉ : ⲉϫⲉ ⲥⲟⲟⲇⲉ *i.e.* ⲉⲛⲟⲩϫⲉ⸗ ⲥⲟϯ "to cast? arrows" ("gettare? frecce") Donadoni | *i.e.* ˢ⟨ⲉ⟩-ⲡⲉ-ϣϥⲉ (haplography) | *i.e.* ˢⲛⲟⲩⲧⲉ ⲉⲩⲕⲱⲧⲉ "gods who encircle" ("dei che circondano") Donadoni, Pernigotti ‖ **16** *i.e.* ˢⲙ̄-ⲡ-ⲕⲱⲧⲉ | *i.e.* ταχύ (twice).

|*front, first hand* ☧ I walked by the door of *hell, I found a beauty, white with black eyes, sitting upon a well of stone, a bag? beside her, drawing water with a bronze jar, … of iron. I said to her, "O beauty, |⁵ give me a kiss!"

She said to me, "Get away from me!" She did not return? my heart?... by? the door of hell. I ran away from her. I suffered, I cried, I groaned.

*Isis said to me, "Why do you cry, ⟨why⟩ do you groan?"

⟨I said⟩, "It is not my fault [that I] cry. I found a beautiful woman whom I wanted to kiss, |¹⁰ but she did not return? my heart."

She said to me, "Even if you did not find me, if you did not find my name, if you did not find the name of these three *angels, Kirie, Kirie, prostrate? … you (pl.) shall bring to my feet NN, daughter of NN, that I might be with her, that I might cast my lust at her, and it … |¹⁵ into her womb, ⟨to⟩? the seventy nerves which surround it, quickly, quickly!"

|*back, second hand* Sophia.

KD, EL & MP, edited from photograph.

Horus-Isis Narrative Charms: This is an example of a narrative charm in which the main protagonists are Horus and Isis; for the structure and parallels, see the notes to *PCM* I 7 front. For a discussion of the woman encountered by *Horus in ll. 10–11, see the notes to *PCM* I 6 l. 3.

front **1.** ⲁⲉⲓⲙⲟⲟϣⲉ ϩⲓⲣⲉⲛ ⲉⲡⲉⲣⲉ ⲛⲁⲙⲉⲛⲧⲉ : "I walked by the door of hell" We might expect "I walked through the door of hell" here—this is how it has been translated in all other editions, and is found in the parallels to this narrative charm; see *PCM* I 7 ll. 1–3, *PCM* I 16 ll. 5–9; *cf.* Blumell/Dosoo 2018: 223. If the preposition is indeed ϩⲓⲣⲛ̄ rather than ϩⲓⲧⲛ̄, however, this does not seem possible, unless we are dealing with an idiom otherwise unknown to us.

3. ϥⲉⲥⲉⲕⲓⲛ : "bag" van der Vliet translates "travelling bag", understanding a writing of the Latin *bisaccium*. This is phonologically plausible (*cf.* ⲥⲁⲕⲏⲛ, ⲥⲁⲕⲓⲛ for σάκκιον in Förster WBGW: 715), although the loanword is only attested in modern Greek (as βισάκκι; Dickey 2023: 85). The normal contemporary Greek equivalent is δισάκκιον (Sophocles 1860: 260) which appears in documentary papyri from Egypt. Donadoni does not translate, but suggests a diminutive of βῆσ(σ)α, an Alexandrian word for a type of jar or drinking cup; see *LSJ* s.v., Bonati 2016: 35 (with further references), although the attested diminutive is rather βησ(σ)ίον.

3. ⲉⲕⲁⲧⲉⲥ : "jar" Donadoni translates "water-wheel" (*noria*), understanding a variant of ⲕⲟⲧⲥ̄ ("turning round, circuit"); Pernigotti follows this translation.

11–12. ⲕⲁⲛ ⲙⲡⲉⲕϩⲉ [ⲉⲣⲱ]ⲓ̈ : "even if you did not find me" For this construction, see the notes to *PCM* I 16 o. 2 ll. 15–16.

12. ⲕⲓ̈ⲣⲓ̈ⲉ : "Kirie" Roxanne Bélanger Sarrazin proposes that the final invocation should be understood as beginning here, supplying "(say)" before this word (private communication 26/3/2020). This seems like a promising possibility, since we might expect an invocation to begin here. Perhaps understand with Donadoni the vocative κύριε κύριε, "O Lord, Lord!"

14. ⲉⲡⲉⲉⲃⲙⲓ̈ : "lust" Likely a euphemism for the male genitalia, as in *PCM* I 24 ll. 32–33.

15. [. .]ⲩ : "…" As suggested by Donadoni, ⲛⲟⲩ "to go" (Crum CD 219a–b) would fit well here, although it is better attested in Coptic as an auxiliary verb with the meaning "to be about to" than as an independent verb of motion.

back **1.** ⲥⲟⲫⲓⲁ : "Sophia" Donadoni understood this as a description ("indicazione definitoria") of the content of the text of the front, presumably the Greek word "wisdom" (σοφία), but it seems more likely that we have here the cognate personal name; this may be an indication that the formulary was later re-used as an applied text targeting a woman named Sophia.

PCM I 21–29. The Heidelberg Coptic Magical Library

Arsinoites (Faiyum) X–XI CE

Other references: P.Heid.Inv. Kopt. 678–686 (formerly P.Heid.Inv. Nr. 1678–1686); TM Arch id 421; *P.Bad.* V 122, 137–142; KYP A8.
Bibliography: Bilabel/Grohmann 1934: 392; Seider 1964: 162–163; Quecke 1972; Meyer/Smith 1994: 323–325; Mößner/Nauerth 2015: 302–373; Johnston/Gardner 2018; Gardner/Johnston 2019; Dosoo/Torallas Tovar 2022b: 99–100, 108; Gardner 2023a; Gardner 2023b.
Present location: Heidelberg, Institut für Papyrologie.
Linguistic description: Sahidic with Middle Egyptian features.
Manuscripts belonging to the archive: *PCM* I 21–29; possible relationships with *PCM* I 30–33.

Nine formularies of various formats (6 sheets and 3 codices) on parchment and paper. Seven of the manuscripts were purchased in May 1930 by Prof. Carl Schmidt along with several Greek, Demotic, and Coptic[1] papyri and ostraca for 1575 marks, and subsequently acquired by the University of Heidelberg papyrus collection no later than in 1933.[2] In October 1933, two further manuscripts (*PCM* I 25–26) from the archive were bought for the University of Heidelberg by Carl Schmidt from the Cairo antiquities dealer Maurice Nahman for 90 Egyptian pounds.[3] The presence of several Greek papyri from the Faiyum in the first sale suggests that this was the origin of the lot.[4]

Six of the manuscripts—*PCM* I 21–26—all written on parchment, can be identified as having been written by the same scribe based on palaeographical analysis; these include the two manuscripts of the second sale. The scribe identifies himself in a colophon in one of the manuscripts, *PCM* I 23, as Deacon Iōhannēs, "servant of Michael of Pcellēt". In the colophon, he also provides a date of production of the manuscript, 11th Paopi 684 AM (9th October 967).[5]

---

[1] The only non-magical Coptic papyrus which appears to come from the sale is P.Heid.Inv. Kopt. 296, a continuous list of names written on the horizontal fibres of a papyrus, whose vertical fibres are occupied by a damaged Arabic text of unidentified content.

[2] These initial purchases were *PCM* I 21–24, 27–29; Bilabel/Grohmann 1934: 392; Seider 1964: 163, n. 31; Gardner/Johnston 2019: 31–32. On the Heidelberg papyrus collection, see also Schmelz 2018.

[3] Seider 1964: 163, n. 32*; Gardner/Johnston 2019: 31–32. On Maurice Nahman, see Hagen/Ryholt 2016: 253–255.

[4] From Krokodilopolis: *P.Heid. Gr.* II 239; from Tebtunis: *P.Bad.* VI 169; *P.Heid. Gr.* IV 318; from Theogonis: *SB* VI 9540; from Kerkeosiris: *SB* VI 9537, but *cf.* also *P.Bad.* II 28, aparently from Hermopolis. *Cf.* Seider 1964: 163; Gardner 2023a: 49.

[5] Front ll. 50–52. Bilabel/Grohmann 1934: 393, 396 mistakenly read "21st Paopi" and gave the date as 18th October 967 (as noted in Meyer 1996: 7 n. 5, "8. Oktober" on p. 393 is a misprint).

Iōhannēs likely produced the other manuscripts within (at most) a few decades of this colophon, so that they can be dated with some certainty to between 951 and 1000 CE. The remaining manuscripts (*PCM* I 27–29) are dated palaeographically to either the tenth or the eleventh centuries (*cf.* the discussions of the individual manuscripts).

PCM I 25 & 26 are written as palimpsests, with the codices produced by taking single folios from pre-existing codices and folding them in half to create bifolios. Those of *PCM* I 25 were identified by Hans Quecke in 1974 as pages drawn from a Pauline lectionary which he dated to the ninth century.[6] Although *PCM* I 26 was lost when he made the identification, Bilabel's description of the manuscript as a palimpsest led him to suggest that its leaves belonged to same original manuscript, a hypothesis since confirmed by Gardner.[7]

The remaining parchment manuscripts from the archive are small sheets (*PCM* I 21–24). These are tall, narrow, and oddly shaped, suggesting both that they mimic the format of the rotulus, or vertical roll, and that they are made from scraps left over from the production of larger parchment sheets.[8]

Three of the Library's manuscripts are written on paper; two, *PCM* I 27 & 29, are sheets. *PCM* I 28, by contrast, is a codex of 16 pages, produced from sheets almost exactly the same size as that of *PCM* I 27, suggesting perhaps that they were produced in the same mould;[9] both of these manuscripts seem to be written in the same hand.

The hand of Iōhannēs is regular, with separate letters written with a rather thick stroke. The script is majuscule, bilinear, and generally upright, though occasionally sloping to the right. The ⲁ is small and triangular, the ⲃ also angular, but quite large, the ⳅ shaped like the numeral 3, and the ⳁ usually shaped like a x with a ⳅ-like tail.[10] There are small serifs on the ascending oblique strokes of ⲗ and ⳋ, curling slightly to the left, and the ⲧ usually has a small serif on the left of its crossbar (more rarely the right). The ⳉ and ⳓ are expansive, the latter with a small bowl and a long, curved ascender which rises from the lower part of the bowl; it thus follows the ductus (though not the form) of the Faiyumic rather than Sahidic

---

Quecke (1972: 5 n. 2) accepted their reading, but corrected this to 19th October, noting that the previous year was a leap year. Meyer/Smith (1994: 179) follow Bilabel/Grohmann's dating, although Meyer 1996: 2 follows that of Quecke. The correct reading was made in Johnston/Gardner 2018: 47–48; *cf.* Gardner 2023a: 51–53. We have confirmed the date using the online *Almagest Ephemeris Calculator* (https://webspace.science.uu.nl/~gent0113/astro/almagestephemeris.htm; accessed 1/3/2023).

[6] Quecke 1974.

[7] Quecke 1972: 6, n. 4; *cf.* Meyer 1996: 5; Gardner 2023a: 66–63. See the manuscript introductions for fuller descriptions of each part of the underlying text.

[8] On such small rotuli, see Dosoo/Torallas Tovar 2022b: 102, 108; on offcuts, see Skinner *et al.* in O'Connell 2022: 54.

[9] Dosoo/Torallas Tovar 2022b: 108.

[10] But *cf. PCM* I 24 l. 23 and *PCM* I 26 p. 16 l. 28, in which it is closer to the canonical form, ⳁ.

ϭ, perhaps another indication of its geographical origin.[11] The † varies between a form with two serifs on the horizontal crossbar, and a sans serif variant. Iōhannēs typically uses dots instead of supralinear strokes, but does use supralineation for *voces magicae, nomina sacra*, abbreviations, and a few other words. Colons and two oblique strokes, sometimes tripuncts and three oblique lines, are used for punctuation. *Paragraphoi* consisting of simple lines are used to separate recipes and textual sections.

The hands of *PCM* I 27 & 28 are so similar that we suggest a single scribe (see the introduction to no. 27 for a discussion). The writing is datable to the tenth or eleventh century (see the introduction to *PCM* I 27). *PCM* I 29 is written in a hand unrelated to the other hands, but of a similar date.[12]

The ink of Iōhannēs and the scribe of *PCM* I 27 & 28 is brown in colour, with different manuscripts displaying different degrees of darkness; in each case, the ink is visible under ultraviolet light, and almost entirely transparent under near-infrared light, suggesting the use of a plant-based ink. The ink of the front of *PCM* I 29 is black, and shows similar opacity under visible, ultraviolet and near-infrared light, suggesting it to be a carbon-based ink; the back is plant based like that of the other manuscripts.[13]

The dialect of all of the manuscripts can be described as a form of Sahidic heavily influenced by a Middle Egyptian dialect of the type likely spoken in the Faiyum,[14] although the lambdicism typical of classical Faiyumic (F4, F5) is rarely apparent.[15] Some of these are typical for non-standard forms of Sahidic: ⲃ for ᔆⳉ; ⲉ in place of the Sahidic supralinear stroke, or more dramatically ⲉ- for ᔆⲛ̄-/ⲙ̄-; interchange of ⲉ/ⲏ and ⲟ/ⲱ; haplography of nasal consonants (ⲙ/ⲛ for ⲙⲙ/ⲛⲛ); lack of ⲛ › ⲙ assimilation before a labial consonant; the simplification of the sequence nasal + stop to the stop alone (ⲙⲡ/ⲛⲧ › ⲡ/ⲧ); the 'strong' article (ⲡⲓ-/ϯ-/ⲛⲓ-) often being used where we would expect the normal definite article in Sahidic. Others are more indicative of a Middle Egyptian dialectal influence: ⲉ/ⲏ for ᔆⲁ;[16] ⲏ for the Sahidic supralinear stroke; ⲓ for unstressed ᔆⲉ; ⲁ for stressed ᔆⲟ; ϩ is occasionally

---

[11] We are grateful to Vincent Walter for pointing this out to us. For the Faiyumic ϭ, see Krall 1886–1887: 111.

[12] *Pace* Dosoo/Torallas Tovar 2022b: 108.

[13] *Cf.* the discussion of inks on p. 28–29. We again thank Krisztina Hevesi for sharing her preliminary work with us.

[14] *Cf.* the discussion in Dosoo/Love/Preininger 2022: 77; we would once again like to thank Ivan Miroshnikov for discussing this dialect with us. In the following notes we provide only a few instances of the rarer dialectal (or idiolectal) features. *Cf.* the briefer characterisations of the dialects in Bilabel/Grohmann 1934: 305, 392; Meyer 1996: 5. Note that 'Middle Egyptian' here refers not to Mesokemic, but rather to the larger family to which Mesokemic, as well as Hermopolitan and Faiyumic belong; see Funk 2020. Jacques van der Vliet (2018b: 100–101) characterises this variety as "Fayoumi-Sahidic".

[15] See, *e.g.*, ⲉϥⲓⲗ (ᔆⲉ-ⲡ-ϩⲓⲣ) and ⲧⲁⲩⲉⲗ (ᔆⲉⲛⲧ-ⲁ⸗ⲩ-ⲡ̄) in *PCM* I 26 p. 15 l. 31, p. 17 l. 10.

[16] See, *e.g.*, ⲥϩⲏⲓ for ᔆⲥϩⲁⲓ in *PCM* I 21 l. 4; ⲛⲉⲱ (ᔆⲛⲁ-ⲱ̄) in *PCM* I 26 p. 16 l. 17.

omitted,[17] and we sometimes find distinctive Faiyumic forms;[18] double vowels are not usually written, but occasionally Sahidic single vowels are doubled;[19] the prefixes ⲉⲕⲉ-, ⲉⲣⲉ- *etc.* (circumstantial/future III) are quite consistently written as ⲕⲉ-, ⲣⲉ-; as a result of the treatment of ⲛ̄, ⲉϥ regularly appears as the conjunctive prefix; the abbreviation ⲟ̄ⲥ̄ is used for ˢⲭⲟⲉⲓⲥ. None of these features appear with complete consistency within any of the manuscripts, but some are found in all of them, and in manuscripts produced by all three scribes. Similar features have been described by Ivan Miroshnikov in an acrostic hymn to the Archangel Michael dated to the tenth or eleventh century,[20] and can also be found in various documentary texts and inscriptions from the Faiyum from this period.[21]

All of the manuscripts (with the sole exception of *PCM* I 27) display the (often extensive) use of Arabic loanwords, albeit almost exclusively in the recipes rather than in the spoken formulae. The Coptic of all three scribes, and in particular Iōhannēs, is so non-standard at times as to suggest that it may not have been their first language—gender is confused, pronouns and conjugation bases may be absent, and entire clauses occasionally seem to have dropped out in the process of copying.[22]

The likely findspot in the Faiyum, and the dialectal features, have led Gardner and Johnston to tentatively suggest a possible relationship to the monastery of the Archangel Michael in Phantoou, near modern Hamuli.[23] As Gardner has observed, the original lectionaries lying beneath the palimpsests resemble those produced at this monastery,[24] and the self-identification of Iōhannēs as "servant of Michael" would be consistent with an attachment to a monastery dedicated to the archangel.[25]

We should note that several other Coptic magical manuscripts from the Institut für Papyrologie in Heidelberg contain marked similarities of dialect, content, and hands to the 'Heidelberg Library' which, although they cannot be as directly connected to the main archive, may nonetheless have once belonged to it, or at

---

[17] See, *e.g.*, ϩⲁⲣⲉ (ˢϩⲁⲣⲉϩ) in *PCM* I 25 p. 10 ll. 3, 26; ⲥⲓⲙⲓ (ˢⲥϩⲓⲙⲉ) in *PCM* I 26 p. 16 l. 11, p. 17 l. 21. For more on the interchange of ⲓ and ⲉ, see the notes to *PCM* I 25 p. 3 ll. 1–2.

[18] See, *e.g.*, ⲓⲱⲛⲁⲙ̄ (ˢⲟⲩⲛⲁⲙ) in *PCM* I 25 p. 13 l. 29; ⲱⲛⲁϩ (ˢⲱⲛϩ̄) in *PCM* I 28 p. 10 l. 5.

[19] See, *e.g.*, ϩⲱⲱⲃ (ˢϩⲱⲃ) in *PCM* I 28 p. 1 l. 1.

[20] Miroshnikov 2022: 402–407.

[21] As noted in Dosoo/Love/Preininger 2022: 77 n. 134, documentary parallels include *P.Fay. Copt.* 15; *P.Lond.Copt.* 592, 659; *SB Kopt.* III 1279, 1413 (this last dated to 986–987 CE). For inscriptions, see van der Vliet 2018b: 100–104. On the linguistic features of letters from the Faiyum, see Garel 2018: 203–206; Walter 2022: 106–108.

[22] On the complex question of the decline of Coptic as a spoken language between the ninth and fourteenth centuries, see Richter 2009: 417–434.

[23] Gardner/Johnston 2019: 50–51. On the toponomy of the monastery and the surrounding region, see Depuydt 1993: ciii–cxii.

[24] Gardner 2023a: 61.

[25] Gardner 2023a: 53; Gardner/Johnston 2019: 49–53.

least derive from a similar context.²⁶ The most notable of these are *PCM* I 30 & 31, both of which contain the same dialectal features as the main Library, and which contain reference to "three evil incenses" (ⲅ̄ ⲉⲑⲟⲟⲩ *etc.*),²⁷ also attested in *PCM* I 27 from the Library. While the manuscript of *PCM* I 31 is lost, the hand of *PCM* I 30 resembles that of *PCM* I 29, although it is not close enough to suggest a single scribe with any certainty. *PCM* I 32 & 33 also display notable similarities in terms of their content to the manuscripts of the Heidelberg Library, although to a less marked degree.

---

²⁶ We should also note here P.Heid.Inv. Kopt. 392 a–b and 994, identified by Krisztina Hevesi as part of the same manuscript as *BKU* I 26 (KYP M525); this manuscript has very similar linguistic features to the Heidelberg Coptic Magical Archive. A new edition of the full manuscript is in preparation by Krisztina Hevesi and Anne Grons.

²⁷ See the glossary under *three evil incenses.

PCM I 21. Parchment formulary containing curse (?)

Arsinoites (Faiyum) 16.3 (H) × 7 (W) cm late X CE

Other references: P.Heid.Inv. Kopt. 680 (formerly P.Heid.Inv. Nr. 1680); TM 102078; *P.Bad.* V 141; KYP M313; Bélanger Sarrazin #180.
Editions: Bilabel/Grohmann 1934: no. 141 (*ed. pr.*); Johnston/Gardner 2023: 86–93.
Translations: Bilabel/Grohmann 1934: no. 141 (German); Johnston/Gardner 2023: 86–93; Gardner 2023b: 86–93.
Additional commentary: Untermann (ed.) 2011: 33; Mößner/Nauerth 2015: 309–310, 329–330; Gardner/Johnston 2019: 51–52; Love 2022b: 701–702.
Present location: Heidelberg, Institut für Papyrologie.
Image: https://doi.org/10.11588/diglit.39748
Linguistic description: Sahidic with Middle Egyptian features.
Contents:
  1. Front ll. 1–23: Curse (?) (KYP T229)

A narrow, irregularly cut sheet of parchment, completely preserved and inscribed with brown ink on the front only. The first three lines of text are written in linear kufic and Coptic, followed by a figure flanked by a description of the ritual procedure as part of which it is to be copied. Below is the invocation, marked on top and bottom by a separation line. The purpose of the formulary seems to perhaps be a curse, since there is space for the naming of two targets in the final lines; it may specifically be a separation spell, since two individuals are mentioned.

The manuscript belongs to the group known as the 'Heidelberg Coptic Magical Library', and is part of the 1930 purchase; it was written in the hand of Deacon Iōhannēs, whose scribal and linguistic features are more fully described in the introduction to this archive (see pp. 259–263). Several recognisable features of his style can be seen in his use of a wide range of paratextual markers, simple horizontal lines to separate text sections, and of brown ink.

Our line numbering of this manuscript diverges from that in Bilabel/Grohmann; they number our ll. 9–11 as ll. 1–3, with our ll. 4–8 numbered 2–6 (overlapping with our ll. 9–11). The line numbered here as 12 corresponds to l. 7 in Bilabel/Grohmann, with the following lines numbered sequentially.

front (flesh?)

ⲁⲣⲣⲣϩϩϩ

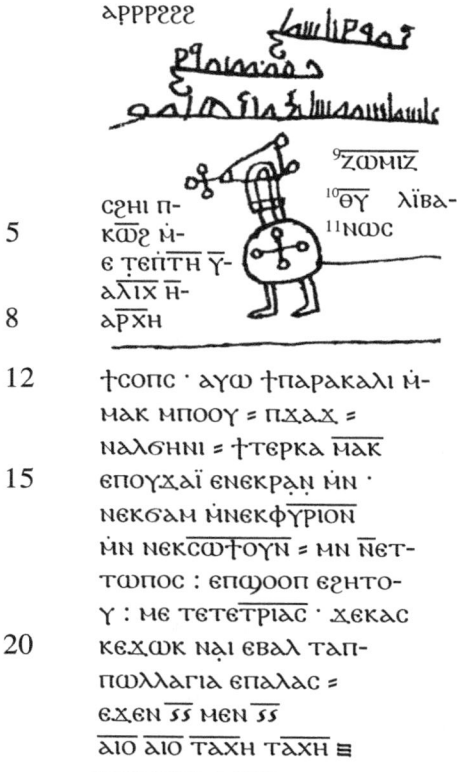

⁹ⲍⲱⲙⲓⲍ
¹⁰θ̄ⲩ̄ ⲗⲓⲃⲁ-
¹¹ⲛⲱⲥ

5 ⲥϩⲏⲓ ⲡ-
ⲕⲱ̄ϩ ⲙ̄-
ⲉ ⲧⲉⲡ̄ⲧⲏ̄ ⲅ̄-
ⲁⲗⲓ̄ⲭ ⲛ̄-
8 ⲁⲣ̄ⲭⲏ

12 †ⲥⲟⲡⲥ · ⲁⲩⲱ †ⲡⲁⲣⲁⲕⲁⲗⲓ ⲙ̄-
ⲙⲁⲕ ⲙⲡⲟⲟⲩ ⸗ ⲡⲭⲁⲝ ⸗
ⲛⲁⲗϭⲏⲛⲓ ⸗ †ⲧⲉⲣⲕⲁ ⲙⲁ̄ⲕ̄
15 ⲉⲡⲟⲩⲭⲁⲓ̈ ⲉⲛⲉⲕⲣⲁⲛ̣ ⲙ̄ⲛ ·
ⲛⲉⲕϭⲁⲙ ⲙ̄ⲛⲉⲕⲫ̄ⲩ̄ⲣ̄ⲓ̄ⲟ̄ⲛ̄
ⲙ̄ⲛ ⲛⲉⲕⲥ̄ⲱ̄†ⲟⲩⲛ ⸗ ⲙⲛ ⲛ̄ⲉⲧ-
ⲧⲱⲡⲟⲥ : ⲉⲡϣⲟⲟⲡ ⲉϩⲏⲧⲟ-
ⲩ : ⲙⲉ ⲧⲉⲧⲉⲧ̄ⲣ̄ⲓ̄ⲁ̄ⲥ̄ · ϫⲉⲕⲁⲥ
20 ⲕⲉϫⲱⲕ ⲛⲁⲓ ⲉⲃⲁⲗ ⲧⲁⲡ-
ⲡⲱⲗⲗⲁⲅⲓⲁ ⲉⲡⲁⲗⲁⲥ ⸗
ⲉϫⲉⲛ ⲥ̄ⲥ̄ ⲙⲉⲛ ⲥ̄ⲥ̄
ⲁⲓⲟ̄ ⲁⲓⲟ̄ ⲧⲁⲭⲏ̄ ⲧⲁⲭⲏ ≡

---

1 First ⲣ corrected from ⲡ by overwriting ‖ **4** *i.e.* ˢⲥϩⲁⲓ ‖ **5** *i.e.* ˢⲉ-ⲡ-ⲕⲟⲟϩ : "jealousy" ("Eifersucht") Bilabel/Grohann : "corner" ("Zipfel") Mößner/Nauerth : "top (*i.e.* the protective script)" Gardner ‖ **5–6** *i.e.* ˢⲙ̄ⲛ̄ ⲧ-ⲃⲏⲧⲉ ? cf. note : ⲙⲉⲧⲉⲅⲓⲧⲏⲩ Gardner ‖ **6** ⲡ̄ⲧ̄ⲏ̄ ⲅ̄- : ⲡ̄ⲧ̄ⲏ̄ⲩ̄ "wind" ("Wind") Bilabel/Grohann, Mößner/Nauerth ‖ **6–7** *i.e.* ورق *waraq* : understand as name Bilabel/Grohann, Mößner/Nauerth ‖ **7–8** *l.* ⲛ̄-ⲁⲣⲭⲏ : or name ? Bilabel/Grohann, Mößner/Nauerth ‖ **10** *i.e.* θυ(σία) ‖ **10–11** *i.e.* λίβανος ‖ **12** *i.e.* παρακαλεῖν ‖ **12–13** *i.e.* ˢⲙ̄ⲙⲟ⸗ⲕ ‖ **13** *i.e.* ˢⲡ-ϫⲱϫ : "bird" ("Vogel") Mößner/Nauerth ‖ **14** *i.e.* الجني *al-ǧinniyy* : *i.e.* ἀλκή "defence" ("Abwehr") Bilabel/Grohmann, "help" ("Hilfe") Mößner/Nauerth | *i.e.* ˢ†-ⲧⲁⲣⲕⲟ : ˢⲙ̄ⲙⲟ⸗ⲕ ‖ **16** *l.* ⲙⲛ ⲛⲉⲕ-φυ(λακτή)ριον ‖ **17** *i.e.* ζῴδιον ‖ **18** *i.e.* τόπος : *i.e.* ˢⲉⲧ⸗ⲕ̄-ϣⲟⲟⲡ : ˢⲉ⸗ⲕ-ϣⲟⲟⲡ Bilabel/Grohmann ‖ **18–19** *i.e.* ˢⲛ̄ϩⲏⲧⲟⲩ ‖ **19** *l.* ⲧⲉ-ⲧⲣⲓⲁⲥ : or *l.* ⲙ̄ⲛⲧ-ⲧⲣⲓⲁⲥ "triple-fold" or "in a trinitarian way" Gardner ‖ **20** ⲛⲁⲓ ⲁ corrected from ϩ by overwriting ‖ **21–22** *i.e.* ἀπολογία : or *i.e.* ἀπαλλαγή ? Gardner ‖ **22** *i.e.* (δεῖνα) (δεῖνα) (twice) ‖ **23** *i.e.* ταχύ (twice)

|above tableau Arrrhhh (*linear kufic*)

|4, left of tableau Write ‹on› the |5 piece? and the metal plate?, paper with ‹wine› of the *first fruits.

|9, right of tableau Zōmiz

|10 Offering: *frankincense.

|12, below tableau I entreat and I invoke you today, O leader of the djinn! I adjure you |15 by the *wellbeing of your *names and your *powers and your *phylacteries and your *images and the *places in which you dwell and the Trinity, that |20 you complete the request of my tongue against NN, child of NN, and NN, child of NN, yea, yea, quickly, quickly!

KD, EL, MP & JS, edited from photograph; tracing by JS.

1–3: As recognised by Gardner (2023b: 88–89), these '*kharaktēres*' represent a form of stylised Arabic called by Casanova (1921: 52–53) 'linear kufic' ("koufique linéaire"). As the name suggests, it is based on the Arabic calligraphic style of the same name used in the early centuries of Islam. 'Linear kufic' exaggerates the angularity of kufic, adding a continuous baseline, and generally neglecting the diacritic marks that distinguish similar letters. Porter (2010: 133) notes that similar stylised kufic appears in non-magical contexts from the ninth century, and in eighth/ninth century Arabic magical papyri (*cf.* Bsees 2019: 203–204). In later periods the style came to be used for amulets, with early examples being found in twelfth-century magical bowls; it may also be found in pseudo-al-Būnī's *Šams al-Ma'ārif* (Porter 2010; Porter 2011: 176–180; for pseudo-al-Būnī see Gardiner 2012: 100–105, 123–30; Coulon 2017: 225–229). In principle the script can be read (see the alphabet in BnF arabe 2676 fol. 5v, reproduced in Porter 2010: 137 as fol. 90), but in practice the degree of stylisation makes this difficult, and so we do not attempt decipherment in this volume. Other examples of linear kufic may be found in *PCM* I 25 p. 17 ll. 1–10, *PCM* I 31 (front tableau), *PCM* I 35 (back), *PCM* I 37 (back), and perhaps *PCM* I 33 (back). Linear kufic may also be found in the Armenian amulet San Lazzaro degli Armeni Ms. 3042 (1779 CE; Feydit 1986: no. VIII, see fig. 81), associated with a procedure for favour before social superiors.

5–6. ne тєптн : "**metal plate**" We tentatively propose to read пth as an unusual writing of the word вhтe "metal plate" (Crum CD 45b), but *cf. PCM* I 24, in which пth appears in a list of ingredients, and we interpret it as п-ет-тнс (c lost to haplography), with the sense "that which is dried", which would not seem to fit here. Alternatively, perhaps understand мєүєпт as ˢn-oy-єiвт "with a nail"

9. ẓωmiẓ : "**Zōmiz**" Gardner (2023b: 89–90) notes a possible connection to Semesilam (from Northwest Semitic *šms 'lm* "Eternal Sun"; Bonnet 1989: 98–99), but a more likely derivation from Semyaz/Shemhazai or Shamhurish, respectively the leaders of the fallen angels in 1 Enoch 6–10, and the leader of the *ifrit* in Egyptian popular tradition (*cf.* Viaud 1978: 26–27). We note that ẓωmiẓ could readily be derived from the Greek form Σεμιαζά (*Semiaza*), the original of the Ge'ez ሰምያዛ (*Sämyaza*, etc.; Langlois 2010: 146).

14. пхаа ⲥ naⲗϭhni : "**leader of the djinn**" As recognised by Gardner (2023b: 86) and Love (2022b: 702), this word is certainly the Arabic loanword جني (*ǧinniyy*; "djinn"). We follow Gardner in understanding the meaning as "chief djinn"; Love suggests "the djinn-swallow" or "the djinn-headed". Mößner and Nauerth suggest, based on their translation of "bird of help", a reference to the Holy Spirit (Mößner/Nauerth 2015: 329).

PCM I 22. Parchment sheet with procedures for favour and cursing

Arsinoites (Faiyum) 29.5 (H) × 10.5 (W) cm late X CE

Other references: P.Heid.Inv. Kopt. 681 (formerly P.Heid.Inv. Nr. 1681); TM 99609; *P.Bad.* V 139; KYP M293; Bélanger Sarrazin #178.
Editions: Bilabel/Grohmann 1934: no. 139 (*ed. pr.*) [B/G].
Translations: Bilabel/Grohmann 1934: no. 139 (German); Frankfurter in Meyer/Smith 1994: no. 105 [F]; Mößner/Nauerth 2015: 330–333 (German); Gardner 2023b: 93–100 [G].
Additional commentary: Untermann (ed.) 2011: 28; Gardner/Johnston 2019: 31–32; Love 2022b.
Present location: Heidelberg, Institut für Papyrologie.
Image: https://doi.org/10.11588/diglit.39866
Linguistic description: Sahidic with Middle Egyptian features.
Contents:
1. Front ll. 1–41: Spell for favour (KYP T231)
2. Front ll. 41–63: Curse to make a woman hated (KYP T232)

Tall, narrow parchment sheet, complete and well-preserved, containing one procedure for favour and one curse. The manuscript is part of the archive known as the 'Heidelberg Coptic Magical Library' and was acquired by Carl Schmidt in the 1930 purchase. The hand is that of the copyist who identifies himself in *PCM I 23* as the Deacon Iōhannēs; see the description of the archive (pp. 259–263) as a whole for this hand and its characteristic linguistic features.

The text is divided into several sections by simple horizontal lines, and contains two image tableaux associated with each of the procedures. The manuscript appears not to have been folded.

Here we count the initial line of *kharaktēres* as a line, whereas the texts of Bilabel/Grohmann and Frankfurter treat the following line as line 1, so that our l. 2 corresponds to their l. 1, and so on, until our l. 11–23, which they number again as ll. 1–13; our ll. 24 and following then correspond to their ll. 10 and following.

front (flesh?)

```
       ⲁⲣⲱⲙ = ⲁⲣⲱⲙ =                    ¹¹ⲓⲁⲱ ⲥⲁⲃⲁⲱⲑ
       ⲁⲣⲱⲙⲁⲱ =                         ⲉⲗⲱⲉⲓ ⲉⲗⲏⲙⲁᶜ
       ⲁⲣⲱⲙⲁⲛⲁ                          ⲙⲁⲭⲏⲡⲱⲧ =
  5    ⲁⲣⲱⲙⲁⲛⲁⲏⲗ ·                      ⲥⲁⲗⲁⲃⲁⲟⲱⲑ
       ⲁⲣⲁⲕⲁ =                          ¹⁵ⲙⲁⲣⲭⲏⲭⲟⲩ —
       ⲁⲣⲁⲧⲁⲙⲟⲩ =                       ⲡⲁⲛⲓⲉⲓⲗⲟⲩ —
       ⲁⲣⲓⲱ · ⲁⲣⲓⲛⲁ                     ⲭⲁⲏⲗ —
       ⲁⲣⲁⲧⲁⲃⲛⲏ                         ⲁⲭⲁⲏⲗ —
 10    ⲁⲣⲁⲕⲥⲁ =                         ⲑⲩ ⲙⲁⲥϯⲭⲓ
 24    ϫⲉ                               ²⁰ⲁⲗⲟⲩⲑ =
       † ⲉⲣⲁ=ⲕ                          ⲥⲧⲏⲣⲝ =
       ⲡⲟⲟⲩ =                           ⲙⲟⲩⲥϯⲁ-
       ⲁⲣⲓⲱ =                           ⲧⲉⲛ
       ⲡⲛⲟϭ ⲛ̄-
       ⲭⲉⲣⲟⲩⲃⲓⲛ
 30    ⲉⲡⲓⲱⲧ =
       ⲡⲁⲛⲧⲱⲣ = ⲧⲉ-
```

ⲫⲱⲏⲛ : ⲧⲁⲥ : ⲉⲓ ⲉⲃⲁⲗ ϩⲛ ⲣⲱⲃ : ⲉⲡⲓⲱⲧ · ⲡⲁⲛⲧⲟⲣ =
ϫⲉ : ⲉⲓⲥ ϩⲏⲏⲧⲉ : ⲧⲉⲛⲁϫⲟⲟⲩ : ⲙⲡⲁⲅⲅⲉⲗⲟⲥ ϩⲁⲭⲟ-
ⲟⲩ ⲥ̄ⲥ̄ † ⲟⲩⲭⲁⲣⲓⲥ ⲛⲉϥ : ⲙⲡⲉⲙⲧⲁ ⲉⲃⲁⲗ = ⲙⲓⲭⲁⲏⲗ
35 ⲁϩⲉⲣⲁⲧⲟⲩ ϩⲓ ⲟⲩⲛⲁⲙ : ⲙⲁⲓ : ϣⲁⲧⲁϯ ⲭⲁⲣⲓⲥ ⲛⲉϥ
ϫⲉⲕⲁⲥ ⲕⲉϫⲁⲕⲟⲩ ⲉⲃⲁⲗ ⲕⲁ ⲟⲩⲭⲁⲣⲓⲥ : ⲕⲁ · ⲟⲩⲕⲁⲣⲱϥ : ⲕⲁ ⲛⲟⲩⲉⲓⲣⲏⲛⲉ = ⲕⲁ· ⲛⲟⲩϩⲩⲡⲟⲥⲧⲓⲥⲙⲟ-
ⲥ = ⲕⲁ ⲛⲟⲩⲥⲟⲟⲩϩⲥ = ⲕⲁ ⲛⲟⲩⲱϣ ⲕⲁ· ⲟⲩⲁⲡⲓ ⲛⲓ-
ⲙ : ⲕⲉϫⲁⲕⲟⲩ ⲛⲁⲓ ⲉⲃⲁⲗ· ϩⲛ ⲟⲩϭⲉⲡⲏ ⲁⲓⲱ ⲧⲁⲭⲓ

```
 40    ⲁⲣⲓⲱ : ⲁⲣⲓⲛⲁ = ⲁⲣⲱⲙⲁ : ⲁⲣⲱⲙⲁⲛⲁⲏⲗ : ⲁⲣⲁⲥⲁ -
       ⲁⲣⲱⲙⲁⲱ : ⲑⲁⲣⲙⲁⲱⲑ = ⲙⲁⲣⲙⲁⲣⲓⲱⲑ = ϫⲉ †
```

13 ⲙⲁⲭⲏⲡⲱⲅ B/G || **19** *i.e.* θυ(σία) | *i.e.* μαστίχη || **20** *i.e.* العود *al-ʿūd* || **22–23** *l.* ⲙⲟⲩⲥⲭⲁⲧⲉⲛ *i.e.* μοσχάτον || **25** *l.* †(ⲱⲣⲕ) ⲉⲣⲁ=ⲕ ? ⲙ̄-ⲡⲟⲟⲩ | *i.e.* στύραξ || **29** *i.e.* χερουβίμ || **30** *i.e.* ˢⲙ̄-ⲡⲓⲱⲧ || **31** *i.e.* ˢⲡ-ⲡⲁⲛⲧ(ⲟⲕⲣάⲧ)ⲱⲣ *cf.* note to *PCM* I 25 p. 2 l. 2 | *i.e.* ˢⲛ̄-ⲧⲉ : *l.* ⲉⲧⲉ B/G || **32** *i.e.* φωνή | *i.e.* ˢⲉⲛⲧⲁ=ⲥ-ⲉⲓ | *i.e.* ˢⲙ̄-ⲡⲓⲱⲧ | *i.e.* ˢⲡ-ⲡⲁⲛⲧⲟ(ⲕⲣάⲧⲱ)ⲣ *cf.* note to *PCM* I 25 p. 2 l. 2 || **33** l. ⲙ̄-ⲡⲁ-ⲁⲅⲅⲉⲗⲟⲥ *i.e.* ἄγγελος *cf.* note || **33–34** *i.e.* ϩⲁⲭⲱⲛ- or ϩⲁⲭⲱ=ⲟⲩ || **34** *i.e.* (δεῖνα) (δεῖνα) | *i.e.* χάρις || **35** *i.e.* ˢⲙ̄ⲙⲟ=ⲓ̈ : "Stand me on the right" ("Stehe mir zur Rechten") B/G, F || **36** *i.e.* ˢⲉ=ⲕⲉ-ϫⲁⲕ=ⲟⲩ | *i.e.* χάρις || **37** *i.e.* ˢⲕⲱ ⲛ̄- | *i.e.* εἰρήνη | *i.e.* ˢⲕⲱ ⲛ̄- ||**37–38** *i.e.* ὑποδεσμός *cf.* LBG s.v. : ὑποθεσμός B/G, F || **38** *i.e.* ˢⲕⲱ ⲛ̄- (twice) | *i.e.* ˢⲟⲩ-ⲟⲩⲱϣ : or ⲟⲩ-ⲱϣ B/G || **39** *i.e.* ˢⲉ=ⲕⲉ-ϫⲁⲕ=ⲟⲩ | *i.e.* ταχύ

PCM I 22 (P.Bad. V 139) : Parchment sheet with procedures for favour and cursing

|within tableau Ariō (*kharaktēres*: ΑΕΗΙΥΥѠ)

|1, above tableau (*kharaktēres*: X|X|X|X|X|X|X| ★★★★★★★)

|2, left of tableau Arōm, Arōm, Arōmaō Arōmana, |5 Arōmanaēl, Araka, Aratamou, Ariō, Arina, Aratabnē, |10 Araksa.

|11, right of tableau *Iao *Sabaoth *Eloei *Elēmas, Makhēpōt, Salabaoōth, |15 Markhēkhou, Panieilou, Khaēl, Akhaēl.

|19 Offering: *mastic, |20 *agarwood, *storax, *musk incense.

|24, below tableau Say: |25 "I ⟨adjure⟩ you today Ariō, the great *cherub |30 of the Father Almighty, by the voice which came from the mouth of the Father Almighty: 'Behold, I shall send my? *angel before NN, child of NN!' Give grace to him in the presence of *Michael! |35 Stand them at my right hand and I will give favour to him, so that you (s.) complete them! Give favour! Give silence! Give peace! Give suppression! Give a gathering! Give desire! Give every skill!
   May you complete them for me quickly! Yea! Quickly!"
|40 Ariō, Arina, Arōma, Arōmanaēl, Arasa, Arōmaō, Tharmaōth, Marmariōth.

Image: Apparently a representation of the cherub Ariō, with the Greek vowels (ΑΕΗΙΥΩ) written on his body as *kharaktēres*; *cf.* Dosoo 2022a: 142; Gardner 2023b: 94–96.
1–23. These lines are divided by horizontal strokes, represented here as supralineation.
28-29. ⲡⲛⲟϭ ⲛ̄ⲭⲉⲣⲟⲩⲃⲓⲛ : "the great cherub" For this title, *cf. PCM* I 18 l. 3 and the accompanying note.
33-34. ⲉⲓⲥ ϩⲏⲏⲧⲉ : ⲧⲉⲛⲁϫⲟⲟⲩ : ⲙⲡⲁⲅⲅⲉⲗⲟⲥ ϩⲁϫⲟⲟⲩ : "Behold, I shall send my? angel before" A citation of Mark 1.2: "As it is written in the prophet Isaiah, 'Behold, I will send my angel before you and he will prepare your way'" (ⲕⲁⲧⲁ ⲑⲉ ⲉⲧⲥⲏϩ ϩⲛ̄ ⲏⲥⲁⲓⲁⲥ ⲡⲉⲡⲣⲟⲫⲏⲧⲏⲥ ϫⲉ ⲉⲓⲥ ϩⲏⲏⲧⲉ ϯⲛⲁϫⲉⲩ ⲡⲁⲁⲅⲅⲉⲗⲟⲥ ϩⲁⲧⲉⲕϩⲏ ⲡⲁⲓ ⲉⲧⲛⲁⲥⲟⲃⲧⲉ ⲛ̄ⲧⲉⲕϩⲓⲏ; Horner 1911: I 354). This passage occurs in scriptural amulets (*e.g., P.Oxy.* LXXVI 5073), probably being understood as a guarantee of angelic protection (*cf.* Sanzo 2014: 141–142).
36-38. ⲕⲁ and ⲕⲁ ⲛ- : "give" Here we consistently translate ⲕⲁ and ⲕⲁ ⲛ- (Sahidic ⲕⲱ and ⲕⲱ ⲛ̄-) as "give" rather than the usual "place" to make the meaning clearer in English.

front (flesh?) (continued)

42 ⲡϣⲁϩ ⲉⲛⲉⲧⲁⲁⲩ ⲛ̄-
ϭⲱⲛⲧ ⸗ ⲉⲡϣⲁⲣⲃⲁ ⸗ ⲡⲙⲁⲥⲧⲓ ⲛ̄ⲡⲉⲑ̄-
ⲗⲁ ⲃⲁⲗ · ⲱⲑⲱⲣ ⸗ ⲡ̅ⲅ̅ ⲛ̄ⲁⲅⲅⲉⲗⲱⲥ ≡
45 ⲙⲙⲁⲥϯ ⸱ ϩⲓ †ⲧⲱⲛ ⸗ ϩⲓ ⲃⲁⲥⲑⲁ ⸗ ⲉⲡϩⲁ ⲥ̅ⲥ̅ ⸗
ϫⲉⲕⲁⲥ ϩⲛ ⲧⲉⲩⲛⲟⲩ ⲛ̄ϣⲁⲥϩⲁⲓ ⲛ̄ⲛⲉ⸗ⲧⲉⲛ-
ⲣⲁⲛ ⸗ ⲙⲛ ⲛⲉⲧⲉⲛⲥⲱ̄ⲧⲟⲩⲛ ⸗ ⲙⲛ ⲛⲉ-
ⲧⲉⲛⲫ̄ⲩ̄ ≡ ⲉⲡⲃⲓⲧ ⸗ ⲡϭⲁⲗⲉϩ ⸱ ⲧⲁⲥⲁϩ-
ϯ ϩⲁⲣⲁⲥ ⸱ ϣⲁⲛⲧⲉⲥϫⲱⲣ ⸱ ⲕⲉϫⲱⲣ ⸗
50 ⲉⲡϩⲁ ⲥ̅ⲥ̅ ⲙ̄ⲡⲉⲙⲧⲁ ⲉⲃⲁⲗ · ⲙⲡⲕⲉⲛⲟⲥ
ⲧⲏⲣϥ ⸗ ⲛⲁ̄ⲇ̄ⲁ̄ⲙ̄ ⸗ ⲙⲛ ⸱ ⲛⲉϣⲏⲣⲉ ⲧⲏⲣ︦ⲟⲩ̣
ⲛ̄ⲥⲱⲏ ⸗ ⲛⲉⲕⲟⲩⲓ ⲙⲛ ⲛⲉⲛⲟϭ
ⲛⲉⲁⲣⲭⲏ ⲙⲛ ⲛⲉⲝⲟⲩⲥⲓⲁ · ⲙ̄ⲛⲉⲣⲟ ⲙⲛ
ⲛⲉⲣⲉϥϯϩⲁⲡ ϫⲉ ϩⲛ ⲧⲉⲩⲛⲟⲩ ⸱ ϣⲁⲩ-
55 ⲛⲁⲩ · ⲉⲡϩⲁ ⲥ̅ⲥ̅ ⸗ ⲉⲩⲙⲉⲥⲧⲱϣϥ · ⲙⲛ
ⲡⲉⲥϣⲁϫⲉ ⲛⲉⲡⲉⲥϩⲁ ϫⲓ ⲭⲁⲣⲓⲥ ⸱ ⲟⲩⲧⲉ ⲡⲉⲥϩⲱⲃ · ⲛⲉϥⲥⲁⲩⲧⲉⲛ ⸱ ϣⲁ ⲛ̄-
ⲛⲉϩ ⸱ ϩⲛ ⲟⲩⲁⲉⲓϣ ⲛⲓⲙ ⲁⲓⲟ ⲧⲁⲭⲏ

ⲥϩⲁⲓ ⲡⲁϣⲣⲱ ⸱ ⲉⲡⲃⲓⲧ ⸱ ⲟⲩϭⲁⲗⲉϩ̄ⲧ ⸗
60 ⲛ̄ⲕⲱⲧ ⲥⲁⲡⲉϩⲟⲩ ⸱ ⲟⲩⲁϩ ⸱ ϩⲓϫⲉⲛ ⲅ̄
ⲛ̄ⲧⲱⲃⲓ ⸱ ⲛⲁⲙⲓ ⸱ ⲥⲁϩϯ ϩⲁⲣⲁⲥ ⲧⲁⲙⲥ
ϩⲓ ⲟⲩϩⲓⲣ ⲉⲥ̄ϯⲣ̄ⲟⲥ ⲟⲩ ⲕⲁⲥ ϫⲁⲉⲓⲧ ≡
ⲟⲩⲱϣⲉ ⲡⲕⲱϩⲧ · ⲁϥϫⲟⲕ ⲉⲃⲁⲗ

---

42 *i.e.* ˢⲛ̄-ⲛ-ⲧⲟⲟⲩ : ⲛ̄-ⲛ-ⲉⲧ-ⲁⲁ⸗ⲩ "the flame of those who make (magic)" ("die Flamme denen, die sie (die Zaubereien) machen" B/G : "the flame from which they are made" F ∥ **43** *i.e.* ˢⲙ̄-ⲡ-ϣⲁⲣⲃⲁ ∥ **43–44** *i.e.* ⲑⲗⲟ ⲉⲃⲟⲗ ∥ **44** *i.e.* ἄγγελος ∥ **45** *i.e.* ˢⲙ̄-ⲙⲟⲥⲧⲉ : *i.e.* ˢⲃⲁⲥⲧ-ϩⲟ *cf.* note | *i.e.* (δεῖνα) (δεῖνα) ∥ **46** *i.e.* ˢⲉ-ϣⲁ⸗ⲓ-ⲥϩⲁⲓ ∥ **47** *i.e.* ζῴδιον ∥ **48** *i.e.* φυ(λακτήριον) | ⲡⲃⲓⲧ ⲙ̄-ⲡϭⲁⲗⲉϩ : "on the potsherd" (auf die Scherbe eines Kruges") B/G, F : "the palm leaf (and put it in) a pot" G ∥ **49** *i.e.* ˢⲉ⸗ⲕ-ⲉ-ϫⲱⲣ : *i.e.* ˢϫⲟ(ⲟ)ⲣ B/G ∥ **50** *i.e.* ˢⲙ̄-ⲡ-ϩⲟ | *i.e.* (δεῖνα) (δεῖνα) | *i.e.* γένος ∥ **51** ⲟⲩ ligatured ⲟ+ⲩ ∥ **53** *i.e.* ἀρχή | *i.e.* ἐξουσία | *i.e.* ˢⲙⲛ ⲛ-ⲣ̄ⲣⲟ (haplography) ∥ **55** *i.e.* (δεῖνα) (δεῖνα) | *i.e.* ˢⲉ⸗ⲩ-ⲉ-ⲙⲉⲥⲧⲱ⸗ϥ ∥ **56** *l.* ⲙⲛ ⲡⲉ⸗ⲥ-ϩⲁ ⲛ corrected from ⲙ by overwriting | *i.e.* χάρις ∥ **58** *i.e.* ταχύ ∥ **59** *i.e.* ˢⲡ-ⲥⲛⲟϥ ⲛ̄-ϣⲣⲱ | *i.e.* ˢⲡ-ⲃⲓⲧ ⲛ-ⲟⲩ-ϭⲁⲗⲁϩⲧ *cf.* Crum CD xvib : *i.e.* ˢⲃⲏⲧ ? B/G | ϭⲁⲗⲁϩ B/G ∥ **60** *i.e.* ˢⲛ̄⸗ⲅ-ⲕⲟⲧ⸗ⲥ ⲥⲁⲡⲉϩⲟⲩ (haplography) : *l.* ⲛⲕⲟⲧⲕ̄ ⲥⲁⲡⲉϩⲟⲩ B/G : "sleep behind it" F : "sleep afterwards" G ∥ **61** *i.e.* ˢⲟⲙⲉ : "correctly" G | *l.* ⲧⲁⲙⲥ⸗ⲥ (haplography) ∥ **62** *i.e.* ˢϩⲓⲣ ⲛ̄-σ(ταυ)ρός | *i.e.* θυ(σία) | *i.e.* ˢⲕⲁⲥ ⲛ-ϫⲟⲉⲓⲧ ∥ **63** *l.* ⲟⲩⲱϣⲉ ⲉⲡⲕⲱϩⲧ *i.e.* ˢⲟⲩⲱϣⲉ ⲙ̄-ⲡⲕⲱϩⲧ (haplography) | *i.e.* ˢϫⲱⲕ

|*captions for figures* Bōk Baroukh
|*inside figures* Ō, Oukhoumar, Uu

|⁴¹ Say: "Give |⁴² the flame of the deserts, the wrath of the scorching heat, the hatred of the scattering—Othōr, O three *angels of |⁴⁵ hatred and strife and hatefulness—to the face of NN, child of NN, so that in the moment that ⟨I⟩ write your *names and your *images and your *phylacteries on the edge ⟨of⟩ the *pot, and I kindle ⟨fire⟩ under it until it blackens, you will blacken |⁵⁰ the face ⟨of⟩ NN, child of NN, in the presence of the entire race of Adam and all the children of Zoe, the small and the great, the rulers and the *authorities and the kings and the judges so that in the moment that they |⁵⁵ see the face ⟨of⟩ NN, child of NN, they will hate it and her speech! Her face will not receive favour neither will her work be successful ever, at any time, yea, quickly!"

Write ⟨in⟩ menstrual ⟨blood⟩ on the edge ⟨of⟩ a *pot. |⁶⁰ Turn it on its back?. Place ⟨it⟩ upon three mud bricks. Kindle ⟨fire⟩ under it. Bury it at a crossroads. Offering: olive pit. Consume ⟨it⟩ in the fire. It is finished.

KD, EL & MP, edited from photograph and autopsy; tracings by KD and JS.

Image: We may note that the central figure is without a face, perhaps symbolising the concept of "hatefulness", or loss of "face" described in the curse. The figure's hand is placed at its mouth, perhaps representing the act of silencing the victim (*cf.* the notes to the image of *PCM* I 24).

45. ⲃⲁⲥϩⲁ : "hatefulness" For this expression, meaning literally a "burnt/dry face", see van der Vliet 1991: 217; for other instances see *PCM* I 27 front l. 2; *PCM* I 31 back ll. 4, 5–6, 12; *P.Bad.* V 123 (KYP M315) front l. 65; Cairo JdE 42573 (KYP M44) p. 2 l. 10. This is one of a number of expressions in Coptic which draw upon the idea of the face as the locus of the social self; *cf.* Nyord 2015: 257–259; Dosoo 2023a: 174–175; Preininger forthcoming c: chapter 2.

49–50. ⲕⲉⲭⲱⲣ = ⲉⲛϩⲁ : "you will blacken the face" A metaphor drawing on the "blackened" cooking pot as a symbol of an indesirable or socially excluded person; compare Pseudo-Athanasius of Alexandria, *On the Mercy of the Father* (CC 51): "and as for the impious, they stand on the left of the place of judgement, their faces black like a blackened pot" (ⲛⲁⲥⲉⲃⲏⲥ ⲇⲉ ϩⲱⲟⲩ ⲉⲩⲁϩⲉⲣⲁⲧⲟⲩ ⲛⲥⲁϩⲃⲟⲩⲣ ⲙ̄ⲡⲙⲁ ⲛ̄ϯϩⲁⲡ ⲉⲣⲉⲛⲉⲩϩⲟ ⲕⲏⲙ ⲛ̄ⲑⲉ ⲛ̄ⲟⲩϭⲁⲗⲁϩⲧ̄ ⲉⲥⲭⲏⲣ; Bernardin 1937: 126.33); for Jewish parallels, see Weingarten 2014: 345.

50–52. ⲙ̄ⲡⲕⲉⲛⲟⲥ ⲧⲏⲣϥ = ⲛ̄ⲁⲇⲁⲙ = ⲙⲛ = ⲛⲉϣⲏⲣⲉ ⲧⲏⲣⲟⲩ ⲛ̄ⲥⲱⲏ : "the entire race of Adam and all the children of Zoe" For this expression, see the notes to *PCM* I 25 p. 7 ll. 12–14.

59. ⲡϣⲣⲱ : "menstrual ⟨blood⟩" The word ϣⲣⲱ ("menstrual blood") is feminine, so the masculine definite article used here must indicate that the masculine word ⲥⲛⲟϥ "blood" has been omitted. Menstrual blood is often used in curses, in particular separation spells, in the Coptic magical corpus; *cf. PCM* I 27 front l. 3; *PCM* I 27 front l. 2; *PCM* I 31 back l. 15; *PCM* I 37 back l. 19; *P.Bad.* V 123 (KYP M315) front ll. 1, 26, 50, 82, back ll. 89, 101. This use seems to draw upon ancient Mediterranean ideas of menstrual blood as a powerful and dangerous substance; see Dosoo 2023a: 173 n. 247, 175–176; Preininger forthcoming a and c: chapter 4. Gardner (2023b: 96–97) prefers to understand an otherwise unattested word with the meaning "curse".

59. ⲉⲛⲃⲓⲧ : "on the edge" For the word ⲃⲓⲧ see Jernstedt 1959: 161–162, who links it to the word βῖτος, "wheel", hence "rim", in turn from Latin *uitus* (Ivan Miroshnikov is thanked for this reference).

62. ⲕⲁⲥ ⲭⲁⲉⲓⲧ : "olive pit?" For this interpretation, see Crum CD 120a.

PCM I 23. Parchment sheet with two curses

Arsinoites (Faiyum)　　　　　　30.5 (H) × 9.8 (W) cm　　　　　　9 October 967 CE

Other references: P.Heid.Inv. Kopt. 682 (formerly P. Heid. Inv. Nr. 1682); TM 99576; *P.Bad.* V 137; KYP M291; Bélanger Sarrazin #176.

Editions: Bilabel/Grohmann 1934: no. 137 (*ed. pr.*) [B/G]; Gardner/Johnston 2019 (colophon) [G/J]; Gardner 2023b: 74–85 [G]; Miroshnikov 2022: 407–408 (colophon) [Mi]; Richter 2023: 161–164 (ll. 1–10; 43–47) [R].

Translations: Bilabel/Grohmann 1934: no. 137 (German); Meyer in Meyer/Smith 1994: no. 86 [M]; van der Vliet 2000: 277 (colophon) [V]; Gardner/Johnston 2019; Gardner 2023b: 74–85; Miroshnikov 2022: 407–408 (colophon); Richter 2023: 161–164 [R] (German).

Additional commentary: Mößner/Nauerth 2015: 310; Love 2022b; Gardner 2023a: 51–53; Preininger forthcoming c: chapter 5.

Present location: Heidelberg, Institut für Papyrologie.

Image: https://doi.org/10.11588/diglit.39750

Linguistic description: Sahidic with Middle Egyptian features.

Contents:

Original use:

1. Front ll. 1–5: Witness testimonies (Arabic, unpublished; KYP T265)

Re-use:

2. Back ll. 1–20: Separation spell to undo a couple (KYP T22)
3. Back ll. 21–49: Curse to bind male virility and female virginity (KYP T23)
4. Back ll. 50–52: Colophon (KYP T24)

A completely preserved tall, narrow parchment sheet. Two curses are inscribed on one side (the back), aimed at preventing romantic or sexual relationships between men and women. A dated colophon, one of only two known among surviving Coptic magical manuscripts,[1] identifies the copyist as the Deacon Iōhannēs.[2] The manuscript was bought by Carl Schmidt in 1930 and is part of the archive known as the 'Heidelberg Coptic Magical Library', six of whose manuscripts were copied by Iōhannēs (*cf.* pp. 259–263 for a description of his hand and linguistic features). Two sets of images and multiple instances of simple horizontal dividing lines appear on the manuscript.

The remains of an unpublished Arabic text is written on the front of the sheet

---

[1] The other colophon is found on the recipes for using the Psalms for various purposes, contained in the manuscript we refer to as Collège de France Ms. 3 (KYP M597), dated to 27th Mesore 427 A.H. (20th August 1035).

[2] Front ll. 50–52; *cf.* the more detailed discussion on pp. 259–260.

at 180° to the Coptic text. This text represents the original use of the sheet, the majority of it having been lost when the parchment was cut down to its current size. Five faded lines are visible, preserving what appear to be the testimonies of witnesses to a legal transaction, one named Saʿīd b. ʿAbd Allāh.[3]

Note that the edition in Bilabel/Grohmann (followed by other editors) numbers our ll. 8–9 as l. 8, and does not count the line of *kharaktēres* in l. 44, resulting in a divergent line numbering.

[3] We are very grateful to Ursula Hammed for making this preliminary identification.

front (flesh)

ⲥϩⲁⲓ ⲛⲉⲛ-
ⲓⲣⲁⲛ ⲉⲩϫⲉ-
ⲕ ⲛⲟⲩⲙⲁⲩ
ⲛⲁⲙⲉ ⸗
⁵ⲛⲁⲗⲙⲓⲧⲉ
ⲛⲁⲗⲭⲱⲃⲓⲁ ⸗
ⲉⲟⲟⲩ ⲉⲃⲁⲗ · ⲛ-
ⲛⲉϩ ⸗ ϯⲁⲥⲙⲉ ⸗
ⲧⲁϩⲥ ⸗ ⲡⲉϩⲁ
10 ⲡϩⲟⲟⲩⲧ: ⲙ̄ⲛ ⲥ̄ⲓ̄ⲙ̄ⲓ̄ ⸗ ⲥϩⲁⲓ ⲡⲥ̄ⲱ̄ϥ̄-
ⲟⲩⲛ ⸗ ⲉⲩⲁⲣⲏⲕ ⲙ̀ⲁⲣⲉϥϫⲱϥ ⸗
ⲡⲱⲧⲁⲭⲏ ⸗ ⲃⲱⲗ ⲉⲃⲁⲗ ⲥ̄ⲥ̄ ⲙⲉⲛ ⲥ̄ⲥ̄
ⲁⲓⲱ̄ⲥ̄ ⸗ ⲃ̄ⲁ̄ⲓ̄ⲱ̄ⲧ̄ ⸗ ⲁ̄ⲧ̄ⲱ̄ⲛ̄ⲁ̄ⲥ̄ · ⲃⲱⲗ
ⲉⲃⲁⲗ ⲥ̄ⲥ̄ ⲛ̄ⲓ̄ⲑ̄ⲁ̄ ⸗ ⲃ̄ⲁ̄ⲣ̄ ⸗ ⲃ̄ⲁ̄ⲩ̄ ⸗
15 ⲙ̄ⲁ̄ⲣ̄ ⸗ ⲙ̄ⲁ̄ⲣ̄ϯ̄ : ⲥ̄ⲱ̄ⲡ̄ⲟ̄ⲥ̄ : ϫ̄ⲁ̄ⲃ̄ⲏ̄ⲥ̄ ⸗
ⲥ̄ⲁ̄ⲣ̄ⲁ̄ⲫ̄ⲱ̄ⲥ̄ ⸗ ⲃ̄ⲏ̄ⲣ̄ ⸗ ⲃ̄ⲁ̄ⲣ̄ ⸗ ϩ̄ⲏ̄ϯ̄ⲱ̄ⲥ̄ ⸗
ⲱ̄ϩ̄ⲉ̄ⲓ̄: ⲫ̄ⲏ̄ⲅ̄ ⸗ ⲃ̄ⲁ̄ⲃ̄ ⸗ ⲙ̄ⲟ̄ⲩ̄ⲣ̄ⲁ̄ⲧ̄ ⸗ ⲧ̄ⲉ̄ⲣ̄ⲓ̄-
ⲕ̄ ⸗ ⲉ̄ⲥ̄ⲭ̄ⲉ̄ⲩ̄ ⸗ ⲕ̄ⲉ̄ⲧ̄ⲁ̄ · ⲃⲱⲗ ⲉⲃⲁⲗ ⲥ̄ⲥ̄
ⲁ̄ⲭ̄ⲏ̄ ⸗ ⲫ̄ⲉ̄ⲣ̄ ⸗ ⲫ̄ⲁ̄ ⸗ ⲭ̄ⲏ̄ⲩ̄ⲙ̄ⲉ̄ ⸗ ⲣ̄ⲟ̄ⲩ̄ⲭ̄ ⸗
20 ϫⲉⲕⲁ ⲉⲕⲉⲃⲱⲗ · ⲉⲃⲁⲗ ⲥ̄ⲥ̄ ⲙⲉⲛ ⲥ̄ⲥ̄ ⸗
ⲙⲟⲩⲣ ⸗ ⲉⲡⲧⲡⲉ ⸗ ⲙⲟⲩⲣ ⲉⲡⲕⲁϩ ⸗ ⲡ-
ⲙⲟⲩⲣ · ⲉⲡⲧⲁⲩ : ⲡⲙⲟⲩⲣ ⲉⲡⲙⲟⲟⲩ ⸗
ⲡⲙⲟⲩⲣ · ⲡⲉⲕϩⲟⲩⲣ ⸗ ⲉⲡⲓⲱⲧ⸗ ⲡⲙⲟⲩⲣ ·
ⲉⲡⲕⲉⲗⲉⲃⲓⲛⲓ ⸗ ⲉⲧϩⲉ ϭⲓϫ ⸗ ⲥⲁⲣϩ ⸗ ⲡⲙⲟ-
25 ⲩⲣ : ⲧⲁⲩⲙⲟⲩⲣ ⸗ ⲡ̄ⲭ̄ⲥ̄ · ϩⲓϫⲉⲛ ⲡϣⲏ ⸗
ⲡⲉⲥϯⲟⲩ - ⲕⲉⲙⲟⲩⲣ ⸗ ⲡⲁⲣⲁⲑⲉⲛⲓⲁ ⲥ̄ⲥ̄
ⲛⲉⲥ̄ⲥ̄ ⲛⲁⲉϣ ⲃⲱⲗ ⲉⲃⲁⲗ ⲡⲁⲣⲑⲉⲛⲓ̄ⲁ̄
ϣⲁⲛⲧⲟⲩⲃⲱⲗ ⲉ̄ⲃ̄ⲁ̄ⲗ̄ · ⲡⲁⲣⲑⲉⲛ̄ⲓ̄ⲁ̄ ⲡ-
ⲡⲁⲣⲑⲉⲛⲟⲥ ⲉⲧⲟⲩⲁⲁⲃ ⸗

1–2 *i.e.* ˢⲛ̄-ⲛ̄- or ᶠⲛⲉⲛ- : "our" M || **2** no initial ⲓ R || **2–4** ⲉⲩϫⲉⲕ ⲛⲟⲩⲛ ⲉⲛⲁⲙⲉ "with a seashell in truth (?)" "mit einer Meermuschel (?) in Wahrheit (?)" B/G : ⲉⲩϫⲉⲕ ⲛⲟⲩⲛ⟨ⲁⲙ⟩ ⲛⲁⲙⲉ "correctly on a right-hand palm" G/J, G : "on a sherd of clay" M : ⲛⲟⲩⲙⲁ R || **5–6** *i.e.* المداد الكوفي *al-midād al-kūfī* : *i.e.* الخفية *al-ḫufya* "secret ink" G/J, G : "Nalmite, Nalchobia" B/G, M : ⲛⲁⲗⲙⲓⲧⲉ/ⲇ\ ⲛⲁⲗⲭⲱⲃⲓ R || **7** *i.e.* ˢⲉⲓⲁⲁ=ⲟⲩ || **8** *i.e.* ˢⲛ̄-ⲧ-ⲓ́ⲁⲥⲙⲏ : ⲙⲙⲏ "genuine (*i.e.*, olive) (oil)" ("echtem (Öl)") B/G, M : ϯ.ⲥⲙⲉ "make the chant" G/J || **9** ⲛⲧⲁϩⲁ B/G || **10** *i.e.* ˢⲙ̄-ⲡ-ϩⲟⲟⲩⲧ || **10–11** *i.e.* ζῴδιον || **11** *i.e.* ورق *waraq* || **12** *i.e.* ὑποταγή : *l.* ⲡⲱⲧ ⲧⲁⲭⲏ *i.e.* ταχύ ? "go quickly" ("Laufe schnell") B/G, M || **12–27** *i.e.* (δεῖνα) (δεῖνα) || **20** *i.e.* ˢϫⲉⲕⲁⲥ || **21** *i.e.* ˢⲛ̄-ⲧ-ⲡⲉ : *l.* ⲉⲧⲡⲉ B/G | *i.e.* ˢⲙ̄-ⲡ-ⲕⲁϩ || **22** *i.e.* ˢⲙ̄-ⲡ-ⲧⲟⲟⲩ | *i.e.* ˢⲙ̄-ⲡ-ⲙⲟⲟⲩ || **23** *i.e.* ˢⲙ̄-ⲡⲉ=ϩⲟⲩⲣ ⲙ̄-ⲡ-ⲓⲱⲧ || **24** *i.e.* ˢⲙ̄-ⲡ-ⲕⲉⲗⲉⲃⲓⲛⲓ | *i.e.* ˢⲛ̄-ⲥⲁ́ⲣⲝ || **25** *i.e.* ˢⲛⲧⲁ=ⲩ-ⲙⲟⲩⲣ | *i.e.* χ(ριστό)ς || **26** *i.e.* ˢⲙ̄-ⲡⲉ-ⲥ(ⲧⲁⲩⲣ)ⲟ́ⲥ | *i.e.* ˢⲉ=ⲕ-ⲉ-ⲙⲟⲩⲣ || **26, 27, 28** *i.e.* ˢⲧ-παρθένια *cf.* note to *PCM* I 25 p. 2 l. 2 || **28–29** *i.e.* ˢⲛ̄-ⲧ-παρθένος *cf.* note to *PCM* I 25 p. 2 l. 2

Write these names on a shell from muddy? water |⁵ with *kufic ink. Wash them off with jasmine oil. Anoint the face ⟨of⟩ the male and the female. Draw the image |¹⁰ on paper. Have it burn.

Subjection?: "Undo NN, child of NN, and NN, child of NN! Aiōs, Baiōt, Atōnas, undo NN, child of NN! Nitha, Bar, Bau, |¹⁵ Mar, Marti, Sōpos, Čabēs, Saraphōs, Bēr, Bar, Hētiōs, Ōhei, Phēg, Bab, Mourat, Terik, Eskheu, Keta, undo NN, child of NN! Akhē, Pher, Pha, Khēume, Roukh, |²⁰ that you undo NN, child of NN, and NN, child of NN!"

|²¹ "*Binding of the sky, binding of the earth, the binding of the mountain, the binding of the water, the binding of the ring of the Father, the binding of the axe which is in ⟨a⟩ fleshly hand, the binding |²⁵ ⟨with⟩ which they bound Christ upon the wood ⟨of⟩ the cross; you shall bind ⟨the⟩ virginity ⟨of⟩ NN, child of NN! NN, child of NN, will not be able to release ⟨the⟩ virginity, until ⟨the⟩ virginity ⟨of⟩ the Holy Virgin is released!

Image: We do not propose an interpretation of the image here. Gardner/Johnston (*cf.* Gardner 2023b) suggest that the image represents an animal effigy standing in for the victim with his mouth and penis bound, and that the *kharaktēres* to the right represent a magic square used to generate the "names" referred to in ll. 1–2 by overlaying them with the *kharaktēres* in l. 43, as planetary sigils are generated in the later work of Cornelius Agrippa (1486–1535; *cf.* Lehrich 2003: 99–110). We rather understand ll. 1–19 and 20–48 to represent two unrelated practices; the *kharaktēres* in l. 43 are paralleled in another text (see the note to ll. 21–43 below). The use of magic squares (*awfāq*, sing. *waqf*) is attested in Arabic magic from the ninth century, but almost exclusively in the form of the 3 × 3 square in which each row, column, and diagonal adds up to 9. Later, more complex, squares are attested from the late eleventh century, but in these the property of equal sums is still respected (Hallum 2020), which would not be the case here. We rather understand the "names" to refer simply to the *kharaktēres* themselves (*cf.* Dosoo 2022a: 121 n. 14).

9. ⲧⲁϩⲥ ⸗ ⲡⲉϩⲁ : "anoint the face" As in *PCM* I 27 front ll. 15–23, it may be that the "face" here is that of an effigy standing in for the curse's target; see Dosoo 2022d: 176–177.

20. ϫⲉⲕⲁ : "that" Note the absence of a preceding speech act of request, adjuration, or invocation.

21–43. Binding Curse: This invocation has a near exact parallel in Chicago OIM E13767 (Stefanski 1939; KYP M7), an applied curse against a man named Pharaouō, the son of Kiranpales, to prevent him from having intercourse with Touaein, the daughter of Kamar. Stefanski dates the text to the ninth to eleventh century, although, based on the use of paper, we can assume a tenth-century date at the earliest. As discussed in Gardner/Johnston 2019: 36–37 (*cf.* Gardner 2023b: 76–78), the two texts are nearly identical, both verbally and in reproducing the same sequence of *kharaktēres*. Compare P.Stras. K 135 (Crum 1922b; KYP M474) for a less direct parallel with the same goal. Gardner/Johnson identify the "finger ring of the Father" as the ring given by Michael to Solomon allowing him to bind demons (*cf.* the introduction to *PCM* I 30), while the reference to Elijah may be to the prayer of Elijah upon mount Carmel to bring down fire from heaven (1 Kings 18.36–38) or else to the revelation to Elijah on mount Horeb in 1 Kings 19.1–18 (*cf.* Frankfurter 1993: 63–64). They also understand the "binding of Jesus" to represent the binding of the Devil made possible by Jesus' crucifixion, but this would not seem to be possible grammatically; rather it seems that the binding is mentioned as having been powerful enough to bind Jesus to the cross. For a similar text in Syriac, see Cherkashina/Kuzin 2022.

22. ⲉⲓⲧⲁⲩ : "of the mountain" The word could be translated as either "mountain" or "desert"; here we opt for "mountain" since this more clearly evokes a single object which could be bound; *cf.* l. 30.

front (flesh) (continued)

30 πμογρ επϣαχε : ταϩηλιας πεπρο-
    φητης · χοογ ⳿ ϩιχεν ταογ ετογααβ ⳿
    ετ ναι νεγραν χακογρι ⳿ χαβνει ⳿
    χαβνα ⳿ ϣωρανι ⳿ ϣογρωναϩ
    μαρεπμογρ επαι πε ϣωπ · ϩιχε-
35 μ πςωμα νϩοογτ ⳿ ςς εϩογν ςς ν-
    νεϥεϣι βωλ · εβαλ παρθενια ⳿ ςς ⳿
    νεϥτως ⳿ νεϥτωογν ⳿
    νεϥϯ ςπερμα ⳿ νεϥναϣε βωλ
    εβαλ · παρθενια ςς αλλα εϥ-
40 ϣωπι ⳿ ϩεν ςαρϩ ςς ⳿ μαρε⟦ςα⟧-
    ςαρϩ ςς ⳿ ϣωπε · ⲛ̇θε ταγρεϥ-
    μαογτ : νεϥνεϣ χ εβαλ ⳿
    ϩεν πταφως · αιο αιο ταχη ⳿

45 ςϩαι ναλ-
    μιτετ ναλχωβι νι ⳿ θγ :
    ϣαλ νϩοογτ : ναλεγ : ϩι λιβ-
    ανος ⳿ πκεμθητι αϥχοκ
    εβολ καλος

50 ανακ πⲇⲓ̄ ⲓ̄ⲱ̄ ϩμϩαλ μιχαηλ
    επϭελλητ αεςϩαϊ ςογⲓ̄ⲁ επαα-
    vac. πι μεν ⲭ̅ⲡ̅ⲇ̅ εραμπι ⳿

---

30 *i.e.* ˢⲙ̄-π-ϣαχε | *i.e.* ˢντα-ϩηλιας || 30–31 *i.e.* προφήτης || 31 *l.* χοοϥ B/G | *i.e.* ˢτοογ || 32 *i.e.* ˢετε ναι νε νεⲉ̱γ-ραν || 33 ϣογρωναϩ : ϣογιωνα B/G || 34 *l.* ε⟨τ⟩ παι πε B/G | ϣωπι B/G || 35 *i.e.* σῶμα | *i.e.* (δεῖνα) (δεῖνα) (twice) || 36 εϣ: βωλ B/G | *i.e.* ˢⲧ-παρθενια *cf.* note to *PCM* I 25 p. 2 l. 2 | *i.e.* (δεῖνα) (δεῖνα) || 37, 38 *i.e.* ⲛ̄ⲛⲉ=ϥ- (four times) || 39 *i.e.* ˢⲧ-παρθενία *cf.* note to *PCM* I 25 p. 2 l. 2 | *i.e.* (δεῖνα) (δεῖνα) | *i.e.* ἀλλά | *i.e.* ˢⲉ=ϥ-ⲉ- || 40 *i.e.* ˢϩⲙ̄ π-σάρξ ν-(δεῖνα) (δεῖνα) | μαρε⟦ςα⟧ deletion by erasure : μαρε τ- B/G || 41 *i.e.* ˢπ-σάρξ ν-(δεῖνα) (δεῖνα) || 41–42 *i.e.* (δεῖνα) (δεῖνα) | *l.* εντ-αγ-ⲣ̄ ρεϥ-μοογτ ? || 42 *i.e.* ⲛ̄ⲛⲉ=ϥ- | *l.* χι or χι εβαλ B/G *cf.* note || 43 *i.e.* τάφος | *i.e.* ταχύ || 45–46 *i.e.* الكوفي المداد *al-midād al-kūfī* : *i.e.* الخفية *al-ḫufya* "secret ink" G/J, G : ⲛⲁⲗⲙⲓⲧⲉⲧ ⲛⲁⲗⲭⲱⲃⲓⲛⲓ "Nalmitet, Nalchobini" B/G, M || 46 *l.* νι⟨ραν⟩ ? : *l.* ναι ? R | *i.e.* θυ(σία) || 47–48 *i.e.* λίβανος || 48 *i.e.* ᶠπ-κεμτ-ϩεϯ ? || 49 *i.e.* καλῶς || 50 *i.e.* δι(άκονος) : B/G do not translate : "Pdi" M | *i.e.* ιω(ϩαννης) : B/G do not translate : "Yo" M || 51 *i.e.* ˢⲙ̄-πϭελλητ α=ϊ-ςϩαι : πεϭελλητα εςϩαι "(son) of Pcelleta, have written" ("(Sohn) des Pgelleta, habe (es) geschrieben") B/G, M : πεϭελλητα εςϩαι *i.e.* ˢⲁ=ϊ̄-ςϩαι van der Vliet : *i.e.* ˢπετ-ϭαλⲏⲩⲧ ⲉ-ςϩαι "the one entrusted to write" G/J || 51–52 *i.e.* ˢⲙ̄ⲡⲁⲟⲡⲉ : *l.* μπααπι Bilabel/Grohmann || 52 *i.e.* ⲙ̄ⲛ or *l.* μήν "month" ? *cf.* Förster WBGW 521–522 | *i.e.* ˢⲛⲣⲟⲙⲡⲉ

|³⁰ The *binding of the word which Elijah the prophet spoke upon the holy mountain, whose *names are these: Khakouri, Khabnei, Khabna, Šōrani, Šourōnae; let this binding be upon |³⁵ the male body of NN, child of NN, towards NN, child of NN! He will not be able to release ⟨the⟩ virginity ⟨of⟩ NN, child of NN! He will not become hard! He will not become erect! He will not ejaculate! He will not be able to release ⟨the⟩ virginity ⟨of⟩ NN, child of NN, but it will |⁴⁰ be in ⟨the⟩ flesh ⟨of⟩ NN, child of NN! Let ⟨the⟩ flesh ⟨of⟩ NN, child of NN, become as ⟨though⟩ they [sic] were dead! He will not be able to beget? from the tomb, yea, yea, quickly!

(*kharaktēres*: EX*+)

|⁴⁵ Write with *kufic ink these ⟨names⟩. Offering: white male *myrrh, *frankincense. The movement? of hearts?. It is completely finished.

|⁵⁰ I, the Deacon Iōhannes, servant of Michael of Pcellēt, I wrote on the 11ᵗʰ of Paopi and? ⟨in the⟩ 684ᵗʰ year.

KD, EL & MP, edited from photograph and autopsy; tracings by JS.

---

32. Bilabel/Grohmann believe something is missing at the beginning of the line, but this is not apparent to us.

35. ⲡⲥⲱⲙⲁ ⲛ̄ϩⲟⲟⲩⲧ : **"male body"** A euphemism for the penis; see Till 1951: 26–27, and *cf.* Cairo JdE 42573 (Chassinat 1955; KYP M44) p. 4 l. 19. A similar binding of the penis is found in the Syriac text edited in Cherkashina/Kuzin 2022.

42. ⲛⲉϥⲛⲉϣ ϫ ⲉⲃⲁⲗ : **"he will not be able to beget?"** We might expect ⲛⲉϥⲛⲉϣ ⲉⲓ ⲉⲃⲁⲗ "he will not be able to come out", as translated by Meyer. Bilabel/Grohmann suggest that the verb might be ϫⲓ ("receive") or ϫⲟ ("put forth"). The latter is the word used for "sowing (seed)", equivalent to Greek σπείρειν, which also has the sense of "beget"; although we have been unable to find a parallel for this in Coptic, this would see to be the most plausible interpretation.

47. ⲛ̄ϩⲟⲟⲩⲧ : **"male"** The term "male" here seems to refer to the quality of the ingredient. In Greek and Latin, the highest grade of frankincense is regularly described as "male" (ἄρρην, *masculum*) in medical, botanical, and magical texts (LiDonnici 2001: 69). Alternatively, we might translate ϩⲟⲟⲩⲧ as "wild" as Meyer does; Pliny the Elder (*Natural History* 12.35) notes that some types of myrrh are "wild" (*silvestrium*) rather than cultivated, but he describes the best kind of wild myrrh as "troglodytic" (*troglodytic*), that is, from Ethiopia, and it is the Greek form of this adjective (τρωγλῖτις) which usually describes high-quality myrrh in the Graeco-Egyptian magical papyri rather than "wild" (*e.g.*, *GEMF* 31/*PGM* I (KYP M153) ll. 71–72).

48. ⲡⲕⲉⲙⲉⲛⲧⲓ : **"the movement of hearts?"** We follow Gardner/Johnston 2019: 46 in suggesting a compound of ˢⲕⲉⲙⲧ ϩⲉⲧⲉ; compare *PCM* I 32 p. 1 l. 15: "move her heart" (ⲕⲓⲙ ⲉⲡⲉⲥϩⲏⲧ), referring to the act of making someone fall in love, although its meaning here would be more obscure, perhaps serving as an end title.

50–52. For discussions of the colophon, see van der Vliet 2005b: 277; Gardner/Johnston 2019: 47–48; Miroshnikov 2022: 407–408; Gardner 2023a: 51–54; Gardner 2023b: 74–75. Bilabel/Grohmann understand Pcellēt to be the name of the father of Iōhannes, van der Vliet and Miroshnikov understand it as his place of origin, while Gardner/Johnston understand "the one assigned to write". For phraseological parallels, see *e.g.*, Lantschoot 1929: nos. 1d, 11c, 15b. Note that in these cases the placename seems to refer to the location of the *topos* of the saint rather than the place of origin of the scribe, *e.g.*, no. 11 l. 35: ⲙⲓⲭⲁⲏⲗ ⲉⲡϩⲁⲛⲧⲁⲩ ("Michael of Phantoou"). For the writing ⲁⲉⲥϩⲁⲓ compare *P.Teschlot* l. 18 ⲁⲉⲣ ⲙⲉⲧⲣⲉ (for Sahidic ⲁⲓⲣ ⲙⲛ̄ⲧⲣⲉ), dated to 1027 CE. On the dating of this colophon, see pp. 259–260, with n. 5.

PCM I 24. Parchment sheet with silencing curse and a love spell

Arsinoites (Faiyum)   21.8 (H) × 14.5 (W) cm   late X CE

Other references: P.Heid.Inv. Kopt. 683 (formerly P.Heid.Inv. Nr. 1683); TM 100000; *P.Bad.* V 140; KYP M312; Bélanger Sarrazin #179.

Editions: Bilabel/Grohmann 1934: no. 140 (*ed. pr.*).

Translations: Bilabel/Grohmann 1934: no. 140 (German).

Additional commentary: Polotsky 1935: 423–424; Untermann (ed.) 2011: 18; Mößner/Nauerth 2015: 310–311, 333–336; Gardner/Johnston 2019: 51–53; Dosoo 2022a: 163–164; Love 2022b: 648–649; Gardner 2023b: 100–103.

Present location: Heidelberg, Institut für Papyrologie.

Image: https://doi.org/10.11588/diglit.39751

Linguistic description: Sahidic with Middle Egyptian features.

Contents:

1. Front ll. 1–18: Silencing curse (KYP T47)
2. Front ll. 19–36: Love spell (KYP T48)

Complete and well-preserved parchment sheet containing a silencing curse and a love spell. The manuscript is part of the 'Heidelberg Coptic Magical Library', acquired in the 1930 purchase, and is written by the Deacon Iōhannēs; a discussion of his hand and linguistic characteristics can be found in the description of the archive (see pp. 259–263).

The text is written on the front only, divided with simple horizontal lines into several registers, and contains two sets of images, one associated with each procedure.

front (flesh)

†сопс ayω †паракa-
λι nмaк ⸗ мпооу ⸗
ⲃⲁⲣⲟⲩⲭ ⸗ ⲡⲛⲟϭ · ⲇⲉ-
ⲛⲁⲧⲱⲥ ϫⲉⲕⲁⲟⲥ · ϩⲉⲛ
ⲧⲉⲩⲛⲟⲩ ⲛ̅ϣⲁⲓⲧⲱⲙ ⲉ̅ⲥ̅   5
ⲙⲁⲕ ⸗ ϩⲓ ⲡⲣⲟ ⲉⲡⲏⲓ ⲥ̅ⲥ̅
ⲁⲩⲱ ⲧⲁⲙⲟⲩⲣ ⲙⲁⲕ ⸗
ϩⲓⲭⲉⲛ ⲡⲉϥⲛⲁϩ : ⲥ̅ⲥ̅ ⸗

ⲕⲉ† ⲛⲟⲩⲕⲁⲣⲱⲃ

10 ⲉⲧⲧⲁⲡⲣⲟ ⲥ̅ⲥ̅ ⲉϩⲟⲩⲛ ⲥ̅ⲥ̅ : ⲁⲩⲱ ⲡⲉⲙⲧⲁ ⲉⲃⲁⲗ ⸗
ⲉⲛⲣⲱⲙⲉ ⲛⲓⲙ ⸗ ⲛⲉⲕⲟⲩⲓ : ⲙⲛ ⲛⲉⲛⲟϭ ⸗ ⲙⲛ̅ ⲙⲏⲧⲉⲛ̅ⲡⲟ ⸗
ⲙⲛ̅ ⲟⲩⲭⲁⲗⲓⲛⲟⲥ ⲙⲛ ⲟⲩϣⲁⲙⲉ : ⲉⲧⲧⲁⲡⲣⲟ ⲥ̅ⲥ̅ ⲭ̅ ⲥ̅ⲥ̅
ⲉϩⲟⲩⲛ : ⲥ̅ⲥ̅ ⲙⲛ ⲟⲩⲱϣ ⲙⲛ ⲟⲩⲕⲱ ⲛⲧⲏⲩ ⸗ ϩⲛ ⲧⲉⲩⲛⲟⲩ : ⲡⲁⲧⲉ:ⲕⲉ:ⲑⲓⲁⲛⲉⲓ : ⲡⲉⲥⲙⲁ ⲛ⸗ⲑⲉ ⲛⲧⲁⲕ-

15 ϣⲧⲁⲙ ⲉⲣⲱϥ : ⲛⲉⲛⲙⲟⲩⲓ : ϩⲓⲑⲏⲛ ⲇⲁⲛⲓⲏⲗ ⸗
ⲡⲉⲡⲣⲱ·ⲫⲏⲧⲏⲥ ⸗ ⲕⲉϣⲧⲁⲙ ⲉⲣⲱϥ : ⲉⲛ ⲥ̅ⲥ̅ ⲭ̅ ⲥ̅ⲥ̅
ⲉϩⲟⲩⲛ ⲥ̅ⲥ̅ ⲛⲉϩⲟⲟⲩ ⲧⲏⲣⲟⲩ ⲡⲉϥⲱⲛⲁϩ ⸗ ⲁⲓⲱ ⲁⲓⲱ ⲧⲁⲭⲏ

ⲁⲥⲟⲩⲭ · ϩⲓ ⲁⲣⲭⲏ : ⲑⲩ · ⲗⲓⲃⲁⲛⲟⲥ : ⲁⲗⲟⲩⲑ · ⲉⲣⲉⲡⲟⲟϩ ⲙⲟⲩϩ · ⲕⲁⲗⲟⲥ ⸗

1–2 *i.e.* παρακαλεῖν || **2** *i.e.* ˢⲙ̅ⲙⲟⲕ || **3–4** *l.* ⲛ̅-δυνατός || **4** *i.e.* ˢϫⲉⲕⲁⲁⲥ || **5** *i.e.* ˢⲧⲱⲙ̅ⲥ̅ || **6** *i.e.* ˢⲙ̅ⲙⲟⲕ | *i.e.* ˢⲙ̅-ⲡ-ⲏⲓ ⲛ̅-(δεῖνα) (δεῖνα) || **7** *i.e.* ˢⲙ̅ⲙⲟⲕ || **8** *i.e.* (δεῖνα) (δεῖνα) || **9** *i.e.* ˢⲉ⸗ⲕ-ⲉ-† || **10** *i.e.* (δεῖνα) (δεῖνα) || **11** *i.e.* ˢⲙⲛ̅ⲧ-ⲙⲡⲟ || **12** *i.e.* χαλινός | *i.e.* (δεῖνα) (δεῖνα) (twice) | *i.e.* (υἱός) || **13** *i.e.* (δεῖνα)(δεῖνα) | *l.* ⲟⲩ-ϣⲁϫⲙ⟩ ? (haplography) || **14** *i.e.* ˢⲙ̅ⲡⲁⲧⲉ⸗ | *i.e.* διανέμειν ? *cf.* Förster WBGW 185–186 : *i.e.* θιγγάνειν "touched" ("berührt") Bilabel/Grohmann || **15** ϣⲧⲁⲙⲉ ⲣⲱϥ ? Bilabel/Grohmann || **16** *i.e.* προφήτης | *i.e.* ˢⲉⲕⲉϣⲧⲁⲙ | *i.e.* (δεῖνα) (δεῖνα) (twice) | *i.e.* (υἱός) || **17** *i.e.* (δεῖνα) (δεῖνα) | *i.e.* ˢⲙ̅-ⲡⲉ⸗ϥ-ⲱⲛϩ | *i.e.* ταχύ || **18** *i.e.* السك *as-sukk* : "Asuch" (name) Bilabel/Grohmann : "sugar", "*sukk*" or error for "musk" Gardner | *i.e.* ἀρχή : "Archê" Bilabel/Grohmann : "newly-pressed oil" Gardner | *i.e.* θυ(σία) | *i.e.* λίβανος | *i.e.* العود *al-ʿūd* | *i.e.* καλῶς *l.* ⲁϥϫⲱⲕ ⲉⲃⲟⲗ ⲕⲁⲗⲱⲥ ?

"I entreat and I invoke you today, Baroukh, the great mighty one, that as |⁵ soon as I bury you at the door of the house ⟨of⟩ NN, child of NN, and I bind you upon the forearm ⟨of⟩ NN, child of NN, you shall give silence |¹⁰ to the mouth ⟨of⟩ NN, child of NN, concerning NN, child of NN—and before every person, the small and the great—and ⟨a⟩ dumbness and a bridle and a closing to the mouth of NN, the child of NN, before NN, child of NN, and a parching and a loss of breath at once, before you have divided? her place, just as you |¹⁵ closed the mouths of the lions before Daniel the prophet, you shall shut the mouth of NN, son of NN, concerning NN, child of NN, all the days of his life. Yea, yea! Quickly!"

Sukk with ⟨wine of the⟩ *first fruits. Offering: *frankincense, *agarwood. When the moon is full. Good.

Image: The central feature of the image is a bird-like figure with its hand to its mouth, apparently symbolising silence. Similar figures with hands to their mouths illustrate other silencing curses; see, for example, *GEMF* 73/*PGM* IX (KYP M748) back; Louvre E 14251 (unpublished; KYP M3734), and compare the image above *PCM* I 22 l. 29, although this seems to be primarily a curse of separation rather than silence.

12. ⲟⲩⲭⲁⲗⲓⲛⲟⲥ : "**a bridle**" The concept of placing a bridle on one's human or demonic enemies in order to control them is recurrent in the Coptic magical corpus, often associated with silencing curses, as is the case here. Compare *PCM* I 25 p. 9 l. 30; *PCM* I 34 p. 4 ll. 23–25; P.Würzburg inv. 42 (Brunsch 1978; KYP M494) l. 17.

14–16. ⲛ̅ⲑⲉ ⲛⲧⲁⲕ ϣⲧⲁⲙ ⲉⲣⲱϥ : ⲛⲉⲛⲧⲙⲟⲩⲓ : ϩⲓⲑⲏⲛⲛ ⲇ̅ⲁⲛⲓⲏⲗ̅ ⳇ ⲡⲉⲡⲣⲟ·ⲫⲏⲧⲏⲥ : "**as you closed the ⟨mouths⟩ of the lions before Daniel the prophet**" A straightforward reference to Daniel 6, which describes how the prophet Daniel was cast into a den of lions for worshipping the Jewish god and not King Darius the Mede, but survived when an angel of God was sent to shut the mouths of the lions. References to the salvation of Daniel by the closing of the mouths of the lions (assimilated to the curse's enemies) appear in several Coptic curses; see also *BKU* III 389 (KYP M338) ll. 6–7; *P.HengstenbergCopt.* 5 (KYP M532) ll. 13–14; Bodleian MS. Copt. c (P) 4 (Crum 1896; KYP M412) ll. 23–24.

18. ⲁⲥⲟⲩⲭ : "***Sukk***" As tentatively suggested by Gardner (2023b: 102), this ingredient is certainly *sukk* (سُكّ), a substance produced through a range of recipes, but often involving cooking fruit or fruit juice (dates, raisins, or grape) with pounded gall nuts and then drying the product. Recipes are preserved by al-Kindi (801–873 CE) and Moses Maimonides (1138–1204 CE) (Lane 1863: 1387b; Gottheil 1935: 137–138; Groom 1997: 228; Amar/Lev 2017: 117–118; King 2017: 152–53; King 2020: 460). It could be ingested for medicinal purposes, worn as a perfume (sometimes mixed with *musk or ambergris), and used to dye fabric or darken facial hair. Here it is probably mixed with wine of the first fruits and used to copy the tableau onto a support which is then to be buried at the door of the curse's target. The same word likely appears in P.Vindob. K 8303 (Stegemann 1933–1934: no. 51; KYP M279) front l. 10 as [ⲁ]ⲥⲟⲩⲭ. It appears as a loanword (סוך or סך) in texts from the Cairo Genizah as the ink to be used to copy text onto applied objects in love spells (Naveh/Shaked 1998: Geniza 5 p. 4 l. 4; Geniza 6 p. 2 l. 8). In the eleventh-century Arabic *Ġāyat al-ḥakim* (known in Latin as the *Picatrix*) it is used as an ingredient in burnt offerings for Venus and the moon, and as part of a soporific mixture to be ingested by the target (Ritter 1933: 220.1, 4 275.7, 299.7, 306.12; German translation in Ritter/Plessner 1962: 231, 232, 281, 312, 319).

front (continued) (flesh)

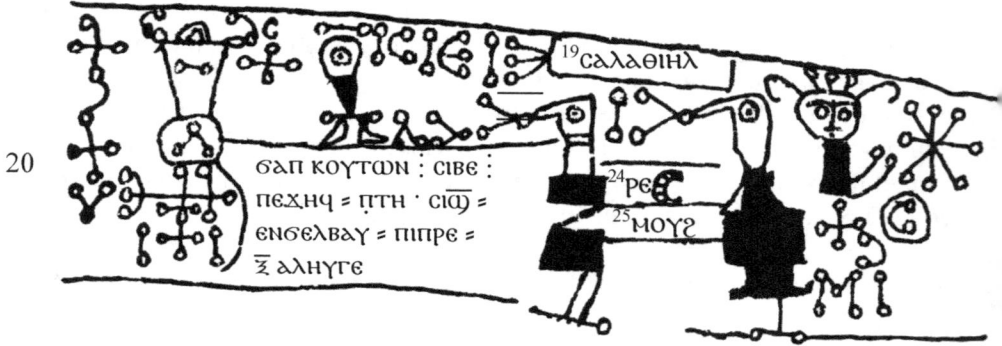

```
20        ϭⲁⲡ ⲕⲟⲩⲧⲱⲛ : ⲥⲓⲃⲉ :
          ⲡⲉⲭⲏⲛϥ ⸗ ⲡⲧⲏ · ⲥⲓⲱ ⸗
          ⲉⲛⲑⲉⲗⲃⲁⲩ ⸗ ⲡⲓⲡⲣⲉ ⸗
          ⲝ̄ ⲁⲗⲏⲩⲅⲉ
```

26 †ⲥⲟⲡⲥ ⲁⲩⲱ †ⲡⲁⲣⲁⲕⲁⲗⲓ ⲟⲛ ⲙⲁⲕ ⲙⲡⲟⲟⲩ ⲥⲁⲗⲁⲑⲓⲏⲗ
    ⲡⲉϭⲱϣ ⲛⲉⲛⲇ̄ ⲛⲉⲧⲉⲛⲁⲙⲓⲥ : ⲉⲧⲉ ⲛⲁⲓ ⲛⲉⲩⲣⲁⲛ ⸗
    ⲁ̄ⲣ̄ⲁ̄ⲝ̄ ⸗ ⲃ̄ⲁ̄ⲣ̄ⲁ̄ⲝ̄ : ⲥ̄ⲁ̄ⲝ̄ : ⲑ̄ⲁ̄ⲝ̄ : ⲡⲉⲛⲧⲁϥ·ⲃⲱⲕ ⸗ ϣⲁ · ⲉⲩ-
    ϩⲁ : ⲥⲉⲛ·ⲉϩⲟⲩ̄ⲛ̄ · ⲉ̄ⲡ̄ⲭⲁⲗⲭⲉⲗ · ⲁⲃⲁⲡⲁⲧⲁ ⲛⲡⲉⲥ-
30 ⲛⲟⲩⲥ ⸗ ϣⲁⲛⲧⲉ·ⲥⲟⲩⲱⲙ ⲉⲃⲁⲗ · ⲡϣⲏ:ⲛ ⲛⲉⲥⲕⲱⲕ-
    ⲕⲁϩⲏⲩ ⸗ ⲛ†ϩⲉ ⲛⲧⲉ ⲱⲛ : †ⲥⲟⲡⲥ ⲛ̄ⲙⲁⲕ ⲙⲡⲟ-
    ⲟⲩ ⲭⲉⲕⲁⲥ : ⲕⲉⲃⲱⲕ : ϣⲁ ss̄ ⲛⲕⲁⲧⲁⲣⲁⲥⲥⲉ ⲛ:ⲡⲉ-
    ⲥⲛⲟⲩⲥ ⸗ ϣⲁⲛⲧⲉⲥⲙⲟⲟϣⲉ ⲛ:ⲛⲉⲥⲟⲩⲉⲣⲏⲧⲉ ⸗
    ⲛⲥⲉⲓ ⲉⲣⲁ · ⲉⲡⲏⲓ ⸗ ⲉⲛ ss̄ ⲧⲉϥ† ⲛⲧⲉϥⲉⲡⲉⲑⲉⲙⲓⲁ : ⲛ-
35 ϩⲟⲟⲩⲧ ⸗ ⲉϩⲟⲩⲛ : ⲧⲉⲥ:ⲉⲡⲉⲑⲉⲙⲓⲁ : ⲛⲥⲓⲙⲉ : ϩⲉⲛ ⲟⲩ-
    ϩⲁ ⲛⲁⲧϣⲓⲡⲉ ⲙ̄ ⲁⲓⲱ : ⲁⲓⲟ ⲧⲁⲭⲏ ⲧⲁⲭⲏ ⸗

---

20 ⲕⲁⲡⲕ ‹ ⲕⲱⲡ "hide yourself" ("verbirg dich") Bilabel/Grohmann | *i.e.* قطن *quṭun* | *i.e.* ᔆⲟⲩⲧⲱ⸗ⲛ "among us" ("zwischen uns") Bilabel/Grohmann ‖ **21** *i.e.* ᔆⲡ-ⲉⲧ-ⲭⲏϥ : "which devastates" ("das verwüstet") Bilabel/Grohmann : "ash" Gardner | *i.e.* ᔆⲡ-ⲉⲧ-ⲧⲏⲥ : ⲅⲓⲧⲏ *i.e.* κιττώ "cassia-bark" ? Gardner | π(ⲉ)-ⲧ-† ⲥⲛⲁϣⲉ "that wounds" ("das verwundet") Bilabel/Grohmann ‖ **22** *i.e.* ϭⲗⲃⲟⲟⲩ *cf.* Crum CD s.v. ⲃⲟⲟⲩ (no translation) Bilabel/Grohmann : "*gelbay*-herbs" Gardner | *i.e.* πέπερι ‖ **23** *i.e.* ἁλυκή ? *cf.* note : λευκή Bilabel/Grohmann ‖ **24** *i.e.* ᔆⲉⲣⲉ-(ⲡ-ⲟⲟϩ) ‖ **26** *i.e.* παρακαλεῖν | *i.e.* ᔆⲙ̄ⲙⲟ⸗ⲕ ‖ **27** *l.* ⲡ-ϫⲱϫ "head" ("Haupt") Bilabel/Grohmann | *i.e.* δύναμις ‖ **28–29** *i.e.* ⲉ-ⲩ-ⲁ̔ⲅⲓⲟⲥ Bilabel/Grohmann ‖ **29** *i.e.* ᔆⲉ⸗ⲥ-ⲛ̄-ϩⲟⲩⲛ | *i.e.* ἀπατᾶν corrected from ⲁⲃⲁⲡⲁⲣⲁ by overwriting | *i.e.* ᔆⲙ̄ⲡⲉ⸗ⲥ ‖ **30** *i.e.* νοῦς ‖ **30–31** *i.e.* ᔆⲛ⸗ⲥ-ⲕⲱ ⲕⲁϩⲏⲩ ‖ **31** *i.e.* ᔆⲛ-†-ϩⲉ δέ ⲟⲛ : *i.e.* αἰδοῖον Bilabel/Grohmann | *i.e.* ᔆⲙ̄ⲙⲟⲕ ‖ **32** *i.e.* ᔆⲉ⸗ⲕ-ⲉ-ⲃⲱⲕ | *i.e.* (δεῖνα) (δεῖνα) | *i.e.* ᔆⲛ⸗ϥ̄-ⲧⲁⲣⲁⲥⲥⲉⲓⲛ : *i.e.* ᔆⲛ⸗ ϥ̄-ⲕⲁⲧⲁⲣⲁ́ⲥⲥⲉⲓⲛ Bilabel/Grohmann ‖ **33** *i.e.* νοῦς | ⲛ:ⲛⲉⲥⲟⲩⲉⲣⲏⲧⲉ corrected from ⲛ:ⲛⲉⲥⲟⲩⲉⲣⲏⲁⲉ by smudging and overwriting ‖ **34** *i.e.* ᔆⲉ-ⲡ-ⲣⲁ | *i.e.* ᔆⲙ̄-ⲡ-ⲏⲓ | *i.e.* (δεῖνα) (δεῖνα) | *i.e.* ᔆⲛ̄⸗ϥ-† | *i.e.* ἐπιθυμία ‖ **35** *l.* ⲛ-ⲧⲉⲥ-ⲉ̓ⲡⲓⲑⲩⲙⲓⲁ ‖ **36** *i.e.* (ἀ)πο(λογία) : πολύ or πονωηρῶς ? Bilabel/Grohmann | *i.e.* ταχύ (twice)

|[19, above image] Salathiēl

|[20] Take cotton, tar that is burnt ⟨and⟩ dried, gall of silurus, pepper, sixty salted fish?.
|[24, to right] When the moon is full.

|[26, below image] "I entreat and I invoke you again today, Salathiēl, the Ethiopian of the Four *Powers—whose names are these: Arax, Barax, Sax, Thax—the one who went to Eve when she was within the enclosure and deceived her |[30] mind so that she ate from the tree, and she stripped naked! Thus again I entreat you today that you go to NN, child of NN, and trouble her mind so that she walks on her feet and goes to ⟨the⟩ door of the house of NN, child of NN, and he puts his male lust |[35] into her female lust with a shameless face—request—yea, yea, quickly, quickly!"

KD, EL & MP, edited from photograph and autopsy; tracings by JS.

Image: This is apparently a depiction of Salathiēl and his four powers. The name 'Salathiēl' seems to be derived from Satanael (via /n/-/t/ metathesis and then a shift of nasal /n/ to liquid /l/), the name of the Devil before his fall (cf. *PCM* I 26 note to p. 4 l. 3). As the chief demon, he is probably the figure depicted on the upper right with a crown; his face seems to have been deliberately painted slightly darker than the others to indicate that he is an "Ethiopian", a common description of dark-skinned demonic figures in Egyptian Christian texts; see Dosoo 2022a: 162–164; Love 2022c: 648–649. For Satanael, cf. the note to *PCM* I 26 p. 4 l. 3. In other cases (*e.g.*, *PCM* I 25 p. 15 l. 27; *PCM* I 26 p. 14 ll. 13–14, 21) Salathiēl is clearly the name of an unfallen angel.
23. ⲁⲗⲏⲩⲅⲉ : "salted fish" Here we follow Gardner (2023b: 104 n. 102) in tentatively proposing to read the Greek word ἀλυκή, apparently referring to a type of fish pickled by salting (see Morelli 1996: 82–88). Perhaps compare *GEMF* 15/*PGM* XII (KYP M160) 415 (366), a separation spell which makes use of an ostracon from a pot for salted fish (ταρείχου ὄστρακον) to create an applied text, although the goal—separation rather than attraction—is the opposite of that here. Bilabel/Grohmann understand instead the word λευκή ("white"), modifying "pepper".
29. ⲉⲡⲭⲁⲗⲭⲉⲗ : "the enclosure" This refers to "the enclosure" of the Garden of Eden; cf. *e.g.*, Pseudo-Timothy of Alexandria, *Institution of Abbaton* (CC 405; Budge 1914: 236.25, 485 (trans.)). The reference is to the Devil's temptation of Eve, which could be understood as a kind of seduction paralleling the love spell described here; compare the notes to *PCM* I 32 p. 1 ll. 32–34.
34–35. ⲛⲧⲉϥⲉⲡⲓⲑⲉⲥⲙⲓⲁ : ⲛ̄ϩⲟⲟⲩⲧ ⲉϩⲟⲩⲛ : ⲧⲉⲥ:ⲉⲡⲓⲑⲉⲥⲙⲓⲁ ⲛ̇ⲥϩⲓⲙⲉ : "his male lust into her female lust" A euphemism for the genitalia; cf. the note to *PCM* I 20 l. 14 and Preininger forthcoming c: chapter 5.

PCM I 25. Book of Mary and the Angels

Arsinoites (Faiyum)　　　　　　23.4 (H) × 17.3 (W) cm　　　　　　late X CE

Other references: P.Heid.Inv. Kopt. 685 (formerly P.Heid.Inv. Nr. 1685); TM 102074; TM 129732 (original text); *Pap.Heid.N.F.* IX; KYP M186; Bélanger Sarrazin #235; CLM 1488.

Editions: Meyer 1996 (*ed. pr.*).

Translations: Kropp 1965: no. d (p. 2 ll. 1–25, p. 8 l. 1; German); Meyer 1996; Johnston/Gardner 2023.

Additional commentary: Seider 1964; Quecke 1972; Meyer 2003; Untermann (ed.) 2011: 44–47; Meyer 2013; Mößner/Nauerth 2015: 311, 338–348; Burns 2018: 153–254; Gardner/Johnston 2018: 139–148; Gardner/Johnston 2019: 31–32; Piwowarczyk 2020: 110–112; Beshay 2020: 147–159, 194–205; Johnston/Gardner 2023; Richter 2023: 166–68 (p. 16 ll. 8–9); Bélanger Sarrazin forthcoming a: chapter 4; Preininger forthcoming c: chapter 4.

Present location: Heidelberg, Institut für Papyrologie.

Image: https://doi.org/10.11588/diglit.39753

Linguistic description: Sahidic with Middle Egyptian features.

Contents:

Original Use: Lectionary of Pauline Epistles (Quecke 1972: 11–12; Meyer 1996: 3)

1. Bifolio 1 hair (pp. 1 + 20): Hebrews 5.3–6; 2 Timothy 2.3–13 (no. 11, day 15 Hathor?)
2. Bifolio 1 flesh (pp. 19 + 2): 2 Timothy 2.13–15; Philippians 4.1–9 (no. 12, day 16)
3. Bifolio 2 hair (pp. 18 + 3): Hebrews 9.7–10; Hebrews 2.11b–[17] (no. [.]6, day 2[.])
4. Bifolo 2 flesh (pp. 17 + 4): Hebrews 2.17–18; Hebrews 12.1–6 (no. [.]7, day 2)
5. Bifolio 3 flesh (pp. 16 + 5): 2 Corinthians 5.17–6.4 (no. [1], day 1 Thout); Hebrews 6.9 (no. [2], day 2 Thout?)
6. Bifolio 3 hair (pp. 15 + 6): Hebrews 6.9–20 (continuation of no. 2 day 2)
7. Bifolio 4 hair (pp. 14 + 7): Hebrews 11.32–40; Titus 2.11–12 (no. [.], day 11? Tobi?)
8. Bifolo 4 flesh (pp. 13 + 8): Titus 2.12–3.7
9. Bifolio 5 flesh (pp. 12 + 9): Hebrews 1.13–2.8
10. Bifolio 5 hair (pp. 11 + 10): Hebrews 2.8–11; Hebrews 4.14–5.3

Re-use:

11. p. 2 ll. 1–25 – p. 9 ll. 1–23: Prayer of Mary (KYP T238)
12. p. 9 ll. 24–31: Recipe for exorcism (KYP T239)
13. p. 10 ll. 1–18: Instructions for an amulet calling upon the protector of Solomon (KYP T240)
14. p. 10 ll. 19–27: Invocation of Sator names for help and protection (KYP T241)
15. p. 11 ll. 1–11: Recipe against bleeding (KYP T242)
16. p. 12 l. 1–29 – p. 16 ll. 1–15: Adjuration of the Nine Guardians (KYP T243)
17. p. 16 ll. 16–27 – p. 17 ll. 1–10: Formulary against bleeding (KYP T245)
18. p. 17 ll. 11–45: Recipe for good business (KYP T244)
19. p. 18 ll. 1–17: Recipe to heal fever (KYP T1138)

Complete, single quire parchment codex of 20 pages. The codex is part of the archive known as the 'Heidelberg Library' (see pp. 259–263) and belongs to the 1930 purchase. The manuscript was written by Deacon Iōhannēs (see pp. 260–263).

Only pages 2–18 are inscribed, while pages 1 and 20 served as blank outer covers. The manuscript is a palimpsest of a lectionary of Pauline epistles in which each of the readings is given its number in the sequence, and the day of the month on which it is read. The names of the months themselves are lost, but comparison with other lectionaries shows that it may have covered the months of Thout, Hathor, and Tobi.[1] Five single sheets from the original lectionary were folded in half and trimmed to create five bifolios.[2] As a result, the lectionary is written in two columns at right angles to the re-used text. Before the re-used codex was disassembled for conservation in the twentieth century, it was bound in a single quire with three parchment strings which were tied on the outer side.[3] These strings of parchment likely came from the same codex.[4] Other leaves from the same lectionary were used to produce *PCM* I 26.

Each page of the re-used text contains a maximum of 31 lines, with about 25 letters (roughly 20 to 30) per line. Besides the hand of Iōhannēs, we recognise other characteristics typical for his manuscripts, such as simple horizontal lines used to divide recipes and recipe sections (including one line at the very beginning of the manuscript) and various paratextual markers, including the mid-point, colon, and two oblique strokes. The text contains the same dialectal and grammatical features typical of this scribe (see pp. 261–262). This manuscript is exceptional for having been partially personalised; at two points, a personal name (Iōsēph, son of Paraseu; *cf.* notes to p. 13) replaces the generic name marker; it is unclear if this is because the manuscript was copied to be used by him, or if this particular text was copied from a personalised exemplar.

The nine texts contained in this manuscript are primarily concerned with healing, exorcism, and good fortune; most of these are discussed in the accompanying notes, but it is worth giving here a fuller introduction to the first text. The so-called *Prayer of Mary 'in Bartos'* is a prayer attributed to the Virgin Mary which calls upon God to protect the patient from disease, sorcery, and demons.[5] This text may be one of the earliest composed of the surviving Christian magical texts, perhaps dating to shortly after the confirmation of Mary as the Mother of God (*theotokos*)

---

[1] See Quecke 1972: 12–16, but *cf.* the discussion in the introduction to *PCM* I 26, which problematises this assumption.

[2] Meyer 1996: 4.

[3] Meyer 1996: 4. On the same page, Meyer notes, following Quecke 1972: 6, n. 4: "Two perforations (1–1.5 cm. apart) near the top, middle, and bottom of the fold in the parchment accommodated the thongs (themselves 7.2 x 0.6–0.9 cm., 5.5 x 0.4–0.6 cm., and 7.1 x 0.3–0.5 cm.)".

[4] Quecke 1972: 6, n. 4.

[5] On this text, see Kropp 1965; Meyer 1999, 2001, 2003, 2004, & 2013; Łajtar/van der Vliet 2017: 80–202; van der Vliet 2019b: 330, 338.

at the Council of Ephesus in 431, which led to the production of dormition narratives describing her powers of healing and exorcism, linked to a prayer given to her by Jesus.[6] A Greek copy, from the tomb of the Archishop Georgios in Old Dongola (*ca.* 1113 CE),[7] probably represents the original language of the text, but there are at least 6 other copies in Coptic,[8] making it the most common Coptic magical text after the Abgar Correspondence,[9] although each copy displays significant variation. Close verbal parallels in several otherwise unrelated Coptic magical texts are suggestive of the influence of the *Prayer of Mary* on the genre as a whole.[10] Early modern (and more standardised) versions of this prayer survive in Arabic and Ge'ez.[11] In the modern tradition, the text is known as the *Prayer of Mary 'in Bartos'*—Bartos probably referring to Parthia (Πάρθος)—and the prayer is said to have been spoken by her to free the Apostle Matthias from imprisonment.[12] An extended literary narrative, *The Miracles of the Virgin Mary in Bartos* (CC 885), whose Arabic version is attributed to Cyril of Jerusalem, survives fragmentarily in Coptic, and fully in Arabic, and describes Mary's use of the prayer to free prisoners and heal the suffering.[13] The highly repetitive nature of this narrative may suggest that it is posterior to the *Prayer*; it seems to focus on the *Prayer*'s capacity to melt iron, which appears in the early part of the text (here p. 2 ll. 24–25). The connection to 'Bartos', however, is absent in any of the Coptic versions of the prayer, and seems to be a later accretion; the version here describes the prayer as that which Mary spoke on her deathbed, creating a connection to the dormition narratives, which link the prayer given to her by Jesus to her "falling asleep" (*i.e.*, death).[14]

---

[6] Łajtar/van der Vliet 2017: 141–142; Dosoo 2021a: 693–694.

[7] Burial vault, Tomb of Archbishop Georgios (Łajtar/van der Vliet 2017: no. 9; KYP M501).

[8] *P.Lond.Copt.* 368 (KYP M117); BL Ms. Or. 6796 (1–3) (Kropp 1931: I no. G, II nos. XL, XLI); *BKU* I 6 (KYP M119); P.Iand. inv. 9 (Kropp 1965; KYP M134); Collège de France Ms. 2 (KYP M 573; unpublished); Coptic Museum 4958 (KYP M130; unpublished).

[9] For a discussion of which, see *PCM* I 11 notes to p. 20 l. 6–p. 25 l. 23.

[10] For some of these parallels, see Łajtar/van der Vliet 2017: 148–149; Bélanger Sarrazin 2020: 190–194.

[11] For a translation of the Arabic version, see Viaud 1978: 75–78; a fragmentary mediaeval Arabic version with angel names written in Coptic script is held in the National Library of Egypt as ID 4562/inv. 768; we are grateful to Abdoulaye Ba for sharing his preliminary edition of this piece, which enabled us to make the identification. For a translation of the Ge'ez version, see Basset 1894: 600–610, 694–700.

[12] For the argument that Bartos (برتوس) represents Πάρθος, "Parthia", rather than the previously-hypothesised Beirut, see Guidi 1888: 9. Euringer (1929a) has argued instead that it represents Tortosa in Syria, but this relies on a hypothetical Arabic writing of Tortosa as ترتوس (subsequently miscopied as برتوس) rather than the usual طرطوس.

[13] For a discussion of this text, see Graf 1944: 253–255; for the fragmentary Bohairic version, see van Lantschoot 1951; the fragmentary Sahidic version is published in Robinson 1896: 20–25; for a translation of the Arabic version, see Basset 1894: 769–789.

[14] Łajtar/van der Vliet 2017: 128–133; Dosoo 2021a: 692–694.

page 2 (flesh)

```
     ταɪ τε τμεϩ:κ̄ᾱ : μπροϲεγχΗ μᾱρ-
     ῑᾱ ⸗ μ̇παρθενοϲ : χοοϲ ⸗ πεϩοογ · π̄ε̄ϲ-
     ενκατε · ϲνερΓεɪ : νεϭαμ : ΝΙ̇Μ τε-
     παν†κɪμενοϲ ⸗ ϲερ παϩρε ϣωΝι
5    ΝΙΜ ⸗ ϩι λαϭλεϭ ΝΙΜ ϩΝ ογεɪρΗΝΗ ϩ̄ᾱ̄ᴹ
     μαρια : δε · αϲβɪ ΝΝεϲβαλ · εϩραι
     ετεπΗ : ϣα πνογτε ⸗ π̄ᾱ̄ν̄τ̄ω̄ρ̄ ⸗
     πεχεϲ χε †ϩωΝχ ερακ μποογ :
     πετϣοοπ ⸗ ϣα ινεϩ ⸗ †ϲμογ ερακ ⸗
10   μποογ ⸗ ιᾱω̄ ⸗ πετΗΝγ ⸗ ϩιχεΝ : Νε-
     ϭΗΝε : Νετπε ≡ ϲ̄ᾱ̄β̄ᾱ̄ω̄θ̄ ≡ πετϭεμ-
     ϭαμ ⸗ εϩογο εραογ ⸗ τΗρογ ⸗ πετϣοοπ
     ϩα·θΗ · Νεων τΗρογ ⸗ ϩαθΗ Νπατε-
     τεπΗ ⸗ μΝ πκαϩ ⸗ ογωναϩ εβαλ ⸗
15   τπε : αϲϣωπε ⸗ Νακ ⸗ Νθρονοϲ ⸗
     αγω ⸗ πκαϩ ⸗ Νϩγπω†ωΝ ⸗ Νε-
     κογερΗ† ≡ ϲωτμ εραι μ̇ποογ ⸗
     ϩεΝ πεκνοϭ ⸗ Νραν ⸗ ετϲμαϲμα-
     ατ : μ̄ᾱ̄ρεϩωβ ΝΙΜ ⸗ κεχϣογ ΝΑΙ ⸗
20   πεϲΗτ ⸗ χε ⸗ ανακ : μ̄ᾱ̄ρ̄ῑᾱ̄ : ανακ
     τε μαρɪϩαμ ⸗ ανακ πε τμααγ
     μπωΝαϩ πκωϲμοϲ τΗρϥ ⸗
     ανακ ϩωωτ ⸗ ⎯ϲ̄ϲ̄⎯ ⸗ πωΝι μαρεϥ- :
     πωϩ ⸗ ϩα ταϩε ποογ ≡ πενιπε ⸗ μα-
25   ρεϥ⸗βωλ εβαλ ⸗ ϩα ταϩε ποογ ≡
```

1 τμεϩ:κ̄ᾱ "24th" Kropp | *i.e.* προσευχή ‖ 1–2 *i.e.* ᔆν̄τα-μ̄ᾱ̄ρ̄ῑᾱ̄ ‖ 2 *i.e.* ᔆτ-παρθένος *cf.* note | *i.e.* ᔆμ̄-πεϩοογ ‖ 2–3 *i.e.* ᔆμ̄-πε⸗ϲ-ν̄κοτ̄κ̄ ‖ 3 *i.e.* (ἐ)νεργεῖν : *i.e.* ἀνείργειν Meyer | *i.e.* ᔆν̄-ϭομ | *i.e.* ᔆΝτε- ‖ 4 *i.e.* ἀντικείμενος | *i.e.* ᔆϣωνε ‖ 5 *i.e.* εἰρήνη | *i.e.* ἀμ(ήν) : ϩ̄ᾱ̄μ̄ Meyer ‖ 6 *i.e.* δέ ‖ 7 *i.e.* ᔆπ-παντ(οκράτ)ωρ *cf.* note to l. 2 ‖ 9 *i.e.* ᔆενεϩ ‖ 10 *i.e.* πετ-ΝΗγ ‖ 11 *i.e.* ϭΗπε ‖ 12 εραογ corrected from ερακ by erasure and overwriting ‖ 13 *i.e.* ᔆν̄-ν̄-αἰών ‖ 13–14 *i.e.* ᔆμ̄πατε-τ-πε ‖ 15 *i.e.* θρόνος ‖ 16 *i.e.* ὑποπόδιον ‖ 18–19 *i.e.* ᔆϲμαμααατ ‖ 19 *i.e.* ᔆκολχ⸗ογ ? ‖ 20 *i.e.* ᔆεπεϲΗτ | *i.e.* ᔆανοκ (twice) ‖ 21 *i.e.* ᔆανοκ τε τ-μααγ ‖ 22 *i.e.* ᔆμ̄-π-κόσμος ‖ 23 l. (δεῖνα) (δεῖνα) ‖ 24 *i.e.* ᔆμ̄-ποογ ‖ 25 *i.e.* ᔆμ̄-ποογ

This is the twenty-first prayer of Mary the Virgin, ⟨that she⟩ spoke on the day of her falling asleep. It works on every power of the Adversary; it heals every sickness |⁵ and every disease, in peace, amen.

And Mary lifted her eyes up to heaven, to God Almighty, saying: "I beseech you today, you who have always existed, I praise you, |¹⁰ today, *Iao, who comes upon the clouds of heaven, *Sabaoth, the one who is mightier than them all, you who existed before all of the aeons, before the heavens and the earth had appeared; |¹⁵ heaven became a throne for you and the earth ⟨a⟩ footstool for your feet! Listen to me today, in your great, blessed name: let every thing bow? down to me, |²⁰ for I am Mary, I am Mariham, I am the mother of the life of the whole world, I myself, NN, child of NN! Stone, let it break before me today! Iron, let |²⁵ it melt before me today!

1–5. ⲧⲁⲓ ⲧⲉ ⲧⲙⲉϩ︤ⲕ︤ⲁ︥ : ⲙ̄ⲡⲣⲟⲥⲉⲩⲭⲏ : "**This is the twenty-first prayer of Mary the Virgin**" For a discussion of the tradition of the *Prayer of Mary 'in Bartos'*, see the introduction to this manuscript.

2. ⲙ̄ⲡⲁⲣⲑⲉⲛⲟⲥ : "**the virgin**" The copyist often seems to treat the initial π of certain Greek words as the Coptic definite article (ⲡ-), consistently omitting the expected article; this is the case even when the word itself is feminine and we would expect an initial ⲧ-. Compare *PCM* I 23 l. 28–29, and the similar treatment of παρθενία in *PCM* I 23 ll. 26, 27, 28, 36, 39, and of other words such as παντοκράτωρ in *PCM* I 22 ll. 31, 32; *PCM* I 26 p. 11 l. 4; *PCM* I 28 p. 9 l. 5, p. 12 ll. 10–11. Compare also the better-known reanalysis of the Greek θάλασσα ("sea") as ⲧ-ϩⲁⲗⲁⲥⲥⲁ (*cf.* Clackson/Papaconstantinou 2010: 81).

11–12. ⲡⲉⲧϭⲙ̄ϭⲁⲙ ⲉ ⲉϩⲟⲩⲟ ⲉⲣⲁⲟⲩ ⲉ ⲧⲏⲣⲟⲩ : "**the one who is mightier than them all**" The parallel versions have a phrase here referring to God's judgement of all mankind, so that we might understand an earlier version of this passage contained something like "to judge them all"; *cf. Tomb of Georgios* North Wall col. 1, l. 4 (Łajtar/van der Vliet 2017: no. 9; KYP M501): καὶ δικάζων παντὶ γένει; British Library MS Or 6796 (1–3) l. 12 (Kropp 1965: no. c; KYP M118): ⲉⲧⲃⲉ ⲅⲉⲛⲟⲥ ⲛⲓⲙ [ⲛ̄ⲛ̄ⲣ]ⲱⲙⲉ; Collège de France Ms. 2 p. 23 l. 14 (KYP M573): ⲉϯϩⲁⲡ ⲉⲅⲉⲛⲟⲥ · ⲛⲓⲙ ⲛ̄ⲣⲱⲙⲉ.

15–17. ⲧⲡⲉ : ⲁⲥϣⲱⲡⲉ ⲉ ⲛⲁⲕ ⲉ ⲛⲑⲣⲟⲛⲟⲥ ⲉ ⲁⲩⲱ ⲉ ⲡⲕⲁϩ ⲉ ⲛϩⲩⲡⲟϯⲫⲱⲛ ⲉ ⲛⲉⲕⲟⲩⲉⲣⲏϯ : "**heaven became a throne for you and the earth ⟨a⟩ footstool for your feet**" *Cf.* Isaiah 66.1: "Thus speaks the Lord, 'Heaven is my throne and earth the footstool of my feet'" (ⲧⲁⲓ ⲧⲉ ⲑⲉ ⲉⲧⲉⲣⲉⲡϫⲟⲉⲓⲥ ϫⲱ ⲙ̄ⲙⲟⲥ ϫⲉ ⲧⲡⲉ ⲡⲉ ⲡⲁⲑⲣⲟⲛⲟⲥ ⲡⲕⲁϩ ⲇⲉ ⲡϩⲩⲡⲟⲡⲟⲇⲓⲟⲛ ⲛ̄ⲛⲁⲟⲩⲉⲣⲏⲧⲉ; Kasser 1965: 180).

19–20. ⲙⲁⲣⲉϩⲱⲃ ⲛⲓⲙ ⲉ ⲕⲉϫⲱⲟⲩ ⲛⲁⲓ ⲉ ⲡⲉⲥⲏⲧ : "**let every thing bow? down to me**" We propose to read here a form of the verb ⲕⲱⲗϫ̄ ("bend") with the ⲗ having been dropped, although the subject of this construction is usually knee (ⲡⲁⲧ). Compare Isaiah 45.23: "every knee shall bow to me" (ⲉⲣⲉⲡⲁⲧ ⲛⲓⲙ ⲛⲁⲕⲱⲗϫ̄ ⲛⲁⲓ; Pierpont Morgan M 568 fol. 47r, col. II, ll. 12–13). The parallels in *Tomb of Georgios*, North wall, col. 1, l. 6 (Łajtar/van der Vliet 2017 no. 9; KYP M501), British Library MS Or 6796 (1-3) ll. 19–20 (Kropp 1965 no. c; KYP M118) and Collège de France Ms. 2 p. 23 l. 19 (KYP M573) use instead the Greek verb ὑποτάσσειν, "be obedient, subservient" here. Meyer translates "submit" but does not discuss his reasoning.

page 3 (hair)

ⲛⲉⲇⲉⲙⲱⲛⲓⲱⲛ ⸗ ⲙⲁⲣⲟⲩⲛ̇ⲁⲭⲱⲣⲓ
ⲉⲓⲛⲁⲩ ≡ ϩⲁ ⲧⲁϩⲉ ⲡⲟⲟⲩ ≡ ⲛⲉⲍⲟⲩ-
ⲥⲓⲁ ⲙ̇ⲡⲟⲩ̇ⲉⲓⲛ ⸗ ⲙⲁⲣⲟⲩⲟ̇ⲩⲱⲛⲁϩ
ⲛⲁⲓ ⲉⲃⲁⲗ ⸗ ⲛⲁⲅⲅⲉⲗⲟⲩ ⲙⲛ ⵓ ⲛⲁⲣ-
5   ⲭⲏ̇ⲁⲅⲅⲉⲗⲱⲥ ⸗ ⲙⲁⲣⲟⲩ·ⲱⲛⲁϩ ⸗
ⲛⲁⲓ ⲉⲃⲁⲗ ⲙ̇ⲡⲟⲟⲩ ≡ ⲛⲉⲣⲟ · ⲉⲧϩⲏⲕ ⸗
ⲁⲩ̇ⲱ ⸗ ⲉⲧϣⲟⲧⲙ̇ ⸗ ⲙⲁⲣⲟⲩⲱⲛϩ ⸗ ⲛⲁⲓ ⸗
ϩⲉⲛ ⲟⲩⲧⲁⲭⲏ ⸗ ⲙⲛ · ⲟⲩϭⲉⲡⲏ ⸗ ϫⲉ ⲣⲉ-
ⲡⲉⲕ·ⲣⲁⲛ ⸗ ϣⲱⲡⲉ · ⲛⲁⲓ ⸗ ⲛⲃⲱⲓⲑⲟⲥ ⸗
10 ⲁⲩⲱ ⲛⲱⲛⲁϩ ⸗ ⲉⲓⲧⲉ · ϩⲙ ⲡⲉϩⲟⲟⲩ ⸗
ⲧⲏⲣⲟϥ ⸗ ⲉⲓⲧⲉ ⵓ ϩⲛ ⲧⲉⲩϣⲏ - ⲧⲏⲣⲥ ⸗
ⲁⲧⲱⲛⲁⲓ ⸗ ⲭⲉⲣⲉⲙ ⸗ ⲁⲧⲱⲙⲁ ⸗ ο
ⲭⲓⲁⲗⲁⲥ ≡ ⲃⲁⲃⲱⲑ ≡ ⲥⲧⲓⲉⲫ ⸗
ⲃⲁ ⸗ ⲥⲁⲑⲁ ⸗ ⲭⲓⲑⲓ ≡ ⲑⲁ ⸗ ⲥⲁⲃⲁⲱⲑ ≡
15 ⲡⲛⲟⲩⲧⲉ ⸗ ⲥⲱⲧⲙ ⲉⲣⲁⲓ ⲙ̇ⲡⲟⲟⲩ ⸗
ⲡⲉⲧϩⲙⲟⲟⲥ ⸗ ⲉϩⲣⲁⲓ ϩⲓϫⲉⲛ ⲡⲉϥ·ⲑ-
ⲣⲱⲛⲟⲥ ⸗ ⲉⲧϫⲟⲥⲉ ⸗ ⲉⲩⲥⲧⲱⲧ · ϩⲁ ⲧ-
ⲉϥϩⲉ ⲛ̇ϭⲓ ⲡⲛⲁ ⲛⲓⲙ ⸗ ⲛⲁ ⲧⲉⲡⲉ ⸗
ⲙⲛ ⵓ ⲛⲁ ⲡⲕⲁϩ ⸗ ⲙⲛ ⸗ ⲛⲉⲧⲥⲁⲡⲉ-
20 ⲥⲏⲧ ⲡⲕⲁϩ ⸗ ⲙⲛ ⵓ ⲛⲉⲧϩⲁ ⲡⲁⲏⲣ ⵓ ⲉⲩ-
ϣⲧⲉⲣⲧⲱⲣ ⸗ ϩⲁⲑⲏ ⲙ̇ⲡⲉⲕⲛⲟϭ
ⲛ̇ⲣⲁⲛ ⸗ ⲉⲧⲟⲩⲁⲁⲃ ⸗ ⲉⲧⲉ ⲡⲁⲓ ≡

---

1 *i.e.* δαιμόνιον | *i.e.* ἀναχωρεῖν || **2** *i.e.* ˢⲛⲁ⸗ⲩ || **2–3** *i.e.* ἐξουσία || **3** ⲙⲛ, ⲛ corrected from ⲁ by overwriting || **4** *i.e.* ἄγγελος || **4–5** *i.e.* ἀρχάγγελος || **5** *i.e.* ˢⲙⲁⲣ⸗ⲟⲩ-ⲟⲩⲱⲛϩ̄ : ⲙⲁⲣⲟⲩⲱⲛⲁϩ Meyer || **7** *l.* ⲙⲁⲣ⸗ⲟⲩ-ⲟⲩⲱⲛ || **8–9** *l.* ⲉⲣⲉⲡⲉⲕⲣⲁⲛ (haplography) || **9** *i.e.* βοηθός || **10** *i.e.* εἴτε || **16–17** *i.e.* θρόνος || **18** *i.e.* πν(εῦμ)α || **20** *i.e.* ἀήρ

The demons, let them withdraw themselves before me today! The *authorities of light, let them appear to me! The *angels and |⁵ *archangels, let them appear to me today! The doors that are braced and shut, let them be opened to me, quickly and in haste, so that your name might become for me a helper |¹⁰ and life, whether in all the day or in all the night!

*Adonai, Kherem, Atōma, Khialas, Babōth, Stieph, Ba, Satha, Khithi, Tha, *Sabaoth, |¹⁵ God, listen to me today, you who sit upon your exalted *throne, every spirit trembling before you, those of the heaven and those of the earth and those below |²⁰ the earth and those under the air, who are disturbed before your great holy name, which is:

1–2. ⲙⲁⲣⲟⲩⲛ̄ⲁⲭⲱⲣⲓ ⲉⲓⲛⲁⲩ : **"let them withdraw themselves"** ⲉⲓ at the beginning of l. 2 poses a problem for parsing; it might be understood either as the ending of ⲛ̄ⲁⲭⲱⲣⲓ, or else as a short prothetic vowel added before ⲛⲁⲩ. Here we opt for the latter, since Greek verbs ending in -εῖν are usually written with final -ⲓ or -ⲉ by this scribe, while a short prothetic vowel (usually ⲉ-) is often written before ⲛⲁⲩ (see, *e.g.*, p. 5 ll. 3, 9 of this manuscript). The writing ⲉⲓ is a result of the often surprising interchange of (ⲉ)ⲓ/ⲉ found in this variety of Coptic (*cf. e.g.*, p. 2 l. 9 of this manuscript; *PCM* I 26 p. 15 l. 26; *PCM* I 27 front l. 19; *PCM* I 31 back l. 16).

12. o This letter differs from the normal form of omicron, and seems instead be some kind of punctuation or lectional mark; compare the similar sign at p. 6 l. 11. Since both appear at similar line positions, it is possible that the copyist used it to keep track of the line count, marking the vertical halfway point of certain pages.

page 4 (flesh)

ⲡⲉ ⲓⲁⲱ ⸗ ⲥⲁⲃⲁⲱⲑ ≡ ⲁⲧⲱⲛⲁⲉⲓ ⸗
ⲉⲗⲟⲉⲓ ⸗ ⲡⲉⲧⲃⲱⲗ ⲉⲃⲁⲗ ⲛϩⲱⲃ
ⲛⲓⲙ ⸗ ⲣⲉⲡⲑⲟⲛⲟⲥ ⸗ ⲛϩⲏⲧϥ ⸗ ⲙⲁⲅⲓⲁ
ⲙⲛ ⲫⲁⲣⲙⲁⲅⲓⲁ · ⲛⲓⲙ ⸗ ⲛⲁⲓ̈ ϣⲁϣⲱ-
5 ⲡⲉ : ϩⲉⲛ̇ ⲣⲱⲙⲉ ⸗ ⲡⲱⲛⲉⲣⲱⲛ ⸗ ⲁⲩⲱ ⸗
ⲡⲉⲣⲓⲕⲟⲩⲣⲅⲟⲥ ⸗ ⲉⲓⲧⲉ · ⲟⲩⲙⲉⲧⲃⲉⲗ-
ⲗⲏ ⸗ ⲉⲓⲧⲉ · ⲟⲩⲙⲉⲧϭⲁⲗ ⸗ ⲉⲓⲧⲉ · ⲟⲩⲙⲉ-
ⲧⲁⲧϣⲁϫⲉ ⸗ ⲉⲓⲧⲉ ⲟⲩⲙⲉⲕⲁϩ ≡ ⲛⲧⲉϥ-
ⲁⲡⲉ ⸗ ⲉⲓⲧⲉ · ⲟⲩϣⲱⲕ ⸗ ⲛ̇ⲧⲉ ⲛⲇⲉⲙⲟ-
10 ⲛⲓⲱⲛ ⸗ ⲉⲓⲧⲉ : ⲟⲩⲁ̈ ⲉϥϩⲏⲙ ⸗ ⲉⲓⲧⲉ ⲟⲩⲁ̈
ⲉϥϣ̇ⲧⲉⲣⲧⲱⲣ ⸗ ⲉⲓⲧⲉ · ⲟⲩⲁ̈ ⲉϥⲗⲁϫ ⸗
ⲉⲓⲧⲉ ⲟⲩⲥⲛⲟⲃ ⸗ ⲁⲩⲕⲁⲟⲩ ϩⲁ · ⲟⲩ:ⲁ̄ : ⲉⲓⲧⲉ ⸗
ⲟⲩᵃⲉ̈ⲁϥϯⲕⲉⲥ ⸗ ⲉⲃⲁⲗ · ϩⲉⲛ ⲛⲉⲇⲉⲙⲱ-
ⲛⲓⲟⲛ ⸗ ⲉⲓⲧⲉ ⲟⲩⲛⲉϩ ⸗ ⲉⲓⲧⲉ · ϩⲩⲡⲱⲣⲁ ⸗
15 ⲉⲓⲉ ⲟⲩⲙⲁ ⲛ⸗ⲥⲱ ⸗ ⲉⲓ̈ ⲕⲉⲧⲱⲥ ⸗ ϩⲁⲡⲗⲟⲥ ⸗
ⲡⲉⲧⲉⲛ:ⲧⲁϥ ⸗ ⲙⲁⲣⲉϥⲃⲱⲗ · ⲉⲃⲁⲗ ⸗ ϩⲓⲧⲉⲛ ⲡⲉⲕⲛⲟϭ ⲛ̇ⲣⲁⲛ ⸗ ⲉⲧⲟⲩⲁⲁⲃ ⸗ ϩⲁ
ⲉⲃⲁⲗ : ⲇ̅ⲇ̅ ⸗ ⲙⲁⲣ:ⲇ̅ⲇ̅ ϣⲱⲡⲉ ⸗ ⲉϥⲟⲩ·ⲁϫ ⸗
ϩⲙ ⲡⲉϥⲥⲱⲙⲁ ⸗ ⲁⲩⲱ ⲡⲉⲃ:ⲥⲱⲙⲁ ⲧ-
20 ⲏⲣϥ : ϣⲱⲡⲉ ϩⲉⲛ ⲟⲩⲧⲁϫⲣⲁ ⸗ ⲛⲉϥⲙⲟⲩ-
ⲧ : ⲙⲛ : ⲛⲉϥⲕⲁⲥ ⸗ ⲛⲉϥⲁⲃⲟⲩϩⲉ ⸗ ⲉⲩϣ-
ⲱⲡⲉ ⸗ ⲉϥⲟⲩⲁϫ ⸗ ϩⲁ ⲉⲃⲁⲗ · ⲙⲁⲅⲓⲁ ⸗
ⲛⲓⲙ ⸗ ⲧⲉⲛⲣⲱⲙⲉ ⸗ ⲙⲛ ϣⲓⲕ ⲛⲓⲙ ⲧⲉⲛ-
ⲇⲉⲙⲟⲛⲓⲟⲛ ⸗ ⲛⲁ ⲡⲉϩⲟⲟⲩ ⸗ ⲙⲛ ⲧⲉⲩϣ-
25 ⲏ ⸗ ⲟⲩⲇⲉ ⲙⲉⲣⲣⲁ ⸗ ⲟⲩⲧⲉ ⲛⲑⲏⲣ ⸗⟦ⲟⲩ⟧

---

3 *i.e.* φθόνος | *i.e.* μαγεία ‖ **4** *i.e.* φαρμακεία ‖ **5** *i.e.* ˢⲙ̄-ⲡⲟⲛⲏⲣⲟⲛ *i.e.* πονηρόν | **6** *i.e.* ˢⲙ̄-ⲡⲉⲣⲓⲟⲩⲣⲅⲟⲥ *i.e.* περιουργός | *i.e.* ⲉⲓⲧⲉ ‖ **7** *i.e.* ⲉⲓⲧⲉ (twice) | *i.e.* ˢⲟⲩ-ⲙⲛⲧ-ⲕⲟⲩⲣ ? ‖ **8** *i.e.* ⲉⲓⲧⲉ | *i.e.* ˢⲙⲕⲁϩ ‖ **9** *i.e.* ⲉⲓⲧⲉ | *i.e.* ˢϣⲱϣϭ (?) : "attack", "intrusion" Meyer ‖ **9–10** *i.e.* δαιμόνιον ‖ **10** *i.e.* ⲉⲓⲧⲉ (twice) ‖ **11** *i.e.* ⲉⲓⲧⲉ | ⲉϥⲗⲁϫ : "depressed" Meyer ‖ **12** *i.e.* ⲉⲓⲧⲉ (twice) | *i.e.* ˢⲟⲩ-ⲥⲛⲟϥ ⲉ-ⲁ⸗ⲩ-ⲕⲁ⸗ϥ ϩⲁ ⲟⲩⲁ ‖ **13** *i.e.* ˢⲉ-ⲁ⸗ϥ-ϯⲕⲁⲥ ⲉⲃⲟⲗ : ⲉ{ⲁ}ϥϯ ⲕⲉⲥ Meyer : or "who has (or, uses) a bone," *i.e.* "makes use of a bone in a spell" Meyer ‖ **14** *i.e.* ⲉⲓⲧⲉ (twice) | *i.e.* ὑπώρα ‖ **15** *i.e.* ἤ | ⲟⲩⲙⲁ ⲛ⸗ⲥⲱ ⸗ ⲉⲓ̈ ⲕⲉⲧⲱⲥ : "a potion in a jar (?)" Meyer | ⲉⲓ̈ ⲕⲉⲧⲱⲥ ⸗ ϩⲁⲡⲗⲟⲥ : or "then I make a drinking place absolutely dry" ? Meyer | *i.e.* κάδος | *i.e.* ἁπλῶς ‖ **16** *i.e.* ˢⲡ-ⲉⲧⲉ-ⲟⲩⲛⲧⲁ⸗ϥ ‖ **18** (δεῖνα) (δεῖνα) (twice) ‖ **19** *i.e.* σῶμα (twice) ‖ **21** *i.e.* ˢⲁϥⲟⲩⲓ : *i.e.* ˢⲟⲃϩⲉ Kropp ‖ **22** *i.e.* μαγεία ‖ **23** *i.e.* ˢⲛⲧⲉ- (twice) | *i.e.* ˢϣⲱϣϭ (?) : "attack", "intrusion" Meyer : "abyss" ("Abgrund") Kropp ‖ **24** *i.e.* δαιμόνιον ‖ **25** *i.e.* οὐδέ | *i.e.* μοῖρα *cf.* note : or *i.e.* ˢⲙⲡ̄ⲣⲉ ? Meyer | *i.e.* οὐδέ | *i.e.* ˢⲉⲛⲧⲏⲣ *cf.* note | ⟦ⲟⲩ⟧ deleted by smudging

*Iao *Sabaoth *Adonai *Eloei, you who undo work which has envy in it, magic and every sorcery, the things that |⁵ come about through evil and meddlesome men, whether blindness, or deafness, or speechlessness, or pain of his head or a strike? of the demons, |¹⁰ or someone who has a fever, or someone who is disturbed, or someone who is crushed, or blood that was loosened under someone, or someone who was given pain by the demons, or ⟨caused by⟩ some oil, or some fruit, |¹⁵ or a banquet, or ⟨a⟩ vessel, in short, whatever he has, let it be undone through your great, holy name, away from NN, child of NN! Let NN, child of NN, be sound in his body and his entire body |²⁰ be strong, his sinews and his bones, his flesh be healthy, away from every magic of men and every crushing? of the demons, those of the day and of the night, |²⁵ neither fates, neither deities!

3–4. ⲙⲁⲅⲓⲁ ⲙⲛ ⲫⲁⲣⲙⲁⲅⲓⲁ · ⲛⲓⲙ : "magic and every sorcery" We might expect "every magic and sorcery", but this would normally require the repetition of ⲛⲓⲙ (cf. Layton 2000: 51 §60(e)). Compare a similar phrase found in another copy of the *Prayer of Mary*: "whether any sorcery or any magic" (ⲉⲓⲇⲉ ⲫⲁ[ⲣⲙ]ⲁⲅⲓⲁ ⲛⲓⲙ ⲉⲓⲧⲉ ⲙⲁⲅⲓⲁ ⲛⲓⲙ; P.Iand.inv. 9 p. 1 ll. 6–7 (Kropp 1965; KYP M134)).

12. ⲉⲓⲧⲉ ⲟⲩⲥⲛⲟⲃ ⲁⲩⲕⲁⲟⲩ ϩⲁ · ⲟⲩ:ⲁ̄ : "blood that was loosened under someone" A reference to a curse to cause bleeding, for which see the notes to *PCM* I 3 front col. 1.

16. ⲡⲉⲧⲉⲛ:ⲧⲁϥ : "whatever he has" For this unusual writing of ˢⲡⲉⲧⲉⲩⲛⲧⲁϥ, compare *PCM* I 31 front l. 23, and ⲉⲧⲁⲥ for ˢⲟⲩⲛⲧⲁⲥ found in the contemporary Teshlot archive (Richter 2000: 120–121).

25. ⲟⲩⲇⲉ ⲙⲉⲣⲣⲁ ⲟⲩⲧⲉ ⲛⲉⲏⲣ : "neither fates, neither deities" The word "fate" (μοῖρα) referred originally to the personified Greek goddesses of fate—Clotho, Lachesis, and Atropos—who were believed to decree the fate of mortals, thus coming to be understood also as goddesses of death. A singular Moira appears in a list of Greek deities in the adjuration P.Carlsberg 52 (Lange 1932; KYP M125) p. 3 l. 18, likely inspired by mentions in Greek literature (cf. Blumell/Dosoo 2018: 249–250 n. 132). In this text, as well as a roughly contemporary amulet to protect a pregnant woman (*P.Lond. Copt.* 524 (KYP M359) front l. 21) the "fates" seem to represent a specific type of malevolent spirit. Likewise, "deities" translates the Coptic ⲉⲛⲧⲏⲣ, the largely obsolete plural of ⲛⲟⲩⲧⲉ "god", treated as an independent singular noun in standard Coptic (Crum CD 725b; Vycichl DELC 145–146). Like "fates", the word seems to have come to refer to a type of demonic being in the context of Christian Egypt; cf. Krueger 2021: 130–132. We find "deities" listed among harmful demons in the Coptic magical corpus in *PCM* I p. 41 ll. 8–9; *P.Lond.Copt.* 524 (KYP M359) front l. 22 (alongside "fates"); Columbia inv. 554 ll. 18–19 (Schiller 1928; KYP M2); P.Berol. 11347 (Beltz 1985: no. II 42) back ll. 8–9. The word also appears in *PCM* I 4 ll. 4, 10 and Mich.Ms. 136 (Zellmann-Rohrer/Love 2022; KYP M128) p. 5 l. 3, albeit referring in these cases to Pharaonic deities (Amun, *Osiris, *Isis, *Apis) rather than harmful demonic beings.

page 5 (flesh)

```
     ⲃⲁⲥⲁⲛⲓⲍⲉ ≡ ⲛⲉⲇⲉⲙⲟⲛⲓⲱⲛ ⸗ ⲛⲁ ⲡⲉ·-
     ϩⲟⲟⲩ · ⲙⲛ ⲛⲁ ⲧⲉⲩϣⲏ · ϫⲉⲕⲁⲥ : ⲉⲩⲛⲁ⸗
     ϣⲱⲣⲓ · ⲉⲛⲁⲩ : ϩⲁ ⲉⲃⲁⲗ : ⲥⲥ ⸗ ⲉϥϣⲱ-
     ⲡⲉ ⲧⲏⲣϥ ⸗ ⲉϥⲟⲩⲁϫ · ϩⲉⲛ ⲡⲉϥⲥⲱⲙⲁ ⸗
 5   ⲙⲛ ⲧⲉϥⲯⲩⲭⲏ ⸗ ⲙⲛ ⲡⲛⲁ ⸗ ⲙⲁⲣⲉϥⲉⲓ-
     ⲙⲉ ⸗ ϫⲉ ⲛⲧⲁⲕ ⸗ ⲧⲉ ⲡⲛⲟⲩⲧⲉ ⸗ ⲁⲩⲱ ⲙⲛ
     ⲕⲉⲟⲩⲁ̇ · ⲛⲃⲉⲗ:ⲗⲁⲕ ⸗ ⲙⲛ·ⲡⲱⲧⲛ ⲥⲉⲭ-
     ⲟⲟⲥ · ϭⲓ ⲛⲉϩⲑⲛⲟⲥ ⸗ ϫⲉ ⲙⲉⲛ ⲃⲱⲓⲑⲓ ⸗
     ϣⲟⲟⲡ ⲉⲛⲁⲩ ⸗ ⲛⲧⲁⲕ · ⲅⲁⲣ ⲡⲉ ⲡⲟⲥ
10   ⲥⲁⲃⲁⲱⲑ ≡ ⲡⲛⲟϭ : ϩⲛ ⲙⲡⲏⲩ ⸗ ⲁⲩⲱ · ϩⲓ-
     ϫⲉ ⲡⲕⲁϩ ⸗ ϩⲱⲃ ⲛⲓⲙ ⸗ ⲧⲉⲕⲟⲩⲟϣⲟⲩ
     ϣⲁⲕⲁⲟⲩ ⸗ ϯⲱⲣⲕ ⲉⲣⲁⲕ ⸗ ⲙ̇ⲡⲟⲟⲩ ⸗ ⲙ̇-
     ⲡⲟⲩϫⲁⲓ : ⲡⲉⲕⲕⲇ ⸗ ⲙ̇ⲡⲉⲣⲉⲥⲃⲩⲧⲉⲣⲟⲥ ⸗
     ⲉⲛⲁⲥⲱⲙⲁⲧⲱⲥ ⸗ ⲉⲧⲉ ⲛⲁⲓ ⲉⲩⲣⲁⲛ ⸗
15   ⲃⲏⲑ ⸗ ⲃⲏⲑⲁ ⸗ ⲣⲟⲩⲏⲗ ⸗ ⲙⲁⲧⲁϯⲏⲗ ·
     ⲣⲓⲏⲗ · ⲣⲓⲭⲁⲏⲗ : ⲭⲱⲃⲁⲛⲧⲁ ⸗ ⲭⲱⲙⲏ ⸗
     ⲉⲓⲭⲁⲙ · ⲙⲁⲙ · ⲥⲁⲃⲁⲱⲑ ≡ ⲣⲱⲏⲗ ⸗
     ⲛⲱⲏⲗ : ⲛⲱⲏⲗ · ⲩⲙⲓⲏⲗ · ⲧⲁⲧⲓⲏⲗ ⸗
     ⲕⲁⲧⲁϯⲏⲗ · ⲍⲁⲣⲓⲏⲗ · ⲁⲣⲓⲏⲗ · ⲓⲁⲱ ⸗
20   ⲃⲏⲑⲁ · ⲡⲁⲧⲣⲟⲩⲏⲗ · ⲥⲁⲕⲓⲁ ≡ ⲁⲣⲓⲏⲗ ⸗
     ⲕⲱ ⲛⲁⲓ ⲉⲃⲁⲗ · ⲙ̇ⲡⲟⲟⲩ : ⲥⲥ : ϯⲥⲟⲡⲥ : ⲁⲩⲱ ·
     ϯⲡⲁⲣⲁⲕⲁⲗⲓ ⲉⲙⲁⲕ ⲙ̇ⲡⲟⲟⲩ ⸗ ⲁⲛⲁⲕ : ⲥⲥ
     ϫⲉⲕⲁⲥ : ⲕⲉⲧⲉⲛ:ⲛⲟⲟⲩ ⲛ̇ⲁⲓ : ⲛ̇ⲧⲉⲕϭⲁⲙ ⸗
     ⲉⲧⲟⲩⲁⲁⲃ ⸗ ⲉⲥⲕⲁⲑⲁⲣⲓⲍⲉ ⸗ ⲙ̇ⲡ·ⲛⲁ ⲛⲓⲙ ⸗
25   ⲛϣⲱⲛⲉ ⸗ ⲉⲧϭⲁⲗⲉⲩ : ⲉⲡⲥⲱⲙⲁ ⲥⲥ ⲙⲁⲣⲟ-
     ⲩⲡⲱⲧ ϩⲁ ⲉⲃⲁⲗ · ⲙⲁⲅⲓⲁ ⲛⲓⲙ ⸗ ⲉϥϣⲱⲡⲉ
     ϩⲉⲛ ⲟⲩⲧⲁⲭⲣⲁ · ⲡⲉϥⲥⲱⲙⲁ · ⟦ⲙⲛ⟧
```

---

1 *i.e.* βασανίζειν | *i.e.* δαιμόνιον ‖ 2–3 *i.e.* (ἀ)ναχωρεῖν ‖ 3 *l.* (δεῖνα) (δεῖνα) ‖ 3–4 *i.e.* ˢⲛ̅⸗ϥ-ϣⲱⲡⲉ : *i.e.* ˢⲉ⸗ϥ-ϣⲱⲡⲉ Meyer ‖ 4 *i.e.* σῶμα ‖ 5 *i.e.* ψυχή | *l.* πν(εῦμ)α ‖ 6 τε *i.e.* ˢⲡⲉ ‖ 7 *i.e.* ˢⲛ̅ⲃⲗ̅ⲕ̅⸗ⲕ | *i.e.* μήποτε : ⲙⲛⲡⲱⲧⲏ Meyer ‖ 8 *i.e.* ἔθνος ‖ *i.e.* βοήθεια ‖ 9 *i.e.* ˢⲛⲁ⸗ⲩ | *i.e.* γάρ | *l.* π-ⲭ(ⲟⲉⲓ)ⲥ ‖ 10 *i.e.* ˢⲡⲏⲩⲉ ‖ 11 *i.e.* ˢⲉⲧ⸗ⲕ̅-ⲟⲩⲁϣ⸗ⲟⲩ ‖ 12 *i.e.* ˢϣⲁ⸗ⲕ-ⲁⲁ⸗ⲟⲩ ‖ 13 *i.e.* πρεσβύτερος ‖ 14 *i.e.* ἀσώματος | *i.e.* ˢⲛⲉ⸗ⲩ-ⲣⲁⲛ ‖ 21 *l.* (δεῖνα) (δεῖνα) ‖ 22 *i.e.* παρακαλεῖν ‖ *i.e.* ˢⲙ̅ⲙⲟ⸗ⲕ | *l.* (δεῖνα) (δεῖνα) ‖ 23 *i.e.* ˢⲉ⸗ⲕ-ⲉ-ⲧⲛ̅ⲛⲟⲟⲩ ‖ 24 *i.e.* ˢⲛ̅⸗ⲥ-ⲕⲁⲑⲁⲣⲓⲍⲉ *i.e.* καθαρίζειν | *l.* πν(εῦμ)α ‖ 25 *i.e.* ˢϣⲱⲛⲉ ⲛ̅-ϭⲁⲗⲉ "paralysis" ("Lähmungskrankheit") Kropp | *i.e.* ˢⲉⲧ-ϭⲁⲗⲏϭ, ϭ corrected from unclear letter by overwriting | *i.e.* σῶμα | *l.* (δεῖνα) (δεῖνα) ‖ 25–27 *i.e.* ˢⲙⲁⲣ⸗ⲟⲩ-ⲡⲱⲧ ϩⲁ ⲉⲃⲟⲗ ⲛ̅ϭⲓ ⲙⲁⲅⲓⲁ ⲛⲓⲙ ⲛ⸗ϥ-ϣⲱⲡⲉ ϩⲛ̅ ⲟⲩ-ⲧⲁⲭⲣⲟ ⲡⲉ⸗ϥ-ⲥⲱⲙⲁ : "let them flee from all magic and let him become strong (in) his body" Meyer ‖ 26 *i.e.* μαγεία | *i.e.* ˢⲛ̅⸗ϥ-ϣⲱⲡⲉ ‖ 27 *i.e.* ˢⲙ̅-ⲡⲉ⸗ϥ-ⲥⲱⲙⲁ | ⟦ⲙⲛ⟧ erased by smudging

Torture the demons, those of the day and those of the night, so that they withdraw themselves from NN, child of NN, and he becomes wholly sound in his body |⁵ and his soul and spirit!

Let him know that you are God and there is no other except you, lest the nations say, "There is no help for them", for you are the Lord |¹⁰ *Sabaoth, the great one in heavens and upon the earth; every thing that you wish you do. I adjure you today by the *wellbeing of the incorporeal *Twenty-Four Presbyters, whose names are Bēth, Bētha, Rouēl, Matatiēl, |¹⁵ Riēl, Rikhaēl, Khōbanta, Khōmē, Eikham, Mam, Sabaoth, Rōēl, Noēl, Nōēl, Umiēl, Tatiēl, Katatiēl, Zariēl, Ariēl, *Iao, |²⁰ Bētha, Patrouēl, Sakia, Ariēl; forgive me, NN, child of NN, today!

I entreat and I invoke you today, I, NN, child of NN, that you send to me your holy power so that it cleanses every spirit |²⁵ of sickness that dwells in the body of NN, child of NN! Let every magic flee away, so that he becomes strong in his body

---

5–7. ⲙⲁⲣⲉϥⲉⲓⲙⲉ ⳽ ϫⲉ ⲛⲧⲁⲕ ⳽ ⲧⲉ ⲡⲛⲟⲩⲧⲉ ⳽ ⲁⲩⲱ ⲙⲛ ⲕⲉ ⲟⲩⲁ · ⲛⲃⲉⲗ:ⲗⲁⲕ : **"Let him know that you are God and there is no other except you"** *Cf.* *e.g.*, Deuteronomy 4.35: "so that you know that the Lord, your God, this one is God, with no other beside him" (ϩⲱⲥⲧⲉ ⲉⲧⲣⲉⲕⲉⲓⲙⲉ ϫⲉ ⲡϫⲟⲉⲓⲥ ⲡⲉⲕⲛⲟⲩⲧⲉ ⲡⲁⲓ ⲡⲉ ⲡⲛⲟⲩⲧⲉ ⲉⲙⲛⲕⲉⲟⲩⲁ ⲛⲃⲗⲗⲁϥ; Kasser 1962: 114, 116).

7–9. ⲙⲛ'ⲡⲱⲧⲛ ⲥⲉϫⲟⲟⲥ · ϭⲓ ⲛⲉϩⲉⲑⲛⲟⲥ ⳽ ϫⲉ ⲙⲉⲛ ⲃⲱⲓⲑⲓ ⳽ ϣⲟⲟⲡ ⲉⲛⲁⲩ : **"lest the nations say: "There is no help for them"** *Cf.* Psalm 78 (79) 10: "lest they say among the nations, 'Where is their God?'" (ⲙⲏⲡⲟⲧⲉ ⲛⲥⲉϫⲟⲟⲥ ϩⲛ ⲛϩⲉⲑⲛⲟⲥ ϫⲉ ⲉϥⲧⲱⲛ ⲡⲉⲩⲛⲟⲩⲧⲉ; Budge 1898: 86); Psalm 113.10 (115.2): "Lest the nations say, 'Where is their God?'" (ⲙⲏⲡⲟⲧⲉ ⲛⲧⲉⲛϩⲉⲑⲛⲟⲥ ϫⲟⲟⲥ ϫⲉ ⲉϥⲧⲱⲛ ⲡⲉⲩⲛⲟⲩⲧⲉ; Budge 1898: 123).

page 6 (hair)

ⲙⲛ ⲯⲩⲭⲏ ⳉ ⲙⲛ ⲡⲉϥ·ⲛ̅ⲁ̅ ⵑ ⲙⲁⲣⲉϥⲉⲓⲙⲉ · ϫⲉ ⲥϣⲟⲟⲡ ⲛⲁϥ ⵑ ⲛϬⲓ ⲃⲱⲓⲑⲓ ⳉ
ⲉⲡⲓⲱⲧ ⵑ ϩⲛ ⲧⲡⲉ ⵑ ϩ̅ⲁ̅ⲙ̅ⲏ̅ⲛ̅ ⳉ ⲉⲓ̅ⲥ̅ ϩ̅ⲁ̅-
ⲙ̅ⲏ̅ⲛ̅ ⳉ ⲓ̅ⲥ̅ ⲡ̅ⲭ̅ⲥ̅ ϩ̅ⲁ̅ⲙ̅ⲏ̅ⲛ̅ ⳉ ⲓ̅ⲥ̅ ϩ̅ⲁ̅ⲙ̅ⲏ̅ⲛ̅
ⲉⲓ̅ⲥ̅ ⲡ̅ⲭ̅ⲥ̅ ⵑ ϩ̅ⲁ̅ⲙ̅ⲏ̅ⲛ̅ ⳉ ⲡ̅ⲉ̅ⲡ̅ⲓ̅ⲥ̅ⲧ̅ⲓ̅ⲥ̅ ⲛ̇·ⲛⲉⲛⲓ-
ⲕⲉⲁ ϩ̅ⲁ̅ⲙ̅ⲏ̅ⲛ̅ ϩ̅ⲁ̅ⲙ̅ⲏ̅ⲛ̅ ⳉ ϩ̅ⲁ̅ⲙ̅ⲏ̅ⲛ̅ ⲥϣⲟⲟᵖ
ⲁ̅ⲅ̅ⲓ̅ⲟ̅ⲥ̅ ⳉ ⲁ̅ⲅ̅ⲓ̅ⲟ̅ⲥ̅ ⳉ ⲁ̅ⲅ̅ⲓ̅ⲟ̅ⲥ̅ ⳉ ⲕⲓⲣⲓⲟⲥ ⳉ ⲥⲁⲃⲁⲱⲑ ⵑ ⲡ̅ⲗ̅ⲓ̅ⲣ̅ⲓ̅ⲥ̅ ⳉ ⲛⲟⲩⲣⲁⲛⲟⲩⲥ ⳉ ⲕⲉ ⲉⲓ ⲕⲏ
ⲧⲏⲥ ⳉ ⲁ̅ⲅ̅ⲓ̅ⲁ̅ⲥ̅ ⳉ ⲟⲩⲧⲟⲝⲓⲱⲥ ⳉ ⲕⲟⲩⲁⲁⲃ ⳉ
ⲕⲟⲩⲁⲁⲃ ⳉ ⲕⲟⲩⲁⲁⲃ ⳉ ⲡⲉⲧⲙⲟⲟⲥ ⲉϩⲣⲁⲓ ⵑ ϩⲓϫⲉⲛ ⵑ ⲛⲉϩⲁⲣⲙⲁ ⲛⲛⲉⲭⲉⲣⲟⲩ-ⲟ
ⲃⲓⲛ ⳉ ⲉⲩⲥⲱⲕ · ⲛ̇Ϭⲓ ⲛⲉⲓⲛⲟϬ ⳉ
ⲛⲥⲱⲛⲧ ⲣⲉ̅ϥ̅ ⲛⲧⲉⲛⲁϩ ⳉ ⲉⲡⲟⲩⲁ ⲡⲟⲩⲁ
ⲙⲁⲁⲩ ⳉ ⲃ̅ⲁ̅ⲑ̅ⲟ̅ⲩ̅ⲣ̅ⲓ̅ⲏ̅ⲗ̅ · ⲉⲡⲓⲱⲧ ⵑ ⲛⲁ ⲧⲡⲉ ⳉ
ⲙⲛ ⵑ ⲛⲁ ⲡⲕⲁϩ ⳉ ⲡⲉⲧⲙⲟ̅ⲟ̅ⲥ̅ ⳉ ϩⲙ ⲡϫⲓⲥⲉ ⳉ
ⲉⲩⲟⲩⲱⲛⲁϩ ⳉ ⲛⲁⲓ ⲉⲃⲁⲗ ⳉ ⲙ̅ⲁ̅ⲣ̅ⲙ̅ⲁ̅ⲣ̅ⲟ̅ⲩ̅-
ⲏ̅ⲗ̅ ⳉ ⲙ̅ⲁ̅ⲣ̅ⲙ̅ⲁ̅ⲣ̅ⲟ̅ⲩ̅ⲛ̅ⲓ̅ⲏ̅ⲗ̅ ⳉ ⲙ̅ⲁ̅ⲣ̅ⲙ̅ⲁ̅ⲣ̅ⲟ̅ⲩ̅ⲏ̅ⲗ̅·
ⲙ̅ⲁ̅ⲣ̅ⲙ̅ⲁ̅ⲣ̅ⲟ̅ⲩ̅ⲛ̅ⲓ̅ⲏ̅ⲗ̅ · ⲙ̅ⲁ̅ⲣ̅ⲙ̅ⲁ̅ⲣ̅ⲟ̅ⲩ̅ⲛ̅ ⳉ
ⲙ̅ⲁ̅ⲣ̅ⲙ̅ⲁ̅ⲣ̅ⲟ̅ⲩ̅ ⳉ ⲙ̅ⲁ̅ⲣ̅ⲙ̅ⲁ̅ⲣ̅ ⳉ ⲙ̅ⲁ̅ⲣ̅ⲙ̅ⲁ̅ⲙ̅ ⳉ
ⲡⲉⲛⲧⲁϥⲣⲱϩⲧ ⳉ ⲑⲁⲗⲁⲥⲥⲁ ⳉ ϩⲛ ⲧⲉϥϬⲁ̅ⲙ̅
ⲉⲧⲟⲩⲁⲁⲃ ⵑ ⲁⲙⲟⲩ ϣⲁⲣⲁⲓ ⲙ̇ⲡⲟⲟⲩ ⳉ ⲡⲛⲟϬ
ⲙ̇ⲡⲛⲟⲩⲧⲉ · ⲉⲧϩⲙ ⲡⲉ ⳉ ϯⲱⲣⲕ ⲉⲣⲁⲕ ⲙ̇ⲡⲟⲟⲩ ⳉ
ⲡⲟⲩϫⲁⲓ · ⲡⲉⲕⲍ̅ ⲛⲁⲣⲭⲁⲅⲅⲉⲗⲱⲥ ⳉ
ⲛⲁⲓ ⵑ ⲉⲧϣⲟⲟⲡ ⳉ ⲛⲉⲙⲁⲕ ⳉ ϩⲁⲑⲉ · ⲙ̇ⲡⲁⲧⲉⲕ̅-
ⲧⲁⲙⲓⲁ ⵑ ⲛⲁⲇⲁⲙ ⲡⲓϣⲁⲣⲡ ⲉⲣⲱⲙⲉ ⳉ
ⲧⲟⲩⲉⲓ ϣⲁⲣⲟⲓ ⵑ ⲙ̇ⲡⲟⲟⲩ ⳉ ⲧⲟⲩⲣⲁⲉⲓⲥ ⳉ
ⲁⲩⲱ ⲧⲟⲩⲥⲕⲉⲡⲁⲥⲉ ⲙ̇·ⲉⲡⲥⲱⲙⲁ ⳉ ⲥ̅ⲥ̅ ⳉ

---

1 *i.e.* ψυχή | *i.e.* (π)ν(εῦμ)α || **2** *i.e.* ˢⲛ̅Ϭⲓ | *i.e.* βοήθεια || **3** *i.e.* ἀμήν | *l.* ι(ησου)ς ? || **3–4** *i.e.* ἀμήν || **4** *l.* ι(ησου)ς | *l.* χ(ριστό)ς | *i.e.* ἀμήν (twice) | *l.* ι(ησου)ς || **5** *l.* ι(ησου)ς | *l.* χ(ριστό)ς | *i.e.* ἀμήν | *i.e.* πίστις || **6** *i.e.* ἀμήν (three times) || **7–9** *i.e.* ἅγιος ἅγιος ἅγιος κύριος Σαβαώθ πλήρης ὁ οὐρανὸς καὶ ἡ γῆ τῆς ἁγίας σου δόξης || **10** *i.e.* ˢⲡⲉⲧ-ϩⲙⲟⲟⲥ || **11** *i.e.* ἅρμα || **11–12** *i.e.* χερουβίμ || **13** *i.e.* ˢⲉⲣⲉ-ϥ̅ || **14** *i.e.* ˢⲙ̅ⲙⲁⲩ (?) | *i.e.* ˢⲛ̅-ⲛⲁ || **15** *i.e.* ˢⲡⲉⲧ-ϩⲙⲟⲟⲥ || **16** ⲉⲩⲟⲩⲱⲛⲁϩ ⳉ ⲛⲁⲓⲉⲃⲁⲗ ⵑ "[Bathouriel] Appear to me!" ("[Bathouriel] erscheine mir!") Kropp || **18** ⲙ̅ⲁ̅ⲣ̅ⲙ̅ⲁ̅ⲣ̅ⲟ̅ⲩ̅ⲛ̅ Meyer || **20** *i.e.* θάλασσα || **20–21** ϩⲛ ⲧⲉϥϬⲁ̅ⲙ̅ ⲉⲧⲟⲩⲁⲁⲃ: "by his holy power" Meyer || **23** *i.e.* ˢⲙ̅-ⲡ-ⲟⲩϫⲁⲓ | *l.* ⲙ̅-ⲡⲉ-ⲕ-ⲍ̅ ἀρχάγγελος || **26** ⲧⲟⲩⲉⲓ *i.e.* ˢⲛ̅-ⲥⲉ-ⲉⲓ | *i.e.* ˢⲛ̅-ⲥⲉ-ⲣⲟⲉⲓⲥ || **27** *l.* ⲛ̅-ⲥⲉ-ⲥⲕⲉⲡⲁⲍⲉⲓⲛ | *i.e.* ˢⲙ̅-ⲡ-ⲥⲱⲙⲁ | *l.* (δεῖνα) (δεῖνα)

and soul and his spirit, let him know that there is for him the help of the Father in heaven, amen! Jesus?, amen! Jesus Christ, amen! Jesus, amen! |⁵ Jesus Christ, amen! The faith of Nicea, amen, amen, amen, it is so! |⁷, ᴳʳᵉᵉᵏ *Holy, holy, holy, Lord *Sabaoth, heaven and earth are full of your holy glory! |⁹, ᶜᵒᵖᵗⁱᶜ You are holy, |¹⁰ you are holy, you are holy, you who who sit upon the chariot of the *cherubim, who fly under them, namely these great creatures, each one having six wings, Bathouriēl of the Father ⟨of⟩ those of heaven |¹⁵ and those of earth, the one who sits in on high, as they appear to me: Marmarouēl, Marmarouniēl, Marmarouēl, Marmarouniēl, Marmaroun, Marmarou, Marmar, Marmam, |²⁰ the one who struck the sea with his holy power!

Come to me today, O great God, who is in heaven! I adjure you today, ⟨by⟩ the *wellbeing ⟨of⟩ your seven *archangels—these who were with you since before you |²⁵ created Adam, the first man—so that they come to me today, and they protect and shelter the body of NN, child of NN,

---

11. ⲟ See note to p. 3 l. 12.

20. ⲡⲉⲛⲧⲁϥⲣⲱϩⲧ ⸗ ⲑⲁⲗⲁⲥⲥⲁ ⸗ ϩⲛ ⲧⲉϥϭⲟⲙ : "the one who struck the sea with his holy power" Compare Job 26.12: "He fixed the sea with his power and he spread the sea monster with his wisdom" (ⲁϥⲥⲙⲛ ⲑⲁⲗⲁⲥⲥⲁ ϩⲛ ⲧⲉϥϭⲟⲙ ⲁϥⲡⲉⲣϣ ⲡⲕⲩⲧⲟⲥ ⲇⲉ ϩⲛ ⲧⲉϥⲥⲃⲱ; Amélineau 1893: 450). The Greek rather has "he struck down" (ἔτρωσε) rather than "spread", corresponding to "struck" (ⲣⲱϩⲧ) in the text here, and suggesting that this text is independent of the surviving Sahidic translation of Job, as we would expect if it were translated directly from Greek.

page 7 (hair)

ϯⲱⲣⲕ ⲉⲣⲁⲕ · ⲙ̇ⲡⲟⲟⲩ ⳿ ⲙⲓⲭⲁⲏⲗ · ⲙⲛ
ⲅⲁⲃⲣⲓⲏⲗ · ϩⲣⲁⲫⲁⲏⲗ ⲥⲟⲩⲣⲓⲏⲗ
ⲥⲁⲗⲁⲫⲟⲏⲗ · ⲁⲍⲟⲩⲏⲗ · ⲙⲛ ⲡⲣⲁⲛ ⲧ̅ⲉⲛ-
ⲧⲉⲩⲛⲁⲙⲓⲥ : ⲛ̇ⲧⲁⲓⲁ̅ⲛⲱⲙⲁⲍⲉ ⲙ̇ⲙⲟⲟⲩ
5 ⲙⲓⲭⲁⲏⲗ ⲙⲁⲣⲉϥϣⲱⲡⲉ · ϩⲓ ⲟⲩⲛⲁⲙ ÷
ⲙⲁⲃ ⳿ ϣⲁⲛϯ ⲡⲟⲩⲭⲁⲓ : $\overline{ss}$: ⲁ̅ⲓ̅ⲱ̅ ⲁ̅ⲓ̅ⲱ̅ ⲧⲁⲭⲏ
ⲅⲁⲃⲣⲓⲏⲗ · ϣⲱⲡⲓ · ϩⲓ ⲃⲟⲩⲣ ⲙⲁⲓ ⳿ ϣⲁⲛ:ⲧⲁ-
ⲃⲓ · ϩⲁ ⲉⲃⲁⲗ ⲙⲁϥ ⲕⲁϩ : ⲙⲛ ϩⲁⲧⲉ ⲛⲓⲙ ⳿
ϩⲣⲁⲫⲁⲏⲗ ⲙⲁⲣⲉϥϯ ⲕⲗⲁⲙ ϩⲓⲭⲉⲛ ⲧⲉϥ-
10 ⲁⲡⲉ ⳿ ⲥⲟⲩⲣⲓⲏⲗ · ⲙⲁⲣⲉϥ·ⲥⲁⲗⲡⲓⳓ·ⲉ · ϩⲓⲑⲏ
ⲙⲁϥ ⳿ ϩⲣⲁⲕⲟⲩⲏⲗ · ⲙⲁⲣⲉϥϯ ⲉⲟⲟⲩ ⳿ ϩⲓ
ⲭⲁⲣⲓⲥ : ⲛⲉϥ · ⲙ̇ⲡⲉⲛⲧⲁ ⲉⲃⲁⲗ · ⲙ̇ⲡⲅⲉⲛ-
ⲛⲟⲥ ⳿ ⲧⲏⲣϥ ⳿ ⲛⲁⲇⲁⲙ ⳿ ⲛⲉϣⲏⲣⲉ ⲧⲏⲣⲟ̄ⲩ̄
ⲛ̇ⲥⲱⲏ ⳿ ϩⲙ̇ ⲡⲣⲁⲛ ⳿ ⲓ̅ⲁ̅ⲱ̅ ⳿ ⲥⲁⲃⲁⲱⲑ ⳿
15 ⲙⲁⲣⲉϥ·ⲟⲩⲭⲁⲓ : ϩⲙ̇ ⲡⲣⲁⲛ ⲛⲁⲧⲱⲛⲁⲉⲓ ⳿
ⲉⲗⲱⲉⲓ ⲙⲁⲣⲉϥⲟⲩⲭⲁⲓ ⳿ ϩⲙ̇ ⲡⲣⲁⲛ : ⲓ̅ⲁ̅ⲱ̅ ⳿
ⲥⲁⲃⲁⲱⲑ : ⲟⲩⲣⲓⲏⲗ · ⲡⲛⲟⳓ ⲛⲉⲛⲟⲩⲧⲉ ⳿
ϩⲉⲛ ⲧⲡⲉ ⳿ ϯⲉⲣⲁⲕ ⲙⲁⲕ ⲙ̇ⲡⲟⲟⲩ : ⲡⲁ ⲛⲓ-
ⲛⲟⳓ ⲛ̇ⲧⲉⲛⲁⲙⲓⲥ ≡ ⲉⲧⲟⲩⲁⲁⲃ ⳿ ⲙⲏⲥ ⳿ ⲃⲏⲑⲁ
20 ⲫⲣⲁⲅⲅⲓⲥ ⳿ ϯ ⲉⲣⲁⲕ ⲙ̇ⲡⲟⲟⲩ · ⲙ̇ⲡⲉⲕ-
ⲕ̅ⲁ̅ ⳿ ⲕⲁⲧⲁⲡⲉⲧⲓⲥⲙⲁ ⲛ̇ⲧⲁⲕ·ⲧⲁⲙⲓⲁ ⳿ ϩⲛ
ⲧⲉⲕⲥⲱⲫⲓⲁ ⳿ ⲁ̅ⲓ̅ⲱ̅ · ⲁ̅ⲓ̅ⲱ̅ ⳿ ϯ ⲉⲣⲁⲕ ⲙ̇ⲡⲟⲟⲩ ⳿
ⲙ̇ⲡⲁⲡⲁⲧ ⲛⲉⲥⲛⲟⲃ ⳿ ⲡⲁⲓ ⲧⲁⲛⲁⲅⲅⲉⲗⲟⲥ ⳿
ⲥⲱ ⲛ̇ϩⲏⲧϥ ⳿ ϣⲁⲛⲧⲟⲩⲭⲓ ⲛⲁ̄ · ⲉⲧⲟⲩⲁⲁⲃ ⳿
25 ϫⲉⲕⲁⲥ : ⲧⲉⲛ·ⲛⲟⲟⲩ ⲛ̇ⲁⲓ ⳿ ⲧⲉⲕⳓⲓϫ : ⲉⲧⲟⲩⲁⲁⲃ ⳿ ⲉϩⲣⲁⲓ ϫⲉⲙ ⲡ:ⲙⲟⲟⲩ ⳿ ⲙⲛ ⲡⲓⲛⲉϩ
ⲉⲧⲕⲏ ⲙ̇ⲡⲁⲙⲧⲁ ⲉⲃⲁⲗ ⳿ ⲁⲛⲁⲕ ⲇⲉ : $\overline{ss}$ ⳿
ⲁⲩⲱ · ⲙ̇ⲁⲣ·ⲉⲓ:ⲥ ⲉϩⲣⲁⲓ · ⲉϫⲱⲟⲩ ⳿

---

3 ⲛⲣⲁⲛ Meyer | *i.e.* ^{S}ⲛ̅ⲧⲉ || **3–4** ⲧⲉⲛⲧⲉⲩⲛⲁⲙⲓⲥ, ⲛ corrected from ⲙ by overwriting *l.* ⲛ̅-ⲛ̅-δύναμις, or ⲛ̅ⲧⲉ ⲧ⸗ⲉⲩ-δύναμις (haplography) ? || **4** *i.e.* ὀνομάζειν || **6** *i.e.* ^{S}ⲙ̅ⲙⲟ⸗ϥ | *i.e.* ^{S}ϣⲁⲛ⸗ϥ⸗ϯ ⲟⲩⲭⲁⲓ ⲛ̅-$\overline{ss}$ Meyer | *i.e.* ταχύ | **7** ⲙⲁⲣⲉϥϣⲱⲡⲓ Meyer | *i.e.* ^{S}ⲙ̅ⲙⲟ⸗ⲓ : ⲙ̅ⲙⲟ⸗ϥ Meyer || **8** ^{S}ⲙ̅ⲙⲟ⸗ϥ | *i.e.* ^{S}ⲙⲕⲁϩ || **10** *i.e.* σαλπίζειν || **11** *i.e.* ^{S}ⲙ̅ⲙⲟ⸗ϥ | ⲉⲟⲟⲩ, ⲉ corrected by overwriting ? || **12** *i.e.* χάρις | **12–13** *i.e.* γένος || **13** *i.e.* ^{S}ⲙⲛ̅ ⲛ̅-ϣⲏⲣⲉ || **18** ^{S}ϯ-ⲧⲁⲣⲕⲟ ⲙ̅ⲙⲟ⸗ⲕ confused with ϯ-ⲱⲣⲕ̅ ⲉⲣⲟ⸗ⲕ || **18–19** *i.e.* ^{S}ⲡⲁ ⲛ̅-ⲛⲓ-ⲛⲟⳓ ⲛ̅-ⲇⲩⲛⲁⲙⲓⲥ *i.e.* δύναμις : "you of (?) these great, holy powers" or "⟨by⟩ these great holy powers" Meyer || **20** *i.e.* ^{S}ϯ-ⲱⲣⲕ ⲉⲣⲟ⸗ⲕ || **21** ⲕⲁⲧⲁⲡⲉⲧⲓⲥⲙⲁ, ⲓ corrected by overwriting from ⲁ ? *i.e.* καταπέτασμα : ⲕⲁⲧⲁⲡⲉⲧⲁⲥⲙⲁ Meyer || **22** *i.e.* σοφία | *i.e.* ^{S}ϯ-ⲱⲣⲕ ⲉⲣⲟ⸗ⲕ || **23** ⲡⲁⲡⲁⲧ ⲛⲉⲥⲛⲟⲃ : "cup of blessing" ("Becher des Segens") Kropp | *i.e.* ^{S}ⲉⲛⲧ-ⲁ-ⲛ̅-ἄγγελος || **24** *i.e.* (π)ν(εῦμ)α : ⲛⲁ̄ "grace" ("Gnade") suggests Kropp || **25** *i.e.* ^{S}ⲉ⸗ⲕⲉ-ⲧⲉⲛⲛⲟⲟⲩ || **26** ^{S}ⲉϫⲉⲙ || **27** *i.e.* ^{S}ⲙ̅ⲡⲉⲙⲧⲟ ⲉⲃⲟⲗ | *i.e.* ^{S}ⲧⲉ | *l.* (δεῖνα) (δεῖνα) || **28** *i.e.* ^{S}ⲙⲁⲣⲉ⸗ⲥ-ⲉⲓ ⲉϩⲣⲁⲓ

I adjure you today, *Michael and *Gabriel, *Raphael, *Suriel, Salaphuēl, Azouēl, and the name of the powers that I named! |⁵ Michael, let him be on his right so that I may heal NN, child of NN, yea, yea, quickly! Gabriel, be on my left, so that I take away from him pain and every fear! Raphael, let him put a crown upon his |¹⁰ head! Suriel, let him trumpet before him! Raguel, let him give glory and favour to him in the presence of all the generation of Adam ⟨and⟩ all the children of Zoe, in the name of *Iao *Sabaoth! |¹⁵ Let him be sound in the name of *Adonai *Eloei! Let him be sound in the name of Iao Sabaoth! Uriel, the great god in heaven, I adjure you today by he of these great holy powers, Mēs Bētha |²⁰ Phraggis! I adjure you today by the twenty-four *veils which you created in your wisdom, yea, yea! I adjure you today by the *cup of blood, that which the *angels drank from so that they received the Holy Spirit, |²⁵ that ⟨you⟩ send to me your holy hand upon the water and this oil that are placed before me, I, NN, child of NN, and let ⟨it⟩ come down upon them,

---

5–7. "Michael, let him be on his right... Gabriel, be on my left" Invocations to angels to surround an individual for protection are extensively attested in Jewish and Christian contexts. The motif likely originated in Mesopotamia, where similar invocations to deities are found by the early second millennium BCE. By the ninth century CE, it is found in Jewish liturgical texts—notably the 'Bedtime *Shema*', a prayer read before sleep—but its presence in Jewish Aramaic incantation bowls from the sixth to eighth centuries CE demonstrates that its use is older. For discussions, see Levene/Marx/Bhayro 2014; Łajtar/van der Vliet 2017: 162–165. Similar calls for protection may be found in a few pre-Coptic Egyptian-language texts: "Isis before me, Nephthys behind me" (*3s.t tp ꜥwy≠i Nb.t-Ḥw.t imy ḥ.t≠i*; BM EA 10761 (Meyrat 2019: no. VIII col. 9 l. 9; XVIII–XVII BCE); "Horus is before me; Isis is behind me; Nephthys is as my diadem" (*Ḥr ḥ⟨t⟩.t 3s.t m-s3≠y Nb.t-Ḥ.t n t3y(≠y) gr[p3(.t)]*; *GEMF* 16/(*PDM* xiv) l. 257; II CE).

12–14. "all the generation of Adam ⟨and⟩ all the children of Zoe" Humankind is commonly referred to collectively as the "children of Adam and Eve (ζωή *Zōē*), especially in favour spells and curses to remove favour from their targets. For other examples, see p. 17 ll. 39–41 of this manuscript, as well as *PCM* I 22 ll. 37–39; *BKU* 1 10 (KYP M112) l. 6; *P.Bad.* V 123 (KYP M315) front ll. 72–74; *P.Lond.Copt.* 369 (KYP M123) ll. 10–11; BL Ms. Or. 6796 (2), (3) verso ll. 51–52 (Kropp 1931: I no. H; KYP M); BM EA 10122 ll. 26–28 (Zellmann-Rohrer 2022a: no. 4; KYP M297) ll. 32–34; BM EA 10414a back ll. 4–5 (Zellmann-Rohrer 2022a: no. 3; KYP M287); P.Iand. inv. 9 p. 7 ll. 5–6 (Kropp 1965; KYP M134); P.Köln Inv. 1470 ll. 6–7 (Weber 1975; KYP M353); P.Stras. K 204 + 205 + 282 §2.1 l. 2 (Hevesi 2018; KYP92); P.Vindob. K 5024 (KYP M356) ll. 4–5; *cf. PCM* I 11 p. 19 ll. 8–9. For examples from Jewish magical texts from the Cairo Genizah; see Schiffman/Schwartz 1992: T-S K1.6 l. 18, T-S K1.24 ll. 16–17, T-S K1.152 l. 22 (discussion on pp. 41–42); Naveh/Shaked 1993: Geniza 12 ll. 16–17; Geniza 15 p. 2 ll. 9–10; Geniza 18 p. 3 ll. 7–8; Geniza 28 p. 4 ll. 9, 11; *MTKG* I Or. 1080.15.81 l. 94; *MTKG* II 42 ll. 12, 18, 22, 32, 39; *MTKG* III 56 p. 1a l. 10; *MTKG* III 71 p. 1a l. 5; *MTKG* III 73 p. 1b ll. 11–12. *Cf.* Bélanger Sarrazin fc. a: ch. 4.

23–24. ⲙⲡⲁⲡⲁⲧ ⲛⲉⲥⲛⲟⲃ : " by the cup of blood" Kropp translates "cup of blessing" ("Becher des Segens"), likely the original text of the *Prayer*; *cf. Tomb of Georgios,* North wall, col. 1, l. 33 (Łajtar/van der Vliet 2017 no. 9; KYP M501): τοῦ ποτηρίου τῆς εὐλογάς; British Library MS Or 6796 (1-3) l. 105 ((Kropp 1965 no. c; KYP M118): [π]ⲁⲡⲟⲧ ⲙ̄ⲡⲉⲥⲙⲟⲩ; likewise in P.Iand.inv. 9 p. 8 l. 11 (Kropp 1965; KYP M134). These other versions also describe the apostles drinking from the cup, rather than the angels as is the case here. Reference to angels drinking a cup in order to receive the Holy Spirit is also found in *PCM* I 12 p. 35 ll. 14–16; *PCM* I 26 p. 4 ll. 17–20, implying a heavenly eucharistic ritual which predated its earthly form (*cf.* Dosoo 2021d: 419).

page 8 (flesh)

ⲛϭⲓ ⲑⲁⲅⲓⲁ ⲙⲁⲣⲓⲁ - ⲡⲁⲣⲑⲉⲛⲟⲥ ⲉⲧⲟⲩⲁⲁⲃ ⳽ ⲛⲉⲥⲙⲟⲩ ⲡⲙⲁⲟⲩ ⵌ ⲉϥϣⲱⲡⲉ ⲛ-
ⲟⲩϫⲁⲓ ⳽ ⲙⲛ ⲟⲩⲧⲃⲃⲁ ⳽ ϫⲉ ϩⲛ ⲧⲉⲩⲛⲟⲩ ⳽ ⲉⲧⲉⲛⲁϫⲱⲕⲉⲙ ⲉ⳽⳽ ⲛϩⲏⲧϥ ⳽
5   ⲙⲁⲣⲉϥⲟⲩϫⲁⲓ ⳽ ⲁⲓⲁ · ⲁⲓⲁ ⲧⲁⲭⲏ ⲧⲁⲭⲏ
ϯⲱⲣⲕ ⲉⲣⲁⲕ ⳽ ⲙⲡⲟⲟⲩ ⳽ ⲡⲉⲃ·ⲇ̄ · ⲙⲉⲥⲧⲏⲣⲓⲱⲛ ⳽ ⲛⲁⲧⲱϫⲉⲛ ⲉⲧⲉ ⲛⲁⲓ ⳽ ⲛ
ⲇⲁⲅⲉⲓⲑⲉⲁ ≡ ⲉⲗⲉⲗⲉⲑ ≡ ⲱⲣⲉⲙ ⳽
ⲙⲱⲥⲓⲏⲗ ⵌ ⲧⲉ ⲛⲁⲓ ⵌ ⲡⲁⲣⲱ · ⲉⲃⲁⲗ ⳽ ϩⲓ-
10 ϫⲉⲛ ⲡⲉⲇ̄ · ⲛ̄ⲥⲁ ⲧⲡⲉ ⳽ ϯ ⲉⲣⲁⲕ ⲙⲡⲟⲟⲩ
ⲙ̄ⲡⲓⲱⲧ ⲡⲁⲛⲧⲱⲣ ⳽ ⲧⲉⲛ·ⲫⲱⲛⲏ ⳽ ⲉⲧⲟⲩⲁⲁⲃ ⳽ ⲧⲉ ⲛⲁⲓ ⵌ ⲛⲉⲣⲁⲛ ⲁⲭⲓ ≡ ⲁⲭⲁ ≡ ⲁⲭⲁⲙ
ⲣⲁ ⳽ ϯⲱⲣⲕ ⲉⲣⲁⲕ ⲙⲡⲟⲟⲩ ⳽ ⲙ̄ⲡⲓϣⲁⲣⲡ ⲉ-
ⲛϣⲁϫⲉ ⲛⲧⲁϥⲉⲓ ⵌ ⲉϩⲣⲁⲓ ⳽ ϩⲙ ⲡⲉⲕϩⲏⲧ
15 ⲁϥϣⲱⲡⲓ ⵌ ⲛⲁⲕ ⳽ ⲛⲟⲩϣⲏⲣⲉ ⵌ ⲙⲱⲛⲟⲅⲉⲛⲏⲥ ⳽ ⲧⲉ ⲡⲁⲓ ⵌ ⲓ̄ⲥ̄ ⲡⲉⲭ̄ⲥ̄ ⳽ ⲙⲛ ⲛⲉϥ- ⳽
ⲧⲉⲛⲁⲙⲓⲥ ⳽ ⲉⲧⲟⲩⲁⲁⲃ ⳽ ⲛⲧⲁⲓ:ⲁⲛⲱⲙ-
ⲁⲍⲉ ⲙ̄ⲙⲁⲩ ⵌ ϫⲉⲕⲁⲥ ⳽ ⲉⲕⲉⲛⲧⲉⲛⲟⲟⲩ ⳽
ⲛⲁⲓ ⳽ ⲛ̄ⲧⲉⲛⲑⲉⲟⲧⲱⲕⲟⲥ ⳽ ⲉⲧⲟⲩⲁⲁⲃ ⳽
20 ⲑⲁⲅⲓⲁ ⲙⲁⲣⲓⲁ ⳽ ⲡⲁⲣⲑⲉⲛⲟⲥ ⵌ ⲉⲥⲁⲁⲃ ⳽
ⲉⲥⲙⲟⲩ ⳽ ⲉⲣⲟⲟⲩ ⲙ̄ⲛ ⲡⲙⲁⲟⲩ ⳽ ⲉⲥϩⲁⲅⲓⲁ-
ⲍⲉ ⲙⲙⲁⲁⲩ ⵌ ⲛⲥⲫⲁⲣⲁⲅⲓⲁⲍ ⵌ ⲙⲟⲟⲩ ⵌ ⲡ̄ⲛⲉϩ
ϫⲉⲕⲁⲥ ϩⲛ ⲧⲉⲩⲛⲟⲩ ⳽ ⲉⲧⲓⲛⲁⲡⲱϩ ⵌ ⲡⲙⲟⲟⲩ
ⲉϫⲉⲛ ⵌ ⳽⳽ ⲛⲉϥϣⲱⲡⲓ ⳽ ϩⲛ ⲟⲩⲧⲁϩⲣⲁ ⳽
25 ⲙⲛ ⵌ ⲟⲩⲧⲁⲗϭⲁ ⳽ ⲙⲛ · ⲟⲩⲉⲙⲧⲁ ⳽ ⲛⲓⲙ ⳽
ⲛ̄ⲧⲉⲛ ϩⲓⲧⲉⲛ ϭⲁⲙ ⲙⲡⲓⲱⲧ ⲙⲛ ⲡ-
ϣⲏⲣⲉ ⲙⲛ ⲡⲉⲡⲛ̄ⲁ̄ ⲉⲧⲟⲩⲁⲁⲃ ⳽ ϣⲁ ⲛⲉ-
ⲛⲉϩ ⵌ ⲛⲉϩ ⳽ ϩⲁⲙⲏⲛ ϩⲁⲙⲏⲛ ϩⲁⲙⲏⲛ
ⲁⲓⲱ ⲁⲓⲱ ⲧⲁⲭⲏ ⲧⲁⲭⲏ ⳽ ⲓ̄ⲥ̄ ⲡⲭ̄ⲥ̄

---

1 *l.* τ-ἅγια | *i.e.* τ-παρθένος *cf.* note to p. 2 l. 2 ‖ **2** *i.e.* ˢⲛ̄-ⲥ-ⲥⲙⲟⲩ : or ˢⲉ⳽ⲥ-ⲥⲙⲟⲩ ? Meyer ‖ **3** *i.e.* ˢⲧⲃⲃⲟ ‖ **4** *i.e.* ˢⲉ⳽ϯ⳽ⲛⲁ-ϫⲱⲕⲙ ? | *l.* (δεῖνα) (δεῖνα) ‖ **5** *i.e.* ταχύ (twice) ‖ **6** *l.* ⲡⲉⲃ(ⲧⲟⲟⲩ) ‖ **6–7** *i.e.* ˢⲙ̄-ⲙⲩⲥⲧⲏⲣⲓⲟⲛ ‖ **7** ⲛ *i.e.* ˢⲛⲉ ‖ **9** *i.e.* ˢⲛⲁⲓ ⲉⲧ- ‖ **10** *l.* ϯ-ⲱⲣⲕ ⲉⲣⲟ⳽ⲕ ‖ **11** *i.e.* παντ(οκράτ)ωρ | *i.e.* ˢⲛ̄-ⲧⲉ-ⲫⲱⲛⲏ : ⲫⲱⲛⲏ Meyer ‖ **12** *i.e.* ˢⲛⲉ⳽ⲩ-ⲣⲁⲛ ‖ **15–16** *i.e.* μονογενής ‖ **16** *i.e.* ˢⲉⲧⲉ | *l.* ⲓ(ⲏⲥⲟⲩ)ⲥ *i.e.* χ(ριστό)ς ‖ **17** *i.e.* δύναμις ‖ **17–18** *i.e.* ὀνομάζειν ‖ **18** *i.e.* ˢⲉ⳽ⲕⲉ-ⲛⲁ-ⲧⲛⲛⲟⲟⲩ ‖ **19** *i.e.* θεοτόκος ‖ **20** *i.e.* ἅγια | *i.e.* παρθένος | *i.e.* ˢⲉⲥⲟⲩⲁⲁⲃ ‖ **21** ⲉⲥⲙⲟⲩ Meyer | *i.e.* ˢ *i.e.* ˢⲉⲣⲟ⳽ϥ {ⲙ̄ⲛ̄} ‖ **21–22** *i.e.* ˢⲛ̄-ⲥ-ⲁⲅⲓⲁⲍⲉⲓⲛ ‖ **22** *i.e.* ˢⲙ̄ⲙⲟ⳽ⲩ | *i.e.* ˢⲛ̄-ⲥ-ⲥⲫⲣⲁⲅⲓⲁⲍⲉ *i.e.* σφραγίζειν : ⲛⲥⲥⲫ(ⲁ)ⲣⲁⲅⲓ(ⲁ)ⲍⲉ or the like Meyer | *i.e.* ˢⲙ̄ⲙⲟ⳽ϥ : *l.* ⲡ-ⲙⲟⲟⲩ "the water" Meyer ‖ **23** *i.e.* ˢⲉ⳽ϯ⳽ⲛⲁ-ⲡⲱϩⲧ ‖ **24** *l.* (δεῖνα) (δεῖνα) | *i.e.* ˢⲛ̄⳽ϥ-ϣⲱⲡⲉ ? : or ˢⲉ⳽ϥ-ⲛⲁ-ϣⲱⲡⲉ ? Meyer ‖ **25** *i.e.* ˢⲟⲩ-ⲙ̄ⲧⲟⲛ ‖ **27** *i.e.* πν(εῦ)α ‖ **27–28** *i.e.* ˢϣⲁ ⲉⲛⲉϩ ⲛ-ⲉⲛⲉϩ : ϣⲁ (ⲛⲓ)ⲉⲛⲉϩ (ⲛ)ⲉⲛⲉϩ or the like Meyer ‖ **28** *i.e.* ἀμήν (three times) ‖ **29** *i.e.* ταχύ (twice) | *l.* ⲓ(ⲏⲥⲟⲩ)ⲥ | *i.e.* χ(ριστό)ς

namely, Saint Mary the holy virgin, that she might bless the water so that it becomes a healing and a purification, so that in the moment that I will wash NN, child of NN, with it |⁵ let him heal, yea, yea, quickly quickly!

I adjure you today by the four imperishable mysteries, which are Daueithea, Eleleth, Ōrem, Mōsiēl, who are the ones spread out |¹⁰ upon the four sides of heaven! I adjure you today by the Father Almighty, by the holy sounds whose names are Akhi, Akha, Akhamra! I adjure you today by the first word that came out from your heart |¹⁵ and became for you an only son, that is Jesus Christ, and his holy powers that I have named, that you will send to me the holy mother of God, |²⁰ Saint Mary the holy virgin, so that she blesses them, and the water, and she sanctifies them, and she seals them, this oil, so that in the moment that I will pour the water upon NN, child of NN, ⟨NN, child of NN,⟩ will become strong |²⁵ and healed and at total peace ... through the power of the Father and the Son and the Holy Spirit, forever and ever and ever, amen, amen, amen, yea, yea, quickly, quickly, Jesus Christ!

8–9. ⲇⲁⲩⲉⲓⲑⲉⲁ ≡ ⲉⲗⲉⲗⲉⲑ ≡ ⲱⲣⲉⲙ ⳽ ⲙⲱⲥⲓⲏⲗ : "**Daueithea, Eleleth, Ōrem, Mōsiēl**" As noted by Meyer (1996: 79) these are the Four Luminaries (φωστῆρες), divine beings known from Sethian Gnostic cosmologies who rule over divisions of the divine realm. In the Berlin version of the *Apocryphon of John* their names are Harmozēl, Ōrōiēl, Daueithe and Ēlēlēth (ϩⲁⲣⲙⲟⲍⲏⲗ ⲱⲣⲱⲓⲁⲏⲗ ⲇⲁⲩⲉⲓⲑⲉ ⲏⲗⲏⲗⲏⲑ; CC 0648; ed. Robinson 2000: II 54–57), but we find slight variation in each text mentioning them. The parallel versions of the prayer use the word φωστήρ ("luminary") where this text has μυστήριον ("mystery", ll. 6–7), suggesting that this version is corrupt (*cf.* Łajtar/van der Vliet 2017: 170–171). On the Luminaries in Coptic magical texts more generally, see Burns 2018; Piwowarczyk 2021: 56–59, 105–109, 134–137, 230–232.

21–22. Probably understand "so that she blesses it, this water... and she seals it, this oil".

25–26. ⲟⲩⲉⲙⲧⲁ ⳽ ⲛⲓⲙ ⳽ ⲛⲧⲉⲛ : "**total peace ...**" This passage seems to be ungrammatical; ⲉⲙⲧⲁ is doubly determined by ⲟⲩ- and ⲛⲓⲙ, and ⲛⲧⲉⲛ would seem to be either a conjugation base or genitive marker missing a following noun. It seems likely that this is the result of miscopying or textual corruption; Meyer does not comment but simply translates "completely well".

page 9 (flesh)

ⲧϭⲓⲛⲉⲣϩⲱⲃ Ⲍ ⲛϭⲱⲃⲉ ⲛⲧⲁⲫⲉⲛ ⸗ Ⲍ ⲛϭⲱⲃⲉ ⲡϣ-
ⲟⲩⲡϣⲁⲡ : ⲛⲌ ⲛⲧⲉⲣ ⲥⲁⲩⲃⲟⲩ ⲙⲁⲣⲓⲁ ⸗ ⲡⲌ ⲛⲧⲉⲣ
ⲛϩⲁϭⲓⲛ ⲛⲉϭⲱϣ ⸗ ⲛⲌ ⲛϭⲱⲃⲉ ⲛ̇ϭⲓⲧⲣⲁ ⸗ ⲡⲌ ⸗
ⲛⲧⲉⲣ ⲛϣⲏ ⸗ ⲁⲃⲣⲁϩⲁⲙ ⸗ ⲟⲩϭⲁⲗⲉϩ ⲃⲏⲣⲓ ⸗
5 ⲙⲁⲁⲩ : ⲛⲁⲑⲏⲗⲓⲕⲱⲛ : ⲉⲕⲛⲏⲥⲧⲉⲩ · ⲉⲣⲉ 𝆺
ⲙⲟⲩϩ ⸗ ⲉⲕϯ ϣⲁⲗ · ⲉⲡϣⲱⲓ : ϩⲁⲓ ⲛ̇ⲁⲗⲏⲭⲧⲁⲙ
ⲉⲃⲉⲣⲓ : ⲛⲉϩ ⲙ̇ⲉ : ϩⲏⲃⲥ · ⲙⲟⲩϩ : ϣⲁⲛ̇ⲧⲉⲕϯ ⲟⲩⲱ ⸗

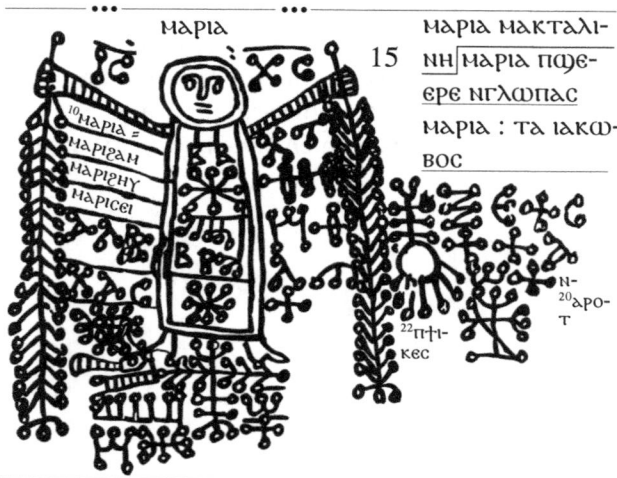

ⲓⲁⲙⲗⲓⲭⲟⲥ ⸗ ⲙⲁⲣϯⲁⲛⲟⲥ ⸗ ⲙⲁⲣⲝⲓⲙⲟⲥ ⸗ ⲁⲛϯⲛⲓⲁⲥ ⸗
25 ⲉⲃⲥⲁⲓⲙⲏⲥ ⸗ ⲟⲩⲁⲥⲓⲕ ⸗ ⲙⲁⲣⲟⲩⲉⲣ ⸗ ϯⲧⲣⲁ ⲙⲁϣ ⲧⲁⲡ̄ⲕⲉϩ ⸗ ϯⲧⲣⲁ ⸗ ⲑⲁⲡⲁⲥ ⸗ ϯⲧⲣⲁ ⲑⲁⲡⲁϩ ⸗ ⲉⲑⲟⲟⲩ ⸗
ϫⲉⲕⲁⲥ ⲧⲉⲣⲃⲱⲕ ⸗ ⲥⲁ · ⲉⲃⲁⲗ · ⲡⲧⲁⲙⲓⲁ · ⲡ̇ⲛⲟⲩⲧⲉ
ⲁⲡ̄ⲡ̄ⲟ̄ⲥ̄ ϫⲟⲟⲥ : ϩⲓ ⲧⲉⲩⲧⲁⲡⲣⲁ ⲛⲓⲙ ⲙⲁⲩ ϫⲉ ⲛⲉ-
ⲣⲃⲱⲕ · ⲉϩⲟⲩⲛ ⸗ ⲉⲡⲧⲁⲙⲓⲁ · ⲛⲉⲣϣⲁⲛⲉⲣ ⲁⲧⲥ-
30 ⲱⲧⲙ ⲉⲥⲱⲓ ⸗ ϣⲁⲓⲧⲱⲃⲓ ⲣⲱ ⲛⲟⲩⲭⲁⲗⲓⲛⲟⲩⲥ
ⲧⲁⲭⲁ ⲗⲓⲥⲙⲟⲥ : ⲉⲣⲁ ⲧⲁⲭⲁⲩϯ ⲛ̇ⲉⲧⲁⲩ : ⲁⲓⲟ ⲁⲓⲟ

---

1 *i.e.* δάφνη : or ˢⲧⲁⲡⲉⲛ "cumin" Gardner 2023b || **1–2** *i.e.* ˢϣⲟⲡϣⲟⲡ || **2** *i.e.* ˢⲙ̄-ⲙⲁⲣⲓⲁ ||
3 *i.e.* ˢϭⲓⲧⲣⲉ *cf.* note to *PCM* I 37 back l. 4 || **4** *i.e.* ˢϭⲁⲗⲁϩⲧ | *i.e.* ˢⲃⲣⲣⲉ || **5** *i.e.* *ἀνθηλιακόν/
ἀνατολικόν ? see note p. 17 ll. 25–27 : "spell-free" Meyer | *i.e.* νηστεύειν | *l.* (ⲡⲟⲟϩ) || **6** *i.e.* ˢϩϩⲁⲓ ?
ⲛ̇ⲁⲗⲏⲭⲧⲁⲙ *see note* || **9** *l.* ⲓ(ⲏⲥⲟⲩ)ⲥ ⲭ(ⲣⲓⲥⲧⲟ́)ⲥ || **15** *i.e.* ˢⲧ-ϣⲉⲉⲣⲉ || **19–20** *i.e.* ˢⲛ̄-ⲁⲧ-ⲗⲟ Meyer ||
22–23 *i.e.* ˢⲡ-ⲧⲕⲁⲥ || **25** *i.e.* ˢϯ-ⲧⲁⲣⲕⲟ ⲙ̄ⲙⲟ⸗ø : understand as name ? Meyer || **26** *i.e.* ˢϯ-ⲧⲁⲣⲕⲟ
ⲙ̄ⲙⲟ⸗ø : understand as name ? Meyer | or "Ethoou" as name ? Meyer || **17** *i.e.* ˢⲛ̄ⲧⲉ⸗ⲣ-ⲃⲱⲕ |
i.e. ˢⲥⲁⲃⲟⲗ ⲛ- | *i.e.* ˢⲙ̄-ⲡ-ⲛⲟⲩⲧⲉ || **28** *i.e.* ˢⲁ-ⲡ-ϫⲟⲉⲓⲥ | *i.e.* ˢⲙⲙⲓⲛ ⲙ̄ⲙⲟ⸗ϥ || **29** *i.e.* ˢⲛ̄ⲛⲉ⸗ⲣ-ⲃⲱⲕ |
i.e. ˢⲉⲛⲉ ⲉⲣ-ϣⲁⲛ-ⲣ̄ | *i.e.* ˢⲉⲣ-ϣⲁⲛ-ⲣ̄ Meyer || **30** *i.e.* ˢⲛ̄ⲥⲱ⸗ⲓ | *i.e.* χαλινός *cf.* notes to *PCM* 24 l. 12 ||
31 *i.e.* ˢⲧⲁ-ⲕⲁ ⲟⲩ-ⲇⲉⲥⲙⲟ́ⲥ ? *cf.* Meyer 1996: 48 | *i.e.* ˢⲉ-ⲣⲟ⸗ø | *i.e.* ˢⲉⲣⲁⲧ⸗ø Meyer | ˢⲧⲁ-ⲭⲟⲟⲩ⸗ø : ⲁⲭⲁⲩ
i.e. ˢⲁ⸗ⲓ-ϫⲟⲟ⸗ⲩ Meyer | *i.e.* ˢⲉ-ⲛ̄-ⲧⲟⲟⲩ or ⲉ-ⲛ-ⲉⲧ-ⲁⲁ⸗ⲩ ? : ϯⲛ̇ⲉⲧⲟⲩ *i.e.* ˢϯ-ⲛⲁ-ⲁⲁ⸗(ⲟ)ⲩ Meyer

The procedure: 7 bay leaves, 7 leaves of marjoram, 7 branches of grass ⟨of⟩ Mary, 7 branches of Nubian mint, 7 leaves of *citron tree, 7 branches of wood ⟨of⟩ Abraham. A new pot, |⁵ *sun-facing? water, while you are fasting, while the moon is full, while you offer up *myrrh, write with new *katam*?, olive oil; a burning lamp until you finish.

|⁸, *above image* Mary, (*kharaktēres*: Jesus Christ) |¹⁰, *left* Mary, Miriam, Marihēu, Marisei (*kharaktēres*: AAⅨXAC✱) |¹⁴, *right* Mary Magdalene, |¹⁵ Mary the daughter of Clopas, Mary of James. (*kharaktēres*: ⇋E+C++AѠ+*) the … |²² The pain.

Iamlikhos, Martianos, Marximos, Antinias, |²⁵ Ebsaimēs, Ouasik, Marouer; I adjure you (f.s.), Tapkeh! I adjure ⟨you⟩, Thapas! I adjure ⟨you⟩, Thapaoh, who are evil, that you you go out of God's creature! The Lord said with his own mouth, "You will not enter the creature!" If you are disobedient |³⁰ to me, I shall seal your mouth with a bridle, and I will place a bond? on your mouth, and I will send you to the deserts?, yea, yea! oooooooooo ōōōōōōōōōōōōōō (*kharaktēres*: ΦΦΦ) aaaaaaa (*kharaktēres*: YYYYMCNETT TT+ ✱✱✱) eeeeeee ⁊⁊⁊⁊⁊⁊

2, 4. "grass ⟨of⟩ Mary", "wood ⟨of⟩ Abraham" *Cf.* the "Tree of Mary" (شجرة مريم *sağara Maryam*, cyclamen) found in an eleventh-century Judaeo-Arabic recipe from the Cairo Genizah (Bohak 2022: 49) as well as the *Guide to the Psalms* (Psalms 19, 20, 70; Henein/Bianquis 1975). "Wood of Abraham" appears in similar lists of ingredients for preparing the water in a pot in British Library MS Or 6796 (2, 3) (Kropp 1931: I no. H; KYP M118) back l. 107; BL Ms. Or. 6796 (Kropp 1931: I no. J; KYP M363) front l. 51; based on parallel names in Arabic and Aramaic, Crum (CD 546a; *cf.* Kropp 1930: III 108) suggests it to be the simpleleaf chastetree (*Agnus castus* (=*Vitex trifolia* L.)).

6. ⲛⲁⲗⲏⲭⲧⲁⲙ : "alēkhtam" Perhaps الكتم (*al-katam*), African boxwood (*Myrsine africana*, L.), from which a dark dyeing agent is extracted (El Shamsy 2020: 191). Gardner proposes to parse ⲛⲁⲗⲏⲭ ⲧⲁⲙⲃⲉⲣⲓ "on paper (ورق), prepare..." (دبر; *cf.* Richter 2015b: 228), although the preposition ⲉ- usually precedes the writing material. Meyer suggests several unconvincing possibilities.

8–18. The names of Mary: Meyer (1996: 80) suggests that we see here a coalescence of different Marys from the Gospels—the mother of Jesus; Mary Magdalene (John 20.1 *etc.*); Mary, daughter of Clopas (John 19.25); Mary (mother) of James (Mark 16.1 *etc.*)—into a "composite universal Mary". But the identification of the mother of Jesus with the mother of James is known from Greek patristic sources (*e.g*, John Chrysostom, *Homily 88 on the Gospel of Matthew* (PG 58: 777)). The appropriation of all of these names by the mother of Jesus is attested in Coptic pseudepigrapha more broadly. In Pseudo-Cyril of Jerusalem's *On the Passion (a)* (CC 116; Campagnano 1980: 26.26–29.5) and *On Mary* (CC 119; Campagnano 1980: 158.26–161.1), the Virgin Mary is born in Magdala (hence, 'Magdalene'), while her father Joachim is also known as Clopas, and James is one of the children of Joseph the carpenter whom she adopted (see Suciu fc.).

24–26. "Iamlikhos, Martianos, Marximos, Antinias, Ebsaimēs, Ouasik, Marouer" Graham (2022) points out that these are the names of the Seven Sleepers of Ephesus (*cf.* p. 167). The initial four names correspond to Iamblichos, Martinos, Maximilios, and Antoninos in the Byzantine Synaxarium, while Ebsaimēs and Ouasik might be versions of Stephanos and Kyriakos known from other lists; Marouer may begin with Syriac *mār* ("Lord"); *cf.* Tondello 2019: 72 n. 1; Grysa 2010: 49 n. 3). Meyer (1996: p. 81) instead understands Iamblichus and Antinous as two famous "pagan" figures here turned into demonic names, and Ouasik as Coptic "a fever", used as a demonic name.

25–26. "Tapkeh... Thapas... Thapaoh" As Meyer (1996: 81–82) notes these might be understood as names for the addressed being, "she of the earth... she of old age... she of the moon".

page 10 (hair)

```
         †ⲥⲁⲡⲥ ⲁⲩⲱ †ⲡⲁⲣⲁⲕⲁⲗⲓ
         ⲙⲁⲕ ⲙ̇ⲡⲟⲟⲩ : ⲛ̄ⲁⲥⲥⲕⲗⲏⲏ
         ⲡⲁⲓ ⲉⲧⲉⲣⲁⲉⲓⲥ : ⲁⲩⲱ ⲅⲁⲣⲉ : ⲉⲡ⸗-
         ⲥⲱⲙⲁ ⸗ ⲛ̄ⲥ̄ⲱ̄ⲗ̄ⲱ̄ⲙ̄ⲟ̄ⲛ̄ ⸗ ⲡⲉ-
5        ⲣⲟ : ⲛⲉϩⲟⲟⲩ ⲧⲏⲣⲟⲩ ⲡⲉϥⲱϩ
         †ⲧⲉⲣⲕⲁ ⲙⲁⲕ ⲙ̇ⲡⲟⲟⲩ : ⲛⲉⲕ-
         ϭⲁⲙ ⸗ ⲙ̇ⲛⲉⲕⲣⲁⲛ ⸗ ⲙⲛ:ⲉⲕ-
         ⲥ̄ⲱ̄†ⲟ̄ⲩ̄ⲛ̄ ⸗ ϫⲉ ϩⲉⲛ ⲧⲉⲩⲛⲟⲩ
         ϣⲁ 𐆖 ϥⲱⲣⲓ ⸗ ⲡⲉⲕⲥ̄ⲩ̄ : ⲕⲉ-
10       ϣⲱⲡⲓ ⲉⲕⲣⲁⲉⲓⲥ ⲣⲁⲃ ⲛⲉ-
         ϩⲟⲟⲩ ⲧⲏⲣⲟⲩ ⲡⲉϥⲱⲛⲁϩ
         ϩⲁⲉⲃⲁⲗ ⲡ̄ⲛ̄ⲁ̄ ⲛⲓⲙ ⲡⲱⲛⲉⲣⲱ̄ⲛ̄ : ⲙⲛ
         ⲡ̄ⲛ̄ⲁ̄ ⲛⲁⲕⲁⲑⲁⲣⲧⲱⲛ ⸗ ⲙⲉⲛ ⲧⲉⲛⲁⲙⲓ̄ⲥ̄
         ⲛⲓⲙ ⲧⲉ ⲡⲇⲉⲁⲃⲱⲗⲟⲥ ⸗ ⲙⲛ ⲁⲗⲟⲅⲁⲥⲓ-
15       ⲟⲩⲁⲥ ⲛⲓⲙ ⸗ ⲙⲛ ⲛⲉⲣⲱϩⲧ ⲙ̄ⲛ̄ ϩⲓⲕ ⲛ̄-
         ⲓⲙ ⸗ ⲙⲛ ⲛⲅ ⲫⲁⲣⲙⲁⲅⲓⲁ ⲛⲓⲙ · ⲙⲛ ⲛ̄-
         ⲧⲉⲡⲇⲓⲁⲃⲟⲗⲟⲥ ⸗ ⲡⲱⲧ ⲛⲉⲩ ⲥⲁⲉⲃⲟ-
         ⲗ 𐆖 - ⲁ̄ⲓ̄ⲁ̄ ⲁ̄ⲓ̄ⲟ̄ ⲧⲁⲭⲏ ≡ ⲁⲃϫⲱⲕ ⲉⲃⲟⲗ
         ⲥⲁⲧⲱⲣ ⸗ ⲁⲣⲉⲧⲱ ⸗ ⲧⲉⲛⲏⲧ ⸗ ⲱⲧⲉⲣⲁ ⸗ ⲣⲱ-
20       ⲧⲁⲥ ⲛ̇†ⲟⲩ ⲉⲓⲃ ⸗ ⲡⲉⲛⲥ̄ⲱ̄ⲣ̄ ⸗ ⲉⲓ̄ⲥ̄ ⲡⲭ̄ⲥ̄
         
                        ⲱⲣⲱⲣⲱⲣϥϥϥϥϥ
                        ⲱⲣⲱⲣ : ⲣϥϥ
         ⲙⲓⲭⲁⲏ̄ⲗ̄ ⲅⲁⲃⲣⲓⲏ̄ⲗ̄ · ⲥⲟⲩⲣⲓⲏ̄ⲗ̄ · ⲣⲁϥ-
25       ⲁ̄ⲏ̄ⲗ̄ · ⲍⲉⲧⲉⲕⲓⲏ̄ⲗ̄ · ⲥⲁⲙⲫⲟⲏ̄ⲗ̄ · ⲁⲛⲁⲏ̄
         ⲁ̄ⲛ̄ⲁ̄ⲏ̄ⲗ̄ ⲃⲱⲓⲑⲓ ⸗ ϩⲁⲣⲉ 𐆖 ⲃⲁⲣⲭ · ⲃⲁⲥ ≡
         ⲓⲓⲓⲓⲓⲓⲓ ⲭⲭⲭⲭⲭⲭⲭ
```

Above figure *l.* δ(εῖνα) δ(εῖνα) ? || **1** *i.e.* παρακαλεῖν || **2** ⲛ̄ⲁⲥⲥⲕⲗⲏⲏ Meyer || **3** ⲉⲧⲉⲣⲁⲉⲓⲥ corrected from ⲉⲧ . ⲣⲁⲉⲓⲥ by overwriting | *i.e.* ˢϩⲁⲣⲉϩ || **4** *i.e.* σῶμα || **5** *i.e.* ˢⲛ̄-ⲛ-ϩⲟⲟⲩ | *i.e.* ˢⲙ̄-ⲡⲉ⸗ϥ-ⲱⲛϩ̄ || **6** *i.e.* ˢⲛ̄-ⲛⲉ⸗ⲕ- (haplography) || **7** *i.e.* ˢⲙⲛ̄ ⲛⲉ⸗ⲕ-ⲣⲁⲛ (haplography) | *i.e.* ˢⲙⲛ̄ ⲛⲉ⸗ⲕ- (haplography) || **8** *i.e.* ζῴδιον || **9** *l.* (δεῖνα) (δεῖνα) | *i.e.* φορεῖν | *i.e.* ζῴ(διον) ? || *i.e.* ˢⲉ⸗ⲕ-ⲉ- || **10** *i.e.* ˢⲉ⸗ⲕ-ⲉ-ⲣⲟⲉⲓⲥ | ⲣⲁⲃ *i.e.* ˢⲉⲣⲟ⸗ϥ || **10–11** *i.e.* ˢⲛ̄-ⲛ-ϩⲟⲟⲩ || **11** *i.e.* ˢⲙ̄-ⲡⲉ⸗ϥ-ⲱⲛϩ̄ || **12** *i.e.* ˢϩⲁⲃⲟⲗ | *l.* πν(εῦμ)α | *i.e.* ˢⲙ̄-ⲡⲟⲛⲏⲣⲟ́ⲛ || **13** *l.* πν(εῦμ)α | *i.e.* ἀκάθαρτον first ⲛ corrected from ⲙ by overwriting | *i.e.* ˢⲙⲛ | *i.e.* ˢⲇⲩⲛⲁⲙⲓⲥ || **14** *i.e.* ˢⲛ̄ⲧⲉ ⲡ-ⲇⲓⲁ́ⲃⲟⲗⲟⲥ || **14–15** *i.e.* الوسواس *al-waswās cf.* note || **15** ⲛⲉⲣⲱϩⲧ, ⲛ corrected from ⲟ or ⲣ by overwriting || **16** *l.* ⲛ-ⲡⲗⲏⲅⲏ́ ⲙⲛ̄ ⲫⲁⲣⲙⲁⲕⲉⲓ́ⲁ ? : ⲛⲅ ⲫⲁⲣⲙⲁⲅⲓⲁ *l.* ⲛ̄-ⲫⲁⲣⲙⲁⲅⲓⲁ Meyer || **16–17** *i.e.* διάβολος : ⲙⲛ [missing noun] ⲛ̄ⲧⲉ ⲡⲇⲓⲁⲃⲟⲗⲟⲥ Meyer || **17–18** *i.e.* ˢⲡⲱⲧ ⲛⲁ⸗ⲩ ⲥⲁⲃⲟⲗ : ⲡⲱⲧ ⲛⲉⲩ ⲥⲁ ⲉⲃⲟⲗ "drive them from" Meyer || **18** *l.* δ(εῖνα) δ(εῖνα) | *i.e.* ταχύ | *i.e.* ˢⲁ⸗ϥ-ϫⲱⲕ || **20** *i.e.* ˢⲡ-ϯⲟⲩ ⲉⲓϥⲧ : ⲛ̇ϯⲟⲩⲉⲓⲃ *i.e.* ˢⲡ-ⲉⲧ-ⲟⲩⲁⲁⲃ Meyer | *l.* σω(τή)ρ | *l.* ⲉⲓ̄(ⲥⲟⲩ)ⲥ̄ χ(ριστό)ς || **26** *i.e.* βοηθεῖν | *i.e.* ˢϩⲁⲣⲉϩ ⲉ- | *l.* (δεῖνα) (δεῖνα)

|^(above figure) (*kharaktēres*: ΔΔ, i.e., NN)

|^(beside figure) Masbēn

|^(p. 10) I entreat and I invoke you today, Nassklnē, the one who guards and protects the body of Solomon the |⁵ king ⟨for⟩ all the days ⟨of⟩ his life! I adjure you today ⟨by⟩ your powers and your *names and your *images that as soon as NN, child of NN, will wear your *image, you will |¹⁰ protect him ⟨for⟩ all the days ⟨of⟩ his life from every evil spirit and unclean spirit and every power of the Devil and all whisperers |¹⁵ and blows and all magic and wounds? ⟨and⟩? all sorcery, so that the Devil flees? from NN, child of NN, yea, yea, quickly! It is finished.

*Satōr, Aretō, Tenēt, Ōtera, Rōtas, |²⁰ the five nails of our saviour, Jesus Christ. (*kharaktēres*: +++++++ ΘΥΘЖЕЕ +++++++ I ꓱ##) ōrōrōrōfffff ōrōrōr rff
*Michael, *Gabriel, *Suriel, |²⁵ *Raphael, Zetekiel, Samphoēl, Anaēl, Anaēl, help, protect NN, child of NN!
Barkh, Bas IIIIIII XXXXXXX (*kharaktēres*: +>ꓳ+)

Image: Gardner (2023b: 114) and Love (2022c: 637) read the label as ⲙⲁⲥ ⲃⲏⲛⲓ, "swallow chick"; Gardner suggests that it is a representation of the manipulation of a bird to be carried out in the course of the ritual. The manipulation of animal effigies in the context of the creation of an amulet would be otherwise unattested in the corpus, however; we instead understand the tableau as that as intended to be copied onto the amulet, with Masbēn representing a variant of the name Nassklnē (note the relatively frequent confusion of ⲏ, ⲙ, ⲛ demonstrated by this scribe). The depiction of the figure is comparable to that on *PCM* I 30, front, another bird-like Solomonic demon with a cross on its head.

2. ⲛ̄ⲁⲥⲥⲕⲗⲛⲏ : "Nassklnē" Meyer (1996: 82) suggests that this may name may be derived from Onoskelis (Ὀνοσκελίς), a female demon with the legs of a donkey who appears in the *Testament of Solomon* 4.2 (McCown 1922).

14–15. ⲁⲗⲟⲅⲁⲥⲓⲟⲩⲁⲥ : "whisperers" As recognised by Helmut Satzinger (Meyer 1996: 49), this is the Arabic الوسواس *al-waswās*, "the whisperer", found in the Qur'an 114.4 as one of a number of beings from which the speaker asks protection from God. The Whisperer is generally understood to be another name for Satan, who tempts humankind by whispering "what is vain, or unprofitable, and destitute of good" (Lane 1863: 2939–2940 s.v. وس; *cf.* Amir-Moezzi/Dye 2019: 2346-2347). Here the originally singular Whisperer seems to be understood as a category of demonic being.

16–18. ⲙⲛ ⲛⲅ ⲫⲁⲣⲙⲁⲅⲓⲁ ⲛⲓⲙ · ⲙⲛ ⲛ̄ⲧⲉⲡⲇⲓⲁⲃⲟⲗⲟⲥ ⸗ ⲡⲱⲧ ⲛⲉⲩ ⲥⲁⲃⲟⲗ : "⟨and⟩? all sorcery, so that the Devil flees? from" This part of the recipe seems to be corrupt. Meyer translates "and all sorcery {and} of the devil. Drive them from NN". Here we propose that another noun, perhaps ⲡⲗⲏⲅⲏ ("wound") stood before ⲫⲁⲣⲙⲁⲅⲓⲁ, paralleling ⲛⲉⲣⲱϩⲧ ⲙⲛ ϩⲓⲕ in the preceding line; a definite article (ⲛ̄-) would be unexpected preceding a noun defined by ⲛⲓⲙ, as would its writing as ⲛⲅ. The form we would expect for Meyer's translation would be ⲡⲱⲧ ⲛⲥⲱⲟⲩ ⲉⲃⲟⲗ, quite unlike the form we find in the text. Rather we understand the ⲛ̄ⲧⲉ- preceding ⲡⲇⲓⲁⲃⲟⲗⲟⲥ to be a conjunctive prefix, but this does lead to the problem of the plural indirect object (expressing the reflexive "he flees (himself)") in ⲛⲉⲩ (i.e. ᔆⲛⲁ⸗ⲩ), where we would expect the third-person singular, ⲛⲁϥ, although compare the use of the third-person plural for the singular on p. 8 ll. 21–22. For the use of ⲙⲛ̄ + conjunctive, *cf.* the note to *PCM* I 26 p. 5 l. 6

page 11 (hair)

ⲃⲁⲗⲉⲑⲁⲣⲟⲓ ⸗
ⲥⲁⲣⲓⲱⲓⲛⲓ ⸗
ⲙⲓⲭⲁⲏⲗ · ⲅⲁⲃⲣⲓⲏⲗ · ⲅⲣⲁⲫⲁⲏⲗ · ⲥⲟⲩⲣⲓⲏⲗ ⸗
ⲥⲁⲣⲁⲑⲓⲏⲗ · ⲍⲉⲧⲉⲕⲓⲏⲗ · ⲁⲛⲁⲏⲗ ⸗
5 ⲥⲁⲧⲱⲣ ⲥⲁⲃⲁⲱⲑ ⸗ ⲡⲁⲛⲧⲱⲣ : ⲓ̅ⲥ̅ : ⲓ̅ⲥ̅ : ⲓ̅ⲥ̅ :
ⲡⲥⲱⲧⲏⲣ ⸗ ⲉⲙⲙⲁⲛⲟⲩⲏⲗ ⸗ ⲁⲣⲉⲧⲱ ⸗
ⲁⲇⲱⲛⲁⲓ ≡ ⲙⲉⲑⲉⲙⲟⲛ ⸗ ⲕⲉⲃⲱⲗ : ⲡ-
ⲡⲉⲥⲛⲟⲃ ⲥⲥ ⲁⲓⲟ ⸗ ⲧⲉⲛⲏⲧ ⸗ ⲉⲗⲱⲉⲓ ⸗ ⲱⲧⲉⲣⲁ
ⲉⲗⲏⲙⲁⲥ ⸗ ⲧⲱⲣⲁⲥ ⸗ ⲥⲁⲃⲁⲱⲑ ⸗
10 ⲃⲱⲓⲑⲓ ⸗ ⲉⲩⲣⲁⲉⲓⲥ · ⲧⲉⲩⲃⲱⲗ · ⲡⲉⲥⲛⲟⲃ ⸗
ⲥⲥ ⲁⲓⲱ ⲁⲓⲱ ⲧⲁⲭⲏ ⲧⲁⲭⲏ ⲁϥϫⲟⲕ ⲉⲃⲟⲗ

---

2 ⲥⲁⲣⲓⲱⲓⲛⲉ Meyer ‖ **5** *l.* παντ(οκράτ)ωρ | *i.e.* ˢⲓ(ⲏⲥⲟⲩ)ⲥ (three times) ‖ **7** ⲙⲉⲑⲉⲙⲟⲛ from μεθ' ἡμῶν *cf.* note | *i.e.* ˢⲉ⸗ⲕ-ⲉ-ⲱⲗ ? ‖ **7–8** *i.e.* ˢⲙ-ⲡ-ⲥⲛⲟϥ ‖ **8** *i.e.* (δεῖνα) (δεῖνα) ‖ **9** ⲉⲗⲏⲙⲟⲥ Meyer | ⲧⲱⲣⲁⲥ corrected from ⲧⲱⲧⲁⲥ by erasure and overwriting? ‖ **10** *i.e.* βοηθεῖν | *i.e.* ˢⲉⲩ-ⲉ-ⲣⲟⲉⲓⲥ ? | *i.e.* ˢⲛ̄⸗ⲥⲉ-ⲱⲗ ? | *i.e.* ˢⲡⲉ-ⲥⲛⲟϥ ‖ **11** *i.e.* (δεῖνα) (δεῖνα) | *i.e.* ταχύ (twice) | *i.e.* ˢⲁ⸗ϥ-ϫⲱⲕ (*kharaktēres*: MKXXX+++++) Baletharoi, Sariōini

|³ *Michael, *Gabriel, *Raphael, *Suriel, Sarathiēl, Zetekiel, Anaēl, |⁵ *Satōr, *Sabaoth, the Almighty, Jesus, Jesus, Jesus the Savior, Emmanuel, Aretō, *Adonai, Methemōn, may you contain? the blood of NN, yea! Tenēt, *Eloei, Ōtera, *Elēmas, Tōras, Sabaoth, |¹⁰ help! May they protect and contain? the blood of NN, yea, yea, quickly, quickly!

It is finished.

1–11. This text is quite similar in content to the previous one (p. 10, ll. 19–27; KYP T241), and may constitute with it a single recipe.

7. ⲙⲉⲑⲉⲙⲟⲛ : **"Methemōn"** For this name, *cf.* Matthew 1.23 "and they will call his name 'Emmanuel', which interpreted means 'God is with us' (*meth'ēmōn*)" (καὶ καλέσουσιν τὸ ὄνομα αὐτοῦ Ἐμμανουήλ, ὅ ἐστιν μεθερμηνευόμενον Μεθ' ἡμῶν ὁ θεός; Horner 1911: I 6,8).

7, 10. ⲕⲉⲃⲱⲗ, ⲧⲉⲩⲃⲱⲗ : **"may you contain?", "and contain?"** The word ⲃⲱⲗ means "undo", but it is likely, given the context, that ⲱⲗ "gather, contain" is intended, since this is the verb usually used in reference to stopping the flow of blood; *cf.* PCM I 3 ll. 33–34; P.Macq. I 1 (KYP M167) p. 16 ll. 1–4; P.Méd.Copt.IFAO (Chassinat 1921; KYP M941) l. 334; P. Vindob. K 11088 (Hevesi 2015; KYP M374) ll. B 4–7.

10. ⲃⲱⲓⲑⲓ ⸗ ⲉⲩⲣⲁⲉⲓⲥ · ⲧⲉⲩⲃⲱⲗ : **"help! May they protect and contain?"** Here we translate an imperative followed by a third future with a third person plural subject, then a conjunctive with a third person plural subject. Meyer (1996: 49) suggests as possibilities three imperatives (ⲃⲱⲓⲑⲓ ⲣⲁⲉⲓⲥ ⲃⲱⲗ), an imperative followed by two circumstantials (?) (ⲃⲱⲓⲑⲓ ⲉⲕⲣⲁⲓⲥ (ⲧ)ⲉⲕⲃⲱⲗ), or else a "word of power" followed by the third person plural forms of circumstantial or conjunctive verb forms.

page 12 (flesh)

1 ϨⲘ ⲠⲢⲀⲚ ⲠⲒⲰⲦ ⲘⲚ ⲠϢⲎⲢⲈ ⁼ ⲠⲈⲠ͞Ⲛ͞Ⲁ ⲈⲦⲞⲨⲀ-
                                              ⲀϤ

1 *i.e.* ˢⲘ̄-ⲠⲈⲒⲰⲦ | *l.* πν(εῦμ)α ‖ **3, 10** *l.* ι(ησου)ς | χ(ριστό)ς ‖ **14** *l.* (δεῖνα) (δεῖνα) ‖ **15** *i.e.* ˢⲠ-ϢⲈ ‖ **17** *i.e.* ˢⲦ-ⲢⲞⲞⲨⲚⲈ ? ‖ **18–19** ⲀⲖⲔⲀⲢⲔⲀⲢϨⲀ Arabic loanword ?

In the name of the Father and the Son ⟨and⟩ the Holy Spirit.

|²⁻³ Manix, Jesus Christ

|⁴⁻⁵ Phourat

|⁶ Phouranei

|⁷ Abiouth

|⁸ Garnabiouth

|⁹ Mosos

|¹⁰ Jesus Christ

|¹¹⁻¹⁴ Iōkap, the Father, *Iao *Sabaoth *Adonai, protect NN, child of NN!

|¹⁵⁻¹⁹ The son of Mary ⟨the⟩ virgin, Alkar Karha.

|²⁰ Garnabiēl

|²¹⁻²² Ssisos, s

|²³⁻²⁴ Bēth, |²⁴ Sabaoth

|²⁵ Bēthaei

|²⁶⁻²⁸ Ssssssssssssssssssss, Bēthaf

---

p. 13 l. 1–p. 16 l. 15: The adjuration contained in these pages addresses the "Nine Guardians" who protect the body of the Trinity, with three each attached to each person, Father, Son, and Holy Spirit. As recognised by Mößner/Nauerth (2015: 344) their forms depicted on p. 12 likely imitate the person they guard, with those who protect the Father and Son being anthropomorphic, and those who protect the Holy Spirit being avian in reference to the Holy Spirit's appearance as a dove. The Nine Guardians appear in several other texts, including *BKU* I 24 (KYP M206); *BKU* III 387 (KYP M 336); BM EA 10391 (Zellmann-Rohrer 2022a: no. 1 front ll. 1–12; KYP M302; BM EA 10122 (Zellmann-Rohrer 2022a: no. 4; KYP M289). There is a similar depiction in the last of these, but with iconography combining the human and birdlike imagery. The figures here are depicted with crosses upon their heads, suggesting their divine nature, and carrying staffs topped with crosses. They are surrounded by *kharaktēres* derived primarily from the Greek vowels (ⲁ, ⲉ, ⲓ, ⲏ, ⲱ), in particular Alpha and Omega in reference to Revelation 22.13. Sequences of names beginning *beth-* are common in Coptic magical texts, and are associated both with the Nine Guardians and the *Twenty-Four Presbyters; for discussions, see Łajtar/van der Vliet 2017: 181–85; Dosoo 2022a: 157–159; Zellmann-Rohrer 2022a: 94–95.

page 13 (flesh)

ⲙⲁⲛⲓⲍ = ⲫⲟⲩⲣⲁⲧ = ⲫⲟⲩⲣⲁⲛⲉⲓ = ⲡⲉⲓⲅ ⲛ̄-
ϩⲟⲩⲣⲓⲧⲉ = ⲉⲧⲣⲁⲉⲓⲥ ⲉⲡⲥⲱⲙⲁ ⲡⲓⲱⲧ ⲡ̄ⲁⲛⲧⲟⲣ
ⲕⲉⲣⲁⲉⲓⲥ = ⲡⲁⲥⲱⲙⲁ : ⲁⲛⲁⲕ ⲓⲱⲥⲏⲫ ⲭ̄ ⲡⲁⲣⲁⲥⲩ̣ᵉ
ⲁⲃⲓⲟⲩⲑ = ⲅⲁⲣⲛⲁⲃⲓⲟⲩⲑ = ⲅⲁⲣⲛⲁⲃⲓⲏⲗ =
5 ⲡⲉⲓⲅ̄ ϩⲟⲩⲣⲓⲧ ≡ ⲉⲧⲣⲁⲉⲓⲥ ⲉⲡⲥⲱⲙⲁ ⲛⲉⲓ̄ⲥ ⲭ̄ⲥ -
ⲡϣⲏⲣⲉ ⲡⲛⲟⲩⲧⲉ ⲕⲉⲣⲁⲉⲓⲥ ⲡⲁⲥⲱⲙⲁ · ⲁⲛⲁⲕ ⲥ̄ⲥ̄ =
ⲃⲏⲑ = ⲃⲏⲑⲁϥ = ⲃⲏⲑⲁⲉⲓ = ⲡⲉⲓⲅ̄ ϩⲟⲩⲣⲓⲧ = ⲉⲧⲣⲁⲉⲓⲥ = ⲉⲡⲥⲱⲙⲁ ⲡⲉⲡ̄ⲛ̄ⲁ̄ · ⲉⲧⲟⲩⲁⲁⲃ = ⲕⲉⲣⲁⲉⲓⲥ ⲉⲡⲥⲱⲙⲁ · ⲁⲛⲁⲕ ⲓⲱⲥⲏⲫ ⲡ̄ⲭ̄ ⲡⲁⲣⲁⲥⲉⲩ · ⲁⲓⲟ = ⲁⲓⲟ :
10 ϯⲧⲉⲣⲕⲟ ⲙⲙⲱⲧ : ⲡⲑ̄ ϩⲟⲩⲣⲓⲧ : ⲛ̄ⲧⲉϣⲁⲣⲡ
ⲛⲁⲕⲓ = ⲧⲁⲙⲁⲣⲓⲁ = ⲧⲁⲟⲥ : ϣⲁⲛⲧⲉⲥⲡ̄ⲭⲡⲟ ⲙ̄-
ⲡ̄ⲭ̄ⲥ̄ ⲡϣⲏⲣⲉ ⲙⲡⲛⲟⲩⲧⲉ = ⲕⲉⲣⲁⲉⲓⲥ ⲥ̄ⲥ̄ ⲁⲓⲁ ⲧⲁⲭⲏ =
ϯⲧⲉⲣⲕⲟ ⲙ̄ⲙⲱⲧ : ⲡⲑ̄ ϩⲟⲩⲣⲓⲧ : ⲛⲉϩⲓⲥ ⲛ̄ⲧⲁⲡϣ-
ⲏⲣⲉ ⲡⲛⲟⲩⲧⲉ = ϣⲁⲡⲟⲩ : ϩⲓⲭⲉⲛ̄ ⲡϣⲏ ⲡⲉⲥ†ⲣ̄ⲟⲥ
15 ⲕⲉⲣⲁⲉⲓⲥ ⲡⲥⲱⲙⲁ ⲥ̄ⲥ̄ ⲡ̄ⲭ̄ ⲥ̄ⲥ̄ ⲁⲓⲱ ⲁⲓⲱ ⲧⲁⲭⲏ
ϯⲧⲉⲣⲕⲟ ⲙ̄ⲙⲱⲧ ⲡ̄:ⲑ̄ : ϩⲟⲩⲣⲓⲧ = ⲉⲡⲧⲟⲩ ⲛⲓⲃⲧ ⲛ̄-
ⲧⲁⲩⲧⲁϩⲟⲩ = ⲛⲉϭⲓⲭ : ⲙⲛ ⲛⲉϥⲟⲩⲉⲣⲏⲧ† = ⲛ̄-
ⲓ̄ⲥ̄ ⲡ̄ⲭ̄ⲥ̄ ⲡϣⲏⲣⲉ ⲙⲡⲛⲟⲩⲧⲉ · ⲧⲉ ⲛⲁⲓ ⲛⲉⲣⲁⲛ =
ⲥⲱⲧⲱⲣ : ⲁⲣⲉⲧⲱ = ⲧⲉⲛⲏⲧ = ⲱⲧⲉⲣⲁ =
20 ⲣⲱⲧⲁⲥ = ⲕⲉⲣⲁⲉⲓⲥ = ⲉⲡⲥⲱⲙⲁ ⲥ̄ⲥ̄ · ⲁⲓⲁ : ⲧⲁⲭⲏ =
ϯⲧⲉⲣⲕⲟ ⲙ̄ⲱⲧ ⲡ:ⲑ̄ : ϩⲟⲩⲣⲓⲧ = ⲡ̄ⲣ̄ⲏ̄ⲙ̄ⲭ̄ = ⲙⲛ :
ⲡⲥⲓϣⲓ = ⲧⲁ·ⲉⲓⲥ ⲡϣⲏⲣⲉ ⲙⲡⲛⲟⲩⲧⲉ : ⲭⲓ †ⲡ-
ⲉ ⲙⲁϥ = ⲉϥⲁⲗⲏⲩ ⲡⲉⲥ†ⲣ̄ⲟⲥ = ⲕⲉⲣⲁⲉⲓⲥ ⲥ̄ⲥ̄ ⲁⲓⲟ ⲟⲓⲟ
ϯⲧⲉⲣⲕⲟ ⲙ̄ⲙⲱⲧ ⲡⲑ̄ ϩⲟⲩⲣⲓⲧ : ⲉⲡⲅ̄ ⲉⲣⲟⲟⲩ =
25 ⲛ̄ⲧⲁⲉⲓ̄ⲥ̄ = ⲱϣ : ⲙⲁⲩ · ⲉⲃⲁⲗ = ϣⲁⲛ† ⲡⲉⲡ̄ⲛ̄ⲁ̄ =
ⲛⲉϭⲓⲭ ⲙ̄ⲡⲓⲱⲧ = ⲛⲁⲕⲁⲑⲱ̄ⲥ̄ = ⲕⲉⲣⲁⲉⲓⲥ ⲥ̄ⲥ̄ ⲁⲓⲟ
ϯⲧⲉⲣⲕⲟ ⲙ̄ⲙⲱⲧ · ⲡ:ⲑ̄ : ϩⲟⲩⲣⲓⲧ ⲛ̄ⲧⲉϣⲥ ⲧⲏ-
ⲗⲱⲅⲭⲓ = ⲛ̄ⲧⲁⲩⲧⲁⲁⲥ = ⲉϩⲟⲩⲛ : ⲡⲉⲥⲡⲓⲣ : ⲛ̇:-
ⲓⲱⲛⲁⲙ : ⲛⲓ̄ⲥ̄ ⲡϣⲏⲣⲉ ⲙⲡⲛⲟⲩⲧⲉ = ⲉϥⲁⲗ-
30 ⲉⲩ ⲡⲉⲥ†ⲣ̄ⲟⲥ : ⲁⲩϩⲁⲧⲉ : ⲉⲃⲁⲗ · ⲛ̄ϭⲓ ⲟⲩⲙⲟⲟⲩ =
ⲙⲛ ⲟⲩ:ⲥⲛⲟⲃ · ⲕⲉⲣⲁⲉⲓⲥ ⲥ̄ⲥ̄ ⲁⲓⲟ

---

2 i.e. σῶμα | i.e. ˢⲙ̄-ⲡ-ⲉⲓⲱⲧ | l. παντο(κράτω)ρ || **3** i.e. ˢⲉ=ⲕ-ⲉ-ⲣⲟⲉⲓⲥ | i.e. ˢⲉ-ⲡⲁ-ⲥⲱⲙⲁ || **3–15** i.e. (υἱός) : ⲓ̄ⲥ̄ Meyer || **5** i.e. σῶμα | l. ⲓ(ⲏⲥⲟⲩ)ⲥ i.e. χ(ριστό)ⲥ || **6** i.e. ˢⲙ̄-ⲡ-ⲛⲟⲩⲧⲉ | i.e. ˢⲉ=ⲕ-ⲉ-ⲣⲟⲉⲓⲥ | i.e. ˢⲉ-ⲡⲁ-σῶμα || **6–31** l. (δεῖνα) (δεῖνα) || **8** i.e. σῶμα | l. ⲙ̄-ⲡⲉ-πν(εῦμ)ⲁ | i.e. ˢⲉ=ⲕ-ⲉ-ⲣⲟⲉⲓⲥ || **8–9** l. ⲉⲡ‹ⲁ›ⲥⲱⲙⲁ ? || **10** i.e. ˢⲙ̄ⲙⲱ=ⲧⲛ̄ || **11** i.e. ˢⲛ̄-ⲛⲁⲁⲕⲉⲉⲛⲧ-ⲁ-ⲙⲁⲣⲓⲁ ⲧⲁⲁⲥ ϣⲁⲛⲧⲉ=ⲥ-ⲭⲡⲟ || **12** i.e. χ(ριστό)ⲥ | i.e. ˢⲉ=ⲕ-ⲉ-ⲣⲟⲉⲓⲥ || **12–20** i.e. ταχύ || **13** i.e. ˢⲙ̄ⲙⲱ=ⲧⲛ̄ | i.e. ˢϩⲓⲥⲉ || **14** i.e. ˢⲙ̄-ⲡ-ⲛⲟⲩⲧⲉ | l. ⲙ̄-ⲡⲉ-σ(ταυρ)ⲟ́ⲥ || **15** i.e. ˢⲉ=ⲕ-ⲉ-ⲣⲟⲉⲓⲥ | i.e. σῶμα | i.e. ταχύ || **16** i.e. ˢⲙ̄ⲙⲱ=ⲧⲛ̄ || **16–17** i.e. ˢⲉⲛⲧ-ⲁ=ⲩ-ⲧⲉⲕⲥ=ⲟⲩ || **17** i.e. ˢⲛⲉ=ϥ-ⲟⲩⲣⲏⲧⲉ : ⲛⲉⲟⲩⲣⲏⲧ† ? Meyer || **18** l. ⲓ(ⲏⲥⲟⲩ)ⲥ χ(ριστό)ⲥ || **20** i.e. ˢⲉ=ⲕ-ⲉ-ⲣⲟⲉⲓⲥ | i.e. σῶμα || **21** i.e. ˢⲙ̄-ⲡ-ϩⲙ̄ⲭ | i.e. ˢⲙ̄ⲙⲱ=ⲧⲛ̄ || **22** i.e. ˢⲥⲓϣⲉ | i.e. ˢⲛ̄ⲧ=ⲁ-ⲓ(ⲏⲥⲟⲩ)ⲥ || **23** i.e. ˢϩⲙ̄ ⲡⲉ-σ(ταυρ)ⲟ́ⲥ | i.e. ˢⲉ=ⲕ-ⲉ-ⲣⲟⲉⲓⲥ | ⲟⲓⲟ i.e. ˢϩⲁⲉⲓⲟ || **24** i.e. ˢⲙ̄ⲙⲱ=ⲧⲛ̄ | ϩⲟⲩⲣⲓⲧ, o corrected to p by overwriting | i.e. ˢϩⲣⲟⲟⲩ || **25** i.e. ˢⲉⲛⲧ-ⲁ-ⲓ(ⲏⲥⲟⲩ)ⲥ | i.e. ˢⲙ̄ⲙⲟ=ⲟⲩ | i.e. ˢϣⲁⲛⲧⲉ=ϥ-† | i.e. ˢⲙ̄-ⲡⲉ-πν(εῦμ)ⲁ || **26** i.e. ˢⲉ-ⲛ-ϭⲓⲭ | i.e. ἀγαθός | i.e. ˢⲉ=ⲕ-ⲉ-ⲣⲟⲉⲓⲥ || **27** i.e. ˢⲙ̄ⲙⲱ=ⲧⲛ̄ || **27** i.e. ˢⲛ̄-ⲧ-ϣⲱⲥ || **27–28** i.e. ˢⲛ̄ⲧⲉ-ⲧ-λόγχη || **29** l. ⲓ(ⲏⲥⲟⲩ)ⲥ | i.e. ˢⲁⲗⲏⲩ || **30** i.e. σ(ταυρ)ⲟ́ⲥ || **31** i.e. ˢⲉ=ⲕ-ⲉ-ⲣⲟⲉⲓⲥ

Manix, Phourat, Phouranei, O Three Guardians who protect the body ⟨of⟩ the Father Almighty, may you (s.) protect my body, me, Iōsēph, son ⟨of⟩ Paraseu! Abiouth, Garnabiouth, Garnabiēl, |⁵ O Three Guardians who protect the body of Jesus Christ, the son ⟨of⟩ God, may you (s.) protect my body, me, NN, child of NN! Bēth, Bēthaf, Bēthaei, O Three Guardians who protect the body of the Holy Spirit, may you (s.) protect ⟨my⟩ body, me, Iōsēph, son ⟨of⟩ Paraseu, yea, yea!

|¹⁰ I adjure you, O Nine Guardians, by the first labour pang that Mary suffered until she gave birth to Christ, the Son of God that you (s.) protect NN, child of NN, yea, quickly! I adjure you, O Nine Guardians, by the suffering that the son of God experienced upon the wood ⟨of⟩ the cross |¹⁵ that you (s.) protect the body ⟨of⟩ NN, the son ⟨of⟩ NN, yea, yea, quickly! I adjure you, O Nine Guardians, by the five nails which pierced the hands and feet of Jesus Christ, the Son of God— whose names are *Sōtōr, Aretō, Tenēt, Ōtera, |²⁰ Rōtas—that you (s.) watch over the body of NN, child of NN, yea, quickly! I adjure you, O Nine Guardians, ⟨by⟩ the vinegar and the gall that Jesus, the Son of God, tasted when he was upon the cross, that you (s.) protect NN, child of NN, yea, yea! I adjure you, Nine Guardians, by the three sounds |²⁵ that Jesus cried out until ⟨he⟩ gave the spirit ⟨into⟩ the hands of the good Father, that you (s.) watch over NN, child of NN, yea! I adjure you, O Nine Guardians, by the wound ⟨from⟩ the spear which was thrust in the right side of Jesus, the Son of God, when he |³⁰ he was upon the cross—water and blood poured out—that you (s.) protect NN, child of NN, yea!

3, 9. ⲁⲛⲁⲕ ⲓⲱⲥⲏⲫ ⲡ̄ ⲡⲁⲣⲁⲥⲉⲩ : "**Iōsēph, son ⟨of⟩ Paraseu**" The mention of a particular individual here offers a striking exception to the usual presence of the generic name marker NN elsewhere. There are a two obvious possibilities that might explain this; the first is that this text was copied from an applied amulet or personalised formulary (*cf.* Saar 2007), and the second is that this manuscript is itself a (partially) personalised copy—if this is the case, Iōsēph would be the individual for whom this manuscript, and perhaps the other manuscripts of the Heidelberg Coptic Magical Library produced by Deacon Iōhannēs, was copied.

11. ⲛⲁⲕⲓ : "**labour pang**" The labour pangs of Mary are also evoked in the *Endoxon of Michael*, *PCM* I 26 p. 12 ll. 19–24.

19–20. ⲥⲱⲧⲱⲣ : ⲁⲣⲉⲧⲱ ⸱ ⲧⲉⲛⲏⲧ ⸱ ⲱⲧⲉⲣⲁ ⸱ ⲣⲱⲧⲁⲥ : "**Sōtōr, Aretō, Tenēt, Ōtera, Rōtas**" This is a writing of the *Sator names, whose canonical Latin form is *Sator Arepo Tenet Opera Rotas*.

page 14 (hair)

ϯⲧⲉⲣⲕⲟ ⲙⲱⲧ ⲡⲉ ϩⲟⲩⲣⲓⲧ : ⲛⲧⲉ ⲛ·ⲧ̅ ⲝ
ⲛⲧⲉⲗϯⲗ ⲉⲛⲝⲣ̅ⲙ̅ⲉⲓⲏ ⲛ:ⲧⲁⲩ·ⲉⲓ ⲉⲃⲁⲗ ⲛ̅-
ϩⲛ ⲛⲉⲃⲁⲗ ⲝ ⲉⲡⲓⲱⲧ ⲛⲁⲕⲁⲑⲟⲥ ⲝ ϩⲓⲭⲉⲛ ⲧⲁⲡⲏ ⲝ ⲡⲉϥϣⲏⲣⲉ ⲝ ⲓ̅ⲥ̅ ⲉϥⲁⲗⲏⲩ ⲡ̅-
5 ⲡⲉⲥ̅ⲧ̅ⲟ̅ⲥ̅ · ϫⲉⲕⲁⲥ ⲣⲁⲉⲓⲥ ss ⲁⲓⲱ ⲧⲁⲭⲏ ⲝ
ϯⲧⲉⲣⲕⲟ ⲙ̅ⲙ̅ⲱ̅ⲧ̅ ⲝ ⲡⲉ ϩⲟⲩⲣⲓⲧ ⲉⲛⲉⲗ-
ⲓⲯⲁⲛⲟⲛ ⲉⲧⲟⲩⲁⲁⲃ ⲝ ⲉⲧⲁⲩⲕⲱ ⲉϩⲣⲁⲓ
ϩⲓϫⲱⲟⲩ ⲡⲥⲱⲙⲁ · ⲙⲛ ⲡⲉ·ⲥⲛⲟⲃ ≡ ⲛ̅ⲓ̅ⲥ̅
ⲡϣⲏⲣⲉ ⲙ̇ⲡⲛⲟⲩⲧⲉ ≡ · ϩⲉⲛ ⲧⲉⲕⲗⲏⲥⲓⲁ ≡
10 ⲛⲉϣⲏⲣⲉ·ⲉⲡⲙⲓⲥⲉ ⲝ ϩⲉ ⲛⲉⲡⲏⲅⲉ ⲕ̅ⲉⲣⲁⲉⲓ
ϯⲧⲉⲣⲕⲟ ⲙ̅ⲙ̅ⲱ̅ⲧ̅ · ⲡⲉ ϩⲟⲩⲣⲓⲧ : ⲛ̅ⲱ̅ⲫⲁ
ⲡⲥⲱⲙⲁ · ⲉⲡⲓⲱⲧ ⲝ ⲙⲛ ⲱ̅ⲣⲫⲁⲙⲓⲏⲗ ⲝ
ⲡⲛⲟϭ ⲛ̅ⲧ̅ⲏ̅ⲏ̅ⲃ̅ ⲝ ϩⲉⲛ ⲟⲩⲛⲁⲙ ⲝ ⲉⲡⲓⲱⲧ ⲝ
ⲙⲛ ⲝ ⲁ̅ⲃⲣⲁⲥⲁ̅ⲝ̅ ⲝ ⲉⲧⲉϣⲓ ⲝ ⲉⲧϭⲓⲭ ⲝ ⲟⲩⲛⲁⲙ ⲝ
15 ⲉⲡⲓⲱⲓⲧ ⲝ
ⲕⲉⲣⲁⲉⲓⲥ · ⲉⲡⲥⲱⲙⲁ s̄s̄ ⲝ ⲁⲓⲟ ⲁⲓⲟ ⲧⲁⲭⲏ
ϯⲧⲉⲣⲕⲟ ⲙ̅ⲙ̅ⲱ̅ⲧ̅ ⲡⲉ ϩⲟⲩⲣⲓⲧ ⲝ ⲉⲧϭⲓⲭ ⲝ
ⲥⲛⲏⲩ : ⲧⲉ ⲡⲓⲱⲧ ⲝ ⲡ̅ⲁ̅ⲛⲧⲱⲣ ⲝ ⲉⲧⲉ ⲛⲁⲓ
ⲛⲉⲣⲁⲛ ⲝ ⲁ̅ⲛ̅ⲇⲣⲁⲙⲓⲏⲗ ⲝ ⲉⲧⲉϥⲟⲩⲛⲁⲙ̅
20 ⲇ̅ⲣⲁⲭⲁⲏⲗ ≡ ⲉⲧⲉ ⲧⲉϥ:ⲃⲟⲩⲣ ⲝ ⲕⲉⲣⲁⲉⲓⲥ s̄s̄ ⲟ̅ⲓ̅ⲟ̅
ϯⲧⲉⲣⲕⲟ ⲙ̅ⲙ̅ⲱ̅ⲧ̅ ⲡⲉ ϩⲟⲩⲣⲓⲧ : ⲛⲧⲟⲩⲏⲣϯ
ⲥⲛⲏⲩ ⲧⲉ ⲡⲓⲱⲧ ⲡ̅ⲁ̅ⲛⲧⲱⲣ ⲝ ⲉⲧⲉ ⲛⲁⲓ ⲛⲉ ⲛⲓ-
ⲣⲁⲛ ⲑ̅ⲁ̅ϣ̅ⲑ̅ ≡ ⲉⲧⲉϥⲓⲱⲛⲁⲙ ⲝ ⲧⲉ · ⲑ̅ⲁ̅ϣ̅ⲑⲁ ⲝ
ⲉⲧⲉϥⲃⲟⲩⲣ ϫⲉⲕⲁⲥ ⲣⲁⲉⲓⲥ s̄s̄ ⲁⲓⲱ ⲧⲁⲭⲏ
25 ϯⲧⲉⲣⲕⲟ ⲙ̅ⲙ̅ⲱ̅ⲧ̅ ≡ ⲡⲉ ϩⲟⲩⲣⲓⲧ ⲙⲡⲉϥ·ⲇ̅ -
ⲛⲥⲧⲏⲗⲟⲥ ⲝ ⲉⲧⲧⲱⲟⲩ ⲝ ⲉϩⲣⲁⲓ ⲝ ϩⲁ ⲧⲉⲡⲏ
ⲉⲧⲉ ⲛⲁⲓ ⲛⲉⲩⲣⲁⲛ ⲝ ⲥ̅ⲏ̅ⲧ̅ ⲝ ⲥ̅ⲏ̅ⲛⲧⲁⲥ ≡

---

1 i.e. ˢⲙ̅ⲙ̅ⲱⲝⲧ̅ⲛ̅ ‖ **2** i.e. ˢⲧ̅ⲗ̅ⲧ̅ⲗ̅ | i.e. ˢⲣⲙⲉⲓⲏ ‖ **3** i.e. ἀγαθός ‖ **4** l. ι(ⲏⲥⲟⲩ)ⲥ ‖ **4–5** l. ˢⲙ-ⲡⲉ-ⲥ(ⲧⲁⲩⲣ)ⲟⲥ ‖ **5** i.e. ˢⲉⲝⲕ-ⲉ-ⲣⲁⲓⲥ | l. (δεῖνα) (δεῖνα) | i.e. ταχύ ‖ **6** i.e. ˢⲙ̅ⲙ̅ⲱⲝⲧ̅ⲛ̅ ‖ **6–7** i.e. ˢⲛ-ⲛⲉ-ⲗⲉⲓⲯⲁⲛⲟⲛ ‖ **7** i.e. ˢⲛ̅ⲧ-ⲁⲝⲩ ⲕⲱ ‖ **8** i.e. σῶμα | l. ι(ⲏⲥⲟⲩ)ⲥ ‖ **9** i.e. ἐκκλησία ‖ **10** i.e. ˢⲙ-ⲡ-ϣⲟⲣⲡ | i.e. ˢϩⲛ ⲙ-ⲡⲏⲩⲉ | i.e. ˢⲉⲝⲕ-ⲉ-ⲣⲟⲉⲓⲥ : ⲕⲉⲣⲁⲉⲓⲥ Meyer ‖ **11** i.e. ˢⲙ̅ⲙ̅ⲱⲝⲧ̅ⲛ̅ | ⲱ̅ⲫⲁ : "Ō(r)pha" Meyer ‖ **12** i.e. σῶμα ‖ **14** i.e. ˢⲛ-ⲧ-ϭⲓⲭ | ⲟⲩⲛⲁⲙ, ⲟ corrected from ⲝ (?) by overwriting ‖ **15** i.e. ˢⲡ-ⲉⲓⲱⲧ : ⲉⲡⲓⲱⲧ Meyer ‖ **16** i.e. ˢⲉⲝⲕ-ⲉ-ⲣⲟⲉⲓⲥ | i.e. σῶμα | l. (δεῖνα) (δεῖνα) | i.e. ταχύ ‖ **17** i.e. ˢⲙ̅ⲙ̅ⲱⲝⲧ̅ⲛ̅ | ˢⲛ-ⲧ-ϭⲓⲭ ‖ **18** i.e. ˢⲥⲛⲁⲩ for ⲥⲛ̅ⲧⲉ | ⲧⲉ i.e. ˢⲛ̅ⲧⲉ | l. παντ(οκράτ)ωρ ‖ **19** i.e. ˢⲉⲧⲉ-ⲧⲉϥ-ⲟⲩⲛⲁⲙ ‖ **20** i.e. ˢϩⲃⲟⲩⲣ | i.e. ˢⲉⲝⲕ-ⲉ-ⲣⲟⲉⲓⲥ | l. (δεῖνα) (δεῖνα) | ⲟ̅ⲓ̅ⲟ̅ i.e. ˢϩⲁⲉⲓⲟ ‖ **21** i.e. ˢⲙ̅ⲙ̅ⲱⲝⲧ̅ⲛ̅ ‖ **22** i.e. ˢⲥⲛⲁⲩ for ⲥⲛ̅ⲧⲉ | i.e. ˢⲛ̅ⲧⲉ | l. παντ(οκράτ)ωρ ‖ **23** i.e. ˢⲉⲧⲉ-ⲧⲉϥ-ⲟⲩⲛⲁⲙ ‖ **24** i.e. ˢϩⲃⲟⲩⲣ | l. (δεῖνα) (δεῖνα) | l. ⲉⲝⲕ-ⲉ-ⲣⲁⲓⲥ | i.e. ταχύ ‖ **25** i.e. ˢⲙ̅ⲙ̅ⲱⲝⲧ̅ⲛ̅ ‖ **25–26** l. ⲙ-ⲡⲉϥ-(ⲧⲟⲟⲩ) : perhaps l. ⲙ-ⲡⲉ-ⲇ̅ Meyer ‖ **26** i.e. στῦλος | i.e. ˢⲧⲱⲟⲩⲛ

I adjure you, O Nine Guardians, by the three teardrops which came from the eyes of the good Father upon the head of his son, Jesus, when he was upon |⁵ the cross, that ⟨you⟩ watch over NN, child of NN, yea, quickly! I adjure you, O Nine Guardians, by the holy remains that were placed upon them, the body and the blood of Jesus, the Son of God, in the Church of |¹⁰ ⟨the⟩ Firstborn in the heavens, that you protect ⟨NN⟩!

I adjure you, O Nine Guardians, by Ōpha, the body of the Father, and Ōrphamiēl, the great finger on the right hand of the Father, and Abrasax, who measures the right hand |¹⁵ of the Father, that you (s.) protect the body ⟨of⟩ NN, child of NN, yea, yea, quickly! I adjure you, O Nine Guardians, by the two hands of the Father Almighty, whose names are Andramiēl, which is his right, |²⁰ Drakhaēl, which is his left, that you watch over NN, child of NN, yea! I adjure you, O Nine Guardians, by the two feet of the Father Almighty, whose names are Thaōth, which is his right, Thaōtha, which is his left, that ⟨you⟩ watch over NN, child of NN, yea, quickly! |²⁵ I adjure you, O Nine Guardians, by the four pillars that bear heaven, whose names are Sēt, Sēntas,

---

1–2. ⲛ̄ⲧ̄ ⸗ ⲛⲧⲉⲗϯⲗ ⲉⲛ⸗ⲡ̄ⲙⲓⲏ : "**the three teardrops**" Other references to God the Father's tears provoked by Jesus' crucifixion are found in *Rossi's Tractate* (*PCM* I 26 p. 18 ll. 1–2) and the *Love Spell of Cyprian* (*PCM* I 28 p. 8 ll. 14–17).

11–24. The body of God the Father: See the discussion in the notes to *PCM* I 12 p. 31.

12. ⲱⲣⲫⲁⲙⲓⲏⲗ : "**Ōrphamiēl**" For the angel Orphamiel, see the note to *PCM* I 12 p. 31 ll. 4–5.

21–22. ⲛⲧⲟⲩⲏⲣϯ ⲥⲛⲏⲩ ⲧⲉⲡⲓⲱⲧ : "**by the two feet of the Father**" The names of the feet of the Father, *Thaōth* and *Thaōtha*, find a precise parallel in the *Endoxon of Michael* (*PCM* I 26 p. 8 ll. 16–17).

page 15 (hair)

ⲥⲏⲛⲧⲁⲗⲁⲗⲁⲥ ⳾ ⲥⲏⲛⲧⲁⲗⲁⲗⲓⲁ ⳾
ϫⲉⲕⲁⲥ ⲉⲧⲣⲁⲉⲓⲥ ≡ ⲉⲡⲥⲱⲙⲁ ⲥⲥ ⲇⲓⲟ
ⲧ̄ⲧⲉⲣⲕⲟ ⲙ̄ⲙⲱⲧ ⳾ ⲡⲑ̄ ϩⲟⲩⲣⲓⲧ · ⲛ̄ⲉⲛ-
ⲉⲓⲣⲁⲛ ⳾ ⲉⲧⲥⲙⲁⲙⲁⲁⲧ ⳾ ⲛⲁⲓ · ⲉⲧⲥⲁ ⲓⲱⲛⲁⲙ
5   ⲉⲡⲉⲑⲩⲥⲁⲧⲏⲣⲓⲱⲛ ⳾ ⲙ̄ⲡⲓⲱⲧ ⳾ ⲉⲧⲉ ⲛⲁⲓ ⳾
ⲛⲉ ⲥⲁⲃⲁⲱⲑ ⳾ ⲙⲏⲑⲏⲙⲱⲛ ⳾ ⲥⲟⲩⲙⲓⲑⲓⲟⲛ ⳾
ⲡⲉⲣⲓⲭⲏ ⳾ ⲁⲕⲣⲁⲙⲁⲧⲁ ⳾ ⲧⲁⲉⲕⲧⲱⲣ ⳾
ϥⲙⲓⲏⲗ ⳾ ⲥⲁⲛⲧⲁⲗⲁⲗⲓⲁ ≡ ⲕⲉⲣⲁⲉⲓⲥ ⲥⲥ ⲁⲓⲱ ⳾
ⲁⲅⲓⲟⲥ ⳾ ⲁⲅⲓⲟⲥ ⳾ ⲁⲅⲓⲁⲥ ⳾ ⲕⲩⲣⲓⲱⲥ ⳾ ⲥⲁⲃⲁⲱⲑ ⳾
10 ⲡ̄ⲗⲏⲣⲟⲥ ⳾ ⲟⲩⲣⲁⲛⲟⲩⲥ ⳾ ⲕⲉ ⲉⲓ ⲕⲏ ⲧⲏⲥ ⳾ ⲁⲅⲓⲟⲥ
ⲉⲩⲇⲱⲝⲟⲥ ⳾ ϩⲁⲙⲏⲛ ⳾ ⲓ̄ⲥ̄ ⲡⲉⲭ̄ⲥ̄ ⲃⲱⲓⲑⲓ ⲉⲗⲁϥ
ϩⲛ̄ ⲉⲛϭⲁⲙ ⲛⲉⲛⲓⲣⲁⲛ ⳾ ⲉⲧⲥⲙⲁⲙⲁⲁⲧ ⲉⲧⲉ ⲛⲁⲓ
ⲛⲉ ⲁⲃⲓⲁ ⳾ ⲉϥⲓⲭⲏ ⳾ ⲁⲣⲑⲁⲥⲁ ⳾ ⲁⲃⲁⲕⲧⲁⲛⲓ ⳾ ⲟⲩⲣⲓⲟⲛ
ⲉⲗⲉⲱⲑ ⳾ ⲁⲗⲁⲃⲓⲁ ⳾ ⲁⲑⲁ ⳾ ⲁⲃⲁⲑⲓⲑⲁⲗ ≡ ⲓ̄ⲥ̄ ⲡ̄ⲭ̄ⲥ̄ ⳾
15 ⲡⲉⲡⲱⲣⲕ ⳾ ⲙⲁⲛⲟⲩⲱⲣⲟⲥ ≡ ⲕⲟⲙⲟⲩⲏⲗ ⳾
ⲥⲁⲣⲁⲕ ⳾ ⲙⲉⲑⲁ ≡ ϥⲁⲣⲙⲁⲣⲟⲥ ⳾ ϥⲁⲣⲁⲣⲁ ⳾
ⲉϩⲧⲱⲣⲱ ≡ ⲱⲙⲁⲣ ⳾ ⲁⲇⲱⲛⲁⲓ ⳾ ⲡⲁⲱⲣⲁⲧⲟⲥ ⳾
ⲡⲁⲙⲓⲁⲛⲧⲱⲥ ⳾ ⲡⲁⲙⲏⲧⲣⲁⲧⲱⲥ ⳾ ⲟⲩϥⲁⲙⲓⲏⲗ ⳾
ⲱⲣϥⲁⲛⲓⲗ ⳾ ⲓ̄ⲥ̄ ⲡ̄ⲭ̄ⲥ̄ ⲃⲱⲓⲑⲓ ⲥⲥ ⲙⲛ ⲟⲩⲁ ⲛⲓ̄ⲙ̄
20 ⲉⲧⲛⲁⲫⲱⲣⲓ ⳾ ⲙ̄ⲡⲉⲑ̄ ϩⲟⲩⲣⲓⲧ ≡ ⲉⲧⲉ ⲛⲁⲓ ⲛ-
ⲉⲩⲣⲁⲛ ⳾ ⲁⲃⲓⲏⲗ ⳾ ⲃⲏⲑ ⳾ ⲃⲏⲑⲁ ⳾ ⲃⲏⲑⲁⲛⲉⲓ ⳾
ⲁⲛⲁⲏⲗ · ⲉⲣⲓⲏⲗ ⳾ ⲭⲟⲩⲙⲁⲭⲁ ≡ ⲙⲁⲛⲟⲛ ⳾
ⲙⲁⲛⲁⲃⲁ ≡ ⲓ̄ⲥ̄ ⲡⲉⲭ̄ⲥ̄ : ⲣⲁⲉⲓⲥ ⲥⲥ ⳾ ⲁⲓⲱ ⲧⲁⲭⲏ
ⲥⲁⲃⲁⲭⲱⲣⲓⲏⲗ ⳾ ⲥⲁⲣⲓⲏⲗ ⳾ ⲥⲏⲣⲓⲏⲗ ⳾
25 ϩⲣⲟⲩⲏⲗ ⳾ ⲙⲁⲣⲙⲁⲣⲟⲩⲏⲗ ⳾ ⲥⲁⲃⲁⲱⲑ ⳾
ⲃⲁⲑⲟⲩⲏⲗ ⳾ ⲙⲓⲭⲁⲏⲗ · ⲅⲁⲃⲣⲓⲏⲗ · ϩⲣⲁⲫⲁⲏⲗ · ⲥⲟⲩⲣⲓⲏⲗ · ⲍⲉⲧⲉⲕⲓⲏⲗ · ⲥⲁⲗⲁⲑⲓⲏⲗ

---

2 *l.* ⲉ⳾ⲧⲉⲧⲛ-ⲉ-ⲣⲟⲉⲓⲥ | *i.e.* σῶμα | *l.* (δεῖνα) (δεῖνα) ‖ **3** *i.e.* ˢⲙ̄ⲙⲱ⳾ⲧⲛ ‖ **3–4** *i.e.* ˢⲛ̄-ⲛⲉⲓ-ⲣⲁⲛ ‖ **5** *i.e.* ˢⲙ̄-ⲡⲉ-ⲑⲩⲥⲓⲁⲥⲧⲏⲣⲓⲟⲛ *i.e.* θυσιαστήριον ‖ **8** *i.e.* ˢⲉ⳾ⲕ-ⲉ-ⲣⲟⲉⲓⲥ | *l.* (δεῖνα) (δεῖνα) ‖ **9–11** *i.e.* ἅγιος ἅγιος ἅγιος κύριος Σαβαώθ πλήρης ὁ οὐρανὸς καὶ ἡ γῆ τῆς ἁγίας δόξης σου ‖ **11** *i.e.* ἀμήν | *l.* ι(ⲏⲥⲟⲩ)ⲥ | *l.* χ(ⲣⲓⲥⲧό)ⲥ | *i.e.* βοηθεῖν ‖ **12** *i.e.* ˢⲛ̄-ⲛⲓ-ⲣⲁⲛ ‖ **14** *l.* ι(ⲏⲥⲟⲩ)ⲥ | *i.e.* χ(ⲣⲓⲥⲧό)ⲥ ‖ **18** ⲱⲣϥⲁⲛⲏⲗ Meyer | ⲡⲁⲙⲏⲧⲣⲁⲧⲱⲥ second ⲁ corrected from ⲓ by erasure and overwriting ? ‖ **19** *l.* ι(ⲏⲥⲟⲩ)ⲥ ⲡⲉ-χ(ⲣⲓⲥⲧό)ⲥ | *i.e.* βοηθεῖν | *l.* (δεῖνα) (δεῖνα) ‖ **20** *i.e.* φορεῖν ‖ **23** *l.* ι(ⲏⲥⲟⲩ)ⲥ ⲡⲉ-χ(ⲣⲓⲥⲧό)ⲥ | *l.* (δεῖνα) (δεῖνα) | *i.e.* ταχύ ‖ **25** ϩⲣⲟⲩⲏⲗ : "Ruēl" Meyer

Sēntalalas, Sēntalalia, that you protect the body ⟨of⟩ NN, child of NN, yea! I adjure you, O Nine Guardians, by these blessed *names, which are on the right side |⁵ of the altar of the Father, which are *Sabaoth, Mēthēmōn, Soumithion, Perikhē, Akramata, Taektōr, Fmiēl, Santalalia, may you protect NN, child of NN, yea!

|^Greek *Holy, holy, holy Lord Sabaoth, |¹⁰ heaven and earth are full of ⟨your⟩ holy glory, amen!

|^Coptic Jesus Christ, help him, by the power of these blessed names, which are Abia, Ephikhē, Arthasa, Abaktani, Ourion, Eleōth, Alabia, Atha, Abathithal, Jesus Christ, |¹⁵ Pepōrk, Manoušros, Komouēl, Sarak, Metha, Farmaros, Pharara, Ehtōrō, Ōmar, *Adonai, Paōratos, Pamiantōs, Pamētratōs, Ouphamiēl, Ōrphanil! Jesus Christ, help NN, child of NN, and all |²⁰ who will carry the Nine Guardians, whose names are Abiēl, Bēth, Bētha, Bēthanei, Anaēl, Eriēl, Khoumakha, Manon, Manaba! Jesus Christ, watch over NN, child of NN, yea, quickly! Sabaxōriēl, Sariēl, Sēriēl, |²⁵ Hrouēl, Marmarouēl, Sabaoth, Bathouēl, *Michael, *Gabriel, *Raphael, *Suriel, Zedekiēl, Salathiēl,

---

6–7. ⲙⲏⲑⲏⲙⲱⲛ, ⲥⲟⲩⲙⲓⲑⲓⲟⲛ, ⲡⲉⲣⲓⲭⲏ, ⲁⲕⲣⲁⲙⲁⲧⲁ : **"Mēthēmōn, Soumithion, Perikhē, Akramata"** Apparently variants of the names of the *Four Living Creatures of Revelation 4.6–8, often given in the Coptic and Nubian tradition as variants of ⲙⲉⲗⲓⲧⲱⲛ, ⲥⲟⲩⲣⲟⲩⲑⲓⲟⲛ, ⲁⲅⲣⲁⲙⲙⲁⲧⲁⲡ, and ⲡⲁⲣⲁⲙⲩⲣⲁ; cf. Tsakos 2014. For the specific form of the first name, cf. the notes to p. 11 l. 7.

13–14. ⲁⲣⲑⲁⲥⲁ ⁓ ⲁⲃⲁⲕⲧⲁⲛⲓ : **"Arthasa, Abaktani"** Cf. σαβαχθανί (sabakhthani), one of the last words of Jesus on the cross in Mark 15.34, Matthew 27.46.

17–18. ⲱⲙⲁⲣ ⁓ ⲁⲇⲱⲛⲁⲓ, ⲡⲁⲱⲣⲁⲧⲟⲥ, ⲡⲁⲙⲓⲁⲛⲧⲱⲥ, ⲡⲁⲙⲏⲧⲣⲁⲧⲱⲥ : **"Ōmar, Adonai, Paōratos, Pamiantōs, Pamētratōs"** Perhaps understand the Greek words ἀόρατος ("unseen"), ἀμίαντος ("undefiled"), ἄμετρος or ἀμέτρητος (both "immeasurable"; or less likely, ἄμητρος, "without mother"), prefixed by the definite article π-. The initial word may be "mār" (Aramaic for "Lord"), preceded by the Greek or Aramaic vocative particle ō (ὦ, ⲁⲓ), i.e., "O Lord Adonai" (see Meyer 1996: 94–95; Gardner 2023b: 118).

18–19. ⲟⲩⲫⲁⲙⲓⲏⲗ, ⲱⲣⲫⲁⲛⲓⲗ : **"Ouphamiēl, Ōrphanil"** Cf. ⲱⲣⲫⲁⲙⲓⲏⲗ (Ōrphamiēl), described as the "great finger on the right hand of the Father" on p. 14 l. 13 of this text.

page 16 (flesh)
ⲁⲛⲁⲏⲗ ⸗ ⲓ̅ⲥ̅ ⲡⲉⲭ̅ⲥ̅ ⵁ ⲃⲱⲓⲑⲓ ⲥ̿ⲥ̿
ϩⲓⲧⲉⲛ ϭⲁⲙ ⸗ ⲛⲉⲩⲛⲓⲣⲁⲛ ⸗ ⲧⲁⲣⲁⲙⲓⲏⲗ · ⲉⲥⲕⲉϩⲱⲏⲗ ⸗ ⲙⲉⲥⲱⲃ ⸗
ⲙⲉⲙⲟⲓ ⸗ ⲓ̅ⲥ̅ ⲡⲉⲭ̅ⲥ̅ · ⲕⲉⲣⲁⲉⲓⲥ ⲥ̿ⲥ̿ ⲁⲓⲱ ⲁⲓⲱ
5 ⲙⲛ ⲟⲩⲁ ⲛⲓⲙ · ⲉⲧⲛⲁϥⲱⲣⲓ ⵁ ⲡⲉⲥⲱ†ⲟⲩⲛ
ⲙⲁⲣⲉϥϣⲱⲡⲉ ⸗ ⲛⲑⲉ ⲙ̇ⲡϣⲏⲛ ⸗
ⲉⲡⲱⲛⲁϩ ⸗ ϩⲉⲛ ⲙⲏⲧⲉ ⲡⲁⲣⲁ†ⲱⲥ ⸗ ⲁⲓⲱ
ⲧⲉⲛϭⲓⲛⲉⲣϩⲱⲃ ⵁ ⲥϩⲁⲓ ⵁ ⲛⲁⲥⲁⲃⲣⲁⲛ ⸗ ϩⲓ ⲁⲣⲭⲏ ⲛⲉⲣ̄ⲡ
ϩⲓ ⲁⲗⲙⲁⲁⲩⲁⲣⲧ ⲉⲩⲁⲣⲣⲏⲕ ⵁ ⲙⲁⲣⲟⲩ ⲉϫϩⲟⲩ
10 ⲥϩⲁⲓ ⲟⲛ ⲉⲩⲁⲗϭⲉⲉⲙ ⸗ ⲓⲁⲁⲩ ⲉⲃⲁⲗ · ϣⲁⲩ·ⲁϥ · ⲉⲧ
ⲡⲙⲟⲁⲩ ⲛⲁⲧⲑⲉⲗⲓⲕⲟⲛ ⸗ ⲓ̅ⲩ̅ ⲟⲛ ⵁ ⲁⲣⲭⲏ · ⲉϫⲱⲱⲙⲓ
ⲉⲡⲙⲁ† ⲉⲛϭⲁⲗⲉϩ ⸗ ⲟⲩⲗⲁⲙⲉ ⲕⲱⲭⲱⲥ ⸗
ⲃⲏⲑ ⲉ†ⲉⲣⲟⲟⲩⲛⲓ ⸗ ⲉⲡⲙⲁ† ⲉⲛ·ϭⲁⲗⲉϩ ⸗ ⲑⲩ ⸗
ⲙⲁⲥ†ⲭⲓ ⵁ ⲁⲗⲟⲩⲑ ⵁ ⲥⲧⲏⲣ̇ⲝ ⵁⵁ 〚 . 〛 ⲙⲟⲩⲥⲭⲁⲧⲉⲛ ≡ ⲙⲟⲟⲩ
15 ⲁⲗⲙⲉⲁⲣⲧⲉ 〚ⲉ〛 ⲁϥϫⲱⲕ ⲉⲃⲟⲗ · ⲕⲁⲗⲱⲥ ⵁ ϩⲁⲙⲏⲛ

ⲁⲡⲁϩⲏⲧ ⲧⲁⲟⲩⲁ ⲉⲃⲁⲗ ⲛⲟⲩϣⲁϫⲉ · ⲉⲛⲁⲛⲟⲩϥ
†ⲛⲁϫⲱ ⲁⲛⲁⲕ ⵁ ⲉⲛⲁϩⲣⲃⲏⲩⲉ ⵁ ⲉⲡⲉⲣⲣⲟ ⵁ ⲡⲁⲗⲁⲥ
ⲟⲩⲕⲁϣ ⲛⲕⲣⲁⲙⲙⲁⲧⲉⲩⲥ ⵁ ⲣⲉϥϭⲉⲡⲏ ⲉϥⲥϩⲁⲓ
ⲛⲉⲥⲱϥ ⲡⲁⲣⲁ ⲛⲉϣⲏⲣⲉ ⲧⲏⲣⲟⲩ ⲛ̅ⲣⲱⲙⲉ ⲕⲉⲱⲗ
20 ⲡⲉⲥⲛⲟⲃ ⸗ ⲥ̿ⲥ̿ ⲙⲓⲭⲁⲏⲗ · ⲅⲁⲃⲣⲓⲏⲗ · ϩⲣⲁⲫⲁⲏⲗ ⸗
ⲥⲟⲩⲣⲓⲏⲗ · ⲥⲁⲣⲁⲑⲓⲏⲗ · ⲍⲉⲧⲉⲕⲓⲏⲗ · ⲁⲛⲁⲏⲗ ⸗
ⲥⲱⲧⲱⲣ ⸗ ⲥⲁⲃⲁⲱⲑ ⵁ ⲡⲁⲛⲧⲱⲣ ⸗ ⲓ̅ⲥ̅ ⲓ̅ⲥ̅ ⲓ̅ⲥ̅ ⲡⲭ̅ⲥ̅ ⲡ-
ⲥⲱⲧⲏⲣ ⸗ ⲉⲙⲙⲁⲛⲟⲩⲏⲗ ⸗ ⲁ·ⲣⲉⲧⲱ ⸗ ⲁⲇⲱⲛⲁⲓ ⸗
ⲙⲉⲑⲉⲙⲱⲛ ⸗ ⲕⲉⲱⲗ · ⲡⲉ·ⲥⲛⲟⲃ ⲥ̿ⲥ̿ ⲁⲓⲱ ⲁⲓⲱ
25 ⲧⲉⲛⲏⲧ ⵁ ⲉⲗⲱⲉⲓ ⵁ ⲱⲧⲉⲣⲁ ⵁ ⲉⲗⲏⲙⲁⲥ ⸗
ⲧⲱⲣⲁⲥ ⸗ ⲥⲁⲃⲁⲱⲑ ⸗ ⲃⲱⲓⲑⲓ ⸗ ⲉⲩⲣⲁⲉⲓⲥ · ⲉⲕ† ⸗
ⲛⲟⲩⲧⲁⲗϭⲁ ϩⲉⲛ ⲥ̿ⲥ̿ ⲁⲓⲁ ⲁⲓⲁ ⲧⲁⲭⲏ ⲧⲁⲭⲏ ⸗

---

1 *l.* ⲓ(ⲏⲥⲟⲩ)ⲥ ⲡⲉ-χ(ριστό)ς | *i.e.* βοηθεῖν | *l.* (δεῖνα) (δεῖνα) double supralinear stroke in papyrus ‖ **2** *i.e.* ᔆⲡ-ϭⲁⲙ | *i.e.* ᔆⲛ̄-ⲛⲓ-ⲣⲁⲛ : *i. e.g.* ⲛ(ⲉ)ⲛⲓⲣⲁⲛ Meyer ‖ **4** *l.* ⲓ(ⲏⲥⲟⲩ)ⲥ ⲡⲉ-χ(ριστό)ς | *i.e.* ᔆⲉ⸗ⲕ-ⲉ-ⲣⲟⲉⲓⲥ | *l.* (δεῖνα) (δεῖνα) ‖ **5** *i.e.* φορεῖν | *i.e.* ζῴδιον | **7** *i.e.* ᔆϩⲛ̄ ⲧ-ⲙⲏⲧⲉ ⲙ̄-ⲡ-ⲡⲁⲣⲁⲇⲉⲓⲥⲟⲥ *i.e.* παράδεισος ‖ **8** *i.e.* ᔆⲧ-ϭⲓ-ⲛ-ⲣ̄-ϩⲱⲃ, ϭ corrected from ⲟ by overwriting | *i.e.* الزعفران *az-zaʿfarān* | *l.* ἀρχή ⲛ̄-ⲏⲣⲡ : ⲁⲣⲭⲏ ⲛⲉϩ, ⲁⲣⲭⲏ ⲛⲉⲣⲡ less likely Meyer ‖ **9** *i.e.* الماورد *al-māward* | ورق *waraq*, second ⲣ corrected from ⲏ by overwriting ‖ **10** *i.e.* الجام *al-ǧām* : "a cup (?)" Meyer | *l.* (ⲁⲡⲉ) ? *cf.* note ‖ **11** *i.e.* *ἀνθηλιακόν or ἀνατολικόν ? see note p. 17 ll. 25–27 : "spell-free (?)" Meyer | ⲓ̅ⲩ̅ *l.* γρ(άφειν) ? : "write (?)" or *l.* ἴδιον Meyer | *l.* ἀρχή (ⲛ̄-ⲏⲣⲡ) : probably (ⲛ) ⲁⲣⲭⲏ (ⲛⲉϩ?) Meyer ‖ **12** *i.e.* ᔆⲛ̄-ⲧ-ϭⲁⲗⲁϩⲧ | *i.e.* ᔆⲟⲩ-χλαμύς ⲛ̄-κόκκος ? : "... linen thread (?)" or *i.e.* ᔆ(ⲙⲟⲣ)ⲟⲩ ⲙⲁϩⲕⲱⲕ ϩⲱⲥ Meyer ‖ **13** ⲃⲏⲑ ⲉ†ⲉⲣⲟⲟⲩⲛⲓ corrected from ⲃⲏⲟ by overwriting *i.e.* ᔆⲃⲏⲧ ⲛ̄-ⲣⲟⲟⲩⲛⲉ | ⲉⲡⲙⲁ† flourish on left part of † resembling ϲ | *i.e.* ᔆⲛ̄-ⲧ-ϭⲁⲗⲁϩⲧ | *l.* θυ(σία) ‖ **14** *i.e.* μαστίχη | *i.e.* العود *al-ʿūd* | *i.e.* στύραξ | *i.e.* μοσχάτον | ⲙⲟⲁⲩ Meyer ‖ **15** *i.e.* الماورد *al-māward* | *i.e.* καλῶς | *i.e.* ἀμήν ‖ **18** *i.e.* γραμματεύς ‖ **19** *i.e.* παρά | *i.e.* ᔆⲉ⸗ⲕⲉ-ⲱⲗ | **19–20** ⲕⲉⲱⲗ ⲡⲉⲥⲛⲟⲃ : "you must stop the flow of blood" Meyer ‖ **20** *l.* (δεῖνα) (δεῖνα) ‖ **22** *i.e.* σωτήρ | *l.* παντ(οκράτ)ωρ | *l.* ⲓ(ⲏⲥⲟⲩ)ⲥ (three times) | *l.* χ(ριστό)ς ‖ **23** *i.e.* σωτήρ ‖ **24** *i.e.* ᔆⲉ⸗ⲕⲉ-ⲱⲗ | ⲕⲉⲱⲗ · ⲡⲉ·ⲥⲛⲟⲃ : "you must stop the flow of blood" Meyer | *l.* (δεῖνα) (δεῖνα) ‖ **26** *i.e.* βοηθεῖ ‖ **26–27** *i.e.* ᔆⲛ̄⸗ⲅ-† ⲛ̄-ⲟⲩ-ⲧⲁⲗϭⲟ ‖ **27** *l.* (δεῖνα) (δεῖνα) | *i.e.* ταχύ (twice)

Anael! Jesus Christ, help NN, child of NN, by the power of these names, Taramiēl, Eskehōēl, Mesōb, Memoi! Jesus Christ, may you protect NN, child of NN, yea, yea, |⁵ and all who will carry this image! May he be like the Tree of Life in ⟨the⟩ middle ⟨of⟩ Paradise, yea!"

The procedure: draw with saffron and wine of the *first fruits and rose water on paper. Bind them upon them. |¹⁰ Draw again upon a platter, wash them off, pour it on the head?; sun-facing? water. Draw? again ⟨with wine of the⟩ first fruits upon a sheet, upon the shoulder of ⟨the⟩ *pot. ⟨Wear⟩ a scarlet cloak?. ⟨A⟩ virgin palm branch on the shoulder of ⟨the⟩ pot. Offering: *mastic, *agarwood, *styrax, *musk incense, water, |¹⁵ rose water. It is completely finished. Amen.

My heart has uttered a good word. I, myself, will speak of my works to the king, my tongue ⟨like⟩ a scribe's pen writing quickly: he is more beautiful than all the children of men! May you contain |²⁰ the blood ⟨of⟩ NN, child of NN! *Michael, *Gabriel, *Raphael, *Suriel, Sarathiēl, Zetekiēl, Anaēl, Sōtōr, *Sabaoth, Almighty, Jesus, Jesus, Jesus Christ the saviour, Emmanuel, Aretō, *Adonai, Methemōn, may you contain the blood ⟨of⟩ NN, child of NN, yea, yea! |²⁵ Tenēt, *Eloei, Ōtera, *Elēmas, Tōras, Sabaoth, help with protection, and give healing to NN, child of NN, yea, yea, quickly, quickly!

---

8. ⲛⲁⲥⲁⲃⲣⲁⲛ : **"with saffron"** For the use of ink made from saffron in Coptic magic, see Richter 2023: 166–68.

10. ⲁⲗⲟϭⲉⲙ : **"platter"** We understand this to be a writing of Arabic الجام *al-ǧām*, *cf.* *platter in the glossary, and Richter 2016a: 155. Meyer suggests that the word is perhaps related to the word "alchemy". Meyer also notes a suggestion by Beltz that it comes from ⲕⲁⲙ/ϭⲉⲙ ("reed, rush") and to a suggestion by Emmel of ϭ(ⲉ)ⲗⲙⲁⲓ ("jar, vase"; Meyer 1996: 50, n. 16, 10).

10. ☉ (ⲁⲡⲉ) : **"head"** We follow Gardner 2023b: 119 in understanding this as a drawing of a round face with two triangular ears on top, to represent the word ⲁⲡⲉ ("head"). Such an ideographic writing would seem to be unparalleled in the Coptic magical corpus, but would fit the context well. Meyer suggests that the drawing is rather "a pot or other vessel with two handles". Perhaps compare *GEMF* 34/*PGM* LXII col. 1 l. 1, in which a drawing of a lamp stands in for the Greek λύχνος ("lamp").

11. ⲛⲁⲧⲟⲉⲗⲓⲕⲟⲛ : **"sun-facing?"** *Cf.* the note to p. 17 ll. 25–27.

12. ⲉⲡⲙⲁϯ ⲉⲛϭⲁⲗⲉϩ : **"on the shoulder of the pot"** Alternatively understand an unexpected writing of ⲙⲁⲁϫⲉ, "ear", but with the specific sense of "handle (of the pot)" (Crum CD 212b–213a).

12. ⲟⲩⲗⲁⲙⲉ ⲕⲱⲭⲱⲥ : **"scarlet cloak"** *Cf.* Matthew 27.28 in which Jesus is dressed in a scarlet cloak (ⲛⲟⲩⲭⲗⲁⲙⲩⲥ ⲛⲕⲟⲕⲕⲟⲥ; Horner 1911a: 330), a symbol of royal status, by the Roman soldiers mocking him.

16–19. "My heart has uttered a good word. I, myself, will speak of my works to the king, my tongue ⟨like⟩ a scribe's pen writing quickly: he is more beautiful than all the children of men!" A direct citation of Psalm 44 (45) 2–3: ⲁⲡⲁϩⲏⲧ ⲧⲁⲩⲟ ⲉⲃⲟⲗ ⲛⲟⲩϣⲁϫⲉ ⲉⲛⲁⲛⲟⲩϥ ϯⲛⲁϫⲱ ⲁⲛⲟⲕ ⲛⲛⲁϩⲃⲏⲩⲉ ⲙⲡⲣⲣⲟ ⲡⲁⲗⲁⲥ ⲟⲩⲕⲁϣ ⲛ̄ⲅⲣⲁⲙⲙⲁⲧⲉⲩⲥ ⲡⲉ ⲛⲣⲉϥϭⲉⲡⲏ ⲉϥⲥϩⲁⲓ ⲉⲛⲉⲥⲱϥ ϩⲙ ⲡⲉϥⲥⲁ ⲡⲁⲣⲁ ⲛϣⲏⲣⲉ ⲛ̄ⲛⲣⲱⲙⲉ (Budge 1898: 49 as verses 1–2).

22–26. c̄ⲱⲧⲟⲣ, ⲁ̄ⲣⲉⲧⲱ, ⲧⲉⲛⲏⲧ, ⲱ̄ⲧⲉⲣⲁ, ⲧⲱⲣⲁⲥ̄ : **"Sōtōr, Aretō, Tenēt, Tōras"** Variants of the *Sator names, whose canonical Latin forms are *Sator Arepo Tenet Opera Rota*s.

24. ⲙ̄ⲉⲑⲉⲙⲱ̄ⲛ : **"Methemōn"** *Cf.* the note to p. 11 l. 7.

page 17 (flesh)

[magical text and figures]

²ΑΝΑΛΜΕΑ · ΜΕΝ ΙΔ :

²⁵ϩΙ ΜΑΟΥ
²⁶ΝΑΘΕ-
²⁷:ΛΙΚΟΝ =

¹¹ⲱⲱⲱⲱ
¹²ⲱⲱⲱ

Χ̅Ⲥ̅

¹⁷ΜΟΥⲤ-
¹⁸ΧΑΤ-
¹⁹-ⲈΝ
²⁰ⲤΝΟⲂ
²¹ⲈⲖⲈ-
²²Υ
²³ΚΟ-
²⁴Ν

²⁸ΠΙ-
²⁹ΝΑΤ
³⁰ΝΑⲂ-
³¹ⲈⲤⲎ́
³²ⲈⲒⲚ́
³³ΜΟΥϨ
³³ⲈⲢⲈⲠΟΟϨ|

⳨ ⳨ Χ̅ Χ̅ Χ̅
⳨ ⳨ Χ̅ Χ̅ Χ̅ †
† ⳨ † Χ ΜΑⲤΧΙ =
ΑⳈⲞΘ : ⲤⲦⲎⲢϤ̅

ⲠⲞⲤ Ⲓ̅Ⲥ̅ Ⲡ̅Χ̅Ⲥ̅ = † ⲚⲞΥⲤⲞⲞΥⲤ : ⲚⲈⲚⲞΥ · ⲤⲰⲔ ⲈⲤⲀ-
35 ⲐⲎ Ⲛ̅=ⲚⲒⲘ = 55 ⲘⲈ ⲠⲈϤⲘⲀⲚⲈⲢϨⲰⲂ = ⲀⲚⲀⲚⲒ-
    ⲀⲤ = ⲀⲌⲀⲢⲒⲀⲤ = ⲘⲒⲤⲀⲎⲖ = ⲀⲐⲀⲚⲀⲎⲖ = ⲘⲀⲚⲞΥ-
    ⲎⲖ = ⲀⲔⲞΥⲎⲖ = ⲀⲀⲀⲀⲀⲀⲀ = ⲀⲀⲀⲀⲀⲀⲀ ≡
    ⲖⲀⲂⲀⲚⲎⲖ = ⲞΥⲢⲒⲎⲖ = ⲂⲘⲤⲀⲎⲖ = ⲂⲈⲤⲞⲞΥⲤ Ⲉ-
    ϨⲞΥⲚ = ⲚⲈⲚ̅ⲄⲀ ⲚⲒⲘ = ⲈⲒⲦⲈ ϨⲀⲒ† = ⲈⲒⲦⲈ · ⲚⲞΥⲂ
40 ⲈⲒⲦⲈ ϨⲀⲦ ⲈⲒⲦⲈ ⲖⲀⲀΥ Ⲛ̇ⲀⲔⲀⲐⲰⲚ : ⲈⲒ ⲈϨⲞΥ-
    Ⲛ : ⲈⲠⲎⲒ = 55 Χ̅ 55 ⲘⲈ ⲄⲈⲚⲞⲤ ⲦⲎⲢϤ = ⲚⲀⲆⲀⲘ =
    ⲚⲈϤϢⲎⲢⲈ ⲦⲎⲢⲞΥ ⲚⲌⲰⲎ = Ⲙ̇Ⲛ Ⲡ̅Χ̅ⲠⲞ ⲦⲎⲢⲂ
    ⲚⲒⲤⲘⲀⲎⲖ · ⲢⲈⲚⲈϬⲒΧ · ⲘⲈϨ ⲚⲀⲔⲀⲐⲞⲚ ⲚⲒⲘ̅
    ⲈΥⲈⲒⲚⲈ ⲘⲞΟΥ = ⲈΥ† ⲘⲞΟΥ = ⲚⲈϬⲒΧ 55 =
45 ⲀⲒⲞ ⲀⲒⲀ ⲦⲀΧⲎ =

---

3 ⲡⲡⲡⲁⲗⲁⲣϩⲡ Meyer || *above central figure:* l. χ(ριστό)ς || 15 *i.e.* μαστίχη || 16 *i.e.* العود al-'ūd | *i.e.* στύραξ || 17–19 *i.e.* μοσχάτον || 20–24 *i.e.* ˢⲤⲚⲞϤ (Ⲛ-ΟΥ-ϬⲢⲞⲘⲠⲈ) Ⲛ-ⲖⲈΥⲔⲞⲚ see note : "limpid blood" Meyer || 26–27 *i.e.* *ἀνθηλιακόν or ἀνατολικόν ? see note : "spell-free (?)" Meyer || 28–29 *i.e.* πίναξ (?) : or else ⲠⲒⲚⲞΥⲦ 'the (or, this) receptacle" Meyer || 34 *l.* ⲡ-ϫⲞⲈⲒⲤ | *l.* ⲓ(ⲎⲤⲞΥ)Ⲥ ⲡⲉ-χ(ριστό)ς |*i.e.* ˢⲞΥⲤⲞⲞΥⲢⲤ ⲈⲦ-ⲚⲈⲚⲞΥ=Ⲥ || 35 *l.* (δεῖνα) (δεῖνα) "shop" Meyer || 38–39 *i.e.* ˢⲈ=ϥ-ⲉ-ⲤⲰⲞΥϨ=Ⲥ ⲈϨⲞΥⲚ Ⲛ-Ⲛ̅ⲔⲀ || 39 *i.e.* εἴτε (twice) | *i.e.* ˢϨⲞⲒⲦⲈ | *i.e.* εἴτε (twice) || 40 *i.e.* ἀγαθόν || 41 *l.* (δεῖνα) (δεῖνα) (twice) | *i.e.* (υἱός) : ȳc Meyer | *i.e.* γένος || 43 Meyer "of Ismael" or "(of) Nismael" | *i.e.* ˢⲈⲢⲈ-ⲚⲈΥ-ϬⲒΧ | *i.e.* ἀγαθόν || 44 *i.e.* ˢⲈ=Υ-ⲉ-ⲈⲒⲚⲈ Ⲙ̅ⲘⲞ=Υ | *i.e.* ˢⲈ=Υ-ⲉ-† Ⲙ̅ⲘⲞ=Υ | *i.e.* ˢⲈ-Ⲛ-ϬⲒΧ | *l.* (δεῖνα) (δεῖνα) || 45 *i.e.* ταχύ

|¹⁻¹⁰ (*linear kufic*)

|² Analmea Men 14 (*kharaktēr*: Ɔ)

|¹¹ ō ō ō ō ō ō ō, ps ps kh kh kh, ps ps kh kh kh, |¹⁵ ps ps ps kh |*above central figure* Christ

|¹⁵ *Mastic, *agarwood, *styrax, *musk incense. |²⁰ ⟨Write with⟩ blood of ⟨a⟩ white ⟨dove⟩? |²⁵ and sun-facing? water ⟨upon a⟩ glass plate. |³³ When the moon is full.

Lord Jesus Christ, grant a good gathering! Draw before |³⁵ NN, child of NN, and his workshop, Ananias, Azarias, Misaēl, Athanaēl, Manouēl, Akouēl, AAAAAAA, AAAAAAA, Labaēl, Uriel, Bmsaēl! May he gather inside every thing, whether garment or gold |⁴⁰ or silver, or anything ⟨else⟩ good! Come inside the house of NN, son of NN, with all the race of Adam ⟨and⟩ all the children of Zoe and all the offspring of Ishmael, with their hands filled with every good thing! May they bring them, may they put them ⟨into⟩ the hands ⟨of⟩ NN, child of NN, |⁴⁵ yea, yea, quickly!

1–10. An example of 'linear kufic'; see the note to *PCM* I 21 ll. 1–3.

20–24. ⲥⲛⲟⲃ ⲉⲗⲉⲩⲕⲟⲛ : "**blood of ⟨a⟩ white ⟨dove⟩?**" See the note to *PCM* I 17 back ll. 1–5.

25–27. ⲙⲁⲟⲩ ⲛⲁⲑⲉ:ⲗⲓⲕⲟⲛ "**sun-facing water**" This phrase poses problems for editors: in addition to the attestation here and on p. 9 l. 5, p. 16 l. 11, we find the same ingredient as ⲙⲙⲟⲟⲩ ⲛⲁⲑⲉⲗⲉⲕⲟⲛ (BM EA 10414a back ll. 24–25, 43–44; Zellmann-Rohrer 2022a: no. 3; KYP M287); ⲙⲟⲟⲩ ⲛⲁⲛⲑⲏⲗⲓⲟⲛ (*P.Macq.* I 1, p. 13.26–7; KYP M167); ⲙⲟⲩ ⲛⲁⲛⲑⲉⲓⲗⲓⲁⲕⲟ[ⲛ] (unpublished text cited in Drescher 1958: 59); ⲙⲟⲩⲟ ⲁⲛⲑⲏⲣⲓⲕⲟⲛ (Coptic Museum 4959 l. 7 (unpublished; trans. Meyer/Smith 1994: no. 119; KYP M300)); ⲙⲁⲟⲩ ⲛⲁⲑⲗⲏⲧⲟⲛ (P.Monts.Roca.inv. 478 (unpublished; KYP M 409)); perhaps *cf.* ⲙⲟⲟⲩ ⲛⲁⲙⲫⲟⲧⲓⲕⲟⲛ (P.Stras. K 204 + 205 + 282 §2.22 l. 7 (Hevesi 2018; KYP M92)). We follow Drescher (1958: 59–60; *cf.* Zellmann-Rohrer 2022a: 139–140) in understanding a word derived from the Greek ἀντήλιος "opposite the sun", perhaps *ἀνθηλικός or *ἀνθηλιακός; less likely we might understand a form of ἀνατολικόν. As Drescher points out, several early modern Greek texts refer to the use of water drawn from springs flowing east (βρύσις ἀνατολική/τρέχουσα ἄντικρυς τοῦ Ἡλίου; Delatte 1927: 40.13, 43.15; 45.23; 51.12; 430.6–7). Water from a well which has never seen the sun is used in the rituals for Psalms 7, 9, 15, 27, 112 of the *Guide to the Psalms* (Henein/Bianquis 1975); in a Syriac healing text (Cherkashina (Nurullina) 2012: 102)); and a Judaeo-Arabic curse (Naveh/Shaked 1993: Geniza 9 p. 1 l. 15), perhaps offering an alternative understanding of this term. As noted by Zellmann-Rohrer (2022: 140), the final form, ⲁⲙⲫⲟⲧⲓⲕⲟⲛ could be derived from *ἀφωτικόν ("without light"). Alternative derivations for ⲁⲑⲉⲗⲓⲕⲟⲛ and its variants include Preisendanz's (ap. Crum 1934b: 197; *cf.* Meyer 1996: 80) suggestion of ἄθελκτον ("spell free (water)"); Kropp's (1931: II 100; 1930: III 154) suggestion of ἀτ-ὑλικόν ("immaterial (water)"); and Smith's (Meyer/Smith 1994: 241; *cf.* Choat/Gardner 2013: 100–101) suggestion of ἀνθέρικον ("flower (water)").

36–37. ⲙⲁⲛⲟⲩⲏⲗ : "**Manouēl**" *Cf. PCM* I 11 p. 16 ll. 2–4 and accompanying note.

41–43. ⲅⲉⲛⲟⲥ ⲧⲏⲣϥ ⲛⲁⲇⲁⲙ ⲛⲉϣⲏⲣⲉ ⲧⲏⲣⲟⲩ ⲛⲍⲱⲏ ⲙⲛ ⲡⲭⲡⲟ ⲧⲏⲣⲃ ⲛⲓⲥⲙⲁⲏⲗ : "**all the race of Adam ⟨and⟩ all the children of Zoe and all the offspring of Ishmael**" For this phrase, see the notes to p. 7 ll. 12–14. Note that here Adam and Zoe are joined by Ishmael, the son of Abraham and Hagar and ancestor of the Arabs, making it clear that the composer wanted to explicitly include Arabs among the people targeted by the ritual, and perhaps suggesting that he or she was uncertain if they belonged to the category of the "children of Adam and Zoe".

page 18 (hair)

```
ⲥⲁⲃⲁⲱⲑ ⳾ ⲡⲁⲛⲧⲱⲣ ⳾ ϯⲧⲉⲣⲕⲁ ⲙⲙⲁⲕ ⲙⲡⲟ-
ⲟⲩ ⳾ ⲛⲉⲧⲉⲛⲣⲁⲛ ⲙ̅ⲛ ⲧⲉⲛϭⲁⲙ ⳾ ⲙⲛⲉⲧⲉⲛ-
ⲫⲟⲩⲣⲓⲱⲛ ⳾ ⲙⲛ ⲛⲉⲧⲉⲛⲧⲱⲡⲟⲥ ⳾ ⲉⲧⲉⲛϣⲟⲟⲡ
ⲉⲛϩⲏⲧⲟⲩ ⲙⲉ ⲑⲏ ⲧⲁⲧⲉⲛⲱϣⲙ ⲉⲡⲕⲱϩ-
5  ⲧ ⲧⲉⲛⲣⲱ ⲥⲁⲧⲉ ⳾ ⲛⲁⲃⲟⲩⲭⲱⲧⲱⲛ⳾ⲱ-
ⲥⲱⲣ ⳴ ⲡⲉⲣⲟ ⳴ ⲃⲁⲃⲓⲗⲱⲛ ⳾ ϩⲉⲛ ⲧⲉⲛϭⲁⲙ ⳾
ⲙⲓⲭⲁⲏⲗ ⲡⲁⲣⲭⲛⲁⲅⲅⲉⲗⲱⲥ ⳾ ϫⲉⲕⲁⲥ ⳾
ⲧⲉⲧⲉⲛⲱϣⲙ ⲉϣⲉⲙ · ⲡⲕⲱϩⲧ ⲙⲉ ⲧⲉⲩ⳾-
ϩⲉⲙ ϩⲉⲛ ⲥⲥ ⲁⲓⲱ ⲧⲁⲭⲏ ⳾ ⲁⲛⲁⲛⲓⲁⲥ ⳾
10 ⲁⲍⲁⲣⲓⲁⲥ ⳾ ⲙⲓⲥⲁⲏⲗ ⳾ ⲥⲉⲧⲣⲁⲕ ⳴ ⲙⲓⲥⲁⲕ
ⲁⲃⲧⲉⲛⲁⲕⲱ ⳾ ⲗⲁⲗ · ⲃⲟⲩⲗⲁⲗ ⳾ ⲙⲟⲩⲗⲁⲗ ⳾
ⲃⲟⲩⲑⲁ ⳾ ⲃⲁⲕⲉ ≡ ⲁⲩⲗⲉⲥ ⳾ ⲉⲩⲗⲉⲥ ⳾ ⲉⲱ ⳾
ⲥⲱ ⳾ ⲗⲉⲕⲧⲏⲥ ⳾ ⲙⲏⲧⲉ ⳾ ⲃⲓⲧⲉⲃⲟⲓⲑⲓ ≡ ⲛⲉ-
ⲇⲱⲗⲉ ≡ ⲃⲱⲓⲑⲱⲛ ⳾ ⲉⲑⲏ
15
```

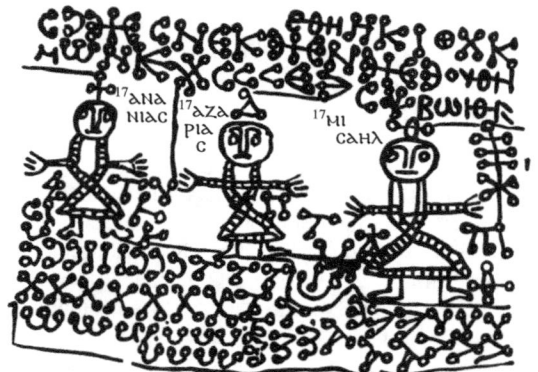

1 *l.* παντ(οκράτ)ωρ ‖ **2** *i.e.* ˢⲛⲉ⳾ⲧⲛ-ⲣⲁⲛ | *i.e.* ˢⲛⲉ⳾ⲧⲛ-ϭⲁⲙ ‖ **2–3** *i.e.* ˢⲙ̄ⲛ̄ ⲛⲉ⳾ⲧⲛ-ⲫⲩⲣⲓⲱⲛ *i.e.* φυ(λακτή)ριον | *i.e.* τόπος ‖ **4** ⲙⲉ ⲑⲏ *i.e.* ˢⲙ̅ⲛ ⲧ-ϩⲉ : "that just as you" Meyer | *i.e.* ˢⲛ̄ⲧⲁ⳾ⲧⲉⲧⲛ̄-ⲱϣⲙ̅ ‖ **5** *i.e.* ˢⲛ̄ⲧⲉ ⲛ-ϩⲣⲱ ⲛ-ⲥⲁⲧⲉ or ⲛ̄ⲧⲉ ⲧ-ϩⲣⲱ ⲛ-ⲥⲁⲧⲉ ‖ **6** *i.e.* ˢⲛⲉⲧⲛ-ϭⲁⲙ | *i.e.* ˢⲛ-ⲃⲁⲃⲩⲗⲱⲛ ‖ **7** *i.e.* ἀρχάγγελος ‖ **8** *i.e.* ˢⲛ̄⳾ⲧⲉⲧⲛ-ⲱϣⲙ̅ | *i.e.* ˢϣⲙ̅- *i.e.* haplography or omission of a section ? ‖ **8–9** *i.e.* ˢⲧ-ϩⲙ̅ⲙⲉ : *i.e.* ˢⲧⲏⲩ ⲙ̄ⲛ ⲧ- "fume (and)" Meyer ‖ **9** *l.* (δεῖνα) (δεῖνα) | *i.e.* ταχύ

*Sabaoth Almighty, I adjure you today by your (pl.) *names and your *powers and your *phylacteries and your *places in which you dwell, and the manner in which you quenched the fire |⁵ of the burning furnaces of Nebuchadnezzar, the king ⟨of⟩ Babylon by the power ⟨of⟩ *Michael the *archangel, that you quench {quench} the fire and the fever in NN, child of NN, yea, quickly! Hananiah, |¹⁰ Azariah, Mishael, Shadrach, Meshach, Abednego, Lal, Boulal, Moulal, Boutha, Bake, Aules, Eules, Eō, Sō, Lektēs, Mēte, Biteboithi, Nedōle, Bōithōn, Ethē!

|*above tableau,* 15 Outhē, Bōithi

|*above three figures,* 17 Hananiah, Azariah, Mishael.

KD, EL, MP & JS, edited from photograph and autopsy; tracings by JS, KD & EL.

---

page 18 ll. 1–17: This page contains a ritual for healing fever which probably consisted of speaking the formula and copying the tableau in order to create an amulet. Both elements draw upon the story of the Three Youths in the Fiery Furnace in Daniel 3, in which the three companions of Daniel were thrown into a burning furnace by Nebuchadnezzar, king of Babylon, for refusing to worship a golden statue he had made, only to be saved by the intervention of an angel who prevented the fire from burning them. The common conception of fever as fire led to the story becoming a popular reference in Christian fever amulets, which often repeat the story or include the names of the Three Youths (Mihálykó 2018a: 53–55; Bélanger Sarrazin forthcoming b); this text finds a particularly close parallel in the applied amulet P.Heid.Inv. Kopt. 564a (Quecke 1963b; KYP M513). Usually we find their original Hebrew names—Hananiah, Azariah, and Mishael—followed by their Chaldaean names—Shadrach, Meshach, and Abednego—and finally a series of names known only from magical texts, here Lal, Boulal, and Moulal (van der Vliet 1991: 236–239). This last series is also found in the *Testament of Solomon* 7.6 (for which see the introduction to *PCM* I 30) as βουλταλά θαλλάλ μελχάλ (*Boultala Thallal Melkhal*), where they are associated with healing fever, but not explicitly with the Three Youths (McCown 1922: 30* ll. 5–6; van der Vliet 1991: 237–239). The image below likewise draws upon the iconography of the Three Youths, depicting them as three figures praying in the orant position with their arms extended to their sides, and three *kharaktēres* (+, Δ, Θ) on their heads where their hats would be in more canonical depictions (cf. Dosoo 2022a: 154–156). The repeated names of the form 'Bōithi' are probably derived from the Greek βοήθει "help".

PCM I 26. *Endoxon* of the Archangel Michael

Arsinoites (Faiyum)　　　　　　　21.1 (H) × 26.9 (W) cm　　　　　　　late X CE

Other references: P.Heid.Inv. Kopt. 686 (formerly P.Heid.Inv. Nr. 1686); TM 100022; KYP M166; Bélanger Sarrazin #137.

Editions: Kropp 1966 (*ed. pr.*) [K].

Translations: Kropp 1966 (German); Meyer in Meyer/Smith 1994: no. 135 [M].

Additional commentary: Bilabel/Grohmann 1934: 392; Quecke 1963b: 247, n. 3; Camplani 2010: 146; Untermann (ed.) 2011: 42–43; Tsakos 2014: 259–261; Mößner/Nauerth 2015: 312, 348–350; Johnston/Gardner 2018; Gardner/Johnston 2019: 51–53; van der Vliet 2020: 273–274; Gardner 2023a: 56–63; Gardner 2023b: 123–134 [G]; Bélanger Sarrazin forthcoming a: chapter 4; Preininger forthcoming c: chapter 7.

Present location: Heidelberg, Institut für Papyrologie.

Image: https://doi.org/10.11588/diglit.39754

Linguistic description: Sahidic with Middle Egyptian features.

Contents:

Original use: Lectionary containing Pauline Epistles, including:

1. Bifolio 1 flesh (pp. 2 + 19): col. 1 ll. 1–7: Philippians 4.9 (no. 12; day 16)
2. Bifolio 1 flesh (pp. 2 + 19): col. 1 ll. 8–36, col. 2 ll. 1–10: 1 Corinthians 1.18–24 (no. 13; day 17 of Thout?)
3. Bifolio 1 flesh (pp. 2 + 19): col. 2 ll. 11–36: 1 Timothy 6.11–13 (no. 14; day 20)
4. Bifolio 1, hair (pp. 1 + 20): col. 1 ll. 1–29: 1 Timothy 6.13–16 (no. 14; day 20)
5. Bifolio 1, hair (pp. 1 + 20): col. 1 ll. 29–36, col. 2 ll. 1–36: Hebrews 9.2–7 (no. 15)
6. p. 9, flesh col. 1 ll. 1–18, col. 2 ll. 1–2: 2 Corinthians 10.4–9 (no. 19; day 25)
7. Bifolio 2, flesh (pp. 11 + 18): col. 1 ll. 1–4: Hebrews 13.6 (no. 20?)
8. Bifolio 2, flesh (pp. 11 + 18): col. 1 ll. 5–36, col. 2 ll. 1–36: Philippians 3.6–14? (no. 21; day 26)

Re-use (palimpsest):

9. p. 2, l. 1–p. 15, l. 26 (1–249): *Endoxon* of the Archangel Michael (KYP T17)
10. p. 15, ll. 27–29 (250–251): Instructions for using the formula as an exorcism (KYP T312)
11. p. 15, ll. 29–31 (252): Instructions to free someone from prison (KYP T313)
12. p. 15, ll. 32–33 (253): Instructions for favour (KYP T314)
13. p. 16, ll. 1–2 (254): Instructions for healing (KYP T315)
14. p. 16, ll. 3–5 (255): Instructions for reconciliation (KYP T905)
15. p. 16, ll. 6–8 (256): Instructions to unbind a man cursed with impotence (KYP T311)
16. p. 16, ll. 9–12 (257): Instructions for someone who has been given a potion (KYP T316)
17. p. 16, ll. 13–14 (258): Instructions for healing pain (KYP T1316)
18. p. 16, ll. 15–17 (259): Instructions for protection in the desert (KYP T1317)
19. p. 16, ll. 18–20 (260): Instructions to ensure a woman's fidelity (KYP T1318)
20. p. 16, ll. 21–23 (261): Instructions for reconciliation (KYP T752)
21. p. 16, ll. 24–25 (262): Instructions to make a criminal unrecognised (?) (KYP T1319)
22. p. 16, ll. 26–27 (263): Instructions for treating sleeplessness (KYP T1320)

23. p. 16, ll. 28–30 (264): Instructions for favour before superior (KYP T1321)
24. p. 16, ll. 31–32 (265): Instructions for making a village inhabited (KYP T1322)
25. p. 16, ll. 33–36 (266): Instructions to curse a workshop (KYP T1323)
26. p. 17, ll. 1–3 (267): Instructions for a curse of unconsciousness (KYP T1324)
27. p. 17, ll. 3–6 (268): Instructions for reconciliation (KYP T1325)
28. p. 17, ll. 7–9 (269): Instructions to ensure a man's fidelity (KYP T1326)
29. p. 17, ll. 10–12 (270): Instructions for the protection of livestock from magic (KYP T1327)
30. p. 17, ll. 13–16 (271): Instruction to prevent death of children (KYP T1328)
31. p. 17, ll. 17–23 (272), ll. 24–29 (273): Instructions for creating an amulet (KYP T1329)
32. p. 17, ll. 30–35 (272–274): Image of Michael accompanied by two Powers (KYP T331)

Complete and undamaged single-quire parchment codex of 20 pages, containing the *Endoxon of the Archangel Michael*, an invocation for protection from sickness and evil influences, followed by a series of ritual prescriptions. The codex is part of the archive known as the 'Heidelberg Library', written in the hand of Deacon Iōhannēs, allowing it to be dated to the late tenth century (see pp. 259–263).

The manuscript was acquired as part of the lot purchased for the University of Heidelberg by Carl Schmidt from the Cairo antiquities dealer Maurice Nahman in October 1933.[1] An edition was initially planned by Friedrich Bilabel,[2] who apparently kept the manuscript (along with many others) in his home. This edition was never completed; Bilabel, an active member of the Nazi Party from 1935, was involved in military service from 1939 to 1942, having volunteered in 1937. He was killed in 1945 during the American advance after retirement to the town of Wallerstein.[3] The manuscript subsequently passed into the hands of his family. Karl Preisendanz, head of the Heidelberg papyrus collection, contacted Bilabel's son-in-law in 1950 to enquire about its whereabouts, but without success.[4] Fortunately, Schmidt had initially offered the manuscript to his student Kropp (together with *PCM* I 25), who had made a transcription of it; this transcription was published in 1966 as *Der Lobpreis des Erzengels Michael*.[5] From the 1980s, Bilabel's estate began to sell some of the manuscripts which he had taken, and in 1998, his grandson offered the *Endoxon* to the University of Heidelberg for 100,000 Deutsche Marks. A second offer of 80–100,000 (apparently euros) was made in 2008. The legal claims of the University of Heidelberg were judged to be too difficult to enforce, and in 2010 the manuscript was bought back by the University for €12,000.[6] It is now, once again, in the University's papyrus collection.[7]

The manuscript is a palimpsest written over a lectionary of Pauline epistles written in two columns—still clearly visible on pages 1, 18, 19, and 20, the blank

---

[1] Seider 1964: 163; Gardner/Johnston 2019: 31–32.
[2] Bilabel/Grohmann 1934: 392.
[3] Préaux 1948; Seider 1982; Chaniotis/Thaler 2006; Bierbrier 2012: 58.
[4] Jayme 2009; Jördens 2010a: 142.
[5] Kropp 1966: 5.
[6] For the history of the recovery, see Jayme 2009; Jayme 2010; Jördens 2010a & b.
[7] *Cf.* Jördens in Untermann 2011: 5; Schmelz 2018: 3.

pages of the re-used text. As recognised by Gardner, this older lectionary is the same as that used to create *PCM* I 25, written the same formal bimodular and bilinear literary hand, perhaps datable to the ninth century.[8] Each section of the lectionary is marked off by *ekthesis* of the first letter. The dates on which the passages are to be read are decorated with horizontal lines, although these are identified only by the ordinal number of the day of the month, and the month is not named. The identification of all passages of the lectionary is necessary before a full reconstruction can be attempted, but bifolio 1 flesh of *PCM* I 26 seems to continue bifolio 1 flesh of *PCM* I 25, since it concludes the passage from Philippians. This is then followed by the hair side of bifolio 1, then by page 9 (the lower half of an original folio), directly followed by bifolio 2 flesh and then hair. The reading of 1 Corinthians 1.18–24 on the seventeeth day of the month corresponds to the reading on the 17th Thout in the lectionary Pierpont Morgan M573 from Hamouli, dating to the ninth or early tenth century, both geographically and temporally close to this lectionary.[9] Certain other readings identifiable in *PCM* I 25 also seem to correspond to those in M573,[10] even though this latter manuscript contains only the readings for the major feasts, while that of *PCM* I 25 & 26 contains the readings from the Pauline epistles for nearly every day. The reading of Hebrews 9.2–7, although the date is lost, might correspond to the reading of verses 2–8 on the 21st Tobi in M573.[11] However, 2 Corinthians 10.4–8 is associated in M573 with the 15th Hathor, while verses 4–9 (and perhaps more of the chapter) in this manuscript are listed for the 25th day of a month.[12] There are further problems—as noted by Quecke, the reading of 2 Timothy 2.3–13 on the 15th day of a month on *PCM* I 25 bifolio 1 hair would correspond well with the reading of the same passage (to verse 14a) on the 15th Hathor in M573.[13] This reading must shortly precede in the cycle that of 1 Corinthians 1.18–24 on *PCM* I 26 bifolio 1 flesh col. 1 ll. 8–36, associated with 17th Thout. Yet Thout is the first month, and Hathor the third, so that the sequence is impossible. It may be safer to assume that all of the surviving passages were for the month of Thout, although more work on this question is required.

The present codex is made of 3 bifolios and 4 sheets, formed from either folding the original codex sheets in two, or cutting them in half.[14] Only pages 2–17 are written, in brown ink of plant origin.[15] Each page has between 25 and 36 lines and there are roughly 25–30 characters per line. The script, dialectal features, and ink

---

[8] Gardner 2023a: 55–56; *cf.* Quecke 1972: 6 on the underlying text of *PCM* I 25.
[9] Depuydt 1993: 70.
[10] Quecke 1972: 12–16.
[11] Depuydt 1993: 73.
[12] Depuydt 1993: 71.
[13] Depuydt 1993: 71; *cf.* Quecke 1972: 16–17.
[14] The bifolios are: pp. 1 + 20/2 + 19; 11 + 18/12 + 17; 13 + 16/14 + 15. The individual sheets are: pp. 3/4, 5/6, 7/8, 9/10.
[15] For the ink used by this copyist, see the discussion on p. 261.

are all those typical of Iōhannēs (see pp. 260–262). The writing is very dense, and the margins extremely narrow.

The *Endoxon* itself is a prayer attributed to the archangel Michael, written on the first 14 pages of the codex (pp. 2–15).[16] It begins with a brief narrative in which Michael greets and praises God, before calling upon the angelic powers to help him sing his praises. This is followed by recurrent sequences of adjurations of and calls to God to come and send his power over water and oil to be used in the following procedure, interspersed with the invocation of various authorities—heavenly beings and the body parts and attributes of God—and a recounting of salvation history, from the creation of Adam to the resurrection of Jesus. It ends with a blessing formula, followed by 22 ritual prescriptions (pp. 15–17). These generally involve the speaking of the *Endoxon* over water, oil, or the image of Michael and his powers which appears at the end of the manuscript, which then become the "applied objects" used to transfer the power of the ritual. An unpublished copy of the *Endoxon* belongs to the Collège de France (KYP M573),[17] containing only a single procedure, directly related to the healing/exorcistic goals explicit in the text of the prayer, making it clear that the multiple prescriptions in the Heidelberg copy are a later accretion. This 'polypractical' format—a single long prayer with multiple recipes which make use of the same prayer—is quite common in the Coptic magical corpus (*cf.* p. 22). In terms of its content, the *Endoxon* recalls the account of salvation history which appears following the *Sanctus in liturgical anaphoras of the 'West Syrian' or 'Antiochene' type, which likewise recounts salvation history from fall of Adam and Eve. Particularly close is an anonymous anaphora contained in the Euchologium of the White Monastery.[18] The presence of this type in Egypt is likely a result of the influence of the Syrian Church, particularly under the patriarchate of Severos of Antioch (r. 512–538),[19] suggesting a date of composition for the *Endoxon* not earlier than the sixth century.

Kropp's original edition is numbered by sentence rather than page or line number; we indicate the equivalent sentence number in Kropp's edition at the beginning of each page. In their editions, Kropp and Meyer omit line p. 5 l. 30, and p. 11 ll. 11, 13, & 15. Corrections made by reference to the Collège de France manuscript are marked 'CdF' in the apparatus.

---

[16] The *Coptic Magical Papyri* project has also produced a podcast episode about this text, which includes a reading of the full *Endoxon*: https://www.coptic-magic.phil.uni-wuerzburg.de/index.php/2021/06/29/podcast-7-praise-of-the-archangel-michael-a-case-study/ (accessed 17/4/2023).

[17] Collège de France Ms. 2 (KYP M573), pp. 1–21. One of the associated manuscripts, CdF 3 (KYP M597), is dated by its colophon to the 27th of Mesore 427 (=20th August 1035). The codex is largely unpublished, but pp. 24–26, containing *Prayer of Shenoute*, was edited by Pezin (1988). For more on the group, see Pezin 1983; Boud'hors/Tardieu 2006: 16.

[18] This is in pp. 113.1–137 l. 21 of the euchologium published in Lanne 1958. Compare the less elaborate form in the Anaphora of Basil in Budde 2004: 146–152; *cf.* the discussion of the development of this sequence in Budde 2004: 273–319.

[19] Budde 2004: 580–582.

page 2 (= Kropp 1) (flesh)

ⲙⲓⲭⲁⲏⲗ · ⲧⲉ ⲁⲃⲟⲩⲱϣⲧ · ϩⲁ ⲛⲉⲟⲩⲣⲏϯ ⳽
ⲙⲡⲓⲱ̄ⲧ ⲛⲁⲅⲁⲑⲱⲥ ⳽ ⲁⲃⲁϩⲉⲣⲁⲧⳇϥ ⳽ ⲁϥ-
ⲧⲱϩ ⲉⲡⲉⲃϩⲣⲁⲃⲧⲱ̄ⲥ ⳽ ϩⲓⲑⲏ ⲙⲁϥ ⳽ ⲁϥⲕⲁ
ⲡⲉⲡϩⲁⲣⲙⲁ · ϩⲓ ⲡⲁϩⲟⲩ ⲙⲁⲃ ⳽ ⲁϥⲡⲱⲣϣ
5 ⲉⲃⲟⲗ ⲛ̄ⲛⲉϥⲧⲉⲛⲁϩ ⲛⲟⲩⲁⲉⲓⲛ ⳽ ⲁⲃⲱ-
ϣ ⲉⲃⲁⲗ · ⲉϥϫⲱⲱ ⲙⲁⲥ ⳽ ϫⲉ ⲭⲉⲣⲉ ⳽
ⲡⲓⲱⲧ ⳽ ⲭⲉⲣⲉ ⲡϣⲏⲣⲉ ⲙⲉⲣⲓⲧ ⳽
ⲭⲉⲣⲉ ⲡⲉⲡⲛ̄ⲁ̄ ⲉⲧⲟⲩⲁⲁⲃ ⳽ ⲭⲉⲣⲉ ≡
ⲡⲉⲛⲧⲁⲃⲧⲁⲙⲓⲁ ⳽ ⲧⲡⲏ ⳽ ⲭⲉⲣⲉ ⲡⲉⲛ-
10 ⲧⲁϥⲥⲉⲙⲉ ⲥⲏⲛϯ ⲙ̄ⲡⲕⲁϩ ⳽ ϩⲓⲭⲉⲛ
ⲛⲉⲙⲁⲟⲩ ⳽ ⲭⲉⲣⲉ ⲡⲉϥⲧⲁϥⲥⲱⲣ ⲉⲃⲁ-
ⲗ ⲛⲍ̄ ⲉⲡⲏⲩ ⳽ ⲙⲉⲛ ⲡⲍ̄ⲃ ⲛ̄ⲧⲉⲣⲉⲩⲙⲁ
ⲭⲉⲣⲉ ⲡⲉⲛⲧⲁⲃ⳽ⲧⲁⲙⲓⲁ · ⲡⲣⲏ ⳽ ⲁⲃϯ ⲧ-
ⲉⲃϩⲏⲙⲙⲉ · ⲉⲣⲁϥ ⳽ ⲭⲉⲣⲉ ⲡⲉⲛⲧⲁⲃⲧⲁ-
15 ⲙⲓⲁ ⲡⲟⲟϩ ⳽ ⲁⲃϯ ⲡⲉⲟⲩⲁⲉⲓⲛ ⳽ ⲉⲣⲁⲃ ⳽
ⲭⲉⲣⲉ ⲡⲉⲛⲧⲁⲃ⳽ⲧⲁⲙⲓⲁ ⲛⲉⲥⲓⲩ ⲁⲃϯ ⲣⲁⲛ
ⲉⲣⲟⲟⲩ ⳽ ⲭⲉⲣⲉ ⲡⲉⲛⲧⲁⲃⲧⲁⲙⲓⲁ ⳽ ⲛⲁⲅⲅⲉⲗⲱⲥ ⳽ ⲁⲃϯ ⲡⲛⲉⲩⲙⲁ ⲉⲣⲟⲟⲩ ⳽ ⲭⲉⲣⲉ · ⲡⲉⲛⲧⲁⲃϯ ⲡⲧⲱϣ ⳽ ⲛⲁⲣⲭⲁⲅⲅⲉⲗⲱⲥ ⳽
20 ⲭⲉⲣⲉ ⲡⲉⲛⲧⲁⲃ⳽ⲧⲁⲙⲓⲁ ⲛⲉⲭⲉ-
ⲣⲱⲃⲓⲛ ⳽ ⲙⲛ ⲛⲉⲥⲉⲣⲁⲫⲓⲛ̄ ⳽
ⲁⲃⲧⲉ ⲋ̄ ⲛ̄ⲧⲉⲛⲁϩ ⳽ ⲉⲡⲟⲩⲁ ⳽
ⲡⲟⲩⲁ ⲙⲁⲩ ⳽
ⲭⲉⲣⲉ · ⲡⲉⲛⲧⲁⲃϯ ⲧⲱϣ ⲛⲛⲉⲧⲉⲛⲁ-
25 ⲙⲓⲥ ⳽ ⲉⲧⲟⲩⲁⲁⲃ ⳽ ⲭⲉⲣⲉ ⲡⲉⲛⲧⲁⲃ-

---

1 *l.* δέ ᴿⲁ⳽ϥ-ⲟⲩⲱϣⲧ̄ : *i.e.* ᴿⲛ̄ⲧⲁ⳽ϥ-ⲟⲩⲱϣⲧ Κ | *i.e.* ᴿⲟⲩⲉⲣⲏⲧⲉ ‖ **2** *i.e.* ἀγαθός | *i.e.* ᴿⲁ⳽ϥ-ⲁϩⲉ-ⲣⲁⲧ⳽ϥ ‖
3 *i.e.* ᴿⲧⲱⲕⲥ̄ : ⲧⲱⲃⲉ *i.e.* ᴿⲧⲱϣⲃⲉ or ⲧⲱⲕⲥ Κ | *i.e.* ᴿⲡⲉ⳽ϥ- | *i.e.* ῥάβδος | *i.e.* ᴿⲙ̄ⲙⲟ⳽ϥ ‖
4 *i.e.* ᴿⲡⲉ⳽ϥ- | *i.e.* ἅρμα | *i.e.* ᴿⲙ̄ⲙⲟ⳽ϥ ‖ **5** *i.e.* ᴿⲁ⳽ϥ- ‖ **6** *i.e.* ᴿⲭⲱ ‖ **7–24** *i.e.* χαῖρε ‖ **8** *l.* πν(εῦμ)α ‖
10 *i.e.* ᴿⲥⲙⲛ- : ⲥⲙⲉⲛ Κ | *l.* ⲛ̄-ⲥⲛ̄ⲧⲓ : ⲥⲏⲛϯ Κ ‖ **11** *i.e.* ᴿⲙⲟⲟⲩ | *l.* ⲡⲉⲛⲧⲁϥⲥⲱⲣ ‖ **12** *i.e.* ᴿⲡⲏⲩⲉ : ⲡⲏⲩ Κ |
l. ⲡ-(ϣⲉϣ)ⲃ *i.e.* ᴿⲡ-ⲥⲁϣϥ : "twice seven" ("zweimal Sieben") Κ, Μ | *i.e.* στερέωμα ‖
13 *i.e.* ᴿⲡ-ⲉⲛⲧⲁ⳽ϥ | *i.e.* ᴿⲁ⳽ϥ-ϯ- ‖ **13–14** *i.e.* ᴿⲧⲉ⳽ϥ- ‖ **14** *i.e.* ᴿϩⲙⲙⲉ | *i.e.* ᴿⲡ-ⲉⲛⲧⲁ⳽ϥ- ‖ **15** *i.e.* ᴿⲁ⳽ϥ-ϯ- |
i.e. ᴿⲡⲉ⳽ϥ- | *i.e.* ᴿⲉⲣⲟ⳽ϥ ‖ **16** *i.e.* ᴿⲡ-ⲉⲛⲧⲁ⳽ϥ- | *i.e.* ᴿⲥⲓⲟⲩ | *i.e.* ᴿⲁ⳽ϥ- ‖ **17** ⲉⲣⲟⲟⲩ first ⲟ corrected
from ⲁ by overwriting | *i.e.* ᴿⲡ-ⲉⲛⲧⲁ⳽ϥ- | *i.e.* ἄγγελος ‖ **18** *i.e.* ᴿⲁ⳽ϥ- | *i.e.* πνεῦμα ‖
18–19 *i.e.* ᴿⲡ-ⲉⲛⲧⲁ⳽ϥ- ‖ **19** *l.* ⲛ-ⲛ-ἀρχάγγελος (haplography of ⲛ) ‖ **20** *i.e.* ᴿⲡ-ⲉⲛⲧⲁ⳽ϥ- ‖
20–21 *i.e.* χερουβίμ ‖ **21** *i.e.* σεραφίμ ‖ **22** *i.e.* ᴿⲁ⳽ϥ- | ⲡⲟⲩⲁ Κ ‖ **23** *i.e.* ᴿⲙ̄ⲙⲁⲩ ‖ **24** *i.e.* ᴿⲡ-ⲉⲛⲧⲁ⳽ϥ- ‖
24–25 ⲛⲛⲉⲩⲉⲛⲁⲙⲓⲥ Κ | *i.e.* δύναμις ‖ **25** *i.e.* ᴿⲡ-ⲉⲛⲧⲁ⳽ϥ-

And *Michael did obeisance at the feet of the good Father. He stood up, he fixed his staff before him, he set his chariot behind him, he spread |⁵ his wings of light, and he cried out, saying:

"Hail, O Father! Hail, O Beloved Son! Hail, O Holy Spirit! Hail, you who created the sky! Hail, you |¹⁰ who established ⟨the⟩ foundations of the earth upon the waters! Hail, you who spread out the seven heavens and the seven firmaments! Hail, you who created the sun and gave its warmth to it! Hail, you who |¹⁵ created the moon and gave its light to it! Hail, you who created the stars and gave names to them! Hail, you who created *angels and gave them spirit! Hail, you who appointed the *archangels! |²⁰ Hail, you who created the *cherubim and the *seraphim and gave six wings to each one of them! Hail, you who appointed the holy *Powers! |²⁵ Hail, you who

---

page 2–15. The *Endoxon* of Michael: The word ἔνδοξον was intepreted by Kropp as meaning "praise" ("Lobpreis"), and this translation is followed by Meyer and Gardner. Kropp (1966: 5) specifically understood it as a hymn sung by Michael at the reconciliation of God with Adam, parallel to the hymns of praise sung by the angels after the resurrection of Jesus described in the *Book of Bartholomew* (CC 27; see Westerhoff 1999: 125–129; Budge 1913: 195–196 (English translation)), although in form and content these are rather different, and this context is not explicit in the text itself. Kropp also prints at the beginning of the text a title, ⲡⲉⲛⲇⲱⲝⲟⲛ ⲙⲙⲓⲭⲁⲏⲗ ⲡⲁⲣⲭⲏⲁⲅⲅⲉⲗⲟⲥ, "The *Endoxon* of Michael the Archangel", not present in the Heidelberg manuscript, but the Collège de France manuscript, of which Kropp was apparently unaware, does indeed contain the end title ⲡⲉⲛⲇⲱⲝⲱⲛ ⲉ·ⲙⲓⲭⲁⲏⲗ ("The *Endoxon* of Michael"), confirming that this is the name of the text. The term appears as a self-reference within the text at several points (p. 3 l. 18, p. 4 ll.13–14, p. 14 ll. 16, 18, 20). The meaning of the word ἔνδοξον is less clear; the LSJ *s.v.* gives its primary meaning as "(something) held in high esteem or honour, of high repute". As noted in Lampe *s.v.* it may be used as an adjective to describe divine things, such as the name of God, Christ's second coming, saints, and angels. We have been unable to find a reference to the term being used to describe a genre of hymn in either Greek or Coptic. The closest term might be δοξολογία ("doxology, laudation"), but in the Christian tradition this typically refers to much briefer praise formulae than that present here.

page 3 (= Kropp 18) (flesh)

ⲧⲁⲙⲓⲁⲛ : ⲁϥϯ ⲡⲛⲁ̄ ⲉⲣⲁⲛ : ϯⲥⲙⲟⲩ ⲉⲣⲁⲕ
ⲉⲙⲡⲟⲟⲩ : ⲡⲉⲛⲧⲁⲃⲧⲓ ⲛⲁⲓ ⸗ ⲙⲡⲓⲛⲟϭ ⲛ⸗
ⲧⲁⲓⲟ : ⲛ̇ⲁⲅⲅⲉⲗⲱⲥ · ⲉⲡⲭⲓⲥⲓ ⲁ:ⲙⲱⲓⲛⲓ ⸗
ⲥⲙⲟⲩ ⲉⲡⲓⲱⲧ ⲛⲉⲙⲁⲓ ⲉⲙⲡⲟⲟⲩ ⸗ ⲛⲉⲭⲉ-
5 ⲣⲱⲃⲓⲛ : ⲉⲡ̇ⲭⲓⲥ · ⲁⲙⲱⲓⲛⲓ ⸗ ϯ ⲉⲟⲟⲩ ⲙⲡ-
ϣⲏⲣⲉ · ⲛⲉⲙⲁⲓ ⲙⲡⲟⲟⲩ ⸗ ⲉⲧⲉⲛⲁⲙⲓⲥ : ⲉⲡⲭ-
ⲓⲥ · ⲁⲙⲱⲓⲛⲓ : ⲭⲱⲣⲉⲅⲉⲓ ⸗ ⲉⲡⲉⲡⲛⲁ̄ · ⲉⲧⲟⲩⲁⲁⲃ ⲛⲉⲙⲁⲓ ⲙⲡⲟⲟⲩ ⸗ ⲙⲁⲣⲉⲡ̇ⲣⲏ · ⲙⲛ ⲡⲟⲟϩ ⸗
ⲙⲛ ⲛⲉⲥⲓⲟⲩ ⲧⲏⲣⲟⲩ ⲁϩⲉⲣⲁⲧⲟⲩ ⲛⲉⲙⲁⲓ ⲉ-
10 ⲡⲟⲟⲩ : ϣⲁⲛⲧⲁⲭⲱ ⲙⲡⲉⲟⲟⲩ ⲙ̇ⲡⲓⲱⲧ ⲙⲉ
ⲡϣⲏⲣⲉ · ⲙⲛ ⲡⲉⲡⲛⲁ̄ ⲉⲧⲟⲩⲁⲁⲃ ⸗ ⲛⲉϩⲉⲙ:-
ⲛⲉⲩⲧⲏⲣⲓⲱⲛ · ⲉⲡⲓⲱⲧ : ϩⲉⲙⲛⲉⲥⲓ : ⲉⲡⲓⲱⲧ ≡
ⲛⲉⲙⲁⲓ ⲉⲙⲡⲟⲟⲩ ⸗ ⲙⲁⲣⲉⲡⲕⲁϩ · ⲟⲩⲱⲛ ⲉⲣⲱⲃ : ⲉⲃⲱⲛⲕ ⲉⲡⲇⲓⲁ̄ⲃⲟⲗⲟⲥ ⸗ ⲙⲛ ⲛⲉⲃⲉⲛ-
15 ⲉⲣⲕⲓⲁ ⲧⲏⲣⲟⲩ ⸗ ⲙⲁⲣⲉⲛⲉⲡⲓⲗⲓ ⲙⲡⲏ ⸗
ⲟⲩⲱⲛ ⲉⲛ̇ⲥⲉⲉⲓ ϣⲁⲣⲁⲓ : ⲛ̇ϭⲓ ⲛⲉⲁⲅⲅⲉⲗⲟⲥ
ⲉⲡⲟⲩⲁⲉⲓ̇ⲛ ⸗ ϣⲁⲛⲧⲁⲭⲱⲕ ⲉⲃⲁⲗ · ⲙ̇ⲡⲓⲉⲛ-
ⲇⲱⲕⲍⲱⲛ ≡ ⲉⲧⲟⲩⲁⲁⲃ ⸗ ⲥⲱⲧⲉⲙ ⲣⲁⲓ ⸗
ⲙⲡⲟⲟⲩ : ⲡⲓⲱⲧ ⲙⲡⲟⲩⲁⲉⲓⲛ ⸗ ⲁⲛⲁⲕ ⲡⲉ
20 ⲙⲓⲭⲁⲏⲗ̄ · ⲡⲁⲣⲁⲛ ⸗ ⲡⲛⲟⲩⲧⲉ · ϩⲓ ⲣⲱⲙⲉ ⸗
ⲕⲁ ⲙⲉⲉⲭⲉ ⲣⲁⲓ ⸗ ⲙⲡⲟⲟⲩ : ⲡⲉⲣⲟ : ⲛⲉⲣⲱⲟⲩ ≡
ⲁⲛⲁⲕ ⲡⲉ ⲙⲓⲭⲁⲏⲗ̄ · ⲁⲛⲁⲕ ⲟⲛ ⲡⲉⲟⲩⲁϩ ⲉⲡⲍ̄ ⸗
ⲙⲉⲥⲧⲏⲣⲓⲱⲛ ⸗ ⲉⲑⲏⲙⲡ ϩⲉ ⲫⲏⲧ ⲉⲡⲓⲱⲧ ≡
ⲛⲁⲓ ⲛⲧⲁⲃⲁⲟⲩ ⲙⲉⲡⲉϩⲁⲟⲩ ⲛⲧⲁⲃⲧⲁⲙⲓⲁ ⸗
25 ⲡⲣⲱⲙⲉ · ⲕⲁⲧⲁ ⲡⲉⲃⲓⲛⲓ : ⲙⲉⲛ ⲧⲉϥϩⲓⲕⲱ-
ⲛ ⸗ ⲛⲧⲉⲣⲉⲃⲧⲁⲙⲓⲁ ⸗ ⲫⲁⲩⲥⲓⲏⲗ̄ : ⲁ̇ⲓⲉⲓ ⸗
ⲁⲛⲁⲕ ⲡⲉ ⲙⲓⲭⲁⲏⲗ̄ ⲙⲉ ⲛⲉⲧⲟⲩⲉϩ ⲉⲥⲱⲓ ⸗
ⲧⲏⲣⲟⲩ ⸗ ⲁⲛⲟⲩⲱϣⲧ : ⲛⲁⲧⲱⲣⲁⲛ̄ ⸗

---

1 *i.e.* ᔆⲧⲁⲙⲓⲟ | *i.e.* πν(εῦμ)α ‖ **2** *i.e.* ᔆⲙ̄-ⲡⲟⲟⲩ | *i.e.* ᔆⲡ-ⲉⲛⲧⲁ⸗ϥ- | ⲙⲡⲓⲛⲟϭ ⲛ- : ⲙⲡⲓⲛⲟⲟⲛ *i.e.* νοῦς "sense" ("Einsicht") K, M ‖ **3** ⲧⲁⲓⲟ "praise" ("Lobpreiset") K | *i.e.* ἄγγελος | *i.e.* ᔆⲙ̄-ⲡ-ϫⲓⲥⲉ ‖ **4** *i.e.* ᔆⲙ̄-ⲡⲟⲟⲩ ‖ **4–5** *i.e.* χερουβίμ | *i.e.* ϫⲓⲥⲉ ‖ **6** *l.* ⲛ̄-δύναμις ‖ **6–7** *i.e.* ᔆϫⲓⲥⲉ ‖ **7** *i.e.* χορεύειν | *i.e.* πν(εῦμ)α ‖ **9–10** *i.e.* ᔆⲙ̄-ⲡⲟⲟⲩ ‖ **10** *i.e.* ᔆϣⲁⲛⲧ-ⲭⲱ ‖ **11** *i.e.* πν(εῦμ)α ‖ **11–12** *i.e.* ὑμνητήριος : ⲛⲉϩⲩⲙⲛⲏⲧⲣⲓⲟⲥ K ‖ **12** *l.* ὑμνεῖν *cf.* ϩⲉⲙⲛⲉⲩⲉ in CdF : ϩⲩⲙⲛⲉⲩⲉⲓ K | *i.e.* ᔆⲙ̄-ⲡⲓⲱⲧ ‖ **13** *i.e.* ᔆⲙ̄-ⲡⲟⲟⲩ ‖ **13–14** *i.e.* ᔆⲉ-ⲣⲱ⸗ϥ ‖ **14** *i.e.* ᔆⲉ⸗ϥ-ⲱⲛⲕ ⲙ̄-ⲡ- : *i.e.* ᔆⲉ⸗ϥ-ⲱⲛⲕ "pounces on" ("springe los auf") K : "burst forth against" M | *i.e.* διάβολος | *i.e.* ᔆⲛⲉ⸗ϥ- ‖ **14–15** *i.e.* ἐνέργεια : "powers" ("Mächte") K | *l.* πύλη : ⲡⲩⲗⲏ K ‖ **16** *i.e.* ἄγγελος ‖ **17** *i.e.* ᔆϣⲁⲛⲧ-ⲭⲱⲕ ‖ **17–18** *i.e.* ἔνδοξον *cf.* note p. 1 | *i.e.* ᔆⲉⲣⲟ⸗ⲓ ‖ **19** ⲡⲟⲩⲁⲓⲛ K ‖ **20** *l.* ⲡⲁⲣⲁⲛ ⲡⲉ ‖ **21** *i.e.* ᔆⲙⲁⲁⲭⲉ | *i.e.* ᔆⲉⲣⲟ⸗ⲓ ‖ **22** ⲁⲛⲟⲕ K | *i.e.* ᔆⲡ-ⲉⲧ-ⲟⲩⲏϩ : ⲡⲉ ⲡⲉⲧⲟⲩⲁϩ K ‖ **23** *i.e.* ᔆⲙ̄-μυστήριον | *i.e.* ᔆⲉⲧ-ϩⲏⲡ ϩⲙ̄ ⲡ-ϩⲏⲧ ⲙ̄-ⲡ-ⲉⲓⲱⲧ : ⲉⲑⲏⲡ ϩⲙ ⲫⲏⲧ ⲙⲡⲓⲱⲧ K ‖ **24** *i.e.* ᔆⲛ̄ⲧⲁ⸗ϥ-ⲟⲩⲱ | *i.e.* ᔆⲙ̄-ⲡ-ϩⲣⲟⲟⲩ : ⲙⲡϩⲣⲁⲟⲩ K | *i.e.* ⲛ̄ⲧⲁ⸗ϥ- ‖ **25** *i.e.* κατά | **25–26** *i.e.* ᔆⲡⲉ⸗ϥ-εἰκών ‖ **26** ⲁⲓⲱ "yea!" ("Wohlan!") K, M | *i.e.* ᔆⲛ̄ⲧⲉⲣ⸗ϥ- ‖ **27** *i.e.* ᔆⲛⲉⲧ-ⲟⲩⲏϩ ⲛ̄ⲥⲱ⸗ⲓ ‖ **28** ⲁⲧⲱⲣⲁⲛ̄ K

created us, and gave us spirit!

I praise you today, you who gave me this great honour! O *angels on high, come! Praise the Father with me today! O *cherubim |⁵ on high, come! Give glory to the Son with me today! O *Powers on high, come! Dance for the Holy Spirit with me today! Let the sun and the moon and all the stars stand with me |¹⁰ today so that I may sing of the glory of the Father and the Son and the Holy Spirit! O singers of hymns to the Father, sing hymns to the Father with me today! Let the earth open its mouth and swallow the Devil and |¹⁵ all his works! Let the gates of heaven open and the angels of the light come to me, until I complete this holy *endoxon*!

Listen to me today, O Father of light! I am |²⁰ *Michael, my name ⟨is⟩ God and man! Lend your ear to me today, O King of kings! I am Michael, I am also the one set over the seven mysteries that are hidden in the heart of the Father, those that he made on the day that he created |²⁵ Man according to his likeness and his image. After he created Phausiēl, I came, I, Michael, and all those who follow me, and we made obeisance to Atōram,

---

13–15. ⲙⲁⲣⲉⲡⲕⲁϩ · ⲟⲩⲱⲛ ⲉⲣⲱⲃ : ⲉⲃⲱⲛⲕ ⲉⲡⲇⲓⲁⲃⲟⲗⲟⲥ ⲍ ⲙⲛ ⲛⲉⲃⲉⲛⲉⲣⲕⲓⲁ ⲧⲏⲣⲟⲩ : "let the earth open its mouth and swallow the Devil and all his works!" *Cf.* the description of the deaths of the rebellious Israelites Dathan and Abiram in Numbers 16.30: "and the earth opened its mouth and swallowed them and their houses and their tents and everything that belonged to them, and they went down to hell still alive" (ⲛ̄ⲧⲉⲡⲕⲁϩ ⲟⲩⲱⲛ ⲉⲣⲱϥ ⲛ̄ϥⲱⲙ̄ⲕ ⲙ̄ⲙⲟⲟⲩ ⲙⲛ̄ ⲛⲉϩⲓ ⲙⲛ̄ ⲛⲉⲩⲥⲕⲩⲛⲏ ⲙⲛ̄ ⲛⲉⲧϣⲟⲟⲡ ⲛⲁⲩ ⲧⲏⲣⲟⲩ ⲛ̄ⲥⲉⲃⲱⲕ ⲉⲡⲉⲥⲏⲧ ⲉⲁⲙⲛ̄ⲧⲉ ⲉⲩⲟⲛϩ̄; *Sahidic Bible 2*).

19. ⲡⲓⲱⲧ ⲙ̄ⲡⲟⲩⲁⲉⲓⲛ : "O Father of light" *Cf.* James 1.17: "father of lights"·(ⲡⲉⲓⲱⲧ ⲛ̄ⲛⲉⲟⲩⲟⲉⲓⲛ; Horner 1924: 192).

20. ⲡⲁⲣⲁⲛ ⲍ ⲡⲛⲟⲩⲧⲉ · ϩⲓ ⲣⲱⲙⲉ : "my name ⟨is⟩ God and Man" *Cf.* the note to *PCM* I 11 p. 9 ll. 17–18.

25–26. ⲕⲁⲧⲁ ⲡⲉⲃⲓⲛⲓ : ⲙⲉⲛ ⲧⲉⲩϩⲓⲕⲱⲛ ⲍ ⲛⲧⲉⲣⲉⲃⲧⲁⲙⲓⲁ : "according to his likeness and his image" *Cf. PCM* I 10 ll. 2–3 and accompanying notes.

page 4 (= Kropp 35) (hair)

ετε παι πε πϩωβ ⸗ ενεϥϭιχ ⸗ ντερνογωϣ-
τ ναρωμαχριμ ⸗ ετε παι πε αδαμ : αβ-:
ερ ατϲωτεμ εϲωκ ενϭι ϲαϧαταηλ ⸗
παρχηπλαϲμα ⸗ ακϣανεβ ϩεμ πεκ-
5   εοογ ετογααβ ⸗ πϣηρε : πτακα ακ:ϣα-
νεϥ ϩεμ πεκεοογ ετογααβ ⸗ ακϣτερ-
τωρ ⸗ νεβϲηητ ⸗ αβινι εϩραι ϩιχω-
ογ νογναϭ νϣωνε : ϣαντογερ πεβ-
ογωϣ ⸗ μενεϲωϲ : αβχι νερωμε ν-
10   νϭανϲ ντακταμια ⸗ μενεϲωϲ ⸗ ϣακ-
τελϭαγ ⸗ †νογ ϭε παϲϲ : ϣαναϩτηκ ⸗
ϩα πεκινι ⸗ μεν τεκϩικων ⸗ κε† νο-
γτελϭα ν⸗ρωμε νιμ ⸗ ετναφωρι᾽ μ-
πεπιενδωκϩων ⸗ ετογααβ : ηϩογο
15   τε ⸓⸓ ειοϩ : ειοϩ ⸗ ϣαραεϩ αιω αιω ταχη
τωρκ εραϰ επο⸗ογ : κεϲωτεμ εραι
εμπο⸗ογ : ω παρχων ⸗ να τπε ⸗ με να πκαϩ
παπατ νταπιωτ : ϲμογ εραϥ ⸗ αναγγε-
λοϲ : ϲω ντϩητϥ ⸗ ϣαντογχι πνα ετο-
20   γααβ †τερκα μακ εποαγ μπϲαϣβ ν-
λογοϲ ντακτειτογ : ετεκμη† μεν
πεκμεριτ νϣηρε ⸗ ιϲ πχϲ μπ-
ναγ ⸗ εβνηγ ⸗ επκωϲμοϲ ⸗ μπεϩογ ν-
ταβταμια : ναδαμ νϩητϥ ≡
25   †τερκα μακ μπαγ ⸗ μπεκνοϭ ⸗
νραν : ντακτϲαβα νεγγελωϲ εραβ ⸗
ϣαντογ†εοογ ⸗ νακ νϩητϥ : ετε
παι πε μεθεμων ⸗ πνοϭ νραν : επϲϲ ⸗
ϲαβαωθ ⸗ †νογ ϭε παϲϲ ϣαναϩτηκ ⸗

---

1 *i.e.* ˢɴ̄-ɴeϥ- ‖ **2** *i.e.* ˢaϥ- ‖ **3** *i.e.* ˢɴ̄cω⸗ĸ | *i.e.* ˢɴ̄ϭi ‖ **4** *i.e.* ἀρχίπλασμα : αρχηπλαϲμ Κ | *i.e.* ˢϣοοɴ⸗ϥ ‖ **5** *i.e.* ˢπϣηρε μ̄-π-τακο : πϣηρε μπτακα Κ ‖ **5–6** *i.e.* ˢϣοοɴ⸗ϥ ‖ **6** *i.e.* ˢϣτορτρ̄ ‖ **7** *i.e.* ˢɴeϥ- | *i.e.* ˢaϥ- ‖ **8** *i.e.* ϣωɴε "robbing" ("Beraubung") Κ | *i.e.* ˢπeϥ- ‖ **9** *i.e.* ˢμ̄ɴɴcω⸗c | *i.e.* ˢaϥ- ‖ **10** *l.* ταμιαγ Κ *cf.* ταμιοο[γ] CdF | *i.e.* ˢμ̄ɴɴcωc | ϣακ- κ partly effaced : ϣα Κ ‖ **11** *l.* *ϭ(ωi)c *i.e.* ˢχοeιc ‖ **12** *i.e.* εἰκών | *i.e.* ˢeϰκ-e-† : *l.* εκ† Κ ‖ **13** *i.e.* φορεῖν ‖ **13–14** *l.* μ̄-πι-ἔνδοξον *cf.* note p. 1 : *l.* μπι- Κ ‖ **14–15** *l.* ɴ-ογ-ϩοτε "in fear" ("in Furcht") Κ, Μ ‖ **15** *i.e.* δέ | *i.e.* δ(εῖνα) δ(εῖνα) : ⸌ Κ | *i.e.* ˢϣα ενeϩ ? : *l.* ϣαρα ενϩ Κ | *i.e.* ταχύ ‖ **16** *i.e.* ˢερο⸗κ | *i.e.* ˢμ̄-ποογ | *i.e.* ˢeϰκ-e-ϲωτμ̄ : *l.* εκϲωτμ Κ ‖ *i.e.* ˢερο⸗i corrected from εραĸ by erasure of legs of κ ‖ **17** *i.e.* ἄρχων | *l.* ɴ̄ɴατπε μɴ ɴαπκαϩ Κ ‖ **18** *l.* μ̄-π-απατ | *i.e.* ˢερο⸗ϥ : εaϥ *l.* εραϥ Κ ‖ **18–19** *i.e.* ἄγγελος ‖ **19** *l.* ϲω ɴϩητϥ Κ | *i.e.* πν(εῦμ)α ‖ **20** *i.e.* ˢ†-ταρκο μ̄μο⸗κ | *i.e.* ˢμ̄ποογ : ποογ Κ | *i.e.* ˢϲaϣϥe ‖ **21** *i.e.* λόγος | *i.e.* ˢταa⸗ ‖ **22** *l.* ι(ηϲογ)ϲ π-χ(ριϲτό)ϲ ‖ **23** *i.e.* ˢeϥ- | κοϲμοϲ Κ ‖ **23–24** *i.e.* ˢɴ̄τa⸗ϥ- ‖ **25** *i.e.* ˢ†-ταρκο μ̄μο⸗κ | *i.e.* ˢμ̄-ποογ ‖ **26** *i.e.* ˢτϲαβο | *i.e.* ἄγγελος | *i.e.* ˢερο⸗ϥ ‖ **27** ɴϩητϥ ɴ corrected from e by addition of stroke ‖ **28, 29** *l.* *ϭ(ωi)c *i.e.* ˢχοeιc

who is the work of his hands. After we had made obeisance to Arōmakhrim—who is Adam—Satanaēl, the First-Formed One, disobeyed you, and you excluded him from your |⁵ holy glory. The son of perdition, you deprived him of your holy glory. You disturbed his foundations. He brought down upon them a great sickness, until they fulfilled his wish. After that, he did violence to the men |¹⁰ whom you created; after that, you would heal them.

Now, my Lord, have pity upon your likeness and your image, and may you give healing to all men who will bear this holy *endoxon*, and in particular |¹⁵ NN, child of NN, month after month, forever?, yea yea, quickly!

I adjure you today that you listen to me today, O, ruler of those of heaven and those of the earth, by the *cup that the Father blessed; the *angels drank from it so that they received the Holy Spirit! |²⁰ I adjure you today by the seven words that passed between you and your beloved son, Jesus Christ, in the hour that he came into the world on the day in which you created Adam! |²⁵ I adjure you today by your great *name, which you taught the angels so that they gave you glory by it, which is Methemōn, the great name of the Lord *Sabaoth! Now, my Lord, have pity

---

3. C̄ⲀⲚⲀⲦⲀⲎⲖ : "Satanaēl" In the pseudepigraphal 2 Enoch and 3 Baruch (surviving in full only in Slavonic), Satanael is given as the name of Satan as an angel before his fall (Gaylord 1982). The name is also found in Coptic sources, such as Pseudo-Theodosius of Alexandria, *On Michael* (CC 387; Budge 1915: 336.6 *etc.*, 904 (trans)); Pseudo-John Chrysostom, *On Raphael* (CC 176; Budge 1915: 529.6 *etc.*, 1036 (trans.)).

4. ⲠⲀⲢⲬⲎⲠⲖⲀⲤⲘⲀ : "the First-Formed One" For this title, *cf.* the note to *PCM* I 12 p. 15 l. 17.

5. ϢⲎⲢⲈ ⲚⲦⲀⲔⲀ : "the son of perdition" *Cf.* John 17.12.

12. ⲠⲈⲔⲒⲚⲒ ⲘⲈⲚ ⲦⲈⲔϨⲒⲔⲰⲚ : "your likeness and your image" *Cf. PCM* I 10 ll. 2–3 and accompanying notes.

15. ⲈⲒⲞϨ : ⲈⲒⲞϨ : "month after month" Literally "moon, moon" (*i.e.* ˢⲞⲞϨ, *cf.* ᴮⲒⲞϨ), that is "every lunar month". Kropp translates "moon for moon" ("Mond für Mond"). For the doubling of a noun to mean "every", see Layton 2000: 53 §62 (b).

18. ⲠⲀⲠⲞⲦ ⲚⲦⲀⲠⲒⲰⲦ : ⲤⲘⲞⲨ ⲈⲢⲀϤ : "the cup blessed by the Father" *Cf. PCM* I 25 p. 7 ll. 23–24 and note.

28. ⲘⲈⲐⲈⲘⲰⲚ : "Methemōn" *Cf. PCM* I 25 p. 11 l. 7 and accompanying note.

page 5 (= Kropp 53) (hair)

ϩⲁ ⲡⲉⲕⲓⲛⲓ ⹎ ⲙⲛ ⲧⲉⲕϩⲓⲕⲱⲛ ⹎ ⲕⲉⲥⲱⲧⲙ ⲉ-
ⲡⲁⲁϣⲁϩⲁⲙ : ⲉⲕⲃⲓ ⲛϩⲓⲥⲓ ⲛⲓⲙ ≡ ϩⲁⲃⲁⲗ ⲛ̄ⲛ ⹎
ⲉϣⲱⲡⲓ ⲟⲩϣⲱⲛⲉ ⹎ ⲉⲃϩⲁⲟⲩ ˙ ⲡⲉ : ⲉⲓ ⲟⲩⲣⲉϩ̇ⲧⲥ ⹎
ⲛⲧⲉ ⲇⲓⲙⲱⲛⲓⲟⲛ ⹎ ⲙⲁⲣⲟⲩⲉⲓ ⲉⲃⲁⲗ ˙ ⲛ̇ϩⲏⲧϥ ⹎
5 ϩⲛ ⲧⲉⲩⲛⲟⲩ : ⲉⲧⲟⲩⲛⲁϫⲁⲕⲙⲉⲃ ⹎ ϩⲉⲛ ⲡⲓⲙⲁⲩ
ⲙⲛ : ⲛⲥⲉⲧⲁϩ̇ⲥⲉⲃ ˙ ϩⲉⲙ ⲡⲓⲛⲉϩ ⹎
†ⲧⲉⲣⲕⲁ ⲙⲁⲕ ⲙⲡⲟⲟⲩ : ⲛⲧⲉⲥⲁϣⲃⲓ ⲛ̄ϭⲏⲛ†
ⲛⲧⲉ ⲡⲕⲁϩ ⹎ ⲙⲉⲛ ⹎ ⲧⲥⲁϣⲃⲓ ⲙⲡⲏⲗⲓ ⲉⲩϩⲉ-
ⲙⲟⲟⲥ ϩⲓϫⲱⲟⲩ : ⲛ̇ϭⲓ ⲙ̇ⲉⲛⲧⲁⲃ†ⲛⲧⲃⲁ ⲟⲩϭⲁⲥ ⹎
10 ⲛⲁⲅⲅⲉⲗⲱⲥ ⹎ †ⲱⲣⲕ ⲉⲣⲁⲕ ⲉⲙ̇ⲡⲟⲟⲩ ⹎ ⲉⲙ-
ⲍ̄ ⹎ ⲛⲁⲕⲧⲓⲛ ⹎ ⲉⲡⲣⲏ ⲙ̇ⲉⲛ ⲡⲟⲟϩ ≡
†ⲧⲉⲣⲕⲁ ⲙⲁⲙⲁⲕ ⲉⲡⲟⲟⲩ ⹎ ⲙⲡⲉⲭⲱⲣⲱⲥ ⹎
ⲛ̇ⲛⲉⲥⲓⲩ ⲛ̇ⲧⲉⲡⲏ ⹎ ϫⲉⲕⲁⲥ ⲉⲧⲉⲛⲧⲉⲛⲛⲁⲩ
ⲛⲁⲓ ⲙ̇ⲡⲁⲣⲭⲁⲅⲅⲉⲗⲱⲥ ⹎ ⲙⲓⲭⲁⲏⲗ ˙ ϩⲓϫⲛ̄
15 ⲡⲓⲙⲁⲩ : ⲙⲛ̄ ⲡⲓⲛⲉ̄ϩ ⹎ ⲉⲧⲕⲏ ⲙⲡⲁⲙⲉⲧⲁ ⲉ-
ⲃⲁⲗ ˙ ⲉⲩⲥⲙⲟⲩ ⲉⲣⲟⲟⲩ ⹎ ⲉⲃϩⲁⲅⲓⲁⲥⲥⲉ ⲙⲁⲩ ⹎
ϫⲉⲕⲁⲥ ⲉⲩϣⲁⲛⲡⲁϩⲧⲟⲩ ⲉϫⲱ ⲡⲥⲱⲙⲁ ⹎
ⲛ̄ⲛ ⲛⲥⲉⲃⲓ ⲛ⹎ϩⲓⲥⲓ ⲛⲓⲙ ⹎ ⲥⲁⲃⲁⲗ ⲉⲙⲁⲃ ⹎
ⲛⲉ ⲛⲁⲓ ⲉⲧϩⲉ ⲡⲉ⹎ⲃⲉⲥⲱⲙⲁ ⹎ ⲉⲕⲉⲟⲩⲱⲃ-
20 ⲥ ⲉ:ⲧϭⲁⲙ ⲧⲏⲣⲉⲥ ⹎ ⲙⲡⲉⲛⲧⲓⲕⲓⲙⲉⲛ-
ⲱⲛ ⲉⲕⲧⲣⲉⲧⲉⲃϭⲁⲙ ⲧⲏⲣⲏⲥ ⹎ ϣⲱⲡⲓ ⹎
ⲛⲑⲏ ⲛⲧϭⲁⲙ ⹎ ⲛⲟⲩϣⲁⲗ⹎ⲙⲉⲥ ⹎ ϩⲓⲧⲉⲛ
ⲡⲱϣⲣ ⲉⲃⲁⲗ ⲛ̇ⲛⲁⲧⲉⲛⲁϩ ≡ †ⲱⲣⲕ ⲉ-
ⲣⲁⲕ : ⲉⲙⲡⲟⲟⲩ ⲛⲉⲛ̇ⲧⲁⲝⲓⲥ̇ ⲧⲏⲣⲟⲩ ⹎ ⲛⲧⲁⲛ-
25 ⲅⲉⲗⲓⲕⲏ ⲧⲏⲣⲉⲥ ⹎ ⲛ̇ⲁ ⲙⲡⲏⲩⲉⲓ ⹎ ⲛⲁⲓ ⲛⲧⲁⲩ-
ⲉⲓ : ⲁⲩⲟⲩⲱϣⲧ : ⲛⲁⲇ̄ⲁⲙ̄ ˙ ⲙⲡⲉϩⲟⲟⲩ ⲛ-
ⲧⲁⲕⲧⲁⲙⲓⲁⲃ ⲛ̇ϩⲏⲧϥ ≡ †ⲱⲣⲕ ⲉⲣⲁⲕ ⲉⲙ̄-
ⲡⲟⲟⲩ ⲛⲛⲉⲕⲣⲁⲛ ⹎ ⲙⲉⲛ : ⲛⲉⲕϭⲁⲙ ⹎ ⲙⲛ ⲛⲉ-
ⲕⲥⲱ†ⲟⲩⲛ̄ ≡ ⲙⲛ ⲛⲉⲕ:ⲫ̄ⲩ̄ ⹎ ⲛⲁⲓ ⲉⲧⲥϩ̄ϩ ⹎
30 ϩⲛ ⲧⲉⲕⲗⲏⲥⲓⲁ ⲛ̇ⲛⲉϣⲏⲣⲉⲡⲙⲓⲥⲓ ⲉⲧϩⲉ-
ⲛ ⲁⲙⲡⲏⲩⲉⲓ : ⲛⲁⲓ ⲛϣⲁⲩ† ≡

---

1 *i.e.* εἰκών | *i.e.* ˢⲉ=ⲕ-ⲉ- || 2 *i.e.* ˢⲛ̄=ⲅ-ϥⲓ | *i.e.* ˢϩⲁⲃⲟⲗ ⲛ̄- || 3 *i.e.* ἤ | *i.e.* ˢⲣⲁϩⲧⲥ || 4 *i.e.* δαιμόνιον || 5 *i.e.* ˢⲉⲧ=ⲟⲩ-ⲛⲁ-ϫⲟⲕⲙ̄=ϥ || 6 *i.e.* ˢⲧⲁⲣⲥ= | 7 *i.e.* ˢ†-ⲧⲁⲣⲕⲟ ⲙ̄ⲙⲟ=ⲕ || 7, 8 *i.e.* ˢⲥⲁϣϥ *cf.* ᶠϣⲉⲙⲃ || 8 *i.e.* πύλη || 9 *i.e.* ˢⲙⲛ̄ⲧ-ⲁϥⲧⲉ ⲛ̄-ⲧⲃⲁ || 10 *i.e.* ἄγγελος | *i.e.* ˢⲙ̄-ⲡⲟⲟⲩ | *i.e.* ˢⲛ̄- || 11 *i.e.* ἀκτίν | *i.e.* ˢⲙ̄-ⲡⲣⲏ | *i.e.* ˢⲙⲛ̄- || 12 *i.e.* ˢ†-ⲧⲁⲣⲕⲟ ⲙ̄ⲙⲟ=ⲕ | *i.e.* ˢⲙ̄-ⲡⲟⲟⲩ | *i.e.* χορός || 13 *i.e.* ˢⲛ̄-ⲛ-ⲥⲓⲟⲩ | *i.e.* ˢⲛ̄-ⲧ-ⲡⲉ | *i.e.* ˢⲉ=ⲧⲉⲧⲛ̄-ⲉ- : ⲉⲧⲉⲧⲛⲉ- Κ || 14 *i.e.* ἀρχάγγελος || 15 ⲙⲧⲁ Κ || 16 *i.e.* ˢⲛ̄=ϥ-ⲥⲙⲟⲩ | *i.e.* ˢⲛ̄=ϥ-ἁγιάζειν | *i.e.* ˢⲙ̄ⲙⲟ=(ⲟ)ⲩ || 17 *i.e.* σῶμα || 18 *i.e.* ˢⲛ̄-δ(εῖνα) δ(εῖνα) | *i.e.* ˢⲥⲁⲃⲟⲗ ⲙ̄ⲙⲟ=ϥ || 19 *i.e.* ˢⲡⲉ=ϥ- | *i.e.* σῶμα | *l.* ⲛⲁⲓ || 19–20 *i.e.* ˢⲟⲩⲱⲥϥ ⲛ̄- *cf.* ⲟⲩⲱⲥϥ CdF : ⲟⲩⲱⲥϥ Κ || 20 *i.e.* ˢⲧⲏⲣ=ⲥ | 20–21 *i.e.* ἀντικείμενος || 21 *i.e.* ˢⲛ̄=ⲅ-ⲧⲣⲉ-ⲧⲉ- ϥ-ϭⲟⲙ | *i.e.* ˢⲧⲏⲣ=ⲥ || 22 *i.e.* ˢϣⲟⲗⲙⲉⲥ || 23 *i.e.* ˢⲡ-ⲡⲱϣ (haplography of ⲡ) || 24 *i.e.* ˢⲙ̄-ⲡⲟⲟⲩ | *i.e.* ˢⲛ̄-ⲛ-τάξις || 24–25 *i.e.* ἀγγελική || 25 *i.e.* ˢⲧⲏⲣ=ⲥ̄ | *i.e.* ˢⲙ̄-ⲡⲏⲩⲉ || 27 *i.e.* ˢⲛ̄ϩⲏⲧ=ϥ || 27–28 *i.e.* ˢⲙ̄-ⲡⲟⲟⲩ || 29 *i.e.* ζῴδιον | *l.* φυ(λακτήριον) || 30 *i.e.* ἐκκλησία | *i.e.* ˢⲙ̄-ⲡⲉ-ϣⲣⲡ-ⲙⲓⲥⲉ || 31 ⲙ̄-ⲡⲏⲩⲉ

upon your likeness and your image, and listen to my sighing and take all suffering away from NN, child of NN, whether it is a wicked sickness or a demonic strike! Let them leave him |⁵ in the moment in which he will be washed in this water and he will be anointed with this oil!

I adjure you today by the seven foundations of the earth and ⟨by⟩ the seven gates, upon which sit one hundred and forty-five thousand |¹⁰ *angels! I adjure you today by the seven rays of the sun and the moon! I adjure you today by the chorus of the stars of heaven, that you (pl.) send to me the *archangel *Michael upon |¹⁵ this water and this oil that is set before me so that he blesses them and sanctifies them, so that when they are poured over the body of NN, child of NN, they take all suffering away from him, that which is in his body! You will bring to naught |²⁰ all the power of the Adversary, causing all his power to become like the power of a gnat through the spreading of my wings!

I adjure you today by all the angelic ranks |²⁵ of the heavens, they who came and greeted Adam on the day in which you created him! I adjure you today by your *names and your *powers and your *images and your *phylacteries, those which are written |³⁰ in the church of the Firstborn which is in the heavens, those that

---

1. ⲡⲉⲕⲓⲛⲓ ⸗ ⲙⲛ ⲧⲉⲕϩⲓⲕⲱⲛ : "your likeness and your image" *Cf. PCM* I 10 ll. 2–3 and accompanying notes.

6. ⲙⲛ : ⲛⲥⲉⲧⲁϩ·ⲥⲉⲃ : "and he will be anointed" Verbal coordination with ⲙⲛ̄ would be unexpected in Sahidic, but as noted in Crum CD 170a, it is found in Bohairic; the use here may indicate Bohairic influence, or else that the phenomenon is not restricted to Bohairic. We are grateful to Vincent Walter for pointing this out to us.

22. ⲛⲑⲏ ⲛⲧϭⲁⲙ ⸗ ⲛⲟⲩϣⲁⲗⲙⲉⲥ : "like the power of a gnat" For similar analogies using small animals to express weakness, see the notes to *PCM* I 28 p. 2 l. 12–13.

page 6 (= *Kropp 71*) (flesh)

ϩⲁ† ⲛⲛⲉⲕⲋⲟⲩⲥⲓⲁ ⲙⲡⲕⲁⲕⲉ : ϫⲉⲕⲁⲥ ⲉⲕⲉ-
ⲧⲉⲛⲛⲁⲩⲥⲟⲩ ϩⲓϫⲉⲛ ⲡⲓⲙⲁⲩ ⲙ̄ⲛ ⲡⲛⲛⲉϩ ⸗
ⲉⲕⲥⲙⲟⲩ ⲉⲣⲁⲩ : ⲉⲕϩⲁⲅⲓⲁⲥⲥⲉ ⲙⲁⲩ : ϫⲉⲕⲁⲥ : ⲉⲩϣⲁⲛⲡⲁϩⲧⲟⲩ : ϩⲓϫⲱ ⲥ̄ⲥ̄ ⸗ ⲛⲥⲉⲉⲓ ·
5 ⲉⲃⲁⲗ · ⲛ̄ϩⲏⲧϥ : ⲛ̄ϭⲓ ϩⲓⲥⲓ ⲛⲓⲙ : ⲉⲧϩⲉ ⲡⲉϥⲥⲱⲙⲁ ≡
ⲉⲃⲙⲟⲩϩ : ⲉⲙⲟⲩⲧ : ϩⲓ ϭⲁⲙ ⲉⲃ† ⲟⲩⲱ ⲃⲁⲗ ⸗
ⲛ̄ⲑⲉ ⲙ̄ⲡϣⲏⲛ · ⲉⲡⲱⲛⲁϩ : ⲉϥⲣⲏ† ϩⲉⲛ ⲧ-⸗
ⲙⲏ† ⲙ̄ⲉⲡⲁⲣⲁⲇⲓⲥⲱⲥ ⸗ †ⲱⲣⲕ ⲉⲣⲁⲕ ⲉⲡⲟⲟⲩ
ⲙⲡⲥⲁϣⲃ : ⲛ̄ⲁⲅⲅⲉⲗⲟⲥ : ⲉⲧⲱϩⲉ ⲣⲁⲧⲟⲩ ⸗
10 ϩⲓϫⲉⲛ · ⲙ̄ⲡⲥⲁϣ̄ⲃⲉ ⲗⲟⲩⲧⲏⲣ ⲛ̄ⲧⲉⲕⲗⲏⲥⲓⲁ
ⲛⲉϣⲏⲣⲉ:ⲡⲙⲓⲥⲓ : ⲉⲧ:ϩⲉⲛ ⲁⲙⲡⲏⲅⲉⲓ ⸗ ⲉⲧⲉ
ⲛⲁⲓ ⲇⲉ ⲛⲉⲩⲣⲁⲛ : ⲓⲁⲱ · ⲓⲁⲕ : ⲡⲓⲁⲕ ⸗ ⲥⲓⲁⲕ ⸗
ⲁⲣⲧⲱⲗⲏ ⸗ ⲁⲣⲧⲱⲗⲁⲛ ≡ ⲁⲣⲧⲱⲗⲁⲣ ⸗ ≡
†ⲱⲣⲕ ⲉⲣⲁⲕ ⲉⲡⲟⲟⲩ : ⲛ̄ⲧⲉϣⲁⲣⲡ ⲛ̄ⲑⲏⲥⲓⲁⲥ
15 ⲛ̄ⲧⲁⲩⲧⲁⲗⲁⲥ ⲛⲁⲕ : ⲉϩⲣⲁⲓ ⲛ̄ϩⲏⲧⲥ ⲙⲛ ⲡⲉ-
ⲑⲉⲥⲓⲁⲥⲧⲏⲣⲓⲱⲛ ⸗ ⲉⲧⲟⲩϩϩ : ϩⲛ ⲧⲉⲥⲙⲏ†
† ⲉⲙⲡⲁⲟⲩ ⲙ̄ⲡⲉⲃⲇ̄ · ⲛ̄ⲥⲧⲏⲗⲟⲥ : ⲉⲧⲧⲱ-
ⲟⲩⲛ̄ ϩⲁⲣⲁϥ ⸗ ⲉⲧⲉ ⲛⲉⲓ : ⲛⲉⲩⲣⲁⲛ : ⲉⲕⲧⲉⲣⲓⲥⲁⲛ ⸗ ⲥⲁⲛⲧⲁⲥ ⸗ ⲥⲁⲛⲧⲁⲗ ⲧⲁⲗⲓⲁⲥ ⸗ † ⲉⲙ-
20 ⲙⲁⲕ ⲉⲡⲟⲟⲩ ⲛ̄ⲉⲡⲉⲥⲛⲟⲃ : ⲉⲛⲉϣⲏⲣⲉⲡ-
ⲙ̄ⲓⲥⲓ ⲧⲁⲩⲡⲁϩⲧϥ ⸗ ⲉⲃⲁⲗ · ϩⲉⲛ ⲟⲩⲭⲓⲛϭⲁ-
ⲛⲥ ⸗ ϫⲉⲕⲁⲟⲥ ⲕⲓⲛⲓⲉⲓ ϣⲁⲣⲁⲓ ⲙⲡⲟⲟⲩ ⲛ : ⲁ-
ⲛⲁⲕ ⲥ̄ⲥ̄ ⸗ ⲣⲉϣⲏⲣⲉⲡⲙ̄ⲓⲥⲓ ⲉⲥⲱⲕ : ϩⲁⲧⲉⲃ-
ϩⲏ ⸗ ⲉⲣⲉⲓⲇ̄ · ⲧⲃⲉ : ⲟⲩϭⲁⲥ ⸗ ϩⲉ ⲧⲉⲩⲏⲡⲓ ⸗
25 ⲁⲙⲟⲩ ⲕⲁⲗⲱⲥ ⸗ ⲁⲕⲓ ϩⲓϫⲉⲛ ⲡⲓⲙⲁⲁⲩ
ⲙⲛ ⲡⲓⲛⲉϩ : ⲉⲕⲓⲛⲓⲃⲓ ⲉⲣⲟⲟⲩ ⸗ ⲉⲕⲙⲁⲩϩⲟⲩ ·
ⲙ̄ⲡⲛ̄ⲁ ⲉⲧⲟⲩⲁⲁⲃ ‖ ϫⲉⲕⲁⲥ ⸗ ⲕⲉ⟦.⟧ϣⲁⲛⲡⲁ-
ϩⲟⲩ=ⲧⲃ ϩⲉϫⲱ ⲥ̄ⲥ̄ ⸗ ⲉⲩⲉⲓ ⲉⲃⲁⲗ · ⲛ̄ϩⲏⲧϥ
ⲛ̄ϭⲓ ϩⲓⲥⲓ ⲛⲓⲙ ⸗ ⲉⲧϩⲉ ⲡⲉⲃⲥⲱⲙⲁ ≡ ⲙⲁⲣⲉ-
30 ⲛⲇⲓⲁⲃⲱⲗⲱⲥ ⸗ ϫⲓ ϣⲓⲡⲉ ⲙⲛ ⲧⲉϥϭⲁⲙ

1 *i.e.* ἐξουσία | *i.e.* ˢⲧⲛⲛⲟⲟⲩⲥ⸗ⲟⲩ ‖ **2** ⲡⲙⲁⲩ K | *i.e.* ˢⲙ̄ⲛ̄- | *i.e.* ˢⲡ-ⲛⲉϩ ‖ **3** *i.e.* ˢⲛ̄⸗ⲅ-ⲥⲙⲟⲩ | *i.e.* ˢⲛ̄ⲅ-ἁγιάζειν | *i.e.* ˢⲙ̄ⲙⲟ⸗ⲟⲩ ‖ **4, 24, 28** (δεῖνα) (δεῖνα) ‖ **5** *i.e.* σῶμα ‖ **6** *i.e.* ˢⲛ̄⸗ϥ-ⲙⲟⲩϩ | *cf.* ⲙⲟⲩⲧ CdF | *i.e.* ˢⲛ̄⸗ϥ-†ⲟⲩⲱ | *i.e.* ˢⲉⲃⲟⲗ ‖ **7** *i.e.* ˢⲙ̄- ‖ **8** *i.e.* ˢⲙⲏⲧⲉ ⲙ̄- | *i.e.* παράδεισος | *i.e.* ⲙ̄-ⲡⲟⲟⲩ ‖ **9–10** *i.e.* ˢⲥⲁϣϥ ‖ **9** *i.e.* ἄγγελος ‖ **10** *i.e.* λουτήρ | *i.e.* ἐκκλησία ‖ **11, 20–21** *i.e.* ⲙ̄-ⲡⲉ-ϣⲣⲡ-ⲙⲓⲥⲉ | *i.e.* ˢⲙ̄-ⲡⲏⲅⲉ ‖ **12** *i.e.* δέ or *l.* ⲛⲉ ? : ⲛⲉ K ‖ **14** *i.e.* ˢⲙ̄-ⲡⲟⲟⲩ | *i.e.* θυσία ‖ **16** ⲑⲉⲥⲓⲁⲥⲧⲏⲣⲓⲱⲛ ⲓ corrected from ⲅ by smudging and overwriting *i.e.* θυσιαστήριον ‖ **17–20** ˢ†-(ⲧⲁⲣⲕⲟ ⲙ̄ⲙⲟ⸗ⲕ) ⲙ̄-ⲡⲟⲟⲩ *cf.* CdF : †ⲱⲣⲕ ⲉⲙⲙⲁⲕ K | *i.e.* ˢⲙ̄-ⲡⲉ⸗ϥⲧⲟⲟⲩ | *i.e.* στῦλος ‖ **19** *i.e.* ˢⲉ⸗ⲕ-ϩⲙⲟⲟⲥ ‖ **20** *i.e.* ˢⲙ̄-ⲡⲟⲟⲩ | *i.e.* ˢⲙ̄-ⲡⲉ- | ⲛ⸗ ⲛⲉ ⲉⲡⲉ·ⲥⲛⲟⲃ K ‖ **22** *i.e.* ϫⲉⲕⲁⲥ | *i.e.* ˢⲉ⸗ⲕ-ⲛⲁ-ⲉⲓ ? *cf.* ⲉⲕⲉⲉⲓ CdF : K see notes ‖ **22–23** *l.* ⲛⲡⲉⲕϣⲣⲉⲡ ⲙⲓⲥⲉ K ‖ **23** *l.* ⲉⲣⲉ-ⲛ-ϣⲣⲉⲡ ⲙⲓⲥⲉ ? *cf.* CdF : *l.* ⲛ̄-ⲡⲉ⸗ⲕ ϣⲣⲉⲡ ⲙⲓⲥⲓ K, M | *i.e.* ˢⲥⲱⲕ ? : *l.* ⲉϥⲉ ⲧⲁⲅⲅⲉⲗⲓⲕⲏ ⲧⲏⲣⲥ⸗ ⲥⲱⲕ ϩⲁⲧⲉϥϩⲏ K ‖ **23–24** K, M see notes ‖ **24** *i.e.* ˢⲏⲡ ‖ **25** *i.e.* καλῶς | *l.* ⲉ⸗ⲕ-ⲉ-ⲉⲓ "may you come" ("Du mögest herabkommen") K : "come!" M ‖ **26** *i.e.* ˢⲛ̄⸗ⲅ-ⲛⲓϥⲉ | *i.e.* ˢⲛ̄⸗ⲅ-ⲙⲁϩ⸗ⲟⲩ corrected from ⲙⲟⲩϩⲟⲩ by overwriting ‖ **27–28** *i.e.* ˢⲉ⸗ⲕ-ϣⲁⲛ-ⲡⲁϩ-ⲧⲟⲩ ? *cf.* ⲉⲩϣⲁⲛⲡⲁϩⲧⲟⲩ CdF ‖ **27** *i.e.* πν(εῦ)α ‖ **28** *i.e.* ˢϩⲓϫⲛ̄- ‖ **29** *l.* ˢⲡⲉ⸗ϥ-ⲥⲱⲙⲁ ‖ **30** *l.* ⲡ-διάβολος | *i.e.* ˢϣⲓⲡⲉ.

terrify the authorities of darkness, so that you shall send them upon this water and this oil, and you bless them and sanctify them, so that when they are poured over NN, child of NN, |⁵ all suffering which is in the body of NN, child of NN, will come out of him, and he will be filled with sinew and power, blossoming like the Tree of Life which grows in the middle of Paradise!

I adjure you today by the seven *angels who stand |¹⁰ upon the seven baptistries of the Church of the Firstborn, which is in the heavens, and whose names are these: *Iao, Iak, Piak, Siak, Artōlē, Artōlan, Artōlar! I adjure you today by the first sacrifice |¹⁵ that was offered up to you in it and the altar that is placed in its middle! I adjure you today by the four pillars which bear it, whose names are these: Ekterisan, Santas, Santal, Talias! I adjure |²⁰ you today by the blood of the firstborn that was spilled in violence, that you come to me today, I, NN, child of NN, while ⟨the⟩ firstborn go before him, one hundred and forty-five thousand in number!

|²⁵ Come well; you came upon this water and this oil, and you breathed upon them, and you filled them with the Holy Spirit, so that when you pour them over NN, child of NN, they will come out of him, namely every suffering which is in his body! Let |³⁰ the Devil be ashamed, and all his power

---

15. n̄ghtc̄ : "in it" That is, in "the church" (tekⲗhcia in l. 30). Kropp understands this as part of a missing invocation ending with "in it" ("in ihr").

22. kinibi : "that you come" Kropp translates "that you bring down to me, NN, today, (your) Firstborn" ("dass du heute zu mir, NN, herabbringest (deinen) Erstgeborenen"), apparently understanding a form of the verb eine ("to bring").

23-24. peϣhpen m̄ici ecⲱk : ϩateⲃeh : "while ⟨the⟩ firstborn go before him" Kropp and Meyer understand the "firstborn" as the being asked to be sent, translating "(send...) the firstborn, before whom there submit one hundred forty-five thousand in number" ("Erstgeborenen, während vor ihm herziehen 145.000 in ihrer Zahl"). The equivalent passage in the Collège de France manuscript, however, reads ereneϣhpen mice [c]ⲱk · etekeh... ("while the firstborn (pl.) go before *you*"), confirming the interpretation given here. The reference to the "firstborn" here is therefore not to Jesus, but rather to a group of several beings whose blood has been spilled; the most obvious reference is to Revelation 7.4 & 7.14, which describes one hundred and forty-four thousand of the Children of Israel who have been sealed after having undergone tribulations, that is, martyrs. In P.Berol. 11347 (Beltz 1985: no. II 42; KYP M220) l. 38 these seem to be associated with the 'Holy Innocents', the children killed by Herod (Matthew 2.16–18): "your one hundred and forty-four thousand, those whom Herod killed" (м̄пекр̄м̄ⲇ̄ nϣo nai taϩhpⲱⲇhc ϩatⲃoy).

27-28. ke⟦.⟧ϣanпaϩoy=tⲃ : "when you pour them" Kropp translates "when one (!) pours it out" ("wenn man (!) sie ausgiesst").

page 7 (= *Kropp 85*) (hair)

ⲧⲏⲣⲏⲥ ⳾ ⲉⲥϣⲱⲡⲓ ⲛⲑⲏ ⲛ̇ⲧϭⲁⲙ ⳾ ⲛⲟⲩϣⲁⲗⲙⲉⲥ ⲁⲓⲱ ⲁⲓⲱ ⳾ † ⲉⲙⲙⲁⲕ ⲉⲡⲁⲟⲩ · ⲙ̇ⲡⲉⲕ ⲅ̅ ·
ⲛⲣⲁⲛ ⳾ ⲉⲧⲟⲩⲁⲁⲃ ⳾ ⲛⲁⲓ ⲛⲧⲁⲕⲟⲩⲁⲛⲁϩⲟⲩ
ⲉⲃⲁⲗ · ⲉⲡⲕⲱⲥⲙⲟⲥ ≡ ϫⲉⲕⲁⲥ ⲉⲩⲉⲥⲟⲩⲉⲥⲟⲩ-
5 ⲱⲛⲅ ⲡⲛⲟⲩ† : ⲙⲉ · ⲙⲁⲟⲩⲁⲁⲃ ≡ ⲉⲧⲉ ⲡⲁⲓ ⲡⲉ
ⲡⲓⲱⲧ ⲙ̇ⲉ ⲡϣⲏⲣⲉ · ⲙ̇ⲉ ⲡⲉⲡⲛⲁ̅ ⲉⲧⲟⲩⲁⲁⲃ ⳾
ⲡⲗⲏⲙⲏⲛ ⲉⲙⲡⲟⲩϫⲁⲓ ⳾ ⲡⲓⲱⲧ : ⟦ⲃ⟧
ⲛ̇ⲧⲉⲥⲫⲣⲁⲅⲓⲥ ⲑⲁ ⲉⲁⲩ · ⲙ̇ⲡⲓⲱⲧ : ⲡ-
ϣⲁⲣϣⲉⲣ ⳾ ⲁⲩⲱ ⲡϩⲏⲓ ⳾ ⲛ̇ⲧϭⲁⲙ ≡
10 ⲧⲏⲣⲉⲥ · ⲙ̇ⲡⲇⲓⲁⲃⲱⲗⲟⲥ ⳾ ⲡⲓⲱⲧ · ⲙⲉ
ⲡϣⲏⲣⲉ ⳾ ⲙⲛ ⲡⲉⲡⲛⲁ̅ ⲉⲓⲧⲟⲩⲁⲁⲃ ⳾
†ⲱⲣⲕ ⲉⲣⲁⲕ ⲙⲡⲟⲟⲩ ≡ ⲛ̇ⲧⲛⲁϫ ⲛ̇-
ⲃⲁⲥⲓⲥ ⲛ̇ⲛⲟⲩⲃ ⳾ ⲉⲣⲉⲡⲉⲕⲑⲣⲱⲛⲟⲥ ⳾
ϩⲓϫⲱⲥ ⳾ ϯ ⲉⲙⲁⲕ ⲡⲟⲟⲩ ⲛ̇ⲉⲙ ⲡⲧⲁⲩ-
15 ⲉⲓ ⲛ̇ⲛⲟⲩⲃ ⳾ ⲉⲧϩⲉ ⲛⲉⲕⲩⲉⲣⲡ†̇ ⳾
ⲡⲉⲩⲣⲁⲛ ⲡⲉ ⲑⲁⲑⲁ ≡ † ⲉⲙⲡⲟⲟⲩ ⳾ ⲙ̇ⲡ-
ⲫⲉⲣⲙⲁ ⲛⲉⲛ̇ⲛⲟⲩⲃ ⳾ ⲉⲧϩⲓϫⲉⲛ ⲧⲁⲡⲏ ⳾
ⲙ̇ⲡⲉⲕⲑⲣⲱⲛⲟⲥ ⳾ ⲉⲧⲉ ⲡⲁⲓ ⲡⲉ ⲑⲓⲏⲗ̅ ⳾
† ⲉⲙⲡⲟⲟⲩ ⲛ̇†ⲡⲱⲣⲫⲱⲣⲁ : ⲉⲧⲁⲉⲓ
20 ⲡⲉⲥⲣⲁⲛ ⳾ ⲡⲉ ⲙⲁⲣⲓⲏⲗ̅ ⳾ † ⲉⲙⲡⲟⲟⲩ ≡
ⲙ̇ⲡⲓⲉⲙⲡⲏⲧⲏⲥ ⳾ ⲛⲟⲩⲁⲉⲓⲛ ⳾ ⲉⲧϭⲁⲁⲗⲓ ⳾
ⲙⲁⲕ · ⲡⲉϥⲣⲁⲛ ⳾ ⲡⲉ ⲑⲱⲏⲗ̅ ⳾ ϯ ⲉⲙⲡⲁⲟⲩ ⳾
ⲡⲓⲛⲁϭ ⲛ̇ϫⲱⲙⲉ ⳾ ⲉⲧϩⲉ ⲧⲉⲕ:ϭⲓϫ ⳾ ⲉⲣ-
ⲉⲧⲓ ⲍ̅ : ⲛ̇ⲥⲫⲣⲁⲅⲓⲥ : ϩⲓϫⲱⲃ ≡ ⲉⲣⲉⲡⲧⲱ-
25 ϣ ⲛ̇ⲛⲁ ⲡⲏ : ⲙⲉ : ⲛⲁ ⲡⲕⲁϩ ⳾ ⲥⲛϩ ⲉⲣⲁⲃ ⳾
† ⲉⲙⲡⲟⲟⲩ ⲙ̇ⲡⲉⲕϭⲉⲃⲁⲓ ⳾ ⲉⲧϫⲟⲥⲓ ⳾
ⲡⲁⲓ ⲉⲧⲁⲙⲁϩ† ⲛⲉⲥⲏⲛ† ⲙ̇ⲡⲕⲁϩ · ⲙⲛ ⳾
ⲛⲉⲡⲏⲗⲓ ⲙ̇ⲡⲏ ⳾ † ⲉⲙⲡⲟⲟⲩ ⲙ̇ⲡⲥⲓⲩ ⲉ-
ⲡⲟⲩⲁⲉⲓⲛ ⳾ ⲉⲙⲡⲉⲕⲥⲛⲉⲩ ⲃⲉⲗ ⳾
30 ⲑⲱⲗ̅ · ⲙ̇ⲛ ⲑⲱⲣⲁ⳾ⲛ

---

1 *i.e.* ˢⲧⲏⲣ⳾ⲥ | *i.e.* ˢⲛ̅⳾ⲥ-ϣⲱⲡⲉ || 1–2 *i.e.* ˢϣⲟⲗⲙⲉⲥ || 2–26 *i.e.* ˢ†-(ⲧⲁⲣⲕⲟ) ⲙ̅ⲙⲟ⳾ⲕ ⲙ̅-ⲡⲟⲟⲩ *cf.* CdF : †ⲱⲣⲕ ⲉⲙⲙⲁⲕ K || 2 *i.e.* ˢⲙ̅-ⲡⲉⲕ || 4 *i.e.* κόσμος || 4–5 *l.* ⲉ⳾ⲩ-ⲉ-ⲥⲟⲩⲱⲛ⳾ⲕ : ⲉⲩⲉⲥⲟⲩⲉⲥⲟⲩⲱⲛⲅ K || 5 *i.e.* ˢⲙ̅-ⲙⲉ ⲙⲁⲩⲁⲁ⳾ϥ || 6 *i.e.* ˢⲙⲛ̅- (twice) | *i.e.* πν(εῦμ)α || 7 *i.e.* λιμήν | or *i.e.* πλησμονή K | *i.e.* ⲙ̅-ⲡ-ⲟⲩϫⲁⲓ | ⟦ⲃ⟧ erased by washing : absent in K, M || 8 *i.e.* σφραγίς | *i.e.* ˢⲉⲧ-ϩⲁ ⲡ-ⲉⲟⲟⲩ ⲙ̅-ⲡ-ⲉⲓⲱⲧ ? : *l.* ⲉⲑⲁ ⲉⲁⲩ ⲙⲡⲱⲧⲛ "that is (full) of the glory of those of yours (pl.) (?)" ("das voll der Herrlichkeit von dem Eurigen (?) ist") or *l.* ⲉⲑⲁ ⲉⲁⲩ ⲡⲓⲱⲧ K || 9 *i.e.* ˢϣⲟⲣϣⲉⲣ | *i.e.* ˢϩⲉ || 10 *l.* ⲧⲏⲣ⳾ⲥ̅ | *i.e.* διάβολος || 11 *l.* πν(εῦμ)α | *i.e.* ˢⲉⲧ- || 13 *i.e.* ˢⲛ̅-βάσις | *i.e.* ˢⲛ̅-ⲛⲟⲩⲃ | *i.e.* θρόνος || 14–15 *i.e.* ˢⲧⲟⲟⲩⲉ || 15 ⲃⲁⲑⲁ K || 16 *i.e.* ˢⲡⲉ⳾ϥ- || 17 *i.e.* ˢⲡ-ἅρμα *cf.* ⲡϩⲁⲣⲙⲁ CdF : ἕρμα K, M | *i.e.* ˢⲛ̅-ⲛⲟⲩⲃ || 18 *i.e.* θρόνος : ⲑⲣⲟⲛⲟⲥ K || 19 *i.e.* πορφύρα | *i.e.* ˢⲉⲧⲉ ? : ⲉⲧⲥⲁⲉⲓ "beautiful (?)" ("schönen") K, M || 20 *i.e.* ˢⲉⲧⲉ || 21 *i.e.* ἐπενδύτης K | *i.e.* ˢϭⲟⲟⲗⲉ^Q || 22 *i.e.* ˢⲙ̅ⲙⲟ⳾ⲕ | *l.* ⲡⲉ ⲡⲉⲑⲱⲏⲗ̅ (haplography) || 23 *i.e.* ˢⲙ̅-ⲡ-ⲛⲟϭ ⲛ̅-ϫⲱⲙⲉ || 24 *i.e.* σφραγίς | *i.e.* ˢϩⲓϫⲱ⳾ϥ || 25 *l.* ⲛⲁ-ⲧ-ⲡⲉ | *i.e.* ˢⲉⲣⲟ⳾ϥ | *i.e.* ˢϫⲟⲥⲉ || 26 *i.e.* ˢϭⲃⲟⲓ ⲉⲧ-ϫⲟⲥⲉ || 27 *i.e.* ˢⲁⲙⲁϩⲧⲉ | *i.e.* ˢⲛ̅-ⲛ-ⲥⲛ̅ⲧⲉ || 28 *l.* πύλη | *i.e.* ˢⲡ-ⲥⲓⲟⲩ : ⲡⲓⲩ *l.* ⲡ-ⲥⲓⲩ K, M | *i.e.* ˢⲙ̅- || 29 *i.e.* ˢⲙ̅-ⲡⲉ⳾ⲕ-ⲥⲛⲁⲩ

become like the power of a gnat, yea, yea!

I adjure you today by your (s.) three holy *names, those that you revealed to the world so that they might know |⁵ you, only true God, that is the Father, and the Son and the Holy Spirit, the harbour of salvation, the Father of the seal which bears the glory of the Father?, the destruction and fall of the entire power |¹⁰ of the Devil, the Father and the Son and the Holy Spirit!

I adjure you today by the great base of gold upon which your throne is! I adjure you today by the shoes |¹⁵ of gold which are on your feet; their name is Thatha! I adjure you today by the chariot of gold which is upon the head of your throne, which is Thiēl! I adjure you by the purple robe whose |²⁰ name is Mariēl! I adjure you today by the garment of light which covers you; its name is Thōēl! I adjure you today by the great book which is in your hand which has the seven seals upon it, which has the ordinance |²⁵ of the things of the heaven and of the earth written in it! I adjure you today by your exalted arm, that which rules the foundations of the earth and the gates of heaven! I adjure you by the star of light of your two eyes, |³⁰ Thōl and Thōran!

1–2. ⲉⲥϣⲱⲡⲓ ⲛⲟⲏ ⲛ̄ⲧϭⲁⲙ ⸗ ⲛⲟⲩϣⲁⲗⲙⲉⲥ : **"become like the power of a gnat"** An example of the common use of small animals as metaphors for powerlessness; *cf.* the notes to *PCM* I 28 p. 2 ll. 11–12, and Dosoo 2022c: 531.

p. 7 l. 12–p. 8 l. 15. The body of God: *Cf.* the note to *PCM* I 12 p. 31 ll. 3–6.

19. ⲛ⸗ϯⲡⲱⲣⲫⲱⲣⲁ : **"by the purple robe"** Kropp translates "fine (?) purple rug" ("schönen (?) Purpurteppich"), while Meyer translates "purple covering."

24. ⲧⲓⲍ̄ : ⲛⲥⲫⲣⲁⲅⲓⲥ : **"the seven seals"** *Cf.* Revelation 5.1: "And I saw a book in the right hand of the one who sat upon the throne, written on the front and back, sealed with seven seals" (ⲁⲩⲱ ⲁⲓⲛⲁⲩ ⲉⲩϫⲱⲱⲙⲉ ϩⲛ ⲧⲟⲩⲛⲁⲙ ⲙⲡⲉⲧϩⲙⲟⲟⲥ ϩⲓ ⲡⲉⲑⲣⲟⲛⲟⲥ ⲉϥⲥⲏϩ ϩⲓⲑⲏ ⲁⲩⲱ ϩⲓⲡⲁϩⲟⲩ ⲉϥⲧⲟⲃⲉ ⲛⲥⲁϣϥⲉ ⲛⲥⲫⲣⲁⲅⲓⲥ; Budge 1912: 283).

27. ⲉⲧⲁⲙⲁϩϯ : **"that which rules"** Kropp translates "that which encloses" ("der [...] umfasst").

28. ⲙⲡⲥⲓⲩ : **"by the star"** Meyer translates as plural "the stars."

page 8 (= Kropp 98) (flesh)

ϯ ⲙ̄ⲡⲟⲟⲩ ⲉ́ⲙⲡⲛⲓⲃⲓ ⲱⲛⲁϩ ⲉⲧⲛⲏⲩ · ⲉⲃⲁⲗ =
ϩⲛⲉⲕ·ϭⲉⲃϣⲁⲁⲛⲉ : ⲡⲉⲃⲣⲁⲛ ⲡⲉ̄ ⲥⲧⲱⲏⲗ̄ =
ϯ ⲉⲙ̄ⲡⲟⲟⲩ : ⲙ̄ⲡⲓⲫⲉⲙⲉⲣⲁⲛⲓⲱⲛ = ⲡⲁⲓ ⲡⲉ =
ⲡⲉⲕⲗⲁⲥ = ϯ ⲉⲙ̄ⲡⲟⲟⲩ ⲛⲧⲉⲕⲁⲩⲣⲓⲏⲗ · ⲉⲧ-
5 ⲉ ⲧⲁⲓ ⲧⲉⲕⲧⲁⲡⲣⲁ ☰ ϯ ⲉⲙ̄ⲡⲟⲟⲩ = ⲛⲉⲕ-
ϣⲁⲗ · ⲉⲧⲉ : ⲛⲁⲓ · ⲛⲉ ⲱ̄ⲣⲓⲥⲕⲱⲥ =
ϯ ⲉⲙ̄ⲡⲟⲟⲩ = ⲛⲧⲉⲕⲁⲡⲏ ⲉⲧⲉ ⲧⲁⲓ · ⲱⲣⲁⲥⲓⲏⲗ̄
ϯ ⲉⲙ̄ⲡⲟⲟⲩ = ⲙ̄ⲡⲧⲏⲡⲱⲥ ⲉⲡⲉⲥ̄ⲣ̄ⲟⲥ ⲛⲟⲩⲁⲉⲓ-
ⲛ ⲉⲧϩⲓϫⲉⲛ ⲧⲉⲕⲁ̄ⲡ̄ⲏ̄ : ⲧⲉ ⲡⲁⲓ ⲡⲉ ⲥⲓⲧⲱⲣⲓⲏⲗ̄ ·
10 ϯ ⲉⲙ̄ⲡⲟⲟⲩ = ⲡⲉⲕⲗⲁⲙ : ⲛⲟⲩⲁⲉⲓⲛ = ⲉⲧϩⲉ
ⲡⲉⲕⲙⲁϩⲕ = ⲡⲉⲃⲣⲁⲛ = ⲡⲉ̄ ⲗⲉⲗⲁⲏⲗ̄ =
ϯ ⲉⲙ̄ⲡⲟⲟⲩ = ⲛⲱⲣⲫⲁⲙⲓⲏⲗ̄ · ⲉⲧⲉⲕ ⲡⲉⲕ-
ⲛ̄ⲧⲏⲏⲃⲓ : ⲛⲧⲉⲕϭⲓⲝ · ⲛⲟⲩⲛⲁⲙ : ϯ ⲉⲙ̄-
ⲟⲟⲩ ⲛⲧⲉⲕϭⲓⲝ : ⲥⲏⲛϯ = ⲁⲛⲁⲣⲁⲙⲟⲩⲏⲗ̄ =
15 ⲧⲉⲕϭⲓⲝ ⲛⲟⲩⲛⲁⲙ = ⲁⲛⲧⲣⲁⲕⲟⲩⲏⲗ̄ =
ⲛⲧⲉⲕϭⲓⲝ · ⲛⲉϩⲃⲟⲩⲣ = ϯ ⲉⲙ̄ⲡⲟⲟⲩ ⲧⲉⲕ-
ⲕⲟⲩⲉⲣⲏϯ · ⲥⲏⲛϯ = ⲑⲁϣⲑ ☰ ⲑⲁϣⲑⲁ =
ϯ ⲉⲙⲡⲟⲟⲩ ⲡⲉⲑⲣⲟⲛⲟⲥ ⲛ̇ⲟⲩⲁⲉⲓⲛ
ⲉⲕⲙⲟⲟⲥ ⲉϩⲣⲁⲓ : ϩⲓϫⲱⲃ = ⲉⲕϯ ϩⲉⲡ ⲉⲡⲥⲱ̄ⲛ̄
20 ⲧⲏⲣϥ = ⲛⲧⲁⲕⲧⲁⲙⲓⲁⲃ = ϯ ⲉⲙ̄ⲡⲟⲟⲩ ⲛϯ-
ⲛⲟϭ ⲛⲧⲉⲛⲁⲙⲓϭ ⲉⲧϩⲉⲣⲁⲧⲥ ϩⲓϫⲛ ⲧⲉⲕⲁⲡⲏ = ⲡⲉⲥⲣⲁⲛ · ⲙⲉ̄ⲣⲟⲩⲏⲗ̄ = ⲧⲁⲓ ⲉⲛⲧⲁⲥϯ
ϩⲓϫⲱⲕ · ⲡⲉⲕⲗⲁⲙ ☰ ϩⲉⲛ ⲛⲉⲕⲗⲁⲧⲟ̄ⲥ̄
ⲙ̄ⲡϣⲏⲛ ⲉⲡⲱⲛⲁϩ = ⲁ̄ⲥⲁϥ = ⲁ̄ⲥⲁⲙⲁ =
25 ⲁ̄ⲥⲁⲙⲗⲱⲗ̄ = ϯ ⲉⲙ̄ⲡⲟⲟⲩ · ⲛⲧⲉⲕⲛⲟϭ · ⲛⲧⲉⲛⲁⲙⲓϭ ⲉⲩⲉⲓⲣⲓ ⲙⲁⲃ = ⲙⲉⲛⲧⲏ ⲙⲉ ⲛ̇ⲁⲁⲃ-
ⲧⲁⲥⲉ : ⲣⲉⲟⲩⲉⲓ · ϩⲓ ⲟⲩⲛⲁⲙ ⲉⲙⲁⲕ · ⲉⲣⲉ-
ⲕⲉⲟⲩⲉⲓ ϩⲓⲃⲟⲩⲣ ⲛ̇ⲁⲕ = ⲉⲣⲉϩⲛⲥⲏⲃⲓ = ⲛⲥⲁϯ =
ⲛⲧⲁⲁⲧⲟⲩ ⲉⲩⲥⲉⲃⲧⲱⲧ ⲉⲩⲉⲓⲣⲓ ⲡⲉⲕⲟⲩⲉϩ-
30 ⲥⲁϩⲛⲓ = ϯ ⲉⲙ̄ⲡⲟⲟⲩ ⲙ̄ⲡⲉⲕ·ⲇ̄· ⲛⲥⲱⲛⲧ ⲉⲧ-

1–30 *i.e.* ˢϯ-(ⲧⲁⲣⲕⲟ ⲙ̄ⲙⲟ=ⲕ) ⲙ̄-ⲡⲟⲟⲩ *cf.* CdF : ϯⲱⲣⲕ ⲉⲣⲁⲕ ⲉⲙⲡⲟⲟⲩ K ‖ **1** *i.e.* ˢⲙ̄- | *i.e.* ˢⲛ̄-ⲱⲛϩ ‖ **2** *i.e.* ˢϩⲛ ⲛⲉ=ⲕ-ϭⲃ-ϣⲁⲁⲛⲉ=ⲕ ? *cf.* ϩⲛ ⲛⲉⲕϣⲁⲁⲛⲕ CdF | *i.e.* ˢⲡⲉ=ϥ-ⲣⲁⲛ : ⲡⲉϥⲣⲁⲛ K ‖ **3** ἐφήμερος K ‖ **5** *i.e.* ˢⲧⲁⲡⲣⲟ | *i.e.* σεραφίμ : M omits ‖ **6** *i.e.* ˢϣⲟⲗ | **8** *i.e.* τύπος | *l.* σ(ταυ)ρός ‖ **9** *i.e.* ˢⲉⲧⲉ ⲡⲁⲓ ⲡⲉ ‖ **11** *i.e.* ˢⲙⲁⲕϩ : ⲙⲁⲕϩ K | *i.e.* ˢⲡⲉ=ϥ- ‖ **12–13** *l.* ⲉⲧⲉ ⲡⲁⲓ ⲡⲉ ⲡⲉⲕⲧⲛⲏⲏⲃⲓ : ⲉⲧⲉⲕⲛⲧⲏⲏⲃⲓ *l.* ⲉⲧⲉ ⲡⲁⲓ ⲡⲉ ⲡⲛⲟϭ ⲛ̄ⲧⲏⲏⲃⲓ K ‖ **13** *i.e.* ˢⲧⲏⲏⲃⲉ ‖ **15** *i.e.* ˢⲟⲩⲛⲁⲙ ‖ **16** *l.* ⲧⲉⲕϭⲓⲝ | *i.e.* ˢⲛ̄-ϩⲃⲟⲩⲣ ‖ **16–17** *i.e.* ˢⲛ̄-ⲧⲉ=ⲕ- ‖ **17** *i.e.* ˢⲟⲩ(ⲉ)ⲣⲏⲧⲉ ‖ **18** *i.e.* θρόνος ‖ **19** *i.e.* ⲉⲧ=ⲕ-ϩⲙⲟⲟⲥ : ⲉⲕⲙⲟ[ⲟⲥ] K | *i.e.* ˢϩⲓϫⲱ=ϥ | *i.e.* ˢⲥⲱⲛⲧ (haplography with following ⲧ) ‖ **20** *i.e.* ˢⲛ̄ⲧⲁ=ⲕ-ⲧⲁⲙⲓⲟ=ϥ : ⲛⲧⲁⲧⲁⲙⲓⲁⲃ *l.* ⲛⲧⲁⲕⲧⲁⲙⲓⲁⲃ K ‖ **21** *i.e.* δύναμις | *i.e.* ˢⲉⲧ-ⲁϩⲉ ⲣⲁⲧ=ⲥ : ⲉⲧⲁϩⲉ K ‖ **22** *l.* ⲡⲉⲥⲣⲁⲛ ⲡⲉ ⲙⲉ̄ⲣⲟⲩⲏⲗ̄ | *l.* ⲧⲁⲓ ⲛ̄ⲧⲁ=ⲥ- ‖ **23** *i.e.* κλάδος ‖ **24** *i.e.* ˢⲙ̄-ⲡ-ⲱⲛⲁϩ ‖ **26–27** *i.e.* δύναμις | *i.e.* ˢⲙⲁⲁⲃ ⲙⲛ̄ ϯ : ⲙⲛ̄ⲧⲏ K ‖ **27** *i.e.* ˢⲙ̄ⲙⲟ=ⲕ ‖ **28** *i.e.* ˢⲙ̄ⲙⲟ=ⲕ | *i.e.* ˢⲉⲣⲉ-ϩⲉⲛ-ⲥⲛϥⲉ

I adjure you today by the breath of life which comes out from your nose; its name is Stōēl! I adjure you today by Piphemeraniōn, that is your tongue! I adjure you today by Tekauriēl, which is |⁵ your mouth! I adjure you today by your molars, which are Ōriskōs! I adjure you today by your head, which is Ōrasiēl! I adjure you today by the form of the cross of light which is upon your head, which is Sitōriēl! |¹⁰ I adjure you today by the wreath of light which is on your neck, its name is Lelaēl! I adjure you today by Ōrphamiēl, which is your finger of your right hand! I adjure you today by your two hands, Anaramouēl, |¹⁵ your right hand, Antrakouēl, your left hand! I adjure you today by your two feet, Thaōth, Thaōtha! I adjure you today by the throne of light upon which you sit, judging all of the creatures |²⁰ which you have created!

I adjure you today by the great *power that stands above your head, her name ⟨is⟩ Merouēl, she who put upon your head the wreath ⟨made⟩ from the shoots of the Tree of Life, Asaf, Asama, |²⁵ Asamlōl! I adjure you today by your great power which is thirty, fifteen, and thirty-six ⟨in number⟩, one on your right, the other one on your left, with swords of fire in their hands, ready, doing your command! |³⁰ I adjure you today by your *Four Creatures who

---

12. ⲛⲱⲣⲫⲁⲙⲓⲏⲗ : **"by Ōrphamiēl"** For this name, see *PCM* I 12 p. 31 ll. 4–5 and accompanying note.

19–20. ⲉⲡⲥⲱⲛ ⲧⲏⲣϥ : **"all of the creatures"** Kropp and Meyer translate "the whole creation" ("die ganze Schöpfung").

26–27. ⲉⲩϣⲓⲡⲓ ⲙⲁⲃ ⳰ ⲙⲉⲛⲧⲏ ⲙⲉ ⲙⲁⲁⲃⲧⲁⲥⲉ : ⲡⲥⲟⲩⲉⲓ : **"thirty, fifteen, and thirty-six ⟨in number⟩"** Kropp translates "which amounts to 30 times 15 and 30" ("die 30 mal 15 und 30 beträgt").

page 9 (= *Kropp 112*) (flesh)

ⲥⲱⲕ ϩⲁ ⲡⲉⲕⲑⲣⲱⲛⲟⲥ ⸗ ⲉⲧⲉ ⲛⲁⲓ ⲛⲉⲩⲣⲁⲛ
ⲙⲉⲗⲓⲧⲟⲛ ⸗ ⲁⲕⲣⲁⲙⲁⲧⲁ · ⲡⲥⲟⲩⲣⲟⲩⲑⲓⲟⲩⲛ ⸗
ⲡⲁⲣⲁⲙⲏⲣⲁ ≡ ⲉⲩⲥⲙⲟⲩ ⲉⲣⲁⲕ ⸗ ⲡⲉϩⲟⲟⲩ ⲙⲛ
ⲧⲉⲩϣⲏ ⸗ ⲉⲩϫⲱⲱ ⲙⲟⲥ ⸗ ϫⲉ ⲁⲅⲓⲁⲥ ⁚ ⲁⲅⲓⲁⲥ
5 ⲁⲅⲓⲁⲥ ⲕⲏⲣⲓⲱⲥ ⸗ ⲥⲁⲃⲁⲱⲑ ⸗ ⲛⲁ ⲙⲡⲏⲩⲉⲓ ⲙⲛ ⸗
ⲛⲁ ⲡⲕⲁϩ ≡ ⲙⲉϩ ⁚ ⲉⲃⲁⲗ ⁚ ϩⲉⲙ ⲡⲉⲕ·ⲉⲟⲟⲩ ⲉⲧⲟⲩⲁⲁⲃ ⸗
☦ ⲉⲙⲡⲟⲟⲩ ⲛⲙⲡⲓⲥⲉⲣⲁⲫⲓⲛ ⸗ ⲃ̄ ⸗ ⲉⲧϩⲱⲃⲥ ⲉⲡⲉⲩ-
ϩⲁ ⲉⲧⲉ ⲛⲁⲓ ⲡⲉⲩⲣⲁⲛ ⸗ ⲫⲱⲣⲁⲉⲓⲙ ⸗ ⲱⲗⲁⲃⲱⲣⲓⲙ ≡
☦ ⲉⲙⲡⲟⲟⲩ ⸗ ⲕⲉⲥⲛⲁⲩ ⁚ ⲉⲑⲱⲃⲥ ⲛⲉⲩⲉⲣⲏϯ ⲉⲧⲉ
10 ⲛⲁⲓ ⲡⲉⲃⲣⲁⲛ ⲥⲱⲗⲱⲙⲱⲛ ⸗ ⲧⲱⲣⲱⲑⲱⲣⲁ
☦ ⲉⲙⲡⲟⲟⲩ ⲙ̄ⲡⲓⲥⲛⲉⲩ ⁚ ⲉⲧϩⲱⲃⲥ ⲉⲡⲉⲩⲥⲱⲙⲁ ⸗
ⲉⲧⲉ ⲛⲁⲓ ⲡⲉⲩⲣⲁⲛ ⲥⲱⲭⲱⲧ ≡ ⲁⲭⲱⲣⲃⲟⲩ ≡
ⲧⲉⲩⲗⲁⲗⲓⲁ ⸗ ⲧⲉ ⲧⲁⲓ ⸗ ϫⲉ ⲕⲟⲩⲁⲁⲃ ⸗ ⲕⲟⲩⲁⲁⲃ ⸗
ⲕⲟⲩⲁⲁⲃ ⸗ ⲡⲟⲥ ⸗ ⲥⲁⲃⲁⲱⲑ ⸗ ⲉⲧⲡⲉ ⸗ ⲙⲛ ⲉⲧⲡⲕⲁϩ ⸗
15 ⲙⲏϩ ⲉⲃⲁⲗ · ϩⲉ ⲡⲉⲕⲉⲟⲟⲩ ⸗ ⲉⲧⲟⲩⲁⲁⲃ ⸗
☦ ⲉⲙⲡⲟⲟⲩ ⸗ ⲙⲡⲉⲕⲇ̄ ⸗ ⲉⲙⲡⲉⲣⲉⲥⲃⲏⲣⲟⲥ ≡ ⲉⲧϩⲁ ⲧⲉⲕⲉⲡⲓⲥⲕⲱⲡⲏ ⸗ ⲛⲁⲓ ⲧⲁⲕⲧⲁϩⲁⲩ ⲉⲣⲁⲧⲟⲩ ≡
ⲉⲙⲡⲉϩⲟⲟⲩ ⲉⲡⲧⲁⲕⲧⲁⲙⲓⲁⲩ ⁚ ⲉϫⲓⲛ ⲁⲗⲫⲁ ϣ ⲟⲱ
☦ ⲉⲙⲡⲟⲟⲩ ⲛ̄ⲧⲛⲟϭ ⲛ̄ϭⲓⲭ ⲛ̄ⲧⲁⲕⲧⲁⲁⲥ ⲉϫⲱⲟⲩ ⸗
20 ☦ ⲉⲙⲡⲟⲟⲩ ⸗ ⲡⲉⲕⲇ̄ ⲛ̇ⲑⲣⲱⲛⲟⲥ ⸗ ⲉⲩϩⲉⲙⲁⲁⲥ
ϩⲓϫⲱⲃ ⸗ ⲙⲛ ⁚ ⲛⲉⲩϭⲉⲣⲏⲡⲏ ⲛ̇ⲟⲩⲃ ⸗ ⲉⲩϩⲓϫⲉ-
ⲛ ⲛ̇ⲉⲩ·ⲁⲡⲏⲩⲉⲓ ⸗ ⲙ̇ⲛ ⲛⲉⲕ·ⲗⲁⲙ ⸗ ⲉⲧϩⲛ
ⲡⲉⲩⲙⲁϯ ⸗ ⲙⲛ ⲛⲉⲩⲫⲓⲁⲗⲓ ⲛ⸗ⲛⲟⲩⲃ ≡ ⲉⲧ-
ⲛⲉⲩϭⲓⲭ ⸗ ⲙⲛ ☦ᶜⲛⲟⲩⲃⲓ ⲉⲧ⸗ⲛⲉⲩ ⲡϣⲱⲓ ⸗
25 ϩⲁ ⲫⲁ ⲙⲡⲓⲱⲧ ⁚ ⲙⲛ ⲡϣⲏⲣⲉ ⸗ ⲙⲛ ⲡⲉⲡⲛ̄ⲁ̄
ⲉⲧⲟⲩⲁⲁⲃ ⸗ ⲥⲱⲧⲙ ⲉⲣⲁⲓ ⲡⲁⲟⲩ ⁚ ⲱ ⲣⲉϥⲥⲱⲧⲙ ⸗ ϫⲉ ⲥⲙⲏ ⲉⲣⲁⲓ ⁚ ⲱ ⲡⲣⲉⲃ⁚ⲭⲓⲥ⸗ⲙⲏ ⸗
ⲙⲁⲣⲉ⸗ⲡⲁⲥⲁⲡⲥ ⸗ ⲉⲓ ⲉϩⲣⲁⲓ ⸗ ϣⲁⲣⲁⲕ ⸗ ⲛⲧⲉ-
ⲧⲁⲥⲙⲏ ⸗ ⲉⲓ ⲡϣⲱⲓ ⁚ ϣⲁ ⲡⲉⲉⲑⲣⲱⲛⲟⲥ
30 ⲉⲕϣⲁⲛⲁϩⲧⲏⲕ ⁚ ϩⲁ ⲡⲉⲕⲓⲛⲓ ⁚ ⲙⲛ ⲧⲉⲕϩⲓⲕⲱⲛ ⸗ ϫⲓ ⲛⲁⲡⲱⲗⲟⲅⲓⲁ ⲛⲧⲁⲁⲧ ⸗
ⲱ ⲡⲁⲟⲥ ⸗ ⲉⲕⲓ ⁚ ϩⲓϫⲛ ⲡⲓⲙⲁⲟⲩ ⸗ ⲙⲛ

---

1 *i.e.* θρόνος | *i.e.* ˢⲉⲧⲉ ⲛⲁⲓ ⲛⲉ ⲛⲉ⸗ⲩ-ⲣⲁⲛ || **2** ⲁⲕⲣⲁⲙⲁⲧⲁ K || **3** *i.e.* ˢⲙ̄-ⲡⲉ-ϩⲟⲟⲩ || **4** *i.e.* ˢⲛ̄-ⲧ-ⲉⲩϣⲏ : ⲧⲉⲩϣⲏ K | *i.e.* ˢⲉ⸗ⲩ-ϫⲱ ⲙ̄ⲙⲟ⸗ⲥ || **4–5** *i.e.* ἅγιος (twice) || **5** *i.e.* κύριος | *i.e.* ˢⲛⲁ-ⲙ̄-ⲡⲏⲩⲉ || **7–20** *i.e.* ˢϯ-(ⲧⲁⲣⲕⲟ ⲙ̄ⲙⲟ⸗ⲕ) ⲙ̄-ⲡⲟⲟⲩ *cf.* CdF : ϯⲱⲣⲕ ⲉⲣⲁⲕ ⲉⲙⲡⲟⲟⲩ K || **7** *i.e.* σεραφίμ || **8, 12** *i.e.* ˢⲉⲧⲉ ⲛⲁⲓ ⲛⲉ ⲛⲉ⸗ⲩ-ⲣⲁⲛ || **9** *i.e.* ˢⲙ̄-ⲡ-ⲕⲉ-ⲥⲛⲁⲩ / *l.* ⲉⲧ-ϩⲱⲃⲥ | *i.e.* ˢⲛⲉ⸗ⲩ-ⲟⲩⲉⲣⲏⲧⲉ || **9–10** *i.e.* ˢⲉⲧⲉ ⲛⲁⲓ ⲛⲉ ⲛⲉ⸗ϥ-ⲣⲁⲛ || **11** *i.e.* σῶμα | **12** *l.* ⲛⲁⲓ K || **13** *i.e.* λαλιά || **14** *l.* ⲡ-ϭ(ⲱ)ⲥ | *i.e.* ˢⲉⲧⲉⲣⲉ-ⲧ-ⲡⲉ | *i.e.* ˢⲉⲧⲉⲣⲉ-ⲡ-ⲕⲁϩ || **15** *i.e.* ˢⲙⲏϩ ⲉⲃⲟⲗ ϩⲙ̄-ⲡⲉ⸗ⲕ- || **16** *i.e.* ˢⲙ̄- | *i.e.* πρεσβύτερος || **17** *i.e.* ἐπισκοπή | *i.e.* ˢⲛ̄ⲧⲁ⸗ⲕ-ⲧⲁϩⲟ⸗ⲟⲩ || **18** *i.e.* ˢⲙ̄- | *i.e.* ˢⲉⲛⲧ-ⲁ⸗ⲕ-ⲧⲁⲙⲓⲟ⸗ⲩ : ⲡⲧⲁⲕⲧⲁⲙⲓⲁⲩ K | *i.e.* ˢϫⲓⲛ ⲁⲗⲫⲁ ϣⲁ ⲱ *cf. e.g.* Crum CD ϣⲟⲩ || **20** *i.e.* θρόνος : ⲑⲣⲟⲛⲟⲥ K | *i.e.* ˢϩⲙⲟⲟⲥ || **21** *i.e.* ˢϩⲓϫⲱ⸗ϥ | *i.e.* ˢϭⲣⲏⲡⲉ | *i.e.* ˢⲛ̄-ⲛⲟⲩⲃ || **22** *i.e.* ˢⲁⲡⲏⲩⲉ | *i.e.* ˢⲛⲉ⸗ⲩ-ⲕⲗⲟⲙ || **23** *i.e.* φιάλη || **23–24** *i.e.* ˢⲉⲧ-ϩⲛ̄ ⲛⲉ⸗ⲩ-ϭⲓⲭ || **24** *i.e.* ˢⲧ̄ⲛⲟⲩϥⲉ : ϯⲥⲛⲟⲩⲃⲓ *l.* ⲥⲧⲛⲟⲩϥⲓ K | *i.e.* ˢⲛⲏⲩ || **25** *i.e.* ˢⲡ-ϩⲟ | *i.e.* πν(εῦμ)α || **26** *i.e.* ˢⲙ̄-ⲡⲟⲟⲩ | *i.e.* ὤ || **29** corrected from ⲡⲉⲓⲉⲣⲱⲛⲟⲥ by overwriting where ⲓ may be unfinished ⲕ *i.e.* θρόνος : ⲡⲉ[ⲕ]ⲑⲣⲱⲛⲟⲥ K || **30** *i.e.* ˢⲉ⸗ⲕ-ⲉ-ϣⲁⲛ ϩⲧⲏ⸗ⲕ *cf.* ⲉⲕⲉϣⲁⲛⲉ ϩⲧⲏⲕ CdF | *i.e.* ˢⲉⲓⲛⲉ || **31** *i.e.* εἰκών | *l.* ⲛⲁ-ἀπολογία (haplography) || **32** *i.e.* ὤ | *i.e.* ˢⲡⲁ-ϫ(ⲟⲉⲓ)ⲥ | *i.e.* ˢⲉ⸗ⲕ-ⲉⲓ.

draw your throne, whose names are Meliton, Akhramata, Psourouthioun, Paramēra, blessing you by day and by night, saying, |^(Greek) "*Holy, holy, |⁵ holy, Lord *Sabaoth, |^(Coptic) those of the heavens and those of the earth are full of your holy glory'! I adjure you today by the two *seraphim who cover their face, whose names are Phōraeim, Ōlalbōrim! I adjure you today ⟨by the⟩ other two who cover their feet, whose |¹⁰ names are Solōmōn, Thōrōthōra! I adjure you today by the two who cover their body, whose names are Sōkhōt, Akhōrbou! This is their song: 'You are holy, you are holy, you are holy, Lord Sabaoth, of whose holy glory the heaven and the earth |¹⁵ are full!' I adjure you today by the *Twenty-Four Presbyters, who are under your episcopacy, those whom you appointed on the day that you created them, from alpha to omega! I adjure you today by the great hand that you put upon them! |²⁰ I adjure you today by the twenty-four thrones that they sit upon and their diadems of gold which are upon their heads and their wreaths which are upon their necks and their golden bowls which are ⟨in⟩ their hands and the incense that rises up |²⁵ under the face of the Father and the Son and the Holy Spirit!

Listen to me today, O you who listen, heed my voice today, O you who heed voices, let my prayer go up to you and let my voice go up to the *throne, |³⁰ that you might take pity upon your likeness and your image! Receive my requests from me, O my lord, come upon this water and

---

2–3. ⲙⲉⲗⲓⲧⲟⲛ ⳽ ⲁⲕⲣⲁⲙⲁⲧⲁ · ⲡⲥⲟⲩⲣⲟⲩⲑⲓⲟⲩⲛ ⳽ ⲡⲁⲣⲁⲙⲏⲣⲁ : "Meliton, Akhramata, Psourouthiou" For these names of the Four Living Creatures, see the glossary under *Angelic Beings.

9. ⲕⲉⲥⲛⲁⲩ : "the other two" Following the previous line, Kropp adds in his translation the specification "seraphim" ("den beiden anderen Seraphim").

18. ⲉⲭⲓⲛ ⲁⲗⲫⲁ ϣ ⲟⲱ : "from alpha to omega" A reference to the names of the Twenty-Four Presbyters, which often each begin with one the twenty-four letters of the Greek alphabet (cf. glossary s.v. *Twenty-Four Presbyters). At the equivalent passage, the Collège de France copy includes their names in full, beginning ⲁⲭⲁⲏⲗ · ⲃⲁⲛⲟⲩⲏ[ⲗ] ⲅⲁⲣⲇⲓⲏⲗ · ⲇⲁⲑⲓⲏⲗ. The version in this manuscript thus seems to represent an abbreviation.

26–27. ⲣⲉϥⲥⲱⲧⲙ, ⲡⲣⲉϥ:ⲭⲓ ⲥⲙⲏ : "he who listens, he who heeds voices" Kropp, followed by Meyer, misunderstand the agentive prefix ⲣⲉϥ- as an abbreviation for the word (π)ρε(σ)β(ύτερος) "presbyters/elders" ("Ältesten"), translating instead, "O elders, listen... O elders, hear my voice" ("Hört mich heute, ihr Ältesten... horchet auf mich, ihr Ältesten").

30–31. ⲡⲉⲕⲓⲛⲓ : ⲙⲛ ⲧⲉⲕ ϩⲓⲕⲱⲛ : "your likeness and your image" Cf. PCM I 10 ll. 2–3 and accompanying notes.

31. ⲛⲁⲡⲱⲗⲟⲅⲓⲁ : "my requests" Kropp translates "my defence" ("meine Verteidigung"), Meyer as "spell"; cf. the discussion on p. 34.

page 10 (=Kropp 132) (hair)

ⲡⲛⲉϩ : ⲉⲕⲡⲱϣⲧ ϩⲓⲭⲱⲟⲩ ⲙⲡⲉⲕⲛⲁ ⲉⲧ⸗
ⲧⲟⲩⲁⲁⲃ ⸗ ⲉⲕⲥⲙⲟⲩ ⲉⲣⲟⲟⲩ ⸗ ⲉⲕϩⲁⲅⲓⲁⲥ⸗
ⲥⲉ ⲙⲁϥ ⸗ ⲉⲃⲙⲁϩⲟⲩ ⲛⲧⲉⲗϭⲁ ⲛⲓⲙ
ϫⲉⲕⲁⲁⲥ ⸗ ϩⲉ ⲧⲉⲩⲛⲟⲩ ⲉⲓⲛⲁⲡⲱϣⲧ ϩⲓⲭ-
5 ⲱ ⲡⲙⲁⲁⲩ : ⲥⲥ ⸗ ⲉⲛⲥⲉⲓ ⲉⲃⲁⲗ ⲛϩⲏⲧϥ —
ⲛϭⲓ ϣⲱⲛⲓ · ⲛⲓⲙ : ⲉⲧϩⲉ ⲡⲉⲃⲥⲱⲙⲁ ⲥⲥ ⲁⲓⲟ
ⲉϣⲱⲡⲓ ⲟⲩϣⲱⲛⲓ ⲉⲃϩⲁⲩ ⲡⲉ ⲉⲓⲉ ⲟⲩ-
ⲣⲁϩⲧⲥ ⲧⲉⲙⲱⲛⲓⲟⲛ ⸗ ⲉⲓⲉ ⲟⲩⲉⲛⲉⲣⲅⲓⲉ
ⲉⲓⲉ ⲟⲩϩⲓⲕ ⲡⲉ ⸗ ⲙⲁⲣⲟⲩ⸗ⲡⲱⲧ ⸗ ⲉⲓϯ ϩⲓⲕ
10 ⲛⲥⲱϣ : ⲉⲓⲉϯ ⲕⲁⲕⲟⲩⲣⲕⲱⲥ ⸗ ⲉⲓⲧⲉ : ⲧⲉⲭⲛⲓ ⲛⲓⲙ ⸗ ⲛⲧⲉⲙⲱⲛⲓⲟⲛ ⸗ ⲉⲓⲧⲉ ⲥⲱϣⲃ ⸗
ⲉⲓⲧⲉ ⲛⲉⲣⲅⲓⲁ · ⲛϩⲣⲓⲙⲉ ⸗ ⲉⲓⲧⲉ ⲕⲁⲛⲧⲁⲕⲗⲏϯⲕⲟⲛ ⸗ ⲉⲓⲧⲉ ⲇⲉⲛⲁⲙⲓⲥ ⸗ ⲉⲑⲁⲟⲩ
ⲉⲓⲧⲉ : ⲛⲁ ⲡⲁⲏⲣ ⸗ ⲉⲓⲧⲉ ⲛⲁ ⲧⲉⲩϣⲁⲩⲉⲓ ⸗
15 ⲛⲉⲧⲉϣⲁⲩ⸗ⲉⲩ ⲛϭⲓ ⲛⲉⲙⲁⲅⲟⲥ ⸗ ⲛϩⲟⲁⲩⲧ
ⲉⲓⲧⲉ ⲟⲩⲙⲁⲅⲟⲥ ⸗ ⲛⲥⲓⲙⲓ ⸗ ⲙⲁⲣⲟⲩⲉⲓ ⲉⲃⲁⲗ ⸗
ϩⲉ ⲥⲥ ⸗ ⲡⲁⲛⲁⲑⲉⲙⲁ ⸗ ⲉⲧⲛⲏⲩ ⲉⲃⲁⲗ ⸗
ϩⲉⲛ ⲧⲁⲡⲣⲟ ⸗ ⲙⲡⲓⲱⲧ ⲙⲛ ⲡϣⲏⲣⲉ ⲙⲉ ⸗
ⲡⲉⲡⲛⲁ ⲉⲧⲟⲩⲁⲁⲃ ⸗ ⲉⲃⲉⲉⲓ · ϩⲓⲭⲉⲛ ⲑⲏⲩ-
20 ⲧⲉⲛ ⲉⲃ⸗ⲃⲁⲧⲧⲏⲩⲧⲉⲛ ⲉⲃⲁⲗ : ⲁⲓⲟ ⲧⲁⲭⲏ
ϯ ⲉⲙⲡⲟⲟⲩ ⸗ ⲙⲅ ⲛⲓⲃⲓ ⲛⲧⲁⲕⲧⲟⲩ ⲉϩ⸗
ⲟⲩⲛ : ⲉⲡϩⲁ ⲛⲁⲇⲁⲙ ⸗ ⲙⲡⲉϩⲟⲟⲩ ⲛⲧⲁⲕⲧⲁⲙⲓⲁⲃ ⸗ ϣⲁⲛⲧⲉⲃϫⲓ ⲡⲉⲛⲁ ⲉⲧⲟⲩⲁⲁⲃ ⸗
ϫⲉⲕⲁⲥ : ⲉⲕⲥⲱⲧⲙ ⲉⲛⲁⲡⲱⲗⲟⲅⲓⲁ ⲙⲡⲟⲟⲩ ⸗
25 ⲙⲉ ⲛⲁⲭⲡⲓⲁ · ⲉⲕⲓ ⲉϩⲣⲁⲓ ϩⲓⲭⲉⲛ ⲡⲓⲙⲁⲟⲩ ⲙⲛ
ⲡⲓⲛⲉϩ ⸗ ⲁⲙⲟⲩ : ⲕⲁⲗⲟⲥ ⸗ ⲁⲕⲓ ⸗ ⲉⲕϩⲓⲭⲛ ⲉⲧ-
ⲉⲛⲁϩ : ⲛⲁⲥⲁⲣⲱⲑ ≡ ⲡⲛⲟϭ ⲛⲭⲉⲣⲟⲩⲃⲓⲛ ⲉⲛⲉⲣ-
ⲉⲣⲉⲙⲁⲟⲃ ⲙⲛ ⲟⲩⲁ ⸗ ⲟⲩϭⲁⲥ ⲛⲧⲃⲁ ⲛⲁⲅⲅⲉⲗⲱⲥ ≡ ϩⲓ ⲛⲁⲣⲭⲏⲁⲅⲅⲉⲗⲱⲥ ≡ ⲥⲱⲕ
30 ϩⲓⲑⲏ ⲙⲁⲃ ⲕⲁⲧⲁ ⲑⲏ : ⲛⲧⲁⲕⲡⲱⲧⲉ ⟦.⟧

---

1 *l.* ⲡⲓⲛⲉϩ | ⲙⲡⲉⲕ[ⲡ]ⲛⲁ K | *i.e.* ˢⲛⲅ̄-ⲡⲱϩⲧ | *i.e.* (π)ν(εῦμ)α || **1–2** *l.* ⲉⲧ-ⲟⲩⲁⲁⲃ || **2–3** *i.e.* ἁγιάζειν || **3** *i.e.* ˢⲙ̄ⲙⲟ⸗ϥ : ⲙⲁⲟⲩ K | *i.e.* ˢⲛ̄ϥ-ⲙⲁϩ⸗ⲟⲩ || **4** *l.* ϩⲛ ⲧⲉⲩⲛⲟⲩ || **4–5** *l.* ϩⲓⲭⲱ⸗ϥ : *l.* ⲡⲙⲁⲁⲩ ϩⲓⲭⲱ K || **5** *i.e.* (δεῖνα) (δεῖνα) | *l.* ⲛ̄ⲥⲉ-ⲉⲓ || **6** *i.e.* ˢⲡⲉ⸗ϥ-ⲥⲱⲙⲁ | *i.e.* (δεῖνα) (δεῖνα) || **7** *i.e.* ˢⲉ⸗ϥ-ϩⲟⲟⲩ || **8** *i.e.* δαιμόνιον | *l.* ⲟⲩⲣⲉϩⲧⲥ ⲛⲧⲉ ⲇⲓⲙⲱⲛⲓⲟⲛ K | *l.* ἐνέργεια (haplography) || **9–14** *i.e.* ⲉⲓⲧⲉ || **10** *i.e.* κακοῦργος | **10–11** *i.e.* τέχνη || **11** *i.e.* δαιμόνιον | *i.e.* ˢⲥⲱⲱϥ K || **12** *i.e.* ἐνέργεια || **12–13** *i.e.* κατακλιτικόν *cf.* note : κατακ[η]λητικός K || **13** *i.e.* δύναμις | *l.* ⲉⲧ-ϩⲟⲟⲩ || **14** *i.e.* ἀήρ || **14–15** *i.e.* ˢⲛ-ⲉⲧⲉ-ϣⲁ⸗ⲩ-ⲁⲁ⸗ⲩ *cf.* ⲧⲁ ⲛⲉⲧϣⲁⲩⲉⲓⲧⲟⲩ CdF : ˢⲛⲁⲓ ⲉⲧ-ϣⲟⲩⲉ [ⲉⲓ] ⲛ-ⲉⲧ-ϣⲟⲩⲟ "what is dry [and] what is flooding (?)" ("Austrocknende und Überflutende (?)") K, M || **15–16** *i.e.* μάγος || **16** *i.e.* ˢϩⲟⲟⲩⲧ || **17** *i.e.* (δεῖνα) (δεῖνα) | *i.e.* ἀνάθεμα || **18** *l.* ⲧ-ⲧⲁⲡⲣⲟ (haplography) || **19** *i.e.* πν(εῦμ)α | *i.e.* ˢⲉ⸗ϥ-ⲉ-ⲉⲓ || **20** *i.e.* ˢⲉ⸗ϥ-ϫⲟⲧ⸗ⲧⲏⲩⲧⲛ̄ : ⲃⲁⲧ⸗ *l.* ϣⲱⲧⲉ "to destroy you" ("er zerstöre euch!") K | *i.e.* ταχύ || **21** *i.e.* †-(ⲧⲁⲣⲕⲟ ⲙ̄ⲙⲟ⸗ⲕ) ⲙ̄-ⲡⲟⲟⲩ : ϯⲱⲣⲕ ⲉⲣⲁⲕ ⲙⲡⲟⲟⲩ K | *i.e.* ˢⲛⲧⲁ⸗ⲕ ⲧⲁⲁ⸗ⲩ K || **23** *i.e.* ˢⲧⲁⲙⲓⲟ⸗ϥ : (π)ν(εῦμ)α : ⲡⲛⲁ K || **24** *i.e.* ˢⲉ⸗ⲕ-ⲉ-ⲥⲱⲧⲙ *cf.* ⲉⲕⲁⲥⲱⲧⲙ CdF | *l.* ⲛⲁ-ἀπολογία (haplography) || **25** *i.e.* ˢⲉ⸗ⲕ-ⲉ-ⲉⲓ *cf.* CdF || **26** *i.e.* καλῶς || **26–27** *l.* ⲉ-ⲧ-ⲉⲛⲁϩ (haplography) : ⲛⲧⲉⲛⲁϩ K || **27** *i.e.* χερουβίμ | *i.e.* ˢⲛ̄-ⲁⲏⲣ ? K || **27–28** *l.* ⲉⲛⲉⲣⲉⲙⲁⲟⲃ || **28** *i.e.* ˢⲙⲁⲁⲃ | ⲛⲧⲃ K, M || **28–29** *i.e.* ἄγγελος : ⲁⲅⲅⲉⲗⲱⲥ K || **29** *i.e.* ἀρχάγγελος || **30** *i.e.* ˢⲙ̄ⲙⲟ⸗ϥ | *i.e.* κατά | ⲛⲧⲁⲕⲡⲱⲧ K

this oil, pour your Holy Spirit upon them, bless them, sanctify it, so that he fills them with every healing, so that as soon as I pour upon ⟨him⟩ |⁵ the water, NN, child of NN, they will come out of him, namely every sickness which is in his body, NN, child of NN, yea, whether it is a wicked sickness or a demonic strike or a force or it is a magic! Let them flee, whether |¹⁰ shameful magic or evil-doing or any demonic craft or pollution or female force or striking-down spells or evil power or those of the air or the things which they do, |¹⁵ namely male magicians or a female magician, let them come out of NN, child of NN! The anathema that comes forth from the mouth of the Father and the Son and the Holy Spirit, may it come upon |²⁰ you (pl.), obliterating you, yea, quickly! I adjure you today by ⟨the⟩ three breaths that you gave to the face of Adam on the day that you created him, so that he received the Holy Spirit, that you listen to my requests today, |²⁵ and my reproaches! May you come upon this water and this oil!

Come well; you came upon ⟨the⟩ wing of Asarōth, the great *cherub, as three hundred and fifteen thousand *angels and *archangels were going |³⁰ before him, you went

---

1–2. ⲉⲕⲡⲱⲣⲧ ϩⲓⲭⲱⲟⲩ ⲙⲡⲉⲕⲛⲁ̅ ⲉⲓ:ⲧⲟⲩⲁⲁⲃ : **"pour your Holy Spirit upon them"** Meyer and Kropp translate "through which you pour out your holy spirit" ("dass du darüber ausgiessest deinen heiligen Geist").

3. ⲉⲃⲏⲁϩⲟⲩ ⲛⲧⲉⲗϭⲁ ⲛⲓⲙ̅ : **"so that he fills it with every healing"** Kropp translates "that they are filled with all healing" ("dass sie mit aller Heilung erfüllt werden").

12–13. ⲕⲁⲛⲧⲁⲕⲗⲏϯⲕⲟⲛ : **"striking-down spells"** Greek κατακλιτικόν, a technical term drawn from Graeco-Egyptian magic for curses which cause their victims to be bedbound (κατακλίνω) with disease; for an example, see *PCM* I 18, and *cf.* the brief discussion in Dosoo 2022d: 218 n. 40.

24. ⲛⲁⲡⲱⲗⲟⲅⲓⲁ : **"my requests"** Kropp translates "my defence" ("meine Verteidigung"), Meyer as "spell" (*cf.* the comments in the introduction, p. 5).

27. ⲛ̅ⲁⲥⲁⲣⲱⲑ ≡ ⲡⲛⲟϭ ⲛ̅ⲭⲉⲣⲟⲩⲃⲓⲛ : **"Asarōth, the great cherub"** *Cf.* *PCM* I 18 l. 3 and the accompanying note.

page 11 (= *Kropp 150*) (flesh)

ⲙⲡⲓⲟⲩⲁⲉⲓⳉ ϣⲁ · ⲁⲇⲁⲙ ⸗ ϩⲉ ⲡⲁⲣⲁⲧⲥⲱⲥ ⸗
ⲛ̄ⲧⲉⲣⲉϩⲁⲃ⸗ⲡⲁⲧⲁ ⲙⲁⲃ ⸗ ⲉⲩϣϣ ⲉⲃⲁⲗ ⲉⲩ-
ϫⲱϣ ⲙⲟⲥ ⸗ ϫⲉ ⲡⲉⲉⲟⲩ ⲛ̀ⲁⲕ ⲡⲉⲣⲟ ⲡⲭ̄ⲥ̄ ⸗
ⲡⲁⲛⲧⲱⲣ ⸗ ⲧⲡⲉ ⲙ̄ⲛ ⲡⲕⲁϩ ⸗ ⲙⲉϩ : ⲉⲃⲁⲗ · ϩⲉ ⲡ- ⸗
5   ⲡⲉⲕⲉⲟⲁⲩ ⲉⲧⲟⲩⲁⲁⲃ ⸗ ⲁⲙⲟⲩ ⲕⲁⲗⲟⲥ ≡ ⲁⲕⲓ ⸗ ⲡ̀-
ⲥⲁϣⲃ ⲛ̄ⲥⲧⲉⲣⲉⲩⲙⲁ ⸗ ⲥⲱⲕ ϩⲁ ⲧⲉⲕϩⲏ ≡ ⲡ̄ⲣ̄ⲏ̄ ⸗
ⲙⲛ ⲡⲁⲟϩ ⸗ ⲙⲛ ⲛⲉⲥⲓⲟⲩ ⲉⲣ ⲟⲩⲁⲉⲓⲛ ⲉⲣⲁⲕ ⸗ ⲛⲉ-
ⲛⲟϭ:ⲁⲙ ⲧⲏⲣⲟⲩ ⲛ̄ⲧⲡⲉ ⸗ ⲙⲛ ⲡⲕⲁϩ ⸗ ⲁϩⲉⲣⲁⲧⲟ̄ⲩ̄
ⲉⲣⲉⲧⲥⲁⲗⲡⲓⳉ ⸗ ⲥⲱⲕ ϩⲁ ⲧⲉⲕϩⲏ : ⲉⲥϫⲱ ⲙ̄ⲙⲟⲥ ⸗
10 ϫⲉ ⲛⲉⲧⲙⲁⲟⲩⲧ ⸗ ⲧⲱⲟⲩⲛ ⸗ ⲧⲉϩⲓⲏ ⲉⲧⲭ̄ⲓ ⲙⲁⲓ- ⸗
ⲉⲓⲧ : ⲉϩⲟⲩⲛ ⲡⲱⲛⲁϩ ⸗ ⲁⲙⲟⲩ : ⲉϩⲣⲁⲓ ⸗ ⲛ̄ϩⲏⲧⲥ ⸗
ⲉⲕⲁϩⲉⲣⲁⲕ · ϩⲓⲭⲛ ⲡⲓⲙⲁⲩ ⸗ ⲙⲛ ⲡⲓⲛⲉ̄ϩ̄ ⸗ ⲉⲕⲥⲙⲟⲩ ⲉⲣⲁⲩ : ⲉⲕϩⲁⲅⲓⲁⲥⲥⲉ ⲙⲁⲩ ⸗ ϫⲉⲕⲁⲟ̄ⲥ̄ ⸗
ⲉⲩϣⲁⲛⲡⲱϩⲧ ⲙⲁⲩ ⸗ ϫⲱ : ⲛ̄ⲛ̄ ⸗ ⲉⲩⲟⲩⲉⲓ ⲉⲃⲁⲗ ⸗
15 ⲛ̄ϩⲏⲧϥ ⲛ̄ϭⲓ ϩⲓⲥⲓ ⲛⲓ̄ⲙ̄ ⸗ ⲉⲧϩⲉ ⲡⲉⲃⲥⲱⲙⲁ ⸗
ⲓⲉϩ̄ ⸗ ϩⲁ̄ⲕ̄ ⸗ ϩⲁⲕ ⲧⲉⲩⲛⲟⲩ ϭⲉ ⲡⲁ̄ⲥ̄ⲥ̄ ⸗ ϣⲁⲛⲁϩⲧⲏⲕ
ϩⲁ ⲡⲉⲕⲓⲛⲓ ⲙ̄ⲛ ⲧⲉⲕϩⲓⲕⲱⲛ ⸗ ⲙⲡⲣⲉⲕⲉ ⲡ-
ϩⲱⲃ ⲉⲛⲉⲕϭⲓⳉ ⲉⲃⲡⲱⲧ ⲉⲡⲧⲁⲕⲟ
ϯⲱⲣⲕ ⲉⲣⲁⲕ ⸗ ⲉⲡϣⲁⲣⲉⲡ ⲉϫⲱⲕ⸗ⲉⲙ ⲉⲛ̄-
20 ⲧⲁⲕϫⲓ ϫⲱⲕⲉⲙ ⲛ̄ϩⲏⲧϥ ⸗ ϩⲉⲛ ⲧⲡⲓⲕⲏ ⲙⲁⲩ
ⲛⲱⲛⲁϩ ⸗ ⲉⲥⲉ̇ⲛ ⲧⲙⲏϯ ⲙⲡⲁⲣⲁⲧⲥⲱⲥ ⸗ ≡
ϯ ⲉⲙⲡⲟⲟⲩ ⸗ ⲛ̄ⲛⲓⲧⲉⲛⲁⲙⲓⲥ̄ ⲡⲉⲥⲣⲁⲛ ⲡⲉ ⸗
ⲡⲁⲣⲃⲓⲱ̄ⲛ̄ⲁ̄ ⸗ ⲧⲙⲉϩ:ⲥⲛⲏϯ ⲡⲉⲥⲣⲁⲛ ⸗ ϯⲙⲉⲥ̄
ⲣⲱⲕϩⲁⲑⲓⲁⲣⲓ ≡ ⲧⲙⲉϩⲅ̄ ⲡⲉⲥⲣⲁⲛ ⸗ ⲡⲉ ϯ-
25 ϩⲣⲁⲭⲁⲏⲗ̄ · ⲧⲙⲉϩ:ⲇ̄ : ⲡⲉⲥⲣⲁⲛ ⲡⲉ̄ ⲧⲁⲗⲗⲱⲉⲓ ⸗
ⲧⲙⲉϩ:ⲉ̄ : ⲡⲉⲥⲣⲁⲛ ⸗ ⲡⲉ̄ ⲟⲩⲁⲛⲱⲛ ⸗ ⲧⲙⲉϩ⸗ⲋ̄ ≡
ⲡⲉⲥⲣⲁⲛ ⸗ ⲡⲉ̄ ⲥⲁⲣⲓⲏⲗ̄ ≡ ⲧⲙⲉϩ⸗ⲍ̄ ⸗ ⲡⲉⲥⲣⲁⲛ ⸗
ⲡⲉ̄ ⲧⲁⲩⲣⲓⲏⲗ̄ ⸗ ϯ ⲉⲙⲡⲟⲟⲩ ⲙⲡⲁⲙⲁϩϯ ⸗
ⲡⲉⲕⲛⲟϭ : ⲛ̄ϭⲉⲃⲁⲓ ⲉⲧϫⲟⲥⲓ ⸗ ⲕⲉⲭⲟⲟⲩ ⲛⲁⲓ ⸗
30 ⲛⲉⲛⲓⲧⲉⲛⲁ *vac* ⲙⲓⲥ ⲉⲧⲟⲩⲁⲁⲃ ⸗
ⲉϩⲣⲁⲓ ⸗ ϩⲓϫⲉⲛ ⲡⲓⲙⲁⲩ ⲙ̀ⲛ ⲡⲓⲛ̄ⲉ̄ϩ̄ ≡

---

1 *i.e.* παράδεισος ‖ **2** *i.e.* ˢⲡ-ϩⲟϥ | *i.e.* ἀπατᾶν | ˢⲙ̄ⲙⲟ⸗ϥ ‖ **3** *i.e.* ˢϫⲱ | *i.e.* ˢⲙ̄ⲙⲟ⸗ⲥ | *i.e.* ˢⲡ-ⲉⲟⲩ | *i.e.* χ(ριστό)ς ‖ **4** *i.e.* ˢⲡ-ⲡⲁⲛⲧⲟⲕⲣⲁⲧⲱⲣ *cf.* note to *PCM* I 25 p. 2 l. 2 ‖ **4–5** *l.* ϩⲉ ⲡⲉⲕⲉⲟⲁⲩ (dittography) | *i.e.* ˢⲉⲟⲟⲩ ‖ **6** *i.e.* ˢⲥⲁϣϥ | *i.e.* στερέωμα | *l.* ⲉⲩ-ⲥⲱⲕ ? ‖ **7** ˢⲟⲟϩ ‖ **8** ˢⲛⲟϭ ⲛ̄-ϭⲁⲙ (haplography) K ‖ **9** *i.e.* σάλπιγξ ‖ **10** *l.* ⲧ-ϩⲓⲏ ⲉ⸗ⲧ-ⲕϫⲓ ⲙⲁⲓⲧ (?) "that is the way which leads (?)" ("Das sei der Weg, der herführt (?)") K : "may this be the way you lead" (?) M ‖ **10–11** *i.e.* ˢⲙⲟⲉⲓⲧ ‖ **11** *i.e.* ˢⲱⲛϩ ‖ **12** *i.e.* ˢⲛ̄-ⲅ-ⲁϩⲉⲣⲁⲧ⸗ⲕ ‖ **13** K omits line, restores ⲉⲕ⸍ⲥⲙⲟⲩ ⲉⲣⲟⲟⲩ ⲉⲕϩⲁⲅⲓⲁⲥⲥⲉ ⲙⲁⲩ ϫⲉⲕⲁⲁⲥ *cf.* p. 4, l. 16 | *i.e.* ἁγιάζειν | *i.e.* ˢⲙ̄ⲙⲟ⸗ⲟⲩ | *i.e.* ˢϫⲉⲕⲁⲁⲥ ‖ **14** *i.e.* ˢⲙ̄ⲙⲟ⸗ⲟⲩ | *i.e.* ˢϩⲓϫⲛ̄- *cf.* ϩⲓϫⲱ- | *i.e.* (δεῖνα) (δεῖνα) ‖ **15** *i.e.* ˢⲡⲉ⸗ϥ-σῶμα ‖ **16** *l.* (ⲭ)ⲟ(ⲉⲓ)ⲥ | *l.* ϩⲛ ⲧⲉ-ⲩⲛⲟⲩ | *i.e.* ˢϣⲛ̄ϩⲏⲧ⸗ⲕ ‖ **17** *i.e.* εἰκών | *i.e.* ˢⲙⲡⲣ̄⸗ⲕⲁ ‖ **18** *i.e.* ˢⲛ̄-ⲛⲉ⸗ⲕ-ϭⲓϫ | *i.e.* ˢⲉ⸗ϥ-ⲡⲱⲧ ‖ **20** *i.e.* πηγή K | *i.e.* ˢⲙ̄-ⲙⲟⲟⲩ ‖ **21** *i.e.* ˢⲱⲛϩ | *i.e.* παράδεισος ‖ **22–28** *i.e.* ˢϯ-(ⲧⲁⲣⲕⲟ ⲙ̄ⲙⲟ⸗ⲕ) ⲙ̄-ⲡⲟⲟⲩ : ϯⲱⲣⲕ ⲉⲣⲁⲕ ⲉⲙⲡⲟⲟⲩ K | *i.e.* δύναμις ‖ **24** ϩⲁⲑⲛⲁⲣⲓ K ‖ **28** *i.e.* ˢⲁⲙⲁϩⲧⲉ ‖ **29** *i.e.* ˢⲙ̄-ⲡⲉ⸗ⲕ- | *i.e.* ˢϭⲃⲟⲓ | *i.e.* ˢϫⲟⲥⲉ | *i.e.* ˢⲉ⸗ⲕ-ϫⲟⲟⲩ ‖ **30** ⲧⲉⲛⲁ *vac.* ⲙⲓⲥ *pap.* (avoiding pre-existing damage) *i.e.* ˢⲛ̄-ⲛⲉⲓ-δύναμις | *l.* ⲡⲓ-ⲛⲉϩ

at that time to Adam in Paradise, after ⟨the⟩ snake deceived him, as they cried out, saying: 'Glory to you, King Christ Almighty! Heaven and earth are filled with |⁵ your holy glory!'

Come well; you came, the seven firmaments going under your path, the sun and the moon and the stars shone upon you, all the great powers of the heaven and of the earth standing, as the trumpet went before your path, saying, |¹⁰ 'O dead, rise!' The path that leads to life, come down upon it, and stand over this water and this oil, and bless them and sanctify them, so that when they are poured upon NN, child of NN, they retreat |¹⁵ from him, namely every suffering that is in his body, Ieh, Hak, Hak!

At once, therefore, my Lord, have pity upon your likeness and your image! Do not allow the work of your hands to go towards destruction!

I adjure you by the first cleansing in |²⁰ which you were cleansed, in the well ⟨of the⟩ water of life that is in the middle of Paradise! I adjure you today by these *powers: her name is Parbiōna, the second, her name is Timesrōkhathiari, the third, her name is |²⁵ Tihrakhael, the fourth, her name is Tallōei, the fifth, her name is Ouanōn, the sixth, her name is Sariēl, the seventh, her name is Tauriēl! I adjure you today by the power ⟨of⟩ your great outstretched arm that you send to me |³⁰ these holy powers down upon this water and this oil

---

5–6. ⲁⲕⲓ ⲥ ⲛ̄ⲥⲁϣⲃ : **"you came, the seven"** Kropp translates "may you come with the seven" ("Du mögest kommen, während die sieben"). Meyer/Smith translate "come, with the seven."

17. ⲡⲉⲕⲓⲛⲓ ⲙⲛ̄ ⲧⲉⲕϩⲓⲕⲱⲛ : **"your likeness and your image"** *Cf. PCM* I 10 ll. 2–3 and accompanying notes.

page 12 (= *Kropp 168*) (hair)

ⲛⲉⲥⲉⲙⲁϩⲃ ⲉⲧⲁⲗϭⲁ ⲛⲓⲙ ⸗ ⲁⲩⲱ : ϣⲁⲛⲡⲁϩ̅ⲃ̅ ⸗
ϩⲉϫⲉⲛ ⲓ̅ⲥ̅ ⲛⲥⲉⲉⲓ ⲉⲃⲁⲗ ⲛ̇ϩⲏⲧⲃ ⲛ̇ϭⲓ ϩⲓϭⲓ ⸗
ⲛⲓⲙ ⲉⲧϩⲉ ⲡⲉⲩⲥⲱⲙⲁ ⲧⲉⲃ† ⲟⲩⲱ ⲉⲃⲁⲗ ⸗ ⲛ-
ⲑⲏ ⲙⲡϣⲏⲛ : ⲉⲡⲱⲛϩ ⸗ ⲉⲧϩⲛ ⲧⲙⲏⲧ † ⲙⲡⲁ-
5   ⲣⲁ†ⲥⲱⲥ ⸗ ⲁⲓⲟ̅ ⲧⲁⲭⲏ̅ ⸗ † ⲉⲙⲡⲟⲟⲩ ⲙ̇ⲡϣⲁⲣ-
ⲡ ⲛⲗⲟⲅⲟⲥ ⸗ ⲛⲧⲁⲃⲓ : ⲉⲃⲁⲗ : ϩⲉⲙ ⲡⲉⲕϩⲏⲧ
ⲁⲃϣⲱⲡⲓ ⲛⲁⲕ ⲛⲟⲩϣⲏⲣⲉ ⸗ ⲙⲱⲛⲟⲅⲉ-
ⲛⲏⲥ ⲉⲧⲉ ⲡⲁⲓ ⲡⲉ ⲓ̅ⲥ̅ ⲡⲉⲭ̅ⲥ̅ ⸗ † ⲉⲙⲡⲟⲟⲩ ⸗
ⲛⲧⲉⲣⲏⲛⲏ ⲛ̇ⲧⲁⲕⲧⲁⲁⲥ ⸗ ⲛⲁⲃ ⸗ ⲉⲃⲛⲏⲩ ⸗
10   ⲡⲉⲥⲛⲧ ⲉⲡⲕⲱⲥⲙⲟⲥ ⸗ ⲉⲃⲟⲩⲱϩ ⲉϩⲏⲧ ⸗
ⲥ ⲛⲟⲩ̇ⲥϩⲓⲙⲉ ⸗ ϫⲉ ⲙⲁⲣⲓⲁ̅ ⸗ ⲙⲁⲣⲓϩⲁⲙ
ⲁⲕⲟⲩⲁⲛⲁϩ ⸗ ⲡⲉⲕⲣⲁⲛ : ⲉⲃⲁⲗ · ϩⲉ ⲡⲕⲱ-
ⲥⲙⲟⲥ ⸗ ⲉⲧⲉ ⲡⲁⲓ ⲡⲉ : ⲙⲁⲛⲟⲩⲏⲗ̅
† ⲉⲙⲡⲟⲟⲩ ⸗ ⲡⲑ̅ ⲛⲉⲃⲁⲧ ⸗ ⲛⲧⲁⲕⲁⲁⲩ ⸗
15   ϩⲛ ⲧⲕⲁⲗⲁϩⲏ : ⲙⲁⲣⲓⲁ̅ ⸗ ⲧⲉⲕⲙⲁⲁⲩ ⸗
† ⲉⲙⲡⲟⲟⲩ ⸗ ⲉⲡⲅ̅ ⲛ̇ⲇⲩⲛⲁⲙⲓⲥ ⸗ ⲛ̇ϫⲱ-
ⲱⲣⲉ : ⲉⲧⲣⲁⲉⲓⲥ ⸗ ⲣⲁⲥ ⸗ ⲧⲉ ⲛⲁⲓ ⲧⲉ ⲛⲉⲣⲁⲛ ⲅⲁⲣⲙⲁⲛⲓⲏⲗ̅ ⸗ ⲉⲝⲓⲏⲗ̅ ⸗ ⲗⲟⲩⲗⲟⲩ-
ⲕⲁⲕⲥⲁⲥ̣ ≡ † ⲉⲙⲁⲕ ⲡⲟⲟⲩ ⲛϣⲁⲣⲡⲓ ⲛ-
20   ⲛⲏⲕⲏ ⸗ ⲛⲧⲁⲥⲧⲁⲁⲥ ⸗ ⲉⲡⲉⲕⲙⲱⲛⲱ-
ⲅⲉⲛⲏⲥ ⸗ ⲛϣⲏⲣⲉ ⲡⲉϩⲟⲟⲩ ⲛⲧⲁⲥⲙⲓⲥⲓ
ⲙⲁⲃ ⸗ ⲡⲉⲥⲣⲁⲛ ⸗ ⲡⲉ ⲭⲱⲣϣⲉⲓ̅ ⸗ ⲧⲙⲉϩ≡-
ⲥⲛⲏ† ⲛⲁⲁⲅⲓ : ⲡⲉ ⲁⲃⲕⲱ̅ ⸗ ⲧⲙⲉϩⲅ̅ ⲛⲁⲁⲅⲓ
ⲡⲉ ϩⲁⲛⲁⲩⲧⲱⲥ ⸗ † ⲉⲣⲁⲕ ⲡⲟⲟⲩ ⲙⲛⲉⲛⲙⲁ-
25   ⲉⲓⲁ ⲙ̇ⲛⲉϣⲡⲏⲣⲉ ⸗ ⲛⲧⲁⲃⲁⲁⲩ ⸗ ϩⲛ ⲧⲙⲏⲧ †
ⲛ̇†ⲕⲟⲩⲙⲏⲛⲉ ⲧⲏⲣⲥ ⸗ ϩⲉⲙ ⲡⲣⲁⲛ ⲛ̇ⲓ̅ⲥ̅ ⸗
ⲉⲧⲙⲟⲁⲩⲧ ⸗ ⲧⲱⲟⲩⲛ ⸗ ϩⲉⲛ ⲡⲣⲁⲛ : ⲓ̅ⲥ̅ ⸗
ⲛⲉⲧⲓⲙⲱⲛⲓⲱⲛ : ⲛⲉⲩ ⲉⲃⲁⲗ ϩⲉⲛ ⲉⲩ⸗
ⲣⲱⲙⲉ ⸗ ϩⲉⲙ ⲡⲣⲁⲛ ⸗ ⲓ̅ⲥ̅ ⸗ ⲛⲉⲧⲕⲏⲕ · ⲉⲡ-
30   ⲥⲱϩⲃ ⲧⲉⲃⲛⲩ ⸗ ϩⲉⲛ ᵛᵃᶜ ⲡⲣⲁⲛ ⸗
ⲓ̅ⲥ̅ ⲛⲉⲃⲉⲗⲏ ⸗ ⲛⲁⲩ ⲉⲃⲁⲗ · ϩⲉⲛ ⲡⲣⲁⲛ ⸗

---

1 *i.e.* ˢⲛ̅⸗ⲥⲉ-ⲙⲁϩ⸗ϥ ⲛ̅- K | ⲁⲩⲱ superfluous K | *i.e.* ˢⲉ⸗ⲩ-ϣⲁⲛ-ⲡⲁϩⲧ⸗ϥ : ⲉⲩϣⲁⲛⲡⲁϩⲧⲟⲩ K || **2** *i.e.* ˢϩⲓϫⲛ̅ | *i.e.* (δεῖνα) (δεῖνα) | *i.e.* ˢⲛ̇ϩⲏⲧ⸗ϥ | *i.e.* ˢⲛ̇ⲥⲉ-ⲉⲓ ‖ **3** *i.e.* ˢⲡⲉ⸗ϥ- | *i.e.* ˢⲛ̇ⲧⲉ⸗ϥ-† ⲟⲩⲱ : *i.e.* ˢⲉⲧ⸗ϥ-† ⲟⲩⲱ K ‖ **4** *i.e.* ˢⲙ̅-ⲡ-ϣⲛϩ ‖ **4–5** *i.e.* παράδεισος | *i.e* ταχύ ‖ **4–18** *i.e.* ˢ†-(ⲧⲁⲣⲕⲟ ⲙ̅ⲙⲟ⸗ⲕ) ⲙ̅-ⲡⲟⲟⲩ *cf.* CdF : †ⲱⲣⲕ ⲉⲣⲁⲕ ⲙⲡⲟⲟⲩ K || **6** *i.e.* λόγος | *i.e.* ˢⲛ̇ⲧⲁ⸗ϥ-ⲉⲓ ‖ **7** *i.e.* ˢⲁ⸗ϥ-ϣⲱⲡⲉ ‖ **7–8** *i.e.* μονογενής ‖ **8** *l.* ⲓ(ⲏⲥⲟⲩ)ⲥ ⲡⲉ-ⲭ(ⲣⲓⲥⲧⲟ́ⲥ) ‖ **9** *i.e.* εἰρήνη | *i.e.* ˢⲛⲁ⸗ϥ | *i.e.* ˢⲉ⸗ϥ-ⲛⲏⲩ corrected from ⲉⲃⲛⲏⲩ by overwriting ‖ **10** *i.e.* ˢⲉⲡⲉⲥⲛⲧ | *i.e.* κόσμος | *i.e.* ˢⲛ⸗ϥ-ⲟⲩⲱϩ ⲛ̅ϩⲏⲧ⸗ ‖ **12** *i.e.* ˢⲁ⸗ⲕ-ⲟⲩⲉⲛϩ ‖ **12–13** *i.e.* κόσμος ‖ **14** *i.e.* ˢⲙ̅-ⲡ-ⲑ̅ ‖ **15** *i.e.* ˢⲧ-ⲕⲁⲗⲁϩⲏ ⲙ̅-ⲙⲁⲣⲓⲁ ‖ **16** *i.e.* ˢⲙ̅-ⲡ-ⲅ̅ | *i.e.* δύναμις ‖ **17** *i.e.* ˢⲉⲧⲉ ⲛⲁⲓ ⲛⲉ ⸗ ⲣⲁⲥ ⸗ | *i.e.* ˢⲉⲣⲟ⸗ⲥ ‖ **17–18** *l.* ⲉⲧⲉ ⲛⲁⲓ ⲛⲉ ⲛⲉⲩⲣⲁⲛ K ‖ **19** ⲕⲁⲕⲥⲁ K ‖ **20** *i.e.* ˢⲛⲁⲁⲕⲉ *s.v.* Crum CD 223a ‖ **20–21** *i.e.* μονογενής ‖ **21** *i.e.* ˢⲙ̅-ⲡ-ϩⲟⲟⲩ ‖ **22** *i.e.* ˢⲙ̅ⲙⲟ⸗ϥ ‖ **23** ⲛⲁⲁⲕⲉ K (twice) ‖ **24** *i.e.* ˢ†-(ⲱⲣⲕ) ⲉⲣⲟ⸗ⲕ (ⲙ̅)-ⲡⲟⲟⲩ | *i.e.* ˢⲛ̅- ‖ **24–25** ‖ *i.e.* ˢⲙⲁⲉⲓⲛ ‖ **25** *i.e.* ˢⲙⲛ̅ ⲛⲉ-ϣⲡⲏⲣⲉ | *i.e.* ˢⲛ̇ⲧⲁ⸗ϥ-ⲁⲁ⸗(ⲟ)ⲩ ‖ **26** *i.e.* ˢⲧ-ⲟⲓⲕⲟⲩⲙⲉⲛⲏ : †ⲕⲟⲩⲙⲉⲛⲏ {ⲛⲉ} K | *l.* ⲓ(ⲏⲥⲟⲩ)ⲥ ‖ **27** *i.e.* ˢⲛ̅-ⲉⲧ-ⲙⲟⲟⲩⲧ | *l.* ⲛ̅-ⲓ(ⲏⲥⲟⲩ)ⲥ ‖ **28** *i.e.* δαιμόνιον | *i.e.* ˢⲛⲏⲩ ‖ **29** *l.* ⲛ̅-ⲓ(ⲏⲥⲟⲩ)ⲥ ‖ **29–30** *i.e.* ˢⲙ̅-ⲡ-ⲥⲱϩⲃ ‖ **30** *i.e.* ˢⲧⲃⲛⲩ | ϩⲉⲛ vac. ⲡⲣⲁⲛ *pap.* ‖ **31** *l.* ⲛ̅-ⲓ(ⲏⲥⲟⲩ)ⲥ | *i.e.* ˢⲃⲗ̅ⲗⲉⲉⲩ

so that it is filled with all healing, and when it is poured upon NN, son of NN, every suffering that is in his body will come out from him, and he will blossom like the Tree of Life that is in the middle of |⁵ Paradise, yea, quickly!

I adjure you today by the first word which came forth from your heart; it became for you a first-born child, that is Jesus Christ! I adjure you today by the peace that you gave to him as he came |¹⁰ down to the world and he dwelt in the womb of a woman, namely Mary Miriam; you revealed your name in the world, that is Manouēl! I adjure you today by the nine months which you passed in |¹⁵ the womb ⟨of⟩ Mary, your mother! I adjure you today by the three strong powers that protect her, whose names are Garmaniēl, Exiēl, Louloukaksas! I adjure you today by ⟨the⟩ first |²⁰ pang of labour that she had for your first-born child ⟨on⟩ the day on which she gave birth to him; its name is Khōrōei; the second pang, Abkō, the third pang is Hanautōs! I adjure you today by the |²⁵ signs and the wonders that he did in the midst of the entire inhabited world! In the name of Jesus, the dead arise; in the name ⟨of⟩ Jesus, the demons come out of a man; in the name ⟨of⟩ Jesus, the lepers |³⁰ are clean; in the name ⟨of⟩ Jesus, the blind see; in the name

---

12. ⲁⲕⲟⲩⲁⲛⲁϩ : **"you revealed"** Kropp translates "he revealed" ("Er offenbarte").

13. ⲙⲁⲛⲟⲩⲏⲗ : **"Manouēl"** As suggested by the context, this is a name for Jesus, derived from Emmanuel; *cf.* PCM I 11 p. 16 ll. 2–4 and accompanying note.

19–24. Labour of Mary: Compare P.Vindob. K 10335 (Crum 1942; KYP M264), a brief text containing the names of the bricks upon which Mary squatted when she gave birth, Ouakramak, Ouararmak, and Ouakra[...] (ⲟⲩⲁⲕⲣⲁⲙⲁⲕ ⲟⲩⲁⲣⲁⲙⲁⲕ ⲟⲩⲁⲕⲣⲁ[, ll. 3–5); *cf.* Preininger forthcoming c: chapter 4.

p. 12 l. 29–p. 13 l. 3. Healing miracles of Jesus: Apparently based upon the very similar list of Jesus' works in Matthew 11.5, Luke 7.22.

page 13 (= *Kropp 184*) (hair)

ⲛⲓⲥ̅ ⲛⲉϭⲁⲗⲏ ⲙ̇ⲁⲁϣ = ϩⲉⲙ ⲡⲣⲁⲛ ⲓ̅ⲥ̅ ⲡⲉⲧⲥⲏϭ —
ⲧⲱⲟⲩⲃⲓⲛ : ⲡⲉⲃϭⲁⲗⲁϫ̣ ⲙⲁⲟϣ = ϩⲉⲙ ⲡⲣⲁⲓⲛ ≡
ⲓ̅ⲥ̅ ⲛ̇ⲓⲉⲙⲡⲟ ϣⲁϫⲉ = ϩⲉⲙ ⲡⲣⲁⲛ = ⲓ̅ⲥ̅ ϣⲁⲣⲕⲱϩ-
ⲧ ϣⲱϩⲙⲉ = ϣⲁⲣⲙⲁⲩ ϣⲁⲟⲩⲉⲓ = ϩⲉⲙ ⲡⲣⲁⲛ
5 ⲛⲓ̅ⲥ̅ ϣⲁⲣⲉ̇ⲡⲉⲧⲣⲁ = ⲡⲱϩ = ϩⲉⲙ ⲡⲣⲁⲛ = ⲓ̅ⲥ̅ =
ⲡⲉⲭ̅ⲥ̅ = ϣⲁⲣⲉϩⲓⲥⲓ ⲛⲓⲙ = ⲉⲓ ⲉⲃⲁⲗ ⲉⲡⲥⲱⲙⲁ = ⲥ̅ⲥ̅ = ⲛ̇ⲧⲉⲡⲉⲃⲥⲱⲙⲁ = † ⲟⲩⲱ ⲉⲃⲁⲗ = ⲛ̇-
ⲑⲏ ⲙ̇ⲡϣⲏⲛ ⲛ̇ⲉⲡⲱⲛϩ = ϩⲉⲛ ⲧⲙⲏⲧ ⲙ̇ⲡⲁ-
ⲣⲁ†ⲥⲱⲥ ≡ † ⲉⲙⲡⲟⲟⲩ = ⲡⲧⲏⲡⲟⲥ ⲡⲉⲥ̅†̅ⲟ̅ⲥ̅ =
10 ⲛ̇ⲧⲁⲩⲧⲁⲗⲁⲕ = ϩⲓϫⲱⲃ = ϩⲁ ⲡⲟⲩϫⲁⲓ = ⲙ̇ⲡ-
ⲅⲉⲛⲟⲥ = ⲧⲏⲣϥ = ⲛ̇ⲧⲙⲉⲧⲣⲱⲙⲉ ≡ ⲧⲉ ⲡⲁⲓ ⲡⲉ
ⲡⲉⲛⲧⲁϥⲟⲩⲱⲃⲥ ⲛ̇ⲧϭⲁⲙ ⲧⲏⲣⲉⲥ : ⲡⲇⲓⲁⲃⲟⲗ-
ⲱⲥ = ⲙⲛ̇ ⲧ̇ⲉⲙⲱⲛⲓⲱⲛ = ⲧⲏⲣⲟⲩ = ⲧⲉ ⲛⲁⲓ ⲛ̇ⲉⲧ-
ⲣⲱϩⲧ ⲉ=ⲛ̇ϣⲏⲣⲉ ⲛ̇ⲉⲣⲱⲙⲉ = † ⲉⲙⲡⲟⲟⲩ ≡
15 ⲛ̇ⲧϣⲁⲣⲉⲡⲓ ⲛ̇ⲣⲉⲙⲓⲉ = ⲛ̇ⲧⲁⲥⲓ ⲉⲃⲁⲗ ϩⲛ ⲛ̇ⲉ-
ⲃⲉⲗ ⲉⲡⲓⲱⲧ : ⲁⲥⲓ ϩⲓϫⲉⲛ ⲧⲁⲡⲏ ⲙ̇ⲡⲉⲕϣⲏⲣⲉ
ⲉⲧⲟⲩⲁⲁⲃ = ⲓ̅ⲥ̅ ⲡⲉⲭ̅ⲥ̅ = ⲡⲛⲁⲩ ⲉⲃⲁϣⲉ : ⲉⲡⲉⲥ̅†̅ⲟ̅ⲥ̅
ϩⲁ ⲡⲟⲩϫⲁⲓ ⲉⲧⲛ̇ⲙⲉⲧⲣⲱⲙⲉ = ⲧⲏⲣⲉⲥ = † ⲉⲙⲡⲟⲟⲩ ⲡⲉⲕⲗⲁⲙ ⲉϣⲁⲛ† ⲛ̇ⲧⲁⲩⲧⲁⲗⲁⲃ ϩⲓϫⲉⲛ
20 ⲧⲉⲕⲁⲡⲏ = ⲙⲛ : ⲉ̅ = ⲛⲓⲃⲧ ⲛ̇ⲧⲁⲩⲧⲁϩⲟⲩ ⲉⲡⲉⲕ-
ⲥⲱⲙⲁ ⲙⲛ ⲧⲉⲥⲧⲉ ⲛ̇ⲗⲟⲛⲭⲓ ⲛ̇ⲧⲁⲩⲧⲁⲁⲥ ⲉⲡⲉⲃ-
ⲥⲡⲉⲣ = ⲙⲛ ⲡⲉⲃⲥⲛⲟⲃ = ⲙⲛ ⲡⲙⲁⲩ · ⲛ̇ⲧⲁⲃ-
ⲓ ⲉⲃⲁⲗ = ⲛ̇ϩⲏⲧϥ = ϩⲓϫⲉ ⲡⲉⲥ̅†̅ⲟ̅ⲥ̅ =
† ⲉⲙⲡⲟⲟⲩ = ⲙ̅ⲅ̅ ⲛⲓⲃⲓ ⲛ̇ⲧⲁⲕⲧⲁⲁⲩ ⲉⲛⲉϭⲓϫ =
25 ⲉⲡⲉⲕⲓⲱⲧ ϩⲓϫⲉ ⲡⲟ✝ⲟ ⲉⲧⲉ ⲛⲁⲓ = ⲛⲉ ⲉ̅ⲗ̅ⲱ̅ⲉ̅ⲓ̅ =
ⲉ̅ⲗ̅ⲏ̅ⲙ̅ⲁ̅ⲥ̅ = ⲁ̅ⲃ̅ⲁ̅ⲕ̅ⲧ̅ⲁ̅ⲛ̅ⲓ̅ = ⲥ̅ⲁ̅ⲃ̅ⲁ̅ⲱ̅ⲑ̅ = † ⲉⲙⲡⲟⲟⲩ =
ⲡⲅ̅ ⲛ̇ⲉϩⲟⲟⲩ ⲛ̇ⲧⲁⲃⲁⲁⲩ ϩⲉⲙ ⲡⲧⲁⲫⲟⲥ · ⲙⲛ ⲧ-
ⲉⲃϭⲓⲛⲧⲱⲟⲩⲛ ⲉⲃⲁⲗ ϩⲛ̇ⲉⲧⲙⲟⲟⲩⲧ = ⲙⲛ ⲡⲥⲟⲩ-
ⲧⲁⲣⲓⲱⲛ = ⲛ̇ⲧⲁⲩϭⲁⲁⲗⲉⲃ ⲉⲙⲁⲃ = ⲓ̅ⲥ̅ ⲡⲉⲭ̅ⲥ̅ ⲡ-
30 ϣⲏⲣⲉ ⲡⲛⲟⲩⲧⲉ · ϩⲉⲛ ⲟⲩⲙⲉ ≡ † ⲉⲙⲡⲟⲟⲩ ⲛ̇-
ⲧⲉⲅⲁⲛⲁⲥⲧⲁⲥⲓⲥ : ⲉⲧⲟⲩⲁⲁⲃ = ⲙⲛ̇ ⲡⲅ̅ ⲛⲓⲃⲓ ⲛ̇-
ⲱⲛⲁϩ : ⲛ̇ⲧⲁⲕⲧⲉⲓⲧⲟⲩ ⲉϩⲟⲩⲛ ⲉⲫⲁ ⲛ:ⲛⲉⲕ-
ⲁⲡⲱⲥⲧⲟⲗⲟⲥ = ⲉⲧⲟⲩⲁⲁⲃ = ⲁⲙⲟⲩ ϣⲁⲣⲁⲓ ⲡⲟⲟⲩ ≡
ⲱ ⲡⲟⲥ ⲓ̅ⲥ̅ ⲡⲉⲭ̅ⲥ̅ · ϩⲛ ⲧⲥⲁⲣⲉϩ =

1–29 *l.* ⲓ(ⲏⲥⲟⲩ)ⲥ ‖ 1 *i.e.* ⁵ⲙⲟⲟϣⲉ | *l.* ⲡⲣⲁⲛ K ‖ 2 *l.* ⲧⲱⲟⲩⲛ K | *i.e.* ⁵ⲙⲟⲟϣⲉ | *l.* ⲡⲣⲁⲛ : ⲡⲣⲁⲛ K ‖ 4 *i.e.* ⁵ϣⲱⲙ | ⲙⲁⲩ corrected from .ⲁⲩ by overwriting | *i.e.* ⁵ϣⲟⲟⲩⲉ *cf.* ᶠϣⲁⲩⲉⲓ K ‖ 5 *i.e.* πέτρα ‖ 6–34 *i.e.* χ(ριστό)ς ‖ 6–7 *i.e.* σῶμα ‖ 7 *i.e.* (δεῖνα) (δεῖνα) | ⲡⲉϥⲥⲱⲙⲁ K | *i.e.* σῶμα ‖ 7–8 *l.* ⲛ-ⲧ-ϩⲏ ‖ 8–9 *i.e.* παράδεισος ‖ 9–30 *i.e.* ⁵†-(ⲧⲁⲣⲕⲟ ⲙ̅ⲙⲟ=ⲕ) ⲙ̅-ⲡⲟⲟⲩ *cf.* CdF : †ⲱⲣⲕ ⲉⲣⲁⲕ ⲉⲙⲡⲟⲟⲩ K ‖ 9 *i.e.* τύπος ‖ 9–25 *l.* στ(αυρ)ός ‖ 10 *i.e.* ϩⲓϫⲱ=ϥ ‖ 11 *i.e.* γένος | *i.e.* ⁵ⲙⲛ̅ⲧ-ⲣⲱⲙⲉ | *l.* ⲉⲧⲉ ‖ 12 *i.e.* ⁵ⲟⲩⲱⲥϥ | *i.e.* ⁵ⲧⲏⲣ=ⲥ ‖ 12–13 *i.e.* διάβολος ‖ 13 *i.e.* δαιμόνιον | *l.* ⲛ̇ⲧⲉⲙⲱⲛⲓⲱⲛ K | *l.* ⲉⲧⲉ ‖ 14 *i.e.* ⁵ⲛ̅-ⲛ̅-ϣⲏⲣⲉ ‖ 15 *i.e.* ⁵ϣⲱⲣⲡ | *i.e.* ⁵ⲣⲙⲉⲓⲏ | *i.e.* ⁵ⲛ̇ⲧⲁ=ⲥ-ⲉⲓ ‖ 16 *i.e.* ⁵ⲁ=ⲥ-ⲉⲓ ‖ 17 *i.e.* ⁵ⲙ̅-ⲡ-ⲛⲁⲩ ‖ 18 *l.* ⲛ̇ⲧⲙⲉⲧ- | *i.e.* ⁵ⲙⲛ̅ⲧⲣⲱⲙⲉ | *i.e.* ⁵ⲧⲏⲣ=ⲥ ‖ 19 *i.e.* ⁵ⲙ̅-ⲡⲉ-ⲕⲗⲟⲙ | *i.e.* ⁵ϣⲱⲛⲧⲉ ‖ 20 *i.e.* ⁵ⲉⲓϥⲧ | *i.e.* ⁵ⲉⲛⲧ-ⲁ=ⲩ-ⲧⲉⲕⲥ=ⲟⲩ : ⲛ̇ⲧⲁⲩⲧⲁⲃⲟⲩ *l.* ⲛ̇ⲧⲁⲩⲧⲁϩⲟⲩ K ‖ 21 *i.e.* σῶμα | *i.e.* ⁵ⲥⲱ- Crum CD 374b *cf.* ⲧⲉⲥϥⲧⲉ CdF | *i.e.* λόγχη | 21–22 *i.e.* ⁵ⲡⲉϥ-ⲥⲡⲓⲣ | *i.e.* ⁵ⲡⲉϥ-ⲥⲛⲟϥ ‖ 22–23 *i.e.* ⁵ⲛ̇ⲧⲁ=ϥ-ⲉⲓ ‖ 23 *i.e.* ⁵ϩⲓϫⲛ̅ : ϩⲓϫⲉⲛ K ‖ 25 *i.e.* ⁵ϩⲓϫⲛ̅ | *i.e.* (σταυρός) ‖ 27 ⲛ̅ⲅ̅ K

of Jesus, the lame walk; in the name ⟨of⟩ Jesus, the paralyzed arises, his feet walking; in the name of Jesus, the dumb speak; in the name of Jesus, fire is extinguished, water dries up; in the name |⁵ of Jesus, stone breaks; in the name of Jesus Christ, every suffering comes out of the body of NN, son of NN, and his body blossoms like the Tree of Life in the middle of Paradise.

I adjure you today by the symbol of the cross, |¹⁰ upon which you were set up for the salvation of all the race of humankind, that is, that which brought all the power of the Devil to naught and of all the demons, those who strike the children of men! I adjure you today |¹⁵ by the first tear which came from the eyes of the Father; it came upon the head of your holy Son, Jesus Christ, ⟨in⟩ the hour that he hung upon the cross for the salvation of all humankind! I adjure you today by the crown of thorns which was lifted upon |²⁰ your head and by the five nails which pierced your body and by the blow of the spear which was put in his side, and by his blood and the water which came forth from it upon the cross! I adjure you today by the three breaths which you gave to the hands |²⁵ of your Father upon the cross, that are these: *Elōei, *Elēmas, Abaktani, *Sabaoth! I adjure you today by the three days that he was in the tomb, and by his resurrection from the dead and by the shroud that he was covered with, Jesus Christ, the |³⁰ Son of God in truth! I adjure you by your holy resurrection and by the three breaths of life, which you gave in the faces of your holy apostles!

Come to me today, O Lord Jesus Christ in the flesh

---

20. ē̄ : ⲛⲓⲃⲧ : **"five nails"** *Cf.* *Sator Square in the glossary.
25. ⲡⲉ⳨ : **"the cross"** The word "cross" is written as a *kharaktēr* resembling a staurogram.
25–26. ⲉⲗⲱⲉⲓ ⸗ ⲉⲗⲏⲙⲁⲥ ⸗ ⲁⲃⲁⲕⲧⲁⲛⲓ ⸗ ⲥⲁⲃⲁⲱⲑ ⸗ : **"Elōei, Elēmas, Abaktani"** *Cf.* the note to p. 22 ll. 17–18.

i.e. ˢⲧⲁ⸗ϥ-ⲁⲁ⸗ⲟⲩ | *i.e.* τάφος || **27–28** *i.e.* ˢⲧⲉ⸗ϥ-ϭⲓⲛ-ⲧⲱⲟⲩⲛ : ⲧⲉϥϭⲓⲛⲧⲱⲟⲩⲛ K || **28–29** *i.e.* σουδάριον || **29** *i.e.* ˢⲛⲧⲁⲩ-ϭⲁⲗ⸗ϥ | *i.e.* ˢⲙ̄ⲙⲟ⸗ϥ || **31** *l.* ⲧⲉⲕ-ⲁⲛⲁⲥⲧⲁⲥⲓⲥ || **32** *l.* ⲉ-ⲡ-ϩⲁ || **33** *i.e.* ἀπόστολος | *i.e.* ˢⲙ̄-ⲡⲟⲟⲩ : ⲙⲡⲟⲩ K || **34** *l.* *ϭ(ⲱ)ⲥ *i.e.* ˢⲭⲟⲉⲓⲥ | *i.e.* σάρξ

page 14 (= *Kropp 208*) (flesh)

ⲛ ᵛᵃᶜ ⲧⲁⲕⲫⲱⲣⲓ ⲙ̣ⲁⲥ̣ ⲉⲕⲥⲙⲟⲩ ⲉⲡⲙⲁⲩ ⲙⲛ ⲡⲓⲛⲉϩ ⸗
ⲉⲧⲙⲡⲉⲙⲧⲁ ⲉⲃⲁⲗ ⲉⲕⲛⲓⲃⲓ ⲉⲡⲉⲥⲏⲧ ⲉⲣⲁⲩ ⁚ ⲉⲕ-
ⲙⲁϩⲟⲩ ⲙⲡⲉⲡⲛ̅ⲁ̅ ⲉⲧⲟⲩⲁⲁⲃ ⸗ ϫⲉⲕⲁⲥ · ⲉⲓ ⲉⲃⲁⲗ ϩⲉ ⲛ̅-
ϩⲏⲧϥ ss̅ ⸗ ⲛϭⲓ ϩⲓⲥⲓ ⲛⲓⲙ · ⲉⲧ ⲡⲉⲃⲥⲱⲙⲁ ⸗ ⲉⲩϣⲁⲛ-
5 ϫⲁⲕⲙⲉⲃ ⸗ ⲛϩⲏⲧϥ ⸗ ⲁⲙⲟⲩ ⲕⲁⲗⲱⲥ · ⲁⲕⲓ ⲧϭⲁⲙ ⲉ-
ⲡⲉⲕⲓⲱⲧ ⲛⲁⲕⲁⲑⲱⲥ ⲙⲁⲟⲩϣⲉ ⲛⲉⲙⲁⲕ ⲑⲁⲓ-
ⲃⲱⲥ ⲙⲡⲉⲡⲛ̅ⲁ̅ ⲉⲧⲟⲩⲁⲁⲃ · ϩⲓϫⲱⲕ ⸗
† ⲉⲙⲡⲟⲟⲩ ⲡϥ̅ ⲛϩⲟⲟⲩ ⲛ̇ⲧⲁⲕⲁⲁⲩ ⸗ ⲉⲣⲉⲣ ϩⲱⲃ
ⲉⲧⲡⲏ ⲙ̇ⲛ ⲡⲕⲁϩ ⸗ ⲁⲕⲉⲙⲧⲁⲛ ⲉⲙⲁⲕ —
10 ⲉⲡⲙⲉϩⲍ̅ ⲛϩⲟⲟⲩ ⸗ † ⲉⲙⲡⲟⲟⲩ ⲛⲧⲉⲕⲁⲡⲏ ⸗ ⲙⲓ-
ⲛ ⲉⲙⲁⲕ ⸗ ⲙⲛ ⲧⲁϭⲓⲛⲁϩ⁚ⲉⲣⲁⲧ ⲉⲣⲁⲕ ⸗ ⲙⲛ
ⲧⲁⲍ̅ ⲛⲥⲧⲉⲣⲁ†ⲗⲁⲧⲏⲥ ⁚ ⲉⲧⲉⲣⲁⲛ ⲅⲁⲃⲣⲓⲏⲗ̅ ⸗
ⲣⲁⲫⲁⲏⲗ̅ ⸗ ⲥⲟⲩⲣⲓⲏⲗ̅ [[.]] ⲥⲉⲧⲉⲕⲓⲏⲗ̅ ⸗ ⲥⲁⲗⲁⲑⲓ-
ⲏⲗ̅ ⲁⲛⲁⲏⲗ̅ ⸗ † ⲉⲡⲟⲟⲩ ⲅⲁⲃⲣⲓⲏⲗ̅ ⸗ ⲡⲃⲁⲓϣⲉ-
15 ⲛⲟⲩⲃⲓ ⲁⲙⲟⲩ ⸗ ϣⲁⲣⲁⲓ ⲉϥⲁⲛⲧⲁϫⲱⲕ ⲉⲃⲟⲗ ⸗
ⲡⲓⲉⲛⲇⲱϩⲱⲛ ⸗ ⲉⲧⲟⲩⲁⲁⲃ ⁚ † ⲉⲡⲟⲟⲩ ϩⲣⲁⲫⲁⲏⲗ̅
ⲡⲁⲅⲅⲉⲗⲱⲥ ⸗ ⲡⲣⲁϣⲉ · ⲁⲙⲟⲩ ϣⲁⲣⲁⲓ ⲙ̅ⲡⲟⲟⲩ⸗
ϣⲁⲛⲧⲁϫⲱⲕ ⲉⲃⲁⲗ ⲡⲓⲛⲇⲱϩⲱⲛ ⲉⲧⲟⲩⲁⲁⲃ
ⲥⲟⲩⲣⲓⲏⲗ̅ ⸗ ⲡⲁⲅⲅⲉⲗⲟⲥ ⲛⲉϭⲁⲙ ⲁ̇ⲙⲟⲩ ϣⲁⲣ-
20 ⲁⲓ ϣⲁⲛⲧⲁϫⲱⲕ ⲉⲃⲁⲗ ⲡⲓⲧⲱϩⲱⲛ ⲉⲧⲟⲩⲁⲃ
ⲥⲁⲗⲁⲑⲓⲏⲗ̅ ⸗ ⲡⲁⲅⲅⲉⲗⲟⲥ · ⲁⲙⲟⲩ ϣⲁⲣⲁⲓ ⸗ ⲉⲕⲓ
ⲉⲟⲟⲩ ⲉⲡⲓⲱⲧ ⲛⲉⲙⲁⲓ ⲡⲟⲟⲩ ⸗ ⲥⲉⲧⲉⲕⲓⲏⲗ̅ · ⲡⲁⲅⲅⲉⲗⲟⲥ ⲛ̅ⲇⲓⲕⲉⲱⲥⲏⲛⲉ ⸗ ⲁⲙⲟⲩ † ⲉⲟⲟⲩ ⲉⲡϣⲏⲣⲉ ⲛⲉⲙⲁⲓ ⲉⲡⲟⲟⲩ ⲁⲛⲁⲏⲗ̅ ⸗ ⲙⲛ ⲡⲛⲁ ⲡⲉⲧ-
25 ⲉⲣⲉⲡⲛⲁ ⲙ̇ⲡⲱⲧ ⸗ ⲡϩⲏⲡ ⲛϩⲏⲧⲃ ϩⲛ ⲧⲉⲃⲕⲁ-
ⲗⲁϩⲛ ⸗ ⲁⲙⲟⲩ ⲭⲱⲣⲉⲅⲉⲓ ⲛ̇ⲉⲙⲁⲓ ⸗ ⲙⲛ ⲡⲉⲡⲛ̅ⲁ̅ ⲉⲧⲟⲩⲁⲁⲃ ⲛⲁⲓ ⲉⲩⲁϩⲉⲣⲁⲧⲟⲩ ⸗ ⲙⲡⲉϩⲟⲟⲩ ⲛⲧⲁⲕⲧⲁ-
ⲙⲓⲁ ⲛⲁⲇⲁⲙ ⸗ ⲛϩⲏⲧⲃ ⸗ ϫⲉⲕⲁⲥ ⁚ ⲉⲩⲉⲓ ϣⲁⲣⲁⲓ ⸗ ⲡⲟⲟⲩ
ⲉⲣⲉⲛⲉⲩⲥϩⲃⲓ ⲛⲥⲁ† ϩⲛ ⲛⲉⲩϭⲓϫ ⸗ ⲛⲥⲉⲁϩⲉⲣⲁⲧⲟⲩ
30 ϩⲓϫⲉⲛ ⲡⲓⲙⲁⲩ ⲙⲛ ⲡⲓⲛⲉϩ ⁚ ⲛⲉⲥⲉⲡⲱⲧ ⸗ ⲛⲥⲁ ⲛⲉ-
ⲍⲟⲩⲥⲓⲁ ⲧⲏⲣⲟⲩ ϣⲁⲛⲧⲟⲩⲁⲛⲁϫⲱ ⲛⲁⲩ ⲥⲁⲉⲃ-
ⲗ ⲉss̅ ⲁⲓⲁ̅ ⲁⲓⲁ̅ ⲧⲁⲭⲏ ⲧⲁⲭⲏ · † ⲉⲡⲟⲟⲩ ⲛⲛⲓϣⲁ̅ ⲛ-
ϣⲁ ⲙⲉ ⲛⲓⲧⲃⲁ ⲛⲧⲃⲁ ⁚ ⲛⲁⲓ ⲉⲩϩⲛⲁ ⲉⲃⲁⲗ · ϫⲉ
ⲡⲁⲏⲣ ⁚ ⲉⲩⲧⲱⲕⲓ ⲛⲥⲁ ⲛⲉϩⲟⲩⲥⲓⲁ ⲧⲏⲣⲟⲩ
35 ⲙⲡⲕⲁⲕⲉ ⲁⲙⲟⲩ ⲉⲃⲁⲗ ϩⲓⲑⲏ ⲙ̇ⲡⲱⲧ ϣⲁⲛ-
ⲛⲧⲉⲃⲓ ⲉⲃⲁⲉϩⲣⲁⲧϥ ⸗ ϫⲉⲛ ⲡⲓⲙⲁⲩ ⲙⲛ ⲡⲓ-

---

1 ⲛ vac. ⲧⲁⲕⲫⲱⲣⲓ *pap.* : *i.e.* φορεῖν | *i.e.* ˢⲙ̅ⲙⲟ⸗ⲥ | *i.e.* ˢⲛ⸗ϥ̅-ⲥⲙⲟⲩ *cf.* CdF ‖ **2** *i.e.* ˢⲙⲡⲉⲙⲧⲟ ⲉⲃⲟⲗ | *i.e.* ˢⲛ⸗ϥ̅-ⲛⲓϥⲉ *cf.* CdF | *i.e.* ˢⲉⲣⲟ⸗ⲟⲩ | **2–3** ⲉⲕⲙⲁϩⲟⲩ *i.e.* ˢⲛ⸗ϥ̅-ⲙⲉϩ⸗ⲟⲩ ‖ **3** *l.* πν(εῦμ)α | *l.* ⲉ⸗ⲩ-ⲉ-ⲉⲓ ‖ **3–4** *i.e.* ˢϩⲛ̅ or ⲛ̅ϩⲏⲧ⸗ϥ̅ ⲛ̅- ‖ **4–32** *i.e.* (δεῖνα) (δεῖνα) ‖ **4** *l.* ⲉⲧ ϩⲉ *i.e.* ˢⲉⲧ-ϩⲙ̅- | *i.e.* ˢⲡⲉ⸗ϥ- | *i.e.* σῶμα ‖ **4–5** *i.e.* ˢⲉ⸗ⲩ-ϣⲁⲛ-ϫⲁⲕⲙⲉ⸗ϥ ‖ **5** *i.e.* καλῶς | *i.e.* ˢⲁ⸗ⲕ-ⲉⲓ | *l.* ⲉⲣⲉ-ⲧ-ϭⲁⲙ ? ‖ **5–6** *i.e.* ˢⲙ̅-ⲡⲉ⸗ⲕ-ⲉⲓⲱⲧ ‖ **6** *i.e.* ἀγαθός | *i.e.* ˢⲙⲟⲟϣⲉ ‖ **6–7** *i.e.* ˢⲧ-ϩⲁⲓⲃⲉⲥ ‖ **7–26** *i.e.* πν(εῦμ)α ‖ **8–32** *i.e.* ˢ†-(ⲧⲁⲣⲕⲟ ⲙ̅ⲙⲟ⸗ⲕ) ⲙ̅-ⲡⲟⲟⲩ *cf.* CdF : ⲧⲱⲣⲕ ⲉⲣⲁⲕ ⲉⲙⲡⲟⲟⲩ K ‖ **8** *l.* ⲉ⸗ⲕ-ⲉⲣ ϩⲱⲃ *cf.* CdF : ⲉⲡⲉⲣϩⲱⲃ K ‖ **9** *i.e.* ˢⲛ̅-ⲧ-ⲡⲉ | *i.e.* ˢⲙ̅ⲙⲟ⸗ⲕ ‖ **10–11** *i.e.* ˢⲙⲙⲓⲛ ‖ **11** *i.e.* ˢⲙ̅ⲙⲟ⸗ⲕ | *i.e.* ˢⲉⲣⲟ⸗ⲕ | *l.* ⲧⲁ-ϭⲓ-ⲛ-ⲁϩⲉ-ⲣⲁⲧ ⲉⲣⲁⲕ ‖ **12** *i.e.* στρατηλάτης | *i.e.* ˢⲉⲧⲉ-ⲛⲉϩ⸗ⲩ-ⲣⲁⲛ ⲛⲉ : ⲉⲧⲉⲛⲁⲓ ⲛⲉ ⲛⲉⲩⲣⲁⲛ K ‖ **14–15** *i.e.* ˢϥⲁⲓ-ϣⲙ-ⲛⲟⲩϥⲉ ‖ **15** *i.e.* ˢϣⲁⲛⲧ-ϫⲱⲕ | ⲉⲃⲁⲗ K ‖

that you bore, and bless the water and this oil that are before me, and breathe down into them and fill them with Holy Spirit, so that ⟨they⟩ come out of from inside NN, son of NN, namely every suffering that is ⟨in⟩ his body, |⁵ when he is washed in it!

Come well; you came, the power of your good Father walking with you, the shadow of the Holy Spirit upon you! I adjure you today ⟨by⟩ the six days you spent working on the heaven and the earth; you rested |¹⁰ on the seventh day!

I adjure you by your own head and ⟨by⟩ my standing before you and ⟨by⟩ my seven generals, whose names ⟨are⟩ *Gabriel, *Raphael, *Suriel, Setekiēl, Salathiēl, Anaēl—I adjure you today, Gabriel, O bearer of good news |¹⁵ come to me, so that I complete this holy *endoxon*! I adjure you today Raphael, O *angel ⟨of⟩ joy, come to me today, so that I complete this holy *endoxon*! Suriel, O angel of power, come to me, |²⁰ so that I complete this holy *endoxon*! Salathiēl, O angel, come to me, and give glory to the Father with me today! Setekiēl, O angel of righteousness, come, give glory to the Son with me today! Anaēl and the mercy, the one in whose |²⁵ womb the mercy of the Father is hidden, come, dance with me and the Holy Spirit—they who stood on the day in which you created Adam, so that they will come to me today, with their swords of fire in their hands, and they will stand |³⁰ upon this water and this oil, and they will pursue every authority until they withdraw? from NN, child of NN, yea, yea, quickly, quickly!

I adjure you today by the thousands of thousands and ten thousands of ten thousands—they who fly in the air, pursuing all the authorities |³⁵ of darkness— come out before the Father, so that he comes and stands upon this water and this

---

16–20 *i.e.* ἔνδοξον *cf.* note p. 1 | † ∈ⲡⲟⲟⲩ K omits || **17–23** *i.e.* ἄγγελος || **17** ⲁⲅⲅⲉⲗⲟⲥ K | *i.e.* ˢⲙ̄-ⲡ-ⲣⲁϣⲉ || **19** *i.e.* ˢⲛ̄-ⲧ-ϭⲟⲙ || **20** *i.e.* ˢⲟⲩⲁⲁⲃ || **21** *i.e.* ἄγγελος | *l.* ˢⲛ̄ⲉⲕ-ϯ ? : ⲉⲕϯ K || **22** *i.e.* ˢⲙ̄-ⲡⲟⲟⲩ || **23** *i.e.* δικαιοσύνη || **24–25** *i.e.* ˢⲡ-ⲉⲧ-ⲉⲣⲉ-ⲡ-ⲛⲁ ⲙ̄-ⲡ-ⲓⲱⲧ ϩⲏⲡ ⲛ-ϩⲏⲧ⸗ϥ *cf.* CdF || **25** *l.* ⲉⲧϩⲏⲡ (?) K | *i.e.* ˢⲛ̄ϩⲏⲧ⸗ϥ || **25–26** *i.e.* ˢⲧⲉ⸗ϥ-ⲕⲁⲗⲁϩⲏ || **26** *i.e.* χορεύειν || **28** *i.e.* ˢⲛ̄ϩⲏⲧ⸗ϥ | *i.e.* ˢⲙ̄-ⲡⲟⲟⲩ || **30** *i.e.* ˢⲛ̄ⲥⲉ-ⲡⲱⲧ: ⲛⲥⲉⲡⲱⲧ K || **31–34** *i.e.* ἐξουσία || **31** ⲁⲛⲁⲭⲱ ⲝ corrected from or to ⲭ *i.e.* ἀναχωρεῖν || **31–32** *i.e.* ˢⲥⲁⲃⲟⲗ : ⲥⲁⲉⲃⲗⲉ *l.* ⲥⲁ⟨ⲛ⟩ⲃⲁⲗ ⲉ- K || **32** *i.e.* ταχύ (twice) || **34** *i.e.* ἀήρ | *i.e.* διώκειν : "may they pursue" ("sie mögen verfolgen") K || **35–36** *i.e.* ˢϣⲁⲛⲧⲉ⸗ϥ-ⲉⲓ ⲉ⸗ϥ-ⲁϩⲉ ⲣⲁⲧ⸗ϥ || **36** *i.e.* ˢⲛ̄⸗ϥ-ⲁϩⲉ ⲣⲁⲧ⸗ϥ *cf.* CdF | *i.e.* ˢⲉϫⲛ̄ or ˢϩⲓϫⲛ̄ *cf.* ϩⲓϫⲉⲛ CdF

page 15 (= *Kropp 234*) (flesh)

ⲛⲉϩ : ⲉⲃⲙⲟⲩϩⲟⲩ ⲛϭⲁⲙ ϩⲓ ⲧⲁϭⲁ ⲇⲉⲕⲁⲥ · ⲉⲩ-
ϣⲁⲛⲡⲁϩⲧⲃ ϩⲉⲭⲱ 𝜎𝜎 = ⲉⲩⲉⲓ ⲉⲃⲁⲗ ⲛϩⲏⲧⲃ ⲛ̄-
ϭⲓ ϩⲓⲥⲓ = ⲛⲓⲙ ⲉⲡⲉⲃⲥⲱⲙⲁ ≡ ⲉⲩϣⲁⲛⲡⲉϩ : ⲡⲓ=ⲙⲁ̄ⲩ̄
ϩⲓⲭⲉⲛ ⲟⲩϣⲏⲛ = ⲧⲁⲃⲉⲣ ϩⲁⲁⲗⲓ = ϣⲁⲃ†ⲟⲩⲱ
5 ⲉⲃⲁⲗ ⲉⲩϣⲁⲛⲡⲉϩⲧⲃ = ϩⲓⲭⲉⲛ ⲟⲩⲡⲓⲛⲓⲡⲓ ϣⲁⲃⲃⲱⲗ · ⲉⲃⲁⲗ = ⲉⲃⲉⲣ ⲙⲁⲩ = ⲉⲩϣⲁⲛⲡⲉϩⲧⲃ =
ϩⲉⲭⲉⲛ ⲟⲩⲡⲉⲧⲣⲁ · ϣⲁⲥⲡⲱϭⲓ = ⲉⲥⲧⲁⲟⲩⲁ ⲙⲁ-
ⲩ ⲉⲃⲁⲗ · ⲉⲩϣⲁⲛⲡⲉϩⲧⲃ ϩⲓⲭⲉ ⲛⲉⲧⲙⲁⲟⲩⲧ =
ϩⲉⲛ ⲟⲩⲡⲓⲥⲧⲓⲥ = ⲥⲉⲛⲁⲧⲱⲟⲩⲛ = ⲧⲁⲡⲣⲁ ⲡⲟ̄ⲥ̄
10 ⲓ̄ⲥ̄ ⲡⲭ̄ⲥ̄ : ⲥⲁⲃⲁⲱⲑ = ⲧⲉⲛⲧⲁⲥⲭⲉ ⲛⲁⲓ = †ⲥⲙⲟⲩ =
ⲉⲣⲁⲕ = ⲙⲉ ⲛⲥ̄ⲱ̄ⲛ̄ⲧ̄ ⲧⲏⲣⲟⲩ = ⲛⲧⲁⲕ=ⲧⲁⲙⲓⲁ =
ⲛⲉⲑⲉⲣⲓⲱⲛ ⲧⲏⲣⲟⲩ = ⲙ̇ⲡⲕⲁϩ = ⲙⲛ ⲛⲉϩⲁⲗ-
ⲁ†ⲛⲧⲡⲏ = ⲉⲩⲥⲙⲟⲩ ⲉⲣⲁⲕ = ⲁ̄ⲣ̄ⲁ̄ⲙ̄ = ⲁ̄ⲣ̄ⲁ̄ⲙ̄ =
ⲁ̄ⲣ̄ⲁ̄ⲙ̄ = ⲁ̄ⲛ̄ⲫ̄ⲟ̄ⲩ̄ = ⲡⲛⲟⲩⲧⲉ = ⲉⲑⲏⲡ ⲥⲱⲧⲉ-
15 ⲙ : ⲉⲣⲁⲓ ⲁⲛⲁⲕ ⲡⲉ ⲙ̄ⲓ̄ⲭ̄ⲁ̄ⲏ̄ⲗ̄ · ⲡⲁⲣⲭⲁⲅⲅⲉⲗⲟ̄ⲥ̄ =
ⲙⲁⲣⲉⲡⲁⲥⲙⲟⲩ = ⲉⲓ ⲉϩⲟⲩⲛ · ⲡⲉⲙⲧⲁ ⲉⲃⲁⲗ =
ⲉⲧⲉⲕⲙⲉⲧⲛⲟϭ = ⲙⲁⲣⲉⲧⲁⲙⲓⲧⲁⲛⲅ : ⲡⲱϩ =
ϣⲁ ⲡⲉⲕⲑⲣⲱⲛⲟⲥ = ⲉⲧⲟⲩⲁⲁⲃ = †ⲛⲟⲩ ϭⲉ =
ⲡⲁ̄ⲟ̄ⲥ̄ = ϣⲁⲛⲁϩⲧⲏⲕ = ϩⲁ ⲡⲉⲕⲓⲛⲓ = ⲙⲛ : ⲧⲉⲕ- =
20 ϩⲓ̄ⲕ̄ⲱ̄ⲛ̄ = ⲉⲕ†ⲛⲟⲩⲧⲉⲗϭⲁ · ⲛⲟⲩⲁⲛ ⲛ̇ⲓⲙ =
ⲉⲧⲛⲁⲫⲱⲣⲓ ⲉⲙ̇ⲡⲓⲛⲉⲇⲱϫⲱⲛ = ⲙⲁⲗⲓⲥⲧⲁ =
𝜎𝜎 : ⲉⲕⲃⲓ ϩⲁⲃⲁⲗ = ⲉⲙⲁⲃ = ⲛϣⲱⲛⲓ ⲛⲓⲙ = ⲙⲉⲛ :
ϣⲧⲁⲣⲧⲉⲣ = ⲛ̄ⲓ̄ⲙ̄ = ⲙⲉⲛ ⲣⲱϩⲧⲥ ⲛⲓⲙ = ϫⲉ ⲛ-
ⲧⲁⲕ ⲡⲉⲧⲉⲣⲉⲁⲩ ⲛ̄ⲓ̄ⲙ̄ ⲙ̇ⲡⲣⲉⲡⲉ ⲛⲁⲕ = ⲙ-
25 ⲡⲓⲱⲧ ⲙⲛ ⲡϣⲏⲣⲉ ⲙⲛ : ⲡⲉⲡ̄ⲛ̄ⲁ̄ ⲉⲧⲟⲩⲁⲁⲃ =
ⲡϣⲁ ⲓⲛⲉϩ ⲛⲓⲛⲉϩ ≡ ϩⲁⲙⲏⲛ : ϩⲁⲙⲏⲛ : ϩⲁⲙⲏⲛ =

ⲟⲩⲣⲱⲙⲓ : ⲣⲉⲟⲩⲧⲙⲱⲛⲓⲟⲛ: ϩⲓⲧ ⲙⲁⲃ : ⲧⲁⲟⲩⲁ †ⲟⲩⲭⲏ ϩⲓⲭⲓ-
ⲛ ⲟⲩⲁ̇ⲙ̇ⲡⲟⲩⲗⲗⲓ : ⲛⲁⲗⲙⲁⲅⲁⲣⲧ ⲡⲉϩⲧⲥ ϩⲓⲭⲱⲃ : ϣⲁⲗⲟ
ⲟ̄ⲩ̄ ⲙⲁⲥ†ⲭⲓ | ⲟⲩⲣⲱⲙⲉ : ⲉⲃϩⲛ ⲡⲉϣ†ⲕⲁ : ϩⲣⲁⲓ †ⲇⲉⲛⲁⲙⲓᶜ
30 ⲉⲓ̄ ⲛⲃⲏⲗϫⲓ ⲛⲕⲗⲱⲗ · ⲃⲏⲣⲓ ϩⲁⲗⲟⲩ ϣⲁⲣⲁⲃ = ϣⲁⲩⲕⲟⲟⲃ =
ⲉⲫⲓⲗ · ϩⲉ ⲡⲟⲩⲱϣ ⲡⲛⲟⲩⲧⲉ : ⲟ̄ⲩ̄ ⲙⲁⲥ†ⲭ · ⲁⲗⲟⲩⲑ ⲕ̄ⲟ̄ⲩ̄ϣ̄ =
ⲟⲩⲭⲁⲣⲓⲥ = ϩⲣⲁⲓ : ⲡⲓⲥⲱ†ⲟⲩⲛ : ⲛⲥⲛⲟⲃ : ϭⲉⲣⲁⲙⲡⲉ : ⲛⲁⲣⲉⲩ =
ⲙ̄ⲁ̄ⲣ̄ⲉ̄ⲃ̄ = ⲉϫⲱⲕ : ⲟ̄ⲩ̄ : ⲙⲟⲩⲥⲭⲁⲧⲉⲛ =

1 *i.e.* ˢⲛ̄=ϥ-ⲙⲉϩ=ⲟⲩ ‖ 1–2 *i.e.* ˢⲉⲩϣⲁⲛ-ⲡⲁϩⲧ=ϥ : ⲉⲩϣⲁⲛⲡⲁϩⲧⲟⲩ K ‖ 2 *i.e.* ˢϩⲓⲭⲛ̄- ‖ 2–22 *i.e.* (δεῖνα) (δεῖνα) | *i.e.* ˢⲛ̄ϩⲏⲧ=ϥ̄ ‖ 3 *i.e.* ˢⲙ̄-ⲡⲉ=ϥ-ⲥⲱⲙⲁ · ˢⲡⲉϩⲧ- ‖ 4 *i.e.* ˢⲉⲛⲧ-ⲁ=ϥ-ⲣ̄ ϩⲟⲟⲗⲉ | *i.e.* ˢϣⲁ=ϥ-†ⲟⲩⲱ ‖ 5 *i.e.* ˢⲃⲉⲛⲓⲡⲉ ‖ 5–8 *i.e.* ˢⲉⲩϣⲁⲛ-ⲡⲁϩⲧ=ϥ ‖ 5–6 *i.e.* ˢϣⲁ=ϥ-ⲃⲱⲗ ‖ 6 *i.e.* ˢⲛ=ϥ-ⲣ̄ ‖ 7 *i.e.* ˢϩⲓⲭⲛ̄- | *i.e.* πέτρα | *i.e.* ˢⲡⲱϭⲉ ‖ 7–8 *i.e.* ˢⲛ=ⲥ-ⲧⲁⲩⲉ ⲙ̄ⲙⲟⲟⲩ ‖ 8 *i.e.* ˢϩⲓⲭⲛ̄ ⲛ-ⲉⲧ-ⲙⲟⲟⲩ (haplography) ‖ 9 *i.e.* πίστις | *l.* ⲧ-ⲧⲁⲡⲣⲁ ‖ 9–19 *l.* *ϭ(ⲱⲓ)ⲥ ‖ 10 *l.* ⲓ(ⲏⲥⲟⲩ)ⲥ ⲡ-ⲭ(ⲣⲓⲥⲧⲟ)ⲥ | *i.e.* ˢⲛ̄ⲧⲁ=ⲥ-ⲭⲉ ⲛ̄ⲛⲁⲓ ‖ 11 *l.* ⲧⲁⲙⲓⲁⲩ *i.e.* ˢⲧⲁⲙⲓⲟ=(ⲟ)ⲩ K ‖ 12 ⲙⲉ K | *i.e.* θηρίον : ⲑⲏⲣⲓⲱⲛ K ‖ 15 *i.e.* ἀρχάγγελος ‖ 17 *i.e.* ˢⲛ̄-ⲧⲉ=ⲕ-ⲙⲛ̄ⲧ-ⲛⲟϭ | *i.e.* μετάνοια : ⲙⲓⲧⲁⲛⲓ K ‖ 18 *i.e.* θρόνος ‖ 20 *i.e.* εἰκών | *i.e.* ˢⲛ=ⲅ-† ‖ 21 *i.e.* φορεῖν | *i.e.* ἔνδοξον | *i.e.* μάλιστα ‖ 22 *i.e.* ˢⲛ=ⲅ-ϥⲓ ⲉⲃⲟⲗ ⲙ̄ⲙⲟ=ϥ | ⲙⲛ K ‖ 24 *i.e.* ˢⲡ-ⲉⲧⲉⲣⲉ-ⲉⲟⲟⲩ : ⲡⲉⲧⲉⲣⲉ-ⲉⲁⲩ K | *i.e.* πρέπειν : *i.e.* ἐμπρέπειν K ‖ 25 *i.e.* πν(εῦμ)α ‖ 26 ⲛϣⲁ K | *i.e.* ˢϣⲁ ⲉⲛⲉϩ ⲛ̄-ⲉⲛⲉϩ | *i.e.* ἀμήν (three times) ‖ 27 *i.e.* ˢⲉⲣⲉ-ⲟⲩ-ⲇⲁⲓⲙⲟⲛⲓⲟⲛ ϩⲓⲧⲉ ⲙⲙⲟ=ϥ | *i.e.* εὐχή ‖ 27–28 *i.e.* ˢϩⲓⲭⲛ̄ ‖ 28 *i.e.* ἀμπύλλη | *i.e.* الماورد *al-māward* | *i.e.* ˢϣⲁ=ϥ-ⲗⲟ ‖ 29–33 *i.e.* θυ(σία) : "make an offering"

oil, and he fills them with power and healing, so that when they are poured upon NN, child of NN, they will come out of him, namely every suffering of his body! If this water is poured upon a tree that has withered, it will blossom. |⁵ If it is poured upon iron, it will dissolve and become water. If it is poured upon a stone, it will break and put forth water. When it is poured upon the dead, in faith, they will arise. It is ⟨the⟩ mouth ⟨of⟩ the Lord, |¹⁰ Jesus Christ *Sabaoth that has said these things.

I bless you with all the creatures that you created, all the beasts of the earth and the birds of heaven who bless you, Aram, Aram, Aram, Anphou. God who is hidden, listen |¹⁵ to me! I am *Michael, the *archangel! Let my praise come in before your greatness! Let my repentance reach your holy *throne! Now, my Lord, take pity on your likeness and your |²⁰ image and give healing to everyone that will carry this *endoxon*, especially NN, son of NN, and take away from him every disease, and every disturbance and every strike! For you are the one to whom all glory is fitting, |²⁵ the Father and the Son and the Holy Spirit, forever and ever, amen, amen, amen!"

A man tormented by a demon. Pronounce the prayer over a flask of rose-water. Pour it on him. He will be healed. Offering: *mastic.

A man in prison. Draw the *power |³⁰ on three new pottery ostraca. Bring? it to him. He will be set free on the street, God willing. Offering: mastic, *agarwood, *costus.

Favour. Draw this image with ⟨the⟩ blood ⟨of a⟩ white dove. Bind it upon yourself. Offering: *musk incense.

19–20. ⲡⲉⲕⲓⲛⲓ ⸗ ⲙⲛ : ⲧⲉⲕ⸗ϩⲓⲕⲱ̄ⲛ̄ : "your likeness and your image" *Cf.* PCM I 10 ll. 2–3 and accompanying notes.
27–33. The first three recipes are not numbered in the manuscript, but Kropp numbers them ⲁ (1), ⲃ (2), and ⲅ (3) in his edition.
32. ⲛ̄ⲥⲛⲟϥ : ϭⲉⲣⲁⲙⲡⲉ : "with ⟨the⟩ blood ⟨of a⟩ white dove" For this substance, *cf.* the note to PCM I 25 p. 17 ll. 20–24.

---

29 *i.e.* μαστίχη | *i.e.* ˢⲱⲧⲉⲕⲟ | *i.e.* δύναμις ‖ **30** *i.e.* ˢⲕⲉⲗⲱⲗ | *i.e.* ˢⲛ̄-ⲃⲏⲣⲉ | *i.e.* ˢⲱⲁ-ⲩ-ⲕⲁⲁ⸗ϥ : "they force him onto the street" ("Sie zwingen ihn auf die Straße") K, M, G ‖ **31** *i.e.* ˢϩⲙ̄ | *i.e.* ˢⲙ̄-ⲡⲛⲟⲩⲧⲉ : "by the will of God" ("nach dem Willen Gottes") K, M, G | *i.e.* μαστίχη | *i.e.* العود al-ʿūd | *i.e.* ˢⲕⲟⲩⲱⲧ ‖ **32** *i.e.* χάρις | *i.e.* ζῴδιον | *i.e.* ˢⲁⲗⲁⲩ ‖ **33** *i.e.* ˢⲙⲟⲣ⸗ϥ | *i.e.* μοσχάτον : "muscat wine" (Muskatwein) K : "muscatel" M : "mastic" Gardner.

page 16 (= *Kropp 254*) (hair)

ⲁ̅ : ⲟⲩⲣⲱⲙⲉ ⲉⲃⲱ ⲛ̄ⲕⲏⲛ̄ⲕⲃ · ⲥϩⲁⲓ ⲡⲓⲥⲱϯⲟⲩⲱⲛ̄ ⲉⲛⲥⲛⲟⲃ ⸗
ⲉⲛⲟⲩⲣⲓ · ⲙⲁⲣⲉⲃ ⲭⲱϥ ⸗ ϣⲁⲩⲗⲟ ⲡ̀ⲟⲩⲱϣ ⲡⲛⲟⲩϯ · ⲙⲁⲥϯⲭⲓ

ⲉ̅ : ⲟⲩⲣⲱⲙⲉ ⲣⲉⲟⲩⲙⲉⲧⲭⲉⲭⲓ ϩⲉ ⲧⲉⲃⲙⲏϯ ⲙⲉ ⲧⲉⲃⲥⲓⲙⲓ ⸗
ⲧⲁⲟⲩⲁ̀ ϯⲟⲩⲭⲏ ϩⲓⲭⲉ · ⲛ̄ⲉϩ ⸗ ⲉⲥⲧⲁϩⲥ ⲡⲉϩⲁ · ϣⲁ ⲉⲓⲣⲏⲛⲓ

5   ⲗⲓⲃⲁⲛⲟⲥ

ⲋ̅ ⸗ ⲟⲩⲣⲱⲙⲉ̀ ⲛ̄ⲧⲁⲩⲙⲁⲣⲉⲃ ⲛ̀ⲉϣ ⲧⲉⲭⲓ ⲧⲉϥⲥⲓⲙⲓ : ⲧⲁⲟⲩ-
ⲁ ϯⲟⲩⲭⲏ ⲭⲉ ⲁⲣⲭⲏ ⲛ̄ⲉϩ : ⲟⲩϭⲁⲗⲉϩⲧ ⲉⲙⲁⲩ : ⲡⲉϩⲧⲥ
ⲭⲱϥ ϣⲁⲃⲱⲗ ⲉⲃⲁⲗ : ⲕⲁⲗⲟⲥ ⲑ̄ⲩ ⲕⲟⲩϣ ϩⲓ ⲥⲧⲏⲣ

ⲍ̅ : ⲟⲩⲣⲱⲙⲉ : ⲛ̄ⲧⲁⲩϯ ⲟⲩⲁⲡⲁⲧ ⲛⲉⲃ ⲧⲁⲟⲩⲁ ϯⲟⲩⲭⲏ : ⲛ:ⲅ̄
10 ⲉⲥⲟⲡ ϩⲓⲭⲉⲛ ⲟⲩⲁⲙⲡⲟⲩⲗⲗⲓ ⲛⲁⲃⲓ:ϭⲏⲛⲛⲓ ⲉⲥⲙⲉϩ : ⲛⲁ-
ⲗⲙⲁⲟⲩⲁⲣⲧ ϩⲓ ⲙⲁⲩ ⲛ̀ⲗⲁⲯⲁⲛ ⲧⲥⲁⲃ ⲛⲉⲥϯⲕⲟⲥ ⸗
ϣⲁⲃϩⲏⲛⲉ ⸗ ⲑ̄ⲩ ⸗ ⲕⲟⲩϣ ⸗ ⲛⲁⲗⲏⲩ

ⲏ̅ ⸗ ⲟⲩⲣⲱⲙⲉ · ⲉⲃϯⲕⲁⲥ ⲧⲁⲟⲩⲁ ϯⲟⲩⲭⲏ · ϩⲓ ⲁⲣⲭⲏ ⲛⲉϩ ⸗
ⲧⲥⲟⲃ : ⲗⲉⲃ ⸗ ϣⲁⲗⲟ ⸗ ⲑ̄ⲩ ⸗ ⲁⲥⲫⲁⲗⲧⲱⲛ ⸗

15 ⲑ̅ : ⲟⲩⲣⲱⲙⲉ · ⲉⲃⲙⲁⲁϣⲓ ϩⲓ : ⲟⲩⲧⲁⲩ ⸗ ⲛ̄ϣⲁⲣⲉⲡⲣ̄ⲏ ⸗
ⲭⲁⲗⲓ ⲗⲁⲃ · ⲙⲁⲣⲉⲃ ⲡⲓⲥⲱϯⲟⲩⲱⲛ ⸗ ⲛ̄ⲧⲁⲁⲃ · ⲙⲁⲛ ⲙ̀ⲉⲣ-
ⲉⲥⲁⲁⲛⲓ : ϩⲉ ⲑⲩⲣⲓⲱⲛ ⸗ ⲛⲉϣ ⲭⲱϩ ⲉⲣⲁⲃ ⸗ ⲁⲗⲟⲩⲁⲥ ⸗

---

1 *i.e.* ˢⲉ⸗ϥ-ⲟ ⲛ̄-ϭⲛ̄ϭⲉϩ ? : ⲉϥⲃⲱⲛⲕ ⲏ ⲛ̄ⲕⲃ⟨ⲱⲛⲕ⟩ or ⲉϥ-ⲱ-ⲛ̄ⲕⲏⲛⲕⲃ ? "A man who is …", perhaps "angry" ("Ein Mann der ist…", "zürnen") K, M : "someone who spasms" Gardner | *i.e.* ζῴδιον || **2** *i.e.* ⲙⲟⲣ⸗ϥ̄ | *i.e.* ˢϩⲙ̄ ⲡ-ⲟⲩⲱϣ ⲙ̄-ⲡⲛⲟⲩⲧⲉ | *i.e.* μαστίχη || **3** *i.e.* ˢⲉⲣⲉ- | *i.e.* ϩⲛ̄ || **4** *i.e.* εὐχή : ⲟⲩϣⲏ K | *i.e.* ˢϩⲓⲭⲛ̄ ⲟⲩ-ⲛⲉϩ | *i.e.* ˢⲛ̄-ⲧⲉϩⲥ | *i.e.* ϣⲁ⸗ⲩ-ⲡ̄ | *i.e.* εἰρήνη : "for peace" ("zum Frieden") K, G : "for the sake of peace" M | **5** *i.e.* λίβανος || **6** ⲟⲩⲣⲱⲙ K | *i.e.* ˢⲉ-ⲙⲉ⸗ϥ-ϩⲉⲛ⸗ϥ ⲧⲱⲱϭⲉ ⲉ- or ⲛ̄-ϥ̄-ϣ ⲧⲱⲱϭⲉ ⲁⲛ ⲉ- ? : *i.e.* ˢⲛ̄ⲛⲉ⸗ϥ-ϣ ⲧⲉⲭⲓ K || **7** *i.e.* εὐχή | *i.e.* ˢⲉⲭⲛ̄ | *i.e.* ἀρχή | *i.e.* ˢⲛ̄-ⲛⲉϩ | *i.e.* ˢⲙ̄-ⲙⲟⲟⲩ | ⲟⲩ-ϭⲁⲗⲉϩⲧ ⲙ̄-ⲙⲁⲩ : "recite this prayer over newly-pressed oil in a water pot" Gardner || **8** *i.e.* καλῶς | *i.e.* ˢϣⲁ⸗ϥ-ⲃⲱⲗ | *i.e.* θυ(σία) | *i.e.* ˢⲕⲟⲩϣⲧ | *i.e.* στύραξ || **9** *i.e.* εὐχή || **10** *i.e.* ˢⲛ̄-ⲥⲟⲡ | *i.e.* ἀμπύλλη | *i.e.* ˢⲁⲃⲁϭⲏⲉⲓⲛ || **10–11** *i.e.* الماورد al-māward || **11** *i.e.* λαψάνη | *i.e.* νηστικῶς see LBG s.v. : *i.e.* ˢⲥϯ-ⲕⲱⲱⲥ "funerary incense" ("Toteninzenz") K, M || **12** *i.e.* ϣⲁ⸗ϥ-ϩⲉⲛ⸗ϥ̄ (< ϩⲓⲛⲉ) ⲉⲃⲟⲗ ? : ϣⲟⲩϩⲏⲛⲉ K : "he shall retch (?)" G | *i.e.* θυ(σία) | *i.e.* ˢⲕⲟⲩϣⲧ : *i.e.* κόστος K : "koush" M || **13** *i.e.* ˢϯⲧⲕⲁⲥ | *i.e.* εὐχή | *i.e.* ἀρχή : "virgin oil" M | *i.e.* ˢⲛ̄-ⲛⲉϩ || **14** *i.e.* ⲉⲣⲟ⸗ϥ : "by mouth" Gardner : *i.e.* λίβανος K, M | *i.e.* ˢϣⲁ⸗ϥ-ⲗⲟ | *i.e.* θυ(σία) | *i.e.* ἄσφαλτος || **15** *i.e.* ˢⲉ-ϣⲁⲣⲉ-ⲡⲣⲏ : *i.e.* ˢⲛ̄ϣⲱⲣⲡ ⲛ̄ⲡⲣⲏ K || **16** *i.e.* ˢϭⲱⲱⲗⲉ Crum 809a : *i.e.* καλεῖν ? K : as K, or else ϭⲟ(ⲉ)ⲓⲗⲉ M | *i.e.* ˢⲉⲣⲟ⸗ϥ || **15–16** "at sunrise summon him" G : "at sunrise visit him" M : "at the first ray of sunshine you stay with him (or call after him)" ("Beim ersten Sonnenstrahl weilst du bei ihm (oder: rufst du nach ihm")) K | *i.e.* ζῴδιον | *i.e.* ˢⲛ̄ⲧⲟⲟⲧ⸗ϥ || **16** "tie it (to him)! When the image is in his hand…" ("Binde es (ihm) an! Wenn das Bildchen in seiner Hand ist…") K || **17** *i.e.* θηρίον | *i.e.* ˢⲛⲁ⸗ⲩ-ϣ-ⲭⲱϩ | ⲁⲗⲟⲩⲁⲥ *i.e.* ᴮἀλουσις ? see note : K, M, G do not translate

4. A man who has elephantiasis?. Draw this *image with ⟨the⟩ blood ⟨of a⟩ vulture. Bind it to him. They will heal, God willing. ⟨Offering:⟩ *mastic.

5. A man with an enmity between him and his wife. Pronounce this prayer upon oil, and she anoints the face. They will reconcile. |⁵ ⟨Offering:⟩ *frankincense.

6. A man who has been *bound, unable to join with his wife. Pronounce the prayer over oil of the *first fruits. A pot of water, pour it upon him. He will be completely released. Offering: *costus and *storax.

7. A man who has been given a *cup. Pronounce the prayer three |¹⁰ times over a glass *flask filled with rose-water and charlock-water. Have him drink while fasting. It will remove ⟨itself⟩. Offering: white costus.

8. A man who is in pain. Pronounce the prayer over oil of the *first-fruits. Have him drink ⟨it⟩. It will cease. Offering: bitumen. |¹⁵

9. A man walking in the desert when the sun is covered. Bind this figure to his hand. Certainly, no robbers or beasts will be able to touch him. ⟨Offering:⟩ pig's senna?.

---

1. ⲛⲕⲏⲛ̄ⲕⲃ : "elephantiasis?" Here we propose a variant of ⲟⲛ̄ⲟⲉϩ; the alteration of ⲕ to ϭ does not pose a problem, although the shift from ϩ to ⲃ would be more unexpected; perhaps *cf.* ⲙⲟⲭϩ/ⲙⲟⲭϥ ("girdle"; Crum CD 213b), although in that case there is also an intermediate form ⲙⲟⲭϩϥ.

9. ⲟⲩⲁⲡⲁⲧ : "a cup" Likely a 'magical potion' administered in a cup; *cf. e.g.,* Cairo JdE 42573 (Chassinat 1955; KYP M44), p. 4, ll. 11–17, a drink from a cup to separate a couple; similar recipes are found in *PCM* I 33 front ll. 1-5; P.Méd.Copt.IFAO (Chassinat 1921; KYP M941) no. 229.

17. ⲁⲗⲟⲩⲁⲥ̄ : "pig's senna?" The initial ⲁⲗ- would seem to suggest an Arabic loanword, but we have not found a good candidate. Instead we suggest that this may be the word found in the *Scala Magna* as ⲁⲗⲟⲩⲥⲓⲥ (4.2.339; Macomber 2020: I 142) with the translation شِشْم مكة ⟨م⟩ مكة *šišm makka*, referring to the seed of *Cassia absus* L. (=*Chamaecrista absus* (L.) H.S. Irwin & Barneby), known in English as pig's senna or *chaksh* (*cf.* Kuczkiewicz-Fraś 2003: 165). The seeds are black, and used in various medical preparations, including eye medicine (Meyerhof 1931: 24, 46; Kuczkiewicz-Fraś 2003: 165; *cf.* Lev/Amar 2008: 554). The Coptic name seems to come from Greek ἀλουσία "unwashed", perhaps in reference to the blackness of the seeds.

28. ⲟⲩⲉⲝⲟⲩⲥⲓⲁ : ⲉⲕⲡⲏⲧ ⲉϩⲟⲩⲛ ϣⲁⲣⲁⲥ : "An authority to whom you are going" Here we understand the "authority" to be a human in a position in authority, a translation also adopted by Meyer. Justification for this may be found in the *Scala Magna*, in which ϯⲉⲝⲟⲩⲥⲓⲁ is translated as "the sultan" (السلطان; Macomber 2020: 70). The term "sultan" is used in several Arabic (including Judaeo- and *Copto-Arabic) recipes to refer to one possible authority a client might need to approach; *cf. e.g.,* ʿĪsā ibn ʿAlī, *Book on the Useful Properties of Animal Parts* (IX CE) 1.10, 2.2, 4.6–7, 18.1, 56.10, 59.22, 67.2 (Raggetti 2018); Geniza 24 l. 10 (Naveh/Shaked 1993); *Guide to the Psalms* Psalms 19, 20, 26, 34, 40, 42, 53, 54, 57 (Henein/Bianquis 1975). Compare also Förster WBGW 272 *s.v.* ⲉⲝⲟⲩⲥⲓⲁ, although these instances tend to refer the abstract quality of power in general rather than specific individuals. Both terms, *exousia* and "sultan", would seem to refer, at this time, to "the person who at a particular time is the personification of the impersonal governmental power" (Kramers *et al.* 2012: §1). Kropp and Gardner understand this to refer to a supernatural being who has confronted the patient of the ritual, specifically a "ghost" ("Totengeist"); Kropp seems to suggest a confusion with οὐσία, "essence", the term often used for materials from a human body used in rituals, sometimes taken from dead bodies. Ἐξουσία in reference to a supernatural being is best attested as a rank of angel, however, which would not seem to fit here.

29. ⲙⲁⲣⲉⲥ ⲉϫⲱϥ : "Bind it to him" Kropp suggests that "him" here might be the dead person whose ghost is being encountered, but on this interpretation see the note to l. 28 above.

page 16 continued (= *Kropp 261*) (hair)

ι̅ ⲟⲩⲣⲱⲙⲉ · ⲉⲃⲟ ⲛⲭⲱⲗⲏ ⸗ ⲭⲉ ⲧⲉⲃⲥⲓⲙⲓ ⸗ ⲉⲣ ⲛⲁⲃⲓ : ⲉⲣⲁⲃ ⸗
ⲥϩⲁⲓ ⲡⲓⲥⲱ†ⲟⲩⲛ · ⲓⲁⲟⲩ ⲉⲃⲁⲗ · ⲉⲛⲉϩ · †ⲁⲥⲙⲏ : ⲙⲁⲃ ⲛ̅ⲟⲩ-
20   ⲁ ⲛⲉϣ ⲕⲁⲧ ⲛⲉⲙⲁⲥ ⸗ ⲙⲁⲣⲉⲧⲱϩⲥ ⲛⲉϩⲣⲁⲥ ⸗ ⲙⲁⲥ†ⲭⲓ

ⲓ̅ⲁ̅ ⸗ ⲟⲩⲥⲓⲙⲓ : ⲣⲉⲡⲉⲥϩⲁⲓ ⲧⲉ ⲃⲏⲭ ⲉⲣⲁⲥ ⸗ ⲥϩⲁⲓ ⲡⲓⲥⲩ ⸗
ⲉⲩϫⲉⲕ : ⲙⲁϩⲃ ⲛⲉϩ : †ⲁⲥⲙⲏ ⸗ ⲁϣ †ⲟⲩⲭⲏ ϩⲓϫⲟⲃ
ⲧⲁϩⲥ ⲡⲉⲥϩⲁ ⸗ ϣⲁ ⲉⲓⲣⲏⲛⲏⲓ ⲣⲁⲥ ⲑⲩ̅ ⲙⲁⲥ†ⲭⲓ ⲁⲗⲟⲩⲑ

ⲓ̅ⲃ̅ ⸗ ⲟⲩⲣⲱⲙⲉ ⲉⲃⲡⲏⲧ : ⲉⲩⲙⲉⲧⲁⲭⲉⲩ · ⲥϩⲁⲓ ⲡⲓⲥⲱ†ⲟⲩⲱⲛ ⸗
25   ⲙⲁⲣⲉϥ ⲉⲣⲁϥ · ⲛⲉⲣⲱⲙⲉ ⸗ ⲉⲓⲙⲓ ⲉⲣⲁⲃ ⲑⲩ̅ ⲥⲧⲏⲣⲝ ⸗

ⲓ̅ⲅ̅ ⸗ ⲟⲩⲣⲱⲙⲓ : ⲉϭⲏⲛⲧ ⲉⲃϩⲁⲣⲕ ⲉⲛ : ⲥϩⲁⲓ
ⲡⲓⲥⲩ̅ ⲟⲩⲁϩϥ ϩⲁϫⲱⲃ · ϩⲓⲛⲏⲃ ⲑⲩ̅ ⲙⲁⲥ†ⲭⲓ ⸗

ⲓ̅ⲇ̅ ⸗ ⲟⲩⲉⲝⲟⲩⲥⲓⲁ : ⲉⲕⲡⲏⲧ ⲉϩⲟⲩⲛ ϣⲁⲣⲁⲥ ⸗ ⲥϩⲁⲓ ⲡⲓ-
ⲧⲉⲛⲁⲙⲓⲥ : ⲉⲧⲥⲁ ⲓⲟⲩⲛⲁⲙ ⸗ ⲙⲁⲣⲉⲥ ⲉϫⲱϥ : ⲡⲱⲧ ⲉ-
30   ϩⲟⲩⲛ ⲡⲉⲣϣⲁϫⲉ ⲙⲁⲛ ϩⲛⲕϣⲁⲛ:ⲙⲟⲩⲭⲁⲅⲉⲓ ⸗

ⲓ̅ⲉ̅ ⸗ ⲟⲩ†ⲙⲓ ⲕⲟⲩⲱϣ ⲧⲉϥ⸗ϭⲱⲣϭ ⲥϩⲁⲓ ⲡⲓⲥⲩ̅ ⸗ ⲧⲁⲙⲥⲉⲃ
ϩⲓ ⲟⲩϩⲣⲓ ⲥⲧⲁⲩⲣⲟⲥ ⸗ ⲙⲁⲛ ϣⲁϭⲱⲣϭ ⲙⲟⲩⲥⲭⲁⲧⲉⲛ

ⲓ̅ⲋ̅ ⸗ ⲟⲩⲙⲁⲛⲉⲣϩⲱⲃ ⸗ ⲉⲃϣⲁϥ : ⲟⲩϭⲁϩⲉⲗ ϭⲙⲁⲩ · ⲉⲧⲥⲱⲕ · ⲧⲁⲟⲩⲁ †ⲟⲩⲭⲏ · ϫⲱⲥ ⲛ̅ⲍ̅ ⲥⲟⲡ · ⲣⲉϩⲁⲓ† ⲡⲏ-
35   ϩ : ϩⲓⲱⲱⲕ · ⲉⲕⲥⲱⲕ · ⲉⲥⲁⲡⲉϩⲟⲩ ϣⲁⲛⲡⲉⲣⲧⲥ ⸗
ⲉⲡⲉⲣⲟ · ⲡⲏⲓ ⲑⲩ̅ ⲭⲁⲃⲁⲛⲓ ⸗

---

18 *i.e.* χολή || **19** *i.e.* ζῴδιον | *i.e.* ˢⲉⲓⲁⲁ⸗ⲟⲩ | *i.e.* ˢⲛⲉϩ ⲛ̅-ⲧ-ⲓⲁⲥⲙⲏ *i.e.* ἰάσμη : *i.e.* ὀσμή translate "fumigate him" ("Beräuchere ihn") K : "disperse fragrance on it" Meyer | *l.* ˢ⟨ⲧⲱϩⲥ̅⟩ ⲙ̅ⲙⲟ⸗ϥ ? || **19–20** *i.e.* ˢⲛ̅ⲛⲉ-ⲟⲩⲁ ? || **20** *i.e.* ˢⲛⲁ-ϣ ⲛ̅ⲕⲟⲧⲕ ⲛ̅ⲙ̅ⲙⲁ⸗ⲥ | *i.e.* ˢⲙⲁⲣⲉ⸗ϥ | *i.e.* ˢⲛ̅-ϩⲣⲁ⸗ⲥ : "with the oil" ("mit Öl") K, M, G | *i.e.* μαστίχη || **21** *i.e.* ˢⲉⲣⲉ | *i.e.* ˢ† : *i.e.* δέ K | *i.e.* ˢϥϭⲟϭⲉ : "whose husband jumps against her" ("deren Gatte gegen sie springt") K | *i.e.* ζῴδιον || **22** "palm (of hand)" Gardner | ⲙⲁϩⲃ ϩ corrected from ⲓ by overwriting | *i.e.* ˢⲛ̅-ⲛⲉϩ ⲛ̅-ⲧ-ⲓⲁⲥⲙⲏ *i.e.* ἰάσμη : *i.e.* ὀσμή ("disperse fragrance") K, M | *i.e.* εὐχή || **23** *i.e.* ˢϣⲁ⸗ϥ-ⲣ̅ ⲉⲓⲣⲏⲛⲓ *i.e.* εἰρήνη : ϣⲁ ⲉⲓⲣⲏⲛⲏⲓ "for peace for her" ("zum Frieden für sie") K, G, M | *i.e.* θυ(σία) | *i.e.* μαστίχη | *i.e.* العود al-ʿūd || **24** "hastening (towards)" M : "running (to)" G : "running to" or "fleeing from" ("von… flieht, zu… eilt") K | *i.e.* ˢⲙⲛ̅ⲧ-ⲁⲧ-ϣⲁⲩ "ruin" G, M : "abomination" ("Abscheulichkeit") K | *i.e.* ζῴδιον || **25** *i.e.* ˢⲛ̅ⲛⲉ- | *i.e.* θυ(σία) | *i.e.* στύραξ || **26** *i.e.* ˢⲉ-ϥ-ϭⲏⲛⲧ (< ϭⲱ) ⲉ⸗ϥ-ϩⲟⲣⲕ ⲁⲛ : or ⲉϭⲏⲛⲧ ⟨ ϭⲓⲛⲉ "a man who cannot find his rest" ("der seine Ruhe nicht finden kann"), "someone who cannot find respite" K, G || **27** *i.e.* ζῴδιον | "place it on him" ("Leg es ihm auf") K, M | *l.* ⟨ϣⲁⲃ⟩ϩⲓⲛⲏⲃ *i.e.* ˢϣⲁ⸗ϥ-ϩⲓⲛⲏⲃ ? : "he will sleep" ("er findet Schlaf") K : "(lay it by his) sleeping (head)" G || **27** *i.e.* θυ(σία) | *i.e.* μαστίχη || **28** *i.e.* ἐξουσία : *cf.* οὐσία K || **29** *i.e.* δύναμις | *i.e.* ˢⲥⲁ | *i.e.* ˢⲛ̅-ⲟⲩⲛⲁⲙ || **30** *i.e.* ˢⲙ̅ⲡⲣ haplography with preceding ⲛ ? | *l. e.g.*, ⲙⲁⲛ ϣⲁⲕⲟⲩϫⲁⲓ || **31** *i.e.* ˢⲉ⸗ⲕ-ⲟⲩⲱϣ | *i.e.* ˢⲉ-ⲧⲣⲉ⸗ϥ-ϭⲱⲣϭ̅ | *i.e.* ζῴδιον || **32** *i.e.* ˢϩⲓⲣ | *i.e.* ˢⲛ̅- | *i.e.* σταυρός | *i.e.* ˢϣⲁ⸗ϥ-ϭⲱⲣϭ̅ | *i.e.* μοσχάτον || **33** *i.e.* ˢⲉ-ϣⲟϥ⸗ϥ ? : ⲉⲃϣⲏϥ K | *i.e.* ˢϭⲁⲗⲁϩⲧ, *cf.* ϭⲁⲗⲉϩ (p. 17 l. 24) with metathesis : *l.* ϫⲱⲗϩ̅ K | *i.e.* ˢⲛ̅-ⲙⲟⲟⲩ || **34** *i.e.* εὐχή | *i.e.* ˢⲉⲣⲉ-ϩⲟⲉⲓⲧⲉ, *cf.* ᶠϩⲁⲓⲧⲓ : ⲣⲉϩ† *l.* ⲉⲣⲉ-ⲟⲩ-ⲣⲁϩⲧⲉ K || **35** *i.e.* ˢⲛ̅-ⲅ-ⲥⲱⲕ=ⲥ haplography ? | *i.e.* ˢⲛ̅-ⲥⲁ-ⲡⲁϩⲟⲩ | *i.e.* ˢϣⲁⲛⲧ=ⲕ-ⲡⲁϩⲧ=ⲥ || **36** *i.e.* ˢⲉ-ⲡ-ⲣⲟ | *i.e.* ˢⲙ̅-ⲡⲏⲓ | *i.e.* θυ(σία) | *i.e.* κάρβων or χαλβάνη ? : "ebony" ("Ebenholz ?) *i.e.* from Egyptian *hbny* ? K : "chabani" M : "coal" Gardner

10. A man who is angry because his wife is sinning against him. Draw the image. Wash them off with jasmine oil. ⟨Anoint⟩ him. No-one |²⁰ will be able to sleep with her. Let ⟨him⟩ anoint her face. ⟨Offering:⟩ *mastic.

11. A woman whose husband is violent? towards her. Draw the image on a shell. Fill it ⟨with⟩ jasmine oil. Recite the prayer over it. Anoint her face. He will make peace with her. Offering: mastic, *agarwood.

12. A man who is going to an unworthy act. Draw the image. |²⁵ Bind it to him. No-one will recognise him. Offering: *storax.

13. A man who is unable to rest. Draw the image. Place it before him. ⟨He will⟩ sleep. Offering: mastic.

14. An authority to whom you are going. Draw the power which is on the right. Bind it to him. Go |³⁰ to ⟨the authority⟩. Do not speak. Certainly, you ⟨will be⟩ well?.

15. A village you desire to make inhabited. Draw the image. Bury it at a crossroads. Certainly, ⟨it⟩ will be inhabited. ⟨Offering:⟩ *musk incense.

16. A workshop, to destroy it?. A pot of flowing water. Pronounce the prayer over it 7 times, wearing torn clothes, |³⁵ and draw ⟨it⟩ backwards until ⟨you⟩ pour it out at the door of the house. Offering: charcoal?.

29–30. ⲡⲱⲧ ⲉϩⲟⲩⲛ ⲡⲉⲣϣⲁⲭⲉ : "Go to ⟨the authority⟩. Do not speak." Gardner translates "Confront, but do not speak".

30. ⲙⲁⲛ ϩⲏⲕ ϣⲁⲛ : ⲙⲟⲩⲭⲁⲩⲉⲓ : "Certainly, ⟨you will be⟩ well?" Kropp understands ˢⲙⲛ̄ ϩⲓⲕ ϣⲱⲛⲕ or ˢⲙⲁⲛ ϩⲓⲕ ϣⲱⲛⲉ followed by ⲙ̄ⲡⲟⲩϫⲁⲓ or ⲙⲟⲟⲩ ⲉⲧ-ϣⲟⲩⲱⲟⲩ "no magic can harm you" ("Kein Zauber kann dich schädigen") or "certainly, magic will become powerless" ("sicherlich wird Zauber kraftlos werden"), suggesting in his notes as "of wellbeing" or "dry water" ("trockenes Wasser") for the following words. Meyer translates "no sorcery will deprive (you) of well-being (?)" or "surely sorcery will be powerless…". Gardner translates "truly the sorcery is rendered impotent". None of these seem to fit the context, in which "magic" is not mentioned, while ϣⲱⲛⲉ ("to be sick") in reference to "magic" becoming powerless is unattested. We assume that here, as in many of the other recipes, the copyist has omitted elements which would normally be gramatically necessary.

33. ⲟⲩⲙⲁ ⲛⲉⲣϩⲱⲃ ≠ ⲉⲃϣⲁϥ : "A workshop, to destroy it?" Here we interpret this as a curse, since this is usually the purpose of rituals that consist of pouring liquids at doors; previous translations have rather understood this as a practice to aid a workplace which is suffering from some kind of problem, being either deserted or flooded by water. Kropp and Meyer translate "a workplace that is deserted when a flow of water streams in" ("ein Arbeitsplatz, der wüst liegt, da eine Wasserflut herzieht"), while Gardner translates "a barren workplace (*i.e.* small-holding)".

34–35. ⲣⲉϩⲁⲓⲧ ⲡⲏϩ : ϩⲓϣⲱⲕ : "wearing torn clothes" Kropp and Meyer understand this as referring to a "broken basin" ("einen zersprungenen Kessel").

35. ⲉⲕⲥⲱⲕ · ⲉⲥⲁⲡⲉϩⲟⲩ : "and walk? backwards" Kropp translates "drag behind you" ("du hinter dir herziehst"); Meyer, "let it stream out behind you"; Gardner, "while you draw (the water) back". We understand an omitted direct object (ⲉⲕⲥⲱⲕⲥ) with the sigma omitted via haplography with the following -ⲉⲥ, where the pronoun refers to the pot (ϭⲁⲗⲁϩⲧ). *Cf.* Gregory of Nyssa *In Ecclesiasten V* (CC 197): "I drew it back with the bridle of my faculties of reason" (ⲁⲓⲥⲟⲕⲥ ⲛⲥⲁ ⲡⲁϩⲟⲩ ϩⲓⲧⲛ ⲡⲉⲭⲁⲗⲓⲛⲟⲥ ⲛⲛⲁⲗⲟⲕⲓⲥⲙⲟⲥ; Amélineau 1911: 432 l. 13; *cf.* Orlandi 1981: 337–338).

p. 17 (= Kropp 267) (hair)

ιζ ⲟⲩⲥⲗⲁⲙ ⲧⲉⲕⲉⲛⲧⲃ · ϩⲓϫⲉⲛ ⲟⲩⲣⲱⲙⲉ ⲧⲁⲩⲟⲩⲁ †ⲟⲩⲭⲏ ⲡ
ϩⲓϫⲉⲛ ⲟⲩⲙⲁⲩ ⲛⲁϫⲉⲃ ϩⲓϫⲱⲃ · ⲉϣⲱⲡⲓ ⲑⲏ ⲟⲩⲣⲉⲃ-
ⲙⲟⲟⲩⲧ ⲗⲓⲃⲁⲛⲟⲥ ιⲏ ⲟⲩⲣⲱⲙⲓ · ϣⲁⲛϭⲁⲓ ⲉⲣⲁⲕ ⲃⲓ
ⲟⲩⲧⲏⲥ ⲛⲧⲏⲕ ⲥϩⲁⲓ ⲡⲥⲓⲩ ⲙⲁⲣⲉⲃ · ⲡⲙⲁϩϯ ⲛⲟⲩϫⲉ-
ϫ ⲛⲃⲏⲛⲛⲓ ϩⲁⲗϥ ⲉⲃⲁⲗ ⲡϫⲱⲕ ⲅ̅ ⲉϩⲟⲟⲩ ⲙⲁ ⲛⲓ-
ⲙ ⲉⲣⲉⲡⲣⲱⲙⲉ ⲛϩⲏⲧϥ ϣⲁⲃⲓ ⲙⲛ ⲡϫⲉϫ ⲛⲃⲏⲛⲛⲓ

ιⲑ ⲟⲩⲣⲱⲙⲉ ⲉⲃⲏⲧ ⲉⲩⲥⲓⲙⲓ ⲥϩⲁⲓ · ⲥⲓⲩ ⲙⲁⲣⲉⲧⲉ-
ⲥⲓⲙⲓϩⲓ ⲧⲁⲙⲥⲉⲃ · ⲉϩⲟⲩⲛ ⲡⲉⲥϩⲓ · ⲙⲁⲛ ⲙⲉⲃⲏⲧ
ⲥϩⲓⲙⲓ ⲛϣⲉⲙⲁ ⲑⲩ ⲙⲁⲥϯϫ ⲁⲗⲟⲩⲑ

ⲕ̅ ⲟⲩⲁϩⲓ ⲛⲧⲉⲃⲛⲏ ⲛⲧⲁⲩⲉⲗ ⲟⲩⲥⲓⲕ ⲉⲣⲁⲕ · ⲥϩⲁⲓ
†ⲧⲉⲛⲁⲙⲓⲥ ⲛϩⲁ ⲛϩⲁⲗⲏⲧ · ⲧⲁⲙⲥ · ⲉϩⲟⲩⲛ ⲉ-
ⲣⲁⲃ ϣⲁⲃⲃⲱⲗ ⲉⲃⲁⲗ · ⲕⲁⲗⲟⲥ ⲑⲩ ⲙⲁⲥϯϫⲓ

ⲕ̅ⲁ ⲟⲩⲥⲓⲙⲓ ⲣⲉⲛϣⲏⲣⲉ ⲙⲁⲟⲩⲧ ⲥϩⲁⲓ †ⲍ̅ ⲛⲧⲉⲛⲁⲙⲓⲥ ⲉⲩⲭⲱⲙⲉ · ⲙⲁⲣ ⲉⲡⲉⲥⲭⲉⲛⲉϩ ⲛⲓⲱⲛⲁ-
ⲙ ⲙⲁⲣⲉⲕⲉⲟⲩⲉⲓ ⲡⲉⲥⲭⲉⲛⲉϩ ⲃⲟⲩⲣ · ⲙⲁⲛ ⲣⲉ-
ⲡⲉⲥϣⲏⲣⲉ ⲙⲟⲩ ⲑⲩ · ⲙⲁⲥϯϫⲓ

ⲡⲣⲁⲉⲓⲥ · ⲥϩⲁⲓ ϩⲓ
ⲁⲣⲭⲏ ⲡϫⲱⲙⲉ
ⲙⲁⲣⲉϥ ⲉⲣⲁⲕ
ⲛⲁⲥⲃ-
ⲣⲁⲛ
ⲙⲁⲥϯϫⲓ
ⲁⲗⲟⲩⲑ

²⁴ⲟⲩϭⲁⲗⲉϩ ⲉⲧ ⲉⲙⲉⲭⲓ ⲟⲩ-
²⁵ⲙⲟⲁⲩ ⲛⲑⲏⲡ ⲥⲧⲁⲓ · ⲍ̅
²⁶ⲃⲏⲧ ⲉⲣⲟⲟⲩⲛⲓ · ⲁⲑⲁⲃ
²⁷ϣⲁ ⲣⲟⲩϩⲉ · ⲡⲉⲧϣⲱ-
²⁸ⲛⲓ
²⁹ⲛⲉⲥϯⲁ

ϣⲁⲉⲉ
ϣⲁⲉⲉ
ϣⲁⲉⲉ
ϣⲁ
ϣⲁ

ⲅⲉⲛⲛⲁ ⲏⲥ

ⲙⲓⲭⲁⲏⲗ
ⲅⲁⲃⲣⲓⲏⲗ
ϩⲣⲁⲫⲁⲏⲗ
[ϣ]ⲟⲩⲣⲓⲏ[ⲗ]   ⲥⲉⲧ[ⲉⲕⲓⲏⲗ]

---

1 *i.e.* ᴮⲥⲣⲟⲙ | *i.e.* ˢⲉⲧ=ⲕ-ⲛ̅ⲧ=ϥ̅ | *i.e.* ˢⲧⲁⲩⲉ- : ⲧⲁⲟⲩⲁ K | *i.e.* ˢⲧ-ⲉὐχή ‖ **2** *i.e.* ˢⲉ=ϥ-ⲉ-ϣⲱⲡⲉ | *i.e.* ˢⲛ-ⲧ-ϩⲉ ⲛ- ‖ **3** *i.e.* λίβανος ‖ **3** *i.e.* ˢⲉ-ϣⲁ=ϥ-ⲧϭⲁⲉⲓⲟ ‖ **4** *i.e.* ˢⲟⲩ-ⲧⲟⲉⲓⲥ | ⲛⲧⲏⲕ *i.e.* ˢⲛⲧⲁ=ⲕ | *l.* ζ(ῴδ)ιο(ν) | *i.e.* ˢⲉ-ⲡ-ⲙⲟⲧⲉ : *i.e.* ˢⲙⲁϩⲧ "entrails" ("Eingeweide") K, M ‖ **5** *i.e.* ˢⲃⲏⲛⲉ | ⲡϫⲱⲕ see note | *i.e.* ˢⲛ̅-ϩⲟⲟⲩ | *i.e.* ˢⲙ̅-ⲙⲁ ? ‖ **7** *l.* ζ(ῴδ)ι(ο)ν (twice) ‖ **7** *i.e.* ˢⲉ-(ⲟ)ⲩ-ⲥϩⲓⲙⲉ ‖ **8** *i.e.* ˢⲥϩⲓⲙⲉ | *i.e.* ˢⲧⲟⲙⲥ=ϥ̅ | *i.e.* ˢⲛ̅-ϩⲟⲩⲛ ⲙ̅-ⲡⲉ=ⲥ-ϩⲏ ‖ **9** *i.e.* ˢⲉ-(ⲟ)ⲩ-ⲥϩⲓⲙⲉ | **9, 12, 16** *i.e.* θυ(σία) | **9, 12, 16, 22** *i.e.* μαστίχη | *i.e.* العود *al-ʿūd* ‖ **10** ⲧⲉⲃⲛⲏⲏ K ‖ **11, 13, 30, 31** *i.e.* δύναμις | *i.e.* ˢⲧⲟⲙⲥ=ⲥ ⲛ̅-ϩⲟⲩⲛ ‖ **12** *i.e.* καλῶς ‖ **13** *i.e.* ˢⲉⲣⲉ-ⲛⲉ=ⲥ-ϣⲏⲣⲉ ‖ **14–15** *i.e.* ˢⲙⲉⲣ=ⲥ ⲉ-ⲡⲉ=ⲥ-ⲭⲛⲁϩ ⲛ̅-ⲟⲩⲛⲁⲙ ‖ **15–16** *i.e.* ˢⲙⲉⲣ ⲕⲉ-ⲟⲩⲉⲓ ⲉ-ⲡⲉ=ⲥ-ⲭⲛⲁϩ ⲛ̅-ϩⲃⲟⲩⲣ | *i.e.* ˢⲉⲣⲉ-, error for ⲙⲉⲣⲉ- ? : ⲙⲁⲛ ⲉⲣⲉ *i.e.* ˢⲙⲉⲣⲉ- K ‖ **17** πραξις *i.e.* πρᾶξις K, M ‖ **18** *i.e.* ἀρχή : "first, (copy...)" ("zuerst") K, M | *i.e.* ˢⲉ-ⲡ-ϫⲱⲙⲉ ‖ **20–21** *i.e.* الزعفران *az-zaʿfarān* : *i.e.* ˢⲛ-*ⲟⲥⲉ=ϥ ⲣⲁⲛ "for its release (?), names" ("zu seiner Entlassung: Namen") K, M ‖ **23** *i.e.* العود *al-ʿūd* ‖ **24** *i.e.* ˢϭⲁⲗⲁϩⲧ | *i.e.* ˢⲙ̅-ⲙⲁⲁⲭⲉ Crum CD 212b : ϊ ⲟⲩ- : ϊⲟⲩ *i.e.* ˢⲉⲓⲱⲧ "three measures) of barley" ("drei Mass Gerste") K, M : "for three measures" G *i.e.* Crum CD 213a ‖ **25** *i.e.* ˢⲙⲟⲟⲩ ⲉⲧ-ϩⲏⲡ ‖ **26** *i.e.* ˢⲣⲟⲟⲩⲛⲉ ‖ **27–28** *i.e.* ˢⲉⲣⲉ-ⲡ-ⲉⲧ-ϣⲱⲛⲉ ⲛⲏⲥⲧⲉⲩⲉ ? : ⲡⲉⲧϣⲱⲛ K ‖ **29** *i.e.* νηστεία : ⲛⲉϯⲁ K ‖ **35** [[ϣ]] overwritten by image

17. An unconsciousness which you bring upon a man. Pronounce the prayer over some water. Throw it on him. He will be like a dead man. ⟨Offering:⟩ *frankincense.

18. A man ⟨who⟩ condemns you. Take a piece of cloth that belongs to you. Draw the *image. Bind it to the neck? of a swallow. |⁵ Bring? it outside. After three days, from? any place in which the man is, he will go? with the swallow.

19. A man who chases after a woman. Draw ⟨the⟩ image. Let the wife bury it in her house. Certainly, he will not pursue ⟨a⟩ strange woman. Offering: *mastic, *agarwood.

|¹⁰ 20. An enclosure of livestock to which an act of sorcery has been done against you. Draw the bird-faced power. Bury it inside it. It will be completely undone. Offering: mastic.

21. A woman whose children have died. Draw the seven *powers on a sheet. Bind ⟨it⟩ to her right forearm. |¹⁵ Bind another ⟨to⟩ her left forearm. Certainly, her child will ⟨not⟩ die. Offering: mastic.

The amulet. Draw with ⟨wine of⟩ the *first fruits on a sheet. Bind it to yourself. |²⁰ ⟨Offering:⟩ saffron, mastic, agarwood. A *pot with three handles, some |²⁵ hidden water. Incense. Seven virgin palm leaves. Unleavened bread until evening. The one who is sick, fast.

|*Around figures, 30–31* Power. Power. Michael, Gabriel, Raphael, |³⁵ Suriel, Setekiēl.

KD, EL, MP & JS, edited from photograph and autopsy; tracings by KD.

---

3. ϢⲀⲚϬⲀⲒ : "who condemns" Kropp suggests a translation of "someone who has been granted to you through a sentence (?)" ("der dir durch Richterspruch zugesprochen ist ?"); he may have considered a word related to ϬⲀⲨⲞⲚ ("slave"), and have understood this as a spell to return an escaped slave (*cf. e.g., PGM* CIX; KYP M830). Meyer translates "a person who is at odds with you", and Gardner "someone estranged (?) from you".

4–5. ⲚⲞⲨⲬⲀⳠ ⲚⲂⲎⲎⲚⲒ : "swallow" Previous editors translate "swallow-sparrow" ("Schwalbenspatze" Meyer & Kropp), "swallow or sparrow" (Gardner; *cf.* Crum CD 40a. *s.v.* ⲂⲎⲚⲈ), but the *Scala Magna*, gives the meaning as simply السنونو *as-sunūnū* "swallow" (Macomber 2020: 123; *s.v.* ⲠⲒϬⲀⲬⲘⲂⲒⲢⲒ).

5. ⲠⲬⲰⲔ ⲚⳠⲞⲘⲚⲦ ⲈϨⲞⲞⲨ : "After three days" *Cf. Life of Macarius* (CC 0419) "after three days, she died" (ⲠⲬⲰⲔ ⲚⲦ ⲚⲈϨⲞⲞⲨ ⲀⲤⲘⲞⲨ; Amélineau 1894: 240 l.10). Kropp/Meyer translate "Completion" ("Die Vollendung"), understanding it to mark the outcome of the ritual.

6. ϢⲀⲂⲒ : "He will go" The usual translation of ⲈⲒ is "to come", but we understand this as a ritual to get rid of an enemy, so the outcome is that the victim "goes away" with the bird. Alternatively, we might understand that the bird returns to the client, bringing the target with it.

7–8. ⲘⲀⲢⲈⲦⲈⲤϨⲒⲘϢ : "let the wife" ˢⲤϨⲒⲘⲈ can be translated as "woman" or "wife". We opt for "wife" to distinguish the woman who must bury the object in her house from the "(strange) woman" whom the first woman's husband or male partner is "chasing after".

13–14. ⲦⲌ ⲚⲦⲈⲚⲀⲘⲒⲤ : "the seven powers" Kropp & Gardner suggest that these "seven powers" may be the angels mentioned in p. 6 ll. 8–13; *cf.* also the powers mentioned in p. 11 ll. 23–29. Kropp wonders if "seven" (Ⲍ̄) is an error for "two" (Ⲃ̄), then referring to the two powers in the tableau.

25. ⲘⲞⲨ ⲚϨⲎⲠ : "hidden water" Perhaps referring to water from an underground source; *cf.* Meyer/Smith 1994: 385; Gardner 2023b: 133. Smith cites Crum CD 696a *s.v.* ϨⲎⲠ; *cf.* p. 321.

Image: The "Powers" are six-winged *angels; the names of several of the *archangels in ll. 32–35 may indicate that the central angel is to be copied multiple times. The figures below him likely represent the human patient, and the reptile-like demon being cast out of him; *cf.* Dosoo 2022a; Mößner/Nauerth 2015: 348–350.

PCM I 27. Curses of hatefulness and separation

Arsinoites (Faiyum)   19.5 (H) × 14.2 (W) cm   X–XI CE

Other references: P.Heid.Inv. Kopt. 679 (formerly P. Heid. Inv. Nr. 1679); TM 102079; *P.Bad.* V 142; KYP M296; Bélanger Sarrazin #181.

Editions: Bilabel/Grohmann 1934: no. 142 (*ed. pr.*) [B/G]; Polotsky 1935: no. 142 [P]; Dosoo 2023a: 171–177 [D].

Translations: Bilabel/Grohmann 1934: no. 142 (German); Meyer in Meyer/Smith 1994: no. 110 [M]; Dosoo 2023a: 173.

Additional commentary: Polotsky 1935; van der Vliet 1991: 226–227; Untermann (ed.) 2011: 32; Mößner/Nauerth 2015: 327–329; Gardner/Johnston 2019: 31–32.

Present location: Heidelberg, Institut für Papyrologie.

Image: https://doi.org/10.11588/diglit.39747

Linguistic description: Sahidic with Middle Egyptian features.

Contents:

1. Front ll. 1–26, back ll. 1–9 (?): Curse for removing favour with ritual variants (KYP T225)

Complete paper sheet, with minor damage along creases. The manuscript is a formulary, carrying a curse with two variant procedures, the first to remove favour from a person so that they are hated, the second a separation spell; the relationship of the text on the back to those on the front is not clear. The manuscript is part of the 'Heidelberg Coptic Magical Library' and belongs to the 1930 purchase (see pp. 259–263).

The text is written on both front and back in a brown ink, likely of plant origin (see p. 261). As in other manuscripts in this archive, the text is divided into sections using simple horizontal lines, with tableaux consisting of images, *voces magicae*, and *kharaktēres* on either side; the back consists almost entirely of a tableau similar to, but much more elaborate than, that of the front. 5 horizontal and 1 vertical creases are apparent, indicating folding.

The hand of this manuscript is not that of Deacon Iōhannēs, responsible for the majority of the Heidelberg Library (*PCM* I 21–26), but it does seem to be the same as that of *PCM* I 28, a codex made from sheets of paper the same size as that used for this manuscript. Although the letter heights of this manuscript are larger than those of *PCM* I 28, the forms of the letters are generally identical. The ⲛ of *PCM* I 27 measures approximately 0.6 cm, as opposed to *ca.* 0.3 cm in the case of *PCM* I 28, with correspondingly thicker strokes. *PCM* I 28 also gives the impression of having been written more slowly and with greater care, with greater variation in shading and more extensive use of flourishes and serifs.

The hand is much more formal and consistent than that of Iōhannēs, writing in an elegant bimodular, largely bilinear majuscule. There is a slight rightward slope, more marked in *PCM* I 27 than 28, and controlled variation in stroke thickness. The letters are generally written separately, although certain letters (such as ⲁ, ⲧ) often extend to touch the following letter. The ⲁ has a slightly angular bowl, with a long tail. ⲃ is angular, ⲉ and ⲥ thin, the former with a slightly detached, but short, middle stroke. ⲗ, ⳉ, and ⳅ have generous descending strokes; most of the letters have short serifs at the end of strokes, notably the ⲧ, which always has a serif on the left, and often also on the right side of its horizontal bar. Notably, ⳉ does not have the distinctive form used by Iōhannēs (namely, a x with a long ⳅ-like tail), so that ⲍ and ⳉ can look quite similar (for majuscule ⲍ, see *PCM* I 28 p. 8 l. 20), the difference being that the tail of the former curls to the left like the numeral 3, whereas that of the latter recurves to the right. This seems to have led the copyist to alter the form to a more typical majuscule form (ⲍ) on l. 15 of the front of this manuscript to reduce ambiguity. ⲫ in *PCM* I 28 generally has a large, angular bowl, and a short vertical stroke, although the form in *PCM* I 27 is somewhat different. ⲩ in *PCM* I 27 is generally y-shaped, while in *PCM* I 28 its form is Y; *PCM* I 28 also uses an elaborate ⲋ with a recurved ascender not present in *PCM* I 27. Nonetheless, the ritual instructions of *PCM* I 28 (p. 12 l. 19–p. 13), written in a slightly less mannered style, uses forms of both ⲩ and ⲋ closer to *PCM* I 27, demonstrating that these divergent letterforms are a deliberate stylistic choice. Supralineation is primarily used for abbreviations and names, but short strokes are also used to mark the schwa/autosyllabic consonants, and sometimes to mark an omitted final ⲛ. Mid-points, colons, two short oblique lines (⸕), and three dots (∴) are used to mark paratextual divisions (the last only in *PCM* I 27). Notably, this copyist generally uses the minuscule forms of Greek letters to write numerals, a feature which posed problems to previous editors.[1] Bilabel/Grohmann (1934: 305, 410) dated this hand to the eleventh century, albeit without identifying the same copyist in both manuscripts. We opt for a slightly wider range; we have found similar hands in manuscripts dated from 917/918 to 1023, leading us to propose a tenth to eleventh century date.[2]

While this copyist seems to be more highly trained than Iōhannēs, the dialectal features are the same—Sahidic heavily influenced by a Middle Egyptian dialect, likely that of the Faiyum. There are fewer grammatical errors, but we still find some unexpected features (see, *e.g.*, *PCM* I 28 p. 4 ll. 7–8).

---

[1] For examples in these manuscripts, see *PCM* I 27 front l. 23; *PCM* I 28 p. 3 l. 12, p. 8 ll. 10, 14, 20, p. 12 ll. 20, 21, p. 13 l. 6. For the cursive Greek forms used for Coptic numerals, see Stern 1880: 131; Hasitzka 1990: 232. The ⲍ (7) is usually somewhat different from that in Stern, though closer to that reproduced by Hasitzka, resembling a mirrored majuscule epsilon (϶).

[2] Similar hands include the colophon on fol. 155r of Vat.Copt. 66.5 (CLM 135; 917/918 CE); the colophon and reader's note of Vat.Copt. 68, fol. 162r & 162v (CLM 153; 957 & 1014 CE); the colophon of Vat.Copt. 58.4–5 fol. 35v (CLM 76; 1017 CE); and the hands of *P.Teschlot* 1 & 2 (Richter 2000; 1022 and 1023 CE respectively); *cf.* the comments of Miroshnikov 2022: 408.

front

ⲛⲉⲃϣⲱⲡ ⲛⲉⲃϯ : ⲛⲉϥⲁⲡⲱⲕⲣ̅ⲥ̅ : ⲛⲧⲁⲃⲥⲙⲓ-
ⲛⲓ ⲛⲁⲃ : ⲉⲓⲙⲏϯ ⲟⲩⲃⲁⲥⲑⲁ : ⲉⲥⲕⲱϯ ⲉⲣⲟϥ ·
ϩⲓ ϣⲟϥ ϩⲓ ⲙⲟⲥϯ : ϩⲓ ⲑⲁⲗⲟ ⲉⲃⲟⲗ : ϩⲓ ⲕⲟϯ ⲉⲡⲁϩⲟⲩ : ϩⲓ ϫⲟⲣⲓ ⲉⲃⲟⲗ ⲛⲓⲙ : ϯⲣ ⲉⲣⲟⲧⲛ̅ : ⲙⲡⲟⲩ
5 ⲛⲓⲁⲛⲅⲉⲗⲟⲥ : ⲛϫⲟⲣⲓ : ⲛ̅ⲛⲉⲧⲁϩⲉⲣⲟⲧⲟⲩ ⲉⲣⲟⲕ ·
ⲛⲟⲩⲟⲉⲓϣ ⲛⲓⲙ : ⲉⲧⲉ ⲛⲁⲓ ⲛⲉ ⲛⲉⲩⲣⲁⲛ : ⲓ̅ⲟ̅ϩ̅ⲁ̅ⲩ̅ : ·
ⲗ̅ⲱ̅ϩ̅ⲉ̅ⲡ̅ ⲁ̅ⲭ̅ⲁ̅ⲃ̅ⲁ̅ ⲟⲩⲁⲥⲏⲗ ⲁⲕⲁⲗⲁⲧⲁ ⲕⲁⲥⲓⲥ : ·
ⲕⲉⲣⲓⲁ ⲁⲭⲁⲣⲁϩ : · ⲥⲁⲗⲁⲛⲓ ⲡⲁⲡⲗⲓⲛ : ⲧⲟⲧⲛ
ⲛⲉⲧⲛⲁϣⲱⲡⲓ : ⲙ̅ⲛ̅ : ⲛ̅ⲛ̅ : ⲧⲉⲧⲛ̅:ⲃⲓ ⲧⲉⲭⲁⲣⲓⲥ
10 [ⲉ]ⲡⲉⲃϩⲁ : ⲧⲉⲕϯ ⲛⲁⲃ ⲉⲧⲉⲭⲁⲣⲓⲥ ⲉⲡⲉⲃⲙⲁⲛϩⲉ-
ⲙⲁⲁⲥ : · ϩⲓ ϣⲟϥ ϩⲓ ⲙⲁⲥϯ · ϩⲓ ⲑⲁ ⲉⲃⲟⲗ ϩⲓ ⲕⲟⲧ
ⲉⲡⲁϩⲟⲩ : · ⲛⲉⲗⲟⲟⲩ ⲛⲣⲱ̅ⲙ̅ⲓ · ⲉⲛⲓⲃⲓ ⲛ[ⲱ]ⲛⲁϩ : ·
ⲛϩⲏⲧϥ ⲛⲉϣ ϭⲱϣⲧ ⲉⲣⲟϥ : ⲉⲡϩⲁ ⲛⲓⲙ :
ⲁⲓⲁ ⲓⲁ ⲧⲁⲭⲏ ⲧⲁⲭⲏ : ⲁⲃϫⲟⲕ ⲉⲃⲟⲗ :—
15 ⲥϩⲁⲓ ⲡⲓⲍ̅ ⲙⲛ ⲛⲓⲫ̅ⲩ̅ ⲉⲩⲃⲉϯ ⲥⲁⲡⲟⲩ ⲃⲁⲧⲟⲩ ⲛⲉϩ
ⲉⲡϩⲁ ⲡⲉⲕϫⲁϫⲓ : ⲧⲁⲙⲥⲟⲩ ⲉⲡⲣⲁ : ⲥϩⲁⲓ ⲟⲛ :—
ⲧⲁⲃ ⲉϩⲟⲩⲛ ⲉⲩⲧⲟⲩⲧ ⲙⲟⲩⲗⲁ ⲛⲁⲧⲕⲟϩᵀ :
ⲟⲩⲁϩϥ : ⲉⲡⲣⲁ ⲛⲟⲩⲁⲗⲧⲓⲕⲉⲟⲛⲟⲥ ⲕⲉϯ ⲉⲡⲓⲏⲃᵀ
ⲟⲩⲑⲗⲁ ⲉⲃⲟⲗ ⲡⲓ : ⲟⲩϣⲟϥ ⲡⲓ : ⲟⲩⲡⲟⲣϫ ⲡⲓ : ⲕ̅ⲁ̅ⲧⲁ
20 ϯϩⲉ : ⲧⲁⲁϥ ⲉϩⲟⲩⲛ ⲉⲥⲛⲏⲩ ⲛⲧⲟⲩⲟⲧ ⲙⲟⲩⲗⲁ
ⲡⲁⲛⲉ ⲡⲉⲩⲥⲁⲓ ⲉⲛⲉⲣⲉⲩ : ⲗⲉⲙⲗⲟⲙⲟⲩ · ⲉⲩ-
ⲧⲁⲓⲥ ⲓⲕⲟⲟⲥ : · ⲭⲁᵉ ⲡⲉⲩϩⲁ : ϣⲣⲟ : ⲡⲛⲉϩ ⲉⲧ-
ⲃⲉϯ : ⲉⲡϩⲁ : ⲟ̅ⲩ̅ : ⲅ ⲉⲑⲟⲟⲩ ⲁⲃϫⲱⲕ ⲉⲃⲟⲗ :—
―――― >> ――――
ϫⲟⲁⲥⲁⲗ ⲥⲁⲁⲃⲉⲗ ⲥ̅ⲟ̅ⲩ̅ⲭ̅
25 . ⲁⲁϩ

26

1 *i.e.* ᔆⲛ̅ⲛⲉ=ϥ- (twice) | *i.e.* ἀπόκρισις ? : ⲁⲩⲱ ⲕ̅ⲣ̅ⲥ̅ *i.e.* ᔆⲉⲟⲩⲱ ... "his ... pledges" ("seine .... -Pfänder") B/G, M || **2** *i.e.* ᔆⲛⲁ=ϥ | *i.e.* εἰμήτι | *i.e.* ᔆⲃⲁⲥⲧ-ϩⲟ cf. note to *PCM* I 22 l. 45 || **3** *i.e.* ᔆⲑⲗⲟ | *i.e.* ᔆⲕⲱⲧⲉ : ⲕⲟⲧ B/G || **4** *i.e.* ᔆϫⲱⲡⲣⲉ | *l.* ⲧⲱⲣⲕ ⲉⲣⲱⲧⲛ̅ | *i.e.* ᔆⲙ̅-ⲡⲟⲟⲩ || **5** *i.e.* ἄγγελος | *i.e.* ᔆϫⲱⲡⲣⲉ | *i.e.* ᔆⲛ-ⲉⲧ-ⲁϩⲉⲣⲁⲧ=ⲟⲩ (dittography?) B/G, M | ⲉⲣⲟϥ B/G || **8** *i.e.* ᔆⲛ̅ⲧⲱⲧⲛ̅ || **9** *i.e.* (δεῖνα) (δεῖνα) | *i.e.* ᔆⲛ=ⲧⲉⲧⲛ̅-ϥⲓ | *i.e.* χάρις || **10** *i.e.* ᔆⲡⲉ=ϥ-ϩⲁ | *l.* ⲧⲉⲧⲛ̅-ⲕⲧⲟ ? B/G, M | *i.e.* ᔆⲛⲁ=ϥ | *i.e.* χάρις || **10–11** *i.e.* ᔆⲙⲁ ⲛ̅-ϩⲙⲟⲟⲥ : "dwelling place" ("(Wohn)sitzes") B/G, M || **11** *i.e.* ᔆⲑⲗⲟ | ⲉⲃ[ⲟⲗ =] B/G || **12** *i.e.* ᔆⲛ̅ⲛⲉ-ⲗⲁⲁⲩ | *i.e.* ᔆⲉⲣⲉ-ⲡⲛⲓϥⲉ ? P : *i.e.* ᔆⲛ-ⲛⲓⲙ B/G | ⲛ[ⲉⲧⲟ]ⲩⲁϩ B/G || **13** *i.e.* ᔆⲙ̅-ⲡ-ϩⲁ || **14** *i.e.* ταχύ (twice) | *i.e.* ᔆⲁ=ϥ-ϫⲱⲕ || **15** *i.e.* ζ(ῴδιον) | *i.e.* φυ(λακτήριον) | *i.e.* ᔆⲃⲛⲧⲉ | ⲃⲁⲧ ⲟⲩⲛⲉϩ B/G || **16** *i.e.* ᔆⲙ̅-ⲡⲉ=ⲕ-ϫⲁϫⲉ || **17** *i.e.* ᔆⲧⲁⲁ=ϥ | *i.e.* ᔆⲙ̅-ⲙⲟⲩⲗϩ ⲛ̅-ⲁⲧ-ⲕⲱϩⲧ̅ : ⲙⲟⲩⲗϩ ⲛⲁⲧⲡⲟⲣ/ⲧ/ *i.e.* ᔆⲁⲧ-ⲡⲁⲣⲧ B/G, M || **18** *i.e.* ἀντικείμενος ? : ⲛⲉⲓⲁⲗⲧ̅ⲛⲕⲉⲟⲛⲟ̅ⲥ̅ⲕ̅ † (no translation) B/G, M : ⲛⲉⲧⲁⲗⲟⲛⲕⲉⲟⲛⲟⲥⲕ *l.* ⲛⲉⲧϯ ⲁⲛⲁⲅⲕⲁⲓⲟⲛ ⲛⲁ=ⲕ "the ones who give you the necessity" ? D | ⲉⲡⲓⲏⲃ = B/G || **19** *i.e.* ᔆⲑⲗⲟ | *i.e.* ᔆⲡⲉ (three times) | *i.e.* κατά || **20** ϯϩⲁ *i.e.* ᔆϩⲉ B/G | *i.e.* ᔆⲉ-ⲥⲛⲁⲩ | *i.e.* ᔆⲧⲟⲩⲱⲧ | *i.e.* ᔆⲙⲟⲩⲗϩ || **21** *i.e.* ᔆⲡⲉ=ⲩ-ⲥⲁⲉⲓⲉ "their beauty" ("ihre Schönheit") B/G | *i.e.* ᔆⲉ-ⲛⲉ=ⲩ-ⲉⲣⲏⲩ | *i.e.* ᔆϭⲗⲙⲗⲱⲙ=ⲟⲩ || **22** *i.e.* ᔆⲧⲟⲃⲓⲥ | *i.e.* ᔆⲛ̅-ⲕⲱⲥ || **23** *i.e.* ᔆⲃⲛⲧⲉ : "(which) destroys" (welches zerstört) B/G | *i.e.* θυ(σία) | ⲅ : B/G, M do not translate | *i.e.* ᔆⲁ=ϥ-ϫⲱⲕ || **25** omitted by B/G

"He will not buy?, he will not make his payments? that he has contracted for himself, except for a hatefulness which surrounds him, and devastation and hatred and scattering and reversal and every annihilation. I adjure you today, |⁵ O mighty *angels, by those who stand before you (s.) at all times, whose names are these: Iohau, Lōhep, Akhaba, Ouasēl, Akalata, Kasis, Keria, Akharah, Salani, Paplin; you (pl.) are the ones who will be with NN, child of NN; you will take the favour |¹⁰ [from] his face and you (s.) will give to him the favour of his backside, and devastation and hatred and scattering and reversal! No person in whom is the breath of life will be able to look at the face ⟨of⟩ NN yea, yea, quickly, quickly!"

It is finished.

|¹⁵ Draw the image and the phylacteries on a metal plate. Dip them. Wipe them off. ⟨Put the⟩ oil on the face ⟨of⟩ your enemy. Bury them at the door. Write again. Put it into a figurine of unsmoked wax. Set it at the door of an opponent?. You apply the nail. It is a scattering. It is a destruction.

It is a separation, according to |²⁰ this manner. Put it in two wax figurines. Turn their backs to each other. Wrap them in cloth from a burial shroud. Smear their face ⟨with⟩? menstrual blood ⟨and⟩ the oil from the metal plate on the face.

Offering: *three evil ⟨things⟩. It is finished.

|around image Xoasal Saabel Soukh |²⁵ .aah Soukh

---

1. ⲛⲉϥⲁⲡⲱⲕⲣⲥ : **"he will not make his payments?"** For the sense "make a payment" see Förster WBGW p. 81 *s.v.* ἀπόκρισις sense 2. The exact meaning of this statement remains obscure.

9–10. ⲧⲉⲧⲛ̅:ⲃⲓ ⲧⲉⲭⲁⲣⲓⲥ [ⲉ]ⲡⲉϥϩⲁ : **"you will take the favour [from] his face"** For the concept of favour being given to or taken from the face, see the note to *PCM* I 22 l. 32.

15–23. Ritual Instructions: Options are provided here for two rituals. For a curse of destruction, the tableau is copied onto a metal plate and washed off with oil. The oil is then applied to an effigy made from wax representing the ritual's target, into which a second copy of the tableau (written on folded paper?) has been placed. The effigy is then is pierced with a nail before being left at the target's door. The second ritual is for a separation curse, in which two wax effigies representing the targets are placed back to back before being anointed with the oil used to wash off the metal plate and menstrual blood, then wrapped in a burial shroud. For the long history of the manipulation of such figurines going back to pre-Christian Egypt, Mesopotamia, and Greece, see Dosoo 2023a. A separation curse very close to the second ritual here which involves placing effigies back to back can be found in the eleventh-century *Ġāyat al-ḥakim* (Latin *Picatrix*; Ritter 1933: 261.5–263.4; German translation in Ritter/Plessner 1962: 269–271), along with the opposite manipulation, placing figurines face to face. For discussions, see Dosoo 2018: 23–51; Dosoo 2023a: 171–177.

17. ⲙⲟⲩⲗⲁ ⲛⲁⲧⲕⲱϩⲧ : **"unfired wax"** Here ⲁⲧⲕⲱϩⲧ seems to be the equivalent of ἀκάπνιστον, used to describe the wax used to make effigies in *GEMF* 84/*PGM* CXXIV (KYP M840; V–VI CE) l. 12, and the Historical and Ethnographic Society of Athens Codex 115 (XVIII CE; Delatte 1927: 77.8). It would seem to refer to a high quality of wax collected without smoking the bees out of their hive; *cf.* Strabo, *Geography* 9.1.23 on unsmoked honey, and BL Ms. Or. 6794 l. 56 (Kropp 1931: I no. E; KYP M306) for an instance of "unsmoked honey" (ⲉϥⲉⲓⲱ... ⲛⲁⲧⲕⲱϩⲧ) in Coptic.

22. ϣⲣⲟ : **"menstrual blood"** For a discussion, see the note to *PCM* I 22 l. 46.

Image: See the discussion of the image on the back.

back

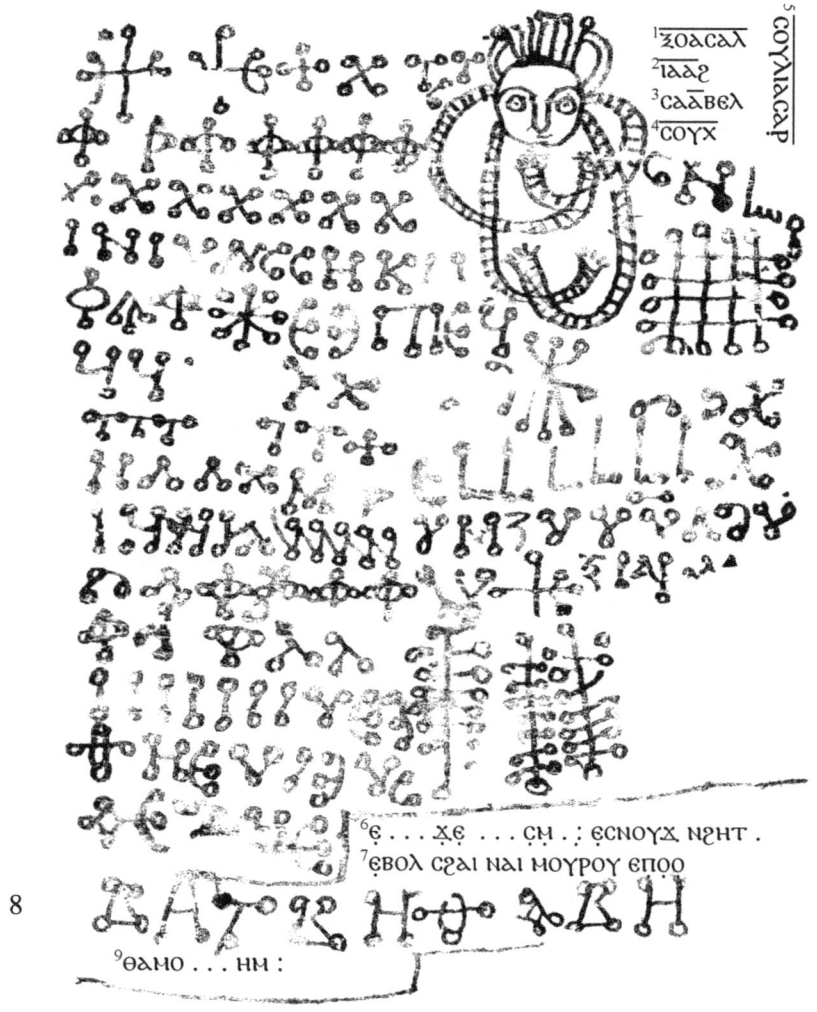

¹ⲝⲟⲁⲥⲁⲗ
²ⲓⲁⲁⲣ̄
³ⲥⲁⲁ̄ⲃⲉⲗ
⁴ⲥⲟⲩⲭ
⁵ⲥⲟⲩⲗⲓⲁⲥⲁⲣ̣

⁶ⲉ . . . ⲭⲉ . . . ⲥ̣ⲙ .᷄ ⲉⲥⲛⲟⲩⲭ ⲛϩⲏⲧ .
⁷ⲉⲃⲟⲗ ⲥϩⲁⲓ ⲛⲁⲓ ⲙⲟⲩⲣⲟⲩ ⲉⲡⲟⲟ

8

⁹ⲑⲁⲙⲟ . . . ⲏⲙ :

---

5 ⲥⲟⲩⲗⲓⲁⲥⲁⲣ̣- B/G ‖ **6** ⲥ̣ .... ⲭⲛ .. ⲉⲥⲛⲟⲩⲭ ⲛϩⲏⲧ . B/G ‖ **7** ⲉⲃⲟⲗ ⲥϩⲁⲓ ⲛⲁⲓ ⲙⲟⲩⲣⲟⲩ ⲉ ... B/G ‖ **9** ⲑⲁⲙⲟ ... ϥⲏⲙ B/G

|^back^ Xoasal, Iaah, Saabel, Soukh, |⁵ Souliasar

|⁶ … it being put … write these things, bind them to the …

(*kharaktēres:* BHT BHΘ ABH)

|⁹ …

KD, EL & MP edited from photograph and autopsy; tracings by KD and JS.

Image: The image here, like that on the front, seems to represent an *angel, perhaps one of the "mighty angels" mentioned in front l. 5. The angel is depicted with the iconography of the *cherubim and *seraphim, a crowned head surrounded by six wings. Here only two wings, resembling long hands, are clearly visible, while the sixth pair may have merged with the crown; see the discussion in Dosoo 2022a: 144–147. Compare Mößner/Nauerth 2015: 328, who refer to the figure as a "snake-woman" ("Schlangenfrau"). Compare the similar image of an angel on *PCM* I 32 p. 2. It is unclear whether this is a fuller version of the same tableau which could not be fully copied onto the front, or if this is a similar but different tableau to be used with the ritual instructions in ll. 6–9, which are too fragmentary to clearly understand.

PCM I 28. Love spell of Cyprian

Arsinoites (Faiyum)　　　　　　14.3 (H) × 9 (W) cm　　　　　　X–XI CE

Other references: P.Heid.Inv. Kopt. 684 (formerly P.Heid. Inv. Nr. 1684); TM 98064; *P.Bad.* V 122; KYP M148; Bélanger Sarrazin #167.

Editions: Bilabel/Grohmann 1934: no. 122 (*ed. pr.*); Polotsky 1935: no. 122.

Translations: Bilabel/Grohmann 1934: no. 122 (German); Jackson in Meyer/Smith 1994: no. 73.

Additional commentary: Seider 1964: 162–163; Camplani 2010: 145–146; Untermann (ed.) 2011: 48–49; Mößner/Nauerth 2015: 311, 336–338; Dosoo 2018: 34–37; Johnston/Gardner 2018; Gardner/Johnston 2019: 31–32; Preininger forthcoming c: chapter 5.

Present location: Heidelberg, Institut für Papyrologie.

Image: Plates IV–XI.

Linguistic description: Sahidic with Middle Egyptian influence.

Contents:

1. Front p. 1–13 (ll. 1–275): Love spell attributed to Cyprian of Antioch (KYP T15)

Single-quire paper codex of 16 pages, consisting of 1 quaternion (4 bifolios), once bound with a thread. The codex is inscribed only on the first 13 pages, the last 3 pages being left blank. The manuscript belongs to the archive known as the 'Heidelberg Coptic Magical Library', being part of the 1930 purchase. Like the other manuscripts from this collection, it was probably produced in the Faiyum and is written in a form of Sahidic heavily influenced by the dialect of that region.[1]

In addition to the centrefolds in the bifolios that we would expect in a codex, the manuscript shows signs of having been further folded, once vertically and once horizontally to form a small package.[2] All of the pages except 12 & 13 show considerable marginal decoration, consisting of a vertical line made up of short horizontal lines in the left margin, broken at intervals by elaborate (but purely decorative) diplai (>) and dotted obeloi (÷), generally four to a page. A decorative double horizontal line also appears at the end of the prayer, separating it from the ritual procedure. The ink on page 13 is darker due to discolouration of the page as a whole, perhaps as the result of staining from either mud or oil following deposition or in the course of use.[3]

The hand is very regular, the script a bilinear and unimodular majuscule, with a

---

[1] For a discussion of the archive, including the process of acquisition and dialect, see the introduction to the archive on p. 259–263. We note that the translation of this piece significantly benefited from the help of Ivan Miroshnikov, Michael Zellmann-Rohrer, Alexandros Tsakos, and So Miyagawa, with whom we read this text in an online reading group in 2021.

[2] For other codices demonstrating folding, see *PCM* I 4 & 34

[3] Bilabel/Grohmann 1934: 304; Johnston/Gardner 2018: 144–145.

slight slope to the right. Interlinear space is well respected, although the margins are very narrow. Supralinear strokes are used above abbreviations and *voces magicae*, as well as to indicate the schwa or autosyllabic letters, but in this last case we find them as very short lines above or between one or more letters. The use of paper suggests a tenth century date at the earliest, and this impression is confirmed by the letterforms; despite the difference in letter height size (*cf.* pp. 362–363), we propose that the copyist of this text is the same as that of *PCM* I 27, and so a fuller discussion of the hand may be found in the introduction to that manuscript.

Cyprian of Antioch, the putative author of this text, is a legendary magician turned bishop and then martyr.[4] His legend developed in the decades prior to 379 CE, when a sermon by Gregory of Nazianzus conflated him with the historical Cyprian of Carthage (*ca.* 210–258 CE).[5] His hagiographical dossier consists of three primary works, the *Conversion*, the *Confession*, and the *Martyrdom of Cyprian*;[6] a synthesis of the three sources of his legend in a single hexameter poem was composed by the Empress Aelia Eudocia (*ca.* 401–460 CE).[7] Versions of his legend survive in most of the languages of Mediaeval Christianity,[8] including Coptic versions of the *Confession* (CC 95) and *Martydrom* (CC 619).[9] His story, most fully told in the first-person *Confession*, describes his initiation into all of the mystery cults of the pagan world (Delphi, Eleusis, Memphis, Chaldaea, and so on), in the process becoming a master magician and a disciple of the Devil. Coming to Antioch, he sets himself up as a philosopher-magician, performing various services for clients and teaching students of his own. Among his clients is a wealthy young man named Aglaïdas, who hires him to use a love spell on a Christian virgin named Justina, but the demons sent by Cyprian, first for Aglaïdas, and then on his own behalf, are thwarted by her simple faith and her use of the sign of the cross. Cyprian finally confronts the Devil with the failure of his magic, and discovering that Jesus is more powerful than he, converts to Christianity, eventually becoming a bishop before being martyred in the Great Persecution of Diocletian (303–313 CE), on the 21st Thouth (18th September) according to the Coptic Synaxarium.[10]

---

[4] On the hagiographical dossier of Cyprian, and related material, see Bilabel/Grohmann 1934: 32–41; Bailey 2009: 2–31; Bailey 2017a: 3–106.

[5] *Oration* 24.8–12; *cf.* Bailey 2009: 18–19; Bailey 2017a: 11–17.

[6] Critical editions of all three parts of the dossier may be found in Bailey 2017a: 110–262; an earlier edition of the *Confession* may be found in Bailey 2009: 34–105.

[7] Ludwich 1897: 16–79; *PG* 85: 831–864; Bevegni 1982; translation in Kastner 1981; *cf.* Bailey 2009: 21–22; Bailey 2017a: 110–261.

[8] See the discussion in Bilabel/Grohmann 1934: 33–38.

[9] von Lemm 1899; Crum 1905: 151–152 no. 220; Bilabel/Grohmann 1934: 43–230.

[10] Basset 1904: 285–287; in the Catholic Church the martyrdom of Cyprian and Justina was commemorated on the 26th September until 1969, when they were expunged from the *Calendarium Romanum* (1969: 140) as fictional personnages.

Cyprian's pre-conversion reputation as a magician led to him becoming a 'patron saint' of magic in some popular Christian traditions; there is evidence of books of magic attributed to him in Germany by the sixteenth century, when their existence is commented on by Johannes Trithemius (1462–1516) and Cornelius Agrippa (1486–1535),[11] although he is particularly important as the pseudonymous author of many such works in early modern Iberia and Scandinavia.[12] The text here, though, seems to have a slightly different origin.

The first-person narrative of the *Love Spell* follows that of the *Confession*, and, in turn, that of the dependent amuletic text known as the *Prayer of Cyprian*. Likely originally a Greek composition, copies of this *Prayer* survive in several other languages, including Arabic, Armenian, Ge'ez, and Syriac, as well as several vernacular European languages.[13] The Coptic *Love Spell* would seem to be the oldest surviving part of this tradition, although a possible sixth-century parallel may allow us to push this back several centuries (see the note to p. 2 ll. 4–5 below). Despite differences in wording, these versions manifestly all belong to a common tradition, and begin with Cyprian boasting of his former magical powers before confessing his realisation of the supremacy of Jesus Christ and invoking God to protect the user of his prayer from misfortune, particularly that caused by harmful magic. While this prayer is not (yet) attested in Coptic, the survival of the *Copto-Arabic version makes the existence of a lost Coptic intermediary virtually certain. The *Love Spell* seems best understood as having been inspired by this text, following as it does the same basic structure. In adapting an older, originally amuletic prayer for aggressive purposes, it resembles other texts from the Coptic magical corpus, including *PCM* I 31, two curses based on the model of the *Testament of Solomon*, and an as yet unpublished love spell which seems to draw on the textual tradition of the *Prayer of Mary 'in Bartos'*.[14]

In this edition we provide the continuous line numbering from Bilabel/Grohmann on the right of the column in grey from page 2 onwards.

---

[11] Ohrvik 2018: 114–115.

[12] For Cyprian in the Iberian tradition, see Coelho 1887–1889; Leitão 2015 & 2017; Smid 2019a & 2019b; for the Scandinavian tradition, see Gårdbäck 2017; Ohrvik 2018: 112–120; *cf.* Richter 2014a.

[13] For an overview, see Bilabel/Grohmann 1934: 38–41; for the Arabic tradition, see Bilabel/Grohmann 1934: 250–295; Basset 1982: 6–24; for the Armenian tradition, see Wingate 1930: 183–187; Feydit 1986: 326–331; for the Ge'ez tradition, see Grohmann 1917–1918; Strelcyn 1955; Basset 1982: 38–52; for the Greek tradition, see Schermann 1903; Bilabel/Grohmann 1934: 232–249, 296–303; for the Syriac tradition, see Hunter 1987: 100–103; Cherkashina (Nurullina) 2012: 48–53, 122–125. Two early (8th- and 10th-century) Latin prayers attributed to Cyprian survive, but they are quite far removed in content from the other versions, lacking the opening confession and explicit request for protection against magic; see Leclercq 1936: 2330–2334, with further references.

[14] Montserrat, Abadia Inv. 604 + 1235 (KYP M30). For the *Prayer of Mary*, see *PCM* I 25.

page 1

ϯⲥⲁⲟⲩⲛ ϫⲉ ⲁϩⲱⲃ ⲛⲓⲙ ⲟⲩⲉⲓⲛⲉ
ⲛⲁϩⲣⲁⲓ
ⲁⲩϣⲓⲃⲓ ϩⲛ̄ ⲧⲁⲯⲩⲭⲏ ⲁⲩϣⲓⲃⲓ
ϩ̣ⲛ ⲧⲁⲫⲩⲥⲓⲥ ⲁⲩⲥⲓϣⲓ ϭⲓ ⲛⲁⲥⲡⲗⲁ-
5   ⲭⲁⲛⲱⲛ ⲁⲓϣⲓⲃⲓ ϩⲙ̄ ⲡⲁⲁⲅⲁⲛ
ⲁⲓⲛⲉϩϣⲗⲏⲃ · ϩⲛ ⲧⲁⲥⲁⲣⲏϩ
ⲁⲩⲅⲓⲙ ⲉⲛϭⲓ ⲡⲃⲱ ⲛⲧⲁⲁⲡⲏ ⸗ ⲁⲓ-
ⲙⲟⲩϩ ⲉⲛⲕⲱϩⲧ ⲁⲓⲉⲛⲕⲁⲧⲕ
ⲉⲙⲡⲓϩⲓⲛⲏⲃ ⲁⲓⲧⲱⲟⲩⲛ ⲙ̄ⲡⲓϫⲓ
10 ⲉⲙⲧⲁⲛ ⲁⲓⲟⲩⲱⲙ ⲁⲩⲱ ⲁⲓⲥⲱ
ϩⲛ̄ ⲟⲩⲗⲏⲡⲓ ⲙⲉⲛ · ⲟⲩⲁϣⲁϩⲁⲙ ⸗
ⲡⲓϩⲏⲛ ⲟⲩⲉⲙⲧⲁⲛ ϩⲛ ⲧⲁⲯⲩⲭ̣ⲏ
ⲟⲩⲧⲉ ⲡⲁⲡⲛ̄ⲁ̄ ⲉⲧⲃⲉ ⲡⲉϩⲟⲩⲁ
ⲧⲁⲉⲡⲓⲑⲉⲙⲓⲁ ⲁⲧⲁⲥⲱⲫⲓⲁ ⲉⲣ
15 ⲕⲁⲕⲉ ⲁⲧⲁϭⲁⲙ ⲱϫⲏⲛ ⲁⲓⲟⲩⲱ-
ⲥⲃ ϩⲉⲛ ⲧⲁⲧⲉⲭⲛⲓ ⲁⲛⲁⲕ ⲡⲉ ⲕⲉⲡⲣⲓⲁⲛⲟⲥ ⲡⲛⲁϭ ⲉⲙⲙⲁⲕⲟⲥ ⲡⲉⲛ-
ⲧⲁⲃⲉⲣ ϣⲃⲏⲣ ⲉⲡⲉⲧⲣⲁⲕⲱⲛ ⲉⲡⲛⲟⲩ͞
ⲁⲃⲙⲟⲩϯ ⲉⲣⲁⲓ ϫⲉ ⲡⲁϣⲏⲣⲉ ⲁⲓⲙⲟ-
20 ϯ ⲉⲣⲁⲃ ϫⲉ ⲡⲓⲱⲧ ⲁⲃϯ ⲡⲉⲃⲕⲗⲁⲙ
ⲙⲉ ⲧⲉⲃϭⲣⲏⲡⲓ ϩⲓϫⲉⲛ ⲧⲁⲁⲡⲏ

---

1 *i.e.* ^{S}ϩⲱⲃ ∥ **3** *i.e.* ψυχή ∥ **4** *i.e.* φύσις | *i.e.* ^{S}ⲥⲓϣⲉ | *i.e.* ^{S}ⲛϭⲓ | *i.e.* σπλάγχνον ∥ **5** *i.e.* ^{S}ϣⲓⲃⲉ ∥ **6** *i.e.* ^{S}ⲛⲉϩ-ϣⲗϩ̄ϥ̄ | *i.e.* σάρξ ∥ **7** *i.e.* ^{S}ⲁ⸗ϥ-ⲕⲓⲙ ⲛ̄ϭⲓ ? : ⲁⲩⲅⲓ ⲙⲉⲛ ϭⲓ *i.e.* κυμαίνει "waved" or "trembled" ("gewogt, gezittert") Bilabel/Grohmann ∥ **11** *i.e.* λύπη ∥ **12** *i.e.* ^{S}ⲙ̄ⲡ⸗ⲓ-ϭⲛ̄ : ⲙ̄ⲡⲓϭⲓ ⲛ- *i.e.* ^{S}ⲙ̄ⲡ⸗ⲓ-ϫⲓ ⲛ- Bilabel/Grohmann | *i.e.* ψυχή ∥ **13** *i.e.* π(νεῦ)μα | ⲡⲉϩⲟⲩⲁ[ⲛ] Bilabel/Grohmann ∥ **14** *i.e.* ^{S}ⲛ̄-ⲧ⸗ⲁ-ἐπιθυμία | *i.e.* σοφία ∥ **15** *i.e.* ^{S}ⲱϫⲛ̄ ∥ **15–16** *i.e.* ^{S}ⲁ⸗ⲓ-ⲟⲩⲱⲥϥ̄ : "I laboured" ("ich bemühte mich") Bilabel/Grohmann ∥ **16** *i.e.* τέχνη ∥ **17** *i.e.* μάγος ∥ **18** *i.e.* δράκων | *l.* ⲉⲡⲛⲟⲩ(ⲛ) *i.e.* ^{S}ⲙ̄-ⲡ-ⲛⲟⲩⲛ : ⲉⲡⲛⲟ\ⲩ͞/[ⲛ] Bilabel/Grohmann

I know that everything has left me. Everything has been changed in my soul. Everything has been changed in my nature. My innards have become like gall. |⁵ My appearance has changed. I have been terrified in my flesh. The hair of my head has moved?. I have burned with fire. I have lain down but I have not slept. I have arisen but I have not |¹⁰ rested. I have eaten and I have drunk in grief and sighing. I have not found rest in my soul or my spirit because of the greatness of my desire. My wisdom has |¹⁵ darkened. My power has perished. I have been undone in my craft.

I am Cyprian the great magician, the one who was companion to the Serpent of the *Abyss. He called me "my son" and I called |²⁰ him "father". He put his crown and his diadem upon my head;

---

1. ⳁⲥⲁⲟⲩⲛ : "**I know**" A small fold in the paper conceals the upper part of the ⳁ in photographs, but autopsy confirms its presence.

1–2. ⲁϩⲱⲱⲃ ⲛⲓⲙ ⲟⲩⲉⲓⲛⲉ ⲛⲁϩⲣⲁⲓ : "**I know that everything has left me**" The exact meaning of this phrase is difficult to determine; Bilabel/Grohmann and Jackson translate the phrase literally as "everything has passed me by" ("jedes Ding vor mir vorübergegangen ist"). The meaning seems to be either that all of Cyprian's powers have left him or that he has been hitherto entirely unaware of the true state of things. For the first interpretation, compare the Greek ἀπέρχομαι (for the equivalence, see Crum CD 483b), and the negative ⲁⲧⲟⲩⲉⲓⲛⲉ ("(that) which does pass away"), and cf. p. 2 l. 9; for the second compare the Greek παρέρχομαι LSJ sense V (cf. Crum CD 438b).

18. ⲉⲡⲉⲧⲣⲁⲕⲱⲛ ⲉⲡⲛⲟⲩ̄ : "**the Serpent of the Abyss**" For consistency we translate δράκων as "serpent", but this word is often translated in English as "dragon". The Serpent here is the Devil; cf. the description of him being cast out of heaven in Revelation 12.7–9.

page 2

```
       αιτcαι νερωϯ ϩⲛ̄ τⲉⲃ[ⲉ]ⲕⲓⲃⲓ
       ⲛⲟⲩⲛⲁⲙ ⲁⲃⲑⲉⲙⲥⲁⲓ ⲥⲁ ⲓⲟⲩⲛⲁ[ⲙ]
       ⲉⲙⲁⲃ ⲁⲃⲧⲣⲉⲧⲉⲃϭⲁⲙ ⲧⲏⲣⲥ
       ϩⲉⲡⲱⲧⲁϩⲥⲓ ⲛⲁⲓ ⲁⲓⲁⲗⲏ ϩⲓⲭⲉⲛ ⲕ-            25
 5     ⲙϩⲟⲩⲧ ⲁⲥⲥⲱⲕ ϩⲁⲣⲁⲓ ⲛ̄ⲑⲉ ⲛⲟⲩ-
       ⲭⲁⲓ ⲁⲓⲉⲓⲙⲓ ⲉⲡⲕⲁⲥⲕⲏⲥ ⲉⲛⲛⲉⲥⲓ[ⲟ]ᵘ
       ⲁⲓⲁⲙⲁϩⲧⲓ ⲛⲁϩϣⲱⲣ ⲉⲛⲛⲉⲧⲏⲩ
       ⲁⲓⲉⲓⲙⲓ ⲉⲧⲁⲥⲧⲣⲁⲛⲱⲙⲓⲁ ⲧⲏⲣⲥ
       ⲁⲛⲁⲓ ⲧⲏⲣⲟⲩ ⲟⲩⲉⲓⲛⲓ ⲧⲁⲁⲧ ⲉⲧⲃⲉ          30
10     ⲟⲩⲡⲁⲣⲑⲉⲛⲟⲥ ϫⲉ ⲓⲟⲩⲥϯⲛⲁ ⲁⲥ-
       ⲉⲣ ⲧⲁϭⲁⲙ ⲙⲉ ϭⲁⲙ ⲉⲡⲥⲁⲧⲁⲛ[ⲁ]ⲥ
       ⲉⲛⲑⲉ ⲛⲟⲩⲭⲁⲭ ϩⲛ̄ ϭⲓϫ ⲛⲟⲩᵘϣⲏⲣⲉ
       ϣⲏⲙ ⲁⲓⲉⲓⲙⲓ ϩⲙ̄ ⲡϣⲓⲕⲉ ⲙⲡⲁϩⲏⲧ
       ⲙⲉⲛ ⲛⲉⲙⲁⲕⲙⲏⲕ ⲛ̄ⲧⲁⲯⲩⲭⲏ             35
15     ⲙⲉ ⲡϣⲓ ⲙⲡⲁⲛⲟⲩⲥ ϫⲉ ⲙⲉⲛ ⲗⲁⲁⲩ
       ⲛⲉϣ ⲉⲣⲡⲣⲱⲫⲉϯ ⲛ̄ⲡⲁϩⲏⲧ ϩⲛ̄ ϯ-
       ⲁⲡⲱⲕⲣⲉⲥⲓⲥ ⲧⲁⲓ ⲟⲩⲧⲉ ⲁⲛⲅⲉⲗⲟⲥ
       ⲟⲩⲧⲉ ⲁⲣˣⲁⲛⲅⲉⲗⲟⲥ ⲟⲩⲧⲉ ⲭⲉⲣⲱⲃⲓ̄
       ⲟⲩⲧⲉ ⲥⲉⲣⲁⲫⲓⲛ ⲟⲩⲧⲉ ϭⲁⲙ ⲟⲩ-            40
20     ⲧⲉ ⲧⲉⲛⲁⲙⲓⲥ ⲟⲩⲧⲉ ⲁⲥⲱⲙⲁⲧⲟⲥ
       ⲟⲩⲧⲉ ⲉϩⲟⲩⲥⲓⲁ ⲛⲁⲉϣ
       ⲟⲩⲧⲉ ⲉϫⲱⲕ ⲉⲃⲟⲗ ⲙ̄ⲡⲁⲟⲩ-
       ϩⲥⲁϩⲛⲉ ⲉⲓⲙⲉϯ ⲡⲓⲱⲧ ⲉⲛⲛⲉⲟⲛ
```

---

1 *l.* ⲁⲃⲧⲥⲁⲓ Polotsky ‖ **2–3** *i.e.* ˢⲁ=ϥ-ⲑⲙⲥⲟ=ⲓ ⲛⲥⲁ ⲟⲩⲛⲁⲙ ⲙ̄ⲙⲟ=ϥ : ⲁⲃϯ ⲉⲙⲥⲁⲓ ⲥⲁⲓ ⲟⲩⲛⲁ[ⲙ] Bilabel/Grohmann ‖ **3** *i.e.* ˢⲧⲏⲣ=ⲥ̄ ‖ **4** *i.e.* ὑποτάσσειν ‖ **4–5** *i.e.* ˢⲧ-ϭⲓⲛⲙⲟⲩⲧ : ⲧ[ϭ]ⲙϩⲟⲩⲧ Bilabel/Grohmann ‖ **5** *i.e.* ˢϩⲁⲣⲟ=ⲓ ‖ **6** *i.e.* ˢⲕⲁⲥⲕ̄ⲥ̄ ‖ **8** *i.e.* ἀστρονομία | *i.e.* ˢⲧⲏⲣ=ⲥ̄ ‖ **10** *i.e.* παρθένος ‖ **11** *l.* ⲧ-ϭⲁⲙ | *i.e.* ˢⲙ̄-ⲡ-ⲥⲁⲧⲁⲛⲁ̂ⲥ ‖ **12** *l.* ⲧ-ϭⲓϫ ‖ **14** *i.e.* ˢⲙⲟⲕⲙⲉⲕ | *i.e.* ψυχή ‖ **15** *i.e.* ϣⲓ "circumference" (CDO) or ϣⲓ(ⲛⲓ) "enquiry" ? : "judgement" ("Ermessen") Bilabel/Grohmann | *i.e.* νοῦς ‖ **16** *i.e.* προφητεύειν ‖ **17** *i.e.* ἀπόκρισις | *i.e.* ἄγγελος ‖ **18** *i.e.* ἀρχάγγελος | *l.* χερουβί(μ) ‖ **19** *i.e.* σεραφίμ ‖ **20** *i.e.* δύναμις ‖ **21** *i.e.* ἐξουσία | *l.* ⲛⲁⲉϣ ⟨ⲉⲣ ⲡⲣⲱⲫⲉϯ⟩ ‖ **23** *i.e.* εἰ μήτι | *i.e.* ˢⲛ̄-ⲛ̄-αἰών

I caused me to drink milk from his right breast, and he sat me at his right hand. He made all of his power subject to me. I mounted on ⟨the⟩ |⁵ Pleiades, and it sailed under me like a ship. I knew the whisper of the stars. I possessed the treasuries of the winds. I knew all astronomy.

All these things left me because of |¹⁰ a maiden named Justina. She made my power and ⟨the⟩ power of Satan like a sparrow in ⟨the⟩ hand of a small child. I knew in the depths of my heart and the thoughts of my spirit |¹⁵ and the bounds of my mind that none would be able to prophesy to my heart in this affair, neither *angel nor *archangel nor *cherubim nor *seraphim nor force nor |²⁰ *power nor bodiless one nor *authority would be able to ⟨prophesy⟩, nor to fulfil my command, except the Father of the Aeons

---

1. ⲁⲓⲧⲥⲁⲓ: **"I caused me to drink"** Polotsky notes that we would expect "he caused me to drink" (ⲁϥⲧⲥⲁⲓ) here, with "he" referring to the Devil; "I" here may be the result of a copying error.

4–5. ⲉⲓϫⲉⲛ ⲕⲙ̄ⲣⲟⲩⲧ : **"on ⟨the⟩ Pleiades"** As noted by Crum (CD 821a) a close parallel to this passage may be found in the *Martyrdom of Phoibammon* §§225–226 (CC 297), in which it is said of a magician named Alexandros: "Many times he had stopped the sun in middle of the sky, and conversed with the moon like two men speaking with one other. Many times he had mounted the Pleiades. He had examined the whole region of the air, and the demons were subject to him, obeying him like servants. These were the things that he had done by his magic" (ⲟⲩⲙⲏⲏϣⲉ ⲅⲁⲣ ⲛⲥⲟⲡ ⲁϥⲥⲱϥⲧ ⲙ̄ⲡⲣⲉ ϩⲛ̄ ⲧⲙⲏⲧⲉ ⲛⲧⲡⲉ · ⲁϥϣⲁϫⲉ ⲙ̄ⲡⲟⲟϩ ⲛ̄ⲑⲉ ⲛ̄ⲣⲱⲙⲉ ⲥⲛⲁⲩ ⲉⲩϣⲁϫⲉ ⲙ̄ⲛ̄ⲉⲩⲉⲣⲏⲩ · ⲟⲩⲙⲏⲏϣⲉ ⲛⲥⲟⲡ ⲁϥⲁⲗⲉ ⲉⲧϭⲓⲛⲙⲟⲩⲧ ⲁϥⲙⲟⲩϣⲧ ⲙ̄ⲡⲕⲱⲧⲉ ⲧⲏⲣϥ̄ ⲙ̄ⲡⲁⲏⲣ · ⲁⲩⲱ ⲛⲉⲣⲉⲛⲇⲁⲓⲙⲱⲛ ϩⲩⲡⲟⲧⲁⲥⲍⲉ ⲛⲁϥ ⲉⲩⲥⲱⲧⲙ̄ ⲛ̄ⲥⲱϥ ⲛ̄ⲑⲉ ⲛ̄ⲛⲉⲓϩⲙ̄ϩⲁⲗ · ⲛⲁⲓ ⲛⲉ ⲛⲁϥⲁⲁⲩ ϩⲛ̄ ⲧⲉϥⲙⲛ̄ⲧⲙⲁⲅⲟⲥ; Müller/Uljas 2019: 68 (Coptic text), 108 (translation); note that Müller/Uljas mistakenly translate ϭⲓⲛⲙⲟⲩⲧ as "death"). The earliest version of this text would seem to be Chester Beatty Library 2029, dated by the PAThs Project to the sixth century (CLM 1163). This passage seems in turn to be dependent on the Greek amuletic *Prayer of Cyprian* (see introduction): "I would bind the moon and the stars and they would not move", "And I did all of this magic, and all the evil spirits served (me)" (τὴν σελήνην τὴς ἀστέρας ἔδενα καὶ οὐκ ἐκινοῦντο; πάσας τε καὶ μαγίας εἰργασάμην, καὶ πάντα τὰ πονηρὰ πνεύματα ἐδούλευον; Schermann 1903: 312, with Ms. V; for the addition of the sun *cf.* Joshua 10.12–13). These parallels imply an older tradition concerning Cyprian upon which the *Love Spell*, the *Martyrdom*, and the *Prayer* are all dependent, perhaps an earlier version of the *Prayer*.

7. ⲛⲁϩⲱⲱⲣ ⲉⲛⲛⲉⲧⲏⲩ : **"the treasuries of the wind"** Bilabel/Grohmann translate "took (*i.e.* carried off) the treasures with the wind" ("die Schätze mit den Winden ergriffen (d.h. entführt)").

12–13. ⲉⲛⲑⲉ ⲛⲟⲩϫⲁϫ ϩⲛ̄ ϭⲓϫ ⲛⲟⲩϣⲏⲣⲉ ϣⲏⲙ : **"like a sparrow in ⟨the⟩ hand of a small child"** For other examples of metaphors which use small animals to express powerlessness, see *PCM* I 26 p. 5 l. 22, p. 7 l. 1. Close parallels to this passage may be found in Athanasius, *Life of Anthony* 24.5: "And indeed he (the Devil) was bound by the Lord like a sparrow for our sport" (καὶ δέδεται μὲν παρὰ τοῦ Κυρίου ὡς στρουθίον εἰς τὸ καταπαίζεσθαι παρ' ἡμῶν; Bartelink 1994: 202); Pseudo-Eustathius of Tracia, *On Michael* (CC 148): "he (the Devil) was gripped fast in the hand of the holy Archangel Michael, like a bird in the hand of a little child, and when the archangel had made him suffer greatly he set him free in great disgrace" (ⲉϥⲥⲟⲛϩ ⲛ̄ⲧⲟⲧϥ̄ ⲙ̄ⲡⲓⲁⲣⲭⲏⲁⲅⲅⲉⲗⲟⲥ ⲉⲑⲟⲩⲁⲃ ⲙⲓⲭⲁⲏⲗ ⲙ̄ⲫⲣⲏϯ ⲛ̄ⲟⲩϭⲁϫ ϧⲉⲛ ⲧϫⲓϫ ⲛ̄ⲟⲩⲕⲟⲩϫⲓ ⲛ̄ⲁⲗⲟⲩ ⲟⲩⲟϩ ⲉⲧⲁϥⲁⲓϥ ⲛ̄ⲟⲩⲭⲱⲃ ⲉⲙⲁϣⲱ ⲁϥⲭⲁϥ ⲉⲃⲟⲗ ϧⲉⲛ ⲟⲩⲛⲓϣϯ ⲛ̄ϣⲓⲡⲓ; Budge 1894: 99 (trans.), 124, l. 11–15); *cf.* Dosoo 2022c: 531.

page 3

ⲙⲉ ⲡⲉⲃⲙⲱⲛⲱⲕⲉⲛⲏⲥ ⲉⲛϣⲏⲣⲉ
ⲓ̅ⲥ̅ ⲡⲉⲭ̅ⲥ̅ ⲙⲉ ⲡⲉⲡ̅ⲛ̅ⲁ ⲛⲁⲅⲓⲁ̣ ⲡ- 45
ⲉⲧⲟⲩⲁⲁⲃ ⲁⲓⲑⲉⲣϣⲁ ⲛ̅ⲡⲁ̣ϭⲱⲛ̣ⲧ
ⲁⲓⲕⲱ ⲧⲁⲱⲣⲕⲏ ⲁⲓϭⲙϭⲛ̣ ⲛ̅ⲧⲁ-
5 ⲙⲁⲛⲓⲁ ϩ̅ⲛ̅ ⲟⲩⲛⲁϭ ⲙ̣ⲙⲉⲧⲭⲁⲥⲓ-
ϩⲏⲧ ⲁⲓⲱϩⲓⲣⲁⲧ ϩⲓⲭⲉⲛ ⲛⲁⲡⲁⲧ 50
ⲁⲓⲡⲱⲱⲛⲓ ⲙⲡⲁϩⲁ ⲉⲡⲉⲙⲏⲛⲧ
ⲁⲓⲃⲓ ⲧⲁⲓⲟⲩⲛⲁⲙ ⲉϩⲣⲁⲓ ⲉⲡⲡⲏ ⲁⲓ-
ⲕⲉⲑⲁⲗⲓⲥⲓ ⲙ̅ⲡⲕⲁϩ ϩⲉⲛ ⲧⲁⲟⲩⲉⲣⲏ-
10 ⲧⲉ ⲁⲓⲥⲉⲕ ϩⲣⲁⲩ ⲉⲃⲁⲗ ϩ̅ⲛ̅ ϣⲁ ϣ-
ⲛⲧ ⲁⲓⲧⲁⲩⲁ ⲛⲛⲓⲁⲡⲱⲗⲱⲅⲓⲁ 55
ϩⲣⲁⲓ ⲉⲧⲓ:ⲍ: ⲡⲏ ϣⲁ ⲧⲉⲥⲕⲉⲛⲏ
ⲙⲡⲓⲱⲧ ⲉϩⲟⲩⲛ ⲉⲥⲁϣⲃ ⲉⲛⲕⲁ-
ⲧⲁⲡⲉϯⲥⲙⲁ ⲁⲓⲱϣ ⲉⲃⲁⲗ ⲙ̅-
15 ⲡⲓⲱⲧ ⲉⲛⲛⲉϣⲛ ⲡ̅ⲟ̅ⲥ̅ ⲉⲁⲣⲭⲏ
ⲛⲓⲙ̣ ⲙⲉ ⲉⲝⲟⲩⲥⲓⲁ ⲛⲓⲙ ⲙⲉ ⲑⲣⲱ- 60
ⲛⲟⲥ ⲛⲓ *vac* ⲙ ⲉⲓⲭⲱ ⲛⲛⲓⲁⲡⲱⲗⲟ̣-
ⲅⲓⲁ ⲭ⁶ ⲉⲣⲓⲥⲓ ⲧⲱⲛⲁⲓ
ⲭⲁⲣⲓⲙ ⲃⲁⲗⲓⲙ ⲃⲁⲥⲓⲗⲉⲟⲥ
20 ⲁⲩⲧⲟⲩⲗ ⲱⲃⲓⲁ ⲕⲁⲕⲓⲕⲉⲫⲁⲗⲓ̣
ⲁⲙⲟⲩ ⲁⲙⲟⲩ ϭⲱⲡⲓ ⲡⲉⲡ̅ⲛ̅ⲁ
ⲉⲛⲧⲁϭⲁⲗⲱϣⲃ ⲉⲣⲁⲓ ⳽ 65

---

1 *i.e.* μονογενής || **2** *l.* ι(ησου)c πε-χ(ριστό)c | *i.e.* πν(εῦμ)α | *i.e.* ἅγια : ⲁⲅⲓⲱⲛ Bilabel/Grohmann || **4** *i.e.* ὀργή | *i.e.* ˢϭⲙ̅ϭⲟⲙ || **5** *i.e.* μανία || **8** *i.e.* ˢⲟⲩⲛⲁⲙ || **9** *i.e.* καθαρίζειν || **11** *i.e.* ἀπολογία || **12** *i.e.* σκηνή | ⲉⲧⲓ:ⲋ: Bilabel/Grohmann || **13** *i.e.* ˢⲛ̅-ⲥⲁϣϥ || **13–14** *i.e.* καταπέτασμα || **15** *i.e.* ˢⲛ̅-ⲛ̅-ⲁⲓών | *i.e.* ˢⲛ̅-ἀρχή || **16** *i.e.* ἐξουσία || **16–17** *i.e.* θρόνος || **17** ⲛⲓⲙ ⲙ written after *vac.* due to tail of ⲍ of previous line | *i.e.* ἀπολογία || **18** ⲧⲱⲛⲁⲓ from Adonai ? || **19** from βασιλεύς ? || **20** from ὅ βία κακὴ κεφαλή ? Polotsky, see note || **21** *i.e.* πν(εῦμ)α || **22** ⲁ[ⲓⲁ] ⲁⲓⲁ Bilabel/Grohmann, Jackson

and his only-begotten Son, Jesus Christ, and the Holy Spirit, the hallowed one. I suppressed my wrath, I set aside my anger, and I mastered my |⁵ madness with great audacity. I stood on my feet, I turned my face to the west, I raised my right hand to the sky, I purified the earth from my feet, |¹⁰ I snorted through my nose, and I sent these requests up to the seventh heaven, to the *tabernacle of the Father within ⟨the⟩ seven *veils. I called upon |¹⁵ the Father of Aeons, the Lord of all *principalities and all *authorities and all *thrones, saying these requests: "Erisi Tōnai Kharim Balim Basileos |²⁰ Autoul Ōbia Kakikephali Amou Amou, seize the spirit which you have entrusted to me,

---

10. ⲁⲓⲥⲉⲕ ϩⲣⲁⲩ ⲉⲃⲁⲗ ϩⲛ̄ ϣⲁⲁⲛⲧ : "**I snorted through my nose**" For a discussion of the practice of "snorting through one's nose" in Greek and Coptic, see Drescher 1969: 91–93. In Coptic literary texts it is most often associated with the Devil, as a rude and insolent action; cf. van der Vliet 1995: 411.

20. ⲱⲃⲓⲁ ⲕⲁⲕⲓⲕⲉⲫⲁⲗⲓ : "**Ōbia Kakikephali**" As Polotsky notes, these *voces* seem to be the Greek words ὦ βία! κακὴ κεφαλή! ("O violence! Idiot!"). These oaths may be found in numerous Greek and Coptic literary texts; see, for example, in the *Apophthegmata Patrum* (Alphabetic Collection) Daniel 3, in which an exorcised demon exclaims, "O violence! The command of Jesus casts me out!" (Ὦ βία! ἡ ἐντολὴ τοῦ Ἰησοῦ ἐκβάλλει με); Pseudo-Eustathius of Tracia, *On Michael* (CC 148) in which the Devil cries out "O violence, what would I do to you, Euphemia, if I could reach you!" (ⲱ ⲃⲓⲁ ⲟⲩ ⲡⲉ ϯⲛⲁⲁⲁⲓϥ ⲛⲉ ⲉⲩⲫⲏⲙⲓⲁ ⲁⲁⲓ ⲉϩⲟⲩⲛ ϣⲁⲣⲟ; Budge 1894: 111.14–15); Herodotus, *Histories* 3.29, in which Cambyses stabs the Apis bull, taunting the priests: "O idiots, are these gods, creatures of blood and flesh who feel iron?" (Ὦ κακαὶ κεφαλαί, τοιοῦτοι θεοὶ γίνονται, ἔναιμοί τε καὶ σαρκώδεες καὶ ἐπαΐοντες σιδηρίων;); *Martyrdom of Lacaron* (CC 284), in which a governor says to soldiers who have defied him: "O idiots! I speak well with you, and you speak badly with me!" (ⲕⲁⲅⲉ ⲕⲉⲫⲁⲗⲏ †ⲥⲁⲝⲓ ⲛⲉⲙⲱⲧⲉⲛ ⲛⲕⲁⲗⲱⲥ ⲧⲉⲧⲉⲛⲥⲁⲝⲓ ⲛⲉⲙⲏⲓ ⲛ̄ⲕⲁⲕⲱⲥ; Balestri/Hyvernat 1908: 18.12–13).

21. ⲁⲙⲟⲩ ⲁⲙⲟⲩ : "**Amou Amou**" Alternatively, we might translate this not as *voces magicae* but as comprehensible Coptic—"come, come".

21–22. ϭⲱⲡⲉ ⲡⲉⲡⲛⲁ ⲉⲛⲧⲁⲕϭⲁⲗⲱⲱⲃ ⲉⲣⲁⲓ ⸗ : "**seize the spirit which you have entrusted to me**" For this construction, compare the *Martyrdom of George* Sa 2 (Borg.Copt. 109, cass. XXVIII, fasc. 152, fol. 5v col. II ll. 23–27): "I will come to you on the clouds so as to receive the deposit [I] have entrusted to [your] body—namely, [your] soul" (ⲧⲁⲭⲓ ⲛ̄ⲧⲡⲁⲣⲁⲑⲏⲕⲏ [ⲛ̄ⲧⲁⲓ̈]ϭⲁⲗⲱ{ⲟⲩ}⸗ⲥ⸗ ⲉⲡⲉ[ⲕ]ⲥⲱⲙⲁ ⲉⲧⲉ [ⲧⲉⲕ]ⲯⲩⲭⲏ ⲧⲉ; Miroshnikov/Marjanen/Iacono (forthcoming)). Ivan Miroshnikov is thanked for this reference. The sense seems to be that unless God sends Gabriel, Cyprian will no longer want to live, in which case his spirit should be taken from him. Jackson understands this as a request to God to seize Justina's spirit.

page 4

ⲛϯⲉⲣ ⲭⲣⲓⲁ ⲉⲙⲙⲁⲃ ⲁⲛ ⲱⲛ
ⲡⲉⲕⲭⲁⲁⲩ ⲛⲁⲓ ⲙⲡⲁⲁⲩ ⲛ̄ⲡ-
ⲛⲁϭ ⲛ̄ⲗⲓⲧⲟⲩⲣⲕⲟⲥ ⲛ̄ⲱⲁϩ
ⲛⲥⲁϯ ⲅⲁⲃⲣⲓⲏⲗ ⲡⲁ ϯ- 70
5 ⲛⲁϭ ⲉⲛϭⲁⲙ ⲉⲛⲕⲱϩⲧ ⲉⲃ-
ⲙⲟⲩϩ ⲉⲡⲉⲃϩⲁ ⲉⲛⲕⲱϩⲧ ϩⲙ̄ ⲡⲓ-
ⲕⲱϩⲧ ⲉⲧⲟⲩⲱⲙ ⲉⲡⲕⲱϩⲧ ⲛ̄ⲙ
ⲉⲧⲉ ⲡⲁⲓ ⲧⲉⲕⲱϩⲧ ⲉⲧⲉⲕⲙⲉⲧ-
ⲛⲟⲩⲧⲉ ⲕⲓⲣⲓⲟⲥ ⲑⲉⲟⲥ ⲁⲩⲱ ⲉⲃ- 75
10 ⲙⲟⲩϩ ⲉⲧⲉⲃⲫⲓⲁⲗⲗⲉ ⲛⲟⲩⲱϣ
ϩⲓ ⲉⲡⲓⲑⲉⲙⲓⲁ ⲁⲩⲱ ⲉⲃⲙⲟⲩϩ
ⲉⲛⲉⲃⲧⲉⲛⲁϩ ⲉⲛⲕⲱϩⲧ ϩⲙ̄ ⲡⲓ-
ⲉⲣⲁ ⲛⲕⲱϩⲧ ⲉⲧⲙⲟⲩϩ ϩⲛ̄
ϭⲁⲙ ⲉⲧⲉⲕⲙⲉⲧⲙⲉⲧⲛⲟⲩⲧⲉ 80
15 ⲡⲁⲓ ⲉⲧⲉⲣⲉⲯⲩⲭⲏ ⲛⲓⲙ ⲛⲁⲭⲱ-
ⲕⲏⲙ ⲉⲛϩⲏⲧⲃ ⲙⲡⲁⲧⲟⲩⲱϣ-
ⲧ ⲉⲡⲉⲕⲙⲧⲱ ⲉⲃⲁⲗ ⸗ ⲉⲃⲓ
ϩⲛ̄ ⲑⲱⲣⲙⲏ ⲛ̄ⲧⲉⲃϭⲁⲙ ϩⲓⲧⲉ
ⲡⲉⲕⲟⲩⲉϩⲥⲁϩⲛⲉ ⲱ ⲡⲓⲱⲧ ⲉⲛ- 85
20 ⲛⲉϭⲱⲛ ⲉⲃⲱⲕ ϣⲁ ⲁ̄ⲁ̄ ⲧⲩ ⲁ̄ⲁ̄
ⲉⲃⲁⲡⲱⲫⲁⲛⲓ ϩⲓⲭⲱⲥ ϩⲛ̄ ⲟⲩ-
ⲛⲁϭ ⲛⲁⲡⲱⲫⲁⲛⲓⲁ

---

1 *i.e.* χρεία | *i.e.* ⁵ⲟⲛ : {ⲉ}ⲟⲛ Bilabel/Grohmann ‖ **2** *i.e.* ⁵ⲙ̄ⲡⲉ⸗ⲕ-ⲭⲟⲟⲩ ‖ ⲡⲛⲧⲭⲁⲁⲩ *l.* ⲡⲛⲧⲁⲕⲭⲁⲁⲩ "the one who (you?) send to me today" ("der (du?) mir heute… schick(s)t") Bilabel/Grohmann : "he who sent out" Jackson ‖ **3** *i.e.* λειτουργός ‖ **7** *l.* ⁵ⲛ̄-ⲕⲱϩⲧ ⲛ(ⲓ)ⲙ ‖ **8** *l.* ⲡⲉ ⲡⲕⲱϩⲧ ? Till *ap.* Bilabel/Grohmann : (ⲉ)ⲧⲧⲉ-ⲕⲱϩⲧ *i.e.* (ⲉ)ⲧϯ-ⲕⲱϩⲧ Bilabel/Grohmann | ⲉⲧⲉⲕ- *i.e.* ⁵ⲛ̄ⲧⲉⲕ- ‖ **9** *i.e.* κύριος θεός ‖ **10** *i.e.* φιάλη ‖ **11** *i.e.* ἐπιθυμία ‖ **14** *i.e.* ⲧ-ϭⲁⲙ | *i.e.* ⁵ⲛ̄-ⲧⲉⲕ-ⲙⲛ̄ⲧ-ⲛⲟⲩⲧⲉ ‖ **15** *i.e.* ψυχή ‖ **16–17** *i.e.* ⁵ⲙ̄ⲡⲁⲧ⸗ⲟⲩ-ⲟⲩⲱϣⲧ (haplography) ‖ **17** *i.e.* ⁵ⲉ-ⲡⲉⲕ-ⲙ̄ⲧⲟ | *i.e.* ⁵ⲛ⸗ϥ-ⲉⲓ ‖ **18** *l.* ⲧ-ϩⲣ̄ⲙⲏ | *l.* ϩⲓⲧⲉ(ⲛ) ‖ **20** *i.e.* αἰών | *i.e.* δ(ε)ῖ(να) δ(ε)ῖ(να) (twice) | *i.e.* (υἱός) ‖ **21** *i.e.* ἀποφαίνειν ‖ **22** *i.e.* ἀποφάνεια

I do not need it anymore, until you send me today the great servant of flaming fire, *Gabriel—he of |⁵ great fiery power, who fills his face with fire from the fire that consumes every fire, which is the fire of your divinity, Lord God, and who |¹⁰ fills his bowl with desire and lust and fills his wings with fire from that river of fire that burns with ⟨the⟩ power of your divinity, |¹⁵ that which every soul will wash within before they worship in your presence—so that he comes on the impulse of his power at your command, O Father of |²⁰ Aeons, to go to NN, the daughter of NN, appearing to her in a great appearance,

---

7–8. ⲉⲡⲕⲱϩⲧ ⲛⲓⲙ ⲉⲧⲉ ⲡⲁⲓ ⲧⲉ ⲕⲱϩⲧ : "every fire, which is the fire" In standard Coptic grammar, the first ⲕⲱϩⲧ should not have the definite article ⲡ-, since it is already defined by ⲛⲓⲙ, while the second should; the ⲧⲉ may represent a miscopied ⲡ(ⲉ)-.

10. For the motif of an angel with a bowl, compare Revelation 16 in which seven angels pour out "the bowls of God's wrath" (ⲛⲉⲫⲓⲁⲗⲏ ⲙ̄ⲡϭⲱⲛⲧ ⲙ̄ⲡⲛⲟⲩⲧⲉ, 16.1) upon the earth, and the note to *PCM* I 3 front col. 2 ll. 30–32; *cf.* Dosoo 2021d: 432–433.

12–13. ⲡⲓⲉⲣⲁ ⲛⲕⲱϩⲧ : "that river of fire" For the concept of the river of fire in Coptic Christian eschatology, see Zandee 1960: 307–310; specifically, this is the river of fire which flows before the throne of judgement, which must be crossed by the dead, and which burns the sinful but spares the just; *cf.* the notes to *PCM* I 12 p. 27 l. 20–p. 29 l. 3.

page 5

	ⲛⲁϯ ⲥⲁ ⲛⲁⲧⲕⲁⲧⲏⲭⲏ ⲛⲁⲧⲁ-	
	ⲙⲉⲗⲓ ⲉⲃⲙⲉϩ ⲡⲉⲥϩⲏⲧ ⲙⲉ ⲧⲉⲥϯ̄-	90
	ⲭⲏ ⲙⲉ ⲡⲉⲥⲡ̄ⲛ̄ⲁ̄ ⲙⲉ ⲡⲉⲥⲛⲟⲩⲥ	
	ⲛⲉⲡⲓⲑⲉⲙⲓⲁ ⲛ̄ⲕⲱϩⲧ ϩⲓ ⲟⲩ-	
5	ⲱϣ ⲉⲧϫⲏⲃ ϩⲓ ϣⲧⲁⲣⲧⲏⲣ	
	ϩⲓ ⲧⲁⲣⲁⲭⲏ ⲉⲃⲙⲁϩⲥ ⲉϭⲏⲛ ⲛⲉ-	
	ⲓⲏⲃ ⲉⲣⲁⲧⲥ ϣⲁ ⲡⲃⲱ ⲛⲧⲉⲥⲁⲡⲏ	95
	ⲛⲉⲡⲓⲑⲉⲙⲓⲁ ϩⲓ ⲟⲩⲱϣ ϩⲓ ⲡⲱⲣⲛⲓⲁ	
	ⲉⲃⲥⲱⲣⲏⲙ ⲉϭⲓ ⲡⲉⲥⲛⲟⲩⲥ ⲉⲃⲉⲣ ⲕⲁ-	
10	ⲕⲓ ϭⲓ ⲡⲉⲥⲟⲩⲁⲉⲓⲛ ⲉⲣⲉⲛⲉⲥⲙⲁⲁ-	
	ϫⲓ ⲧⲱⲙ ⲉⲛⲛⲉⲥⲟⲩⲱⲙ ⲟⲩⲧⲉ ⲛ̄-	
	ⲛⲉⲥⲥⲱ ⲛⲛⲉⲥⲉⲛⲕⲁⲧ ⲟⲩⲧⲉ ⲛ̄-	100
	ⲛⲉⲥϩⲓⲛⲏⲃ ⲉⲣⲉⲛⲉⲥϩⲁⲓⲧⲓ ⲉⲣ	
	ⲕⲱϩⲧ ⲉⲡⲉⲥⲥⲱⲙⲁ ⲉⲣⲉⲧⲡⲏ †	
15	ⲕⲱϩⲧ ⲛⲁⲥ ⲉⲣⲉⲡⲕⲁϩ ⲥⲁϩϯ ϩⲁ-	
	ⲣⲁⲥ ⲛ̄ⲛⲉⲡⲓⲱⲧ ⲛⲁ ⲛⲁⲥ ⲉⲛⲛⲉ-	
	ⲡϣⲏⲣⲓ ϣⲉⲛⲉϩⲧⲏⲃ ϩⲁⲣⲁⲥ ⲉⲛⲛⲉ-	105
	ⲡⲉⲡ̄ⲛ̄ⲁ̄ ⲉⲧⲟⲩⲁⲁⲃ ϯ ϩⲓⲛⲏⲃ	
	ⲉⲛⲉⲥⲃⲁⲗ ⲉⲣⲉⲡⲙⲉⲉⲩⲉ ⲉⲙⲡ̄ⲛ̄ⲟ̄-	
20	ⲧⲉ ⲙⲉ ⲧⲉⲃϩⲁⲧⲓ ⲡⲱⲧ ⲥⲁⲃⲁⲗ	
	ⲉⲙⲙⲁⲥ ⲧⲉⲛⲉⲥⲙⲉⲉⲩⲉ ⲙⲉ ⲛⲉⲥ-	
	ⲙⲁⲕⲙⲏⲕ ⲙⲉ ⲡⲉⲥⲛⲟⲩⲥ ⲉⲣ ⲙⲉ-	110
	ⲟⲩⲉ ⲛ̄ⲧⲓⲁⲃⲱⲗⲓⲕⲱⲛ	

---

1 *i.e.* ˢⲛ̄-ⲁⲧ-ϯ ⲥⲟ | *i.e.* κατέχειν || **1–2** *i.e.* ἀμελεῖν || **2** *i.e.* ˢⲛ≠ϥ̄-ⲙⲉϩ || **2–3** *i.e.* ψυχή || **3** *l.* πν(εῦμ)α | *i.e.* νοῦς || **4** *i.e.* ἐπιθυμία || **5** *l.* ⲭⲱⲃ or ⲭⲟϥϥ/ⲭⲟϥϥ Bilabel/Grohmann | *i.e.* ˢϣⲧⲟⲣⲧⲣ || **6** *i.e.* ταραχή | *i.e.* ˢⲉ-ϫⲓⲛ || **7** *i.e.* ˢⲛ̄-ⲣⲁⲧ≠ⲥ̄ || **8** *i.e.* ἐπιθυμία | *i.e.* πορνεία || **9** *i.e.* ˢⲥⲱⲣⲙ̄ | *i.e.* ˢⲛ̄ϭⲓ | *i.e.* νοῦς || **14** *i.e.* σῶμα || **18** *l.* πν(εῦμ)α || **20** *i.e.* ˢϩⲟⲧⲉ || **22** *i.e.* ˢⲙⲟⲕⲙⲉⲕ | *i.e.* νοῦς || **23** *i.e.* διαβολικόν

without delay, without waiting, without negligence, and he fills her heart and her soul and her spirit and her mind with burning lust and |⁵ scorching desire and disturbance and tumult, filling her from the nails of her feet to the hair of her head with lust and longing and fornication, as her mind goes astray, as |¹⁰ her light darkens, as her ears shut! She shall not eat nor drink nor lie down nor sleep, her clothes will burn her body, the sky will |¹⁵ burn her, the earth will kindle under her! The Father will not have mercy on her, the Son will not have pity on her, the Holy Spirit will not give sleep to her eyes! The thought of God |²⁰ and fear of Him will leave her, and her thoughts and her counsel and her mind will have devilish thoughts,

---

9–10. ⲉⲃⲉⲣ ⲕⲁⲕⲓ ⲛ̄ϭⲓ ⲡⲉⲥⲟⲩⲁⲉⲓⲛ : **"as her light darkens"** "Her light" here probably refers to the "light of her eyes", so that as it darkens she becomes blind, in analogy with her ears shutting; *cf.* Crum CD 101b, 480b.

11–16. Symptoms of Love: This description draws upon two recurrent motifs, LOVE IS ABSTINENCE and LOVE IS FIRE; for the first, see the notes to *PCM* I 17 back l. 44–front l. 36; for the second, see the note to *PCM* I 3 front col. 2 ll. 33–38.

page 6

	ⲉⲥϣⲱⲡⲓ ⲉⲥⲓⲱϯ ⲉⲃⲁⲗ ϩⲛ ⲟⲩⲉⲡⲓ-	
	ⲑⲉⲙⲓⲁ ⲙⲉⲛ ⲟⲩⲱϣ ⲙⲉⲛ ⲟⲩϣ-	
	ⲧⲁⲣⲧⲏⲣ ⲉⲧⲃⲉ ⲇ̅ⲇ̅ ⲡⲭ̅ ⲇ̅ⲇ̅ ⲛ̄ⲑⲉ	
	ⲛⲟⲩⲓⲱ ⲉⲥϩⲁ ⲡⲓϣ ⲟⲩⲙⲟⲩⲧⲥⲉ	115
5	ϩⲁ ⲡϫⲉⲩ ⲟⲩⲟⲩϩⲁⲁⲣⲓ ϩⲁ ⲡⲟⲩ-	
	ϩⲁⲣ ⲉⲥϩⲙ̄ϩⲙ̄ ⲉⲛⲑⲉ ⲛⲟⲩⲉϩⲧⲁⲁⲣⲓ	
	ⲉⲥⲃⲏⲕⲃⲏⲕ ⲛ̄ⲑⲉ ⲛⲟⲩϭⲁⲙⲉⲩⲗⲓ	
	ⲉⲥⲗⲓⲃⲓ ⲛ̄ⲑⲉ ⲛⲟⲩⲗⲁⲃⲁⲓ ⲙⲉⲛ ⲟⲩ-	
	ⲉⲙⲥⲁϩ · ⲉⲥⲓϣⲓ ⲉⲃⲁⲗ ϩⲁ ⲧⲉⲡⲓⲑⲉ-	120
10	ⲙⲓⲁ ⲙⲉ ⲡⲟⲩⲱϣ ⲉⲛ ⲇ̅ⲇ̅ ⲡⲭ̅ ⲇ̅ⲇ̅	
	ⲛ̄ⲑⲉ ⲛⲟⲩⲧⲉⲗⲧⲓⲗⲓ ⲙⲁⲩ ⲉⲥⲁϣⲓ	
	ⲉⲡⲃⲓⲧ ⲛⲟⲩⲕⲉⲧⲟⲩⲥ ⲉⲣⲉⲟⲩⲁ	
	ϭⲱϣⲧ ⲉⲛⲥⲱⲥ ⲉⲃⲛⲉⲥⲧⲉⲩⲉ	
	ϩⲙ ⲡⲕⲁⲩⲥⲱⲛ ⲉⲡϣⲱⲙ ⲁⲓⲁ	125
15	ⲧⲓⲱⲣⲕ ⲉⲣⲁⲕ ⲱ ⲅⲁⲃⲣⲓⲏⲗ̅ ⲝ	
	ⲃⲱⲕ ϣⲁ ⲇ̅ⲇ̅ ⲧⲭ̅ ⲇ̅ⲇ̅ ⲁϣⲧⲥ ⲉⲛⲥⲁ	
	ⲡⲃⲱ ⲛ̄ⲧⲉⲥⲁⲡⲏ ⲙ̄ⲛⲉⲃⲟⲩⲓ-	
	ϩⲓ ⲛⲉⲥⲃⲁⲗ ⲁⲛⲓⲧⲥ ⲉⲣⲁⲧⲃ ⲉ-	
	ⲇ̅ⲇ̅ ⲡⲭ̅ ⲇ̅ⲇ̅ ϩⲛ ⲟⲩⲱϣ ⲙⲉⲛ ⲟⲩ-	130
20	ⲉⲡⲓⲑⲉⲙⲓⲁ ⲉⲥⲙⲏⲛ ⲉⲃⲟⲗ ϣⲁ ⲉ-	
	ⲛⲉϩ ⲛ̄ⲑⲏ ⲛ̄ⲧⲁⲕϫⲓ ⲙⲡϣⲉ-	
	ⲛⲟⲩⲃⲉ ⲙ̄ⲡⲓⲱⲧ ϣⲁ ⲙⲁⲣⲓⲁ	
	ⲡⲁⲣⲑⲉⲛⲱⲥ ⲉⲧⲟⲩⲁⲁⲃ	

---

1 *i.e.* ˢⲛⲥ̄ⲥ-ϣⲱⲡⲉ ‖ **1–2** *i.e.* ἐπιθυμία ‖ **2–3** *i.e.* ˢϣⲧⲟⲣⲧⲣ̄ ‖ **3** *l.* δ(ε)ῖ(να) δ(ε)ῖ(να) (twice) | *l.* (υἱός) ‖ **4** ⲟⲩⲙⲟⲩⲧ ⲉⲥ- Bilabel/Grohmann ‖ **6** *i.e.* ˢⲛⲥ̄ⲥ-ϩⲙ̄ϩⲙ̄ ‖ **7** *i.e.* ˢⲛⲥ̄ⲥ-ⲟⲩⲟϭⲟⲩⲉϭ ‖ **8** *i.e.* ˢⲛⲥ̄ⲥ-ⲗⲓⲃⲉ ‖ **9** *i.e.* ˢⲛⲥ̄ⲥ-ⲉⲓϣⲉ *cf.* the qualitative ⲉⲥⲁϣⲓ in l. 11 ‖ **9–10** *i.e.* ἐπιθυμία ‖ **11** *i.e.* ˢⲙ̄ⲙⲟⲟⲩ ‖ **12** *i.e.* κάδος : *i.e.* κῆτος "whale" Bilabel/Grohmann : *i.e.* κύτος "vessel" ("Gefäß") Till *ap.* Bilabel/Grohmann ‖ **13** *i.e.* ˢⲉⲥⲧ̄-ⲛⲏⲥⲧⲉⲩⲉⲓⲛ : *l.* ⲉⲃⲉⲛⲉⲥⲧⲉⲩⲉ Bilabel/Grohmann ‖ **14** *i.e.* καύσων ‖ **16** *l.* δ(ε)ῖ(να) δ(ε)ῖ(να) (twice) | *l.* (υἱός) ‖ **17** *l.* ˢⲙ̄ⲛ ⲛⲉ- ‖ **17–18** *i.e.* ˢⲃⲟⲩϩⲉ ‖ **18** *i.e.* ˢⲛ̄-ⲛⲉⲥ-ⲃⲁⲗ ‖ **19** *l.* δ(ε)ῖ(να) δ(ε)ῖ(να) (twice) | *l.* (υἱός) | *i.e.* ˢⲟⲩ-ⲟⲩⲱϣ (haplography) ‖ **20** *i.e.* ἐπιθυμία ‖ **21–22** *i.e.* ˢϣⲙ-ⲛⲟⲩϥⲉ ‖ **23** *i.e.* παρθένος so that she clings to lust and desire and disturbance because of NN, the son of NN, like a female donkey under the male donkey, a female cat |⁵ under the male cat, a female dog under the male dog, and she whinnies like a mare, and she chews like a she-camel, as she is crazed like a she-bear and a crocodile, and she clings to lust |¹⁰ and desire for NN, the son of NN, as for a drop of water clinging to the edge of a jar when one looks at it while fasting in the burning heat of summer, yea!

|¹⁵ I adjure you, O *Gabriel, go to NN the daughter of NN, hang her from the hair of her head and the lids ⟨of⟩ her eyes, bring her to the feet of NN, the son of NN, in desire and |²⁰ ever-lasting lust, just as you took the good news of the Father to Mary, the Holy Virgin,

---

3–14. For the reference to animals and a drop of water as metaphors for passionate love and desire, see the notes to *PCM* I 7 ll. 32–36. For the word ⲃⲓⲧ, *cf.* the note to *PCM* I 22 l. 46. Bilabel/Grohmann and Meyer/Smith understand the final clause as an independent phrase, translating "when one looks at her, he shall faint for the burning summer heat" ("wenn einer nach ihr blickt, (so) soll er verschmachten (oder: ernüchtert sein) in der Sommerhitze"), that is, the victim is so full of the fire of love that she will cause those who look upon her to faint. The correct translation, given here, is suggested by Stephen Emmel in Meyer/Smith 1994: 366, note to text 73 l. 125.

4–5. ⲟⲩⲙⲟⲩⲧⲥⲉ ϩⲁ ⲡⲭⲉⲩ : "a female cat under a male cat" For these rare words, with the probable meanings "female cat" and "male cat" respectively, see Drescher 1961–1962: 288; *cf.* Macomber 2020: I 120 *s.v.* ⲡⲓϣⲁⲩ. Compare ⲙⲟⲩⲧⲥⲉ as a female personal name in *P.MoscowCopt.* 34 (KYP M733).

page 7

	ϩⲛ̄ ⲟⲩϣⲉⲛⲟⲩⲃⲓ ⲉⲙⲙⲉⲓ ⲙⲁⲣⲉⲡⲓ-	135
	ϣⲉⲛⲟⲩⲃⲉ ⲱⲛ ϣⲱⲡⲓ ⲙ̄ⲙⲉ ⲉⲩ-	
	ϫⲱⲕ ⲉⲃⲁⲗ ⲛ̄ϭⲓ ⲛⲓⲁⲡⲱⲗⲱⲅⲓⲁ	
	ϩⲓⲧⲁⲁⲧⲕ ⲛ̄ⲧⲁⲭⲏ ⲙ̄ⲡⲉⲣϣⲱⲡⲓ	
5	ⲛⲁⲧⲥⲱⲧⲏⲙ ⲛ̄ⲑⲏ ⲙⲡⲉϩⲁⲁⲩ	
	ⲧⲁⲡⲟ̅ⲥ̅ⲧⲁⲅⲁⲕ ⲉⲡⲕⲁϩ ⲛⲉⲧⲏⲙ	140
	ⲁⲕⲕⲧⲁⲕ ϣⲁⲣⲁϥ ⲛⲁⲧⲕⲁϩ	
	ⲉⲣⲉⲛⲉⲕϭⲓϫ [[ⲓ̣ϥ̣]] ϣⲟⲩⲉⲓⲧ ⲁⲗⲗⲁ	
	ϫⲱⲕ ⲛⲁⲓ ⲉⲃⲁⲗ ϩⲱⲧ ⲉⲙⲡⲁ-	
10	ⲁⲩ ⲁⲛⲁⲕ ⲧⲉ ⲁ̅ⲇ̅ ⲡ̅ⲭ̅ ⲁ̅ⲇ̅ ⲙⲡⲓϣⲉ-	
	ⲛⲟⲩⲃⲓ ⲡⲁⲓ ⲙⲉⲛ ⲧⲓⲁⲡⲱⲕⲣⲉ-	145
	ⲥⲓⲥ ϩⲛ̄ ⲟⲩⲥⲱⲧⲏⲙ ⲛⲁⲧⲕⲁ-	
	ⲧⲏⲭⲏ ⲁⲓ ⲁⲓ ⲧ̅ⲁ̅ ⲧ̅ⲁ̅ ⲧⲱ̅ⲣⲕ ⲉⲣⲁⲕ	
	ⲱ ⲅⲁⲃⲣⲓⲏⲗ ⲙ̄ⲡⲟⲩⲭⲁⲓ ⲛ̄ⲧⲉⲧ-	
15	ⲣⲓⲁⲥ ⲛ̄ϩⲱⲙⲁⲩⲥⲓⲱⲛ ⲧⲱ̅ⲣⲕ	
	ⲉⲣⲁⲕ ⲱ ⲅⲁⲃⲣⲓⲏⲗ ⲛ̄ⲧⲉⲥⲅⲓⲛⲏ	150
	ⲙ̄ⲡⲓⲱⲧ ⲙⲉ ⲛⲉⲧϣⲁⲁⲡ ⲉⲛϩⲏⲧⲥ	
	ⲧⲱⲣⲕ ⲉⲣⲁⲕ ⲱ ⲅⲁⲃⲣⲓⲏⲗ ⲙ̄ⲡⲉⲑⲣⲱ-	
	ⲛⲱⲥ ⲛ̄ⲡⲁⲛⲧⲱⲕⲣⲁⲧⲱⲣ ⲙⲉ ⲡ-	
20	ⲉⲧϩⲙⲁⲁⲥ ⲉϩⲣⲁⲓ ⲉϫⲱⲃ ⲧⲱⲣⲕ	
	ⲉⲣⲁⲕ ⲱ ⲅⲁⲃⲣⲓⲏⲗ ⲛ̄ϭⲁⲙ ⲛ̄ⲛⲡⲟ̆-	
	ⲣⲁⲛⲓⲱⲛ ⲙⲉ ⲧϭⲓⲛϩⲱⲥ ϩⲓ ⲥⲙⲟⲩ	155
	ⲉⲛⲛⲉϭⲁⲙ - ⲉⲧⲡⲏ	

1, 2 *i.e.* ˢϣⲙ-ⲛⲟⲩϥⲉ ‖ **2** *i.e.* ˢⲟⲛ ‖ **3** *i.e.* ἀπολογία ‖ **4** *i.e.* ταχύ ‖ **5** *i.e.* ˢⲥⲱⲧⲙ̄ | *l.* ⲡ‹ⲡ›ⲉ‹ⲧ›ϩⲁⲁⲩ Bilabel/Grohmann ‖ **6** *i.e.* ˢⲛ̄ⲧⲁ-ⲡ-ⲭ(ⲟⲉⲓ)ⲥ ‖ **8** ⲓϭ Bilabel/Grohmann | *i.e.* ἀλλά ‖ **10** ⲧⲉ *l.* ⲡⲉ ? : *i.e.* ϫⲉ Bilabel/Grohmann | *l.* δ(ε)ῖ(να) δ(ε)ῖ(να) (twice) | *l.* (υἱός) ‖ **10–11** *i.e.* ˢϣⲙ-ⲛⲟⲩϥⲉ ‖ **11** *l.* ι(ⲏⲥⲟⲩ)ⲥ ‖ **11–12** *i.e.* ἀπόκρισις ‖ **12** *i.e.* ˢⲥⲱⲧⲙ̄ ‖ **12–13** *i.e.* κατέχειν ‖ **13** *l.* ταχύ (twice) ‖ **14–15** *i.e.* τριάς ‖ **15** *i.e.* ὁμοούσιον ‖ **16** *i.e.* σκηνή ‖ **18–19** *i.e.* θρόνος | *i.e.* ˢⲙ̄-‹ⲡ›-ⲡⲁⲛⲧⲱⲕⲣⲁⲧⲱⲣ ‖ **21** *l.* ⲛ̄ϭⲁⲙ : ⲛ̄ⲛϭⲁⲙ Bilabel/Grohmann ‖ **21–22** *i.e.* ˢⲛ̄-ⲛ-ἐπουράνιον ‖ **23** *i.e.* ˢⲛ̄-ⲧ-ⲡⲉ

as true good news, may this good news also be true, as they are completed, namely these requests, through you, quickly! Do not be |⁵ disobedient as you were on the day that the Lord sent you to the land of Eden and you returned to him without earth, with your hands empty, but complete for me, myself, today, |¹⁰ me, NN, the son of NN, this good news, and this commission in unhesitating obedience, yea, yea, quickly, quickly!

I adjure you, O *Gabriel, by the *wellbeing of the |¹⁵ consubstantial Trinity! I adjure you, O Gabriel, by the *tabernacle of the Father and those who dwell within it! I adjure you, O Gabriel, by the throne of the Almighty and he |²⁰ who sits upon it! I adjure you, O Gabriel by ⟨the⟩ heavenly powers and the song and praise of the powers of heaven!

4–8. ⲘⲠⲈⲢϢⲰⲠⲒ ⲚⲀⲦⲤⲰⲦⲎⲘ ⲚⲐⲎ ⲘⲠⲈϨⲀⲀⲨ ⲦⲀⲠⲞⲤ ⲦⲀⲨⲀⲔ ⲈⲠⲔⲀϨ ⲚⲈⲐⲎⲘ ⲀⲔⲔⲦⲀⲔ ϢⲀⲢⲀϤ ⲚⲀⲦⲔⲀϨ ⲈⲢⲈⲚⲈⲔϬⲒⲬ [[ⲓⲟ̣]] ϢⲞⲨⲈⲒⲦ : "Do not be disobedient as you were on the day that the Lord sent you to the land of Eden and you returned to him without earth, with your hands empty" A reference to a version of the story of the origin of mankind in which God sends seven angels to fetch earth from Eden in order to create Adam. As it is being gathered, the earth cries out, predicting mankind's future sins and the punishment that they will receive for them, adjuring the angels in the name of the Lord to be left in the ground. Bound by the adjuration and frightened by the name of the Lord, the seven angels return emptyhanded. Only the eighth angel, Muriel— the future Abbaton, angel of Death—unafraid and unpitying, dares to take the earth from the ground. By implication, one of the seven angels sent would have been Gabriel (the second of the seven archangels), who refused to take earth back to God. For a discussion of the idea and its development see Swanson 1996: 218–219, and for the surviving Coptic account, see Pseudo-Timothy of Alexandria, *Institution of Abbaton* (CC 405; Budge 1914: 232–233: trans. 481–482).

8. ⲓⲟ̣ These letters are faint, and thus perhaps were effaced. Bilabel/Grohmann (1934: 322) suggest that the scribe was unsure whether to write ϬⲒⲬ or ⲬⲒⲞ.

page 8

```
     ϯⲱⲣⲕ ⲉⲣⲁⲕ ⲱ ⲅⲁⲃⲣⲓⲏⲗ ⲙⲡϣⲁϫⲓ
     ⲁⲩⲱ ⲡⲛⲓⲃⲓ ⲙ̄ⲡⲱⲧ ⲡⲁⲓ ⲉⲛⲧⲁ-
     ⲃⲱⲕ ϣⲁ ⲙⲁⲣⲓⲁ ⲡⲁ̅ⲣ̅ⲛⲟⲥ · ⲁⲕϩⲓ                  160
     ϣⲉⲛⲟⲩⲃⲓ ⲉⲙⲙⲁⲃ ⲛⲁⲥ ϣⲁⲛ-
5    ⲧⲉⲃⲟⲩⲱϩ ⲉⲛϩⲏⲧⲥ ⲉⲃⲉⲣ ⲛⲟⲩϯ
     ϩⲓ ⲣⲱⲙⲉ ⲧⲉⲥϫⲡⲁⲃ ⲧⲉⲃⲁⲗⲏ
     ⲉⲡⲉⲥ̅ⲧ̅ⲟⲥ ⲧⲉⲃⲥⲱϯ ⲙⲁⲛ ⸗ ϯⲱⲣⲕ
     ⲉⲣⲁⲕ ⲱ ⲅⲁⲃⲣⲓⲏⲗ ⲛ̄ⲛϩⲓⲥⲓ ⲉⲧⲟ̅ⲁⲁⲃ
     ⲛⲧⲁⲓ̅ⲥ̅ ⲡⲉⲭ̅ⲥ̅ ϣⲁⲡⲟⲩ ϩⲁⲣⲁⲛ ϩⲓ-         165
10   ϫⲉⲙ ⲡϣⲏ ⲙⲡⲉⲥ̅ⲧ̅ⲟⲥ ⲙⲉ ⲡⲅ ⲉⲛⲓ-
     ⲃⲓ ⲛ̄ⲧⲁⲃⲧⲁⲁⲩ ⲉⲛⲉϭⲓϫ ⲉⲡⲉⲃ-
     ⲓⲱⲧ ⲉⲧⲉ ⲛⲁⲓ ⲛⲉ ⲉⲗⲱⲉⲓ ⲉⲗⲱⲉⲓ
     ⲉⲗⲉⲙⲁⲥ ⲁⲃⲁⲕⲧⲁⲛⲏ ϯⲱⲣⲕ
     ⲉⲣⲁⲕ ⲱ ⲅⲁⲃⲣⲓⲏⲗ ⲛ̄ⲅ ⲣⲉⲙⲓⲏ             170
15   ⲧⲁⲡⲓⲱⲧ ⲧⲁⲁⲩ ϩⲓϫⲛ ⲧⲁⲡⲏ
     ⲛⲓ̅ⲥ̅ ⲡⲉϥⲙⲱⲛⲱⲅⲉⲛⲏⲥ ⲛ̄ϣⲏⲣⲉ ϩⲓ-
     ϫⲙ ⲡϣⲏ ⲙⲡⲥ̅ⲧ̅ⲟⲥ ϯⲱⲣⲕ ⲉⲣⲁⲕ ⲉⲛ-
     ⲧⲉⲕⲥⲛⲃⲓ ⲧⲁⲓ ⲉⲛⲧⲁⲕⲡⲱϩ ⲉⲛⲕⲁ-
     ⲧⲁⲡⲉⲧⲥⲙⲁ ⲉⲙⲡⲉⲣⲡⲏ ⲉⲛϩⲏⲧⲥ             175
20   ϯⲱⲣⲕ ⲉⲣⲁⲕ ⲙ̄ⲡϩ̅ ⲉⲛⲭⲉⲣⲉ ⲧⲁⲡⲓ-
     ⲱⲧ ⲧⲁⲁⲩ ⲛⲓ̅ⲥ̅ ⲡⲉⲃϣⲏⲣⲓ ⲉⲛ-
     ϣⲱⲣⲏⲡ ⲉⲧⲕⲏⲣⲓⲁⲕⲏ ϣⲁⲛⲧϥ̄-
     ⲧⲱⲟⲩⲛ ϩⲓ ⲛⲉⲧⲙⲁⲟⲩⲧ ⸗
```

---

1 *i.e.* ˢⲙ-ⲡ-ϣⲁϫⲉ ‖ **2** *l.* ⲡ⟨ⲱ⟩ⲱⲧ ‖ **2–3** *l.* ⲉⲛⲧⲁⲃⲃⲱⲕ ‖ **3** *l.* ⟨ⲧ⟩-παρθ⟨έ⟩νος *cf.* note to *PCM* I 25 p. 2 l. 2 ‖ **4** *i.e.* ˢϣⲙ-ⲛⲟⲩϥⲉ ‖ **7** *l.* στ(αυρ)ός ǀ *i.e.* ˢⲙ̄ⲙⲟⲛ *cf.* ᶠⲉⲙⲙⲁⲛ ‖ **9** *l.* ⲓ(ⲏⲥⲟⲩ)ⲥ ⲡⲉ-χ(ριστό)ς ‖ **10** *l.* στ(αυρ)ός ǀ ⲡⲅ Polotsky : ⲡⲛ√ Bilabel/Grohmann ‖ **10–11** *i.e.* ˢⲛ̄-ⲛⲓϥⲉ : ⲙⲉ ⲡⲅ ⲉⲛⲓⲃⲓ : ⲙⲉⲡⲛⲉⲛⲓⲃⲓ *l.* ⲙⲉ{ⲡ}ⲛⲉⲛⲓⲃⲓ Bilabel/Grohmann ‖ **14** *i.e.* ˢⲙ̄ⲡⲅ ǀ ⲛⲅ Polotsky : ⲛⲛ√ *l.* ⲛⲛ- Bilabel/Grohmann ǀ *i.e.* ˢⲣⲙⲉⲓⲏ ‖ **15** *i.e.* ˢⲛ̄ⲧⲁ-ⲡ-ⲉⲓⲱⲧ ‖ **16** *l.* ⲓ(ⲏⲥⲟⲩ)ⲥ ǀ *i.e.* μονογενής ‖ **17** *l.* στ(αυρ)ός ‖ **18–19** *i.e.* καταπέτασμα ‖ **19** *i.e.* ˢⲣⲡⲉ ‖ **20** *i.e.* χαῖρε ǀ *i.e.* ˢⲛ̄ⲧⲁ- ‖ **21** *l.* ⲓ(ⲏⲥⲟⲩ)ⲥ ‖ **22** *i.e.* ˢϣⲱⲣⲡ ǀ *i.e.* ˢⲛ̄-ⲧ-κυριακή

I adjure you, O *Gabriel, by the word and the breath of the Father, that which went to Mary the Virgin; you brought good news of him to her so that |⁵ he dwelt within her, and he became god and man, and she gave birth to him, and he mounted upon the cross and saved us! I adjure you, O Gabriel, by the holy sufferings which Jesus Christ received for us |¹⁰ upon the wood of the cross and the three breaths that he sent to the hands of his father, which are "*Eloei Eloei *Elemas Abaktanē"! I adjure you, O Gabriel, by the three tears |¹⁵ that the Father shed over the head of Jesus, his only-begotten son upon the wood of the cross! I adjure you by your sword, that with which you rent the *veil of the Temple! |²⁰ I adjure you by the seven greetings that the Father spoke to Jesus, his son, on the Sunday morning so that he rose from the dead

---

10–13. For the last words of Jesus on the cross, *cf.* Matthew 27.46: "In the ninth hour, Jesus cried out in a great voice, saying, 'Elōi, Elōi, lama sabaktanei', that is, 'My God, my God, why have you forsaken me?'" (ϩⲙ ⲡⲛⲁⲩ ⲇⲉ ⲛ̄ϫⲡ︦ⲯⲓⲧⲉ ⲁϥϫⲓϣⲕⲁⲕ ⲉⲃⲟⲗ ⲛ̄ϭⲓ ⲓⲏ̄ⲥ ϩⲛ ⲟⲩⲛⲟϭ ⲛ̄ⲥⲙⲏ ⲉϥϫⲱ ⲙ̄ⲙⲟⲥ ϫⲉ ⲉⲗⲱⲉⲓ ⲉⲗⲱⲉⲓ ⲗⲁⲙⲁ ⲥⲁⲃⲁⲕⲧⲁⲛⲉⲓ ⲉⲧⲉ ⲡⲁⲓ ⲡⲉ ⲡⲁⲛⲟⲩⲧⲉ ⲡⲁⲛⲟⲩⲧⲉ ⲉⲧⲃⲉ ⲟⲩ ⲁⲕⲕⲁⲁⲧ ⲛ̄ⲥⲱⲕ; Horner 1911: I 338); Mark 15.34: "And in the ninth hour Jesus cried out in a great voice, 'Elōi, Elōi, lama sakhthanei' (sic), whose translation is, 'My God, my God, why have you forsaken me?'" (ⲁⲩⲱ ⲙ̄ⲡⲛⲁⲩ ⲛ̄ϫⲡ ⲯⲓⲧⲉ ⲁϥϣϣ ⲉⲃⲟⲗ ⲛ̄ϭⲓ ⲓⲏ̄ⲥ ϩⲛ ⲟⲩⲛⲟϭ ⲛ̄ϩⲣⲟⲟⲩ ϫⲉ ⲉⲗⲱⲉⲓ ⲉⲗⲱⲉⲓ ⲗⲁⲙⲁ ⲥⲁⲭⲑⲁⲛⲉⲓ ⲉⲧⲉ ⲡⲁⲓ ⲡⲉ ϣⲁⲩϩⲉⲣⲙⲉⲛⲉⲩⲉ ⲙ̄ⲙⲟϥ ϫⲉ ⲡⲁⲛⲟⲩⲧⲉ ⲡⲁⲛⲟⲩⲧⲉ ⲉⲧⲃⲉ ⲟⲩ ⲁⲕⲕⲁⲁⲧ ⲛ̄ⲥⲱⲕ; Horner 1911: I 627–628); Luke 23.46: "Jesus cried out in a great voice, saying 'My father, I give my spirit into your hands!', and when he had said this he gave up his breath" (ⲁⲓⲏ̄ⲥ ϫⲓϣⲕⲁⲕ ⲉⲃⲟⲗ ϩⲛ ⲟⲩⲛⲟϭ ⲛ̄ⲥⲙⲏ ⲡⲉϫⲁϥ ϫⲉ ⲡⲁⲓⲱⲧ ϯϯ ⲙⲡⲁⲡⲛ̄ⲙⲁ ⲉⲛⲉⲕϭⲓϫ ⲛ̄ⲧⲉⲣⲉϥϫⲉ ⲡⲁⲓ ⲇⲉ ⲁϥⲕⲁ ⲡⲧⲛⲟⲩ; Horner 1911: II 452); the first two citing Psalm 21 (22) 2: "God, my God, attend to me; why have you forsaken me?" (ⲡⲛⲟⲩⲧⲉ ⲡⲁⲛⲟⲩⲧⲉ ⲙⲁϯϩⲧⲏⲕ ⲉⲣⲟⲓ ⲉⲧⲃⲉ ⲟⲩ ⲁⲕⲕⲁⲁⲧ ⲛ̄ⲥⲱⲕ; Budge 1898: 22). For the concepts of "three breaths", *cf.* PCM I 26 p. 10 l. 21, p. 12 ll. 24–26, ll. 31–32, where Jesus gives up three breaths to his Father upon the cross, but three breaths are also given by God to Adam on the day of his creation, and by Jesus to his apostles.

14–15. ⲛ̄ⲅ ⲣⲉⲙⲓⲏ ⲧⲁⲡⲓⲱⲧ ⲧⲁⲁⲩ : **"the three tears that the Father shed"** For the tears shed by God the father at the moment of death of Christ, compare *PCM* I 12 p. 18 ll. 1–2; *PCM* I 25 p. 14 ll. 2–5.

18–20. ⲧⲉⲕⲥⲏⲃⲓ ⲧⲁⲓ ⲉⲛⲧⲁⲕⲡⲱϩ ⲉⲛⲕⲁⲧⲁⲡⲉϯⲥⲙⲁ ⲉⲙⲡⲉⲣⲡⲏ ⲉⲛϩⲏⲧⲥ : **"your sword, that with which you rent the veil of the Temple"** A reference to the rending of the veil before the Holy of Holies in the Jerusalem temple at the death of Jesus, described in Matthew 27.51, Mark 15.38, and Luke 23.45. The gospels do not describe an angel carrying out the act, but in Pseudo-Evodius of Rome, *Dormition of the Virgin Mary*, we find a description of an unnamed "mighty angel" (ⲟⲩⲁⲅⲅⲉⲗⲟⲥ ⲛ̄ϫⲱⲣⲓ) who comes down from heaven and cuts the veil in two with his sword (de Lagarde 1883: 53.5–9; Robinson 1986: 57 (trans.)). Here, as on p. 7 ll. 4–8, Gabriel takes on the identity of an angel who is an anonymous in the surviving literary tradition.

page 9

ⲙⲉⲛ ⲧⲉⲑⲉⲥⲓⲁ ⲉⲛⲗⲱⲕⲓⲕⲏ : ⲙ̄ⲛ	180
ⲧⲁⲛⲁⲫⱳⲣⲁ ⲉⲧⲟⲩⲁⲁⲃ ⲙⲉ ⲛⲉ-	
ⲙⲉⲥⲧⲏⲣⲓⱳⲛ ⲛⲓ̄ⲥ̄ ⲡⲉⲭ̄ⲥ̄ ⲉⲣⲉⲛⲉ-	
ⲧⲟⲩⲁⲁⲃ ϫⲓ ⲉⲃⲁⲗ ⲉⲛϩⲏⲧⲟⲩ ⲙⲉ	
5 ⲡϩⲁⲡ ⲉⲧⲉⲣⲉⲡⲁⲛⲧⱳⲕⲣⲁⲧⱳⲣ	
ⲛⲁⲧⲁⲁⲃ ⲉϯⲕⱳⲙⲏⲛⲓ ⲧⲏⲣⲥ	185
ϩ̄ⲙ ⲡⲓⲁ ⲓⱳⲥⲁⲫⲁⲧ ϫⲉⲕⲁⲁⲥ ⲉ-	
ⲛⲉⲕⲕⲁⲧⲏⲭⲓ ⲟⲩⲧⲉ ⲛⲛⲉⲕⲁ-	
ⲙⲉⲗⲓ ⲛⲟⲩⲥⲟⲩⲥⲟⲩ ⲉⲛⲟⲩⱳⲧ	
10 ⲟⲩⲧⲉ ⲟⲩⲣⲓⲕⲓ ⲛⲃⲁⲗ ϣⲁⲛⲧⲉⲕⲓ	
ϩⲓϫⲉⲛ ⲡⲉⲕⲥ̄ⲱ̄ⲧ̄ ϩ̄ⲛ ⲧⲉⲩⲛⲟⲩ ⲛ̄-	190
ϣⲁⲓϯ ⲕⲱϩⲧ ⲉⲣⲁϥ ⲃⱳⲕ ϣⲁ ⲇ̄ⲇ̄	
ⲧ̄ϫ̄ ⲇ̄ⲇ̄ † ⲛⲟⲩⲕⱳϩⲧ ⲙⲉⲛ ⲟⲩϣⲱ	
ⲙⲉⲛ ⲟⲩⲉⲡⲓⲑⲉⲙⲓⲁ ⲙⲉ ⲩϣⲧⲁⲣⲧⲣ̄	
15 ⲙⲉⲛ ⲟⲩⲧⲁⲣⲁⲭⲏ ⲉⲡⲉⲥⲏⲧ ⲉⲡⲉⲥ-	
ϩⲏⲧ ⲉϩⲟⲩⲛ ⲉ̄ⲇ̄ⲇ̄ ⲡ̄ϫ̄ ⲇ̄ⲇ̄ ⲁⲛⲓⲧⲥ	195
ⲛⲁϥ ϩⲉⲛ ⲟⲩⲑⲉⲃⲓⲁ ⲙⲉⲛ ⲟⲩϩⲉ-	
ⲡⲱϯⲥⲙⲟⲥ · ⲉⲃⲛⲁⲩ ⲉⲡⲉⲥⲕⱳⲕⲁ-	
ϩⲏⲩ ⲛⲉⲩⲛⲟⲩ ⲛⲓⲙ · ⲉⲃⲧⱳϩ ⲉ-	
20 ⲧⲉⲃⲉⲡⲓⲑⲉⲙⲓⲁ ⲙⲉ ⲧⲱⲥ ⲉⲃⲉⲛ-	
ⲕⲁⲧ ⲛⲉⲙⲥ ⲉⲛⲛⲉⲥⲥⲓ ⲙ̄ⲙⲁⲃ	200
ⲃⲓ ⲡϣⲓⲡⲓ ⲡⲉⲥϩⲁ ⲙⲉ ⲛⲉⲥⲃⲁⲗ	

---

1 *i.e.* θυσία | *i.e.* λογική ‖ **2** *i.e.* ἀναφορά ‖ **3** *i.e.* μυστήριον | *l.* ι(ησου)ς πε-χ(ριστό)ς ‖ **5** *i.e.* ᶳπ-παντοκράτωρ *cf.* note to *PCM* I 25 p. 2 l. 2 ‖ **6** *i.e.* οἰκουμένη| *i.e.* ᶳⲧⲏⲣ=ⲥ̄ ‖ **8** *i.e.* κατέχειν ‖ **8–9** *i.e.* ἀμελεῖν ‖ **11** *l.* ζῴδι(ον) ‖ **12–13** *l.* δ(ε)ῖ(να) δ(ε)ῖ(να) (twice) ‖ **13** *l.* (υἱός) ‖ **14** *i.e.* ἐπιθυμία | *i.e.* ᶳⲟⲩ-ϣⲧⲟⲣⲧⲣ̄ ‖ **15** *i.e.* ταραχή ‖ **16** *l.* δ(ε)ῖ(να) δ(ε)ῖ(να) (twice) | *l.* (υἱός) ‖ **17–18** *i.e.* ὑποδεσμός *cf.* LBG *s.v.* ‖ **18** *i.e.* ᶳⲛ=ϥ̄-ⲛⲁⲩ ‖ **19** *i.e.* ᶳⲛ-ϥ̄-ⲧⲱϩ ‖ **20** *i.e.* ἐπιθυμία ‖ **22** *i.e.* ᶳϥⲓ ⲡ-ϣⲓⲡⲉ ⲙ-ⲡⲉ=ⲥ-ϩⲟ

and the rational sacrifice and the holy offering and the mysteries of Jesus Christ which the saints receive and |⁵ the judgement which the Almighty will pronounce over the whole world in the Valley of Josaphat that you shall not delay nor shall you be neglectful for a single moment |¹⁰ nor a blink of the eye, until you come upon your image; in the moment that I put fire to it go to NN, the daughter of NN, put fire and desire and lust and disturbance |¹⁵ and tumult down into her heart for NN, the son of NN!

Bring her to him in humiliation and *bound, so that he sees her nakedness in every moment and he mingles |²⁰ his lust with hers! He will lie with her, she will not be sated with him! Take the shame ‹from› her face and her eyes,

---

1. ⲧⲉⲑⲩⲥⲓⲁ ⲉⲛⲗⲱⲕⲓⲕⲏ : "the rational sacrifice" The "rational" or "reasonable sacrifice" (λογικὴ θυσία) is a term for the Christian Eucharist; *cf.* Romans 12.1 and Mikhail 2015: 196–197.

7. ⲡⲓⲁ ⲓⲱⲥⲁⲫⲁⲧ : "Valley of Josaphat" *Cf.* Joel 3.2, 3.12: "and I will bring together all the nations and lead them down to the valley of Josaphat and judge them there concerning my people and my share, Israel" (καὶ συνάξω πάντα τὰ ἔθνη καὶ κατάξω αὐτὰ εἰς τὴν κοιλάδα Ιωσαφατ καὶ διακριθήσομαι πρὸς αὐτοὺς ἐκεῖ ὑπὲρ τοῦ λαοῦ μου καὶ τῆς κληρονομίας μου Ισραηλ), "Let all the nations rise themselves and come to the valley of Josaphat, for there I will sit to judge all the nations from all around" (ἐξεγειρέσθωσαν καὶ ἀναβαινέτωσαν πάντα τὰ ἔθνη εἰς τὴν κοιλάδα Ιωσαφατ, διότι ἐκεῖ καθιῶ τοῦ διακρῖναι πάντα τὰ ἔθνη κυκλόθεν).

11. ⲥⲱⲧ̄ : "image" Understand with Bilabel/Grohmann "image", referring to the image of Gabriel from the end of the text, copied onto an ostracon (*cf.* note p. 13), rather than "sign of the zodiac", as translated by Jackson in Meyer/Smith.

20. ⲧⲉⲃⲉⲡⲓⲑⲉⲙⲓⲁ ⲙⲉ ⲧⲱⲥ : "his lust with hers" "Lust" (ἐπιθυμία) here probably serves as a euphemism for the genitalia; *cf.* the notes to *PCM* I 20 l. 14.

page 10

	ⲙⲁⲣⲉⲃⲉⲣ ⲟ̅ⲥ̅ ⲉⲣⲁⲥ ⲙⲁⲣⲉⲃⲱⲡⲓ ⲛ-	
	ⲁⲥ ⲛⲟ̅ⲥ̅ ⲉⲥϣⲱⲡⲓ ⲛⲁⲃ ⲉⲛϩⲙ̅ϩⲁⲗ	
	ⲙⲁⲣⲉϣⲓⲛⲓ ⲥⲱϥ ⲉⲛⲥⲏⲩ ⲛⲓⲙ	
	ⲙⲉ ⲩⲁⲉⲓϣ ⲛ̅ⲙ̅ ⲙⲉ ⲭⲣⲱⲛⲟⲥ ⲛⲓⲙ	205
5	ⲙⲉ ⲉⲛⲟⲩ ⲛⲓⲙ ⲙⲉ ⲡⲉⲥⲱⲛⲁϩ ⲧⲏ-	
	ⲣⲏⲃ ⲙⲉ ⲡⲱⲃ ⲙⲁⲣⲉⲣⲱⲙⲓ ⲛⲓⲙ	
	ⲙⲉ ⲯⲩⲭⲏ ⲛⲓⲙ ⲙⲉ ⲛⲓⲃⲉ ⲛⲓⲙ	
	ⲉⲣ ⲃⲁϯ ϩⲓ ⲗⲱⲙⲥ̅ ϩⲓ ⲕⲛⲁⲥ ϩⲓ ⲙ ⲁ ᶜᵗ	
	ⲛⲁⲥ ⲉⲓⲉⲙⲉϯ ⲁ̅ⲁ̅ ⲡ̅ⲭ̅ ⲁ̅ⲁ̅ ⲙⲁⲃⲟⲕ	210
10	ⲉⲃⲁⲗ ϩⲓⲧⲁⲁⲧⲥ ⲙⲁⲣⲉⲥⲉⲣ ϩⲏⲃⲓ	
	ⲉⲥⲉⲣ ⲁϣⲁϩⲁⲙ ⲉⲥⲣⲓⲙⲓ ϩⲉⲛ ϭⲥⲓϣⲓ	
	ⲙⲁⲥⲛⲁⲩ ⲉⲣⲁⲃ ⲉϭⲓⲛ ⲡⲁϩⲟⲩ ⲙⲁ-	
	ⲣⲉⲥϣϩⲓⲣⲁⲧⲥ ϩⲓϫⲉⲛ ⲛⲉⲥⲡⲁⲧ	
	ⲉⲥⲡⲣⲟⲥⲕⲏⲛⲓ ⲉⲙⲙⲁⲃ ϩⲛ̅ ⲟⲩϩⲁϯ	215
15	ⲙⲉⲛ ⲟⲩⲑⲉⲃⲓⲁ ⲛⲁϥϣⲁϫⲓ ⲙⲁ-	
	ⲣⲉⲥⲕⲁⲣⲱⲥ ⲙⲁⲃϭⲱⲛⲧ ⲙⲁⲣⲉⲥ-	
	ⲁⲁⲃ ⲛⲓⲣⲏⲛⲏ ⲉⲥⲗⲁⲕⲁⲡⲁ ⲛⲏ-	
	ⲙ̅ⲙⲁⲃ ⲉⲥϯ ⲛⲁⲃ ⲉⲡⲉⲥⲛⲟⲩⲃ ⲙⲉ	
	ⲡⲉⲥϩⲁⲧ ⲙⲉ ⲛⲉⲥϩⲁⲓϯ ⲙⲉ ⲛⲉⲥ-	220
20	ⲥϯⲛⲟⲩⲃⲉ ⲙⲉ ⲛⲉⲥⲟⲩⲱⲙ ⲙⲉ	
	ⲛⲉⲥⲥⲱ ⲙⲉ ⲛⲉⲥⲧⲱⲣⲱⲛ	

1 *l.* ϭ(ⲱ)ⲥ | *l.* ⲙⲁⲣⲉⲣⲃϣⲱⲡⲓ ‖ **2** *l.* ϭ(ⲱ)ⲥ | *i.e.* ˢⲛ⸗ⲥ̅-ϣⲱⲡⲉ ‖ **3** *i.e.* ˢⲛ̅ⲥⲱϥ ‖ **4** *i.e.* ˢⲟⲩⲟⲉⲓϣ | *l.* ⲛⲓⲙ | *i.e.* χρόνος ‖ **5** *i.e.* ˢⲟⲩⲛⲟⲩ ‖ **7** *i.e.* ψυχή ‖ **8** *i.e.* ˢⲕⲛⲟⲥ ‖ **9** *i.e.* εἰ μήτι | *l.* δ(ε)ῖ(να) δ(ε)ῖ(να) (twice) | *l.* (υἱός) | *l.* ⲙⲁⲃⲃⲱⲕ *cf.* note ‖ **12** *i.e.* ˢⲉ-ϫⲓⲛ ? ‖ **11** ⲟ\ⲩ/ⲥⲓϣⲓ corrected from ⲟⲓϣⲓ by overwriting ‖ **14** *i.e.* προσκυνεῖν ‖ **17** *i.e.* εἰρήνη ‖ **17–18** *i.e.* ˢⲛ̅⸗ⲥ-ⲣ̅-ἀγαπᾶν ⲛⲙ̅ⲙⲁ⸗ϥ : ⲁⲕⲁⲡⲁ ⲛⲏ ⲙ̅ⲙⲁϥ *i.e.* ἀγαπᾶν ναί ? "treating him truly (?) lovingly" ("und ihn fürwahr (?) liebreich behandeln") Bilabel/Grohmann, Jackson ‖ **18** *i.e.* ˢⲛ̅⸗ⲥ̅-ϯ ‖ **19** *i.e.* ˢϩⲟ(ⲉ)ⲓⲧⲉ ‖ **20** *i.e.* ˢⲛⲟⲩϥⲉ ‖ **21** *i.e.* δῶρον

may he rule over her, may he become master to her, and she become slave to him! May she seek him in all seasons and all moments and all times |⁵ and all hours and all of her life and his! May every man and every soul and every breath become abominable and foul and putrid and hateful to her except NN, son of NN!

If he goes |¹⁰ away from her, let her mourn, groaning, crying bitterly! If she sees him from? behind, let her kneel in obeisance to him in fear |¹⁵ and humiliation! If he speaks let her be silent! If he is angry let her make peace ‹with him› and love him and give him her gold and her silver and her clothes and her |²⁰ perfume and her food and her drink and her gifts

---

9, 12, 15, 16. ⲛⲁ- : "if..." For this verbal prefix, see Crum 1930; Crum CD 155b; we thank Vincent Walter for the former reference.

page 11

```
       ⲙⲉ ⲛⲉⲥⲧⲁⲓⲁ ⲛⲟⲩⲁⲉⲓⲱ ⲛⲓⲙ
       ⲙⲉ ⲥⲏⲩ ⲛⲓⲙ ⲙⲉ ⲛⲉⲥϩⲁⲁⲩ ⲧⲏⲣⲟ̇ⲩ
       ⲙⲉ ⲡⲉⲥⲱⲛⲁϩ ⲧⲏⲣϥ · ⲉⲩⲉ-                      225
       ϣⲱⲡⲓ ⲉⲩⲙⲏⲛ ⲉⲃⲁⲗ ⲛⲉⲙⲁⲃ
5      ⲕⲁⲧⲁ ⲛⲓⲁⲡⲱⲗⲱⲅⲓⲁ ⲉⲥⲧⲓ ⲉⲡ-
       ⲥⲁ ϩⲓ ⲉⲡⲁⲛⲁⲓ ⲉⲙⲙⲏⲛⲓ ϫⲉ ⲡⲉⲥϩⲏ-
       ⲧ ⲙⲉ ⲡⲉⲥⲛⲟⲩⲥ ⲙⲉ ⲛⲉⲥⲙⲉⲉⲩⲉ
       ⲙⲉ ⲛⲉⲥⲙⲁⲕⲙⲕ ⲙⲉ ⲛⲉⲥⲃⲁⲗ ⲉⲣⲉ-           230
       ⲟⲩϩⲁⲟⲩ ϣⲱⲡⲓ ⲛⲁⲥ ⲉⲃⲛⲁϣⲧ
10     ⲡⲁⲣⲁ ⲟⲩϩⲁⲟⲩ ⲙⲉⲛ ⲉⲛⲟⲩ ⲛⲙ
       ⲙⲉ ϩⲁⲁⲩ ⲛⲓⲙ ⲙⲉ ⲉⲩϣⲏ ⲛⲓⲙ ⲁⲓ ⲁⲓ ⲧⲁ̇
       ⲁϩⲁ ⲙⲡⲉⲕⲓⲣⲓ ⲱ ⲅⲁⲃⲣⲓⲏⲗ ⲙⲡⲁⲟⲩ-
       ⲱϣ ⲉⲕϫⲱⲕ ⲉⲃⲟⲗ ⲉⲙⲡⲁⲟⲩⲉϩ-           235
       ⲥⲁϩⲛⲓ ϣⲁⲓⲥⲁϣⲕ ⲉⲃⲟⲗ ⲧⲁ-
15     ϣⲉⲉⲧⲕ ⲉⲃⲟⲗ ⲧⲁⲁⲛⲁⲑⲉⲙⲁ ⲉ-
       ⲙⲙⲁⲕ ⲧⲁⲥⲁϣⲕ ⲧⲁⲃⲁⲃⲱⲕ
       ⲉⲛⲛⲉⲡⲓⲱⲧ †ⲙⲁ ⲛⲁⲕ ϩⲛ ⲧⲡⲏ
       ⲉⲛⲛⲉⲡϣⲏⲣⲉ † ⲧⲁⲝⲓⲥ ⲛⲁⲕ              240
       ϩⲛ ⲧⲡⲏ ⲛⲛⲉⲡⲉⲡⲛⲁ ⲉⲧⲟⲩⲁⲁⲃ
20     ⲕⲉ ⲧⲧⲉⲕⲯⲁⲗⲗⲉ ⲟⲩⲧⲉ ⲛⲉⲧⲉ-
       ⲣⲱ ⲛⲉϩⲓⲁⲙⲓ ⲙⲁⲣⲓⲁ ⲡⲁ̇ⲣⲛⲟⲥ
       ϣⲁⲡⲕ ⲉⲣⲁⲥ ⲟⲩⲧⲉ ⲧⲟⲩⲙⲟⲩ†
       ⲉⲣⲁⲕ ϫⲉ ⲃⲁⲓϣⲉⲛⲟⲩⲃⲉ                  245
```

---

3 *i.e.* ˢⲧⲏⲣⲍϥ ‖ **5** *i.e.* κατά | *i.e.* ἀπολογία | *i.e.* ˢⲛⲍⲥ̄-† ‖ **7** *i.e.* νοῦς ‖ **10** *i.e.* παρά | *l.* ⲟⲩⲛⲟⲩ ⲛⲓⲙ ‖ **11** ϩⲁⲁⲩ corrected from ⲡⲁⲁⲩ by overwriting | *l.* ⲛⲓⲙ | *l.* ταχ(ύ) ‖ **15** *i.e.* ἀνάθημα, apparently treated as verb ‖ **16** *i.e.* ˢⲃⲁⲃⲱⲍ ‖ **17** *i.e.* τιμᾶν : † ⲙⲁ "assign (you) a place in heaven" ("Platz im Himmel geben") Bilabel/Grohmann, Jackson ‖ **18** *i.e.* τάξις ‖ **19** *l.* πν(εῦμ)α ‖ **20** *i.e.* ˢⲕⲁ ⲉ-ⲧⲣⲉⲍⲕ-ψάλλειν : *l.* ⲕⲉ(ⲉ)ⲕ ⲉⲕϫⲁⲗⲗⲉ or ⲕⲉ ⲧⲣⲉⲕϫⲁⲗⲗⲉ "(not) encourage your hymns of praise" ("deinen Psalmengesang nicht ermuntern") Bilabel/Grohmann, Jackson ‖ **21** *l.* ‹ⲧ›-παρθ(έ)νος cf. note to *PCM* I 25 p. 2 l. 2 ‖ **22** *l.* ⲉⲧⲟⲩⲙⲟⲩⲧⲉ ? (haplography) *i.e.* ˢⲛ̄-ⲥⲉⲙⲟⲩⲧⲉ | *l.* ⲛⲟⲩⲙⲟⲩⲧ Till ‖ **23** *i.e.* ˢϣⲙ-ⲛⲟⲩϥⲉ

and her presents at all times and all seasons and all her days and all her life; they will remain with him |⁵ according to these requests, and she will make ‹herself› beautiful and pleasing every day in her heart and her mind and her thoughts and her thinking and her eyes, ‹even› if a day comes for her more difficult |¹⁰ than any day and hour, and every day and every night, yea, yea, quickly!

If you have not done my desire, O *Gabriel, fulfilling my command, I will despise you, and I will |¹⁵ cut you off, and I will anathematise you and I will despise you and I will abhor you! The Father will not honour you in heaven! The Son will not give you rank in heaven! The Holy Spirit |²⁰ will not allow you to sing, nor will the queen of women, Mary the Virgin receive you unto herself, nor will they call you the bringer of good news,

---

1. ⲧⲁⲓⲁ : "**presents**" For the translation as "present" (*i.e.*, a synonym of "gift") *cf.* Meyer/Smith and Crum CD 391a. Compare the Coptic marriage contract P.Gardiner (Thompson 1912: 175, 177), in which ⲧⲁⲓⲟ seems to refer to a payment which a bride might receive, apparently separate from her bridal gift, usually called the ⲥⲭⲁⲧ (Richter 2008: 272; *cf.* the term ⲃⲉⲭⲉ, "wage" used for the bridal gift in the *Scala Magna*; see Macomber 2020: I 68).

12. ⲁϩⲁ : "**if**" Probably to be understood as Sahidic ⲉϩⲉ, which appears with conditional phrases; *e.g.*, 1 Kings (=1 Samuel) 25.8: "if it is the case, ask your servants, and they will tell you these things" (ⲉϣⲱⲡⲉ ⲁϩⲉ ϫⲛⲉ ⲛⲉⲕϩⲙ̄ϩⲁⲗ ⲁⲩⲱ ⲥⲉⲛⲁⲧⲁⲙⲟⲕ ⲉⲛⲁⲓ, Drescher 1970: 77; *cf.* Crum CD 64b for further examples). It may be that a preceding ⲉϣⲱⲡⲉ or ⲉϣϫⲉ has dropped out here, or else that ⲁϩⲁ has been reanalysed as a conditional particle itself.

20. ⲕⲉ ⲡⲧⲉⲕϯⲁⲗⲗⲉ : "**allow you to sing**" For this construction with the inflected infinitive base ⲧⲉ⸗ (here apparently ⲡⲧⲉ⸗), see Funk 2017: 59–63, *cf.* Crum CD 439 *s.v.* ⲧⲧⲟ.

page 12

```
     ϣⲁⲧⲉⲕϫⲱⲕ ⲉⲃⲁⲗ ⲛⲁⲡⲟⲗⲟ-
     ⲅⲓⲁ ⲛⲓⲙ ⲉⲛⲧⲁⲓϫⲁⲁⲩ ϩⲛ̄ ϯ-
     ⲡⲣⲱⲥⲉⲩⲭⲏ ⲟⲩⲧⲉ ⲛⲛⲉⲕⲁ-
     ⲡⲱⲫⲁⲛⲓ ϩⲓϫⲱⲓ ϩⲱⲱⲧ ⲛⲟⲩ-
5    ⲡⲉⲑⲁⲩ ⲟⲩⲧⲉ ⲛⲉⲕϥⲱⲃⲓ                  250
     ⲛⲁⲓ ⲟⲩⲧⲉ ⲧⲉⲕⲧ . ⲁ . . ⲏ ⲛⲁⲓ
     ⲟⲩⲧⲉ ⲧⲉⲕϫⲱϩ ⲉⲣⲁⲓ ϩⲛ̄ ⲟⲩ-
     ⲡⲉⲑⲁⲩ ⲓⲉ ⲟⲩϩⲓⲥⲓ ⲁⲗⲗⲁ ϩⲛ̄
     ⲣⲁϣⲉ ⲛⲓⲙ ⲙⲉⲛ ⲧⲁⲓⲁ ⲛⲓⲙ ⲧⲁⲥ-
10   ⲙⲟⲩ ϩⲱⲱⲧ ⲉⲡⲓⲱⲧ ⲡⲁⲛⲧⲟⲕ-            255
     ⲣⲁⲧⲱⲣ ⲧⲁϯ ⲉⲁⲩ ⲛ̄ⲓ̄ⲥ̄ ⲡⲙⲱ-
     ⲛⲱⲕⲉⲛⲏⲥ ⲧⲁϩⲉⲙⲛⲉⲩⲉ ⲉⲡⲉ-
     ⲡ̄ⲛ̄ⲁ̄ ⲉⲧⲟⲩⲁⲁⲃ ⲧⲁϯ ⲉⲁⲩ
     ⲛⲁⲕ ϩⲱⲱⲕ ⲱ ⲅⲁⲃⲣⲓⲏⲗ ϫⲉ
15   ⲁⲕϣⲱⲡⲓ ⲛⲁⲓ ⲉⲛⲣⲉϥⲥⲱⲧⲙ̄            260
     ϩⲛ̄ ⲛⲁⲁⲡⲱⲕⲣⲉⲥⲓⲥ ⲁⲙⲟⲩ
     ⲁⲙⲟⲩ ⲙ̄ⲡⲉⲣⲕⲁⲧⲏⲭⲉ . . .
     ⲛⲓ ⲛⲁⲕ ϣⲁ ⲉⲛⲉϩ ϩⲁⲙⲏⲛ
     ─── ))) ─── )))
     ooo        ooo         ooo    ooo
          ))) ─── )))
     ϯ ϯ ⲑ̄ⲩ̄ ϩⲁⲣⲁⲃ ⲙⲙⲁⲥⲧⲭⲏ ⲁⲗ[ⲟ]ⲩⲑ ⲥ-
20   ⲧⲓⲣⲏⲝ ⲙⲟⲩ̈ⲥⲥ ⲅ ⲉⲛϩⲁⲟⲩ · ⲍ ⲛⲉⲩⲭⲏ   265
     ⲉⲙⲏⲛⲉ ⲉϭⲏⲛ ⲡⲅ ⲉⲕⲉⲣⲓⲁⲕⲏ ϣⲁ
     ⲡⲟⲩⲱϣ ⲉⲕⲛⲉⲥⲧⲉⲩⲉ ⲉⲙⲏⲛⲉ
```

1–2 *i.e.* ἀπολογία || **3** *i.e.* προσευχή || **3–4** *i.e.* ἀποφαίνειν || **5** ....ⲟ̣ⲃⲓ Bilabel/Grohmann || **6** ⲧⲉⲕⲧⲱ[...]. Bilabel/Grohmann || **7** ⲧⲉⲕϫⲱ[ϩ] Bilabel/Grohmann || **8** *i.e.* ἀλλά || **10–11** *i.e.* ˢⲡ-ⲡⲁⲛⲧⲟⲕⲣⲁⲧⲱⲣ *cf.* note to *PCM* I 25 p. 2 l. 2 || **11–12** *i.e.* μονογενής || **12** *i.e.* ὑμνεῖν || **13** *l.* πν(εῦμ)α | ⲧ[ⲁ]ⲧ̣[*ca.* 5] Bilabel/Grohmann || **14** ⲭ[ⲉ] Bilabel/Grohmann || **15** ⲉⲛⲣⲉϥ[....]ⲧ̣ⲏ̣ⲛ Bilabel/Grohmann || **16** *i.e.* ἀπόκρισις | ⲁ̣[. . .] . . [.] Bilabel/Grohmann || **17** *i.e.* κατέχειν : ⲙ̄ⲡⲉⲣⲕⲁⲧⲕ [*ca.* 5]ⲩ̣ Bilabel/Grohmann || **19** *l.* θυ(σία) | *i.e.* μαστίχη : ⲉⲙⲙⲁⲥϯⲉⲏ *i.e.* μαστίχη Bilabel/Grohmann | *i.e.* العود al-ʿūd : Bilabel/Grohman do not translate : transliterate "alouth" Jackson || **19–20** *i.e.* στύραξ || **20** *l.* μόσχ(ο)ς | *i.e.* εὐχή : for this line ⲧⲓⲣⲏⲝ ⲙⲟⲩⲥⲥⲥ̣ⲉⲛ ϩⲁ:·϶ ⲛⲉⲩⲭⲏ "styrax... (daily) prayers" ("Styrax... die Gebete") Bilabel/Grohmann, Jackson || **21** *i.e.* ˢⲉ-ϫⲓⲛ | *i.e.* κυριακή : ⲡⲛ√ ⲉⲕⲉⲣ . ⲁⲭⲏ Bilabel/Grohmann || **22** *i.e.* νηστεύειν | *i.e.* ˢⲙ̄-ⲙⲏⲛⲉ

until you complete every request that I have spoken in this prayer, nor shall you impose on me, myself |⁵ anything evil, nor shall you mock? me, nor shall you ... to me nor shall you touch me with evil, or suffering, but rather with all joy and all honour, and I will |¹⁰ myself praise the Almighty Father and I will give glory to Jesus, the only-begotten son, and I will sing hymns to the Holy Spirit, and I will give glory to you, yourself, O *Gabriel, for |¹⁵ you have been obedient to me in my affairs! Come?, come, do not delay ... to you forever, amen!

☩ Make an offering for him of *mastic, *agarwood?, |²⁰ *styrax, *musk. Three days, seven prayers daily, from Tuesday until Thursday, while you fast daily,

---

3–4. ⲛⲛⲉⲕⲁⲡⲱⲫⲁⲛⲓ : **"shall you [not] impose"** For the sense of "impose", see Förster WBGW 91, s.v. ἀποφαίνω.

5–6. ⲛⲉⲕϭϣⲱⲃⲓ ⲛⲁⲓ : **"nor shall you mock? me"** We propose this restoration very tentatively; the object would usually be expressed with ⲙ̄ⲙⲟⲓ or ⲛ̄ⲥⲱⲓ rather than ⲛⲁⲓ.

19. ☩ ⲟⲩ ϩⲁⲣⲁⲃ : **"make an offering for him"** Or "for it"; the pronoun here may be taken to refer either to the angel Gabriel or the ritual as a whole.

21–22. ⲡⲅ ⲉⲕⲉⲣⲓⲁⲕⲏ ϣⲁ ⲡⲟⲩⲱϣ : **"from Tuesday until Thursday"** For the Coptic names of the week, see Till 1947 & 1953. Tuesday is designated as the third day of the week (ⲡϣⲟⲙⲛ̄ⲧ ⲛ̄ⲧⲕⲩⲣⲓⲁⲕⲏ) following the ordinal system (cf. Ast 2012: 10–16), with the week beginning on Sunday, while Thursday is referred to as "the pause" (ⲡⲟⲩⲱϣ) between the "little" and "great" fasts of Wednesday and Friday (ⲧⲕⲟⲩⲓ ⲛ̄ⲛⲏⲥⲧⲓⲁ/ⲧⲛⲏⲥⲧⲓⲁ ϣⲏⲙ, ⲧⲛⲟϭ ⲛ̄ⲛⲏⲥⲧⲓⲁ/ⲧⲛⲏⲥⲧⲓⲁ ⲱ). For this reading, cf. Polotsky 1939: 112. Bilabel/Grohmann and Jackson in Meyer/Smith translate as "as long as you like" ("bis zu dem Wunsch").

page 13

ⲉⲕⲟⲩⲁⲙ ⲁⲡⲟⲩⲱϣ . . ⲧⲁⲙⲟⲩⲛϩ . .
ⲓⲱⲥⲏⲫ ϩⲓ ⲛⲉϩ ⲉⲙⲙⲉ ⲉⲣⲁⲃ ⲉⲣ ⲕⲃ . .
ⲉⲑⲉ . † ⲉⲕⲛⲉⲥⲧⲉⲩⲉ ⲉⲕⲧⲃⲃⲏⲩ ⲉⲕ-   270
ⲫⲱⲣⲓ ⲛϩⲉⲛϩⲁⲓ† ϣⲁϩⲗⲏⲃ ⲉⲩⲃⲏ-
5   ⲗϫⲓ ⲛⲁⲙⲓ ⲉⲛⲃⲱ† ⲡⲣⲟⲥⲉ̄ⲩ͞ : ⲕⲁ ⲛ̄-
ⲅ ⲉⲥⲁⲡ ϩⲁⲣⲉϩ ⲉⲣⲁⲕ ⲉⲣⲁⲃ ⲙⲁⲣ
ⲟⲩⲣⲁⲉⲓⲥ ϩⲓϫⲱⲕ ⲛⲁⲧϣⲣⲁϩⲕ

[8]ⲅⲁⲃⲣⲓⲏⲗ
[9]ⲁⲛⲓ ⲁ . . . .

ⲱⲱ
ⲱⲱ

[10]ϣⲁⲓⲣⲁϩ-
[11]ⲕⲓ ϩⲓ ⲡⲕⲱ-
[12]ϩⲧ ⲡⲁⲓ

[13]ⲁⲓ ⲁⲓ
[14]ⲧⲁ ⲧⲁ
[15]ⲁⲛⲓⲛⲓ
[15]ⲇ̄ⲇ̄ ⲧ͞ⲩ ⲇ̄ⲇ̄
[16]ⲉⲣⲁⲧ-
[17]ⲃ ⲉⲇ̄ⲇ̄ ⲡ͞ⲩ
[18]ⲉⲇ̄ⲇ̄ ⲉⲛ
----

20   ⲗ . . .
ⲕⲉⲭⲁⲣⲓ
. . . ⲟ . .
[19]ⲅⲁⲃⲣⲓⲏⲗ ⲗⲓⲧⲟⲩⲣⲕⲟⲥ
ⲱ ⲕⲓⲣⲓⲟⲥ ⲙⲁⲧⲛⲟⲟⲩ ⲅⲁⲃⲣⲓⲏⲗ
ⲁⲩⲱ . . . . ⲁⲫⲁ

---

1 for this line Bilabel/Grohmann read ⲉⲕⲟⲩ . . ⲛ̄ⲁⲧⲟⲩ . . . . ⲧⲁⲙⲟⲩ ⲛ . . . ‖ **2** for this line Bilabel/Grohmann read ⲁϣⲥⲏⲫ ϩⲓ ⲛⲉϩ . [. . . .] ⲉⲕϩⲱ . . ⲕⲁ ‖ **3** ⲉⲑⲉ . . Bilabel/Grohmann | *i.e.* νηστεύειν ‖ **4** *i.e.* φορεῖν | *i.e.* ˢϩⲟⲓⲧⲉ | *i.e.* ˢϣⲟⲗϩ=ϥ̄ ? : ϣⲁ . ⲗⲏⲃ Bilabel/Grohmann ‖ **5** *i.e.* ˢϥⲱⲧⲉ : ⲃⲱ †- "with a hair (brush?)" ("mit Haar(?-Pinsel?)") Bilabel/Grohmann, Jackson | *i.e.* προσευχή : π[ⲣⲟⲥ]ⲉⲩ\ⲭ/⁼.. Bilabel/Grohmann ‖ **6** ⲅ : √ (untranslated) Bilabel/Grohmann | ϩⲁⲣϩ ϩⲉ[.]ⲣⲁⲛ Bilabel/Grohmann ‖ **7** ϩⲓϫⲱ . [.] Bilabel/Grohmann | ⲛⲁⲧϣⲣⲁϩⲛ Bilabel/Grohmann ‖ **11** ⲡⲁⲓ : . . ⲏ Bilabel/Grohmann ‖ **14** *l.* ταχ(ύ) (twice) ‖ **15** *l.* δ(ε)ῖ(να) δ(ε)ῖ(να) (twice) | *l.* (υἱός) ‖ **17** *l.* δ(ε)ῖ(να) δ(ε)ῖ(να) | *l.* υ(ἱός) ‖ **18** *l.* δ(ε)ῖ(να) δ(ε)ῖ(να) ‖ **19** ⲱ ⲅⲁⲃⲣⲓⲏⲗ Bilabel/Grohmann ‖ **20** ⲗ . . . : ⲗⲁ . . . . Bilabel/Grohmann ‖ **22** . . ⲟ . . : . . ⲣⲏ . . Bilabel/Grohmann ‖ **23** *i.e.* ὦ κύριος : ⲱⲕⲧⲣⲓⲟⲥ Bilabel/Grohmann | ⲙ . ⲧ . ⲁⲥⲟ . . [ⲅ]ⲁⲃⲣⲓⲏⲗ Bilabel/Grohmann ‖ **24** . . . . ⲁⲫⲁ : . . . . ⲛ . . . . . Bilabel/Grohmann

and you eat? on? Thursday? ... Joseph? and olive oil on it? ... while you fast, being pure, wearing clothes. Mark? it on a |⁵ clay ostracon with sweat. ⟨The⟩ prayer twenty-one times on three occasions. Beware of him. Bind a ... amulet on yourself.

|above image *Gabriel
|10, around image I will burn in this flame! Yea, yea, quickly, quickly! Bring |¹⁵ NN, daughter of NN, to him, NN, the son of NN, ... Gabriel, ⟨the⟩ minister |²⁰ ... Kekhari ... O Lord, send Gabriel and ...

KD, EL & MP, edited from photograph and autopsy; tracing by JS.

---

2. ιⲱⲥⲏⲫ : **"Joseph"** Perhaps understand this as a reference to an ingredient named after Joseph; compare the "grass of Mary" and "wood of Abraham" (ⲥⲁⲩⲃⲟⲩ ⲙⲁⲣⲓⲁ, ϣⲏ : ⲁⲃⲣⲁϩⲁⲙ) mentioned in *PCM* I 25 p. 9 ll. 2, 4 (KYP M186).

5–6. ⲕⲁ ⲛ̄ⲅ ⲉⲥⲁⲡ : **"twenty-one times on three occasions"** *Cf.* p. 12 ll. 20–21, which prescribes saying the prayer seven times daily for three days, giving a total of twenty one times across three days. We may alternatively understand multiplication, although this would make it harder to square with the instructions on the previous page; *cf.* Matthew 18.22: "seventy times seven times" (ⲥⲁϣϥ̄ ⲛ̄ϣϥⲉ ⲛ̄ⲥⲟⲡ; Horner 1911: I 194);

6. ϩⲁⲣⲉϩ ⲉⲣⲁⲕ ⲉⲣⲁⲃ : **"Beware of him"** For the understanding "beware of him", with two objects expressed with ⲉⲣⲟ=, *cf.* 2 Timothy 4.15: "beware of him, for he has opposed our words very much" (ϩⲁⲣⲉϩ ⲉⲣⲟⲕ ⲉⲣⲟϥ ⲁϥϯ ⲅⲁⲣ ⲉⲙⲁⲧⲉ ⲟⲩⲃⲉ ⲛⲁϣⲁϫⲉ; Thompson 1932: 244). It is unclear exactly who "him" refers to here—perhaps it should be translated as "it" and understood as the ritual as a whole, but it seems more likely the fiery angel Gabriel who might pose a danger to the practitioner without an amulet. While this is concept otherwise unknown to us in the Coptic magical corpus, the use of such amulets for protection against beings invoked during rituals is common in Graeco-Egyptian practice; see *GEMF* 31/*PGM* I.271–272 (KYP M153): "Be careful that you do not lose a leaf (of the branch being used as a phylactery) and injure yourself" (βλέπε δὲ μὴ ἀπολέσῃς φύλλον [κ(αὶ)] σεαυτὸν βλάψῃς); *GEMF* 57/*PGM* IV.2508–2510 (KYP M3): "the goddess lifts those without phylacteries into the air and casts them down from aloft" (ἡ θεὸς τοὺς ἀφυλακτηριαστοὺς τοῦτο πράσσοντας ἀεροφ⟨ερ⟩εῖς ποιεῖν καὶ ἀπὸ τοῦ ὕψους ἐπὶ τὴν γῆν ῥῖψαι) *GEMF* 74/*PGM* VII.231–232 (KYP M156): "wear the cloth around your neck so that (the god) will not strike you" (τὸ δὲ ῥάκος περίθου περὶ τὸν τράχηλον ἵνα μή σε πλήξῃ).

6–7. ⲙⲁⲣ ⲟⲩⲣⲁⲉⲓⲥ ϩⲓϫⲱⲕ ⲛⲁⲧⲱⲣⲁϩⲕ : **"bind a ... amulet on yourself"** Bilabel/Grohmann and Jackson in Meyer/Smith translate "let them watch over" ("mögen sie wachen über"), but do not offer a translation for the final word. Perhaps understand a negation of the verb ϣⲗⲁϩ ("to be afraid"; Crum CD 562; *cf.* ϣⲗⲁϩϥ in the following column), in an otherwise unattested pre-pronominal form, giving the sense "bind an amulet on yourself so that you are not afraid".

7. ⲟⲩⲣⲁⲉⲓⲥ : **"an amulet"** For the translation "amulet" see Crum CD 301b.

Image: As the label 'Gabriel' suggests, this image seems to represent the angel in a schematic form, apparently with multiple eyes. Across his chest, his name, ⲅⲁⲃⲣⲓⲏⲗ, is written in *kharaktēres*, and he seems to be holding to small figures in his hands, likely representing the target and the user of the ritual, bringing them together in the love spell as if they were effigies. The image is to be copied onto an ostracon (apparently with sweat; see ll. 4–5 of this page), before being thrown onto a fire as part of the ritual (*cf.* p. 9 l. 11–12). For similar rituals and a discussion of the motif LOVE IS FIRE, see *PCM* I 3 front column 2 ll. 33–38. For this image, *cf.* Mößner/Nauerth 2015: 337–338; Dosoo 2018: 34; Dosoo 2022a: 150–151.

PCM I 29. Curse using narrative charm concerning Jesus and further prescription(s)

Arsinoites (Faiyum)   27.8 (H) × 18 (W) cm   X–XI CE

Other references: P.Heid.Inv. Kopt. 678 (formerly P.Heid.Inv. Nr. 1678); TM 102077; *P.Bad.* V 138; KYP M311; Bélanger Sarrazin #177.

Editions: Bilabel/Grohmann 1934: no. 138 (*ed. pr.*); Polotsky 1935: no. 138.

Translations: Bilabel/Grohmann 1934: no. 138 (German).

Additional commentary: Polotsky 1935; Mößner/Nauerth 2015: 309; Gardner/Johnston 2019: 31–32.

Present location: Heidelberg, Institut für Papyrologie.

Image: https://doi.org/10.11588/diglit.39746

Linguistic description: Sahidic with Middle Egyptian influence.

Contents:

1. Front ll. 1–22: Curse including Jesus-Serpent narrative charm (KYP T310)
2. Back ll. 1–13: One or more prescriptions for unclear purposes (KYP T46)

Sheet of paper, complete except for some damage to the upper right and along the folds. The front is well legible, the text of the back, written at 180° to the front, has been significantly abraded. 1 vertical and 8 horizontal creases are visible. The front of the manuscript consists of a curse structured around a narrative charm in which Jesus encounters a worm,[1] while the back contains a text of unclear purpose. The manuscript belongs to the archive known as the 'Heidelberg Coptic Magical Library' and was purchased in 1930 by Carl Schmidt (see p. 259–263).

    Both sides are written in the same hand, but likely on different occasions; the ink of the front is black, while that of the back is brown; respectively, they seem to be carbon and plant-based.[2] The text on both sides is written in an informal but rather regular right-sloping majuscule. The bilinear letters are quite compact, while the ascenders and descenders of the ⲣ, ⲧ, ⲩ, ϣ, ϩ, ⳉ, † are often very elongated. The bowl of the ⲁ is either rounded or flattened to a single stroke, so that it at times resembles a small majuscule ⲗ. ⲧ and † have consistent serifs on the horizontal bars, and ⲙ is quite flat, with the middle stroke nearly horizontal. The ⲕ usually has a small serif on its lower oblique stroke, making it resemble the Greek abbreviation for καί (ϗ), or even a ⲃ. Like the second Heidelberg copyist (responsible for *PCM* I 27–28; *cf.* p. 362–363), the scribe of this manuscript makes

---

[1] For the genre of narrative charm, see pp. 24–25.

[2] As with all of the ink descriptions of the Heidelberg papyri, we are grateful to Krisztina Hevesi for sharing her unpublished work with us. For further discussions of the ink, see p. 261.

use of the minuscule forms of letters as numerals (front l. 3, perhaps also 21). The copyist uses supralinear dots instead of strokes, so that true supralineation is only used for numbers, abbreviations, and *voces magicae*. The hand of this manuscript is close to that of *PCM* I 30, also written in a black ink, but the letterforms are not identical; most notably, the latter manuscript lacks the distinctive κ. While these hands' idiosyncracies makes dating them difficult, broadly similar styles can be seen in *SB Kopt* III 1285 (TM 109891), P.Monts.Roca inv. 524 (Torallas Tovar 2007; TM 140969), and, to a lesser extent, P.Stras. K 332 (D) (Walter 2022: no. 2). All of these are dated by their editors to the tenth or eleventh centuries. Given that the document is written on paper, and that the other Heidelberg Library manuscripts with more readily datable hands are likewise dated to this range, this seems reasonable for *PCM* I 29 & 30 too. Bilabel and Grohmann (1934: 397) suggested an eleventh century date for the manuscript, crediting Viktor Stegemann.

The text on the front of the manuscript differs significantly from other texts from the archive; it is written in a single column of 22 lines, undivided by horizontal lines. The final two lines, which we interpret here as the ritual instructions, seem to be separated only by a slightly larger interlinear space. Alternatively, it might be possible to interpret these final lines instead as part of the spoken formula, perhaps explaining the lack of dividing lines. The layout of the back is closer in style to the other manuscripts from the archive—with simple horizontal lines used to divide recipes and sections within them (formulae and ritual instructions), and *kharaktēres*, absent from the front. The brown ink is also closer to the other manuscripts from the archive.

Like the other manuscripts from the Heidelberg Coptic Magical Library, the manuscript is written in a variety of Sahidic strongly influenced by a Middle Egyptian dialect, likely that of the Faiyum (see p. 261–262). This copyist shows occasional features not found in the other manuscripts, such as the writing of ˢoγ as γ (*e.g.*, front l. 11; perhaps also present in *PCM* I 35 front l. 4). The grammar of both front and back is also highly divergent from the literary standard; in front l. 9, for example, the negative imperative (ⲙ̄ⲡⲉⲣ-) seems to be confused with the negative first perfect (ⲙ̄ⲡⲉ-).

front

+ ⲓ̅ⲥ̅ ⲛⲉⲃⲙⲁⲁϣⲉ ⲙ̇ⲛ ⲙⲓⲭⲁⲏⲗ · ⲙ̇[ⲛ]
ⲅⲁⲃⲣⲓⲏⲗ · ⲙ̇ⲛ ϩⲣⲁⲫⲁⲏⲗ · ⲙⲛ ⲡⲓⲙ̇[ⲉⲧ-]
ⲓ̅ⲃ̅ ⲛ̅ⲁ̅ⲡⲱⲥⲧⲱⲗⲱⲥ · ⲙⲛ ⲡⲓⲭⲟⲩⲧⲁ̇[ϥⲧⲉ]
ⲛ̇ⲡ̇ⲣⲉⲥⲃⲏⲧⲉⲣⲟⲥ · ϩⲓⲭⲛ̇ ⲛ̇ⲣⲁ ⲙ̇ⲡ̇ⲡⲁ-
5   ⲣⲁ†ⲥⲟⲥ · ⲁⲃϭⲓⲛ ⲟⲩⲃⲏⲛⲧ · ⲉⲃⲛ̇ⲕⲁⲧ
ⲉ̇ⲃⲁⲃⲱ̇ · ⲡⲁϫⲁⲃ ⲛⲁⲃ · ⟦ⲡⲁϫⲁⲃ⟧ ϫⲉ ⲁϩ-
ⲣⲁⲕ · ⲡⲉϫⲁ ⲛⲁⲃ ϫⲉ ⲡⲁⲡ̅ⲟ̅ⲥ̅ ⲓ̅ⲥ̅ ⲡⲉⲭ̅ⲥ̅
ⲛⲧⲁⲟⲩⲛⲟⲟⲩ ⲉ̇ⲣⲁⲕ ⲁⲓⲉⲣ ϩⲁ† · ⲡⲉϫⲁ-
ⲁⲃ ⲛⲁⲃ · ϫⲉ ⲙ̇ⲡⲱⲣ ⲙ̇ⲡⲉⲕⲉⲣ ϩⲁ†
10   ⲁⲗⲗⲁ ⲧⲱⲛ ⲉⲕⲃⲱⲕ · ⲉⲕⲗⲱⲕⲥ · ⲛ̅ⲓ̅ⲙ̅ ⲁ̅
†ⲱⲣⲕ ⲉⲣⲁ · ⲙ̇ⲡⲟⲟⲩ ⲧⲟⲩϩⲁϩⲓ · ⲛ̇ϩⲩⲧ
ⲧⲟⲩϩⲁϩⲓ ⲛ̇ϭϩⲓⲙⲓ · ⲙ̇ⲡ̇ⲣⲁⲛ ⲙ̇ⲡ̇ⲣⲁⲛ ⲙ̇-
ⲡⲓⲱⲧ ⲙ̇ⲛ ⲡϣⲏⲣⲓ ⲙⲛ ⲡ̅ⲛ̅ⲁ̅ ⲉ̅ⲧⲟⲩⲁⲁⲃ ·
†ⲱⲣⲕ ⲉⲣⲁⲕ̇ ⲛ̇† ⲛⲓⲃⲧ ⲛ̇ⲧⲁⲩⲧⲁⲕⲥ ·
15   ⲉ̇ⲡⲉⲭ̅ⲥ̅ ⲉ̇ⲧⲉ ⲛⲁⲓ ⲛⲉ ⲛⲉⲩⲣⲁⲛ · ⲥⲁⲧⲱⲣ
ⲁⲣⲉⲧⲱ ⲧⲉⲛⲏ̇ⲧ ⲱⲧⲉⲣⲁ ⲣⲱⲧⲁⲥ ⲁⲩ-
⟦ⲉⲛⲧⲁϥ⟧ \ ⲧⲉⲣϫⲁⲧϥ · ⲛ̇ⲑⲉ ⲛⲟⲩⲕⲱϩⲧ
ⲉⲕϭⲁⲁϭⲓ ⲙ̇ⲙⲁϥ - ⲛ̇ⲑⲉ ⲛⲟⲩⲥⲧⲉⲗⲟⲩⲥ
ⲧⲣⲉⲓⲛⲓ ⲉⲣⲁⲃ ⲉ̇ϫⲓⲛ ⲡⲣⲏⲥ ⲙ̇ⲡⲕⲁϩ ⲙ̇-
20   ⲡⲉⲣⲡⲓⲥⲧⲉⲩ ⲉ̇ⲣⲟⲟⲩ ϣⲁⲛⲧⲁⲟⲩⲱϣ ⲁⲛⲁ̇ᵏ

vac.

ⲑⲩ . . ⲕ̅ⲁ̅ ⲕⲱⲕⲏⲥ ⲉ̇ⲕⲗⲁⲙ ⲛⲁⲗⲁⲣⲱⲱⲥ ⲙ̇ⲡⲁⲧⲉϥⲃⲱⲕ ϣⲁ ⲧⲉϥⲧⲉϥⲥⲓⲙⲓ

---

1 *l.* ⲓ̅(ⲏⲥⲟⲩ)ⲥ̅ : ⲁⲕ Bilabel/Grohmann | *i.e.* ˢⲙⲟⲟϣⲉ ‖ **2** ⲡⲓⲙ̇[ⲉⲧ-] Polotsky : ⲡⲓⲙ[ϩ ⲙⲛ ·] Bilabel/Grohmann ‖ **3** ⲓ̅ⲃ̅ written in miniscules : ⲓ̣̅ⲃ̣̅ Bilabel/Grohmann | *i.e.* ἀπόστολος ‖ **4** *i.e.* πρεσβύτερος | ⲙ̇ⲡ̇ⲣⲁⲛ̇ ⲛ Bilabel/Grohmann ‖ **4–5** *i.e.* παράδεισος | ⲡ̇ⲣⲁⲛ̇ ⲛ̅ⲡⲁⲣⲁ†ⲥⲟⲥ Bilabel/Grohmann ‖ **5** *i.e.* ˢⲁ=ϥ-ϭⲛ̅ ⲟⲩ-ϥⲛ̅ⲧ : ⲁⲃϭⲓ ⲛⲟⲩⲃⲏⲛⲧ *i.e.* ˢⲁ=ϥ-ϫⲓ ⲛ̅-ⲟⲩ-ϥⲛ̅ⲧ Bilabel/Grohmann ‖ **6** *i.e.* ˢⲡⲉϫⲁ=ϥ | ⟦ⲡⲁϫⲁⲃ⟧ deleted with horizontal scribbles ‖ **7** *i.e.* ˢⲡⲉϫⲁ=ϥ : *l.* ⲡⲁ-*ϭ(ⲱ)ⲓⲥ *i.e.* ˢⲡⲁ-ϫⲟⲉⲓⲥ : *l.* ⲡⲁ ⲡ̅ⲟ̅ⲥ̅ "you, (son) of the Lord" ("Du (Sohn) des Herrn") Bilabel/Grohmann | *l.* χ(ριστό)ς ‖ **8** *i.e.* ˢⲛ̅ⲧ-ⲁ=ⲩ-ⲛⲁⲩ ? ‖ **8–9** *i.e.* ˢⲡⲉϫⲁ=ϥ (dittography) ‖ **9** *l.* ⲙⲡⲉⲣⲉⲣ ϩⲁ† Polotsky ‖ **10** *i.e.* ἀλλά | *i.e.* ˢⲛ̅-ⲅ̅-ⲃⲱⲕ | *i.e.* ˢⲛ̅-ⲅ̅-ⲗⲱⲕⲥ : ⲉⲕⲗⲱⲕⲉ *i.e.* ˢⲛ̅-ⲅ̅-ⲗⲏⲕ ? "and be fresh" ("und sei frisch") Bilabel/Grohmann | *l.* δ(εῖνα) : ⲛⲉⲙⲗⲁ̅ Bilabel/Grohmann, Polotsky : or *l.* ⲛ̅ ⲉⲙⲗⲁ "(bite) Emla!" Polotsky ‖ **11** *l.* ⲉⲣⲁⲕ Bilabel/Grohmann | *i.e.* ˢⲟⲩⲟⲟϩⲉ | *i.e.* ⲛ̅-ϩⲣⲟⲟⲩⲧ : ⲛ̇ϩⲟⲧ Bilabel/Grohmann ‖ **12** *i.e.* ˢⲟⲩⲟⲟϩⲉ | *l.* ⲙ̇ⲡ̇ⲣⲁⲛ (dittography) ? ‖ **13** *l.* πν(εῦμ)α ‖ **14** *i.e.* ˢⲡ-†ⲟⲩ | *i.e.* ˢⲉⲛⲧ-ⲁ=ⲩ-ⲧⲟⲕⲥ : ⲛ̇ⲧⲁⲩⲧⲁⲕⲁ[ⲩ] Bilabel/Grohmann : ⲛ̇ⲧⲁⲩⲧⲁⲕⲥ[ⲟⲩ] Polotsky ‖ **15** *l.* χ(ριστό)ς ‖ **17** ⟦ⲉⲛⲧⲁϥ⟧ deleted with horizontal scribbles : ⟦ⲉⲛⲧⲟⲁϥ⟧ Bilabel/Grohmann | ⲛⲉⲧⲭⲁⲧϥ Bilabel/Grohmann ‖ **18** *i.e.* ˢⲛ̅-ⲅ̅-ϭⲱϭ | *i.e.* στῦλος for ξύλον ? *cf.* note ‖ **19** ⲟⲧⲟⲣ ⲉⲓⲛⲓ Bilabel/Grohmann ‖ **20** *i.e.* πιστεύειν (haplography) | ϣⲁⲛⲧⲁⲟⲩϣ Bilabel/Grohmann | ⲁⲛⲁ\ⲕ/ : ⲛ̇ⲙⲁ- Bilabel/Grohmann ‖ **21** *l.* θυ(σία) : ⲟⲩ Bilabel/Grohmann | . . ⲕ̅ⲁ̅ : . . ⲕ̅ⲓ̅ⲁ̅ Bilabel/Grohmann : ⲕⲱⲕⲏⲥ ⲉ̇ⲕⲗⲁⲙ *i.e.* ᴮⲕⲏⲕⲥ̅ ?, ˢⲛ̅ -ⲕⲗⲟⲙ : ⲕⲱⲕ ⲛⲥⲉⲕⲗⲁⲙ (no translation) Bilabel/Grohmann ‖ **21–22** *l.* ⲛ̅-ⲟⲩ-ⲁⲗⲁⲣⲱⲱⲥ *i.e.* العروس *al-ʿarūs* : . . ⲗⲁⲣⲱⲱⲥ Bilabel/Grohmann ‖ **22** *l.* ⲧⲉϥⲥⲓⲙⲓ (dittography)

+ Jesus was walking with *Michael and *Gabriel and *Raphael and the Twelve Apostles and the *Twenty-[Four] Presbyters by the doors of |⁵ Paradise. He found a worm lying, sleeping.

He said to him, "What is the matter with you?"

He said to him, "My Lord Jesus Christ, you were seen, and I was afraid."

He said to him, "By no means, you were not afraid, |¹⁰ but rather arise and go and bite NN ‹child of› NN!"

I adjure you (f.) today, O male scorpion, O female scorpion, in the name {the name} of the Father and the Son and the Holy Spirit! I adjure you (m.) ‹by› the five *nails which pierced |¹⁵ Christ—whose names are *Satōr, Aretō, Tenēt, Ōtera, Rōtas …—that you (f.) pierce him like fire, and you (m.) roast him like firewood?, bring (f.) to him from the south of the earth, do not |²⁰ believe them until I, myself, desire!

Offering?: … 21? scales? from ‹the› crown of a bridegroom ‹who› has not yet gone to his wife.

---

5. ⲟⲩⲃⲏⲛⲧ : **"a worm"** This text seems to be a curse calling upon a worm to attack the victim. The word "worm" (ϥⲛⲧ) has a variety of referents, including the "undying worm" of Mark 9.44–48 which devours sinners after their death, and the worms linked to sickness which consume or are produced by the diseased body. While a scorpion is mentioned later, both scorpions and worms belong to the category of ϫⲁⲧϥⲉ, noxious crawling creatures, creating a fluidity between the two agents of the curse not apparent in the English translation; cf. Dosoo 2022c: 506–508, 526–527.

8–9. Polotsky plausibly proposes to restore the equivalent of the Sahidic ⲛ̄ⲧⲉⲩⲛⲟⲩ ⲛⲧⲁⲓⲛⲁⲩ… ⲙⲡⲉⲣⲣ̄ ϩⲁϯ "the moment I saw (you, I was afraid)… do not be afraid…".

11–12. ⲧⲟⲩⲁϩⲓ · ⲛ̇ϩⲩⲧ ⲧⲟⲩⲁϩⲓ ⲛ̇ⲥ̇ϩⲓⲙⲓ : **"O male scorpion, O female scorpion"** Bilabel/Grohmann translate "the one who loves men, the one who loves women" ("der die Männer liebt, der die Frauen liebt"). For another magical text addressing a scorpion, see *P.MoscowCopt.* 33 (KYP M664).

14. ⲡ̇ϯ ⲛⲓⲃⲧ ⲛ̇ⲧⲁⲩⲧⲁⲕⲥ : **"the five nails which pierced"** Bilabel/Grohmann translate "you who gives the nails which were destroyed (by Christ)".

18. ⲛⲟⲩⲥⲧⲉⲗⲟⲩⲥ : **like firewood?"** The word as written seems to be στῦλος ("pillar"); we suggest an error for the phonetically similar ξύλον ("wood"), defined with the sense of "firewood" in the *Scala Magna* (Macomber 2020: I 129 s.v. ϩⲩⲗⲁ).

19. ⲧⲣⲉⲓⲛⲓ ⲉⲣⲁⲃ ⲉ̇ϫⲓⲛ ⲡⲣⲏⲥ ⲙ̇ⲡⲕⲁϩ : **"bring (f.) to him from the south of the earth"** The object to be brought from the south seems to be missing here, but it may be that ⲉ/ⲉⲣⲟ⸗ is being used to indicate the direct object of ⲉⲓⲛⲉ, contrary to the normal grammar of standard Coptic; in this case, the translation would be "bring him from the south of the earth".

20. ϣⲁⲛⲧⲁⲟⲩⲱϣ ⲁⲛⲁ\ⲕ/ : **"until I, myself, desire"** ⲟⲩⲱϣ here may be an error for ⲱϣ; cf. Kasser CDC 81b s.v. ⲱϣ, and compare Chicago OIM E13767 (Stefanski 1939; KYP M7) ll. 10–11: "until I read ‹it›, myself!" (ϣⲁⲛⲧⲁⲱϣ ⲁⲛⲟⲕ). The idea in this case would be that reading a deposited curse undoes it; cf. Dosoo 2023a: 169.

21–22. ⲕⲱⲕⲏⲥ ⲉ̇ⲕⲗⲁⲙ ⲛⲁⲗⲁⲣⲱⲱⲥ : **"scale from ‹the› crown? of a bridegroom?"** ᴮⲕⲏⲕⲥ̄ may refer to a piece of metal; cf. Numbers 17.3 (16.38; de Lagarde 1867: 358.28) which describes plates (λεπίς, ˢⲃⲏⲧⲉ; Crum CD 101a) made by hammering out bronze pans. The reference here may be to a hammered-out wedding crown from which an applied text is created. The word العروس ("bridegroom") also seems to appear in *PCM* I 33 front l. 10. The crowning of couples during wedding ceremonies is well attested in Mediterranean Christianity (e.g., Burmester 1967: 132–140; Parani 2000: 197–198, 208–210). Presumably the reference to the bridegroom not having gone to his wife means that the marriage has not yet been consummated.

back (at 180° to front)

ⲁⲁⲁ . . . . ⲁ̣ ⲁ̣ⲧⲓⲣⲏⲑⲁ . .
ⲧⲉⲥⲟⲩⲕⲟⲩ ⲡⲣⲕ ⲉⲧϣⲓⲣⲓⲣⲁⲩⲣⲉ
ⲟ . . [ⲉ]ⲧⲉ ⲧⲁⲓ ⲧⲉⲥⲟ̇ⲩ ⲙⲡ ⲉ . ⲟⲗ .
. ⲉ ⲡⲥⲙⲟⲩ ⲉⲡⲏⲣⲡ ⲕ⳨ ⲥⲟⲟⲩ ϩⲉ . ⲉⲛ . ⲧ-
5   ⲃⲧ · ⲛⲁⲓ ⲛⲉ ⲛⲉⲣⲁⲛ ⲱϩⲧ̇ · ⲙⲁⲣⲏ .
ⲙ̣ⲁⲕⲑⲁⲓ ⲥⲉⲑⲣⲟ . . ϥϩⲁⲓ ⲛⲁⲓ ⲉⲡⲃⲓⲧⲉ
ⲕⲥϩⲁⲓ ⲉⲛⲁ̣ⲥ̣ ⲕⲟⲩϣⲧ ⲛⲁⲣⲉⲩ ϣⲏ ⲕⲁⲣⲩ
ⲥⲉⲧ ⲙⲟⲟⲩ ⲥϩⲁⲓ ⲛⲁⲓ ⲙⲁⲣⲟⲩ ⲉⲣⲁⲥ

10

ϭⲱⲃⲓ ⲛ̄ⲕⲏⲧ
ϩⲁ ⲧⲉϥⲁⲡⲏ
ⲟⲩϭⲱⲃⲓ ⲛ̄ϣ
ⲛ̄ⲭⲁⲓⲉⲓⲧ

1–8 Bilabel/Grohmann do not transcribe ‖ **3** *i.e.* ˢⲧ-ⲥⲟⲉ ? ‖ **4** *i.e.* ˢⲛ̄=ⲅ-⳨ ? ‖ **6** *i.e.* ˢⲃⲏⲧⲉ ‖ **7** *i.e.* ˢⲉ=ⲕ-ⲥϩⲁⲓ ? (haplography) or ⲛ=ⲕ̄-ⲥϩⲁⲓ | *i.e.* ˢⲛ̄-ⲁⲗⲁⲩ | *i.e.* ˢϣⲉ ⲛ-ⲕⲁⲣⲩⲁ ? ‖ **8** *l.* ⲉⲛⲁⲥ(ⲥⲁϥⲣⲁⲛ) *i.e.* الزعفران *az-zaʿfarān* ? *cf.* PCM I 25 p. 16 l. 8 ‖ **10** *i.e.* ˢⲕ̄ⲛⲧⲉ ? : ⲛⲕⲛⲧ[ⲉ] Bilabel/Grohmann ‖ **12–13** ⲛ̄ϣ ⲛⲭⲁⲓⲉⲓⲧ perhaps understand ⲛ̄ϣ as error for ⲛⲭ(ⲁⲓⲉⲧ) ? : ⲛⲕⲛ[ⲧⲉ] ⲉⲭⲛ ⲉⲣ . . Bilabel/Grohmann

|^back^ Aaa? ...a? Atirētha ... Tesoukou Prk Etširiraure ... that is, the six? ... the prayer to the wine, and have them drink from? ... |⁵ ... these are the names?: Ōhti Marē... Makthai Sethro ...

Write these ‹things› on the ‹metal› plate and write? with saffron?. White *costus, wood ‹of a› nut? tree?. Pour? water. Write these ‹things›. Bind them to her.

(*kharaktēres*: Z+B♯ΠΛXKΠ K3+ΠCKΛ ⌥)
|¹⁰ ‹A› fig leaf? under his head.

(*kharaktēres*: M+CAMNΛ)
An olive? leaf.

KD, EL, MP & JS, edited from photograph and autopsy; tracings by JS.

Back: The text of the back poses many problems of interpretation; it is unclear how many recipes there are, and how they relate to one another. Lines 1–6 seem to be the spoken formula, which may go with the ritual instructions in ll. 6–8. The mention of binding an object to someone suggests some kind of healing ritual; the use of a female pronoun rather than the generic male referent may suggest a specifically gynecological concern, such as childbirth or uterine bleeding (*cf.* the notes to *PCM* I 2 l. 1). The references to leaves placed under the head of a male individual in ll. 10–13, by contrast, would seem to find their closest parallels in recipes for dream divination found in the second century, such as *GEMF* 16/*PDM* xiv (KYP M162) ll. 1073–1074: "write these things on a reed leaf and place it under your head when you go to sleep; it causes dreams and it sends dreams" (*i-ir≠k sẖ n3y r w^c.t gb3.t n 3qyr mtw≠k ḥ3^c ḥr tp≠k i-ir≠k in qte.t≠k ḥr ir≠f rswe.t mtw≠f hb rswe.t*); *cf.* the similar instructions in *GEMF* 18/*PDM* lxi (KYP M183) ll. 64–67 (albeit with a laurel leaf), and the instructions to place a leaf under the head of a corpse in the dream sending ritual in *GEMF* 17/*PDM* Suppl. (KYP M163) ll. 55–56. These recipes are significantly earlier than that here, however, so it is uncertain how seriously the parallels should be taken.

PCM I 30. Two destructive curses drawing on the *Testament of Solomon*

Arsinoites (Faiyum) ? 22 (H) × 18 (W) cm X–XI CE

Other references: P.Heid.Inv. Kopt. 408; TM 832290; *P.Heid.Kopt.* 4; KYP M43.
Editions: Beck 2018 (*ed. pr.*).
Translations: Beck 2018 (German).
Additional commentary: Seider 1964: 164; Mößner/Nauerth 2015: 305; Love 2022b.
Present location: Heidelberg, Institut für Papyrologie.
Image: https://doi.org/10.11588/diglit.39773
Linguistic description: Sahidic with Middle Egyptian features.
Contents:
 1. Front ll. 1–21: Curse to destroy tools or a workshop (KYP T174)
 2. Front ll. 22–25, back ll. 1–6: Curse to destroy tools or a workshop (KYP T175)

Complete paper sheet preserved in two fragments with the bottom left side missing due to folding. The manuscript is inscribed on the front and back, however most of the back was left blank. The sheet was folded multiple times horizontally; at least 4 horizontal creases and 4 vertical creases are visible.[1] The manuscript was written in a black ink with equal opacity under visible, ultraviolet, and near-infrared light, suggesting a carbon ink.[2] Simple horizontal lines are used to create divisions within the manuscript: a vertical line to divide the tableau (left) from the ritual procedure (right), and two horizontal lines, to divide the instructions from the first formula, and the two formulae from one another. Supralinear strokes are used to indicate *voces magicae* and a few other words, and a colon is occasionally used to separate phrases.

The text is written in a right sloping majuscule, in a largely unimodular and bilinear script. The ⲙ has the very deep curve typical of the "flat μ",[3] and the upper curve of the ⲉ is often reduced or absent. ⲗ, x and ⳉ have decorative serifs on their ascenders, while ⲧ has a serif on the left part of its horizontal bar. ⲥ and ⲗ have very long ascenders, while the ⲩ, ϣ, and ϩ have similarly long descenders. The right vertical stroke of the ⲛ is shorter than the left. The hand is notably similar

---

[1] Beck (2018: 46, n. 8) seems to be in agreement with this analysis, noting that it was folded to form around 16 sections of the same size, with the back on the inside, although as many as 12 horizontal creases seem to be visible on the photograph.

[2] As with all of the information on the inks of the Heidelberg manuscripts, we are grateful to Krisztina Hevesi for sharing her preliminary work on this point with us. For a discussion of inks, see pp. 28, 261.

[3] Mihálykó 2019: 16–18.

to that of *PCM* I 29, leading us to suspect some connection to the Heidelberg Library, even if this cannot be proven. As suggested by Beck,[4] it should probably likewise be dated to the tenth or eleventh century; see the discussion of the very similar hand of *PCM* I 29 for parallels. This manuscript likewise shares the same dialectal features as this group, a form of Sahidic with considerable influence from a Middle Egyptian dialect, likely indicating an origin in the Faiyum.[5]

The manuscript was sold along with a collection of Arabic administrative records and magical texts offered for sale to the Heidelberg University Library by Adolf Grohmann in March 1935 for the price of 175 marks.[6] The items from this collection came from the Faiyum, El-Ashmunein (Hermopolis), and Old Cairo (Al-Fustat); as noted, the linguistic features of this piece make the Faiyum the most likely source of this manuscript.

In terms of contents, the text contains two formulae consisting of curses against property preceded by the instructions for using them. The formulae take the form of dialogues between King Solomon and demons, with the king demanding their names and/or activity, and receiving in response a description of their destructive acts, which are then wished upon the targets of the curses. A comparable question–answer interaction between a Jewish king (in this case, Solomon's father David) and demons is first attested in a fragmentary first-century CE Hebrew manuscript from Qumran containing exorcistic psalms.[7] A developed motif of Solomon's confrontation with Asmodeus, King of the Demons, appears in the Babylonian Talmud (Skolnik 2007: 592a–593b), while a Christian (or christianised) version of the encounter is found in the textual tradition known as the *Testament of Solomon*.[8] The *Testament* describes Solomon's creation of the Jerusalem Temple, in the course of which he receives from the Archangel Michael a ring which enables him to submit demons to him, whom he binds and puts to work on the construction of the temple. In the course of this narrative, he questions the demons as to their names and activities, with the exchanges demonstrating a repetitive structure in which they reveal the diseases or misfortunes they cause, followed by how they may be thwarted; the text thus serves as a handbook for healing and exorcising various conditions of demonic origin. The earliest stages of this composition have

---

[4] Beck 2018: 46

[5] See the introduction to this archive, pp. 261–262 for a fuller description of dialectal features, and pp. 398–399 for a brief discussion of the hand and parallels.

[6] The group consisted of 23 papyri, 4 parchment manuscripts and 3 paper documents; see Seider 1964: 164.

[7] This is 11QPsAp^a; see Puech 2000; Torijano 2002: 43–53. A mention of Solomon in col. 2 l. 2 suggests that similar texts may have already been attributed to him by this time.

[8] For an introduction to the tradition, descriptions and editions of the principal Greek manuscripts, see McCown 1922, with Bailey 2017b for further manuscripts. For a recent English translation with helpful notes, see Duling in Charlesworth 1983: 935–987. For further literature on the *Testament*, see Torijano 2002; Klutz 2005; Busch 2006; Busch 2013; Boustan/Beshay 2015. For Solomon more generally in early ('Gnostic') Coptic texts, see van der Vliet 2013.

been dated as early as the first century CE,⁹ but the first concrete evidence for its existence is in a sixth to seventh-century Greek manuscript preserving chapter 18,¹⁰ in which Solomon questions the stellar demons known as decans. Variant recensions of the Greek text are fully preserved in manuscripts dating from the twelfth to seventeenth centuries, and there are unpublished versions in Arabic (including one in Syriac Garshuni).¹¹ A few other Coptic manuscripts attest to the use of texts extracted from, or based on the *Testament*, albeit in the form of healing prescriptions,¹² and we find similar, albeit much later, texts in Ge'ez and Syriac.¹³ This particular example, in which the original healing purpose has been subverted to create curses, would seem to be unique, but parallels other cases in which the Coptic magical tradition adapts the structure of healing/exorcistic prayers to create agressive spells—compare the love spell based on the *Prayer of Cyprian* (*PCM* I 28); another, as yet unpublished love spell seems to draw on the textual tradition of the *Prayer of Mary 'in Bartos'*.¹⁴ An interesting, albeit very brief, partial parallel to this text is held in the Oxford Griffith Institute; see the notes to the image on the front for a discussion.

---

⁹ Klutz 2005: 108–110; Hartman 2017; *cf.* Schwarz 2007 for a more sceptical perspective, but see the counterargument in Bailey 2017b: 210.

¹⁰ This is *P.Rain.Cent.* 39; see Daniel 1983 & 2013; a re-edition is forthcoming as *GEMF* 87.

¹¹ For the Greek manuscripts, see McCown 1922; Bailey 2017b. For the unpublished Arabic and Syriac Garshuni manuscripts, see Charlesworth 1981: 197; Busch 2013: 11 n. 4.

¹² For Solomon in other Coptic magical texts, see *PCM* I 25 p. 10 ll. 1–18; *PCM* I 36 front col. 1 ll. 13–15; BM EA 10414a (Zellmann-Rohrer 2022a: no. 3 with notes *ad loc.*),

¹³ For Ge'ez texts related to the *Testament*, see *e.g.*, the "Net of Solomon" (መርበብት፡ ሰሎሞን፡ *märbäbtä Sälomon*) and the "Mirror of Solomon" (መጽሔት፡ ሰሎሞን፡ *mäṣḥetä Sälomon*) in Euringer 1929b & 1937 respectively; *cf.* the discussion in Witakowski/Balicka-Witakowska 2013: 225–228. For Syriac, see the "Anathema of King Solomon" (ܚܪܡܐ ܕܡܠܟܐ ܫܠܝܡܘܢ *ḥermā d-malkā Šlēmōn*) in Cherkashina 2021: 148–162.

¹⁴ Montserrat, Abadia Inv. 604 + 1235 (KYP M30). For the Prayer of Mary, see *PCM* I 25.

front

ϭⲓⲛⲉⲣϩⲱⲃ ⲥⲛⲁⲃ ⲉ-
ϣⲣⲱ ⲡⲡⲓⲛⲁϩ ⲛⲁⲗⲉⲥⲟⲩ-
ⲉⲛⲓ ⲓⲁⲁⲩ ⲉⲃⲁⲗ ⲙⲙⲁⲩ
ϭⲓⲁⲩⲛⲓ ⲡⲁⲧϥ ⲉⲡⲣⲁ
5 ⲡⲅ̅ ⲉⲑⲁⲩ ⲁϥϫⲱⲕ
ⲉⲃⲁⲗ

ⲁϥⲉⲝⲥⲱⲙⲱⲗⲱⲕⲉ ⲛϭⲓ ⲥⲱⲗⲱⲙⲱⲛ ⲁϥⲓ ⲛⲁϥ ⲉϩⲟⲩⲛ ⲉϭⲓ ⟦ⲭ⟧
ⲭⲟⲩⲃⲓⲛ ϩⲁⲣⲡⲁⲝ ⲡ[ⲉⲭ]ⲉ̅ ⲥⲱⲗⲱ : ⲛⲁϥ ϫⲉ ⲟⲩ ⲡⲉ ⲡⲉⲕϩⲱⲃ
ⲡⲉϫⲁϥ ⲛⲁϥ ϫⲉ ⲡ[ⲁ]ϩ̣[ⲱⲃ ⲡⲉ ⲡ]ⲧ̅ⲁⲕⲁ ⲙⲡⲓⲉⲣ ⲟⲩⲡⲉⲧⲛⲁⲛ[ⲟⲩϥ]
10 [ⲉ]ⲛⲏϩ ⲉⲣⲉⲛⲉⲑⲁⲩ ⲧ[ⲏⲣⲟ]ⲩ ⲟⲩⲉϩ ⲛⲥⲱⲓ̈ : ⲟⲩⲁⲛⲁⲩⲣⲏϣ
[ϣ]ⲁⲓⲧⲁⲕⲁϥ ⲟⲩⲙⲉⲧ[. .]ⲏ ϣⲁⲓⲧⲁⲕⲁⲥ ⲟⲩⲁⲗⲙⲉⲣⲉ̣ ϣⲁⲓ̈-
[ϣⲁ]ⲃⲉϥ ⲟⲩϣⲁⲗⲁⲩ ϣⲁ[ⲓⲧ]ⲁ̣ⲕⲁϥ ⲟ̣ⲩϭⲱⲙ ϣⲁⲓⲧⲁⲕⲁϥ ⲧⲉⲭ[. ?]-
[ca. 13] ϣⲁⲧⲁⲕⲁϥ ⲟⲩⲁⲡⲱⲑⲏⲕⲉ ϣⲁⲓ̈[ⲧⲁⲕ-]
[ⲁⲥ ca. 13] ⲉⲡⲉⲥⲣⲁ ⲟⲩⲥⲁⲙⲉⲧ ϣⲁⲓⲧⲁⲕⲁⲥ ⲟⲩⲁ-
15 [ca. 16] ⲛ̣ⲡⲣⲟⲙⲉ ϩⲱⲃ ⲛⲓⲙ ⲉⲑⲁⲩ ϣⲁⲉⲓⲛⲧϥ
[ca. 16] ϩ̣ⲁⲙ ⲉ̅ⲥⲁⲛⲁ̅ ⲡⲛⲁϭ ⲧⲁⲛⲁϭ ⲉϭⲁⲙ
[ca. 16 ⲭ]ⲟ̅ⲩⲃⲓⲛ ⲁ̅ⲣ̅ⲡ̅ⲁ̅ⲭ̅ ⲡⲉ ⲡⲁⲣⲁⲛ ⲱ̅ⲣ̅ⲛⲉⲑⲁⲩ
[ⲡⲉ ⲡⲁⲣⲁⲛ ca. 9] : ⲡⲉ ⲡⲁⲣⲁⲛ ⲁ̅ⲣ̅ ⲡⲉ ⲡ̅ⲁ̅ⲣ̅ⲁ̅ⲛ̅ ⲱ̅ⲣ̅ ⲡⲉ ⲡ-
[ⲁⲣⲁⲛ ca. 11 ϩ]ⲱⲃ ⲛⲓⲙ ⲑⲁⲩ ⲉⲧⲉⲕⲉϯ ⲙⲙⲁⲩ ⲙⲙⲁⲓ̈ ϣⲁⲓ̈-
20 [ca. 14 ⲥⲱ]ⲧⲙ ⲉⲣⲁⲓ̈ ⲥ̅ⲁ̅ⲛ̅ⲁ̅ⲧ̅ⲁ̅ⲛ̅ⲗ̅ ⲙⲛ ⲥ̅ⲉⲧⲣⲁⲕ̅
[ca. 16] ⲁ̅ⲓ̅ⲁ̅ ⲓ̅ⲁ̅ ⲧⲁⲭⲏ ⲧⲁⲭⲏ
[ca. 8 ⲥⲱⲗⲱ]ⲙⲱⲛ ⲁϥⲓ ⲛⲁϥ ⲛϭⲓ ⲡⲁⲣⲭⲱⲛ ⲛⲛⲉ-
[ⲇⲁⲓⲙⲱⲛ ⲡⲉϫⲁϥ] ⲛ̣ⲁϥ ϫⲉ ⲛⲓⲙ ⲡⲉ ⲡⲉⲕⲣⲁⲛ ⲡⲉϫⲁϥ ϫⲉ
[ⲃⲉⲣⲥⲉⲃⲟⲗ ⲡⲉ ⲡⲁⲣⲁⲛ] ⲙⲡⲓⲉⲣ ⲟⲩⲡⲉⲧⲛⲁⲛⲟⲩϥ ⲉⲛⲏϩ ⲁ̅ⲗ̅ⲗ̅ⲁ̅
25 [ⲛⲉⲡⲉⲑⲁⲩ ⲧ]ⲏⲣⲟⲩ ⲟⲩⲉϩ ⲛⲥⲱⲓ̈ ⲛⲉⲕⲗⲉⲥⲓⲁ ϣⲁⲓϣⲁⲃⲟⲩ

---

1 *i.e.* ᴱⲥⲛⲟϥ ‖ **1–2** *i.e.* ᴱⲛ̅-ϣⲣⲱ ‖ **2** *i.e.* πίναξ ‖ **2–3** *i.e.* الاسواني *al-aswānī* ‖ **3** *i.e.* ᴱⲉⲓⲁ=ⲩ ‖
4 *i.e.* ᴱⲥⲓⲟⲟⲩⲛ : ⲭⲓⲁⲩⲛⲓ *i.e.* كيواني *kaywānī* "of Saturn" ? *i.e.* lead water ? Beck | *i.e.* ᴱⲡⲁϩⲧϥ |
ⲉⲡⲣⲉ Beck ‖ **5** *i.e.* ᴱⲉⲧ-ϩⲟⲟⲩ ‖ **7** *i.e.* ἐξομολογεῖν | *i.e.* ᴱⲛϭⲓ | ⟦ⲭ⟧ deleted by smudging : ϯ Beck ‖
8 *l.* ⲥⲱⲗⲱ(ⲙⲱⲛ) ‖ **9** ⲟⲩⲧ̅ⲁⲕⲁ Beck ‖ **10** *i.e.* ᴱⲉⲛⲉϩ | *i.e.* النورج *an-nawraǧ* ‖ **11** *i.e.* المرّ *al-marr* ‖
12 *i.e.* ᴱϣⲟϥ= ‖ **13** *i.e.* ἀποθήκη ‖ **15** *i.e.* ᴱⲙ̅-ⲡ-ⲣⲱⲙⲉ ‖ **16** *i.e.* ᴱⲛϭⲟⲙ ‖ **18** *l.* ⲁ̅ⲣ̅(ⲡⲁⲭ) ? | *l.* ⲱ̅ⲣ̅ⲛⲉⲑⲁⲩ ? ‖
19 *l.* ⲉⲑⲁⲩ *i.e.* ᴱⲉⲧ-ϩⲟⲟⲩ | -ⲉϯ *i.e.* αἰτεῖν ‖ **19–20** *i.e.* ϣⲁⲓ̈[ⲁⲁϥ] ? Beck ‖ **21** *i.e.* ταχύ (twice) ‖
22 *l.* [ⲁϥⲉⲝⲥⲱⲙⲱⲗⲱⲕⲉ ⲛϭⲓ ⲥⲱⲗⲱ]ⲙⲱⲛ ? *cf.* l. 7 : [...]ⲟⲛ Beck | *i.e.* ἄρχων ‖ **23** *i.e.* δαίμων ‖
24 *i.e.* ᴱⲉⲛⲉϩ | *i.e.* ἀλλά ‖ **25** *i.e.* ἐκκλησία | *i.e.* ᴱϣⲟϥ= Crum CD 609B

|inside tableau (*kharaktēres*: Ͻ+CXXШΩ⸓) Arpakh (*kharaktēres*: HCΛΑΝⲬ)

Procedure: menstrual blood, *Aswan dish. Wash them off ⟨with⟩ bathwater, pour it at the door. |⁵ The *three evil things. It is finished.

Solomon gave thanks. Khoubin Harpak came in to him. Solomon said to him, "What is your work?" He said to him "My work is destruction. I have never done a good thing, |¹⁰ ever. All evil things follow in my wake. A thresher, I destroy it; a […] I destroy it; a shovel, I lay waste to it; a water-wheel, I destroy it; a garden, I destroy it; … I destroy it; a storehouse; I destroy it; … to its door. A water-tank, I destroy it; a… |¹⁵ […] of the man, everything that is evil, I bring it […] power, Esana the great, my? great power […] Khoubin Arpakh is my name, Ōrnethau [is my name …] is my name, Ar⟨pakh?⟩ is my name, Ōr⟨nethau?⟩ is [my name …] everything that is evil that you ask of me, I … |²⁰ […] listen? to me, *Sanataēl and Setrak […] Yea, yea! Quickly, quickly!

[…] Solomon. The ruler of the [demons] came to him […] he said, "What is your name?" He said, ["Beelzebub is my name,] I have never done a good thing, ever, but rather |²⁵ all [evil things] follow in my wake. Churches, I lay waste to them,

Image, 8 et al. (H)arpakh: A similar name, Ἅρπαξ (Harpax) appears in the Greek *Testament of Solomon* (18.32P; McCown 1922: 57*) and the Coptic *Confession of Cyprian* (Bilabel/Grohmann 1934: 75 II.26–29). The demon is depicted here as a stylised bird-like figure within a circle (*cf.* Love 2022b: 697–699), perhaps representing the dish upon which it is to be copied using menstrual blood in the following procedures. For the cross on its head, *cf.* Masbēn on *PCM* I 25 p. 10, another Solomonic demon. A similar bird-headed, three-toed (*cf.* Vilozny 2015: 142) figure with an axe appears in Crum 23.2.2 (Love 2022b; KYP M570), surrounded by *voces magicae* with parallels to the text discussed here, including ⲭⲱⲃⲓⲛ (2.1), ⲁⲗⲡⲁⲕ (2.2), and the phrase ⲁⲃⲉϩⲟⲙⲟⲗⲟⲅⲓ ("he gave thanks"; 3.6; *cf.* l. 7 of this text); see Love 2022b; Dosoo 2022a: 127–128.

7. ⲁϥⲉⲭⲥⲱⲙⲱⲗⲱⲕⲉ ⲛϭⲓ ⲥⲱⲗⲱⲙⲱⲛ : "Solomon gave thanks" *Cf. Testament of Solomon* 1.5: "And on hearing this I, King Solomon, went into the sanctuary of God and prayed with all my soul, giving thanks to him night and day, that the demon might be delivered into my hands and I might gain authority over him" (Καὶ ταῦτα ἀκούσας ἐγὼ ὁ βασιλεὺς Σολομῶν εἰσῆλθον εἰς τὸν ναὸν τοῦ θεοῦ καὶ ἐδεήθην ἐξ ὅλης μου τῆς ψυχῆς ἐξομολογούμενος αὐτῷ νύκτα καὶ ἡμέραν ὅπως παραδοθῇ ὁ δαίμων εἰς τὰς χεῖράς μου καὶ ἐξουσιάσω αὐτόν; McCown 1922: 9*–10*); *cf.* the note to the image.

3–4. ⲙⲙⲁⲩ ⲥⲓⲁⲅⲛⲓ̈ : "bathwater" "Bath" (ⲥⲓⲟⲟⲩⲛ) likely refers to a collective bathhouse (Greek βαλανεῖον, Arabic حمام *ḥammām*; *cf.* Macomber 2020: I 110; Crum CD 369b); *cf.* Cairo JdE 45060 (Kropp 1931: I no. K; KYP M303) front ll. 25, 37–38, which mentions the "furnace" (ⲉⲛⲧⲱⲕⲉ *cf.* Crum CD 404b) of a bath. Bathwater is used in several other Coptic and *Copto-Arabic curses; see BM EA 10391 (Zellmann-Rohrer 2022a: no. 1; KYP M302) back l. 95; Cairo JdE 42573 (Chassinat 1955; KYP M44) p. 2 l. 7; *Guide to the Psalms* Psalms 7, 17, 51, 78, 88, 98, 108 (Henein/Bianquis 1975); *cf.* drainwater in *PCM* I 31 back ll. 16–17; *PCM* I 32 p. 1 l. 23; *PCM* I 37 back ll. 5, 20. For bathhouses as liminal spaces inhabited by demons, see Bonner 1932; Dunbabin 1989; Alfayé 2016.

14. List of evil works: For similar curses against work equipment, see *PCM* I 37 back 21–23 (for a furnace), Cairo JdE 42573 (Chassinat 1955; KYP M44) p. 1 ll. 21–23 (for a water-wheel), and the Syro- and Judaeo-Arabic curses against mills edited in Cherkashina/Cherkashin/Saar 2022.

17. ⲱⲣⲛⲉⲑⲁⲩ : "Ōrnethau" *Cf.* Ornias (Ὀρνίας), the first demon encountered by Solomon in the *Testament*, perhaps modified by the relative phrase "who is evil" (ˢⲉⲧ-ϩⲟⲟⲩ).

22–24. Compare the *Testament of Solomon* 3.6V: "I am Beelzebub, the ruler of the demons" (ἐγώ εἰμι ὁ Βεελζεβοὺλ τῶν δαιμονίων ὁ ἄρχων; McCown 1922: 17*).

back

[ca. 10]ϣⲁⲓϣⲁⲃⲟⲩ ⲛⲉⲙⲁⲛⲉⲣϩⲱⲃ ϣⲁⲓϣⲁⲃⲟⲩ
[ca. 5 ⲡⲑⲣⲟⲛ]ⲟⲩ ⲛⲟⲩⲁⲗⲁⲙⲡⲉ ⲡⲉϫⲁϥ ⲛϭⲓ ⲃⲉⲣⲥⲉⲃⲟⲗ
[ⲡⲁⲣⲭⲱⲛ ⲛⲛⲉⲇⲁⲓ]ⲙⲱⲛ : ϯⲱⲣⲕ ⲉⲣⲁⲕ ⲙⲡⲟⲩϫⲁⲓ ⲙⲡⲓⲥⲟⲩ
[ca. 8 ϫⲉⲕⲁ]ⲁⲥ ⲉⲕⲃⲱⲕ ϣⲁ ⲛⲓⲙ ⲡⲭ̄ⲥ̄ ⲛⲓⲙ ⲉⲕⲓⲛⲉ
5 [ca. 12]ⲁⲩ ⲁⲣⲁⲕ ⲙⲛ ⲟⲩϣⲱⲃ ⲙⲛ̄ ⲟⲩϫⲱⲱⲣⲉ ⲃⲁⲗ
[ca. 12]ⲕ ⲉⲣⲁϥ ⲇⲓⲁ ⲓⲁ ⲧⲁⲭⲏ ⲧⲁⲭⲏ

---

1 [*ca.* 14] Beck | *i.e.* ᔆϣⲟϥ= Crum CD 609B ‖ **2** *i.e.* θρόνος | [*ca.* 15] ⲟⲩ Beck | *i.e.* الأنبا *al-anbā* : Beck does not translate ‖ **3** *i.e.* δαίμων : [*ca.* 16] ⲛ̄ⲱⲛ Beck | ⲙⲡⲓⲥⲟⲩ *i.e.* ᔆⲙ̄-ⲡ-ⲥⲟⲟⲩ c corrected from unclear letter by overwriting : ⲙⲡⲕⲟⲩ Beck ‖ **4** [*ca.* 16]ⲁⲥ Beck | ⲉⲕ- *i.e.* ᔆⲛ̄=ⲅ- (twice) | *i.e.* (υἱός) ‖ **5** [*ca.* 16] Beck | *i.e.* ᔆⲉⲃⲟⲗ (haplography of ⲉ) : ⲃ Beck ‖ **6** [*ca.* 16] Beck | *i.e.* ᔆⲁⲓⲟ (twice) (haplography of ⲁ) | *i.e.* ταχύ (twice)

[...] I lay waste to them; workshops, I lay waste to them; [... the] seat? of an *anba*. Beelzebub, [the ruler of the demons,] said "I adjure you by the *wellbeing of the six? [...] that you go to NN, the son of NN, and you bring |⁵ [...] to you?, and devastation and annihilation [...] to him, yea, yea, quickly, quickly!"

KD, EL & MP, edited from photograph.

---

2. [ⲡⲉⲣⲟⲛ]ⲟⲩ ⲛⲟⲩⲁⲗⲁⲙⲡⲉ : "[the] seat? of an *anba*" We are grateful to Marijn van Putten for his suggestion to read الأنبا (*al-anba*) here. This title derives from the Coptic ⲁⲡⲁ (*apa*, Greek ἄπα), in turn from the Aramaic אבא ('*abbā*, "father") via Greek ἀββᾶ (cf. Mark 14.36; Romans 8.15; Galatians 4.6). Originally a title of respect for ecclesiastical and monastic figures, by the sixth century *apa* was also applied to important secular individuals (Wipszycka/Derda 1994). The Arabic *anba* has a narrower meaning, being used as only for bishops (including metropolitans and the patriarch) and saints (Graf 1954: 14; Badawi/Hinds 1986: 34). A form close to the Arabic is attested in Coptic as ⲁⲛⲃⲁ by the tenth/eleventh century, when it is found in P.Col.inv. 597 l. 25 (Walter 2022: no. 4) and P.CtYBR inv. 2123 l. 6 (unpublished; we thank Vincent Walter for bringing this text to our attention). In the latter manuscript the addressee is explicitly a bishop (ⲉⲡⲓⲥⲕⲱⲡⲟⲥ, l. 4), and the referent here should probably likewise be understood as such. The preceding word is likely a Greek loanword whose nominative form ends in -ος or -ον; compare ἄγγελος as ⲁⲅⲅⲉⲗⲟⲩ in *PCM* I 25 p. 3 l. 4 (we thank Frederic Krueger for discussing this point with us). If we understood *anba* as referring to a saint here, we might restore ⲧⲟⲡⲟⲩ ("place, shrine") or ⲙⲟⲛⲁⲥⲧⲏⲣⲓⲟⲩ ("monastery"), but in this case we would expect the Coptic ⲡⲉⲧⲟⲩⲁⲁⲃ or ϩⲁⲅⲓⲟⲥ to more clearly designate a saint. We propose θρόνος "throne, seat", used to refer to the throne upon which bishops were seated during their ordination, representing their authority; compare καθέδρα (*kathedra*), "seat", whence "cathedral", the church in which the bishop's throne is situated. For instances of ⲑⲣⲟⲛⲟⲥ used to refer to the episcopal seat in Coptic, see the *Life of Aaron* (VI–VII CE; CC 255; Dijkstra/van der Vliet 2019: 108.5, 112.31, cf. discussion on p. 224–225, and pp. 57–60 for the dating); John the Presbyter, *Life of Pisentius* (VII CE?; CC 238; Budge 1913: 91.34, 92.8 *etc*.), 280 (trans)); Pseudo-Flavianus of Ephesus, *On Demetrius and Peter of Alexandria* (VII–VIII CE?; CC 155; Budge 1914: 140.21, 23 *etc.*, translation p. 393); *SB Kopt.* I 719 l. 11 (862 CE). The threat posed to the throne by the demon would offer a parallel to the mention of the church (ἐκκλησία) on front l. 25.

2. ⲃⲉⲣⲥⲉⲃⲟⲗ : "Beelzebub" *Cf.* the notes to front ll. 22–24.

PCM I 31. Two separation spells

Arsinoites (Faiyum) ?	45 (H) × 9.5 (W) cm	X–XI CE

Other references: P.Heid.Äg.Slg.inv. Kopt. 1030; TM 113762; KYP M366; Bélanger Sarrazin #147.
Editions: Stegemann 1938 (*ed. pr.*) [S].
Translation: Stegemann 1938 (German).
Additional commentary: Grumach 1970: 173; Dosoo 2018: 31–46.
Present location: Formerly belonged to the Ägyptologische Sammlung, Heidelberg.
Image: Lost, only tracings of images survive (Stegemann 1938: 77, 79).
Linguistic description: Sahidic with Middle Egyptian influence.
Contents:
   1. Front ll. 1–47: Separation spell (KYP T188)
   2. Back ll. 1–28: Separation spell (KYP T185)

A formulary written on a paper rotulus, acquired for the Egyptological Institute of the University of Heidelberg by Carl Schmidt in 1934, but since lost; it may have been one of the manuscripts which went missing following the Second World War.[1] Stegemann describes some abrasion to the first three lines of front, and some damage on the left side of the manuscript. Stegemann dated the text to the eleventh century based on the other manuscripts from the Heidelberg collection (*PCM* I 21–33) with which it shares several notable similarities. We suggest a more cautious tenth- to eleventh-century dating. The hand—insofar as can be gauged from the surviving letters in the tableaux—is an informal, undecorated sloping majuscule, with a very flat ϻ and y-shaped ϥ, perhaps broadly similar to the hands of *PCM* I 29 & 30. The copyist uses supralineation primarily to mark abbreviations, and frequently uses diaeresis on ι, ϥ, and even some consonants, in this last case alternating with single dots. The mid-dot, sparely used, is the only other form of punctuation, although decorated dividing lines are used to separate text sections. Frequent words (such as ⲁⲓⲟ, ⲧⲁⲭⲏ) often have their final letters raised, a trait also seen in *PCM* I 28 (*e.g.*, p. 13 ll. 12–13). The dialect is the same form of Sahidic, heavily influenced by a Middle Egyptian dialect, found in the 'Heidelberg Coptic Magical Library' (see the description on pp. 261–262), suggesting a similar Faiyumic origin for this manuscript.

As the manuscript is lost, we rely almost entirely on the edition of Stegemann for the Coptic text, occasionally suggesting alternative readings where these seem plausible to us. The images are likewise reproduced from Stegemann's tracings.

---

[1] Stegemann 1938: 74; Seider 1964: n. 85; Jördens 2015: 11 n. 55; *cf.* p. 325.

front

[. ?] . . . ⲛⲉϣⲡⲉⲣⲉⲛⲗ
[. ?]ⲡⲉⲣϩⲓⲛⲉⲃ · ⲃⲉⲗⲥⲟ-
[ⲃⲟ]ⲩⲗ ⲡⲉϫ̄ⲱⲣ † ⲙⲟⲥ†
[. ?] ⲡⲱⲣⲝ † ϫⲱⲣ ⲉⲃⲟⲗ
5 † ⲙⲉⲧⲁⲧⲥⲙⲟⲩ † ⲙⲉⲧ-
ⲟⲩⲁϩⲥ ϩⲓⲧⲉ ⲧⲙⲉ† ⲁ̄ⲁ̄
ⲓ̄ⲥ̄ ⲁ̄ⲁ̄ ⲉⲃⲙⲉⲥⲧⲱⲱⲥ
ⲉⲛⲑⲉ ⲣⲉⲇⲓ̈ⲁⲃⲱⲗⲱⲥ
ⲙⲁⲥ† ⲙⲟⲩⲇⲓⲕⲏⲱⲥ
10 ⲁⲩⲱ ⲉⲕⲡⲱⲣⲝ ⲉⲛⲙⲟⲟⲩ
ⲉⲃⲟⲗ ⲉⲛ̄ⲛⲉⲩⲉⲣⲉⲩ ⲉⲛⲑ ⲛ̄-
ⲓⲱⲥⲛ̇ϥ · ⲙⲛ̄ⲃⲥⲛⲏⲩ ⲉⲕ-
ⲡⲱⲣⲝ ⲉⲃⲟⲗ ⲛⲓⲙ ⲓ̄ⲥ̄ ⲙⲛ
ⲁ̄ⲁ̄ ⲉⲛⲑⲉ ⲛ̄ⲡⲇⲓ̈ⲁⲃⲱⲗ-
15 ⲱⲥ ⲉⲛⲧⲁϥ̄ⲡⲁⲣⲝⲉⲃ
ⲉⲃⲟⲗ ⲉⲡⲛⲟⲩⲧⲉ ⲙⲛ ⲛ-
[[ⲡ]]ⲁⲅⲅⲉⲗⲟⲥ ⲉⲕⲉⲧⲟⲩⲛ-
ⲟⲩⲥ ϩⲓϫⲱϥ ⲛⲟⲩⲭⲓⲙⲟⲛ
ⲉⲛⲑⲉ ⲛ̄ⲛⲉⲓⲟⲩⲇⲁⲓ ⲉⲛ̄-
20 ⲙⲡⲓⲟⲩⲁⲉⲓϣ ⲉⲕϣⲱⲃ
ⲉⲡⲉϥⲛⲓ ⲉⲑ ⲛ̄ⲡⲁ ⲓ̈ⲩⲟⲩ-
ⲧⲁⲥ ⲧⲉⲕϫⲱⲣ ⲉⲃⲟⲗ
ⲉⲛⲡⲉⲧⲉⲛⲧⲉⲃ ⲉⲛ-
ⲑ ⲛ̄ⲡϣⲁⲉⲓϣ ⲉⲙⲡⲁⲥ-
25 ⲉⲃⲏⲥ ⲉⲕⲓⲛⲉ ϫⲱϥ
ϩⲉⲛϩⲓⲥⲉ ⲙⲛ ϩⲛⲉⲙ-
ⲕⲁϩ ⲉⲙⲉϩⲁⲟⲩ ⲧⲉ . . ⲩ̄
ⲉⲛ ⲉⲛⲡⲉⲃⲱⲛⲁϩ̄ ⲁ[. .]
ⲙⲁⲣⲉⲡⲁϣⲗⲏⲗ ⲉⲓ ⲉ-
30 ϩⲣⲁⲓ ϣⲁⲣⲁⲕ ⲧⲁⲙⲓ-
[ⲧ]ⲁ̇ⲛⲓⲁ ⲉⲓ ⲡⲉⲕⲉ[ⲙ]ⲧⲟ

---

2 *i.e.* ˢⲙ̄ⲡⲉⲣ-ϩⲓⲛⲏⲃ ? || **3**]ϫ̣ⲗ S | *i.e.* ˢⲡ-ⲉⲧ-ϫⲱⲱⲣⲉ : "scattering" ("Zerstreuung") S || **4** *i.e.* ˢⲡⲱⲣ̄ⲝ || **5–6** *i.e.* ˢⲙⲛ̄ⲧ-ⲱϩ̄ⲥ̄ ? || **6** *i.e.* ˢϩⲓⲧⲛ | *i.e.* ˢⲙⲏⲧⲉ | *l.* δ(ε)ῖ(να) δ(ε)ῖ(να) || **7** *l.* υ(ἰό)ς | *l.* δ(εῖνα) δ(εῖνα) | *i.e.* ˢⲛ̄=ϥ-ⲙⲉⲥⲧⲱ=ⲥ || **8** *i.e.* ˢⲛ-ⲧ-ϩⲉ ⲉⲣⲉ-ⲡ-ⲇⲓάβολος (haplography) || **9** *i.e.* ˢⲛ-ⲟⲩ-δίκαιος || **10** *i.e.* ˢⲛ̄=ⲅ-ⲡⲱⲣ̄ⲝ : *i.e.* ˢⲉ=ⲕ-ⲉ-ⲡⲱⲣ̄ⲝ S | *i.e.* ˢⲙ̄ⲙⲟⲟⲩ || **11** *i.e.* ˢⲛ̄-ⲧ-ϩⲉ || **12** *i.e.* ˢⲙⲛ ⲛⲉ=ϥ-ⲥⲛⲏⲩ (haplography) || **12–13** *i.e.* ˢⲛ̄=ⲅ-ⲡⲱⲣ̄ⲝ || **13** *i.e.* υ(ἰό)ς || **14** *l.* δ(ε)ῖ(να) δ(ε)ῖ(να) | *i.e.* ˢⲛ-ⲧ-ϩⲉ || **14–15** *i.e.* διάβολος || **15** *i.e.* ˢⲡⲣ̄ⲝ=ϥ || **17** *i.e.* ἄγγελος || **18** *i.e.* χειμών || **19** *i.e.* ˢⲛ̄-ⲧ-ϩⲉ | *i.e.* Ἰουδαῖος || **20** *i.e.* ˢⲛ̄=ϥ-ϣⲱⲃ || **21** *i.e.* ˢⲛ̄-ⲧ-ϩⲉ || **21–22** *i.e.* Ἰούδας || **23** *i.e.* ˢⲙ̄-ⲡⲉⲧⲉ-ⲟⲩⲛⲧⲁ=ϥ : ˢⲙ̄-ⲡⲉⲧ=ⲛ̄ⲧ=ϥ "the one who brought him" ("den, der ihn brachte") S || **23–24** *i.e.* ˢⲛ̄-ⲧ-ϩⲉ || **24–25** *i.e.* ἀσεβής || **25** *i.e.* ˢⲉ=ⲕ-ⲉ-ⲉⲓⲛⲉ || **26–27** *i.e.* ˢϩⲉⲛ-ⲙ̄ⲕⲁϩ || **27** *i.e.* ˢⲛ̄-ⲛ̄-ϩⲟⲟⲩ | *l.* ⲧⲉ[ⲣⲟ]ⲩ || **28** *i.e.* ˢⲙ̄-ⲡⲉϥ-ⲱⲛϩ (dittography) || **30–31** *i.e.* ˢⲛⲧⲉ-ⲧⲁ-μετάνοια *cf. PCM* I 26 p. 15 ll. 17–18 || **31** *i.e.* ˢⲉ-ⲡⲉ=ⲕ-ⲙ̄ⲧⲟ

... do not⁷ sleep! Beelzebub⁷, you who annihilates, cause hatred! ... separation! Cause annihilation! |⁵ Cause unblessedness! Cause a reaping⁷ between NN, son of NN, ⟨and NN, child of NN,⟩ so that he hates her like ⟨the⟩ Devil hates a righteous man, |¹⁰ and separate them from one another like Joseph and his brothers, and separate NN, son ⟨of NN⟩, and NN, child of NN, like the Devil, |¹⁵ who separated himself from God and the angels! You will raise a storm upon him like the Jews |²⁰ in that time, and lay waste to his house like that of Judas, and annihilate his possessions like the dust of the impious, |²⁵ and bring upon him sufferings and pains for all the days of {of} his life! Let my prayer come to |³⁰ you, and my⁷ repentance⁷ come before you,

---

4. ⲡⲱⲣⲉϫ : "**separation**" We might expect to restore † before this word, but Stegemann notes that the traces do not allow such a restoration.

13. ⲛⲓⲙ ⲩ̄ⲥ : "**NN, son**" The scribe has omitted a second ⲛⲓⲙ. Note that in this manuscript we reproduce the abbreviation for "son" (υἱός) as ⲩ̄ⲥ, following Stegemann's transcription, but it likely resembled the sign ⲩ̄ used in the other manuscripts of similar date (cf. p. 33–34 and the index of abbreviations s.v. υἱός).

23. ⲉⲛⲡⲉⲧⲉⲛⲧⲉϥ : "**his possessions**" For this unusual form, see the notes to *PCM* I 25 p. 4 l. 16.

front (continued)

32 ⲉⲃⲟⲗ ⲉⲓⲥ ï̈ⲏⲓϩⲥⲭⲟ[...]
ⲡⲉⲗϩⲱⲃ ⲉⲛⲧё[...]
ⲙⲛ ⲛⲉⲥⲁϩ[...]
35 ⲁⲓ° ⲁⲓ° ⲧⲁ︦ⲭ︦ⲏ ⲧⲁⲭⲏ
ⲅⲣ ⲙⲟⲩ ⲛⲉϭⲉï̈ ⲥⲛⲉϥ
ⲙϭⲱⲗϭⲉ̅ⲗ̅ⲱ̅ ϫⲱⲙⲉ
ⲛⲁⲛⲙ̅ⲟ̅ⲩ̅ ϭⲱϣ ⲩ̅ ⲉϑⲱ .
ⲉⲁⲁⲃ ⲉⲃⲟⲗ ⲙⲙⲟⲟⲩ ⲛⲉ[..]
40 ⲡⲁϩⲧⲏϥ ⲡ̅ⲣ̅ⲟ̅ ⲧⲁⲙⲉϥ

41 ϣⲁⲣϣⲁⲣ
42 ⲟⲩⲙⲁ-
43 ⲥ†ⲟⲩ-
44 ⲭⲱⲣ
45 ⲉⲃⲟⲗ
46 ⲉϥϣⲱϥ
47 ⲡⲁⲡⲉϩⲁⲩ

---

32 *l.* ⲉ-ⲓ(ⲏⲥⲟⲩ)ⲥ ⲡⲉ-ⲭ(ⲣⲓⲥⲧⲟ)ⲥ ? : "behold" ("Siehe") S || ï̈ⲏⲓ : *l.* ⲁⲓⲟ ? S || **33** *i.e.* ᔆⲙ̅ⲡⲉⲣ-ϩⲱⲃ or ᔆⲙ̅ⲡⲉⲣ-ⲣ̅ ϩⲱⲃ ? || **34** ⲛⲉⲥⲁϩ or ⲛⲉⲥⲁϩ ? S || **35** *i.e.* ταχύ || **36** *l.* γρ(άφειν) | *i.e.* ᔆⲛ̅-ⲛϭⲉ : *i.e.* ᔆϭⲁⲓ followed by ⲓⲥ S || **38** *i.e.* ᔆⲛ̅-ἀμνός ⲛ̅-ⲉϭⲱϣ ? *cf.* note : S does not translate || *i.e.* ⲅ ᔆⲉⲧ-ϩⲟⲟⲩ ? : S does not translate || **39** *i.e.* ᔆⲉⲓⲁⲁ=ϥ | *l.* ⲛⲉ[ϭⲉⲓⲓ] ? || **40** *i.e.* ᔆⲡⲁϩⲧ=ϥ̅ | *i.e.* ᔆⲉ-ⲡⲣⲟ || **47** ⲡⲁⲡⲉϩⲁⲩ *l.* ⲡⲉⲧϩⲁⲩ or ⲡⲁ ⲡⲧϩⲁⲩ ?

Jesus? Christ? ... do not send? ... and the ... |³⁵ yea, yea, quickly, quickly!

Write ‹with› leek? water ‹and› bat blood ‹on a› sheet of Ethiopian? lamb?‹skin›. ‹Offering:› *three? evil? ‹things›. Wash off with [leek?] water. |⁴⁰ Pour it ‹at› the door. Bury it.

|⁴¹, *above left figure* Šaršar

|⁴², *inside right figure* A hatred, a separation |⁴⁶, *below right figure* which is laid waste, which is evil?.

---

38. ⲛⲁⲛⲙⲟⲩ ⲋⲱϣ : "Ethiopian? lamb?‹skin›" Here we tentatively propose to understand ⁵ⲛ̄-ἀμνός ⲛ̄-ⲉϭⲱϣ. ⲁⲙⲛⲟⲥ with the meaning of a "lamb" (الخروف *al-ḥarūf*) occurs in the *Scala Magna* (Macomber 2020: I 121). For "Ethiopian animals", *cf.* ϭⲁⲓⲙⲉ ⲛⲉϭⲱϣ in Crum CD 818a. The use of parchment made from the skin of a lamb or kid (ἀρνίον, ἐρίφιον) is attested in Mediaeval Greek magic; *e.g.*, Athens, National Library of Greece 1265 fol. 15r (XVI/XVII CE; Delatte 1927: 14.8).
Image: The image here follows a common construction for curses of separation, in which two figures are depicted standing back to back, symbolising their regard being turned away from each other; this seems to represent visually in two dimensions a ritual process known from Coptic and Arabic texts, as well as Greek archaeological remains. *Cf.* the image on the back of this manuscript, and the ritual described in *PCM* I 27 front ll. 19–22, and the discussions in Dosoo 2018: 23–51; Dosoo 2023a: 164, 174, 178. There seem to be two short strings of linear kufic to the left of the left-hand figure; see the notes to *PCM* I 21 ll. 1– for a discussion. Note that the letter † here, and in the tableau on the back, seems to have decorations resembling the circles often used to decorate *kharaktēres*.

back

::==::==::————·

ⲡⲣⲓⲙⲡⲣⲓⲙ ⲡϣⲏ[ⲣⲉ ⲛ]
ⲕⲛⲱⲫⲟⲥ ⲡⲣⲉϥⲙ[ⲁⲥϯ]
ⲡⲣⲉϥϯⲧⲱⲛ ⲡⲣⲉϥ-
ϯ ⲃⲁⲧⲥϩⲁ ⲧⲟⲟⲩⲛ ϯ
5 ⲧⲟⲩⲧⲱⲛ ϯ ⲙⲓϣⲉ ϯ ⲃⲁⲧ-ᶜ
ϩⲁ ⲉⲧⲙⲉϯ ⲇ̅ⲇ̅ ⲉϥⲙⲉⲥ-
ⲧⲱⲟⲥ ⲉⲛⲑⲏ ⲛⲟⲩⲣ̇ⲓⲣ̇ ⲙⲛ
ⲟⲩϩⲁⲣ̇ ⲉⲛⲑⲉ ⲛ̅ⲙⲧⲁⲡⲗⲁ-
ⲟⲥ ⲙ̅ⲛⲓⲟⲩⲇⲁⲓ̈ ⲙⲓⲉⲥⲧ ⲓ̅ⲥ̅
10 ⲉⲕⲉϯ ⲙⲁⲥϯ ⲙⲛ ⲟⲩⲡ-
ⲱⲣⲉⲭ ⲉⲧⲙⲉϯ ⲙ̅ⲇ̅ⲇ̅
ⲩ̅ⲥ̅ ⲇ̅ⲇ̅ ⲙⲛ ⲟⲩⲃⲁⲥⲧϩⲁ
ⲛⲉⲃϩⲁ ⲧⲏⲣⲟⲩ ⲁⲓᵒ ⲁⲓᵒ
ⲧⲁⲭᴴ ⲧⲁⲭᴴ ——··—··——
15 ⲅ̅ⲣ̅ ⲥⲛⲟϥ ⲉϣⲣⲱ ⲉⲩⲡⲓ-
ⲛⲁⲕⲉⲥ ⲓⲥⲟⲩⲉⲛ ⲙⲟᵒⲩ
ⲛⲁⲟⲩⲉⲛ ⲑⲁⲟⲩ ⲟ̅ⲩ̅ ⲅ̅
ⲉⲑⲟⲟⲩ ⲅⲣ ⲉⲩⲭⲱⲱⲙⲉ ·
ⲛⲁⲩⲭⲟⲥ ⲧⲁⲙⲥⲉϥ ϩⲉ ⲡⲣᵒ
20 ⲉⲣⲉ☙ ⲭⲁⲭⲉϥ

2 or ⲡⲣⲉϥⲙ[ⲟⲥϯ] ? S || **4** *i.e.* ˢⲃⲁⲥⲧ-ϩⲟ *cf.* note to *PCM* I 22 l. 45 | *i.e.* ˢⲧⲱⲟⲩⲛ ? ||
5 *l.* ϯⲧⲱⲛ ? || **6** *i.e.* ˢⲉ-ⲧ-ⲙⲏⲧⲉ || **5–6** *i.e.* ˢϯ ⲃⲁⲥⲧ-ϩⲟ *cf.* l. 4 : *l.* ⲃⲁⲧⲥ ϩⲁⲧⲟⲟⲩ *i.e.* ᴮⲃⲱⲧⲥ
+ ϩⲁ ? S || **6, 12** *l.* δ(ε)ῖ(να) δ(ε)ῖ(να) || **6–7** *i.e.* ˢⲛ̅-ϥ-ⲙⲉⲥⲧⲱ=ⲥ : *i.e.* ˢⲉ=ϥ-ⲉ-ⲙⲉⲥⲧⲱ=ⲥ S ||
7 *i.e.* ˢⲛ̅-ⲧ-ϩⲉ || **8** *i.e.* ˢⲟⲩ-ⲟⲩϩⲟⲣ | *i.e.* ˢⲛ̅-ⲧ-ϩⲉ || **8–9** *i.e.* ˢⲉⲛⲧ-ⲁ-ⲡ-ⲗⲁⲟⲥ || **9** *i.e.* ˢⲛ̅-ⲛ-Ἰⲟⲩⲇⲁⲓⲟⲥ |
i.e. ˢⲙⲉⲥⲧⲉ- | *l.* Ἰ(ⲏⲥⲟⲩ)ⲥ̅ || **11** *l.* δ(εῖνα) δ(εῖνα) || **11** *i.e.* ˢⲙⲏⲧⲉ || **12** *l.* υ(ἱό)ς | *i.e.* ˢⲃⲁⲥⲧ-
ϩⲟ *cf.* l. 4 : *l.* ⲃⲁⲧⲥ ϩⲁⲧⲟⲟⲩ *i.e.* ᴮⲃⲱⲧⲥ + ϩⲁ ? S || **13** *i.e.* ˢϩⲟⲟⲩ ? || **14** *i.e.* ταχύ (twice) ||
15 *l.* γρ(άφειν) || **15–16** *i.e.* πίναξ || **16** *i.e.* ˢⲛ̅-ⲥⲟⲩⲁⲛ : ⲓⲥ ⲟⲩⲟⲛ "... something" ("... etwas") ? S ||
17 *i.e.* ˢⲛ̅-ⲟⲩⲉⲓⲛ | *i.e.* ˢⲉⲧ-ϩⲟⲟⲩ | *l.* θυ(σία) | ⊢ S || **18** *l.* γρ(άφειν) || **18–19** *i.e.* ἤ ˢⲉ-ⲩ-ⲕⲉⲥ ? *cf.* note to
PCM I 37 front l. 2 : S does not translate || **19** *i.e.* ˢϩⲓ || **20** *l.* (ⲡⲟⲟϩ) || **27–28** ϯ ·· ⲥϯ S

Primprim, the son of Knōphos, the hater, the quareller, the giver of hatefulness, arise, cause |⁵ quarrel, cause conflict, cause hatefulness between NN, child of NN, ⟨and NN, child of NN⟩, so that he hates her like a pig and ⟨a⟩ dog, like the Jewish people hated Jesus! |¹⁰ May you cause hatred and separation between NN, son of NN, ⟨and NN, child of NN⟩, and hatefulness all his days, yea, yea, quickly, quickly!

|¹⁵ Write ⟨with⟩ menstrual blood on an *Aswan dish. Putrid drain water. Offering: *three evil ⟨things⟩. Write on a sheet or a bone?. Bury it at the door |²⁰ when the moon wanes.

|²¹, *above two left figures* Prim Prim

|²², *above right figure* Baroukh

|²³ *inside figures* Cause hatred! |²⁵ Cause hatred! Cause hatred!

KD, EL & MP, edited from Stegemann's transcript, tracings from Stegemann.

7–8. ⲉⲛⲉϩ ⲛⲟⲩⲣⲓⲣ ⲙⲛ ⲟⲩϩⲁⲣ : "**like a pig and ⟨a⟩ dog**" This analogy finds a parallel in a separation spell from the Cairo Genizah, T-S K 1.73, p. 4 ll. 17–18: "and he shall hate NN, son of NN, as the dog hates the pig and the pig the dog" (ויסני ית פ׳ ב׳ פ׳ הך מא דכלבה סני לחיירה וחזירה לכלבה; Naveh/ Shaked 1998: no. Geniza 6; Saar 2017: 191–192). As discussed by Saar (2017: 192) conflicts between dogs and pigs are already attested in Hurro-Hittite texts, suggesting a possible Near Eastern origin for this analogy, perhaps deriving from the status of both animals as scavengers which competed for food waste; *cf.* Dosoo 2022c: 532; Peled/Saar forthcoming. Compare the discussions of animal analogies used in love spells in the notes to *PCM* I 7 ll. 35–36 and *PCM* I 28 p. 2 ll. 12–13

Image: *Cf.* the discussion of the image on the front. Here, in addition to the two figures represented back to back, we have a third figure, perhaps with its arms raised in the orant position, likely representing the practitioner or superhuman being who causes the separation between the two targets. As already noted, the letter † here, as in the tableau on the front, seems to have decorations resembling the circles often used to decorate *kharaktēres*. A similar circle decorates the left part of the supralinear stroke of the word ⲡⲣⲓⲙ above the left-hand figure.

PCM I 32. Parchment bifolio with two preserved love spells

Arsinoites (Faiyum) ? 21.4 (H) × 16.4 (W) cm X CE

Other references: P.Heid.Inv. Kopt. 518; TM 99553; *P.Bad.* V 131; KYP M285; Bélanger Sarrazin #170.

Editions: Bilabel/Grohmann 1934: no. 131 (*ed. pr.*) [B/G].

Translations: Bilabel/Grohmann 1934: no. 131 (German); Frankfurter in Meyer/Smith 1994: no. 77 [F].

Additional commentary: Polotsky 1935: no. 131; Seider 1964; Mößner/Nauerth 2015: 307–308; Bélanger Sarrazin forthcoming a: chapter 3.

Present location: Lost; formerly Heidelberg, Institut für Papyrologie.

Image: Plate XII.

Linguistic description: Sahidic with inconsistent Middle Egyptian influence.

Contents:

Original Use:

1. p. 2: Jeremiah (including 41 (34) 8)

Re-use (palimpsest):

2. p. 1 ll. 1–27: Love spell (KYP T204)
3. p. 1 ll. 28–35, p. 2 ll. 1–38: Love spell (KYP T1559)
4. p. 3 ll. 18–19 (?): Traces of lost text

Parchment bifolio with the first folio (pages 1 & 2) almost complete, but only a tiny fragment of what would have been the second folio preserved, with a few letter traces from page 3 visible to the right of ll. 18–19 on the photograph;[1] it is possible that this bifolio was once part of a larger codex. Pages 1 and 2 are damaged on all sides, with the outer margin being the text preserved.

The manuscript was acquired from a dealer in 1896 by Carl Reinhardt (1856–1903), then dragoman (interpreter) at the German consulate in Cairo, as part of the first major purchase of the University of Heidelberg papyrus collection, consisting of at least 579 papyrus, parchment, and wooden manuscripts, written in six languages.[2] Karl Zangemeister, the head librarian of the University of Heidelberg, arranged to buy the collection, with the process beginning on the 30th May 1897 when Adolf von Öchelhäuser—who was in contact with Reinhardt—sent Zangemeiser a letter informing him of the collection in Reinhardt's possession. Several professors from the University of Heidelberg met on the next

---

[1] Bilabel/Grohmann (1934: 375) read ⲛ̄ to the right of l. 18 of p. 2.

[2] Greek, Pahlavi, Egyptian (Hieratic, Demotic, and Coptic), Hebrew, Arabic, Latin; Seider 1964: 168. For the life of Reinhardt, see Köpstein 1996.

day to formulate a letter to Öchselhauser stressing the importance of the collection for the university library, as it would make it comparable to the Berlin papyrus collection or that of Erzherzog Rainer in Vienna. Thanks to the support of the Minister of Justice, Wilhelm Nokk, arranged by Öchelhäuser, Friedrich I, Grand Duke of Baden (r. 1858–1907), approved the purchase. A telegram confirming the purchase was sent by Reinhardt to Zangemeister shortly thereafter. On the 30th June 1897, Zangemeister confirmed that the collection, bought for 6,280 marks, had arrived in Heidelberg.[3] The manuscript belonged to the collection of the University of Heidelberg Library until it was lost in the Second World War.[4]

The manuscript is a palimpsest; the underlying text, written in two columns at right angles to the later text, is visible on the lower part of page 2, where Jeremiah 41 (34) 8 can be read; the original manuscript may date to around the sixth century.[5] As with *PCM* I 25 & 26, therefore, this manuscript was produced by cutting the bifolios of the older Biblical codex into individual folios, which were folded to produce the smaller bifolios of the later manuscript.

Bilabel and Grohmann describe the colour of the ink as being brown,[6] like the manuscripts of the Heidelberg Library produced by the Deacon Iōhannēs and the second copyist (*PCM* I 21–28); this suggests that it was written in a plant ink (*cf.* p. 261). The hand is close to, but not the same as, the second copyist, who produced *PCM* I 27–28, a regular, bilinear and bimodal sloping majuscule. Several letters have serifs at the ends of strokes, notably the ⲧ and ⲧ̇ (on the left side of the horizontal bar) and the ⲁ (at the top of the oblique stroke). The oblique strokes of the ⲕ are separated from its vertical stroke, and the ⲙ is very flat, with a slight upwards curve in the middle. The ⲉ is bilinear. With a few exceptions, the use of the supralinear stroke is limited to names and abbreviations. The mid-dot is the only punctuation, and a decorated double horizontal line is used to separate the two recipes on page 1.

Very similar hands can be found in the colophons to several manuscripts belonging to the White Monastery near Akhmim in Upper Egypt, but copied in Touton in the Faiyum; these are BnF 132.1 (CLM 5353), dated by its colophon on fol. 67v to 927/8 CE, and Vienna K 351 (CLM 5857) and BnF Copte 13.3 fol. 39v (CLM 578), both datable to 939–940 CE. Based on these parallels, a tenth century dating seems most likely, even if a late ninth or early eleventh century date cannot be excluded.

The dialect of the majority of the text is a very standard form of Sahidic, but in the instructions accompanying the first recipe (p. 1 ll. 19–7) we find some suggestive non-standard features, notably ⲉ for ⁵ⲛ̄; this is a feature typical of the

---

[3] For the account of the sale given here, see Seider 1964: 143–145, 168–173.
[4] Mößner and Nauerth 2015: 307; *cf.* p. 325.
[5] We are very grateful to Alin Suciu for his help in identifying this underlying text, and for providing us with his estimate of the date.
[6] Bilabel/Grohmann 1934: 375.

texts of the Heidelberg Coptic Magical Library, which show the strong influence of a Middle Egyptian dialect (likely that of the contemporary Faiyum; see pp. 261–262). Several of the other manuscripts from the 1897 purchase came from the Faiyum,[7] including other Coptic magical texts, leading us to tentatively suggest that this manuscript too may come from the Faiyum, even if not from the Heidelberg Library itself.

Because the manuscript was lost during the Second World War, we are reliant upon Bilabel and Grohmann's readings for page 1. For page 2 we have been able to check readings using a black and white photograph produced before the manuscript's disappearance, kindly provided by Elke Fuchs of the University of Heidelberg.[8] Here we follow Bilabel/Grohmann in numbering the pages as 1 and 2; since the beginning of page 2 is damaged, there is no absolute indication in the text as to which side came first, but the fact that page 2 ends with an image and instructions suggests that it represents the end of the recipe which begins on page 1 l. 28. Note that Bilabel and Grohmann do not transcribe ll. 36–38 of page 2. We number the lines on page 2 from l. 1 to l. 41, whereas Bilabel/Grohmann number the second page continuously from page 1, so that page 2 l. 1 is numbered l. 36 in Bilabel/Grohmann.

The exact form of the δεῖνα sign used in this manuscript is unclear. In their transcription, Bilabel and Grohmann often place a dot under the sign (ⲁ̣̄), but at other times mark it without a dot (ⲁ̄) and in still other places depict the sign with a descender (ⲁ̣̄). In the case of the dotted sign, it is unclear if they are marking uncertainty or a small descender in the form of a dot. Because of the low quality of the preserved photo, it not possible for us to resolve the question with certainty. On p. 2 ll. 8, 33, 34, there seems to be no descender (as Bilabel and Grohmann correctly note), but on ll. 14 & 25 two dots seem to be present below ⲁ̄ⲁ̄ (where Bilabel and Grohmann indicate descenders), although these may be ink smudges or another form of discolouration. In our transcription, we follow the form provided in Bilabel/Grohmann, except where the sign is clear to us; in every one of these instances, we use a simple delta with supralinear stroke (ⲁ̄).

---

[7] These include PCM I 33; P.Heid.Inv. Kopt. 544b (KYP M365) & P.Heid.Inv. Kopt. 564a (KYP M513; both in Quecke 1963b), all three of which show dialectal features suggestive of a Faiyumic origin. Of the 148 inventory numbers from the sale listed in the database of the Heidelberg Papyrus Collection (https://www.ub.uni-heidelberg.de/papyri/; consulted 16/3/2023) which have provenances listed, 34 are listed as coming from the Faiyum; a larger proportion (92) is described as coming from the Hermopolitan nome, although we should note that it is only generally the Greek manuscripts which have provenances listed.

[8] This is the same image reproduced in Bilabel/Grohmann 1934: Tafelband, plate 10b.

page 1

[*ca.* 18 ca]ⲃⲁⲱⲑ ϩⲙⲟⲟⲥ ⲉϫ[ⲱϥ]
[*ca.* 20]ⲛ ⲛϥⲁϩⲉⲣⲁⲧϥ ⲙⲛ [...]
ⲣⲟⲙⲡⲓ [*ca.* 10] ϣⲁⲛⲧⲉϥⲧⲛⲛⲟⲟⲩ ⲛ[ⲁ]ⲩ
ⲙⲡⲟⲟⲩ ⲙⲡⲛⲟϭ [ⲛϭⲟⲙ] ⲛⲛⲁⲣⲭⲁⲅⲅⲉⲗⲟⲥ · ⲙⲓⲭⲁⲏⲗ
5   ⲙⲛ ⲅⲁⲃⲣⲓⲏⲗ · ⲧⲟ[ⲩ]ⲃⲱⲕ ϣⲁ ⲙⲁ ⲛⲓⲙ ⲉⲣⲉⲇ̅ⲇ̅ ϣⲟⲟⲡ
ⲛ̅ϩⲏⲧϥ · ⲧⲟⲩⲙⲉϩ ⲡⲉⲥϩⲏⲧ ⲛⲟⲩⲱϣ ⲛⲓⲙ ⲛⲕⲱϩⲧ ·
ϩⲓ ⲉⲡⲓⲑⲩⲙⲓⲁ ⲛⲓⲙ · ϩⲓ ⲡⲁⲑⲟⲥ ⲛⲓⲙ · ϩⲓ ⲙⲉ ⲛⲓⲙ · ⲧⲟⲩ-
ϩⲁⲣⲡⲁⲍⲉ ⲙⲙⲟⲥ ⲛⲑⲉ ⲛⲟⲩϩⲁϩ ⲛⲕⲱϩⲧ · ⲧⲟⲩⲉⲓⲛⲉ
ⲙⲙⲟⲥ ⲉⲣⲁⲧϥ ⲛⲇ̅ⲇ̅ · ⲁⲓⲟ · ⲁⲓⲟ · †ⲧⲁⲣⲕⲟ ⲙⲙⲱⲧⲛ ⲙⲡⲟⲩ-
10 ϫⲁⲓ ⲛⲛⲉⲧⲛⲛⲟϭ ⲛϭⲟⲙ · ⲙⲛ ⲛⲉⲧⲛⲣⲁⲛ · ϣⲁⲛⲧⲉⲧ-
ϣⲧⲟⲣⲧⲣ ⲙⲡⲗⲟⲅⲓⲥⲙⲟⲥ ⲧⲏⲣϥ ⲉⲧϩⲓϩⲟⲩⲛ ⲉⲡϩⲏⲧ ⲉⲇ̅ⲇ̅ ·
ⲛⲛⲉⲥϣ ⲟⲩⲱⲙ · ⲟⲩⲧⲉ ⲛⲛⲉⲥϣ ⲥⲱ · ⲟⲩⲧⲉ ⲛⲛⲉⲥϣ ϭⲱ
ϩⲛ ⲗⲁⲁⲩ ⲙⲙⲁ · ϣⲁⲛⲧⲉⲥⲧⲱⲟⲩⲛ ⲛⲥⲙⲟⲟϣⲉ ⲛⲛⲉⲥ-
ⲟⲩⲉⲣⲧⲏⲉ · ⲛⲥⲉⲓ ⲉⲣⲁⲧϥ ⲛⲇ̅ⲇ̅ ⲛϥϫⲉⲕ ⲡⲉϥⲟⲩⲱϣ ⲛ-
15 ϩⲏⲧ ⲉⲃⲟⲗ ⲛⲙⲙⲁⲥ ⲧⲁⲭⲏ ⲧⲁⲭⲏ ⲕⲓⲙ ⲉⲡⲉⲥϩⲏⲧ ϩⲛ ⲟⲩ-
[ⲛ]ⲟϭ ⲛⲟⲩⲱϣ ⲛ̅ⲑⲉ ⲉϣⲁⲣⲉⲡⲕⲱϩⲧ ⲕⲓⲙ ⲉⲣⲱⲧⲛ ·
ⲧⲁⲓ ϩⲱⲱϥ ⲧⲉ ⲑⲉ · ⲉⲧⲁⲉⲓⲛⲉ ⲛⲇ̅ⲇ̅ ⲉⲣⲁⲧϥ ⲛⲇ̅ⲇ̅ · ⲁϫⲛ̅
ⲕⲁ†ϫⲉ ⲙⲙⲟⲥ ⲁⲓⲟ ⲁⲓⲟ · ⲧⲁⲭⲏ ⲧⲁⲭⲏ ·

---

1 [ⲡⲉⲑⲣⲟⲛⲟⲥ ⲉⲧⲉⲣⲉⲓⲁⲱ ⲥⲁ]ⲃⲁⲱⲑ B/G, F ∥ **3** [ⲛⲓⲙ ϩⲓ ⲉⲃⲟⲧ ⲛⲓⲙ ⲙⲛ ϩⲟⲟⲩ ⲛⲓⲙ] "[any] year, [any month and any day]" ("[jedes] Jahr, [jeden Monat und jeden Tag]") B/G, F | *l.* ⲛ[ⲁ]ⲓ ? ∥ **4** *i.e.* ἀρχάγγελος ∥ **5** *i.e.* ᔆⲛ̅=ⲥⲉ-ⲃⲱⲕ ∥ **5, 9, 11, 17** *i.e.* δ(εῖνα) δ(εῖνα) ∥ **6** *i.e.* ᔆⲛ̅=ⲥⲉ-ⲙⲉϩ ∥ **7** *i.e.* ἐπιθυμία | *i.e.* πάθος ∥ **7–8** *i.e.* ᔆⲛ̅=ⲥⲉ-ἁρπάζειν ∥ **8** *i.e.* ᔆⲛ̅=ⲥⲉ-ⲉⲓⲛⲉ ∥ **10–11** *i.e.* ᔆϣⲁⲛ=ⲧⲉⲧⲛ̅-ϣⲧⲟⲣⲧⲣ̅ ∥ **11** *i.e.* λογισμός | *i.e.* ᔆϩⲓϩⲟⲩⲛ ⲛ̅- ∥ **12** *i.e.* οὔτε (twice) ∥ **14** *l.* δ(ε)ῖ(να) δ(ε)ῖ(να) | *i.e.* ᔆⲟⲩⲉⲣⲏⲧⲉ ∥ **15** *i.e.* ταχύ (twice) ∥ **17** *i.e.* ᔆⲉ=ⲧⲉⲧⲛ̅-ⲛⲁ-ⲉⲓⲛⲉ | *l.* ⲉⲧⲁⲥⲉⲓⲛⲉ "which has brought" ("welche die... gebracht hat") B/G ∥ **18** *i.e.* κατέχειν | *i.e.* ταχύ (twice)

[" ...] *Sabaoth? sits upon? ... and he stands with ... year? ... until he sends to me? today the great [power?] of the *archangels, *Michael |⁵ and *Gabriel, so that they go to every place in which NN, child of NN, is and fill her heart with every fiery desire and every lust and every passion and every love, and seize her like a fiery flame and bring her to NN, child of NN, yea, yea! I adjure you (pl.) by the |¹⁰ *wellbeing of your great *powers and your *names so that you disturb all the reason which is in the heart of NN, child of NN! May she be unable to eat and unable to drink and unable to stay in any place until she rises and walks on her feet and comes to NN, child of NN, so that he fulfils the desire of his |¹⁵ heart with her, quickly, quickly! Move her heart in a great desire, just as the fire moves you, this is the same way in which you will bring NN, child of NN, to NN, child of NN, without delay, yea, yea, quickly, quickly!"

---

1. [*ca.* 18 ca]ʙⲁⲱⲑ : [" ... Sa]baōth Bilabel/Grohmann, followed by Frankfurter in Meyer/Smith, plausibly suggest [ⲡⲉⲑⲣⲟⲛⲟⲥ ⲉⲧⲉⲣⲉⲓⲁⲱ ⲥⲁ]ʙⲁⲱⲑ, rendering "the throne upon which Iao Sabaoth sits".
2. ⲛϥⲁϩⲉⲣⲁⲧϥ : **"and he stands"** Bilabel/Grohmann translate "he shall not stand" ("er soll nicht stehen").
3. ϣⲁⲛⲧⲉϥⲧⲛⲛⲟⲟⲩ : **"until he sends"** Frankfurter translates "until he tramples them".
9–10. ϯⲧⲁⲣⲕⲟ ⲙⲙⲱⲧⲛ ⲙⲡⲟⲩϫⲁⲓ̄ : **"I adjure you by the wellbeing"** Frankfurter translates "I adjure you and your healing".
11–12. ⲛⲉⲥϣ ⲟⲩⲱⲙ · ⲟⲩⲧⲉ ⲛⲛⲉⲥϣ̄ ⲥⲱ : **"may she be unable to eat and unable to drink"** An example of the motif LOVE IS ABSTINENCE, for which see the note to *PCM* I 17 back l. 44–front l. 36.
16. ⲛ̄ⲑⲉ ⲉϣⲁⲣⲉⲡⲕⲱϩⲧ ⲕⲓⲙ ⲉⲣⲱⲧⲛⲧ : **"just as the fire moves you"** Both of the rituals in this manuscript seem to involve placing an applied object in the fire in order to apply the burning of love to the rituals' targets by persuasive analogy; for a discussion of the motif LOVE IS FIRE, see the notes to *PCM* I 3 l. front col. 2 33–38.

page 1 (continued)

```
      ⲅⲣ ⲛⲉⲍⲱ͞ ⲉ͞ⲃ ⲉⲥⲕⲱⲧⲉ̀ ⲉⲥⲟⲩⲁⲛ ⲉⲛⲁ̀ · ⲅⲣ ⲧⲉⲩ̀ ⲙⲉ ⲡⲍⲱ͞ ⲉⲡⲉϣⲁⲕ-
20   [ⲛⲧϥ] ⲥϩⲁⲓ ⲡϩⲟⲟⲩⲧ ⲟⲩⲁⲁⲃ · ⲅⲣ ⲟⲛ ⲉⲩⲁⲣⲣⲁⲕ ⲟⲩⲣⲟⲉⲓⲥ
     [.]ⲧⲉ ⲙⲡⲉϣⲁⲕⲛⲧϥ̄ · ⲅⲣ ⲙⲡⲁ ⲡϩⲟⲟⲩⲧ ⲉⲧⲁⲗϭⲉⲉⲙⲓⲁ ⲁϥ-
     [ⲉ..]ⲛ̄ ⲡⲡⲛⲟⲉⲓ ⲧⲉⲡⲣⲟⲥⲫⲟⲣⲁ ⲟⲩϣⲙⲉϥ ϩⲓ ⲧⲁⲣⲭⲏ ⲛ̄-
     [ⲡⲉϣⲁ]ⲕ̣ⲛⲧϥ ⲟⲛ ⲉⲩⲁⲗϭⲉⲉⲙⲓⲁ ⲁϥⲉ ⲙⲟⲩ ⲛⲁⲩⲉⲓⲛ ⲧⲁⲛⲟ
     [...]ⲧ ϩⲓⲱⲱϥ ⲟⲛ ⲑⲉ · ⲧⲁⲗⲟ ⲡϩⲟⲟⲩⲧ ϩⲓϩⲣⲁⲓ · ⲧⲁⲁⲩⲟ ·
25   [...]ⲉⲗⲉⲛ ⲙⲟⲣⲟⲩ ⲙⲙⲁϩ ⲕⲱⲕ · ⲥⲟⲗϭⲟⲩ ⲛⲟⲙⲉ ⲙ̄[ⲟ]ⲩ̀-
     [ⲟⲩ ϩ]ⲙ ⲡⲕⲱϩⲧ · ⲟⲩ͞ ⲙⲁ͞ⲥ · ⲁⲗⲁⲱⲑ · ⲥ͞ⲧ͞ⲩ͞ⲣ͞ⲍ · ⲉϥ · [.?ⲡⲉ-]
     [ϣⲁⲕ]ⲛⲧϥ ⲉⲡⲧⲏⲩ : ⲉⲕⲥϩⲁⲓ ⲉⲛⲁⲥⲥⲁⲁⲃⲣⲁⲛ ϩⲣⲁ̣ⲓ [.] .. ⲉϭⲟⲩ

     [.?]ⲛ̣ · ϣ͞ⲟⲩⲣⲁⲛ · ϣ͞ⲟⲩⲧⲁⲃⲓⲛ · ϣ͞ⲟⲩⲣⲁⲃⲁⲧⲁⲛ ϣ͞ⲟⲩⲣⲁⲭⲁⲛ
     [.?]ⲃⲁⲛ · ϣ͞ⲟⲩϣ̣ϥ · ϣ͞ⲟⲩⲣⲁⲭⲁⲛⲗ · ⲡⲣⲓⲙ · ⲡⲣⲓⲙⲡⲉ · ⲁ ...
30   [.?] . ⲡ͞ⲁⲧⲃⲟⲩⲕⲁⲛⲓⲁⲁ · ⲡ͞ⲍⲉⲩⲥ · ⲡ͞ⲇⲓⲁⲃⲟⲗⲟⲥ · ⲡⲁⲡⲟ[ⲗⲗⲱⲛ]
     [.?]ⲁ̣ ⲡ͞ⲕⲟⲛⲟⲥ · ⲡ͞ϣⲟⲩϣϥ · ⲡⲁⲛ†ⲛⲟⲥ · ⲡⲁⲛ†ⲧⲟⲥ ·
     [.?] ⲁⲕϩⲓ ⲧⲟⲟⲧⲕ ϫⲓⲛ ⲉϣⲟⲣⲡ̄ · ⲁⲕⲃⲱⲕ ⲉϩⲣⲁⲓ ⲉ-
     [.?] ⲛⲉⲓⲉⲣⲟ · ⲁⲕⲙⲁϩⲟⲩ ⲙⲡⲁⲑⲟⲥ ϩⲓ ⲉⲡⲓⲑⲩⲙⲓⲁ
     [ϩⲓ ....] ϩⲓ ⲡⲟⲛⲏⲣⲓⲁ · ϩⲓ ⲙⲉ · ϩⲓ ⲟⲩⲱϣ · ϩⲓ ⲗⲓⲃⲉ · †ⲱⲣ[ⲕ]
35   [ⲉⲣⲟⲕ ϩⲓ ⲧⲁⲡⲟ]ⲗⲟⲅⲓⲁ · ϫⲉⲕⲁⲥ ⲙⲁ ⲛⲓⲙ ⲉⲧⲉⲩⲛⲁⲕⲱ · [ⲙ̄ⲙⲟⲕ]
```

19, 21 *i.e.* γρ(άφειν) ‖ **19** *i.e.* ζῴδ(ιον) (twice) | *i.e.* ˢⲛ̄-ⲃ̄ : F does not translate | *i.e.* σκουτέλ(λιον) | *i.e.* ˢⲛ̄-ⲥⲟⲩⲁⲛ | *i.e.* ˢⲛ̄ⲁⲗⲁⲩ | *l.* ⲉⲥⲕⲱⲧⲉ (ⲉ)ⲗ(ⲁⲁⲩ) ⲉⲥⲟⲩⲁⲛ(-ⲱⲛ) ⲉⲛⲁⲗ(ⲟϫ) ? "when she turns, when she..." ("indem sie sich wendet..., indem sie ...") B/G, F | *i.e.* εὐχ(ή) | **20** *l.* ⲡϩⲟⲟⲩ ⲧⲟⲩⲁⲁⲃ "the holy day" ("den heiligen Tag") B/G, F | *i.e.* ˢⲉ-(ⲟⲩ)-(ⲟ)ⲩⲁⲣⲣⲁⲕ *i.e.* ورق *waraq* : F does not translate, but notes possibility | "a guardian" F ‖ **21** ⲙⲡⲁ ⲡϩⲟⲟⲩⲧ translate "male member" ("was dem Manne gehört (=penis)") B/G, F ‖ **21, 23** *i.e.* الجام *al-ǧām* : B/G, F do not translate ‖ **21–22** *i.e.* ˢⲱϥⲉ ‖ **22** *l.* ⲡ-ⲛⲟⲉⲓ ? *cf.* Crum CD 219a *s.v.* | *i.e.* προσφορά | *i.e.* ˢⲟⲩⲟϣ=ϥ | *i.e.* ἀρχή : "rulership" ("Herrschaft") B/G : "principle" F ‖ **23** *i.e.* ˢⲱϥⲉ : B/G, F do not translate | *i.e.* ˢⲛ̄-ⲟⲩⲉⲓⲛ : B/G do not translate : "colours" F | ⲧⲁⲛⲟ : "create", ("schaffe") B/G : "destroy" F ‖ **24** *i.e.* ˢϩⲓⲱⲱ=ϥ ⲟⲛ ⲛ̄-ⲧ-ϩⲉ : ϩⲓⲱⲱ ϥⲟ ⲛⲑⲉ "and he is similar" ("indem er ähnlich ist") B/G, F | ⲧⲁⲗⲟ ⲡϩⲟⲟⲩⲧ ϩⲓϩⲣⲁⲓ : "put the male (=penis) on it" (" lege den männlichen (=penis) darauf" B/G : "offer up the male ‹member›" F | *i.e.* ˢⲧⲁⲩⲟ- or ⲧⲁⲁ=ⲩ ⲟ- ‖ **25** *i.e.* ˢⲙ-ⲙⲁϩⲉ ⲛ-ⲕⲱⲕ *cf.* Crum CD 211a ‖ **25–26** ⲙ[ⲟ]ⲩ\ⲭ/[ⲟⲩ] *l.* ⲛⲟϫⲟⲩ ? : "burn them" ("[brenne sie]") *i.e.* ⲣⲟⲕϩ=ⲟⲩ ? B/G, F ‖ **26** *i.e.* θυ(σία) μασ(τίχη) : transcribe "thumas", or translate as CMPT B/G, F | *i.e.* العود *al-ʿūd* : "alaôth" B/G, F | *i.e.* στύραξ ? ‖ **27** *i.e.* الزعفران *az-zaʿfarān* : B/G do not translate : "(when you write) ⲉⲛⲁⲥⲥⲁⲁⲃⲣⲁⲛ" F ‖ **32** ⲁⲕ ϩⲓⲧⲟⲟⲧⲕ "through you" ("durch dich") B/G : "in your hand" F ‖ **33** *i.e.* πάθος | *i.e.* ἐπιθυμία ‖ **34** *i.e.* πονηρία ‖ **35** *i.e.* ἀπολογία : [ϩⲓ ⲧⲁⲡⲟ]ⲗⲟⲅⲓⲁ "(I adjure you) through this adjuration" ("Ich beschwöre dich durch diese Beschwörung") B/G, F | ⲙⲁ ⲛⲓⲙ ⲉⲧⲉⲩⲛⲁⲕⲱ · [ⲙ̄ⲙⲟⲕ] : ⲙⲁ ⲛⲓⲙ ⲉⲧⲉⲩⲛⲁⲕⲱ · [.?] "in every place, in which they will be" ("jeder Ort, an den sie sich stellen werden") B/G, F

Draw the *images on two white? *Aswan dishes. Write the prayer and the image on what you will [bring]. |²⁰ Draw the man alone. Draw again on paper. An amulet. … of? what you will bring. Draw that of the male on the *platter, gather? … the storage place? of? the offering. Knead it with ‹wine of the› *first fruits? on? what you bring, again, in a platter. Gather drain water. Pound … upon it again in this manner?. Lift up the male. Pronounce? |²⁵ … bind them with fine flax. Smear them with clay, place? [them] in the fire. Offering: *mastic, *agarwood, *storax … [what you] bring to the wind?. You write with saffron upon?…

[…] Šouran, Šoutabin, Šourabatan, Šourakhan, …ban, Šoushf, Šourakhaēl, Prim, Primpe, A… |³⁰ …patboukaniaa, Zeus, the Devil, Apollo, …a, Pkonos, Šoušf, Antinoos, Pantitos, … you began? from the beginning, you went down in … rivers, you filled them with passion and lust [and …] and wickedness and love and desire and madness. I adjure [you] |³⁵ [by my?] request?, that every place [in which you] will be placed …

---

19. ⲅⲣ/ ⲛⲉⲍⲱ\ⲁ/ : **"draw the images"** These instructions seem to describe the creation and manipulation of a pair of two-dimensional figures, one male, on plates, with the two perhaps being bound together with linen. This is similar to other Coptic and Arabic recipes describing the use of effigies to represent the male and female targets of love spells, which are usually brought together, facing one another as part of the ritual; *cf.* Dosoo 2018: 25–46; Dosoo 2023a. Bilabel/Grohmann do not note any image on this first page that might have served as a model.

19–20, 21, 23. ⲡⲉϣⲁⲕⲛⲧϥ : **"what you will bring"** The meaning is obscure; it may refer to an object belonging to the target, known in Greek as οὐσία (*ousia*, "essence"). Often pieces of hair or fingernails are used, but the fact that it must be drawn on would imply a piece of clothing or another intimate possession. For the concept of *ousia*, *cf.* Gager 1992: 16–18; Faraone 2020: 4 n. 14. For the construction using a substantivised circumstantial (ⲡⲉϥⲥⲱⲧⲙ̄), common in the later manuscripts of this volume, see Richter 2017b.

27. ⲉⲛⲁⲥⲥⲁⲁⲃⲣⲁⲛ : **"with saffron"** For the use of ink made from saffron in Coptic magic, see Richter 2023: 166–68.

28–31. These names are probably those of demons. Aside from ⲡⲇ̄ⲓⲁⲃⲟⲗⲟⲥ ("the Devil"), we may compare ϣⲟⲩⲣⲓⲛ ϣⲁⲩⲣⲁⲛ ϣⲟⲩⲧⲁⲃⲁⲛ ϣⲟⲩⲧⲁⲃⲉⲛⲉⲓ̈ in *BKU* I 2 (KYP M300), alternative names for ⲥⲁⲧⲁⲛⲁⲥ ⲡⲇ̄ⲓⲁⲃⲟⲗⲟⲥ ("Satan the Devil"). ⲡⲣⲓⲙⲡⲣⲓⲙ in *PCM* I 31 (KYP M366) is a being who causes strife. The rest are the names of pagan deities, likewise understood as demons: ⲡⲍ̄ⲉⲩⲥ̄ ("Zeus"), ⲡⲁⲡⲟ[ⲗⲗⲱⲛ] ("Apollo"), ⲡⲕⲟ̄ⲛⲟ̄ⲥ ("K‹r›onos"), ⲡⲁⲛⲧ̄ⲛⲟⲥ̄ ("Antinous"?); *cf.* Blumell/Dosoo 2018: 249–250, in particular n. 133.

32–34. This is likely a reference to the story of the Devil scraping his sweat into the water of the four rivers of Eden so that Eve would drink it and be filled with desire, allowing her to be deceived into eating the fruit of the Tree of Life, an event mentioned in the *Questions of Bartholomew* IV.59 (Bonwetsch 1987: 26); *cf.* the love spell BM EA 10376 (Zellman-Rohrer 2022a: no. 2; KYP M286) ll. 15–18: "the lust which Mastema scraped? into a bowl and cast into the source of the four rivers, and he bared himself? in it so that the children of men would drink from it and be filled with the lust of the Devil" (ⲧⲉⲡⲉⲑⲓⲙⲓⲁ ⲧⲁⲓ ⲧⲉⲛⲧⲁⲙⲁⲥⲧⲁⲙⲁ ⲉⲏⲣⲉⲥⲥⲉ ⲙⲙⲟⲥ ϩⲛ ⲟⲩⲫⲉⲁⲗⲉ ⲁϥⲛⲟϫⲥ ϩⲣⲁⲓ ϩⲛ ⲧⲁⲣⲭⲏ ⲙⲡⲉϥⲧⲟⲟⲩ ⲛⲉⲣⲟ ⲁϥϭⲱⲕⲁⲕ ⲉⲃⲟⲗ ⲛϩⲏⲧϥ ϫⲉⲕⲁⲥ ⲉⲣⲉⲛϣⲏⲣⲉ ⲛⲛⲣⲱⲙⲉ ⲥⲱ [ⲉ]ⲃⲟⲗ ⲛϩⲏⲧϥ ⲛⲥⲉⲙⲟϩ ⲉⲃⲟⲗ ϩⲛ ⲧⲉⲡⲉⲑⲓⲙⲓⲁ ⲛⲡⲇⲓⲁⲃⲟⲗⲟⲥ ⲁⲗⲗⲁ ⲥⲱ ⲉⲃ[ⲟⲗ] ⲛϩⲏⲧϥ ⲁϥⲙⲟϩ ⲉⲃⲟⲗ ϩⲛ ⲧⲉⲡⲉⲑⲓⲙⲓⲁ ⲛⲡⲇⲓⲁⲃⲟⲗⲟⲥ); see the discussion in Zellman-Rohrer 2022a: 122.

page 2

[ⲛ̄ϩⲏⲧϥ̄ ⲟⲩϣ]ⲧⲟⲣⲧⲣ · ⲙⲛ [ⲟ]ⲩⲗⲓⲃ[ⲉ *ca.* 18–22]
[. . . .] ⲉⲥⲉⲓ ⲉⲣⲁⲧϥ ⲛⲇ̄ⲇ̄ ⲛ̣[ⲥ *ca.* 16–20] . . . .
[. .] . [.] ⲙ̣ⲛ ⲟⲩⲟⲩⲱϣ ⲉⲛⲁⲧⲃⲱ[ⲗ ⲉⲃⲟⲗ] . . . .
[ⲭ]ⲉⲕⲁⲥ ⲉⲕⲉⲃⲱⲕ ϣⲁ ⲙⲁ ⲛⲓⲙ̣ [ⲉⲧⲉⲣ]ⲉ̣ⲇ̄ⲇ̄ ϣⲟⲟⲡ ⲛ̄ϩⲏⲧϥ
5   ⲛⲕϩⲁⲣⲡⲁⲍⲉ ⲙⲙⲟⲥ ⲛⲅⲉⲓⲛⲉ ⲙⲙⲟⲥ ⲉⲣⲁⲧϥ ⲛⲇ̄ⲇ̄ · ϩⲙ   40
ⲙⲁ ⲛⲓⲙ ⲉⲧⲉⲥϣⲟⲟⲡ ⲛ̄ϩⲏⲧϥ · ⲕⲁⲛ ⲉⲥⲟⲩⲱⲙ ⲕⲁⲛ ⲉⲥⲥⲱ
ⲕⲁⲛ ⲉⲥϯ ⲉⲕⲓⲃⲉ̣ ⲕⲁⲛ ⲉⲥϩⲛ ⲛⲧⲟ̣ⲟ̣ⲩ ⲕⲁⲛ ⲉⲥϩⲛ ⲙⲙⲟⲟⲩ
ⲁⲛⲁⲅⲕⲁⲍⲉ ⲙ̄ⲙⲟⲥ ϣⲧⲟⲣⲧⲣ ⲛⲁⲥ̣ ϣⲁⲛⲧⲉⲥⲉⲓ ⲉⲣⲁⲧϥ ⲛ̄ⲇ̄ⲇ̄
ϯⲱⲣⲕ ⲉⲣⲟⲕ ⲙⲓⲭⲁⲏⲗ ⲛⲟⲩⲟⲉⲓⲛ ⲉⲧⲉⲕⲁⲗⲏⲩ ⲉϩⲣⲁⲓ ⲉϫⲱϥ
10   ⲛⲧⲟⲕ ⲙⲛ̣ ⲛⲉⲕϣⲃⲏⲣ ⲉⲧⲛⲙⲙⲁⲕ · ϩⲙ ⲡⲉⲓⲁⲝⲓⲱⲙⲁ ⲛ[ⲟ]ⲩ̣ⲱⲧ ·   45
ϫⲉⲕⲁⲁⲥ ⲛ̄ⲧⲉⲩⲛⲟⲩ ⲉⲓⲛⲁⲟⲛⲟⲙⲁⲍⲉ ⲛⲛⲉⲧⲛⲣⲁⲛ ⲧⲁ-
ⲟⲩⲱϩ ⲙ̄ⲙⲱⲧⲛ ϩⲙ ⲡⲉⲓⲕⲱϩⲧ · ⲏ ⲡⲣⲟ ⲙ̄ⲡⲏⲓ · ⲏ ⲛⲟⲩϭⲁ-
ⲗⲁϩⲧ · ⲏ ϩⲛ ⲟⲩⲛⲉϩ · ϩⲁⲡⲗⲱⲥ ⲙⲁ ⲛⲓⲙ ⲉϣⲁⲓⲟⲛⲟⲙⲁ-
ⲍⲉ ⲛⲛⲉⲧⲛⲣⲁⲛ ⲉ·ϩⲣⲁⲓ ⲉϫⲱϥ · ⲧⲁⲧⲁⲁϥ ⲛ̄ⲇ̄ⲇ̄ ⲉⲥⲉⲓ ⲉⲣⲁ-
15   ⲧϥ ⲛ̄ⲇ̄ⲇ̄ · ⲣⲟⲙⲡⲓ ⲛⲓⲙ · ϩⲓ ⲉⲃⲟⲧ ⲛⲓⲙ · ⲙⲛ ϩⲟⲟⲩ ⲛⲓⲙ ⲉⲕⲉ-   50
ϫⲓ ⲛⲓⲧⲁⲣⲕⲟ ϩⲛ ⲛⲉⲕⲙⲁⲁϫⲉ · ⲛⲧⲟⲕ ⲡⲉⲛⲧⲁⲕⲧⲣⲉⲛⲁ-
ⲁϥ ⲉ̣ⲓ̣ ϭⲉ · ⲁⲕⲧⲣⲉⲛϭⲁⲙⲟ̣ⲩⲗ ⲃⲁⲕⲃⲉⲕ · ⲁⲕⲧⲣⲉⲛⲉϩⲟⲩⲟⲣ
ⲉⲓ ϩⲁ ⲡⲉϩⲟⲩⲟⲣ · ⲁⲕⲧⲣⲉⲛ . . . ⲩⲥ̣ . . ϩⲁ ⲡⲭⲉⲩ ⲛⲧⲁⲕ
ⲙⲛ ⲛⲉⲕⲕⲉϣⲃⲏⲣ · ⲛ̄ⲧⲟⲕ ⲡⲉ ⲡⲉⲧϣⲧⲟⲣⲧⲣ ⲙ̄ⲡⲗⲟⲅⲓⲥ[ⲙⲟⲥ]
20   ⲙⲛ ⲙⲛⲧⲥⲁⲃⲉ ⲛⲇ̄ⲇ̄ ⲛⲕⲉⲓⲛⲉ ⲙⲙⲟⲥ ⲉⲣ[ⲁ]ⲧϥ ⲛ̄ⲇ̄ⲇ̄ . [. . . .]   55

---

1 [. . . . ϣ]ⲧⲟⲣⲧⲣ B/G || **2–20** *i.e.* δ(ε͂ινα) δ(ε͂ινα) || **3** *i.e.* ˢⲛ̄-ⲁⲧⲃⲱⲗ [*ca.* 10] : [*ca.* 7] ⲩ ⲛϭⲓ B/G || **4** ⲉ‹ⲣⲁ›ⲙⲁ B/G || **5** *i.e.* ἁρπάζειν | ⲛⲧⲉⲓⲛⲉ B/G || **6** ⲛϩⲏⲧⲉϥ B/G || **6–7** *i.e.* κἄν || **8** *i.e.* ἀναγκάζω || **10** "bring the companions" ("Bringe du die Gefährten") B/G, F | *i.e.* ἀξίωμα || **11** *i.e.* ὀνομάζειν || **12** *i.e.* ἤ : ⲙⲡⲣⲟ B/G || **12–13** *i.e.* ἤ : ⲏ ⲛⲟⲩϭⲓ ϩⲓ ⲟⲩϣⲛⲉ "and doorpost, on a stone" ("und der Türpfosten... auf einen Stein") B/G, F, *i.e.* Crum CD 803a s.v. ϭⲓⲏ ? || **13** *i.e.* ἁπλῶς || **13–14** *i.e.* ὀνομάζειν || **16–17** "you are the one who caused us to..." ("du, der du veranlaßt hast, daß Wir") B/G : "you are the one who is called. Thus he came" F || **17** "... Abakuk" B/G | *i.e.* ˢⲛ-ⲟⲩϩⲟⲟⲣⲉ "female dogs (?)" ("Hündinnen (?)") B/G || **18** *i.e.* ˢⲡ-ⲟⲩϩⲟⲣ || **18–19** "you have caused that the peasants have also come to... with (?) the great... Friends!" (du hast veranlasst, dass auch die Bauern unter den... gekommen sind... mit (?) dem großen ... Freunde!") B/G : "you have called the little ones to come under the... with the great companion" F || **19** "Come! It was you" ("Komm! Du bist es gewesen") B/G | *i.e.* λογισμός *cf.* p. 1 l. 11 : ⲙⲡⲁ . ⲉ . B/G, F || **20** *l.* ϩⲓⲧⲛ ⲛⲧⲁⲁⲃⲉ "through the seals" ("durch die Seigel") B/G, F | restore *e.g.* ϩⲛ ⲧⲉⲕ- ? : *l.* ⲛⲉⲕⲉⲓⲛⲉ B/G

… disturbance and madness … she will come to NN, child of NN, and [she will] … and an unending desire … that you go to every place in which NN is, |⁵ and you snatch her and bring her to NN, child of NN, from every place in which she is, even if she is eating, even if she is drinking, even if she is breastfeeding, even if she is in the mountains, even if she is in the waters, compel her, disturb her until she comes to NN, child of NN! I adjure you, *Michael, by ⟨the⟩ light upon which you are mounted, |¹⁰ you and your companions who are with you in the same rank, that as soon as I name your names and I place you in this fire or? ⟨at⟩ the door of the house or in a *pot or in oil, in short, every place over which I name your names and give it to NN, child of NN, may she go to |¹⁵ NN, child of NN, every year and every month and every day! May you (s.) take these adjurations in your ears! You are the one who caused bees? to come, indeed you have caused the camel to chew, you caused the female dogs to go under the male dog; you have caused the [female cat?] to come under the male cat, you and also your companions. You are the one who disturbs the reason? |²⁰ and wisdom? of NN, child of NN, so that you may bring her to NN, child of NN, [through your?]

---

1. [ⲚϨⲎⲦϤ ⲞⲨⲰ]ⲦⲞⲢⲦⲢ : "… disturbance" There would seem to be space for only about five letters before the visible Ⲧ, but all of the elements here are necessary; perhaps there was another lost line at the end of the recto.

9. ⲚⲞⲨⲞⲈⲒⲚ ⲈⲦⲈⲔⲀⲖⲎⲨ ⲈϨⲢⲀⲒ ⲈϪⲰϤ : "by ⟨the⟩ light upon which you are mounted" Perhaps restore "⟨chariot⟩ of light" (ⲘⲠⲈⲔϨⲀⲢⲘⲀ ⲚⲞⲨⲞⲈⲒⲚ), compare the chariot of light (ⲠϨⲀⲢⲘⲀ ⲚⲞⲨⲀⲒⲚ) given to Michael in the *Investiture of Michael* (CC 488; Müller 1962: 19.6).

15. ⲢⲞⲘⲠⲒ : "year" This word is very uncertain; the omicron may be inserted above the line.

16–18. For similar descriptions of women maddened in love behaving like animals, *cf.* the note to *PCM* I 7 ll. 32–36. By comparison with *PCM* I 28 p. 6 ll. 4–5, we might perhaps restore at the end ⲀⲔⲦⲢⲈ ⲦⲘⲞⲨⲦⲤⲈ ⲈⲒ ϨⲀ ⲠⲬⲈⲨ ("you caused the female cat to go under the male cat"; *cf.* the notes to *PCM* I 28). Bilabel/Grohmann translate "Abakuk, you caused the female dogs (?) to come under the dog (?), you also caused the peasants to come under the…" ("… Abakuk, du hast veranlaßt, daß die Hündinnen (?) unter den Hund (?) gekommen sind, du hast veranlaßt, daß auch die Bauern unter den… gekommen sind…"). Frankfurter in Meyer/Smith translates "You have called, ⲚⲞⲨⲚⲞⲨ ⲀⲂⲀⲔⲞⲨⲔ, you have called. The dogs come under the dog. You have called the little ones to come under the …".

page 2 (continued)

21 ⲛⲟϭ ⲛϭⲟⲙ ⲧⲁⲭⲏ · ⲟⲩⲣⲓⲭ · ⲙⲁⲣⲓⲭ · ⲃⲁⲧⲱⲗ · . . . [. . . .]
ⲙⲁ ϫⲟⲟⲩ ⲛⲛⲉⲕⲇⲩⲛⲁⲙⲓⲥ ⲛⲥⲉⲃⲱⲕ ⲉϩⲟⲩⲛ ⲉⲡ[ⲏⲓ]
ⲛⲇⲇ ϣⲁⲛⲧⲉⲥϣⲧⲟⲣⲧⲣ ⲛⲥⲣ ϩⲃⲁ · ⲛⲥⲕⲱ ⲛⲥ[ⲱⲥ ⲙⲡⲉⲥⲉⲓⲱⲧ]
ⲙⲛ ⲧⲉⲥⲙⲁⲁⲩ · ⲙⲛ ⲡⲉⲥϩⲁⲓ ⲙⲛ ⲛⲉⲥⲥ̄ⲛ̄ⲥ̄ · ⲛⲥⲛϣ[ⲟⲧ ⲛⲥⲙⲟⲩϩ]
25 ⲛⲟⲩⲱϣ ⲉⲇⲇ · ϩⲛ ⲟⲩⲟⲩⲱϣ ⲉϥϫⲏϥ ⲙⲛ ⲟⲩⲙⲉ ⲛ[. . . .]   60
ⲛ[ⲓⲙ] ϩⲓ ⲉⲡⲓⲑⲩⲙⲓⲁ ⲛⲁⲧⲃⲱⲗ ⲉⲃⲟⲗ ϣⲁ ⲉⲛⲉϩ . . . ⲧⲁ[ⲭⲏ]

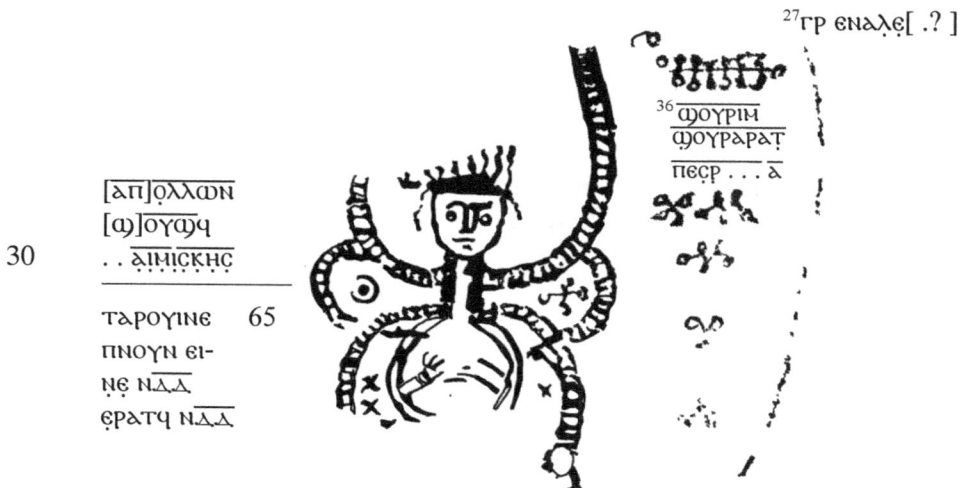

²⁷ⲅⲣ ⲉⲛⲁⲗⲉ[.?]

[ⲁⲡ]ⲟⲗⲗⲱⲛ
[ϣ]ⲟⲩϣϥ
30 . . ⲁⲓⲙⲓⲥⲕⲏⲥ

³⁶ϣⲟⲩⲣⲓⲙ
ϣⲟⲩⲣⲁⲣⲁⲧ
ⲡⲉⲥⲣ . . . ⲁ

ⲧⲁⲣⲟⲩⲓⲛⲉ   65
ⲡⲛⲟⲩⲛ ⲉⲓ-
ⲛⲉ ⲛⲇⲇ
ⲉⲣⲁⲧϥ ⲛⲇⲇ

---

22 *i.e.* δύναμις ‖ **23** *i.e.* δ(εῖνα) δ(εῖνα) ‖ **24** *i.e.* υ(ἱό)ς ‖ **25** *i.e.* ˢⲟⲩ-ⲟⲩⲱϣ : ⲟⲩⲱϣ B/G ‖ *i.e.* δ(εῖνα) δ(εῖνα) ‖ **26** *i.e.* ἐπιθυμία | . . . ⲧⲁ[ⲭⲏ] *i.e.* ταχύ : ⲉ . ⲁ . ⲧⲁ B/G ‖ **27** *i.e.* γρ(άφειν) *cf.* p. 1 l. 19 | *l.* ⲉⲛⲁⲗⲉⲩ ? | ⲅⲣ ⲉⲛⲁ · ⲉⲩ[ⲭⲏ?] Bilabel/Grohmann : "write the [prayer (?)]" F ‖ **sub 27** two lines of illegible text ? ‖ **30** ⲁⲣⲓ ⲙⲓⲥⲓⲧⲏⲥ *i.e.* μεσίτης "be a mediator" ("[seid (?)] Mitler") B/G, F | ⲧⲁⲣⲟⲩⲓⲛⲉ "so that the underworld is brought about" ("damit die Unterwelt herbeigeführt wird") B/G : "illumine" F ‖ **33** *i.e.* δ(εῖνα) δ(εῖνα) ‖ **34** *i.e.* δ(εῖνα) δ(εῖνα)

great power, quickly! Ourikh, Marikh, Batōl ... send your powers so that they go to the [house?] of NN, child of NN, so that she is disturbed and distressed and she abandons [her father] and her mother and her husband and her children and she becomes bold? and is [filled] with |²⁵ desire for NN, child of NN, in burning desire, and every ... love ... and unending desire for ever ... quickly?!

|²⁷ Write on ⟨a⟩ white? ...

Left of tableau: |²⁸ Apollo, Šoušf, |³⁰ Aimiskēs, Tarouine, the abyss?, bring NN to NN!

Right of tableau: |³⁵ *(kharaktēres*: +++++++) Šourim, Šourarat, Pesr...a

(kharaktēres: XM M Y . A)

KD, EL, MP & JS; page 1 edited from Bilabel/Grohmann 1934, page 2 edited from photograph; tracings by KD & JS.

Image: The central image here depicts a crowned angel, with the six wings typical of the iconography of *cherubim and *seraphim, and his arms held against his body. No caption is visible, but the *angel may represent *Michael, who is invoked in the accompanying formula. For a discussion of such images, see Dosoo 2022a: 139–151, and compare the image of Michael on *PCM I* 26 p. 17, accompanied by two such six-winged angels, there labelled as *"powers".

PCM I 33. Formulary with healing procedures

Arsinoites (Faiyum) ?   15 (H) × 16.5 (W) cm   X–XI CE
Other references: P.Heid.Inv. Kopt. 580; TM 102082; *P.Bad.* V 133; KYP M319; Bélanger Sarrazin #172.
Editions: Bilabel/Grohmann 1934: no. 133 (*ed. pr.*) [B/G].
Translations: Bilabel/Grohmann 1934: no. 133 (German).
Additional commentary: Seider 1964: 143–145, 168; Untermann (ed.) 2011: 10; Mößner/Nauerth 2015: 308; Love 2022a: 192–193.
Present location: Heidelberg, Institut für Papyrologie.
Image: https://doi.org/10.11588/diglit.39648
Linguistic description: Sahidic (non-standard).
Contents:
1. Front ll. 1–5: Instructions for amulet for someone given sorcery (KYP T208)
2. Front ll. 6: Instructions stop a child from crying (KYP T209)
3. Front ll. 7–9: Instructions for amulet against uterine bleeding (KYP T210)
4. Front ll. 10–13: Instructions for unbinding a bridegroom (?) (KYP T211)
5. Front ll. 14–18: Instructions for healing amulet (KYP T2075)
6. Back ll. 1–3: *Kharaktēres* (KYP T212)

Sheet of paper with significant damage to the left and lower parts; traces of 3 vertical and 4 horizontal creases demonstrate folding, along which much of the damage has been sustained. The middle-left and bottom left parts are missing.

The manuscript was acquired in 1896 by Dr. Carl Reinhardt as part of a large number of papyri, parchments and wooden tablets and sold in 1897 to the University of Heidelberg, where it remains.[1] Manuscripts aquired within this lot came from the Faiyum, El-Ashmunein (Hermopolis), and Al-Fustat (Old Cairo). Despite the lack of the most prominent dialectal features associated with the group, the similarity in dating and content to the Heidelberg Coptic Magical Library (*PCM* I 21–29) perhaps suggests that this manuscript, like them, originated in the Faiyum.

The text is written with a black carbon ink on the front and back,[2] with *kharaktēres* visible on the back, either connected to one of the texts on the front or to a now lost text which existed below it. The text is written in right-sloping, generally bilinear, bimodal majuscule. The hand is fairly, but not entirely, regular: the lines often slope, and the letter heights show some variation. ⲙ is curved but

---

[1] Seider 1964: 143–145, 168. This manuscript was bought within the same lot as *PCM* I 32; see this introduction to that manuscript on pp. 421–422 for more information on its aquisition.

[2] We are again grateful to Krisztina Hevesi for sharing her work on the inks of the Heidelberg manuscripts; for the process of determining the ink, see pp. 28–29.

not flat, while the descenders of ρ, ϛ, and ϥ reach slightly below the line. There are slight serifs on the lower and left strokes of the τ, but the hand is otherwise undecorated. The ϥ consistently takes the form of a Latin lowercase y. ϭ seems to be written with a counterclockwise stroke, as with other texts of similar date from the Faiyum (*cf.* pp. 260–261). Horizontal dividing lines (both simple and decorated) is used extensively on the front to separate recipes. Supralinear strokes are used above *voces magicae* and other names, which may also be separated by colons.

As discussed in the introduction (p. 27–28), the use of paper suggests a tenth century date at the earliest, and a hand with many similar traits may be found in *CPR* II 1 ll. 29–40 (TM 82031), dated to year 410 of the Hijra (1019–1020 CE). We thus propose a tenth to eleventh century date for this manuscript.

The language of the manuscript is largely Sahidic, but with some surprising features; apart from dittography (ⲙⲙ, ⲉⲉ) and an instance of the absence of ⲛ › ⲙ assimilation, we see some surprising phonological substitutions (ⲉ for ^{S}ⲟⲩ, ⲓ for ^{S}ⲁⲓ). The lambdicistic writing of φαρμακεία as ⲫⲁⲗⲙⲁⲕⲓⲁ (front l. 1) may confirm our proposal that the manuscript originates in the Faiyum.

front

ογρωμε ντaγτaaϥ εaπoτ νφaλмaκιa
cϩaι naι ϩι ερωτε ενεcογ ϩι мacτιχεν : cηκ
caθω : caмην : мενεϊc c̄τ̄c̄ : aρωnaι : caηλ
λaмna : φογcηc : cηc вaρ : вaλιa : γεcaмηc
5   γην

6   [*nothing lost?* ογ]ϣηρε κογι εϥριммε cϩι naм τεn

ογ[cϩιм]ε ερεπεcnoϥ ϩaρoc · cϩaιεcoγ εγaρρaκ
. [..]. ι τι aмιantoν εροϥ мορϥ εροc

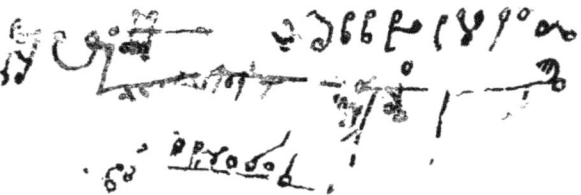

10 ογϭωπεεc aγϭoπϥ oγaλaλωcε πνταϥвωλ εвoλ
.. ν . cϩaιcε nογεϩaλητ εχм νπεϥcωмa νϩooγ̄ᵀ
[*ca.* 6] . νaρκaρτaмa κτaaϥ επcω̄м τεϥ .. γϣ .
[*ca.* 8] .. εν πεϩ επεϥcωмa ϥnaвωλ εвoλ

                    cϩaι νмoρ .. мoρϥ ϩιχω πε
15 [*ca.* 16] . ϥ мaρεϥвωκ ϩaτη ρϥмε ..
    [*ca.* 15] · εnoγηλ : cη.. [....]
    [*ca.* 16] : мιχaηλ [*ca.* 5]
    [*ca.* 16] : .... [...]

----

back

1 *i.e.* ˢn̄-ογ-aπoτ : εγνoc B/G | *i.e.* φαρμακεία ‖ 2 *i.e.* ˢn̄-εcooγ | *i.e.* μαστίχη ‖ 3 *i.e.* σ(ταυρό)c ? : εἰc θc *i.e.* εἰς θεός ? B/G | cαϩη B/G ‖ 4 cηc B/G | вana B/G ‖ 5 γεcaмηc B/G ‖ 6 .. oγι B/G | *i.e.* ˢριмε | *l.* cϩaι n̄-ἀμίαντον ? : ϩιм aмογ "... Come!" ("... Komm!") B/G ‖ 7 [.]n[*ca.* ?]ε B/G | *i.e.* ˢcϩaιc=cογ | *l.* ε-(o)γaρρεκ *i.e.* ورق *waraq* ‖ 8 . ι τι :]nε B/G | *i.e.* ἀμίαντον : αναмιa мτoν *i.e.* ἀνομία "lawlessness! Agree (with him)" ("Gesetzlosigkeiten! Stimme ihm zu") B/G | κορϥ εροc "destroy them!" ("Richte sie zugrunde") B/G ‖ 10 *i.e.* ˢϭoπc̄ ? see Crum 827a : aγϭωπε εc- B/G | *i.e.* العروس *al-ʿarūs* ? : oγa ... πε B/G ‖ 11 *i.e.* ˢ .. cϩaιcε n̄-oγaλητ εχм πε=ϥ-cῶмa n̄-ϩooγτ : [*ca.* ?] . n . [ ]ρaκ cnoγ εϩaλητ εχм {n}πεϥ-cῶмa νϩooγ\τ/ B/G ‖ 12 *i.e.* ال (al-) + κάρδαμον ? | *i.e.* ˢn̄=τ-ταa=ϥ ? | *i.e.* σῶμα ? | for this line [*ca.* ?] . мaρκaρτa . aκτaaϥ επ . ω̄мτεϥ [..] .. B/G ‖ 13 [*ca.* ? ϣ]ωπε ϩε πεϥcωмa B/G ‖ 14 *l. e.g.* μυρ(σίνη) ? : nмoι[B/G | nмoι[.]nορ ... n̄ε B/G ‖ 16 [*ca.* 16] :]ε B/G | εnoγηλ "E(ma)nuêl" B/G | cη .. [....] : coγρ[ιηλ B/G ‖ 17]:мιχaη[λ B/G ‖ 18 B/G do not print.

A man who has been given ⟨a⟩ *cup of sorcery. Write these ⟨names⟩ with sheep's milk and *mastic:

Sēk, Sathō, Samēn, Meneis, cross?, Arōnai, Saēl, Lamna, Phousēs, Sēs, Bar, Balia, Gesamēs, |⁵ Gēn (*kharaktēres*: CCCCCCCIIIIIIIII)

|⁶ [A?] small child who cries. Write with? asbestos?.

|⁷ A [woman] who has blood under her. Write them on paper [...] ... put asbestos on it. Bind it to her. (*kharaktēres*: ✶Ọ✶ⱫⱫⱫⱫⱫⱫⱫ++C[C]CCCCC++)

|¹⁰ A capture?. He has been seized, a bridegroom?, the one who has been released. ... write them on a bird? upon his male member ... in garden cress?, and you put it on his body?, his? ... reaches? his body. He will be released.

Write ... Bind it upon the |¹⁵ [... write?] it, have him go before ⟨the⟩? man ... [...] ... Enouēl ... [...] *Michael [...]

|*back* (*kharaktēres*: ..IIECYI✶)

KD, EL, MP & JS, edited from photograph; tracings by JS.

---

1. ⲉⲁⲡⲟⲧ ⲛ̄ⲫⲁⲗⲙⲁⲕⲓⲁ : "⟨a⟩ cup of sorcery" Probably a reference to some kind of harmful 'potion or 'poison'; *cf.* the note to *PCM* I 26 p. 16 l. 16 and the glossary *s.v.* *cup.

3. ⳨ This letter or sign is uncertain; it may be a *kharaktēr*. Here we read it as the word "cross".

6. This recipe may have been preceded by *kharaktēres* which were to be copied. There are traces to the lower left after this line which may be a letter (perhaps a ⲛ), or part of the elaborate divider.

6. [ⲟⲩ]ϣⲏⲣⲉ ⲕⲟⲩⲓ ⲉϥⲣⲓⲙⲙⲉ : "[a?] small child who cries" For other Coptic procedures for crying children, see *PCM* I 36 front col. 2 ll. 1–10; Mich.Ms. 136 (Zellmann-Rohrer/Love 2022; KYP M220) p. 13 ll. 5–6, and the recipes for Psalms 8, 62, 95, 114 & 130 in the *Guide to the Psalms* (Henein/Bianquis 1975). Those for Psalms 8, 62 & 130 give indications about the possible causes and consequences of "crying": the first adds that the child may also be unable to sleep, the second that the crying may be preventing breathing, and the last that the crying may be due to weaning.

7. ⲟⲩ[ⲥϩⲓⲙ]ⲉ ⲉⲣⲉⲡⲉⲥⲛⲟϥ ϩⲁⲣⲟⲥ : "a [woman] who has blood under her" For other recipes for the healing of uterine bleeding with the use of amulets, see *PCM* I 2 l. 1 and the accompanying note.

10. ⲟⲩϭⲱⲡⲉ ⲉⲥ ⲁⲩϭⲟⲡϥ ⲟⲩⲁⲗⲁⲗⲱⲥⲉ ⲡⲛⲧⲁϥⲃⲱⲗ ⲉⲃⲟⲗ : "A capture?. He has been seized, a bridegroom?, the one who has been released" Perhaps understand "⟨For⟩ a 'seizure' that has seized a bridegroom, in order that he be released" (ⲟⲩϭⲱⲡⲉ ⲉⲛⲧⲁϥϭⲱⲡⲉ ⲛ̄ⲟⲩⲁⲗⲁⲗⲱⲥ ⲉⲧⲣⲉϥⲃⲱⲗ ⲉⲃⲟⲗ). Apparently intended to treat a (newly-married?) husband suffering from magically-induced impotence; *cf. PCM* I 26 p. 16 ll. 6–8; the recipes associated with Psalms 44, 117, and 126 in Henein/Bianquis 1975; with Cherkashina/Kuzin 2022 for the Syriac tradition; and Chassinat 1955 (KYP M44) p. 1 ll. 6–10, this last a Coptic recipe intended to bind a bridegroom.

12. ⲛ̄ⲁⲣⲕⲁⲣⲧⲁⲙⲁ : "garden cress?" The suggestion to read "cardamom" here is very speculative; ⲕⲁⲣⲧⲁⲙⲁ is a plausible Coptic rendering of Greek κάρδαμον, which seems refer to garden cress (*Lepidium sativum* L.), but an Arabised form with an initial *al-* does not seem to be otherwise attested; the normal Arabic name for garden cress is حرف *ḥurf*, given as the equivalent of ⲕⲁⲣⲇⲁⲙⲟⲛ in the *Scala magna* (Macomber 2020: 139). Garden cress is mentioned as an ingredient in several ancient and mediaeval Greek and Arabic medical texts; *cf.* Lev/Amar 2008: 172–174.

PCM I 34. Bifolio with bowl divination procedure and silencing curses

Arsinoites (Faiyum) ? 18.7 (H) × 14.3 (W) cm X–XI CE

Other references: Strasbourg K 550; TM 874130; *P.Stras.Copt.* 9; KYP M106; Bélanger Sarrazin #225.

Editions: Tibet 2014 (*ed. pr*) [T].

Translations: Tibet 2014.

Present location: Strasbourg, Bibliothèque Nationale.

Image: Plates XIII–XIV; *P.Stras.Copt.*: fig. 28, 29.

Linguistic description: Sahidic with Middle Egyptian features.

Contents:
1. p. 1 ll. 1–27 – p. 2 ll. 1–26: Invocation for bowl divination (KYP T1085)
2. p. 3 ll. 1–11: Silencing curse (?) (KYP T1086)
3. p. 4 ll. 1–27: Silencing or binding curse (KYP T1658)

Considerably damaged paper bifolio containing three recipes for various purposes. As David Tibet has suggested, the bifolio may have been part of a larger codex which would have opened from either side, as pages 3 and 4 are written at 180° with respect to pages 1 and 2.[1] The bifolio seems to have been further folded before deposition, with 4 horizontal and 3 vertical creases visible on each page,[2] resulting in symmetrical damage patterns, perhaps due to insects. There is also notable discolouration, particularly on the upper edge of pages 3–4 near the spine.

The manuscript was purchased by the Papyruskartell (German Papyrus Cartel) in 1909, as part of a lot including inventory numbers 550–582.[3] Based on the dialect, similar to that of many manuscripts from the Faiyum dating to the same period (*cf.* below), we propose that it may also have originated from that region.

The manuscript is written rather densely, with thick, consistent strokes in a black or dark brown ink. The script is a right-sloping majuscule, bilinear, with serifs on the horizontal bar of ⲧ and, to a lesser extent, ϯ. The ⲁ has a small and very rounded bowl, while the oblique stroke sometimes extends to the right. The lower belly of ⲃ is markedly larger than the top one. The strokes of ⲉ, ⲕ, and ⲗ consistently do not fully join, and there is some bimodularity in the narrowing of ⲉ, ⲟ, and ⲥ. ⲩ and ϩ are bilinear, and the tail of the ϣ is almost horizontal,

---

[1] Tibet 2014: 131–132. Tibet (2014: 131) also notes "some evidence of holes for a binding-cord in the centre of the leaf, though the damage to the manuscript makes it difficult to be certain of this."

[2] *Cf. PCM* I 4 & 28, codices which also seem to have been folded prior to deposition.

[3] Inventaire des papyrus, Coptes, Coptes-Arabes, IPC, IPCM, Bibliothèque Nationale et Universitaire, Strasbourg.

while the ascender of the ϭ is rather long. The copyist respects spaces between lines and letters; on page 1, the line shows a marked upwards slope. No dividing lines are visible on the preserved sections. Supralinear strokes are used above *voces magicae*, and dots are used above certain letters in a similar manner to the supralinear stroke or later djinkim. Colons are used to separate individual words or phrases. As Tibet (2014: 132) notes, the use of paper suggests a tenth century date at the earliest. A tenth or eleventh century date is likewise likely based on the hand, which notably demonstrates the "flat μ".[4]

The dialect is a form of Sahidic heavily influenced by a Middle Egyptian dialect, likely that of the Faiyum, but lacking in the lambdacism associated with the classical forms of Faiyumic (F4/F5), which is very close to that found in the archive known as the 'Heidelberg Coptic Magical Library'.[5]

We have renumbered the pages assuming that the bifolio was originally written in such as way that two pages in the same orientation followed one another when folded; as a result, our page 1 = Tibet's Verso (1); page 2 = Recto (1); page 3 = Recto (inverted); page 4 here = Verso (inverted). On page 4, we number the lines continuously, whereas Tibet numbers each text area separately. Tibet does not generally mark supralineation in his edition, and so we do not mark divergences in the treatment of supralineation in the apparatus.

---

[4] Mihálykó 2019: 16–18.
[5] See pp. 261–262 for a fuller description.

page 1

```
------------------------------------------------
[ ca. 9 ] . ге̣[ ca. 10 ]
. [ ca. 8 ] . . . c̣ : м̄ . [ ca. 10 ]
. . [ ca. 6 ] . т̄ . ṇaḳ . [ ca. 10 ]
. . [ ca. 8 ] . . . . ·.· т . [ ca. 9 ]
```
5 т . . [ca. 6]ai†ṗeṭ[ca. 10]
..ṇai̇ [. . . .] . ⲁⲉⲡ ⲉⲧ[. . .] . [. .] . [. .]
ⲉⲕϥⲱⲧ[. . . .] ⲛ̄ⲡⲟⲟⲩ ⲧⲉⲧⲉⲛⲉⲓ ⲉϩⲣ[ⲁⲓ]
ⲉϫⲉⲛ ⲡⲁ̇ⲡⲟⲧ ⲉⲙⲙⲁⲟⲩ : ⲉⲧⲕⲏ ⲉϩⲣⲁⲓ̇
ⲉⲛ̄ⲡⲁⲉⲙⲧⲁ ⲉⲃⲁⲗ : ⲧⲉⲧⲛⲙⲁϩϥ ⲉ-
10 [ca. 8] ⲥⲁϣⲃ ⲉⲛⲥⲁⲡ : ϩⲉⲛ . . .
. . . . ⲉi̇ṇ . ⲡⲟⲩⲣⲁⲛⲓⲱⲛ : ⲙⲁⲣⲉϥⲉⲣ ⲟⲩⲁ-
[ⲉⲓⲛ] ⲉⲑⲉ ⲉⲡⲣⲏ : ⲙⲁⲣⲉϥⲉ̄ⲣ̄ ⲟ̄ⲩⲁⲉⲓⲛ
ⲉⲑⲉ ⲉⲡⲁϩ ⲧⲉϥⲟⲩⲱⲛϩ ⲏⲃⲁⲗ ⲉⲣⲁi̇ ⲛ̄-
ⲇⲓⲉⲛⲉ ⲧⲁⲭⲓⲱⲛ . . . . ⲕⲱⲥⲙⲟⲥ ⲙⲁⲣⲉⲡ-
15 ⲕⲁϩ ⲡⲱϣ ⲉⲛⲡⲁⲉⲙⲧⲱ ⲉⲃⲁⲗ ⲉ[ⲧ]ⲙⲉ̣[ϩ-]
ⲯⲓⲥ ⲡⲏ : ϣ : ϣⲁ ⲛⲉⲥⲉⲛ† ⲛ̄ⲡ[ⲕⲁϩ]
ⲧⲉⲧⲉⲛⲙⲟⲩϩ : ⲉⲛⲛⲉⲃⲁⲗ ⲉⲛⲡ[ⲁⲑ]ⲉ̣ⲟ-
ⲣⲓⲥⲧⲱⲥ ⲉⲛⲟⲩⲁⲉⲓⲛ : ⲉⲛ̄ⲍ̄ ⲉⲛ[ⲥⲁ]ⲡ ⲍ̄ ⲉⲛⲥⲁⲡ : ⲉϥϭⲱϣ† ϩⲏⲛ ⲟⲩϭⲓⲉⲛⲑⲉⲱⲣi̇
20 ⲉⲧⲛⲁⲛⲟⲩⲥ : ⲛⲁⲧϭⲁⲗ : ⲛⲁⲧϣⲧⲟⲣⲧⲉⲣ
ⲛⲁⲧⲉⲣϩⲁⲧⲏ : ⲛⲁⲫⲁⲛⲧ[ⲁⲥⲓ]ⲁ ⲧⲉϥ-
ϭⲱⲗⲡ̄ ⲛⲁⲓ ⲉⲃⲁⲗ ⲉⲛϩⲱⲃ [ⲛⲓⲙ] ⲉⲧϣⲓ-
ⲛⲓ ⲉⲛⲥⲱⲩ : ⲉⲃⲁⲗ ϩⲓⲧⲁⲧ[ϥ :] ⲉⲓⲧⲏ ⲛⲟⲩᴮ
ⲉⲓⲧⲏ ϩⲁⲓ† : ⲉⲓ† ⲕⲱⲥⲙⲏⲥ[ⲓⲥ :] ⲉⲓⲧⲏ ⲡ̇ⲛⲓ-
25 ⲡ̣i̇ ⲉⲓⲧⲏ ⲃⲁⲣⲱⲧ : ⲉⲓⲧ[ⲏ] ⲧⲉϥⲛⲏ
ⲉi̇[ⲧⲏ ⲉ]ⲓⲧⲱⲥ ⲛⲓⲙ ⲉⲧ[ϩⲉⲛ ⲡⲕ]ⲱ̣ⲥⲙⲟⲥ
[. .] . ϭⲟ[ⲗ]ⲡⲟⲩ ⲛⲁi̇ . [. . . .] . ⲟⲩ

---

2 м̄ : ẹ T :]ⲉ̣ṭ T ‖ **3** ṇai T ‖ **5** ..† · .ṭ T ‖ **6** ⲡⲁ[T ‖ **7** ⲉⲕ . ϣ T | *i.e.* ˢм̄-ⲡⲟⲟⲩ : ⲉ̣ⲛⲛⲁⲩ T | *i.e.* ˢⲛ̄=ⲧⲉⲧⲛ̄-ⲉⲓ̈ | ⲉⲣⲁi T ‖ **8** .. ϫⲉ ⲛⲛ̣ⲭ[..] ⲉⲧ[ⲉⲙ]ⲙⲁⲟⲩ T | *i.e.* ˢм̄-ⲙⲟⲟⲩ ‖ **9** *i.e.* ˢм̄-ⲡⲁ-м̄ⲧⲟ ⲉⲃⲟⲗ : [ca. 10] T | *i.e.* ˢⲛ̄=ⲧⲉⲧⲛ̄-ⲙⲁϩ=q̄ ‖ **10** *l.* -ⲛⲟⲩⲁⲉⲓⲛ *cf.* note : ca. 7 T | *i.e.* ˢⲥⲁϣϥ ⲛ̄-ⲥⲟⲡ ‖ **10–11** *l. e.g.* ϩⲉⲛ ⲟⲩⲟⲩⲁⲉⲓⲛ ⲉⲡⲟⲩⲣⲁⲛⲓⲟⲛ *i.e.* ἐπουράνιον : [ca. 3 | ca. 7] ⲟⲩⲣⲁⲛⲓⲱⲛ *i.e.* οὐράνιον T ‖ **12** ⲉⲑⲉ : [ⲉϩⲟⲩⲟ] T | ⲙⲁⲣⲉϥⲉⲣ ⲟⲩⲁ̣ⲉ[ⲓⲛ] T ‖ **13** ⲉⲑⲉ : [ⲉϩⲟⲩⲟ] T | [ⲉ]ⲡ[ⲓⲁ]ϩ T | *i.e.* ˢⲛ̄=ϥ-ⲟⲩⲱⲛϩ ⲉⲃⲟⲗ ⲉⲣⲟ=ⲓ̈ : ⲧⲉϥⲟⲩⲱ[ⲛ]ϩ T | *i.e.* ˢⲉⲃⲟⲗ | ⲉ.ⲁ.. : ⲁ[ca. 3] T | **12** ⲉ.. : [ⲉϩⲟⲩⲟ] T ‖ **13–14** *l.* ⲛ̄-ⲛ-ⲇⲓⲉⲛⲉ or ⲛ̄-ⲡ-ⲇⲓⲉⲛⲉ *i.e.* διανοεῖν or διάνοια ? : ⲁ[ca. 4] T | *i.e.* ταχίων T ‖ **14** *i.e.* κόσμος | ⲙⲁⲣⲉⲡ ink trace between ⲙ and ⲁ : [. .]p̣[. . . .] T ‖ **15** *i.e.* ˢм̄-ⲡⲁ-м̄ⲧⲟ | ⲙⲁⲣⲉ- : [....] T ‖ **16** ⲯⲓⲥ : *cf.* ὄψις? T | *i.e.* ˢм̄-ⲡⲉ ϣⲁ : ⲡⲛϣ "being divided" T | [ca. 5] T ‖ **17** *i.e.* ˢⲛ̄=ⲧⲉⲧⲛ̄-ⲙⲟⲩϩ ⲛ̄-ⲛ-ⲃⲁⲗ ‖ **17–18** *i.e.* θεωριστής ? : ⲉⲛⲛⲉ... [ⲉⲩⲭⲁ]ⲣⲓⲥⲧⲱⲥ *i.e.* εὐχάριστος T ‖ **18–19** *i.e.* ˢⲛ̄-ⲍ̄ ⲛ̄-ⲥⲟⲡ ‖ **19** *i.e.* ˢⲛ̄=ϥ-ϭⲱϣⲧ | *i.e.* ˢϩⲛ̄- | *i.e.* ˢⲟⲩ-ϭⲓⲛ-ⲑⲉⲱⲣⲉⲓⲛ : ⲟⲩϭⲓⲉⲛⲑ̣ⲭⲱⲙ T ‖ **20–21** *cf.* p. 2 ll. 8–9, 15–16 ‖ **21** *i.e.* ˢϩⲟⲧⲉ | *i.e.* ˢⲁⲧ-ⲫⲁⲛⲧ[ⲁⲥί]ⲁ *cf.* note to p. 2 ll. 8–9, 15–16 ‖ **21–22** *i.e.* ˢⲛ̄=ϥ-ϭⲱⲗⲡ ‖ **22** *i.e.* ˢⲛ̄-ϩⲱⲃ ‖ **23** *i.e.* ˢⲛ̄ⲥⲱ=ⲩ ‖ **23–26** *i.e.* ⲉⲓ̈ⲧⲉ ‖ **24** *i.e.* ˢϩⲟⲉⲓⲧⲉ | *i.e.* ⲉⲓ̈ⲧⲉ | *i.e.* κόσμης[ⲓⲥ] | *i.e.* ⲉⲓ̈ⲧⲉ ‖ **24–25** *i.e.* ˢⲃⲉⲛⲓⲡⲉ : ⲡ̇ⲛⲓ|[ⲓⲡ]ⲓ̇ T ‖ **25** [ⲡ]ⲓ̣ ink traces after ⲓ | *i.e.* ⲉⲓ̈ⲧⲉ : ⲉⲓ[ⲧⲏ] T | *i.e.* ˢⲧⲃⲛⲏ : ⲧⲉϥⲛⲏ[ⲩ] T ‖ **26** [ⲉⲓⲧⲏ] T | *i.e.* [ⲉ]ⲓ̂ⲇⲟⲥ | *i.e.* [ⲕ]όσμος ‖ **27** [. . . .] . ⲟⲩ *l.* ⲛ̄ⲡⲁⲟⲩ *i.e.* ˢм̄-ⲡⲟⲟⲩ ?

... |⁵... this? ... to his ... today and you come down upon the *cup of water that is placed before me and fill it with |¹⁰ [light?], seven times with heavenly light?. May it shine [like?] the sun, may it shine like the moon, and reveal to me the thoughts? earlier? ... world, may the |¹⁵ earth divide before me from the ninth? heaven to the foundations of the [earth,?] and may you fill the eyes of my scryer? with light, seven [times] seven times, so that he sees in a good vision, |²⁰ without deception, without disturbance, without fear, without illusion, and he reveals for me everything that I enquire about through [him?], whether gold, or clothes, or ornaments, or iron, |²⁵ or bronze, or livestock, or any other thing in [the] world, ... reveal them to me ...

pp. 1–2. Bowl divination procedure: This represents a rare instance of bowl divination ('lecanomancy') in the Coptic magical corpus. The practitioner speaks the formula over a cup of water and a scryer (*cf.* notes to ll. 17–18 below) looks into the water to see a vision in which the answer to a question is revealed by a superhuman being who appears in the water. There is a close parallel with the only other published Coptic bowl divination recipe, BM EA 10391 (Zellmann-Rohrer 2022a: no 1; KYP M302) front ll. 38–49. Particularly close are ll. 41–42: "and you come down upon this cup of water that is placed before me and you fill it for me with light like the sun and the moon seven times seven times" (ⲛⲧⲉⲧⲛⲉⲓ ⲉϩⲣⲁⲓ ⲉϫⲛ ⲡⲉⲁⲡⲟⲧ ⲛⲙⲟⲟⲩ ⲉⲧⲕⲏ ⲉϩⲣⲁⲓ ⲛⲡⲁⲙⲧⲟ ⲉⲃⲟⲗ ⲛⲧⲉⲧⲛⲙⲟⲣϥ ⲛⲁⲓ ⲛⲟⲩⲟⲉⲓⲛ ⲛⲑⲉ ⲛⲡⲣⲏ ⲙⲛ ⲡⲟϩ ⲛⲍ̄ ⲛⲕⲱⲃ ⲛⲥⲟⲟⲡ). Other divination rituals in the Coptic magical corpus are found in Cairo JdE 45060 (Kropp 1931: I no. K; KYP M303) front ll. 38–40; P.Mich.Inv. 593 (Worrell 1930; KYP M9) p. 10 ll. 4–8; P.Mich.Inv. 594 (KYP M9) back ll. 12–14; *P.Macq.* I 1 (KYP M167) p. 15 ll. 20–21 (all dream divination procedures); BM EA 10391 (Zellmann-Rohrer 2022a: no 1; KYP M302) front ll. 50–58: (thumbnail divination (?)); *cf.* *GEMF* 57/*PGM* IV (KYP M3) ll. 11–25 & 88–93, two Old Coptic divination texts (*cf.* Love 2016: 124–149). On bowl divination in general, see Hopfner 1932; Dosoo 2014: 253–257, 398–399 *et passim*; Nagel 2017.

15. ϩ[ⲡ]ⲙⲉ[ϩ]ϯⲥ ⲡⲏ : "**from the ninth? heaven**" If this reading is correct it would represent an unusual example of a nine-heaven scheme in a post-fourth century Coptic-language source; more common in Coptic literature are three- or seven-heaven schemes, *e.g.*, *Apocalypse of Paul* (CC 30) in Lanzillotta/van der Vliet 2022 214.24–25, 215 (trans.); Pseudo-Timothy of Alexandria, *Institution of Abbaton* (CC 405) in Budge 1914: 246.4, 493 (trans.). Nine-heaven schemes are attested, for example, in earlier Hermetic sources (see Robinson 2000: III 342). In such schemes, the first seven heavens correspond to the seven planetary spheres, the eighth may correspond to the sphere of the fixed stars, and the ninth to the supercelestial sphere beyond this.

17–18. ⲛⲡ[ⲁⲑ]ⲉⲟⲣⲓⲥⲧⲱⲥ : "**of my scryer**" This word also appears in the parallel text BM EA 10391 (Zellmann 2022a: no. 1; KYP M302) front ll. 42–48: "(may) you fill my eyes with divinity and those of my scryer? with light ... (may) [you fill] my eyes ‹and› those of my scryer? with light" (ⲛⲧⲉⲧⲛⲙⲉϩ ⲛⲁⲃⲁⲗ ϩⲛ ⲡⲁⲑϩⲉⲱⲣⲏⲥ ⲛⲁⲡⲁⲑⲉⲱⲣⲓⲥⲧⲏⲥ ⲛⲟⲉⲓⲛ ... ⲛ[ⲧⲉⲧⲛⲙⲉϩ] ⲛⲁⲃⲁⲗ ⲛⲁⲡⲁⲑⲉⲱⲣⲓⲥⲧⲏⲥ ⲛⲟⲉⲓⲛ). As noted by Zellmann-Rohrer (2022a: 102), this would seem to be a loan of an otherwise unattested Greek term θεωριστής, formed from the scarcely-attested verb θεωρίζω (*cf.* θεωρέω; see Horrocks 1997: 239 for verb formations of this type) by the addition of the agentive suffix -ιστής. In meaning it would be comparable to θεωρός or θεωρητής "one who observes". Here we understand it as referring to the boy medium who looks into the bowl for the practitioner and receives the vision, comparable to the term ἐπόπτης ("observer") used in older Greek magical and theurgic contexts (see, *e.g.*, Iamblichus, *On the Mysteries* III.13; *PGM* VII/*GEMF* 74.570–572). Zellmann-Rohrer (2022a: 89) translates "vision". On scryers, also known as "child mediums" or "seers", *cf.* Johnston 2001; Dosoo 2014: 329–334, 391–393.

24. ϩⲁⲓϯ : "**clothes**" perhaps correct to ϩⲁⲧ, ᴿϩⲁⲧ "silver", which would fit the context well here.

page 2

[ca. 5 ϩⲉⲛ ⲟⲩ]ϭⲏⲡⲏ [ca. 10]
[ca. 10]ⲁ̣ⲓ ⲡ̣ⲓ ⸱⸱ ⲧⲉ̣ . [ca. 7]ⲏ̣
[ca. 10 ϩⲉ]ⲛ̣ ⲟⲩϭⲏⲡⲏ [ⲙⲉⲛ ⲟⲩ]ⲧⲁ̣ⲭⲏ
[ca. 8] ⲧⲁⲣⲓⲕ ⸱ ⲕ[ca. 5]. ⲟ̣ⲩ̅ⲣ̅ⲓ̣
5   [. . .]ⲕⲁ[ca. 5] . ⲇ̅ⲉ̅ⲁ̅ ⸱ ⲉⲗ . [. . . . ⲁ]ⲧⲟⲛⲁⲓ
[ⲡⲓ]ⲱⲧ ⲡⲛⲟⲩ[ⲧⲉ] ϩⲉⲛ ⲧⲉⲩⲙ[ⲉ]ϯ ⲉⲕϭⲱⲗⲡ̅
ⲛⲁⲓ ⲉⲃⲁⲗ ⲉⲛⲡⲁⲟⲩ ⲉⲛⲡ[ⲉϯ]ϣⲓⲛⲓ ⲉⲛ-
ⲥⲱⲃ ⲉⲛⲧⲁⲧⲉⲩⲧⲉⲛ ⲛⲁϭⲁⲗ ⲛⲁⲧⲉⲣ
ϩⲁϯ ⸱ ⲛⲁⲫⲁⲛⲧⲁⲥⲓⲁ ⸱ ⲑⲁⲣⲁ ⲯⲡⲣⲁ . .
10 ⲙ̅ⲁ̅ⲓ̅ⲑ̅ⲉ̅ⲥ̅ⲁ̅ⲱ̅ ⲙ̅ⲡ̅ⲟ̅ⲩ̅ⲣ̅ⲛ̅ⲱⲥ . . ⲁ̅ⲙ̅ⲁ̅ϩ̣ . . . .
ϩⲣⲁⲃⲁⲗⲧϯ ⲫ̅ϯ̅ ⲓⲱⲧ ϩⲉⲛ ⲧⲉⲩⲙⲉϯ
ⲥⲱⲧⲉⲛ ⲉⲣⲁⲓ ⲉⲛⲡⲁⲟⲩ ⸱ ⲉⲓⲱϣ ⲉϩⲣⲁⲓ ⲉⲣⲁⲕ
ϫⲱⲕ ⲛⲁⲓ ⲉⲃⲁⲗ ⲉⲛⲧⲁⲡⲱⲗⲁⲕⲓⲁ ⲉⲛⲡⲁ-
ⲗⲁⲥ ⸱ ⲉⲛϩⲱⲃ ⲛⲓⲙ ⲉⲧⲉϯ ⲉⲙⲙⲁⲩ ϩⲓⲧⲁ-
15 ⲧⲉⲩⲧⲉ̣ⲛ̣ ⲛⲁϭⲁⲗ ⸱ ⲛⲁⲧⲉⲣ ϩⲁϯ ⸱ ⲛⲁⲧⲫⲁⲛⲧⲁⲥⲓⲁ ⲁⲗⲗⲁ ϩⲛⲛ ⲟⲩⲙⲓⲏ ⲙⲉⲛ ⲟⲩϣⲱⲧ
ⲉⲃⲁⲗ ⸱ ⲙⲉⲛ ⲟⲩⲥⲁⲩⲧⲉⲛ ⸱ ⲙⲁⲣⲉⲡϭⲱ ϭⲱⲡⲓ
ⲧⲉⲡⲉⲧϯ ⲉⲓⲛⲓ ⸱ ⲁⲓⲱ ⲁⲓⲱ ⲧⲁⲭⲏ ⲧⲁⲭⲏ
ⲁ̅ⲛ̅ⲁ̅ⲣ̅ⲭ̅ⲓ̣[. .]ⲛ̅ⲭ̅ⲣ̅ⲁ̅ⲛ̅ⲱ̅ⲥ̅ ⲙ̅ⲡ̅ⲛ̅ⲁ̅ⲅ̅ⲟ̅ⲥ̅
20 ⲙ̅ⲡ̅ⲁ̅ⲣ̅ϯ̅ⲭ̅ⲥ̅ⲱ̅ⲑ̅ⲏ̅ⲛ̅ⲥ̅ ⲙ̅ⲓ̅ⲛ̅ⲁ̅ⲏ̅ⲗ̅ ⲁ̅ⲙ̅ⲟ̅ⲩ̅ ⲛ̅ⲁ̅ⲓ̅
ⲥ̅ⲁ̅ⲃ̅ⲁ̅ⲱ̅ⲧ̅ ⲧ̅ⲁ̅ⲛ̅ⲁ̅ⲏ̅ⲗ̅ ⲧ̅ⲏ̅ⲍ̅ⲟ̅ⲩ̅ⲏ̅ⲗ̅ ⲥ̅ⲏ̅ⲫ̅ⲏ̅ⲃ̅ⲁ̅ⲛ̅
ⲧ̅ⲗ̅ⲏ̅ⲗ̅ ⲥⲁ . [.] . ⲁ̣ⲗ ⲏ̅ⲗ̅ ⲏ̅ⲗ̅ ⲏ̅ⲗ̅ ⲏ̅ⲗ̅ ⲏ̅ⲗ̅ ⲏ̅ⲗ̅
ⲙ̅ⲏ̅ . . . [.] . ⲁ̅ⲧ̅ⲁ̅ⲏ̅ⲗ̅ ⲉⲓⲉⲣϣⲉϩ ⲕ̅ⲁ̅ⲑ̅ⲓ̅ⲏ̅ⲗ̅
ⲗⲁϯⲁ . [. . .]ⲩ̅ⲏ̅ⲗ̅ ⲙ̅ⲓ̅ⲙ̅ⲓ̅ⲏ̅ⲗ̅ ⲥ̅ⲓ̅ⲫ̅ⲓ̅ⲏ̅ⲗ̅ ⲣⲟ̣[.]
25 ⲧϣ . . [. . . .]ⲩ̅ⲛ̅ⲏ̅ ⲥ̅ⲁ̅ⲃ̅ⲁ̅ⲱ̅ⲑ̅ ⲛⲧⲁⲩ[. . . .]
ⲛ̣ⲁ̣ⲛ̣[ca. 6]ⲁ̅ⲛ̅ⲁ̅ⲧ̅ ⲗ̅ⲁ̅ⲗ̅ ⲙ̅ⲓ̅ⲭ̅ⲁ̅ⲏ̅ⲗ̅ [. . . .]

---

1 *i.e.* ᔆϩⲛ ⲟⲩ-ϭⲉⲡⲏ ‖ **2** [ⲡϭⲱϭⲱ]ⲡⲓⲧⲉ̣ *i.e.* ᔆⲕⲁⲕⲟⲩⲡⲁⲧ T ‖ **3** *i.e.* ᔆⲟⲩ-ϭⲉⲡⲏ | *i.e.* ταχύ :] ⲧⲁ̣ⲭⲏ T ‖
4 ⲧⲁⲣ̣ⲓⲕ T ‖ **5** ⲉ̣ⲗ . : ⲅ[T ‖ **7** *i.e.* ᔆⲙ̅-ⲡⲟⲟⲩ ‖ **7–8** *i.e.* ᔆⲛ̅-ⲡ-ⲉⲧ-ϯ-ϣⲓⲛⲉ ⲛ̅ⲥⲱ⸗ϥ ⲛⲧⲟⲟⲧ⸗ⲧⲏⲩⲧⲛ̅ ‖
8 *i.e.* ᔆⲛ̅-ⲁⲧ-ϭⲟⲗ ‖ **9** *i.e.* ᔆⲁⲧ-φαντασία ‖ **12** *i.e.* ᔆⲥⲱⲧⲙ̅ ⲉⲣⲟ⸗ⲓ̈ ⲙ̅-ⲡⲟⲟⲩ ‖ **13** *i.e.* ἀπολογία :
[ⲉ]ⲛⲧⲁⲡⲟⲗⲱⲕⲓⲁ T ‖ **13–14** *i.e.* ᔆⲙ̅-ⲡⲁ-ⲗⲁⲥ ‖ **14** *i.e.* ᔆⲛ̅-ϩⲱⲃ : [ⲉ]ⲛϩⲱⲃ T | *i.e.* ᔆⲉⲧ-ϯ-αἰτεῖν ‖
14–15 *i.e.* ᔆϩⲓⲧⲟⲟⲧ⸗ⲧⲏⲩⲧⲛ̅ ‖ **15** *i.e.* ᔆⲛ̅-ⲁⲧ-ϭⲟⲗ ‖ **15–16** *i.e.* φαντασία ‖ **16** *i.e.* ἀλλά | *i.e.* ᔆϩⲛ :
ϩⲉⲛ T | *i.e.* ᔆⲟⲩ-ⲙⲉ | *i.e.* ᔆⲟⲩ-ϣⲱⲧ ‖ **17–18** *i.e.* ᔆⲙⲁⲣⲉ-ⲡ-ϫⲱ ϭⲱⲡⲉ ⲛ̅ⲧⲉ-ⲡⲉⲧ-ϯ ⲉⲓⲛⲉ ? : or
i.e. ᔆⲙⲁⲣⲉ-ⲡ-ⲕⲁⲕⲟⲩⲡⲁⲧ ϯ ⲉⲓⲛⲉ ? T ‖ **18** *i.e.* ᔆⲛ̅ⲧⲉ-ⲡ-ⲉⲧ-ϯ | *i.e.* ταχύ (twice) ‖ **19** ⲁ̅ⲛ̅ⲁ̅ⲣ̅ⲭ̅ T |
ⲛⲭⲣⲁⲛⲱⲥ T | ⲙⲡⲛⲁⲅⲟⲥ T ‖ **20** ⲛⲡⲁⲣⲧⲭ̣[.]ⲱⲑⲡⲁⲥ T ‖ **21** ⲥⲁⲃⲁⲱⲑ T | [.]ⲁⲛⲁⲏⲗ T ‖ **24** ⲙ̅ⲓ̅ⲙ̅ⲓ̅ⲏ̅ⲗ̅ :
ⲙⲓⲭ[. .] T ‖ **25** ⲧϣ : ⲧⲁ T | ⲩⲡⲏ T ‖ **26** ⲛ̣ⲁ̣ⲛ̣ : [.]ⲁ̣ⲓ T

|p. 2 ... quickly?, ... quickly, swiftly ... |5 ... *Adonai [the] Father, God in their midst, may you reveal to me today that which I enquire about through you (pl.) without deception, without fear, without illusion! Thara Pspra ... |10 Maithesaš Mpoureōs ... amah ... Hrabaltti, God, Father in their midst, listen to me today as I call upon you, fulfil for me the request of my tongue in everything that I ask from |15 you (pl.), without deception, without fear, without illusion, but truthfully, concisely, and rightly! May the *cup? take, and the one who gives bring, yea, yea, quickly, quickly! Anarkhi ...nkhranōs Mpēagos |20 Mpartikhsōthēns Minaēl, come to me, *Sabaoth Tanaēl Tēxouēl Sēphēban Tlēl Sa...al Ēl Ēl Ēl Ēl Ēl Ēl Mē ... ataēl Eieršeh Kathiēl Latia...uēl Mimiēl Sphiēl Ro... |25 Tš...unē Sabaoth Ētau... Nan...anat Lal *Michael...

8–9, 15–16. ⲚⲀϬⲀⲖ ⲚⲀⲦⲈⲢ ϨⲀϮ ⲚⲀⲦⲪⲀⲚⲦⲀⲤⲒⲀ : **"without deception, without disturbance, without fear, without illusion"** *Cf.* p. 1 ll. 20–21. A specification to prevent the revelation of the superhuman being from being either frightening or deceptive. Similar specifications appear in older Graeco-Egyptian divination procedures; see *GEMF* 12/*PGM* LXXXVII (KYP M80; II CE) ll. 20–22: "I have requested a clear oracle without fear or trembling" ([κε]χρημάτισμαι ἀφόβως ἀδρώμως εὔδηλον χρησμὸν); *GEMF* 16/*PDM* xiv (KYP M162; II CE): "without fear, without deceit, truthfully" (ἀφόβως ἀψεύστως ἐπ' ἀληθείᾳ; l. 42), "in truth, truthfully, without lies, without ambiguity, concerning this matter" (ἐπ' ἀληθείας ἀληθῶς ἀψευδῶς ἀναμφιλόγως; ll. 106–107).

16–17. ⲞⲨϢⲰⲦ ⲈⲂⲀⲖ : **"concisely"** For the translation "concisely", *cf. Acts of the Apostles* 24.4 (Thompson 1932: 71), in which ⲞⲨϢⲰⲰⲦ ⲈⲂⲞⲖ phrase translates the Greek συντόμως "concisely, briefly". Tibet translates "decisively".

page 3 (at 180° to pages 1–2)

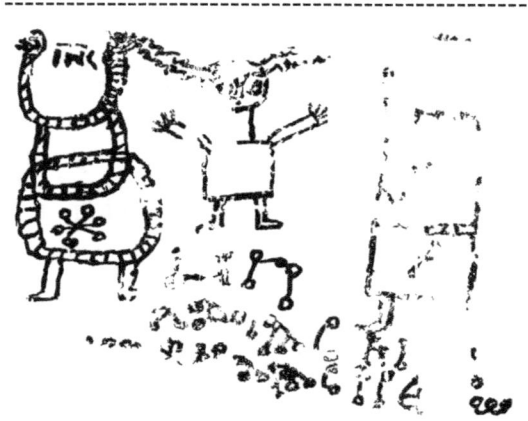

```
     [ ca. 11  ] . ⲁⲱⲗⲓⲁⲙ . [ . . ] ⲛⲁⲩ
     [ ca. 11  ]ⲃⲏⲥⲱⲛ ⲕⲁⲧ[ . . . ] .
     [ ca. 10  ⲓ]ⲁ̣ⲱ ⲥⲁ̣ⲃ̣ⲁ̣ⲱⲑ [ . ]ⲗⲱⲛ
     [ ca. 11  ]ⲁ̣ⲑ ⲙⲓⲭ[ⲁ]ⲏⲗ ⲅ̣ⲁ̣ⲃⲣⲓⲏⲗ
5    [ ca. 11  ]ⲕⲟⲩⲏⲗ ⲥⲁⲣⲁⲫⲟⲩⲏⲗ
     [ ca. 11  ⌈. ⲁ̣ .⌉ ⲡⲓⲍ̣ ⲛⲁⲣⲭⲏⲁⲛ-
     [ⲅⲉⲗⲟⲥ ca. 6  ]ⲙ ⲉⲛⲭⲱⲱⲣⲉ ⲛ
     [ ca. 6  †ⲥⲟⲡⲥ]ⲡ ⲁⲩⲱ †ⲡⲁⲣⲁⲕⲁⲗ-
     [ⲉⲓ ⲙⲙⲱⲧⲉⲛ ⲛⲡ]ⲁⲟⲩ : ⲡⲟⲩⲭⲁⲓ ⲉⲛⲛⲉ̣-
10   [ⲧⲉⲛⲣⲉⲛ ⲙⲉⲛ ⲛⲉ]ⲧⲉⲛϭⲁⲙ ⲙⲉⲛ ⲛⲉ-
     [ⲧⲉⲛ- ca. 9  ] . . . . . . . . . . . .
```

1]ⲱⲗⲓⲁⲙ T ‖ **2** ⲃ̣ⲣⲥⲱⲛ T ‖ **3** *l.* [ⲉ]ⲗⲱⲛ ? *cf. PCM* 10 l. 14 :]ⲁⲱ ⲥⲁ[ⲃ]ⲁⲱⲑ [*ca.* 2] ⲗⲱⲛ T ‖ **4** ⲁ̣ⲑ : ⲑ T ‖
6]ⲁ̣ⲡⲓⲍ̣ T | ⲁⲣⲭⲏⲟⲛ *i.e.* ἄρχων ? T ‖ **6–7** *i.e.* ἀρχάγγελος ‖ **7** ⲉⲛⲭ̣ [. . . .] ⲉⲛ T ‖ **8** [†ⲥⲟⲡⲥ]ⲡ :]† T ‖
8–9 *i.e.* παρακαλ[εῖν] ‖ **9** [ⲡ]ⲁⲟⲩ : T does not transcribe | *i.e.* ⁽ˢ⁾ⲙ̄-ⲡ-ⲟⲩⲭⲁⲓ

PCM I 34 (P.Stras.Copt. 9) : Bifolio with bowl divination procedure and silencing curses 443

|left of figure Iak
|below figure (kharaktēres: IZΓI XΔIAC+N . . . NΛACIIE . Ⲱ)

... aōliam...nau ...bēson Kat ... *Iao *Sabaoth Elōn? ...ath, *Michael, *Gabriel, |⁵ ... kouēl, Saraphouēl, ... the seven *archangels ... mighty ... [I entreat] and I invoke [you] today ⟨by⟩ the *wellbeing of your |¹⁰ [*names and] your *powers and [your] ...

Image: We propose that this page contains a binding or silencing curse based on the presence of a tableau paralleled in the binding/silencing curse in P.Würzburg inv. 42 (Brunsch 1978; M494); a similar, albeit much faded, tableau is found in P.Berol. 20911 (Beltz 1984: no. III 32; KYP M219). These images seem to represent the curse's targets flanked by spirit-beings who threaten and bind them; for a discussion, see Dosoo 2023a: 177–183.
7.]ⲙ ⲉⲛϫⲱⲱⲣⲉ : "... mighty" Perhaps restore [ϭⲟ]ⲙ ⲉⲛϫⲱⲱⲣⲉ, cf. P.KölnÄgypt. I 11 (KYP M413) ll. 11–12: "I adjure you by your names and your mighty powers" (ϯⲧⲁⲣⲕⲟ ⲙⲙⲱⲧⲛ ⲛ̄ⲛⲉⲧⲛ̄ⲣⲁⲛ ⲙ̄ⲛ ⲛⲉⲧⲛ̄ⲇⲩⲛⲁⲙⲓⲥ ⲛ̄ϫⲱⲱⲣⲉ), where ϭⲟⲙ is the native Coptic equivalent of ⲇⲩⲛⲁⲙⲓⲥ; cf. Stegemann 1935.
9–10. We propose here some plausible reconstructions based on parallels; cf. e.g., PCM I 32 ll. 9–10: "I adjure you by the wellbeing of your great powers and your names" (ϯⲧⲁⲣⲕⲟ ⲙⲙⲱⲧⲛ ⲙⲡⲟⲩϫⲁⲓ̈ ⲛⲛⲉⲧⲛⲛⲟϭ ⲛϭⲟⲙ · ⲙⲛ ⲛⲉⲧⲛⲣⲁⲛ); BKU III 387 (KYP M336) ll. 36–39: "I entreat and I invoke you by the wellbeing of your names and your powers" (ϯⲥⲟⲡⲥ ⲁⲩⲱ ϯⲡⲁⲣⲁⲕⲁⲗⲉⲓ ⲙⲟⲧⲛ ⲙⲡⲟⲩϫⲁⲓ ⲉⲛⲉⲧⲛⲣⲁⲛ ⲙⲛ); cf. the glossary s.v. *horkōmotoi.

page 4 (at 180° to pages 1–2)

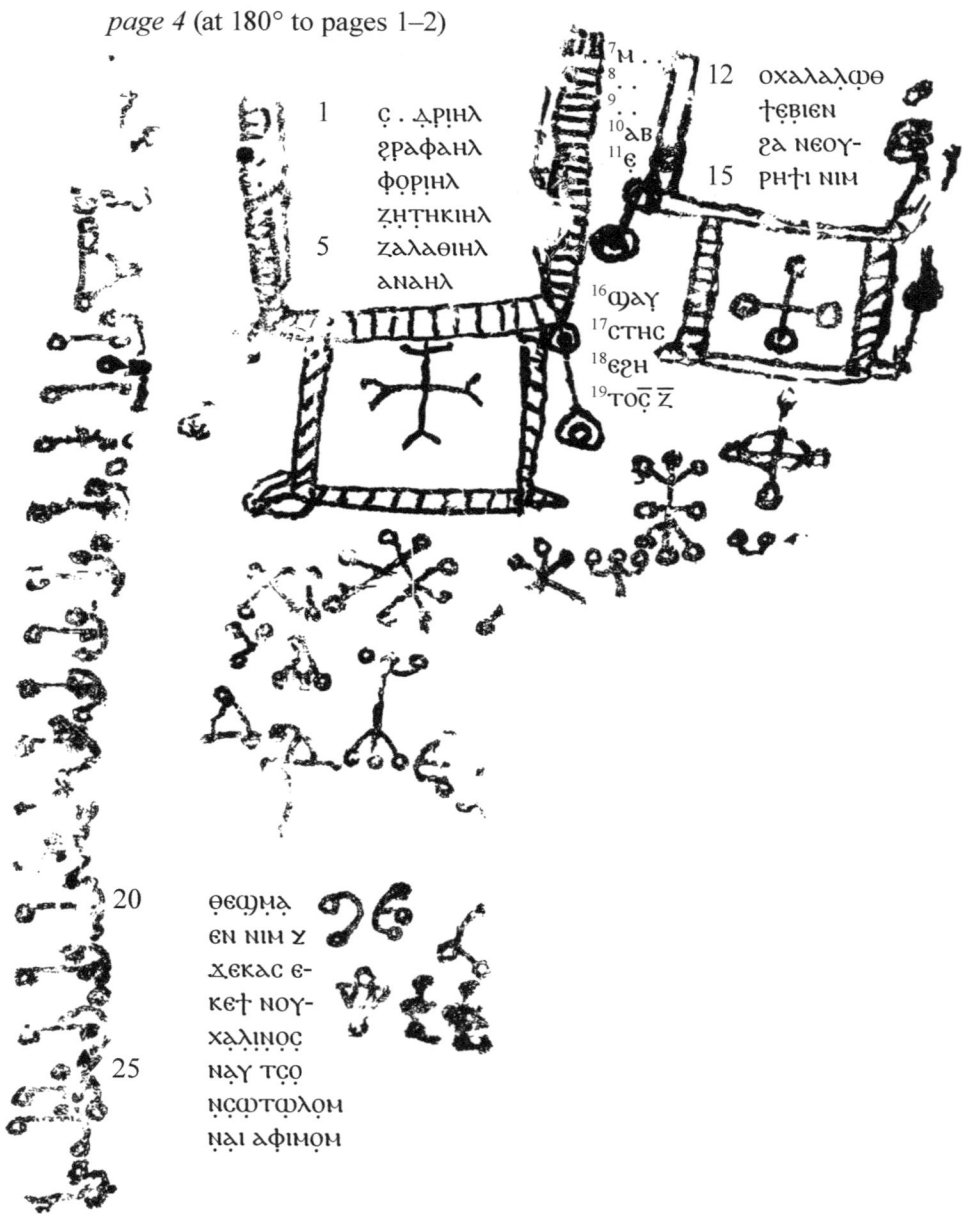

1 ⲥ . ⲇⲣⲓⲏⲗ
ⲉⲣⲁⲫⲁⲛⲗ
ⲫⲟⲣⲓⲏⲗ
ⲍⲏⲧⲏⲕⲓⲏⲗ
5 ⲍⲁⲗⲁⲑⲓⲏⲗ
ⲁⲛⲁⲏⲗ

7 ⲙ . .
8 . .
9 . .
10 ⲁⲃ
11 ⲉ

12 ⲟⲭⲁⲗⲁⲗⲱⲑ
ϯⲉⲃⲓⲉⲛ
ⲉⲁ ⲛⲉⲟⲩ-
15 ⲣⲏϯ ⲛⲓⲙ

16 ϣⲁⲩ
17 ⲥⲧⲏⲥ
18 ⲉⲉⲏ
19 ⲧⲟⲥ ⲍ̅

20 ⲑⲉϣⲙⲁ
ⲉⲛ ⲛⲓⲙ ⲭ
ϫⲉⲕⲁⲥ ⲉ-
ⲕⲉϯ ⲛⲟⲩ-
ⲭⲁⲗⲓⲛⲟⲥ
25 ⲛⲁⲩ ⲧⲥⲟ
ⲛ̄ⲥⲱⲧⲱⲗⲟⲙ
ⲛⲁⲓ ⲁⲫⲓⲙⲟⲙ

---

1 *l.* ⲥⲉⲇⲣⲓⲏⲗ ? |]ⲁⲙⲏⲗ T || **2** ⲫⲁⲫⲁⲛⲗ T || **4** ⲉⲓⲅⲅⲏⲕⲓⲏⲗ T || **5** ⲉⲁⲛⲁⲑⲓⲏⲗ T || **6** ⲉⲁⲛⲁⲏⲗ T || **7–11** T does not transcribe || **12** ⲟⲗⲁⲗⲁⲗⲱⲑ T || **13** *i.e.* ᵠⲉⲃⲓⲏⲛ || **14–15** *i.e.* ᵠⲛ̄-ⲟⲩⲉⲣⲏⲧⲉ ⲛ̄-ⲛⲓⲙ || **16** *i.e.* ᵠϣⲟⲟⲩ ? || **16–18** *i.e.* ᵠϣⲁ=ⲩ-ⲥⲉⲁⲓ=ⲥ "it will be written ?" T || **17** *i.e.* στύ(ραξ) or ᵠⲥⲧⲟⲓ ? || **18–19** *i.e.* εἶδος ? || **19** ⲍ̅ T does not transcribe || **20** ⲑⲉϣⲙⲁ . T || **21** *i.e.* υ(ἱός) || **23** *i.e.* ᵠⲕ-ⲣ̅ ⲧⲉⲛⲟⲩ T || **24** *i.e.* χαλινός : ⲭ[. . . . .] T || **25** ⲛⲟⲩⲧⲉ T || **26** [. . .] ⲧⲁⲗⲟⲙ T || **27** ⲛ̣ⲓⲛⲁⲗⲓⲙⲟⲙ T

|*above left figure* Sedriēl?, *Raphael, Phoriēl, Zetekiēl, |⁵ Zalathiēl, Anaēl...
|*above right figure,* ¹² Okhalalōth, the wretched woman is beneath the |¹⁵ feet of NN!
|*between figures,* ¹⁶ incense?, *storax? ... 7.
|*below figures,* ²⁰ ... NN son of ⟨NN⟩, so that you put a bridle |²⁵ on? them?... for? me?...

KD, EL & MP, edited from photograph and autopsy; tracings by KD.

23–25. ⲕⲉϯ ⲛⲟⲩⲭⲁⲗⲓⲛⲟⲥ ⲛⲁⲩ : "**so that you put a bridle on them**" For the concept of placing a bridle on one's enemies, *cf. PCM* I 24 l. 12 and the accompanying notes.

PCM I 35. Fragmentary formulary with various curses

Arsinoites (Faiyum) ? 22.3 (H) × 17.5 (W) X–XI CE

Other references: P.Heid.Inv. Kopt. 658 (formerly P.Heid.Inv. Nr. 1658); P.Heidelberg Nr. 564a (?); TM 102084; *P.Bad.* V 135; KYP M322; Bélanger Sarrazin #174.
Editions: Bilabel/Grohmann 1934: no. 135 (*ed. pr.*) [B/G].
Translations: Bilabel/Grohmann 1934: no. 135 (German).
Additional commentary: Mößner/Nauerth 2015: 308–309.
Present location: Heidelberg, Institut für Papyrologie.
Image: Plates XV–XVI.
Linguistic description: Sahidic with Middle Egyptian influence.
Contents:
1. Front ll. 1–6: Curse, perhaps separation spell (?) (KYP T1701)
2. Front ll. 7–17: Curse to make woman bleed pus (KYP T217)
3. Front ll. 18–20: Curse (?) (KYP T219)
4. Front ll. 21–23: Curse to make woman bleed pus (KYP T220)
5. Front ll. 24–26: Separation spell/curse to make someone hated (KYP T222)
6. Back ll. 1–17: Curse, perhaps for silencing target (KYP T214)
7. Back ll. 18–19: Separation spell/curse to make someone hated (?) (KYP T216)

Parchment sheet surviving in four fragments organised by Bilabel and Grohmann into three sections—A (composed of two fragments), B, and C.[1] Fragments A and B are very damaged along the edges; the major breaks within the sheet appear to be cuts made with a sharp knife.[2] Most of the fragments are discoloured on the outer rim; the edges are brown, while the inner side is yellowish in colour. The fragments have been considerably deformed, likely as a result of moisture, giving a misleading impression of their shape when photographed in two dimensions. Section A, composed of two fragments, was cut sharply in the middle, where it does not show any discoloration. C is the smallest fragment, discoloured on all sides, and apparently without any sharp cuts. Bilabel and Grohmann observed small crystals on the parchment, leading them to assume that it had been in contact with

---

[1] Fragment A consists of 2 fragments which belong together. Bilabel/Grohmann 1934: no. 135 mention only fragments A and B. The dimensions of the individual fragments are as follows: fragment A: H16 × W9 cm; fragment B: H6.3 × W8.5 cm; fragment C: H9.3 × W4.3 cm (Bilabel/Grohmann 1934: 385; Mößner/Nauerth 2015: 308). The overall dimensions of the sheet have been calculated by adding together the dimensions of fragments A + B, since they do not overlap, and jointly capture the entire height and width of the sheet.

[2] Compare other manuscripts showing similar damage patterns, such as Montserrat Magical Book I (*P.Monts.Roca* II 25–27; KYP M31), Magical Book II (*P.Monts.Roca* II 3–8; KYP M30), Naqlun N. 78/93 (Kalchenko/van der Vliet 2022; KYP M1135).

soil.³ As we show in plates XV–XVI fragment A seems to represent the lower part of the sheet, and fragment B and C the top right and left respectively. Significant fragments are missing from the upper middle, and lower right (viewed from the front). A fragment is missing from the middle. The back (flesh) is written at 180° to the front (hair), and its lower part is left blank. Note that Bilabel and Grohmann refer to our front as the "verso" and our back as the "recto"; we consider the hair side to be the first written, since it is fully covered with text, while the flesh side seems to have had a shorter pair of recipes added at a later moment.

The provenance of the manuscript is unknown. Bilabel and Grohmann noted that the manuscript was in the collection of the University of Heidelberg before 1933. However, they refer to it by two different sigla: "Inv. No. 1658" in the edition, and "P. Heidelberg, Nr. 564a" in the contents.⁴ A different manuscript from Heidelberg with the latter inventory number (564a) was acquired in 1897 by the University of Heidelberg and published by Quecke in 1963.⁵ Unfortunately, we have not been able to find precise aquisition information on this object.⁶

The manuscript is written with black ink, likely by the same scribe in two different styles, likely with two different writing implements. The initial 17 lines of the recto are written in thicker strokes in browner ink, which has run slightly; the remaining lines on the front, and those on the back, are written with thinner strokes, in a darker and sharper ink. Both inks are opaque under visible, near-infrared, and ultraviolet light, but the initial lines of the recto lose some of their opacity under near-infrared; this suggests that the initial 17 lines of the recto are written in iron-gall ink, and the rest of the manuscript in carbon ink.⁷ The two styles seem to display the same ductus, and likely represent the same hand. The text is written in a bimodal, largely bilinear majuscule with a slight rightwards slope. The bowl of the ⲁ is often quite angular, with a long descending tail; the ⲃ is enlarged, with its lower bowl descending below the lower line. There are marked serifs on the left part of the horizontal bar of ⲧ, and on the ascending strokes of ⲗ and ⲭ. ⲙ is curved but not flat, whle ⲱ and ⳑ have long descenders. The ascendent of the ϭ is very long. Horizontal dividing lines are used to separate recipes on the front, but not the back, which seems to rather be organised spatially, with the second recipe (ll. 18–19) written below the first, leaving a small gap, and another recipe, including *kharaktēres*, written at 90° clockwise to the left. Supralineation

---

³ Bilabel/Grohmann 1934: 384.

⁴ Bilabel/Grohmann 1934: xii, 384; *cf.* Seider 1964: 196 n. 79, who repeats the mistake found in the contents.

⁵ Quecke 1963b.

⁶ The manuscript was likely acquired as part one of the acquisitions of the University of Heidelberg which included Coptic texts, made in 1897, 1899, 1904, 1914, 1926 and 1930; see Seider 1964.

⁷ As with all of the discussions of ink for the manuscripts belonging to the University of Heidelberg, we are very grateful to Krisztina Hevesi for sharing her preliminary results with us. For a more detailed discussion of the process of determining inks, see pp. 28–29.

is used very sparingly, only on the back and only on abbreviations and one *vox magica*.

Bilabel and Grohmann suggested a ninth century date for the 'hand' of style 1, and a tenth century date for the 'hand' of style 2.[8] Similar hands can be found in the colophon on fol. 82v of BL Ms. Or 7026 (CLM 192), dated to 1005 CE; *CPR* II 1 ll. 29–40 (TM 82031), dated to year 410 of the Hijra (1019–1020 CE); and *P.Teschlot* 2 (TM 84991), dated to 1023 CE. We thus propose a slightly later date in the tenth or eleventh century.

The fragmentary nature and obscurity of much of the text makes it difficult to be certain of its dialectal features, but it seems to represent for the most part a relatively standard form of Sahidic; the most common deviations from the literary standard are the use of ⲉ for both the supralinear stroke alone and for ⁽ⲛ̄⁾. The latter is characteristic of the Middle Egyptian dialects, so that it is tempting to suggest that this manuscript may come from the Faiyum, like those of the 'Heidelberg Coptic Magical Library' (*PCM* I 21–9), with similar, albeit more marked, dialectal traits (see pp. 261–262); compare also the writing of δεῖνα δεῖνα ("NN") as ⲗ̄ⲗ̄, found also in *PCM* I 27 front l. 9, which is part of the Library.

---

[8] Bilabel/Grohmann 1934: 385.

front (hair)

s¹   ⲟ[ⲩⲣ]ϣⲙⲉ . [. . . ?]ⲁⲁϥ : ⲉⲕⲟⲩⲓ ⲉⲧⲉⲥϩⲓⲙⲉ : ϫⲓ ⲛⲁⲕ
ⲛ[ⲟ]ⲩⲁϩⲟⲟⲩ [. . . ?] ⲕⲁϩ : ϫⲓ ⲛⲁⲕ ⲙⲡⲁⲣϣⲓⲛ ⲉ-
ϥⲗ . . ⲛⲟϭ [. . . ?] : ⲥⲟⲗϥ ⲧⲁⲁϥ ⲉⲩⲛⲟϭ ⲉⲛⲁ .
ϩⲟⲃⲥϥ : ⲛⲧⲟ . [. . . . ?] ⲥⲉⲃⲩⲣⲉ : ϣⲁ ⲡⲉϥϣ . [. . .]
5   ⲡⲉϣⲁⲕϩⲉ ⲣⲟϥ : [. . . ?] ϫⲱϩⲟ ⲡⲁⲣϣⲓⲛ ⲉ[. . . .]
ⲧⲥⲟϥ : ⲁϥϫ[ⲱⲕ ⲉⲃⲟⲗ] ―――――
ⲟⲩⲥϩⲓⲙⲉ ⲉⲕⲁ[ⲙⲟⲩ ⲓⲁ]ⲃⲉ ϩⲁⲣⲟⲥ : ϫⲓ ⲛⲁ[ⲕ
ⲁⲛⲟⲩ[*ca.* 11] . · ⲛⲥⲁ ϫⲱϥ ⲉϫ[ⲛ ⲟⲩ-]
ⲁⲣϣⲓⲛ . [*ca.* 14] . . . . [. .]
10   ϩⲓⲱⲱⲥ [*ca.* 4] . . . [. . ?] . . [*ca.* 12 ?]
ⲟⲩⲛⲟϭ ⲉⲛ . ⲟ . . . . . ⲛⲟ [*ca.* 12 ?]
ⲛⲉ . . . . ⲉϫⲛ ⲟⲩⲧⲁⲫⲟⲥ · ⲣ[*ca.* 7 ?]
ⲟⲩⲟϣⲧ[*ca.* 6]ⲛ̄ⲧⲙ ⲉⲛⲛⲟⲩ[*ca.* 7 ?]
ϩⲓⲧⲙ . . . ⲁⲁⲕ ⲧⲟⲩϣⲟⲟⲩⲉ [*ca.* 7 ?]
15   ⲡⲏⲓ ⲉⲡⲣⲱⲙⲉ : ⲙⲡⲛⲁⲩ ⲉⲡ . [*ca.* 7 ?]
ϩⲁⲧϥ ⲉⲡⲣⲟ :: ϣⲓ ⲥⲁϣⲃⲉ ⲛ[*ca.* 7 ?]
ⲡⲱⲧ ⲛⲁⲕ : ⲁϥϫⲱⲕⲟⲩ [*nothing lost ?*]

s²   ⲟⲩⲙ . . ⲉ ϫⲓ ⲛⲁⲕ ⲛⲟⲩⲁϩⲟⲟⲩ ⲕⲁϩ : [*ca.* 5 ?]
ϩⲛ ⲟⲩϩⲟⲗ[ϥ ? . .]ⲟⲛⲧⲉ : ⲕⲁⲁⲃ ⲉϫⲛ ⲛⲟⲩ . [*ca.* 4 ?]
20   ⲧⲁⲁϥ ⲉⲡⲙⲟⲟⲩ ⲧⲥⲟϥ ⸗
ⲟⲩⲥϩⲓⲙⲉ ⲕⲁ ⲙⲟⲩ ⲓⲁⲃⲉ ϩⲁⲣⲟⲥ : ϫⲓ ⲛ[ⲁⲕ *ca.* 5 ?]
ⲁϣⲧϥ ⲛⲥⲁ ϫⲱϥ ⲉϫⲛ ⲟⲩ:ⲁⲣϣⲓⲛ [*ca.* 6 ?]
ⲡⲉϣⲁⲉⲓ ⲉⲃⲟⲗ ϩⲓⲱⲱϥ : ⲧⲁⲁϥ ⲉⲛ[*ca.* 5 ?]
ⲟⲩⲛⲟϭ ⲉⲙⲟⲥⲧⲉ . ⲁ ―――――
25   [. . .] . ⲧⲉ ⲧⲁⲕⲟⲥ : [. .] . . . . . [?]
[. . . .]ⲟⲛⲛⲥ : ⲣⲟⲕ[

---

1 ⲟ[B/G | [ⲗ?]ⲁⲁⲩ B/G | *i.e.* ˢⲛ̄⸗ⲕ-ⲟⲩⲉ ? | ⲉⲩⲥϩⲓⲙⲉ B/G | ϫⲓ corrected from ϭⲓ by erasure and overwriting ? || **1–2** ϫⲓ ⲛⲁⲕ [ⲛⲟⲩⲁϩⲟⲟⲩ] ⲕⲁϩ B/G || **2** ⲧ[B/G || **3** ϣϥ B/G | ⲉⲛ.[B/G || **4** *i.e.* ˢϩⲟⲃⲥ̄⸗ⲟⲩ : ϩⲟⲃϥ B/G | ⲛⲧⲟ . [*ca.* 4 ?] : [ ] B/G | *i.e.* ˢⲛ̄⸗ⲥⲉ-ⲃⲱϣⲣⲉ ? | ⲡⲉϥ B/G || **5** *i.e.* ˢⲡ(ⲉ)-ⲉ-ϣⲁ⸗ⲕ-ϩⲉ ⲉⲣⲟ⸗ϥ (haplography) : ⲡⲉϣⲁⲥϥ ⲉⲣⲟⲩ B/G | *i.e.* ˢϫⲁϩ ? : ϫⲱϩ · B/G || **6** ⲁϥ . [B/G || **7** ⲟⲩⲥϩⲓⲙⲉ ⲉⲕⲁ[ⲙⲟⲩ ⲓⲁ]ⲃⲉ ϩⲁⲣⲟⲥ : ⲕⲁⲙⲟⲩ ⲓⲁⲃⲉ ϩⲁⲣⲟⲥ B/G || **8** [*ca.* 11] . · ⲛⲥⲁ ϫⲱϥ ⲉϫ[ⲛ ⲟⲩ-] : ⲁϣⲧ]ϥ ⲛⲥⲁ ϫⲱϥ ⲉϫ[ⲛ B/G || **9–10** . [*ca.* 14] . . . . [. .] ϩⲓⲱⲱⲥ : [ⲙⲡⲉϣⲁ ⲉⲓ ⲉⲃⲟⲗ] ϩⲓⲱⲱ[ϥ B/G || **11** ⲟⲩⲛⲟϭ ⲉⲛ . ⲟ *ca.* 5 ⲛⲟ [*ca.* 12 ?] : [ ] ⲕⲟ . ⲃ . . ⲣⲁ[B/G || **12** ⲛⲉ . . . . ⲉϫⲛ ⲟⲩⲧⲁⲫⲟⲥ · ⲣ[*ca.* 7 ?] :] . ⲟⲩⲧⲁⲫⲟⲥ . ⲛ B/G| *i.e.* τάφος || **13** ⲟⲩⲟϣⲧ[*ca.* 6]ⲛ̄ⲧⲙ ⲉⲛⲛⲟⲩ[*ca.* 7 ?] : ϩ[ ]ⲛ ⲧⲙⲉ ⲛⲛⲟⲩ[B/G | *i.e.* ˢⲟⲩⲱϣⲧ ? || **14** ϩⲓⲧⲙ . . . ⲁⲁⲕ ⲧⲟⲩϣⲟⲟⲩⲉ :]ⲁⲁⲕⲧⲟⲩϣⲟⲟⲩ ⲟ | *i.e.* ˢⲛ̄⸗ⲥⲉ-ϣⲟⲟⲩⲉ ? || **15** ⲡⲏⲓ ⲉⲡⲣⲱⲙⲉ : ⲙⲡⲛⲁⲩ ⲉⲡ . [*ca.* 7 ?] : ⲡ . . . . ⲣⲱⲙⲉ : ⲙⲡⲛⲁⲩ ⲉⲛ[B/G || **16** *i.e.* ˢⲡⲁϩⲧ⸗ϥ ? : . ⲁⲧϥ B/G || **17** ⲡⲱϣ B/G || **18** *l.* ⲟⲩⲙⲁⲥⲧⲉ ? :] B/G || **19** ϩⲛ ⲟⲩϩⲟⲗ[ϥ ? . .] :]ⲟⲛⲧⲉ B/G | ⲛⲟⲩ . : ⲛⲟⲩ B/G || **20** ⲧⲁⲁϥ ⲉⲡⲙⲟⲟⲩ : ⲧ . [ⲧ]ⲛ̄ⲛⲟⲟⲩ B/G || **21** *i.e.* ˢⲟⲩ-ⲥϩⲓⲙⲉ ⲉ-ⲕⲁ ⲙⲟⲩ ⲉⲓⲁⲃⲉ ϩⲁⲣⲟ⸗ⲥ (haplography of ⲉ) || **22** [*ca.* 6 ?] : [ⲛⲅϣⲱ? ⲡⲉⲧⲙ] B/G || **23** *i.e.* ˢⲡ-ⲉ⸗ϥ-ϣⲁ-ⲉⲓ ? : "worthy, come out" ("würdiger, komme heraus") B/G || **24** *i.e.* ˢⲙ̄-ⲙⲟⲥⲧⲉ || **25** [. . .] . ⲧⲉ :]ⲙⲟⲥⲧⲉ B/G | [. .] *ca.* 5 [?] : [.] ⲟⲩⲧⲟⲙⲥ · ["spoil them [with] a burial" ("Verdirb sie [mit] einem Begraben") B/G

A man? ... him?, and you remove yourself? from the woman. Take for yourself a ... earth?. Take for yourself the lentil that is ... great?... sieve?. Put it in a big ... cover them with? ... and they swell? to his ... |⁵ that which you find ... smear the lentil on ... Have him drink. It is [finished.]

A woman, to put [pus] under her. Take for [yourself] ... from its head upon [a] lentil ... |¹⁰ upon her ... a great ... upon? a grave ... greet? ... through ... and they dry? ... |¹⁵ the house of the man at the time of ... pour? it at the door. Measure seven ... Go away. It is complete?.

A hatred.? Take for yourself ... earth ... in a sieve. Put it upon a ... |²⁰ Put it in the water. Have him drink it.

A woman, to put pus under her. Take for yourself ... Hang it from its head upon a lentil? ... that? which? comes out of it. Give it to? ...

A great hatred... |²⁵ ... destroy it ...

1–6. Bilabel/Grohmann treat this as two separate texts, not recognising that the two fragments represent the beginning and end of the same lines; they number these lines as verso ll. 20–25, and verso ll. 48–52.

2, 18. ⲛ[ⲟ]ⲩⲁϩⲟⲟⲩ : "a..." The meaning of this word is unclear; ˢⲁϩⲟ ("treasury, storehouse"), ᴮⲁϩⲟ ("dwelling, abode"), and ˢⲉϩⲟⲟⲩ ("cows") are all possibilities, but none would seem to fit the context.

7. ⲟⲩⲥϩⲓⲙⲉ ⲉⲕⲁ[ⲙⲟⲩ ⲓⲁ]ⲃⲉ ϩⲁⲣⲟⲥ : "a woman, to put [pus] under her" This recipe seems consist of one or more curse procedures. The title in l. 7 apparently describes causing a woman to leak pus from her vulva; cf. the parallel phrase in l. 21 below. For [ⲙⲟⲩ ⲓⲁ]ⲃⲉ as pus, cf. ⲙⲱⲟⲩ ⲛ̄ⲓⲁⲃⲓ (Crum CD 76b). The phrase "under her" recalls the common description of uterine bleeding as blood being "under (a woman)"; for this phrase and similar curses to make a woman experience uterine bleeding, see the notes to PCM I 3 front col. 1 ll. 1–34.

10. ϩⲓⲱⲱⲥ : "upon her" Or "upon it".

18, 24. ⲉⲙⲟⲥⲧⲉ : "hatred" In Coptic magical texts, "hatred" usually refers to a quality of "hatefulness" brought upon a curse's target, either to separate them from a particular individual, or to make them generally socially unpopular, the inverse to the quality of "favour" (χαρις) which granted social success. Compare PCM I 22 front ll. 27–50; PCM I 31 front 1–40, back ll. 1–20; PCM I 37 back ll. 18–20; Cairo JdE 42573 (Chassinat 1955; KYP M44) p. 4 ll. 1–2, ll. 11–17; O.Monts.Roca inv. no. 1472 (Martín Hernández/Torallas Tovar 2014a; KYP M22); O.Bélanger Sarrazin (Bélanger Sarrazin 2017b; KYP M502).

21. ⲟⲩⲥϩⲓⲙⲉ ⲕⲁ ⲙⲟⲩ ⲓⲁⲃⲉ ϩⲁⲣⲟⲥ : "A woman, to put pus under her" See the note to l. 7. Bilabel/Grohmann translate "a woman – pour (lit. lay) pus water (?) on her" ("Eine Frau – gieße (wtl. lege) Eiterwasser auf sie").

22. ⲛⲥⲁ ϫⲱϥ ⲉϫⲛ ⲟⲩ:ⲁⲣϣⲓⲛ : "from its head upon a lentil?" Bilabel/Grohmann translate "behind him upon a lentil" ("hinter ihn auf eine Linse").

23. ⲡⲉ ϣⲁ : " ... " Bilabel/Grohmann translate "dignified" ("würdiger").

24. ⲟⲩⲛⲟϭ ⲉⲙⲟⲥⲧⲉ : "a great hatred" It is tempting to consider, as Bilabel/Grohmann do, this to be part of the previous recipe, but it would seem to be a title, so here we take it as beginning a new text, with the horizontal stroke separating title and recipe rather than two recipes.

25. ⲧⲁⲕⲟⲥ : "destroy it" Or "destroy her."

back (flesh)

ⲡⲁ ⲛⲉⲁⲝ

ⲛⲉⲃⲁⲗ ⲙⲉⲩⲛⲁⲩ ⲉⲃⲟⲗ : ⲛ̄ⲛ̄ ⲛ̇ⲉϥ[*ca.* ?]
ⲛⲉϥⲟⲩⲉⲣⲩⲧⲉ ⲙⲙⲟϥ ⲙⲉϥⲙⲟⲟϣⲉ : ⲛⲉϥ[*ca.* ?]
ⲣ̄ⲁⲛ ⲧⲉ . . ⲣⲩⲱϥ ⲉⲙⲙⲟϥ ⲙⲉϥϣⲁϫⲉ ϫ[ⲉ]
5   [*ca.* 6]ⲛⲛⲉⲛ̄ⲛ̄ ⲛⲁ:ⲣ ⲧⲉⲩϩⲉ [*ca.* ?]
ⲙⲉϥ . . ⲧⲟⲛ ϩⲣⲁⲓ ⲛ̄ϩⲏⲧⲟⲩ : ⲉⲣⲉⲁ̄ⲁ̄ [*ca.* ?]
. · ⲉⲧⲙ̄ⲙⲁⲩ : ⲙⲡⲉⲙⲧⲟⲟⲩ ⲉⲃⲟⲗ ⲛ̄[*ca.* ?]
ⲉⲛⲁⲧϣⲁϫⲉ ⲉⲛⲁⲧⲙⲟⲩⲧⲉ : ⲉⲛⲁⲧ[*ca.* ?]
ⲡϣⲏ ⲛ̄ⲁ̄ⲁ̄ ⲁⲓⲟ ⲁⲟ ⲧⲁⲭⲏ ⸗

10 ⲅⲣ/ ⲛⲁ̄[ⲓ *ca.* ?]
ⲁϣ ⲧⲛ̄[*ca.* ?]
†ⲡⲟⲧ . [*ca.* ?]
ⲁⲙⲁϩ[ⲧⲉ *ca.* ?]
ϩⲓⲧⲉⲛ [*ca.* ?]
15 ϩⲓⲧⲉⲛ [*ca.* ?]
ϫⲓⲛ · [*ca.* ?]
[*ca.* ?]. ⲙⲟⲓ · [*ca.* ?]

[*ca.* ?] ⲙⲟⲥⲧⲉ : ⲙⲟⲩⲥ ⲁ . . [*ca.* ?]
[*ca.* ?]ⲡⲟⲕ ⲉⲕⲁϩ · ⲧⲏⲣⲉ[ϥ *ca.* ?]

---

1 *i.e.* ˢⲡⲁ ⲛ̄-δ(εῖνα) (υἱός) ? : "the one who belongs to the powers" ("der den Mächten Gehörige") or understand as name B/G ‖ **2** *l.* ⲛⲉ=ϥ-ⲃⲁⲗ ? | *i.e.* ˢⲙⲉ=ϥ-ⲛⲁⲩ | *i.e.* (δεῖνα) (δεῖνα) | *i.e.* ˢⲛ̄ⲛⲉ=ϥ- ? | ⲛⲉⲃⲁⲗ ⲙⲉⲩⲛⲁⲩ ⲉⲃⲟⲗ : ⲛ̄ⲛ̄ ⲛ̇ⲉϥ[*ca.* ?]] : "the eyes do not see. NN shall not [… It shall not…]" ("Die Augen pflegen nicht sehend zu werden. N.N. soll nicht […Es sollen nicht]") B/G ‖ **3** *i.e.* ˢⲙⲉ=ϥ-ⲙⲟⲟϣⲉ | *i.e.* ˢⲛ̄ⲛⲉ=ϥ- ? | [*ca.* ?] : [ⲙⲟⲩⲧⲉ ⲛⲉ] B/G ‖ **4** *i.e.* ˢⲣⲱ=ϥ ‖ **5** ⲛ̄ⲛⲉ : ⲉ]ⲣⲉ B/G | *i.e.* (δεῖνα) (δεῖνα) ‖ **6** *i.e.* δ(εῖνα) δ(εῖνα) ‖ **9** *i.e.* δ(εῖνα) δ(εῖνα) | *i.e.* ταχύ ‖ **10** *i.e.* γρ(άφειν) ‖ **11** ⲧⲛ̄ : ⲧⲏ̄ B/G ‖ **16** ϫⲓⲛ · B/G ‖ **18** ⲁ . . [: ⲁ . [B/G ‖ **19** ⲧⲏⲣⲉ[ϥ *ca.* ?] : ⲉⲧⲛⲣⲉ B/G

PCM I 35 (P.Bad. V 135) : Fragmentary formulary with various curses

|*tableau* That of NN, child ‹of NN›?.

|² His? eyes do not see, NN, he shall not ... his feet do not walk. He shall not [...] name? ... his ... does not speak, for? ... |⁵ ... NN will not act in their way? ... he does not ... among them, let NN ... those ..., before ... not speaking, not calling out, not ... the son of NN, yea, yea, quickly!

|¹⁰ Write these things? ... take? ... using? ... |¹⁵ using? ... until ...

... hatred. ... all of the? ...

KD, EL, MP & JS, edited from photograph; tracings by JS.

The initial letters of several of the lines are scarcely visible from photographs due to the darkening of the parchment, and so we have often followed the readings of Bilabel/Grohmann (which are undotted), adding dotting to indicate our uncertainty.

1–9. This recipe seems to represent a silencing curse, intended to make the target unable to speak against the beneficiary of the ritual; the specific wording ("his eyes do not see", and so on) are reminiscent of the description of the "idols of the nations" in Psalm 134 (135) 16–17: "they have eyes but do not see, they have ears but do not hear, their mouths do not speak, their noses do not breathe, their hands do not touch, their legs do not walk; they do not cry out with their throats, for there is no breath in their mouths" (ⲟⲩⲛ ⲃⲁⲗ ⲙ̄ⲙⲟⲟⲩ ⲙⲉⲩⲛⲁⲩ ⲉⲃⲟⲗ ⲟⲩⲛ ⲙⲁⲁϫⲉ ⲙ̄ⲙⲟⲟⲩ ⲙⲉⲩⲥⲱⲧⲙ̄ ⲣⲱⲟⲩ ⲙ̄ⲙⲟⲟⲩ ⲙⲉⲩϣⲁϫⲉ ϣⲁⲁⲛⲧⲟⲩ ⲙ̄ⲙⲟⲟⲩ ⲙⲉⲩϣⲱⲗⲙ̄ ⲛⲉⲩϭⲓϫ ⲙ̄ⲙⲟⲟⲩ ⲙⲉⲩϭⲟⲙϭⲙ̄ ⲛⲉⲩⲟⲩⲉⲣⲏⲧⲉ ⲙ̄ⲙⲟⲟⲩ ⲙⲉⲩⲙⲟⲟϣⲉ ⲙⲉⲩⲙⲟⲩⲧⲉ ϩⲛ̄ ⲧⲉⲩϣⲟⲩⲱⲃⲉ ⲙⲛ̄ ⲡ̄ⲛ̄ⲁ ⲅⲁⲣ ϩⲛ̄ ⲣⲱⲟⲩ; Budge 1898: 141). The same imagery is used in the applied curse P.Berol. 8503 (Beltz 1984: III 23; KYP M495) front ll. 61–back l. 5.

10. ⲛⲁ̣[ⲓ] : "these things?" Perhaps alternatively restore ⲛ- + noun, *e.g.*, ⲛ̄-ⲁⲥⲥⲁⲃⲣⲁⲛ "with saffron"; *cf. PCM* I 25 p. 15 l. 8; *PCM* I 32 p. 1 l. 27.

17. Bilabel/Grohmann see this line as belonging to the next recipe, ll. 18–19.

18. For curses of hatred, compare the notes to front ll. 18, 24.

Left of ll. 10–19: Perhaps part of a separate recipe, as well as a zoomorphic figure, this tableau contains instances of linear kufic, for which see *PCM* I 21 ll. 1–3.

PCM I 36. Three healing prescriptions on paper

Arsinoites (Faiyum) or Middle Egypt ? 11 (H) × 16.5 (W) cm   X–XI CE
Other references: Köln Inv. 1850; TM 704888; *P.Köln.* XV 641; KYP M503.
Editions: Schenke 2017 (*ed. pr.*); Richter 2023: 164–65 (col. 1 ll. 1–12).
Translations: Schenke 2017 (German); Richter 2023: 164–65 (German).
Additional commentary: Preininger forthcoming c: chapter 4.
Present location: Cologne, Kölner Papyrussammlung.
Image: https://papyri.uni-koeln.de/stueck/tm704888
Linguistic description: Sahidic with Middle Egyptian influence.
Contents:

1. Front col. 1 ll. 1–12: Prescription to heal uterine bleeding (KYP T1244)
2. Front col. 1 ll. 13–15: Solomonic prescription to heal swelling (KYP T1245)
3. Front col. 2 ll. 1–10: Prescription to treat a crying child (KYP T1246)
4. Back l. 1: Unclear text (KYP T1663)

Incomplete paper sheet; the top and side margins are preserved, but the lower margin is lost to a break along a fold; it is likely that at least half the original height is missing. The manuscript is a formulary containing three surviving healing recipes written in black ink on the front, two of which are completely preserved and one incomplete at the very bottom. The lost lower part of the manuscript likely contained further prescriptions which are now lost. The back is written at 90° to the front and preserves a few letters. Although it is a formulary, it was folded into a small package, 1 horizontal and 6 vertical creases are clearly visible. Based on the acquisition number, the manuscript was likely bought in Egypt between 1957 and 1958 and now belongs to the Papyrus collection of Cologne.[1]

A single hand (m¹) seems to be responsible for all of the text on the front; a second, different hand (m²), may be responsible for the brief text on the back, which shows distinct letterforms. The principal copyist nonetheless makes use of two different styles: the upper parts of the manuscript are written in larger, more upright letters with a thicker implement, showing variation in shading; the lower parts are written in a smaller, more sloping script with more ligatures and little variation in shading. Both styles are right-sloping, bimodular, bilinear majuscules, with consistent decorative serifs on the left stroke of the ⲧ, and the upper left part of the oblique strokes on ⲁ and ⲗ, among others. The ⲙ is rather flat, but not completely so. ⲥ has a distinctive form, with the body being drawn

---

[1] Personal communication from Charikleia Armoni, curator of the Kölner Papyrussammlung (6/10/2022).

counterclockwise and the ascender rising from its lower side, as in several other manuscripts from the Faiyum (*cf.* p. 260–261); the ascender is long and curved, resembling that of *PCM* I 28. The use of paper indicates a tenth century date at the earliest; Schenke (2017: 253 n. 2) proposes a tenth or eleventh century dating by comparison with the hands presented by Stegemann (1936: plates 19 & 21). This dating is certainly correct; similar hands can be seen in the Teshlot Archive, in particular *P.Teschlot* 1, dated to 1032 CE (Richter 2000), as well as the colophon of BL Or. 7033 (CLM 194) fol. 59v, dated to 981 CE.

The recipes are separated by vertical and horizontal lines, creating sections of different sizes based on the shape of the texts. The first prescription, against uterine bleeding, is written in the left side of the sheet and its 13 lines are completely preserved. The second, a recipe for treating swelling, is incomplete, with only 3 lines preserved. The third recipe, for a crying child, is located on the right side and consists of 10 complete lines.

The manuscript is written in a form of Sahidic, with a few non-standard features: ⲙⲉ for ^{S}ⲙⲛ̄, and ⲏ for ^{S}ⲉ (*e.g.*, ϩⲏⲁⲡⲉ for ^{S}ϩⲉⲗⲡⲉ, col. 1 l. 2; ⲏⲣ for ^{S}ⲡ̄, col. 2 l. 3), and ⲉ for where Sahidic would use supralineation (*e.g.*, ⲉⲣⲣⲟ for ^{S}ⲣ̄ⲣⲟ, col. 1 ll. 13–14). While the last of these is common in non-standard Sahidic, the first two are indicative of influence from one of the Middle Egyptian dialects (Faiyumic, Mesokemic, Hermopolitan),[2] suggesting an origin in the Faiyum or somewhere in Middle Egypt.

---

[2] *Cf.* Kahle 1954: 52–54, 55, 70–71, 113–116; Funk 2020; Dosoo/Love/Preininger 2022: 77.

front

m¹, s¹ ετβε ογςϩιμε ερεογςνοϥ ϩαρος ρ ναι μορογ ερος
λοϫκογ ετεςϯπε με τεςϩλπε απγ͞ ογ μας͞
ϣαςωλ ταχη

5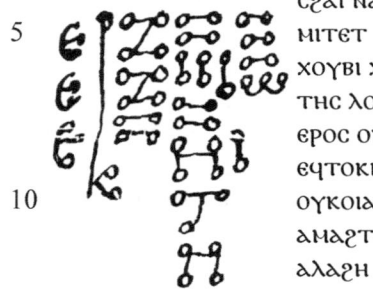
ςϩαι ναι ναλ-
μιτετ ναλ-
χογβι χαρ-
της λοϫκογ
ερος ογςαιη πε
εϥτοκιμων
10 ογκοιανα = ϩα͞μ
αμαϩτε εϫν τκ-
αλαϩη ν͞ΔΔ

s¹ ογροεις εγκογι
cαχο εϥριμε
εϥηρ ϩοτε ·

5

s² ταλϭο μπετϣωνε
ϩι ϯ ϩοτε · ροεις Δ͞Δ
ϩμ πιριμε μν ϯμανι̇ᷓ:
10 αιο αιο :· ταχη ταχη

s² ετβε ογρωμε εϥϣαβε : πεϫε πε-
ρρο ςωλομον · εϩογ̇ν επεϥτημο-
15 νι̇ο̇ν̇ · ϫε ογ πε ππαϩρε επαι ·

- -

back (at 90° to front)

m² ϛγν

---

front col. 1, 2 *i.e.* ˢϩελπε | *i.e.* ἀπολο(γία) | *i.e.* θυ(σία) : *l.* θυ(μίαμα) or θυμ(ί)α(μα) Schenke |
i.e. μασ(τίχη) ‖ **3** *i.e.* ˢϣa≠c-λο ‖ **4–6** *i.e.* المداد الكوفي *al-midād al-kūfī* · includes Persian چوب
čōb "wood", add ⟨ἤ⟩, "on wood ⟨or⟩ papyrus" Schenke ‖ **6–7** *i.e.* χάρτης ‖ **9** *i.e.* δόκιμον ‖
10. *i.e.* κοινά ? : *i.e.* οὐγγία/οὐγκία "uncia" or *l.* οὐγγία/οὐγκία να "an *uncia* is appropriate"
("eine Unze ist angemessen") Schenke | *i.e.* ἀμ(ήν) : ϩα͞ν- "against the" ("gegen die") Schenke ‖
12 *i.e.* δ(εῖνα) δ(εῖνα) ‖ **14–15** *i.e.* δαιμόνιον ‖ **front col. 2, 3** *i.e.* ˢεϥ-ρ̄ ‖ **8** *i.e.* δ(εῖνα) δ(εῖνα) ‖
9 ϩμ corrected from ϩ . | *i.e.* μανία ‖ **10** *i.e.* ταχύ (twice) ‖ **back 1** ϛγν : *i.e.* σὺν [θεῷ], "with [God]"
Schenke.

|*col. 1* For a woman with blood under her. Make these things. Bind them to her. Stick them to her loins and her navel. Request. Offering: *mastic. She will quickly be healed?. Write these things in |⁵ *kufic ink ⟨on⟩ papyrus. Stick them to her. It is a good ⟨procedure⟩, it is tested, |¹⁰ a common? ⟨procedure⟩?, amen!

"Restrain the womb of NN, child of NN!"
(*kharaktēres*: EEEKZZ= = ‖ =HTH≣ⓌⓌ)

For a man with swelling. King Solomon said to his demon, |¹⁵ "What is the remedy for this..."

|*col. 2* An amulet for a little child? who cries, who is afraid.
(*kharaktēres*: ƎEV\+)
|⁵ (*kharaktēres*: IEƎEƎ)
(*kharaktēres*: V\+= =)

"Heal the one who is sick and afraid, protect NN, child of NN, from crying and madness, |¹⁰ yea, yea, quickly, quickly!"

|*back, second hand* ...

KD, EL & MP, edited from photograph; tracings by KD.

---

front col. 1
3. ϢⲀⲤⲰⲖ : **"she will be healed?"** The act of "gathering/containing" (ⲰⲖ) usually refers in recipes of this type to the act of gathering blood back into the body, but the subject here is feminine, so it cannot refer to the blood; here we propose that this is an error for ⲖⲞ "to heal", giving the translation "she will quickly be healed", but it is possible that the use of ⲰⲖ in similar texts conditioned this error. For other recipes against uterine bleeding in Coptic, see *PCM* I 2 l. 1 and the accompanying notes.
6-7. ⲬⲀⲢⲦⲎⲤ : **"papyrus"** *cf.* the note to *PCM* I 37 back l. 13
11. ⲀⲘⲀϨⲦⲈ : **"restrain"** Schenke translates "powers" ("Kräfte").
13–15. This recipe takes a dialogue form clearly modelled on the *Testament of Solomon*; *cf.* the discussion in the introduction to *PCM* I 30.
front col. 2
2. ⲤⲀⲬⲞ: **"child?"** Crum CD 384a gives the meaning of this word as "great scribe, official, craftsman", but the parallels for the patient in recipes to prevent crying cited in Schenke 2017: 257–258—as well as those in Mich.Ms. 136 (Zellmann-Rohrer/Love 2022; KYP M128) p. 13 ll. 5–6: "a little child" (ⲞⲨⲔⲞⲨⲒ ⲚⲔⲈⲔⲈ) and *BKU* I 26 p. 4 l. 12: "a small child" (ⲞⲨϢⲎⲢⲈ ⲔⲞⲨⲒ)—demonstrate that the meaning "small child" would be expected here. This meaning is also suggested by the apparent use of ⲔⲞⲨⲒ ⲤⲀⲬⲞ as the equivalent of ϢⲎⲢⲈ in the funerary stela published by Delattre 2008: 149 (ll. 11–12, 17). For a more detailed discussion of the problem, see Garel 2019: 64–65, 67. For a brief discussion of recipes for crying children, *cf.* the notes to *PCM* I 33, front l. 6.
back
ⲤⲨⲚ : " ... " Schenke proposes to read the beginning of σὺν θεῷ "with God", a common phrase used to open documents following the Arab conquest; it seems to be the equivalent of (and a calque of) the Arabic "in the name of God" (بسم الله *bi-smi llāh*; Cromwell 2022: 359–360 & 2023: 233–234). While this proposal would seem to be the best interpretation, the absence of the ⲑ (usually written above the ⲛ as an abbreviation for θεῷ) and the lack of context lead us to leave this untranslated.

PCM I 37. Parchment sheet with various prescriptions

Middle Egypt ? 23.5 (H) × 19.1 (W) cm XI CE

Other references: Leiden F 1964/4.14; TM 874124; KYP M21; Bélanger Sarrazin #159.
Editions: Green 1987 (*ed. pr.*); Green 1988.
Translations: Green 1987; Green 1988.
Present location: Leiden, National Museum of Antiquities.
Image: https://hdl.handle.net/21.12126/18615
Linguistic description: Sahidic.
Contents:

1. Front ll. 1–35: Love spell (KYP T938)
2. Back l. 1: Title (KYP T1582)
3. Back ll. 2–3: Instructions for favour (KYP T1583)
4. Back ll. 4–5: Instructions for separation (KYP T1584)
5. Back l. 6: Instructions for destruction (KYP T1578)
6. Back ll. 7–8: Instructions for destruction (KYP T1579)
7. Back ll. 9–10: Instructions for love spell (KYP T1581)
8. Back ll. 11–12: Instructions for reconciliation (KYP T898)
9. Back ll. 13–15: Instructions for a love spell (KYP T1576)
10. Back ll. 16–17: Instructions for separation (KYP T899)
11. Back ll. 18–20: Instructions for separation (KYP T900)
12. Back ll. 21–23: Instructions for destroying a furnace (KYP T1577)
13. Back ll. 24–28: Instructions for a love spell (KYP T1580)
14. Back ll. 29–32: Instructions for a love spell (KYP T2087)

A complete parchment sheet, damaged along the folds; 1 vertical and approximately 17 horizontal creases are visible. The sheet is a palimpsest; a single column of the underlying literary text, written in a Biblical majuscule, is clearly visible on the back, albeit less so on the front.[1] The presence of at least one ⲃ indicates that the underlying text was written in Bohairic. The later magical text is written on both sides, with the back at 180° to the front, but apparently in the same hand. The ink, likely plant-based,[2] is a faded brown in colour, making some passages very difficult to read, in particular on the lower half of the back. The parchment is very fine, making it difficult to determine with certainty which side is hair and which flesh, but the darker colour of the back leads us to suggest that this is the hair side.

The manuscript was acquired by the Leiden National Museum from Mr. J. Möger of Soestdijk, the Netherlands, in April 1964 as part of a lot of sixteen

---

[1] Green 1987: 29.
[2] Based on examination with a Dino-Lite microscope by Korshi Dosoo on 22 February 2023. The ink is visible under ultraviolet, but not near-infrared light; *cf.* the discussion on pp. 28–29.

(primarily) Coptic manuscripts.³ Of the sixteen, ten have been published and well-studied, and form an archive of Coptic and Arabic letters and legal documents relating to a man named Raphaēl, son of the Deacon Mina, dating to 1022–1063 CE.⁴ Raphaēl lived in Middle Egypt, first in Bawit and later in Teshlot, leading to the group being as known the Teshlot Archive. The other five manuscripts from the sale, to date unpublished, are literary in nature: a Sahidic fragment containing short passages with Biblical reminiscences;⁵ an Arabic-Bohairic Coptic liturgical manuscript;⁶ a series of extracts from the Psalms;⁷ and a leaf from a two-column literary codex used as a palimpsest to write another text in a less formal hand.⁸ As discussed further below, it is possible that these manuscripts have some relationship to the magical text beyond their common purchase.

On the front of the magical text, the sheet contains a single recipe to attract a woman, while the back preserves a title and 12 brief prescriptions for favour, separation, love spells, and curses, aimed both at people and property (a furnace). The front contains a large image tableau at the top, and a smaller one consisting primarily of *kharaktēres* at the bottom, while the lower part of the back contains two lines of linear kufic. The copyist uses enlarged initial letters set in *ekthesis* for l. 10 of the front and back, and the beginning of each subsequent recipe; the capital omicrons on the back are decorated with internal circles.

The text is written in a right sloping majuscule with regular serifs on ⲗ, ⲧ, ⲩ, ⲭ, ϥ; letters such as ⲣ, ⲩ, ϕ, ⲱ, ⳉ have long descenders. ⲙ is the 'flat' μ which emerges in the tenth century.⁹ ⲋ often has a long, curved ascender, similar to that of *PCM* I 28. Supralinear strokes are consistently drawn above magical names, and the dipunct is regularly used for punctuation (including between magical names). The numerals two (ⲃ) and twenty (ⲕ) take their miniscule forms (front l. 15, back l. 18) although this is not true of the other numerals. Two oblique strokes are used to mark the ends of recipes on the back. The tail of the ⳉ descends beyond the notional lower line. Within this volume, the hand is comparable to those of the second scribe of the Heidelberg Coptic Magical Library (*PCM* I 27 & 28), as well as to *PCM* I 32, which also use minuscule letterforms for numerals ($\overline{\text{ⲕⲁ}}$ front l.

---

³ Private communication Daniel Soliman, 21/10/2020 & 14/7/2023. The manuscripts purchased in this sale have the inventory numbers Leiden F 1964/4.1–16.

⁴ We are very grateful to Vincent Walter for suggesting a possible connection to the Teshlot Archive. For the core group, see Richter 2003 (*P.Teschlot*), as well as the older treatments in Green 1983; MacCoull 1989. Further texts from the Teshlot Archive are published in *P.Köln* XI 466 and *P.Köln ägypt.* II 64, and Thung 1996.

⁵ Leiden F 1964/4.9; the side glassed as the recto contains in the middle a passage adapting Revelation 3.19.

⁶ Leiden F 1964/4.13.

⁷ Leiden F 1964/4.15; the manuscript contains numbered full lines of each psalm, followed by two shorter passages from the same psalm labelled ⲁ and ⲃ.

⁸ Leiden F 1964/4.16.

⁹ *Cf.* Mihálykó 2019: 16–18.

15).

Broadly similar hands can be seen in the colophons of BnF Copte 129.14 fol. 95v and BnF Copte 131.5 fol. 28v, dated to 1002–1003 and *ca.* 1091 CE respectively.[10] Green suggested a more precise eleventh century date,[11] and in support of this we may note that the hand of *PCM* I 37 shows similarities with other manuscripts from the 1964 purchase, in particular *P.Teschlot* 7 & 8, both written by Iōsaphat, son of the Deacon Pisrael, in 1062 CE, as well as the unpublished and undated literary text Leiden F 1964/4.9. The letterforms are very close without being identical: ⲁ, ⲕ, ⲗ, ⲧ, ⲭ, ϩ are notably similar across the four manuscripts, while ⲩ, ϣ, and ⲝ are markedly different in *PCM* I 37. We thus suggest an eleventh century date for this manuscript, even if the late tenth century cannot be entirely excluded.

The dialect is a highly standard Sahidic. The only non-standard features are the common interchange of ϥ and ⲃ, the use of ⲉ for the schwa, normally indicated by a supralinear stroke in the literary dialect, and a few surprising forms, such as ⲉⲁϩⲥⲉ for ⁵ϩⲓⲥⲉ? (front l. 22), ⲧⲉϥⲁϣⲉⲕ for ⁵ⲉ-ⲧⲣⲉϥ-ⲟⲩⲁϣⲕ (back l. 13), and ⲥⲛⲁϥ for ⁵ⲥⲛⲟϥ (back l. 6); these last two features would point to an origin in the Faiyum or Middle Egypt.[12] As with the other texts from the tenth and eleventh centuries in this volume, there are many Arabic loanwords, not all of which have been convincingly identified. Once again, these features—standard Sahidic with Middle Egyptian vocalism and Arabic loanwords—are present in the manuscripts from the Teshlot Archive.[13] For these reasons, it seems very likely that this manuscript also originated in Middle Egypt, perhaps in the region of Bawit or Teshlot. It is tempting to imagine that this manuscript, like the documentary texts, once belonged to the archive of Raphaēl, son of Mina, but more work on all of the manuscripts from the 1964 sale will be necessary to determine whether a relationship between them all can be reconstructed, and the exact nature of any relationship.

Green begins numbering the recto from our l. 10, which thus corresponds to l. 1 in his edition. Our ll. 1, 25–32 are not assigned line numbers in Green's edition, while ll. 2–9 correspond to his ll. 24–31. Our ll. 33–35 correspond to his ll. 32–34. Green's line numbers are indicated to the right of the column in grey.

---

[10] Lantschoot 1929: fasc. I 116–117, 131; *cf.* fasc. II 52 n. 3.
[11] Green 1987: 29.
[12] Funk 2017: 59–63.
[13] See Richter 2003: 98–102 *et passim*; MacCoull 1989: 204–205.

front (flesh)

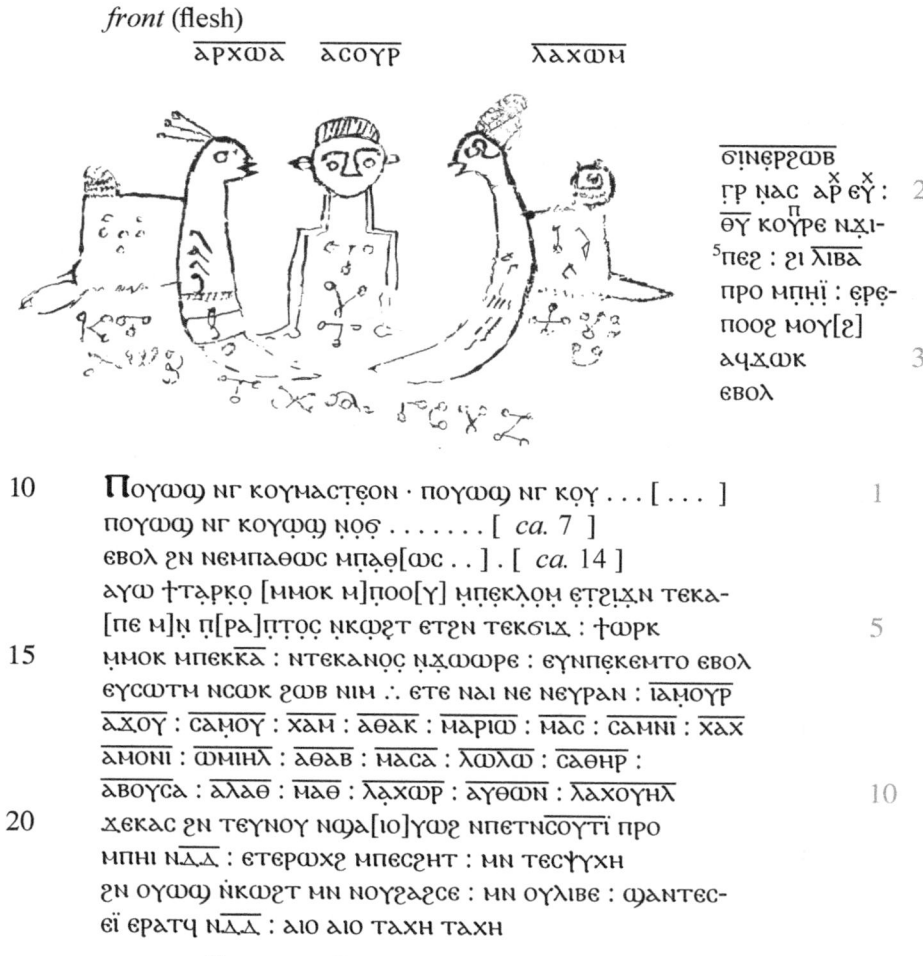

ⲁⲣⲭⲱⲁ   ⲁⲥⲟⲩⲣ   ⲗⲁⲭⲱⲙ

ⲟ̄ⲓⲛⲉⲣϩⲱⲃ
ⲅⲣ ⲛⲁⲥ ⲁ̇ⲣ̇ ⲉⲩ̇ :   25
ⲟ̄ⲩ ⲕⲟⲩⲣⲉ ⲛⲭⲓ-
⁵ⲡⲉϩ : ϩⲓ ⲗ̄ⲓⲃⲁ
ⲡⲣⲟ ⲙⲡⲏⲓ̈ : ⲉⲣⲉ-
ⲡⲟⲟϩ ⲙⲟⲩ[ϩ]
ⲁϥϫⲱⲕ   30
ⲉⲃⲟⲗ

10 Ⲡⲟⲩⲱϣ ⲛⲅ ⲕⲟⲩⲙⲁⲥⲧⲉⲟⲛ · ⲡⲟⲩⲱϣ ⲛⲅ ⲕⲟⲩ . . . [. . .]   1
    ⲡⲟⲩⲱϣ ⲛⲅ ⲕⲟⲩϣϣ ⲛ̇ⲟ̇ⲥ̇ . . . . [*ca.* 7]
    ⲉⲃⲟⲗ ϩⲛ ⲛⲉⲙⲡⲁⲑⲱⲥ ⲙⲡⲁⲑ[ⲱⲥ . .] . [*ca.* 14]
    ⲁⲩⲱ ϯⲧⲁⲣⲕⲟ̣ [ⲙⲙⲟⲕ ⲙ]ⲡⲟⲟ[ⲩ] ⲙⲡⲉⲕⲗⲟⲙ ⲉⲧϩⲓϫⲛ ⲧⲉⲕⲁ-
    [ⲡⲉ ⲙ]ⲛ ⲡ[ⲣⲁ]ⲡ̣ⲧⲟⲥ ⲛⲕⲱϣⲧ ⲉⲧϩⲛ ⲧⲉⲕϭⲓϫ : ϯⲱⲣⲕ   5
15 ⲙ̄ⲙⲟⲕ ⲙⲡⲉⲕⲕ̄ⲁ̄ : ⲛⲧⲉⲕⲁⲛⲟⲥ ⲛ̄ϫⲱⲱⲣⲉ : ⲉⲩⲛⲡⲉⲕⲉⲙⲧⲟ ⲉⲃⲟⲗ
    ⲉⲩⲥⲱⲧⲙ ⲛⲥⲱⲕ ϩⲱⲃ ⲛⲓⲙ ∴ ⲉⲧⲉ ⲛⲁⲓ ⲛⲉ ⲛⲉⲩⲣⲁⲛ : ⲓ̄ⲁ̇ⲙⲟⲩⲣ
    ⲁ̄ⲭⲟⲩ : ⲥⲁ̇ⲙⲟⲩ : ⲭⲁⲙ : ⲁⲑⲁⲕ : ⲙⲁⲣⲓⲱ : ⲙⲁⲥ : ⲥⲁⲙⲛⲓ : ⲭⲁⲭ
    ⲁⲙⲟⲛⲓ : ⲱⲙⲓⲏⲗ : ⲁⲑⲁⲃ : ⲙⲁⲥⲁ : ⲗⲱⲗⲱ : ⲥⲁⲑⲏⲣ :
    ⲁⲃⲟⲩⲥⲁ : ⲁⲗⲁⲑ : ⲙⲁⲑ : ⲗⲁⲭⲱⲣ : ⲁⲩⲑⲱⲛ : ⲗⲁⲭⲟⲩⲏⲗ   10
20 ϫⲉⲕⲁⲥ ϩⲛ ⲧⲉⲩⲛⲟⲩ ⲛϣⲁ[ⲓⲟ]ⲩⲱϣ ⲛⲡⲉⲧⲛⲥⲟⲩⲧⲓ ⲡⲣⲟ
    ⲙⲡⲏⲓ ⲛ̄ⲁ̄ⲇ̄ : ⲉⲧⲉⲣⲱϩ ⲙⲡⲉⲥϩⲏⲧ : ⲙⲛ ⲧⲉⲥⲯⲩⲭⲏ
    ϩⲛ ⲟⲩⲱϣ ⲛ̄ⲕⲱϣⲧ ⲙⲛ ⲟⲩϩⲁⲣⲥⲉ : ⲙⲛ ⲟⲩⲗⲓⲃⲉ : ϣⲁⲛⲧⲉⲥ-
    ⲉⲓ̈ ⲉⲣⲁⲧϥ ⲛ̄ⲁ̄ⲇ̄ : ⲁⲓⲟ ⲁⲓⲟ ⲧⲁⲭⲏ ⲧⲁⲭⲏ

---|||| ———— |||| ———— |||| ———— |||| ———

1 i.e. الحاوي *al-ḥāwi* "the magician" Green | *l.* ⲁⲥ(ⲥ)ⲟⲩⲭ(ⲁⲣⲉ) i.e. السحر *as-sāḥir* "the magic" Green | i.e. الحمى *al-ḥummā* "the fever" Green || **3** i.e. γρ(άφειν) | *l.* ⲛ̄-ⲁⲥ(ⲥⲁⲃⲣⲁⲛ) i.e. الزعفران *az-za'farān* cf. PCM I 25 15.8 or ⲛ̄-ⲁⲥ(ⲥⲟⲩⲕ) السكّ *as-sukk* cf. PCM I 24 l. 18 ? : ⲧⲟⲙⲁⲥ Green | *i.e.* ἀρχή | *l.* ⲉⲩⲭ(ⲟⲥ) *i.e.* ˢⲉ-(ⲟ)ⲩ-ⲕⲁⲥ ? cf. note : *i.e.* εὐχή Green || **4** *i.e.* θυ(σία) | **4–5** *i.e.* ˢϫ(ⲉ)ⲙⲡⲉϩ | **5, 8** *i.e.* λίβα(νος) || **6** ⲡⲣⲟⲙ ⲉⲓⲛ Green || **10** ⲡ enlarged | ⲛ ⲧⲁⲕⲟ [ⲟ]ⲩⲙⲁⲥⲧⲓ Green | ⲛ ⲧⲁⲕⲟ [ⲟ]ⲩ[...] Green || **11** ⲛ ⲧⲁⲕⲟ ⟨ⲟ⟩ⲩϣⲱⲛⲉ [. ?] Green || **12** *i.e.* ἐμπαθῶς : ⲛⲉⲙⲡⲁⲑⲱⲥ Green || **13** ϯⲧⲁ̣[...]ⲧⲟ̣[...]ⲙⲟⲕ (or ⲡⲉⲕ) ϩⲉⲡⲟ...[..]ⲛ Green | *i.e.* πάθος ? || **13–14** ⲧⲉⲕⲁ[ⲛ]ⲟⲥ *i.e.* δεκανός Green || **14** ⲛⲧⲕ (or ⲛⲉⲕ) [....]ⲙⲟⲕ.ⲥ̣..ⲉ̣.ⲧ̣ⲉ̣ⲩ̣ⲧⲁ̣ or ⲧⲉϥⲡ) Green | *i.e.* ῥάβδος ? || **15** ⲙⲟⲕ ⲙⲡⲉⲕⲣⲁ[ⲛ] Green | *i.e.* δεκανός : "(and also) the decans" Green | ⲛⲉⲧϫⲱⲱⲣⲉ Green | *i.e.* ˢⲙ̄-ⲡⲉ=ⲕ-ⲙ̄ⲧⲟ || **16** *i.e.* ⲛ̄-ϩⲱⲃ ⲛⲓⲙ | ⲓ̄ⲁ̇ⲙⲟⲩⲣ Green || **17** ⲙⲁⲣⲙⲱ Green || **20** *i.e.* ˢⲉ-ϣⲁ=ⲓ-ⲟⲩⲱϣ : ⲛϣⲁⲓ [ⲟ]ⲩⲱϣ Green | *i.e.* ζῴδιον | *i.e.* ⲉ-ⲡ-ⲣⲟ || **21** *i.e.* δ(εῖνα) δ(εῖνα) | *i.e.* ˢⲉ=ⲧⲉⲧⲛ̄-ⲉ-ⲣⲱⲕϩ ⲙ̄-ⲡⲉ=ⲥ-ϩⲏⲧ | ⲉⲧⲉⲣⲱⲭ (or ⲡⲱⲭ) ϩⲙ ⲡⲉⲥϩⲛⲧ parse as CMPT "burning will be in her heart" or "bewitching will be in her heart" ? Green | *i.e.* ψυχή || **22** *i.e.* ˢϩⲛ̄ ⲟⲩ-ⲟⲩⲱϣ | *i.e.* ˢϩⲓⲥⲉ ? || **23** *i.e.* δ(εῖνα) δ(εῖνα) | *i.e.* ταχύ (twice)

|*above tableau* Arkhōa Asour Lakhōm

|*right of tableau* Procedure: Write ‹with› saffron? ‹and wine of the› *first fruits on a bone. Offering: apple-hued henna |⁵ and *frankincense. ‹Place it at› the door of the house when the moon is full. It is complete.

|¹⁰, *below tableau* "The desire of three?... The desire of three?... The desire of three?... in passionate? passion ... and I adjure [you] today by your crown that is upon your head and the staff? of fire that is in your hand! I adjure |¹⁵ you by your twenty-one mighty decans who are in your presence, obeying you ‹in› all things—whose names are these: Iamour, Ačou, Samou, Kham, Athak, Mariō, Mas, Samni, Khakh, Amoni, Ōmiēl, Athab, Masa, Lōlō, Sathēr, Abousa, Alath, Math, Lakhōr, Authōn, Lakhouēl |²⁰—that as soon as [I] place your (pl.) image ‹by› the door of the house of NN, child of NN, you will burn her heart and her soul with burning desire and suffering? and madness until she comes to the feet of NN, child of NN, yea, yea, quickly, quickly!"

Image: Images with facing figures in Coptic magical texts are associated with love spells, as opposed to those in which they are depicted back to back, which are associated with separation spells (*cf.* the notes to the images of *PCM* I 31). The two facing bird-like figures may represent the two targets of the spell, who are made to face one another by the practitioner or invoked being, represented by the front-facing figure in the middle; this depiction would parallel rituals involving the manipulation of effigies, which may be artificial (clay, wax, and so on), or else in the form of animal bodies (Dosoo 2018: 25 *et passim*; *cf.* Dosoo 2023a: 164). The image was probably to be copied onto a bone using a mixture of saffron (or *sukk*, *cf. PCM* I 24 l. 18) and wine as ink, and placed at the target's door (ll. 2–6). Green 1987: 30 suggests that the two bird-like figures are female, and the central figure male, but acknowledges that he has no "concrete evidence" for this. He suggests that the three figures are labelled (left-to-right) in Arabic "the magician", "the magic", and "the fever", but these proposals seem phonologically unlikely (*cf.* Richter 2017a: 518).

3. ⲉⲩⲭⲟⲥ : "on a bone" Here and elsewhere (back ll. 2, 6, 9, 16, 24), Green understands ⲉⲩⲭⲟⲥ and its abbreviations as writings of the Greek εὐχή "prayer", but the syntax of the passages in this manuscript regarding writing lead us to expect the writing surface here, preceded by the preposition ⲉ-, *cf.* back ll. 3, 4, 7, 11, 13. The form ⲭⲱⲥ for ⲕⲁⲥ is unexpected, but might be explained as a hypercorrection by a speaker of a ⲥⲁⲛ/ⲡⲉⲛ dialect (likely a form of Faiyumic) writing in Sahidic, or as a result of a confusion with ⲕⲱⲱⲥ "corpse". For bones in Coptic magic, *cf.* Dosoo 2021e.

10–11. ⲡⲟⲩⲱϣ ⲛⲅ... : This initial sequence is difficult to understand; Green translates "the desire for the destruction of a hatred. Also, the desire for a destruction of a... the desire for destruction of a sickness", but this does not match the surviving traces. "Desire" as a heading would make sense (*cf.* back l. 9), but repetition of this type is unexpected in such a heading. Perhaps understand, *e.g.*, "the desire of three scourges" (ⲡⲟⲩⲱϣ ⲛⲅ ⲙ̄ⲙⲁⲥⲧⲓⲍ), but this would leave much unexplained.

14. ⲡ̣[ⲣⲁ]ⲡⲧⲟⲥ ⲛ̄ⲕⲱϩⲧ : "the staff of fire" For the form of ῥάβδος here, *cf.* ⲣⲁⲡⲧⲟⲥ in P.Berol. 8503 (Beltz 1894: no. III 23; KYP M495) l. 57. Compare the "staff of fire" (ⲛ̄ϭⲣⲱⲱϣ ⲛ̄ⲥⲁⲧⲉ) possessed by a being invoked in l. 11 of the unpublished curse P.CtYBR inv. 846 (KYP M371).

15. ⲛ̄ⲧⲉⲕⲁⲛⲟⲥ : "decans" The "decans" were originally thirty-six asterisms each representing 10° of the ecliptic; compare the signs of the zodiac, each representing 30°. As stars, they were associated in astrology with the concept of fate, and in Christian literature come to be seen as demonic beings often associated with death; *cf.* Gundel 1936; Dosoo 2022a: 152–156.

22. ⲟⲩⲱϣ ⲛ̄ⲕⲱϩⲧ : "burning desire": For the motif of LOVE IS FIRE, see the notes to *PCM* I 3 front col. 2 ll. 33–38.

25 ⲟⲩⲕⲧⲟⲩⲭⲟⲥ 15   29 ⲟⲩⲃⲕⲟⲩⲛⲟⲩⲏⲗ 19   ⲣⲣⲣⲱⲫⲟⲛ 20
    ⲙⲉⲛⲁⲥⲱⲧⲟⲥ   30 ⲕⲁⲧⲟⲩⲟⲥⲭⲟⲥ
    ⲁⲥⲉⲛⲁⲕⲱⲥ   ⲕⲉⲛⲁⲕⲱⲥ
    ⲧⲥⲃⲱⲕ   Ⲃ ✠ Ⲃ ✸   ⲁ̅ⲙ̅ᵛ

right of the bottom tableau (text at 90°)

                    ⲁⲩ̇ ⲙⲡⲉⲣ†ⲥⲧⲁⲥⲥⲉ   32
                    ⲉⲣⲟⲥ ⲙⲙⲟⲛ ⲥⲁⲛ ⲧⲉ
             35   ⲛⲁⲗⲙⲟⲩⲅⲁⲣⲣⲏⲡ ⸗

back (hair), at 180° to front

Ⲧⲁⲓ ⲧⲉ ⲧϭⲓⲛⲉⲣϩⲱϥ : ⲛ† ⲁⲥⲥⲟⲩⲭⲁⲣⲉ :
Ⲟⲩⲭⲁⲣⲓⲥ ⲅ̅ⲣ̅ ⲛ̅ⲁ̅ⲥ̅ ⲁ̇ⲣ̇ˣⲥ ⲉⲩ̅ⲭⲟ̅ⲥ̅ : ⲙⲁⲣϥ ⲉⲧⲉⲕⲟⲩⲛⲁⲙ
ⲅ̅ⲣ̅ ⲟⲛ ⲉⲩⲁⲗⲥⲉⲙⲉ : ⲛⲉϩ ⲛ[ⲁ]ⲥⲥⲁⲛⲧⲉⲗ : ⲧⲱϩⲥ ⲉⲡⲉⲕϩⲟ ⲑ̅ⲩ̅ ⲙ̅ⲁ̅ⲥ̅
Ⲟⲩⲭⲱⲣⲉ ⲉⲃⲟⲗ : ⲅ̅ⲣ̅ ⲉⲩⲡⲓⲛⲁⲝ : ⲛⲉⲣⲱⲧⲉ ⲛϭⲓⲧⲣⲉ ⲛⲧⲟⲟⲩ — ⲁ̅ⲗⲱⲑ̅
5   ⲓⲁⲁⲩ ⲙⲙⲟⲟⲩ ⲛⲁⲟⲩⲉⲓⲛ ⲡⲣⲟ ⲑ̅ⲩ̅ ⲗⲓⲃⲁⲛⲟⲥ //
Ⲟⲩⲧⲁⲕⲟ: ⲅ̅ⲣ̅ ⲛⲥⲛⲁϥ ⲛⲅⲣⲟⲩⲣ : ⲉⲩ̅ˣ̇ᵒ̇ˢ : ⲑ̅ⲩ̅ ⲕⲟⲩⲱⲧ //
Ⲟⲩⲧⲁⲕⲟ : ⲅ̅ⲣ̅ ϩⲓ ⲥⲛⲟϥ : ⲛⲉⲗⲁ̣ⲓ ⲛϩⲟⲟⲩⲧ ⲉⲩⲡⲓⲛⲁⲝ ⲓⲁⲁⲩ ⲉⲃⲟⲗ :
ⲙⲙⲟⲟⲩ ⲛⲥⲟⲩⲣⲉⲥ : ⲡⲣⲱ ⲑ̅ⲩ̅ ⲗⲓⲃⲁ //
Ⲟⲩⲱϣ : ⲅ̅ⲣ̅ ⲡⲉⲥⲛⲁϥ ⲛⲁϩⲟⲟⲩ · ϥⲓ ⲡⲉϥⲙⲁⲁϫⲉ ⲛϭⲁⲛⲁϩⲉ : ⲉⲩ̇ˣ
10 ⲙⲁⲣϥ ⲉⲧⲉⲕⲟⲩⲛⲁⲙ : ⲑ̅ⲩ̅ [ⲙ̅]ⲁ̣ⲥ̅ ⲁⲗⲱ̅ᶿ //
Ⲟⲩⲥϩⲓⲙⲉ ⲉⲣⲉⲡⲉⲥϩⲁⲓ ⲙⲁⲥⲧⲉ ⲙⲙⲟⲥ : ⲅⲣ ⲛ̅ⲁ̅ⲥ̅ : ⲥⲛⲁϥ ⲉⲥ-
ⲕⲟⲩⲧⲉⲗⲗⲉ : ⲛⲁⲗⲁⲁⲩ : ⲛⲉϩ ⲛⲁⲣⲭⲏ : ⲡϩⲟ ⲙ̅ⲁ̅ⲥ̅ //

front 25 cf. κάτοχος ? || **26** cf. ⲙⲛ̅ + ἄσωτος ? || **28** cf. ˢⲧⲃⲃⲟⲕ ? || **30** cf. κάτοχος ? || **32** i.e. ἀπολ(ογία) || **33** i.e. διστάζειν ? : ⲛⲡⲉⲣⲧ ⲥⲧⲁⲥⲥⲉ i.e. στύραξ ? Green || **35** i.e. المجرب al-muǧarrib cf. note || **back 1–18** enlarged initial letters at the beginning of each recipe || **1** ⲧϭⲓ Green : i.e. ˢⲧ-ϭⲓⲛⲣϩⲱⲃ : or ⲡϭⲓ ⲛⲉⲣ ϩⲱϥ Green | i.e. الساحر ? : السكر i.e. as-sāḥir ? Green || **2** i.e. χάρις | i.e. γρ(άφειν) | l. ⲛ̅-ⲁⲥ(ⲥⲁⲃⲣⲁⲛ) i.e. الزعفران az-zaʿfarān ? : ⲙ̅ⲁ̅ⲥ̅ i.e. μασ(τίχη) Green | i.e. ἀρχ(ή) | i.e. ˢⲕⲁⲥ ? cf. note front l. 2 : ⲉⲩⲭ ⲛⲟ̅ⲥ̅ i.e. εὐχ(ή) (λίβα)νος Green || **3** i.e. γρ(άφειν) | i.e. الجام al-ǧām : ⲁⲩⲁⲁⲥϭⲙⲉ Green | ⲙⲉϩ "(the) content (is)" Green | i.e. الصندل aṣ-ṣandal : [ⲧ]ⲉ ⲥⲁ ⲛⲧⲉⲗ "of (a) part of fenugreek" Green | i.e. θυ(σία) | i.e. μασ(τίχη) | i.e. العود al-ʿūd || **4** i.e. γρ(άφειν) | i.e. πίναξ | i.e. ˢⲙⲉⲣⲟⲥ (or ⲙⲁⲩⲣⲉⲥ) ⲛ̅ⲧⲉ-ϭⲓⲧⲣⲉ i.e. μέρος "portion of mountain lemon" Green || **5** i.e. ˢⲛ̅-ⲟⲩⲉⲓⲛ | i.e. θυ(σία) | i.e. λίβανος | **6** i.e. γρ(άφειν) || i.e. ˢⲉ-(ⲟ)ⲩ-ⲕⲁⲥ ? cf. note front l. 2 : i.e. εὐχή Green | i.e. θυ(σία) || **7** i.e. γρ(άφειν) | ⲛⲉⲗⲁⲓ cf. note | i.e. πίναξ. || **8** ⲛ̇ⲥⲟⲩⲣⲉⲥ cf. note : cf. الساحر as-sāḥir "enchanted" ? Green | i.e. ˢⲡ-ⲣⲟ | i.e. θυ(σία) | i.e. λίβα(νος) || **9** i.e. γρ(άφειν) | ⲛⲁϩⲟⲟⲩⲧ Green | i.e. ˢⲉϩⲟⲟⲩ | i.e. ˢⲉ-ϥ-ϩⲓ | i.e. ˢϭⲁⲛⲁϩ cf. note | i.e. ˢⲉ-(ⲟ)ⲩ-ⲕⲁⲥ cf. note front l. 2 : i.e. εὐχή Green || **10** i.e. θυ(σία) | i.e. μαστίχη | i.e. العود al-ʿūd || **11** i.e. γρ(άφειν) | l. ⲛ̅-ⲁⲥ(ⲥⲁⲃⲣⲁⲛ) i.e. الزعفران az-zaʿfarān ? : ⲛⲁ=ⲥ Green | i.e. ˢⲛ̅-ⲥⲛⲟⲩ : ⲥⲛⲁⲩ Green || **11–12** i.e. ˢⲛ̅-ⲟⲩ-ⲥⲕⲟⲩⲧⲉⲗⲗⲓⲟⲛ : i.e. σκυτάλη "sticks" Green || **12** i.e. ˢⲁⲗⲁⲩ | i.e. ἀρχή | i.e. μασ(τίχη)

|*around tableau* Oubkounouēl |²⁵ Ouktoukhos, Menasōtos, Asenakōs, Tsbōk, Rrrōphon, |³⁰ Katouoskhos, Kenakōs—request.

And do not doubt it, verily, it is ⟨a⟩ good |³⁵ and tested ⟨procedure⟩!

|*back* This is the procedure of giving enchantment?.

Favour. Write it ⟨with⟩ saffron? ⟨and wine of the⟩ *first fruits on a bone. Bind it to your right arm. Write again on a *platter. Sandalwood oil. Anoint your face. Offering: *mastic, *agarwood.

A separation. Write on a tablet with milk of a desert citron. |⁵ Wash them ⟨off⟩ with water from a drain. ⟨Pour? it at⟩ the door. Offering: *frankincense.

A destruction. Write with frog blood on a bone. Offering: *costus.

A destruction. Write with blood of ⟨a⟩ male *elsai* on a tablet. Wash them off with water of Soures. ⟨Pour? it at⟩ the door. Offering: frankincense.

Desire. Write ⟨with⟩ cow blood, from his left ear, on a bone. |¹⁰ Bind it to your right. Offering: mastic, agarwood.

A woman whose husband hates her. Write ⟨with⟩ saffron? ⟨and⟩ blood on ⟨a⟩ white *dish. Oil of ⟨the⟩ first fruits. ⟨Anoint⟩ the face. ⟨Offering:⟩ mastic.

---

35. ⲛⲁⲗⲙⲟⲩϭⲁⲣⲣⲏⲡ : "tested" As Green (1987: 37) notes, this is the Arabic المجرّب (*al-muǧarrib*); *cf.* back l. 28; the same word is used of a love spell in Cairo JdE 42573 (Chassinat 1955; KYP M44) p. 4 l. 6. For such statements in Greek and Demotic (*e.g.*, GEMF 57/*PGM* IV.3007: δόκιμον; GEMF 16/*PDM* xiv.115: *iw=f dnt*) *cf.* Dosoo 2014: 343–344. For Judaeo-Arabic and Hebrew examples, *cf.* MTKG III no. 57 1b l. 5 (likewise מגרב *muǧarrib*), and the discussion in MTKG I: 146–147.

back 1. ⲁⲥⲥⲟⲩⲭⲁⲣⲉ : "..." Green (1987: 37) proposes الساحر (*as-sāḥir*), translating "bewitching", but the writing of ح as ⲭ is unlikely (*cf.* Richter 2017a: 518). The initial ⲁⲥ- does suggest an Arabic loanword. The word resembles Coptic writings of the word "sugar" (السكر *as-sukkar*; *cf.* Richter 2017a: 520, 525), but this would not make sense in context; perhaps understand *sukr* "intoxication", with the extended sense of "enchantment" (Lane 1863: 1391a *s.v.* سُكْر).

4. ⲛⲉⲣⲱⲧⲉ ⲛϭⲓⲧⲣⲉ ⲛⲧⲟⲟⲩ : "with milk of a desert citron" The citron, also 'cedrate', or 'sweet lime' (*Citrus medica* L.) is a large, bitter, citrus fruit, known in Greek as κίτρον and in Arabic as ترنج (*turunǧ*). References to plant "milk" are known in other Coptic texts, and likely refer simply to the juice. *Cf.* PCM I 25 p. 9 l. 3; Macomber 2020: I 132; Lev/Amar 2008: 147–149; Till 1951: 76, 104.

7. ⲛⲉⲗϭⲁⲓ ⲛϩⲟⲟⲩⲧ : "of ⟨a⟩ male *elsai*" As Green (1987: 37) notes, this must be some kind of animal; the initial ⲉⲗ- might suggest an Arabic loanword, although the /l/ would be expected to assimilate to the following /s/. Perhaps understand a word related to ⲉⲓⲟⲩⲗ ("deer"); for the use of deer (in particular its skin) in Greek magic, see Delatte 1927: 447.6, 483.14, 493.2, 552.1, 13, 553.11 *etc*.

8. ⲛⲥⲟⲩⲣⲉⲥ : "Soures" Green (1987: 39) suggests again a word related to السحر (*as-siḥr*; "magic"), hence "enchanted (water)", or alternatively a derivation from σύρειν, thus "flowing water", but neither is close to the expected form form. Perhaps understand the personal name Sourēs (ⲥⲟⲩⲣⲏⲥ), from Latin *Severus*, the name of one or more saints venerated in Middle Egypt (Papaconstantinou 2001: 205–206 *s.v.* Σουροῦς; Suciu 2017b: 147–48); "water of Soures" might therefore be blessed water from a shrine of the saint.

9. ⲛϭⲁⲛⲁϩⲉ : "left" Green reads "namely, from (an) ox" (*i.e.*, ⁽ⲛϭⲓ ⲛ̄-ⲟⲩ-ⲉϩⲉ), but more plausible is a form of ϭⲁⲛⲁϩ, whose basic meaning is "maimed" (Crum CD 824a), but *cf.* British Library MS Or. 6794 l. 8 (Kropp 1931: I no. E; KYP M306/T361) in which it clearly means "left": "he with the golden bell in his right hand, the spirit lute in his *left* hand" (ⲡⲉⲧⲉⲣⲉ ⲡⲉϣⲕⲗⲕⲓⲗ ⲛ̄ⲛⲟⲩϥ ϩⲛ̄ ⲧⲉϥϭⲓⲝ ⲛⲟⲩⲛⲁⲙ ⲉⲣⲉⲧⲕⲓⲑⲁⲣⲁ ⲙ̄ⲡⲛ̄ⲁ ϩⲛ̄ ⲧⲉϥϭⲓⲝ ⲛϭⲁⲛⲁϩ; *cf.* Vycichl DELC 343a). A reconciliation spell in Cairo JdE 42573 p. 2 ll. 1–5 (Chassinat 1955; KYP M44) uses the blood of the right ear of a cow.

back (hair) (continued)

13 ⲞⲨⲢⲰⲘⲈ : ⲈⲔⲞⲨⲰϢ ⲦⲈϤⲀϢⲈⲔ : ⲄⲢ ⲈⲚⲀⲠⲈ ⲚⲬⲀⲢⲦⲎⲤ
    ⲒⲀⲀⲨ ⲈⲂⲞⲖ : ⲚⲚⲈϨ ⲦⲀⲀⲨ ⲈⲠⲈⲤⲎⲦ ⲈⲨⲀⲚⲠⲞⲨⲖⲖⲈ † ⲚⲈϨ ⲈⲬⲰϤ
15 ⲚⲞⲨⲈⲨϢⲎ : ⲦⲰϨⲤ ⲈⲠⲈⲔϨⲞ ⲘⲠⲚⲀⲨ ϢⲰⲢⲠ ⲘⲎⲚⲈ : ⲐⲨ ⲖⲒⲂⲀ //
    ⲞⲨⲠⲰⲢⲔ : ⲈⲂⲞⲖ : ⲄⲢ ⲚⲤⲚⲀϤ ⲚⲀⲂⲰⲔ ⲚⲦⲞⲞⲨ ⲈⲨⲬ̅ ⲀⲘ̅ ⲘⲀⲢϤ
    . . . . . . [.] . ⲂϢⲔ ⲬⲞⲞⲤ ⲚⲀϤ ⲬⲈ ⲂϢⲔ ⲚⲀⲔ : ⲐⲨ [ⲘⲀ]Ⲥ̅ //
    ⲞⲨⲘⲀⲤⲦⲈ : ϨⲚ ⲦⲘⲎⲦⲈ Ⲃ ⲚⲢⲰⲘⲈ ⲄⲢ ⲚⲤⲚ[ⲞϤ ⲚⲞⲨⲔ]ⲀⲔⲞⲨⲠⲀⲦ
    ϨⲒ ᶜⲚⲞϤ ⲚⲞⲨϨⲀⲢ ⲚⲔⲀⲘⲈ : ϢⲢϢ ⲠϢⲀⲢ ⲚⲈⲖⲤⲀ[Ⲓ ⲒⲀⲀⲨ Ⲉ]Ⲃ[ⲞⲖ]
20 ⲘⲀⲞⲨ ⲚⲀⲞⲨⲈⲒⲚ ⲠⲢⲞ : ⲐⲨ Ⲅ ⲠⲦⲀⲔⲞ ⸗

ⲞⲨϨⲢⲰ ⲈⲦⲀⲔⲞⲤ : ⲤϨⲀⲒ ⲚⲚⲒⲢⲀⲚ : ⲈⲨ . . Ⲍ . . ⲚⲀⲘⲈ : ⲚⲀⲬⲤ
ⲂⲀⲢⲂⲎⲤ : ⲞⲨⲀⲢⲂⲎⲤ : ⲐⲨ ⲖⲒⲂⲀⲚⲞⲤ   ⲈⲢⲞⲤ ⸗
ⲂⲀⲢⲂⲎⲤ : ⲂⲀⲢⲂⲀⲢⲀⲔ

   ⲄⲢ ⲀⲢⲬ ⲈⲨⲬⲞⲤ   27   [. ?] ⲞⲨⲰϢ ⲠⲈ ⲚⲤⲀⲎ
25 . . [. . Ⲉ]Ⲩ[ⲀⲚ]ⲠⲞⲨⲖⲖ[Ⲉ]   ⲚⲀⲖⲘⲞⲨϨⲀⲢ
   . . . ⲡ .

29 ✢ [[ⲚⲈⲚϬ]] ⲠⲒⲘⲈϨⲤⲚⲀⲨ ᶜⲤϨⲀⲒ ⲚⲀⲖⲘⲒⲤⲒⲬ ⲈⲨⲀⲖϬⲈⲘⲈ ⲂⲀⲦⲞⲨ ⲚⲚⲈϨ ⲚⲞⲨⲎⲢⲈⲦ
30   ⲞⲨⲬⲀⲢⲒⲤ   31   ⲦⲰϨⲤ ⲘⲠⲈⲔϨⲞ
32   ⲠⲤⲦⲨ ⸗

---

13 *i.e.* ˢⲈ-ⲦⲢⲈ=ϥ̄-ⲞⲨⲀϢ=Ⲕ̄ : *cf.* ˢϢⲰⲔ "bury" ? Green | *i.e.* γρ(άφειν) | *i.e.* χάρτης ‖ **14** *i.e.* ἀμπύλλη ‖ **15** *i.e.* ˢⲚ̄-ⲞⲨϢⲎ | *i.e.* ˢⲚ̄-ϢⲰⲢⲠ | *i.e.* ˢⲘ̄-ⲘⲎⲚⲈ | *i.e.* θυ(σία) | *i.e.* λίβα(νος) ‖ **16** *i.e.* γρ(άφειν) | *i.e.* ˢⲈ-(Ⲟ)Ⲩ-ⲔⲀⲤ ? *cf.* note front l. 2 | *i.e.* ἀπ(ολογία) ‖ **17** ⲈⲦⲈⲔ ⲞⲞ[....] ⲂϢⲔ Ⲭ[.]ⲀⲤ Green | or ⲚⲞϤ *l.* ⲤⲚⲞϤ ? Green | *i.e.* θυ(σία) | *i.e.* μασ(τίχη) ‖ **18** *i.e.* γρ(άφειν) | ⲘⲠⲢⲰⲘⲈ or Ϣ ⲠⲢⲰⲘⲈ Green | [ⲚⲞⲨⲔⲀⲔ]ⲞⲨⲠⲀⲦ Green ‖ **19** *i.e.* ˢⲚ̄-ⲞⲨ-ⲞⲨϨⲞⲢ ‖ ϢⲢϢ *cf.* note : ϨⲒⲬⲰ Green | ⲚⲈⲖⲤⲀ[Ⲓ] *cf.* note l. 7 : ⲚⲈⲬⲞⲨ [ca. 12–13] Green ‖ **20** ϨⲒⲬⲞⲨ Green | *i.e.* ˢⲚ̄-ⲞⲨ-ⲞⲨⲈⲒⲚ | *i.e.* θυ(σία) | *i.e.* ˢⲘ̄-Ⲡ-ⲦⲀⲔⲞ ? ‖ **21** . . Ⲍ . . restore ˢⲂⲖ̄ⲬⲈ ? : *i.e.* φυλακτήριον Green | corrected from ⲚⲀⲬⲤⲈ Green ‖ **22** *i.e.* θυ(σία) | *i.e.* λίβανος ‖ **23** ⲘⲀⲢ[ϤⲈ]Ⲩ Green ‖ **24** *i.e.* γρ(άφειν) | *i.e.* ἀρχ(ή) | *i.e.* ˢⲈ-(Ⲟ)Ⲩ-ⲔⲀⲤ *cf.* note front l. 2 : *i.e.* εὐχή Green ‖ **25** *i.e.* ἀμπύλλη : ⲘⲀⲢ[Ϥ Ⲛ]⟨Ⲟ⟩Ⲩ[ⲀⲚ]ⲠⲞⲨⲖⲖⲈ Green ‖ **26** Ⲁ . . Ⲡ Ⲭ ⲠⲦⲎⲢ[. ?] or Ⲁ . . Ⲓ Ⲣ ⲠⲦⲎⲢ[. ?] Green ‖ **27** *i.e.* ˢⲞⲨ-ⲞⲨⲀϢ ‖ **28** *l.* ⲀⲖⲘⲞⲨϨⲀⲢ(ⲢⲎⲠ) *i.e.* المجرب al-muǧarrib *cf.* note front l. 35 ‖ **29** ✢ [[ⲚⲈⲚϬ]] omitted in Green | *i.e.* المسك al-misk | *i.e.* الجام al-ǧām : *i.e.* الجماع al-ǧamā "sexual intercourse" Green | ⲒⲂ Ϛ ϤⲦⲞⲨ "twelve as well as four (parts) of" Green ‖ **30** *i.e.* χάρις ‖ **31** ϨⲘ ⲦⲈⲤϨⲞ Green ‖ **32** ⲠⲤϨⲀⲒ ? "the writing" Green

A man whom you wish to desire you. Write on the upper parts of ⟨a⟩ papyrus sheet. Wash them off with oil. Put them into a *flask. Put oil upon it |¹⁵ at night. Anoint your face at the first hour, daily. Offering: *frankincense.

A removal. Write with desert raven blood on a bone. Request. Bind it to your … say to him, "Go!" Offering: mastic?.

A hatred between two people. Write with hoopoe blood and blood of a black dog ⟨and⟩ menstrual? ⟨blood on⟩ the skin of an *elsai* [wash it off with] |²⁰ water from a drain. ⟨Place at⟩ the door. Offering: *three of destruction?.

A furnace, to destroy it. Write these names on a clay [ostracon?]. Throw it at it. "Barbēs Ouarbēs, Barbēs Barbarak." Offering: frankincense.

Write ⟨with wine of the⟩ *first fruits on a bone. |²⁵ […] to a flask?. It is a good, tested desire ⟨procedure⟩.

|³⁰ Favour. |²⁹ The second one. Write with *musk on a bowl. Wipe it with rose oil. |³¹ Anoint your face. …

KD, EL & MP, edited from photograph and autopsy; tracings by KD & JS.

Kharaktēres: An example of linear kufic, for which see the notes to *PCM* I 21 ll. 1–3. These symbols are probably those to be copied onto various materials as part of the rituals described on the back of the sheet.

13. ⲛⲭⲁⲣⲧⲏⲥ : "papyrus sheet" Green translates χάρτης as papyrus plant. If it does indeed refer to papyrus, it should be understood as a papyrus sheet used as a writing surface (*cf.* Lewis 1974: 70–74). Given the late date of the manuscript however, we might perhaps understand a more generic sense of a sheet of writing material, made of either paper or parchment; *cf.* LBG *s.v.* χαρτί(ν); Richter 2023: 165.

19. ϣⲣⲱ : "menstrual? ⟨blood on⟩" *Cf.* the notes to *PCM* I 22 l. 46.

20. Ⲅ̄ ⲡⲧⲁⲕⲟ : "three of destruction" See glossary *s.v.* *three evil things.

21. ⲟⲩϩⲣⲱ ⲉⲧⲁⲕⲟⲥ : "a furnace, to destroy it" For similar curses against work equipment, see the note to *PCM* I 30 front ll. 10–14.

24. ⲁⲣⲭ : "⟨with wine of the⟩ first fruits" Green understands ⲁⲣⲭ as referring to "freshly-pressed (oil)", but here we translate as ⲁⲣⲭ(ⲏ ⲛ̄ⲏⲣⲡ), *i.e.* "wine of the first fruits"; *cf.* the glossary *s.v.* *first fruits.

24–32. The text in these lines is significantly smaller than that aabove, and may have been added later, in the gaps between the linear kufic.

Indices

Glossary

The Glossary offers brief discussions of words marked with an asterisk (*) elsewhere in the volume, as well as references to discussions on other pages.

Abra see *Abrasax*

Abrasax

The name Abrasax and its variants (*Abra*, *Abrasaxael*, *Abraxas*, *Abrazakh*, perhaps also *Abrax*, *Atrakh*, *Ax*) was likely produced through Greek isopsephy, with the letters of the name Αβρασαξ (1 + 2 + 100 + 1 + 200 + 1 + 60) adding up to 365, the number of days in the solar year. The number of letters, seven, was also a significant one in the ancient Mediterranean, equalling, for example, the number of planets (*cf.* Barb 1957). In the corpus of Graeco-Egyptian magical papyri, it appears as a name associated at times with the supreme solar deity, at others with the Jewish deity *Iao (see, *e.g.*, *GEMF* 11/*PGM* LXIX.1, 2 (II CE); *GEMF* 15.254–257/*PGM* XII.205–206 (II CE); *GEMF* 18.195/*PGM* LXI.33 (III CE)), although we equally find him in the company of the Jewish angels *Michael and *Gabriel (*e.g.*, *GEMF* 31/*PGM* I.302 (III CE); KYP M154/*PGM* III.150). Abrasax appears in several of the Sethian 'Gnostic' treatises of the Nag Hammadi Library (Piwowarczyk 2021: 9–10), albeit not with a systematic role, and is mentioned by Irenaeus of Lyons (II CE) and the other heresiologists dependent on him, as the ruler of the three hundred and sixty-five heavens within the Gnostic system of Basilides (Piwowarczyk 2021: 10). Within Jewish and Christian magical texts, Abrasax appears as the, or an, angel of the sun, or, less often, as one of the names of God, with the name borrowed from Graeco-Egyptian sources (Bohak 2008: 247–250; Dosoo 2021d: 416). Note that Abrasax is often associated with the 'anguipede', a figure with snake legs, and usually a rooster's head, whip, and shield, depicted on many magical gems. This association is mistaken; both the figure of the anguipede and the name 'Abrasax' are independently associated with Iao, one of the names of the Jewish God, and so when the name 'Abrasax' appears with the image of the anguipede it is probably due to their mutual association with Iao, rather than because of a meaningful independent connection (Bonner 1950: 133–134; Shandruk 2022: 105–106).

Abrazakh see *Abrasax*

Abyss

In Coptic literature, the "abyss" (Coptic ⲛⲟⲩⲛ *noun*, often translating the Greek ἄβυσσος, *abussos*), is associated both with the depths of the earth (that is, *hell) and the primordial waters which lie below the earth. In biblical contexts, the Greek word designates "a bottomless place" (Lambert 1916). In the Septuagint, it is used to translate to the Hebrew תהום (*təhôm*), referring to the primordial waters which covered the earth before creation and which were subsequently shut up in subterranean storehouses. Augustine, for instance, understands 'abyss' as a term for primordial deep waters, associated with caves as the source of all water, in which serpents (Greek δράκοντες) live (*Expositions on Psalms*, 148.9). The Devil, likewise described as a serpent, is said to have been cast bound into the abyss for a thousand years (Revelation 20.1–3), and this association of the abyss or hell as the dwelling place or prison of fallen angels is found in other texts (*e.g.*, T.Varie.13 (KYP M107) front ll. 26–27). In the Coptic magical texts, the abyss often occurs in association with cosmic beings whose head is in heaven and whose feet are in the abyss, understood as being beneath the earth (*cf. PCM* I 8 front ll. 12–3; see Dosoo 2022c: 502). The four pillars of the abyss are said to support the first heaven (*PCM* I 12 p. 43 ll. 1–3), and God, called in this passage Thrakai, is said to have covered the abyss with the earth and suspended heaven like a vault (*PCM* I 12 p. 11 ll. 13–15; *cf.* Genesis 1.7).

Adam and Eve, children of *see the notes to PCM I 25 p. 7 ll. 12–14*
Adjuration *see pp. 32–33; cf. Horkōmotoi*
Adonai see *Iao Sabaoth Adonai Eloei Elemas*

Agarwood

Agarwood or aloes (Coptic ⲁⲗⲟⲅⲉ, from Arabic العود *al-ʿūd*, Greek ἀγάλοχον *agalokhon*) is the wood of aquilaria trees (*Aquilaria* sp.), which secrete an oleoresin in response to parasitic infection, making the infected parts of the wood highly aromatic. It was generally imported to Egypt from eastern India and other parts of Southeast Asia, such as Cambodia and Indochina, and should be distinguished from Greek ἀλόη (*aloē*), bitter aloes (*Aloe* sp.). Agarwood was known to Dioscorides (*Materia Medica* I.22) in the first century CE, who describes it as "fragrant" (εὐώδης), but it seems only to have become commonly imported into the Mediterranean after the Islamic conquests. Agarwood is regularly found as an element of offerings in Coptic magical texts; see, for example, *PCM* I 22 l. 11; *PCM* I 24 l. 18; *PCM* I 25 p. 16 l. 14, p. 17 l. 16; *PCM* I 26 p. 15 l. 31, p. 16 l. 23, p. 17 ll. 9, 23; *PCM* I 28 p. 12 l. 19; *PCM* I 32 p. 1 l. 26; *PCM* 37 back ll. 3, 10; P. Stras. K 204 + 205 + 282 §2.5 l. 1(Hevesi 2018; KYP M92); P.Vindob. K 8303 l. 10 (Stegemann 1934: no. 51; KYP M279).

Sources and further reading: Lev/Amar 2008: 97–98; Amar/Lev 2013: 22; King 2017: 63–65; López-Sampson/Page 2018.

Angelic Beings

Angels are omnipresent in Christian literature and cult, as well as in magical texts, in which they serve as agents of higher powers, usually the Jewish-Christian God. As Mihálykó (2022: 725) points out, in early liturgical prayers from Egypt, the congregation asked God for protection through "angelic powers", or to appoint an angel as a guide. Angels were also believed to appear at the altar during the service, although, as incorporeal heavenly beings, they were not visible to the congregation (Mihálykó 2022: 725; Müller 1962: 77).

Angels were often divided into multiple ranks, including cherubim (ⲭⲉⲣⲟⲩⲃⲓⲙ), seraphim (ⲥⲉⲣⲁⲫⲓⲙ), powers (ⲇⲩⲛⲁⲙⲓⲥ, ⲇⲩⲛⲁⲧⲟⲥ, or ϭⲟⲙ), thrones (ⲑⲣⲟⲛⲟⲥ), principalities (ⲁⲣⲭⲏ), and authorities (ⲉⲝⲟⲩⲥⲓⲁ) (*cf.* Dosoo 2021d: 407). The best-known of such systems is found in Pseudo-Dionysius the Areopagite's *On the Celestial Hierarchy* (6.7), but we find similar lists in other authors, such as Cyril of Alexandria (*On the Mysteries* 5.6; V CE). The seven archangels are often understood to be the highest rank, who directly serve and stand in the presence of God; only three are named in the canonical books of the Bible: Michael (in Daniel 10.13, 10.21, 12.1; Jude 9.1; Revelation 12.7–12), Gabriel (in Daniel 18.16, 9.21; Luke 1.19, 26), and Raphael (in Tobit 3.17 *etc.*). We find a full list of seven archangels in 1 Enoch 20: Suriel (or Uriel), Raphael, Raguel, Michael, Sarakael, Gabriel, and Remiel (Isaac in Charlesworth 1983: 23–24). The names in the Coptic magical papyri are inconsistent, but those of the angels from the Bible, including 1 Enoch, tend to recur (*cf.* Dosoo 2021d: 414–415). For the names of the archangels, *cf.* the notes to *PCM* I 11 p. 9 ll. 12–24.

Michael is generally understood as the most foremost of the archangels, the general of the angelic armies who took over the rank of the Devil after his fall (Müller 1959: 8–35).

Seraphim and cherubim in the Egyptian tradition are understood as high-ranking six-winged angels who stand in the presence of God, and recite the *Sanctus before him. The chariot-throne of God is understood as being drawn by the Four Living Creatures (ϥⲧⲟⲟⲩ ⲛ̄ⲍⲱⲟⲛ): four cherubim (or two cherubim and two seraphim) with human, lion, ox, and eagle faces (Müller 1959: 83–84; Stevenson 2001; de Grooth/van Moorsel 1977–1978; *cf.* Ezekiel 1; Revelation 4.6–8), and are associated with two sets of names—the first a palindromic square ⲁⲗⲫⲁ ⲗⲏⲱⲛ ⲫⲱⲛⲏ ⲁⲛⲏⲣ, the second variants of ⲙⲉⲗⲓⲧⲱⲛ, ⲁⲅⲣⲁⲙⲙⲁⲧⲁ, ⲡⲁⲣⲁⲙⲩⲣⲁ, ⲥⲟⲩⲣⲟⲩⲑⲓⲟⲛ (Tsakos 2014; Dosoo 2022c: 522–523). The tradition of associating the Four Living Creatures with the Four Evangelists, common in the Latin West (*cf.* Stevenson 2001: 474–486), is less prominent, but not unattested in Coptic texts; see *e.g.*, Pseudo-John Chrysostom, *On the Four Bodiless Living Creatures* (CC 177). The Four Living Creatures, and sometimes other angels, are sometimes described as "bodiless" or "incorporeal" (ⲁⲥⲱⲙⲁⲧⲟⲥ).

Animal Analogies see the notes to *PCM I 7 ll. 35–36; PCM I 28 p. 2 ll. 12–13; PCM I 31 back ll. 7–8*

Apis see *Pharaonic deities*

Aswan Dish

"Aswan dish" translates Coptic ⲥⲕⲟⲩⲧⲉⲗⲓⲟⲛ/ⲡⲓⲛⲁⲝ ⲛ̄ⲥⲟⲩⲁⲛ and variants thereof, the former from the Greek σκουτέλλιον (in turn from Latin *scutella*; *cf.* Förster WBGW 739), the latter from the Greek πίναξ. This term seems to be equivalent to the Arabic *ṣaḥfa* (صحفة; *cf.* *P.Bad.* V 123 front l. 1, back 17 (KYP M315); *Scala Magna* 2.6, 1255 *s.v.* ⲃⲓⲛⲁⲝ (Macomber 2020: I 106)). In modern Egypt this refers to a broad dish of *ca.* 30 cm in diameter with raised edges (van der Vliet 1991: 224–225). An example of an object labelled an "Aswan dish" (ⲡⲓⲛⲁⲝ ⲛⲥⲟⲩⲁⲛ) can be found in the British Museum under inventory no. EA 27718 (TM 82637). Although fragmentary, it would seem to be a very similar object to the modern *ṣaḥfa*. "Aswan" here refers to the place of manufacture. It seems that the pottery was usually red, but we also find reference to "white" dishes (*PCM* I p. 1 l. 19; *PCM* I 37 back ll. 11–12) and even "glass dishes" (*PCM* I 21 p. 17 ll. 26–30). In Coptic magical papyri, dishes are usually used as supports to copy texts and images, which may be washed off during rituals; see *PCM* I 30 front ll. 2–3, *PCM* I 31 back l. 16; *PCM* I 32 p. 1 l. 19; *PCM* I 37 back ll. 11–12.

Atrakh see *Abrasax*

Authorities see *Angelic Beings*; for temporal authorities, *cf.* the notes to *PCM I 26 p. 16 l. 28*

Ax see *Abrasax*

Bathwater see notes to *PCM I 30 front ll. 3–4*

Binding and Releasing

The concept of binding (ⲙⲟⲩⲣ *mour*) and releasing (ⲃⲱⲗ ⲉⲃⲟⲗ *bōl ebol*) is at the centre of many Coptic magical texts. "Binding" translates Greek terms such as καταδέω ("I bind"), and the concept appears frequently in binding curses and love spells, and relates to binding an individual through a curse so that they are unable to act in specific ways—speaking against someone, or having sexual intercourse, for example. The act of unbinding (ⲃⲱⲗ ⲉⲃⲟⲗ, translating Greek λύω) refers to rituals to undo such binding procedures (*cf.* Eidinow 2007: 142–152; Dosoo 2020: 267–272). ⲙⲟⲩⲣ is used in a second, unrelated sense, to refer to the act of binding an amulet to the body, equivalent to the Greek περιάπτω.

Bond see *Binding and Releasing*
By the power see notes to *PCM I 16 p. 3 ll. 7–8*
Chaksh see note to *PCM I 26 p. 16 l. 17*
Cherubim see *Angelic Beings*

Citron *see note to PCM I 37 back l. 4*

Copto-Arabic
"Copto-Arabic" generally refers to Arabic-language texts produced by Copts, the indigenous Christian community of Egypt. Some of these are translations of older Coptic-language texts, others are original compositions; *cf.* Swanson 2014.

Costus
Costus (Coptic ⲕⲟⲩϣⲧ *koušt*, Greek κόστος *kostos*, Arabic قسط *qusṭ*) is a term used to refer to two different plants, *Dolomiaea* (or *Saussurea*) *costus* (Falc.) and *Hellenia speciosa* (J. Koenig, formerly *Cheilocostus speciosu*s or *Costus speciosus)*. Although authors do not clearly or consistently distinguish between the two, the original referent was probably to the former, referred to as *kuṣṭha-* in Sanskrit, whence the names in the other languages derive. The former grows in the mountainous far north of India, while the latter is found in both northern India (including modern Pakistan) and the Near East, leading to them being at times referred to as, respectively, "Indian" and "Arabian" costus, the former being black and the latter white (*e.g.*, Dioscorides, *Materia Medica* 1.16). Both are used primarily for their root, although an oil may be extracted from the Indian variety. Costus was already being imported into the Mediterranean area in the fourth century BCE (see, *e.g.*, Theophrastus, *Enquiry into Plants* 9.7), and its medical use is attested in Greek, Coptic, Jewish, and Arabic texts from antiquity to the Middle Ages. Dioscorides (*Materia Medica* 1.16) describes the Arabian costus as being the best, with a pleasant (ἡδεῖα) smell. Other Greek and Latin sources consider it as dry, pungent, heating, and bitter. In the magical papyri it is used in burnt offerings, although it is usually unclear which plant it refers to. Since we sometimes find instructions to use white costus (ⲕⲟⲩϣⲧ ⲛ̄ⲁⲗⲁⲩ *koušt n-alau*, *e.g.*, *PCM* I 26 p. 16 l. 12 *cf.* l. 8), likely the Arabian costus, it may be that *koušt* on its own refers to Indian costus, although further work is needed on this point. Costus is found occasionally in the Graeco-Egyptian magical papyri (*e.g.*, *GEMF* 16/*PDM* xiv.336 (?) (KYP M162); *GEMF* 57/*PGM* IV.2680; *GEMF* 60/*PGM* XIII.18, 353 (KYP M161)). For Coptic examples, see *PCM* I 17 ll. 11, 27; *PCM* I 26 p. 15 l. 31, p. 16 ll. 8, 12; *PCM* I 29 back l. 7; *PCM* I 37 l. 6; *P.Ryl. Copt.* 109 (KYP M328); BM EA 10391 (Zellmann-Rohrer 2022a: no. 1) front l. 60.

Sources and further reading: Till 1951: 69–70; Greppin 1999; Lev/Amar 2008: 157–158; Piperakis 2022: 265.

Cup
The word 'cup' (Coptic ⲁⲡⲟⲧ *apot*) is the equivalent of the Greek ποτήριον (*potērion*), referring to a small drinking vessel. The same term is used for the liturgical chalice used for the wine which becomes the blood of Christ during the anaphora (the Eucharistic prayer), as part of the *epiclesis*, when the priest asks

God to fill the wine in the chalice with the Holy Spirit (Mihálykó 2019: 61). In the context of curses and love spells, it can be used to refer to a "potion", which may have a negative effect on the one who drinks it; see, for example *PCM* 10 ll. 16–17, in which a woman might be barren because "someone has given her an enchanted cup"; *PCM* I 26, recipe number 7, for a man "who has been given a cup"; *PCM* I 33 front ll. 1–5. In magical rituals, cups may be used to contain various liquids, such as water, oil, wine, and blood. Often, an invocation was to be spoken over the liquid, following the pattern of the epiclesis in the anaphora (see *PCM* I 6 ll. 15–18; *PCM* I 10 l. 10; *PCM* I 17 ll. 21–22; *cf.* Dosoo 2021b: 76–77).

Dish see *Aswan Dish*
Dwelling places see *Horkōmotoi*
Elemas see *Iao Sabaoth Adonai Eloei Elemas*
Eloei see *Iao Sabaoth Adonai Eloei Elemas*
Eve and Adam, Children of see note to *PCM I 25 p. 7 ll. 12–14*

First Fruits (*wine* or *oil of the*)

The "first fruits" (Greek/Coptic ἀπαρχή/ⲁⲡⲁⲣⲭⲏ *aparkhē*, translating Hebrew ראשית *rēʾšīt*) are the first products of the harvest. Numbers 18.12 specifies that the Israelites are to dedicate the first fruits of oil, wine, and grain to the priestly tribe, the Levites, and in early Christianity this prerogative was understood to have been transferred to the Christian clergy. Canonical collections from around the fourth century onwards specify that the first fruit offerings were to be taken to the church and blessed by the bishop to serve three purposes—first, the production of the bread and wine used in the communion, second, the maintenance of the clerics, and finally, the remainder was to be used for the care of the sick and poor (Wipszycka 1972: 70–71; Madey/Amatowni 1982: 13–14, 18–19; Wipszycka 2009: 559–561; Arabic *Canons of Athanasius* §§63–65, 82, 107 in Riedel/Crum 1904; Bohairic *Apostolic Constitutions* §§54, 74 in Tattam 1848).

In Coptic, the word *aparkhē* came to refer specifically to the wine used for communion, with the word being transliterated into Arabic as ابارکة *abārka* (Worrell 1942: 329; Burmester 1967: 82; Madey/Amatowni 1982: 18–19; Macomber 2020: I 91, 174).

Coptic magical texts regularly make use of wine and oil of the first fruits ((ⲁⲡ)ⲁⲣⲭⲏ ⲛ̄ⲏⲣⲡ, (ⲁⲡ)ⲁⲣⲭⲏ ⲛ̄ⲛⲉϩ), likely referring to wine and oil from the first fruit offering which had been blessed by the bishop and which could therefore serve as liturgical wine and oil. *Aparkhē* is usually abbreviated to *arkhē* in the corpus, but we should probably understand this as being the same word (*cf.* Zellmann-Rohrer 2022a: 96–97, 101). The long form is best attested in the Michigan manuscripts (KYP M9 & 15) edited by Worrell (1930: 246.11, 13; 248.15; 249.9). In one text we find both forms, the longer (and more "correct") form in the spoken formula, and the shorter ('abbreviated') form in the ritual instructions (BM EA 10391 front ll. 35, 37; Zellmann-Rohrer 2022a: no. 1; KYP M302). The shorter form also appears as a variant of the full writing in some copies of the *Scala Magna* (Macomber 2020: II 393).

Since the primary referent of the *(ap)arkhē* is wine, we translate it as "⟨wine of the⟩ first fruits" where it is not specified as being oil. Support for this is found in the instructions for creating an amulet in the *Endoxon of Michael* in which the Heidelberg copy has *arkhē* alone (*PCM* I 26 p. 17 l. 18), but the equivalent instructions in the unpublished Collège de France copy specifies the use of wine (ⲁⲣⲭⲏ ⲛⲏⲣⲡ, p. 21 ll. 5–6). Note that this means, almost paradoxically, that when the product is specified, oil is more common, since no specification is necessary to refer to wine. In this volume, wine of the first fruits is used in *PCM* I 21 l. 8; *PCM* I 24 l. 18; *PCM* I 25 p. 16 ll. 8, 11; *PCM* I 26 p. 17 l. 18; *PCM* I 32 l. 22; *PCM* I 37 front l. 3, back l. 2 and oil in *PCM* I 26 p. 16 ll. 7, 13, 24; *PCM* I 37 back l. 12.

Flask
'Flask' in this volume translates the Greek ἀμπύλλη (*ampullē*; from Latin *ampulla*), borrowed into Coptic. The Latin term refers to small bottles with rounded bodies and short necks used to store oil, ointment, but also wine; they are often made out of glass (TLL *s.v. ampulla*). This description would seem to hold true also for the Greek loanword (*cf.* Remondon 1952: 203). In Coptic texts, the eighth-century monk Frange mentions flasks (ⲁⲙⲡⲟⲩⲗⲉ) in two letters, in one case to be filled with fish sauce (ϫⲓⲣ *čir*; *O.Frange* 53.14, 15; O.Bâle inv. Lg Ae BJF 31c ll. 5, 8 (Boud'hors 2011: 105–106); Boud'hors/Heurtel 2015: 71). The *Scala Magna* (*s.v.* ⲟⲩⲁⲙⲡⲟⲩⲗⲓⲁ, Macomber 2020: I 108) defines the *ampullē* as a جفنة *ǧafna*, referring rather to a large bowl (see Lane 1863: 434 *s.v.* جَفْنَةٌ, جَفَنَ نَاقَةً). It is possible the word could have both meanings simultaneously, depending on context, or that the meaning had changed by the time of the writing of the *Scala* in the fourteenth century. In the Coptic magical papyri, the word appears as a container of water or oil in *PCM* I 26 p. 15 l. 28, p. 16 l. 10; *PCM* I 37 back ll. 14, 25; British Library MS Or 6796 (2), (3) verso l. 111 (Kropp 1931: I no. H; KYP M118).

Four Living Creatures see *Angelic Beings*

Frankincense
Frankincense (Greek/Coptic λίβανος/ⲗⲓⲃⲁⲛⲟⲥ *libanos*) is the resin of evergreen trees of the genus *Boswellia*, imported to Egypt from South Arabia and the Horn of Africa. It is found regularly in the Hebrew Bible and New Testament among offerings to the Jewish god (*e.g.*, Leviticus 2.16), and was famously one of the gifts of the *magoi* to Jesus, along with gold and myrrh (Matthew 2.11). Like *costus and *saffron, it continued to be popular after the Islamic conquests, but became less prestigious with the arrival as newer fragrances such as *agarwood

and *musk became more readily available. Frankincense regularly appears as an offering in the Graeco-Egyptian magical papyri (LiDonnici 2001: 68–77), as well as the Coptic examples; see λίβανος in the index for attestations in this volume. As well as being burned as an incense, we regularly find it used for various complaints in Coptic, Arabic, and Jewish medicine.

Sources and further reading: Till 1951: 101; Asensi Amorós 2003: 2–4; Lev/Amar 2008: 168–171; Amar/Lev 2013: 27; Piperakis 2022: 265.

Gabriel *see Angelic Beings*
Grass of Mary *see note to PCM I 25 p.9 ll. 2–4*

Hell

"Hell", Greek ᾅδης (*hadēs*), Coptic ⲁⲙⲛⲧⲉ (*amente*), refers in popular Egyptian Christianity to the underworld. Prior to the resurrection of Jesus, nearly all the human dead were confined in hell, but after his resurrection, only the evil were kept there, while the righteous were taken to Paradise (ⲡⲁⲣⲁⲇⲉⲓⲥⲟⲥ *paradeisos*) to await final judgement. Hell is overseen by angels who punish sinners, whose ruler is known as *Temeluchus* or *Tartaruchus* ("ruler of Tartarus"), and is also the place to which the fallen angels, or demons, are confined as punishment. There is often a conflation between the angels of hell and the demons, and thus the ruler of hell and the Devil (Rosenstiehl/Ménard 1986; Zandee 1960: 338–332). The deepest and most terrible part of hell is referred to as Tartarus (Τάρταρος) (Zandee 1960: 317–318). Hell may also be referred to as the *abyss, a term originally referring to the primordial waters below the earth (Zandee 1960: 318–319).

The Coptic term *amente* derives from the older Egyptian 𓇋𓏠𓈖𓏏𓏏 *imn.t.t*, literally "western land" (DELC: 11), referring to the other realm of the dead ruled over by *Osiris, but in Christian texts the original signification seems to have been almost entirely lost (*cf.* Zandee 1960: 305–307, 310–316).

Horkōmotoi

The speech acts of invoking, adjuring, and requesting are often strengthened by the use of authorities (*horkōmotoi* in Shauf 2005), introduced using the preposition "by" (ⲛ̄). A particularly extensive example is "I adjure you today, by the wellbeing of your names and your powers and your phylacteries and your images and the places in which you dwell and the Trinity" (*PCM* I 21 ll. 14–19). According to Shauf (2005), these authorities are understood as entities with a special relationship to the addressed being, of such a nature that, when they are called upon, the being cannot refuse the request (*cf.* Shauf 2005: 203, 214; Dosoo 2022a: 131–132). Common *horkōmotoi* in Coptic magical texts are the "name" (ⲣⲁⲛ), "dwelling place(s)" (ⲙⲁ/ⲧⲟⲡⲟⲥ ⲉⲧ(ⲕ̄)ϣⲟⲟⲡ ⲛ̄ϩⲏⲧϥ), "image" (ⲍⲱⲇⲓⲟⲛ ‹ ζῴδιον), "phylacteries" (ⲫⲩⲗⲁⲕⲧⲏⲣⲓⲟⲛ ‹ φυλακτήριον), "power" (ϭⲟⲙ), and "wellbeing" (ⲟⲩϫⲁⲓ). "Image" here seems to refer to the images of superhuman beings which are often found in magical texts, understood as having an ontologically significant relationship to the being which they depict, and "phylacteries" may be the accompanying *kharaktēres* (Dosoo 2022a: 132). "Wellbeing" refers to the health and fortune of the being, equivalent to Latin *salus* or Greek σωτήρια, with its use probably deriving from oaths sworn by the 'wellbeing' of emperors, found from the sixth century onwards (Dosoo 2022a: 131–132). The wellbeing mentioned as a *horkōmotos* is usually that of another being than the one addressed.

Images see *Horkōmotoi*
Holy, Holy, Holy see *Sanctus*
Horus see *Pharaonic Deities*
Horus-Isis Narrative Charms see *notes to PCM I 7*

Iao Sabaoth Adonai Eloei Elemas

Names for the Jewish-Christian deity, drawn from Hebrew and Aramaic. **Iao** (Ιαω/ιαω) is a Greek rendering of the personal name of the deity, either the Tetragrammaton, 'four-letter name' יהוה (*YHWH*) or the shorter three-letter name יהו (*YHW*), the latter found in names such as "Elijah" (Hebrew ʾĒlīyyāhū; Weippert 1980: 249–250; Vasileiadis 2013: 6–8; Vasileiadis 2015: 68; Vasileiadis 2017: 34–39).

In Egypt, the form *Yahō* seems to have been commonly in use among the Jewish population of Elephantine from the fifth-century BCE (Weippert 1980: 249; van der Toorn 2019: 102–107), and is likely the form represented by *Iao*, the most common writing in Greek. Writings in Demotic, Old Coptic, and Latin suggest that this would originally have been pronounced as *Yaho*, even though the /h/ could not be clearly written in Greek (Vasileiadis 2017: 49 n. 72; *GEMF* 16/ *PDM* xiv.169 etc.; *GEMF* 57/*PGM* IV.92). Other forms attested in Greek suggest that the full Tetragrammaton was pronounced as *Yahwe* (Weippert 1980: 249; Marjanen 2004), implying that 'Iao' may be the three-letter name.

Nonetheless, 'Iao' is the usual form in which the name appears in the Greek magical papyri. It is one of, if not the, most common divine names in this corpus, although it is often unclear if it is understood as the name of the specifically Jewish-Christian deity, or rather as another name for a different powerful god (such as the sun god), or simply a powerful word (Fauth 2014: 17–62). In Second Temple and Rabbinic Judaism, speaking of the name was avoided, being replaced with **Adonai** ("my lord") in reading the scriptures; this taboo surrounding the name likely increased its sense of power (Skehan 1980; Bohak 2000: 5; Vasileiadis 2015: 57–58).

Early Christian authors show awareness of the pronunciation of the personal name of the Jewish-Christian god as *Iao*, even if they did not use it extensively (Vasileiadis 2013: 9–13; Vasileiadis 2015: 57–59). It notably appears as a secret name of Jesus in the Coptic apocryphal *Book of Bartholomew* (CC 27; Westerhoff

1999: 76–77).

Sabaoth (Σαβαώθ) is the Greek rendering of the biblical epithet, "(of) hosts" (צבאות, *ṣəḇā'ôṯ*), usually found after the Tetragrammaton, with the sequence thus commonly rendered in English translation as "Lord of Hosts". Unlike the Tetragrammaton, 'Sabaoth' was transliterated into Greek, and appears in the Septuagint (*e.g.*, Joshua 15.17) and in the *Sanctus in liturgical texts (*e.g.*, Johnson 2010: 24), so would certainly have been very familiar to most Christians.

Eloei comes from the Aramaic אלהי (*elōhāi* "my god"), rendered in Mark (15.34) as Ἐλωΐ *Elōi* in the citation of Psalm 21 (22) 2 "God, my god, listen to me, why have you forsaken me?"

Elemas seems to derive from a reinterpretation of λεμὰ σαβαχθανί (*lema sabakhthani*), the following part of the citation of Psalm 21.2 (22.2) as given in Matthew 27.46, from Aramaic למה שבקתני (*ləmā šəḇaqtanī* "why have you forsaken me"). In the absence of knowledge of Aramaic, it seems likely that the whole sequence was understood by the Christian composers of the magical papyri as part of the name of God (*cf.* Kropp 1930: III: 128 (§218); Piwowarczyk 2021: 159–182, 241–261).

Examples of these names in sequence can be seen in, for example, *PCM* I 11 p. 2 ll. 9–10, p. 5 ll. 5–6, p. 16 ll. 14–15; *PCM* I 12 p. 10, ll. 17–18; *PCM* I 22 front ll. 11–12; *PCM* I 26 p. 13 ll. 25–26.

Invocation *see pp. 22–24 (genre of magical text), 32–33 (speech act)*
Isis see *Pharaonic Deities*
Katam *see note to PCM I 25 l. 6*

Kufic Ink

As recognised by Richter (2023), the Coptic ⲁⲗⲙⲓⲧⲉⲧ ⲛⲁⲗⲭⲱⲃⲓ (*almitet n-alkhōbi*, from Arabic المداد الكوفي *al-midād al-kūfī*), refers to a type of ink known as 'kufic', for which recipes are attested in Arabic from the eleventh century CE. It is a type of black carbon ink, produced by the pyrolysis (prolonged heating in the absence of oxygen) of organic matter—including, depending on the recipe, cloth, pomegranate rind, gallnuts, and date seeds—mixed with gum arabic and formed into solid cakes which would be moistened by the scribe when writing (Richter 2023; Levey 1962: 7, 16, 31, 34). The word ⲁⲗⲙⲓⲧⲉⲧ ("ink") also appears, but without the specification 'kufic', in P.Vindob. K 11088 (Hevesi 2015; KYP M374) B l. 5).

Linear Kufic *see note to PCM I 21 ll. 1–3*
Love is Abstinence (motif) *see note to PCM I 17 back l. 44–front l. 36*
Love is Fire (motif) *see note to PCM I 3 front col. 2 ll. 33–38*

Mastic

Greek/Coptic μαστίχη/ⲙⲁⲥⲧⲓⲭⲏ (*mastikhē*), or σχῖνος/ⲥⲭⲓⲛⲟⲥ (*skhinos*), Arabic مصطكاء (*maṣṭakāʾ*) refers to the resin of the lentisk or mastic tree (*Pistacia lentiscus* L.), common around the Mediterranean, and, at least in the eleventh century, imported to Egypt from the Greek islands. It seems to be very rare in the Graeco-Egyptian magical papyri; in the Betz *PGM* and volume 1 of *GEMF*, we find it only in *GEMF* 57/*PGM* IV (KYP M3) ll. 2582, 2648 (as σχῖνος), in descriptions of hypothetical offerings in spoken formula, but not in ritual instructions. In the Coptic corpus, however, it is very common (see the index of Greek words, *s.v.* μαστίχη). As with many of the items used as offerings, it is also attested in Greek, Coptic, Jewish, and Arabic medicine.

Sources and further reading: Till 1951: 75; Lev/Amar 2008: 203–205.

Menstrual Blood *see note to PCM I 22 l. 59*
Michael see *Angelic Beings*

Musk (Incense)

In Coptic the word for "musk" or "musk incense" is usually that derived from the Greek μοσχάτον (*moskhaton*); as noted by Fournet (2008), the translation of "muscat wine", originally proposed by Crum, is incorrect. In other texts, we find (ⲁⲗ)ⲙⲓⲥⲕ from the Arabic المسك (*al-misk*). More rarely we find ⲙⲁⲥⲭⲉ (*maskhe*), which may be derived from the Greek μόσχος (*moskhos*), or else represent a miswriting of ⲙⲁⲥϯⲭⲉ (*mastikhe*), that is, *mastic. Musk is a pungent substance produced in the scent glands of male musk deer (*Moschus moschiferus*), found in the Himalayas and Tibet, during the mating season. After extraction it is black in colour and may be sold as a liquid or a solid. The earliest mentions of musk in the Mediterranean region are found in the fourth century, but it did not become widely available until new trade routes to India were set up following the Arab conquests, and so is absent from magical texts from Egypt before the seventh century. Technically *moskhaton* probably refers to a compound perfume whose primary ingredient is musk, leading us here to translate it as "musk incense". While commonly used as a component of perfumes, musk was also used in medicine, and in the Coptic magical papyri we find it, usually used in burnt offerings, in *PCM* I 7 back l. 9; *PCM* I 22 ll. 13–14; *PCM* I 25 p. 16 l. 14, p. 17 ll. 17–18; *PCM* I 26 p. 15 l. 33, p. 16 l. 32; *PCM* I 28 p. 12 l. 19; *PCM* I 37 back l. 29; *BKU* I 26 (KYP M525) l. 8; BM EA 10391 (Zellmann-Rohrer 2022a: no. 1; KYP M302) front l. 57; *P.Köln Kopt.* 3 back l. 5; P. Stras. K 19 (Fournet 2008; KYP M188) l. 2.

Sources and further reading: Till 1951: 76; Fournet 2008; Lev/Amar 2008: 215–217; Amar/Lev 2013: 23–24; King 2017; Dosoo 2018: 17–18.

Myrrh

Coptic ϣⲁⲗ (*šal*) refers to the resin of the tree *Commiphora myrrha* (T. Nees);

ⲥⲧⲁⲕⲧⲏ (from Greek στακτή, both *staktē*) refers to the liquid form, considered to be of a higher quality. The names ⲥⲙⲏⲣⲛⲏⲥ (*smērnēs*, from Greek σμύρνα *smurna*) and ⲙⲱⲣ (from Arabic مُرّ *murr*) are more common in Coptic medical texts (Till 1951: 64). Like frankincense, the plant is native to the Horn of Africa and southern Arabia, and was imported to Egypt and the Mediterranean from pre-Christian times. Dioscorides (*Materia medica* 1.60, 64) describes myrrh as "bitter" (πικρά), "fragrant" (εὐώδης, in particular *staktē*), "sharp" (δριμεῖα), and "warming" (θερμαντική). The name in most languages derives from the Semitic root *m-r-r*, meaning "bitter", a quality noted in some Greek magical papyri (Klein 1987: 380; *cf.* LiDonnici 2001: 77). Myrrh in the Jewish Scriptures and New Testament is generally used for anointing (*e.g.*, Exodus 30.23; Luke 7.46), and, along with *frankincense and gold, was one of the gifts of the *magoi* to the infant Jesus in Matthew 2.11. Like frankincense, myrrh is regularly used in the Graeco-Egyptian magical papyri, with the soot produced by burning it often being used to make ink (LiDonnici 2001: 66–77). As with many other fragrant objects, its use is also attested in Greek, Coptic, Jewish, and Arabic medicine (Till 1951: 78; Lev/Amar 2008: 221–223); *cf.* Asensi Amorós 2003: 4–7. For instances in this volume, see the index under ϣⲁⲗ.

Names see *Horkōmotoi*
Nails see *Sator Square*
Narrative Charm see pp. 24–25
NN (*nomen nescio*) see pp. 33–34
Osiris see *Pharaonic Deities*
Petbe see *Pharaonic Deities*

Pharaonic Deities
Between the third and fifth centuries, most traditional Egyptian temple cults ceased to operate (see p. 2), but certain Pharaonic Egyptian deities are continuously mentioned in Coptic magical texts up to the eighth or ninth century (*cf.* Dosoo/Blumell 2018; Bélanger Sarrazin forthcoming a). Most commonly, the texts contain narrative charms in which the main protagonists are **Isis** (ⲏⲥⲉ) and her son **Horus** (ϩⲱⲣ). Isis and Horus are both deities with wide ranging associations—Isis is associated with motherhood, queenship, and magic (Griffiths 2001), among other phenomena, and Horus with kingship, the sky, and the sun (Meltzer 2001). In these Coptic texts, however, their most important characteristic is their nature as archetypal mother and son. In Pharaonic narrative charms, Horus is often injured or sick, and Isis must heal him. The Coptic-language charms continue this pattern, with Horus often being afflicted by the burning 'sickness' of love.

Rarer in the Coptic magical papyri are **Osiris** (ⲟⲩⲥⲓⲣⲓ)—the king of the dead, husband of Isis and father of Horus—and **Nephthys** (ⲛⲉⲃⲑⲱ)—the sister of Isis and Osiris (Kitchen 2001). In *PCM* I 9, Nephthys is referred to as ⲥⲃ̄ⲑⲱ *Sbthō*

("Sephthys") a contraction of the name Isis-Nephthys (ⲥⲉⲛⲉⲃⲉⲱ, Ἡσενεφθυς). This combined form of the name represents a case in which the two goddesses are assimilated to one another as a result of Nephthys' primary role as Isis' companion (Quaegebeur 1991).

In *PCM* I 4 (p. 4 ll. 12, p. 5 ll. 2, 5) we find three other deities mentioned: Apis (ϩⲁⲡⲉ *hape*), Petbe (ⲡⲉⲧⲃⲉ), and Seth (ⲥⲏⲑ). **Apis** was the sacred bull who lived in the temple of Ptah at Memphis from the Old Kingdom to the Roman period (Vercoutter 1975; Dodson 2005). **Petbe**, "the avenger" was a deity (or sometimes, plural deities) worshipped in the Ptolemaic and Roman period as a god of justice, often depicted as a griffin (and more vaguely, as a hybrid monster) (Quaegebeur 1983; Brashear 1991: 24–34; Aufrère 2005). **Seth** is the brother and killer of Osiris, a god of storms and the desert understood as powerful and lawless, associated in the Greek tradition with the giant Typhon, and often called upon in the Graeco-Egyptian magical corpus (te Velde 1967; Fabre 2001; Cruz–Uribe 2009). Note that within Judaism and Christianity, 'Seth' is also the name of an unrelated figure, the third son of Adam and Eve (Genesis 4.25).

Phylacteries see *Horkōmotoi*
NB: Outside the context of *horkōmotoi*, the word "phylactery" refers simply to an amulet.

Pig's senna *see note to PCM I 26 p. 16 l. 17*

Platter
In this volume we use "platter" to translate the Coptic ⲁⲗⲟⲉⲙⲉ (*alceme*) and variants, from the Arabic الجام *al-ǧām*, following Richter 2016a: 155, who suggests the translation "cup". While this word can refer to a cup, it seems more often to refer to a tray or platter; see Lane 1863: 490b *s.v.* جوم; Nasrallah 2017: 581. The word is masculine in Arabic, but apparently treated as feminine in Coptic; this may be because of its plural form, which resembles that of a feminine noun (جامات *ǧāmāt*; we thank Marijn van Putten for this suggestion).

Pot
The Coptic word ϭⲁⲗⲁϩⲧ (*calaht*, Demotic *glḫt*) refers to a pot or cauldron, usually made out of terracotta and with one or more handles (referred to as "ears" in Coptic), although examples made of bronze and glass, and without handles, are also recorded. The word is used, in both magical and literary contexts to translate the Greek χύτρα (*khutra*; Crum CD 813b–814a; *cf.* Łajtar/van der Vliet 2017: no. 9 l. 39), a word with the same meaning. The *calaht/khutra* was used for cooking both meat and vegetables, being placed directly on the fire so that its bottom became blackened (Richter 2020: 174–175; Bonati 2016: 197–229), but it could also be used for storage and transporting goods, such as bread and pickled fish

(O. Sarga 188.5–6). The Coptic word was borrowed from a Semitic language around the time of the 19th Dynasty (1295–1069 BCE), and is cognate with the Hebrew *qallaḥat* (קלחת). This Semitic word was itself a loanword from the older Egyptian word *ḳrḥ.t* ("pot"), which survives in Coptic only as ⲕⲁⲗⲁϩⲏ (*kalahē*), with the sense of "womb" (Sauneron 1961; CED: 329; DELC: 339–340; Hoch 2014: 331–332; Richter 2020: 174–175; Vitmann 2021: 286). In magical texts, the *calaht* serves two purposes: first, its blackening on a fire may serve as a metaphor for someone becoming hated (*PCM* I 22 ll. 35–36: *cf.* Bernardin 1937: 126.33; Weingarten 2013: 345); secondly, and more commonly, it may serve as a container for liquid to be activated in rituals, often with the addition of other ingredients, and the practitioner speaking a formula over it. For attestations, see ϭⲁⲗⲁϩⲧ in the glossary, and *cf.* BL Ms Or. 6795 l. 48 (Kropp 1931: I no. f; KYP 307); BL Ms Or. 6796 (1 verso) ll. 13, 14 (Kropp I 1931: no. H'; KYP M118); BL Ms Or 6796 (2–3) l. 105 (Kropp 1931: I no. H; KYP M118); BL Ms Or. 6796 (4) + Ms Or. 6796 ll. 49, 61 (Kropp 1931: I no. J; KYP M308); *P.Macq.* I 1 l. 20 (KYP M167); P. Stras. K 204 + 205 + 282 §2.5 l. 3 (Hevesi 2018; KYP M92); BM EA 10414a l. 19 (Zellmann-Roher 2022a: no. 3).

Powers see *Angelic Beings* & *Horkōmotoi*
Presbyters see *Twenty-Four Presbyters*
Principalities see *Angelic Beings*
Raphael see *Angelic Beings*
Releasing see *Binding and Releasing*
Request see pp. 32–34, and note to PCM I 12 p. 9 l. 7
River of Fire see note to PCM I 12 p. 27 l. 20–p. 29 l. 3
Sabaoth see *Iao Sabaoth Adonai Eloei Elemas*
Sanataēl i.e., Satanael; see note to PCM I 26 p. 4 l. 3
Satanael see note to PCM I 26 p. 4 l. 3

Sanctus
The term 'Sanctus' or 'Trishagion' refers to the modified version of a phrase taken from Isaiah 6:3 which describes how the seraphim, flying around the throne of God, hymn him by singing "Holy, holy, holy, Lord Sabaoth, heaven and earth are full of your glory" (ἅγιος, ἅγιος, ἅγιος, κύριος Σαβαώθ, πλήρης ὁ οὐρανὸς καὶ ἡ γῆ τῆς ἁγίας δόξης σου). In many Christian traditions, including the Orthodox churches, this phrase is part of the anaphora, the Eucharistic prayer, spoken both by the celebrant and the congregation. In Egypt, this passage is usually in Greek, although the repetition by the priest may spoken in Coptic (Mihálykó 2019: 374; de Bruyn 2017: 193). The speaking of this praise in the liturgy was seen as bringing together the faithful and the angelic hosts in the act of worship (de Bruyn 2017: 191). Witnesses of the Sanctus as part of the anaphora from Egypt survive from as early as the fourth century, in the Euchologion of Serapion of Thmuis (Johnson

1995: 46–47) and a book of liturgical prayers now kept in Monserrat (P.Monts. Roca fol. 154b–155a in Roca-Puig 1996); de Bryun 2017: 6.1.2.). The phrase is commonly borrowed in the Coptic magical corpus (*cf.* Kropp 1930: III 190–242), in which we find it in various genres of texts—most commonly in invocations for healing and protection (*PCM* I 11 p. 18 l. 27 – p. 19 l. 3; *PCM* I 12 p. 4, ll. 17–21; *PCM* I 25 p. 6 ll. 7–9, p. 15 ll. 9–10; *PCM* I 26, p. 9 ll. 4–6; British Library MS Or 6796 2, 3 (verso)=KYP M118, ll. 38–40), but also in a curse (Bodleian MS. Copt. c (P) 4; Crum 1896 (KYP M412) front ll. 13–14), and in a spell for a good singing voice (*BKU* I 8 (KYP M81) front ll. 6–7). For the Sanctus in Greek amulets, see de Bruyn 2006: 18–19.

Sator Square

The Sator square is a sequence of names which, when written in a square, form an acrostic which can be read in any direction. Likely Latin in origin, their original form is *sator arepo tenet opera rotas*, while the standard Greek form is σατωρ αρεπω τενετ ωπερα ρωτας. Most of the individual words have a meaning in Latin: *sator* "sower", *tenet* "he holds", *opera* "work", *rotas* "wheels". The letters can be rearranged to read *pater noster* ("our Father") (*cf.* Matthew 6.9), leading some to suggest a Christian origin for the square, but the earliest clear attestation is found in an inscription from Pompeii predating the eruption of 79 CE, and thus the sequence may also predate the Christian Lord's Prayer, which begins with the words "our Father".

The Sator square is attested several times in the Coptic magical corpus, *e.g.* P.Vindob K 2435 (Stegemann 1934: no. 48; KYP M276); P.Vindob K 2436 (Stegemann 1934: no. 49; KYP M277); P.Berol. 8096 (Beltz 1984: no. III 17; KYP M210); P.Berol. 982 (Beltz 1985: no. IV 1031; KYP M226); *BKU* III 387 (KYP M336) ll. 24–28 (in which they are written as *kharaktēres*).

The sequence also occurs in Coptic magical texts as individual names (*e.g.* P.Vindob. K 8638 (Stegemann 1934: no. 28; KYP M362)), sometimes as part of longer lists of *voces magicae* and names (*e.g.*, *PCM* I 25 p. 16 ll. 23–26), while at other times we find the word *Sator* standing alone (*e.g.*, *P.Ryl.Copt.* 105 (KYP M325) l. 1).

In Coptic, the sequence is often written in such a way that it would no longer form a palindrome even if arranged in a square, with, for example, *opera* written as ⲱⲧⲉⲣⲁ (a visual confusion of ⲡ and ⲧ), or *rotas* written as ⲣⲱⲇⲟⲥ (interchange of unvoiced ⲧ with voiced ⲇ and of unstressed vowels).

By the eighth century, we have evidence of a tradition common to Nubia and Egypt according to which the Sator names were understood as those of the five nails which pierced Jesus on the cross (*e.g.*, *PCM* I 25 p. 10 ll. 19–20; *PCM* I 29 front ll. 15–16; Griffith 1927: no. 25 (KYP M91); EES 39 5B.125/A (Alcock 1982; KYP M280) ll. 3–19). These "five nails" may have been understood as his five wounds—the four nails (one in each hand and foot) and the spear with which he was pierced in the side (John 19.34; *cf.* Worrell 1909: 169 n. 8; Schiller 1971–1972: II 91), although in *PCM* I 13 ll. 20–22 the five nails and the spear are mentioned separately. This association of the Sator-names with the nails of Christ is also well-attested in Ethiopian Christianity. As recognised by Basset (1894: 517) the surprising forms that they take in Ethiopian texts—such as *Sador Alador Danat Adera Rodas* (ሳዶር ፡ ኣላዶር ፡ ዳናት ፡ ኣደራ ፡ ሮዳስ ፡ from Griaule 1930: 27)—is partially explicable by the changes already found in Coptic (*cf.* Worrell 1915: 88–89 n. 7), while a *Copto-Arabic intermediary would explain many of the rest.

Sources and further reading: Grosser 1926; Carcopino 1948; Hofmann 1977; Marcovich 1983; Sheldon 2003; Hofmann 2006.

Sephthys see *Pharaonic deities*
Seraphim see *Angelic Beings*
Seth see *Pharaonic Deities*

Storax

Storax (Coptic ⲥⲧⲏⲣⲝ *stērx* from Greek στύραξ *sturax*) is the term used for the resin of the trees *Styrax officinalis* (L.) and *Liquidambar orientalis* (Mill.), the latter found in a range from southern Europe to the Levant, the latter in Rhodes and southwest Asia Minor. The first of these produces solid styrax, more expensive and rarer, while the second produces a liquid. It is often described by Greek authors as "heavy" (βαρύ) in scent. Storax is common in the Graeco-Egyptian magical papyri, *e.g. GEMF* 31/*PGM* I.285; *GEMF* 16/*PDM* xiv.330 (?), 417, 913; *GEMF* 55/*PGM* III.23; *GEMF* 57/*PGM* IV.1213, 1832, 2460, 2462, 2872; *GEMF* 60/ *PGM* XIII.17, 353; *GEMF* 74/*PGM* VII.434. In the Coptic magical papyri, it is found in *PCM* I 22 l. 12; *PCM* I 26 p. 16 ll. 8, 25; *PCM* I 32 l. 26; *PCM* I 34 p. 4 l. 17 (?); BL Ms Or. 6796 (1–3) (Kropp 1931: I no. H; KYP M118) back l. 103; BM EA 10391 (Zellmann-Rohrer 2022a: no. 1) front l. 11.

Sources and further reading: Till 1951: 96; Ghica 2006; Amigues 2007; Bellini 2019: 17–18. Piperakis 2022: 266–267.

Sukk see note to *PCM I 24 l. 18*
Sun-Facing Water see note to *PCM I 25 p. 17 ll. 25–27*
Suriel see *Angelic Beings*

Tabernacle and Veils

In the Hebrew Bible, the term "tabernacle" (Greek/Coptic σκηνή/ⲥⲕⲏⲛⲏ *skēnē* translating Hebrew משכן *miškān*) refers to a large tent which served as the sanctuary of the Jewish god, within which was kept the Ark of the Covenant (Exodus 25–30). Within the tabernacle (as in the later Temple of Solomon and Second Temple), the innermost part, the Holy of Holies, was separated from the rest of the temple, and by extension the outer world, by a curtain or veil (Greek/Coptic καταπέτασμα/ⲕⲁⲧⲁⲡⲉⲧⲁⲥⲙⲁ *katapetasma* translating Hebrew פרכת *pōreket*). In the Coptic magical papyri, the term is used in a sense derived from later Judaism and Christianity in which the tabernacle on earth has a counterpart in the heavenly tabernacle (*cf.*, Revelation 15.5), which designates the highest heaven in which God resides. Since the heavenly dwelling place of God was the equivalent of the Holy of Holies, it was likewise understood as being separated from the world by veils, often seven in number, likely inspired by the seven planetary spheres understood to separate earth from the highest heaven in Late Antique cosmological schemes. In this volume, the heavenly tabernacle and its veils are mentioned in *PCM* I 12 p. 1 ll. 1–2, p. 21 ll. 5–6; *PCM* I 15 p. 7 l. 21 (?); *PCM* I 17 front l. 4; *PCM* I 18 l. 4; *PCM* I 28 p. 3 ll. 12–14, p. 7 l. 16. For the rending of the veil of the temple, see the notes fo *PCM* I 28 p. 8 18–20.

Sources and further reading: Charlesworth 1983: 249, 296 n. 45a; Westerhoff 1999; Lajtar/van der Vliet 2017: 166–167; Suciu 2017a: 49–50; 249–251.

Tartaruchus see *Hell*
Tartarus see *Hell*
Temeluchus see *Hell*

Three Evil Things
The term "three evil things" (ⲡϣⲟⲙⲛ̄ⲧ ⲉⲧϩⲟⲟⲩ *p-šomnt et-hoou*) appears in several ritual prescriptions as part of burnt offerings in tenth and eleventh century texts (*PCM* I 27, front l. 23; *PCM* I 30 front l. 5; *PCM* I 31 front l. 38, back 17–18). It is probably to be associated with the "three of destruction" (ⲅ̄ ⲡⲧⲁⲕⲟ), found in a text of a similar date (*PCM* I 37 back l. 20). These are all curses of separation or destruction. The burnt offerings found in other curses and separation spells are not consistent enough to suggest what these three items were—common incenses (such as *mastic or myrrh) or other objects (such as menstrual blood or carbon). "Evil" in this context should probably be understood primarily in the sense of "causing harm" rather than as metaphysical evil (*cf.* Dosoo 2023a: 174 n. 254; Young 1970: 195 for the case of Ethiopia), although the two can easily blur together; in *PCM* I 30, for example, "doing evil" is associated with the demons and their ruler, Beelzebub.

Thrones see *Angelic Beings*
Tobi Water see *note to PCM I 17 back l. 20.*

Twenty-Four Presbyters
The Twenty-Four Presbyters (Greek/Coptic πρεσβύτερος/ⲡⲣⲉⲥⲃⲩⲧⲉⲣⲟⲥ *presbuteros*) first appear in the vision of heaven in Revelation 4–5. They are described as sitting on twenty-four thrones surrounding that of God, dressed in white and wearing golden crowns, holding harps and bowls of incense. The term

presbuteros in Greek originally meant "elder", and is often translated as such in English, but in the context of the Christian church it came to refer to the clerical rank whose primary task was the performance of the divine liturgy, in English, the "priest" (a word ultimately derived from *presbuteros*). In the Christian Egyptian tradition, they are thus understood as the angelic priests whose role it is to transmit the prayers of the faithful to God, and carry out the liturgy in the church which exists in heaven. The number twenty-four led to a secondary association with the letters of the Greek alphabet, so that in some schemes the names of the Twenty-Four Presbyters each began with a different letter of the alphabet—Akhaēl, Banouēl, Ganaēl, and so on. In this volume, the Twenty-Four Presbyters are mentioned in *PCM* I 12 p. 41 ll. 16–17; *PCM* I 17 front l. 9; *PCM* I 25 p. 5 ll. 13–20; *PCM* I 26 p. 9 l. 16.

Sources and further reading: Müller 1959: 85–87; Łajtar/Vliet 2017: 181–190; Dosoo 2021d: 414; Mihálykó 2022; Richter forthcoming.

Veils see *Tabernacle*
Wellbeing see *Horkōmotoi*
Water from the Month of Tobi *see note to PCM I 17 back l. 20*
Wood of Abraham *see note to PCM I 25 p. 9 ll. 2–4*

Concordance of texts in this volume

Ancient Christian Magic
(ACM=Meyer/Smith 1994)

ACM no. 47	PCM I 9
ACM no. 48	PCM I 6
ACM no. 66	PCM I 3
ACM no. 71	PCM I 12
ACM no. 72	PCM I 7
ACM no. 73	PCM I 28
ACM no. 74	PCM I 17
ACM no. 77	PCM I 32
ACM no. 82	PCM I 8
ACM no. 83	PCM I 10
ACM no. 86	PCM I 23
ACM no. 105	PCM I 22
ACM no. 106	PCM I 18
ACM no. 110	PCM I 27
ACM no. 122	PCM I 17
ACM no. 134	PCM I 11
ACM no. 135	PCM I 26
ACM appendix 2	PCM I 17
ACM appendix 3	PCM I 17
ACM appendix 4	PCM I 18

Ausgewählte koptische Zaubertexte
(AKZ=Kropp 1930–1931)

AKZ I no. A	PCM I 6
AKZ I no. B	PCM I 7
AKZ I no. R	PCM I 12
AKZ II no. 1	PCM I 6
AKZ II no. 2	PCM I 7
AKZ II no. 4	PCM I 9
AZK II no. 18	PCM I 15
AKZ II no. 22	PCM I 11
AKZ II no. 23	PCM I 11
AKZ II no. 27	PCM I 11
AKZ II no. 45	PCM I 11
AKZ II no. 46	PCM I 11
AKZ II no. 47	PCM I 12
AKZ II no. 63 B	PCM I 11
AKZ II no. 64 A	PCM I 11

Kyprianos Manuscript Number (KYP M)

KYP M8	PCM I 14
KYP M21	PCM I 37
KYP M43	PCM I 30
KYP M72	PCM I 3
KYP M106	PCM I 34
KYP M109	PCM I 16
KYP M120	PCM I 6
KYP M121	PCM I 7
KYP M122	PCM I 9
KYP M126	PCM I 4
KYP M127	PCM I 20
KYP M129	PCM I 8
KYP M148	PCM I 28
KYP M166	PCM I 26
KYP M171	PCM I 11
KYP M176	PCM I 1
KYP M186	PCM I 25
KYP M213	PCM I 5
KYP M241	PCM I 2
KYP M283	PCM I 12
KYP M284	PCM I 17
KYP M285	PCM I 32
KYP M290	PCM I 10
KYP M291	PCM I 23
KYP M293	PCM I 22
KYP M294	PCM I 18
KYP M296	PCM I 27
KYP M311	PCM I 29
KYP M312	PCM I 24
KYP M313	PCM I 21
KYP M319	PCM I 33
KYP M322	PCM I 35
KYP M335	PCM I 15
KYP M366	PCM I 31
KYP M503	PCM I 36
KYP M574	PCM I 19
KYP M3723	PCM I 13

Collection Inventory Numbers

Ann Arbor, Michigan University Library
P.Mich.Inv. 1190   PCM I 3
P.Mich.Inv. 4932f   PCM I 8

Berlin, Staatliche Museen
P.Berol. 11918   PCM I 5
P.Berol. 5565   PCM I 9

Cologne, Papyrussammlung
P.Köln Inv. 1850   PCM I 36

Heidelberg, Ägyptologisches Institut
P.Heid.Äg.Slg.inv. Kopt. 1030
                          PCM I 31

Heidelberg, Institut für Papyrologie
P.Heid.Inv. Kopt. 408   PCM I 30
P.Heid.Inv. Kopt. 518   PCM I 32
P.Heid.Inv. Kopt. 580   PCM I 33
P.Heid.Inv. Kopt. 658   PCM I 35
P.Heid.Inv. Kopt. 678   PCM I 29
P.Heid.Inv. Kopt. 679   PCM I 27
P.Heid.Inv. Kopt. 680   PCM I 21
P.Heid.Inv. Kopt. 681   PCM I 22
P.Heid.Inv. Kopt. 682   PCM I 23
P.Heid.Inv. Kopt. 683   PCM I 24
P.Heid.Inv. Kopt. 684   PCM I 28
P.Heid.Inv. Kopt. 685   PCM I 25
P.Heid.Inv. Kopt. 686   PCM I 26

Leiden, National Museum of Antiquities
AMS 9 (P.Leiden I 385)   PCM I 11
F 1964/4.14   PCM I 37

London, British Museum
BM EA 29528   PCM I 5

Los Angeles, County Museum of Art
M.80.202.214   PCM I 14

Milan, Università Statale
P.Mil.Vogl.Copt. 16   PCM I 4

New Haven, Yale University, Beinecke Library
P.CtYBR inv. 1791   PCM I 17
P.CtYBR inv. 1800 qua   PCM I 18

New York, Pierpont Morgan Library
MS M.662B.22   PCM I 10
B1 363 D MS M.0662 Box 3 PCM I 10

Provo, Brigham Young University
Harold B. Lee Library
inv. 76, 77, 81   PCM I 16

San José, Rosicrucian Museum
RC-2643   PCM I 19

Strasbourg, Bibliothèque Nationale
Strasbourg K 550   PCM I 34

Turin, Biblioteca Nazionale
a.IV.27   PCM I 12, 13

Vienna, Nationalbibliothek
P.Vindob. K 5520 Pap   PCM I 2

Published Sigla

Cited after the *Checklist of Editions of Greek, Latin, Demotic, and Coptic Papyri, Ostraca, and Tablets*, founding editors John F. Oates and William H. Willis (continually updated) <https://papyri.info/docs/checklist>.

BKU I 22 9
O.Brit.Mus.Copt. 27   PCM I 15
P.Heid.Kopt. 4   PCM I 30
P.Bad. V 122   PCM I 28
P.Bad. V 13   PCM I 32
P.Bad. V 133   PCM I 33
P.Bad. V 135   PCM I 35
P.Bad. V 137   PCM I 23
P.Bad. V 138   PCM I 29
P.Bad. V 139   PCM I 22
P.Bad. V 140   PCM I 24
P.Bad. V 141   PCM I 21
P.Bad. V 142   PCM I 27
P.Kellis V 35   PCM I 1
P.Köln XV 641   PCM I 36
P.Stras.Copt. 9   PCM I 34
Pap.Heid. N.F. IX   PCM I 25
SB Kopt. V 2356   PCM I 10

Index locorum

References within editions are to the notes and/or apparatus relating to the relevant line(s).

Books of the Hebrew Bible and New Testament

Hebrew Bible

Genesis
1.7   p. 472
1.26   **10** 2–3
4.25   p. 483
5.24   **15** f.4–5
10.6   **9** f.1–2
17.15–18.15   **10** f.5
21.1–3   **10** f.5

Exodus   **1** f.6
8.15 (8.19)   **12** 15.4–5
13.16   **11** 7.10–12
13.19   **11** 28.3–6
13.21–22   **12** 31.23–24
25–30   p. 486
26.32   **12** 33.1
30.23   p. 482
31.11   **11** 7.10–12

Leviticus
2.16   p. 477

Numbers
16.30   **26** 3.13–15
17.3   **29** f.21–22
18.12   p. 476

Deuteronomy
4.35   **25** 5f.5–7

Joshua
10.12–13   **28** 2.4–5
24.15   **11** 11.19–20

Judges
2.13   **3** f.II.25–26

Samuel
2   **9** 4
25.8   **28** 11.12

1 Kings
18.36–38   **23** f.20–42
19. 1–18   **23** f.20–42

Tobit
3.8   **18** f.19–20
3.17   p. 473

Psalms
3   **17** b.20
4 (5)   **17** b.20
7 (8)   **17** b.20
8   **33** f.6
9 (10)   **17** b.20
15 (16)   **17** b.20
21 (22) 2   **28** 8.10–13; p. 480
21 (22) 16   **9** 4
27 (28)   **17** b.20
31 (32)   **17** b.20
35 (36)   **17** b.20
43 (44)   **33** f.6
44 (45) 2–3   **25** 16.16–19
60 (61)   **33** f.6
74 (75)   **17** b.20
88 (89)   **17** b.20
78 (79) 10   **25** 5f.7–9
90 (91)   pp. 23, 25; **11** 29.23–30.28
90 (91) 1–2   **11** 30.21–28
93 (94) 8   p. 110
95 (96)   **33** f.6
96 (97)   p. 109
106 (107) 14–16   **7** f.2–3
112 (113)   **17** b.20
113 (114)   **33** f.6
113.10 (115.2)   **12** 9.13–14; **25** 5f.7–9
115 (117)   **33** f.10
125 (126)   **33** f.10
129 (130)   **33** f.6

134 (135) 7 **1** f.4–5
134 (135) 16–17 **35** b.1–9

Job
26.12 **25** 6.20
40.19 **12** 15.17

Ecclesiasticus (Sirach)
22.16 **11** 19.15–16

Joel
3.2 **28** 9.7
3.12 **28** 9.7

Isaiah
7.14 **11** 10.6, 8, 11–12, 17, 23–24, 11. 2–3,
      18–19, 25–26,16.2–4
8.18 **11** 11.21–23
9.2 **11** 11.23–25
9.6–7 **11** 12.1–4
14.12 **11** 2.7–8
40.15 **17** b.44–f.36
40.22 **12** 11.14–15
45.23 **25** 2.15–17

Jeremiah
10.13 **1** f.4–5
27 (50).1–46 **1** f.6–7
51.16 **1** f.4–5
41.8 p. 414
41 (37).1–21 **1** f.6
44 (37).5 **1** f.6–7
45–46 (38–39) **6** 20

Lamentations
2.19 **1** f.1
4.1 **1** f. 1

Ezekiel
1 p. 473
16.25 **1** f.1
21.24 **1** f.1

Daniel
3 **25** 18.1–17
7.9 **12** 16.8–12
7.9–10 **12** 27.20–29.3
9.21 p. 473
10.13 p. 473
10.21 p. 473

12.1 p. 473
18.16 p. 473

New Testament

Matthew
1.1 **11** 29.25–26
1.23 **25** 11.6–7
1.22–23 **11** 16.2–4
2.11 p. 477
4.16 **11** 11.23–25
6.9 p. 485
8.26 **1** f.4–5
9.20 **2** f.1
9.29 **11** 24.13–14
11.5 **26** 12.29–13.3
18.6 **3** f.I1–34
27.28 **25** 16.12
27.46 **12** 10.17–18; **25** 15.13–14; **28** 8.10–13
27.51 **28** 8.18–20

Mark
1.1 **11** 30.1–7
1.2 **22** f. 20–21
4.29 **1** f.4–5
9.42 **3** f.I 1–34
18.22 **28** 13.5–6
15.34 **12** 10.17–18; **25** 15.13–14; **28** 8.10–13
15.38 **28** 8.18–20

Luke
1.1 **11** 30.10–13
1.19 p. 473
1.26 p. 467
7.22 **26** 12.29–13.3
7.46 p. 482
8.24 **1** f.4–5
8.43 **2** 1
11.20 **12** 15. 4–5
17.2 **3** f.I 1–34
23.45 **28** 8.18–20
23.46 **28** 8.10–13

John
1.1 **11** 30.16–20
19.34 p. 485
20.16 **11** 18. 22–24
20.29 **11** 24.12–13

Index Locorum

Acts
   24.4   **34** 2.16–17

Romans
   12.1   **28** 9.1
   15.13   **16** 3.17–18
   15.19   **16** 3.17–18

1 Corinthians
   1.18–24   p. 326
   2.5   **16** 3.17–18
   10.4–9   p. 324

2 Corinthians
   5.17–6.4   p. 283
   6.7   **16** 3.7–8

Ephesians
   4.5   **11** 12.12–26

Philippians
   3.6–14?   p. 325
   4.1–9   p. 288
   4.9   p. 325

2 Timothy
   2.3–13   p. 287
   2.13–15   p. 287
   4.1   **11** 8.11–13
   4.15   **28** 13.6

Titus
   2.11–12   p. 287
   2.12–3.7   p. 287

Hebrews
   1.13–2.8   p. 287
   2.8–11   p. 287
   2.11b–[17]   p. 287
   2.13   **11** 11.21–23
   2.17–18   p. 287
   4.14–5.3   p. 287
   5.3–6   p. 287
   6.9   p. 287
   6.9–20   p. 287
   9.2–7   p. 324
   9.7–10   p. 287
   11.32–40   p. 287
   12.1–6   p. 287

   13.6   p. 324

James
   1.17   **26** 2.19

1 Peter
   2.8   **11** 10.18–19

Jude
   9.1   p. 473

Revelation
   1.8   **11** 17.28–29
   1.14   **12** 16.8–12
   4–5   p. 487
   4.6–8   **25** 15 6–7; p. 473
   5.1   **26** 7.24
   5.6   **12** 19.12–13
   7.4   **26** 6.23–24
   7.14   **26** 6.23–24
   12.7–9   **28** 1.18
   12.7–12   p. 473
   15.5   p. 486
   16.1   **28** 4.14
   20.1–3   p. 472
   22.16   **11** 2.7–8

Manuscripts and Papyri

By Collection

Present Location Unknown/In situ
Nahman Amulet   **12** 31.3–6
Naqlun N. 45/95   p. 233
Naqlun N. 78/93   pp. 15, 24, 447
   ll. 22–26   **16** 2.15–16
P.Gardiner   **28** 11.1
Qasr Ibrim 80.3.11/2 (NI 113)   p. 24

Ann Arbor, University of Michigan Library
Mich.Ms. 136
   p. 43   **11** 26.1–2
   p. 2 l. 4   **3** f.2.12–14
   pp. 5–6   p. 24
   p. 5 l. 1–p. 6 l. 5   **8** f.3–4
   p. 5 l. 3   **25** 4.25
   p. 5 ll. 3–4   **4** 4.4–6
   p. 5 ll. 18–19   **16** 3.15–16
   p. 6 l. 5   **16** 3.7–8
   p. 13 ll. 5–6   **33** f.6; **36** f.II

Mich.Ms.Copt. 166   **11** 20.6–25.23
P.Mich.Copt. 18   p. 26
P.Mich.Inv. 593   p. 21
   p. 6 l. 5–7   **17** b.20
   p. 9 l. 3   **2** 1
   p. 10 ll. 4–8   **34** 1–2
P.Mich.Inv. 593   p. 21; **2** 1
   f. l. 3–4   **17** b.20
   b. l. 3   **2** 1
   b. ll. 12–14   **34** 1–2
P.Mich.Inv. 594   p. 21
P.Mich.Inv. 595   p. 21
P.Mich.Inv. 596   p. 21
P.Mich.Inv. 597   p. 21
P.Mich.Inv. 598   p. 21
P.Mich.Inv. 599   p. 21
P.Mich.inv. 4949 ro   **15** f.2
P.Mich.Inv. 6213   **11** 20.6–25.23

Athens, Historical and Ethnographic Society of Athens
Codex 115   **27** f.17

Athens, National Library of Greece
Codex 1265 fol. 15r   **31** f.38
Pap.Athen.Nat.-Bibl. 1826   **12** 37.18–20

Baarn, Private collection Moen
Moen Inv. no 34/607   **12** 31.3–6

Basel, Antikenmuseum
O.Bâle inv. Lg Ae BJF 31c
   ll. 5, 8   p. 477

Bawit, Courtyard 47
East wall, text IV   **11** 20.6–25.23

Berlin, Berliner Papyrussamlung
P.Berol. 982   p. 485
P.Berol 3027   **11** 5.176.7
P.Berol. 5731 + 5732   **11** 25.24–28.21
P.Berol. 8096   p. 485
P.Berol. 8503
   f. l. 57   **37** f.14
   f. ll. 61–b.l. 5   **35** b.1–9
P.Berol. 10587 ll. 3–7   **8** b.3
   I ll. 21–23   **18** 15
P.Berol. 11347
   f. l. 38   **26** 6.23–24
   b. ll. 8–9   **25** 4.25

P.Berol. 20911   **34** 3.7
cf. BKU in *"By Papyrological Siglum" below*

Berlin, Staatsbibliothek
Berlin Ms. or. fol. 1605 fol. 1v col. 1 ll. 10–15
   10 2–3

Cairo, Coptic Museum
Al-Suryan MS 383/ Al-Suryan MS 266 Lit
   11 20.6–25.23
Coptic Museum 4959 l. 7   **25** 17.25–27

Cairo, Egyptian Museum
Cairo JdE 42573
   p. 1, ll. 6–10   **34** 1–2
   p. 1, ll. 21–23   **30** f.10–14
   p. 2, ll. 1–5   **37** b.9
   p. 2, l. 7   **30** f.3–4
   p. 2, l. 10   **22** 32
   p. 4, l. 6   **37** f.35
   p. 4, ll. 1–2   **35** f.18,24
   p. 4, ll. 11–17   **26** 16.16; **35** f.18,24
   p. 4, l. 19   **23** 34
Cairo JdE 45060   pp. 15, 21
   l. 3   p. 71
   l. 25   **30** f.ll.3–4
   ll. 37–38   **30** f.ll.3–4
   ll. 38–40   **34** 1–2
   l. 59   **17** b.1–5
Cairo JdE 49547   p. 69
   ll. 29–32   **3** f.II.30–32
   ll. 23–24   **17** f.19

Cairo, IFAO
IFAO P.Edfou Jarre 13, 19   p. 229
IFAO Pap.Méd.Copt. l. 334   **25** 11.7,10

Cambridge, Taylor-Schechter Cairo Genizah Collection
T-S K1.6 l. 18   **25** 7.12–14
T-S K1.24 ll. 16–17   **25** 7.12–14
T-S K 1.73, p. 4 ll. 17–18   **31** b.7–8
T-S K1.152 l. 22   **25** 7.12–14
T-S K 1.168 ll. 108–112   **11** 4.3–20
cf. *MTKG, Naveh/Shaked in "By Papyrological Siglum" below*

Cambridge, University Library
Cambridge UL T-S 12.207   p. 11

Chicago, Oriental Institute Museum
Chicago OIM E13767   **23** 20–42; **29** f.20

Cologne, Papyrussammlung
P.KölnÄgypt. I 11, ll. 11–12   **34** 3.9–10
P.Köln Inv. 1470
   ll. 1–2   **13** 1–3
   ll. 6–7   **5** 7.12–14
P.Köln Kopt. 3 b. l. 5   p. 481

Copenhagen, Carlsberg Papyrus Collection
P.Carlsberg 52
   p. 2 ll. 2–3   **4** 3.1
   p. 3 l. 18   **25** 4.25

Durham (NC), Duke University
P. Duke inv. 460   p. 8

Egypt, Thebes, MMA 1152, Polish excavations 2003-2013
O.Gurna Górecki 108   **11** 20.6–25.23

Fribourg, Bibel + Orient Museum
Fribourg AeT 2006.5 f. II, ll. 18–21   **12** 31.3–6

Giessen, Universitätsbibliothek
P.Iand. Inv. 9   p. 289
   p. 1 ll. 6–7   **25** 4.3–4
   p. 7 ll. 5–6   **25** 7.12–14
   p. 8 l. 11   **25** 7.23–24

Heidelberg, University Library
P.Heid. Gr. II 239   p. 259
P.Heid. Gr. IV 318   p. 259
P.Heid.Inv. Kopt. 544b   p. 423
P.Heid.Inv. Kopt. 564a   **25** 18.1–17; pp. 419, 448
   l. 11   **2** 5
cf. P.Bad. in "By Papyrological Siglum" below

London, British Library
BL Ms. Or. 6794   **12** 31.11–13
   f. l. 8   **37** b.9
   f. ll. 56–58   **17** b.18–19
BL Ms. Or. 6795
   l. 36   **4** 2.7–13
   l. 48   p. 484
BL Ms. Or. 6796
   (1v)
      ll. 13, 14   p. 484
   (1–3)   p. 289
      l. 12   **25** 2.11–12
      ll. 19–20   **25** 2.19–20
      l. 105   **25** 7.23–24
   (1–3) b. l. 103   p. 486
   (2)   **17** b.20; p. 470
   (2–3) l. 105   p. 484
   (2), (3) verso
      ll. 38–40   p. 484
      ll. 51–52   **25** 7.12–14
      l. 112   **17** b.1–5
   (3) verso   **17** b.20
      ll. 104–105   **17** b.20
      l. 103   p. 479
      l. 105   p. 477
      l. 111   p. 477
   (4)
      l. 21   **11** 16.2–4
      ll. 41–42   **12** 31.3–6
      l. 49   p. 34; p. 484
      l. 61   p. 484
BL Ms. Or. 7026, fol. 82v   p. 449
BL Ms. Or. 7033, fol. 59v   p. 455

London, British Museum
BM EA 5892   p. 229
BM EA 10122   **25** 13. 1–16.15
   f. ll. 20–24   **7** f.19
   ll. 26–28   **25** 7.12–14
   ll. 32–34   **34** 1–2
BM EA 10376
   l. 1   **4** 3.1
   ll. 15–18   **32** 1.28–31
BM EA 10391   pp. 24, 49
   f. ll. 1–12   **25** 13.1–16.15
   f. l. 11   p. 486
   f. ll. 12–27   p. 24
   f. ll. 12–16   **7** n.
   f. l. 13   **4** 3.1
   f. ll. 14–15   **7** f.2–3
   f. ll. 23–24   **3** f.I 7–9
   f. l. 24   **3** f.I.15–16
   f. l. 35   p. 476
   f. l. 37   p. 476
   f. ll. 38–49   **34** 1–2
   f. ll. 41–42   **34** 1–2
   f. ll. 42–48   **34** 1.17–18
   f. ll. 50–58   **34** 1–2
   f. l. 57   p. 481

f. l. 60   p. 475
b. ll. 76–78   p. 49
b. ll. 79–80   p. 49
b. ll. 80–82   **18** 5
b. ll. 82–84   p. 49
b. ll. 94–95   p. 49
b. l. 95   **30** f.3–4
BM EA 10414a   p. 407
 f. l. 19   p. 484
 b. ll. 4–5   **17** b.1–5
 b. l. 19   **17** b.1–5
 b. l. 24–25   **25** 17.25–27
 b. l. 43–44   **25** 17.25–27
BM EA 10688   **12** 37.18–20
BM EA 10808   p. 2
BM EA 14241   p. 228
BM EA 19967   **11** 20.6–25.23
BM EA 71005   pp. 110, 111

Montserrat, Abadia
Inv. 604 + 1235   pp. 9, 371, 407
O.Monts.Roca inv. 1472   **35** f.18,24
P.Monts.Roca inv. 154b–155a   p.484
P.Monts.Roca.inv. 478   **25** 17.25–27
P.Monts.Roca inv. 524   p. 399

Naqlun, Storehouse of the Excavation
Naqlun N. 78/93   pp. 15, 24, 447; **16** 2 15–16

New Haven, Yale University, Beinecke Library
P.CtYBR inv. 846, l. 11   **37** f.14

New York, Columbia University
Columbia inv. 554 ll. 18–19   **25** 4.25

New York, Metropolitan Museum of Art
P.MMA 34.1.226   **2** 5

New York, Pierpont Morgan Library
Pierpont Morgan M573   p. 326
Pierpont Morgan M568 fol. 47r   **25** 2.15–17
Pierpont Morgan M636   p. 251

Oxford, Bodleian Library
Bodleian MS. Copt. c (P) 4
 f. ll. 13–14   p. 484
 f. l. 23–24   **24** 14–16
 b. l. 6   **18** 15

Oxford, Griffith Institute
Crum 23.2.2   **30** n. to image, 8 *et al.*

Oxford, Sackler Library
EES 39 5B.125
 ll. 3–19   p. 485
 l. 19   **11** 16.2–4

Paris, Bibliothèque Nationale de France
BnF Arabe 2676 fol. 5v   **21** 1–3
BnF Copte 13.3, fol. 39v   p. 422
BnF Copte 132.1, fol. 67v   p. 422
BnF Copte 129.14 fol. 95v   p. 451
BnF Copte 129.20 fol. 178   p. 15
 ll. 1–5   p. 44
BnF Copte 131.5 fol. 28v   p. 461
BnF Gr. 2316 fol. 435v l. 14   **11** 4.14–16
BnF Suppl.Grec. 1340, l. 9   **19** 1

Paris, Collège de France
Collège de France Ms. 1   **5** b.3
Collège de France Ms. 2   p. 289; **26** 2.2–15;
 26 6.23–24
 pp. 1–21   p. 327
 p. 23 l. 19   **25** 2.19–20
Collège de France Ms. 3   pp. 8, 18, 274, 323

Paris, Louvre
Louvre E 14251   **24** n. to image

Saqqara, Storehouse
Saqqara F.17.10 (SA.03/141)   p. 44

Strasbourg, Bibliothèque Nationale
P.Stras. K 19 l. 2   p. 481
P.Stras. K 135   **19** 2; **23** 20–42, **25** 7.12–14
P.Stras. K 204 + 205 + 282   pp. 472, 484; **11** 16.2–4; **17** b.1–5; **25** 7.12–14, 17.25–27
P.Stras.K. 332 (D)   p. 399

Turin, Biblioteca Nazionale
Mss. Peyron 158–159   p. 174

Vatican, Biblioteca Apostolica Vaticana
Vat.Copt. 58.4–5 fol. 35v   p. 363
Vat.Copt. 66.5, fol. 155r   p. 363
Vat.Copt.68, fol. 162r   p. 363
 162v   p. 363

Venice, St. Lazzaro Monastery
San Lazzaro degli Armeni Ms. 3042   **21** 1–3

Vienna, Nationalbibliothek
P.Vindob. K 78   **11** 20.6–25.23
P.Vindob. K 351   p. 422
P.Vindob. K 880 l.49   **11** 4.14–16
P.Vindob. K 2435   p. 485
P.Vindob. K 2436   p. 485
P.Vindob. K 3151a   **11** 20.6–25.23
P.Vindob. K 5024 ll.4–5   **25** 7.12–14
P. Vindob. K 8301
   ll.1–5   **18** 3
   l.6   **11** 16.2–4
P.Vindob. K 8302   **11** 20.6–25.23
P.Vindob. K 8303, l.10   **24** 18; p. 472
P.Vindob. K 8636   **11** 20.6–25.23
P.Vindob. K 8638   p. 485
P.Vindob. K 10335   **26** 12.19–24
P.Vindob. K 11088   p. 480
   B ll.4–7   **2** 1; **25** 11.7,10

Würzburg, Papyrussammlung
P.Würzburg inv. 42   **34** 3 n.
   l. 17   **24** 12

By Papyrological Siglum

Where possible cited after the *Checklist of Editions of Greek, Latin, Demotic, and Coptic Papyri, Ostraca, and Tablets*, founding editors John F. Oates and William H. Willis (continually updated) <https://papyri.info/docs/checklist>.

BKU
BKU I 1   pp. 24, 44
   f.II   **7** n.
   l. 19   **4** 3.1
   f.II & b.   **8** f.3–4
BKU I 2   **32** 1.28–31
BKU I 3   **7** ll.2–3
   l. ll.8–9   **7** f.35–36
   ll.21–24   **3** f.I 7–9
BKU I 6   p. 289
   l.l 22–25   **11** 18.11–14
BKU I 7   p. 24; **7** n.; **7** f.2–3
   f. ll. 10–11   **3** f.I.15–16
   f. ll. 20–21   **3** f.I 7–9
   f. ll. 21–24   **3** f.I 7–9
   f. ll. 29–30   **16** 2.15–16
   b. ll. 3–4   **16** 2.15–16
BKU I 8   **11** 29.1–22; **17** f.19
   f. ll. 6–7   p. 484
   f. ll. 1–39   p. 241
   f. l. 33   **17** b.20
   f. ll. 33, 39   **17** b.18–19
   f. l. 39   **17** b.18–19
BKU I 10 l. 6   **25** 7.12–14
BKU I 11   **3** f.I.1–34
BKU I 19 f.   **11** 29.1–22
BKU I 20   **11** 29.1–22
BKU I 23   p. 174
BKU I 24   **25** 13.1–16.15
BKU I 25 f.l. 13   **2** 1
BKU I 26   p. 263
   p. 1 l. 8   p. 481
   p. 4 l. 12   **36** f.II.2
BKU III 387   **25** 13.1–16.15
   ll. 24–28   p. 485
   ll. 36–39   **34** 4.23–25
BKU III 389 ll. 6–7   **24** 14–16

CPR
CPR II 1 ll. 29–40   pp. 433, 449
CPR II 226   p. 104
CPR II 233   p. 104
CPR IV 55   p. 254
CPR IV 66   p. 254
CPR IV 88   p. 254

Crum ST
Crum ST 399   **3** f.I.1–34

Defixionum Tabellae (Audollent 1904)
270 ll.21–24   **4** 4.4–6

GEMF (Faraone/Torallas Tovar 2022–)
GEMF 4 ll. 31–32   **8** f.3–4
GEMF 8. l. 47   **4** 4.4–6
GEMF 11 1, 2   p. 465
GEMF 12 ll. 20–22   **34** 2.8–9, 15–16
GEMF 14   p. 2
GEMF 15
   l. 254–257   p. 472
   l. 127 (78)   p. 39
   l. 415 (366)   **24** 23
GEMF 16   pp. 2, 14
   l. 42   **34** 2.8–9, 15–16
   ll. 106–107   **34** 2. 8–9, 15–16
   l. 115   **37** f.35

l. 169   p. 479
l. 330   p. 486
l. 336   p. 475
l. 417   p. 486
ll. 451–458   **4** 4. 4–6
ll. 497–498   **1** 1
l. 772   **7** 31
ll. 610–620   **8** 3–4
l. 913   p. 486
ll. 1029–1031   **7** 35–36
ll. 1073–1074   **29** b.
ll. 1197–1198   **2** 1
GEMF 17 ll. 55–56   **29** b.
GEMF 18 III
  ll. 64–67   **29** b.
  ll. 174–177   **3** f.I.15–16
  ll. 159–196   **8** f.2–3
  l. 195   p. 471
GEMF 30 l. 77 (30)   p. 39
GEMF 31
  ll. 71–72   **23** 46
  l. 271–272   **28** 13.6
  l. 285   p. 486
  l. 302   p. 472
GEMF 34
  ll. 75–105 I   **3** f.I.1–34
  I 1 l. 1   **25** 16.10
GEMF 42 I ll. 10–11   **3** f.I.15–16
GEMF 55   p. 14
  l. 23   p. 486
  ll. 410–423   p. 2
  ll. 633–731   p. 2
GEMF 57   p. 14
  ll. 1–21   p. 2
  ll. 11–25   **34** 1–2
  ll. 81–153   p. 2
  ll. 88–93   **34** 1–2
  l. 92   p. 479
  l. 109   **4** 3.1
  l. 1213   p. 486
  l. 1832   p. 486
  ll. 1227–1264   p. 3
  ll. 1505–1508   **3** f.I.15–16
  l. 2460   p. 486
  l. 2462   p. 486
  ll. 2508–2510   **28** 13.6
  l. 2582   p. 481
  l. 2648   p. 481
  l. 2680   p. 475
  l. 2872   p. 486

l. 3007   **37** f.35
GEMF 60
  l. 17   p. 486
  l. 18   p. 475
  l. 289   p. 39
  l. 353   pp. 469, 486
GEMF 70 l. 266   **4** 4.4–6
GEMF 73 b.   **24** n.
GEMF 74
  l. 231–232   **8** 13.6
  l. 434   p. 486
  l. 570–572   **34** 2.8–9, 15–16
  l. 643–651   **8** f.2–3
GEMF 82   pp. 68, 69
GEMF 84   p. 69
  f. l. 12   **27** f.17
  f. ll. 10–33   **4** 3.4–6
GEMF 156, ll. 643–65   **18** f.2–3

Lantschoot (1929)
fasc. I 116–117   p. 461
fasc. I 131   p. 461
fasc. II 52 n. 3   p. 461

MTKG (Schäfer/Shaked 1994–1999)
MTKG I Or. 1080.15.81 l. 94   **25** 7.12–14
MTKG I T.-S. NS 322.10 1a   **10** 5n.
  ll. 11–33
MTKG I T-S NS 322.10 p. 2b l. 13   **5** b.3
MTKG II 42
  ll. 12   **25** 7.12–14
  ll. 18   **25** 7.12–14
  ll. 22   **25** 7.12–14
  ll. 32   **25** 7.12–14
  ll. 39   **25** 7.12–14
MTKG III 56 p. 1a l. 10   **25** 7.12–14
MTKG III 71 p. 1a l. 5   **25** 7.12–14
MTKG III 73 p. 1b ll. 11–12   **25** 7.12–14

Naveh/Shaked 1993
Geniza 9 p. 1 l. 15   **25** 17 ll.25–27
Geniza 12 ll. 16–17   **25** 7.12–14
Geniza 15 p. 2 ll. 9–10   **25** 7.12–14
Geniza 18 p. 3 ll. 7–8   **25** 7.12–14
Geniza 22 p. 1 ll. 1–6   **3** f.II33–38
Geniza 28   **25** 7.12–14

Naveh/Shaked 1998
Amulet 10   **3** f.II 33–38

O.Bachit.
O.Bachit. 929   p. 228

O.Bawit IFAO
O.BawitIFAO 31   p. 104
O.BawitIFAO 33   p. 104
O.BawitIFAO 34   p. 104
O.BawitIFAO 35   p. 104
O.BawitIFAO 36   p. 104
O.BawitIFAO 37   p. 104
O.BawitIFAO 40   p. 104
O.BawitIFAO 42   p. 104

O.Bélanger Sarrazin (Bélanger Sarrazin 2017b)
O.Bélanger Sarrazin   **35** f.18,24

O.Crum
O.Crum 22   **11** 20.6–25.23

O.CrumST
O.Crum ST 36   **11** 20.6–25.23

O.Frangé
O.Frange 53   p. 477
O.Frange 247–262   p. 233
O.Frange 265   p. 233
O.Frange 266   p. 233
O.Frange 294–318   p. 233
O.Frange 317   p. 233
O.Frange 318   p. 233

O.Saint-Marc
O.Saint-Marc 398   **11** 20.6–25.23

O.Sarga/P. Sarga
O.Sarga 188.5–6   p. 483

P.Bad.
P.Bad. II 28   p. 259
P.Bad. V 123
    f. l. 1   **22** 46; p. 478
    f. l. 26   **22** 46
    f. l. 34   **2** 1
    f. l. 41   **11** 16.2–4
    f. l. 49   **2** 1
    f. l. 50   **22** 46
    f. ll. 52–84   **11** 8.19
    f. l. 65   **22** 32
    f. ll. 72–74   **25** 7.12–14
    f. l. 76   **3** f.2 l].12–13, 25–26
    f. l. 82   **22** 46
    f. l. 89   **22** 46
    f. l. 101   **22** 46
    b. 17   p. 474
P.Bad. VI 169   p. 259

P.Brux.Bawit
P.Brux.Bawit 5   p. 104
P.Brux.Bawit 9   p. 104
P.Brux.Bawit 22   p. 104
P.Brux.Bawit 28   p. 104
P.Brux.Bawit 30   p. 104

P.CLT
P.CLT 1   p. 239

PDM (Betz 1986)
PDM xiv   pp. 2, 14
    l. 42   **34** 2.8–9, 15–16
    l. 106–107   **34** 2. 8–9, 15–16
    l. 115   **37** f.35
    l. 169   p. 479
    l. 330   p. 486
    l. 336   p. 475
    l. 417   p. 479
    ll. 451–458   **4** 4.4–6
    l. 772   **7** 31
    ll. 610–620   **8** 3–4
    l. 913   p. 486
    ll. 1029–1031   **7** 35–36
    ll.1073–1074   **29** b.
    ll. 1197–1198   **2** 1
PDM lxi ll. 64–67   **29** b.
PDM Suppl. ll. 55–56   **29** b.

P.Eleph.Wagner
O.Eleph.Wagner 322   **11** 29.1–22

P.Fay.Copt.
P.Fay.Copt. 15   p. 262

PGM (Preisendanz/Henrichs 1973–1974)
PGM I
    ll. 71–72   **23** 46
    l. 271–272   **28** 13.6
    l. 302   p. 471
PGM II l. 77 (30)   p. 39
PGM III   p. 14
    l. 23   p. 486

l. 150   p. 471
ll. 410–423   p. 2
ll. 633–731   p. 2
PGM IV   p. 14
  ll. 1–21   p. 2
  ll. 11–25   **34** 1–2
  ll. 81–153   p. 2
  ll. 88–93   **34** 1–2
  l. 92   p. 479
  l. 109   **4** 3.1
  l. 1213   p. 486
  ll. 1227–1264   p. 3
  ll. 1505–1508   **3** f.I.15–16
  l. 1832   p. 486
  l. 2460   p. 486
  l. 2462   p. 486
  ll. 2508–2510   **28** 13.6
  l. 2582   p. 481
  l. 2680   p. 475
  l. 2648   p. 481
  l. 2872   p. 486
  l. 3007   **37** f.35
PGM V l. 266   **4** 4.4–6
PGM VI b. l. 3   p. 39
PGM VII
  l. 231–232   **28** 13.6
  l. 570–572   **34** 2.8–9, 15–16
  l. 643–651   **8** f.2–3
PGM IX b.   **24** n. to image
PGM XII
  l. 127 (78)   p. 39
  l. 205–206   p. 471
  l. 415 (366)   **24** 23
PGM XIII
  l. 17   p. 479
  l. 18   p. 475
  l. 289   p. 39
  l. 353   pp. 475, 486
PGM LVII l. 47   **4** 4.4–6
PGM LXI III ll. 174–177   **3** f.I.15–16
PGM LXI
  l. 33   p. 465
  ll. 159–196   **8** f.2–3
  III. ll. 174–177   **3** f.I.15–16
PGM LXII
  ll. 75–105 I   **3** f.I.1–34
  I l l. 1   **25** 16.10
PGM LXIX.1, 2   p. 471
PGM LXXXVII l. 20–22   **34** 2.8–9, 15–16
PGM LXXXIX, l. 5   p. 39

PGM CXXII ll. 31–32   **8** f.3–4
PGM CXXIII   pp. 68, 69
PGM CXXIIIb–f   p. 68
PGM CXXIIIa   p. 69
PGM CXXIV
  f. ll. 10–33   **4** 4.4–6
  f. l.12   **27** f.17
PGM CXXVa–f   p. 68, 69
PGM CXXVI   p. 49

P.HengstenbergCopt.
P.HengstenbergCopt. 5 ll. 13–14 5 ll. 13–14 **24** 14–16

P. Herm.Copt.
P.Herm.Copt. 55 + 71, p. 5 ll. 2–5   **7** f.35–36
P.Herm.Copt. 59   p. 24
P.Herm.Copt. 67   pp. 24, 44
P.Herm.Copt. 161   **22** 46
*P.Herm.Copt.*162   **22** 46

P.Kell.
P.Kell. I *Gr.* 44   p. 49
P.Kell. I *Gr.* 85–88   p. 48
P.Kell. II *Copt.* 53   p. 49
P.Kell. V *Copt.* 12 ll. 17–18   **1** 23–24
P.Kell. V *Copt.* 15   p. 49
P.Kell. V *Copt.* 17   p. 49
P.Kell. V *Copt.* 22   p. 49
P.Kell. V *Copt.* 19 ll. 68–69   **1** 23–24
P.Kell. V *Copt.* 20   p. 48
P.Kell. V *Copt.* 21 ll. 30–31   **1** 23–24
P.Kell. V *Copt.* 22 ll. 51–52   **1** 23–24
P.Kell. V *Copt.* 25   p. 48
P.Kell. V *Copt.* 26   p. 48
P.Kell. V *Copt.* 31   p. 48
P.Kell. V *Copt.* 36   pp. 48, 42
P.Kell. V *Copt.* 39   p. 48
*P.Kell.*V *Copt.* 43   p. 48
P.Kell. V *Copt.* 50   p. 48
  50 ll. 2–3   **1** 23–24
P.Kell. VII *Copt.* 72 ll. 4–5, 7–8   **1** 23–24
P.Kell. VII *Copt.* 78   p. 49
P.Kell. VII *Copt.* 97 ll. 5–8   **1** 23–24
P.Kell. VII *Copt.* 103 ll. 50–51   **1** 23–24

P.L.Bat.
P.Lat.Bat. XIII 25   **11** 29.1–22

Index Locorum

P.Lond.Copt.
P.Lond.Copt. 275   p. 110
P.Lond.Copt. 279   p. 110
P.Lond.Copt. 317   **11** 20.6–25.23
P.Lond.Copt. 325   p. 110
P.Lond.Copt. 368   p. 289
   p. 4 ll. 4–6   **3** f.I 7–9
P.Lond.Copt. 369 ll. 10–11   **25** 7.12–14
P.Lond.Copt. 514   p. 251
P.Lond.Copt. 524   pp. 11, 21
   f. l. 21   **25** 4.25
   f. l. 22   **25** 4.25
   f. l. 115   **18** 3
   f. l. 116–119   **11** 9.12–27
P.Lond.Copt. 592   p. 262
P.Lond.Copt. 659   p. 262
P.Lond.Copt. 1007 l. 8   p. 22
P.Lond.Copt. 1008   p. 174
   l. 50   **4** 2.7–13
P.Lond.Copt. 1223 l. 10   **3** f.I.1–34; **11** 16.2–4

P.Macq. I 1
P.Macq. I 1   pp. 14, 21, 174, 233; **3** f.2 ll. 12–13
   p. 1 l. 14   **11** 16.2–4
   p. 1 l. 20   p. 484
   p. 2 l. 16   **11** 16.2–4
   p. 15 ll. 20–21   **34** 1–2
   p. 16 l. 1   **5** f.12
   p. 16 ll. 1–4   **25** 11.7,10

P.Méd.Copt.IFAO
P.Méd.Copt.IFAO   **26** 16.9

P.Mon.Apollo
P.Mon.Apollo I 47   p. 97

P.Mon.Epiph.
P.Mon.Epiph. 50   **11** 20.6–25.23
P.Mon.Epiph. 592+49   p. 77

P.Mon.Phoib.Test. (Garel 2020)
   P.Mon.Phoib.Test. 2   p. 229

P.Monts.Roca
P.Monts.Roca II
   3–8, 25–27   p. 447

P.MoscowCopt.
P.MoscowCopt. 33   **29** f.11–12
P.MoscowCopt. 34   **28** 6.4–5
P.MoscowCopt. 88   **11** 20.6–25.23

P.Oxy.
P.Oxy. LXV 4469   **11** 20.6–25.23
P.Oxy. LXXVI 5073   **22** 20–21

P.PalauRib.
P.PalauRib.Copt. 5   **11** 20.6–25.23
P.PalauRib. 137   p. 241
   f. l. 3   **17** b.18–19

P.Pisentius
P.Pisentius 21   p. 229
P.Pisentius 35   p. 225

P.Rain.Cent.
P.Rain.Cent. 39   p. 407

P.Ryl.Copt.
P.Ryl.Copt. 101   **11** 29.1–22
P.Ryl.Copt. 105, l. 1   p. 485
P.Ryl.Copt. 109   p. 475
P.Ryl.Copt. 175   p. 248
P.Ryl.Copt.Suppl. no. 50   **11** 20.6–25.23

PSI
PSI inv. C 55   **11** 20.6–25.23

PSI Com.
PSI Com. XI 2   p. 247

P.Stras.Copt.
P.Stras.Copt. 6a, ll. 7–8   **2** 5
P.Stras.Copt. 6b, ll. 7–8   **2** 5

SB
SB VI 9537   p. 259
SB VI 9540   p. 259
SB VI 9615   **11** 29.1–22
SB XVIII 13422   p. 104
SB XVIII 13423   p. 104
SB XVIII 13448   p. 104
SB XVIII 13477   p. 104
SB XVIII 13478   p. 104
SB XVIII 13504   p. 104
SB XVIII 13505   p. 104
SB XVIII 13542   p. 104
SB XVIII 13371   p. 104
SB XXVIII 17249   **11** 29.1–22

SB Kopt.
SB Kopt. I 36   p. 81
SB Kopt. II 946   p. 239
SB Kopt. III 1279   p. 262
SB Kopt III 1285   p. 395
SB Kopt. III 1413   p. 262
SB Kopt. V 2344   p. 104

SM/Suppl.Mag.
SM 13 l. 5   p. 39
SM I 45   **3** f.II.33–38
SM I 48   **3** f.II.33–38
SM II 95   p. 49
SM II 98.3   p. 69

Stud.Pal.
Stud.Pal. 20 294   p. 26

P. Teschlot (Richter 2000)
P.Teschlot 1   pp. 363, 455
P.Teschlot 2   pp. 363, 449
P.Teschlot 3 l. 18   **23** 50–52
P.Teschlot 7   p. 461
P.Teschlot 8   p. 461

T.Varie (Pintaudi/P.J. Sijpesteijn 1989)
T.Varie 13   p. 472; **11** 25.24–28.21, 25.27–28.7; 26.8–27.3, 27.8–13, 27.13–21, 28.1, 28.19–20

Literary Works

CC (*Clavis coptica*) numbers are provided for Coptic works where possible.

Anonymous
   Acts of Andrew and Philemon (CC 562)   **17** f. 19; **25** 8.8–9
   Anaphora of Basil   p. 327
   Apocalypse of Paul (CC 30)   **34** 1.15
   Apocryphon of John (CC 0648)   **25** 8.8–9
   Apophthegmata Patrum (Alphabetic Collection)   **28** 3.20
   Apostolic Constitutions
      54   p. 476
      74   p. 476
   3 Baruch   **26** 4.3
   4 Baruch/Paraleipomena Ieremiou   **6** 20
   Book of Bartholomew (CC 27)   p. 479; **11** 9.12–27; **17** f.19; **26** 2.2–15

Book of Mary's Repose 32–35   **11** 28.3–6
Confession of Cyprian (CC 95)   pp. 370, 371; **30** f. 8
Conversion of Cyprian   p. 370
Coptic Synaxarium   p. 370; **17** f.19
Difnar (*Antiphonarium*)   **11** 25.24–28.21
1 Enoch
   20   p. 473
   12.4   **15** f.6–7
2 Enoch   **26** 4.3
Euchologium of the White Monastery (CC 758)   p. 328
Finding of the Holy Cross (*Inventio sanctae crucis*)   **11** 25.24–28.21, 26.8–27.3, 27 8–13, 13–21, 28.1, 19–21
Guide to the Psalms (ed. Henein/Bianquis 1975)   p. 8, 17; **25** 9.2, 4, 17.25–27; **26** 16.28; **30** f.3–4; **33** 6;
Gospel of Judas (CC 894)   p. 18; **30** f. 3–4
History of the Captivity in Babylon (CC 576) 6.20; **12** 31.23–24
Instruction of the 318 Nicene Fathers (*Didascalica CCCXVIII Patrum Nicaenorum*) (CC 19)   **11** 12.12–26
Investiture of Gabriel (CC 378)   **17** f.19; **32** 2.9
Letter of Jesus to Abgar   **11** 20.6–25.23
Life of Macarius (CC 419)   **26** 17.5
Maqlû Ritual (ed. Abusch 2015)   **11** 4.3–20, 5.17–6.7; **12** 37.18–20
Martyrdom of Lacaron (CC 284)   **28** 3.21–22
Martyrdom of Phoibammon (CC 297)   **28** 2.4–5
The Miracles of the Virgin Mary in Bartos (CC 885)   p. 289
On Peter of Alexandria (CC 15)   **11** 12.12–26
Prayer of Cyprian (Greek)   **11** 1.1–14.14; **28** 2.4–5; pp. 371, 407
Prayer of Mary in Bartos   **25** 2.1–5, 11–12, 19–20, 7.23–24
Questions of Bartholomew IV.59   **32** 1.28–31
Second Book of Ieou (CC 675)   **12** 1.2–5
Shepherd of Hermas 23.4–5   1 1
Shi'ur Qomah   **12** 31.3–6
Testament of Levi 16.3   **16** 3.17–18
Testament of Solomon   pp. 5, 371, 406–407; **30** f. 8, f.17; **36** f.I.13–15

1.5   **30** f.7
3.6   **30** f.22–24
4.2   **25** 10.2
5   **18** 18–19
7.6   **25** 18.1–17

Aḥmad al-Būnī (Pseudo-)
    al-Būnī's Šams al-Maʿārif   **21** 1–3

Athanasius of Alexandria
    Life of Anthony   **28** 2.12–13

Athanasius of Alexandria (Pseudo-)
    Canons of Athanasius (Arabic)   p. 477
    On the Mercy of the Father (CC 51)   **22** 36–37

Augustine
    City of God 22.8   **10** 15
    Expositions on Psalms 148.9   p. 472

Basil of Caesarea
    On the Forty Martyrs   **11** 29.1–22

Cyril of Alexandria
    On the Mysteries 5.6   p. 473

Cyril of Jerusalem (Pseudo-)
    On Mary Magdalene (CC 118)   **17** f.19
    On Mary (CC 119)   **25** 9.8–18
    On the Passion (a) (CC 116)   **25** 9.8–18

Dionysius the Areopagite (Pseudo-)
    On the Celestial Hierarchy 6.7   p. 473

Dioscorides
    De materia medica (ed. Wellmann 1907–1914)
        I.16   p. 475
        I.22   p. 471
        I.60   p. 482
        I.64   p. 482
        III.83   **5** b.2–3
        III. 6–7   **5** b.3
        IV.69   **12** 1.2–5

Epiphanius of Salamis
    Panarion 31.5.2   **1** 1
    Ancoratus 118.3–4   **11** 12.12–26

Etheria
    Itinerary 17.1, 19.19   **11** 20.6–25.23

Eusebius
    Ecclesiastical History 13.1–20   **11** 20.6–25.23

Eustathius of Tracia (Pseudo-)
    On Michael (CC 387)   **28** 2.12–13, 3.20

Evodius of Rome (Pseudo-)
    Dormition of the Virgin Mary   **28** 8.18–20

Gelasius I/Damasus I. (Pseudo-)
    Gelasian Decree   p. 5

Gregory of Nazianzus
    In Ecclesiasten V (CC 197)   **26** 16.35
    Oration 24.8–12   p. 370

Iamblichus
    On the Mysteries III.13   **34** 1.17–18

John Chrysostom
    Exposition of Psalm 7   **9** 4
    Homily 88 on the Gospel of Matthew   **25** 9.8–18

John Chrysostom (Pseudo-)
    On Raphael (CC 176)   **26** 4.3
    On the Four Bodiless Living Creatures (CC 177)   **15** f.6–7; **18** 3; p. 473
    On Susannah 26 (CC 178)   **7** f.7

Herodotus
    Histories 3.29   **28** 3.20

Homer
    Illiad 8.15   **7** f.2–3

Īsā ibn ʿAlī
    Book on the Useful Properties of Animal Parts   **26** 16.28

Justin Martyr
    Dialogue with Trypho 131.3   **12** 31.23–24

Maslama Ibn-Aḥmad al-Maǧrīṭī (Pseudo-)
    Ġāyat al-ḥakim (Picatrix)   **24**18; **27** f.15–23

Michael the Syrian
  Chronicle   **11** 12.12–26
Origen
  Against Celsus 1.6.29, 38–41, 68   p. 3

Qur'an 114.4   **25** 10 14–15

Shams al-Ri'asah Abu al-Barakat Ibn Kabar
  Scala Magna   **11** 9.17–18; **26** 16.17, 16.28, 17.5; **28** 11.1; **29** f. 18; **31** f.38; pp. 468, 470

Serapion of Thmuis
  Euchologion   p. 484

Strabo
  Geography 9.1.23   **27** f.17

Theodosius of Alexandria (Pseudo-)
  On Saint Michael (CC 387)   **15** 2; **26** 4.3

Theophrastus
  Enquiry into Plants 9.7   p. 475

Timothy of Alexandria (Pseudo-)
  Discourse on Abbaton (CC 405)   **24** 27; **28** 7.4–8; **34** 1.17–18

Bibliography

Abbreviations

B	Bohairic (Coptic dialect)
b.	back
Bélanger Sarrazin#	R. Bélanger Sarrazin, "Catalogue des textes magiques coptes" (2017)
CAVT	J-C Haelewyck, *Clavis Apocryphorum Veteris Testamenti* (1998)
CC	*Clavis coptica*, for which see Buzi *et al.*, *PAThs Archaeological Atlas of Coptic literature*, online at https://atlas.paths-erc.eu
CDO	Koptische/Coptic Electronic Language and Literature International Alliance (KELLIA) (ed.), *Coptic dictionary Online*, online at https://coptic-dictionary.org
Crum CD	W.E. Crum, *A Coptic Dictionary* (1939)
CED	J. Černý, *Coptic Etymological Dictionary* (1976)
CLM	*Coptic Literary Manuscript* number, for which see Buzi *et al.*, *PAThs Archaeological Atlas of Coptic literature*, online at https://atlas.paths-erc.eu
CMPT	*Coptic Magical Papyri Team*, indicates the readings adopted in this volume
D	depth
DBMNT	G. Ochała, *Database of Medieval Nubian Texts* (2011–2022), online at http://www.dbmnt.uw.edu.pl
DELC	W. Vycichl, *Dictionnaire étymologique de la langue copte* (1984)
ed. pr.	*editio princeps* (first edition)
EL	Edward O.D. Love (editor)
F	Faiyumic (Coptic dialect)
f.	feminine (grammatical gender) or front (in index)
fc.	forthcoming
fem.	feminine (grammatical gender)
Förster WBGW	H. Förster, *Wörterbuch der griechischen Wörter in den koptischen dokumentarischen Texten* (2002)
GEMF	C.A. Faraone & S. Torallas Tovar (eds.), *Greek and Egyptian Magical Formularies*, 2022 & forthcoming.
H	height
JS	Julia Schwarzer (editor)
Kasser CDC	R. Kasser, *Compléments au dictionnaire copte de Crum* (1964)
KD	Korshi Dosoo (editor)

KYP M	*Kyprianos Database of Ancient Ritual Texts and Objects* Manuscripts number, online at https://www.coptic-magic.phil.uni-wuerzburg.de/index.php/manuscripts-search/
KYP T	*Kyprianos Database of Ancient Ritual Texts and Objects* Texts number, online at https://www.coptic-magic.phil.uni-wuerzburg.de/index.php/texts-search/
l.	*lege*, "read" (in italics), line (in Roman)
Lampe	G.W.H. Lampe, *A Patristic Greek Lexicon* (1961)
LBG	E. Trapp (ed.), *Lexikon zur byzantinischen Gräzität* (2020), online at http://stephanus.tlg.uci.edu/lbg.
LSJ	Liddell-Scott-Jones Greek-English Lexicon, online at http://stephanus.tlg.uci.edu/lsj/
m	*manus*, scribal hand (in text editions)
m.	masculine (grammatical gender) (in word indices)
MP	Markéta Preininger (editor)
MTKG	P. Schäfer & S. Shaked, *Magische Texte aus der Kairoer Geniza*, 3 vols. (1994–1999).
pap.	papyrus
PDM	*Papyri demoticae magicae*, numbering from H.D. Betz (ed.), *The Greek Magical Papyri in Translation* (1986).
PG	J.P. Migne, *Patrologiae Cursus Completus. Series Graeca* (1857–1866).
PGM	*Papyri graecae magicae*, numbering from K. Preisendanz & A. Henrichs, *Papyri Graecae Magicae: Die Griechischen Zauberpapyri* (1973–1974), and H.D. Betz (ed.), *The Greek Magical Papyri in Translation* (1986).
pl.	plural
Q	qualitative (verb form)
r.	reigned (used of politcal and religious leaders)
RBS	Roxanne Bélanger Sarrazin (editor)
S	Sahidic (Coptic dialect)
s	style (in text editions)
s.	singular
SM	R.W. Daniel & F. Maltomini, *Supplementum Magicum* (1990–1992).
SVS	Selina Schuster (editor)
TLL	*Thesaurus linguae latinae*, online at https://tll.degruyter.com
TM	*Trismegistos* text number, online at https://www.trismegistos.org/tm/
TM arch id.	*Trismegistos* archive identified, online at https://www.trismegistos.org/arch/
W	width
Westendorf HWB	W. Westendorf, *Koptisches Handwörterbuch* (1965–1977)

Works Cited

Calendarium Romanum ex decreto sacrosancti œcumenici concilii Vaticanii II instauratum auctoritate Pauli PP. VI Promulgatum. 1969. Vatican: Typis Polyglottis.

"Distribution of Papyri bought 1922." 1922. Michigan University Library, https://apps.lib.umich.edu/files/libraries/papyrology/acq-reports/Distribution%20of%20Papyri%20Bought%201922.pdf (accessed 21/6/2023).

Expositions on the Book of Psalms by S. Augustine, Bishop of Hippo. Expositions on the Book of Psalms. Translated, with Notes and Indices in Six Volumes. Vol. VI, Psalm CXXVI.-CL. London: John Henry Parker; F. and J. Rivington, 1859.

"Guide to the Yale Papyrus Collection." *Beinecke Rare Book and Manuscript Library*, https://beinecke.library.yale.edu/research-teaching/doing-research-beinecke-library/introduction-yale-papyrus-collection/guide-yale (accessed 17/10/2022).

Sahidic Bible 2, edited by the Digital Edition of the Coptic Old Testament in Göttingen (CoptOT) and Institut für Neutestamentliche Textforschung (INTF), online at http://crosswire.org/study/fulllibrary.jsp?show=CopSahBible2 (consulted 28/7/2023)

'Abd Al-Masiḥ, Yassā. 1947. "An Unedited Bohairic letter of Abgar." *Bulletin de l'Institut français d'archéologie orientale* 45: 65–80.

—1954. "An Unedited Bohairic Letter of Abgar (continued)." *Bulletin de l'Institut français d'archéologie orientale* 54: 13–43.

Abusch, Tzvi. 2011. "The Revision of Babylonian Anti-Witchcraft Incantations: The Critical Analysis of Incantations in the Ceremonial Series Maqlû." In *Continuity and Innovation in the Magical Tradition*, edited by Gideon Bohak, Yuval Harari, and Shaul Shaked, 11–42. Leiden/Boston: Brill.

—2015. *The Magical Ceremony Maqlû: A Critical Edition*. Leiden/Boston: Brill.

Afentoulidou, Eirini. 2021. "Between Incantation and Prayer: Guardian Angels in Amulets, Euchologia, and Canonical Texts." In *Papers Presented at the Eighteenth International Conference on Patristic Studies held in Oxford 2019. Volume 5: Euchologia*, edited by Markus Vinzent and Claudia Rapp, 77–87. Studia Patristica 108. Leuven: Peeters.

Aland, Barbara, Kurt Aland, Johannes Karavidopoulos, Carlo M. Martini, Bruce M. Metzger, Luc Herren, Marie-Luise Lakmann, Beate von Tschischwitz, Klaus Wachtel, and Holger Strutwolf. 2017. *Novum Testamentum Graece*. 28th revised edition. Stuttgart: Deutsche Bibelgesellschaft.

Alcock, Anthony. 1982. "A Coptic Magical Text." *Bulletin of the American Society of Papyrologists* 19, nos. 3–4: 97–103.

Alfayé, Silvia. 2016 "Mind the Bath! Magic at the Roman Bath-Houses." In *From Polites to Magos. Studia György Németh sexagenario dedicata*, edited by Ádám Szabó, 28–37. Budapest: Kódex Könyvgyártó Kft.

Allen, James P. 2013. *The Ancient Egyptian Language: An Historical Study*. Cambridge: Cambridge University Press.

Altenmüller, Hartwick. 1977. "Götterbedrohung." In *Lexikon der Ägyptologie* 2, edited by Wolfgang Helck, Eberhard Otto, and Wolfhart Westendorf, 664–669. Wiesbaden: Harrassowitz.

Amar, Zohar, and Efraim Lev. 2013. "Trends in the Use of Perfumes and Incense in the Near East after the Muslim Conquests." *Journal of the Royal Asiatic Society* 23, no. 1: 11–30.

—2017. *Arabian Drugs in Early Medieval Mediterranean Medicine*. Edinburgh Studies in Classical Islamic History and Culture 4. Edinburgh: Edinburgh University Press.

Amélineau, Émile C. 1888. "Fragments de la version thebaine de l'Écriture (Ancien Testament)." *Recueil de travaux relatifs à la philologie et à l'archéologie égyptiennes et assyriennes* 10, no. 1/2: 67–96.

—1891. *Notice sur le papyrus gnostique Bruce: Texte et traduction*. Paris: Imprimerie Nationale.

—1893. "The Sahidic Translation of the Book of Job." *Society of Biblical Archæology* 9: 405–475.

—1894. *Histoire des monastères de la Basse-Égypte*. Paris: Ernest Leroux.
—1895. *Le nouveau traité gnostique de Turin*. Paris: Chamuel.
—1911. *Œuvres de Schenoudi: Texte copte et traduction française* 2. Paris: Ernest Leroux.
Amigues, Suzanne. 2007. "Le styrax et ses usages antiques." *Journal des savants* 97, no. 2: 261–318.
Amir-Moezzi, Mohammad Ali, and Guillaume Dye. 2019. *Le Coran des historiens. Volume 2b. Commentaire et analyse du texte coranique. Sourates 27 à 114*. Paris: Les éditions du Cerf.
Amory, Yasmine. 2023. "Usi intratestuali dei simboli cristiani nei papiri documentari di epoca bizantina e araba." In *Segni, sogni, materie e scrittura dall'Egitto tardoantico all'Europa carolingia* 221, edited by Maria Boccuzzi, Antonella Ghignoli, Anna Monte, 51–69. Rome: Edizioni di Storia e Letteratura.
—Forthcoming. "More than a Simple Intuition. Towards a Categorization of Paleographical Features in Greek Documentary Papyri." In *Neo-Paleography: Analysing Ancient Handwritings in the Digital Age*, edited by Isabelle Marthot-Santaniello.
André, Jacques. 1985. *Les noms de plantes dans la Rome antique*. Paris: Les Belles Lettres.
Asensi Amorós, Victoria. "Essences à brûler en Egypte ancienne: une enquête ethnobotanique du coté de la Corne de l'Afrique". *Memnonia, cahier supplémentaire* 1: 1–19.
Askeland, Christian. 2018. "Dating Early Greek and Coptic Literary Hands." In *Nag Hammadi Codices and Late Antique Egypt*, edited by Hugo Lundhaug and Lance Jenott, 457–489. Studien und Texte zu Antike und Christentum/Studies and Texts in Antiquity and Christianity 110. Tübingen: Mohr Siebeck.
Ast, Rodney. 2013. "Schedule of Work Days." In *Papyrological Texts in Honor of Roger S. Bagnall*, edited by Rodney Ast, Hélène Cuvigny, Todd M. Hickey, and Julia Lougovaya, 9–16. American Studies in Papyrology 53. Durham: American Society of Papyrologists.
Atiya, Aziz S. 1991. *The Coptic Encyclopedia*. 8 vols. New York: Macmillan.
Audollent, Auguste. 1904. *Defixionum tabellae: Quotquot innotuerunt, tam in Graecis Orientis quam in totius Occidentis partibus praeter Atticas in Corpore inscriptionum atticarum editas*. Paris: Fontemoing.
Aufrère, Sydney H. 2005. "ⲕⲣⲟⲛⲟⲥ, un crocodile justicier des marécages de la rive occidentale du Panopolite au temps de Chénouté?" In *Encyclopédie religieuse de l'univers végétal: Croyances phytoreligieuses de l'Égypte ancienne* 3, edited by Sydney H. Aufrère, 77–93. Orientalia Monspeliensia 15. Montpellier: Université Paul-Valéry, Montpellier III.
Austin, John L. 1962. *How to do Things with Words: The William James Lectures Delivered at Harvard University in 1955*. London: Oxford University Press.
Awad, Magdi, and Samuel Moawad. 1999. "A Response to the Article 'Monophysitism' by W.H.C. Frend in the Coptic Encyclopedia, vol. 5, pp. 1669–1678." In *Claremont Coptic Encyclopedia*. https://ccdl.claremont.edu/digital/collection/cce/id/1959/rec/1.
Badawi, El-Said, and Martin Hinds. 1986. *A Dictionary of Egyptian Arabic: Arabic-English*. Beirut: Librairie du Liban.
Bagnall, Roger S. 1988. "Combat ou vide: Christianisme et paganisme dans l'Égypte romaine tardive." *Ktèma* 13: 285–296.
—2008. "Models and Evidence in the Study of Religion in Late Roman Egypt." In *From Temple to Church: Destruction and Renewal of Local Cultic Topography in Late Antiquity*, edited by Johannes Hahn, Stephen Emmel, and Ulrich Gotter, 24–42. Religions in the Graeco-Roman World 163. Leiden: Brill.
—2009a. *Early Christian Books in Egypt*. Princeton: Princeton University Press.
—2009b. "Practical Help: Chronology, Geography, Measures, Currency, Names, Prosopography and Technical Vocabulary." In *Oxford Handbook of Papyrology*, edited by Roger S. Bagnall, 179–196. Oxford: Oxford University Press.
Bailey, Ryan. 2009. "The Confession of Cyprian of Antioch: Introduction, Text, and Translation." MA Thesis, McGill University. https://escholarship.mcgill.ca/downloads/gm80hv700?locale=en.

—2017a. "The Acts of Saint Cyprian of Antioch: Critical Editions, Translations, and Commentary." PhD Diss., McGill University. https://escholarship.mcgill.ca/downloads/gm80hv700?locale=en.
—2017b. "Greek Manuscripts of the Testament of Solomon in the Biblioteca Apostolica Vaticana." In *The Embroidered Bible: Studies in Biblical Apocrypha and Pseudepigrapha in Honour of Michael E. Stone,* edited by Lorenzo DiTommaso, Matthias Henze, and William Adler, 170–212. Studia in Veteris Testamenti Pseudepigrapha 26. Leiden: Brill.
Bąk, Tomasz B. 2019. "A Critical Edition and Philological Analysis of the First Chapter of Deutero-Isaiah (Isa 40) on the Basis of the Coptic Manuscript sa 52 (M 568) in Light of Other Coptic Manuscripts Written in the Sahidic Dialect and the Greek Text of the Septuagint." *The Biblical Annals* 9, no. 1: 73–100.
—2020. *Proto-Isaiah in the Sahidic Dialect of the Coptic Language. Critical Edition Based on the Coptic Manuscript sa 52 (M 568) and Other Witnesses.* Turnhout: Brepols.
Balestri, Giuseppe, and Henri Hyvernat. 1908. *Acta Martyrum* 1. Corpus Scriptorum Christianorum Orientalium 43–44. Leipzig: Harrassowitz.
Barb, Alphons A. 1957. "Abraxas-Studien." In *Hommages à Waldemar Deonna,* 67–86. Collection Latomus 28. Brussels: Latomus.
Barkay, Gabriel, Marilyn J. Lundberg, Andrew G. Vaughn, and Bruce Zuckerman. 2014. "The Amulets from Ketef Hinnom: A New Edition and Evaluation." *Bulletin of the American Schools of Oriental Research* 334, no. 1: 41–71.
Bartelink, Gerhardus J. M. 1994. *Vie d'Antoine. Introduction, texte critique, traduction, notes et index.* Sources chrétiennes 400. Paris: Les éditions du Cerf.
Basset, René. 1894. "Les apocryphes éthiopiens." *La haute science* 2: 54–92, 193–207, 271–281, 351–353, 513–521, 600–610, 694–704, 759–789.
—1904. "Le synaxaire arabe Jacobite 1: Mois de Tout et de Babeh." *Patrologia Orientalis* 1: 223–379.
—1909. "Le Synaxaire arabe Jacobite 2: Mois de Hatour et de Kihak." *Patrologia Orientalis* 3: 243–545.
—1915. "Le Synaxaire arabe Jacobite 3: Les mois de Toubeh et d'Amchir." *Patrologia Orientalis* 11, no. 5: 505–825.
—1982. *Les Prières de S. Cyprien et de Théophile. Les Apocryphes éthiopiens 6.* Paris: Librairie de l'Art Indépendant, 1896. Facsimile reprint of the first edition. Milan: Archè.
Beck, Susanne. 2018. "4. Ein Rezept und zwei Beschwörungen (P.Heid. Inv. Kopt. 408)." In *Coptica Palatina: Koptische Texte aus der Heidelberger Papyrussammlung (P.Heid.Kopt.); Bearbeitet auf der Vierten Internationalen Sommerschule für Koptische Papyrologie, Heidelberg, 26. August – 9. September 2012,* edited by Anne Boud'hors, Alain Delattre, Tonio Sebastian Richter, Gesa Schenke, and Georg Schmelz, 45–52. Studien und Texte aus der Heidelberger Papyrussammlung 1. Heidelberg: Heidelberg University Publishing.
BeDuhn, Jason D. 2000. *The Manichaean Body: In Discipline and Ritual.* Baltimore: John Hopkins Press.
Behlmer, Heike, and Anthony Alcock. 1996. *A Piece of Shenoutiana from the Department of Egyptian Antiquities (EA 71005).* British Museum Occasional Paper 119. London: British Museum.
Bélanger Sarrazin, Roxanne. 2017a. "Catalogue des textes magiques coptes." *Archiv für Papyrusforschung und verwandte Gebiete* 63.2: 367–408.
—2017b. "Une malédiction copte sur un ostracon d'Antinoupolis." *Analecta Papyrologica* 29: 119–122.
—2020. "Les appels au 'Jésus guérisseur' dans les formules iatromagiques coptes." In *Études coptes 16. Dix-huitième journée d'études (Bruxelles, 22–24 juin 2017),* edited by Anne Boud'hors, Esther Garel, Catherine Louis, and Naïm Vanthieghem, 187–204. Cahiers de la bibiothèque copte 23. Paris: Éditions de Boccard.

—Forthcoming a. *Les divinités gréco-égyptiennes dans les textes magiques coptes: Une étude du syncrétisme religieux en Égypte tardo-antique et médiévale.* Leuven: Peeters.
—Forthcoming b. "'Just as You Quenched the Fiery Furnace of Nebuchadnezzar, Also Quench Every Fever.' The Three Holy Children in Coptic Magic."
—Forthcoming c. "Appropriating the Gods: Magic in the Changing Contexts of Late Antique Egypt." In *Appropriation: A New Approach to Religion in Antiquity*, edited by Jitse Dijkstra and Andreas Bendlin. Cambridge: Cambridge University Press.
Bell, Harold I. 1922. "Report on Papyri, etc., Brought by Nahman, July, 1922." University of Michigan Library, https://apps.lib.umich.edu/files/libraries/papyrology/acq-reports/Report%20on%20Papyri%20Brought%20by%20Nahman%2C%20July%2C%201922.pdf (accessed 21/6/2023).
—1927, May 9. "Report on the Papyri in the Season 1926–1927." University of Michigan Library, https://apps.lib.umich.edu/papyrus-collection/report-papyri-season-1926-1927 (accessed 21/6/2023).
Bell, Harold I., Arthur Darby Nock, and Herbert Thompson. 1932. *Magical Texts from a Bilingual Papyrus in the British Museum.* London: Milford.
Bellini, Davide. 2019. "Due papiri medici della collezione dell'Università Cattolica del Sacro Cuore di Milano". *Aegyptus* 99: 3–20
Bellusci, Alessia. 2016. "A Genizah Finished Product for She'elat Ḥalom based on Sefer Ha-Razim." *Journal of Jewish Studies* 67, no. 2: 305–326.
Beltz, Walter. 1980. "Die koptischen Zauberostraka der Papyrus-Sammlung der Staatlichen Museen zu Berlin." *Hallesche Beiträge zur Orientwissenschaft* 2: 59–75.
—1983. "Die koptischen Zauberpapyri der Papyrus-Sammlung der Staatlichen Museen zu Berlin." *Archiv für Papyrusforschung und verwandte Gebiete* 29: 59–86.
—1984. "Die koptischen Zauberpergamente der Papyrus-Sammlung der Staatlichen Museen zu Berlin." *Archiv für Papyrusforschung und verwandte Gebiete* 30: 83–104.
—1985. "Die koptischen Zauberpapiere und Zauberostraka der Papyrus-Sammlung der Staatlichen Museen zu Berlin." *Archiv für Papyrusforschung und verwandte Gebiete* 31: 31–41.
Berger, Adolf. 1968. *Encyclopedic Dictionary of Roman Law.* Transactions of the American Philosophical Society, n.s. 43, pt. 2. Philadelphia: American Philosophical Society.
Berkes, Lajos, Alain Delattre, and Naïm Vanthieghem. 2021. "A Ninth-Century Coptic Tax Refund Document. Reedition of *CPR* IV 197." *Chronique d'Egypte* 96, no. 191: 164–172.
Bernardin, Joseph B. 1937. "A Coptic Sermon Attributed to St Athanasius." *The Journal of Theological Studies* 38, no. 150: 113–129.
Betz, Hans D., ed. 1986. *The Greek Magical Papyri in Translation.* Chicago: University of Chicago Press.
Beshay, Michael. 2020. "The Virgin Mary in Ritual in Late Antique Egypt: Origins, Practice, and Legacy." PhD Diss., Ohio State University. http://rave.ohiolink.edu/etdc/view?acc_num=osu15888899395967 (accessed 21/6/2023).
Bevegni, Claudio. 1982. "Eudociae Augustae Martyrium S. Cypriani I 1–99." *Prometheus* 8, no. 3: 249–262.
Bhayro, Siam. 2021. "Syriac Magic and Medicine: A Near-Eastern Paradigm of Priestcraft." In *Studies in the Syriac Magical Traditions*, edited by Marco Moriggi and Siam Bhayro, 31–56. Magical and Religious Literature of Late Antiquity 9. Leiden: Brill.
Bierbrier, Morris L. 2012. *Who Was Who in Egyptology.* London: Egypt Exploration Society.
Bilabel, Friedrich, and Adolf Grohmann. 1934. *Griechische, koptische und arabische Texte zur Religion und religiösen Literatur in Ägyptens Spätzeit.* Veröffentlichungen aus den badischen Papyrus-Sammlungen 5. Heidelberg: Verlag der Universitätsbibliothek.

Blid, Jesper, Maximous El-Antony, Hugo Lundhaug, Jason Zaborowski, Meira Polliack, Mengistu Gobezie Worku, and Samuel Rubenson. 2016. "Excavations at the Monastery of St. Antony at the Red Sea." *Opuscula: Annual of the Swedish Institutes at Athens and Rome* 9: 133–215.

Bloom, Jonathan M. 2001. *Paper Before Print: The History and Impact of Paper in the Islamic World*. New Haven: Yale University Press.

Blumell, Lincoln. 2012. *Lettered Christians: Christians, Letters, and Late Antique Oxyrhynchus*. New Testament Tools, Studies and Documents 39. Leiden: Brill.

—2013. "Two Coptic Ostraca in the Brigham Young University Collection." *Chronique d'Égypte* 88, no. 175: 182–187.

—2017. "P. Mich. inv. 4461KR: The Earliest Fragment of the *Didascalia CCCXVIII Patrum Nicaenorum*." *Journal of Theological Studies* 68.2: 607–620.

Blumell, Lincoln, and Korshi Dosoo. 2018. "Horus, Isis, and the Dark-Eyed Beauty: A Series of Magical Ostraca in the Brigham Young University Collection." *Archiv für Papyrusforschung und verwandte Gebiete* 64: 199–259.

—2021. "A Coptic Magical Text for Virginity in Marriage: A Witness to the Practice of Celibate Marriage from Christian Egypt?" *Harvard Theological Review* 114, no. 1: 118–142.

Boberg, Charles, John Nerbonne, and Dominic Watt. 2018. "Introduction." In *The Handbook of Dialectology*, edited by Charles Boberg, John Nerbonne, and Dominic Watt, 1–5. Hoboken, NJ/Oxford: Wiley Blackwell.

Boeser, Pieter A. A. 1922. "Deux textes coptes du musée d'antiquités des Pays-Bas à Leide." In *Recueil d'études égyptologiques dédiées à la mémoire de Jean-François Champollion*, 529–535. Paris: E. Champion.

Bohak, Gideon. 1999. "Greek, Coptic, and Jewish Magic in the Cairo Genizah." *The Bulletin of the American Society of Papyrologists* 36, no. 1/4: 27–44.

—2000. "The Impact of the Jewish Monotheism on the Greco-Roman World." *Jewish Studies Quarterly* 7, no. 1: 1–21.

—2003. "Hebrew, Hebrew Everywhere? Notes on the Interpretation of Voces Magicae." In *Prayer, Magic, and the Stars*, edited by Scott Noegel and Brandon Wheeler, 69–82. University Park: Pennsylvania State University Press.

—2005. "Reconstructing Jewish Magical Recipe Books from the Cairo Genizah." *Ginzei qedem: Genizah Research Annual* 1: 9–29.

—2008. *Ancient Jewish Magic: A History*. Cambridge: Cambridge University Press.

—2009. "Prolegomena to the Study of the Jewish Magical Tradition." *Currents in Biblical Research* 8, no. 1 (2009): 107–150.

—2016. "The Diffusion of the Greco-Egyptian Magical Tradition in Late Antiquity." In *Greco-Egyptian Interactions: Literature, Translation, and Culture, 500 BCE – 300 CE*, edited by Ian Rutherford, 366–374. Oxford: Oxford University Press.

—2019. "An Ancient Babylonian Text on a Modern Jewish Amulet". In *Windows on Jewish Worlds: Essays in Honor of William Gross Collector of Judaica, on the Occasion of his Eightieth Birthday*, edited by Shalom Sabar, Emile Schrijver, and Falk Wiesemann, 350–361. Zutphen: Walburg Pers.

—2022. "Specimens of Judaeo-Arabic and Arabic Magical Texts from the Cairo Genizah." In *Amulets and Talismans of the Middle East and North Africa in Context*, edited by Marcela A. Garcia Probert and Petra M. Sijpesteijn, 15–46. Leiden Studies in Islam and Society 13. Leiden/Boston: Brill.

Bohak, Gideon, and Ortal-Paz Saar. 2015. "Genizah Magical Texts Prepared for or against Named Individuals." *Revue des études juives* 174, no. 1–2: 77–110.

Bonati, Isabella. 2016. *Il lessico dei vasi e dei contenitori greci nei papiri: Specimina per un repertorio lessicale degli angionimi greci*. Archiv für Papyrusforschung und verwandte Gebiete – Beihefte 37. Berlin: De Gruyter.

Bonwetsch, Nathanael G. 1897. "Die Apokryphen Fragen des Bartholomäus." In *Nachrichten von der Königl. Gesellschaft der Wissenschaften zu Göttingen*, 1–42. Göttingen: Commissionsverlag der Dieterich'schen Universitätsbuchhandlung.

Bonner, Campbell. 1932. "Demons of the Bath." In *Studies presented to F. Ll. Griffith*, 203–208. London: Oxford University Press.

—1950. *Studies in Magical Amulets Chiefly Graeco-Egyptian*. University of Michigan Studies: Humanistic Series 49. Ann Arbor: University of Michigan Press.

Bonnet, Corinne. 1989. "Le dieu solaire Shamash dans le monde phénico-punique." *Studi epigrafici e linguistici sul Vicino Oriente antico* 6: 97–115.

Booth, Phil. 2017. "Towards the Coptic Church: The Making of the Severan Episcopate." *Millennium* 14, no. 1: 151–190.

Borgehammar, Stephan. 1991. *How the Holy Cross Was Found: From Event to Medieval Legend*. Bibliotheca Theologicae Practicae, Kyrkovetenskapliga Studier, 47. Stockholm: Almquist & Wiksell International.

Borghouts, Joris F. 1978. *Ancient Egyptian Magical Texts*. Leiden: Brill.

Boud'hors, Anne. 1997. "L'onciale penchée en copte et sa survie jusqu'au XVe siècle en Haute Égypte." In *Scribes et Manuscrits du Moyen-Orient*, edited by François Déroche and Francis Richard, 117–133. Paris: Bibliotheque Nationale de France.

—1999. "Manuscrits coptes de papier (XIe-XIVe siècle) : quelques éléments de caractérisation." In *Le papier au Moyen-Age: histoire et techniques*, edited by Monique Zerdoun Bat-Yehouda, 75–84. Paris: Turnhout.

—2008. "Copie et circulation des livres dans la région thébaine (VIIe–VIIIe siècles)." In *'Et maintenant ce ne sont plus que des villages...' Thèbes et sa région aux époques hellénistique, romaine et byzantine. Actes du colloque tenu à Bruxelles les 2 et 3 décembre 2005*, edited by Alain Delattre and Paul Heilporn, 149–162. Papyrologica Bruxellensia 34. Brussels: Association Égyptologique Reine Élisabeth.

—2011. "Pièces supplémentaires du dossier de Frangé." *Journal of Coptic Studies* 13: 99–112.

—2017a. "À la récherche des manuscrits coptes de la région thebaine." In *From Gnostics to Monastics: Studies in Coptic and Early Christianity in Honor of Bentley Layton*, edited by David Brakke, Stephen J. Davis, and Stephen Emmel, 175–212. Orientalia Lovaniensia Analecta 263. Leuven: Peeters.

—2017b. "Greek loanwords in Fayyumic documentary texts." In *Greek Influence on Egyptian-Coptic: Contact-Induced Change in an Ancient African Language*, edited by Eitan Grossman, Peter Dils, Tonio Sebastian Richter, and Wolfgang Schenkel, 423–439. Lingua Aegyptia : Studia monographica 17. DDGLC working papers 1. Hamburg: Widmaier Verlag.

—2020. "Issues and Methodologies in Coptic Palaeography." In *The Oxford Handbook of Egyptian Epigraphy and Palaeography*, edited by Vanessa Davies and Dimitri Laboury, 618–633. New York: Oxford University Press.

Boud'hors, Anne, Alain Delattre, Catherine Louis, and Tonio Sebastian Richter. 2014. *Coptica Argentoratensia: Textes et Documents de la Troisième Université d'Été de Papyrologie Copte (Strasbourg, 18-25 juillet 2010) (P.Stras.Copt.)*. Cahiers de la Bibliothèque copte 19. Paris: De Boccard.

Boud'hors, Alain Delattre, Tonio Sebastian Richter, Gesa Schenke, and Georg Schmelz. 2018. *Coptica Palatina: Koptische Texte aus der Heidelberger Papyrussammlung (P.Heid.Kopt.); Bearbeitet auf der Vierten Internationalen Sommerschule für Koptische Papyrologie, Heidelberg, 26. August–9. September 2012*. Studien und Texte aus der Heidelberger Papyrussammlung 1. Heidelberg: Heidelberg University Publishing.

Boud'hors, Anne, and Esther Garel. 2016. "Que reste-t-il de la bibliothèque du monastère de Saint-Phoibammon à Deir el-Bahari?" In *Aegyptus et Nubia Christiana: The Włodzimierz Godlewski*

Jubilee Volume on the Occasion of His 70th Birthday, edited by Adam Łajtar, Artur Obłuski, and Iwona Zych, 47–60. Warsaw: Agade.

Boud'hors, Anne, Esther Garel, Catherine Louis, and Naïm Vanthieghem, eds. 2020. *Études coptes 16. Dix-huitième journée d'études (Bruxelles, 22–24 juin 2017)*. Cahiers de la bibiothèque copte 23. Paris: Éditions de Boccard.

Boud'hors, Anne, and Chantal Heurtel. 2015. *Ostraca et papyrus coptes du topos de Saint-Marc à Thèbes*. Bibliothèque d'études coptes 24. 2 vols. Cairo: Institut français d'archéologie orientale du Caire.

Boud'hors, Anne and Michel Tardieu. 2006, December. "Retour des parchemins coptes au Collège de France." *La lettre du Collège de France* 18: 16.

Boustan, Ra'anan, and Michael Beshay. 2015. "Sealing the Demons, Once and For All: The Ring of Solomon, the Cross of Christ, and the Power of Biblical Kingship." *Archiv für Religionsgeschichte* 16: 99–130.

Bowen, Gillian E. 2015. "The Environment Within: The Archaeological Context of the Texts from House 3 at Kellis in Egypt's Dakhleh-Oasis." In *Housing and Habitat in the Ancient Mediterranean*, edited by A. Andrea Di Castro and Colin A. Hope, 231–241. Bulletin antieke beschaving Supplement 26. Leuven/Paris/Bristol, CT: Peeters.

Bozóky, Edina. 2013. "Medieval Narrative Charms." In *The Power of Words: Studies on Charms and Charming in Europe*, edited by Jonathan Kapaló, Éva Pócs, and William Ryan, 101–116. Budapest: Central European University Press.

Brakke, David. 2010. *The Gnostics. Myth, Ritual, and Diversity in Early Christianity*. Cambridge, MA.: Harvard University Press.

Brakke, David, Stephen J. Davis, and Stephen Emmel, eds. 2017. *From Gnostics to Monastics: Studies in Coptic and Early Christianity in Honor of Bentley Layton*. Orientalia Lovaniensia Analecta 263. Leuven/Paris/Bristol, CT: Peeters.

Brand, Mattias. 2022. *Religion and the Everyday Life of Manichaeans in Kellis*. Nag Hammadi and Manichaean Studies 102. Leiden: Brill.

Brashear, William M. 1991. *Magica Varia*. Papyrologica Bruxellensia 25. Brussels: Fondation Égyptologique Reine Élisabeth.

—1995. "The Greek Magical Papyri: An Introduction and Survey; Annotated Bibliography (1928–1994)." In *Aufstieg und Niedergang der römischen Welt (ANRW) / Rise and Decline of the Roman World. Band 18/5. Teilband Religion. Heidentum*, edited by Wolfgang Haase, 3380–3684. Berlin/Boston: De Gruyter.

Bremmer, Jan N. 2002. "Magic in the Apocryphal Acts of the Apostles." In *The Metamorphosis of Magic from Late Antiquity to the Early Modern Period*, edited by Jan N. Bremmer and Jan R. Veenstra, 51–70. Groningen Studies in Cultural Change 1. Leuven: Peeters Publishing.

Brunsch, Wolfgang. 1978. "Ein koptischer Bindezauber." *Enchoria* 8, no. 1: 151–157.

Bsees, Ursula. 2019. "Dokumentarische Materialien zur Magie aus der Frühzeit des Islams: Forschungsfragen und Forschungsansätze." In *Die Geheimnisse der oberen und der unteren Welt: Magie im Islam zwischen Glaube und Wissenschaft*, edited by Sebastian Günther and Dorothee Pielow, 195–222. Islamic History and Civilization 158. Leiden: Brill.

Budde, Achim. 2004. *Die ägyptische Basilios-Anaphora: Text, Kommentar, Geschichte*. Jerusalemer Theologisches Forum 7. Münster: Aschendorff.

Budelli, Rosanna. 2014. *Il Sigillo di Salomone. In tre manoscritti di magia copta in lingua araba*. Milan: Edizioni Terra Santa.

Budge, Wallis E.A. 1894. *Saint Michael the Archangel: Three Encomiums by Theodosius, Archbishop of Alexandria, Severus, Patriarch of Antioch, and Eustathius, Bishop of Trake. The Coptic Texts with Extracts from Arabic and Ethiopian Versions*. London: Kegan Paul, Trench, Trübner.

—1898. *The Earliest Known Coptic Psalter. The Text, in the Dialect of Upper Egypt*. London: Kegan Paul, Trench, Trübner.

—1910. *Coptic Homilies in the Dialect of Upper Egypt. Edited from the Papyrus Codex Oriental 5001 in the British Museum*. London: British Museum.
—1912. *Coptic Biblical Texts in the Dialect of Upper Egypt*. London: Oxford University Press.
—1913. *Coptic Apocrypha in the Dialect of Upper Egypt*. London: Trustees of the British Museum.
—1914. *Coptic Martyrdoms etc. in the Dialect of Upper Egypt* 1. London: Trustees of the British Museum.
—1915. *Miscellaneous Coptic Texts in the Dialect of Upper Egypt*. London: Oxford University Press.
—1929. *The Bandlet of Righteousness: An Ethiopian Book of the Dead*. Luzac's Semitic Text and Translation Series 19. London: Luzac.
Bulliet, Richard W. 1979. *Conversion to Islam in the Medieval Period: An Essay in Quantitative History*. Cambridge, MA: Harvard University Press.
Bülow-Jacobsen, Adam. 2009. "Writing Materials in the Ancient World." In *Oxford Handbook of Papyrology*, edited by Roger S. Bagnall, 3–29. Oxford: Oxford University Press.
Burke, Tony, and Brent Landau, eds. 2016–2023. *New Testament Apocrypha: More Noncanonical Scriptures*. 3 vols. Grand Rapids: William B. Eerdmans.
Burmester, Oswald H.E. 1967. *The Egyptian or Coptic Church: A Detailed Description of her Liturgical Services and the Rites and Ceremonies Observed in the Administration of her Sacraments*. Publications de la Société d'Archéologie Copte, Textes et documents. Cairo: The French Institute of Oriental Archaeology.
Burns, Dylan M. 2014. *Apocalypse of the Alien God: Platonism and the Exile of Sethian Gnosticism*. Divinations: Rereading Late Ancient Religion 31. Philadelphia: University of Pennsylvania Press.
—2018. "Magical, Coptic, Christian: The Great Angel Eleleth and the 'Four Luminaries' in Egyptian Literature of the First Millenium CE." In *The Nag Hammadi Codices and Late Antique Egypt*, edited by Hugo Lundhaug and Lance Jenott, 141–162. Studien und Texte zu Antike und Christentum/Studies and Texts in Antiquity and Christianity 110. Tübingen: Mohr Siebeck.
—2019. "Gnosticism, Gnostics, and Gnosis." In *The Gnostic World*, edited by Garry W. Trompf, Gunner B. Mikkelsen, and Jay Johnston, 9–25. London/New York: Routledge.
Busch, Peter. 2006. *Das Testament Salomos: Die älteste christliche Dämonologie, kommentiert und in deutscher Erstübersetzung*. Texte und Untersuchungen zur Geschichte der altchristlichen Literatur 153. Berlin: De Gruyter.
—2013. "Solomon as a True Exorcist: The Testament of Solomon in Its Cultural Setting." In *The Figure of Solomon in Jewish, Christian, and Islamic Tradition: King, Sage, and Architect*, edited by Joseph Verheyden, 183–195. Themes in Biblical Narrative 16. Leiden: Brill.
Buzi, Paola. 2015–2016. "Amedeo Peyron and the Coptic Codices from This." *Egyptian & Egyptological Documents, Archives & Libraries* 5: 59–80.
—2016. "From Single-Text to Multiple-Text Manuscripts: Transmission Changes in the Coptic Literary Tradition. Some Case-Studies from the White Monastery Library." In *One-Volume Libraries: Composite and Multiple-Text Manuscripts*, edited by Michael Friedrich and Cosima Schwarke, 93–110. Studies in Manuscript Cultures 9. Berlin: De Gruyter.
—2018. "The Coptic Papyrus Codices Preserved in the Museo Egizio, Turin: New Historical Acquisitions, Analysis of Codicological Features, and Strategies for a Better Understanding and Valorization of the Library from Thi(ni)s." *Adamantius* 24: 39–57.
—2019. "The Ninth-Century Coptic 'Book Revolution' and the Emergence of Multiple-Text Manuscripts." In *The Emergence of Multiple-Text Manuscripts*, edited by Alessandro Bausi, Michael Friedrich, and Marilena Maniaci, 125–142. *Studies in Manuscript Cultures* 17. Berlin: De Gruyter.

—2021. "Literature, Coptic: Update." In *Claremont Coptic Encyclopedia*, edited by Karen J. Torjesen, Gawdat Gabra, and Hany N. Takla. The Claremont Colleges Digital Library, https://ccdl.claremont.edu/digital/collection/cce/id/2175/rec/1 (accessed 21/6/2023).

—2023. "From Bernardino Drovetti's Collection to Amedeo Peyron's Classification. The Coptic Literary Codices Held in the Museo Egizio: An Overview." In *The Coptic Codices of the Museo Egizio, Turin. Historical, Literary, and Codicological Feature*, edited by Paola Buzi and Tito Orlandi, 9–26. Studi del Museo Egizio 4. Modena: Franco Cosimo Panini.

Campagnano, Antonella. 1980. *Ps. Cirillo di Gerusalemme: Omelie copte sulla passione, sulla croce e sulla vergine*. Testi e documenti per lo studio dell'Antichità 66 = Serie copta 9. Milan: Cisalpino – Goliardica.

Camplani, Alberto. 2010. "'Eli, Eli, lema sabachthani'. Pluralità dei linguaggi religiosi e loro rielaborazione rituale in alcune preghiere magiche copte." *Studi e Materiali di Storia delle Religioni (Magia e tecnica grafica)* 76, no. 1: 139–150.

Capasso, Mario, Paola Davoli, and Natascia Pellé. 2022. *Proceedings of the 29th Congress of Papyrology, Lecce, 28 July–3 August 2019*. Quaderni dell' Istituto superiore universitario di formazione interdisciplinare 2. Lecce: Centro di Studi Papirologici dell'Università del Salento.

Carcopino, Jérôme. 1948. "Le Christianisme secret du « carré magique »." *Museum Helveticum* 5, no. 1: 16–59.

Carlig, Nathan. 2020. "Les symboles chrétiens dans les papyrus littéraires et documentaires grecs: forme, disposition et fonction (IIIe–VIIe/VIIIe siècles)." In *Signes dans les textes. Recherches sur les continuités et les ruptures des pratiques scribales en Égypte pharaoniques, gréco-romaine et byzantine*, edited by Nathan Carlig, Guillaume Lescuyer, Aurore Motte, Nathalie Sojic, 271–281. Liège: Presses Universitaires de Liège.

Casanova, M. 1921. "Alphabets magiques arabes." *Journal Asiatique* 11th series, no. 18: 37–55.

Casey, Christian. 2022. "Egyptian Phonology Beginning from the End." In *In the House of Heqanakht: Text and Context in Ancient Egypt; Studies in Honor of James P. Allen*, edited by M. Victoria Almansa-Villatoro, Silvia Štubňová Nigrelli, and Mark Lehner, 188–202. Harvard Egyptological Studies 16. Leiden: Brill.

Černý, Jaroslav. 1976. *Coptic Etymological Dictionary*. Cambridge: Cambridge University Press.

Chaniotis, Angelos, and Ulrich Thaler. 2006. "Altertumswissenschaften." In *Die Universität Heidelberg im Nationalsozialismus*, edited by Wolfgang U. Eckart, Volker Sellin, and Eike Wolgast, 391–434. Heidelberg: Springer.

Chapa, Juan. 2011. "Su demoni e angeli. Il Salmo 90 nel suo contesto." In *I papyri letterari cristiani: Atti del convegno internazionale di studi in memoria di Mario Naldini, Firenze, 10–11 giugno 2010*, edited by Guido Bastianini and Angelo Casanova, 59–90. Studi e testi di papirologia n.s. 13. Firenze: Istituto Papirologico "G. Vitelli."

Charles, Robert H. 1908. *The Greek Versions of the Testaments of the Twelve Patriarchs*. Oxford: Clarendon Press.

Charlesworth, James H. 1981. *The Pseudepigrapha and Modern Research*. Septuagint and Cognate Studies 7. Reprint with supplement of the 1976 edition. Chico, CA: Scholars Press.

—, ed. 1983. *The Old Testament Pseudepigrapha* 1: *Apocalyptic Literature and Testaments*. Garden City, New York: Doubleday.

Chassinat, Émile. 1921. *Un papyrus médical copte*. Mémoires publiés par les membres de l'Institut français d'archéologie orientale 32. Cairo: IFAO.

—1955. *Le manuscrit magique copte no. 42573 du Musée Égyptien du Caire*. Bibliothèque d'études coptes 4. Cairo: L'Institut français d'archéologie orientale.

Chepel, Elena. 2017. "Invocations of the Blood of Christ in Greek Magical Amulets." *Scrinium* 13, no. 1: 53–71.

Cherkashina (Nurullina), Anna. 2012. Сирийские заклинания как продолжение арамейской заклинательной традиции поздней античности: исследование на материале рукописи

ЦНБ КНЦ РАН 4 (*Syriac Charms as a Continuation of the Aramaic Magical Tradition: A Research Based on the Manuscript CNB KNC RAN 4*). MA Thesis, Russian State University for the Humanities.

—2021. "Соломон и демоны в заклинаниях сирийских христиан (Solomon and the Demons in the Charms of the Syriac Christians in Christian Orient)." *Христианский Восток* (*Christian East*) 9, no. 15: 141–170.

Cherkashina, Anna, Dmitry Cherkashin, and Ortal-Paz Saar. 2022. "Syriac Spells for a Mill and Their Historical Context." *Scrinium* 18, no. 1: 49–84.

Cherkashina, Anna, and Nikita Kuzin. 2022. "'Binding of a Husband': A Syriac Erotic Binding Spell." *Aramaic Studies* 20, no. 2: 154–195.

Cherkashina (Nurullina), Anna, and Alexey Lyavdansky. 2017. "Сирийская версия Сисиниевой легенды" ("The Syriac Versions of St. Sisinnius' Legend"). In Сисиниева легенда в фольклорных и рукописных традициях Ближнего Востока, Балкан и Восточной Европы (*St. Sisinnius' Legend in Folklore and Handwritten Traditions of the Near East, Balkans, and Eastern Europe*), edited by A. L. Toporkov, 203–241. Moscow: Ndrik.

Cherkashina, Anna, and Alexey Lyavdansky. 2021. "Syriac Love Charms. Part I. The Recipe-Type." *Scrinium* 17, no. 1: 68–91.

—2022. "Syriac Love Charms: Part II. The Prayer-Type." *Scrinium* 18, no. 1: 22–48.

Chernetsov, Sevir. 2005. "Ethiopian Magic Texts." Translated by Catriona Kelly. *Forum for Anthropology and Culture* 2: 188–200.

—2006. "Ethiopian Magic Literature." *Scrinium* 2, no. 1: 92–113.

Choat, Malcolm. 2006. *Belief and Cult in Fourth-Century Papyri*. Studia Antiqua Australiensa 1. Turnhout: Brepols.

—2012a. "Christianity." In *Oxford Handbook of Roman Egypt*, edited by Christina Riggs, 474–490. Oxford: Oxford Univeristy Press.

—2012b. "Coptic." In *Oxford Handbook of Roman Egypt*, edited by Christina Riggs, 581–593. Oxford: Oxford Univeristy Press.

—2019. "Gnostic Elements in Ancient Magical Papyri." In *The Gnostic World*, edited by Garry W. Trompf, Gunner B. Mikkelsen, and Jay Johnston, 217–224. London/New York: Routledge.

Choat, Malcolm, and Iain Gardner. 2013. *A Coptic Handbook of Ritual Power (P. Macq. I 1)*. The Macquarie Papyri 1. Turnhout: Brepols.

Chrysikopoulos, Vasilis. 2015. "À l'aube de l'Égyptologie hellénique et de la constitution des collections égyptiennes: Des nouvelles découvertes sur Giovanni d'Anastasi et Tassos Néroutsos." In *Proceedings of the Tenth International Congress of Egyptologists, University of the Aegean, Rhodes, 22–29 May 2008*, vol. 2, edited by Panagiotis E. M. Kousoulis and Nikolaos Lazaridis, 2147–2162. Orientalia Lovaniensia Analecta 241. Leuven: Peeters.

Ciasca, Augustinus. 1889. *Sacrorum Bibliorum Fragmenta Copta-Sahidica Musei Borgiana* 2: *Iussu et sumptibus S. Congregationis de Propaganda Fide*. Rome: Typius Eiusdem S. Congregationis.

Clackson, Sarah J. and Arietta Papaconstantinou. 2010. "Coptic or Greek? Bilingualism in the Papyri." In *The Multilingual Experience in Egypt from the Ptolemies to the Abbasids*, edited by Arietta Papaconstantinou, 73–104. Farnham: Ashgate.

Clarysse, Willy. "A Coptic Invocation to the Angel Orphamiel." *Enchoria* 14 (1986): 155.

Clédat, Jean. 1999. *Le Monastère et la nécropole de Baouit*, edited by Dominique Bénazeth and Marie-Hélène Rutschowscaya, with contributions by Anne Boud'hors, René-Georges Coquin, Éliane Gaillard. Mémoires de l'Institut français d'archéologie orientale du Caire 111. Cairo: Institut français d'archéologie orientale.

Coelho, Francisco A. 1887–1889. "Notas e Parallelos Folkloricos: I – Tradições relativas a S. Cypriano." *Revista Lusitana* 1: 166–174.

Cohen, Martin S. 1983. *The Shi'ur Qomah, Liturgy and Theurgy in Pre-Kabbalistic Jewish Mysticism*. Lanham, MD: University Press of America.

—1985. *The Shi'ur Qomah: Texts and Recensions*. Texte und Studien zum antiken Judentum 9. Tübingen: Mohr/Siebeck.
Colin, Gérard. 1988. "La version éthiopienne de la prière de Pachôme." In *Mélanges Antoine Guillaumont. Contributions à l'étude des christianismes orientaux*, 57–61. Cahiers d'orientalisme 20. Geneva: Patrick Cramer.
Connor, Andrew. 2022. *Confiscation or Coexistence: Egyptian Temples in the Age of Augustus*. New Texts from Ancient Cultures 10. Ann Arbor: University of Michigan Press.
Coquin, René-Georges, and Gérard Gordon. 1990. "Un encomion copte sur Marie-Madeleine attribué à Cyrille de Jérusalem." *Bulletin de l'Institut français d'archéologie orientale* 90: 169–212.
Coulon, Jean-Charles. 2017. *La Magie en terre d'islam au Moyen Âge*. CTHS Histoire 61. Paris: Éditions du Comité des travaux historiques et scientifiques.
Coulon, Jean-Charles, and Korshi Dosoo. 2022. *Magikon Zōon: Animal et magie dans l'Antiquité et au Moyen Âge | Animal and Magic from Antiquity to the Middle Ages*. Bibliothèque d'histoire des textes 2. Paris: Institut de recherche et d'histoire des textes.
Crégheur, Éric. 2019. *Les « deux Livres de Iéou » (MS Bruce 96, 1-3). Les Livres du grand discours mystérique – Le Livre des connaissances du Dieu invisible – Fragment sur le passage de l'âme. Textes établis, traduits et présentés*. Québec: Les Presses de l'Université Laval. Bibliothèque copte de Nag Hammadi, Section Textes 38.
Cribiore, Raffaella. 1996. *Writing, Teachers, and Students in Graeco-Roman Egypt*. American Studies in Papyrology 36. Atlanta: Scholars Press.
Crisci, Edoardo, and Paola Degni. 2011. *La scrittura greca dall'antichità all'epoca della stampa. Una introduzione*. Rome: Carocci.
Cromwell, Jennifer. 2017. *Recording Village Life: A Coptic Scribe in Early Islamic Egypt*. Ann Arbor: University of Michigan Press.
—2022. "Scribal Networks, Taxation, and the Role of Coptic in Marwanid Egypt." In *Egypt and the Eastern Mediterranean World: From Constantinople to Baghdad, 500–1000 CE*, edited by Jelle Bruning, Janneke H. M. De Jong, and Petra M. Sijpesteijn, 353–378. Cambridge: Cambridge University Press.
—2023. "Religious Expression and Relationships Between Christians and Muslims in Coptic Letters from Early Islamic Egypt." In *Religious Identifications in Late Antique Papyri: 3rd–12th Century Egypt*, edited by Mattias Brand and Eline Scheerlinck, 232–247. London: Routledge.
Crum, Walter E. 1896. "Eine Verfluchung." *Zeitschrift für Ägyptische Sprache und Altertumskunde* 34: 85–89.
—1899. "Besprechung – Manuscripts coptes du Musée d'Antiquités des Pays-Bas à Leide." *Orientalistische Literaturzeitung* 1: 17–21.
—1897–1898. "Coptic Studies." *Archaeological Report (Egypt Exploration Fund), 1897–1898*: 55–70.
—1902. "A Bilingual Charm." *Proceedings of the Society of Biblical Archaeology* 24: 329–331.
—1904. Hand-written notes on p. 21 of the copy of *Aegyptische Urkunden aus den Koeniglichen Museen zu Berlin: Koptische Urkunden* 1. Berlin: Weidmannsche Buchhandlung, by Adolf Erman in the Sackler Library, Oxford. Consulted by Edward O. D. Love.
—1905. *Catalogue of the Coptic Manuscripts in the British Museum*. London: British Museum.
—1922. "La Magie copte: nouveaux textes." In *Recueil d'études égyptologiques dédiées à la mémoire de Jean-François Champollion à l'occasion du centenaire de la lettre à M. Dacier relative à l'alphabet des hiéroglyphes phonétiques*, 537–544. Bibliothèque de l'École des Hautes Études 234. Paris: Champion.
—1930. "Ein neues Verbalpräfix im Koptischen." *Zeitschrift für Ägyptische Sprache und Altertumskunde* 65: 124–127.
—1934a, June. "Magical Texts in Coptic I." *Journal of Egyptian Archaeology* 20, no. 1/2: 51–53.

—1934b, November. "Magical Texts in Coptic II." *Journal of Egyptian Archaeology* 20, no. 3/4: 195–200.

—1939. *A Coptic Dictionary*. Oxford: Clarendon Press.

—1942. "Bricks as Birth-Stool." *Journal of Egyptian Archaeology* 28: 69–69.

Cruz-Uribe, Eugene. 2009. "*Stḫ ꜥꜣ Pḥty* 'Seth, God of Power and Might.'" *Journal of the American Research Center in Egypt* 45: 201–226.

Curbera, Jaime B. 1999. "Maternal Lineage in Greek Magical Texts." In *The World of Ancient Magic: Papers from the First International Samson Eitrem Seminar at the Norwegian Institute at Athens, 4 – 8 May 1997*, edited by David R. Jordan, Hugo Montgomery, and Einar Thomassen, 195–203. Bergen: The Norwegian Institute at Athens.

Daniel, Robert W. 1983. "The Testament of Solomon XVIII 27–28, 33–40." In *Papyrus Erzherzog Rainer (P.Rainer Cent.): Festschrift zum 100-jährigen Bestehen der Papyrussammlung der Österreichischen Nationalbibliothek* 1: *Textband*, 294–306. Wien: Hollinek.

—2013. "Testament of Solomon: Addendum to P.Rain.Cent. 39." *Tyche* 28: 37–40.

Daniel, Robert W., and Franco Maltomini. 1990–1992. *Supplementum Magicum*. 2 vols. Abhandlungen der Rheinisch-Westphälischen Akademie der Wissenschaften 16. Sonderreihe Papyrologica Coloniensia. Opladen: Westdeutscher Verlag.

Davidson, Gustav. 1994. *A Dictionary of Angels. Including the Fallen Angels*. New York: Simon and Schuster.

de Bruyn, Theodore S. 2006. "The Use of the Sanctus in Christian Greek Papyrus Amulets." In *Papers presented at the Fourteenth International Conference on Patristic Studies held in Oxford 2003*, edited by Frances M. Young, Mark J. Edwards, and Paul M. Parvis, 15–19. Studia Patristica 40. Leuven: Peeters.

—2017. *Making Amulets Christian: Artefacts, Scribes, and Contexts*. Oxford Early Christian Studies 101. Oxford: Oxford University Press.

de Bruyn, Theodore S., and Jitse Dijkstra. 2011. "Greek Amulets and Formularies from Egypt Containing Christian Elements. A Checklist of Papyri, Parchments, Ostraka, and Tablets." *Bulletin of the American Society of Papyrologists* 48: 163–216.

Dekker, Renate. 2018. *Episcopal Networks and Authority in Late Antique Egypt: Bishops of the Theban Region at Work*. Orientalia Lovaniensia Analecta 264. Leuven: Peeters.

de Lagarde, Paul A. 1867. *Der Pentateuch koptisch*. Leipzig: B.G. Teubner.

—1883. *Aegyptiaca*. Göttingen: Arnoldi Hoyer.

Delatte, Armand. 1927. *Anecdota Atheniensia* 1: *Textes grecs inédits relatifs à l'histoire des religions*. Bibliothèque de la Faculté de philosophie et lettres de l'Université de Liège 36. Liège: H. Vaillant-Carmanne.

Delattre, Alain. 2003. "Les graffitis coptes d'Abydos et la crue du Nil." In *Études Coptes 8. Dixième journée d'études Lille 14–16 juin 2001*, edited by Christian Cannuyer, 133–146. Cahiers de la Bibliothèque Copte 13. Lille: Association francophone de coptologie.

—2007. *Papyrus coptes et grecs du monastère d'apa Apollô de Baouît conservés aux Musées royaux d'art et d'histoire de Bruxelles*. Mémoires de la Classe des lettres, Collection in-8°, 3ᵉ série, tome XLIII, no 2045. Brussels: Académie Royale de Belgique.

—2008. "Textes coptes et grecs d'Antinoé." In *Antinoupolis* I, edited by Rosario Pintaudi, 131–162. Scavi e Materiali 1. Florence: Istituto Papirologico "G. Vitelli."

Delattre, Alain, Perrine Pilette, and Naïm Vanthieghem. 2015. "Papyrus coptes de la Pierpont Morgan Library I: Cinq documents du monastère de Baouît." *Journal of Coptic Studies* 17: 33–53.

Denysenko, Nicholas E. 2016. *The Blessing of Waters and Epiphany: The Eastern Liturgical Tradition*. London: Routledge.

Depauw, Mark, and Willy Clarysse. 2013. "How Christian Was Fourth Century Egypt? Onomastic Perspectives on Conversion." *Vigiliae Christianae* 67, no. 4: 407–435.

—2015. "Christian Onomastics: A Response to Frankfurter." *Vigiliae Christianae* 69.3: 327–329.

Depuydt, Leo. 1993. *Catalogue of Coptic Manuscripts in the Pierpont Morgan Library* 1. Corpus van verluchte handschriften uit de Nederlanden 4–5. Leuven: Peeters.

—2017. "A New Verb Form in Coptic." In *From Gnostics to Monastics. Studies in Coptic and Early Christianity in Honor of Bentley Layton*, edited by David Brakke, Stephen J. Davis, and Stephen Emmel, 213–244. Orientalia Lovaniensia Analecta 263. Leuven/Paris/Bristol, CT: Peeters.

Derchain, Philippe. 1964. "Intailles magiques du Musée de Numismatique d'Athènes." *Chronique d'Égypte* 39, no. 77–78: 177–193.

Derillo, Eyob. 2019. "Traveling Medicine: Medieval Ethiopian Amulet Scrolls and Practitioners Handbooks." In *Toward a Global Middle Ages: Encountering the World Through Illuminated Manuscripts*, edited by Bryan C. Keene, 121–124. Los Angeles: J. Paul Getty Museum.

Dieterich, Albrecht. 1903. *Eine Mithrasliturgie*. Leipzig: B.G. Teubner.

Dickens, Mark, and Natalia Smelova. 2021. "A Rediscovered Syriac Amulet from Turfan in the Collection of the Hermitage Museum." *Written Monuments of the Orient* 7, no. 2: 107–147.

Dickey, Eleanor. 2023. *Latin Loanwords in Ancient Greek: A Lexicon and Analysis*. Cambridge: Cambridge University Press.

Dickie, Matthew W. 2001. *Magic and Magicians in the Greco-Roman World*. London: Routledge.

Dieleman, Jacco. 2005. *Priests, Tongues and Rites: The London-Leiden Magical Manuscripts and Translation in Egyptian Ritual (100–300 CE)*. Religions in the Graeco-Roman World 153. Leiden: Brill.

—2006. "A Coptic Magical Text From the Los Angeles County Museum of Art (LACMA): Ostracon LACMA MA 80.202.214." *Coptica* 5: 20–31.

—2010. "What's in a Sign? Translating Filiation in the Demotic Magical Papyri." In *Multilingual Experience in Egypt, from the Ptolemies to the Abbasids*, edited by Arietta Papaconstantinou, 127–152. Farnham: Ashgate.

—2011. "Scribal Practices in the Production of Magic Handbooks in Egypt." In *Continuity and Innovation in the Magical Tradition*, edited by Gideon Bohak, Yuval Harari, and Shaul Shaked, 85–118. Jerusalem Studies in Religion and Culture 15. Leiden: Brill.

—2019. "The Greco-Egyptian Magical Papyri." In *Guide to the Study of Ancient Magic*, edited by David Frankfurter, 283–321. Religions in the Graeco-Roman World 189. Leiden: Brill.

Dijkstra, Jitse H. 2008. *Philae and the End of Ancient Egyptian Religion: A Regional Study of Religious Transformation (298–642 CE)*. Orientalia Lovaniensia Analecta 173. Leuven: Peeters.

Dijkstra, Jitse, and Jacques van der Vliet. 2019. *The Coptic Life of Aaron: Critical Edition, Translation and Commentary*. Supplements to Vigiliae Christianae 155. Leiden: Brill.

Dobschütz, Ernst von. 1900. "Der Briefwechsel zwischen Abgar und Jesus." *Zeitschrift für wissenschaftliche Theologie* 43, no. 3: 422–86.

—1912. *Das Decretum Gelasianum: De libris recipiendis et non recipiendis*. Texte und Untersuchungen zur Geschichte der altchristlichen Literatur 38, no. 4. Leipzig: J. C. Hinrichs'sche Buchhandlung.

Dodson, Aidan. 2005. "Bull Cults." In *Divine Creatures: Animal Mummies in Ancient Egypt*, edited by Salima Ikram, 72–105. Cairo: American University in Cairo Press.

Donadoni, Sergio. 1965–1966. "Un incantesimo amatorio copto." *Atti della Reale Accademia delle Scienze di Torino, scienze morali, storiche e filologiche* 100: 285–292.

—1986. *Cultura dell'antico Egitto*. Rome: Dipartimento di scienze storiche archeologiche e antropologiche dell'antichità.

Dosoo, Korshi. 2014. "Rituals of Apparition in the Theban Magical Library." PhD thesis, Macquarie University.

—2016. "A History of the Theban Magical Library." *Bulletin of the American Society of Papyrologists* 53: 251–274.

—2018. "Zōdion and Praxis: An Illustrated Coptic Magical Papyrus in the Macquarie University Collection." *Journal of Coptic Studies* 20: 11–56.

—2020. "Circe's Ram: Animals in Ancient Greek Magic." In *Animals in Ancient Greek Religion*, edited by Julia Kindt, 260–288. Abingdon: Routledge.

—2021a. "Auteur et autorité, tradition et révélation: Études de cas de la magies gréco-égyptienne et chrétienne copte." *Revue de l'histoire des religions* 238, no. 4: 673–697.

—2021b. "Healing Traditions in Coptic Magical Texts." *Trends in Classics* 13, no. 1: 44–94.

—2021c. "Isis in Christian Egypt: The Cultural Context of Michigan Ms. Copt. 136 ll.17–34". In *Hymnen und Aretalogien im antiken Mittelmeerraum: Von Inana bis Isis*, edited by Laurent Bricault and Martin Stadler, 195–232. Philippika 154. Wiesbaden: Harrassowitz Verlag.

—2021d. "Ministers of Fire and Spirit: Knowing Angels in the Coptic Magical Papyri." In *Inventer les anges de l'Antiquité à Byzance: Conception, representation, perception*, edited by Delphine Lauritzen, 403–434. Travaux et mémoires 25, no. 2. Paris: Association des Amis du Centre d'Histoire et Civilisation de Byzance.

—2021e. "The Powers of Death: Memory, Place, and Eschatology in a Coptic Curse." *Religion in the Roman Empire* 7, no. 1: 167–194.

—2022a. "Heathen Serpents and Wingless Angels? Some Notes on Images in Coptic Magical Texts." In *The Iconography of Magic: Images of Power and the Power of Images in Ancient and Late Antique Magic*, edited by Raquel Martín Hernández, 117–168. Leuven: Peeters.

—2022b. "'Magical' Adjuration." In *Coptica Sorbonensia. Textes de la 6ᵉ école d'été de papyrologie copte, Paris, 2–11 juillet 2018 (P.Sorb.Copt.)*, edited by Anne Boud'hors and Alain Delattre, 27–39. Studia Papyrologica et Aegyptiaca Parisina 4. Paris: Association des amis du Centre de l'histoire et civilisation de Byzance.

—2022c. "Suffering Doe and Sleeping Serpent: Animals in Christian Magical Texts from Late Roman and Early Islamic Egypt." In *Magikon Zōon: Animal et magie dans l'Antiquité et au Moyen Âge | Animal and Magic from Antiquity to the Middle Ages*, edited by Jean-Charles Coulon and Korshi Dosoo, 495–544. Paris-Orléans: Institut de recherche et d'histoire des textes.

—2022d. "The Composition of the Demotic Magical Papyrus of London and Leiden (*GEMF* 16= *PGM/PDM* XIV)." In *The Greco-Egyptian Magical Formularies: Libraries, Books and Recipes*, edited by Christopher A. Faraone and Sofía Torallas Tovar, 3–233. Ann Arbor: The University of Michigan Press.

—2023a. "Two Body Problems: Binding Effigies in Christian Egypt." In *Drawing Spirit: The Role of Image and Design in the Magical Practice of Late Antiquity*, edited by Jay Johnston and Iain Gardner, 135–184. Berlin/Boston: De Gruyter.

—2023b. "Horus, Sabaoth, Satanas: La 'Bibliothèque de Berlin' et autres fonds d'archives magiques de l'Égypte romaine et les premiers siècles de la période islamique." In *La magie et les sciences occultes dans le monde islamique*, edited by Jean-Charles Coulon, 28–125. Marseille: Diacritiques Éditions.

—Forthcoming a. "(Post-)Colonialism and Ancient Magic." In *Handbook of Classics and Postcolonial Theory*, edited by Ben Akrigg and Katherine Blouin. London: Routledge.

—Forthcoming b. "Magic as Cultural Cross-Roads." In *A Cultural History of Magic: Antiquity*, edited by Esther Eidinow and Richard Gordon. London: Bloomsbury.

—Forthcoming c. "Magical Names: Tracing Religious Changes in Egyptian Magical Texts from Roman and Early Islamic Egypt." *Archiv für Religionsgeschichte*.

Dosoo, Korshi, Edward O.D. Love, and Markéta Preininger. 2022. "The Coptic Magical Papyri Project: Progress Report." *Journal of Coptic Studies* 24: 43–100.

Dosoo, Korshi, and Sofía Torallas Tovar. 2022a. "Anatomy of the Magical Archive." In *The Greco-Egyptian Magical Formularies: Libraries, Books and Recipes*, edited by Christopher A. Faraone and Sofía Torallas Tovar, 3–63. Ann Arbor: The University of Michigan Press.

—2022b. "Roll vs Codex: The Format of the Magical Handbook." In *The Greco-Egyptian Magical Formularies: Libraries, Books and Recipes*, edited by Christopher A. Faraone and Sofía Torallas Tovar, 64–120. Ann Arbor: The University of Michigan Press.

Drescher, James. 1948. "A Coptic Malediction." *Annales du Service des antiquités de l'Égypte* 48: 267–276.

—1950. "A Coptic Amulet." In *Coptic Studies in Honor of Walter Ewing Crum*, edited by Aziz S. Atiya, 265–270. Bulletin of the Byzantine Institute 2. Washington: Byzantine Institute.

—1958. "Two Coptic Magical Ingredients." *Bulletin de la Société d'Archéologie Copte* 14: 59–61.

—1961–1962. "The Coptic Dictionary: Additions and Corrections." *Bulletin de la Société d'Archéologie Copte* 16: 285–288.

—1969. "Graeco-Coptica." *Le Muséon* 82: 85–100.

—1970. *The Coptic (Sahidic) Version of Kingdoms I, II (Samuel I, II)*. Corpus Scriptorum Christianorum Orientalium 313. Scriptores Coptici 35. Leuven: Peeters.

Drijvers, Hendrik J. W. 1992. *Helena Augusta: The Mother of Constantine the Great and the Legend of Her Finding of the True Cross*. Brill's Studies in Intellectual History 27. Leiden: Brill.

Drijvers, Han J. W. and Hendrik J. W. Drijvers. 1997. *The Finding of the True Cross. The Judas Kyriakos Legend in Syriac. Introduction, Text and Translation*. Corpus Scriptorum Christianorum Orientalium 565, Subsidia 93. Leuven: Peeters.

Dunbabin, Katherine M.D. 1989. "*Baiarum grata voluptas*: Pleasures and Dangers of the Baths." *Papers of the British School at Rome* 57: 6–46.

Eidinow, Esther. 2007. *Oracles, Curses, and Risk Among the Ancient Greeks*. Oxford: Oxford University Press.

El Shamsy, Ahmed. 2020. "The Curious Case of Early Muslim Hair Dyeing." In *Islam at 250: Studies in Memory of G.H.A. Juynboll*, edited by Petra M. Sijpesteijn and Camilla Adang, 187–206. Leiden/Boston: Brill.

Emmel, Stephen. 1994. "Ithyphallic Gods and Undetected Ligatures: Pan Is Not 'Ours,' He Is Min (Rectification of a Misreading in a Work of Shenute)." *Göttinger Miszellen* 141: 43–46.

Erman, Adolf. 1895a. "Heidnisches bei den Kopten." *Zeitschrift für Ägyptische Sprache und Altertumskunde* 33: 47–51.

—1904. *Aegyptische Urkunden aus den Koeniglichen Museen zu Berlin* 1: *Koptische Urkunden*. Berlin: Weidmannsche Buchhandlung.

Euringer, Sebastian. 1928. "Das Netz Salomons." *Zeitschrift für Semitistik und verwandte Gebiete* 6: 76–100, 178–199, 300–314.

—1929a. "Bartos=Parthien?" *Zeitschrift für Semitistik und verwandte Gebiete* 7: 214–216.

—1929b. "Das Netz Salomons (Schluß)." *Zeitschrift für Semitistik und verwandte Gebiete* 7: 68–85.

—1937. "Der Spiegel Salomons: Ein abessinisches Amulett." *Zeitschrift der Deutschen Morgenländischen Gesellschaft* 91, n. F. 16: 162–174.

Fabre, David. 2001. "De Seth à Typhon et vice versa." *Égypte, Afrique & Orient* 22: 41–55.

Farag, Lois. 2011. "Miaphysitism." In *The Encyclopedia of Christian Civilization*, edited by George T. Kurian. Chichester: Wiley-Blackwell. https://doi.org/10.1002/9780470670606.wbecc0901 (accessed 21/6/2023).

—2014. "Alexandrian Theology from Athanasius the Great to Timothy II: A Historical Survey of Coptic Orthodox Theology." In *Coptic Civilization: Two Thousand Years of Christianity in Egypt*, edited by Gawdat Gabra, 45–54. Cairo: American University in Cairo Press.

Faraone, Christopher A. 2009. *Ancient Greek Love Magic*. Cambridge, MA./London: Harvard University Press.

—2020. "Simaetha got it Right, After All: Theocritus, Idyll 2, A Courtesan's Pantry and a Lost Greek Tradition of Hexametrical Curses." *Classical Quarterly* 70.2: 650–663.

—2022. "The Traffic in Magical Recipes: Single-Sheet Formularies as Prompts for Oral Performance." In *The Greco-Egyptian Magical Formularies: Libraries, Books and Recipes*, edited by Christopher A. Faraone and Sofía Torallas Tovar, 422–455. Ann Arbor: The University of Michigan Press.

Faraone, Christopher A., and Sofía Torallas Tovar, eds. 2022a. *Greek and Egyptian Magical Formularies* 1: *Text and Translation*. California Classical Studies 9. Berkeley: California Classical Studies.

—2022b. *The Greco-Egyptian Magical Formularies: Libraries, Books and Recipes*. New Texts from Ancient Cultures 11. Ann Arbor: University of Michigan Press.

Fauth, Wolfgang. 2014. *Jao-Jahwe und seine Engel: Jahwe-Apellationen und zugehörige Engelnamen in griechischen und koptischen Zaubertexten*. Studien und Texte zu Antike und Christentum / Studies and Texts in Antiquity and Christianity 88. Tübingen: Mohr Siebeck.

Feder, Frank, ed. 2002. *Biblia Sahidica: Ieremias, Lamentationes (Threni), Epistula Ieremiae et Baruch*. Texte und Untersuchungen zur Geschichte der altchristlichen Literatur 147. Berlin/New York: De Gruyter.

Feydit, Frédéric. 1986. *Amulettes de l'Arménie chrétienne*. Saint Lazare, Venice: Mekhitarist Press for Calouste Gulbenkian Foundation Armenian Library.

Fischer-Elfert, Hans-Werner. 2005. *Altägyptische Zaubersprüche*. Stuttgart: Philipp Reclam.

Fodor, Alexander. 1978. "The Use of Psalms in Jewish and Christian Arabic Magic." In *Jubilee Volume of the Oriental Collection, 1951–1976: Papers Presented on the Occasion of the 25th Anniversary of the Oriental Collection of the Library of the Hungarian Academy of Sciences*, edited by Éva Apor, 67–71. Keleti Tanulmanyok (Oriental Studies) 2. Budapest: Library of the Hungarian Academy of Sciences.

Förster, Hans. 2002. *Wörterbuch der griechischen Wörter in den koptischen dokumentarischen Texten*. Texte und Untersuchungen zur Geschichte der altchristlichen Literatur 148. Berlin: De Gruyter.

Förster, Hans, Kerstin Sänger-Böhm, and Matthias H.O. Schulz. 2021. *Kritische Edition der sahidischen Version des Johannesevangeliums*: *Text und Dokumentation*. Arbeiten zur Neutestamentlichen Forschung 56. Berlin/Boston: De Gruyter.

Fossum, Jarl. 1983. "Jewish-Christian Christology and Jewish Mysticism." *Vigiliae Christianae* 37, no. 3: 260–287.

Fournet, Jean-Luc. 2007. "Disposition et réalisation graphique des lettres et des pétitions protobyzantines: pour une paléographie « signifiante » des papyrus documentaires." In *Proceedings of the 24th International Congress of Papyrology: Helsinki, 1 – 7 August, 2004*, vol. 1, edited by Frösen Jaakko, Tiina Purola, and Erja Salmenkivi, 353–367. Commentationes humanarum litterarum 122. Helsinki: Societas Scientarum Fennica.

—2008. "Parfums et magie dans un papyrus copte inédite de Strasbourg (P.Strasb. K 19)." In *Études coptes 10. Douzième journée d'études (Lyon, 19–21 Mai 2005)*, edited by Anne Boud'hors and Catherine Louis, 157–166. Cahiers de la Bibliothèque Copte 16. Paris: De Boccard.

—2009. "Esquisse d'une anatomie de la lettre antique tardive d'après les papyrus." In *Correspondances. Documents pour l'histoire de l'Antiquité tardive. Actes du colloque international, université Charles-de-Gaulle-Lille 3, 20–22 novembre 2003*, edited by Roland Delmaire, Janine Desmulliez, and Pierre-Louis Gatier, 23–66. Collection de la Maison de l'Orient et de la méditerranée 40. Série littéraire et philosophique 13. Lyon: Maison de l'Orient et de la Méditerranée Jean Pouilloux.

—2019. "Anatomie d'un genre en mutation: la pétition de l'Antiquité tardive." In *Proceedings of the 28th Congress of Papyrology; 2016 August 1-6; Barcelona*, edited by Alberto Nodar and Sofía Torallas Tovar, 571–590. Scripta Orientalia 3. Barcelona: Publicacions de l'Abadia de Montserrat, Universitat Pompeu Fabra.

—2020a. "Les signes diacritiques dans les papyrus documentaires grecs." In *Signes dans les textes 2. Continuités et ruptures des pratiques scribales en Égypte pharaonique, gréco-romaine et byzantine*, edited by Nathan Carlig, Guillaume Lescuyer, Aurore Motte, and Nathalie Sojic, 145–166. Papyrologica Leodiensia 9. Liège: Presses Univ. de Liège.

—2020b. "Temples in Late Antique Egypt: Cultic Heritage between Ideology, Pragmatism, and Artistic Recycling." In *Coptic Literature in Context (4th–13th cent.). Cultural Landscape, Literary Production, and Manuscript Archaeology. Proceedings of the Third Conference of the ERC Project "Tracking Papyrus and Parchment Paths: An Archaeological Atlas of Coptic Literature. Literary Texts in their Geographical Context ('PAThs')"*, edited by Paula Buzi, 29–50. Percorsi, Strumenti e Temi di Archeologia 5. Rome: Edizioni Quasar.

—2022. *The Rise of Coptic: Egyptian versus Greek in Late Antiquity*. The Rostovtzeff Lectures 1. Princeton: Princeton University Press.

Fournet, Jean-Luc, Rodney Ast, Amin Benaissa, Willy Clarysse, Hélène Cuvigny, Alain Delattre, Nick Gonis, Jürgen Hammerstaedt, Federico Morelli, Paul Schubert, Joanne Stolk, and Katelijn Vandorpe. 2022. "Guidelines for Editing Papyri," https://aip.ulb.be//PDF/Guidelines_for_editing_papyri.pdf (accessed 4/4/2023).

Frankfurter, David. 1993. *Elijah in Upper Egypt: The Apocalypse of Elijah and Early Egyptian Christianity*. Studies in Antiquity and Christianity. Minneapolis: Fortress Press.

—1995. "Narrating Power: The Theory and Practice of the Magical Historiola in Ritual Spells." In *Ancient Magic and Ritual Power*, edited by Marvin W. Meyer and Paul Mirecki, 457–476. Religions in the Graeco-Roman world 129. Leiden/New York: Brill.

—1997. "Ritual Expertise in Roman Egypt and the Problem of the Category 'Magician.'" In *Envisioning Magic: A Princeton Seminar and Symposium*, edited by Peter Schäfer and Hans Kippenberg, 115–135. Numen Book Series 75. Leiden: Brill.

—1998. *Religion in Roman Egypt: Assimilation and Resistance*. Mythos: The Princeton/Bollingen Series in World Mythology 645. Princeton, NJ: Princeton University Press.

—2001. "The Perils of Love: Magic and Countermagic in Coptic Egypt." *Journal of the History of Sexuality* 10, no. 3/4: 480–500.

—2007. "Demon Invocations in the Coptic Magic Spells." In *Actes du huitième Congrès international d'Études coptes: Paris, 28 juin–3 juillet 2004*, vol. 2, edited by Nathalie Bosson and Anne Boud'hors, 453–466. Orientalia Lovaniensia Analecta 163. Leuven: Peeters.

—2009. "The Laments of Horus in Coptic: Myth, Folklore, and Syncretism in Late Antique Egypt." In *Antike Mythen: Medien, Transformationen und Konstruktionen; Fritz Graf zum 65. Geburtstag*, edited by Ueli Dill and Christine Walde, 229–251. Berlin: De Gruyter.

—2012. "Amente Demons and Christian Syncretism." *Archiv für Religionsgeschichte* 14: 83–101.

—2014. "Onomastic Statistics and the Christianization of Egypt: A Response to Depauw and Clarysse." *Vigiliae Christianae* 68: 284–289.

—2017. *Christianizing Egypt: Syncretism and Local Worlds in Late Antiquity*. Martin Classical Lectures 34. Princeton: Princeton University Press.

—2019. "Spell and Speech Act: The Magic of the Spoken Word." In *Guide to the Study of Ancient Magic*, edited by David Frankfurter, 608–625. Leiden/Boston: Brill.

—2022. "Shenoute and Magic." In *The Rediscovery of Shenoute: Studies in Honor of Stephen Emmel*, edited by Anne Boud'hors with the assistance of David Brakke, Andrew Crislip, and Samuel Moawad, 299–308. Orientalia Lovaniensia Analecta 310. Leuven/Paris/Bristol, CT: Peeters.

Frantz-Murphy, Gladys. 2004. "Conversion in Early Islamic Egypt: The Economic Factor." In *Muslims and Others in Early Islamic Society*, edited by Robert Hoyland, 323–329. The Formation of the Classical Islamic World 18. London: Routledge.

Frazer, James G. 1925. *The Golden Bough: A Study in Magic and Religion*. Abridged Edition. New York: Macmillan.

Friedman, Florence D., ed. 1989. *Beyond the Pharaohs: Egypt and the Copts in the 2nd to 7th Centuries A.D.* Providence, Rhode Island: Museum of Art, Rhode Island School of Design.

Funk, Wolf-Peter. 1988. "Dialects wanting Homes: A Numerical Approach to the Early Varieties of Coptic." In *Historical Dialectology: Regional and Social*, edited by Jacek Fisiak, 149–192. Trends in Linguistics. Studies and Monographs 37. Berlin: De Gruyter Mouton.

—1991. "Dialects, Morphology of Coptic." In *Coptic Encyclopedia* 8, edited by Aziz S. Atyia, 101–108. New York: Macmillan.

—2017. "Some Lesser Known Prospective and Causative Conjugation Forms in Coptic Dialects and the Problem of Their Ancestry." *Journal of the Canadian Society for Coptic Studies* 9: 53–66.

—2020. "Le problème de la variation du copte littéraire en Moyenne Égypte." In *Études coptes 16. Dix-huitième journée d'études (Bruxelles, 22–24 juin 2017)*, edited by Anne Boud'hors, Esther Garel, Catherine Louis, and Naïm Vanthieghem, 219–228. Cahiers de la bibiothèque copte 23. Paris: Éditions de Boccard.

Gabra, Gawdat, ed. 2014. *Coptic Civilization: Two Thousand Years of Christianity in Egypt*. Cairo: American University in Cairo Press.

Gabrieli, Giuseppe. 1930. *Manoscritti e carte orientali nelle biblioteche e negli archivi d'Italia: Dati statistici e bibliografici delle collezioni. Ioro storia e catalogazione*. Bibliotheca di Bibliografia Italiana 10. Florence: Leo S. Olschki.

Gager, John G., ed. 1992. *Curse Tablets and Binding Spells from the Ancient World*. Oxford/New York: Oxford University Press.

Gallazzi, Claudio, and Patrizia Piacentini. 1998. "Testi copti ed arabi dell'Istituto di Papirologia dell'Università degli Studi di Milano." *Acme. Annali della Facoltà di Filosofia e Lettere dell'Università Statale di Milano* 51, no. 3: 3–21.

Gårdbäck, Johannes B. 2017. "Cyprian Books in the Scandinavian Tradition." In *Cypriana: Old World*, edited by Alexander Cummins, Jesse Hathaway Diaz, and Jennifer Zahrt, 51–82, 2nd ed. Folk Necromancy in Transmission. Seattle: Revelore Press.

Gardiner, Noah. 2012. "Forbidden Knowledge? Notes on the Production, Transmission, and Reception of the Major Works of Aḥmad al-Būnī." *Journal of Arabic and Islamic Studies* 12: 81–143.

Gardner, Iain. 2022. "Types of Christianity: History and Spread, Organisation, Practices and Literature." In *Kellis: A Roman-Period Village in Egypt's Dakhleh Oasis*, edited by Colin A. Hope, and Gillian E. Bowen, 289–306. Cambridge: Cambridge University Press.

—2023a. "The Heidelberg Magical Archive: A Discussion of its Origins, Context and Purpose." In *Drawing Spirit: The Role of Image and Design in the Magical Practice of Late Antiquity*, edited by Jay Johnston and Iain Gardner, 45–71. Berlin/Boston: De Gruyter.

—2023b. "An Archive of Coptic Handbooks and Exemplars for the Making of Amulets and the Enacting of Ritual Power from the Tenth Century (P.Heid. Inv. Kopt. 680–683 and 685–686)." In *Drawing Spirit: The Role of Image and Design in the Magical Practice of Late Antiquity*, edited by Jay Johnston and Iain Gardner, 73–134. Berlin/Boston: De Gruyter.

Gardner, Iain, Anthony Alcock, and Wolf-Peter Funk, eds. 1999. *Coptic Documentary Texts from Kellis 1. P. Kell. V; (P.Kell.Copt. 10–52; O.Kell.Copt. 1–2)*. Dakhleh Oasis Project 9. Oxford: Oxbow Books.

Gardner, Iain, Jason D. BeDuhn, and Paul Dilley. 2018. *The Chapters of the Wisdom of My Lord Mani: Part III: Pages 343-442 (chapters 321-347)*. Leiden: Brill.

Gardner, Iain, and Malcolm Choat. 2004. "Towards a Palaeography of Fourth Century Documentary Coptic." In *Coptic Studies on the Threshold of a New Millennium: Proceedings of the Seventh International Congress of Coptic Studies, Leiden, August 27-September 2, 2000*, vol. 2, edited by Mat Immerzeel and Jacques van der Vliet, 495–503. Leuven/Paris/Dudley, MA: Peeters.

Gardner, Iain, and Jay Johnston. 2019. "'I, Deacon Iohannes, Servant Of Michael': A New Look at P. Heid. Inv. Kopt. 682 and a Possible Context for the Heidelberg Magical Archive." *Journal of Coptic Studies* 21: 29–61.

Gardner, Iain, and Sam N. C. Lieu. 1996. "From Narmouthis (Medinet Madi) to Kellis (Ismant El-Kharab): Manichaean Documents from Roman Egypt." *The Journal of Roman Studies* 86: 146–169.

Garel, Esther. 2018. "Éditer et rééditer les documents coptes fayoumiques du début de l'époque arabe, progrès et perspectives." In *Le Fayoum: Archéologie – Histoire – Religion. Actes du sixième colloque international Montpellier, 26–28 octobre 2016*, edited by Marie-Pierre Chaufray, Ivan Guermeur, Sandra Lippert, and Vincent Rondot, 199–216. Wiesbaden: Harrassowitz Verlag.

—2019. "Relire une lettre fayoumique: l'exemple de SB Kopt. I 280." *Journal of Coptic Studies* 21: 63–71.

—2020. *Héritage et transmission dans le monachisme égyptien. Les testaments des supérieurs du topos de Saint-Phoibammôn à Thebes (P.Mon.PhoibTest.)*. Bibliothèque d'études coptes 27. Cairo: IFAO.

Gaster, Moses. 1900. "Two Thousand Years of a Charm against the Child-Stealing Witch." *Folklore* 11, no. 2: 129–162.

Gaylord, Harry E. 1982. "How Satanael Lost His '-el'." *The Journal of Jewish Studies* 33, no. 1/2: 303–309.

Geliot, Louvan. 1664. *La vraye et parfaite science des armoiries, ou L'indice armorial de feu maistre Louvan Geliot, advocat au parlement de Bourgongne*. Paris: Rouveyre.

Gessel, Wilhelm. 1988. "Das Öl der Martyrer. Zur Funktion und Interpretation der Ölsarkophage von Apamea in Syrien." *Oriens Christianus* 72: 185–204.

Ghica, Victor. 2006. "Les désignations de l'alibouffier et du storax en copte." *Bulletin de l'Institut français d'archéologie orientale* 106: 75–88.

Ghigo, Tea, and María J. Albarrán Martínez. 2021. "The Practice of Writing Inside an Egyptian Monastic Settlement: Preliminary Material Characterisation of the Inks used on Coptic Manuscripts from the Monastery of Apa Apollo at Bawit." *Heritage Science* 9, no. 62.

Ghigo, Tea, Ira Rabin, and Paola Buzi. 2020, March. "Black Egyptian Inks in Late Antiquity: New Insights on Their Manufacture and Use." *Archaeological and Anthropological Sciences* 12, no. 70.

Girard, Louis St.-P. 1927. "Un fragment de liturgie magique copte sur ostrakon." *Annales du Service des antiquités de l'Égypte* 27: 62–68.

Given, Gregory J. 2016. "Utility and Variance in Late Antique Witnesses to the Abgar-Jesus Correspondence." *Archiv für Religionsgeschichte* 17, no. 1: 187–222.

Giversen, Søren. 1959. "Ad Abgarem: The Sahidic Version of the Letter of Abgar on a Wooden Tablet." *Acta Orientalia* 24: 71–82.

Gollancz, Hermann. 1912. *The Book of Protection: Being a Collection of Charms*. London: H. Frowde.

Goodwin, Charles W. 1852. *Fragment of a Græco-Egyptian Work upon Magic: From a Papyrus in the British Museum*. Octavo Publications 2. Cambridge: Deighton.

Gordon, Richard L. 2002. "Shaping the Text: Theory and Practice in Graeco-Egyptian Malign Magic." In *Kykeon: Studies in Honour of H. S. Versnel*, edited by Herman F. J. Horstmanshoff, Henk W. Singor, Folkert T. van Straten, and Johan H.M. Strubbe, 69–111. Religions in the Graeco-Roman World 142. Leiden: Brill.

—2011. "*Signa nova et inaudita*: The Theory and Practice of Invented Signs (*charaktêres*) in Graeco-Egyptian Magical Texts." *MHNH: revista internacional de investigación sobre magia y astrología antiguas* 11: 15–44.

—2014. "*Charaktêres* Between Antiquity and Renaissance: Transmission and Reinvention." In *Les savoirs magiques et leur transmission de l'Antiquité à la Renaissance*, edited by Véronique Dasen and Jean-Michel Spieser, 253–300. Micrologus' Library 60. Florence: Sismel.

—2022. "The Rationale of Multi-Purpose Praxeis in the Formulary Tradition." In *The Greco-Egyptian Magical Formularies: Libraries, Books and Recipes*, edited by Christopher Faraone and Sofía Torallas Tovar, 397–421. New Texts from Ancient Cultures 11. Ann Arbor: University of Michigan Press.

Gorrini, Giovanni. 1904. *L'incendio della Biblioteca Nazionale di Torino/L'incendie de la Bibliothèque Nationale de Turin*, translated by A. Mellé. Turin: Renzo Streglio & cia.

Gottheil, Richard J. H. 1935. "A Fragment on Pharmacy from the Cairo Genizah." *Journal of the Royal Asiatic Society* 67, no. 1: 123–144.

Graf, Georg. 1944. *Geschichte der Christlichen Arabischen Literatur* 1: *Die Übersetzungen*. Studi e testi 118. Vatican City: Biblioteca Apostolica Vaticana.

—1954. *Verzeichnis arabischer kirchlicher Termini*. Corpus Scriptorum Christianorum Orientalum 147, no. 8. 2nd ed. Leuven: Imprimerie orientaliste L. Durbecq.

Graham, Lloyd. 2022. "The Exorcism in *The Magical Book of Mary and the Angels* (P. Heid. Inv. Kopt. 685, 9.13–24) Opens with an Invocation of the Seven Sleepers of Ephesus." *Academia.edu*. https:/www.academia.edu/93511358/The_Exorcism_in_The_Magical_Book_of_Mary_and_the_Angels_P_Heid_Inv_Kopt_685_9_13_24_opens_with_an_invocation_of_the_Seven_Sleepers_of_Ephesus (consulted 13/3/2023).

Green, Michael. 1983. "A Private Archive of Coptic Letters and Documents from Teshlot." *Oudheidkundige Mededelingen Leiden* 64: 61–122.

—1987. "A Late Coptic Magical Text from the Collection of the Rijksmuseum van Oudheden, Leiden." *Oudheidkundige Mededelingen uit het Rijksmuseum van Oudheden te Leiden* 67: 29–43.

—1988. "Additional Notes on the Coptic Magical Text Leiden F 1964/4.14." *Oudheidkundige Mededelingen uit het Rijksmuseum van Oudheden te Leiden* 68: 113–115.

Greenfield, Richard P. H. 1988. *Traditions of Belief in Late Byzantine Demonology*. Amsterdam: Adolf M. Hekkart.

—1989. "Saint Sisinnios, the Archangel Michael and the Female Demon Gylou: The Typology of the Greek Literary Stories." *Byzantina* 15: 83–141.

Greppin, John A.C. 1999. "κόστος: A Fragrant Plant and Its Eastern Origin." *Journal of Indo-European Studies* 27.3/4: 395–408.

Gretser, J. 1734. *Opera omnia. Tomus II. De sancta cruce*. Regensburg.

Griaule, Marcel. 1930. *Le livre de recettes d'un dabtara abyssin*. Travaux et mémoires de l'Institut d'ethnologie 12. Paris: Institut d'Éthnologie.

Griffith, Francis L. 1927. "Oxford Excavations in Nubia–continued." *University of Liverpool Annals of Archaeology and Anthropology* 14: 57–116.

Griffiths, John G. 2001. "Isis." In *The Oxford Encyclopedia of Ancient Egypt* 2, edited by Donald B. Redford, 188–191. Oxford: Oxford University Press.

Grob, Eva M. 2010. *Documentary Arabic Private and Business Letters on Papyrus: Form and Function, Content and Context*. Archiv für Papyrusforschung und verwandte Gebiete – Beihefte 29. New York: De Gruyter.

Grohmann, Adolf. 1917–1918. "Studien zur den Cyprianusgebeten." *Wiener Zeitschrift für die Kunde des Morgenlandes* 30: 121–150.

—1922. *Südarabien als Wirtschaftsgebiet* 1. Osten und Orient 4 = Schriften der Philosophischen Fakultät der Deutschen Universität in Prag 13. Wien: Forschungsinstitut für Osten und Orient.

Grons, Anne. 2021. "The Question of the Effectiveness of Coptic Pharmacological Prescriptions." *Trends in Classics* 13.1: 122–153.

—2022. "Coptic Medical Texts: An Overview of the Corpus and the Present State of Research." In *Médecine et christianisme: Sources et pratiques. Actes du colloque international de Paris, septembre 2016*, edited by Alessia Guardasole, Antonio Ricciardetto and Véronique Boudon-Millot, 187–210. Orient et Méditeranée 40. Leuven: Peeters.

—Forthcoming. *Medizinische Rezepttexte in koptischer Sprache*.

Groom, Nigel, ed. 1997. *New Perfume Handbook*. 2nd ed. London: Blackie Academic and Professional.

Grooth, Marjorie de, and Paul van Moorsel. 1977–1978. "The Lion, the Calf, the Man and the Eagle in Early Christian and Coptic Art." *Bulletin antieke beschaving: Annual Papers on Classical Archaeology* 52–53: 233–245.

Grosser, Felix. 1926. "Ein neuer Vorschlag zur Deutung der Sator-Formel." *Archiv für Religionswissenschaft* 24: 165–169.

Grossman, Eitan, and Martin Haspelmath. 2015. "The Leipzig-Jerusalem Transliteration of Coptic." In *Egyptian-Coptic Linguistics in Typological Perspective*, edited by Alexander Sollee and Gábor Takács, 145–154. Empirical Approaches to Language Typology 55. Hamburg: Widmaier Verlag.

Grossman, Eitan, and Tonio Sebastian Richter. 2017. "Dialectal Variation and Language Change: The Case of Greek Loan-Verb Integration Strategies in Coptic." In *Greek Influence on Egyptian-Coptic: Contact-Induced Change in an Ancient African Language*, edited by Eitan Grossman, Peter Dils, Tonio Sebastian Richter, and Wolfgang Schenkel, 207–236. Lingua Aegyptia: Studia monographica 17. DDGLC working papers 1. Hamburg: Widmaier Verlag.

Grossmann, Peter. 1991. "Epiphany Tanks." In *The Coptic Encyclopedia* 3, edited by Aziz S. Atiya, 968. New York: Macmillan.

Gruenwald, Ithamar. 2014. *Apocalyptic and Merkavah Mysticism*. 2nd ed. Leiden: Brill.

Grumach, Irene. 1970. "On the History of a Coptic *Figura Magica*." In *Proceedings of the Twelfth International Congress of Papyrology: Ann Arbor, Michigan, 13–17 August 1968*, edited by Deborah H. Samuel, 169–182. American Studies in Papyrology 7. Toronto: Hakkert.

Grysa, Bartłomiej. 2010. "The Legend of the Seven Sleepers of Ephesus in Syriac and Arab Sources – A Comparative Study." *Orientalia Christiana Cracoviensia* 2: 45–59.

Guidi, Ignazio. 1888. "Gli Atti apocrifi degli Apostoli: Nei testi copti, arabi ed etiopici." *Giornale della Società Asiatica Italiana* 2: 1–66.

Guillaumont, Antoine, ed. 1988. *Mélanges Antoine Guillaumont: Contributions à l'étude des christianismes orientaux; avec une bibliographie du dédicataire*. Cahiers d'Orientalisme 20. Geneva: Patrick Cramer.

Gundel, Hans Georg. 1968. *Weltbild und Astrologie in den griechischen Zauberpapyri*. Münchener Beiträge zur Papyrusforschung und antiken Rechtsgeschichte 53. Munich: Beck.

Gundel, Wilhelm. 1936. *Dekane und Dekansternbilder. Ein Beitrag zur Geschichte der Sternbilder der Kulturvölker*. Studien der Bibliothek Warburg 19. Glückstadt: J. J. Augustin.

Haelewyck, Jean-Claude. 1998. *Clavis Apocryphorum Veteris Testamenti*. Turnhout: Brepols.

Hagen, Fredrik, and Kim Ryholt. 2016. *The Antiquities Trade in Egypt, 1880–1930: The H. O. Lange Papers*. Scientia Danica. Series H. Humanistica 4, vol. 8. Copenhagen: The Royal Danish Academy of Sciences and Letters.

Hagen, Joost L. 2007. "'The Great Cherub' and His Brothers. Adam, Enoch and Michael and the Names, Deeds and Faces of the Creatures in Ps.-Chrysostom, *On the Four Creatures*." *Actes du huitième Congrès International d'études coptes*, edited by Nathalie Bosson and Anne Boud'hors, 467–480. Orientalia Lovaniensia analecta 163. Leuven: Peeters.

Hägg, Tomas. 1993. "Magic Bowls Inscribed with an Apostles-and-Disciples Catalogue from the Christian Settlement of Hambukol (Upper Nubia)." *Orientalia* 62, no. 4: 376–399.

Hanhart, Robert, ed. 2006. *Septuaginta: Id est Vetus Testamentum graece iuxta LXX interpretes*. Edited by Alfred Rahlfs. Editio altera. 2 vols. Stuttgart: Deutsche Bibelgesellschaft.

Hall, Henry R., ed. 1905. *Coptic and Greek Texts of the Christian Period from Ostraka, Stelae, etc. in the British Museum (O.Brit.Mus.Copt.)*. London: British Museum.

Hallum, Bink. 2020. "New Light on Early Arabic *Awfāq* Literature." In *Islamicate Occult Sciences in Theory and Practice*, edited by Liana Saif, Francesca Leoni, Matthew Melvin-Koushki, and Farouk Yahya, 57–161. Handbook of Oriental Studies. Section 1: The Near and Middle East 140. Leiden: Brill.

Hamilton, Alastair. 2006. *The Copts and the West, 1439–1822: The European Discovery of the Egyptian Church*. Oxford-Warburg Studies 13. New York: Oxford University Press.

Hamann, Carolus. 1871. *Adnotationes criticae et exegeticae in librum Rût ex vetustissimis eius interpretationibus depromptae.* Marburg: N.G. Elwert.
Harari, Yuval. 2019. "Ancient Israel and Early Judaism." In *Guide to the Study of Ancient Magic*, edited by David Frankfurter, 139–174. Leiden/Boston: Brill.
Harnett, Benjamin. 2017. "The Diffusion of the Codex." *Classical Antiquity* 36, no. 2: 183–235.
Harrauer, Christine. 2006. "Abraxas." In *Brill's New Pauly*, edited by Hubert Cancik and Helmuth Schneider. English edition by Christine F. Salazar. Classical Tradition volumes, edited by Manfred Landfester. English edition by Francis G. Gentry. First published online: 2006, doi:http://dx.doi.org/10.1163/1574-9347_bnp_e101040 (accessed 28/3/2023).
Hartman, Dorota M. 2017. "La redazione cristiana del Testamento di Salomone." *Koinonia (Napoli)* 41: 579–605.
Hasitzka, Monika, ed. 1990. *Neue Texte und Dokumentation zum Koptisch-Unterricht.* Mitteilungen aus der Papyrussammlung der Österreichischen Nationalbibliothek (Papyrus Erzherzog Rainer) n.s. 18. Wien: Brüder Hollinek.
—2020. *Koptisches Sammelbuch* 5. Mitteilungen aus der Papyrussammlung der Österreichischen Nationalbibliothek (Papyrus Erzherzog Rainer) n.s. 23, no. 5. Berlin: De Gruyter.
Hazard, Willis H. 1893. "A Syriac Charm." *Journal of the American Oriental Society* 15: 284–296.
Heim, Richard. 1892. "Incantamenta magica graeca et latina." *Jahrbuch für classische Philologie* 19: 465–576. Also as separatum: Leipzig: Teubner, 1892.
Henein, Nessim H., and Thierry Bianquis. 1975. *La magie par les Psaumes: Édition et traduction d'un manuscrit arabe chrétien d'Égypte.* Bibliothèque d'études coptes 12. Cairo: L'Institut français d'archéologie orientale.
Henry, Andrew M. 2016. "Apotropaic Autographs: Orality and Materiality in the Abgar-Jesus Inscriptions." *Archiv für Religionsgeschichte* 17, no. 1: 165–186.
Heurtel, Chantal. 2007. "Marc le prêtre de Saint-Marc." In *Actes du huitième congrès international d'études coptes, Paris, 28 juin – 3 juillet 2004*, edited by Nathalie Bosson and Anne Boud'hors, 727–750. Orientalia Lovaniensia Analecta 163, no. 2. Leuven: Peeters.
—2010. "Écrits et écriture de Marc." In *Études coptes 11. Treizième journée d'études (Marseille, 7–9 juin 2007)*, edited by Anne Boud'hors and Catherine Louis, 139–150. Cahiers de la Bibliothèque copte 17. Paris: De Boccard.
Hevesi, Krisztina. 2015. "The Coptic Medico-Magical Text K 11088 from the Papyrus Collection of the Austrian National Library." *Journal of Coptic Studies* 17: 55–83.
—2018. "P. Stras. K 204 and K 205 An Unpublished Coptic Magical Collection from the Bibliothèque nationale et universitaire de Strasbourg." In *Bild und Schrift auf 'magischen' Artefakten*, edited by Sarah Kiyanrad, Christoffer Theis, and Laura Willer, 49–118. Materiale Textkulturen 19. Berlin/Boston: De Gruyter.
—2019. "A Few Remarks on the Persistence of Native Egyptian historiolae in Coptic Magical Texts." In *Current Research in Egyptology 2018: Proceedings of the Nineteenth Annual Symposium, Czech Institute of Egyptology, Faculty of Arts, Charles University, Prague, 25–28 June 2018*, edited by Marie Peterková Hlouchová, Dana Bělohoubková, Jiří Honzl, and Věra Nováková, 42–54. Oxford: Archaeopress Publishing.
—2022. "The Role of Greek Loanwords in Coptic Magical Texts. Mere Technical Terms or Indicators of Scribal Education?" In *Current Research in Egyptology 2021: Proceedings of the Twenty-First Annual Symposium, University of the Aegean, 9–16 May 2021*, edited by Electra Apostola and Christos Kekes, 237–248. Oxford: Archaeopress Publishing.
Hoch, James E. 2014. *Semitic Words in Egyptian Texts of the New Kingdom and Third Intermediate Period.* Course Book ed. Princeton: Princeton University Press.
Hodak, Suzana. 2012. "The Ostraca of Deir el-Bachit and the Anatolios-Zacharias Archive." In *Coptic Society, Literature and Religion from Late Antiquity to Modern Times. Proceedings of*

the Tenth International Congress of Coptic Studies. Volume I, edited by Paola Buzi, Alberto Camplani, and Federico Contardi, 723–738. Leuven: Peeters.

Hofmann, Heinz. 1977. *Das Satorquadrat: zur Geschichte und Deutung eines antiken Wortquadrats.* Bielefelder Papiere zur Linguistik und Literaturwissenschaft 6. Bielefeld: Universität Bielefeld, Fakultät für Linguistik und Literaturwissenschaft.

—2006. "Sator Square." In *Brill's New Pauly, Antiquity,* edited by Hubert Cancik, and Helmuth Schneider. English edition by Christine F. Salazar, Classical Tradition volumes, edited by Manfred Landfester. English edition by Francis G. Gentry, http://dx.doi.org/10.1163/1574-9347_bnp_e1102210. First published online: 2006 (accessed 30/3/2023).

Holl, Karl. 1915. *Epiphanius* 1: *Ancoratus and Panarion Haer. 1–33.* Leipzig: J. C. Hinrischs'che Buchhandlung.

Honigmann, Ernest. 1953. *Patristic Studies.* Studi e testi / Biblioteca Apostolica Vaticana 173. Vatican: Biblioteca Apostoliza Vaticana.

Hope, Colin A., and Gillian E. Bowen, eds. 2022. *Kellis: A Roman-Period Village in Egypt's Dakhleh Oasis.* Cambridge: Cambridge University Press.

Hopfner, Theodor. 1932. "Mittel- und neugriechische Lekano-, Lychno-, Katoptro- und Onychomantien." In *Studies Presented to F. Ll. Griffith*, 218–232. London: Egypt Exploration Society.

Horner, George W. 1911. *The Coptic Version of the New Testament in the Southern Dialect.* 3 vols. Oxford: The Clarendon Press.

—1920. *The Coptic Version of the New Testament in the Southern Dialect. The Epistles of S. Paul (continued)* 5. Oxford: The Clarendon Press.

—1924. *The Coptic Version of the New Testament in the Southern Dialect. The Catholic Epistles and the Apocalypse* 7. Oxford: The Clarendon Press.

Horrocks, Geoffrey. 1997. *Greek: A History of the Language and Its Speakers.* Harlow: Longman.

Hovorun, Cyril. 2008. *Will, Action and Freedom: Christological Controversies in the Seventh Century.* Leiden: Brill.

Hunter, Erica C.D. 1987. "Saints in Syriac Anathemas: A Form-Critical Analysis of Role." *Journal of Semitic Studies* 32, no. 1: 83–104.

—1990. "Genres of Syriac Amulets: A Study of Cambridge Ms. Syr 3086." *Orientalia Christiana Analecta* 236: 355–368.

House, Juliane, and Dániel Z. Kádár. 2021. *Cross-Cultural Pragmatics.* Cambridge: Cambridge University Press.

Hubert, Henri, and Marcel Mauss. 1902–1903. "Esquisse d'une théorie générale de la magie." *L'Année sociologique* 7: 1–146.

Hyvernat, Henri. 1886. *Les actes des martyrs de l'Egypte tirés des manuscrits coptes de la bibliothèque du Vatican et du musée Borgia* 1. Paris: Ernest Leroux.

Immerzeel, Mat, and Jaques van der Vliet, eds. 2004. *Coptic Studies on the Threshold of a New Millennium: Proceedings of the Seventh International Congress of Coptic Studies Leiden, 27 August – 2 September 2000.* Orientalia Lovaniensia Analecta 133. Leuven: Peeters.

Jacobi, Eliza, C.H. Scheper, and E. Menei. Forthcoming. "A Complete Coptic Codex: A Material Study and Conservation Approach of a Relatively Unknown Bound Papyrus Manuscript." In *Suave Mechanicals: Essays on the History of Bookbinding* 8, edited by Julia Miller. Ann Arbor.

Janowitz, Naomi. 2019. "The Magical Elements of Mysticism: Ritual Strategies for Encountering Divinity." In *Guide to the Study of Ancient Magic*, edited by David Frankfurter, 678–693. Religions in the Graeco-Roman World 189. Leiden: Brill.

Jayme, Erik. 2009. "Ersitzung im Kunstrechtsstreit am Beispiel der Heidelberger Papyrussammlung." *Kunstrechtsspiegel* 3: 138–144.

—2010. "Ersitzung im Kunstrechtsstreit am Beispiel der Heidelberger Papyrussammlung." In *Kunst im Markt - Kunst im Recht: Tagungsband des Dritten Heidelberger Kunstrechtstags am 09. und*

10. Oktober 2009, edited by Matthias Weller, Nicolai Kemle, Thomas Dreier, and Peter Michael Lynen, 129–138. Baden-Baden: Nomos Verlagsgesellschaft mbH & Co. KG.

Jernstedt, Peter V. 1929. "Graeco-Coptica." *Zeitschrift für Ägyptische Sprache und Altertumskunde* 64: 122–135.

—1959. Коптские тексты государственного Эрмитажа (*P.Hermitage*). Moskow: Izd-vo Akademii Nauk SSSR.

Johnson, Maxwell E. 1995. *The Prayers of Sarapion of Thmuis: A Literary, Liturgical, and Theological Analysis.* Orientalia Christiana Analecta 249. Rome: Pontificio Istituto Orientale.

—2010. *Liturgy in Early Christian Egypt.* Gorgias Liturgical Studies 33. Piscataway, NJ: Gorgias Press.

Johnson, William A. 2004. *Bookrolls and Scribes in Oxyrhynchus.* Toronto: University of Toronto Press.

Johnston, Jay, and Iain Gardner. 2018. "Relations of Image, Text and Design Elements in Selected Amulets and Spells of the Heidelberg Papyri Collection." In *Bild und Schrift auf 'magischen' Artefakten*, edited by Sarah Kiyanrad, Christoffer Theis, and Laura Willer, 139–148. Materiale Textkulturen 19. Berlin/Boston: De Gruyter.

—2023. *Drawing Spirit: The Role of Image and Design in the Magical Practice of Late Antiquity.* Berlin: De Gruyter.

Johnston, Sarah I. 2001. "Charming Children: The Use of the Child in Ancient Divination." *Arethusa* 34, no. 1: 97–117.

Jones, Brice C. 2015. "Scribes Avoiding Imperfections in their Writing Materials." *Archiv für Papyrusforschung und verwandte Gebiete* 61, no. 2: 371–383.

—2016. "New Testament Texts on Greek Amulets: From Late Antiquity and Their Relevance for Textual Criticism." PhD Diss., Concordia University, Montreal.

Jördens, Andrea. 2010a. "Editorial: Die Rückkehr des Zauberbuches." *Kunstrechtsspiegel* 4: 146.

—2010b. "Die Heidelberger Papyrussammlung." In *Kunst im Markt - Kunst im Recht: Tagungsband des Dritten Heidelberger Kunstrechtstags am 09. und 10. Oktober 2009*, edited by Matthias Weller, Nicolai Kemle, Thomas Dreier, Peter Michael Lynen, 139–143. Baden-Baden: Nomos Verlagsgesellschaft mbH & Co. KG.

—2015. "Magisches und Verwandtes in der Heidelberger Papyrussammlung." In *Ägyptische Magie und ihre Umwelt*, edited by Andrea Jördens, 1–29. Wiesbaden: Harrassowitz.

Kahle, Paul E. 1954. *Bala'izah. Coptic Texts from Deir el-Bala'izah in Upper Egypt* 1. London: Oxford University Press.

Kalchenko, Evgenia, and Jacques van der Vliet. 2022. "'The Burning Months of the Year'. A Coptic Charm against Fever in Double Transmission." *Journal of Coptic Studies* 24: 203–241.

Kapaló, James, Éva Pócs, and William Ryan, eds. 2013. *The Power of Words: Studies on Charms and Charming in Europe.* Budapest: Central European University Press.

Karabacek, Joseph. 1887. "Das arabische Papier: Eine historisch-antiquarische Untersuchung." *Mitteilungen aus der Sammlung Papyrus Erzherzog Rainer* 2–3: 87–178. Also printed as a special print: 1887. *Das arabische Papier: Eine historisch-antiquarische Untersuchung.* Wien: Verlag der Kaiserl. Königl. Hof- und Staatsdruckerei.

Karlin-Hayter, Patricia. 1991. "*Passio* of the XL Martyrs of Sebasteia: The Greek Tradition; The Earliest Account (BHG 1201)." *Analecta Bollandiana* 109, no. 3–4: 249–304.

Kasser, Rodolphe. 1961. *Exode I–XV, 21 en Sahidique.* Papyrus Bodmer 16. Cologny-Geneva: Bibliotheca Bodmeriana.

—1962. *Deutéronome I–X,7 en Sahidique.* Papyrus Bodmer 18. Cologny-Genève: Bibliotheca Bodmeriana.

—1964. *Compléments au dictionnaire copte de Crum.* Bibliothèque d'études coptes 7. Cairo: L'Institut français d'Archéologie Orientale.

—1965. *Esaïe XLVII, 1–LXVI, 24 en Sahidique*. Papyrus Bodmer 23. Cologny-Genève: Bibliotheca Bodmeriana.
—1980a. "Prolégomènes à un essai de classification systématique des dialectes et subdialectes coptes selon les critères de la phonétique." *Muséon (Le) Louvain* 93, no. 1–2: 53–112.
—1980b. "Prolégomènes à un essai de classification systématique des dialectes et subdialectes coptes selon les critères de la phonétique (II)." *Muséon (Le) Louvain* 93, no. 3–4: 237–297.
—1990. "A Standard System of Sigla for Referring to the Dialects of Coptic." *Journal of Coptic Studies* 1: 141–151.
—1991a. "Alphabets, Coptic." In *The Coptic Encyclopedia* 8, edited by Aziz S. Atiya, 32–41. New York: Macmillan.
—1991b. "Alphabets, Old Coptic." In *The Coptic Encyclopedia* 8, edited by Aziz S. Atiya, 41–45. New York: Macmillan.
—1991c. "Dialects." In *The Coptic Encyclopedia* 8, edited by Aziz S. Atiya, 87–97. New York: Macmillan.
—1991d. "Dialects, Grouping and Major Groups of." In *The Coptic Encyclopedia* 8, edited by Aziz S. Atiya, 97–101. New York: Macmillan.
—1991e. "Dialects, Morphology of Coptic." In *The Coptic Encyclopedia* 8, edited by Aziz S. Atiya, 101–108. New York: Macmillan.
Kasser, Rodolphe, Marvin Meyer, Gregor Wurst, and Francois Gaudard, eds. 2008. *The Gospel of Judas*. 2nd ed. Washington: National Geographic Books.
Kastner, G. Ronald. 1981. "Eudokia." In *A Lost Tradition: Women Writers of the Early Church*, edited by Patricia Wilson-Kastner, 135–171. Lanham, MD: University of America Press.
Kebede, Gidena M. 2017. "Ethiopian Abənnät Manuscripts: Organizational Structure, Language Use, and Orality." PhD Diss., Staats- und Universitätsbibliothek Hamburg Carl von Ossietzky.
Khater, A. 1970. "L'emploi des Psaumes en thérapie avec formules magiques cryptographiques." *Bulletin de la Société d'archéologie copte* 19: 123–176.
Kieckhefer, Richard. 1998. *Forbidden Rites: A Necromancer's Manual of the Fifteenth Century*. Magic in History 2. University Park: Pennsylvania State University Press.
—2014. *Magic in the Middle Ages*. 2nd ed. Cambridge: Cambridge University Press.
King, Anya H. 2017. *Scent from the Garden of Paradise: Musk and the Medieval Islamic World*. Islamic History and Civilization 140. Leiden: Brill.
—2020. "Gilding Textiles and Printing Blocks in Tenth-Century Egypt." *Journal of the American Oriental Society* 140, no. 2: 455–465.
Kippenberg, Hans G. 1997. "Magic in Roman Civil Discourse: Why Rituals Could Be Illegal." In *Envisioning Magic: A Princeton Seminar and Symposium*, edited by Hans G. Kippenberg and Peter Schäfer, 137–163. Numen Book Series 75. Leiden: Brill.
Kircher, Athanasius. 1665. *Arithmologia, sive De Abditis Numerorum Mysteriis*. Rome: Varesius.
Kitchen, Kenneth A. 2001. "Osiris." In *The Oxford Encyclopedia of Ancient Egypt* 2, edited by Donald B. Redford, 615–620. Oxford: Oxford University Press.
Klein, Ernest. 1987. *A Comprehensive Etymological Dictionary of the Hebrew Language for Readers of English*. Jerusalem: Carta.
Klutz, Todd. 2005. *Rewriting the Testament of Solomon: Tradition, Conflict, and Identity in a Late Antique Pseudepigraphon*. Library of Second Temple Studies 53. London/New York: T & T Clark.
Köpstein, Sylvia. 1996. "Carl August Reinhardt: Kaufmann, Philologe, Sammler, Konsul." In *Mitteilungen aus der Arbeit am Wörterbuch der Ägyptischen Sprache* 5, edited by Walter F. Reineke, 13–59. Berlin: Altägyptisches Wörterbuch.
Kosack, Wolfgang. 1974. *Lehrbuch des Koptischen*. Graz: Akadem. Druck u. Verlagsanst.
Krall, Jakob. 1886–1887. "Über die Anfänge der koptischen Schrift." In *Mittheilungen aus der Sammlung der Papyrus Erzherzog Rainer* 1, 109–112. Wien: Verlag der K.K. Hof- u. Staatsdr.

Kramers, J.H., C.E. Bosworth, O. Schumann, and Ousmane Kane. 2012. "Sulṭān." In *Encyclopaedia of Islam*, 2nd ed., edited by P. Bearman, Th. Bianquis, C.E. Bosworth, E. van Donzel, and W.P. Heinrichs. Leiden: Brill. http://dx.doi.org/10.1163/1573-3912_islam_COM_1115 (accessed 21/6/2023).

Kraus, Thomas. 2005. "Septuaginta-Psalm 90 in apotropäischer Verwendung: Vorüberlegungen für eine kritische Edition und (bisheriges) Datenmaterial." *Biblische Notizen* 125: 39–73.

Kropp, Angelicus. 1930–1931. *Ausgewählte koptische Zaubertexte*. 3 vols. Brussels: Édition de la Fondation Égyptologique Reine Élisabeth.

—1965. *Oratio Mariae ad Bartos: Ein koptischer Gebetstext aus den Giessener Papyrus-Sammlungen*. Giessen: Universitätsbibliothek.

—1966. *Der Lobpreis des Erzengels Michael (vormals P. Heidelberg Inv. Nr. 1686)*. Brussels: Fondation égyptologique reine Elisabeth.

Krueger, Frederic. 2020. *Andreas von Hermonthis und das Kloster des Apa Hesekiel: Mikrohistorische Untersuchungen zu Kirchengeschichte und Klosterwesen im Gebiet von Armant (Oberägypten) in byzantinischer Zeit anhand der koptischen Ostraka der Universitätsbibliothek Leipzig (O.Lips. Copt. II)*. Archiv für Papyrusforschung und verwandte Gebiete – Beihefte 43. Berlin/Boston: De Gruyter.

—2021. "The Monastery of Apa Posidonios at Hermonthis and an Alleged Local Cult of 'Poseidon' (with Notes on 'Kothos' and the Supposed Fish-Cult at Latopolis)." *Archiv für Papyrusforschung und verwandte Gebiete* 67, no. 1: 110–137.

—2022. "The Angel of the Topos Shall Bless You": Preliminary Report on the Cult of the Altar-Angels in Late Antique Egypt." *Zeitschrift für Antikes Christentum/Journal of Ancient Christianity* 26, no. 2: 284–304.

—Forthcoming "'You Are the Pillar of Light That Supports the Whole World': A Letter to Pesynthios of Koptos, Late Antique Concepts of a 'Pillar of Light' and New Evidence for the Christian Redaction of the *History of the Captivity in Babylon*" *Archiv für Papyrusforschung*.

Kuczkiewicz-Fraś, Agnieszka. 2003. "Medical Terminology of Perso-Arabic Origin in Hindi." In *Zeszyty Naukowe Uniwersytetu Jagiellońskiego*, edited by Stanisław Stachowski, 153–172. Krakow: Wydawnictwo Uniwersytetu Jagiellońskiego.

Kuhn, Karl H. 1970. "A Coptic Jeremiah Apocryphon." *Muséon* 83: 95–135, 291–350.

Kühnel, Bianca. 1986–1987. "Jewish Symbolism of the Temple and the Tabernacle and Christian Symbolism of the Holy Tabernacle and the Heavenly Tabernacle." *Journal of Jewish Art* 12–13: 147–68.

Łajtar, Adam, and Jacques van der Vliet. 2011. "A Late Christian Ostracon from Dongola." In *Nubian Voices: Studies in Christian Nubian Culture*, edited by Adam Łajtar and Jacques van der Vliet, 133–140. Journal of Juristic Papyrology Supplement 15. Warsaw: University of Warsaw.

—2017. *Empowering the Dead in Christian Nubia: The Texts from a Medieval Funerary Complex in Dongola*. Journal of Juristic Papyrology Supplement 32. Warsaw: University of Warsaw.

Lambert, John C. 1916. "Abyss." In *Dictionary of the Apostolic Church* 1, edited by James Hastings, 11–12. New York: Charles Scribner's Sons.

Lampe, Geoffrey W.H. 1961. *A Patristic Greek Lexicon*. Oxford: Oxford University Press.

Lane, Edward W. 1863. *Arabic-English Lexicon*. London: Williams & Norgate.

Lange, Hans O. 1932. "Ein faijumischer Beschwörungstext." In *Studies Presented to F. Ll. Griffith*, 161–166. London: Egypt Exploration Society.

Langlois, Michael. 2010. "Shemihazah et compagnie(s). Onomastique des anges déchus dans les manuscrits araméens du Livre d'Hénoch." In *Aramaica Qumranica: Proceedings of the Conference on the Aramaic Texts from Qumran in Aix-en-Provence 30 June – 2 July 2008*, edited by Katell Berthelot and Daniel Stökl Ben Ezra, 145–180. Studies on the Texts of the Desert of Judah 94. Leiden: Brill.

Lanne, Emmanuel. 1958. *Le grand euchologe du Monastère Blanc*. Patrologia Orientalis 28, no. 2 = 135. Paris: Firmin-Didot.

Lantschoot, Arnold van. 1929. *Recueil des colophons des manuscrits chrétiens d'Égypte: Les colophons coptes des manuscrits sahidiques*. Leuven: Istas.

—1951. "Miracles opérés par la S. Vierge Marie à Bartos". In *Miscellanea Biblica et Orientalia: R. P. Athanasio Miller O.S.B. complexis 70 annis oblata*, edited by Adalberti Metzinger, 504–511. Studia Anselmiana 27–28. Rome: Orbis Catholicus.

Lanzillotta, Lautaro Roig, and Jacques van der Vliet. 2022. *The Apocalypse of Paul (Visio Pauli) in Sahidic Coptic: Critical Edition, Translation and Commentary*. Leiden: Brill, .

Layton, Bentley. 2000. *A Coptic Grammar: With Chrestomathy and Glossary; Sahidic Dialect*. Porta Linguarum Orientalium, n.s., 20. Wiesbaden: Harrassowitz.

Leclercq, Henri. 1936. "Oratio Cypriani." In *Dictionnaire d'archéologie chrétienne et liturgie* 12, no. 2, edited by Fernand Cabrol and Henri Leclercq, 2332–2345. Paris: Letouzey et Ané.

Legendre, Marie. 2014. "Perméabilité linguistique et anthroponymique entre copte et arabe: L'exemple de comptes en caractères coptes du Fayoum fatimide." In *Coptica Argentoratensia: Textes et Documents de la Troisième Université d'Été de Papyrologie Copte (Strasbourg, 18-25 juillet 2010); P. Stras. Copt.*, edited by Anne Boud'hors, Alain Delattre, Catherine Louis, and Tonio Sebastian Richter, 325–440. Cahiers de la Bibliothèque copte 19. Paris: De Boccard.

Lehrich, Christopher I. 2003. *The Language of Demons and Angels: Cornelius Agrippa's Occult Philosophia*. Brill's Studies in Intellectual History 119. Leiden: Brill.

Leitão, José V. 2015. "The Folk and Oral Roots of the Portuguese 'Livro de São Cipriano'." *International Journal of Heritage and Sustainable Development* 4, no. 1: 129–139.

—2017. "Searching for Cyprian in Portuguese Ethnography." In *Cypriana: Old World*, edited by Alexander Cummins, Jesse Hathaway Diaz, and Jennifer Zahrt, 117–162, 2nd ed. Folk Necromancy in Transmission. Seattle: Revelore Press.

Lesses, Rebecca. 1995. "The Adjuration of the Prince of the Presence: Performative Utterance in a Jewish Ritual." In *Ancient Magic and Ritual Power*, edited by Marvin W. Meyer and Paul Mirecki, 185–206. Religions in the Graeco-Roman world 129. Leiden/New York: Brill.

Lev, Yaacov. 2012. "Coptic Rebellions and the Islamization of Medieval Egypt (8th–10th Century): Medieval and Modern Perceptions." *Jerusalem Studies in Arabic and Islam* 39: 303–344.

Lev, Efraim, and Zohar Amar. 2008. *Practical Materia Medica of the Medieval Eastern Mediterranean According to the Cairo Genizah*. Sir Henry Wellcome Asian Series 7. Leiden: Brill.

Levene, Dan, Dalia Marx, and Siam Bhayro. 2014. "'Gabriel is On Their Right': Angelic Protection in Jewish Magic and Babylonian Lore." *Studia Mesopotamica* 1: 185–198.

Levey, Martin. 1962. "Mediaeval Arabic Bookmaking and Its Relation to Early Chemistry and Pharmacology." *Transactions of the American Philosophical Society* 52, no. 4: 1–79.

Lewis, Naphtali. 1974. *Papyrus in Classical Antiquity*. Oxford: Clarendon Press.

Lexa, František. 1925. *La magie dans l'Égypte antique de l'Ancien Empire jusqu'à l'époque copte 2: Les textes magiques.* Paris: Librairie orientaliste P. Geuthner.

LiDonnici, Lynn R. 2001. "Single-Stemmed Wormwood, Pinecones and Myrrh: Expense and Availabitity of Recipe Ingredients in the Greek Magical Papyri." *Kernos* 14: 61–91.

Little, Donald P. 1976. "Coptic Conversion to Islam under the Baḥrī Mamlūks, 692–755/1293–1354." *Bulletin of the School of Oriental and African Studies, University of London* 39, no. 3: 552–569.

Loebenstein, Helene. 1983. "Vom 'Papyrus Erzherzog Rainer' zur Papyrus-sammlung der Österreichischen Nationalbibliothek: 100 Jahre Sammeln, Bewahren, Edieren." In *Festschrift zum 100-jährigen Bestehen der Papyrussammlung der Österreichischen Nationalbibliothek: Papyrus Erzherzog Rainer (P.Rainer Cent.)* 1, edited by Josef Zessner-Spitzenberg, 3–39. Vienna: Hollinek.

López-Sampson, Arlene, and Tony Page. 2018, March. "History of Use and Trade of Agarwood." *Economic Botany* 72, no. 1: 107–129.

Love, Edward O. D. 2016. *Code-Switching with the Gods. The Bilingual (Old Coptic-Greek) Spells of PGM IV (P. Bibliothèque Nationale Supplément Grec. 574) and their Linguistic, Religious, and Socio-Cultural Context in Late Roman Egypt*. Zeitschrift für Ägyptische Sprache–Beihefte 4. Berlin: De Gruyter.

—2021a. *Script Switching in Roman Egypt: Case Studies in Script Conventions, Domains, Shift, and Obsolescence from Hieroglyphic, Hieratic, Demotic, and Old Coptic Manuscripts*. Archiv für Papyrusforschung und verwandte Gebiete – Beihefte 46. Berlin: De Gruyter.

—2021b. "The Nature of Old Coptic I: Approaching and Contextualising Old Coptic (§1–4). Old Coptic at Oxyrhynchus (§5)." *Journal of Coptic Studies* 23: 91–143.

—2022a. "Bilingualism and Mono-/Bigraphia at the Nexus of Magical Traditions: From Egyptian-Greek to Coptic-Arabic Magical Texts." In *Christians and Muslims in Early Islamic Egypt: New Texts and Studies*, edited by Lajos Berkes, 169–201. American Studies in Papyrology 56. Ann Arbor: University of Michigan Press.

—2022b. "'Crum's Chicken': Alpak, Demonised Donkeys, and Avianised Demons among the Figures of Demotic, Greek, and Coptic Magical Texts." In *Magikon Zōon: Animal et magie dans l'Antiquité et au Moyen Âge | Animal and Magic from Antiquity to the Middle Ages*, edited by Jean-Charles Coulon and Korshi Dosoo, 661–726. Paris-Orléans: Institut de recherche et d'histoire des textes.

—2022c. "Apa Baula and The Destroyer: The Embedding of Efficacy in Figural Amulets/Deposits from Roman and Early Islamic Egypt." In *Magikon Zōon: Animal et magie dans l'Antiquité et au Moyen Âge | Animal and Magic from Antiquity to the Middle Ages*, edited by Jean-Charles Coulon and Korshi Dosoo, 621–659. Paris-Orléans: Institut de recherche et d'histoire des textes.

—2022d. "The Nature of Old Coptic II: Old Coptic at Tebtunis (§ 6), Soknopaiou Nesos (§ 7), and Narmouthis (§ 8)." *Journal of Coptic Studies* 24: 243–281.

—2022e. *Petitioning Osiris. The Old Coptic Schmidt Papyrus and Curse of Artemisia in Context among the Letters to Gods from Egypt*. Zeitschrift für Ägyptische Sprache und Altertumskunde – Beihefte 11. Berlin: De Gruyter.

Ludwich, Arthur. 1897. *Eudociae Augustae Procli Lycii Claudiani carminum Graecorum reliqiuiae*. Leipzig: B.G. Teubner.

Luijendijk, AnneMarie. 2008. *Greetings in the Lord: Early Christians and the Oxyrhynchus Papyri*. Harvard Theological Studies 60. Cambridge, MA: Harvard Divinity School.

Luisier, Philippe. 2014. "Il miafisismo, un termine discutibile della storiografia recente: problemi teologici ed ecumenici." *Cristianesimo nella storia* 35, no. 1: 297–307.

Lundhaug, Hugo. 2021. "Dating and Contextualising the Nag Hammadi Codices and Their Texts: A Multi-Methodological Approach Including Radiocarbon Evidence." In *Texts in Context: Essays on Dating and Contextualising Christian Writings of the Second and Early Third Century*, edited by Jos Verheyden, Jens Schröter, and Tobias Nicklas, 117–142. BETL 319. Leuven: Peeters.

Lyavdansky, Alexey. 2011. "Syriac Charms in Near Eastern Context: Tracing the Origin of Formulas." In *Oral Charms in Structural and Comparative Light: Proceedings of the Conference of the International Society for Folk Narrative Research's (ISFNR); Committee on Charms, Charmers and Charming, 27–29 October 2011*, edited by Tatyana A. Mikhailova, Jonathan Roper, Andrey L. Toporkov, and Dmitry S. Nikolayev, 15–21. Moscow: PROBEL-2000.

MacCoull, Leslie S.B. 1975. "Coptic Papyri in the Beinecke Collection at Yale University." In *Proceedings of the XIV International Congress of Papyrologists, Oxford, 24–31 July 1974*, 217–219. Graeco-Roman Memoirs 61. London: Egypt Exploration Society.

—1982. "*P. Morgan Copt.*: Documentary Texts from the Pierpont Morgan Library." *Bulletin de la Société d'archéologie copte* 24: 1–19.

—1989. "The Teshlot Papyri and the Survival of Documentary Coptic in the Eleventh Century." *Orientalia Christiana Periodica* 55: 201–206.

—1997. "Dated and Datable Coptic Documentary Hands Before AD 700." *Le Muséon* 110, no. 3–4: 349–366.

Macomber, William F. 2020. *The Scala Magna of Shams al-Ri'āsah Abū al-Barakāt*. 2 vols. Corpus scriptorum Christianorum orientalium 684. Leuven: Peeters.

Madey, Johannes, and Karapet Amatowni. 1982. *The Eucharistic Liturgy in the Christian East*. Kottyam: Prakasam Publ.

Maguire, Henry, ed. 1995. *Byzantine Magic*. Washington, D.C.: Dumbarton Oaks Research Library and Collection.

Malara, Diego M. 2022. "Sympathy for the Devil: Secrecy, Magic and Transgression among Ethiopian Orthodox Debtera." *Ethnos* 87, no. 3: 444–462.

Malinowski, Bronisław. 1935. *Coral Gardens and Their Magic*. 2 vols. New York: American Book Co.

Marathakis, Ioannis, ed. 2012. *The Magical Treatise of Solomon, Or Hygromanteia: Also Called the Apotelesmatikē Pragmateia, Epistle to Rehoboam, Solomōnikē: Being a Translation of Mss. Harleianus 5596, Bononiensis 3632, Atheniensis 1265, Gennadianus 45, Atheniensis 115, Parisinus 2419, Monacensis Gr. 70, Supplemented by a Number of Other Greek Manuscripts*. Sourceworks of Ceremonial Magic Series 8. Singapore: Golden Hoard Press.

Marcovich, Miroslav. 1983. "Sator Arepo = Γεωργος Ἁρπον (Κνουφι) Ἁρπως, Harpo(crates)." *Zeitschrift für Papyrologie und Epigraphik* 50: 155–171.

Marjanen, Antti. 2004. "A Nag Hammadi Contribution to the Discussion about the Pronunciation of the Tetragrammaton." *Studia Orientalia Electronica* 99: 153–160.

Markschies, Christoph. 2009. "Carl Schmidt und kein Ende: Aus großer Zeit der Koptologie an der Berliner Akademie und der Theologischen Fakultät der Universität." *Zeitschrift für antikes Christentum* 13: 5–28.

Marro, Giovanni. 1952. "Bernardino Drovetti archeologo." *Aegyptus* 32, no. 1: 121–130.

Martín Hernández, Raquel. 2019. "More than a Logos. The Ιωερβηθ Logos in Context." In *Litterae Magicae: Studies in Honour of Roger S. O. Tomlin*, edited by Celia Sánchez Natalías, 187–209. Supplementa MHNH 2. Zaragoza: Libros Pórtico.

Martín Hernández, Raquel, and Arie Shaus. 2022. "New Technologies for Tracing Magical Texts and Drawings: Experience with Automatic Binarization Algorithms." In *The Materiality of Greek and Roman Curse Tablets: Technological Advances*, edited by Sofía Torallas Tovar and Raquel Martín Hernández, 33–43. Chicago: The Oriental Institute.

Martín Hernández, Raquel, and Sofía Torallas Tovar. 2012. "'You Who Impose Sleep Upon Abimelech For Seventy Two Years': An Egyptian Spell Against Insomnia." In *Contesti magici = Contextos mágicos: Convegno internazionale*, edited by Marina Piranomonte and Francisco Marco Simón, 309–312. Rome: L'Erma di Bretschneider.

—2014. "A Magical Spell on an Ostracon at The Abbey of Montserrat." *Zeitschrift für Papyrologie und Epigraphik* 189: 175–184.

—2014. "The Use of the Ostracon in Magical Practice in Late Antique Egypt. Magical handbooks vs. Material Evidence." *Studi e Materiali di Storia delle Religioni* 80, no. 2: 780–800.

Martinez, David G. 1995. "'May She Neither Eat Nor Drink': Love Magic and Vows of Abstinence." In *Ancient Magic and Ritual Power*, edited by Marvin W. Meyer and Paul Mirecki, 335–359. Religions in the Graeco-Roman world 129. Leiden/New York: Brill.

Maspero, Gaston. 1892. *Fragments de la version thébaine de l'Ancien Testament*. Mémoires publiés par les membres de la Mission archéologique française du Caire (=MMAF) 6ème tome, fasc. 1. Paris: Ernest Leroux.

Mastrocinque, Attilio. 2012. "Les *charaktêres*, formes des dieux d'après les papyri et les gemmes magiques." In *La raison des signes : Présages, rites, destin dans les sociétés de la méditerranée ancienne*, Stella Georgoudi, Renée Koch Piettre and Francis Schmidt, 537–546. Religions in the Graeco-Roman World, Volume: 174. Leiden: Brill.

Mauss, Marcel. 1972. *A General Theory of Magic*. Translated by Robert Brain. London: Routledge & Kegan Paul.

Mazza, Roberta. 2019. "Dating Early Christian Papyri: Old and New Methods—Introduction." *Journal for the Study of the New Testament* 42, no. 1: 46–57.

McCown, Chester C. 1922. *The Testament of Solomon: Edited from Manuscripts at Mount Athos, Bologna, Holkham Hall, Jerusalem, London, Milan, Paris and Vienna*. Leipzig: J.C. Hinrichs'sche Buchhandlung.

Meinardus, Otto F.A. 1968. "The Twenty-Four Elders of the Apocalypse in the Iconography of the Coptic Church." *Studia Orientalia Christiana* 13: 141–157.

Meltzer, Edmund S. 2001. "Horus". In *The Oxford Encyclopedia of Ancient Egypt* 2, edited by Donald B. Redford, 119–122. Oxford: Oxford University Press.

Ménonville, Siena de. 2018a. "Approaching the Debtera in Context: Socially Reprehensible Emotions and Talismanic Treatment in Contemporary Northern Ethiopia." *Cahiers d'études africaines* 231–232: 1001–1028.

—2018b. "In Search of the Debtera: An Intimate Narrative on Good and Evil in Ethiopia Today." *Journal of Religion in Africa* 48, no. 1–2: 105–144.

Mercier, Jacques. 1974. "Les peintures des rouleaux protecteurs éthiopiens." *Journal of Ethiopian Studies* 12, no. 2: 107–146.

—1988. *Asrès, le magicien éthiopien. Souvenirs 1895–1985*. Paris: J. C. Lattès.

Merkelbach, Reinhold, and Maria Totti. 1991. *Abrasax. Ausgewählte Papyri religiösen und magischen Inhalts* 2: *Gebete (Fortsetzung)*. Papyrologica Coloniensia 17, no. 2. Opladen: Westdeutscher Verlag.

Meyer, Marvin W. 1988. *Rossi's "Gnostic" Tractate*. Occasional Papers of the Institute for Antiquity and Christianity 13. Claremont: Institute for Antiquity and Christianity.

—1996. *The Magical Book of Mary and the Angels (P.Heid. Inv. Kopt. 685); Text, Translation and Commentary*. Veröffentlichungen aus der Heidelberger Papyrus-Sammlung 9. Heidelberg: Universitätsverlag C. Winter.

—1999. "The Magical Book of Mary and the Angels (*P.Heid. Inv. Kopt. 685*)." In *Ägypten und Nubien in spätantiker und christlicher Zeit: Akten des 6. Internationalen Koptologenkongresses, Münster, 20. – 26. Juli 1996* 2: *Schrifttum, Sprache und Gedankenwelt*, edited by Steven Emmel, Martin Krause, Siegfied G. Richter, and Sofia Schaten, 287–294. Sprachen und Kulturen des christlichen Orients 6, 2. Wiesbaden: Reichert.

—2001. "The Prayer of Mary Who Dissolves Chains in Coptic Magic and Religion." In *Magic and Ritual in the Ancient World*, edited by Paul Mirecki and Marvin Meyer, 405–415. Religions in the Graeco-Roman World 141. Leiden: Brill.

—2003. "The Prayer of Mary in the Magical Book of Mary and the Angels." In *Prayer, Magic, and the Stars*, edited by Scott Noegel and Brandon Wheeler, 57–67. University Park: Pennsylvania State University Press.

—2004. "Mary Dissolving More Chains in Coptic Museum Papyrus 4958 and Elsewhere." In *Coptic Studies on the Threshold of a New Millennium: Proceedings of the Seventh International Congress of Coptic Studies Leiden, 27 August – 2 September 2000*, edited by Mat Immerzeel and Jacques van der Vliet, 369–376. Orientalia Lovaniensia Analecta 133. Leuven: Peeters.

—2013. "The Persistence of Ritual in the Magical Book of Mary and the Angels: *P.Heid. Inv. Kopt. 685*." In *Practicing Gnosis: Ritual, Magic, Theurgy and Liturgy in Nag Hammadi, Manichaean and Other Ancient Literature. Essays in Honor of Birger A. Pearson*, edited by April D. DeConick, Gregory Shaw, and John D. Turner, 359–376. Nag Hammadi and Manichaean Studies 85. Leiden: Brill.

Meyer, Marvin W., and Paul Mirecki. 1995. *Ancient Magic and Ritual Power.* Religions in the Graeco-Roman World 129. Leiden: Brill.

Meyer, Marvin W., and Richard Smith. 1994. *Ancient Christian Magic: Coptic Texts of Ritual Power.* San Francisco: Harper.

Meyerhof, Max. 1931. "Alî at-Tabarî's 'Paradise of Wisdom,' One of the Oldest Arabic Compendiums of Medicine." *Isis* 16, no. 1: 6–54.

Meyrat, Pierre. 2019. "Les papyrus magiques du Ramesseum." *Recherches sur une bibliothèque privée de la fin du Moyen Empire.* Bibliothèque d'étude 182. Cairo: Institut français d'archéologie orientale.

Mihálykó, Ágnes T. 2015. "Christ and Charon: *PGM* P13 Reconsidered." *Symbolae Osloenses* 89: 183–209.

—2018a. "5. Amulet Against Fever: P.Heid. Inv. Kopt. 407." In *Coptica Palatina, Coptica Palatina: Koptische Texte aus der Heidelberger Papyrussammlung (P.Heid.Kopt.); Bearbeitet auf der Vierten Internationalen Sommerschule für Koptische Papyrologie, Heidelberg, 26. August – 9. September 2012,* edited by Boud'hors, Alain Delattre, Tonio Sebastian Richter, Gesa Schenke, and Georg Schmelz, 51–53. Studien und Texte aus der Heidelberger Papyrussammlung 1. Heidelberg: Heidelberg University Publishing.

—2018b. "The Thrice-Blessed Pesynthios of Koptos and the Presanctified Holies: Some Notes on a Coptic Pastoral Letter (P. Berol. 11346)." *Adamantius* 24: 143–149.

—2019. *The Christian Liturgical Papyri: An Introduction.* Studies and Texts in Antiquity and Christianity 114. Tübingen: Mohr Siebeck.

—2021. "Healing in Christian Liturgy in Late Antique Egypt: Sources and Perspectives." In *Trends in Classics* 13, no. 1: 154–194.

—2022. "Mary, Michael and the Twenty-Four Elders: Saints and Angels in Christian Liturgical and Magical Texts." In *Proceedings of the 29th Congress of Papyrology, Lecce, 28 July–3 August 2019,* edited by Mario Capasso, Paola Davoli, and Natascia Pellé, 722–731. Quaderni dell' Istituto superiore universitario di formazione interdisciplinare 2. Lecce: Centro di Studi Papirologici dell'Università del Salento.

Mikhail, Ramez. 2015. "The Presanctified Liturgy of the Apostle Mark in Sinai Ar. 237 (13th c.): Text and Commentary." *Bollettino della Badia Greca di Grottaferrata* 3, no. 12: 163–214.

Mikhail, Maghed S. A. 2016. *From Byzantine to Islamic Egypt: Religion, Identity and Politics after the Arab Conquest.* Library of Middle East History 45. London: I. B. Tauris.

—2017. *The Legacy of Demetrius of Alexandria: 189–232 CE; The Form and Function of Hagiography in Late Antique and Islamic Egypt.* Routledge Studies in the Early Christian World 10. London: Routledge.

Migne, Jacques P. 1857–1866. *Patrologiae Cursus Completus. Series Graeca.* 161 vols. Paris: Imprimerie Catholique.

Milkias, Paulos. 1976. "Traditional Institutions and Traditional Elites: The Role of Education in the Ethiopian Body-Politic." *African Studies Review* 19, no. 3: 79–94.

Minov, Sergey. 2022. "Christians, Jews, and Magic in the Sasanian Realm: Between Confrontation and Cooperation." *Entangled Religions* 13, no. 3.

Mirecki, Paul A. 2001. "Manichaean Allusions to Ritual and Magic: Spells for Invisibility in the Coptic Kephalaia." In *The Light and the Darkness: Studies in Manichaeism and Its World,* edited by Paul Allan Mirecki and Jason David BeDuhn, 173–180. Nag Hammadi and Manichaean Studies 50. Leiden: Brill.

—2013. "Manichaeism, Scribal Magic, and Papyrus Kellis 35." In *Gnostica et Manichaica: Festschrift für Aloïs van Tongerloo Anläßlich des 60. Geburtstages überreicht von Kollegen, Freunden und Schülern,* edited by Michael Knuppel and Luigi Cirillo, 133–146. Wiesbaden: Harrassowitz.

Mirecki, Paul A., Iain Gardner, and Anthony Alcock. 1997. "Magical Spell, Manichaean Letter." In *Emerging from Darkness: Studies in the Recovery of Manichaean Sources*, edited by Paul Allan Mirecki and Jason Beduhn, 1–32. Nag Hammadi and Manichaean Studies 43. Leiden: Brill.

Mirecki, Paul, and Marvin Meyer. 2001. *Magic and Ritual in the Ancient World*. Religions in the Graeco-Roman World 141. Leiden: Brill.

Miroshnikov, Ivan. 2017. "The Acts of Andrew and Philemon in Sahidic Coptic." *Apocrypha* 28: 9–83.

—2022. "A New Fragment of the Acrostic Hymn in Praise of the Archangel Michael (P.MorganLib. 272)." In *Sortieren – Edieren – Kreieren. Zwischen Handschriftenfunden und Universitätsalltag Stephen L. Emmel zum 70. Geburtstag gewidmet*, edited by Frank Feder, Angelika Lohwasser, and Gesa Schenke, 399–417. Aegyptiaca Monasteriensia 8. Düren: Shaker Verlag.

—2023. "The Acts of Andrew and Philemon: A Translation and Introduction." In *New Testament Apocrypha: More Noncanonical Scriptures* 3, edited by Tony Burke, 196–230. Grand Rapids: Eerdmans.

—Forthcoming. "From the Nachlass of Wolf-Peter Funk: The *Visio Constantini* and the *Inventio crucis* in Fayyūmic Coptic (P.Berol. 5731+5732)."

Miroshnikov, Ivan, Antti Marjanen, and Francesca Iacono. Forthcoming. *The Coptic Versions of the Martyrdom of George: A Study on the Coptic Reception of the George Legend, with an Edition of Seven Fragmentary Manuscripts in Sahidic, Bohairic, and Fayyūmic*. Leuven: Peeters.

Monson, Andrew. 2012. *From the Ptolemies to the Romans: Political and Economic Change in Egypt*. Cambridge: Cambridge University Press.

Morelli, Federico. 1996. *Olio e retribuzioni nell'Egitto tardo (V–VII d.C.)*. Florence: Instituto Papirologico "G. Vitelli."

Moriggi, Marco. 2018. "'And the Impure and Abominable Priests Fled for Help to the Names of the Devils': Amulets and Magical Practices in Syriac Christian Culture between Late Antiquity and the Modern World." *Hugoye: Journal of Syriac Studies* 19, no. 1: 371–384.

Moriggi, Marco, and Siam Bhayro. 2021. *Studies in the Syriac Magical Traditions*. Magical and Religious Literature of Late Antiquity 9. Leiden: Brill.

Mößner, Tamara, and Claudia Nauerth. 2015. "Koptische Text und ihre Bilder: Zauber in Wort und Bild." In *Ägyptische Magie und ihre Umwelt*, edited by Andrea Jördens, 302–337. Philippika 80. Wiesbaden: Harrassowitz.

Müller, Caspar D.G. 1959. *Die Engellehre der koptischen Kirche: Untersuchungen zur Geschichte der christlichen Frommigkeit in Ägypten*. Wiesbaden: Harrassowitz.

—1962. *Die Bücher der Einsetzung der Erzengel Michael und Gabriel*. Corpus scriptorum Christianorum orientalium / Scriptores Coptici 31 = 225. Leuven: CorpusSCO.

Müller, Matthias. 2009. "Koptische magische Texte in Fribourg." In *Liber amicorum Jürgen Horn zum Dank*, edited by Antonia Giewekemeyer, 57–65. Göttinger Miszellen 5. Göttingen: Univ., Seminar für Ägyptologie und Koptologie.

Müller, Matthias, and Sami Uljas. 2019. *Martyrs and Archangels: Coptic Literary Texts from the Pierpont Morgan Library*. Studies and Texts in Antiquity and Christianity 116. Tübingen: Mohr Siebeck.

Mulugetta, Meley. 2015. "Some Notes on Binding Magic (*ma'əsärä əgr*) in Ethiopia." *Aethiopica* 18: 183–189.

Murray, Margaret A. 1904. *The Osireion at Abydos*. Egyptian Research Account 9. London: Bernard Quaritch.

Nagel, Svenja. 2017. "'Was im Tempel passiert, bleibt nicht (mehr) im Tempel': Transformationen von agyptischem Tempelritual und rituellem Raum in den Praktiken der demotischen und griechischen magischen Papyri." In *Der ägyptische Tempel als ritueller Raum: Theologie und Kult in ihrer architektonischen und ideellen Dimension; Akten der internationalen Tagung, Haus der Heidelberger Akademie der Wissenschaften, 9.–12. Juni 2015*, edited by Stefan Baumann and Holger Kockelmann, 507–536. Studien zur spätägyptischen Religion 17. Wiesbaden: Harrassowitz Verlag.

Nanos, Mark. 2009. "Paul's Reversal of Jews Calling Gentiles' Dogs (Philippians 3:2): 1600 Years of an Ideological Tale Wagging an Exegetical Dog?" *Biblical Interpretation* 17, no. 4: 448–482.

Nasrallah, Nawal. 2017. *Treasure Trove of Benefits and Variety at the Table: A Fourteenth-Century Egyptian Cookbook; English Translation, with an Introduction and Glossary*. Islamic History and Civilization 148. Leiden: Brill.

Naveh, Joseph, and Shaul Shaked. 1993. *Magic Spells and Formulae: Aramaic Incantations of Late Antiquity*. Jerusalem: Magnes Press, The Hebrew University.

—1998. *Amulets and Magic Bowls: Aramaic Incantations of Late Antiquity*, 3rd ed. Jerusalem: Magnes Press, The Hebrew University.

Nesseris, Ilias. 2021. "First-Person Prayers Attributed to the Church Fathers." In *Papers presented at the Eighteenth International Conference on Patristic Studies held in Oxford 2019. Volume 5: Euchologia*, edited by Markus Vinzent, and Claudia Rapp, 89–102. Studia Patristica 108. Leuven: Peeters.

Nestle, Eberhard. 1895. "Die Kreuzauffindungslegende: Nach einer Handschrift vom Sinai." *Byzantinische Zeitschrift* 4: 319–345.

Neugebauer, Otto, and Richard A. Parker. 1969. *Egyptian Astronomical Texts* 3: *Decans, Planets, Constellations and Zodiacs*. Providence: Brown University Press.

Noegel, Scott, Joel Walker, and Brannon Wheeler, eds. 2003. *Prayer, Magic, and the Stars in the Ancient and Late Antique World*. Magic in History 9. University Park, PA: The Pennsylvania State University Press.

Nongbri, Brent. 2018. *God's Library: The Archaeology of the Earliest Christian Manuscripts*. New Haven: Yale University Press.

Nurullina, Anna *see* Cherkashina (Nurullina), Anna.

Nyord, Rune. 2015. "Conceptualizations of Embodied Space: The Semantics of Body Parts in Sahidic Compound Prepositions." In *Lotus and Laurel: Studies on Egyptian Language and Religion in Honour of Paul John Frandsen*, edited by Rune Nyord and Kim Ryholt, 241–282. CNI Publications 39. Copenhagen: Museum Tusculanum.

O'Connell, Elisabeth. 2018. "Theban Books in Context." *Adamantius* 24: 75–105.

—ed. 2022. *The Hay Archive of Coptic Spells on Leather: A Multi-disciplinary Approach to the Materiality of Magical Practice*. British Museum Research Publications 233. London: British Museum Press.

Ohrt, Ferdinand. 1936. "Über Alter und Ursprung der Begegnungssegen." *Hessische Blätter für Volkskunde* 35: 49–58.

Ohrvik, Ane. 2018. *Medicine, Magic and Art in Early Modern Norway: Conceptualizing Knowledge*. Palgrave Historical Studies in Witchcraft and Magic 32. London: Palgrave MacMillan.

O'Leary, De Lacy. 1926. *The Difnar (Antiphonarium) of the Coptic Church (First Four Months)*. London: Luzac.

Olivieri, A. 1898. "De inventione crucis libellus." *Analecta Bollandiana* 17: 414–420.

Omar, Hussein. 2013. "'The Crinkly-Haired People of the Black Earth': Examining Egyptian Identities in Ibn ʿAbd al-Ḥakam's *Futūḥ*." In *History and Identity in the Late Antique Near East*, edited by Philip Wood, 149–168. Oxford Studies in Late Antiquity 4. New York: Oxford University Press.

Orlandi, Tito. 1974. "Les papyrus coptes du Musée Egyptien de Turin." *Le Muséon* 87: 115–127.

—1981. "Gregorio di Nissa nella letteratura copta." *Vetera Christianorum* 18.2: 333–339.

—1998. "Koptische Literatur." In *Ägypten in spätantik-christlicher Zeit: Einführung in die koptische Kultur*, edited by Martin Krause, 117–147. Sprachen und Kulturen des christlichen Orients 4. Wiesbaden: Reichert.

—2005. "La letteratura copta e la storia dell'Egitto cristiano." In *Le antiche Chiese orientali: Storia e letteratura*, edited by Paolo Siniscalco, 85–117. Roma: Città Nuova.

—2013. "The Turin Coptic Papyri." *Augustunianum* 53, no. 2: 501–530.

Orsenigo, Christian. 2020. "A Life Dedicated to Egypt: Carla Maria Burri & the New Egyptian Section of the Museum of Crema in Italy". *KMT* 3, no. 3: 49–155.

Orsini, Pasquale. 2018. *Studies on Greek and Coptic Majuscule Scripts and Books*. Studies in Manuscript Cultures 15. Boston: De Gruyter.

O'Sullivan, Shaun. 2006. "Coptic Conversion and the Islamization of Egypt." *Mamlūk Studies Review* 10, no. 2: 65–79.

Pachoumi, Eleni. 2013. "The Erotic and Separation Spells of the Magical Papyri and the Defixiones." *Greek, Roman, and Byzantine Studies* 53, no. 2: 294–325.

Papaconstantinou, Arietta. 2001. *Le culte des saints en Egypte: des Byzantins aux Abbassides: l'apport des inscriptions et des papyrus grecs et coptes*. Le monde byzantin. Paris: CNRS Éditions.

—2010. *The Multilingual Experience in Egypt, from the Ptolemies to the Abbasids*. Farnham: Ashgate.

—2015. "Dioscorus and the Qquestion of Bilingualism in Sixth-Century Egypt." In *Languages and Cultures of Eastern Christianity: Greek*, edited by Scott F. Johnson, 249–260. The Worlds of Eastern Christianity, 300-1500, vol. 6. Farnham: Ashgate Variorum.

Parani, Maria. 2000. "Byzantine Bridal Costume." In *Dōrēma: A Tribute to the A.G. Leventis Foundation on the Occasion of Its 20th Anniversary*, edited by Anastasia Serghidou, 185–216. Nicosia: A. G. Leventis Foundation.

Passalis, Haralampos. 2014. "From Written to Oral Tradition. Survival and Transformation of St. Sisinnios Prayer in Oral Greek Charms." *Incantatio* 4: 111–38.

Peled, Ilan, and Ortal-Paz Saar. Forthcoming. *Spells for Separation from Mesopotamia to the Cairo Genizah*.

Pearson, B.A. 2000. "Enoch in Egypt." In *For a Later Generation: The Transformation of Tradition in Israel, Early Judaism, and Early Christianity; Festschrift G. Nickelsburg*, edited by Randal A. Argall, Beverly Bow, and Rodney A. Werline, 216–231. Harrisburg: Trinity Press International.

Pernigotti, Sergio. 1979. "Il codice copto." *Studi classici e orientali* 29: 19–53.

— 1983. "Una tavoletta lignea con un testo magico in copto." *Egitto e Vicino Oriente* 6: 75–92.

—1989. "13. Testo magico. P.Vat.Copt. 7 (già Vat. copt. 114)." In *Tavolette lignee e cerate da varie collezioni (T.Varie)*, edited by Rosario Pintaudi, Pieter J. Sijpesteijn, and Roger S. Bagnall, 59–69. Papyrologica Florentina 18. Firenze: Edizioni Gonnelli.

—1993. "Una rilettura del P.Mil.Vogl. Copto 16." *Aegyptus* 73: 93–125.

—1995. "La magia copta: I testi." In *Aufstieg und Niedergang der römischen Welt* II.18.5, edited by Hildegard Temporini and Wolfgang Haase, 3685–3730. Berlin and New York: Walter de Gruyter.

—2000. *Testi della magia copta*. Piccola biblioteca di egittologia 5. Imola: Editrice La Mandragora.

Petersen, Theodore C. 1954. "Early Islamic Bookbindings and Their Coptic Relations." *Ars Orientalis* 1: 41–64.

—1964. *A Collection of Papyri: Egyptian, Greek, Coptic, Arabic: Showing the Development of Handwriting Mainly from the Second Century B.C. to the Eighth Century A.D*. Catalogue 105. New York: H. P. Kraus.

Petrucci, Armando. 2002. *Prima lezione di paleografia, Universale Laterza, Prime Lezioni*. Roma: Laterza.

Peust, Carsten. 1999. *Egyptian Phonology: An Introduction to the Phonology of a Dead Language* 2. Göttingen: Peust und Gutschmidt.

Peyron, Amedeo. 1824. *Saggio di studi sopra papiri, codici cofti, ed uno stele trilingue del Regio Museo Egiziano*. Memorie della Reale Accademia delle Scienza di Torino 29. Turin: Stamperia Reale.

—1835. *Lexicon linguæ Copticæ*. Turin: Ex Regio Typographeo.
—1841. *Grammatica linguæ Copticæ: Accedunt addimenta ad lexicon copticum*. Turin: Ex Regio Typographeo.
Peyron, Bernardino. 1876. "Notizie ed osservazioni intorno a cinque manoscritti copti della Biblioteca nazionale di Torino, 26 nov. 1876." *Atti della Reale Accademia delle Scienze di Torino*, n.s., 12: 65–74.
Pezin, Michel. 1983. "Les manuscrits coptes inédits du Collège de France." In *Écritures et traditions dans la littérature copte. Journée d'Études coptes, Strasbourg 28 mai 1982*, 23–26. Cahiers de la Bibliothèque copte 1. Louvain: Peeters.
—1988. "Un texte copte de la prière attribuée à Chenouti." In *Mélanges Antoine Guillaumont: Contributions à l'étude des christianismes orientaux*, 63–68. Geneva: Patrick Cramer.
Pharr, Clyde. 1932. "The Interdiction of Magic in Roman Law." *Transactions and Proceedings of the American Philological Association* 63: 269–295.
Phillips, C. Robert III. 1991. "Nullum Crimen sine Lege: Socioreligious Sanctions on Magic." In *Magika Hiera: Ancient Greek Magic and Religion*, edited by Christopher A. Faraone and Dirk Obbink, 260–276. New York: Oxford University Press.
Pietersma, Albert, and Benjamin G. Wright, eds. 2007. *A New English Translation of the Septuagint*. Oxford: Oxford University Press.
Piperakis, Spyros. 2022. "Sacrificing to the Planets: Planetary Incenses and Flowers of P.Leid. I 395 (=*PGM* XIII.16–20, 24–26)." *Symbolae Osloenses* 96: 260–284.
Piovanelli, Pierluigi. 2000. "Le sommeil séculaire d'Abimélech dans l'*Histoire de la captivité babylonienne* et les *Paralipomènes de Jérémie*. Textes–intertextes–contextes." In *Intertextualités: La Bible en échos*, edited by Daniel Marguerat and Adrian H.W. Curtis, 73–96. Le Monde la Bible 40. Geneva: Labor et Fides.
Piwowarczyk, Przemysław. 2020. "Sethians and Their Texts in Christian Egypt in the 4th and 5th Centuries." *Studi e Materiali di Storia delle Religioni* 86, no. 1: 99–116.
—2021. *Lexicon of Spiritual Powers in the Nag Hammadi 'Library' in the Light of the Texts of Ritual Power*. Seria Filologia Klasyczna Uniwersytetu Śląskiego w Katowicach 5. Katowice: Wydawnictwo Uniwersytetu Śląskiego.
Pleyte, Willem, and Pieter A. A. Boeser. 1897. *Manuscrits coptes du Musée d'Antiquités des Pays-Bas à Leide*. Leiden: Brill.
Polański, Tomasz. 2016. "Translation, Amplification, Paraphrase. Some Comments on the Syriac, Greek and Coptic Versions of the Abgar Letter." *Collectanea Christiana Orientalia* 13: 159–210.
Polotsky, Hans J. 1935. "Zu einigen Heidelberger koptischen Zaubertexten." *Orientalia* 4: 416–425.
—1937. "Zwei koptische Liebeszauber." *Orientalia*, n.s., 6: 119–131.
—1939. "Review of 'A Coptic Dictionary' by W. E. Crum." *The Journal of Egyptian Archaeology* 25, no. 1: 109–113.
Popko, Lutz. 2018. "Some Notes on Papyrus Ebers, Ancient Egyptian Treatments of Migraine, and a Crocodile on the Patient's Head." *Bulletin of the History of Medicine* 92, no. 2: 352–366.
Porter, Venetia. 2010. "The Use of the Arabic Script in Magic." In *The Development of Arabic as a Written Language. Proceedings of the Seminar for Arabian Studies* 40: *Papers from the Forty-third Meeting of the Seminar for Arabian Studies Held at the British Museum, London, 23–25 July 2009*, edited by M.C.A. Macdonald, 131–140. Oxford: Archaeopress.
—, ed. 2011. *Arabic and Persian Seals and Amulets in the British Museum*. London: British Museum Press.
Préaux, Claire. 1948. "Friedrich Bilabel." *Chronique d'Égypte* 23, no. 45–46: 247–250.
Preininger, Markéta. 2022. "BnF Copte 129 (20) fol. 178: Three Healing Prescriptions." *Archiv für Papyrusforschung und verwandte Gebiete* 68, no. 2: 344–357.

—Forthcoming a. "Blood in Coptic Magical Texts and Beyond." In Proceedings of the Conference 'Bodily Fluids in Ancient Egyptian and Near Eastern Civilizations' in Montpellier, 2019, to appear in the series *Orbis Biblicus et Orientalis*, Peeters.

—Forthcoming b. "The Jesus-Abgar Correspondence and the Question of Claims of Authenticity." In the Proceedings of the Conference "Briefe, Archive und Kommunikation in der Spätantike" in Heidelberg, 2021, to appear in the series *Kulturelles Erbe: Materialität–Text–Edition* series, Heidelberg.

—Forthcoming c. "The Conceptualization of the Body and its Liquids in Coptic Magical Papyri." PhD Diss., defended at the University of Würzburg in 2022. Awaiting publication.

Preisendanz, Karl, and Albert Henrichs 1973–1974. *Papyri Graecae Magicae: Die griechischen Zauberpapyri*. 2 vols. Stuttgart: Teubner.

Provençal, Philippe. 2010. *The Arabic Plant Names of Peter Forsskål's Flora Aegyptiaco-Arabica*. Biologiske Skrifter 57. Copenhagen: Det Kongelige Danske Videnskabernes Selskab.

Proverbio, Delio V. 1997. "Un nuovo testimone copto del *Responsum Christi ad Abgarum*." *Miscellanea Marciana* 12: 155–169.

Puech, Émile. 1990. "11QPsAp^a : un rituel d'exorcismes. Essai de reconstruction." *Revue de Qumrân* 14, no. 3 = 55: 377–408.

—2000. "Les psaumes davidiques du rituel d'exorcisme (11Q11)." In *Sapiential, Liturgical and Poetical Texts from Qumran: Proceedings of the Third Meeting of the International Organization for Qumran Studies, Oslo 1998; Published in Memory of Maurice Baillet*, edited by James H. Charlesworth, 160–181. Studies on the Texts of the Desert of Judah 35. Leiden: Brill.

Quack, Joachim F. 2017. "How the Coptic Script Came About." In *Greek Influence on Egyptian-Coptic: Contact-Induced Change in an Ancient African Language*, edited by Eitan Grossman, Peter Dils, Tonio Sebastian Richter, and Wolfgang Schenkel, 27–96. Lingua Aegyptia: Studia monographica 17. DDGLC working papers 1. Hamburg: Widmaier Verlag.

Quaegebeur, Jan. 1983. "De l'origine égyptienne du griffon némésis." In *Visages du destin dans les mythologies : mélanges Jacqueline Duchemin ; actes du Colloque de Chantilly, 1er–2 mai 1980*, edited by François Jouan, 41–54. Paris: Société d'édition "Les Belles Lettres".

—1991. "Le théonyme Senephthys." *Orientalia Lovaniensia Periodica* 22: 111–122.

Quecke, Hans. 1963a. "Erhebet euch, Kinder des Lichtes." *Le Muséon* 76: 27–45 and 266 (Nachtrag).

—1963b. "Zwei koptische Amulette der Papyrussammlung der Universität Heidelberg (Inv. Nr. 544b und 564a)." *Le Muséon* 76: 247–265.

—1970. "Untersuchungen zum koptischen Stundengebet." PhD Diss., Univ. Cathol. de Louvain, Inst. Orientaliste. Publications de l'Institut Orientaliste de Louvain 3.

—1971. "Ein saïdischer Zeuge der Markusliturgie (Brit.Mus. Nr. 54 036)." *Orientalia Christiana Periodica* 36: 40–54.

—1972. "Palimpsestfragmente eines Koptischen Lektionars." *Le Muséon* 85: 5–24.

—1973. "Ein neues koptisches Anaphora-Fragment (Bonn, Univ.-Bibl. So 267)." *Orientalia Christiana Periodica* 39: 216–223.

—1984. *Das Johannesevangelium Saïdisch: Text der Handschrift PPalau Rib. Inv.-Nr. 183 mit den Varianten der Handschriften 813 und 814 der Chester Beatty Library und der Handschrift M 569*. Papyrologica Castroctaviana 11. Rome/Barcelona: Papyrologica Castroctaviana.

Rabin, Ira. 2015. "Digital and Scientific Approaches to Oriental Manuscript Studies: Instrumental Analysis in Manuscript Studies." In *Comparative Oriental Manuscript Studies: An Introduction*, edited by Alessandro Bausi, Pier Giorgio Borbone, Françoise Briquel-Chatonnet, Paola Buzi, Jost Gippert, Caroline Macé, Marilena Maniaci, Zisis Melissakis, Laura E. Parodi, and Witold Witakowski, 27–33. Hamburg: Tradition.

Rabin, Ira, and Marcello Binetti. 2014. "NIR Reflectography Reveals Ink Type: Pilot Study of 12 Armenian Manuscripts of the Staatsbibliothek Zu Berlin." Բանբեր Մատենադարանի (*Banber Matenadaran*) 21: 465–470.

Rabin, Ira, and Myriam Krutzsch. 2019. "The Writing Surface Papyrus and Its Materials 1. Can the Writing Material Papyrus Tell Us Where It Was Produced? 2. Material Study of the Inks." In *Proceedings of the 28th Congress of Papyrology; 2016 August 1-6; Barcelona*, edited by Alberto Nodar, and Sofía Torallas Tovar, 773–781. Scripta Orientalis 3. Barcelona: Publicacions Abadia de Montserrat.

Raggetti, Lucia. 2018. *'Īsā ibn 'Alī's Book on the Useful Properties of Animal Parts: Edition, Translation and Study of a Fluid Tradition*. Science, Technology, and Medicine in Ancient Cultures 6. Berlin/Boston: De Gruyter.

Rahlfs, Alfred. 1935. *Septuaginta: id est, Vetus Testamentum graece iuxta LXX interpretes*. Stuttgart: Deutsche Bibelgesellschaft.

Raven, Maarten J. 1982. *Papyrus. Van bies tot boekrol, met een bloemlezing uit de Leidse papyrusverzameling*. Zutphen: Terra.

—1996. *Schrift en schrijvers in het Oude Egypte*. Amsterdam: De Bataafsche Leeuw.

—2010. *Egyptische magie: Op zoek naar het toverboek van Thot*. Zutphen: Walburg Pers.

Reinfandt, Lucian. 2013. "The Political Papyrologist: Adolf Grohmann (1887–1977)." In Sources and Approaches across Disciplines in Near Eastern Studies. Proceedings of the 24th Congress Union Européenne des Arabisants et Islamisants, Leipzig 2008, edited by Verena Klemm and Nuha Al-Sha'ar, 251–269. Leuven: Peeters.

Reitzenstein, Richard. 1904. *Poimandres. Studien zur Griechisch-Ägyptischen und Frühchristlichen Literatur*. Leipzig: B.G. Teubner.

Rémondon, Roger. 1952. "Autour de quelques termes du P. Fouad inédit inv. n° 45." *Chronique d'Égypte* 27, no. 53: 196–204.

Reuvens, Caspar J.C. 1830. *Lettres à M. Letronne sur les papyrus bilingues et grecs et sur quelques autres monumens gréco-égyptiens du Musée d'antiquités de l'Université de Leide*. 2 vols. Leiden: Luchtmans.

Revillout, Eugène. 1875. "Le concile de Nicée. Second série de documents." *Journal asiatique* 7.5: 209–266.

Richter, Tonio Sebastian. 2000. "Spätkoptische Rechtsurkunden neu bearbeitet (II): Die Rechtsurkunden des Teschlot-Archivs." *Journal of Juristic Papyrology* 30: 95–148.

—2003. "Spätkoptische Rechtsurkunden neu bearbeitet (III): P.Lond.Copt. I 487; Arabische Pacht in koptischem Gewand." *Journal of Juristic Papyrology* 33: 213–230.

—2005. "Texte und Riten in koptischer Schrift." In *Altägyptische Zaubersprüche*, edited by Hans-Werner Fischer-Elfert, 167–179. Stuttgart: Philipp Reclam.

—2008. *Rechtssemantik und forensische Rhetorik: Untersuchungen zu Wortschatz, Stil und Grammatik der Sprache koptischer Rechtsurkunden*. Wiesbaden: Otto Harrassowitz Verlag.

—2009. "17. Greek, Coptic, and the 'Language of the Hijra': The Rise and Decline of the Coptic Language in Late Antique and Medieval Egypt." In *From Hellenism to Islam: Cultural and Linguistic Change in the Roman Near East*, edited by Hanna Cotton, Robert G. Hoyland, Jonathan J. Price, and David J. Wasserstein, 401–446. Cambridge: Cambridge University Press.

—2010. "Language Choice in the Qurra Dossier." In *The Multilingual Experience in Egypt, from the Ptolemies to the Abbasids*, edited by Arietta Papaconstantinou, 189–220. Farnham: Ashgate.

—2014a. "Cyprianus und seine Zauberbücher. Zur Herkunft und Überlieferungsgeschichte eines Motivs in Storms Märchen-Novelle 'Der Spiegel des Cyprianus' (1865)." *Storm-Blätter aus Heiligenstadt* 18 (2014): 56–81.

—2014b. "Neue koptische medizinische Rezepte." *Zeitschrift für ägyptische Sprache und Altertumskunde* 141, no. 2: 154–194.

—2015a. "Markedness and Unmarkedness in Coptic Magical Writing." In *Écrire la magie dans l'Antiquité: Actes du colloque international (Liège, octobre 13–15, 2011)*, edited by Magali de Haro Sanchez, 85–110, plates VII–XIII. Papyrologica Leodiensia 5. Liège: Presses universitaires de Liège.

—2015b. "On the Fringes of Egyptian Language and Linguistics. Verb Borrowing from Arabic into Coptic." In *Fuzzy Boundaries: Festschrift für Antonio Loprieno* 1, edited by Hans Amstutz, Andreas Dorn, Matthias Müller, Miriam Ronsdorf, and Sami Uljas, 227–242. Hamburg: Widmaier.

—2016a. "Arabische Wörter in koptischen Texten." In *Zwischen Philologie und Lexikographie des Ägyptisch-Koptischen. Akten der Leipziger Abschlusstagung des Akademienprojekts 'Altägyptisches Wörterbuch'*, edited by Peter Dils and Lutz Popko, 137–163. Abhandlungen der Sächsischen Akademie der Wissenschaften zu Leipzig, Philologisch historische Klasse 84, no. 3. Leipzig: Sächsische Akademie der Wissenschaften zu Leipzig.

—2016b. "Toward a Sociohistorical Approach to the Corpus of Coptic Medical Texts." In *Studies in Coptic Culture: Transmission and Interaction*, edited by Mariam F. Ayad, 33–54. Cairo: American University in Cairo Press.

—2017a. "Borrowing into Coptic, the Other Story: Arabic Words in Coptic Texts." In *Greek Influence on Egyptian-Coptic: Contact-Induced Change in an Ancient African Language*, edited by Eitan Grossman, Peter Dils, Tonio Sebastian Richter, and Wolfgang Schenkel, 513–533. Lingua Aegyptia : Studia monographica 17. DDGLC working papers 1. Hamburg: Widmaier Verlag.

—2017b. "The Pattern ⲡⲉϥⲥⲱⲧⲙ 'The One Who Hears' in Coptic Documentary Texts", in *Labor omnia uicit improbus: Miscellanea in Honorem Ariel Shisha-Halevy*, 315–330. Orientalia Lovaniensia Analecta 256. Leuven: Peeters.

—2020. "P.Berlin P.8316 (=*BKU* I, 21): Ein koptisches Rezept zur Purpur-Imitation durch Krapp-Färbung auf gebeizter Wolle." *Journal of Coptic Studies* 22 (2020): 151–186.

—2023. "Magische Schreibflüssigkeiten zwischen Philologie, Lexikographie und Verfahrenstechnik. Kufische Tinte in P.Heid. Inv. Kopt. 682, safranhaltige Amulett-Tinte in P.Heid. Inv. Kopt. 685." In *Papyrologische und althistorische Studien zum 65. Geburtstag von Andrea Jördens*, edited by Lajos Berkes, W. Graham Claytor und Maria Nowak, 157–173. Wiesbaden: Harrassowitz Verlag.

—Forthcoming. "Die sogenannte 'Apokalypse der 24 Ältesten,' apokrypher Visionsbericht innerhalb einer Cyrill von Jerusalem zugeschriebenen Predigt über die 24 Presbyter am Gottesthron (CC 0560)." In *Antike Christliche Apokryphen. Apokalypsen und Verwandtes* 3, edited by C. Markschies and J. Schröter. Tübingen: Mohr Siebeck.

Riedel, Wilhelm, and Walter E. Crum. 1904. *The Canons of Athanasius of Alexandria: The Arabic and Coptic Versions*. Works Issued by the Text and Translation Society 9. Oxford: Williams and Norgate.

Riedinger, Rudolph, and Hans Thurn. 1985. "Die *Didascalia CCCXVIII patrum Nicaenorum* und das *Syntagma ad monachos* im Codex Parisinus graecus 1115 (a. 1276)." *Jahrbuch der Osterreichischen Byzantinistik Wien* 35: 75–92.

Rist, Martin. 1938. "The God of Abraham, Isaac, and Jacob: A Liturgical and Magical Formula." *Journal of Biblical Literature* 57, no. 3: 289–303.

Ritner, Robert K. 1993. *The Mechanics of Ancient Egyptian Magical Practice*. Studies in Ancient Oriental Civilization 54. Chicago: Oriental Institute of the University of Chicago.

—1998. "The Wives of Horus and the Philinna Papyrus (PGM XX)." In *Egyptian Religion the Last Thousand Years: Studies Dedicated to the Memory of Jan Quaegebeur* 2, edited by Willy Clarysse, Antoon Schoors, and Harco Willems, 1026–1041. Orientalia Lovaniensia Analecta 85. Leuven: Peeters.

Ritter, Hellmut, ed. 1933. *Pseudo-Maǧrīṭī. Das Ziel des Weisen*. Studien der Bibliothek Warburg 12. Leipzig: B.G. Teubner.

Ritter, Hellmut, and Martin Plessner. 1962. *Picatrix: Das Ziel des Weisen, von Pseudo-Maǧrīṭī*. Studien der Bibliothek Warburg 27. London: The Warburg Institute.

Rives, James B. 2003. "Magic in Roman Law: The Reconstruction of a Crime." *Classical Antiquity* 22, no. 2: 313–339.

—2006. "Magic, Religion, and Law: The Case of the *Lex Cornelia de sicariis et veneficiis*." In *Religion and Law in Classical and Christian Rome*, edited by Clifford Ando and Jörg Rüpke, 47–67. Potsdamer Altertumswissenschaftliche Beiträge 15. Stuttgart: Franz Steiner.

Robert, Louis. 1981. "Amulettes grecques." *Journal des Savants* 1981, no. 1: 3–44.

Roberts, Colin H., and Theodore C. Skeat. 1983. *The Birth of the Codex.* London: British Academy.

Robinson, Forbes. 1896. *Coptic Apocryphal Gospels: Translations Together with the Texts of Some of Them.* Texts and Studies: Contributions to Biblical and Patristic Literature 4, n. 2. Cambridge: Cambridge University Press.

Robinson, James M. 2000. *The Coptic Gnostic Library: A Complete Edition of the Nag Hammadi Codices.* 5 vols. Leiden: Brill.

Roca-Puig, Ramón. 1996. *Anàfora de Barcelona i altres pregàries (Missa del segle IV).* 2nd ed. Barcelona: Grafos.

Rodinson, Maxime. 1967. *Magie, médecine et possession à Gondar*. Monde d'outre-mer, passé et présent, série 2, Documents 5. Paris: Mouton et Cie.

Römer, Cornelia, and Heinz J. Thissen. 1990. "Eine magische Anrufung in koptischer Sprache." *Zeitschrift für Papyrologie und Epigraphik* 84: 175–181.

Roper, Jonathan, ed. 2004. *Charms and Charming in Europe.* Basingstoke: Palgrave Macmillan UK.

—2005. *English Verbal Charms.* FF Communications 288. Helsinki: Suomalainen Tiedeakatemia.

—, ed. 2009. *Charms, Charmers and Charming: International Research on Verbal Magic*. Palgrave Historical Studies in Witchcraft and Magic 2. Basingstoke: Palgrave Macmillan UK.

Rosenstiehl, Jean-Marc, and Jacques-E. Ménard. 1986. "Tartarouchos-Temelouchos: Contribution à l'étude de l'Apocalypse apocryphe de Paul." In *Études coptes 2. Deuxième Journée d'Études coptes, Strasbourg 25 mai 1984*, 29–56. Cahiers de la Bibliothèque copte 3. Leuven: Peeters.

Rossi, Francesco. 1894. "Di alcuni manoscritti copti che si conservano nella Biblioteca nazionale di Torino." *Memorie della Reale Accademia delle scienze di Torino*, Serie 2, 44: 21–70.

—1899. "Manoscritti copti esistenti nel Museo Egizio e nella Biblioteca Nazionale di Torino raccolti da Bernardino Drovetti e indicati del prof. Francesco Rossi." *Rivista delle Biblioteche e degli Archivi* 10: 113–122.

Rubensohn, Otto. 1903. "Griechisch-Römische Funde im Ägypten." *Archäologischer Anzeiger* 18: 77–81.

Ruffini, Giovanni R. 2012. "The Meinarti Phylactery Factory: Medieval Nubian Ostraka from the Island of Michael." *Journal for Juristic Papyrology* 42: 273–300.

Russell, James R. 2011. "The Armenian Magical Scroll and Outsider Art." *Iran and the Caucasus* 15, no. 1–2: 5–47.

Saar, Ortal-Paz. 2007. "Success, Protection and Grace: Three Fragments of a Personalized Magical Handbook." *Ginzei qedem: Genizah Research Annual* 3: 101–135.

—2014. "A Genizah Magical Fragment and its European Parallels." *The Journal of Jewish Studies* 65, no. 2: 237–262.

—2017. *Jewish Love Magic: From Late Antiquity to the Middle Ages.* Magical and Religious Literature of Late Antiquity 6. Leiden: Brill.

—2019a. "Geniza Magical Documents." *Jewish History* 32, no. 2–4: 477–484.

—2019b. "Fire Symbolism in Late-Antique and Medieval Jewish Love Magic." *Groniek* 220: 311–321.

Sadock, Jerrold. 2006. "Speech Acts." In *The Handbook of Pragmatics,* edited by Laurence R. Horn and Gregory Ward, 53–73. Malden: Blackwell Publishing.

Saif, Liana, Francesca Leoni, Matthew Melvin-Koushki, and Farouk Yahya. 2020. *Islamicate Occult Sciences in Theory and Practice.* Handbook of Oriental Studies. Section 1: The Near and Middle East 140. Leiden: Brill.

Sanzo, Joseph E. 2014. *Scriptural Incipits on Amulets from Late Antique Egypt: Text, Typology, and Theory.* Studies and Texts in Antiquity and Christianity 84. Tübingen: Mohr Siebeck.

—2015. "The Innovative Use of Biblical Traditions for Ritual Power: The Crucifixion of Jesus on a Coptic Exorcistic Spell (Brit. Lib. Or. 6796[4], 6796) as a Test Case." *Archiv für Religionsgeschichte* 16: 67–98.

—2017. "Magic and Communal Boundaries: The Problems with Amulets in Chrysostom, *Adv. Iud.* 8, and Augustine, *In Io. tra.* 7." In *Dangerous Books. Scribal Activity and Religious Boundaries in Late Antiquity and Beyond*, edited by Flavia Ruani, and Joseph E. Sanzo, 227–246. Henoch, n.s. 39, no. 2.

—2019a. "At the Crossroads of Ritual Practice and Anti-Magical Discourse in Late Antiquity: Taxonomies of Licit and Illicit Rituals in Leiden, Ms. AMS 9 and Related Sources." In *Narrating Witchcraft: Agency, Discourse, and Power* 2: *The Roman Empire: Pagans and Christians*, edited by Esther Eidinow and Richard Gordon. *Magic, Ritual, and Witchcraft* 14, no. 2: 230–254.

—2019b. "Early Christianity." In *Guide to the Study of Ancient Magic*, edited by David Frankfurter, 198–239. Religions in the Graeco-Roman World 189. Leiden: Brill.

—2020. "Deconstructing the Deconstructionists: A Response to Recent Criticisms of the Rubric 'Ancient Magic'." In *Ancient Magic: Then and Now*, edited by Attilio Mastrocinque, Joseph E. Sanzo, and Marianna Scapini, 25–46. Potsdamer Altertumswissenschaftliche Beitraege 74. Stuttgart: Franz Steiner.

Sarri, Antonia. 2017. *Material Aspects of Letter Writing in the Graeco-Roman World*. Materiale Textkulturen 12. Berlin/Boston: De Gruyter.

Satzinger, Helmut. 1991. "Old Coptic." In *The Coptic Encyclopedia* 8, edited by Aziz S. Atiya, 169–176. New York: Macmillan.

—1994. "An Old Coptic Text Reconsidered: PGM 94ff." In *Coptology: Past, Present and Future; Studies in Honour of Rodolphe Kasser*, edited by Rodolphe Kasser, Søren Giversen, Martin Krause, and Peter Nagel, 213–224. Orientalia Lovaniensia Analecta 61. Leuven: Peeters.

Sauneron, Serge. 1951. "Aspects et sort d'un thème magique égyptien: Les menaces incluant les dieux." *Bulletin de la société française d'égyptologie* 8: 11–21.

—1961. "Copte ⲕⲁⲗⲁϩⲏ." In *Mélanges Maspéro*, vol. 1, fasc. 4, 113–20. Cairo: Institut français d'archéologie orientale.

Schäfer, Peter and Shaul Shaked. 1994–1999. *Magische Texte aus der Kairoer Geniza*. 3 vols. Texts and Studies in Ancient Judaism 42; 64; 72. Tübingen: Mohr Siebeck.

Shauf, Scott. 2005. *Theology as History, History as Theology: Paul in Ephesus in Acts 19*. Zeitschrift für die neutestamentliche Wissenschaft und die Kunde der älteren Kirche – Beihefte 133. Berlin/New York: Walter de Gruyter.

Schenke, Gesa. 2017. "P.Köln 641: Heilmittel gegen Blutungen aus dem Unterleib, gegen Schwellungen und Angstzuständen." In *Kölner Papyri (P.Köln)* 15, edited by Thomas Backhuys, Charikleia Armoni, Robert W. Daniel, Jannik Korte, Klaus Maresch, Gesa Schenke, Alkestis A. Spinou, and Wolfgang Wegner, 253–260. Sonderreihe der Abhandlungen Papyrologica Coloniensia 7/15. Leiden: Brill.

Schermann, Theodor. 1903. "Die griechischen Kyprianosgebete." *Oriens Christianus* 3, no. 2: 303–323.

Schiffmann, Lawrence H., and Michael D. Swartz. 1992. *Hebrew and Aramaic Incantation Texts from the Cairo Genizah*. Semitic Texts and Studies 1. London: A&C Black.

Schiller, Arthur A. 1928. "A Coptic Charm. Columbia Coptic Parchment, Numbers 1 and 2." *Journal of the Society of Oriental Research* 12: 25–34.

—1968. "The Budge Papyrus of Columbia University." *Journal of the American Research Center in Egypt* 7: 79–118.

Schiller, Gertrud. 1971–1972. *Iconography of Christian Art*. Translated by Janet Seligman. 2 vols. London: Lund Humphries.

Schmidt, Carl, and Violet MacDermot. 1978. *The Books of Jeu and the Untitled Text in the Bruce Codex*. Nag Hammadi Studies 13. Leiden: Brill.

Schmelz, Georg. 2018. "Einleitung: Koptische Texte in der Heidelberger Papyrussammlung. Erwerbungen – Publikationen – Perspektiven." In *Coptica Palatina: Koptische Texte aus der Heidelberger Papyrussammlung (P.Heid.Kopt.). Bearbeitet auf der Vierten Internationalen Sommerschule für Koptische Papyrologie, Heidelberg, 26. August – 9. September 2012*, edited by Anne Boud'hors, Alain Delattre, Gesa Schenke, Tonio Sebastian Richter, and Georg Schmelz, 1–16. Studien und Texte aus der Heidelberger Papyrussammlung 1. Heidelberg: Heidelberg University Publishing.

Schulz, Regine, and Kamal Sabri Kolta. 1998. "Schlangen, Skorpione und feindliche Mächte." *Biblische Notizen. Beiträge zur exegetischen Diskussion* 93: 89–104.

Schwartz, Martin. 1996. "*Sasm, Sesen, St. Sisinnios, Sesengen Barpharangēs, and... 'Semanglof.'" In *Studies in Honor of Vladimir A. Livshits*, edited by Carol Altman Bromberg and Prods Oktor Skjærvø. Bulletin of the Asia Institute, n.s. 10: 253–257.

Schwartze, Möritz G., and Julius H. Petermann. 1851. *Pistis Sophia: Opus gnosticum Valentino adiudicatum e codice manuscripto Coptico Londinensi*. Berlin: F. Duemmler.

Schwarz, Sarah L. 2007. "Reconsidering the *Testament of Solomon*." *Journal for the Study of the Pseudepigrapha* 16, no. 3: 203–237.

Schwemer, Daniel. 2014. "'Form Follows Function'? Rhetoric and Poetic Language in First Millennium Akkadian Incantations." *Die Welt des Orients* 44, no. 2: 263–288.

Searle, John R. 1969. *Speech Acts: An Essay in the Philosophy of Language*. Cambridge: Cambridge University Press.

—1989. "How Performatives Work." *Linguistics and Philosophy* 12, no. 5: 535–558.

Seider, Richard. 1964. "Aus der Arbeit der Universitätsinstitute: Die Universitäts-Papyrussammlung." *Heidelberger Jahrbücher* 8: 142–203.

—1982. "Bilabel, Friedrich Nikolaus Alexander." In *Badische Biographien. Neue Folge* 1, edited by Bernd Ottnad, 54–56. Stuttgart: Kohlhammer.

Shandruk, Walter. 2022. "The Anguipede, Its Origins and Market Diffusion." In *The Iconography of Magic: Images of Power and the Power of Images in Ancient and Late Antique Magic*, edited by Raquel Martín Hernández, 103–115. Studies in the History and Anthropology of Religion 7. Leuven: Peeters.

Sheldon, Rose M. 2003. "The Sator Rebus: An Unsolved Cryptogram?" *Cryptologia* 27, no. 3: 233–287.

Shisha-Halevy, Ariel. 1989. *The Proper Name: Structural Prolegomena to Its Syntax — A Case Study in Coptic*. Vienna: VWGÖ.

—1991. "Sahidic." In *The Coptic Encyclopedia* 8, edited by Aziz S. Atiya, 194–202. New York: Macmillan.

—1992. "In Memoriam: Hans Jakob Polotsky (1905–1991)." *Orientalia*, N.S. 61, no. 3: 208–213.

—2002. "An Emerging New Dialect of Coptic [Review of *Coptic Documentary Texts from Kellis, Volume 1: P. Kell. V (P. Kell. Copt. 10–52; O. Kell. Copt. 1–2)*, by Iain Gardner, Anthony Alcock, and Wolf-Peter Funk]." *Orientalia*, n.s., 71, no. 3: 298–308.

Shoemaker, Stephen J. 2002. *Ancient Traditions of the Virgin Mary's Dormition and Assumption*. Oxford Early Christian Studies 23. Oxford: Oxford University Press.

Sijpesteijn, Petra M. 2013. *Shaping a Muslim State: The World of a Mid-Eighth-Century Egyptian Official*. Oxford Studies in Byzantium 13. Oxford: Oxford University Press.

—2021. "Loyal and Knowledgeable Supporters: Integrating Egyptian Elites in Early Islamic Egypt." In *Empires and Communities in the Post-Roman and Islamic World, C. 400–1000 CE*, edited by Rutger Kramer, and Walter Pohl, 329–359. Oxford Studies in Early Empires 17. Oxford: Oxford University Press.

Sippel, Benjamin. 2022. "Temples in Decline? The Egyptian Priesthood under Roman Rule." In *Proceedings of the 29th Congress of Papyrology, Lecce, 28 July–3 August 2019*, edited by Mario

Capasso, Paola Davoli, and Natascia Pellé, 905–914. Quaderni dell'Istituto superiore universitario di formazione interdisciplinare 2. Lecce: Centro di Studi Papirologici dell'Università del Salento.

Skeat, Theodore C. 1994. "The Origin of the Christian Codex." *Zeitschrift für Papyrologie und Epigraphik* 102: 263–268.

Skehan, Patrick W. 1980. "The Divine Name at Qumran, in the Masada Scroll, and in the Septuagint." *Bulletin of the International Organization for Septuagint and Cognate Studies* 13: 14–44.

Skemer, Don C. 2021, spring. "The Magic Serpent German Amulet Rolls in Time of War and Pestilence." *Magic, Ritual, and Witchcraft* 16, no. 1: 23–63.

Skolnik, Fred (editor in chief). 2007. *Encyclopaedia Judaica, Second Edition. Volume 2: ALR-AZ*. Detroit: MacMillan Reference USA.

Smid, Mária B. 2019a. "The Magic of Saint Cyprian: Individual Crisis and Historicity in Recent On-line Prayer Texts." In *Present and Past in the Study of Religion and Magic*, edited by Ágnes Hesz and Éva Pócs 341–361. Religious Anthropological Studies in Central Easter Europe 7. Budapest: Balassi Kiadó.

—2019b. "Piety, Practices of Reading, and Inquisition. A Catalan Saint Cyprian Prayer from 1557 and Its Context." *Acta Ethnographica Hungarica* 64, no. 2: 279–310.

Smither, Paul C. 1939. "A Coptic Love-Charm." *Journal of Egyptian Archaeology* 25, no. 2: 173–174.

Sobhy, George P. G. 1915. "The Pronunciation of Coptic in the Church of Egypt." *The Journal of Egyptian Archaeology* 2, no. 1: 15–19.

Sophocles, E. A. 1860. *A Glossary of Later and Byzantine Greek*. Memoirs of the American Academy of Arts and Sciencesa 7.

Sørensen, J. Podemann. 1984. "The Argument in Ancient Egyptian Magical Formulae." *Acta Orientalia* 45: 5–19.

Sørensen, Jesper. 2007. *A Cognitive Theory of Magic*. Cognitive Science of Religion Series. Lanham: Alta Mira.

Sperber, Daniel. 1985. "Some Rabbinic Themes in Magical Papyri." *Journal for the Study of Judaism in the Persian, Hellenistic, and Roman Period* 16, no. 1: 93–103.

Spiegelberg, Wilhelm. 1911. "Die Ägyptischen Namen und Zeichen der Tierkreisbilder in Demotischer Schrift." *Zeitschrift für Ägyptische Sprache* 48: 146–151.

Stefanski, Elizabeth. 1939. "A Coptic Magical Text." *The American Journal of Semitic Languages* 56, no. 3: 305–307.

Stegemann, Viktor. 1933–1934. *Die koptischen Zaubertexte der Sammlung Papyrus Erzherzog Rainer in Wien*. Sitzungsberichte der Heidelberger Akademie der Wissenschaften. Philosophisch-historische Klasse, 1933–34, 1. Abhandlung. Heidelberg: Carl Winters Universitätsbuchhandlung.

—1935. "ⲟⲩϫⲱⲱⲣⲉ ϩⲛ̄ⲧⲉϥϭⲟⲙ = stark." *Zeitschrift für ägyptische Sprache* 71: 81–84.

—1936. *Koptische Paläographie*. Heidelberg: F. Bilabel.

—1938. "Neue Zauber- und Gebetstexte aus koptischer Zeit in Heidelberg und Wien." *Le Muséon* 51: 73–87.

Stern, Ludwig C. 1880. *Koptische Grammatik*. Leipzig: T. O. Weigel.

Stevenson, Kenneth. 2001. "Animal Rites: The Four Living Creatures in Patristic Exegesis and Liturgy." In *Papers Presented to the 13th International Conference on Patristic Studies held at Christ Church, Oxford 1999*, edited by Maurice F. Wiles and Edward J. Yarnold, 470–492. Studia Patristica 34. Leuven: Peeters.

Stratton, Kimberly B. 2007. *Naming the Witch: Magic, Ideology, and Stereotype in the Ancient World*. Gender, Theory, and Religion 5. New York: Columbia University Press.

Strelcyn, Stefan. 1955. *Prières magiques éthiopiennes pour délier les charmes (Maftǝḥe Śǝray)*. Rocznik Orientalistyczny 18. Warsaw: Polska Akademia Nauk.

—1981. "Les mystères des Psaumes, traité éthiopien sur l'emploi des Psaumes (amharique ancien) 1." *Bulletin of the School of Oriental and African Studies* 44, no. 1: 54–84.

Strittmatter, Dom A. 1930. "Ein griechisches Exorcismusbüchlein: Ms. Car. C 143b der Zentralbibliothek in Zürich." *Orientalia Christiana* 20: 169–178.

—1932. "Ein griechisches Exorcismusbüchlein: Ms. Car. C 143b der Zentralbibliothek in Zürich." *Orientalia Christiana* 26: 125–144.

Stroppa, Marco. 2013. "L'uso di rotuli per testi cristiani di carattere letterario." *Archiv für Papyrusforschung und verwandte Gebiete* 59, no. 2: 347–358.

Suárez de la Torre, Emilio. 2014. "Pseudepigraphy and Magic." In *Fakes and Forgers of Classical Antiquity: Ergo decipiatur!*, edited by Javier Martínez, 233–262. Metaforms 2. Leiden: Brill.

Suciu, Alin. 2012. "Rossi's Edition of the Coptic Papyrus Codices in the Egyptian Museum in Turin 1." In *Alin Suciu. Patristics, Apocrypha, Coptic Literature and Manuscripts*, January 27 2012, https://alinsuciu.com/2012/01/27/rossis-edition-of-the-coptic-papyrus-codices-in-the-egyptian-museum-in-turin-1/ (accessed 20/6/2023).

—2017a. *The Berlin-Strasbourg Apocryphon: A Coptic Apostolic Memoir*. Wissenschaftliche Untersuchungen zum Neuen Testament 370. Tübingen: Mohr Siebeck.

—2017b. "Sitting in the Cell: The Literary Development of an Ascetic Praxis in Paul of Tamma's Writings. With an Edition of some Hitherto Unknown Fragments of *De cella*." *The Journal of Theological Studies* 68, no. 1: 141–171.

—Forthcoming. "*Noli me tangere* in Greek, Syriac, and Coptic Literature: From Biblical Exegesis To Apocryphal Narrative."

Swanson, Mark N. 1996. "The Specifically Egyptian Context of a Coptic Arabic Text: Chapter Nine of the *Kitāb al-Īḍāḥ* of Sawīrus ibn al-Muqaffaʿ." *Medieval Encounters* 2, no. 3: 214–227.

—2014. "Copto-Arabic Literature." In *Coptic Civilization: Two Thousand Years of Christianity in Egypt*, edited by Gawdat Gabra, 153–161. Cairo: American University in Cairo Press.

Swartz, Michael D. 1990 "Scribal Magic and Its Rhetoric: Formal Patterns in Medieval Hebrew and Aramaic Incantation Texts from the Cairo Genizah." *Harvard Theological Review* 83, no. 2: 163–180.

—2006. "Ritual Procedures in Magical Texts from the Cairo Genizah." *Jewish Studies Quarterly* 13, no. 4: 305–318.

Szirmai, John A. 1999. *The Archaeology of Medieval Bookbinding*. Aldershot: Ashgate.

Tambiah, Stanley J. 1990. *Magic, Science, Religion, and the Scope of Rationality*. Cambridge: Cambridge University Press.

Tattam, Henry. 1848. *The Apostolical Constitutions: Or Canons of the Apostles in Coptic; With an English Translation*. London: The Oriental Translation Fund.

Teigen, Håkon F. 2021. *The Manichaean Church in Kellis*. Nag Hammadi and Manichaean Studies 100. Leiden: Brill.

Thomas, D. Winton. 1960. "Kelebh 'Dog': Its Origin and Some Usages of It in the Old Testament 1." *Vetus Testamentum* 10, no. 1: 410–427.

Thompson, Herbert. 1911. *A Coptic Palimpsest containing Joshua, Judges, Ruth, Judith and Esther in the Sahidic Dialect*. Oxford: Oxford University Press.

—1912. "A Coptic Marriage Contract." *Proceedings of the Society for Biblical Archaeology* 34: 173–179.

—1932. *The Coptic Version of the Acts of the Apostles and the Pauline Epistles in the Sahidic Dialect*. Cambridge: University Press.

Thung, Michael H. 1966. "An Arabic Letter of the Rijksmuseum van Oudheden, Leiden." *Oudheidkundige mededelingen uit het Rijksmuseum van Oudheden te Leiden* (OMRO) 76: 63–68.

Tibet, David. 2014. "A Magical Request for Revelation: P.Stras. Inv. Kopt. 550." In *Coptica Argentoratensia: Textes et Documents de la Troisième Université d'Été de Papyrologie Copte (Strasbourg, 18-25 juillet 2010); P.Stras.Copt.*, edited by Anne Boud'hors, Alain Delattre, Catherine Louis, and Tonio Sebastian Richter, 131–141. Cahiers de la Bibliothèque copte 19. Paris: De Boccard.

Till, Walter. 1935. "Zu den Wiener koptischen Zaubertexten." *Orientalia* 4: 195–221.
—1942. "Koptische Kleinliteratur 1–4." *Zeitschrift für Ägyptische Sprache und Altertumskunde* 77: 101–111.
—1947. "Neue koptische Wochentagsbezeichnungen." *Orientalia*, n.s., 16, no. 1: 130–135.
—1951. *Die Arzneikunde der Kopten*. Berlin: Akademie-Verlag.
—1953. "Die Wochentagsnamen im Koptischen." In *Tome commémoratif du millénaire de la Bibliothèque Patriarcale d'Alexandrie*, 101–110. Publications de l'Institut d'Études Orientales de la Bibliothèque Patriarcale d'Alexandrie 2. Alexandria.
—1960. "La séparation des mots en copte." *Bulletin de l'Institut français d'archéologie orientale* 60: 151–170.
Tondello, Marco. 2019. "The Story of the Sleepers of Ephesus according to the Oldest Extant Text: Manuscript N.S.S.4." *Journal of Eastern Christian Studies* 71, nos. 1–2: 29–92.
Toorn, Karel van der. 2019. *Becoming Diaspora Jews. Behind the Story of Elephantine*. The Anchor Yale Bible Reference Library. New Haven: Yale University Press.
Töpfer, Susanne. 2018. "The Turin Papyrus Online Platform (TPOP): An Introduction." *Rivista del Museo Egizio* 2: 74–84.
Torallas Tovar, Sofía. 2007. "A Tenth Century List of Payments or Poll Tax Collecting on Paper from the Montserrat Collection." In *From Al-Andalus to Khurasan: Documents from the Medieval Muslim World*, edited by Petra Sijpesteijn, Lennart Sundelin, and Uwe Vagelpohl, 187–197. Islamic History and Civilization 66. Leiden: Brill.
—2021."Resisting the Codex: The Christian Use of the Roll in Late Antiquity." *Early Christianity* 12, no. 1: 61–84.
Torijano, Pablo A. 2002. *Solomon the Esoteric King: From King to Magus, Development of a Tradition*. Journal for the Study of Judaism Supplement 3. Leiden: Brill.
Trompf, Garry W., Jay Johnston, and Gunner B. Mikkelsen, eds. 2019. *The Gnostic World*. The Routledge Worlds. London/New York: Routledge.
Tsakos, Alexandros. 2014. "Miscellanea Epigraphica Nubica V: The Names of the Four Creatures of the Apocalypse in Christian Nubia." *Collectanea Christiana Orientalia* 11: 253–263.
Tuki, Raphael. 1761. ⲡⲓϫⲱⲙ ⲉϥⲉⲣⲁⲡⲁⲛⲧⲟⲕⲧⲓⲛ ⲉϫⲉⲛ ⲛⲓ ⲉⲩⲭⲏ ⲉⲑⲟⲩⲁⲃ ⲡⲓ ⲙⲉⲣⲟⲥ ⲛ̀ ϩⲟⲩⲓⲧ ⲉⲑⲃⲉ ⲛⲓ ϫⲓⲛϥⲱϣ ⲛ̀ⲛⲏ ⲉⲧⲁⲩⲥⲱⲧⲡ ⲛ̀ⲛⲓⲧⲱⲧⲉⲣ ⲛ̀ ⲕⲗⲏⲣⲓⲕⲟⲥ ⲛⲉⲙ ⲛⲓ ⲟⲩⲏⲃ ⲛⲉⲙ ⲡⲓ ⲥⲙⲟⲩ ⲛ̀ⲧⲉ ⲛⲓ ⲉ̀ⲃⲱⲥ ⲙ̀ ⲙⲟⲛⲁⲭⲟⲥ ⲛⲉⲙ ⲛⲓ ⲉⲛⲓⲉⲣⲟⲛⲓⲥⲙⲟⲥ ⲛ̀ⲧⲉ ⲡⲓ ⲉⲡⲓⲥⲕⲟⲡⲟⲥ ⲛⲉⲙ ⲡⲓ ⲁⲅⲓⲁⲥⲙⲟⲥ ⲙ̀ ⲙⲩⲣⲟⲛ ⲛⲉⲙ † ⲉⲕⲕⲗⲏⲥⲓⲁ (Euchologion), vol. 1. Rome.
Turner, Eric G. 1977. *The Typology of the Early Codex*. Haney Foundation Series. Philadelphia: University of Pennsylvania Press.
—1978. *The Terms Recto and Verso: The Anatomy of the Papyrus Roll*. Papyrologica Bruxellensia 16. Brussels: Fondation Égyptologique Reine Élisabeth.
Tuross, Noreen. 2014. "Accelerated Mass Spectrometry Radiocarbon Determination of Papyrus Samples." *Harvard Theological Review* 107, no. 2: 170–171.
Untermann, Matthias, ed. 2011. *Ägyptische Magie im Wandel der Zeiten: Eine Ausstellung des Instituts für Papyrologie in Zusammenarbeit mit dem Institut für Ägyptologie der Universität Heidelberg*. Universitätsmuseum Heidelberg Kataloge 5. Heidelberg: Universitätsmuseum Heidelberg.
Vanderheyden, Loreleï. 2012. "Les lettres coptes des archives de Dioscore d'Aphrodité." In *Actes du 26e Congrès international de papyrologie. Genève, 16–21 août 2010*, edited by Paul Schubert, 793–799. Publications de la Faculté des Lettres de l'Université de Genève 30. Geneva: Librairie Droz.
van der Horst, Pieter W. 2015. "Pious Long-Sleepers in Greek, Jewish, and Christian Antiquity." In *Tradition, Transmission, and Transformation from Second Temple Literature through Judaism and Christianity in Late Antiquity: Proceedings of the Thirteenth International Symposium of the Orion Center for the Study of the Dead Sea Scrolls and Associated Literature, Jointly Sponsored*

by the Hebrew University Center for the Study of Christianity, 22–24 February, 2011, edited by Menahem Kister, Hillel Newman, Michael Segal, and Ruth Clements, 93–111. Studies on the Texts of the Desert of Judah 13. Leiden: Brill.

van der Vliet, Jacques. 1991. "Varia magica coptica." *Aegyptus* 71, no. 1/2: 217–242.

—1995. "Satan's Fall in Coptic Magic." In *Ancient Magic and Ritual Power*, edited by Marvin W. Meyer and Paul Mirecki, 401–418. Religions in the Graeco-Roman world 129. Leiden/New York: Brill.

—1998. "Cologne Coptic Magical Texts: Some Notes and Corrections." *Zeitschrift für Papyrologie und Epigraphik* 122: 119–122.

—2000. "Les Anges du Soleil." In *Études coptes 7. Neuvième Journée d'études (Montpellier, 3-4 juin 1999)*, edited by Nathalie Bosson, 319–337. Cahiers de la bibiothèque copte 12. Leuven: Peeters.

—2005a. "A Coptic Charitesion (P.Gieben Copt. 1)." *Zeitschrift für Papyrologie und Epigraphik* 153: 131–140.

—2005b, May – August. "Review of *Testi della magia copta* by Sergio Pernigotti." *Bibliotheca Orientalis* 62, no. 3–4: 276–279.

—2011. "Literature, Liturgy, Magic: A Dynamic Continuum." In *Christianity in Egypt: Literary Production and Intellectual Trends. Studies in Honor of Tito Orlandi*, edited by Paola Buzi and Alberto Camplani, 555–574. Studia Ephemeridis 'Augustinianum' 125. Rome: Institutum Patristicum Augustinianum.

—2013. "Solomon in Egyptian Gnosticism." In *The Figure of Solomon in Jewish, Christian, and Islamic Tradition: King, Sage, and Architect*, edited by Joseph Verheyden, 197–218. Themes in Biblical Narrative 16. Leiden: Brill.

—2014. "Magic in Late Antique and Early Medieval Egypt." In *Coptic Civilization: Two Thousand Years of Christianity in Egypt*, edited by Gawdat Gabra, 145–152. Cairo: American University in Cairo Press.

—2018a. "Charming a Clogged Nose: A Late Coptic Magical Spell from Saqqara." *Journal of Ancient Near Eastern Religions* 18, no. 2: 145–166.

—2018b. "Reconstructing the Landscape: Epigraphic Sources for the Christian Fayoum." In *The Christian Epigraphy of Egypt and Nubia*, edited by Jacques van der Vliet and Renate Dekker, 99–109. Variorum Collected Studies Series. London/New York: Routledge.

—2019a. "Roman and Byzantine Egypt." In *Guide to the Study of Ancient Magic*, edited by David Frankfurter, 240–276. Religions in the Graeco-Roman World 189. Leiden: Brill.

—2019b. "Christian Spells and Manuals from Egypt." In *Guide to the Study of Ancient Magic*, edited by David Frankfurter, 322–350. Religions in the Graeco-Roman World 189. Leiden: Brill.

—2020. "Tradition and Innovation: Writing Magic in Christian Egypt." In *Rituals in Early Christianity: New Perspectives on Tradition and Transformation*, edited by Nienke M. Vos and Albert C. Geljon, 259–281. Supplement, Vigilae Christianae 164. Leiden/Boston: Brill.

Vandorpe, Katelijn. 1996. "Seals in and on the Papyri of Greco-Roman and Byzantine Egypt." In *Archives et sceaux du monde hellénistique. Archivi e sigilli nel mondo ellenistico, Torino, Villa Gualino, 13–16 Gennaio 1993*, edited by Marie-Françoise Boussac and Antonio Invernizzi, 231–291. Bulletin de correspondance hellénique Supplément 29. Athens: École Française d'Athènes.

Vardanyan, Edda. 2012. "Fragments d'amulettes manuscrites conservés au Musée arménien de France Fondation Nourhan Fringhian: Catalogue et édition." *Revue des Etudes Arméniennes* 34: 333–370.

Vasileiadis, Pavlos D. 2013. "The Pronunciation of the Sacred Tetragrammaton: An Overview of a *Nomen Revelatus* that Became a *Nomen Absconditus*." *Judaica Ukrainica* 2: 5–20.

—2015. "Aspects of Rendering the Sacred Tetragrammaton in Greek." *Open Theology* 1: 56–88.

—2017. "The God Iao and his Connection with the Biblical God, with Special Emphasis on the Manuscript 4QpapLXXLevb." *Vetus Testamentum et Hellas* 4: 21–51.

Velde, Hermann te. 1967. *Seth: God of Confusion: A Study of His Role in Egyptian Myth and Religion.* Probleme der Ägyptologie 6. Translated by G. E. van Baaren-Pape. Leiden: Brill.

Vercoutter, Jean. 1975. "Apis." In *Lexikon der Ägyptologie* 1, edited by Wolfgang Helck and Eberhard Otto, 338–350. Wiesbaden: Otto Harrassowitz.

Versnel, Henk S. 2002. "The Poetics of the Magical Charm." In *Ancient Magic and Ritual Power*, edited by Marvin W. Meyer and Paul Mirecki, 105–158. Religions in the Graeco-Roman world 129. Leiden/New York: Brill.

Viaud, Gérard. 1977. *Les 151 Psaumes de David dans la magie copte avec la Clef.* Paris: Édition Perthuis.

—1978. *Magie et coutumes populaires chez les Coptes d'Egypte.* Le Soleil dans le cœur 12. Saint-Vincent-sur-Jabron: Editions Présence.

Vittmann, Günter. 2021. "Zum ägyptischen Sprachgut im Alten Testament." *Orientalistische Literaturzeitung* 116, no. 4–5: 275–288.

von Lemm, Oscar. 1899. *Sahidische Bruchstücke der Legende von Cyprian von Antiochien.* Mémoires de l'Académie impériale des sciences de St.-Pétersbourg, series 8, vol. 4, no. 6. St. Petersburg: Académie impériale des sciences de St.-Pétersbourg.

—1901. "Kleine koptische Studien XXI–XXV." *Bulletin de l'Académie impériale des sciences de St.-Petersbourg* 14, no. 3: 289–313.

—1908. "Kleine koptische Studien LI–LV." *Bulletin de l'Académie impériale des sciences de St.-Petersbourg* 8, no. 12: 467–534.

—1910. "Koptische Miszellen LXVIII–LXXII." *Bulletin de l'Académie impériale des sciences de St.-Pétersbourg* 6, vol. 4, no. 1: 61–86.

Vilozny, Naama. 2015. "Lilith's Hair and Ashmedai's Horns: Incantation Bowl Imagery in the Light of Talmudic Descriptions." In *The Archaeology and Material Culture of the Babylonian Talmud*, edited by Markham J. Geller, 133–152. IJS Studies in Judaica 16. Leiden: Brill.

Vycichl, Werner. 1984. *Dictionnaire étymologique de la langue copte.* Leuven: Peeters.

Walter, Vincent. 2022. "A Prisoner's Fate in Fatimid Egypt: The Late Coptic Paitos Dossier." In *From Samarqand to Toledo: Greek, Sogdian and Arabic Documents and Manuscripts from the Islamicate World and Beyond*, edited by Andreas Kaplony and Matt Malczycki, 104–138. Islamic History and Civilization 201. Leiden: Brill.

Wasink, Craig S. 1991. "Encomium on the Four Bodiless Living Creatures attributed to John Chyrsostom." In *Homiletica from the Pierpont Morgan Library*, edited by Leo Depuydt, 43:27–46; 44:27–47. Corpus Scriptorum Christianorum Orientalium 525–526: Scriptores Coptici, 43–44 Leuven: De Gruyter.

Wasserstrom, Steven M. 1992. "The Magical Texts in the Cairo Genizah." In *Genizah Research After Ninety Years: The Case of Judaeo-Arabic; Papers Read at the Third Congress of the Society for Judaeo-Arabic Studies*, edited by Joshua Blau and Stefan C. Reif, 160–166. Cambridge: Cambridge University Press.

Weber, Manfred. 1975. "Ein Koptisches Liebeszauber." *Enchoria* 5: 115–118.

Wegner, Joanna. 2016. "The Bawit Monastery of Apa Apollo in the Hermopolite Nome and Its Relations with the 'World Outside'." *Journal of Juristic Papyrology* 46: 147–274.

Weingarten, Susan. 2014. "The Qederah: The Everyday Cooking Pot of Talmudic Times." In *Food and Material Culture: Proceedings of the Oxford Symposium on Food and Cookery 2013*, edited by Mark McWilliams, 344–353. Oxford: Prospect Books.

Weippert, Manfred. 1980. "Jahwe." In *Reallexikon der Assyriologie* 5, edited by Erich Ebeling and Bruno Meissner, 246–253. Berlin: De Gruyter.

Wellmann, Max. 1907–1914. *Pedanii Dioscuridis Anazarbei de materia medica libri quinque.* 3 vols (vol. 1, 1907; vol. 2, 1906; vol. 3, 1914). Berlin: Weidmann.

Westendorf, Wolfhart. 1965–1977. *Koptisches Handwörterbuch: Bearbeitet auf Grund des Koptischen Handwörterbuchs von Wilhelm Spiegelberg.* 9 vols. Heidelberg: C. Winter Universitätsverlag.

Westerhoff, Matthias. 1999. *Auferstehung und Jenseits im koptischen 'Buch der Auferstehung Jesu Christi, unseres Herrn.'* Orientalia Biblica et Christiana 11. Wiesbaden: Harrassowitz Verlag.

Wingate, Jane S. 1930. "The Scroll of Cyprian: An Armenian Family Amulet." *Folklore* 41, no. 2: 169–187.

Winkler, Hans A. 1931. *Salomo und die Ḳarīna. Ein orientalische Legende von der Bezwingung einer Kindbettdämonin durch einer heiligen Helden.* Veröffentlichungen des orientalischen Seminars der Universität Tübingen. Abhandlungen zur Orientalischen Philologie und zur allgemeinen Religionsgeschichte 4. Stuttgart: W. Kohlhammer.

Winlock, Herbert E., and Walter E. Crum. 1926. *The Monastery of Epiphanius at Thebes. Part 1.* New York: Publications of the Metropolitan Museum of Art.

Wipszycka, Ewa. 1972. *Les ressources et les activités économiques des églises en Égypte du IVe au VIIIe siècle.* Papyrologica Bruxellensia 10. Brussels: Fondation Egyptologique Reine Élisabeth.

—2009. *Moines et communautés monastiques en Égypte (VIe–VIIIe siècles).* Journal of Juristic Papyrology Supplement 11. Warsaw: Raphael Taubenschlag Foundation.

—2015. *The Alexandrian Church: People and Institutions.* Journal of Juristic Papyrology Supplement 25. Warsaw: Raphael Taubenschlag Foundation.

Wipszycka, Ewa, and Tomasz Derda. 1994. "L'emploi des titres 'abba', 'apa' et 'papas' dans l'Egypte byzantine." *The Journal of Juristic Papyrology* 24: 23–56.

Wissa, Myriam. 2020. "The Last Revolt of Bashmūr (831 A.D.) in Coptic and Syriac Historiography." In *Migration Histories of the Medieval Afroeurasian Transition Zone: Aspects of Mobility Between Africa, Asia and Europe, 300-1500 C.E.*, edited by Johannes Preiser-Kapeller, Lucian Reinfandt, and Yannis Stouraitis, 247–260. Studies in Global Social History 39, no. 13. Leiden: Brill.

Witakowski, Witold, and Ewa Balicka-Witakowska. 2013. "Solomon in Ethiopian tradition." In *The Figure of Solomon in Jewish, Christian and Islamic Tradition*, edited by Joseph Verheyden, 219–240. Leiden: Brill.

Woolley, Leonard C. 1911. *Karanog. The Town.* Eckley B. Coxe Junior Expedition to Nubia 5. Philadelphia: University Museum.

Worp, Klaas A. 1995. *Greek Papyri from Kellis: I (P.Kell. G.); Nos. 1–90.* Dakhleh Oasis Project 3. Oxford: Oxbow Books.

Worrell, William H. 1909. "Studien zum abessinischen Zauberwesen." *Zeitschrift für Assyriologie und Vorderasiatische Archäologie* 23, no. 1–3: 149–183.

—1910. "Studien zum abessinischen Zauberwesen." *Zeitschrift für Assyriologie und Vorderasiatische Archäologie* 24, Jahresband: 59–96.

—1915. "Studien zum abessinischen Zauberwesen." *Zeitschrift für Assyriologie und Vorderasiatische Archäologie* 29, no. 1–2: 85–141.

—1916. "Ink, Oil and Mirror Gazing Ceremonies in Modern Egypt." *Journal of the American Oriental Society* 36: 37–53.

—1930. "A Coptic Wizard's Hoard." *The American Journal of Semitic Languages and Literatures* 46, no. 4: 239–262.

—1934. *Coptic Sounds: With an Appendix by Hide Shohara.* University of Michigan Studies 26. Ann Arbor: University of Michigan Press.

—1935a. "Coptic Magical and Medical Texts." *Orientalia*, n.s. 4: 1–37.

—1935b. "Coptic Magical and Medical Texts. (Continued)." *Orientalia*, n.s. 4: 184–194.

—1942. *Coptic Texts in the University of Michigan Collection.* University of Michigan Studies 46. Ann Arbor: University of Michigan Press.

Wotke, K. 1891. "Die griechische Vorlage der lateinischen Kreuzauffindungslegende." *Wiener Studien* 13: 300–311.

Yamauchi, Edwin M. 2003. *Pre-Christian Gnosticism: A Survey of the Proposed Evidences*. Reprint. Eugene, Oregon: Wipf and Stock Publishers.

Young, Allan L. 1970. "Medical Beliefs and Practices of Begemder Amhara." PhD Diss., University of Pennsylvania.

—1975. "Magic as a 'Quasi-Profession': The Organization of Magic and Magical Healing among Amhara." *Ethnology* 14, no. 3: 245–265.

Zakrzewska, Ewa D. 2014. "The Coptic Language." In *Coptic Civilization: Two Thousand Years of Christianity in Egypt*, edited by Gawdat Gabra, 79–89. Cairo: American University in Cairo Press.

—2015. "L* as a Secret Language: Social Functions of Early Coptic." In *Christianity and Monasticism in Middle Egypt: Al-Minya and Asyut*, edited by Gawdat Gabra and Hany N. Takla, 185–198. Cairo: American University in Cairo Press.

Zandee, Jan. 1960. *Death as an Enemy According to Ancient Egyptian Conceptions*. Studies in the History of Religions 5. Leiden: Brill.

Zellmann-Rohrer, Michael. 2016. "The Tradition of Greek and Latin Incantations and Related Ritual Texts from Antiquity through the Medieval and Early Modern Periods." PhD diss., University of California, Berkeley.

—2017. "Seth on Mount Sinai: A Coptic Magical Formulary with a Prayer and Theophany of the Biblical Seth." *Zeitschrift für Ägyptische Sprache und Altertumskunde* 144, no. 2: 240–254.

—2018a. "'Psalms Useful for Everything': Byzantine and Post-Byzantine Manuals for the Amuletic Use of the Psalter." *Dumbarton Oaks Papers* 72: 113–168.

—2018b. "Two Greek Amulets." *Zeitschrift für Papyrologie und Epigraphik* 207: 105–114.

—2019. "Incantations in Byzantine and Post-Byzantine Greek: Change and Continuity." In *Cultural Plurality in Ancient Magical Texts and Practices: Graeco-Egyptian Handbooks and Related Traditions*, edited by Ljuba Merlina Bortolani, William D. Furley, Svenja Nagel, and Joachim Friedrich Quack, 276–296. Orientalische Religionen in der Antike 32. Tübingen: Mohr Siebeck.

— 2020. "Lawsuits with Headless Foes: A Greek Incantation Motif." *Archiv für Religionsgeschichte* 21–22, no. 1: 51–83.

—2021. "More on the 'Book of Protection' and the Syriac 'Charms': New Texts and Perspectives for the Study of Magic and Religion." In *Studies in the Syriac Magical Traditions*, edited by Marco Moriggi, and Siam Bhayro, 77–140. Magical and Religious Literature of Late Antiquity 9. Leiden: Brill.

—2022a. "Catalogue: Hay 1–7." In *The Hay Archive of Coptic Spells on Leather: A Multidisciplinary Approach to the Materiality of Magical Practice*, edited by Elisabeth O'Connell, 76–178. London: British Museum Press.

—2022b. "Further Useful Psalms." *Byzantinische Zeitschrift* 115, no. 3: 1115–1124.

—Forthcoming. "Enoch the Cosmic Scribe: A Less Unusual Suspect in Late Ancient Magic." In *Proceedings of the XXXth Congress of Papyrology*.

Zellmann-Rohrer, Michael W., and Edward O. D. Love. 2022. *Traditions in Transmission. The Medical and Magical Texts of a Fourth-Century Greek and Coptic Codex (Michigan Ms. 136) in Context*. Archiv für Papyrusforschung und verwandte Gebiete – Beihefte 47. Berlin: De Gruyter.

Zoëga, Georgius. 1810. *Catalogus codicum Copticorum manu scriptum qui in Museo Borgiano Veltiris adservantur*. Rome: Typis Sacrae Congregationis de Propaganda Fide.

Word Indices for *PCM* I 1

Note that here f. and b. refer to 'front' and 'back' respectively.

I. Personal Names and *Voces Magicae*

ⲁⲁⲙⲉⲕⲧⲱⲗ **11** 26.1
ⲁⲁⲣⲟⲁⲃⲇⲏⲗ **12** 41.11
. ⲁⲁⳅ **27** f.25
ⲁⲃ... **12** 21.24
ⲁⲃⲁⲑⲓⲑⲁⲗ **25** 15.14
ⲁⲃⲁⲑⲟⲩ **12** 37.9
ⲁⲃⲁⲕⲧⲁⲛⲓ **25** 15.13
 ⲁⲃⲁⲕⲧⲁⲛⲏ **28** 8.14
ⲁⲃⲓⲁ **25** 15.13
ⲁⲃⲓⲏⲗ **25** 15.21
ⲁⲃⲓⲛⲓⲭⲟⲭ **4** 1.4
ⲁⲃⲓⲟⲩⲑ **25** 12.7, 13.4
ⲁⲃⲕⲱ **26** 12.23
ⲁⲃⲗⲁⲛ[ⲁⲑ]ⲁⲛⲁⲁⳋⲗⲁ **12** 2.9
ⲁⲃⲟⲑⲏⲗ **12** 41.12
. . ⲁⲃⲟⲩⲏⲗ **12** 7.19
ⲁⲃⲟⲩⲟⲩⲭ **4** 1.4
ⲁⲃⲟⲩⲥⲁ **37** f.19
ⲁⲃⲣⲁⳅⲓⲱ **11** 26.2
ⲁⲃⲣⲁⲥⲁⳅ "Abrasax" **4** 4.13; **12** 45.18, 34; **25** 14.14
 ⲁⲃⲣⲁⲍⲁⲭ **9** 10
 ⲃⲣⲁⲥⲁⳅ **12** 45.19
 ⲣⲁⲥⲁⳅ **12** 45.20
 ⲁⲥⲁⳅ **12** 45.21, 22
 ⲥⲁⳅ **12** 45.36
 ⲁⳅ **12** 45.23
ⲁⲃⲣⲁⳋⲁⲙ "Abraham" **11** 8.7, 29.28; **25** 9.4
ⲁⲃⲧⲉⲛⲁⲕⲱ "Abednego" **25** 18.11
ⲁⲃⲧⲓⲙⲉⲗⲗⲉⲭ "Abdemelech" **9** 11–12
 ⲁⳇⲧⲓⲙⲉⲗⲉⲭ **6** 20
ⲁⲅⲟⲩⲁⲕ **16** 1.5
ⲁⲇⲁⲙ "Adam" **11** 19.9; **12** 35.12; **22** 51; **25** 6.25, 7.13, 17.41; **26** 4.2, 24, 5.26, 10.22, 11.1, 14.28
ⲁⲇⲟⲛⲓⲏⲗ **12** 27.4
ⲁⲇⲣⲁⲥⲁⳋⲁⲏⲗ **12** 9.2
ⲁⲇⲱⲛ[ⲁ]ⲏⲗ **12** 9.5
ⲁⲇⲱⲛⲁⲓ "Adonai" **11** 2.9, 5.5, 16.14, 17.28; **12** 11.4, 13.11, 15, 15.8, 19.12, 21.2, 4, 17, 25.12, 37.7; **13** 2; **25** 11.7, 12.13, 15.17, 16.23
 ⲁⲇⲱⲛⲉ **3** f.II.6; **10** 14
 ⲁⲧⲱⲛⲁⲓ **25** 3.11–12
 ⲁⲧⲱⲛⲁⲉⲓ **25** 4.1, 7.15
 ⲁⲧⲟⲛⲁⲓ **34** 2.5
ⲁⲉⲇⲓⲟⲥ "Aetius" **11** 29.15
ⲁⲉⲓⲣ **11** 25.28
ⲁⲍⲁⲏⲗ **11** 9.23, 17.16
ⲁⲍⲁⲣⲓⲁⲥ "Azariah" **25** 17.36, 18.10, 17
ⲁⲍⲁⲥⲏⲗ **11** 26.1
ⲁⲍⲟⲩⲏⲗ **25** 7.3
ⲁⲏⲗ **11** 17.4; **12** 45.31, 32
[. .] . ⲁⲏⲗ **11** 15.11
...ⲁⲑ **34** 3.4
ⲁⲑⲁ **11** 15.14; **14** 3; **25** 15.14
ⲁⲑⲁ[. . . ?] **14** 4
ⲁⲑⲁⲃ **37** f.18
ⲁⲑⲁⲏⲗ **11** 14.19, 15.15
ⲁⲑⲁⲕ **37** f.17
ⲁⲑⲁⲛⲁⲏⲗ **25** 17.36
ⲁⲑⲁⲛⲁⲥⲓⲟⲥ "Athanasius" **11** 29.18
ⲁⲑⲁⲱⲣ **12** 39.17
ⲁⲑⲉⲥ **18** 20
ⲁⲑⲏⲑⲁⲗ **11** 26.2
ⲁⲑⲓⲏⲗ **12** 27.4
. . . ⲁⲑⲓⲏⲗ **12** 7.20
ⲁⲑⲣⲁⲕ **3** f.I.1
ⲁⲑⲱⲛⲁⲑ **12** 41.17, 45.4
ⲁⲑⲱⲛⲁⲑⲁⲑⲱⲛⲁⲑ **12** 23.11
ⲁ[ⲑ]ⲱ[ⲛ]ⲁⲥ **12** 25.23
ⲁⲓⲟⲩⲑⲁ **11** 14.19
ⲁⲓⲱⲥ **23** 13
[ⲁ]ⲕⲁⲑⲟ[ⲥ] **12** 23.1
ⲁⲕⲁⲕⲓⲟⲥ "Acacius" **11** 29.14
ⲁⲕⲁⲗⲁⲧⲁ **27** f.7
ⲁⲕⲉⲛⲧⲁⲏⲗ **12** 7.9
ⲁⲕⲗⲁⲉⲓⲕⲟⲥ "Aglaius" **11** 29.22
ⲁⲕⲟⲩⲏⲗ **25** 17.37
ⲁⲕⲟⲩⲧⲁⲏⲗ **12** 27.4
ⲁⲕⲣⲁⲃⲉⲓ **11** 25.27
ⲁⲕⲣⲁⲃⲓ **11** 25.27

ⲁⲕⲣⲁⲏⲗ   **12** 7.17
ⲁⲕⲣⲁⲙⲁⲧⲁ   **25** 15.7
ⲁⲕⲣⲁⲙⲁⲭ[ⲁ]ⲙⲁⲣⲓ   **4** 2.10
ⲁⲕⲣ̣ⲁⲙⲁⲧⲁ   **26** 9.2
ⲁⲗⲁⲃⲓⲁ   **25** 15.14
ⲁⲗⲁⲑ   **37** f.19
ⲁⲗⲉⲝⲁⲛⲇⲣⲟⲥ "Alexander"   **11** 29.7
ⲁⲗⲕⲁⲣ   **25** 12.18
ⲁⲗⲗⲁⲧⲓⲟⲥ   **11** 28.25
ⲁⲗⲫⲁⲙⲓⲏⲗ   **11** 17.28
ⲁⲗⲱⲙ   **16** 1.2
ⲁⲙⲁⲓ .   **12** 45.3
ⲁ[ⲙ]ⲁⲙⲓⲏⲗ   **12** 23.2
ⲁⲙⲁⲛⲁⲏⲗ   **14** 15.9–10
ⲁⲙⲁⲣⲁⲏⲗ   **11** 15.10
. . ⲁ̣ⲙⲁ̣ⲣ̣ **34** 2.10
ⲁⲙⲓⲟⲩⲱ   **12** 45.7
. . ⲁ̣ⲓ̣ⲙ̣ⲓ̣ⲥ̣ⲕ̣ⲏ̣ⲥ̣   **32** 2.30
ⲁⲙⲓⲧⲱⲛ   **12** 39.14
ⲁⲙⲓⲱⲏⲗ   **4** 3.3
ⲁⲙⲟⲛⲓ   **37** f.18
ⲁⲙⲟⲩ   **28** 3.21
ⲁⲙⲧⲁⲧⲑ   **5** f.6
…ⲁⲙⲱⲑⲁⲙ   **12** 45.2
ⲁⲙ̣ⲱⲙⲓⲭ   **4** 1.5
ⲁⲛⲁⲏⲗ   **11** 9.22, 17.16; **25** 10.25, 26, 11.4, 15.22, 16.1, 21; **26** 14.14, 24; **34** 4.6
ⲁⲛⲁⲗⲙⲉⲁ ⲙⲉⲛ   **25** 17.2
ⲁⲛⲁⲛⲓⲁⲥ "Hananiah"   **25** 17.35–36, 18.9, 17
ⲁⲛⲁⲛⲓⲏⲗ   **11** 15.11
ⲁⲛⲁⲣⲁⲙⲟⲩⲏⲗ   **26** 8.14
ⲁⲛⲁⲣⲭⲓ . .   **34** 2.19
…ⲁⲛⲁⲧ   **34** 2.26
ⲁⲛⲁⲧⲏⲗ   **11** 16.27;
ⲁⲛⲇⲣⲁⲙⲓⲏⲗ   **25** 14.19
ⲁⲛⲉⲭⲱⲭ   **12** 45.4
ⲁⲛⲗⲏⲗ   **12** 27.2
ⲁⲛⲧⲣⲁⲕⲟⲩⲏⲗ   **26** 8.15
ⲁⲛⲫⲟⲩ   **26** 15.14
ⲁⲛⲱⲱ   **12** 45.2
ⲁⲛϯⲛⲓⲁⲥ   **25** 9.24
ⲁⲛϯⲛⲟⲥ "Antinoos"   **32** 1.31
ⲁⲝ   **9** 10; **12** 45.9
ⲁⲡⲟ[ⲗⲗⲱⲛ] "Apollo"   **32** 1.30, 2.28
[… ?]ⲁⲣ   **13** 3
ⲁⲣⲁⲏⲗ   **11** 15,4
ⲁⲣⲁⲑⲁ   **11** 16.26
ⲁⲣⲁⲑⲁⲏⲗ   **11** 16.27
ⲁⲣⲁⲕⲁ   **22** 6
ⲁⲣⲁⲕⲥⲁ   **22** 10

ⲁⲣⲁⲕⲧⲟⲥ   **12** 13.10
ⲁⲣⲁⲙ   **11** 14.18; **26** 15.13, 14
ⲁⲣⲁⲝ   **24** 28
ⲁⲣⲁⲥⲁ   **22** 40
ⲁⲣⲁⲧⲁⲃⲛⲏ   **22** 9
ⲁⲣⲁⲧⲁⲙⲟⲩ   **22** 7
ⲁⲣⲁⲧⲁⲭⲁⲏⲗ   **11** 15.4–5
ⲁⲣⲁⲭⲁ   **11** 14.24
ⲁⲣⲁⲭⲁⲏⲗ   **11** 14.24, 15.5
ⲁⲣⲉⲧⲱ   **25** 10.19, 11.6, 13.19, 16.23; **29** f.16
ⲁⲣⲑⲁⲙⲓⲏⲗ   **12** 27.12
ⲁⲣⲑⲁⲥⲁ   **25** 15.13
ⲁⲣⲓⲏⲗ   **25** 5.19, 20
ⲁⲣⲓⲙⲁⲑⲁ   **11** 14.18, 15.24
ⲁⲣⲓⲛⲁ   **22** 8, 40
ⲁⲣⲓⲛⲁⲧⲁⲏⲗ   **11** 17.6
ⲁⲣⲓⲱ   **22** [tableau], 8, 27, 40
ⲁⲣⲓⲱⲙⲁ   **4** 2.10
ⲁⲣⲛⲁⲏⲗ   **12** 7.6
ⲁⲣⲟⲏⲗ   **12** 41.9
ⲁⲣⲟⲩⲱⲏⲗ   **12** 41.9
ⲁⲣⲡⲁⲭ   **30** f [tableau], f.17
     ϩⲁⲣⲡⲁⲕ̣   **30** f.8
     ⲁⲣ (?)   **30** f.18
ⲁⲣⲧⲱⲗⲁⲛ   **26** 6.13
ⲁⲣⲧⲱⲗⲁⲣ   **26** 6.13
ⲁⲣⲧⲱⲗⲏ   **26** 6.13
ⲁⲣⲭⲓⲗⲗⲓⲧⲟⲥ "Archillides"   **11** 28.24
ⲁⲣⲭⲱⲁ   **37** f.1
ⲁⲣⲱⲙ   **22** 2
ⲁⲣⲱⲙⲁ   **22** 40
ⲁⲣⲱⲙⲁⲛⲁ   **22** 4
ⲁⲣⲱⲙⲁⲛⲁⲏⲗ   **22** 5, 40
ⲁⲣⲱⲙⲁⲭⲣⲓⲙ   **26** 4.2
ⲁⲣⲱⲙⲁⲱ   **22** 3, 41
ⲁⲣⲱⲛⲁⲓ   **33** 3
ⲁⲣⲱⲫⲧⲏⲃⲏⲗ   **12** 27.12
ⲁⲥⲁⲙⲁ   **26** 8.24
ⲁⲥⲁⲙⲗⲱⲗ   **26** 8.24
ⲁⲥⲁⲣⲱⲑ   **18** 3; **26** 10.27
ⲁⲥⲁϥ   **26** 8.24
ⲁⲥⲃⲓⲏⲧ   **5** f.4
ⲁⲥⲉⲛⲁⲕⲱⲥ   **37** f.27
ⲁⲥⲉⲛⲧⲁⲏⲗ   **12** 7.10
ⲁⲥⲙⲟⲧⲉⲟⲥ "Asmodeus"   **18** 18–19
ⲁⲥⲟⲩⲏⲗ   **3** b.I.4
ⲁⲥⲟⲩⲣ   **37** f.1
ⲁⲥⲫⲟⲩⲏⲗ   **5** f.5
ⲁⲥⲱⲧⲱⲫ   **4** 3.3
[.] . ⲁⲧⲁⲏⲗ   **34** 2.23

ⲁⲧⲓⲣⲏⲑⲁ   **29** b.1
ⲁⲧⲱⲙⲁ   **25** 3.12
ⲁⲧⲱⲛⲁⲥ   **23** 13
ⲁⲧⲱⲣⲁⲙ   **26** 3.28
ⲁⲩⲏⲗ   **12** 41.10
ⲁⲩⲑⲱⲛ   **37** f.19
ⲁⲩⲕⲁⲣⲟⲥ "Abgar"   **11** 20.6, 24.2, 6, 25.23
ⲁⲩⲗⲉⲥ   **25** 18.12
ⲁⲩⲣⲓⲏⲗ   **12** 27.3
ⲁⲩⲧⲟⲩⲗ   **28** 3.20
ⲁⲫⲁⲏⲗ   **12** 7.16
ⲁⲭⲁ   **25** 8.12
ⲁⲭⲁⲃⲁ   **27** f.7
ⲁⲭⲁⲏⲗ   **11** 17.4; **22** 18
ⲁⲭⲁⲙⲣⲁ   **25** 8.12–13
ⲁⲭⲁⲣⲁϩ   **27** f.8
ⲁⲭⲏ   **23** 19
ⲁⲭⲏⲗ   **12** 41.11
ⲁⲭⲓ   **25** 8.12
ⲁⲭⲓⲏⲗ   **5** f.4
ⲁⲭⲗ   **11** 26.4
ⲁⲭⲱⲣⲃⲟⲩ   **26** 9.12
. . . . ⲁⲱⲗⲓⲁⲙ   **34** 3.1
ⲁϥⲃⲟⲩⲣⲉ   **9** 1
ⲁϥⲗⲓⲃⲏⲗⲓⲍⲉ   **5** f.6–7
ⲁϥⲣⲁⲕ   **12** 23.4
ⲁϥⲣⲓⲧⲱⲛ   **12** 39.14
ⲁϥⲣⲱⲙⲱⲑⲁⲙ   **12** 45.3
ⲁϥⲫⲏⲗ   **12** 41.9
ⲁϫⲉ   **12** 41.13
ⲁϫⲏ   **12** 41.13
ⲁϫⲟⲩ   **37** f.17
ⲃⲉⲗⲥⲟ[ⲃⲟ]ⲩⲗ "Beelzebub"   **31** f.2–3
  ⲃⲉⲣⲥⲉⲃⲟⲗ   **30** f.24, b.2
  ⲃ[ⲉ]ⲣⲥⲉⲃⲟⲩⲣ   **17** b.42
ⲃⲁ   **25** 3.14
ⲃⲁⲃ   **23** 17
ⲃⲁⲃⲁⲙ   **12** 37.6
ⲃⲁⲃⲱⲑ   **25** 3.13
ⲃⲁⲏⲗ   **12** 17.14, 41.7, 10
ⲃⲁⲑⲟⲩⲏⲗ   **25** 15.26
ⲃⲁⲑⲟⲩⲣⲓⲏⲗ   **12** 19.1, 23.6, 25.6–7, 37.7, 39.16, 41.1; **25** 6.14
ⲃⲁⲓⲱⲧ   **23** 13
ⲃⲁⲕⲉ   **25** 18.12
ⲃⲁⲗ   **4** 2.15
ⲃⲁⲗⲉⲑⲁⲣⲟⲓ   **25** 11.1
ⲃⲁⲗⲓⲁ   **33** 4
ⲃⲁⲗⲓⲙ   **28** 3.19
[. ?]ⲃⲁⲛ   **32** 1.29
ⲃⲁⲣ   **23** 14, 16; **33** 4
ⲃⲁⲣⲁϩ   **24** 28
ⲃⲁⲣⲃⲁⲣⲁⲕ   **37** b.23
ⲃⲁⲣⲃⲏⲥ   **37** b.22, 23
ⲃⲁⲣⲓⲏⲗ   **12** 27.11
ⲃⲁⲣⲟⲩⲭ   **11** 26.3; **22** [tableau]; **24** 3; **31** b.22
ⲃⲁⲣⲭ   **25** 10.26
ⲃⲁⲥ   **25** 10.26
ⲃⲁⲥⲓⲗⲉⲟⲥ   **28** 3.19
ⲃⲁⲧⲱⲗ   **32** 2.21
ⲃⲁⲩ   **23** 14
ⲃⲁⲭⲱⲱⲗ   **12** 41.8
ⲃⲁⲱⲑ   **2**.1
ⲃⲁⲱⲧⲱⲣ   **4** 5.5
ⲃⲉⲃⲓⲁⲛⲟⲥ "Vibianus"   **11** 29.9
ⲃⲉⲛⲓⲟⲑⲱ   **12** 45.7
ⲃⲉⲛⲓⲭⲱⲭ   **12** 45.27
ⲃⲏⲑ   **25** 5.15, 12.23, 15.21
ⲃⲏⲑⲁ   **25** 5.15, 20, 7.19, 15.21
ⲃⲏⲑⲁⲉⲓ   **25** 12.28, 15.21
ⲃⲏⲑⲁϥ   **25** 12.28
ⲃⲏⲣ   **23** 16
. . . . ⲃⲏⲥⲱⲛ   **34** 3.2
ⲃⲓⲣⲟⲃⲁ   **11** 26.4
ⲃⲓⲧⲉⲃⲟⲓⲑⲓ   **25** 18.13
ⲃⲗⲁⲣⲁⲣⲟ   **12** 17.3
ⲃⲗⲓⲕⲁⲃⲟⲩ   **16** 1.1–2
ⲃⲙⲥⲁⲏⲗ   **25** 17.38
ⲃⲟⲣⲁⲱ   **11** 26.1–2
ⲃⲟⲣ . . . ⲱ   **3** f.II.12
ⲃⲟⲩⲑⲁ   **25** 18.12
ⲃⲟⲩⲗⲁⲗ   **25** 18.11
ⲃⲱⲃⲱⲏⲗ   **12** 39.17
ⲃⲱⲓⲑ   **25** 18.16
ⲃⲱⲓⲑⲱⲛ   **25** 18.14
ⲃⲱⲕ   **22** [tableau]
ⲃⲱⲣⲁⲃⲱⲏⲗ   **4** 2.11
ⲃⲱⲭⲱⲭ   **4** 3.3
ⲅⲁⲃⲣⲓⲏⲗ "Gabriel"   **3** f.II.2, b.I.3; **11** 6.16, 9.17–18, 17.14; **12** 7.5, 21.9; **25** 7.2, 7, 10.24, 11.3, 15.26, 16.20; **26** 14.12, 14, 17 [tableau]; **28** 4.4, 6.15, 7.14, 16, 18, 21, 8.1, 8, 14, 11.12, 12.14, 13.8, 19, 23; **29** f.2; **32** 1.5; **34** 3.4
ⲅⲁⲫⲣⲓⲏⲗ   **12** 35.10
ⲅⲁϥⲣⲓⲏⲗ   **12** 13.4, 13, 15.11, 17.2, 8, 17, 23, 19.3, 14–15, 21.9, 23.12, 25.6, 20, 27.1, 3, 18, 29.4, 9, 31.2, 9, 15, 21, 33.3, 8, 16, 22, 35.2, 7, 19, 23, 37.4, 39.12, 19, 24, 41.3, 43.3, 18, 45.4
ⲕⲁϥⲣⲓⲏⲗ   **12** 27.9, 29.14

ⲅⲁⲣⲙⲁⲛⲓⲏⲗ   **26** 12.18
ⲅⲁⲣⲛⲁⲃⲓⲏⲗ   **25** 12.20, 13.4
ⲅⲁⲣⲛⲁⲃⲓⲟⲩⲑ   **25** 12.8, 13.4
ⲅⲉⲥⲁⲙⲏⲥ   **33** 4
ⲅⲏⲙⲛⲁⲛ   **11** 26.6
ⲅⲏⲛ   **33** 5
ⲅⲣⲏⲅⲟⲣⲓⲟⲥ "Gregory"   **11** 1.2–3, 28, 4.24, 7.27
    ⲉⲅⲟⲣⲓⲟⲩ   **11** 14.13
ⲇⲁⲛⲓⲏⲗ "Daniel"   **12** 37.10; **24** 15
ⲇⲁⲩⲉⲓⲇ "David"   **11** 29.28, 30.21–22
ⲇⲁⲩⲉⲓⲑⲉⲁ   **25** 8.8
ⲇⲁⲩⲗⲁ   **11** 26.5
ⲇⲓⲙⲉⲗⲟⲩⲭⲟⲥ "Temelouchos"   **8** b.3
ⲇⲓⲟⲙⲏⲧⲟⲥ "Diomedes"   **11** 28.24
ⲇⲟⲙⲏⲇⲓⲁⲛⲟⲥ "Domitian"   **11** 29.3
ⲇⲣⲁⲭⲁⲏⲗ   **25** 14.20
ⲉⲃⲥⲁⲓⲙⲏⲥ   **25** 9.25
ⲉⲇⲉⲕⲓⲏⲗ   **11** 15.25, 16.28, 17.5
ⲉⲑⲏ   **25** 18.14
ⲉⲓⲁⲱ   **11** 18.21
ⲉⲓⲁⲱϩ   **11** 18.21
ⲉⲓⲉⲣϣⲉϩ   **34** 2.23
. ⲉⲓⲗⲁⲏⲗ   **12** 7.18
ⲉⲓⲭⲁⲙ   **25** 5.17
ⲉⲕⲇⲓⲕⲁⲓⲟⲥ "Ecdicius"   **11** 29.14
ⲉⲕⲧⲉⲣⲓⲥⲁⲛ   **26** 6.18–19
ⲉⲕⲱⲉ   **12** 25.24
ⲉⲗⲉⲗⲉⲑ   **25** 8.8
ⲉⲗⲉⲙⲁⲥ   **11** 2.9, 5.6, 16.15; **28** 8.13
    ⲉⲗⲉⲙⲁ   **12** 21.17
    ⲉⲗⲏⲙⲁⲥ   **22** 12; **25** 11.9, 16.2; **26** 13.26
ⲉⲗⲉⲱⲑ   **25** 15.14
ⲉⲗⲱⲉⲓ "Eloei"   **11** 2.9, 5.6, 16.15, 17.28, 18.20–21, 25.28; **22** 12; **25** 7.16, 11.8, 16.25; **26** 13.25, 8.12
    ⲉⲗⲱⲏ   **10** 14 cf. [.]ⲗⲱⲛ
    ⲉⲗⲟⲉⲓ   **12** 11.4, 15.8, 13.11, 19.13, 21.2, 5, 17; **13** 3; **25** 4.2; **26** 13.26
ⲉⲙⲙⲁⲛⲟⲩⲏⲗ "Emmanuel"   **25** 11.6, 16.23
ⲉⲙⲟⲩⲃⲓⲕ   **4** 1.7
ⲉⲛⲛⲁⲏⲗ   **18** 1
ⲉⲛⲟⲩⲏⲗ   **33** f.16
ⲉⲛⲱⲭ "Enoch"   **15** f.6
ⲉⲝⲓⲏⲗ   **26** 12.18
ⲉⲣⲓⲏⲗ   **25** 15.22
ⲉⲣⲓⲥⲓ   **28** 3.18
ⲉⲣⲙⲟⲩ   **11** 26.4
ⲉⲥⲁⲉⲥ   **12** 21.23
ⲉⲥⲁⲛⲁ   **30** f.16
ⲉⲥⲕⲉϩⲱⲏⲗ   **25** 16.3
ⲉⲥⲡⲁⲣⲧⲏ   **3** f.II.25–6
ⲉⲥⲭⲉⲩ   **23** 18
ⲉⲧⲱⲁⲕ   **12** 23.4
ⲉⲧϣⲓⲣ ⲓⲣⲁⲩⲣⲉ   **29** b.2
ⲉⲩⲗⲉⲥ   **25** 18.12
ⲉⲩⲛⲟⲉⲓⲕⲟⲥ "Eunoicus"   **11** 29.11
ⲉⲩⲧⲩⲭⲓⲟⲥ "Eutychius"   **11** 29.10
    ⲉⲩⲧⲏⲭⲓⲟⲥ   **11** 29.8
ⲉⲩϩⲁ   **24** 28–29
ⲉⲫⲓⲭⲏ   **25** 15.13
ⲉⲫⲛⲓⲝ   **12** 27.13
ⲉⲱ   **25** 18.12
ⲉϩⲧⲱⲣⲱ   **25** 15.17
ⲍⲁⲣⲓⲏⲗ   **25** 5.19
ⲍⲉⲧⲉⲕⲓⲏⲗ   **25** 10.25, 11.4, 15.27, 16.21
    ⲥⲉⲧⲉⲕⲓⲏⲗ   **26** 14.13, 22
ⲍⲉⲩⲥ "Zeus"   **32** 1.30
ⲍⲓⲁⲙⲟⲩⲣ   **11** 26.3
ⲍⲱⲏ "Zoe"   **25** 17.42
    ⲥⲱⲏ   **22** 52; **25** 7.14
ⲍⲱⲙⲓⲍ   **21** 9
ⲏⲅⲓⲁⲥ "Aggius"   **11** 29.13
ⲏⲗ   **34** 2.22
ⲏⲗⲁⲕⲗⲓⲟⲥ "Heraclius"   **11** 29.6
ⲏⲟⲩⲱ   **12** 45.8
ⲏⲣ   **11** 15.18–19, 16.16–17
ⲏⲣⲓⲏⲗ   **12** 7.14
ⲏⲥⲁⲓⲁⲥ   **11** 30.6
ⲏⲥⲉ "Isis"   **4** 4.5, 12; **6** 5; **7** 12, 15; **8** f.3; **16** 2.3, 14; **20** f.8
    ⲉⲥⲥⲉ   **9** 5, 7, 8
    [[ⲉ]]ⲥⲉ   **16** 1.6
    ⲏⲉ   **16** 2.5
ⲏⲥⲏⲭⲓⲟⲥ "Hesychius"   **11** 29.4
ⲏⲧⲁⲩ[. . . .]   **34** 2.25
ⲑⲁ   **12** 45.2; **25** 3.14
ⲑⲁⲃⲁⲏⲗ   **12** 41.8
ⲑⲁⲃⲟⲃⲩⲭ   **4** 1.5
ⲑⲁⲃⲟⲩⲏⲗ   **12** 41.11
ⲑⲁⲏⲗ   **12** 41.7, 9, 10
ⲑⲁⲑⲁ   **26** 7.16
ⲑⲁⲓⲥⲁⲣⲁ   **12** 17.7
ⲑⲁⲗⲁⲙⲱⲣⲁ   **12** 17.7
ⲑⲁⲙⲓⲏⲗ   **12** 41.12
ⲑⲁⲍ   **24** 28
ⲑⲁⲡⲁⲟϩ   **25** 9.26
ⲑⲁⲡⲁⲥ   **25** 9.26
ⲑⲁⲣⲁ   **34** 2.9
ⲑⲁⲣⲁⲃⲭ   **4** 2.8
ⲑⲁⲣⲓⲙⲓⲏⲗ   **12** 41.10

ⲑⲁⲣⲙⲁⲱⲑ **22** 41
ⲑⲁⲣⲟⲓⲉⲗ **12** 41.13
ⲑⲁⲣⲥⲟⲩⲭ **4** 1.6
ⲑⲁⲩⲏⲗ **12** 41.12
ⲑⲁⲩⲣⲟⲩⲏⲗ **12** 9.1
ⲑⲁⲱⲑ **25** 14.3; **26** 8.17
ⲑⲁⲱⲑⲁ **25** 14.3; **26** 8.17
ⲑⲁⲩⲣⲓⲏⲗ **12** 41.11
ⲑⲉⲃⲱⲏⲗ **12** 41.22
ⲑⲉⲛⲉⲡⲉⲓⲙ **4** 1.7
ⲑⲉⲟⲇⲟⲩⲗⲟⲥ "Theodulus" **11** 29.21
ⲑⲉⲟⲫⲓⲗⲟⲥ "Theophilus" **11** 29.21
ⲑⲉⲱⲑⲁⲛⲁⲩⲧⲏⲣⲓ **12** 39.15
ⲑⲏⲗ **12** 41.11
ⲑⲏⲣⲓⲏⲗ **12** 17.13
ⲑⲏⲥⲟⲣ **12** 17.7
ⲑⲓⲏⲗ **12** 41.8; **26** 7.18
ⲑⲟⲕ **12** 41.10
ⲑⲣⲁⲕⲁⲓ **12** 11.13
ⲑⲣⲁⲕⲁⲓⲙ **12** 13.3
ⲑⲣⲓⲏⲗ **12** 27.4
ⲑⲣⲟⲏⲗ **12** 17.14, 41.7, 10
ⲑⲱⲏⲗ **12** 41.8; **26** 7.22
ⲑⲱⲗ **26** 7.30
ⲑⲱⲣⲁⲑ **4** 2.7
ⲑⲱⲣⲁⲛ **26** 7.30
ⲓⲁⲁⲣ **27** b.2
ⲓⲁⲕ **26** 6.12; **34** 3[tableau]
ⲓⲁⲕⲱⲃ "Jacob" **11** 8.8
ⲓⲁⲙⲗⲓⲭⲟⲥ **25** 9.24
ⲓⲁⲙⲟⲩⲣ **37** f.16
ⲓⲁⲛⲥ **12** 45 [tableau]
ⲓⲁⲭⲁⲟⲓ **12** 37.9
ⲓⲁⲱ "Iao" **3** b.I.12; **4** 6.2; **8** f.2; **11** 18.21; **12** 11.1, 13.10, 21.2, 4, 21, 25.11, 37.7, 43.15; **13**.1; **16** 3.7–8; **22** 11; **25** 2.10, 4.1, 5.19, 7.14, 16, 12.12; **26** 6.12; **34** 3.3
ⲓⲁⲱⲏⲗ **12** 9.3
ⲓⲁⲱⲑ **12** 21.21
ⲓⲉⲣⲉⲙⲓⲏⲗ **12** 7.12
ⲓⲉⲭⲁ **12** 41.15
ⲓⲉⲣ **26** 11.16
ⲓⲏⲗ **11** 26.7
ⲓⲏⲥⲟⲩⲥ ⲡⲉⲭⲣⲓⲥⲧⲟⲥ "Jesus Christ" **11** 2.3, 13, 4.24–25, 8.2, 11.27, 19.28, 20.2, 9, 24.1, 4, 25.23, 28.10, 13, 17, 29.27, 30.4; **12** 31.6; **15** f.1; **23** 25; **25** 6.4–5, 8.16, 29, 10.20, 11.5, 12.3, 10, 13.5, 18, 22, 25, 29, 14.4, 8, 15.11, 14, 19, 23, 16.1, 4, 22, 17.12, 34; **26** 4.22, 11.3, 12.8, 26, 27, 29, 31, 13.1, 3, 5–6, 17, 29, 34, 15.10; **28** 3.2, 8.9, 16, 21, 9.3, 12.11; **29** f.1, 7; **31** f.32, b.9
ⲓⲟⲁⲕ **12** 23.4
ⲓⲟⲩⲥⲧⲛⲁ "Justina" **28** 2.10
ⲓⲟⲣⲁⲩ **27** f.6
ⲓⲥⲁⲕ "Isaac" **11** 8.7
ⲓⲥⲙⲁⲏⲗ "Ishmael" **25** 17.43
ⲓⲩⲟⲩⲧⲁⲥ "Judas" **31** f.21–22
ⲓⲭⲁⲟⲩ **12** 37.9
ⲓⲱ **13** 20
ⲓⲱ ⲁⲣ **13** 20
ⲓⲱ ⲡⲁⲕⲉⲣⲃⲑ **4** 5.3–4
ⲓⲱ ⲡⲁⲫⲩⲗⲁⲝ **4** 5.4
ⲓⲱ ⲥⲏⲑ **4** 5.3
ⲓⲱ ⲫⲉⲛⲓⲝ **4** 5.4
ⲓⲱⲁ **13** 21
ⲓⲱⲃⲏⲑ **14** 5
ⲓⲱⲏⲗ **12** 41.9
ⲓⲱⲓⲣⲓⲏⲗ **12** 19.8
ⲓⲱⲕⲁⲡ **25** 12.11
ⲓⲱⲥⲏⲫ "Joseph" **11** 28.6; **28** 13.2; **31** f.12
  ⲓⲱⲥⲏⲫ ⲡⲩ ⲡⲁⲣⲁⲥⲉⲩ "Iōsēph son of Paraseu" **25** 13.3, 9
ⲓⲱⲫ[. . .] **14** 5
ⲓⲱⲣⲁⲛⲛⲏⲥ "John, Iōhannēs" **11** 29.16, 30.14–15
  ⲓⲱ **23** 50
ⲕⲁⲁⲃ **12** 25.24
ⲕⲁⲛⲥⲁⲥ **12** 25.24
ⲕⲁⲑⲁⲇⲱ **11** 26.4–5
ⲕⲁⲑⲓⲏⲗ **34** 2.23
ⲕⲁⲓⲟⲥ "Gaius" **11** 29.17
ⲕⲁⲕⲓⲕⲉⲫⲁⲗⲓ **28** 3.20
ⲕⲁⲗⲗⲓⲕⲗⲏⲥ "Kalliklēs" **1** f.33–34
ⲕⲁⲙⲟⲩⲥ **5** f.5
ⲕⲁⲛⲧⲓⲧⲟⲥ "Candidus" **11** 29.19
ⲕⲁⲣⲣⲁ **25** 12.19
ⲕⲁⲥⲓⲥ **27** f.7
ⲕⲁⲧ[. . .] . **34** 3.2
ⲕⲁⲧⲁⲧⲏⲗ **25** 5.19
ⲕⲁⲧⲟⲩⲟⲥⲭⲟⲥ **37** f.30
ⲕⲉⲛⲁⲕⲱⲥ **37** f.31
ⲕⲉⲡⲣⲓⲁⲛⲟⲥ "Cyprian" **28** 1.16–17
ⲕⲉⲣⲓⲁ **27** f.8
ⲕⲉⲧⲁ **23** 18
ⲕⲉⲭⲁⲣⲓ **28** 13.21
ⲕⲓⲣⲓⲉ **20** f.12
ⲕⲗⲁⲩⲇⲓⲟⲥ "Claudius" **11** 29.17
ⲕⲛⲱⲫⲟⲥ **31** b.2
ⲕⲟⲙⲟⲩⲏⲗ **25** 15.15

ⲕⲟⲣⲁⲛⲓⲏⲗ   4 2.11
ⲕⲟⲣⲕⲟⲛⲓⲟⲥ "Gorgonius"   11 29.20
ⲕⲟⲩⲏⲗ   4 2.12
...ⲕ̣ⲟⲩⲏⲗ   34 3.5
ⲕⲥⲁⲥ   12 25.23
ⲕⲩⲣⲓⲁⲕⲟⲥ "Cyriacus"   11 28.26
ⲕⲩⲣⲓⲗⲗⲟⲥ "Cyril"   11 29.10
ⲕⲩⲣⲓⲱⲛ "Cyrion"   11 29.7
ⲗⲁⲁⲅⲟⲩⲙ   16 1.4
ⲗⲁⲃⲁⲏⲗ   25 17.38
ⲗⲁⲃⲓⲱ   16 1.2
ⲗⲁⲉⲗⲁⲙⲑ   4 2.7
ⲗⲁⲑⲁⲑ   4 2.9
ⲗⲁⲗ   25 18.11; 34 2.26
ⲗⲁⲙⲛⲁ   33 4
ⲗⲁⲛⲁⲭ   12 27.12
ⲗⲁⲩⲣⲓⲏⲗ   12 13.5
ⲗⲁⲭ   16 1.3
ⲗⲁⲭⲟⲩⲏⲗ   37 f.19
ⲗⲁⲭⲱⲙ   37 f.1
ⲗⲁⲭⲱⲣ   37 f.19
ⲗⲁ†ⲁ.[...]ⲩⲏⲗ   34 2.24
ⲗⲉⲕⲧⲏⲥ   25 18.13
ⲗⲉⲗⲁⲏⲗ   26 8.11
ⲗⲉⲟⲛⲧⲓⲟⲥ "Leontius"   11 29.12
ⲗⲉⲥⲓⲙⲁⲭⲟⲥ "Lysimachus"   11 29.9
ⲗⲟⲩⲕⲁⲥ "Luke"   11 30.8–9
ⲗⲟⲩⲗⲟⲩⲕⲁⲕⲥⲁⲥ   26 12.18
ⲗⲱⲗⲱ   37 f.18
[.]ⲗⲱⲛ   34 3.3 cf. ⲉⲗⲱⲓ
ⲗⲱϩⲉⲡ   27 f.7
ⲙ̣[...?]   14 1
ⲙⲁⲑ   37 f.19
ⲙⲁⲑⲑⲁⲓⲟⲥ "Matthew"   11 29.25
ⲙⲁⲓⲑⲉⲥⲁϣ   34 2.10
ⲙⲁⲕⲑⲁⲓ   29 b.6
ⲙⲁⲗⲁⲭ   16 1.3
ⲙⲁⲗⲁϩⲁ   16 1.3–4
ⲙⲁⲙ   25 5.17
ⲙⲁⲙⲓⲏⲗ   12 23.3
ⲙⲁⲛⲁⲭⲱⲑ   12 11.16
ⲙⲁⲛⲓⲍ   25 12.2, 13.1
ⲙⲁⲛⲟⲛ   25 15.22
ⲙⲁⲛⲟⲩⲏⲗ   11 16.2–4, 27–28, 17.4; 12 31.8, 37.8; 25 17.36–37; 26 12.13
ⲙⲁⲛⲟⲩϣⲣⲟⲥ   25 15.15
ⲙⲁⲣ   23 15
ⲙⲁⲣⲏ̣.   29 b.5
ⲙⲁⲣⲓ   12 37.5
ⲙⲁⲣⲓⲁ "Mary"   11 27.16; 25 2.1–2, 6, 20, 8.1, 20, 9.9, 10, 14, 15, 17, 12.16, 13.11; 26 12.11, 15; 28 6.22, 8.3, 11.21
ⲙⲁⲣⲓⲁ ⲙⲁⲕⲧⲁⲗⲓⲛⲏ "Mary Magdalene"   25 9.14–15
ⲙⲁⲣⲓⲁ ⲡϣⲉⲉⲣⲉ ⲛⲅⲗⲱⲡⲁⲥ "Mary the daughter of Clopas"   25 9.15–16
ⲙⲁⲣⲓⲁ ⲧⲁ ⲓⲁⲕⲱⲃⲟⲥ "Mary of James"   25 9.17–18
ⲙⲁⲣⲓⲏⲕ   12 23.3
ⲙⲁⲣⲓⲏⲗ   12 41.2
ⲙⲁⲣⲓⲏⲗ   26 7.20
ⲙⲁⲣⲓⲛⲑⲁⲏⲗ   11 15.25
ⲙⲁⲣⲓⲥⲉⲓ   15 9.13
ⲙⲁⲣⲓⲭ   32 2.21
ⲙⲁⲣⲓⲱ   37 f.17
ⲙⲁⲣⲓϩⲁⲙ "Miriam"   25 2.21, 9.11; 26 12.11
ⲙⲁⲣⲓϩⲏⲩ   25 9.12
ⲙⲁⲣⲕⲟⲥ "Mark"   11 30.1–2
ⲙⲁⲣⲙⲁⲙ   25 6.19
ⲙⲁⲣⲙⲁⲣ   25 6.19
ⲙⲁⲣⲙⲁⲣⲁⲙⲓ   12 19.11
ⲙⲁⲣⲙⲁⲣⲁⲱⲑ   12 11.7
ⲙⲁⲣⲙⲁⲣⲓⲱⲑ   5 f.7; 22 41
ⲙⲁⲣⲙⲁⲣⲟⲩ   12 37.6
ⲙⲁⲣⲙⲁⲣⲟⲩ   25 6.19
ⲙⲁⲣⲙⲁⲣⲟⲩⲏⲗ   25 6.16, 17, 25 15.25
ⲙⲁⲣⲙⲁⲣⲟⲩⲛ   25 6.18
ⲙⲁⲣⲙⲁⲣⲟⲩⲛⲓⲏⲗ   25 6.17, 18
ⲙⲁⲣⲍⲓⲙⲟⲥ   25 9.24
ⲙⲁⲣⲟⲩⲉⲣ   25 9.25
ⲙⲁⲣⲟⲩⲑⲁ   11 16.20–21
ⲙⲁⲣⲟⲩⲑⲁⲏⲗ   11 16.21
ⲙⲁⲣⲭⲏⲭⲟⲩ   22 15
ⲙⲁⲣ†   23 15
ⲙⲁⲣ†ⲁⲛⲟⲥ   25 9.24
ⲙⲁⲥ   37 f.17
ⲙⲁⲥⲁ   37 f.18
ⲙⲁⲥⲃⲏⲛ   25 10 [tableau]
ⲙⲁⲧⲁ†ⲏⲗ   25 5.15
ⲙⲁⲩⲉ   12 39.17
ⲙⲁⲭⲁ   12 41.1
ⲙⲁⲭⲏⲡⲱⲧ   22 13
ⲙⲅⲣⲁ...   12 45.2
ⲙⲉⲑⲁ   25 15.16
ⲙⲉⲑⲉⲙⲟⲛ   25 11.7, 16.24; 26 4.28
ⲙⲏⲑⲏⲙⲱⲛ   25 15.6
ⲙⲉⲗⲓⲧⲟⲛ   26 9.2
ⲙⲉⲗⲙⲱⲛ   11 26.5
ⲙⲉⲙⲟⲓ   25 16.4
ⲙⲉⲛⲁⲥⲱⲧⲟⲥ   37 f.26

ⲙⲉⲛⲉⲓⲥ 33 3
ⲙⲉⲣⲟⲩⲏⲗ 26 8.22
ⲙⲉⲥⲱⲃ 25 16.3
ⲙⲉⲧⲱⲛ "Meton" 11 29.13
ⲙⲏ... 34 2.23
ⲙⲏⲥ 25 7.19
ⲙⲏⲧⲉ 25 18.13
ⲙⲓⲗⲁⲥ 11 25.27
ⲙⲓⲙⲓⲏⲗ 34 2.24
ⲙⲓⲛⲁⲏⲗ 34 2.20
ⲙⲓⲥⲁⲏⲗ "Mishael" 25 17.36, 18.10, 17
ⲙⲓⲥⲁⲕ "Meshach" 25 18.10
ⲙⲓⲭⲁⲏⲗ "Michael" 3 f.I.35, b.I.2, 5, 13; 11 6.16, 9.14–15, 17.13–14; 12 7.3, 27.2; 15 b.1, 2; 22 34; 23 50; 25 7.1, 5, 10.24, 11.3, 15.26, 16.20, 18.7; 26 2.1, 3.20, 22, 27, 5.14, 15.15; 17. [tableau]; 29 f.1; 32 1.4, 2.9; 33 f.17; 34 2.26, 3.4
ⲙⲁⲙⲟⲩⲑ 11 26.3
ⲙⲟⲥⲟⲥ 25 12.9
...ⲙⲟⲩ 12 21.24
ⲙⲟⲩⲗⲁⲗ 25 18.11
ⲙⲟⲩⲣⲁⲧ 23.17
ⲙⲟⲫⲣⲏⲏⲥ 2 3
ⲙⲡⲁⲣ†ⲭⲥⲱⲑⲏⲛⲥ 34 2.20
ⲙⲡⲛⲁⲅⲟⲥ 34 2.19
ⲙⲡⲟⲩⲣⲱⲥ 34 2.10
ⲙⲱⲥⲓⲏⲗ 25 8.9
ⲙⲱⲩⲥⲏⲥ "Moses" 11 7.15, 28.4–5
ⲛ.ⲛⲁⲣ 4 1.8
ⲛⲁⲃ 12 37.5
ⲛⲁⲃⲟⲩⲭⲱⲧⲱⲛⲱⲥⲱⲣ "Nebuchadnezzar" 25 18.5
ⲛⲁⲛ... 34 2.26
ⲛⲁⲛⲟⲏⲗ 11 15.10
[..]ⲛⲁⲩ 34 3.1
ⲛⲁⲥⲥⲕⲗⲏⲏ 25 10.2
ⲛⲉⲇⲱⲗⲉ 25 18.13–14
ⲛⲉⲫⲁⲏⲗ 12 7.8
ⲛⲉⲭⲓⲏⲗ 12 27.4
ⲛⲓⲏⲗ ⲕⲟⲣⲁⲑⲟⲑ 4 2.9
ⲛⲓⲑⲁ 23 14
ⲛⲓⲕⲟⲗⲁⲟⲥ "Nicholas" 11 29.15
[..]ⲛⲭⲣⲁⲛⲱⲥ 34 2.19
ⲛⲱⲏⲗ 25 5.18
ⲝⲁⲛⲑⲓⲁⲥ "Xantheas" 11 29.12
ⲝⲟⲁⲥⲁⲗ 27 f.24, b.1
ⲟⲃⲙⲓⲏⲗ 12 41.10
ⲟⲛⲟⲉⲣⲟⲥ 12 23.1
ⲟⲣⲓⲥⲉⲕⲉⲣⲩⲃ 4 1.6
ⲟⲣⲫⲁ 12 31.3

ⲟⲣⲫⲁⲙⲓⲏⲗ 12 31.4
  ⲱⲣⲫⲁⲙⲓⲏⲗ 25 14.12; 26 8.12
[...?]ⲟⲥ 14 6
ⲟⲩⲁⲗⲗⲉⲣⲓⲟⲥ "Vibianus" 11 29.8
Οὐάλης "Oualēs, Valens" 1 b.10
  ⲟⲩⲁⲗⲗⲏⲥ 11 29.3
ⲟⲩⲁⲛⲱⲛ 26 11.26
ⲟⲩⲁⲣⲃⲏⲥ 37 b.222
ⲟⲩⲁⲥⲏⲗ 27 f.7
ⲟⲩⲁⲥⲓⲕ 25 9.25
ⲟⲩⲃⲕⲟⲩⲛⲟⲩⲏⲗ 37 f.24
ⲟⲩⲏⲗ 12 41.10, 12
ⲟⲩⲑ 25 18.15
ⲟⲩⲕⲧⲟⲩⲭⲟⲥ 37 f.25
ⲟⲩⲣⲓⲏⲗ "Uriel" 3 b.I.3; 11 6.17, 9.20, 15.5, 17.15; 12 7.7; 25 7.17, 17.38
  ⲟⲩⲣⲓ 3 f.II.9
ⲟⲩⲣⲓⲟⲛ 25 15.13
ⲟⲩⲣⲓⲭ 32 2.21
ⲟⲩⲥⲓⲣⲉ "Osiris" 4 4.6, 12
  ⲩⲥⲓⲣ 8 f.4
ⲟⲩⲫⲁⲙⲓⲏⲗ 25 15.18
ⲟⲩⲭⲁⲛ 12 45.6
ⲟⲩⲭⲟⲩⲙⲁⲣ 22 [tableau]
ⲟⲩⲭⲱⲑⲱⲙⲓⲭ 4 1.8
ⲟⲭⲁⲗⲁⲗⲫⲑ 34 4.12
ⲡⲁⲃⲁⲯⲑⲟⲩ 12 39.14
ⲡⲁⲙⲏⲧⲣ[[ⲁ]]ⲧⲱⲥ 25 15.18
ⲡⲁⲙⲓⲁⲛⲧⲱⲥ 25 15.18
ⲡⲁⲙⲓⲛ 3 f.II.24
ⲡⲁⲛⲓⲉⲓⲗⲟⲩ 22 16
ⲡⲁⲛ†ⲧⲟⲥ 32 1.31
ⲡⲁⲡⲗⲏⲩ 9 5
ⲡⲁⲡⲗⲓⲛ 27 f.8
ⲡⲁⲣⲁⲙⲏⲣⲁ 26 9.3
ⲡⲁⲣⲁⲥⲉⲩ 25 13.3, 9
ⲡⲁⲣⲃⲓⲱⲛⲁ 26 11.23
ⲡⲁⲧⲃⲟⲩⲕⲁⲛⲓⲁⲁ 32 1.30
ⲡⲁⲧⲣⲟⲩⲏⲗ 25 5.20
ⲡⲁⲯⲣⲁⲧⲟⲥ 25 15.17
...ⲡⲁⲫⲱ... 12 45.1
ⲡⲉⲡⲱⲣⲕ 25 15.15
ⲡⲉⲣⲓⲭⲏ 25 15.7
ⲡⲉⲥⲣ...ⲁ 32 2.38
ⲡⲉⲧⲃⲉ 4 5.5
ⲡⲓⲁⲕ 26 6.12
ⲡⲓⲫⲉⲙⲉⲣⲁⲛⲓⲱⲛ 26 8.3
ⲡⲕⲟⲛⲟⲥ "Kronos" ? 32 1.31
ⲡⲕⲩⲃⲁⲕ 14 8
ⲡⲙⲟⲩ 12 21.24

ⲡⲣⲁⲃⲁⲱⲑ **4** 2.1
ⲡⲣⲓⲙ **31** b.22 (twice); **32** 1.29
   ⲡⲣⲓⲙⲡⲣⲓⲙ **31** b.1
ⲡⲣⲓⲙⲡⲉ **32** 1.29
ⲡⲣⲓⲥⲕⲟⲥ "Priscus" **11** 29.19
ⲡⲣⲕ **29** b.2
ⲡⲣⲟⲃⲁⲧⲓⲟⲥ **11** 28.25
ⲡⲣⲱⲟⲏⲙⲁⲥ **4** 1.10
ⲡⲥⲁⲧⲁⲏⲗ **18** 1
ⲡⲥⲟⲩⲣⲟⲩⲑⲓⲟⲩⲛ **26** 9.2
ⲣⲁⲕⲟⲩⲏⲗ **3** b.I.3
ⲣⲁⲙⲱⲑⲁⲙ **12** 45.3
. . . ⲣⲁⲱⲙ **12** 11.21
ⲣⲓⲏⲗ **25** 5.16
ⲣⲓⲭⲁⲏⲗ **25** 5.16
ⲣⲟ[.] **34** 2.24
ⲣⲟⲩⲏⲗ **25** 5.15
ⲣⲟⲩⲭ **23** 19
ⲣⲣⲣⲱⲫⲟⲛ **37** f.29
ⲣⲱⲏⲗ **25** 5.17
ⲣⲱⲧⲁⲥ **25** 10.19-20, 13.20; **29** f.16
ⲥ . ⲁⲣⲓⲏⲗ **34** 4.1
ⲥⲁ . [.] . ⲁⲗ **34** 2.22
ⲥⲁⲁⲃⲉⲗ **27** f.24, b.3
ⲥⲁⲁⲣⲁ **10** 5
ⲥⲁⲃⲁ **12** 21.20
ⲥⲁⲃⲁⲃ **12** 21.20
ⲥⲁⲃⲁⲏⲗ **12** 9.4
ⲥⲁⲃⲁⲱ **12** 37.10
ⲥⲁⲃⲁⲕ **12** 25.23
ⲥⲁⲃⲁⲕⲧⲁⲛⲓ **12** 21.18
ⲥⲁⲃⲁⲭⲱⲣⲓⲏⲗ **25** 15.24
ⲥⲁⲃⲁⲱⲑ "Sabaoth" **3** f.I.17, b.I.12; **4** 6.2; **8** f.3, 10, 14; **11** 2.10, 5.6, 16.15, 18.18–19, 22, 19.1; **12** 2.18, 9.19, 11.2, 13.8, 17.21–22, 21.2, 4, 20–21, 25.11, 31.8, 37.7, 9, 39.17, 41.1; **16** 3.8; **22** 11; **25** 2.11, 3.14, 4.1, 5.10, 18, 6.7–8, 7.14, 16, 11.5, 9, 12.25, 15.6, 9, 15.25, 16.22, 26, 18.1; **26** 4.29, 9.5, 14, 13.26, 15.10; **32** 1.1; **34** 2.25, 3.3
   ⲥⲁⲃⲟⲱⲑ **25** 12.12
   ⲥⲁⲃⲁⲱⲧ **34** 2.21
   cf. ⲥⲁⲃⲁⲱⲑ
ⲥⲁⲃⲃⲁⲧⲓⲟⲥ **11** 28.27
ⲥⲁⲃⲉⲣ **12** 17.3
ⲥⲁⲏⲗ **4** 2.13; **12** 41.10; **33** 3
ⲥⲁⲑⲁ **25** 3.14
ⲥⲁⲑⲏⲣ **37** f.18
ⲥⲁⲑⲱ **33** 3
ⲥⲁⲕⲉⲣⲧⲱⲛ "Sacerdon" **11** 29.20

ⲥⲁⲕⲓⲁ **25** 5.20
ⲥⲁⲗⲁⲃⲁⲱⲑ **22** 14
ⲥⲁⲗⲁⲑⲓⲏⲗ **24** 19, 26; **25** 15.27; **26** 14.13–14, 21
   ⲍⲁⲗⲁⲑⲓⲏⲗ **34** 4.5
ⲥⲁⲗⲁⲛⲓ **27** f.8
ⲥⲁⲗⲁⲫⲟⲩⲏⲗ **3** b.I.4; **25** 7.3
ⲥⲁⲙⲏⲛ **33** 3
ⲥⲁⲙⲓⲏⲗ **12** 41.9
ⲥⲁⲙⲛⲓ **37** f.17
ⲥⲁⲙⲟⲩ **37** f.17
ⲥⲁⲙⲫⲟⲏⲗ **25** 10.25
ⲥⲁⲛⲁⲧⲁⲏⲗ **26** 4.3; **30** f.20
ⲥⲁⲛⲧⲁⲗ **26** 6.19
ⲥⲁⲛⲧⲁⲥ **26** 6.19
ⲥⲁⲝ **24** 28
ⲥⲁⲣⲁⲑⲓⲏⲗ **25** 11.4, 16.21
ⲥⲁⲣⲁⲕ **25** 15.16
ⲥⲁⲣⲁⲙⲓⲏⲗ **4** 2.13
ⲥⲁⲣⲁⲫⲟⲩⲏⲗ **34** 3.5
ⲥⲁⲣⲁⲫⲱⲥ **23** 16
ⲥⲁⲣⲓⲏⲗ **12** 27.2; **25** 15.24; **26** 11.27
ⲥⲁⲣⲓⲛⲁⲏⲗ **11** 17.6-7
ⲥⲁⲣⲓⲱⲓⲛⲓ **25** 11.2
ⲥⲁⲣⲙⲁⲧⲁⲣ **14**.4
ⲥⲁⲣⲟⲁⲏⲗ **12** 41.11
ⲥⲁⲣⲥⲁⲃⲁⲏⲗ **21** 41.14–15
ⲥⲁⲣⲥⲁⲏⲗ **12** 41.14
ⲥⲁⲣⲥⲟⲙⲱⲏⲗ **12** 41.14
ⲥⲁⲥⲁⲏⲗ **12** 27.3
ⲥⲁⲧⲁⲛⲁⲥ "Satan" **11** 18.15–16; **12** 19.17; **28** 2.11
ⲥⲁⲧⲱⲣ **25** 10.19, 11.5; **29** f.15
   ⲥⲱⲧⲱⲣ **25** 13.19, 16.22
ⲥⲃⲉⲱ "Sephthys" **9** 5, 8
ⲥⲉⲇⲉⲕⲓⲏⲗ "Sedekiel" **11** 9.20–21, 17.15
   ⲥⲉⲧ[ⲉⲕⲓⲏⲗ] **26** 17 [tableau]
   ⲍⲏⲧⲏⲕⲓⲏⲗ **34** 4.3
ⲥⲉⲉⲣⲟ **29** b.6
ⲥⲉⲙⲁⲛⲟⲩⲏⲗ **11** 16.3
ⲥⲉⲣⲛⲉⲩⲱ **12** 39.13
ⲥⲉⲥⲏⲛ **11** 26.6
ⲥⲉⲧⲏⲗ **11** 17.16
ⲥⲉⲧⲣⲁⲕ "Shadrach" **25** 18.10; **30** f.20
ⲥⲉⲩⲏⲣⲓⲁⲛⲟⲥ "Severianus" **11** 29.5
ⲥⲏⲑ "Seth" **4** 5.2
   ⲍⲏⲑ **4** 5.3
ⲥⲏⲕ **33** 2
ⲥⲏⲛⲧⲁⲗⲁⲗⲁⲥ **25** 15.1
ⲥⲏⲛⲧⲁⲗⲁⲗⲓⲁ **25** 15.1

ⲥⲁⲛⲧⲁⲗⲁⲗⲓⲁ   **25** 15.8
ⲥⲏⲛⲧⲁⲥ   **25** 14.27
ⲥⲏⲣⲓⲏⲗ   **25** 15.24
ⲥⲏⲥ   **33** 4
ⲥⲏⲧ   **25** 14.27
ⲥⲏⲫⲏⲃⲁⲛ   **34** 2.21
ⲥⲓⲁⲕ   **12** 25.23; **26** 6.12
ⲡⲁⲙⲓⲛ   **3** f.II.24
ⲥⲓⲥⲓⲛⲛⲓⲟⲥ "Sisinnius"   **11** 29.5
ⲥⲓⲧⲱⲣⲓⲏⲗ   **26** 8.9
ⲥⲓⲫⲓⲏⲗ   **34** 2.24
ⲥⲙⲁⲣⲁⲕⲧⲟⲥ "Smaragdus"   **11** 29.4
ⲥⲛⲧⲁⲏⲗ   **11** 17.5
ⲥⲟⲩⲗⲓⲁⲥⲁⲣ   **27** b.5
ⲥⲟⲩⲙⲓⲑⲓⲟⲛ   **25** 15.6
ⲥⲟⲩⲣⲉⲥ   **37** b.8
ⲥⲟⲩⲣⲓⲏⲗ "Suriel"   **3** b.I.4; **25** 7.2, 10, 10.24, 11.3, 15.27, 16.21; **26** 14.13, 19, 17 [tableau]
ⲥⲟⲩⲭ   **14** 1; **27** f.24, **26** b.4
ⲥⲟⲩⲭⲱⲣⲁⲃⲉ **4** 2.12
ⲥⲟⲫⲓⲁ   **20** b.1
ⲥⲥⲓⲥⲟⲥ   **25** 12.21
ⲥⲧⲉⲫⲁⲛⲟⲥ   **11** 28.26
ⲥⲧⲓⲉⲫ   **25** 3.13
ⲥⲧⲱⲏⲗ   **26** 8.2
ⲥⲱ   **25** 18.13
ⲥⲱⲗⲟⲙⲱⲛ "Solomon"   **25** 10.4; **36** f.I.14
ⲥⲱⲗⲱⲙⲱⲛ   **26** 9.10; **30** f.7, 22
ⲥⲱⲗⲱ   **30** f.8
ⲥⲱⲡⲟⲥ   **23** 15
ⲥⲱⲭⲱⲧ   **26** 9.12
ⲧⲁⲉⲕⲧⲱⲣ   **25** 15.7
ⲧⲁⲏⲗⲭⲁⲙⲁⲣⲓⲙⲁ   **12** 45.16
ⲧⲁⲗⲓⲁⲥ   **26** 6.19
ⲧⲁⲗⲗⲱⲉⲓ   **26** 11.25
ⲧⲁⲙⲁⲭ   **12** 23.3
ⲧⲁⲙⲃⲏⲗ   **12** 41.13
ⲧⲁⲛⲁⲏⲗ   **34** 2.21
ⲧⲁⲡⲕⲉⲣ   **25** 9.25–26
ⲧⲁⲣⲁⲙⲓⲏⲗ   **25** 16.2–3
ⲧⲁⲣⲧⲁⲣⲟⲩⲭⲟⲥ ⲛⲁⲙⲉⲛⲧⲉ "Tartaruchus of hell" **3** f.2.20–21, f.2.28
ⲧⲁⲧⲓⲏⲗ   **25** 5.18
ⲧⲁⲩⲣⲓⲏⲗ   **26** 11. 28
ⲧⲁⲭⲁⲏⲗ   **12** 41.13
ⲧⲉⲕⲁⲩⲣⲓⲏⲗ   **26** 8.4
ⲧⲉⲛⲏⲧ   **25** 10.19, 11.8, 13.19, 16.25; **29** f.16
ⲧⲉⲣⲓⲕ   **23** 17–18
ⲧⲉⲥⲟⲩⲕⲟⲩ   **29** b.2
ⲧⲏⲍⲟⲩⲏⲗ   **34** 2.21

†ⲙⲉⲥⲣⲱⲕⲣⲁⲑⲓⲁⲣⲓ   **26** 11.23–24
†ⲣⲣⲁⲭⲁⲏⲗ   **26** 11.24–25
ⲧⲗⲏⲗ   **34** 2.22
ⲧⲟⲙⲛⲟⲥ "Domnus"   **11** 29.22
ⲧⲟⲩⲱⲣⲁ   **12** 23.1
ⲧⲟⲫⲟⲩ   **12** 27.11
ⲧⲥⲃⲱⲕ   **37** f.28
ⲧⲱⲁⲕ   **12** 23.3
ⲧⲱⲛⲁⲓ   **28** 3.18
ⲧⲱⲣⲁⲥ   **25** 11.9, 16.26
ⲧⲱⲣⲱⲑⲱⲣⲁ   **26** 9.10
ⲧⲱ .. [. . . .]ⲩⲛⲏ   **34** 2.25
ⲩⲗⲓⲧⲟⲙⲛⲟⲥ   **11** 29.18
ⲩⲙⲓⲏⲗ   **25** 5.18
ⲫ[. . . ?]   **14** 3
ⲫⲁ   **23** 19
ⲫⲁⲛⲟⲩⲏⲗ   **12** 7.15
ⲫⲁⲣⲁⲣⲁ   **25** 15.16
ⲫⲁⲣⲓⲏⲗ   **12** 27.3
ⲫⲁⲩⲥⲓⲏⲗ   **26** 3.26
ⲫⲉⲗⲗⲱⲑ   **18**.20
] . ⲫⲉⲣ   **2** 3
ⲫⲉⲣ   **23** 19
ⲫⲉⲩ   **2** 3
ⲫⲏⲅ   **23** 17
ⲫⲓⲗⲉⲙⲟⲛ "Philemon"   **17** f.20
ⲫⲓⲗⲟⲕⲧⲏⲙⲱⲛ "Philoctimon"   **11** 29.6
ⲫⲓⲛⲁⲗⲱⲛ   **11** 25.28
ⲫⲓⲱⲟⲩ   **12** 37.6
ⲫⲗⲁⲩⲉⲓⲟⲥ   **11** 29.11
ⲫⲟⲣⲓⲏⲗ   **34** 4.3
ⲫⲟⲩⲣⲁⲛⲉⲓ   **25** 12.6, 13.1
ⲫⲟⲩⲣⲁⲧ   **25** 12.4–5, 13.1
ⲫⲟⲩⲥⲏⲥ   **33** 4
ⲫⲣⲁⲅⲅⲓⲥ   **25** 7.20
ⲫⲣⲓⲍ   **14** 2
ⲫⲣⲱ[. . . ?]   **14** 2
ⲫⲱⲏⲗ   **12** 41.7
ⲫⲱⲣⲁⲉⲓⲙ   **26** 9.8
ⲭⲁⲃⲛⲁ   **23** 33
ⲭⲁⲃⲛⲉⲓ   **23** 32
ⲭⲁⲏⲗ   **22** 17
ⲭⲁⲕⲟⲩⲣⲓ   **23** 32
ⲭⲁⲙ   **37** f.17
ⲭⲁⲙⲁⲣⲓⲏⲗ   **12** 45.31
ⲭⲁⲙⲁⲣⲙⲁⲣⲓⲁⲱ   **12** 11.10
ⲭⲁⲙⲓⲱⲑ   **12** 45.30
ⲭⲁⲣⲓⲙ   **28** 3.19
ⲭⲁⲭ   **37** f.17
ⲭⲁⲭⲁⲩⲫⲁⲛⲉⲭⲱⲭ   **12** 45.28

ϫⲉⲃⲟⲩⲑⲁⲛⲓⲉ   12 23.2
ϫⲉⲣⲉⲙ   25 3.12
ϫⲉⲣⲓⲛⲁⲏⲗ   11 17.6
ϫⲏⲩⲙⲉ   23 19
ϫⲓⲁⲗⲁⲥ   25 3.13
ϫⲓⲑⲓ   25 3.14
ϫⲟⲩⲃⲓⲛ ϩⲁⲣⲡⲁⲕ̣   30 f.8, 17
ϫⲟⲩⲇⲓⲱⲛ "Chudion"   11 29.16
ϫⲟⲩⲙⲁⲭⲁ   25 15.22
ϫⲭⲱⲱⲭⲁⲏ   12 45.29
ϫⲱⲃⲁⲛⲧⲁ   25 5.16
ϫⲱⲙⲏ   25 5.16
ϫⲱⲣⲱⲉⲓ   26 12.22
Ψάις   1 b.10
ϯⲡⲣⲁ̣ . .   34 2.9
ⲱⲃⲓⲁ   28 3.20
. . ⲱⲏⲗ   12 41.22
ⲱⲑⲱⲣ   22 44
ⲱⲗⲁⲗⲃⲱⲣⲓⲙ   26 9.8
ⲱⲙⲁⲣ   25 15.17
ⲱⲙⲓⲏⲗ   37 f.18
ⲱⲣⲁⲥⲓⲏⲗ   26 8.7
ⲱⲣⲉⲙ   25 8.8
ⲱⲣⲓⲥⲕⲱⲥ   26 8.6
ⲱⲣⲛⲉⲑⲁⲩ   30 f.17
    ⲱⲣ (?)   30 f.18
ⲱⲣⲫⲁⲙⲓⲏⲗ   26 8.12
ⲱⲣⲫⲁⲛⲓⲗ   25 15.19
ⲱⲣⲱⲙⲁⲏⲗ   4 2.8
ⲱⲧⲉⲣⲁ   25 10.19, 11.8, 13.19, 16.25
ⲱⲫⲁ   25 14.11
ⲱⲭⲁⲛ   12 45.6
ⲱϩⲉⲓ   23 17
ⲱϩϯ   29 b.5
ϣⲁⲉⲓⲙ   16 1.1
ϣⲁⲣϣⲁⲣ   31 f.21
ϣⲟⲩⲣⲁⲣⲁⲧ   32 2.37
ϣⲟⲩⲣⲁⲭⲁⲏⲗ   32 1.29
ϣⲟⲩⲣⲓⲙ   32 2.36
ϣⲟⲩⲣⲱⲛⲁϩ   23 33
ϣⲟⲩϣϥ   32 1.29, 31, 2.29
ϣⲱⲣⲁⲛⲓ   23 33
ϭⲁⲣⲙⲁⲣⲟⲥ   25 15.16
ϭⲙⲓⲏⲗ   25 15.8
ϭⲡⲁⲕⲁⲗⲉ   12 23.2
ϩⲁ   12 39.15
ϩⲁⲕ   26 11.16
ϩⲁⲛⲁⲩⲧⲱⲥ   26 12.24
ϩⲁⲡⲉ "Apis"   4 4.5, 12
ϩⲏⲗⲓⲁⲥ   23 30

ϩⲏϯⲱⲥ   23 16
ϩⲣⲁⲃⲁⲗⲧϯ   34 2.11
ϩⲣⲁⲃⲟⲩⲛⲉⲓ   11 18.22
ϩⲣⲁⲕⲟⲩⲏⲗ "Raguel"   25 7.11
ϩⲣⲁⲍ   16 1.5
ϩⲣⲁⲫⲁⲏⲗ "Raphael"   11 6.17, 9.19, 17.14–15;
    12 7.4; 25 7.2, 9, 11.3, 12.3, 10, 15.26–27,
    16.20; 26 14.16, 17 [tableau]; 29 f.2; 34 4.2
    ⲏⲣⲁⲫⲁⲏⲗ   12 7.11
    ⲣⲁⲫⲁⲏⲗ   12 13.5, 27.2, 11; 26 14.13
    ⲣⲁϥⲁⲏⲗ   25 10.24–25
ϩⲣⲓⲍ   16 1.4
ϩⲣⲟⲩⲏⲗ   25 15.25
ϩⲱⲣ "Horus"   6 1, 9; 9 7; 16 1.6
ϩⲱⲣⲙⲟⲥⲉⲏⲗ "Hormosiel"   17 f.16
    ϩⲟⲣⲙⲟⲥⲉⲏⲗ   17 f.19
ϫⲁⲃⲏⲥ   23 15

II. Place-names and Ethnonyms

Ἀραβία "Arabia"   1 f.11
Βαβυλῶν "Babylon" (king of)   25 18.6
Ἑβραῖος "Hebrew"   11 6.3–4
Ἔδεσσα "Edessa"
    ⲁⲓⲇⲉⲥⲥⲁ   11 21.25
    ⲉⲧⲉⲥⲥⲁ   11 20.6–7, 24.6, 11, 20
ⲉⲧⲏⲙ "Eden"   28 7.6
Ἔφεσος "Ephesus"   11 28.23
ⲉϭⲱϣ "Kushite, Ethiopian"   24 27; 25 9.3
    ⲉϣⲱ (?)   31 f.38
Ἱερουσαλήμ (cf. Ἱεροσόλυμα) "Jerusalem"
    ⲓ̅ⲗ̅ⲏ̅ⲙ̅   11 26.6
    ⲑⲓ̅ⲗ̅ⲏ̅ⲙ̅   11 28.20
Ἰσραήλ "Israel"   11 28.18
    ⲓ̅ⲏ̅ⲗ̅   11 23.2, 26.7
ⲓⲟⲩⲇⲁⲓ "Jews"   31 f.19, b.9
ⲕⲏⲙⲉ "Egypt"   1 f.6; 11 6.5–6
Νίκαια "Nicea" (faith of)   25 6.5–6
Πέρσης "Persian"   11 5.26–27
ⲡⲓⲁ ⲓⲱⲥⲁⲫⲁⲧ "Valley of Josaphat"   28 9.7
ⲡϭⲉⲗⲗⲏⲧ "Pcellēt"   23 51
Σεβαστή "Sebaste"   11 29.1–2
Σῖναι "Sinai"   11 7.16
ⲥⲟⲩⲁⲛ "Aswan" (dish)   31 b.16; 32 1.19
Χαλδαῖος "Chaldeans"   1 f.7; 11 6.1–2
ϫⲟⲩⲥⲓ "Kush (?)"   9 4
ϩⲁⲃⲓⲛ "Habin" (temple of)   6 6
الاسواني al-aswānī
    ⲁⲗⲉⲥⲟⲩⲉⲛⲓ "Aswan" (dish)   30 f.2–3

III. Numbers

half
   ϫⲉⲥ   **3** f.2.38
   ϭⲁⲥ   **26** 5.9, 6.24, 10.28

one
   ⲟⲩⲁ "one, someone"   **10** 16; **11** 4.2, 5.14 (twice), 20, 21, 9.4 (twice); **12** 29.15 (twice), 18; **25** 4.10, 11, 12, 13, 5.7, 6.13 (twice), 15.19, 16.5; **26** 2.22, 23, 10.28, 16.19–20; **28** 6.12
   ⲟⲩⲉ   **1** f.42, b.1
   ⲟⲩⲉⲓ (fem.)   **6** 4, 5, 13, 14
   ⲩⲉⲓ   **26** 17.15
   ⲙ̅ⲛ̅ⲧⲟⲩⲁ "unity"   **11** 12.14, 15

first
   ϣⲱⲣⲡ   **37** b.15
   ϣⲁⲣⲉⲡ   **26** 11.19
   ϣⲁⲣⲡ   **25** 6.25, 8.13, 13.10; **26** 12.5–6
   ϣⲟⲣⲡ   **10** 2; **12** 11.3, 5, 35.24
   ϣⲱⲣⲏⲡ   **28** 8.22
   ϣⲟⲣⲡⲉ (fem.)   **11** 16.8–9; **12** 31.15–16, 43.3
   ϣⲁⲣⲉⲡⲉ   **26** 13.15
   ϣⲁⲣⲡⲓ   **26** 6.14, 12.19
   ϭⲓⲛⲉϣⲟⲣⲡ   **12** 35.4–5
   cf. s.v. ⲙⲓⲥⲉ in Words of Egyptian Origin

first
   ϩⲟⲩⲉⲓ̈ⲧⲉ   **11** 30.16

two
   ⲃ   **4** 3.2; **26** 9.7; **32** 1.19; **37** b.18
   ⲥⲛⲁⲩ   **6** 19; **11** 26.25; **12** 13.2, 19.18, 29.14, 16, 17, 18, 9.9; **37** b.29
   ⲥⲛⲉⲩ   **26** 7.29, 9.11
   ⲥⲏⲛⲩ   **25** 14.18, 22
   ⲥⲛⲛⲩ   **27** f.20
   ⲥⲛⲟⲟⲥ   **6** 20
   ⲥⲛⲧⲉ (fem.)   **9** 5; **11** 4.15
   ⲥⲉⲛⲧⲉ   **9** 9
   ⲥⲏⲛⲧ   **26** 8.14, 17, 11.23, 12.23

three (also "Tuesday")
   ⲅ   **12** 19.23; **17** b.30; **22** 44; **25** 13.1, 5, 7, 24, 14.1; **26** 7.2, 10.21, 11.24, 12.16, 23, 13.24, 27, 31, 15.30, 16.9, 17.5, 24, 23; **28** 8.10, 14, 12.20, 21, 13.6; **30** f.5; **31** b.17; **37** f.10? (twice), 11?
   ϣⲟⲙⲛ̅ⲧ   **11** 19.7; **12** 17.3–4
   ϣⲙⲧ   **4** 4.4, 10
   ϣⲟⲙⲉⲧ   **20** f.11–12
   ϣⲟⲙⲧ   **12** 35.7
   ϣⲟⲙⲧⲉ (fem.)   **6** 3, 11; **11** 4.15, 12–17

four
   ⲇ̅   **24** 27; **25** 8.10; **26** 8.30, 11.25; **26** 16.1
   ⲃⲧⲟⲟⲩ   **12** 11.19
   ⲃ·ⲇ̅   **25** 8.6; **26** 6.17
   ϥ·ⲇ̅   **25** 14.25
   ϥⲧⲟⲟⲩ   **3** f.1.29–30; **11** 25.10, 26.19, 20, 29.23; **12** 1.1, 17.5, 9, 10, 15, 19.3, 29.5, 39.6, 43.1
   ϥⲧⲟ (fem.)   **6** 4, 12; **11** 16.4; **12** 43.2

five
   ⲉ̅   **26** 11.26, 13.20, 16.3
   ϯⲟⲩ   **25** 10.20, 13.16
   ⲧⲏ   **3** f.2.38
   ϯ   **29** f.14

six
   ⲋ̅   **25** 6.13; **26** 2.22, 11.26, 14.8, 16.6
   ⲥ̅ⲟⲩ   **30** b.3
   ⲥⲟⲟⲩ   **12** 29.15; **29** b.3

seven
   ⲍ   **3** b.1.1; **7** 31; **12** 27.17; **25** 6.23, 9.1 (twice), 2 (twice), 3 (twice); **26** 2.12, 3.22, 5.11, 7.24, 11.27, 14.10, 12, 16.9, 34 17.13, 25; **27** f.15; **28** 3.12, 8.20, 12.20; **34** 1.18 (twice), 3.6, 4.19
   ⲍ̅ⲃ   **26** 2.12
   ⲥⲁϣϥ   **7** 4, 26, 30, 21; **11** 17.19, 28.22; **12** 21.6, 27.10, 39.12
   ⲍⲁϣϥ   **3** b.1.9
   ⲥⲁϣⲃ   **26** 4.20, 6.9, 11.6; **28** 2.13; **34** 1.10
   ⲥⲁϣⲉϥ   **17** f.34
   ⲥⲁϣϥⲉ (fem.)   **6** 2, 7, 8, 13; **7** 20
   ⲥⲁϣⲃⲓ   **26** 5.7, 8
   ⲍⲁϣϥⲉ   **3** b.1.11
   ⲥⲁϣⲃⲉ   **26** 6.10; **35** f.16
   ϭⲁϣⲉ   **17** f.4

eight
   ⲏ̅   **26** 16.13

nine
   ⲑ̅   **25** 13.10, 13, 16, 21, 24, 27, 14.1, 6, 11, 17, 21, 25, 15.3, 20; **26** 12.14, 16.15
   ϯⲥ   **34** 1.16

ten
   ⲓ   **26** 16.18

eleven
   ⲓ̅ⲁ̅   **26** 16.21; **23** 51; **28** 9.7

twelve
   ⲓ̅ⲃ̅   **3** f.2.7, 10, 30, 34; **12** 39.2; **26** 16.24
   ⲙ̅ⲓ̅ⲃ̅   **3** f.2.31
   ⲙ̅[ⲉⲧ]ⲓ̅ⲃ̅   **29** f.2–3
   ⲙ̅ⲛ̅ⲧⲓ̅ⲃ̅   **4** 2.4

ⲙⲏⲧⲥⲛⲟⲟⲥ 17 f.34
ⲙⲏⲧⲥⲩⲛⲟⲟⲥ 17 f.7, 14, 15
thirteen
ⲓⲅ̄ 26 16.26
fourteen
ⲓⲇ 26 6.24, 16.28
ⲙ̄ⲛ̄ⲧⲁϥⲧⲉ 12 11.11, 18, 13.16, 19.4
ⲙⲉⲛⲧⲁⲃ† 26 5.9
fifteen
ⲓⲉ̄ 26 16.31
ⲙⲉⲛⲧⲏ 26 8.26
sixteen
ⲓ̄ⲋ̄ 26 16.33
seventeen
ⲓ̄ⲍ̄ 26 17.1
eighteen
ⲓ̄ⲏ̄ 26 17.3
nineteen
ⲓ̄ⲑ̄ 26 17.7
twenty
ⲕ̄ 26 17.10
twenty-one
ⲕ̄ⲁ 26 17.13; 25 2.1; 28 13.5; 37 f.15
twenty-four
ⲕ̄ⲇ 25 5.13, 7.21; 26 9.16, 20
ϫⲟⲩⲧⲁϥⲧⲉ 12 25.16, 41.15, 16; 29 f.3
ϫⲟⲩⲧⲁⲃⲧⲉ 17 f.8
ϫⲟⲩⲧⲁϥⲧⲏ 12 43.14
thirty
ⲙⲁⲃ 26 8.26
ⲙⲁⲟⲃ 26 10.28
forty
ϩⲙⲉ 7 33, 34; 11 29.1
sixty
ⲥⲉ 12 23.19, 21, 22, 24, 25.1, 2, 4, 39.7, 8, 10
seventy
ϣϥⲉ 20 f.15
ϣⲃⲉ 6 20; 18 13
seventy-five
ⲥϩⲃⲩⲧⲏ 9 12
six hundred and eighty-four
ⲭ̄ⲡ̄ⲇ̄ 23 51
hundred
ϣⲉ 3 f.2.38
one hundred and fifty-five
ϣⲉ ⲙ̄ⲭⲉⲥ ⲧⲏ 3 f.2.38
thousand
ϣⲟ 12 29.11 (twice)
ϣⲁ 26 14.32, 33

ten thousand
ⲧⲃⲁ 12 23.20, 21, 23, 24, 25.1, 3, 4, 25.1–2, 3, 4, 39.7, 9, 10; 26 5.9, 10.28, 14.33 (twice)
ⲧⲃⲉ 26 6.24
one hundred and forty-five thousand
ⲙⲉⲛⲧⲁⲃ† ⲛ̄ⲧⲃⲁ ⲟⲩϭⲁⲥ 26 5.9
ⲓ̄ⲇ̄ · ⲧⲃⲉ : ⲟⲩϭⲁⲥ 26 6.24
three hundred and fifteen thousand
ⲙⲁⲟⲃ ⲙ̄ⲛ ⲟⲩⲁ : ⲟⲩϭⲁⲥ ⲛ̄ⲧⲃⲁ 26 10.28
six hundred thousand
ⲥⲉ ⲛ̄̄ⲧⲃⲁ 12 23.20–21, 21–22, 22–23, 24, 25.1–2, 2–3, 4, 39.7, 8–9, 10

IV. Calendrical Vocabulary

μήν "month"
ⲙⲉⲛ ? 23 52
παοπε "Paopi" (month)
ⲡⲁⲁⲡⲓ 23 51–52
ⲡⲟⲩⲱϣ "Thursday" 28 12.22, 13.1?
ⲧⲱⲃⲉ "Tobi" (month)
ⲧⲱⲃ 17 b.20
χ̄π̄ⲇ̄ "six-hundred and eighty-four" (year) 23 51
ϣⲟⲙⲛ̄ⲧ "Tuesday" (lit. "three") 28 12.21
cf. s.v. κυριακή in Words of Greek Origin; ⲉⲃⲟⲧ, ⲣⲟⲙⲡⲉ, ⲥⲟⲩ-, ϩⲟⲟⲩ, ⲭⲡ- in Words of Egyptian Origin

V. Abbreviations

ἀμήν "amen"
ϩⲁ\ⲙ̄/ 25 2.5
ⲁⲡⲉ "head"
♉ 25 16.10
ἀπολογία "request"
ⲁ̄ⲡⲟⲗ 37 f.32
ⲁ̄ⲡ̄ⲟ̄ⲗⲟ/ 12 9.7, 17.20
ⲁⲡⲟⲗⲟ/ 12 21.16, 23.14, 25.5, 27.9, 29.8, 13, 31.2, 6, 14, 20, 33.2, 7, 15, 21, 35.2, 6, 9, 18, 37.3, 39.11, 41.9, 43.3, 7, 20; 36 f.I.2
π̄ⲟ 24 36
ἀρχή "first fruits"
ⲁⲣ\ⲭ/ⲥ 37 b.2
ⲁⲣⲭ 37 b.24
ⲁⲣⲭⲉ 37 f.3
γράφειν "to write"
ⲅⲣ 31 f.36, b.15, 18; 31 1.19 (twice), 21, 2.27; 37 f.3, b. 4, 11, 18, 24
ⲅ̄ⲣ̄ 37 b.2, 6, 7, 9, 13, 16

ⲅⲣ/ **35** b.10
ⲅⲣ̅ **32** 1.19 (twice), 21
ⲓ̅ⲝ̅ ? **25** 16.11
δεῖνα "NN"
  ⲇ **17** f.21, 32; **20** f.13; **29** 10;
  ⲇⲇ **18** 9, 14, 16; **31** f.7, b.11; **32** 1.6, 9, 11, 17 (twice), 2.2, 8, 14, 15, 20 (twice), 33, 34; **35** b.6, 9; **36** f.I.12, f.II.8; **37** f.21, 23
  ⲇ̅ **1** f.19, 20 (three times); **3** f.I.34; **16** II.1, 13; **17** f.37
  ⲇ̅ⲇ̅ **4** 2.7, 4.17, 5.1, 9, 6. 1, 2; **5** b.1; **6** f.21; **7** f.1; **8** f.8 (twice), b.7; **16** I.10, II.8; **17** f.21, 31, b.41; **18** f.9,14, 16; **19** 3; **28** 4.20 (twice), 6.4 (twice), 10 (twice), 16 (twice), 19 (twice), 7.10 (twice), 9.12, 13, 16 (twice), 10.9 (twice), 13.15 (twice), 17, 18; **31** f.6, 14, b.6, 12; **32** 14
  ⲇ̅ⲥ̅ **17** b.41 (twice), f.37
  ⲭ̅ⲭ̅ **27** f.9; **35** b.1, 5
  ⲥ̅ⲥ̅ **21** 22 (twice); **22** 45, 50, 55; **23** 11 (twice), 13, 19 (twice), 25, 26, 34 (twice), 35, 38–40; **24** 6, 7, 10 (twice), 12 (twice), 13, 16 (twice), 17, 32, 34; **25** 2.23, 4.18 (twice), 5.3, 21, 22, 25, 6.27, 7.6, 26, 8.4, 24, 10.9, 28, 11.8, 11, 12.14, 13.6, 12, 15 (twice), 20, 23, 26, 31, 14.5, 16, 20, 24, 15.2, 8, 19, 23, 16.1, 20, 24, 27, 17.35, 41 (twice), 44, 18.9; **26** 4.15, 5.2, 18, 6.4, 23, 28, 10.5, 6, 17, 11.14, 12.2, 13.7, 14.4, 32, 15.2, 22
διάκονος
  ⲇ̅ⲓ̅ **23** 49
ἐπικαλεῖν "to invoke"
  ⲉ **3** f.II.25, 29; **4** 2.3, 7–13
  ⲉ̅ⲡ̅ **3** f.II.2, 14, b.I.1
  ⲉ̅ⲡ̅ⲓ̅ **3** f.II.9
  ⲉⲡⲓ/ **4** 2.6
εὐχή "prayer"
  ⲉⲩⲭ **32** 1.19
ζῴδιον "image"
  ⲍⲱⲇ **32** 1.19 (twice)
  ⲍ̅ **27** f.15
  ⲥ̅ **3** f.II.5, 9, 11
  ⲥ̅ⲓ̅ⲩ̅ **26** 16.27, 31, 17.4, 7
  ⲥ̅ⲟ̅ⲩ̅ⲧ̅ⲓ̅ **37** f.20
  ⲥ̅ⲩ̅ **25** 10.9, **26** 16.21
  ⲥ̅ⲱ̅ **14** 9
  ⲥ̅ⲱ̅ϥ̅ **28** 9.11
θυσία "offering"
  ⲑ **12** 1.6
  ⲑⲩ **17** b.30; **24** 18; **29** f.21

ⲑ̅ⲩ̅ **21** 10; **22** 19, 62; **23** 45; **25** 16.13; **26** 15.29, 31, 16.8, 12, 14, 23, 25, 27, 36, 17.9, 12, 16; **27** f.23; **28** 12.19; **31** b.17; **32** 1.26; **36** f.I.2; **37** f.4, b.3, 5, 8, 10, 15, 17, 20, 22
Ἰερουσαλήμ "Jerusalem"
  ⲑⲓ̅ⲗ̅ⲏ̅ⲙ̅ **11** 28.20
  ⲓ̅ⲗ̅ⲏ̅ⲙ̅ **11** 26.6
ⲓⲏⲥⲟⲩⲥ "Jesus"
  ⲓ̅ⲥ̅ **11** 2.3, 18, 4.24, 8.6, 11.27, 19.28, 20.9, 24.1, 4, 25.23, 29.27, 30.4; **15** f.1; **25** 6.4 (twice), 5, 8.16, 29, 9.9, 10.20, 11.5 (three times), 12.3, 10, 13.5, 18, 22, 25, 29, 14.4, 8, 15.11, 14, 19, 23, 16.1, 4, 16.22 (three times), 17.34; **26** 4.22, 12.8, 26, 27, 29, 31, 13.1, 3 (twice), 5, (twice), 17, 29, 34, 15.10; **28** 3.2, 7.11, 8.9, 16, 21, 9.3; **29** f.1; **31** f.33 (?), b.9
Ἰσραήλ "Israel"
  ⲓ̅ⲏ̅ⲗ̅ **11** 7.19, 28.18
ⲓⲱϩⲁⲛⲛⲏⲥ "Iōhannēs"
  ⲓ̅ⲱ̅ **23** 50
κοινά "usual"
  ⲕ̅\ⲟ/ (?) **3** b.II.8, 10
  ⲕⲟⲓ/ **4** 2.7, 3.2, 6.2
λίβανος "frankinsense"
  ⲗⲓ/ **12** 1.6
  ⲗ̅ⲓ̅ⲃ̅ⲁ̅ **37** f.5, 8, b.15
μαστίχη "mastic"
  ⲙ]ⲁⲥ **37** b.10, 17
  ⲙ̅ⲁ̅ⲥ̅ **32** 1.26; **36** f. I.2; **37** b.3, 12, 17
  ⲙ̅ⲁ̅ⲥ̅ϯ̅ⲭ̅ **26** 15.31
  ⲙⲁϩ/ ? **12** 1.6
ⲛⲟⲩⲧⲉ "God"
  ϕϯ **34** 2.11
παντοκράτωρ "almighty"
  ⲡ̅ⲁ̅ⲛ̅ⲧ̅ⲟ̅ⲣ̅ **22** 32; **25** 13.2
  ⲡⲁⲛⲧⲱⲣ **22** 31; **25** 2.7, 8.11, 11.5, 14.18, 22; 16.22, 18.1; **26** 11.4
πνεῦμα "spirit"
  ⲛ̅ⲁ̅ **25** 6.1, 7.24; **26** 10.1, 23
  ⲡⲛⲁ **26** 14.24, 25
  ⲡ̅ⲛ̅ⲁ̅ **7** 32; **11** 12.13, 28, 19.25, 26, 23.25, 25.15; **12** 5.16, 9.10, 17, 13.22, 19.12, 16, 37.17, 18, 19, 21, 22, 39.3, 43.6; **15** b.4; **25** 3.18, 5.5, 24, 8.27, 10.12, 13, 12.1, 13.8, 25; **26** 2.8, 3.1, 7, 12, 4.19, 6.27, 7.6, 11, 9.25, 10.19, 14.3, 7, 26, 15.25; **28** 1.13, 3.2, 21, 5.3, 18, 11.19, 12.13; **29** f.13
(ⲡ)ⲟⲟϩ "moon"
  ☾ **24** 24; **25** 9.5; **31** b.20

σκουτέλλιον "dish"
  ⲥⲕⲱⲧⲉⲗ   **32** 1.19
στακτή "myrrh"
  ⲥⲧⲁⲕ/   **12** 1.6
σταυρός "cross"
  ⲥ̄ⲣ̄ⲟⲥ   **12** 37.2
  c̄⳨ⲟⲥ   **22** 62; **25** 13.23, 30, 14.5; **26** 8.8, 13.9, 17, 23; **28** 8.7, 10, 17
  c̄⳨ⲟⲩ   **23** 26
  c̄⳨ⲟⲥ   **11** 28.9, 13, 17
  ⳨   **33** 3 (?)
  ⳨   **26** 13.25
στ(αυρ)οῦν "to crucify"
  c̄⳨ⲟⲩ   **11** 6.15
στύραξ "storax"
  ⲥⲧⲏ/   **12** 1.6
  ⲥⲧⲏⲣ   **26** 16.8
  ⲥⲧⲏⲥ   **34** 4.17 (?)
σύν "with"
  ⲥⲩⲛ   **36** b.1
ⲥⲱⲗⲱⲙⲱⲛ "Solomon"
  ⲥⲱⲗⲱ   **30** f.8
σωτήρ "saviour"
  ⲥⲱⲣ   **25** 10.20
†ⲧⲁⲣⲕⲟ (± ⲉⲣⲟⲕ/ⲉⲣⲟ ± ⲙ̄ⲡⲟⲟⲩ) "I adjure (you today)"
  ⲧⲣⲁ   **25** 9.25, 26 (twice), 9.25, 26
  †   **26** 6.17, 19, 7.2, 14, 16, 19, 20, 22, 26, 8.1, 3, 4, 5, 7, 8, 10, 12, 13–14, 16, 18, 20, 25, 30, 9.7, 9, 11, 16, 19, 20, 10.21, 11.22, 28, 12.5, 8, 14, 17, 19, 13.9, 14, 18–19, 24, 26, 30, 14.8, 10, 14, 16, 32
†ⲱⲣⲕ "I adjure"
  †   **22** 25; **25** 7.20, 22, 8.10; **26** 12.24
  ⲧ̄ⲣ   **27** f.4
υἱός "son, child"
  ⲭ   **34** 4.21
  ⲭ̄   **24** 12, 16; **25** 13.3, 9, 15, 17.41; **28** 4.20, 6.3, 16, 19, 7.10, 9.13, 16, 10.9, 13.15; **30** b.4; **31** f.7; **35** b.1
  ⲩ̄ⲥ   **31** f.7, 13, b.12; **32** 2.24
φυλακτήριον "phylactery"
  ⲫ̄ⲩ   **22** 48; **26** 5.29; **27** f.15
  ⲫⲩⲣⲓⲟⲛ   **21** 16
  ⲫⲟⲩⲣⲓⲱⲛ   **25** 18.3
χριστός "Christ"
  ⲭⲥ   **11** 2.3, 18, 4.25, 8.6, 11.27, 17.10, 19.28, 20.2, 9, 24.1, 4, 25.23, 28.10, 13, 17, 29.27, 30.4; **12** 31.6; **23** 24; **25** 6.4, 5, 8.16, 29, 10.20, 12.3, 10, 13.5, 12, 18, 15.11, 14, 19, 23, 16.1, 4, 22, 17.12, 34; **26** 4.22, 11.3, 12.8, 13.6, 17, 29, 34, 15.10; **28** 3.2, 8.9, 9.3; **29** f.15, 7; **31** f.32 (?)
ϫⲟⲉⲓⲥ "Lord"
  ϫⲥ   **10** 12
  ⲟⲥ   **25** 5.9, 9.28, 17.34; **26** 4.11, 28, 29, 9.14, 32, 11.16, 13.34, 15.9, 19; **28** 3.15, 7.6, 10.1, 2; **29** f.7

VI. Words of Arabic Origin

الاسواني *al-aswānī* "of Aswan"
  ⲁⲗⲉⲥⲟⲩⲉⲛⲓ   **30** f.2–3
الأنبا *al-anbā* "(the) anba" (ecclesiastical title)
  ⲁⲗⲁⲙⲡⲉ   **30** b.2
الجام *al-ǧām* "(the) platter"
  ⲁⲗϭⲉⲉⲙ   **25** 16.10
  ⲁⲗϭⲉⲉⲙⲓⲁ   **32** 1.21 and 23
  ⲁⲗϭⲉⲙⲉ   **37** b.3
  ⲁⲗϭⲉⲙⲉ   **37** b.29
الجني *al-ǧinniyy* "(the) djinn"
  ⲁⲗϭⲏⲛⲓ   **21** f.14
الزعفران *az-za ʿfarān* "(the) saffron"
  ⲁⲥ (?)   **29** b.7; **37** b.2, 11
  ⲁⲥⲁⲃⲣⲁⲛ   **25** 16.8
  ⲁⲥⲃⲣⲁⲛ   **26** 17.20–21
  ⲁⲥⲥⲁⲁⲃⲣⲁⲛ   **32** 1.27
السكّ *as-sukk* "(the) *sukk*"
  ⲁⲥⲟⲩⲭ   **24** f.18 cf. note ad loc.
الساحر *as-sukr* "(the) intoxication, enchantment"
  ⲁⲥⲥⲟⲩⲭⲁⲣⲉ (?)   **37** b.1
الصندل *aṣ-ṣandal* "(the) sandalwood"
  [ⲁ]ⲥⲥⲁⲛⲧⲉⲗ   **37** b.3
العروس *al-ʿarūs* "(the) bridegroom"
  ⲁⲗⲁⲣⲱⲱⲥ   **29** f.21–22
  ⲁⲗⲁⲗⲱⲥⲉ   **33** f.10
العود *al-ʿūd* "(the) agarwood"
  ⲁⲗⲟⲩⲑ   **22** 20; **24** f.18; **25** 17.1626 15.31, 17.23
  ⲁⲗⲁⲱⲑ   **32** 1.26
  ⲁⲗⲱⲑ   **37** b.3
  ⲁⲗⲱ\ⲑ/   **37** b.10
قطن *quṭun* "cotton"
  ⲕⲟⲩⲧⲱⲛ   **24** f.20
الكوفي *al-kūfī* "kufic"
  ⲁⲗⲭⲱⲃⲓⲁ   **23** 6
  ⲁⲗⲭⲱⲃⲓ   **23** 46
  ⲁⲗⲭⲟⲩⲃⲓ   **36** f.I.5–6
الكتم *al-katam* "(the) *katam*"
  ⲁⲗⲏⲭⲧⲁⲙ ?   **25** 9.6

الماورد *al-māward* "(the) rose water"
   ⲁⲗⲙⲁⲁⲩⲁⲣⲧ   **25** 16.9
   ⲁⲗⲙⲉⲁⲣⲧⲉ   **25** 16.15
   ⲁⲗⲙⲁⲩⲁⲣⲧ   **26** 15.28
   ⲁⲗⲙⲁⲟⲩⲁⲣⲧ   **26** 16.10–11

المجرب *al-muğarrib* "tested"
   ⲁⲗⲙⲟⲩϭⲁⲣ   **37** b.28
   ⲁⲗⲙⲟⲩϭⲁⲣⲣⲏⲡ   **37** f.35

المداد *al-midād* "(the) ink"
   ⲁⲗⲙⲓⲧⲉ   **23** 5
   ⲁⲗⲙⲓⲧⲉⲧ   **23** 45–46
   ⲁⲗⲙⲓⲧⲉⲧ   **36** f.I.4–5

المرّ *al-marr* "(the) shovel"
   ⲁⲗⲙⲉⲣⲉ   **30** f.11

المسك *al-misk* "(the) musk"
   ⲁⲗⲙⲓⲥⲓⲭ   **37** b.28

النورج *an-nawrağ* "(the) thresher"
   ⲁⲛⲁⲩⲣⲏϣ   **30** f.10

ورق *waraq* "paper"
   ⲅⲁⲗⲓⲭ   **21** f.6–7
   ⲅⲁⲣⲏⲕ   **23** 11
   ⲅⲁⲣⲣⲁⲕ   **32** 1.20; **33** f.7
   ⲅⲁⲣⲣⲏⲕ   **25** 16.9

الوسواس *al-waswās* "(the) whisperer"
   ⲁⲗⲟⲩⲁⲥⲓⲟⲩⲁⲥ   **25** 10.14–15

VII. Words of Greek Origin

ἀγαθός "good"   **13** 12
   ⲁⲅⲁⲑⲱⲥ   **16** 2.2
   ⲁⲕⲁⲑⲟⲥ   **12** 13.13, 23.1; **27** 19; **25** 14.3
   ⲁⲕⲁⲑⲱⲥ   **25** 13.26; **26** 14.6
   ⲁⲕⲁⲕⲁⲑⲟⲥ   **12** 31.19
   ἀγαθόν (n.)   **11** 10.5
   ⲁⲕⲁⲑⲱⲛ   **25** 17.40

ἀγαπᾶν "to love"
   ⲁⲕⲁⲡⲁ   **28** 10.17

ἀγάπη "love"
   ⲁⲅⲁⲡⲏ   **11** 23.13, 24.25

ἀγγελική "angelic"
   ⲁⲕⲉⲗⲓⲕⲏ   **12** 37.21
   ⲁⲛⲅⲉⲗⲓⲕⲏ   **26** 5.24–25

ἄγγελος "angel"   **3** f.I.3, 36, f.II.2–3, 9, 15; **4** 2.15; **6** 19; **11** 6.17–18, 12.2, 17.21–22, 18.25–26, 27.7–8; **12** 1.1, 2.12–14, 19, 11.8, 15.11, 17.9, 15, 17–18, 19.15, 21–22, 21.9, 23.12, 35.16, 39.19, 41.3, 15–16, 43.4, 12, 18–19; **18** 5; **22** 33; **25** 7.23; **26** 3.16, 4.18–19, 6.9, 14.21; **31** f.17
   ⲁⲅⲅⲉⲗⲟⲩ   **25** 3.4
   ⲁⲅⲅⲉⲗⲱⲥ   **22** 44; **26** 2.17; **27** 3.3; **26** 4.26; **26** 5.10; **26** 10.28–29; **26** 14.21
   ⲁⲅⲅⲓⲗⲟⲥ   **9** 10
   ⲁⲛⲅⲉⲗⲟⲥ   **27** f.5; **28** 2.17

ἅγιος "holy"   **25** 15.10
   ⲁⲅⲓⲁ   **28** 3.2
   ⲁⲕⲓⲱⲛ   **2** 5
   ⲑⲁⲅⲓⲁ   **25** 8.1, 20
   ϩⲁⲅⲓⲁⲥ   **12** 9.20–21, 29.23

ἁγιάζειν "to sanctify"
   ϩⲁⲅⲓⲁⲍⲉ   **25** 8. 21–22
   ϩⲁⲅⲓⲁⲥⲥⲉ   **26** 5.16, 6.3,10.2–3

ἀδελφός "brother"   **1** b.10 (twice)

ἀετός "eagle"   **12** 29.7, 33.19

ἀήρ "air"   **11** 26.13; **12** 15.3, 25.3–4, 20; **26** 10.14, 14.34

ἀθετεῖν "to reject"
   ⲁⲑⲉⲧⲓ   **11** 22.18

αἰτεῖν "to ask"
   ⲉⲁⲓ   **3** f.I.15
   ⲉϯ   **30** f.19; **34** 2.14

αἴτημα "demand"   **11** 18.10–11
   ⲁⲏⲧⲏⲙⲁ   **6** 24
   ⲉⲧⲉⲙⲁ   **18** 18
   ⲉⲧⲏⲙⲁ   **3** b.I.8

αἰών "aion"
   ⲉⲟⲛ   **28** 2.23
   ⲉⲱⲛ   **12** 2.8, 11; **25** 2.13; **28** 3.15, 4.20

ἀκάθαρτον "unclean"   **11** 25.15–16; **12** 9.11, 15.1, 19, 21.13, 37.18, 39.3, 41.6
   ⲁⲅⲁⲑⲁⲣⲧⲟⲛ   **11** 19.26

ἀκτίν "ray"   **26** 5.11

ἀλλά "but"   **3** f.I.16; **8** b.4; **11** 6.27; **12** 21.14–15, 39.2; **23** 39; **28** 7.8, 12.8; **29** f.10; **30** f.24; **34** 2.16

ἀλυκή "salted fish"
   ⲁⲗⲏⲅⲉ (?)   **24** 23

ἄλφα   **11** 19.14–15

ἅμα "also"
   ϩⲁⲙⲁ   **11** 20.25

ἀμελεῖν "to be neglectful"
   ⲁⲙⲉⲗⲉⲓ   **1** f.41, b.2
   ⲁⲙⲉⲗⲓ   **28** 5.1–2, 9.8–9

ἀμήν "amen"
   ϩⲁⲙⲏⲛ   **4** 2.26; **11** 14.12, 20.5, 23.26, 24.2, 25.21, 23, 26.7, 28.21; **12** 15.6, 19.23, 27.17, 37.15, 39.2, 15 (?), 22, 43.20; **25** 6.3, 6.4, 5 (three times), 8.28 (three times), 15.11, 16.15; **26** 15.26 (three times)

ϩⲁ\ⲙ/   25 2.5
ἀμίαντον "asbestos"   32 8
   ⲁⲙⲧⲉⲛ   32 6
ἀμμωνιακός "amoniac"
   ⲁⲙⲟⲩⲛⲓⲁⲕⲟⲩ   12 1.4–5
ἀμνός "lamb"
   ⲁⲛⲙⲟⲩ (?)   31 f.38
ἀμπύλλη "flask"
   ⲁⲛⲡⲟⲩⲗⲗⲉ   37 b.14,25
   ⲁⲙ̇ⲡⲟⲩⲗⲗⲓ   26 15.28
ἀναγαγεῖν "to report"
   ⲁⲛⲁⲛⲁⲅⲉ   11 20.10
ἀναγκάζειν "to compel"
   ⲁⲛⲁⲅⲕⲁⲍⲉ   32 2.8
ἀνάθεμα "anathema"
   ⲁⲛⲁⲑⲉⲙⲁ   26 10.17; 28 11.15
ἀνάστασις "resurrection"
   ⲁⲛⲁⲥⲧⲁⲥⲓⲥ   26 13.31
ἀνατολή "east"
   ⲁⲛⲁⲧⲟⲗⲏ   11 15.1
ἀναφορά "offering"
   ⲁⲛⲁⲫⲱⲣⲁ   28 9.2
ἀναχωρεῖν "to withdraw"
   ⲁⲛⲁⲭⲱⲣⲉⲓ   11 19.28
   ⲁⲛⲁⲭⲱⲣⲏ̣   11 5.8, 8.25
   ⲁⲛⲁⲭⲱⲣⲓ   12 9.11–12
   ⲁⲛⲁⲭⲱ   26 14.31
   ⲛ̇ⲁⲭⲱⲣⲓ   25 3.1, 5.2–3
ἀνθηλιακόν "sun-facing" (?)
   ⲁⲑⲉⲗⲓⲕⲟⲛ (?)   25 17.26–27
   ⲁⲑⲏⲗⲓⲕⲱⲛ (?)   25 9.5
   ⲁⲧⲑⲉⲗⲓⲕⲟⲛ (?)   25 16.11
ἀντίγραφον "copy"   11 24.3
ἀντικείμενος "adversary"
   ⲁⲗⲧⲓ̣ⲕⲉⲟⲛⲟⲥ   27 f.18
   ⲁⲛⲧⲓⲕⲓⲙⲉⲛⲟⲥ   11 25.14
   ⲁⲛ†ⲕⲓⲙⲉⲛⲟⲥ   25 2.4
ἀξιοῦν "to ask"
   ⲁⲍⲓⲟⲩ   1 f.36; 11 21.22
ἀξίωμα "rank"
   ⲁⲍⲓⲱⲙⲁ   32 2.10
ἀόρατος "invisible"
   ⲁϩⲟⲣⲁⲧⲟⲛ   11 23.22–23
ἀπαντᾶν "to meet"
   ⲁⲃⲁⲡⲁⲧⲁ   24 29
   ⲁⲡⲁⲛⲧⲁ   11 19.12; 18.8
ἅπαξ "once"
   ϩⲁⲡⲁⲍ   11 1.18, 6.6
ἀπαρχή ? "first fruits"
   ⲁⲡⲁ.....   12 7.20

cf. sv. ἀρχή
ἀπατᾶν "deceive"
   ⲡⲁⲧⲁ   26 11.2
ἁπλῶς "generally"
   ϩⲁⲡⲗⲟⲥ   25 4.15
   ϩⲁⲡⲗⲱⲥ   11 1.18, 6.6–7
ἀποθήκη "storehouse"
   ⲁⲡⲱⲑⲏⲕⲉ   30 f.13; 32 2.13
ἀπόκρισις "payment"
   ⲁⲡⲱⲕⲣⲉⲥⲓⲥ   28 2.17, 7.11–12, 12.16
   ⲁⲡⲱⲕⲣⲥ   27 f.1
ἀπολογία "request"   28 12.1–2; 32 1.35
   ⲁⲡⲟⲩⲗⲉⲅⲓⲁ   17 f.32
   ⲁⲡⲡⲱⲗⲗⲁⲅⲓⲁ   21.21–22
   ⲁⲡⲱⲗⲁⲕⲓⲁ   34 2.13
   ⲁⲡⲱⲗⲟⲅⲓⲁ   26 9.31, 10.24; 28 3.11, 17
   ⲁⲡⲱⲗⲱⲅⲓⲁ   28 7.3, 11.5
   cf. sv. ἀπολογία in Abbreviations
ἀπόστολος "apostle"
   ⲁⲡⲱⲥⲧⲟⲗⲟⲥ   26 13.33
   ⲁⲡⲱⲥⲧⲱⲗⲱⲥ   29 f.3
ἀποφαίνειν "to appear"
   ⲁⲡⲱⲫⲁⲛⲓ   28 4.21
ἀποφάνεια "appearance"
   ⲁⲡⲱⲫⲁⲛⲓⲁ   28 4.22, 12.3–4
ἄπρακτος "idleness"   11 1.16
ἅρμα "chariot"
   ϩⲁⲣⲙⲁ   4 2.4; 18.2; 25 6.11; 26 2.4
ἁρπάζειν "to snatch"
   ϩⲁⲣⲡⲁⲍⲉ   32 1.8, 2.5
   ϩⲁⲣⲡⲁ[ⲥ]ⲥⲉ   4 6.1
ἀρχάγγελος "archangel"   11 9.26–27, 17.13, 18.26–27; 17 f.4; 26 15.15; 32 1.4; 12 27.10
   ⲁⲣⲭⲁⲅⲅⲉⲗⲱⲥ   26 5.14
   ⲁⲣⲭⲁⲛⲅⲉⲗⲟⲥ   28 2.18
   ⲁⲣⲭⲏⲁⲅⲅⲉⲗⲟⲥ   3 f.II.30, b.I.1–2; 12 2.14, 11.9, 43.14; 17 f.4; 25 3.4–5
   ⲁⲣⲭⲏⲁⲅⲅⲉⲗⲱⲥ   25 6.23, 18.7; 26 2.19, 10.29
   ⲁⲣⲭⲏⲁⲛⲅⲉⲗⲟⲥ   28 2.18
ἄρχειν "to rule"
   ⲁⲣⲭⲉⲓ   11 2.15
   ⲁⲣⲭⲓ 11 23.12
ἀρχή "beginning, source, rule, ruler, Principality"
   1 f.1; 3 f.I.29; 11 12.20, 29.23, 30.3; 17 f.5; 22 53; 28 3.15; 32 1.22; 37 f.12
   "first fruits"   21 8; 24 18; 25 16.8, 11; 26 17.7, 13, 18; 37 b.12
   cf. sv. ἀπαρχή; ἀρχή in Abbreviations
ἀρχίπλασμα "first-formed one"
   ⲁⲣⲭⲏⲡⲗⲁⲥⲙⲁ   12 15.17, 23.15–16, 17–18,

37.22–23, 41.20; **26** 4.4
ἄρχων "ruler"
   ⲁⲣⲭⲱⲛ   **17** f.14–16; **26** 4.17; **30** f.22
ἀσεβής "impious"   **31** f.24–25
ἄσφαλτος "bitumen"
   ⲁⲥⲡⲁⲣⲧⲟⲛ   **17** b.30
ἀσώματος "incorporeal"
   ⲁⲥⲱⲙⲁⲧⲱⲥ   **25** 5.14
ἄσωτος "desperate" (?)
   ⲁⲥⲱⲧⲟⲥ   **37** f.26
ἄτιμος "not honoured"
   ⲁⲧⲙⲉⲥ   **4** 2.15–16
αὐθεντία "authority"
   ⲁⲩⲑⲉⲛⲧⲓⲁ   **11** 21.14
αὐλή "courtyard"
   ⲁⲩⲗⲏ   **11** 3.9, 4.11–12
βάπτισμα "baptism"   **11** 12.25
βασανίζειν "to torture"
   ⲃⲁⲥⲁⲛⲓⲍⲉ   **25** 5.1
βασιλεύς "king"
   ⲃⲁⲥⲓⲗⲉⲟⲥ   **28** 3.19
βάσις "base"   **17** b.16; **26** 7.13
*βισάκκιον "bag" (Latin *bisaccium*)
   ϥⲉⲥⲉⲕⲓⲛ   **20** f.3
βοήθεια "help"
   ⲃⲟⲏⲑⲓⲁ   **11** 10.4, 30.22–23; **12** 2.18, 7.9, 13.20
   ⲃⲱⲓⲑⲓ   **25** 5.8, 6.2
βοηθεῖν "to help"
   ⲃⲟⲏⲑⲓ   **12** 41.17
   ⲃⲟⲏⲑⲓⲁ   **12** 15.15–16, 19.6
   ⲃⲱⲓⲑⲓ   **25** 10.26, 11.10, 15.11, 19, 16.1, 26
βοήθημα "remedy"
   ⲃⲟⲏⲑⲏⲙⲁ   **11** 14.2–3
βοηθός "helper"   **12** 25.9
   ⲃⲱⲓⲑⲟⲥ   **25** 3.9
βοτάνια "herbs"
   ⲃⲏⲧⲁⲛⲓⲁ   **11** 21.1
γάμος "marriage"
   ⲕⲁⲙⲟⲥ   **19**.2, 4
γάρ "for"   **10**.2; **11** 10.9, 24, 22.1, 23.5, 27.3; **12** 2.17, 17.20; **25** 5.9
γενεά "generation"   **11** 20.19, 25.4
γένος "race"
   ⲅⲉⲛⲛⲟⲥ   **25** 7.12–13, 17.41; **26** 13.11
   ⲕⲉⲛⲟⲥ   **11** 19.9; **22** 50
γῆ "earth"
   ⲕⲏ   **12** 9.20, 29.22; **25** 6.8, 15.10
   ⲕⲣ   **12** 9.20
γραμματεύς "scribe"   **15** f.7

   ⲕⲣⲁⲙⲙⲁⲧⲉⲩⲥ   **25** 16.18
γράφειν "to write"
   cf. s.v. γράφειν in *Abbreviations*
δαιμονιακός "demoniac"
   ⲧⲉⲙⲟⲛⲓⲁⲕⲟⲥ   **18**.19
δαιμόνιον "demon"   **11** 11.13–14, 20.8
   ⲇⲉⲙⲟⲛⲓⲟⲛ   **25** 4.24
   ⲇⲉⲙⲱⲛⲓⲱⲛ   **25** 3.1, 4.9–10, 5.1
   ⲇⲏⲙⲟⲛⲓⲟⲛ   **17** b.42
   ⲧⲉⲙⲱⲛⲓⲱⲛ   **26** 10.8, 11, 13.13
   ⲧⲏⲙⲟⲛⲓⲟⲛ   **36** f.I.14–15
   ⲧⲓⲙⲱⲛⲓⲱⲛ   **26** 12.28
   ⲧⲙⲱⲛⲓⲱⲛ   **26** 15.27
δαίμων "demon"   (**30** f.23, b.3)
   ⲧⲉⲙⲟⲛ   **12** 41.6–7
δάφνη "bay"
   ⲧⲁⲫⲉⲛ   **25** 9.1
δέ "but, and"   **1** f.14, 7.8, 28; **11** 11.3, 20.23, 26, 23.7, 26.25; **15** f.1; **25** 2.6; **26** 6.12
   ⲧⲉ   **26** 4.15
δεῖνα "NN"
   cf. δεῖνα in *Abbreviations*
δεκανός "decan"
   ⲧⲉⲕⲁⲛⲟⲥ   **37** f.15
δεσμός "binding"
   ⲗⲓⲥⲙⲟⲥ   **25** 9.31
δεσπότης "lord"   **1** b.9
   ⲇⲉⲥⲡⲟⲧⲁ   **10**.1
δημοσίᾳ "publicly"
   ⲇⲏⲙⲟⲥⲓⲁ   **11** 21.12
διαβολή "slander"
   ⲇⲓⲁⲃⲟⲗⲏ   **11** 13.9
διαβολικόν "devilish"
   ⲧⲓⲁⲃⲱⲗⲓⲕⲱⲛ   **28** 5.23
διάβολος "Devil"   **8** b.6; **11** 13.19, 18.7, 17, 19.22–23; **25** 10.17; **26** 3.14
   ⲇⲉⲁⲃⲱⲗⲟⲥ   **25** 10.14; **26** 7.10
   ⲇⲓⲁⲃⲟⲗⲱⲥ   **26** 13.12–13;
   ⲇⲓⲁⲃⲱⲗⲱⲥ   **26** 6.30; **31** f.8, 14–15
   ⲧⲓⲁⲃⲟⲗⲟⲥ   **3** f.II.26
διάκονος "deacon"
   cf. διάκονος in *Abbreviations*
δίκαιος "just"
   ⲇⲓⲕⲏⲱⲥ   **31** f.9
δικαιοσύνη "justice"   **11** 9.12, 21; **12** 15.11–12, 17.18, 19.15, 22, 21.10, 39.19–20, 43.4, 19; **17** f.3
   ⲇⲓⲕⲉⲱⲥⲏⲛⲉ   **26** 14.23
   ⲧⲓⲕⲁⲓⲟⲥⲏⲛⲏ   **12** 23.12–13, 41.3–4
διστάζειν "to hesitate, doubt"

ⲧⲓⲥⲧⲁⲍⲉ **11** 20.25
†ⲥⲧⲁⲥⲥⲉ **37** f.33
διώκειν "to persecute"
   ⲇⲓ[ⲟⲓⲕⲉⲓ] **12** 2.1–2
   ⲇⲓⲱⲕⲉⲓ **11** 19.28
   ⲧⲓⲱⲕⲓ **26** 14.34
   †ⲟⲩⲕⲉ (?) **13**.16
   †ⲱⲕⲉ **11** 22.21
δόκιμον "tested"
   ⲧⲟⲕⲓⲙⲱⲛ **36** f.I.9
δόξης "glory" **12** 9.21
   ⲧⲟⲝⲓⲱⲥ **25** 6.9
   ⲇⲱⲝⲟⲥ **25** 15.11
δράκων "serpent"
   ⲇⲣⲁⲕⲱ **8** f.14
   ⲧⲣⲁⲕⲱⲛ **28** 1.18
δρόμος "course"
   ⲇⲣⲟⲙⲟⲥ **11** 26.12
δύναμις "power" **26** 12.16; **32** 2.22
   ⲇⲉⲛⲁⲙⲓⲥ **26** 10.13
   ⲇⲏⲛⲁⲙⲓⲥ **11** 25.13
   ⲧⲉⲛⲁⲙⲓⲥ **24** 27; **25** 7.19, 8.17, 10.13, 2.24; **26** 3.6, 8.21, 26–27, 16.29, 17.11, 13–14, 30, 31; **28** 2.20
   ⲧⲉⲩⲛⲁⲙⲓⲥ **25** 7.3–4
   ⲧⲏⲛⲁⲙⲓⲥ **12** 15.18, 17.1, 19.20–21, 23.16, 41.21; **17** f.12–13
   ⲧⲩⲛⲁⲙⲉⲥ **17** f.8
δυνατός "might"
   ⲇⲉⲛⲁⲧⲱⲥ **24** 3–4
δωρεά "gift" **11** 23.6–7
δῶρον "gift"
   ⲧⲱⲣⲱⲛ **28** 10.21
ἔθνος "nation"
   ϩⲉⲑⲛⲟⲥ **11** 22.1, 17
   ⲉϩⲑⲛⲟⲥ **25** 5.8
εἰ μήτι "except"
   ⲉⲓⲉⲙⲉ† **28** 10.9
   ⲉⲓⲙⲉ† **28** 2.23
   ⲉⲓⲙⲏ† **27** f.2
   ⲉⲙⲓⲧⲉ **3** f.I.34
εἶδος "thing"
   ⲉⲓⲧⲱⲥ **34** 1.26
   ϩⲏⲧⲟⲥ **34** 4.18–19 (?)
εἴδωλον "idol" **11** 8.11
εἰκών "image"
   ϩⲓⲕⲱⲛ **10** 3; **16** 3.25–26; **26** 4.12, 5.1, 15.20
   ⲓⲕⲟⲛ **17** f.34
   ϩⲓⲕⲱⲛ **26** 11.17

εἰμί
   ὄντα **1** f.2
εἰρήνη "peace" **11** 25.20–21
   †-ⲣⲏⲛⲏ **11** 9.10
   ⲉⲓⲣⲏⲛⲉ **22** 37; **25** 2.5
   ⲉⲓⲣⲏⲛⲓ **26** 16.4
   ⲉⲓⲣⲏⲛⲛⲓ **26** 16.23
   ⲉⲣⲏⲛⲏ **26** 12.9
   ⲓⲣⲏⲛⲏ **28** 10.17
εἴτε "either... or" **11** 2.28, 3.1, 5.19–22; **12** 15.1–3, 37.18, 19, 20, 22, 41.6, 7, 8; **25** 3.10, 4.6, 7 (twice), 8, 9, 10 (twice), 11 (twice), 14 (twice), 17.39 (twice); **26** 10.9, 10, 11, 12, 13, 14, 16 (twice)
   ⲓⲇⲉ **3** f.30 (twice), 31, 32 (twice)
   ⲉⲓ† **26** 10.9; **34** 1.24
   ⲉⲓⲉ† **26** 10.10
   ⲉⲓⲧⲏ **34** 1.23, 24, 25, 26
ἐκκλησία "church"
   ⲅⲕⲗⲉⲥⲓⲁ **17** f.6–7, 9–10
   ⲉⲕⲗⲏⲥⲓⲁ **25** 14.9; **26** 5.30, 6.10
   ⲉⲕⲗⲉⲥⲓⲁ **30** f.25
ἐλάχιστος "humble" **11** 16.25–26, **17**.3
ἐλευθέρουν "to free"
   ⲉⲗⲉⲩⲑⲉⲣⲟⲩ **11** 19.8
ἐμπαθῶς "passionate" **37** f.12
ἔνδοξον "endoxon (hymn of praise?)"
   ⲉⲛⲇⲱⲕⲍⲱⲛ **26** 3.17–18; **26** 4.14
   ⲉⲛⲇⲱⲝⲱⲛ **26** 14.16
   ⲧⲱⲝⲱⲛ **26** 14.16
   ⲛⲉⲇⲱⲝⲱⲛ **26** 15.21
ἐνέργεια "work, energy"
   ⲉⲛⲉⲣⲅⲓⲁ **11** 1.7, 11.13, 12.21–22, 13.18, 20
   ⲉⲛⲉⲣⲕⲓⲁ **26** 3.15
   ⲉⲛⲉⲣⲅⲓⲉ **26** 10.8
   ⲛⲉⲣⲅⲓⲁ **26** 10.12
ἐνεργεῖν "to work"
   ⲛⲉⲣⲅⲉⲓ **25** 2.3
ἔνθεμα "ornament" **12** 33.13
ἐξομολογεῖν "to praise"
   ⲉⲍⲟⲙⲟⲗⲟⲅⲉⲓ **11** 16.12
   ⲉⲍⲟⲙⲟⲗⲟⲅⲓ **11** 21.10–11
   ⲉⲭⲥⲱⲙⲱⲗⲱⲕⲉ **30** f.7
ἐξορκίζειν "to adjure"
   ⲉⲍⲟⲣⲕⲓⲍⲓ **2** 1
ἐξορκισμός "adjuration"
   ⲉⲍⲟⲣⲅⲓⲥⲙⲟⲥ **11** 1.1–2, 6.9, 14.16, 23, 15.3, 9, 14, 24, 16.1–2, 7, 19–20, 17.12, 18.12
ἐξουσία "authority" **1** f.5; **11** 2.17, 12.22–23, 15.27; **22** 53; **25** 3.2–3; **26** 14.30–31, 16.28;

28 2.21, 3.16
ⲉⲕⲍⲟⲩⲥⲓⲁ   3 f.I.4; 26 6.1
ⲏⲕⲍⲟⲥⲓⲁ   17 f.6
ἐπάνω "over"   1 f.2
ἐπειδή "for"
ⲉⲡⲓⲇⲏ   11 24.12
ἐπειδήπερ "inasmuch"
ⲉⲡⲓⲇⲏⲡⲉⲣ   11 30.10
ἐπενδύτης "garment"
ⲉⲙⲡⲏⲧⲏⲥ   26 7.21
ἐπί "upon"   1 f.1
ἐπιβουλία "treachery"   11 13.21–22
ἐπιθυμία "lust, desire"   32 1.7, 2.33, 26
ⲉⲡⲉⲑⲉⲙⲓ   20.14
ⲉⲡⲉⲑⲉⲙⲓⲁ   24 34, 35
ⲉⲡⲓⲑⲉⲙⲓⲁ   28 1.14; 28 4.11, 5.4, 8, 6.1–2, 9–10, 20, 9.14, 20
ἐπικαλεῖν "to invoke"
ⲉⲡⲓⲕⲁⲗⲉ   3 f.I.1; 3 f.II.12
ⲉⲡⲓⲕⲁⲗⲓ   3 f.I.35; 4 2.1
cf. s.v. ἐπικαλεῖν in Abbreviations
ἐπικαλοῦμαί "to invoke"   1 f.1
ἐπισκοπή "episcopacy"   26 9.17
ἐπιστολή "letter"   11 24.1, 3–4, 25.9, 22
ἐπουράνιον "heavenly"
ⲡⲟⲩⲣⲁⲛⲓⲟⲛ   3 f.I.31
ⲡⲟⲩⲣⲁⲛⲓⲱⲛ   28 7.21–22, 34 1.11
ἔτι "furthermore"
ⲁⲓⲧⲓ   11 7.27,18.14
εὐαγγέλιον "gospel"   11 29.24–25, 30.1, 3, 8, 14
ⲉⲅⲁⲅⲅⲉⲗⲓⲟⲩ   11 29.25
εὐφραίνειν "to rejoice"
ⲉⲅⲫⲣⲁⲛⲉ   11 17.26
εὐχή "prayer"   4 2.2; 11 1.1; 28 12.20
†ⲟⲩⲭⲏ   26 15.27, 16.22, 34, 17.1
ⲉⲩⲭⲟⲥ   37 b.6
cf. s.v. εὐχή in Abbreviations
ζῴδιον "image"
ⲥⲱ†ⲟⲩⲛ   21.17; 22 47; 25 10.8,16.5; 26 5.29, 15.32, 16.19
ⲥⲱ†ⲟⲩⲱⲛ   26 16.24
cf. s.v. ζῴδιον in Abbreviations
ζῷον "living creature"   11 26.20
ⲥⲱⲟⲛ   11 17.22
ⲍⲱⲟⲩⲛ   11 26.10
ἡ (article)
ⲉⲓ   25 6.8, 15.10
ⲧⲏⲥ   12 9.20, 29.22; 25 6.8, 15.10
ἤ "or"   11 2.20, 3.26, 27, 4.5–22, 5.11, 23–27,
6.1–5, 8.10–12, 9.1, 6; 12 29.21; 18.7
ⲉ   12 9.20
ⲉⲓ   25 4.15
ἤδη "now"
ⲉⲧⲓ   4 3.2; 6.25
ⲉⲧⲏ   9.13
ⲉⲧ†   16 2.6
ἡδύνειν "to delight"
ⲏⲧⲟⲩⲛⲏ   17 f.18
ἧπαρ "liver"
ⲏⲡⲁⲣⲟⲛ   3 f.II.37
θάλασσα "sea"   12 7.16; 25 6.20
ⲑⲁⲗⲗⲁⲥ   3 f.I.10
θεός "God"   10.1; 28 4.9
θεοτόκος "Mother of God"
ⲑⲉⲟⲧⲱⲕⲟⲥ   25 8.19
θεωρεῖν "to see"
ⲑⲉⲱⲣⲓ   34 1.19
θεωριστής "scryer (?)"
[ⲑ]ⲉⲟⲣⲓⲥⲧⲱⲥ   34 1.17–18
θηρίον "beast"
ⲑⲉⲣⲓⲱⲛ   26 15.12
θρόνος "throne, seat"   4 5.13; 8 f.2; 11 22.15; 12 21.7, 27.20; 17 f.37; 25 2.15; 26 8.18
[ⲑⲣⲟⲛ]ⲟⲩ ?   30 b.2
ⲑⲣⲱⲛⲟⲥ   25 3.16–17; 26 7.13, 9.20; 27 7.18; 26 9.1, 26, 15.18
ⲑⲣⲱⲛⲱⲥ   28 3.16–17, 7.18–19
θυσία "sacrifice"
ⲑⲉⲥⲓ\ⲁ/   17 b.36
ⲑⲏⲥⲓⲁ   18.7; 28 9.1
ⲑⲏⲥⲓⲁⲥ   26 6.14
cf. s.v. θυσία in Abbreviations
θυσιαστήριον "altar"
ⲑⲏⲥⲓⲁⲥⲧⲏⲣⲓⲟⲛ   18.5
ⲑⲩⲥⲁⲧⲏⲣⲓⲱⲛ   25 15.5
ⲑⲉⲥⲓⲁⲥⲧⲏⲣⲓⲱⲛ   26 6.16
ἰάσμη "jasmine"
(ⲓ)ⲁⲥⲙⲉ   23 8
(ⲓ)ⲁⲥⲙⲏ   26 16.19, 22
Ἰουδαῖος "Jew"
ⲓⲟⲩⲇⲁⲓ   31 f.19, b.9
κάδος "jar"
ⲕⲁⲧⲟⲥ   17 f.36
ⲕⲁⲧⲉⲥ   20.3
ⲕⲉⲧⲟⲩⲥ   28 6.12
ⲕⲉⲧⲱⲥ   25 4.15
καθαρίζειν "to purify"
ⲕⲁⲑⲁⲣⲓⲍⲉ   12 23.19, 20, 22, 23, 25.1–3, 37.16–17, 39.2, 5, 8; 25 5.24

κεθαλιϲι 28 3.9
καθαρόν "pure" 12 33.12
καθέδρα "seat" 12 27.7
κάθημαι "to sit" 1 f.1
καί "and" 1 f.3; 11 22.1, 23.5, 29.21
κε 25 6.8; 25 15.10
κακία "wickedness" 11 22.19–20
κακοῦργος "evil-doing"
  κακουρκωϲ 26 10.10
καλῶς "completely, well" 17 b.29; 25 16.15; 26 6.25
  καλοϲ 23 49; 24 18; 26 10.26,17.12
κἄν "even if, whether" 11 8.9, 22; 20.10; 32 2.6 (twice), 2.7 (twice
  καει (?) 6.14
  ⲅⲁⲛ 10.15–17
καπνός "smoke" 11 28.11, 14–15
κάπρος "boar"
  καπρϲ 7 36
κάρβων "charcoal"
  καρβωνε 12 1.8
  ⲭⲁⲃⲁⲛⲓ 26 16.36
κάρδαμον "garden cress"
  καρταμα 33 12
καρπός "fruit" 11 3.15–17, 4.13, 17; 12 7.15
καρύα "nut, nut tree"
  καιρε 17 b.21
  κᾳⲣⲩ? 29 b.7
κασσίτερος "tin"
  καϲιτηρⲛ 17 b.30
κατά "according to" 10.2; 11 24.14, 28.3, 30.1, 5, 14; 12 17.3, 19.8–9; 26 3.25; 26 10.30; 27 f.19; 28 11.5
κατακλιτικόν "striking-down spells"
  καⲛⲧⲁⲕⲗⲏ†ⲕⲟⲛ 26 10.12–13
καταλαλία "slander" 11 13.1
καταλύειν "to destroy"
  καταλη 11 18.6
καταξιοῦν "to deem worthy"
  καταξιογ 11 23.9
καταπέτασμα "veil" 12 1.2, 21.6
  καταπετιϲμα 25 7.21
  ⲕⲁⲧⲁⲡⲉ†ⲥⲙⲁ 28 3.13–14; 8.18–19
καταχθόνιον "subterranean"
  καταπⲧⲟⲛⲓⲟⲛ 3.f.I.32
κατέχειν "to restrain"
  καⲧⲏⲭⲉ 28 12.17
  κατⲏⲭⲏ 28 5.1, 7.12–13
  καⲧⲏⲭⲓ 28 9.8
  κατιⲭⲉ 4 5.1

κα†ⲭⲉ 32 1.18
κάτοχος "binding curse"
  κατοⲅοϲⲭοϲ? 37 f.30
  κⲧⲟⲅⲭοϲ? 37 f.25
καύσων "burning" 28 6.14
κελεύειν "command"
  κελεⲅⲉ 11 28.10, 14
κενταύριον "centaury"
  κενⲧⲁ\ⲣ/ 5 b.3
κεραυνός "thunderbolt"
  ϭⲉⲣⲁⲅⲛοϲ 1 f.19
κεφαλίς "capital" 12 33.1
κῆπος "garden" 11 4.14
κιννάμωμον "cinnamon" 12 1.7
κλάδος "branch, shoot"
  κ[λ]ατοϲ 12 1.3; 26 8.23
κοινά "usual, common"
  κοιⲁⲛⲁ (?) 36 f.I.10
  cf. sv. κοινά in Abbreviations
κοιτών "bedroom" 11 3.10
κόλασις "punishment" 11 27.12
κόσμησις "ornament" 34 1.24
κόσμος "world" 11 16.13–14, 20.13, 28.19–20; 12 33.6, 35.17
  κⲱϲⲙοϲ 25 2.22; 26 7.4, 12.10, 12–13; 34 1.14, 26
κρίσις "judgement" 8 b.4
κριτής "judge" 18.8
κτίσις "creation"
  κⲧⲏϲιϲ 12 35.9
  ..ⲏϲιϲ? 12 31.23
κυριακή "Sunday, week"
  κεⲣⲓακⲏ 28 12.21
κύριος "lord" 10.1; 11 19.1; 12 9.19, 29.20
  κⲏⲣⲓⲱϲ 26 9.5
  κιⲣⲓοϲ 25 6.7; 28 4.9
  κⲩⲣⲓⲱϲ 25 15.9
κύριε (voc.)
  κῖⲣⲓⲉ 20.12
λαλιά "song" 26 9.13
λαός "people" 11 7.9, 11.23–24, 22.6, 23.2, 16, 24.24; 31 b.8–9
λειτουργεῖν "to serve"
  λιⲧοⲩⲣⲅⲓ 11 26.21
  λιⲧοⲩⲣⲕⲟϲ 28 4.3
λείψανον "remains"
  λιψⲁⲛοⲛ 25 14.6–7
λευκόν "white"
  λεⲅⲕωⲛ 17 b.4–5, 18, 19

λιμήν "harbour"
  ⲗⲏⲙⲏⲛ **26** 7.7
λίμνη "lake"
  ⲗⲏ[ⲙ]ⲛⲏ **12** 7.19
λίβανος "frankincense" **23** 47–48; **24** 18; **26** 17.3; **37** b.5,8
  ⲗⲓⲃⲁⲛⲱⲥ 21.10
  cf. sv. λίβανος in Abbreviations
λογική "rational"
  ⲗⲱⲕⲓⲕⲏ **28** 9.1
λογισμός "reason" **32** 1.11
λόγος "word" **26** 4.21, 12.6
λόγχη "spear"
  ⲗⲟⲛⲭⲓ **26** 13.21
  ⲗⲱⲅⲭⲓ **15** 13.28
λουτήρ "baptistery" **26** 6.10
λυπεῖν "to grieve"
  ⲗⲩⲡⲉ 9.6, 9
λύπη "grief"
  ⲗⲏⲡⲉ **17** b.40
  ⲗⲏⲡⲓ **28** 1.11
μαγεία "magic"
  ⲙⲁⲅⲓⲁ **25** 4.3; **15** 4.22, 5.26
μάγος "magician" **3** f.I.30; **11** 5.25, 8.10; **26** 10.15–16
  ⲙⲁⲕⲟⲥ 18.15; **28** 1.17
μαθητής "disciple" **11** 19.13
μάλιστα "especially" **26** 15.21
μανία "madness" **28** 3.5; **36** f.II.9
μάννα "manna" **11** 7.20
μαργαρίτης "pearl"
  ⲙⲁⲣⲕⲁⲣⲓⲧⲏⲥ **12** 33.13–14
μάρτυρος "martyr"
  ⲙⲁⲣⲧⲏⲣⲟⲥ **11** 29.1
μαστίχη "mastic"
  ⲙⲁⲥⲧⲭ **26** 17.9
  ⲙⲁⲥⲧⲭⲏ **28** 12.19
  ⲙⲁⲥⲧⲭⲓ **22** 19; **25** 16.14, 17.15; **26** 16.20, 23, 17.12, 16, 22
  ⲙⲁⲥⲧⲭⲓ **26** 17.12
  ⲙⲁⲥⲧⲓⲭⲉⲛ **33** 2
  ⲙⲁⲥⲭⲉ (?) **17** b.9
  cf. s.v. μαστίχη in Abbreviations
μεθ' ἡμῶν "with us"
  see ⲙⲉⲑⲉⲙⲟⲛ in Personal Names and Voces Magicae
  cf. s.v. μαστίχη in Abbreviations
μέλαν "ink"
  ⲙⲉⲗⲁ **15** b.1
μέλος "body part" **3** f.II.38; **11** 6.23

μετάνοια "repentance"
  ⲙⲓⲧⲁⲛⲅ **26** 15.17
  ⲙⲓ[ⲧ]ⲁⲛⲓⲁ **31** f.30–31
μήποτε "lest"
  ⲙⲛ·ⲡⲱⲧⲛ **25** 5.7
μήτρα "womb" **3** f.1.21
μοῖρα "fate"
  ⲙⲉⲣⲣⲁ **25** 4.25
μονογενής "only-begotten" **11** 21.19–20
  ⲙⲟⲛⲟⲅⲏⲛⲏⲥ **12** 2.3–4
  ⲙⲱⲛⲟⲅⲉⲛⲏⲥ **25** 8.15–16
  ⲙⲱⲛⲱⲅⲉⲛⲏⲥ **26** 12.7–8, 20–21; **28** 8.16
  ⲙⲱⲛⲱⲕⲉⲛⲏⲥ **28** 3.1, 12.11–12
μορφή "form"
  ⲙⲟⲣⲫⲩ **4** 2.3
μοσχάτον "musk incense"
  ⲙⲟⲩⲥⲧⲁⲧⲉⲛ **22** 22–23
  ⲙⲟⲩⲥⲭⲁⲧⲉⲛ **25** 16.14, 17.17–19; **26** 15.33, 16.32
μόσχος "musk"
  ⲙⲁⲥⲭⲉ **17** b.9
  ⲙⲟⲩⲭⲥⲥ **28** 12.20
μοχλός "bolt"
  ⲙⲟⲩⲭⲗⲟⲥ **11** 27.11
μυρσίνη "myrtle"
  ⲙⲟⲣⲥⲏⲛⲏ **12** 1.4
μυστήριον "mystery"
  ⲙⲉⲥⲧⲏⲣⲓⲱⲛ **25** 8.6–7; **26** 3.23; **28** 9.3
νηστεύειν "to fast"
  ⲛⲉⲥⲧⲉⲩⲉ **28** 6.13, 12.22, 13.3
  ⲛⲉⲥⲧⲁ **26** 17.29
  ⲛⲏⲥⲧⲉⲩ **25** 9.5
νόμος "law" **11** 7.17
νοῦς "mind" **12** 2.6; **24** 30, 33; **28** 2.15, 5.3, 9, 22, 11.7
νυκτέριον "nocturnal"
  ⲛⲉⲕⲣⲏⲕⲧⲏⲣⲓⲟⲛ ? **12** 7.13
ξύλον "wood"
  ⳉⲏⲗ[ⲟⲛ] **12** 1.8–9
  ⲥⲧⲉⲗⲟⲩⲥ (?) **29** f.18
οἰκονόμος "steward"
  ⲉⲕⲟⲛⲟⲙⲟⲥ **12** 13.5, 19–20, 25.8
οἰκουμένη "(inhabited) world"
  ⲕⲟⲩⲙⲏⲛⲏ **3** f.II.23
  †ⲕⲟⲩⲙⲏⲛⲉ **26** 12.26
  †ⲕⲱⲙⲏⲛⲓ **28** 9.6
ὅλως "completely, at all"
  ϩⲟⲗⲱⲥ **11** 7.24
ὁμοούσιον "consubstantial" **11** 14.9
  ϩⲱⲙⲁⲩⲥⲓⲱⲛ **28** 7.15

ὀνομάζειν "name"
 ⲟⲛⲟⲙⲁⲍⲉ **11** 17.23; **32** 2.11, 13–14
 ⲁⲛⲱⲙⲁⲍⲉ **25** 7.4, 8.17–18
ὀποκάλαμος "calamus juice"
 ⲁⲡⲟⲩⲕⲁⲗⲁⲙⲱⲛ **17** b.7–8
ὀργή "anger"
 ⲱⲣⲕⲏ **28** 3.4
ὁρμή "impulse"
 ⲱⲣⲙⲏ **28** 4.18
ὅταν "whenever"
 ϩⲟⲧⲁⲛ **11** 10.9
οὐδέ, οὔτε "neither... nor; and not"
 ⲟⲩⲇⲉ **3** f.I.15–16; **11** 11.1, 25.15, 17; **17** b.44, 45; **18**.6–8, 15, 16; **25** 4.25
 ⲟⲩⲧⲉ **12** 15.5; **16** 2.2, 12–13; **32** 1.12
οὐράνιον "heavenly" **12** 15.2
οὐρανός "heaven" **12** 9.20, 29.21
 ⲟⲩⲣⲁⲛⲟⲩⲥ **25** 6.8, 15.10
οὔτε *see s.v.* οὐδέ
πάθος "passion" **32** 1.33
πάλιν "again" **11** 7.4, 10.10
παντοκράτωρ "almighty" **10**.1; **11** 1.27; **28** 12.10–11
 ⲡⲁⲛⲇⲱⲕⲣⲁⲇⲱⲣ **12** 2.6, 13.11–12, 15.8–9, 13–14, 17.21, 19.13, 19–20, 21.3, 37.8
 ⲡⲁⲛⲇⲱⲕⲣⲁⲧⲱⲣ **12** 11.4–5
 ⲡⲁⲛⲧⲱⲕⲣⲁⲇⲱⲣ **12** 25.12
 ⲡⲁⲛⲧⲱⲕⲣⲁⲧⲱⲣ **11** 2.24, 7.8; **18**.4; **28** 9.6
cf. s.v. παντοκράτωρ *in Abbreviations*
παρά "than" **25** 16.19; **28** 11.10
παραβαίνειν "to transgress"
 ⲡⲁⲣⲁⲃⲉ **11** 27.8
παράγειν "to go by"
 ⲡⲁⲣⲁⲅⲉ **15** f.1
 ⲡⲁⲣⲁⲕⲉ **11** 5.22
παράδεισος "paradise"
 ⲡⲁⲣⲁⲇⲓⲥⲟⲥ 9.11; **11** 26.26–28; **15** f.1
 ⲡⲁⲣⲁⲇⲓⲥⲱⲥ **17** f.11; **26** 6.8
 ⲡⲁⲣⲁϯⲱⲥ **25** 16.7
 ⲡⲁⲣⲁϯⲥⲟⲥ **29** f.4–5
 ⲡⲁⲣⲁϯⲥⲱⲥ **26** 11.1, 21, 12.4–5, 13.8–9
παραδιδόναι "to hand over"
 ⲡⲁⲣⲁⲇⲓⲇⲟⲩ **11** 27.7
παρακαλεῖν "to invoke, entreat"
 ⲡⲁⲗⲁⲕⲁⲗⲓ **5** f.1
 ⲡⲁⲣⲁⲅⲁⲗⲉ **17** f.18
 ⲡⲁⲣⲁⲕⲁⲗⲉⲓ **11** 1.25–26, 2.22–23, 3.17–18, 8.2, 19.16, 14.6 (?); **34** 3.8–9
 ⲡⲁⲣⲁⲕⲁⲗⲓ 10.7; **12** 2.1, 17.14, 21.16, 23.5, 14, 25.5–6, 10, 19, 27.1, 9, 18, 29.4–5, 9, 13, 31.2, 7, 9, 21, 33.3, 8, 16, 22, 35.2, 6, 10, 18–19, 23, 37.3–4, 13, 39.11–12, 21, 23, 43.12–13; 14.6 (?); 21.12; **24** 1–2, 26; **25** 5.22, 10.1
παράκλητος "Paraclete" **1** f.27
παρθενία "virginity" **19**.2, 4; **23** 26, 27, 28, 39
παρθένος "virgin" **7** 5, 26; **12** 35.3; **23** 29; **25** 2.2, 8.1, 20; **28** 2.10
 ⲡⲁⲣⲑⲉⲛⲱⲥ **28** 6.23
 ⲡⲁⲑⲣⲛⲟⲥ **28** 8.3, 11.21
πατάσσειν "to strike"
 ⲡⲁⲧⲁⲥⲥⲉ **11** 7.12–13
πατριά "lineage" **11** 25.5
πείθειν "to persuade, seduce"
 ⲡⲓⲑⲉ **7** 7, 21, 22
πειρασμός "temptation"
 ⲡⲓⲣⲁⲥⲙⲟⲥ **11** 13.16–17
πέπερι "pepper"
 ⲡⲓⲡⲣⲉ **24** 22
περίεργος "meddlesome" **11** 1.23
περιουργός "meddlesome man"
 ⲡⲉⲣⲓⲕⲟⲩⲣⲅⲟⲥ **25** 4.6
πέταλον "leaf"
 ⲡⲉⲧⲁⲗⲱⲛ **17** b.30
πέτρα "stone" **3** f.1.12; **11** 9.19; **26** 13.5, 15.7
πηγή "well" **7** 20
 ⲡⲓⲕⲏ **26** 11.20
 ⲡⲩⲅⲏ **7**.6
πικρία "bitterness" **11** 13.11
πίναξ "dish" **30** f.2; **37** b.4,7
 ⲡⲓⲛⲁⲧ **25** 17.28–29
 ⲡⲓⲛⲁⲕⲉⲥ **31** b.15–16
πιστεύειν "to believe"
 ⲡⲓⲥⲧⲉⲩ **29** f.20
 ⲡⲓⲥⲧⲉⲩⲉ **11** 20.12–13, 24, 24.13, 28.12–13, 16
πίστις "faith" **11** 24.14, 24–25
πιττάκιον "sheet"
 [ⲡⲓ]ⲧⲁⲕⲓⲱⲛ **2** 5
πλάσσειν "to mould"
 ⲡⲗⲁⲥⲥⲉ **12** 35.12
πλατεῖα "street"
 ⲡⲗⲁⲧⲓⲁ **11** 24.26
πλήρης "full"
 ⲡⲗⲏⲣⲟⲥ **12** 9.20, 29.21; **25** 15.10
 ⲡⲗⲓⲣⲓⲥ **25** 6.8
πνεῦμα "spirit" **12** 41.5; **17** f.4; **26** 2.18
 ⲡⲉⲛⲉⲩⲙⲁ **17** f.28
cf. s.v. πνεῦμα *in Abbreviations*
πόλις "city" **11** 20.7, 22.13, 23.11, 24.10–11, 29.2

πονηρία "wickedness"   **32** 1.34
πονηρός "evil"   **11** 1.9, 25, 7.3, 13.21
   πονηρόν (n.)   **11** 13.22–23, 19.25; **12** 13.22, 15.19–20, 43.6
   ⲡⲱⲛⲉⲣⲱⲛ   **25** 4.4, 10.12
πορνεία "fornication"
   ⲡⲱⲣⲛⲓⲁ   **28** 5.8
πορφύρα "purple"
   ⲡⲱⲣⲫⲱⲣⲁ   **26** 7.19
ποταμός "river"   **12** 29.2
πρᾶγμα "matter"   **11** 1.18
πρέπειν "to be fitting"
   ⲡⲣⲉⲡⲓ   **11** 12.12
   ⲙⲡⲣⲉⲡⲉ   **26** 15.24
πρεσβύτερος "presbyter"
   ⲡⲉⲣⲉⲥⲃⲏⲣⲟⲥ   **26** 9.16
   ⲡⲉⲣⲉⲥⲃⲩⲧⲉⲣⲟⲥ   **25** 5.13
   ⲡⲣⲏⲥⲃⲏⲧⲉⲣⲟⲥ   **12** 41.17
   ⲡⲣⲉⲥⲃⲏⲧⲉⲣⲟⲥ   **29** f.4
   ⲡⲣⲉⲥⲃⲏⲧⲏⲣⲟⲥ   **17** f.9
προαίρεσις "good intention"
   ⲡⲣⲟϩⲉⲣⲏⲥⲓⲥ   **11** 24.15–16
προσευχή "prayer"   **11** 2.20, 28, 3.26, 5.10–11, 6.25, 7.26, 8.27, 10.22–23, 25, 27, 11.6–7, 13.28, 14.13, 19.24, 20.3; **25** 2.1
   ⲡⲣⲟⲥⲉⲭⲩ   **28** 13.5
   ⲡⲣⲱⲥⲉⲩⲭⲏ   **28** 12.3
προσκυνεῖν "to prostrate"
   ⲡⲣⲟⲥⲕⲏⲛⲓ   **28** 10.14
   ⲡⲣⲟⲥⲕⲉⲉⲩⲛⲓ̈   **20**.12
   ⲡⲣⲟⲥⲕⲩⲛⲉⲓ   **11** 5.2, 22.6
προσκύνησις "adoration"   **11** 12.10–11
πρόσταγμα "ordinance"   **11** 7.18
προστάτης "benefactor"   **12** 13.19, 25.8
προσφορά "offering"   **32** 1.22
πρόσωπον "person"   **11** 12.23–24; **12** 15.7, 17.4
   ⲡⲣⲟⲥⲟⲡⲟⲛ   **12** 13.4–5, 25.11
προφητεύειν "to prophesy"
   ⲡⲣⲫⲉϯ   **28** 2.16
προφήτης "prophet"   **11** 30.6–7; **32** f. 29–30
πύλη "gate"   **11** 16.4–5, 23, 17.1
   ⲏⲗⲏ   **16** 2.6
   ⲡⲏⲗⲏ   **11** 16.9; **16** 1.8, 2.7
ῥάβδος "staff"
   ⲣⲁⲃⲧⲱⲥ   **16** 2.3
   [ⲣⲁ]ⲡⲧⲟⲥ   **37** f.14
ῥεῦμα "discharge"
   ϥⲣⲉⲩⲙⲁ   **18** 10
σάλπιγξ "trumpet"

ⲥⲁⲗⲡⲓⲍ   **26** 11.9
σαλπίζειν "to trumpet"
   ⲥⲁⲗⲡⲓⲍⲉ   **25** 7.10
σάρξ "flesh"   **11** 2.16, 21.18; **23** 24, 40
   ⲥⲁⲣⲉⲍ   **26** 13.34
   ⲥⲁⲣⲏⲍ   **28** 1.6
Σατανᾶς "Satan"   **11** 18.15–16; **28** 2.11
σεραφίμ "Seraphim"
   ⲥⲁⲣⲟⲩⲫⲓⲛ   **1** f.3
   ⲥⲉⲣⲁⲫⲓⲛ   **11** 3.22, 17.8–9, 27.2–3; **12** 11.6, 29.14–15, 33.5; **26** 2.21
   ⲥⲩⲣⲁⲡⲫⲉⲛ   **17** f.8–9
   ⲥⲉⲣⲁⲫⲓⲛ   **26** 9.7; **28** 2.19
σκάνδαλον "offence"
   ⲥⲕⲁⲧⲁⲗⲟⲛ   **11** 10.19
σκεπάζειν "shelter"
   ⲥⲕⲉⲡⲁⲥⲉ   **25** 6.27
σκηνή "tabernacle"
   ⲥⲅⲓⲛⲏ   **28** 7.16
   ⲥⲕⲉⲛⲏ   **28** 3.12
   ⲥⲕⲩⲛⲏ   **17** f.3; **18**.4
σκουτέλλιον "dish"
   ⲥⲕⲟⲩⲧⲉⲗⲗⲉ   **37** b.11–12
   cf. s.v. σκουτέλλιον in Abbreviations
σκύλλειν "to trouble"
   ⲥⲕⲏⲗⲗⲓ   **11** 22.7, 23.10
σουδάριον "shroud"
   ⲥⲟⲩⲧⲁⲣⲓⲱⲛ   **26** 13.28–29
σοφία "wisdom"
   ⲥⲱⲫⲓⲁ   **25** 7.22; **28** 1.14
σπέρμα "seed"   **10** 12
σπλάγχνον "innards"
   ⲥⲡⲗⲁⲭⲁⲛⲱⲛ   **28** 1.4–5
στακτή "myrrh"
   cf. s.v. στακτή in Abbreviations
σταυρός "cross"   **10**.21; **26** 16.32
   ⲥϯⲟⲥ   **25** 13.23
   cf. s.v. σταυρός in Abbreviations
στερέωμα "foundation"
   ⲥⲧⲉⲣⲉⲩⲙⲁ   **4** 5.12; **12** 11.12, 19.4; **26** 11.6
   ⲧⲉⲣⲉⲩⲙⲁ   **26** 2.12
στήλη "stele"   **17** b.39
στολή "garment"   **12** 33.8–9
   ⲥⲧⲱⲗⲏ   **17** b.38
στρατηλάτης "general"
   ⲥⲧⲉⲣⲁϯⲗⲁⲧⲏⲥ   **26** 14.12
στῦλος "pillar"
   ⲥⲧⲏⲗⲗⲟⲥ   **12** 11.19–20, 17.5, 10–11, 31.22, 43.1; **25** 14.26; **26** 6.17

στύραξ "styrax"
  ⲥⲧⲏⲣⲉⲝ 17 b.6
  ⲥⲧⲏⲣⲝ 22 21; 25 16.14, 17.16; 26 19.25
  ⲥⲧⲓⲣⲏⲝ 28 12.19–20
  ⲥⲧⲩⲣⲍ 32 1.26
  cf. s.v. στύραξ in Abbreviations
συκωτόν "liver"
  ⲥⲓⲕⲟⲩⲧⲟⲛ 3 f.II.37–38
συνευδοκεῖν "to consent"
  ⲥⲩⲛⲉⲩⲇⲟⲕⲉⲓ 11 5.18–19, 9.8
σφραγίς "seal" 11 6.10, 13.26; 26 6.8, 7.34
  ⲫⲣⲁⲕⲓⲥ 12 13.15, 15.13, 25.14, 31.10
σῶμα "body" 1 f.25; 12 31.3, 37.17, 43.15; 18.9, 14; 23 35; 25 4.19 (twice), 5.4, 5.25, 27, 6.27, 10.4, 13.2, 3, 5, 6, 8, 14.8, 12, 16, 15.2; 26 5.17, 19, 6.5, 6.29, 9.11, 10.6, 15, 13.6–7, 21, 14.5, 15.3; 28 5.14
  ⲥⲱⲙ 33 12
σωτήρ "saviour" 25 16.23
  ⲥⲱⲧⲱⲣ 25 16.22
  ⲥⲱⲣ 25 10.20
  cf. s.v. σωτήρ in Abbreviations
τάξις "rank" 26 5.24; 28 11.18
ταράσσειν "to trouble"
  ⲧⲁⲣⲁⲥⲥⲉ 24 32
ταραχή "disturbance" 28 5.6, 9.15
τάρταρος "Tartarus" 11 27.9
ταρταροῦχος "Tartaruchus"
  ⲧⲁ[ⲣ]ⲧⲁⲣⲟⲩⲭⲟⲥ 3 f.II.20–21
τάφος "grave" 34 f.12
  ⲧⲁⲫⲱⲥ 23 43; 26 13.27
τάχα "perhaps" 1 f.36
ταχύ "quickly" 1 f.41
  ⲧⲁⲭⲉ 20 f.16
  ⲧⲁⲭⲏ 3 b.I.19; 4 3.2; 6 25 (twice); 9 13 (twice); 12 19.2, 8, 29.4, 41.18, 16 3.6–7; 17 f.32, 37, b.41; 18 19 (twice), 20 (twice); 21 23; 22 58; 23 43; 24 17, 36 (twice); 25 7.6, 8.5 (twice), 8.29 (twice), 10.18, 11.11 (twice), 13.12, 15, 20, 14.5, 16, 24, 15.23, 16.27, 17.45, 18.9; 26 4.15, 10.20, 12.5, 14.32; 27 f.14 (twice); 28 7.4; 29 f.21 (twice), b.6 (twice); 31 f.35 (twice), b.14 (twice); 32 1.15 (twice), 18 (twice), 2.26; 34 2.3, 18 (twice); 35 b.9; 36 f.II.10 (twice); 37 f.23 (twice)
  ⲧⲁⲭⲓ 22 39
  ⲧⲁⲭ 28 7.13 (twice), 11.11, 13.14 (twice)
ταχύνειν "to hurry"
  ⲧⲁⲭⲩ 1 f.29
τετράς "quaternion" 1 f.37

τέχνη "craft"
  ⲧⲉⲭⲛⲓ 26 10.10–11; 28 1.16
τιμᾶν "to honor"
  ϯⲙⲁ 28 11.17
τιμή "honor"
  ϯⲙⲏ 11 25.3
τολμᾶν "to dare"
  ⲧⲟⲗⲙⲁ 11 10.20
τόπος "place" 11 4.20, 25.18; 12 2.16, 9.4, 13.18, 23.19, 37.12, 39.3; 17 f.30
  ⲧⲱⲡⲟⲥ 21 18
τρίας "trinity" 11 12.15–16, 13.12, 13, 23, 14.5, 8, 20.4; 21 19; 28 7.14–15
τρίκλινον "dining-room" 11 4.11
τροχός "wheel" 17 f.24
τύπος "model"
  ⲧⲉⲡ[ⲟⲥ] 2 5
  ⲧⲏⲡⲱⲥ 26 8.8, 13.9
τύραννος "tyrant"
  ⲇⲏⲣⲁⲛⲟⲥ 17 b.29
υἱός "son, child" see s.v. υἱός in Abbreviations
ὑμνεῖν "to sing"
  ϩⲉⲙⲛⲉⲥⲓ 26 3.12
  ϩⲉⲙⲛⲉⲩⲉ 28 12.12
ὑμνητήριος "singer"
  ϩⲉⲙⲛⲉⲩⲧⲏⲣⲓⲱⲛ 26 3.11–12
ὑπηρεσία "servants"
  ϩⲩⲡⲉⲣⲣⲏⲥⲓⲁ 11 26.18–19
ὑποδεσμός "suppression"
  ϩⲩⲡⲟⲥⲧⲓⲥⲙⲟⲥ 22 37–38
  ϩⲉⲡⲱϯⲥⲙⲟⲥ 28 9.17–18
ὑποπόδιον "footstool"
  ϩⲩⲡⲟⲡⲟⲇⲓⲟⲛ 11 23.18
  ϩⲩⲡⲱϯⲱⲛ 25 2.16
ὑπόστασις "hypostasis"
  ϩⲩⲡⲟⲥⲧⲁⲥⲓⲥ 11 12.18
ὑποταγή "subjection"
  ⲡⲱⲧⲁⲭⲏ 23 12
ὑποτάσσειν "to be subject"
  ϩⲏⲡⲟⲧⲁⲥⲉ 3 f.I.5
  ϩⲩⲡⲟⲧⲁⲥⲥⲉ 12 2.15
ὑπουργεῖν "to serve"
  ϩⲩⲡⲟⲩⲣⲅⲓⲉ 11 15.21
ὑπώρα "fruit"
  ϩⲩⲡⲱⲣⲁ 25 4.14
φαντασία "illusion" 34 1.21, 2.9, 15–16
Φαραώ "Pharaoh" 11 7.13
φαρμακεία "sorcery"
  ⲫⲁⲣⲙⲁⲅⲓⲁ 25 4.4, 10.16
  ⲫⲁⲗⲙⲁⲕⲓⲁ 33 1

φάρμακος "sorcerer"
   ⲫⲁⲣⲙⲁⲅⲟⲥ   **3** f.I.31; **18** 15
φθόνος "envy"   **11** 22.20, 23.14, 20
   ⲡⲑⲟⲛⲟⲥ   **25** 4.3
φιάλη "bowl"
   ⲡⲓⲁⲗⲉ   **3** f.II.31, 34
   ⲫⲓⲁⲗⲉ   **17** b.27
   ⲫⲓⲁⲗⲓ   **26** 9.23
   ⲫⲓⲁⲗⲗⲉ   **28** 4.10
φορεῖν "to bear, carry"
   ⲫⲟⲣⲓ   **11** 20.3; **12** 1.2
   ⲫⲱⲣⲓ   **25** 10.9, 15.20, 16.5; **26** 4.13, 14.1, 15.21; **28** 13.4
φυλακτήριον "phylactery"   **10** 16; **11** 1.5, 2.21–22, 7.1–2, 14.2
   ⲫⲉⲗⲁⲕⲧⲏⲣⲓⲟⲛ   **4** 1.8–9
   ⲫⲏⲗⲁⲕⲧⲏⲣⲓⲟⲛ   **12** 13.16–17, 25.15, 17, 29.10, 31.12; **17** b.37
  cf. s.v. φυλακτήριον *in Abbreviations*
φύσις "nature"   **11** 26.15; **28** 1.4
   ⲫⲏⲥⲓⲥ **12** 2.15–16
φωνή "sound, voice"   **12** 31.16
   ⲫⲱⲛⲏ   **22** 32; **25** 8.11
χαῖρε "hail"
   ⲕⲁⲓⲣⲉ   **17** b.21
   ⲭⲉⲣⲉ   **11** 20.9; **17** f.3–6, 8–9, 11–13, 15–16; **26** 2.7, 8, 9, 11, 14, 16, 17, 18, 20, 24, 25
   ⲭⲉⲣⲉ   **28** 8.20
   ⲭⲁⲓⲣⲉⲧⲉ   **11** 24.7
χαλβάνη "galbanum"
   ⲭⲁⲗⲃⲁⲛⲉⲓ   **5** b.2
χαλινός "bridle"   **24** 12; **34** 4.24
   ⲭⲁⲗⲓⲛⲟⲩⲥ   **25** 9.30
χαρίζειν "to grace"
   ⲭⲁⲣⲓⲥⲍⲉ   **10** 12
χάρις "favour"   **13** 2, 12; **22** 34, 23, 43; **25** 7.12; **26** 15.32; **27** f.9, 10; **37** b.2, 30
χάρτης "papyrus"   **1** f.31; **36** f.I.6–7; **37** b.13
χειμών "storm"
   ⲭⲓⲙⲟⲛ   **31** f.18
χερουβίμ "cherubim"
   ⲭⲉⲣⲟⲩⲃⲓⲛ   **1** f.2; **11** 3.21, 14.20, 17.8, 26.9–10; **12** 11.5–6, 23.5, 33.5; **18** 3; **22** 29
   ⲭⲉⲣⲟⲩⲃⲉⲛ   **17** f.8
   ⲭⲉⲣⲟⲩⲃⲓⲛ   **26** 10.27
   ⲭⲉⲣⲟⲩⲟⲃⲓⲛ   **25** 6.11–12
   ⲭⲉⲣⲱⲃⲓ   **28** 2.18
   ⲭⲉⲣⲱⲃⲓⲛ   **26** 2.21, 3.4–5
   ⲭⲣⲉⲣⲓⲃⲓⲛ   **10** 8
χιών "snow"   **12** 7.16, 33.9

χλαμύς "cloak"
   ⲗⲁⲙⲉ (?)   **25** 16.12
χολή "anger"
   ⲭⲱⲗⲏ   **26** 16.18
χορεύειν "to dance"
   ⲭⲱⲣⲉⲅⲉⲓ   **26** 3.7, 14.26
χορός "chorus"
   ⲭⲱⲣⲱⲥ   **26** 5.12
χρεία "need"
   ⲭⲣⲓⲁ   **1** f.36; **28** 4.1
χριστός "Christ"   **11** 2.3, 13, 4.25, 11.27, 17.10, 19.28, 20.2, 9, 24.1, 4, 25.23, 28.10, 13, 17, 29.27, 30.4; **12** 31.6
  cf. s.v. χριστός *in Abbreviations*
χρόνος "time"   **11** 21.2–3
   ⲭⲣⲱⲛⲟⲥ   **28** 10.4
χώρημα "land"   **11** 3.12
ψάλλειν "to sing"
   ϯⲁⲗⲗⲉ   **28** 11.20
ψυχή "soul"   **3** b.I.8; **11** 12.8; **17** f.37; **18** 18; **25** 5.5, 6.1; **28** 1.3, 12, 2.14, 4.15, 5.2–3, 9.7
   ϯⲭⲏ   **16** 1.13, 2.10
ὤ "O", interjection   **26** 9.26, 32
  ὤ βία κακὴ κεφαλή "O violence! Idiot!"
   ⲱⲃⲓⲁ ⲕⲁⲕⲓⲕⲉⲫⲁⲗⲓ   **28** 3.20
ᾠδή "song"
   ⲱⲇⲏ   **11** 30.21
ὡς "like"
   ϩⲱⲥ   **11** 24.19; **12** 25.18, 43.15
ὥστε "so that"
   ϩⲱⲥⲇⲉ   **12** 13.13–14, 15.8, 23.9, 37.11

VIII. Words of Egyptian Origin

We include here only substantives (including independent pronouns) and verbs (with the exception of the very common ⲉⲓⲣⲉ and ϣⲱⲡⲉ).

ⲁⲃⲱⲕ "crow, raven"   **37** b.16
ⲁⲃⲁϭⲏⲉⲓⲛ "glass"
   ⲁ̄ⲃⲉϭⲏⲉⲓⲛ̄   **25** 17.20–32
   ⲁⲃⲓ:ϭⲏⲏⲛⲓ   **26** 16.10
ⲁⲗ "deaf"   **11** 8.17, 21.5
ⲁⲗⲉ "to mount, go up"
   ⲁⲗⲏ   **28** 2.4, 8.6
   ⲁⲗⲉⲩ   **25** 13.29–30
   ⲁⲗⲏⲩ   **25** 13.23, 14.4; **32** 2.9
ⲁⲗⲟⲩ "child, pupil"
   ⲁⲗ?   **16** 1.12, 2.9
ⲁⲗⲁⲩ "white"   **17** b.28
   ⲁⲗ   **32** 1.19

ⲁⲗⲁⲁⲩ   37 b.12
ⲁⲗⲉ[(?)   32 2.27
ⲁⲣⲁⲩ   20 f.2
ⲁⲗⲉⲩ   23 47
ⲁⲣⲉⲩ   26 15.32; 29 b.7
ⲁⲗⲟϭ "thigh, knees, arms, shoulders"   12 13.1
ⲁⲙⲛⲧⲉ "hell"   8 b.5; 11 27.12
ⲁⲙⲉⲛⲧⲉ   3 f.2.21, 27, 28; 20 f.1, 6–7
ⲁⲙⲁϩⲧⲉ "to prevail, rule, grasp, possess"   11 2.8, 23–8; 17 f.34; 35 b.13; 36 f.I.11
ⲁⲙⲁϩⲧⲓ   28 2.7
ⲁⲙⲁϩⲧ†   26 7.27, 11.28
ⲙⲉϩⲓ   2 2
ⲁⲛⲁⲓ "to be pleasing; beauty"   28 11.6
ⲁⲛⲟⲕ "I, me" (first-person singular independent pronoun)   3 f.1.34; 4 2.6; 7 1, 37; 8 f.8, b.9; 10 9; 11 1.2, 28, 4.23, 7.27, 11.21, 22.5, 23.16, 24.27 (twice), 28, 25.8; 12 23.9, 25.10; 16 1.5; 17 f.21, 30; 18 16
ⲁⲛⲁⲕ   1 b.4; 23 50; 25 2.20 (twice), 21, 23, 5.22, 7.27, 13.3, 6, 9, 16.17; 26 3.19, 22 (twice), 27, 6.22–23, 15.15; 28 1.15, 7.10; 29 f.20
ⲁⲛⲟⲛ "we, us" (first-person plural independent pronoun)   11 27.4
ⲁⲛⲁϣ "oath"   4 2.3
ⲁⲡⲉ "head"   6 22; 11 5.15, 18, 8.4; 12 17.16, 19.1, 23.6, 25.6, 27.1, 31.5, 33.11, 14, 18, 20, 43.2; 17 f.27, 35; 25 4.9, 7.10; 37 f.13–14?, b.13

♉   25 16.10

ⲁⲡⲏ   25 14.4; 26 7.17, 25, 8.7, 9, 22, 13.16, 20, 14.10; 28 1.7, 21, 5.7, 6.17, 17, 8.15; 29 b.11
ⲁⲡⲏⲩⲉⲓ (pl.)   29 9.22
ⲁⲡⲟⲧ "cup"   6 15; 10 10, 17, 22; 12 35.14; 17 f.22, 24; 33 f.1; 34 1.8
ⲁⲡⲁⲧ   9 1; 14 9; 16 2.18–3.1; 25 7.23; 26 4.18, 16.9
ⲁⲁⲡⲟⲧ   17 b.16–17
ⲁⲣϣⲓⲛ "lentil"   35 f.2, 5, 9, 22
ⲁⲣⲏⲭ= "end, limit"   11 10.7, 25.7
ⲁⲧⲁⲣⲏⲭ= "limitless"   11 25.14–15
ⲁⲥⲓⲕ "fever"   18 10
ⲁⲧ- privative prefix   1 f.40; 4 2.15
ⲁⲧⲭⲟⲟⲛϥ̄ "undefiled/ineffable/inaccessible" (?)   11 5.3–4
  cf. s.v. ⲁⲣⲏⲭ=, ⲕⲁϩ, ⲕⲱϩⲧ, ⲛⲓϥⲉ, ⲥⲙⲟⲩ, ϩⲱⲗ, ϩⲟⲧⲉ

ⲁⲩⲁⲛ "colour"   28 1.5
ⲁϣⲁⲓ "to be, become many"   11 24.23
  ⲟϣQ   11 22.10
ⲁϣⲁϩⲟⲙ "to sigh, groan"   6 2, 10, 11; 7 10, 13; 20 7, 8
ⲁϣⲁϩⲁⲙ   26 5.2; 28 1.11, 10.11
ⲁϥ "flesh"
ⲁⲃⲟⲩϩⲉ (pl.)   25 4.21
ⲁϥ "fly, bee"   32 2.17
ⲁⲃ   5 b.3
ⲁϩⲟ "treasury, storehouse"
ⲁϩⲱⲱⲣ   28 2.7
ⲁϩⲣⲟ= "what is wrong?" (interrogative pronoun with suffix)   6 9 (twice); 7 12; 15 f.3; 20 f.8
ⲁϩⲣⲟ=   16 2.4
ⲁϩⲣⲁ=   29 f.6–7
ⲁϩⲣⲱ=   9 7
ⲁϭⲣⲏⲛ "barren woman"
ⲁϭⲛⲏⲛ   10 4
ⲃⲁⲁⲃⲉ "to regard as foolish, despise"
ⲃⲁⲃⲱⲟ=   28 11.16
  cf. s.v. ⲣⲱⲙⲉ
ⲃⲉⲉⲃⲉ "to bubble, well up, to pour forth, rain down"   12 33.17
ⲃⲱⲕ "to go"   7 1, 3, 16, 18, 24; 8 f.7, b.5; 11 4.7, 5.14, 9.3; 16 1.7, 2.6; 18 6; 24 28, 32; 25 9.27, 29; 28 4.20, 6.16, 8.3, 9.12; 29 f.10, 22; 30 b.4; 32 1.5, 32, 2.4, 22; 33 f.16; 37 b.17 (twice)
ⲃⲟⲕ   28 10.9
ϥⲱⲕ   3 f.2.27
ⲃⲏⲕQ   17 f.23?
ⲃⲁⲗ "eye"   4 3.1?; 6 23; 7 11, 14; 11 12.6; 12 37.1, 39.13; 15 f.4, 5, b.2; 16 1.11, 2.9; 25 2.6, 14.3; 28 5.19, 6.28, 9.10, 22, 11.8; 34 1.18; 35 f.2
ⲃⲉⲗ   26 7.29, 13.16
ϥⲁⲣ   20 2
ⲃⲱⲗ "to undo, interpret"   3 f.1.12; 11 1.7, 3.22, 5.7, 6.8, 18.8, 26.8; 15 b.3; 23 12, 13, 18, 27, 28, 36, 38; 25 2.25, 4.2, 16; 26 15.6, 16.8, 17.12; 32 2.3; 33 f.10, 13
ϥⲱⲗ   10 18
ⲃⲏⲗQ   18 6
ⲃⲟⲗ=   3 f.1.8; 8 b.1
ⲁⲧⲃⲱⲗ   32 2.26
ⲃⲟⲗⲃⲗ̄ "to dig up, be undermined"
ⲃⲟⲗⲃⲉⲗ   4 5.6
ⲃⲗⲗⲉ "blind (person)"
ⲃⲉⲗⲏ   26 12.31

ⲃⲉⲗⲉⲉⲅⲉ (pl.) **11** 21.3
ⲙⲉⲧⲃⲉⲗⲗⲏ "blindness" **25** 4.6–7
ⲃⲗϫⲉ "ostracon"
  ⲃⲏⲗϫⲓ **26** 15.30; **28** 13.4–5
  . . ⲍ . .(?) **37** b.21
ⲃⲛⲛⲉ "swallow"
  ⲃⲏⲛⲓ **26** 17.6
  ⲃⲏⲏⲛⲓ **26** 17.5
ⲃⲉⲛⲓⲡⲉ "iron"
  ⲙⲉⲛⲓⲡⲉ **16** 1.9, 2.7–8
  ⲡⲉⲛⲓⲡⲉ **3** f.1.8; **4** 3.1; **7** 3, 18, 25–26; **8** b.1; **25** 2.24
  ⲡ̄ⲛ̄ⲓⲡⲉ **20** 4
  ⲡⲓⲛⲓⲡⲓ **26** 15.5
  ⲡ̄ⲛⲓⲡⲓ **34** 1.24–25
ⲃⲱϣⲣⲉ "to be excrescent"
  ⲃⲩⲣⲉ (?) **35** f.4
ⲃⲣⲣⲉ "new, young"
  ⲃⲏⲣⲓ **25** 9.4; **26** 15.30
  ⲃⲉⲣⲓ **25** 9.7
ⲃⲁⲣⲱⲧ "brass, bronze" **34** 1.25
ⲃⲏⲧ "palm-leaf" **26** 17.26
  ⲃⲏⲑ **25** 16.23
ⲃⲓⲧ "edge" **22** 48, 59; **28** 6.12
ⲃⲏⲧⲉ "metal plate, lamella"
  ⲃⲉϯ **27** f.15, 23
  ⲃⲓⲧⲉ (?) **29** b.6
  ⲡ̄ⲧ̄ⲏ̄ (?) **21** 6
ⲃⲟⲧⲉ "abomination" **11** 5.17
  ⲃⲁϯ **28** 10.8
ⲃⲱϣ "to be unsheathed"
  ⲃⲏϣ^Q **12** 21.11, 41.4
ⲃⲟⲩϩⲉ "eyelid"
  ⲃⲟⲩⲓϩⲓ **28** 6.27–28
ⲉⲃⲓⲱ "honey"
  ⲉⲃⲓⲁ **5** b.3
ⲉⲃⲓⲏⲛ "wretched, miserable person"
  ⲉⲃⲓⲉⲛ **34** 4.13
ⲉⲃⲣⲏϭⲉ "lightning"
  ⲃⲣⲏϫⲉ **12** 9.3
ⲉⲃⲟⲧ "month" **32** 2.15
  ⲉⲃⲁⲧ **26** 12.14
ⲉⲕⲓⲃⲉ "breast" **11** 3.3–4; **32** 2.7
  [ⲉ]ⲕⲓⲃⲓ **28** 2.2
ⲉⲗⲟⲟⲗⲉ "pupil (?)" **15** f.2, 3
ⲉⲙⲛⲧ "west" **1** 17.1; **12** 25.2
  ⲉⲙⲏⲛⲧ **28** 3.7
ⲉⲙⲡϣⲁ "to be worthy" **11** 20.13–14
  ⲁⲧⲉⲙⲡϣⲁ **11** 23.5–6
ⲉⲛⲉϩ "eternity" **11** 14.11–12, 12, 20.21, 23.9, 26, 24.22, 25.2, 20, 27.13, 28.20; **25** 8.27–28; **28** 6.20–21, 12.18; **32** 2.26
  ⲉⲛⲏϩ **30** f.10, 24
  ⲓⲛⲉϩ **25** 2.9; **26** 15.26 (twice)
  ⲛⲉϩ **25** 8.28
  ⲛⲛⲉϩ **22** 57–58
  ⲡⲁ̄ⲉ̄ϩ **26** 4.15
ⲉⲣⲏⲩ "one another" **1** f.11, 14, 16
  ⲁⲣⲏⲟⲩ **4** 5.15
  ⲉⲣⲉⲩ **27** f.21
ⲉⲣⲱⲧⲉ "milk" **33** f.2; **37** b.4
  ⲉⲣⲱϯ **28** 2.1
ⲉⲥⲟⲟⲩ "sheep" **8** f.14
  ⲉⲥⲟⲩ **33** f.2
ⲉⲟⲟⲩ "glory" **11** 2.12–13, 5.1, 7.7, 12.9, 14–6, 19.3, 20.11, 23.21, 22, 24, 24.22–23; **12** 9.21 (twice), 11.1–2, 3–4, 7, 9–10, 12, 15, 20, 13.2, 4, 6 (twice), 8, 9, 10, 11, 15.7, 17.1, 20, 19.7, 21.8, 25.21, 27.19, 31.1, 19; **17** f.5; **25** 7.11; **26** 3.5, 10, 4.5, 6, 27, 8.6, 15, 14.22, 23
  ⲉⲁⲩ **26** 7.8, 15.24; **28** 12.11, 13?
  ⲉⲉⲟⲟⲩ **16** 11.3
  ⲉⲟⲁⲩ **26** 11.5
ⲉϣⲱ "sow (female pig)"
  ϣⲟⲩ **7** 36
ⲉϩⲉ "cow"
  ⲁϩⲟⲟⲩ **37** b.9
ⲉϭⲱϣ "Ethiopian (Kushite)" **24** 27; **25** 9.3
  ϭⲱϣ (?) **31** f.38
ⲏⲓ "house" **1** f.16; **24** 6, 34; **25** 17.41; **26** 16.36, 17.8; **31** f.21; **32** 2.12, 22?; **35** f.15; **37** f.6, 21
ⲏⲣⲡ "wine" **29** b.4
  ⲉⲣ **25** 16.8
  ⲉⲣⲏⲡ **10** 10; **17** b.19
ⲏϭⲉ "leek"
  ⲉϭⲉⲓ̈ (?) **31** f.36
  ⲛⲉ[. .] **31** f.39
ⲉⲓ "to come" **1** f.17; **3** f.2.2, 4, 8, 11, 13, 25, 29; **4** 2.14, 4.15; **7** 2, 4, 17, 19, 25; **11** 22.8, 23.10, 27.22; **12** 9.7, 8, 11.21, 13.18, 17.22, 19.2?, 5, 23.13, 25.4, 27.7, 29.3, 8, 13, 21.1, 31.6, 13, 16, 17, 20, 33.2, 7, 15, 21, 35.1, 5, 17, 20, 22, 39.10, 43.19; **15** b.1, 2; **16** 2.7; **17** f.20, 21, 37, 18 13; **22** 32; **24** 34; **25** 6.26, 8.14, 14.2; **26** 3.16, 26, 5.4, 26, 6.4, 22, 28, 9.28, 29, 10.5, 16, 19, 11.14, 12.2, 13.6, 14.3, 28, 15.2, 16; **31** f.29, 31; **32** 1.14, 2.2, 8, 14, 2.17, 18; **34** 1.7; **35** f.23; **37** f.23
  ⲉ **17** f.30
  ⲉⲓ:ⲥ (sic) **25** 7.28

ι 3 b.1.5; 11 3.6, 7, 4.8; 12 15.12, 17.18,
19.22, 25.13, 37.1, 3, 11; 16 1.8; 26 6.25,
9.32, 10.25, 26, 11.5, 12.6, 13.15, 16, 23,
14.1, 36, 6; 28 4.17, 9.10; 30 f.7, 22
  ⲛⲏⲩQ 11 6.11, 14.14, 21, 25, 15.6, 12, 16,
20, 16.18, 22, 29, 21.9, 14, 25.4, 27.15, 16;
17 f.23; 26 4.23, 8.1, 10.17, 12.9, 28
  ⲏⲛⲩQ 25 2.10
  ⲛⲓ̄Q 11 15.26
  ⲛⲉⲩQ 26 9.24,
  ⲁⲙⲟⲩ (imp.) 12 13.12; 16 2.17; 25 6.21; 26
6.25, 10.26, 11.5, 11, 13.33, 14.5, 15, 19, 21,
23, 35; 28 12.16, 17
  ⲁⲙⲏⲓⲧⲛ (imp. pl.) 11 14.15, 22, 25.1–2,
15.7–8, 22, 23 16.19, 23–24, 17.1–2, 10
  ⲁⲙⲛⲏⲓⲧⲛ 11 15.13, 16.6
  ⲁⲙⲱⲓⲛⲓ 26 3.3, 5, 7
ⲉⲓⲁ "eye"
  ⲉⲓⲧ⸗ (?) 15 f.5
ⲉⲓⲱ "to wash"
  ⲉⲁⲁⲃ 31 f.39
  ⲓ̈ⲱⲉ 1 f.12, 13
  ⲓⲁⲁ⸗ 25 16.10; 37 b.5, 7, 14, 19?; 30 f.3
  ⲉⲟⲟ⸗ 23 7
  ⲓⲁ̄ⲟ̄⸗ 26 16.19
ⲓⲱ "donkey" 28 6.4 (twice)
ⲉⲓⲃ "nail, hoof, claw, sting" 3 f.1.23
  ⲉⲓⲏⲃ 28 5.6–7
ⲉⲓⲁⲃⲉ "pus"
  ⲓⲁⲃⲉ 35 f.7, 21
ⲉⲓⲉⲃⲧ "east" 12 23.22
  ⲓⲏⲃⲧ 11 16.23
ⲉⲓⲙⲉ "to know" 16 2.16; 25 5.5–6, 6.1–2
  ⲉⲓⲙⲓ 26 16.25; 28 2.6, 8, 13
  ⲙ̄ⲙⲉ 1 f.39
ⲉⲓⲉⲣⲟ "river" 32 1.33
  ⲓⲉⲣⲁ 28 4.12–13
  ⲓⲉⲣⲟ 3 f.1.30, b.1.9
  ⲡ̄ⲉⲓⲟ 9 2
  ⲉⲓ̈ⲉⲣⲱⲟⲩ (pl.) 11 4.18
ⲉⲓⲛⲉ "to bring" 8 f.8; 11 9.5; 18 9; 25 17.44; 32
1.8, 17, 2.5, 20, 32–33
  ⲉⲓⲛⲓ 29 f.19; 34 2.18
  ⲓⲛⲉ 3 f.1.14, 23, 2.27–28; 20 13; 30 b.4; 31 f.25
  ⲓⲛⲓ 26 4.7, 5.1, 9.30
  ⲛ̄- 1 f.38
  ⲉⲛ- 11 7.9
  ⲉⲓⲛ- 9 2, 12
  ⲛⲧ⸗ 1 f.33; 8 f.7; 9 4; 26 17.1; 30 f.15; 32
1.20?, 21, 23, 27
  ⲉⲛⲧ⸗ 18 13
  ⲉⲛⲧⲉ⸗ 31 f.23
  ⲛⲧⲧⲁ⸗ (?) 15 f.4
  ⲁⲛⲓⲛⲓ (imp.) 28 13.15
  ⲁⲛⲓⲧ⸗ 4 6.1; 28 6.18, 9.16
ⲉⲓⲛⲉ "likeness"
  ⲓⲛⲉ ? 1 f.11
  ⲓⲛⲓ 26 3.25, 4.12, 11.17, 15.19
  ⲛⲓⲛⲉ 10 3
ⲉⲓⲟⲡⲉ "craft, art, occupation"
  ⲓⲁⲡⲓ 22 48
ⲉⲓⲥ "behold" 9 1, 7
  + ϩⲏⲏⲧⲉ 11 11.21; 22 33
ⲉⲓⲱⲧ "father" 3 b.1.15; 11 2.2, 13, 8.5, 12.13, 16.1, 23.22; 15 b 4; 32 2.23?
  ⲓⲱⲧ 3 f.2.1, 4; 11 2.17, 12.27, 16.13; 12
1.2, 5.5, 7, 9.6, 19.1, 9, 23.7, 25.7, 14, 18,
20, 27.5–6, 14, 29.11, 31.3, 5, 10, 11, 13, 17,
33.1, 4, 10, 14, 18, 20, 35.4, 8, 11, 20, 37.1,
5, 39.13, 16; 17 f.2, 3, 5, 27; 18 3, 4; 22 30,
32; 23 23; 25 6.3, 6.14, 8.11, 8.26, 12.1, 11,
13.2, 26, 14.3, 12, 13, 15, 18, 22, 15.5; 26
2.2, 7, 3.4, 10, 12 (twice), 19, 23, 4.18, 7.6,
7, 9, 9.25, 10.18, 13.16, 25, 14.6, 22, 25, 35,
15.25; 28 1.19, 2.22–23, 3.13, 15, 4.19, 5.16;
28 6.22, 7.17, 8.12, 15, 21, 11.17, 12.10; 29
f.13; 34 2.6?, 11
  ⲓⲱⲑ 12 9.16, 13.15, 15.13, 17.16, 27.20
  ⲱⲧ (sic) 26 7.8; 28 8.2
ⲉⲓϣⲉ "to hang, suspend"
  ⲁϣⲉ 17 f.36 (twice); 26 13.17
  ⲁϣⲓ 28 6.11
  ⲓϣⲓ 28 6.1, 9
  ⲁϣ- 12 11.14; 26 16.22
  ⲁϣⲧ⸗ 28 6.16; 35 f.22
  ⲁϣⲧⲟ⸗ 17 b.25
  ⲁϣⲉQ 7 34, 8 f.15
ⲉⲓϥⲧ "nail"
  ⲉⲓⲃ 25 10.20
  ⲓⲃⲧ 26 13.20; 29 f.14
  ⲓⲏⲃⲧ 27 f.18
ⲕⲉ- "other" 1 f.25, b.1; 10 6; 25 5.7; 26 9.9,
17.15; 32 2.19
  ⲕⲉⲕⲉⲩⲉ (pl.) 1 b.1
  ⲕⲉⲟⲩⲉ 1 f.30
  ⲕⲟⲟⲩⲉ 3 f.1.16; 9 3
ⲕⲱ "to place, leave, permit" 11 2.27, 4.3, 7.25,
7.25, 10.26, 24.19–20, 25.1, 26.25; 17 f.29;
24 13; 25 5.21, 14.7; 28 3.4; 32 1.35, 2.23

ⲅⲟ (?) **16** 2.1
ⲕⲁ **22** 37 (three times)
ⲕⲟ **16** 2.11
ⲕⲁ- **22** 36 (twice); **26** 3.21; **35** f.21
ⲕⲉ- **26** 11.17; **28** 11.20
ϩⲁ- **25** 9.31
ⲕⲁⲁ⸗ **11** 2.21, 5.12; **12** b.44
ⲕⲁ⸗ **1** f.16; **11** 9.1; **16** 3.3; **25** 4.12; **26** 2.3
ⲕⲟⲟ⸗ **26** 15.30, ,
ⲕⲏ^Q **11** 28.8; **17** f.22; **25** 7.27; **34** 1.8
ⲕⲱⲕ "to peal, strip off, divest; bareness, nakedness" **32** 1.25
ⲕⲏⲕ^Q **26** 12.29
ⲕⲱⲕⲁϩⲏⲩ "nakedness" **28** 9.18–29
ⲕⲱⲕⲕⲁϩⲏⲩ **24** 30–31
ⲕⲁⲕⲉ "darkness" **11** 11.24; **26** 6.1, 14.35; **28** 1.15
ⲕⲁⲕⲓ **8** f.15; **28** 5.9–10
ⲕⲏⲕⲥ "strip, scale"
ⲕⲱⲕⲏⲥ (?) **29** f.21
ⲕⲁⲕⲟⲩⲡⲁⲧ "hoopoe" **37** b.18
ⲕⲉⲗⲉⲃⲓⲛ "axe"
ⲕⲉⲗⲃⲓⲛⲓ **23** 24
ⲕⲉⲗⲱⲗ "pitcher, jar"
ⲕⲗⲱⲗ **26** 15.30
ⲕⲗⲟⲟⲗⲉ "cloud" **12** 9.1–2
ⲕⲱⲗⲉⲙ "to hasten"
ϭⲗⲁⲙ **1** b.2
ⲕⲗⲟⲙ "crown" **12** 1.3, 7.8, 33.13; **17** f.35; **37** f.13
ⲕⲗⲁⲙ **25** 7.9; **26** 8.10, 23, 9.22, 13.19; **28** 1.20; **29** f.21
ⲕⲁⲗⲁϩⲏ "womb" **26** 12.15, 14.25–26; **36** f.I.11–12
ⲕⲁⲗⲁϩⲉ **10** 19
ⲕⲱⲗϫ "to bend"
ⲕⲉϫⲱ⸗ (?) **25** 2.19
ⲕⲓⲙ "to move" **3** f.1.11; **4** 5.7, 9, 11; **12** 35.9; **32** 1.15, 16
ⲅⲓⲙ (?) **28** 1.6
ⲕⲉⲙⲉⲛⲧⲓ "movement of hearts" (?) **23** 48
ⲕⲁⲙⲉ "black" **17** b.45; **37** b.19
ⲕ̄ **16** 2.9
ⲕⲁ **16** 1.11
ⲕⲁⲙ **20** 2
ⲕⲁⲙⲏ **17** b.31
ⲕⲙⲟⲙ "to be, become black"
ⲕⲙⲁⲙ **1** f.10
ⲕⲏⲙ^Q **1** f.9
ⲕⲟⲩⲛ⸗ "breast, chest, bosom" **12** 31.11

ⲕⲛⲟⲥ "to stink, be putrid; stink"
ⲕⲛⲁⲥ **28** 10.8
ⲕⲛⲧⲉ "fig"
ⲕⲏⲧ (?) **29** b.10
ⲕⲛⲡⲉ "vault, canopy"
ϭⲛⲡⲉ **12** 19.9
ⲕⲣⲟⲩⲣ "frog"
ⲅⲣⲟⲩⲣ **37** b.6
ⲕⲣⲟϭ "guile; guileful person" **11** 4.4
ⲕⲉⲉⲥ "bone" **4** 4.5, 11; **8** f.3–4, 28.5
ⲕⲁⲥ **22** 62?; **25** 4.21
ⲭ (?) **37** f.3, b.9
ϩⲟⲥ (?) **31** b.19; **37** b.2, 6, 16, 24
ⲕⲱⲥ "corpse, burial"
ⲕⲟⲟⲥ **27** f.22
ⲕⲁⲥⲕⲥ "whisper"
ⲕⲁⲥⲕⲏⲥ **28** 2.6
ⲕⲥⲟⲩⲣ "ring"
ϫⲟⲩⲣ **23** 23
ⲕⲟⲧ "wheel" **6** 22
ⲕⲧⲟ "to turn"
ⲕⲧⲁ⸗ **28** 7.7
ⲕⲓⲧⲉ "sleep" **9** 4, 11, 12
ⲕⲱⲧⲉ "to turn, go around, surround; surroundings" **4** 4.1, 2, 6, 7; **9** 8 (twice); **12** 27.5–6, 29.2, 31.19, 39.6, 7; **17** f.13, 24; **20** 15, 16
ⲕⲟϯ **27** f.3, 11
ⲕⲱϯ **27** f.2
ⲕⲱⲧ⸗ **22** 60
ⲕⲏⲧ^Q **6** 8
ⲕⲉⲧ^Q **6** 7
ⲕⲟⲧⲥ "turning, guile"
ⲥⲁⲛⲕⲟⲧⲥ "guileful, cunning person" **11** 1.24
ⲕⲟⲩⲓ "small" **1** f.30; **6** 16; **11** 3.3, 23.11; **22** 52; **24** 11; **33** f.6; **36** f.II.1
ⲙⲉⲧⲕⲟⲩⲓ "smallness" **18** 11
ⲕⲁϣ "reed, pen" **15** f.7; **25** 16.18
ⲕⲟⲩϣⲧ "costus" **17** b.27; **29** b.7; **37** b.6
ⲕⲟϣ **17** b.11
ⲕⲟⲩϣ **26** 15.31, 16.8, 12
ⲕⲁϩ "earth" **1** f.6; **4** 5.6, 10; **9** 6; **11** 7.10, 10.7, 17.24, 19.2, 22.27, 25.8; **12** 5.2?, 3?, 11.3, 14, 17, 13.7, 15.3, 17.6, 21.20, 29.12, 23; **15** f.4; **17** f.17; **23** 21; **25** 2.14, 16, 3.19, 20, 4.11, 6.15; **26** 2.10, 3.13, 4.17, 6.8, 7.25, 27, 9.6, 14, 11.4, 8, 14.9, 15.12; **28** 3.9, 5.15, 7.6; **29** f.19; **34** 1.15, 16?; **35** f.2
ⲕⲉ[ϩⲓ] **2** 2

ⲁⲧⲕⲁϩ "without earth"   **28** 7.7
ⲕⲟϩ "corner"   **12** 19.4
ⲕⲱϩ "to be envious, zealous; envy, zeal"   **11** 1.15, 13.2, 23.14
ⲕⲱϩⲧ "fire, fiery"   **4** 2.1, 4.3, 9 (twice), 14, 4.16; **12** 27.21, 29.1, 2; **22** 63; **25** 18.4–5, 8; **26** 13.3–4; **28** 1.8, 4.5, 6, 7 (twice), 12, 13, 5.4, 14, 15, 9.12, 13, 13.11–12; **29** f.17, 32 1.6; **32** 1.8, 16, 26, 2.12; **37** f.14, 22
 ⲕⲱⲧϩ   **4** 4.3
 ⲕϩⲱⲧ   **3** f.2.5, 13, 33, 35; **3** b.1.10
ⲁⲧⲕⲟϩⲧ "without fire"   **27** f.17
ⲗⲟ "to cease, heal"   **4** 4.6, 8, 9, 11, 13; **15** 3; **26** 15.28, 16.2; **26** 16.14
 ⲗⲱ   **4** 4.7
ⲗⲁⲃⲟⲓ "lioness, bear"   **8** f.10
 ⲗⲁⲃⲁⲓ   **28** 6.8
ⲗⲓⲃⲉ "to be mad; madness"   **17** b.41; **18** 12; **32** 1.34, 2.1; **37** f.22
 ⲗⲓⲃⲓ   **28** 6.8
 ⲗⲟⲃⲉ   **17** b.47
ⲗⲉⲕⲙⲉ "piece, fragment"   **1** f.30–31
ⲗⲱⲕⲥ "to bite"   **29** f.10
ⲗⲱⲙⲥ̄ "to be foul, stink; foulness, putrescence"   **28** 10.8
ⲗⲁⲙⲁϩⲧ "gluttonous"
 ⲙ̄ⲛ̄ⲧⲗⲁⲙⲁϩⲧ "gluttony"   **11** 13.6
ⲗⲁⲥ "tongue"   **7** 31; **17** f.32?; **21** 21; **25** 16.17; **26** 8.4; **34** 2.14
ⲗⲁⲁⲩ "no one, nothing"   **11** 22.3–4, 25.13, 15; **12** 19.11, 35.5; **25** 17.40; **28** 2.15; **32** 1.13
 ⲗⲟⲟⲩ   **27** f.12
ⲗⲟⲟⲩ "lock of hair"   **3** f.2.21–22
ⲗⲟⲓϩⲉ "filth, mud"
 ⲗ̄ⲩϩϩⲉ   **9** 2
ⲗⲱⲝ "to be sticky; to crush, bruise"
 ⲗⲁⲝ^Q   **25** 4.11
ⲗⲱϫⲕ "to stick, be sticky; to crush, bruise"
 ⲗⲟϫⲕ⸗   **36** f.I.2, 7
ⲗⲟϫⲗϫ "to be sickly; sickness, infirmity"
 ⲗⲁϭⲗⲉϭ   **25** 2.5
 ⲗⲟϭⲗⲉϭ   **18** 10
ⲗⲁϭⲉ "to stop; heal"   **15** b.1
ⲙⲁ "place"   **3** b.1.11, 18?; **5** f.10; **11** 2.27, 3.7, 11, 24, 4.2, 5, 9, 5.10, 8.11, 12, 25–26, 10.26, 28, 25.11, 28.8, 30.28; **12** 19.12; **24** 14; **15** 4.15; **16** 26.32, 17.5; **32** 1.5, 13, 35, 4, 2.13
cf. s.v. ϩⲱⲃ, ϩⲙⲟⲟⲥ
ⲙⲉ "to love; love"   **8** b.8; **11** 19.22, 24.29; **32** 1.7, 34, 2.25

ⲙⲏⲉ   **1** f.28
ⲙⲏ   **8** f.8; **17** b.29, 40
ⲙⲉⲣⲉ   **7** 8, 22, 28
ⲙⲉⲣⲓⲧ   **11** 27.25; **13** 11; **26** 2.7, 4.22
ⲙⲉⲣ.⸗   **3** 10?
ⲙⲉⲣⲓ⸗   **16** 1.13, 2.10
ⲙ̄ⲛ̄ⲧⲙⲁⲓ̈ⲣⲱⲙⲉ "philanthropic"   **11** 20.20–21
cf. s.v. ϩⲟⲙⲛⲧ
ⲙⲉ "truth, true"   **11** 2.13, 27.17; **25** 9.7; **26** 13.30; **28** 7.2, 13.2
ⲙⲉⲓ   **28** 7.1
ⲙⲓⲛ   **34** 2.16
ⲙⲏⲧ   **9** 5; **11** 18.2; **18** 7
ⲙⲟⲩ "to die; death"   **26** 17.16
 ⲙⲁⲟⲩⲧ^Q   **26** 11.10, 15.8, 17.13; **28** 8.23
 ⲙⲟⲟⲩⲧ^Q   **11** 6.13, 19.6–7, 21.13, 23.3, 27.27; **26** 13.28
 ⲙⲟⲁⲩⲧ^Q   **26** 12.27
 ⲣⲉϥⲙⲁⲟⲩⲧ "dead person"   **23** 41–42
 ⲣⲉϥⲙⲟⲟⲩⲧ   **26** 17.2–3
ⲙⲟⲩⲓ "lion"   **12** 29.6; **24** 15
ⲙⲟⲕⲙⲉⲕ "to think; thought"
 ⲙⲁⲕⲙⲏⲕ   **28** 2.14, 5.22
 ⲙⲁⲕⲙ̄ⲕ   **28** 11.8
ⲙⲁⲕϩ "neck"
 ⲙⲁϩⲕ   **26** 8.11
ⲙⲟⲩⲕϩ "to afflict, oppress"
 ⲙⲟⲟⲩⲕ   **9** 6
 ⲙⲟⲟⲩⲕϩ   **9** 9
ⲙⲕⲁϩ "to be painful, difficult; pain, grief"
 ⲉⲙⲕⲁϩ   **31** f.26–27
 ⲕⲁϩ   **25** 7.8
 ⲙⲉⲕⲁϩ   **25** 4.8
 ⲙⲟⲕϩ^Q   **11** 13.17
ⲙⲟⲩⲗϩ "wax"
 ⲙⲟⲩⲗⲁ   **27** f.17, 20
ⲙⲙⲓ̄ⲛ "oneself"
 ⲙ̄ⲙⲓⲛⲉ   **11** 25.10
 ⲙⲓⲛ   **26** 14.10–11
 ⲛⲓⲙ   **25** 9.28
ⲙⲁⲉⲓⲛ "sign"   **11** 28.1
 ⲙⲁⲉⲓⲁ (sic)   **26** 12.24–25
ⲙⲟⲩⲛ "to remain"
 ⲙⲏⲛ   **28** 6.20, 11.4
ⲙⲏⲛⲉ "daily"   **37** b.15; **28** 12.21, 22
 ⲉⲙⲏⲛⲛⲓ   **28** 11.6
ⲙⲓⲛⲉ "sort, type"   **11** 8.20
ⲙⲛⲧ- prefix forming abstract compounds *see s.v.* ⲥⲙⲟⲩ, ⲃⲗⲗⲉ, ⲕⲟⲩⲓ, ⲙ̄ⲡⲟ, ⲛⲟⲩⲧⲉ, ⲛⲟϭ, ⲣⲱⲙⲉ, ⲱϩⲥ, ϣⲁⲩ, ϣⲁϫⲉ, ϫⲟⲉⲓⲥ, ϫⲁϫⲉ, ϭⲁⲗⲉ

ⲙ̄ⲡⲉ "no"   9 3
ⲙ̄ⲡⲟ "dumb (person)"   11 21.4
   ⲉⲙⲡⲟ   26 13.3
   ⲙⲛ̄ⲧⲉⲙⲡⲟ "dumbness"   11 8.17
   ⲙⲛ̄ⲧⲉⲛ̄ⲡⲟ   24 11
ⲙ̄ⲡⲱⲣ "no, by no means"   1 b.2; 8 b.2; 29 f.9
ⲙⲟⲩⲣ "to bind; bond, binding"   10 15; 11 4.2; 23 21 (twice), 22 (twice), 23 (twice), 24–25, 25, 26, 30, 34; 24 7
   ⲙⲁⲣ-   28 13.6
   ⲙⲟⲣ⸗   32 1.25; 33 f.8, 14; 36 f.I.1
   ⲙⲁⲗ⸗   2 5
   ⲙⲁⲣ⸗   25 16.9; 26 17.14; 29 b.8; 37 b.2, 10, 16
   ⲙⲁ̄ⲣⲉ⸗   26 15.33, 16.2, 6, 16, 25, 29, 17.4, 15, 17.19
   ⲙⲟⲩⲣ⸗   27 b.7
   ⲙⲛ̄ⲧⲣⲉϥⲙⲟⲩⲣ "binding"   11 1.12
ⲙⲣⲣⲉ "chain, bond, joint"   11 4.3, 18.8, 16
   ⲙⲉⲣⲉ   10 18
ⲙⲁⲥⲉ "calf"   12 29.7
ⲙⲓⲥⲉ "to give birth"   10 4
   ⲙⲓⲥⲓ   26 12.21
   ϣⲣⲡ̄ⲙⲓⲥⲉ "firsborn"   12 5.7, 11
   ϣⲣⲉⲡⲙⲉⲥⲉ   17 f.7
   ϣⲏⲣⲉⲉⲡⲙⲓⲥⲉ   25 14.10
   ϣⲏⲣⲉⲡⲙⲓⲥⲓ   26 5.30, 6.11, 20–21, 23
ⲙⲟⲥⲧⲉ "to hate; hatred"   11 13.2–3; 35 f.24, b.18
   ⲙⲁⲥⲧⲉ   37 b.20
   ⲙⲁⲥⲧⲓ   22 43
   ⲙⲁⲥⲧ†   22 45; 27 f.11; 28 10.8; 31 f.9, 42–43, b.2?, 10, 23–24, 27–28?
   ⲙⲉⲥⲧ†   31 25–26
   ⲙⲟⲥⲧ†   27 f.3; 31 f.3
   ⲙⲓⲉⲥⲧ-   31 b.9
   ⲙⲉⲥⲧⲱⲟ⸗   31 b.6–7
   ⲙⲉⲥⲧⲱϣ⸗   22 55; 31 f.7
ⲙⲉⲥⲉⲛⲧ "breast, chest"
   ⲙⲛ̄ⲥⲧⲛ̄ϩⲏⲧ   12 21.13
ⲙⲥⲁϩ
   ⲉⲙⲥⲁϩ   28 6.9
ⲙⲟⲉⲓⲧ "road, path"
   ⲙⲁⲓⲉⲓⲧ   26 11.10–11
ⲙⲟⲩⲧ "sinew, vessel"   20 15; 25 4.21–22; 26 6.6
ⲙⲁⲧⲉ "greatly, very"
   ⲉⲙⲁⲧⲉ   11 24.29
   ⲙ̄ⲙⲁⲧⲉ   11 6.26–27, 20.14–15, 21.7
ⲙⲛ̄ⲧⲉ "middle, midst"   4 4.8–9, 13, 16; 9 8

(twice); 11 4.12; 12 13.1, 17.4–5; 25 16.7; 37 b.18
   ⲙⲉⲧ†   31 f.6, b.6, 11; 34 2.6?, 11
   ⲙⲏⲧⲓ   4 4.3
   ⲙⲏⲧ†   26 4.21, 6.8, 16, 11.21, 12.4, 25, 13.8
ⲙⲟⲧⲉ "neck"   17 b.26
   ⲙⲁⲧ†   25 16.13, 14; 26 9.23
   ⲙⲁϩⲧ†(?)   26 17.4
ⲙⲟⲩⲧⲉ "to call, recite, name"   6 18, 37; 8 f.4, 5 (twice), 6, b.10; 10 17; 11 12.1, 27.2
   ⲙⲟⲩⲧ†   28 1.19, 19–20, 11.22
   ⲁⲧⲙⲟⲩⲧⲉ "speechless"   35 b.8
   ⲙⲛ̄ⲧⲣⲉϥⲙⲟⲩⲧⲉ "enchantment"   11 1.11
ⲙⲧⲟ "face, presence"   12 9.15, 15.4–5, 21.14, 27.13–14, 37.24; 31 f.31
   ⲉⲙⲧⲁ   34 1.9
   ⲉⲙⲧⲟ   11 6.19; 12 15.5, 25.22; 37 f.15
   ⲉⲙⲧⲱ   28 4.17; 34 1.15
   ⲙⲧⲁ   22 34, 50; 24 10; 25 7.12, 27; 26 14.2, 15.16
   ⲙⲧⲟⲩ   17 f.22
   ⲙⲧⲟⲟⲩ   35 b.7
   ⲙⲉⲧⲁ   26 5.15
ⲙⲧⲟⲛ "to rest; rest"
   ⲙⲧⲁ   25 8.25
   ⲙ̄ⲧⲁⲛ   1 b.5; 26 14.9; 28 1.10, 12
ⲙⲟⲩⲧⲥⲉ "female cat"   28 6.4
ⲙⲁⲁⲩ "mother"   6 6; 10 5; 25 2.21; 26 12.15; 32 2.24
   ⲙⲁⲟⲩ   16 2.3, 5–6; 34 1.8
ⲙⲟⲟⲩ "water"   3 f.1.9–10, 25, 31; 6 16; 7 6, 21; 9 2; 11 17.26; 12 7.14, 18, 35.21; 14 10; 17 f.36; 23 22; 25 7.26, 8.23, 23; 25 13.30, 16.14; 29 b.8; 31 f.39, b.16; 32 2.7; 35 f.20; 37 b.5, 8
   ⲙⲁⲁⲩ   25 9.5; 26 6.25, 10.5
   ⲙⲁⲩ   23 4; 26 5.5, 15, 6.2, 11.12, 20, 31, 13.4, 22, 14.1, 14.30, 36, 15.3, 6, 7–8, 16.7, 11, 33, 17.2; 28 6.11; 30 f.3
   ⲙⲁⲟⲩ   25 8.2, 21; 25 16.11, 17.25; 26 2.11, 9.32, 10.25; 37 b.20
   ⲙⲟⲁⲩ   26 17.25
   ⲙⲟⲩ   12 33.17; 17 b.20; 20 f.3; 31 f.36; 32 1.23; 35 f.7?, 21
   ⲙⲟⲩⲛⲉⲓⲟⲟⲩⲉ (pl.)   11 4.17–18
ⲙⲉⲉⲩⲉ "to think; thought"   8 b.6; 11 10.13, 13.1, 2, 10, 21.24, 25.2; 28 5.19, 21, 11.7
   ⲙⲉⲟⲩⲉ   28 5.22–23
ⲙⲁⲩⲁⲁ⸗ "alone"   11 2.15; 12 21.5
   ⲙⲁⲟⲩⲁⲁ⸗   26 7.5

ⲙⲟⲩⲟⲩⲧ "to kill"
   ⲙⲟⲟⲩⲧ⸗ **3** f.1.6, 7
ⲙⲉϣⲉ "NN" **8** b.7; **10** 11
   ⲁϣⲉ ? **20** f.13
ⲙⲓϣⲉ "to fight, strike" **1** f.4, 18; **31** b.5
   ⲙⲁϣ⸗ **15** f.4
ⲙⲟⲟϣⲉ "to walk" **20** f.1; **24** 33; **32** 1.13
   ⲙ̄ⲁⲁϣ **26** 13.1
   ⲙⲁⲁϣⲉ **29** f.1
   ⲙⲁⲁϣⲓ **26** 16.15
   ⲙⲁⲟϣ **26** 13.2
   ⲙⲁⲟⲩϣⲉ **26** 14.6
   ⲙⲟϣⲉ **35** f.3
ⲙⲉϩ- ordinal number prefix **25** 2.1; **26** 11.23, 24, 25, 26 (twice), 27, 12.22, 23, 14.10; **34** 1.15; **37** b.29
   ⲙⲉ **3** f.2.7
ⲙⲟⲩϩ "to burn" **12** 29.1; **25** 9.7; **28** 1.8, 4.13
ⲙⲟⲩϩ "to fill, be full" **24** 18, 25; **25** 9.6, 17.33; **26** 6.6; **28** 4.6, 10, 11; **32** 2.24; **34** 1.17; **37** f.7
   ⲙϩⲟⲩ **3** f.2.34
   ⲙⲏϩ **17** f.24; **26** 9.15
   ⲙⲉϩ **11** 4.26, 10.4, 19.2, 29.3; **25** 17.43; **26** 9.6, 11.4, 16.10; **28** 5.2; **32** 1.6
   ⲙϩⲏ **3** f.2.31
   ⲙⲁϩ⸗ **26** 10.3, 12.1, 14.3, 16.22; **28** 5.6; **32** 1.33; **34** 1.9
   ⲙⲁϩⲉ⸗ **17** f.22
   ⲙⲁⲩϩ⸗ **26** 6.26
   ⲙ̄ⲙⲟⲩϩ⸗ **9** 2
   ⲙⲟⲩϩ⸗ **26** 15.1
ⲙⲁϩⲉ "flax"
   ⲙⲁϩ **32** 1.25
ⲙⲁϩⲉ "cubit" **12** 23.20, 21, 23, 24, 39.7, 9, 10
ⲙⲁϩⲧ "bowels, intestines" **5** f.12
ⲙ̄ϩⲓⲧ "north" **11** 16.10; **12** 23.24
ⲙϩⲁⲁⲩ "tomb, cavern" **11** 21.15
ⲙⲁⲁⲭⲉ "ear, handle" **32** 2.16; **37** b.9
   ⲙⲁⲁⲭⲓ **28** 5.10–11
   ⲙⲉⲭⲓ̈ **26** 17.24
   ⲙⲉⲉⲭⲉ **26** 3.21
ⲛⲁ "to take pity; grace" **18** 15, 17; **25** 7.24; **28** 5.16
ⲛⲟⲉⲓ "place where loaves and wine are deposited" **32** 1.22
ⲛⲟⲩⲃ "gold" **9** 1; **25** 17.39; **26** 7.13, 15, 17, 9.21, 23; **28** 10.18; **34** 1.23
   ⲛⲟⲩϥ **12** 33.1
ⲛⲟⲃⲉ "sin" **11** 24.18–19
   ⲛⲁⲃⲓ **26** 16.18

ⲛⲁⲓ̈ⲁⲧ⸗ "to be blessed" **11** 24.8, 10
ⲛⲕⲁ "thing, vessel, property"
   ⲉⲛⲅⲁ **25** 17.39
ⲛⲁⲁⲕⲉ "pain, labour pang"
   ⲛⲁⲁⲅⲓ **26** 12.23 (twice)
   ⲛⲁⲕⲓ **25** 13.11
   ⲛⲏⲕⲏ **26** 12.20
ⲛⲕⲟⲧⲕ "to sleep, lie down; sleep" **11** 4.9–10
   ⲉⲛⲕⲁⲧ **28** 5.12, 9.20–21
   ⲉⲛⲕⲁⲧⲉ **25** 2.3
   ⲕⲁⲧⲛⲉ **26** 26.20
   ⲛ̄ⲕⲁⲧ **29** f.5
   ⲛⲕⲁⲧⲕ **28** 1.8
ⲛⲓⲙ "NN, who" **1** f.9, 10; **3** f.1.34; **4** 5.8 (twice); **7** 8 (twice), 22, 23, 28 (twice), 33; **8** b.7; **9** 3, 4, 12 (twice); **10** 9 (twice), 11 (twice); **17** f.37; **20** f.13; **25** 17.35; **27** f.13; **29** f.10; **30** f.23, b.4 (twice); **34** 4.15, 21
ⲛⲟⲉⲓⲛ "to shake" **11** 17.25
ⲛⲟⲩⲛ "abyss" **3** f.1.6; **8** f.13; **9** 6, 10; **12** 11.14, 17.12, 23.21, 39.8, 43.1?; **32** 2.32
   ⲛⲟⲩ̄ **28** 1.18
ⲛⲟⲩⲛⲉ "root" **11**, 13.7, 18.15
ⲛⲁⲛⲟⲩ⸗ "to be good, beautiful" **11** 20.16, 24.7–8; **25** 16.16; **34** 1.20
   ⲛⲉⲛⲟⲩ⸗ **25** 17.34
   ⲡⲉⲧⲛⲁⲛⲟⲩϥ "what is good" **11** 19.20; **12** 9.5; **30** f.9, 24
ⲛⲟⲩⲣⲉ "vulture"
   ⲛⲟⲩⲣⲓ **26** 16.2
ⲛⲟⲩⲥⲉ "woman (?)" **6** 3, 7, 8, 13
ⲛⲟⲩⲧⲉ "god" **10** 14 (twice); **11** 1.3, 26–27, 2.3, 4, 10, 11, 23–24, 3.18–19, 6.14, 7.7, 8.1, 8.6; **11** 9.9, 10, 11, 12, 14, 17, 18, 9.25, 10.6, 8, 11, 17, 23, 11.2–3, 8, 16–17, 18, 23, 26, 12.3, 4, 27, 20.8, 21.21, 23.4, 24.5, 23, 26.8, 13–14, 27.6, 30.4–5, 19, 20, 25; **12** 9.14, 15.6; **12** 19.19, 21.5, 22, 39.18 (twice); **18** 6; **25** 2.7, 3.15, 5.6, 6.22, 7.17, 9.27, 13.12, 14, 18, 22, 29; **26** 3.20, 13.30, 15.14, 31; **28** 5.19–20; **31** f.16; **34** 2.6
   ϥ̄ⲧ̄ **34** 2.11
   ⲛⲟⲩ† **26** 7.5, 16.2; **28** 8.5
ⲉⲛⲧⲏⲣ "deity" (pl.) **12** 41.8
   ⲉⲧⲏⲣ **4** 4.4, 10
   ⲛⲑⲏⲣ **25** 4.25
ⲙⲛ̄ⲧⲛⲟⲩⲧⲉ "divinity" **11** 12.16, 21.26–27; **12** 23.8
   ⲙⲉⲧⲛⲟⲩⲧⲉ **28** 4.8–9
   ⲙⲉⲧⲙⲉⲧⲛⲟⲩⲧⲉ (sic) **28** 4.14

ⲛⲧⲟⲕ "you" (second-person masculine singular independent pronoun)   **7** 37; **8** b.10; **9** 10 (twice); **10** 1, 3, 4; **11** 21.19, 22.25, 26.17, 27.3; **32** 2.10, 16, 19
 ⲛ̄ⲧⲁⲕ   **1** f.14; **25** 5.6, 9
ⲛⲟⲩⲧⲙ "to be sweet, pleasant; sweet"
 ⲛⲟⲧⲉⲙ   **17** f.20, 23
ⲛ̄ⲧⲟⲥ "she, her" (third-person feminine singular independent pronoun)   **7** 23, 28
 ⲛⲟⲥ   **16** 2.1, 12
 ⲛ̄ⲧⲁⲥ   **1** f.20
 ⲧⲟⲥ   **7** 8
ⲛ̄ⲧⲱⲧⲛ̄ "they, them" (third-person plural independent pronoun)   **1** f.8
ⲛ̄ⲧⲟⲟⲩ "they, them" (third-person plural independent pronoun)   **11** 9.7, 25.11, 27.10
ⲛⲧⲟϥ "he, him" (third-person masculine singular independent pronoun)   **11** 6.7, 28.17–18
ⲛⲁⲩ "hour"   **3** f.2.32; **26** 4.23, 13.17; **35** f.15; **37** b.15
 ⲩⲛⲟⲟⲩⲉ (plural)   **17** f.14
 ⲩⲛⲟⲩⲉ   **17** f.15
ⲛⲁⲩ "to see"   **11** 11.25, 24.13; **13** 25; **14** 2; **17** b.32; **22** 55; **26** 12.31; **28** 9.18, 10.12; **35** b.2
 ⲛⲟ   **1** f.40
 ⲛⲟⲟⲩ   **29** f.8
 ⲁⲧⲛⲁⲩ "invisible"   **12** 27.6
ⲛⲁϣⲉ "to be many, great"   **11** 2.14
ⲛϣⲟⲧ "to be hard, strong, difficult"   **32** 2.24?
 ⲛⲁϣⲧ   **28** 11.9
ⲛⲓϥⲉ "to blow, breathe; breath"   **6** 17
 ⲛⲓⲃⲉ   **6** 16–17, 17; **12** 31.17; **28** 10.7
 ⲛⲓⲃⲓ   **26** 6.26, 8.1, 13.31, 14.2; **27** f.12; **28** 8.2, 10–11
 ⲁⲧⲑⲉⲙⲛⲉϥⲉ "not breathing with difficulty"   **17** f.25
ⲛⲁϩⲧⲉ "to trust, be trustworthy"   **11** 11.15
ⲛⲉϩ "oil"   **8** f.1 (four times), 2, 3, 4; **12** 1.8; **23** 8; **25** 4.14, 7.26, 8.22, 9.7; **26** 5.6, 15, 6.2, 26, 10.1, 26, 11.12, 31, 14.1, 30, 15.1, 16.4, 7, 13, 19, 22; **27** f.15, 22; **28** 13.2; **32** 2.13; **37** b.3, 12, 14 (twice), 29
ⲛⲉϩⲥⲉ "to awake"   **4** 2.13; **4** 5.7
ⲛⲟⲩϫⲉ "to throw, cast, place"   **1** f.6–7; **3** f.2.35; **15** f.7, 8; **20** f.14
 ⲛⲟⲩϫ   **12** 9.10, 21.12; **27** b.6
 [ⲛ̄]ϣⲩϭ   **12** 13.22
 ⲛⲉϫ-   **17** f.26
 ⲙⲟⲩϫ= (?)   **32** 1.25
 ⲛⲁϫⲉ=   **26** 17.2

ⲛⲁϫⲥ=   **37** b.21
ⲛⲟϭ "great"   **3** f.2.6, 9; **4** 5.16; **5** f.2, 9; **7** 32; **10** 20; **11** 4.25, 7.6, 8.4, 10.4, 11.25, 12.3, 5, 12, 14.17, 19, 15.16, 17.27, 18.1, 3, 19.14, 20.8, 27; **12** 5.3, 15.6, 17.15, 19.1, 12, 21.5, 23.6, 25.7, 20, 27.19, 29.14, 31.4, 22, 33.18, 35.3, 39.16, 24; **17** f.16, b.42; **18** 3, 18; **22** 28, 52; **24** 3, 11; **25** 2.18, 3.21, 21, 4.17, 5.10, 6.12, 21, 7.17, 19, 14.13; **26** 3.2, 4.25, 28, 8.21, 25, 9.19, 10.27, 11.8, 29; **32** 1.4, 10; **32** 1.16, 21; **35** f.3, 11, 24
 ⲛ̄ϭⲧ   **17** b.29
 ⲛⲁϫ   **26** 7.12
 ⲛⲟϫ   **3** f.1.2
 ⲛⲁϭ   **1** f.5, 24, b.2, b1.7; **2**.1; **26** 4.8, 23; **28** 1.17, 3.5, 4.3, 5, 22; **30** f.16
 ⲙⲛ̄ⲧⲛⲟϭ "greatness"   **11** 14.7–8
 ⲙⲉⲧⲛⲟϭ   **26** 15.17
ⲟⲙⲉ "clay, mud"   **32** 1.25
 ⲁⲙⲉ   **23** 4; **37** b.21
 ⲁⲙⲓ   **22** 61; **28** 13.5
ⲟⲛ "again"   **10** 3, 7; **11** 7.1; **25** 16.10; **27** f.16; **32** 1.24?
 ō   **11** 7.4
 ⲱⲛ   **24** 31; **28** 4.1, 7.2
ⲟⲟⲧⲉ "womb"   **10** 18
 ⲟⲟⲇⲉ   **20** f.15
ⲟⲟϩ "moon"   **4** 4.2, 7; **8** f.5; **11** 14.15; **15** f.6; **24** 18; **25** 17.33; **26** 2.15, 3.8, 5.11; **37** f.7
 ☾ and similar   **24** 24; **25** 9.5; **31** b.20
 ⲁⲟϩ   **26** 11.7
 ⲁϩ   **34** 1.13
 ⲉⲓⲟϩ   **26** 4.15 (twice)
 ⲟϩ   **9** 8; **12** 13.8
 ⲟϩⲉ   **17** f.13
ⲟϩⲉ "yard, pasture, flock, herd"   **11** 4.10
 ⲁϩⲓ   **26** 17.10
ⲡⲉ "sky, heaven"   **3** b.1.11; **4** 5.12; **8** f.5, 12, 15; **9** 6, 8; **11** 12.8, 14.26, 15.26, 16.5, 9, 30.25; **12** 5.2, 3, 11.3, 14?, 17, 13.6, 17.6, 13, 23.10, 29.11, 23, 39.9, 43.3; **15** f.5, b.1, 2; **17** f.17; **23** 21; **25** 2.11, 15, 3.18, 6.3, 14, 22, 7.18, 8.10; **26** 4.17, 9.14, 11.4, 8
 ⲡⲏ   **2** 2; **25** 2.7, 14, 14.26; **26** 2.9, 3.15, 5.13, 7.28, 14.9, 15.13; **28** 3.8, 12, 5.14, 11.17, 19; **34** 1.16
 ⲡⲏⲩⲉ (pl.)   **11** 6.21, 17.19, 19.2, 22.26; **25** 14.10
 ⲙⲡⲏⲩⲉ   **12** 21.19, 33.6
 ⲡⲉⲩ   **17** f.17?

ⲡⲉⲩⲉ 17 f.10
ⲡⲏⲩ 25 5.10; 26 2.12
ⲡⲏⲩⲉⲓ 26 5.25, 31, 6.11, 9.5
ⲡⲓ "kiss" 7 9, 24, 29; 16 2.1, 2, 11
ⲡⲉ (?) 20 f.5, 9–10
ⲡⲱⲱⲛⲉ "to change, turn; change, removal"
   ⲡⲱⲱⲛⲓ 28 3.7
   ⲡⲁⲛⲉ- 27 f.21
   ⲡⲟⲟⲛⲉ⸗ 12 21.20
ⲡⲱⲛⲕ "to draw, bail out water"
   ⲡⲁⲅⲕⲱ⸗ 9 2
ⲡⲱⲣⲕ "to pluck out" 8 b.5–6; 37 b.16
   ⲡⲟⲣⲕ⸗ 8 b.1
   ⲡⲱⲣⲉⲕ 11 18.14–15
ⲡⲱⲣϣ "to spread, be spread"
   ⲡⲁⲣϣ 25 8.9
   ⲡⲟⲣⲉϣ 3 f.2.22
   ⲡⲟⲣϣ 12 33.19
   ⲡⲱⲱⲣ 26 5.23
ⲡⲱⲣⲭ "to separate, divide"
   ⲡⲟⲣⲭ 27 f.19
   ⲡⲱⲣⲉⲭ 31 f.4, 10, 13, b.10–11
   ⲡ̄ⲁⲣⲭⲉ⸗ 31 f.15
ⲡⲁⲧ "knee, foot, leg, shin" 28 3.6, 10.13
ⲡⲱⲧ "to run, flee, pursue" 3 b.1.10; 4.14; 11 7.21, 30.28; 12 5.20, 7.1–2, 9.15, 21.15, 39.1, 43.6; 20 f.7; 25 5.26, 10.17; 26 10.9, 11.18, 14.30, 16.29; 28 5.20; 35 f.17
   ⲡⲱⲧⲉ 26 10.30
   ⲡⲏⲧᵠ 26 16.24, 28, 17.7, 8
ⲡⲓⲧⲉ "bow" 12 23.15, 41.20
ⲡⲁⲧⲥⲉ "spittle" 12 35.19–20
ⲡⲱⲧϩ "to carve, depict" 2 4
ⲡⲱϣ "to divide, separate; division" 34 1.15
ⲡⲱϣⲛ "to serve; service"
   ⲣⲉϥⲡⲱϣⲛ "servant" 8 f.6
ⲡⲱϩ "to burst, rend" 1 f.40; 25 2.24; 26 13.5; 28 8.18
   ⲡϩⲱ 3 f.1.13
   ⲡⲏϩᵠ 26 16.34–35
ⲡⲱϩ "to reach" 26 15.17
   ⲡⲉϩ 33 f.13
ⲡⲱϩⲧ "to bend, pour" 26 10.1, 4, 11.14
   ⲡⲉϩ- 26 15.3
   ⲡⲱϩ- 25 8.23
   ⲡⲁϩⲧ⸗ 26 5.17, 6.4, 21, 26–27, 15.2
   ⲡⲁⲧ⸗ 30 f.4
   ⲡⲁϩ⸗ 26 12.1
   ⲡⲉϩⲧ⸗ 26 15.5, 6, 8, 28, 16.7, 35
   ⲡⲁϩⲧⲏ⸗ 31 f.40

ⲡⲁϩⲣⲉ "drug, remedy" 11 21.1; 18 16, 25 2.4; 36 f.I.15
ⲡⲁϩⲟⲩ "buttocks, hindpart" 8 f.14
ⲡⲉϫⲉ- "... said" 16 2.3, 13–14; 30 f.8; 36 f.I.13
   ⲙⲉϫⲉ- 20 f.7–8
   ⲙⲉϫⲁ⸗ 20 f.4, 5, 10
   ⲡⲁϫⲁ⸗ 29 f.6 (twice)
   ⲡⲁϫⲉ⸗ 1 b.1, 3
   ⲡⲉϫⲁ⸗ 15 f.2, 3, 5–6, b. 3; 16 1.14, 2.11; 29 f.7; 30 f.9, 23 (twice ?), b.2
   ⲡⲉϫⲁⲁ⸗ 29 f.8–9
   ⲡⲉϫⲉ⸗ 25 2 8
ⲡⲱϭⲉ "to break, burst"
   ⲡⲱϭⲓ 26 15.7
   ⲡⲟϭ⸗ 3 f.1.9
ⲣⲏ "sun" 3 f.1.4, 5; 4 4.1, 7; 8 f.4, 6; 9 4, 8; 11 14.21, 15.13; 12 7.11, 13.7; 15 f.6; 17 f.12; 26 2.13, 8, 5.11, 11.6, 16.15; 34 1.12
   ⲣⲉ 7 13
ⲣⲟ "mouth, door" 7 2, 3, 18, 24, 25; 11 4.8, 21.7, 27.16, 35.1; 15 f.1; 17 b.32; 24 6; 25 3.6; 26 16.36; 31 f.40, b.19; 32 2.12, 12; 35 f.16; 37 f.6, 20, b.5, 20
   ⲣⲁ 27 f.16, 18; 29 f.4; 30 f.4, 14
   ⲣⲉ 20 f.1, 6
   ⲣⲱ 7 17; 37 b.8
   ⲣⲱ⸗ 3 b.1.6; 6 17; 12 1.5, 27.16, 31.16, 35.1, 20; 17 b.31; 22 32; 24 15, 16; 26 3.13–14
   ⲣⲩⲱ⸗ 35 b.4
ⲕⲁⲣⲱϥ "silence" 12 7.2; 22 36–37
   ⲕⲁⲣⲱⲃ 24 9
   ⲕⲁⲣⲱⲥ 28 10.16
ⲣⲓⲕⲉ "to bend, turn; turning, inclination" 8 f.16
   ⲣⲓⲕⲓ 28 9.10
ⲣⲕⲣⲓⲕⲉ "bending, nodding of head (in sleep)"
   ⲣⲉⲕⲣⲓⲕⲉ 6 5, 14
ⲣⲱⲕϩ "to burn, burning"
   ⲣⲁϩⲕⲓ 28 13.19–11
   ⲣⲱⲭϩ 1 f.15; 37 f.21
ⲣⲓⲙⲉ "to cry, weep; tear" 6 1, 9, 10; 7 10, 13, 16; 15 f.2, 3; 16 2.2; 20 f.7, 8 (twice), 9; 36 f.II.2, 9
   ⲣⲓⲙⲓ 28 10.11
   ⲣⲉⲙⲓⲉ 26 13.15
   ⲣⲓⲙⲙⲉ 33 f.6,
   ⲣⲓ̈ⲙⲡⲉ 16 2.4
   ⲣ̄ⲙⲓⲛ (pl.) 25 14.2
   ⲣⲙⲉⲓⲉ 15 f.2, 3
   ⲣⲉⲙⲓⲛ 12 37.1; 28 8.14

ⲣ̄ⲙⲉⲓⲟⲟⲩ   7 14
ⲣⲙⲉⲓⲟⲟⲩⲉ   7 11
ⲣⲱⲙⲉ "person, human, man"   3 f.I.33; 7 12; 10 2, 12, 15; 11 1.9, 13, 22?, 23?, 9.18, 13.14, 22, 20.11, 24.19, 26.16, 29.8; 13 13, 25; 24 11; 25 4.5, 23, 6.25, 16.19; 26 3.20, 25, 4.9, 13, 12.29, 13.14, 15.29, 16.1, 3, 6, 9, 13, 15, 16.18, 24, 25, 17.1, 6; 28 8.6; 30 f.15; 33 f.1, 15; 35 f.1, 15; 36 f.I.13, b.13; 37 b.18
ⲣⲱⲙⲓ   26 15.27, 16.26, 17.3; 27 f.12; 28 10.6
ⲣⲙϩⲉ "free (person)"   11 3.1, 5.23
ⲣⲉⲙϩⲉ   18 7
ⲣ̄ⲙ̄ⲛ̄ⲕⲏⲙⲉ "Egyptian"   11 6.4–5, 5–6
ⲙⲛ̄ⲧⲣⲱⲙⲉ "humanity"   11 21.27
ⲙⲉⲧⲣⲱⲙⲉ   26 13.11, 18
ⲙⲛ̄ⲧⲃⲁⲃⲉⲣⲱⲙⲉ "boastfulness"   11 13.8–9
cf. s.v. ⲙⲉ, ϩⲏⲧ
ⲣⲙⲟⲛⲧ "shivering, ague"
ⲉⲣⲙⲟⲉⲧ   18 11–12
ⲣⲟⲙⲡⲉ "year"   6 20; 10 6
ⲣⲙ̄ⲡⲉ   9 12
ⲣⲁⲙⲡⲓ   23 52
ⲣⲟⲙⲡⲓ   32 1.3?, 2.15
ⲣⲁⲛ "name"   3 f.2.24; 5 f.2, 9; 6 15; 9 5; 10 20; 11 4.25, 5.4, 7.6, 8.4, 24, 9.25, 26, 12.2, 14.17, 16.12, 16, 17.19, 27, 18.1, 2, 3, 19, 21.11, 22.12, 24.11, 25.1, 28.22; 12 5.12, 19.11, 21.1, 16, 22, 23.11, 25.20, 31.3, 33.1, 37.5, 39.24; 15 b.4, 5; 17 b.36; 20 f.11; 21 15; 22 47; 23 2, 32; 24 27; 25 2.18, 3.9, 22, 4.17, 5.14, 7.3, 14, 15, 8.12, 10.7, 13.18, 14.19, 23, 27, 15.4, 12, 21, 16.2, 18.2; 26 2.16, 3.20, 4.26, 28, 5.28, 6.12, 18, 7.3, 16, 20, 22, 8.2, 11, 22, 9.1, 8, 10, 12, 11.22, 23, 24, 25, 26, 27 (twice), 12.12, 18, 26, 27, 29, 30, 31, 13.1, 3, 4, 5, 14.12; 27 f.6; 29 f.12 (twice), 15; 29 b.5; 30 f.17, 18 (three times?), 23, 24?; 32 1.10, 2.11; 37 f.16, 21
ⲣⲁⲓⲛ   26 13.2
ⲣⲉⲛ   1 f.8; 34 3.10?
ⲣⲟⲟⲩⲛⲉ "virgin, virginity"
ⲣⲟⲟⲩⲛⲓ   25 12.17, 16.13; 26 17.26
ⲣⲡⲉ "temple"   6 6
ⲉⲣⲡⲏ   28 8.19
ⲣⲓⲣ "pig"   31 b.7
ⲣⲱⲣ "binding (?)"   15 f.4
ⲣ̄ⲣⲟ "king, emperor"   11 2.4, 11, 3.19, 6.14, 20.6, 8, 22.25, 23.15, 24.6, 28.18; 17 b.42
ⲉⲣⲟ   11 27.15; 22 53; 25 10.4–5, 18.6; 26 3.21, 11.3
ⲉⲣⲣⲟ   11 22.13; 25 16.17; 36 f.I.13–14
ⲉⲣⲱ (f.)   28 11.20–21
ⲣ̄ⲣⲱⲟⲩ (pl.)   11 2.4
ⲉⲣⲱⲟⲩ   26 3.21
ⲣⲏⲥ "south"   11 16.18; 12 15.1; 29 f.19
ⲣⲟⲉⲓⲥ "to be awake, watch, guard; amulet"   11 26.27, 28; 12 39.4; 18 4; 32 1.20; 36 f.II.1, 8
ⲣⲁⲉⲓⲥ   25 6.26, 7.1, 10.3, 10, 11.10, 12.14, 13.2, 3, 5, 6, 7–8, 8, 12, 15, 20, 23, 26, 31, 14.5, 16, 20, 24, 15.2, 23, 16.4, 26; 26 12.17, 17.17; 28 13.7
ⲣⲁⲉⲓ   25 14.10
ⲣⲟⲓⲥ   12 27.7
ⲣⲁϣⲉ "to rejoice; joy"   11 12.8, 19.4; 26 14.17; 28 12.9
ⲣⲉϣⲉ   1 f.26, b 6
ⲣⲱⲧ "to sprout"
ⲣⲏⲧ   26 6.7
ⲣⲟⲟⲩϣ "to have care for; care"   11 21.26, 22.2
ⲣⲱϣⲉ "to suffice"   11 23–12
ⲣⲉϥ- agentive prefix see s.v. ⲙⲟⲩ, ⲡⲱϣⲛ, ⲥⲙⲛ, †, ⲧⲱⲛ, ϣⲱⲡ, ϩⲁⲡ, ϩⲓⲧⲉ
ⲣⲟⲩϩⲉ "evening"   26 17.4
ⲣⲱϩⲧ "to strike; blow"   25 6.20, 10.15; 26 13.14
ⲣⲁϩⲧⲥ "striking, slaughter"   26 10.8
ⲣⲉϩⲧⲥ   26 5.3
ⲣⲱϩⲧⲥ   26 15.23
ⲥⲁⲉⲓⲉ "beautiful/good person/thing"
ⲉⲁⲓⲏ   16 1.10
ⲥⲁⲓ̈ⲉ   20 f.1, 4–5, 9
ⲥⲁⲏ   37 f.34, b.27
ⲥⲁⲓⲏ   16 2.8–9, 36.8
ⲥⲉⲓ "to be filled, satisfied, enjoy"
ⲥⲓ   28 9.21
ⲥⲟ "respite, refrain"   11 13.12, 24
ⲥⲁ   28 5.1
ⲥⲱ "to drink; drink"   13 13; 14 9; 17 b.44?; 15 4.15; 25 7.24; 26 4.19; 28 1.10, 5.12, 10.21; 32 1.12, 2.6
ⲥⲟ⸗   29 b.4
ⲥⲁⲃⲉ "wise (person)"
ⲙⲛ̄ⲧⲥⲁⲃⲉ "wisdom"   32 2.20
ⲥⲱⲃⲉ "to laugh, play, mock, deride; laughter, derision"
ϭⲱⲃⲓ (?)   28 12.5
ⲥⲟⲃⲧⲉ "to ready, prepare"
ⲥⲉⲃⲧⲱⲧ   26 8.29

сѡвϩ "to be, become leprous; leprosy"
    совеϩ   **11** 21.5–6
    сѡϩⲃ̄   **26** 12.29
сѡⳡ "to smear, wipe, obliterate"
    соⳡ⸗   **32** 1.25
сѡк "to draw, flow, fly"   **12** 29.3, 6; **17** f.25; **20** f.3; **25** 6.12, 17.34; **26** 9.1, 10.29, 11.6, 9, 16.33–34, 35; **28** 3.5
    ⲍѡк   **3** f.1.28–29
    сек-   **28** 3.10
сіке "to grind; grinding"   **3** f.1 28; **6** 22
саⲭо "child" (?)   **36** f.II.2
сⲙн "voice"   **4** 5.16; **11** 25.24, 26.22–23; **17** f.20; **26** 9.27, 29
    сеⲙн   **17** f.17
    реваⲓсⲙн "listener, obeyer"   **26** 9.27
сⲙоⲩ "to bless; blessing"   **11** 12.7, 19.3–4, 25.3, 30.21; **25** 2.9, 8.2, 21; **26** 3.1, 4, 4.18, 5.16, 6.3, 9.3, 10.2, 11.13, 14.1, 15.10, 13, 15.16; **28** 7.22, 12.9–10; **29** b.4
    сⲙаⲙ[а]т^Q   **1** f.42
    сⲙаⲙаат^Q   **11** 5.5, 24.21; **25** 2.18–19, 15.4
    ⲙетатсⲙоⲩ "unblessedness"   **31** f.5
сⲙⲓⲛe "to be established, set in order"
    сеⲙе   **26** 2.10
    сⲙⲛ   **12** 11.17
    сⲙ̣ⲓ̣ⲛⲓ   **27** f.1–2
саⲙⲛт "water tank"
    саⲙет   **30** f.14
соⲛ "brother, sibling"   **11** 27.6
    саⲛ   **1** f.33, 37, b. 8
    сѡⲛ   **8** f.10
    сѡⲛе "sister"   **8** f.10; **9** 5, 9
сіⲛе "to pass by, through, bring out of"
    сⲛт⸗   **11** 13.16
соⲟⲛе "robber"
    саⲁⲛⲓ   **26** 16.17
сѡⲛт "creature"   **11** 14.14, 24–25, 15.11–12, 15, 20, 26, 16.10, 17, 22, 28–29, 17.12, 18.3–4, 25, 19.4–5; **12** 5.8, 29.6; **25** 6 13; **26** 8.30, 15.11
    сѡ̄ⲛ   **26** 8.19
    сѡѡⲛ̄т   **11** 15.6
    атсоⲛт⸗   **11** 2.6
сⲛте "foundations"   **4** 5.6, 10; **11** 3.13, 4.5; **12** 11.17, 17.12
    сеⲛⲧ   **34** 1.16
    снⲛⲧ   **26** 2.10, 4.7, 5.7, 7.27
сⲛоϥ "blood"   **3** f.1.24, 34; **11** 20.1; **31** b.15; **33** f.7; **36** f.I.1, b.7, 18, 19

с – о . (?)   **12** 1.7?
сⲏⲛоϥ   **17** b.1
сⲛав   **30** f.1
сⲛов   **25** 4.12, 7.23, 10.8, 11.10, 13.31, 14.8, 16.20, 24, 17.20; **26** 6.20, 13.22, 15.32, 16.1
сⲛаⲩ   **2** 1; **37** b.6, 9, 11, 16
сⲛeϥ   **31** f.36
соп "moment, time"   **11** 8.9, 23.13; **13** 15; **26** 16.10, 34
    саⲡ   **1** f.25; **28** 13.6; **34** 1.10, 18, 19
сѡⲡ "to dip, soak"
    саⲡ⸗   **27** f.15
сⲡⲓр "side, rib"   **3** f.1.13–14, 21, 26; **25** 13.28
    ⲍⲡⲓⲣ   **3** f.1.26
    сⲡер   **26** 13.22
соⲡс "to pray, entreat; entreaty, prayer"   **11** 2.1, 18.18, 22.5; **12** 25.9; **17** f.18; **20** f.12; **24** 1, 25, 31; **25** 5.21
    саⲡс   **25** 10.1; **26** 9.28
    [соⲡс]ⲡ (?)   **34** 3.8
    соⲡоⲡс   **10** 7
сѡр "to score"   **26** 2.11
сроⲙ "unconsciousness, sleep"
    сⲗаⲙ   **26** 17.1
сѡрⲙ "to go astray"
    сѡрⲙ   **28** 5.9
сорт "wool"   **12** 33.12
сате "fire"   **25** 18.5
    сāтⲓ   **28** 4.4
    сат⸗   **26** 8.28, 14.29
сіте "to throw, sow"
    сет-   **29** b.8
    сат⸗   **3** f.1.6, 2.32–33
соте "arrow"   **4** 4.1, 6; **12** 15.17
сѡте "to redeem, rescue"
    сѡ†   **28** 8.7
стоі "incense"
    стаі   **26** 17.25
с†ⲛоⲩве "good smell, perfume"   **28** 10.20
    с†ⲛоⲩві   **26** 9.24
сѡтⲙ "to hear, listen, obey"   **4** 2.5; **6** 1 (twice); **10** 9, 13; **11** 10.6–7, 14.16, 22, 15.2–3, 8, 13, 17–18, 23, 16.1, 7, 25, 17.2, 11, 20, 20.23, 22.17, 28.3–4; **12** 13.14, 15.9, 23.9, 25.13, 18, 27.14, 43.11, 16; **25** 2.17, 3.15, 5.1; **26** 9.26, 10.24; **30** f.20; **37** f.16
    ⲍѡтⲙ   **12** 5.4, 9, 13, 13.12, 27.16
    ϥѡтⲙ̄   **12** 7.7
    сѡтeⲙ   **3** b.1.6; **17** f.17; **26** 3.18, 4.16,

15.14–14
ⲥⲱⲧⲉⲛ   **34** 2.12
ⲥⲱⲧⲙ̄   **28** 7.12
ⲥⲟⲧⲙⲉ⸗   **11** 25.7
ⲁⲧⲥⲱⲧⲙ "heedless"   **25** 9.29–30
ⲁⲧⲥⲱⲧⲉⲙ   **26** 4.3
ⲁⲧⲥⲱⲧⲏⲙ   **28** 7.5
ⲙ̄ⲛⲧⲁⲧⲥⲱⲧⲙ̄ "heedlessness"   **11** 13.5
ⲣⲉϥⲥⲱⲧⲙ "listener, servant"   **26** 9.26–27
ⲣⲉϥⲥⲱⲧⲏⲙ   **28** 12.15
ⲥⲧⲙⲏⲧ "obedient"
ⲙⲛⲧⲥ̄ⲧⲙⲏⲧ "obedience"   **11** 9.22
ⲥⲧⲱⲧ "to tremble"   **11** 4.27, 17.24, 20.10; **12** 9.15, 21.19, 29.12; **25** 3.17
ⲥⲏⲩ "time, season"   **28** 10.3, 11.2
ⲥⲟⲩ- prefix indicating day of month   **23** 51
ⲥⲓⲟⲩ "star"   **8** f.5; **11** 14.26, 15.16–17; **12** 7.10, 13.9; **17** f.13, 34, 35; **26** 3.9, 11.7; **28** 2.6
ⲥⲓⲩ   **26** 2.16, 5.13, 28
ⲥⲟⲩ   **11** 2.7
ⲥⲱⲟⲩⲃⲉⲛ "grass"
ⲥⲁⲩⲃⲟⲩ   **25** 9.2
ⲥⲓⲟⲟⲩⲛ "bath"
ϭⲓⲁⲩⲛⲓ̈   **30** f.4
ⲥⲟⲟⲩⲛ "to know; knowledge"   **11** 1.19, 20, 27.20
ⲥⲁⲟⲩⲛ   **28** 1.1
ⲥⲁⲩⲛⲉ   **1** f.27, 32
ⲥⲟⲩⲱⲛ⸗   **11** 21.18–19
ⲥⲟⲩⲉⲥⲟⲩⲱⲛ⸗ (sic)   **26** 7.4–5
ⲁⲧⲥⲟⲟⲩⲛ "ignorance"   **11** 22.24
ⲥⲟⲩⲥⲟⲩ "point, moment, atom"   **28** 9.9
ⲥⲟⲟⲩⲧⲛ "to be straight, straighten; uprightness"   **12** 15.16
ⲥⲁⲩⲧⲉⲛ   **22** 57; **34** 2.17
ⲥⲱⲟⲩϩ "to gather"
ⲥⲱⲩϩⲉ   **17** f.16
ⲥⲁϣ "stroke, blow"
ⲥⲧⲉ (?)   **26** 13.21
ⲥⲱϣ "to despise, humble; shame"   **26** 10.10
ⲥⲁϣ⸗   **28** 11.14, 16
ⲥⲓϣⲉ "to be bitter; gall, bitterness"
ⲥⲓϣ   **24** 21
ⲥⲓϣⲓ   **25** 13.22; **28** 1.4, 10.11
ⲥⲱϣⲉ "field, meadow, countryside"
ⲥⲱϣⲉ   **11** 4.13
ⲥⲱϣⲧ "to stop, impede; impediment"
ϣⲉϣⲧ⸗   **2** 1
ⲥⲱϥ "to be defile, polluted"
ⲥⲱⲱⲃ   **26** 10.11

ⲥⲏϥⲉ "sword"   **3** f.2.4–5; **12** 13.1
ⲥⲏⲃⲉ   **12** 13.1, 41.4, 43.5
ⲥⲏⲃⲏ   **12** 21.10, 23.17
ⲥⲏⲃⲓ   **26** 8.28, 14.29; **28** 8.18
ⲥⲓϥⲉ "tar"
ⲥⲓⲃⲉ   **24** 20
ⲥⲁϩ "scribe, teacher"   **11** 18.24
ⲥⲟⲟⲩϩⲉ "egg, crown of the head"
ⲥϩ[ⲟ]ⲟⲩ   **3** f.1.22
ⲥⲟⲟϩⲉ "to remove; removal, departure"
ⲥⲁϩⲱ⸗   **20** f.5
ⲥϩⲁⲓ "to write, draw; writing, letter"   **11** 11.28, 20.7, 21.23–24, 24.5–6, 25.8–9, 12, 30.11; **12** 1.1, 25.16–17; **17** b.30; **22** 33, 46; **23** 1, 10, 45, 51; **25** 16.8, 10, 18; **26** 15.29, 32, 16.19, 21, 24, 26, 28, 31, 17.4, 7, 10, 13; **27** f.15, 16, b.7; **29** b.6, 7, 8; **32** 1.20, 27; **33** f.2, 14; **36** f.I.4; **37** b.21, 29
ⲥⲁⲓ   **17** b.13
ⲥϩⲉⲓ   **1** f.37, b.1, 2, 3
ⲥϩⲏⲓ   **21** 4
ϛϩⲓ   **33** f.6
ϩⲁⲓ   **25** 9.6
ⲥⲉϩ-   **1** f.34
ⲥⲁϩ⸗   **1** f.29, 41, b.4
ⲥϩⲁⲓ⸗   **33** f.11,
ⲥϩⲁⲓⲉ⸗   **11** 1.2; **33** f.7
ⲥⲏϩ^Q   **1** f.30, 39; **11** 30.6; **12** 31.12, 33.2; **26** 5.29, 7.25
ⲥϩⲃⲛⲧⲉ "foam"
ⲥⲃⲏⲧⲉ   **17** b.31
ⲥϩⲓⲙⲉ "woman, wife, female"   **11** 3.1, 5.25, 27, 6.2, 4, 6; **12** 15.2, 37.20, 41.7, 8; **16** 1.10; **18** 15; **20** f.9; **26** 9.12, 12.11; **33** f.7; **35** f.1, 721; **36** f.I.1; **37** b.11
ⲥⲓⲙⲉ   **3** f.1.13; **16** 2.8; **17** b.29, 32; **24** 35
ⲥⲓⲙⲓ   **23** 10; **26** 9.16, 16.3, 6, 21, 17.7, 13; **29** f.22
ⲥⲓⲙⲓϩⲓ   **26** 17.8
ⲥϩⲓⲙⲓ   **26** 17.9; **29** f.12
ϩⲓⲟⲙⲉ (pl.)   **8** f.17
ϩⲓⲁⲙⲓ   **28** 11.21
ⲥⲟⲟⲩⲥ "congregation; collection"   **22** 38
ⲥⲟⲟⲩⲥ   **25** 17.34, 38
ⲥⲁϩⲧⲉ "to kindle, heat; fire"   **4** 4.4–5, 11
ⲥⲁϩ†   **22** 48–49, 61; **28** 5.15
ⲥⲟϭ "fool"
ⲥⲉϭⲉ   **1** b.4
ⲥⲱϭ "to become rigid, paralysed"
ⲥⲏϭ   **26** 13.1

ⲧⲁⲉⲓⲟ "to honour; honour"
    ⲧⲁⲓⲁ   **28** 11.1, 12.9
    ⲧⲁⲓⲉⲓ   **10** 4
    ⲧⲁⲓⲟ   **11** 14.7; **26** 3.3
    ⲧⲁïⲏⲩ^Q   **11** 5.1–2, 20.11–12; **12** 21.17, 35.3
† "to give, cause, offer, sell"   **1** f.15, b.5; **8** f.12; **11** 2.25, 3.16, 7.16, 11 13.12, 24, 19.13, 22.27; **12** 9.21 (twice), 11.1, 3, 7, 9, 12, 15, 20, 13.2, 4, 6 (twice), 7 (twice), 8, 9, 10, 11, 15.7; **14** 10; **15** f.1, 3; **22** 34, 35, 41; **23** 38; **24** 9, 34; **25** 7.6, 9, 12, 9.6, 13.25, 16.26, 17.34, 44; **26** 2.13, 15, 16, 18, 19, 24, 3.1, 5, 4.12, 27, 5.31, 6.6, 8.19, 22, 12.3, 13.8, 14.23, 15.4, 20, 16.9; **27** f.1, 10, 18; **28** 1.20, 5.14, 9.12, 10.18, 11.19, 12.11; **29** b.4; **31** f.3, 4, 5 (twice), b.4 (twice), 5, 10; **31** b.23, 25, 27; **32** 2.7; **34** 2.18, 4.21; **35** f.23; 36 f.2.8
    ⲓ (sic)   **26** 14.21
    ⲁⲓ   **12** 7.7; **20** f.5, 9
    ⲧⲓ   **10** 16; **11** 3.15; **26** 3.2; **28** 5.18, 11 5, 12.13
    ⲧⲉ-   **16** 2.1; **26** 2.22, 16.21
    ⲁⲫ- (?)   **20** f.6, 10
    ⲧⲁ⸗   **27** f.17
    ⲧⲁⲁ⸗   **8** b.2; **10** 11; **11** 11.23; **25** 13.28; **26** 9.19, 12.9, 20, 13.21, 24; **27** f.20; **28** 8.11, 15, 21, 9.6; **32** 2.14; **33** f.1, 12; **35** f.20, 23; **37** b.14
    ⲧⲟ⸗   **26** 10.21
    ⲧⲁⲟ⸗   **25** 13.11
    ⲧⲱ⸗ (?)   **1** f.13
    ⲧⲉⲓⲧ⸗   **26** 4.21, 13.32
    ⲙⲁ (imp.)   **11** 11 8; **32** 2.22
    ⲁⲧ† "without giving"   **28** 5.1
    ⲣⲉϥ† "giver"   **31** b.3–4
    cf. s.v. ⲧⲱⲛ, ⲧⲛⲛⲟⲟⲩ, ϩⲁⲡ
ⲧⲏⲏⲃⲉ "finger"   **12** 31.4
    ⲧ̄ⲏⲏⲃ   **25** 11.13
    ⲧⲏⲏⲃⲓ   **26** 8.13
ⲧⲱⲃⲉ "seal"
    ⲧⲱⲃⲓ   **25** 9.30
ⲧⲱⲱⲃⲉ "brick"
    ⲧⲱⲃⲓ   **22** 61
ⲧⲃⲃⲟ "to purify, to be pure; purity, purification"   **11** 2.26, 11.18, 21.6
    ⲧⲉⲃⲟ   **17** f.28
    ⲧⲉⲃⲱ   **19** 2, 5
    ⲧⲃⲃⲁ   **25** 8.3
    ⲧⲉⲃⲟ-   **11** 13.14
    ⲧ̄ⲃⲃⲟ⸗   **11** 11.8

    ⲧⲉⲃⲏⲩ^Q   **26** 12.30
    ⲧ̄ⲃⲃⲏⲩ^Q   **28** 13.3
ⲧⲃⲛⲏ "livestock, (domestic) animal"
    ⲧⲉⲃⲛⲏ   **26** 17.10
    ⲧⲉϥⲛⲏ   **34** 1.25
    ⲧ̄ⲃⲛⲟⲟⲩⲉ (pl.)   **11** 3.4
†ⲙⲉ "village"
    †ⲙⲓ   **26** 16.31
ⲧⲱⲃϩ "to pray, entreat, console; prayer"   **10** 9
ⲧⲱⲕ "to be strong, firm"
    ⲧⲟⲕ⸗   **7** 9, 30
ⲧⲁⲕⲟ "to destroy, perish; perdition"   **26** 11.18; **37** b.6, 7, 20
    ⲧⲁⲕⲁ   **26** 4.5; **30** f.9
    ⲧⲁϭⲟ   **15** f.5
    ⲧⲁⲕⲟ⸗   **35** f.25?; **37** b.21
    ⲧⲁⲕⲁ⸗   **30** f.11 (twice), 12 (twice), 13, 13.14, 14
    ⲁⲧⲧⲁⲕⲟ "imperishable"   **11** 2.5
ⲧⲱⲕⲙ̄ "to pluck, draw, drag"   **12** 23.17, 43.4
ⲧⲱⲕⲥ "to pierce, bite, fix"
    ⲧⲁⲕⲥ   **29** f.14
    ⲧⲱⲝ   **26** 2.3
    ⲧⲁⲝ⸗   **25** 13.17; **26** 12.20
ⲧⲕⲁⲥ "pain"   **11** 8.20, 14.4; **18** 10
    †ⲕⲉⲥ   **25** 4.13, 22–23
    †ⲕⲁⲥ   **26** 16.13
ⲧⲁⲗⲟ "to lift, offer up, mount; offering"   **32** 1.24
    ⲧⲁⲗⲁ⸗   **26** 6.15, 13.10, 19
    ⲧⲁⲗⲏⲩ^Q   **18** 2
    ⲧⲁⲗⲏⲟⲩ^Q   **4** 2.5
ⲧⲉⲗⲏⲗ "to rejoice; joy"   **11** 18.27
ⲧⲱⲗⲙ "to defile; defilement"
    ⲁⲧⲧⲱⲗⲉⲙ "undefiled"   **11** 2.5–6
ⲧⲗ̄ⲧⲗⲉ "drop"
    ⲧⲉⲗⲧⲓⲗ   **17** b.46
    ⲧⲉⲗⲧⲓⲗⲓ   **28** 6.11
    ⲧⲉⲗ†ⲗ   **25** 14.2
ⲧⲁⲗϭⲟ "to heal; healing"   **11** 2.26, 9.11, 19, 14.3, 20.27, 22.10; **36** f.II.7
    ⲧⲁⲗϭⲁ   **25** 8.25, 16.27; **26** 12.1, 15.1
    ⲧⲉⲗϭⲁ   **26** 4.13; **26** 15.20
    ⲧⲁⲗϭⲟ⸗   **11** 24.17
    ⲧⲉⲗϭⲁ⸗   **26** 4.11, 10.3
ⲧⲱⲙ "to shut"   **28** 5.11
ⲧⲁⲙⲓⲟ "to make, create; creation"   **10** 2; **11** 26.18, 27.6
    ⲧⲁⲙⲓⲁ   **25** 6.25, 7.21, 9.27, 29; **26** 2.9, 13, 14–15, 16; **26** 2.17, 20, 3.24, 26, 4.10, 24, 14.27–28, 15.11

ⲧⲁⲙⲓⲉ- **12** 19.10, 35.5
ⲧⲁⲙⲓⲟ= **12** 19.17–18
ⲧⲁⲙⲓⲁ= **26** 3.1, 5.27, 8.20, 9.18, 10.23
ⲧⲁⲙⲟ "to tell, inform" **11** 23.7
ⲧⲱⲙⲥ "to bury"
   ⲧⲱⲙⲉⲥ **17** b.32; **24** 5
   ⲧⲟⲙⲥ= **11** 21.16
   ⲧⲁⲙⲥ= **22** 61; **26** 17.11; **27** f.16
   ⲧⲁⲙⲉⲥ= **31** f.40
   ⲧⲁⲙⲥⲉ= **26** 16.31, 17.8; **31** b.19
ⲧⲱⲛ "where" **12** 9.14
ⲧⲱⲛ "dispute, quarrel" **31** b.5
   †ⲧⲱⲛ **1** f.4, 7, 18–19; **22** 45
   ⲣⲉϥ†ⲧⲱⲛ "quarreller" **31** b.3
ⲧⲛⲛⲟ "to pound, tread down"
   ⲧⲁⲛⲟ **32** 1.23
ⲧⲛⲛⲟⲟⲩ "to send" **32** 1.3
   ⲛⲟⲟⲩ **25** 7.25
   ⲛ:ⲛⲟⲟⲩ **25** 5.23
   ⲧⲉⲛⲉⲩ **11** 9.6–7
   ⲧⲉⲛⲟⲟⲩ **12** 15.10, 17.17, 19.14, 21, 21.8, 23.10, 39.18, 41.2, 43.17; **25** 8.18
   ⲧⲉⲛⲛⲁⲩ **26** 5.13
   ⲧ̄ⲛ̄ⲛⲟⲟⲩ= **11** 23.23–24
   ⲧ̄ⲛⲉⲩ= **11** 5.16, 8.13
   ⲧⲛⲛⲁⲩ= **1** b.2, f.29, 32, 34, 35, 38, 42
   ⲧⲉⲛⲛⲁⲩ= **26** 6.2
   ⲙⲁⲧⲛⲟⲟⲩ (imp.) **28** 13.23
ⲧⲱⲛⲟⲩ "very, greatly"
   ⲧⲟⲛⲟⲩ **1** f.23, b. 5
ⲧⲛϩ "wing"
   ⲍⲱϩ (?) **11** 26.20
   ⲧⲛⲁϩ **12** 29.15
   ⲧⲉⲛⲁϩ **12** 33.19; **25** 6.13; **26** 2.5, 22, 5.23, 10.26–27; **28** 4.12
ⲧⲁⲛϩⲟ "to make alive, preserve; sustenance, salvation"
   ⲧⲁⲛϩⲉ **11** 2.19?
   ⲣⲉϥⲧⲁⲛϩⲟ "life-giver" **11** 14.10
†ⲡⲉ "loins" **36** f.I.2
†ⲡⲉ "taste" **25** 13.21–22
ⲧⲁⲡⲣⲟ "mouth" **24** 10, 12; **26** 10.18
   ⲧⲁⲡⲣⲁ **9** 25.28; **26** 8.5, 15.9
ⲧⲉⲣ "branch" **25** 9.2 (twice), 4
ⲧⲟⲉⲓⲥ "piece of cloth, rag"
   ⲧⲁⲓⲥ **27** f.22
   ⲧⲏⲥ **26** 17.4
ⲧⲁⲣⲕⲟ "to adjure" **11** 4.23, 7.5, 16.8, 18.2; **12** 17.2, 8, 23, 19.3, 8; **32** 1.9, 2.16; **37** f.13
   ⲧⲁⲣⲕⲁ **8** f.12

ⲧⲉⲣⲕⲁ **21** 14; **25** 10.6, 18.1; **26** 4.20, 25, 5.7, 12
ⲧⲉⲣⲕⲟ **25** 13.10, 13, 16, 21, 24, 27, 14.1, 6, 11, 17, 21, 25, 15.3
cf. †ⲧⲁⲣⲕⲟ *in Abbreviations*
ⲧⲱⲣϣ "to be red"
   ⲧ̄ⲱ̄ⲣⲉ (?) **15** f.6
ⲧⲱⲥ "to harden, dry" **23** 37
   ⲧⲏⲥ **24** 21
ⲧⲥⲟ "to cause to drink" **12** 35.15; **26** 16.14; **35** f.20
   ⲧⲥⲟ= **35** f.6
   ⲧⲥⲁ= **26** 16.11; **28** 2.1
ⲧⲥⲁⲃⲟ "to make wise, teach, show"
   ⲧⲥⲁⲃⲁ **26** 4.26
   ⲧⲥⲁⲃⲟ= **11** 28.2, 5
ⲧⲥⲧⲟ "to bring back, repeat, turn back, cause to return" **11** 23.4
ⲧⲱⲧ "to be joined, persuaded, agreeable" **11** 30.13
ⲧⲏⲩ "wind" **17** f.25; **24** 13; **28** 2.7; **32** 1.26
   ⲧⲏⲟⲩ **1** f.5
ⲧⲟⲟⲩ "mountain, desert" **3** f.1.11; **11** 7.16, 17.25; **32** 2.7; **37** b.4, 16
   ⲧⲁⲩ **23** 22; **25** 9.31?; **26** 16.15
   ⲧⲁⲁⲩ **22** 42
   ⲧⲁⲟⲩ **23** 31
ⲧⲟⲟⲩⲉ "shoe"
   ⲧⲁⲩⲉⲓ **26** 7.14–15
ⲧⲁⲩⲟ "to send, recite, proclaim"
   ⲧⲁⲁⲩⲟ (?) **32** 1.24
   ⲧⲁⲟⲩⲟ **11** 2.20, 3.25, 5.10, 6.26
   ⲧⲉⲟⲩⲟ **1** f.8, 20–21
   ⲧⲁⲟⲩⲁ **25** 16.16; **26** 15.7, 27, 16.4, 6–7, 9, 13, 34
   ⲧⲁⲩⲁ **28** 3.11, 7.6
   ⲧⲁⲩⲟⲩⲁ **26** 17.1
   ⲧⲁⲟⲩⲉ- **11** 22.11
   ⲁⲧⲧⲁⲩⲟ= "indescribable" **11** 5.3
ⲧⲱⲟⲩⲛ "to rise, support" **11** 10.2, 19.6, 27.26; **12** 17.6, 13, 41.19, 43.2; **23** 36; **26** 6.17–18, 11.10, 12.27, 15.9; **28** 1.9, 8.23; **32** 1.13
   ⲧⲱⲟⲩ **25** 14.25
   ⲧⲱⲟⲩⲃⲓⲛ **26** 13.2
   ⲧⲟⲟⲩⲛ **31** b.4
   ⲧⲱⲛ **29** f.10
   ⲧⲟⲩⲛⲟⲩ= **31** f.17–18
   ϭⲓⲛⲧⲱⲟⲩⲛ "resurrection" **26** 13.28
ⲧⲟⲩⲛⲟⲥ "to wake, raise, set up; raising"
   ⲧⲟⲩⲛⲟⲩⲥ **1** f.19

ⲧⲟⲩⲱⲧ "figurine, idol"   **27** f.17
   ⲧⲟⲩⲟⲧ   **27** f.20
ⲧⲱϣ "to ordain; ordinance"   **11** 29.23; **26** 2.19, 24, 7.24–25
   ⲧⲏϣ^Q **11** 4.1, 22; **17** f.14, 15
ⲧⲱϩ "to mix, disturb"   **29** 9.29
ⲧⲁϩⲟ "to set up, reach, meet, arrest"
   ⲧⲁϩⲁ⸗   **26** 9.17
ⲑⲁⲃ "leaven"
   ⲁⲑⲁⲃ "unleavened"   **26** 17.26
ⲑⲁⲃ "spittle"   **17** f.26
ⲑⲃⲃⲓⲟ "to humiliate, be humble; humility"
   ⲑⲉⲃⲓⲁ   **28** 10.15
ⲑⲗⲟ "to scatter; scattering"
   ⲑⲗⲁ   **22** 43–44; **27** f.11, 19
   ⲑⲁⲗⲟ   **27** f.3
ⲑⲙⲥⲟ "to cause to sit"
   ⲑⲙⲥⲁ⸗   **28** 2.2
ⲧⲣϣⲟ "to make heavy, terrify"
   ⲑⲉⲣϣⲁ   **28** 3.3
ⲧⲱϩⲥ "to anoint"   **26** 16.20; **37** b.3, 15, 31
   ⲧⲁϩⲥ   **23** 9; **26** 16.4, 23
   ⲧⲁϩⲥ⸗   **8** f.3
   ⲧⲁϩⲥⲉ⸗   **26** 5.6
ⲧⲟⲩϫⲟ "to make whole, save; salvation"
   ⲧⲟⲩϫⲟ⸗   **11** 7.2, 11.11
ⲧⲁϫⲣⲟ "to strengthen, make firm"; firmness, strength"   **12** 11.18
   ⲧⲁϫⲣⲁ   **25** 4.20, 5.27, 8.24
   ⲧⲁϫⲣⲟ⸗   **12** 37.14
   ⲧⲁϫⲣⲏⲩ^Q **11** 19.15; **12** 7.4
   ⲧⲁϫⲣⲏⲟⲩ^Q **12** 17.11
ⲧⲱϭⲉ "to join, affix"
   ⲧⲱϫⲉ   **11** 25.11
   ⲧⲉϫⲓ-   **26** 16.6
   ⲧⲟϭ⸗   **11** 13.29
ⲧϭⲁⲓⲟ "to make ugly; disgrace, condemnation"
   ϭⲁⲓ   **26** 17.3
ⲟⲩ "what"   **7** 15, 25
ⲟⲩⲉ "to be distant"   **9** 7; **11** 7.22
   ⲟⲩⲏⲩ   **11** 8.22–23
   ⲟⲩⲓ (?)   **35** f.1
ⲟⲩⲱ "bud, blossom"   **12** 35.13; **26** 6.6, 12.3, 13.7, 15.4
ⲟⲩⲱ "finish, run out"   **1** b.3; **7** 12; **25** 9.7
ⲟⲩⲱ "reply"   **6** 6; **7** 12
ⲟⲩⲱⲃϣ "white"
   ⲟⲩⲟϥϣ   **12** 33.9
   ⲟⲩⲱϥϣ   **12** 33.12
   ⲟⲩⲟϣⲉ   **16** 1.11

ⲟⲩⲟⲃϣⲉ (f.)   **16** 2.9
ⲟⲩⲗⲗⲉ "melody, music"
   ⲟⲩⲉⲗⲗⲉ   **17** f.24
ⲟⲩⲱⲗⲡ "to damage, break" (?)
   ⲟⲩⲟⲗⲡ⸗   **3** f.1.8
ⲟⲩⲱⲙ "to eat; food"   **4** 4.3–4; **11** 7.20; **16** 3.2; **17** b.44; **24** 30; **28** 1.10, 4.7, 5.11; **28** 10.20; **32** 1.12, 2.6
   ⲟⲩⲁⲙ   **28** 13.1
   ⲟⲩⲟⲙ   **4** 4.10
ⲟⲩⲉⲓⲛ "drain"
   ⲁⲟⲩⲉⲛ   **31** b.17
   ⲁⲟⲩⲉⲓⲛ   **37** b.5, 20
   ⲁⲩⲉⲓⲛ   **32** 1.23
ⲟⲩⲟⲉⲓⲛ "light"   **11** 9.13, 11.25, 14.20, 15.7, 17.27, 24.26, 25.14; **12** 19.9, 31.22, 33.3, 23; **15** f.5; **32** 2.9
   ... ⲉⲓⲛ   **34** 1.11
   ⲟⲩⲁⲉⲓⲛ   **25** 3.3; **26** 2.5, 15, 3.17, 19, 7.21, 29, 8.8–9, 10, 18, 11.7; **28** 5.10; **34** 1.11–12, 12, 18
   ⲟⲩⲉⲓⲛ   **11** 9.17; **17** f.12
ⲟⲩⲟⲛ "someone, something"   **10** 13; **11** 1.5, 2.19, 4.21, 5.9
   ⲟⲩⲛ   **11** 9.5
ⲟⲩⲱⲛ "to open"   **26** 3.13, 16
   ⲟⲩⲛ   **3** f.1.22
   ⲟⲩⲱⲛϩ   **25** 3.7; **34** 1.13
ⲟⲩⲉⲓⲛⲉ "to pass by"   **28** 1.1
   ⲟⲩⲉⲓⲛⲓ   **28** 2.9
ⲟⲩⲛⲁⲙ "right"   **3** f.1.14, 26, 2.1, b.1.14; **12** 13.17, 15.14, 15.15, 21.12, 23.7, 25.16, 31.5, 10, 35.15, 41.5, 43.5; **17** f.26–27, 33; **18** 2; **22** 35; **25** 7.5, 13.13, 14.14, 19; **26** 8.13, 15, 27; **28** 2.2; **37** b.2, 10
   ⲓⲟⲩⲛⲁⲙ   **26** 16.28; **28** 2.2, 3.8
   ⲓⲱⲛⲁⲙ   **25** 13.29, 14.23, 15.4; **26** 17.14–15
   ⲩⲟⲩⲛⲁⲙ̄   **3** f.1.3–4
ⲟⲩⲛⲟⲩ "hour"   **3** f.2.7–8, 10; **11** 18.13, 19.6
   ⲉⲛⲟⲩ   **28** 10.5, 11.10
   -ⲩⲛⲟⲩ   **14** 7?; **15** b.2; **22** 46, 54; **24** 5, 13–14; **25** 8.3–4, 23, 10.8; **26** 5.5, 10.4, 11.15; **28** 9.11, 19; **32** 2.11; **37** f.20
   ⲧⲉⲛⲟⲩ "now"   **11** 14.10, 27.6–7
   ⲧⲓⲛⲟⲩ   **17** f.18
   ϯⲛⲟⲩ   **1** b.1; **26** 4.11, 29, 15.18
ⲟⲩⲱⲛϩ "to reveal, be revealed, appear, show"
   ⲟⲩⲱⲛⲁϩ   **12** 15.20, 21, 17.19, 19.2, 14, 20; **24** 17; **25** 2.14, 22, 3.3; **25** 6.16, 10.11, 11.11
   ⲱⲛⲁϩ   **25** 3.5

ⲟⲩⲁⲛⲁϩ⸗ 26 7.3, 12.12
ⲟⲩⲟⲡ "to be pure, holy"
  ⲟⲩⲁⲁⲃ^Q 8 f.1; 11 5.4, 6.11, 6.18, 21, 12.13–14, 13.12, 14, 23–24, 14.5, 9, 20.4, 23.7, 21, 25; 12 9.17–18, 21.1, 8, 25.21, 31.1, 37.5; 15 b4; 17 f.28, b.36; 18 3, 5; 23 29, 31; 25 3.22, 4.17, 5.24, 6.9, 10 (twice), 21, 7.19, 24, 26, 8.1–2, 11–12, 19, 20, 27, 13.8, 14.7; 26 2.8, 25, 7–8, 3.11, 18, 4.5, 14, 19–20, 6.27, 7.3, 7.6, 11, 8.6, 13 (twice), 15, 26, 10.2, 19, 23, 11.5, 30, 13.17, 31, 33, 14.3, 7, 16, 18, 27, 15.18, 25; 28 3.3, 5.18, 6.23, 8.8, 9.2, 4, 11.19, 12.13; 29 f.13
  ⲟⲩⲁⲃ^Q 26 14.20
  ⲟⲩⲁⲁϥ^Q 12 17.12; 25 12.1
ⲟⲩⲣⲧ "rose"
  ⲟⲩⲉⲣⲧ 12 1.3
  ⲟⲩⲏⲣⲉⲧ 37 b.29
  ⲟⲩⲉⲓⲧ (?) 12 1.8?
ⲟⲩⲉⲣⲏⲧⲉ "foot, leg" 3 f.1.23; 11 23.19; 24 33; 28 3.9–10
  ⲉⲣⲏⲧ 26 9.9
  ⲟⲩⲉⲣⲏϯ 25 2.17, 13.17; 26 7.15, 8.17
  ⲟⲩⲉⲣⲧⲏⲉ 32 1.14
  ⲟⲩⲉⲣⲩⲧⲉ 35 f.3
  ⲩⲉⲣⲏⲧⲉ 12 29.10, 17
  ⲟⲩⲏⲣϯ 25 14.21; 26 2.1
  ⲟⲩⲣⲏϯ 34 4.14–15
ⲟⲩⲱⲥϥ "to be idle, brought to naught"
  ⲟⲩⲱⲃⲥ 26 5.19–20, 13.12
  ⲟⲩⲱⲥⲃ 28 1.15–16
ⲟⲩⲱⲧ "single" 11 12.16–17, 19, 20, 21, 22, 24, 25, 26, 27; 12 19.19; 28 9.9; 32 2.10
ⲟⲩⲱⲧϩ "to pour, make molten"
  ⲟⲩⲟⲑ^Q 6 2
  ⲟⲩⲱⲑ^Q 6 12
ⲟⲩⲱϣ "to want, desire; wish, desire, will" 1 b.1; 3 b.1.7; 4 5.2–3; 6 10, 11, 24; 7 6 (twice), 7, 9, 16, 21, 22, 23, 27 (three times), 29, 32, 38; 8 f.7, 11, b.4, 10; 11 22.23, 27.14; 12 5.17–18, 17.21; 16 2.1, 5, 12, 3.5; 17 f.31; 18 17; 20 f.9; 22 25; 26 4.9, 15.31, 16.2, 31; 28 4.10, 5.4–5, 8, 6.2, 10, 19, 9.13, 11.12–13; 29 f.20; 32 1.6, 14, 15, 34, 2.3; 32 3.25 (twice); 37 f.10 (twice), 11 (twice), 22, b.9, 13, 27
  ⲟⲩⲟϣⲉ 16 1.11
  ⲟⲩⲱϣⲉ 1 f.13
  ⲱ̄ϣ 7 21
  ⲁϣⲉ⸗ 37 b.13
ⲟⲩⲁϣ⸗ 1 f.6; 13 15
ⲟⲩⲟϣⲟ⸗ 25 5.11
ⲟⲩⲟⲉⲓϣ "time, occasion" 11 14.11, 20.14; 27 f.6
  ⲟⲩⲁⲉⲓϣ 22 58; 26 10.1, 11.1; 31 f.20
  ⲟⲩⲁⲓϣ 1 f.24, b.9
  ⲟⲉⲓϣ 10 5
  ⲩⲁⲉⲓϣ 28 10.4
ⲟⲩϣⲏ "night" 7 34
  ⲉⲩϣⲏ 37 b.15
  ⲩϣⲏ 3 f.2.11; 6 4, 12; 17 f.14; 25 3.11, 4.24–25, 5.2, 9.4; 28 11.11
ⲟⲩⲱϣⲉ "to consume" 22 63
ⲟⲩⲱϣⲙ "to knead, bruise; dough"
  ⲟⲩⲟϣⲙⲉ 32 1.22
ⲟⲩⲱϣⲥ̄ "to be/become broad"
  ⲟⲩⲟϣⲥ̄ 11 4.5–6
ⲟⲩⲱϣⲧ "to worship" 11 23.17–18; 26 2.1, 3.28, 4.1–2, 5.26; 28 4.16–17
  ⲟⲩⲱϣⲉⲧ 18 7
  ⲟⲩⲁϣⲧ⸗ 1 f.25
ⲟⲩⲟϥ "lung" "to damage" 3 f.2.36
ⲟⲩⲱϩ "to place, dwell" 6 19, 21; 11 7.22, 26.16; 26 12.10; 28 8.5; 32 2.12; 37 f.20
  ⲁϩϩⲉ ? 9 11
  ⲟⲩⲁϩ- 22 60; 26 3.22
  ⲟⲩⲁϩ⸗ 26 16.27
  ⲟⲩⲏϩ^Q 5 f.11; 11 6.20, 17.18, 30.22
  ⲟⲩⲁϩ^Q 27 f.18
  ⲟⲩⲉϩ^Q 26 3.27, 6.16; 30 f.10, 25
  cf. s.v. ⲟⲩⲉϩⲥⲁϩⲛⲉ
ⲟⲩⲟⲟϩⲉ "scorpion"
  ⲟⲩⲁϩⲓ 29 f.11, 12
ⲟⲩⲱϩⲙ "to repeat, answer; answer"
  ⲟⲩⲁϩⲙⲉ⸗ 11 9.15, 18.23
ⲟⲩϩⲟⲣ "dog" 7 35; 11 23.3
  ⲟⲩϩⲁⲣ 28 6.5–6; 31 b.8; 37 b.19
  ⲟⲩϩⲱⲣ 17 b.45
  ϩⲟⲩⲟⲣ 32 2.17, 18
  ⲟⲩϩⲟⲣⲉ (fem.) 7 35
  ⲟⲩϩⲁⲁⲣⲓ 28 6.5
ⲟⲩⲉϩⲥⲁϩⲛⲉ "to command; command" 11 21.12–13; 28 4.19
  ⲟⲩϩⲥⲁϩⲛⲉ 28 2.22–23
  ⲟⲩⲉϩⲥⲁϩⲛⲓ 26 8.29–30; 28 11.13–14
ⲟⲩϫⲁⲓ "to be whole, safe, sound; health, safety, salvation" 11 2.25, 20.22, 22.9, 25.20, 28.19; 17 b.43; 21 15; 25 5.13, 6.23, 7.6, 15, 16, 8.3, 5; 26 7.7, 13.10, 18; 28 7.14; 30 b.3; 32 1.9–10; 34 3.9

ⲩⲭⲁⲓ   **12** 7.5
ⲟⲩⲭⲉⲓⲧⲉ   **1** f.24, b.7
ⲟⲩⲁⲭ^Q   **25** 4.18, 22, 5.4
ⲟⲩⲱϭⲡ "to break, be broken"
   ⲟⲩⲱϭⲡ   **4** 5.14
ⲟⲩⲟϭⲟⲩⲉϭ "to chew, crush"
   ⲃⲁⲕⲃⲉⲕ   **32** 2.17
   ⲃⲛⲕⲃⲛⲕ   **28** 6.7
ⲱⲱ "to conceive, be pregnant; conception"
   ⲉⲧ   **3** f.1.13
ⲱⲃϣ "to forget, sleep"
   ⲁⲃϣ   **29** f.6
ⲱⲕⲙ "to be dark"
   ⲟⲕⲉⲙ   **3** f.1.25
ⲱⲗ "to gather, contain"   **3** f.1.33; **5** f.12; **25** 16.19, 24; **36** f.I.3
   ⲃⲱ̄ⲗ (?)   **25** 11.7, 10
ⲱⲙⲕ "to swallow"
   ⲱⲛⲕ   **26** 3.14
ⲱⲛⲉ "stone, rock"   **3** f.1.9, 28; **7** 2, 17, 25; **11** 10.18; **16** 1.8, 2.7; **20** f.2
   ⲱⲛⲓ   **25** 2.24
ⲱⲛϩ "to live; life"   **1** b.6; **11** 22.16, 22.27–23.1; **26** 12.4, 13.8
   ⲟⲛϩ   **11** 1.4, 6.12, 8.1–2, 20.9, 23.5, 24.5, 30.5
   ⲱⲛⲁϩ   **12** 27.8, 35.21–22, 37.15–16, 39.5; **25** 3.10, 16.7; **26** 6.7, 8.1, 24, 11.21, 13.32; **27** f.12; **28** 10.5, 11.3; **31** f.28
   ⲱⲛⲉϩ   **18** 14
   ⲱϩ   **25** 10.5
ⲱⲡ "to count, esteem; reckoning"
   ⲏⲡ^Q   **11** 3.12, 5.13, 21, 9.2
   ⲏⲡ^Q   **26** 6.24
ⲱⲣⲕ "to promise, swear, adjure"   **1** f.26; **5** f.8; **10** 19; **17** b.36, 40, 41, 43; **25** 5.12, 6.22, 8.6, 13; **26** 4.16, 5.10, 23, 27, 6.8, 6.14, 7.12, 11.19; **28** 6.15, 7.13, 15, 18, 20, 8.1, 7, 13, 20; **29** f.11, 14; **30** b.3; **32** 1.34, 2.9; **37** f.14
   ⲣ   **27** f.4
   ⲱⲣⲉ   **17** f.28
   ⲱⲣⲉⲕ   **17** f.26, 27, 33; **18** 1, 5; **19** 1
   cf. †ⲱⲣⲕ in Abbreviations
ⲱⲣⲝ "to be firm, secure; firmness"   **11** 20.24
ⲱⲥⲕ "to delay, continue"   **11** 21.2
ⲱⲧ "fat"   **12** 1.7?
ⲱϣ "to call, read"   **4** 2.16, 4.14, 5.16; **10** 13; **11** 8.27, 12.9, 18.12, 26.22; **12** 5.5, 10, 21.3; **25** 13.25; **26** 2.5–6, 11.2; **28** 3.13; **34** 2.12
   ⲱϣⲉ   **12** 29.19

ⲟϣ⸗   **11** 1.6
ⲱϣⲙ "to quench, extinguish"   **25** 18.4, 8
   ⲱϣ (?)   **24** 13
   ⲱϣⲙⲉ   **26** 13.4
   ⲉϣⲉⲙ- (?)   **25** 18.8
   ⲁⲧⲧⲱϣⲉϣⲙ "unquenched"   **17** b.17
ⲱϥⲉ "to press, gather, mop up"
   ⲁϥⲉ   **1** 21–22?, 23
ⲱϩⲉ "to stand"   **26** 6.9
   ⲁϩⲉⲣⲁⲧ⸗   **7** 10, 30; **11** 6.18–19, 7.23–24, 16.11, 17.9, 17, 19.17–18; **12** 9.8–9, 15.4, 35.8; **17** f.5, 21; **22** 35; **26** 2.2, 3.9, 11.8, 14.27, 29; **32** 1.2
   ⲁϩⲉⲣⲁ   **26** 11.12
   ⲁϩⲉⲣⲁⲑ⸗   **3** f.1.2
   ⲁⲁϩⲉⲣⲁⲧ⸗   **12** 21.13–14
   ⲁⲉϩⲣⲁⲧ⸗   **26** 14.36
   ⲁϩⲁⲣⲉⲧ⸗   **1** f.3
   ⲁϩⲉⲣⲁⲧⲉ⸗   **18** 8
   ⲁϩⲉⲉⲣⲁⲧ⸗   **12** 15.15, 17.9–10, 25.22, 27.5, 13, 37.23–24, 41.16
   ⲁϩⲉⲣⲟⲧ⸗   **27** f.5
   ϩⲁⲉⲣⲁ⸗   **3** f.2.1
   ϩⲁⲉⲣⲁⲧ⸗   **3** f.2.3, 7, 10, b.1.14
   ⲱϩⲓⲣⲁⲧ⸗   **28** 3.6, 10.13
   ϩⲉⲣⲁⲧ⸗   **26** 8.21
   ϭⲓⲛⲁϩ:ⲉⲣⲁⲧ "standing"   **26** 14.11
ⲱϩⲥ "to reap; reaping, harvest"
   ⲙⲉⲧⲟⲩⲁϩⲥ "reaping" (?)   **31** f.5–6
ⲱϫⲛ "to cease, perish, destroy; destruction"
   ⲱϫⲏⲛ   **28** 1.15
   ⲁⲧⲱϫⲉⲛ "imperishable"   **25** 8.7
ϣ- "to be able"   **11** 22.3, 25.16, 26.16; **12** 21.13; **32** 1.12 (three times)
   ⲉϣ-   **12** 15.4; **18** 15; **23** 27, 41; **26** 16.6, 17, 20; **27** f.13; **28** 2.16, 21
   ⲉϣⲓ-   **23** 36
   ϣⲉ-   **23** 38
ϣⲁ "to rise"   **15** f.6
ϣⲁ "nose"
   ϣⲁⲛⲧ⸗   **6** 17
   ϣⲁⲁⲛⲧ⸗   **28** 3.10–11
ϣⲉ "to go"
   ϣϣⲉ   **9** 6
ϣⲉ "wood"
   ϣⲏ   **23** 25; **25** 9.4, 13.14; **28** 8.10, 17; **29** b.7
ϣⲏⲓ "cistern"   **11** 3.14
ϣⲓ "to measure; circumference"   **28** 2.15; **35** f.16

ⲉϭⲓ   25 13.14
ϣⲱ "sand"   6 23
ϣⲓⲃⲉ "to change, be strange, fearful; reward"
  1 b.4
  ϣⲓⲃⲓ   28 1.3 (twice), 5
  ϣⲟⲃⲉ   11 1.14; 18 13
ϣⲃⲏⲣ "friend, companion"   28 1.18; 32
  2.10, 19
ϣⲓⲕ "depth"   11 27.9
ϣⲓⲕⲉ "to dig; depths"   28 2.13
ϣⲁⲗ "myrrh"   23 47; 25 9.6
ϣⲟⲗ "molar tooth"
  ϣⲁⲗ   26 8.6
ϣⲱⲗ "to despoil"   11 19.10
ϣⲗⲏⲗ "to pray, prayer"   1 f.23; 11 11.6, 25.25;
  31 f.29
ϣⲟⲗⲙⲉⲥ "gnat"
  ϣⲁⲗⲙⲉⲥ   26 5.22, 7.1–2
ϣⲁⲗⲟⲟⲩ "water–wheel"
  ϣⲁⲗⲁⲩ   30 f.12
  ϫⲁⲗⲁⲩ   9 8
  ϫⲁⲗⲟⲟⲩ   4 4.1, 7
ϣⲱⲗϩ "to make, mark"
  ϣⲁϩⲗⲏ⸗   28 13.4
ϣⲗϩ "fear, terror"
  ϩⲁϩⲗϥ   11 8.15
  ϩϣⲉϩⲗϥ   11 4.27
  ⲛⲉϩϣⲗⲏⲃ "be terrified"   28 1.6
ϣⲗϭⲟⲙ "mustard"
  ϣⲗⲧⲉⲙ   1 f.14
ϣⲏⲙ "small"   11 11.22, 28.23; 28 2.13
ϣⲱⲙ "summer"   28 6.14
ϣⲙⲙⲟ "foreign, strange"   11 5.20
  ϣⲉⲙⲁ   26 17.9
ϣⲙϣⲉ "to serve, worship; service, worship"
  11 8.22–12, 22.14, 23.20
ϣⲏⲛ "tree"   9 11; 11 3.15, 4.16, 27.1; 24 30; 25
  16.6; 26 6.7, 8.24, 12.4, 13.8, 15.4
  ϣⲏ   23 25
ϣⲛⲏ "garden"   11 3.14
ϣⲓⲛⲉ   1 f.23, b.4
  ϣⲓⲛⲓ   28 10.3; 34 1.22–23, 2.7
  ϣⲙ̄ⲛⲟⲩϥⲉ "good news, gospel"   11 19.14
  ϣⲉⲛⲟⲩⲃⲉ   28 6.21–22, 7.2
  ϣⲉⲛⲟⲩⲃⲓ   28 7.1, 10–11, 8.4
  ⲃⲁⲓϣⲉⲛⲟⲩⲃⲉ "messenger"   28 11.23
  ⲃⲁⲓϣⲉⲛⲟⲩⲃⲓ   26 14.14–15
  cf. s.v. ϩⲏⲧ
ϣⲱⲛⲉ "to be sick, ill; sickness, illness"   11
  1.13, 22.10, 24.17; 18 9, 13; 25 5.25; 26 4.8,
  5.3; 36 f.II.7
  ϣⲱⲛⲓ   25 2.4; 26 10.6, 7, 15.22, 17.27–28
ϣⲱⲱⲛⲉ "to exclude"
  ϣⲁⲛⲉ⸗   26 4.4, 5–6
ϣⲱⲡ "to receive, buy, contain, take, suffer"
  27 f.1
  ϣⲁⲡ⸗   25 13.14; 28 8.9, 11.22
  ϣⲟⲡ⸗   10 20
  ⲣⲉϥϣⲟⲡ⸗ "receiver, refuge"   11 30.27
ϣⲓⲡⲉ "to be ashamed; shame"   11 19.11, 21–
  22; 24 36; 26 6.30
  ϣⲓⲡⲓ   28 9.22
ϣⲱⲱⲧ "to cut (off), slay"
  ϣⲱⲧ   34 2.16
  ϣⲉⲉⲧ⸗   28 11.15
ϣⲡⲏⲣⲉ "wonder"   11 12.5, 27.20, 23–24; 26
  12.25
ϣⲟⲡϣⲟⲡ "marjoram"
  ϣⲟⲩⲡϣⲁⲡ   25 9.1–2
ϣⲁⲁⲣ "skin, hide"   37 b.19
ϣⲏⲣⲉ "son, child"   1 f.9; 3 f.1.15; 7 13; 8 f.11;
  9 7; 10 6; 11 3.3, 7.18–19, 11.22, 12.13, 28,
  20.8, 21.20, 24.4, 27.15, 25, 28.23, 29.27, 28,
  30.4; 12 9.17, 37.2; 15 b4; 16 2.4–5; 17 f.s.4,
  f. 27, 33, b.46; 22 51; 25 7.13, 8.15, 27, 12.1,
  13.6, 12, 13–14, 18, 22, 29, 14.4, 9, 16.19,
  17.42; 26 2.7, 3.6, 11, 4.5, 22, 7.6, 11, 9.25,
  10.18, 12.7, 21, 13.14, 16, 30, 14.23–24,
  15.25, 17.13, 16; 28 1.19, 2.12, 3.1, 8.16,
  11.18; 29 f.13; 31 f.1; 33 f.6
  ϣⲉⲣⲉ   3 f.2.26
  ϣⲉⲣⲓ   4 5.8 ϣ 7 8, 23, 28, 33
  ϣⲏⲣⲓ   28 5.17, 8.21,
  ϣⲡⲣⲉ   13 27?
  ϣⲉⲉⲣⲉ "daughter"   13 11; 25 9.15–16
  ϣⲉ (reduced form)   10 9, 11; 16 1.6; 20 f.13
  ϣⲏ   9 4, 12; 25 9.4; 35 b.9
  ϣⲓ   25 12.15
  cf. υἱός in Abbreviations
ϣⲣⲱ "menstruation, menstrual blood"   22 59;
  30 f.2; 31 b.15; 37 b.19
  ϣⲣⲟ   27 f.22
ϣⲁⲣⲃⲁ "scorching heat"   22 43
ϣⲟⲣϣⲣ "to upset, overturn"
  ϣⲁⲣϣⲉⲣ   26 7.9
ϣⲱⲥ "wound"
  ϣⲥ   25 13.27
ϣⲱⲧ "well"   9 1
ϣⲱⲧⲉ "well, cistern, pit"   20 f.2
ϣⲧⲉⲕⲟ "prison"

ϣⲧⲕⲁ   **26** 15.29
ϣⲧⲁⲙ "to shut; shutting"   **24** 15, 16
   ϣⲧⲁⲙⲉ   **24** 12
   ϣⲟⲧⲙ̄^{Q} **25** 3.7
ϣⲧⲟⲣⲧⲣ "to disturb, trouble; disturbance"
   4 5.10, 11; **11** 11.2; **32** 1.11, 2.1, 8, 19, 2.23
   ϣⲧⲁⲣⲧⲣ̄   **28** 9.14
   ϣⲧⲁⲣⲧⲉⲣ   **26** 15.23
   ϣⲧⲁⲣⲧⲏⲣ   **28** 5.5, 6.2–3
   ϣⲧⲉⲣⲧⲱⲣ   **25** 3.21, 4.11; **26** 4.6–7
   ⲁⲧϣⲧⲟⲣⲧⲉⲣ "without disturbance"   **34** 1.20
ϣⲁⲩ "use, value"
   ϣⲉⲩ   **1** b.3
   ϣⲟⲩ   **11** 5.2, 17.20, 20.12
   ⲙⲉⲧⲁϣⲉⲩ "unworthy act" (?)   **26** 16.24
ϣⲁⲩ "male cat"
   ϣⲉⲩ   **28** 6.5; **32** 2.18
ϣⲟⲟⲩ "incense, perfume"
   ϣⲁⲩ (?)   **34** 4.16
ϣⲟⲟⲩⲉ "to be dry"   **3** f.1.10–11; **35** f.14
   ϣⲁⲟⲩⲉⲓ   **26** 13.4
ϣⲟⲩⲟ "to pour"
   ϣⲁⲩⲁ⸗   **25** 16.10
ϣⲟⲩⲉⲓⲧ "to be empty"   **28** 7.8
ϣⲟⲉⲓϣ "dust"
   ϣⲁⲉⲓϣ   **31** f.24
ϣⲟⲩϣⲟⲩ "to boast; boast, pride"
   ⲙⲛ̄ⲧϣⲟⲩϣⲟ "pride"   **11** 13.4–5
ϣⲟⲩϣⲧ "window"   **11** 3.8–9, 4.9
ϣⲱϥ "to be desert, laid waste, destroyed"   **31** f.46
   ϣⲁϥ   **26** 16.33
   ϣⲟϥ   **27** f.3, 11, 19
   ϣⲱⲃ   **30** b.5; **31** f.20
   ϣⲁⲃ⸗   **30** f.25, b.1 (twice)
   [ϣⲁ]ⲃⲉ⸗   **30** f.12
ϣⲁϧⲉ "to swell; swelling"
   ϣⲉⲃⲉ   **18** 12
   ϣⲁⲃⲉ^Q **36** f.II.13
ϣⲁϥⲧⲉ "impious (person), impiety"   **11** 19.27
ϣⲁϩ "flame, fire"   **3** f.2.13; **12** 27.20, 29.1; **22** 42; **28** 4.3; **32** 1.8
ϣⲁϫⲉ "to speak; word"   **10** 21; **11** 7.15, 10.15, 11.18, 16.25, 17.3, 21.7, 24.28, 30.12, 17, 18, 20; **22** 56; **23** 30; **25** 8.14, 16.16; **26** 13.3, 16.30; **35** b.4
   ⲥⲉϫⲉ   **1** b.5
   ϣⲁⲭⲓ   **28** 8.1, 10.15
   ϣⲉⲭⲉ   **1** f.21
   ⲁⲧϣⲁⲭⲉ "speechless"   **35** b.8

ⲙⲛ̄ⲧⲁⲧϣⲁϫⲉ "speechlessness"   **11** 8.18
ⲙⲉⲧⲁⲧϣⲁϫⲉ   **25** 4.7–8
ϣⲟϫⲛⲉ "plan, scheme, counsel"   **11** 10.12, 12.3, 5
ϣⲱⲱϭⲉ "to smite, wound; blow, wound"
   ϣⲓⲕ (?)   **25** 4.23
   ϣⲱⲕ (?)   **25** 4.9
ϥⲓ "to raise, take, carry, lift"   **11** 25.23; **15** f.5
   . . ?   **12** 31.23
   ⲃⲓ   **25** 2.6, 7.8; **26** 5.2, 18, 14.36, 15.22; **27** f.9; **28** 3.8, 9.22
   ⲃⲓⲧ⸗   **4** 5.8
   ϥⲓ̈⸗   **11** 12.6
   cf. s.v. ϣⲓⲛⲉ
ϥⲱ "hair"   **3** f.2.22
   ⲃⲟ   **12** 33.11
   ⲃⲱ   **28** 1.7, 5.7, 6.17
ϥⲛⲧ "worm"
   ⲃⲏⲛⲧ   **29** f.5
ϥⲱⲧⲉ "sweat"
   ⲃⲱⲧⲉ (?)   **5** b.2
   ⲃϥ†   **28** 13.5
ϥⲱⲧⲉ "to wipe (off), obliterate"
   ⲃⲁⲧ⸗   **26** 10.20; **27** f.15; **37** b.29
ϥⲱϭⲉ "to move hastily, seize; violence"
   ⲃⲏϫ   **26** 16.21
ϩⲁⲓ "husband"   **26** 16.21; **32** 2.24; **37** b.11
ϩⲁⲉⲓⲟ "yea"   **17** f.26, 33
   ⲁⲓⲁ   **25** 8.5 (twice); **25** 13.12, 20, 17.45; **26** 14.32 (twice); **27** f.14; **28** 6.14; **30** f.21, b.6
   ⲁⲓⲟ   **8** f.11 (twice); **12** 25.5 (twice), 27.17 (twice), 29.4; **18** 19 (twice); **21** 23 (twice); **22** 58; **23** 43 (twice); **24** 36; **25** 7.6 (twice), 9.31 (twice), 11.8, 13.9 (twice), 23, 26, 31, 15.16 (twice), 15.2, 16.4 (twice), 24, 17.45; **26** 7.2, 10.20, 12.5; **28** 7.13 (twice), 11.11 (twice), 13.13 (twice); **31** f.25 (twice), b.13 (twice); **32** 1.9 (twice), 18 (twice); **35** b.9; **36** f.II.10 (twice); **37** f.23 (twice)
   ⲁⲓⲱ   **10** 12; **22** 39; **24** 17; **25** 11.11 (twice), 13.15, 14.5, 24, 15.8, 16.7, 24, 18.9; **26** 4.15 (twice), 7.2; **34** 2.18 (twice)
   ⲁⲓⲱⲱ̄   **25** 13.15
   ⲁⲟ   **35** b.9
   ⲓ̄ⲁ   **27** f.14; **30** f. 21, b.6
   ⲟⲓ̄ⲟ   **25** 13.23, 14.20
   ϩⲁⲉⲓ   **17** f.26
ϩⲉ "to fall, find"   **11** 19.23; **20** f.1, 10, 11 (twice); **35** f.5
   ϩⲏⲉⲓ   **26** 7.9

ⲉ̅ "way, manner" **10** 7; **11** 25.26, 27.15; **24** 31; **25** 2.24, 25, 3.2, 18; **27** f.20; **35** b.5
ⲛⲑⲉ "like, in the manner" **1** f.5–6, 11–12; **3** f.1.29; **6** 22, 23; **7** 35, 36; **8** f.10?; **11** 8.8; **12** 11.15; **12** 33.9, 11; **17** f.24, b. 46, f.36; **19** 1; **23** 41; **24** 14; **26** 6.7; **28** 2.5, 6.3, 6.7, 8; **29** f.17, 18; **32** 1.8, 16
  ⲉⲑ **31** f.21
  ⲉ̅ⲉ̅ **34** 1.12, 13
  ⲉⲛⲑⲉ **17** f.20; **28** 2.12, 6.6; **31** f.8, 14, 19, b.8
  ⲉⲛⲉⲏ **31** b.7
  ⲉⲛⲉ **31** f.11, 23–24
  ⲑⲉ **11** 30.4; 13.10; **17** f.25, b.45; **32** 1.17, 24
  ⲑⲏ **25** 18.4; **26** 10.30, 16.2
  ⲛⲑⲏ **25** 16.6; **26** 5.22, 12.3–4, 13.7–8; **26** 6.21; **28** 7.5
ⲉ̅ "forepart" **8** f.13; **12** 29.3, 12; **26** 11.6, 9
ⲉⲓⲏ "path, road" **11** 3.6 (twice), 4.6, 7; **26** 11.10
  ⲉ̅ⲉ **11** 4.13?
  ⲉ̅ⲏ **11** 4.16
ⲉ̅ⲟ "face" **3** f.2.13; **6** 7, 9, 14; **11** 17.10; **12** 7.2, 9.10 (twice), 12, 21.15, 29.6, 7 (three times), 16; **37** b.3, 12, 15, 31
  ⲉ̅ⲁ **4** 5.5; **8** f.13; **22** 45, 50, 55, 56; **23** 9; **24** 36; **26** 9.8, 10.22, 16.23, 17.11; **27** f.10, 13, 16, 22, 23; **28** 3.7, 4.6, 9.22; **31** b.13
  ⲫⲁ **26** 9.25, 13.32
  ⲫⲟ **17** f.2
  ⲉ̅ⲣⲁ⸗ **11** 8.19; **26** 16.20
  ⲃⲁⲥⲧⲉ̅ⲁ "hatefulness" **31** b.12
  ⲃⲁⲥⲑⲁ **22** 45 (with note); **27** f.2
  ⲃⲁⲧⲥⲉ̅ⲁ **31** b.4, 5–6
ⲉ̅ⲟⲓ "field" **11** 4.19
ⲉ̅ⲱⲃ "to send" **31** f.33
  ⲉ̅ⲁⲃ⸗ **9** 3
ⲉ̅ⲱⲃ "task, work, matter, thing" **1** b.5, 6; **9** 1; **11** 1.12, 21, 2.12, 7.2; **13** 4; **22** 57; **25** 2.19, 4.2, 5.11; **26** 4.1, 11.18, 14.8; **30** f.8, 9, 15, 19, b.1; **34** 1.22, 2.14; **37** f.16
  ⲉ̅ⲱⲱⲃ **28** 1.1
  ⲉ̅ⲱϥ **12** 23.13, 25.9, 35.1, 37.13, 39.20, 43.20
  ⲉ̅ⲃⲏⲩⲉ (pl.) **11** 21.17, 30.12
  ⲉⲉ̅ⲃⲏⲩⲉ **25** 16.17
  ⲙⲁⲛⲉⲣⲉ̅ⲱⲃ "workshop" **25** 17.35; **26** 16.33; **30** b.1
  cf. s.v. ϭⲓ
ⲉ̅ⲏⲃⲉ "grief, mourning"
  ⲉ̅ⲏⲃⲓ **2** 4; **28** 10.10

ⲉ̅ⲃⲁ "straits, embarrassment, misfortune" **32** 2.23
ⲉ̅ⲃⲟⲩⲣ "left" **3** f.2.3; **12** 35.14
  ⲃⲟⲩⲣ **25** 7.7, 14.20, 24; **26** 17.15
  ⲉⲉ̅ⲃⲟⲩⲣ **3** f.1.27; **26** 8.16
  ⲉ̅ⲓⲃⲟⲩⲣ **26** 8.28
ⲉ̅ⲁⲓⲃⲉⲥ "shade, shadow"
  ⲑⲁⲓⲃⲉⲥ **11** 30.24
  ⲑⲁⲓⲃⲱⲥ **26** 13.6–7
ⲉ̅ⲱⲃⲥ "to cover; covering" **7** 11, 14; **12** 11.13, 29.16, 17; **26** 9.7, 11
  ⲑⲱⲃⲥ̅ **26** 9.9
  ⲉ̅ⲟⲃⲥ⸗ **35** f.4
ⲉ̅ⲃⲥ **25** 9.7
ⲉ̅ⲓⲕ "sorcery, magic" **11** 19.27; **25** 10.15; **26** 10.9 (twice), 17.10
  ⲙⲛ̅ⲧⲣⲉϥⲉ̅ⲓⲕ **11** 1.10
ⲉ̅ⲱⲱⲕ "to gird, brace"
  ⲉ̅ⲏⲕ **25** 3.6
ⲉ̅ⲱⲗ "to fly"
  ⲉ̅ⲏⲗ^Q **11** 26.12; **12** 29.17; **26** 14.33
ⲉ̅ⲱⲗ "to be hoarse"
  ⲁⲧⲑⲱⲗ "not hoarse" **17** f.25
ⲉ̅ⲱⲗ "to throw, bring"
  ⲉ̅ⲁⲗ⸗ **16** 15.30, 17.5?
ⲉ̅ⲟⲟⲗⲉ "moth"
  ⲉ̅ⲁⲁⲗⲓ **26** 15.4
ⲉ̅ⲗⲡⲉ "navel"
  ⲉ̅ⲏⲗⲡⲉ **36** f.I.2
ⲉ̅ⲗⲟⲡⲗⲡ "to be weary, despondent; weariness, distress"
  ⲉ̅ⲗⲟⲡⲗⲉⲡ **18** 11
ⲉ̅ⲗⲟⲥⲧⲛ "mist, darkness" **15** b.3
ⲉ̅ⲁⲗⲏⲧ "bird" **26** 17.11
  ⲉⲉ̅ⲁⲗⲏⲧ **33** f.11
  ⲉ̅ⲁⲗⲁϯ (pl.) **26** 15.12–13
ⲉ̅ⲗⲟϭ "to be sweet, take delight"
  ⲉ̅ⲟⲗⲉϭ **17** f.19, 23, 25
  ⲉ̅ⲟⲗⲟϭ **17** f.20
ⲉ̅ⲙⲟⲙ "to be hot; heat, warmth, fever"
  ⲉ̅ⲉⲙ **25** 18.9
  ⲉ̅ⲏⲙⲙⲉ^Q **26** 2.14
  ⲉ̅ⲏⲙ^Q **25** 4.10
ⲉ̅ⲟⲙⲛⲧ "copper, bronze"
  ⲉ̅ⲟⲙⲉⲧ **20** f.4
  ⲙⲛ̅ⲧⲙⲁⲓⲉ̅ⲟⲙⲛ̅ⲧ "greed" **11** 13.6–7
ⲉ̅ⲙⲟⲟⲥ **3** b.1.12; **4** 5.13; **7** 4; **10** 8; **11** 3.20, 11.24, 26.9; **12** 21.7, 22–23, 23.4; **17** b.37; **20** f.2; **25** 3.16; **32** 1.1
  ⲑⲙ̅ⲙⲟⲟⲥ **4** 2.2

ⲙⲟⲟⲥ   **25** 6.10, 15; **26** 8.19
ϩⲙⲁⲥ   **2** 2 (twice)
ϩⲙⲁⲁⲥ   **28** 7.20
ϩⲉⲙⲁⲁⲥ   **26** 9.20
ϩⲉⲙⲟⲟⲥ   **17** b.45; **26** 5.8–9
ϩⲙⲙⲟⲟⲥ   **9** 11
   ⲙⲁⲛϩⲉⲙⲁⲁⲥ "buttocks, backside"   **27** f.11
ϩⲙϩⲁⲗ "servant, slave"   **11** 1.3, 2.1, 3.2, 4.24, 5.23, 8.1, 28.4; **23** 50; **29** 10.2
ϩⲙϩⲙ "roar, neigh"   **28** 6.6
ϩⲙϫ "vinegar"
   ϩⲙⲙϫ   **25** 13.21
ϩⲱⲛ "to approach"
   ϩⲱⲛⲉ   **11** 10.20–21, 25.17
   ϩⲏⲛ^Q **1** f.28; **11** 8.21
ϩⲱⲛ "to command"   **11** 24.27
ϩⲓⲛⲉ "to move oneself"
   ϩⲏⲛⲉ (?)   **26** 16.12
ϩⲛⲉ= "will, desire"
   ϩⲛⲁ=   **16** 2.2
   ⲛⲁ=   **16** 2.13
ϩⲛⲁⲩ "vessel, thing"
   ϩⲛⲟ   **1** f.12
ϩⲓⲛⲏⲃ   **6** 4; **9** 4; **26** 16.27; **28** 1.9, 5.13, 18
   ϩⲓⲛⲉⲃ   **31** f.2
   ϩⲓⲛⲏϥ   **6** 13, 19–20
ϩⲱⲛϫ "to entreat, exhort"   **25** 2.8
ϩⲁⲡ "judgement"   **28** 9.5
   ϩⲉⲡ   **26** 8.19
   ⲣⲉϥϯϩⲁⲡ "judge"   **22** 54
ϩⲱⲡ "to hide"
   ϩⲏⲡ^Q **11** 4.4; **12** 5.7, 19.10, 37.4; **26** 14.25
   ⲑⲏⲡ^Q **12** 21.22; **26** 15.14, 17.25
   ⲑⲏⲙⲡ^Q **26** 3.23
ϩⲓⲣ "road, street"   **22** 62
   ⲫⲓⲗ   **26** 15.31
   ϩⲣⲓ   **26** 16.32
ϩⲣⲱ "oven"   **37** b.21
   ⲣⲱ̄   **25** 18.5
ϩⲣⲟⲕ "be still; quiet"
   ϩⲁⲣⲕ   **26** 16.26
ϩⲣⲏⲣⲉ "flower"   **12** 35.12–13
ϩⲣⲟⲟⲩ "voice"   **17** f.19
   ⲣⲟⲟⲩ   **25** 13.24
   ϩⲣⲁⲩ   **28** 3.10
   ϩⲉⲣⲟⲟⲩ   **17** f.23
ϩⲟⲩⲣⲓⲧ "watcher, guardian"   **25** 13.5, 7, 10, 13, 21, 24, 27, 14.1, 6, 11, 17, 21, 25, 15.3, 20
   ϩ̄ⲟⲩⲣⲓⲧⲉ   **25** 13.2
ϩⲣⲟϣ "to be slow, heavy, dificult"   **6** 22

ϩⲉⲣⲟϣ   **3** f.1.27
ϩⲁⲣⲉϩ "to guard, protect, watch over"   **11** 3.5, 6.22, 11.10, 20.2, 27.11; **19** 1, 3; **28** 13.6
   ϩⲁⲣⲉ   **25** 10.3
ϩⲱⲥ "to sing, make music"
   ϭⲓⲛϩⲱⲥ "song"   **28** 7.22
ϩⲓⲥⲉ "to suffer; suffering"   **6** 2; **10** 20; **18** 9; **20** f.7; **31** f.26
   ϩⲓⲥ   **25** 13.13
   ϩⲓⲥⲓ   **26** 5.6, 18, 6.5, 29, 11.15, 12.2, 13.6, 14.4, 15.3; **28** 8.8, 12.8
   ϩⲁϩⲥⲉ (?)   **37** f.22
ϩⲟⲥⲙ "natron"
   ϩⲁⲥⲃ   **1** f.11
ϩⲁⲧ "silver"   **3** f.1.7; **25** 17.40; **28** 10.19
ϩⲏⲧ "heart"   **1** f.10, 15, b.5; **3** f.2.36, 37, b.1.8; **6** 24; **8** f.9; **9** 6 (twice), 9 (twice), b.8; **11** 11.15, 19.21, 30.13; **17** f.31, b.41 (twice); **18** 11, 18; **25** 8.14, 16.16; **26** 12.6; **27** b.6; **28** 2.13, 16; **28** 5.2, 9.16, 11.6–7; **32** 1.6, 11, 15 (twice); **37** f.21
   ϩⲉⲧ   **20** f.6?, 10
   ⲫⲏⲧ   **26** 3.23
   ⲙ̄ⲛⲧⲣⲙ̄ⲛ̄ϩⲏⲧ "wisdom"   **17** b.43
   ϣⲁⲛϩ̄ⲧ= "to have pity, mercy"   **26** 4.11
   ϣⲁⲛⲁϩⲧⲏ=   **26** 4.29, 9.30, 11.16, 15.19
   ϣⲉⲛⲉϩⲧⲏ=   **28** 5.17
   ⲙ̄ⲛⲧϣⲁⲛϩ̄ⲧⲏ= "pity, mercy"   **11** 2.14–15, 9.23–24
   ϫⲁⲥⲓϩⲏⲧ "pride, audacity"   **28** 3.5–6
   ⲙ̄ⲛⲧϫⲁⲥⲓϩⲏⲧ   **11** 13.3–4
   cf. s.v. ⲕⲓⲙ
ϩⲟⲧ "presence" (?)   **11** 17.17
ϩⲁⲧⲉ "to flow"   **8** f.2; **12** 33.17; **25** 13.30
ϩⲓⲧⲉ "to convulse"
   ϩⲓⲧ   **26** 15.27
   ⲙ̄ⲛⲧⲣⲉϥϩⲓⲧⲉ "torment"   **11** 8.16
ϩⲟⲉⲓⲧⲉ "garment, clothing"
   ϩⲁⲓⲧⲓ   **28** 5.13
   ϩⲁⲓϯ   **25** 17.39; **26** 16.34; **28** 10.19, 13.4; **34** 1.24?
ϩⲟⲧⲉ "fear"   **11** 4.26, 8.5, 8.23, 10.28, 11.1, 11–12, 21.9, 25.13; **36** f.II.3, 8
   ϩⲁⲧⲉ   **25** 7.8
   ϩⲁⲧⲓ   **28** 5.20
   ϩⲁϯ   **26** 6.1; **28** 10.14; **29** f.8, 9
   ⲁⲧⲉⲣϩⲁⲧⲏ "without fear"   **34** 1.21
   ⲁⲧⲉⲣϩⲁϯ   **34** 2.8–9, 15
ϩⲧⲟ "horse"   **17** b.31
   ⲉϩⲧⲁⲁⲣⲓ (fem.)   **28** 6.6

ϩⲧⲟⲟⲩⲉ "dawn, morning"   **11** 2.7–8
ϩⲟⲟⲩ "day"   **3** f.2.8; **6** 3, 12; **7** 33; **11** 19.8, 22.15; **12** 7.12, 13.20, 15.10, 19.6, 18, 27.8, 35.7, 37.15, 39.4; **17** f.16; **18** 14; **24** 17; **25** 2.2, 3.10, 4.24, 5.2; **25** 10.5, 11; **26** 4.23, 5.26, 9.3, 18, 10.22, 12.21, 13.27, 8, 14.10, 27, 17.5; **32** 2.15
 ϩⲁⲁⲩ   **28** 7.5, 11.2, 11
 ϩⲁⲟⲩ   **26** 3.24, 5.3; **28** 11.9, 10, 12.20; **31** f.27
 ⲡⲟⲟⲩ "today"   **4** 2.6, 15; **10** 9; **11** 15.2, 16.6, 24, 17.11, 19.19; **12** 5.1, 4, 10, 13.14, 15.21 (twice?), 17.2, 22, 19.16, 21.3, 25.13–14, 29.8, 9, 31.6, 14, 20, 33.2, 7, 15, 21, 35.6, 18, 22, 37.3; **17** f.18, 21; **18** 5; **21** 13; **22** 26; **24** 2, 26, 31–32; **25** 2.8, 10, 17, 18, 25, 3.6, 15, 5.12, 21, 22, 6.21, 22, 26, 7.1, 18, 20, 22, 8.6, 10, 13, 10.2, 6, 18.1–2; **26** 3.2, 4, 6, 8, 10, 13, 19, 21, 4.16, 17, 5.7, 5.10, 12, 24, 28, 6.8, 14, 20, 22, 7.12, 14, 16, 19, 20, 26, 28, 8.1, 3, 4, 5, 7, 8, 10, 12, 13–14, 17, 18, 20, 30, 8.7, 9, 11, 16, 19, 20, 10.21, 24, 11.22, 28, 12.58, 14, 16, 19, 24, 13.9, 14, 18–19, 24, 26, 30, 33, 14.8, 10, 14, 16, 17, 22, 24, 28, 32; **29** f.11; **32** 1.4; **34** 1.7; **37** f.13
 ⲡⲁⲁⲩ   **26** 4.25; **28** 4.2, 7.9–10
 ⲡⲁⲟⲩ   **26** 6.17, 7.2, 22, 9.26; **34** 2.7, 12, 3.9
 ⲡⲟⲁⲩ   **26** 4.20
 ⲡⲟⲩ   **27** f.4
 ⲡⲱⲟⲩ   **19** 1
ϩⲟⲟⲩ "evil"
 ⲑⲁⲟⲩ   **26** 10.13; **28** 12.5; **31** b.17
 ⲑⲁⲩ   **28** 12.8; **30** f.5, 10, 15, 19, 25?
 ⲑⲟⲟⲩ   **11** 7.4, 13.8; **12** 39.4; **25** 9.26; **27** f.23; **31** b.18
 ⲑ̄ⲱ̄ (?)   **31** f.38
 ϩⲁⲩ   **26** 10.7; **31** f.37?
ϩⲱⲟⲩ "rain"   **12** 7.18
ϩⲓⲟⲩⲉ "to strike, cast"
 ϩⲓ   **28** 8.3
 ϩⲓ ⲧⲟⲟⲧ "to begin, undertake"   **31** 1.32
ϩⲟⲩⲟ "greater than"   **25** 2.12; **26** 4.14
 ϩⲟⲩⲁ   **28** 1.13
ϩⲟⲟⲩⲧ "male"   **11** 3.1, 5.26; **12** 15.1, 37.19, 41.7, 8; **18** 15; **23** 10, 34, 46; **24** 35; **32** 1.20, 21, 24; **37** b.7
 ϩⲟⲉⲓⲧ (?)   **17** b.10
 ϩⲟⲁⲩⲧ   **26** 9.15
 ϩⲟⲟⲧ   **33** f.11
 ϩⲩⲧ   **29** f.11

ϩⲟϥ "snake"   **17** f.36
 ϩⲁϥ   **26** 11.2
ϩⲁϩ "many"   **11** 24.18, 30.10
ϩⲱⲭⲡ "to shut"   **1** f.4–5
ϩⲁϭⲓⲛ "mint"   **25** 9.3
ϫⲁⲓⲉ "desert"   **1** f.6
ϫⲏ "chip, mote"
 ϫⲓ   **15** b.3
ϫⲓ "to take, receive"   **6** 5, 14, 15; **7** 9, 23, 29; **8** f.11; **11** 3.3, 10.25, 19.11, 21, 24.14; **12** 13.3; **22** 56; **25** 7.24, 13.22; **26** 4.9, 19, 6.30, 10.23, 11.10, 20; **28** 1.9, 6.21, 9.4; **32** 2.16; **35** f.1, 2, 7, 18, 21
 ϫⲉ-   **26** 9.27
 ϫⲓⲧ=   **11** 1.6; **12** 35.11
 cf. s.v. ⲥⲙⲏ, ϭⲟⲛⲥ
ϫⲟ "put forth"
 ϫ (?)   **23** 42
ϫⲟⲓ "boat"
 ϫⲁⲓ   **28** 2.6
ϫⲱ "to say"   **11** 11.20, 12.9, 25.26; **12** 29.19; **25** 16.17; **26** 3.10, 11.9; **28** 3.17
 ϫⲱ   **35**
 ϫⲱⲱ   **26** 2.6, 9.4, 10.3
 ϫⲉ-   **22** 24, 41; **26** 15.10
 ϫⲁⲁ=   **28** 12.2
 ϫⲟ=   **10** 22; **11** 10.16, 20.26
 ϫⲟⲟ=   **10** 5; **11** 30.26; **12** 9.13; **23** 31; **25** 2.2, 5.7–8, 9.28; **26** 11.29; **37** b.17
 ϫⲱ=   **7** 3, 19; **8** f.12
 ϭⲱ=   **3** f.1.22
 ⲁϫⲉ (imp.)   **9** 5
ϫⲱ "cup"
 ϭⲱ (?)   **34** 2.17
ϫⲉⲕ "shell"   **23** 3; **26** 16.22
ϫⲱⲕ "to complete, be perfect; end, completion, perfection"   **1** f.22, 26; **6** 23; **10** 21; **11** 18.11, 18.18, 19.19; **17** f.31; **18** 17; **21** 20; **25** 10.18; **25** 16.15; **26** 3.17, 14.15, 18, 20, 17.5; **27** f.23; **28** 2.22, 7.3, 9, 11.13, 12.1; **30** f.5; **34** 2.13; **35** f.6?; **37** f.8
 ϫⲱ   **16** 3.4
 ϫⲟⲕ   **22** 63; **23** 48; **25** 11.11; **27** f.14
 ϭⲱⲕ   **3** b.1.7
 ϫⲉⲕ-   **32** 1.14
 ϫⲁⲕ=   **22** 36, 39
 ϫⲱⲕ= (?)   **35** f.17
 ϫⲏⲕ^Q **17** b.39
ϫⲱⲕⲙ "to wash, cleanse; washing"   **12** 35.11
 ϫⲱⲕⲉⲙ̄   **25** 8.4; **26** 11.19, 20

ϫⲱⲕⲏⲙ   **28** 4.15–16
ϫⲁⲕⲙⲉ⸗   **26** 5.5, 14.5
ϫⲱⲗ "to sharpen"   **12** 11.21?
ϫⲱⲗⲕ "to extend, draw"   **12** 23.15, 41.19
ϫⲟⲗϫⲗ "to enclose; enclosure"
   ϫⲁⲗϫⲉⲗ   **24** 29
ϫⲱⲱⲙⲉ "book, scroll, sheet"   **11** 29.26; **26**
7.23, 17.14; **31** f.37, b.18
   ϫⲱⲙⲉ   **26** 17.18
   ϫⲱⲱⲙⲓ   **25** 16.11
ϫⲙⲡⲉϩ "apple (coloured)
   ϫⲓⲡⲉϩ   **37** f.4–5
ϫⲛⲁϩ "forearm, strength, violence"
   ϫⲉⲛⲉϩ   **26** 17.14, 15
   ϭⲛⲁϩ   **24** 8
ϫⲡ- "hour"   **6** 3, 11, 12
ϫⲡⲟ "to blame, be ashamed; blame"
   ϫⲡⲓⲁ   **26** 20.25
ϫⲡⲟ "to give birth, beget; generation"   **1** f.9?;
11 29.26; **25** 17.42
   ⲡϫⲡⲟ (sic)   **25** 13.11
   ϫⲡⲁ⸗   **28** 8.6
ϫⲱⲣ "to blacken"   **22** 49 (twice)
ϫⲱⲱⲣⲉ "mighty"   **5** f.2–3; **12** 43.12; **26** 12.16–17; **34** 3.7; **37** f.15
   ϫⲟⲟⲣ   **11** 7.11
   ϫⲟⲣⲓ   **27** f.5
ϫⲱⲱⲣⲉ "to scatter"   **12** 19.16; **30** b.5; **37** b.4
   ϫⲟⲣⲓ   **27** f.4
   ϫⲱⲣ   **31** f.22, 44
   ϫⲱⲱⲣ   **31** f.3, 4
   ϫⲟⲟⲣⲉ⸗   **11** 10.14
ϫⲱⲣⲙ "to urge, drive on"   **4** 4.14, 16–17
ϫⲣⲟⲡ "obstacle, impediment"   **11** 10.18
ϫⲟⲉⲓⲥ "lord"   **8** b.2; **10** 15 (twice); **11** 1.26, 2.2, 18, 2.23, 8.6, 24, 9.13, 10.14, 11.7, 16, 20, 12.26, 16.13, 18.19, 19.5, 21.23, 22.13, 23.8, 24.2, 27.3–4, 20–21, 28.2, 7, 30.26; **12** 19.19, 43.13; **15** f.3; **18** 8
   ϫ̄ⲥ̄   **10** 12
   ⲟ̄ⲥ̄   **25** 5.9, 9.28, 17.34; **26** 4.11, 28, 29, 9.14, 32, 11.16, 13.34, 15.9, 19; **28** 3.15, 7.6, 10.1, 2; **29** f.7
   ϫⲁⲓⲥ   **1** f.27, 37, b.8
   ⲙⲛ̄ⲧϫⲟⲉⲓⲥ "lordship"   **11** 12.19, 22.18–19
ϫⲓⲥⲉ "to be high; height"   **17** f.6; **25** 6.15
   ϫⲓⲥ   **26** 3.5, 6–7
   ϫⲓⲥⲓ   **26** 3.3
   ϫⲟⲥⲉ^Q **11** 6.22, 7.12, 30.23; **12** 21.23; **25** 3.17

ϫⲟⲥⲓ^Q **26** 7.26, 11.29
cf. s.v. ϩⲏⲧ
ϫⲟⲉⲓⲧ "olive"   **12** 1.9
   ϫⲁⲉⲓⲧ   **22** 62
   ϫⲁⲓⲉⲓⲧ   **29** b.13
ϫⲱⲧⲉ "to pierce, traverse"
   ϫⲁⲧ⸗   **3** b.1.9; **29** f.17
ϫⲟⲟⲩ "send"   **22** 33; **32** 2.22
   ϫⲁⲁⲩ   **28** 4.2
   ϫⲟⲩ   **9** 3
   ϫⲁⲩ⸗ (?)   **25** 9.31
   ϫⲟⲟⲩ⸗   **8** f.7; **9** 1, 2, 3; **11** 27.17–18
ϫⲟⲟⲩϥ "papyrus plant"
   ϭⲉⲙⲟϥ   **17** b.22
ϫⲟⲩϥ "to burn"
   ϫⲱⲃ   **16** 1.12
   ϫⲱϥ   **1** f.14, f.15; **23** 11
   ϫⲏⲃ^Q **28** 5.5
   ϫⲏϥ^Q **24** 21?; **32** 2.25
ϫⲉϥϣⲁ "nostrils"   **12** 31.18
   ϭⲉⲃϣⲁⲁⲛⲉ   **26** 8.2
ϫⲱϩ "to smear, anoint"
   ϫⲁϩ-   **27** f.22
   ϫⲱϩⲟ- (?)   **35** f.5
ϫⲱϩ "to touch"   **11** 15.18; **26** 16.17; **28** 12.7
ϫⲱϩⲙ "to defile, pollute; pollution"
   ϫⲁϩ̄ⲙ̄   **11** 13.11
   ϫϩⲁⲙ^Q **3** f.1.24
ϫⲁϫ "swallow"   **28** 2.12
   ϫⲉϫ   **26** 17.4–5, 6
ϫⲱϫ "head"
   ϫⲁϫ   **21** 13
ϫⲁϫⲉ "enemy"   **11** 11.12; **12** 5.21
   ϫⲁϫⲓ   **27** f.16
   ⲙⲛ̄ⲧϫⲁϫⲉ "enmity"   **11** 12.3
   ⲙⲉⲧϫⲉϫⲓ   **26** 16.3
ϭⲓ "type"   **18** 13
ϭⲓⲛⲉⲣϩⲱⲃ "procedure"   **25** 9 1, 16.8; **30** f.1; **37** f.1
ϭⲓⲛⲉⲣϩⲱϥ   **37** b.1
ϭⲓⲉⲛⲑⲉϣⲡⲓ "vision"   **34** 1.19
   from Greek θεωρεῖν
cf. s.v. ⲧⲱⲟⲩⲛ, ⲱϩⲉ
ϭⲱ "to remain"   **11** 10.16, 23.17; **32** 1.12
   ϭⲏⲛⲧ^Q (?)   **26** 16.26
ϭⲁⲓⲉ "ugly (person), ugliness, disgrace"
   ϩⲉⲛⲙⲛ̄ⲧϭⲁⲓⲉ "disgrace"   **11** 8.19
ϭⲱⲱⲃⲉ "leaf"
   ϭⲱⲃⲉ   **25** 9.1 (twice), 3
   ϭⲱⲃⲓ   **29** b.10, 12

ϭⲃⲟⲓ "arm, foreleg"   **11** 7.11
   ϭⲉⲃⲁⲓ   **26** 7.26, 29
ϭⲟⲗ "lie"
   ⲁⲧϭⲁⲗ "without lies"   **34** 1.20
   ⲁϭⲁⲗ   **34** 2.8, 15
ϭⲁⲗⲉ "lame or crippled person"
   ϭⲁⲗⲉⲉⲩⲉ (pl.)   **11** 21.4
   ϭⲁⲗⲉⲩ   **25** 5.25
   ϭⲁⲗⲏ   **26** 13.1
   ⲙⲉⲧϭⲁⲗ "lameness"   **25** 4.7
ϭⲟⲉⲓⲗⲉ "to deposit, entrust"
   ϭⲁⲗⲱ⸗   **28** 3.22
ϭⲟⲟⲗⲉ "to conceal"
   ⲭⲟⲟⲗⲉ   **12** 33.10
ϭⲱⲱⲗⲉ "to swathe, cover, clothe"
   ϭⲁⲁⲗⲓ   **26** 7.21
   ϭⲟⲗⲉ   **17** b.38
   ⲭⲁⲗⲓ (?)   **26** 16.16
   ϭⲁⲁⲗⲉ⸗   **26** 13.29
ϭⲁⲃⲟⲟⲩ "catfish"
   ϭⲉⲗⲃⲁⲩ   **24** 22
ϭⲙⲗⲟⲙ "to be twisted, implicated"
   ⲗⲉⲙⲗⲟⲙ⸗   **27** f.21
ϭⲱⲗⲡ "to uncover"   **34** 1.22, 2.6
   ϭⲟ[ⲗ]ⲡ⸗   **34** 1.27
   ϭⲟⲗⲉⲡ^Q   **11** 3.11
ϭⲗⲱⲧ "kidney"
   ϭⲗⲟⲧⲉ   **5** b.1
ϭⲁⲗⲁϩⲧ "pot"   **32** 2.12–13
   ϭⲁⲗⲉϩ   **22** 48; **25** 9.4, 16.12, 16.13, 17.24
   ϭⲁⲗⲉϩⲧ   **22** 59; **26** 16.7
   ϭⲁϩⲉⲗ   **26** 16.33
ϭⲁⲗⲟϫ "foot, knee"
   ϭⲁⲗⲁϫ   **26** 13.2
ϭⲁⲙ "bull"
   ϭⲉⲙ   **4** 5.5
ϭⲟⲙ "power"   **4** 2.2; **4** 3.2, 5.2, 6.2; **11** 3.19, 7.14, 9.14, 20, 12.21, 14.8, 18.6, 22.3; **12** 7.3, 6, 15.6, 17.20?, 19.7, 21.1, 23.18; **13** 1, 3; **16** 3.7; **17** f.6, b.32, 42, 18; **21** 16; **26** 11.8; **32** 1.4?, 10, 2.21
   ϭⲁⲙ   **25** 2.3, 5.23, 6.20, 8.26, 10.7, 15.12, 16.3, 18.2, 6; **26** 5.20, 21, 22, **28**, 6.6, 30, 7.1, 9, 13.12, 14.5, 19, 15.1; **28** 1.15, 2.3, 11 (twice), 19, 4.5, 14, 18, 7.21, 23; **30** f.16 (twice ?); **34** 3.10
   ϭⲙϭⲟⲙ "find power, be strong, able" **11** 10.10, 12.4, 23.25–26, 25.16; **12** 15.4
   ⲭⲙϭⲟⲙ   **12** 37.24
   ϭⲙϭⲱⲙ   **11** 2.11

ϭⲉⲙϭⲁⲙ   **25** 2.11–12
ϭⲉⲙϭⲟⲙ   **3** f.1.33
ϭⲙϭⲛ   **28** 3.4
ⲁⲧϭⲙ̄ϭⲱⲙⲉ⸗ "untouchable"   **11** 2.6–7
ϭⲱⲙ "garden, vineyard"   **30** f.12
   ϭⲟⲟⲙ   **11** 4.19
ϭⲁⲙⲟⲩⲗ "camel"   **32** 2.17
   ϭⲁⲙⲉⲩⲗⲓ (f.)   **28** 6.7
ϭⲓⲛⲉ "to find"   **6** 15; **7** 4, 19, 26; **16** 1.10
   ϭⲛ-   **1** b.4; **10** 1.17; **16** 2.8, 16
   ϭⲓⲛ-   **20** f.9; **29** f.5
   ϭⲏⲛ-   **28** 1.12
   ϭⲛ̄⸗   **9** 7?
   ϭⲛⲧ⸗   **1** f.28, 31 (twice); **6** 14?
   ϭⲙ̄ⲡϣⲓⲛⲉ "visit, visitation"   **11** 20.15–16
   ϭⲙⲡⲉⲛϣⲓⲛⲉ   **11** 20.18
   cf. s.v. ϭⲟⲙ
ϭⲟⲟⲩⲛⲉ "sack"   **6** 23
ϭⲓⲛⲙⲟⲩⲧ "Pleiades"
   ⲕⲛ̄ⲙⲟⲩⲧ   **9** 8
   ⲕⲙϩⲟⲩⲧ   **28** 2.4–5
   ϭⲓⲙⲟⲩⲧ   **4** 4.2, 8
ϭⲟⲛⲥ "might, violence"
   ϭⲁⲛⲥ   **26** 4.10
   ϫⲓⲛϭⲟⲛⲥ "violence"   **11** 3.23, 4.20–21, 6.8, 7.5–6, 8.3, 18.9
   ϫⲓⲛϭⲁⲛⲥ   **26** 6.21–22
ϭⲱⲛⲧ "to be wroth; wrath"   **22** 43; **28** 3.3, 10.16
   ϭⲁⲛⲁϩⲉ "mutilated, left"   **37** b.9
ϭⲓⲛϭⲗⲱ "bat"   **17** b.31
   ϭⲱⲗϭⲉⲗⲱ   **31** f.37
ϭⲛ̄ϭⲉϩ "elephantiasis"
   ⲕⲏⲛ̄ⲕⲃ (?)   **26** 16.1
ϭⲟⲡ "sole (of foot)"   **7** 11, 15
ϭⲉⲡⲏ "haste"   **12** 5.17, 7.1, 19.23, 25.19, 31.14; **22** 39; **25** 3.8, 16.18
   ϭⲏⲡⲏ   **34** 2.1, 3
ϭⲏⲡⲉ "cloud"
   ϭⲏⲛⲉ   **25** 2.11
ϭⲱⲡⲉ "to seize, take"
   ϭⲱⲡⲓ   **28** 3.31; **34** 2.17
   ϭⲁⲡ-   **24** 20
   ϭⲟⲡ⸗   **33** f.10
ϭⲟⲡⲥ "capture"
   ϭⲱⲡⲉⲉⲥ   **33** f.10
ϭⲉⲣⲱⲃ "staff, rod"
   ϭⲉⲣⲏⲡⲏ   **26** 9.21
ϭⲣⲟⲙⲡⲉ "dove"
   . ⲣⲟⲙ̄ⲡⲉ (?)   **12** 1.7

ϭⲣⲟⲟⲙⲡⲉ   **11** 27.16
ϭⲉⲣⲁⲙⲡⲉ   **26** 15.32
ϭⲉⲣⲟⲡⲉ   **17** b.2–3
ϭⲣⲏⲡⲉ "diadem, sceptre"
   ϭⲣⲏⲡⲓ   **28** 1.21
ϭⲱⲣϭ "to prepare"
   ϭⲱⲣⲉⲭ   **17** b.23
ϭⲱⲣϭ "to be inhabited"   **26** 16.31, 32
ϭⲱⲧⲡ "to be defeated"   **11** 10.11
ϭⲓⲧⲣⲉ "citron"   **37** b.4
   ϭⲓⲧⲣⲁ   **25** 9.3
ϭⲱϣⲧ "to look, see"   **27** f.13; **28** 6.13; **34** 1.19
   ϫⲱϣⲧ   **12** 21.18
ϭⲓϫ "hand"   **10** 10, 22; **11** 2.8, 7.11, 25.10; **12** 13.17, 15.14, 20, 21.11, 23.7, 25.16, 31.5, 9, 35.13, 15, 43.5; **18** 16; **23** 24; **25** 7.25, 13.17, 13.26, 14.14, 17, 17.43, 44; **26** 4.1, 7.23, 8.13, 14, 16, 9.19, 24, 11.18, 13.24, 14.29; **28** 2.12, 7.8, 8.11; **37** f.14
   ϫⲓϭ   **3** f.1.32, 2.32; **12** 1.4
   ϭⲓϭ   **12** 41.5
ϭⲱϫⲃ "to be small, humble, wane"
   ϭⲟϫⲃ̄   **11** 20.19
   ϫⲁϫⲉⲃ^Q **31** b.20
ϭⲱϭ "to roast, bake"
   ϭⲁⲁϭⲓ   **29** f.18.

Plates

Plate II. *PCM* I 20 (P.Donadoni) front. Photography: Massimo Giuseppetti.
Image courtesy of the Donadoni family.

Plate III. *PCM* I 20 (P.Donadoni) back. Photography: Massimo Giuseppetti.
Image courtesy of the Donadoni family.

Plate IV. *PCM* I 28 (*P.Bad.* V 122) pages 16 & 1. Photography: Elke Fuchs
© Institut für Papyrologie, Universität Heidelberg.

Plate V. *PCM* I 28 (*P.Bad.* V 122) pages 2 & 15. Photography: Elke Fuchs
© Institut für Papyrologie, Universität Heidelberg.

Plate VI. *PCM* I 28 (*P.Bad.* V 122) pages 14 & 3. Photography: Elke Fuchs
© Institut für Papyrologie, Universität Heidelberg.

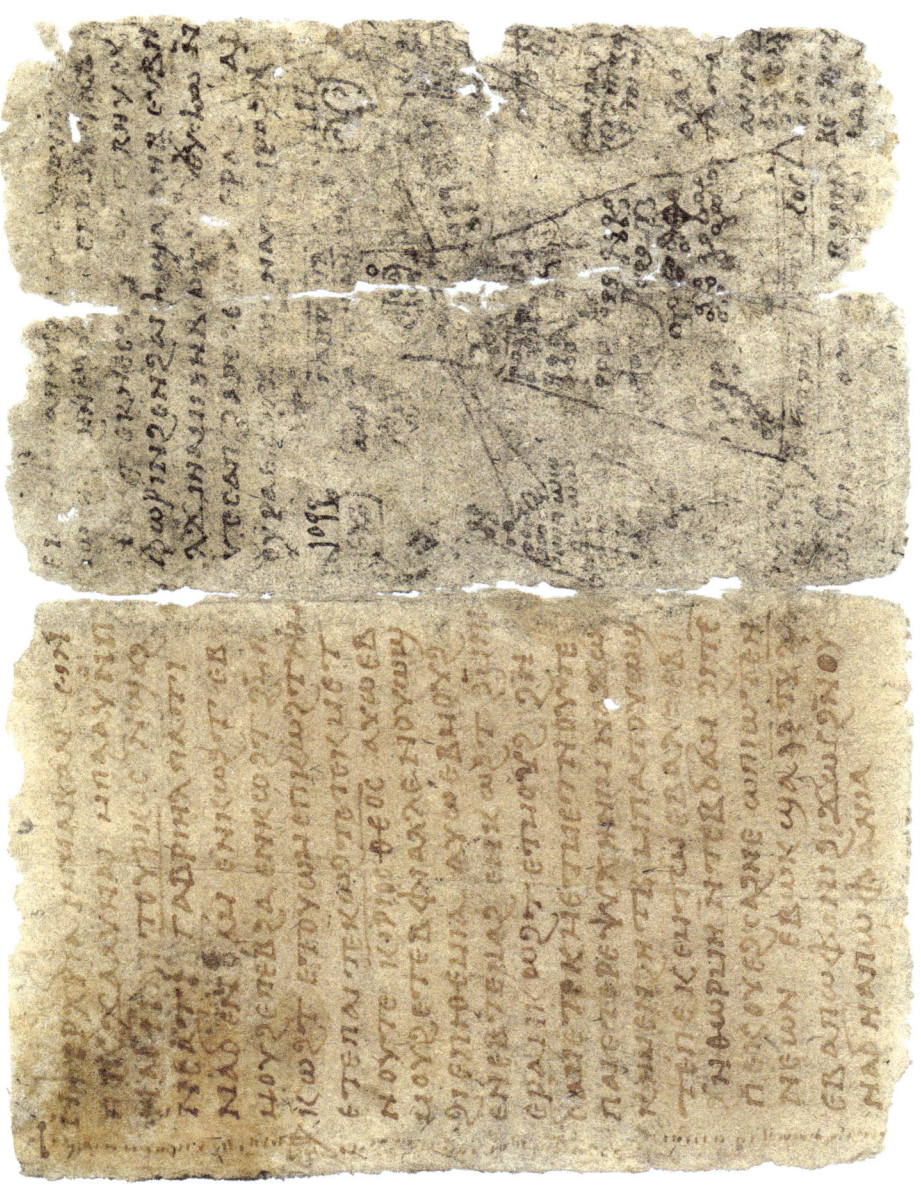

Plate VIII. *PCM* I 28 (*P.Bad.* V 122) pages 12 & 5. Photography: Elke Fuchs
© Institut für Papyrologie, Universität Heidelberg.

Plate IX. PCM I 28 (P.Bad. V 122) pages 6 & 11. Photography: Elke Fuchs
© Institut für Papyrologie, Universität Heidelberg.

Plate X. *PCM* I 28 (*P.Bad.* V 122) pages 10 & 7. Photography: Elke Fuchs
© Institut für Papyrologie, Universität Heidelberg.

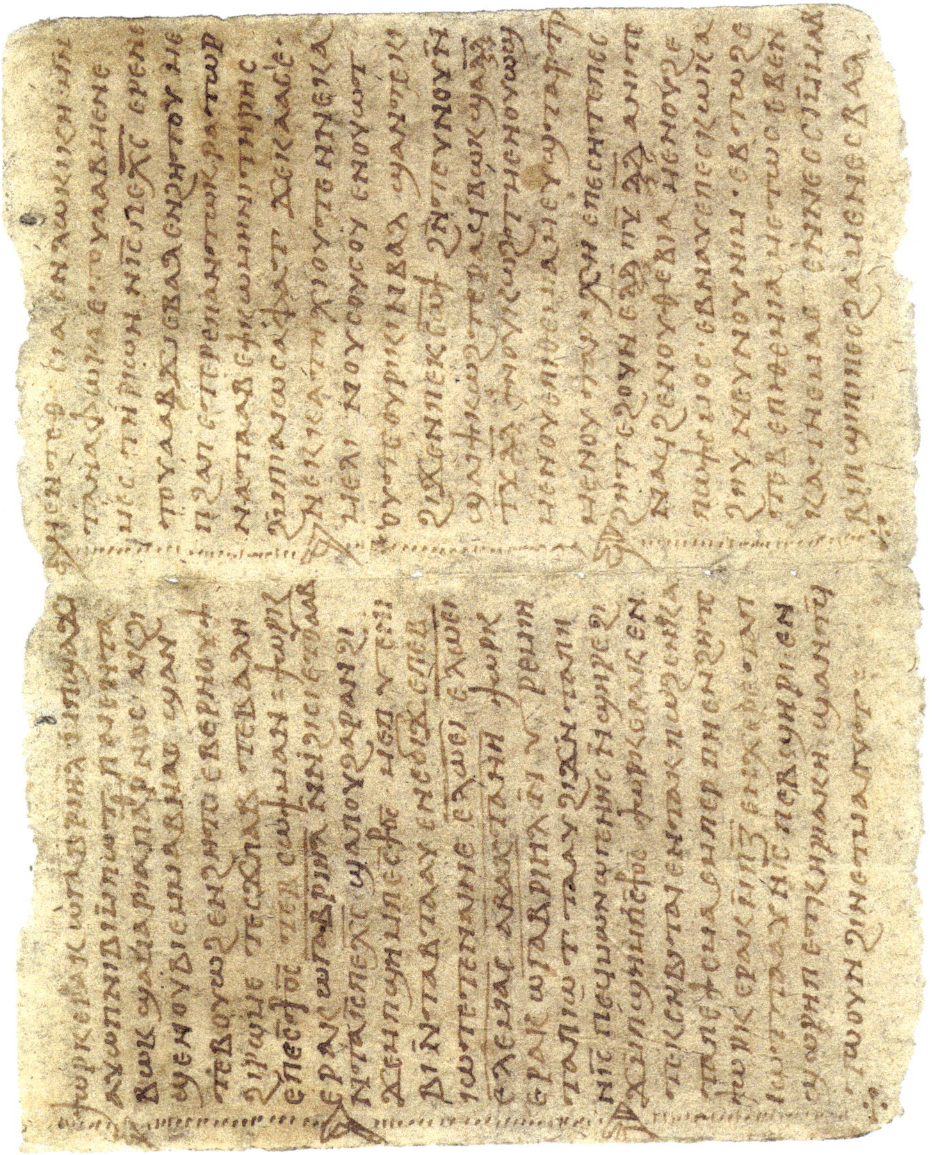

Plate XI. *PCM* I 28 (*P.Bad.* V 122) pages 8 & 9. Photography: Elke Fuchs
© Institut für Papyrologie, Universität Heidelberg.

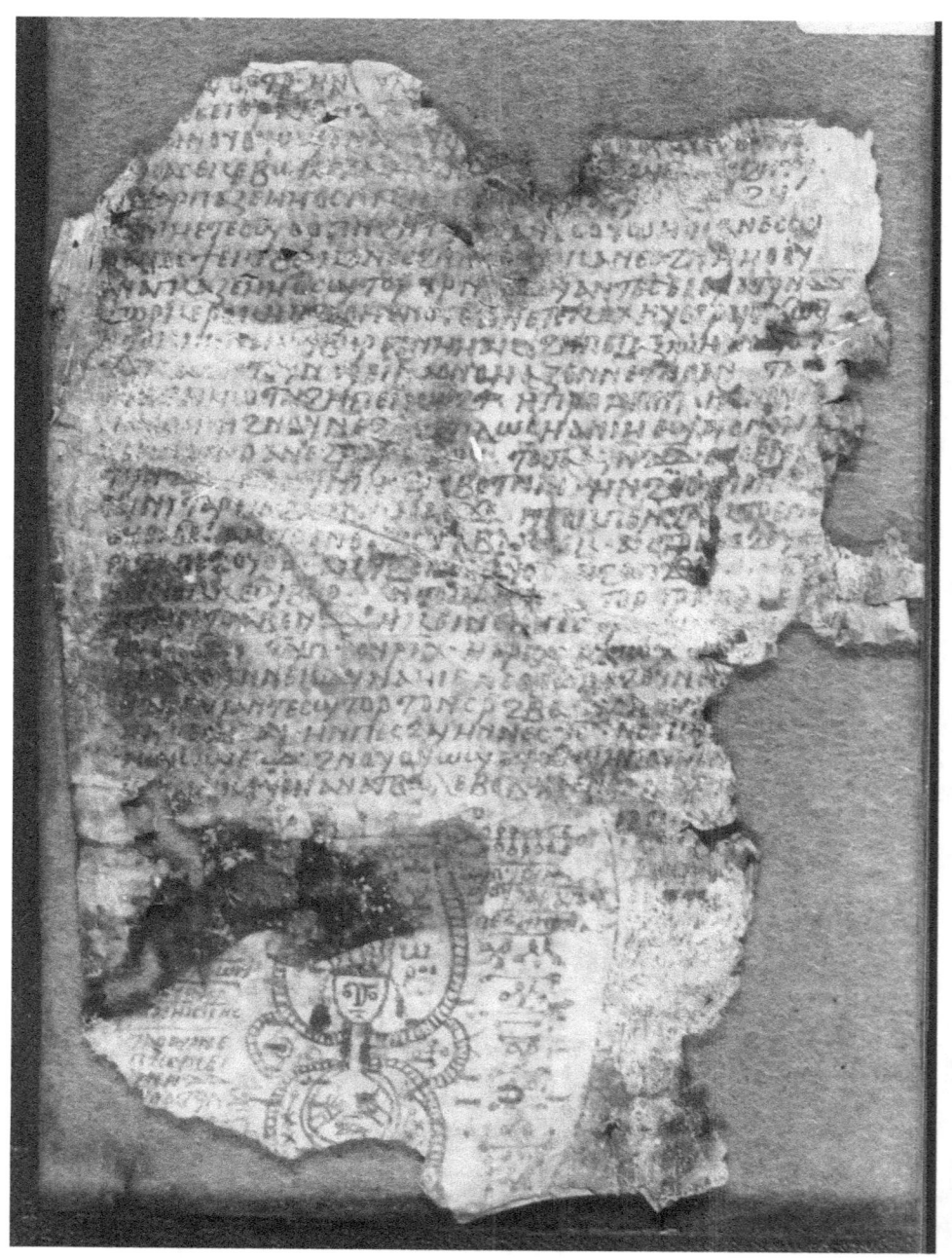

Plate XII. *PCM* I 32 (*P.Bad.* V 131) page 2. Photography: Elke Fuchs
© Institut für Papyrologie, Universität Heidelberg.

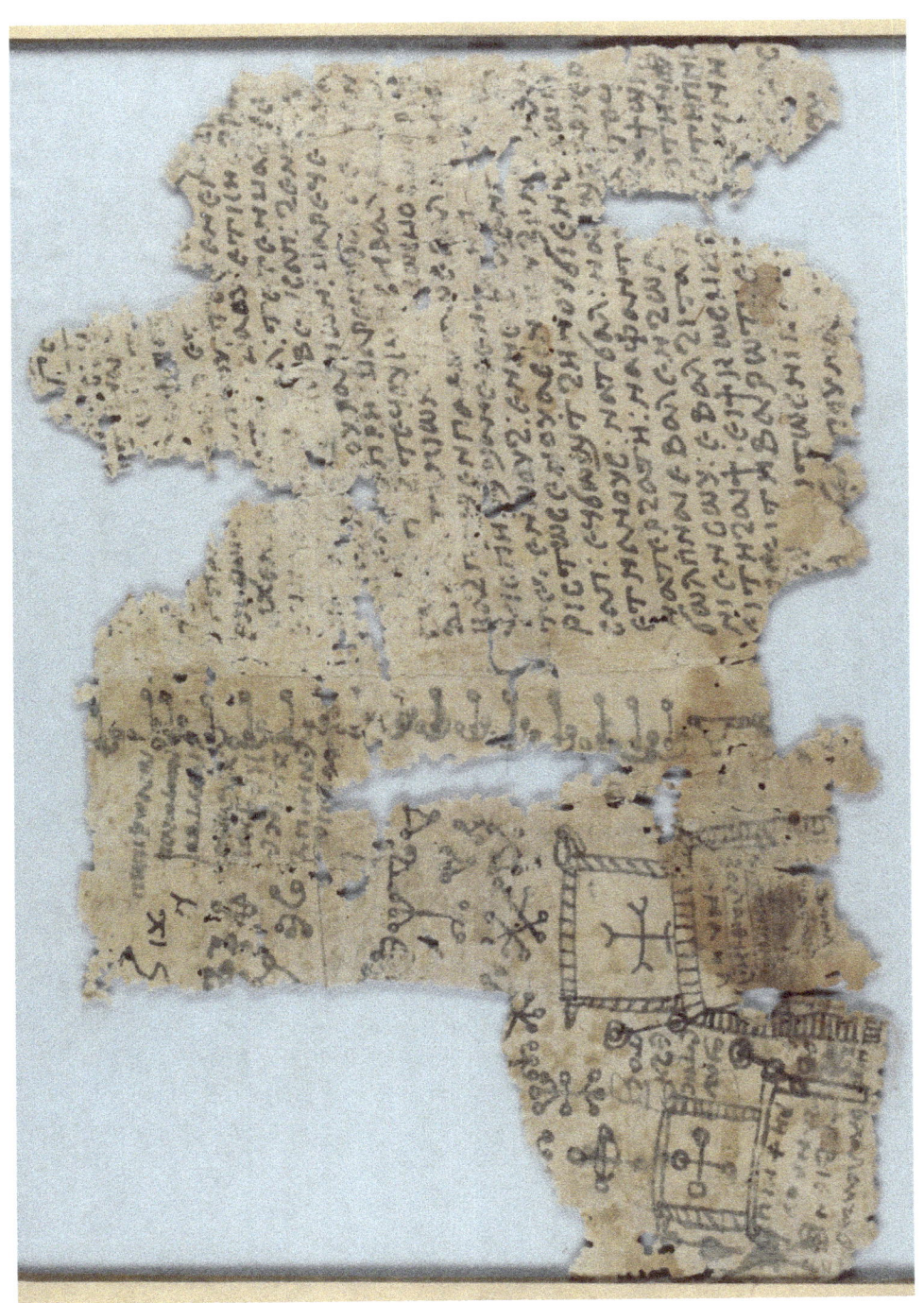

Plate XIII. *PCM I* 34 (*P.Stras.Copt.* 9) pages 4 & 1.
Coll. and photogr. Bnu de Strasbourg.

Plate XIV. *PCM* I 34 (*P.Stras.Copt.* 9) pages 2 & 3.
Coll. and photogr. Bnu de Strasbourg.

Plate XV. *PCM* I 35 (*P.Bad.* V 135) front. Photography: Elke Fuchs
© Institut für Papyrologie, Universität Heidelberg.

Plate XVI. *PCM* I 35 (*P.Bad.* V 135) back. Photography: Elke Fuchs
© Institut für Papyrologie, Universität Heidelberg.

www.ingramcontent.com/pod-product-compliance
Lightning Source LLC
Chambersburg PA
CBHW081942230426
43669CB00019B/2902